Italy

Parra-Bordas/DIAF

I reached the Alps: the soul within me burned
Italia, my Italia, at thy name;
And when from out of the mountain's heart I came
And saw the land for which my life had yearned,
I laughed as one who some great prize has earned.

Oscar Wilde, *Sonnet on Approaching Italy*

Travel Publications

38 Clarendon Road - WATFORD Herts WD1 1SX - U.K.
Tel. (01923) 415 000
www.michelin-travel.com
TheGreenGuide-uk@uk.michelin.com

___

Manufacture française des pneumatiques Michelin

Société en commandite par actions au capital de 2 000 000 000 de francs
Place des Carmes-Déchaux – 63000 Clermont-Ferrand (France)
R.C.S. Clermont-Fd B 855 200 507

© Michelin et Cie, Propriétaires-éditeurs, 2000
Dépôt légal avr. 2000 – ISBN 2-06-000004-1 – ISSN 0763-1383

Printed in Belgique 01- 01/6.2

Compogravure : MAURY Imprimeur S.A., Malesherbes
Impression et brochage : CASTERMAN, Tournai (Belgique).

Maquette de couverture extérieure : Agence Carré Noir à Paris 17e

THE GREEN GUIDE:
The Spirit of Discovery

*The exhilaration of new horizons,
the fun of seeing the world, the
excitement of discovery: this is what
we seek to share with you. To help you
make the most of your travel experience,
we offer first-hand knowledge and turn
a discerning eye on places to visit.
This wealth of information gives
you the expertise to plan your own
enriching adventure. With THE GREEN
GUIDE showing you the way, you can
explore new destinations with confidence
or rediscover old ones.
Leisure time spent with THE GREEN
GUIDE is also a time for refreshing
your spirit, enjoying yourself,
and taking advantage of our selection
of fine restaurants, hotels
and other places for relaxing.
So turn the page and open a window
on the world. Join THE GREEN GUIDE
in the spirit of discovery.*

Contents

Using this guide   8
Key   9
Map of principal sights   10
Suggested touring programmes   14
Map of places to stay   18

Introduction   22

Italy Today   24

Landscape 24 – Political and administrative
organisation 25 – Regions of Italy 26 –
Economy 29

Historical table and notes   30

Ancient civilisations 30 – The Roman Empire 31 –
The Golden Age 35 – Italian unity 35

Architecture   39

Italian art   48

Byzantine 48 – Romanesque and Gothic 49 –
Quattrocento 51 – Cinquecento 53 – Manner-
ism 56 – Naturalism, Classicism and Baroque 56
– Settecento 57 – Ottocento 58 – Novecento 58

Art of Ancient Civilisations   61

Literature   65

Music   69

Cinema   72

Arts and crafts   74

Food and wine   75

Genova, St Andrea Cloisters
and Porta Soprana

W. Buss/HOA QUI

Sights   79

Abruzzo 80 – Amalfi 83-Anagni 86 –
Ancona 87 – Anzio 87 – Aosta 88 –
Aquileia 90 – Arezzo 91 – Promonto-
rio dell'Argentario 92 – Ascoli
Piceno 93 – Assisi 95 – Atri 98 –
Bari 99 – Barletta 101 – Bassano del
Grappa 101 – Belluno 102 – Ben-
evento 103 – Bergamo 103 –
Bologna 108 – Bolsena 115 – Bol-
zano 115 – Riviera del Brenta 116 –
Brescia 117 – Bressanone 119 – Brin-
disi 120 – Calabria 121 – Val
Camonica 124 – Palazzo Farnese di
Caprarola 124 – Capri 125 –
Capua 127 – Carrara 128 – Abbazia
di Casamari 129 – Reggia di
Caserta 130 – Castelfranco
Veneto 130 – Castellammare di Sta-
bia 131 – Castelli Romani 131 –
Cerveteri 132 – Chiavenna 132 – Chi-
eti 133 – Chiusi 134 – Parco Nazion-
ale del Cilento 134 – Cinque Terre 135
– Cividale del Friuli 136 – Civitavec-
chia 136 – Comacchio 137 –
Como 137 – Conegliano 137 – Cor-
tina d'Ampezzo 138 – Cortona 138 –
Cremona 139 – Crotone 140 –
Cuma 141 – Dolomiti 142 – Isola
d'Elba 147 – Ercolano 149 – Fab-
riano 150 – Faenza 151 – Fano 151 –
Fermo 152 – Ferrara 153 – Fie-
sole 156 – Firenze 157 – Forlì 175 –
Abbazia di Fossanova 176 –
Gaeta 176 – Promontorio del Gar-
gano 177 – Genova 178 –
Grado 183 – Grosseto 183 – Gub-
bio 184 – Ischia 186 – Jesi 187 –
Regione dei laghi 188 – L'Aquila 195
– Lecce 196 – Lignano 198 –
Livorno 198 – Loreto 199 – Lucca 200
– Mantova 204 – Massa Marit-

Pasta

Maximilian Stock Ltd/DIAF

tima 207 – Matera 208 – Merano 209 – Milano 210 – Modena 222 – Molise 223 – Abbazia di Montecassino 224 – Montecatini Terme 225 – Montefalco 226 – Abbazia di Monte Oliveto Maggiore 226 – Montepulciano 227 – Monte Sant'Angelo 228 – Monza 228 – Napoli 229 – Golfo di Napoli 242 – Novara 246 – Orvieto 246 – Ostia antica 248 – Otranto 251 – Padova 252 – Paestum 256 – Parma 257 – Pavia 260 – Certosa di Pavia 261 – Perugia 262 – Pesaro 265 – Piacenza 266 – Pienza 267 – Pisa 269 – Pistoia 272 – Golfo di Policastro 273 – Pompei 274 – Abbazia di Pomposa 278 – Promontorio di Portofino 279 – Potenza 280 – Pozzuoli 280 – Prato 280 – Puglia 282 – Ravello 286 – Ravenna 287 – Reggio di Calabria 290 – Reggio Emilia 291 – Rieti 292 – Rimini 292 – Riviera ligure 293 – Roma 297 – Sabbioneta 317 – Salerno 318 – Saluzzo 319 – San Gimignano 321 – Repubblica di Saxxxn Marino 323 – San Remo 323 – Sansepolcro 324 – Siena 325 – Sorrento 330 – Spoleto 330 – Subiaco 331 – Sulmona 331 – Taranto 332 – Tarquinia 333 – Terni 334 – Terracina 334 – Santuario della Madonna di Tirano 335 – Tivoli 335 – Todi 338 – Tolentino 339 – Torino 340 – Isole Tremiti 352 – Trento 353 – Treviso 355 – Trieste 356 – Terra dei Trulli 358 – Tuscania 359 – Udine 360 – Urbino 361 – Venezia 362 – Val Venosta 374 – Verona 375 – Vicenza 378 – Vipiteno 380 – Viterbo 381 – Volterra 382

Le isole 385

La Sardegna 386

Alghero 388 – Arzachena 389 – Barbagia 389 – Barumini 391 – Cagliari 391 – Costa Smeralda 393 – Arcipelago della Maddalena 393 – Nuoro 393 – Oristano 394 – Porto Torres 394 – Isola di Sant'Antioco 394 – Sassari 395 – Tharros 395 – Tortolì 395

La Sicilia 396

Agrigento 399 – Caltagirone 401 – Villa Romana del Casale 402 – Catania 402 – Cefalù 404 – Isole Egadi 404 – Enna 405 – Isole Eolie 405 – Erice 407 – Etna 408 – Marsala 408 – Messina 409 – Monreale 409 – Noto 410 – Palermo 411 – Isola di Pantelleria 417 – Ragusa 418 – Segesta 419 – Antica città di Selinunte 419 – Siracusa 420 – Taormina 423 – Tindari 424 – Trapani 424 – Ustica 425

Practical information 427

Main tourist routes	428
Travelling to Italy	429
Travelling in Italy	430
Accomodation and eating out	433
General and tourist information	434
Recreation	436
Nature parks	437
Further reading, films	438
Vocabulary	440
Calendar of events	442
Admission times and charges	446
Index	492

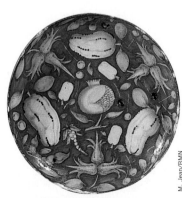

Faenza earthenware, 16C

M. Jean/RMN

Bologna

R. Mazin/DIAF

Maps
and plans

COMPANION PUBLICATIONS

Michelin map 988 Italia
– a practical map on a scale of 1:1 000 000 which shows the whole Italian road network.

Atlas Italia
– a practical, spiral-bound road atlas, on a scale of 1:300 000, with an alphabetical index of places and maps of 70 cities and conurbations.

Regional maps
– five regions maps on a scale of 1:400 000 which give detailed information on the area you wish to tour.

No 428 North-West
No 429 North-East
No 430 Centre
No 431 South
No 432 Sicily
No 433 Sardenia

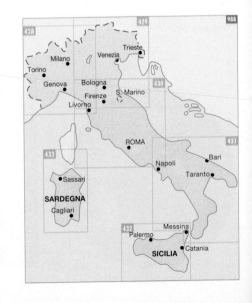

LIST OF MAPS
AND PLANS

Map of principal sights   10
Suggested touring programmes   14
Map of places to stay   18
Main tourist routes   428

Town plans

Arezzo   91
Assisi   96
Bari   99
Bergamo   105
Bologna   111
Brescia   118
Capri   127
Catania   402
Cremona   139
Ferrara   153
Fiesole   156
Firenze   165
Genova   182
Gubbio   185
Lecce   196
Lucca   201
Mantova   205
Milano   211
Milano: dettaglio del centro   214
Napoli   232
Orvieto   247
Padova   253
Palermo   412
Parma   258
Perugia   263
Pisa   270
Prato   281
Ravenna   288
Roma   307
Salerno   319
San Gimignano   321
Siena   329
Siracusa   422
Torino   346
Trieste   356
Venezia   369
Verona   376
Volterra   382

Touring maps

Abruzzo   80
Costiera Amalfitana   84
Valle d'Aosta   89
Gruppo del Brenta   355
Cagliari   391
Capri   126
Dolomiti   142
Isola d'Elba   147
Promontorio del Gargano   177
Isola d'Ischia   187
Regione dei laghi,   191
Golfo di Napoli   242

Promontorio di Portofino   279
Riviera Ligure di Ponente   294
Riviera Ligure di Levante   295
Sardegna   386
Sicilia   398

Maps of archeological zones

Agrigento: Valle dei Templi   399
Ercolano   149
Ostia   249
Paestum   256
Pompei   275
Tivoli: Villa Adriana   337

Using this guide

- The summary maps on the following pages are designed to assist you in planning your trip: the **Map of principal sights** identifies major sights and attractions, the **Touring programmes** propose regional driving itineraries and the **Places to stay map** points out pleasant holiday spots.

- We recommend that you read the **Introduction** before setting out on your trip. The background information it contains on history, the arts and traditional culture will prove most instructive and make your visit more meaningful.

- The main towns and attractions are presented in alphabetical order in the **Sights** section. In order to ensure quick, easy identification, original place names have been used throughout the guide. For Firenze and Siena, we have included a selection of addresses of hotels and restaurants, marked by a blue band. The clock symbol ⊘, placed after monuments or other sights, refers to the **Admission times and charges** section at the end of the guide, in which the names appear in the same order as in the Sights section.

- The **Practical information** section offers more useful addresses for planning your trip, seeking accommodation, indulging in outdoor activities and more; opening hours and admission prices for monuments, museums and other tourist attractions; festival and carnival dates; suggestions for thematic tours on scenic railways and through nature reserves etc.

- The **Index** lists attractions, famous people and events, and other subjects covered in the guide.

Let us hear from you. We are interested in your reaction to our guide, in any ideas you have to offer or good addresses you would like to share. Send your comments to Michelin Tyre PLC, Michelin Travel Publications, 38 Clarendon Road, Watford, Herts WD1 1SX, U.K. or TheGreenGuide-uk @ uk.michelin.com

B. Morandi/DIAF

Key

	Sight	Seaside Resort	Winter Sports Resort	Spa
Worth a journey	★★★	⚲⚲⚲	❋❋❋	⚕⚕⚕
Worth a detour	★★	⚲⚲	❋❋	⚕⚕
Interesting	★	⚲	❋	⚕

Tourism

⊙ Admission Times and Charges listed at the end of the guide

◉⇒ Sightseeing route with departure point indicated

🛉🛉🛉🛉 Ecclesiastical building

✡ 🕌 Synagogue – Mosque

🏛 Building (with main entrance)

■ Statue, small building

⊥ Wayside cross

◎ Fountain

—●—■—■ Fortified walls – Tower – Gate

►► Visit if time permits

AZ B Map co-ordinates locating sights

🛈 Tourist information

⋈ ⁂ Historic house, castle – Ruins

⌣ ☼ Dam – Factory or power station

☆ ⌒ Fort – Cave

▼ Ⅶ Viewing table – View

▲ Miscellaneous sight

Recreation

🏇 Racecourse

⛸ Skating rink

≋ ⊠ Outdoor, indoor swimming pool

⟁ Marina, moorings

⛺ Mountain refuge hut

□-■-■-□ Overhead cable-car

🚂 Tourist or steam railway

🏃 Waymarked footpath

◆ Outdoor leisure park/centre

🎪 Theme/Amusement park

🐃 Wildlife/Safari park, zoo

❀ Gardens, park, arboretum

🐦 Aviary, bird sanctuary

Additional symbols

═══ ══ Motorway (unclassified)

❶ ❶ Junction: complete, limited

⊏═⊐ ══ Pedestrian street

ᴵ══════ᴵ Unsuitable for traffic, street subject to restrictions

⊡⊡⊡ ---- Steps – Footpath

🚆 🚌 Railway – Coach station

□-+-+-+-□ Funicular – Rack-railway

—•— ◉ Tram – Metro, Underground

Bert (R.)... Main shopping street

⊗ ☏ Post office – Telephone centre

✉ Covered market

⁙ Barracks

△ Swing bridge

⋃ ✗ Quarry – Mine

Ⓑ Ⓕ Ferry (river and lake crossings)

⛴ Ferry services: Passengers and cars

⛵ Foot passengers only

③ Access route number common to MICHELIN maps and town plans

Abbreviations and special symbols

H Town hall (Municipio)

J Law courts (Palazzo di Giustizia)

M Museum (Museo)

P Local authority offices (Prefettura)

POL. Police station (Polizia) (in large towns: Questura)

T Theatre (Teatro)

U University (Università)

ⓐ Hotel

🏛 Nuraghe

🏛 Palace, villa

⚏ Temple, Greek and Roman ruins

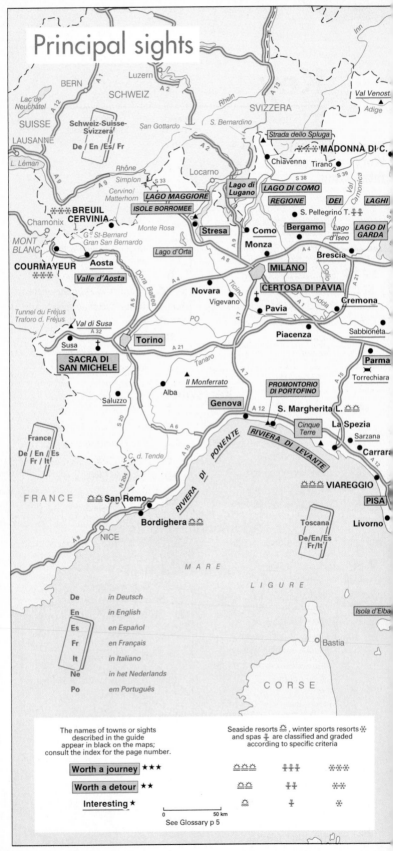

Principal sights

Val Venost
Adige

BERN
SCHWEIZ
Luzern
Schweiz-Suisse-Svizzera
De / En /Es/ Fr
Lac de Neuchâtel
SUISSE
LAUSANNE
L. Léman

Rhein
SVIZZERA
San Gottardo
S. Bernardino
Strada dello Spluga
Chiavenna
Tirano
MADONNA DI C.

Rhône
Simplon
Locarno
Cervino / Matterhorn
BREUIL CERVINIA
Chamonix
Monte Rosa
Gᵒ St-Bernard
Gran San Bernardo
MONT BLANC
COURMAYEUR
Aosta
Valle d'Aosta

LAGO MAGGIORE
ISOLE BORROMEE
Lago di Lugano
LAGO DI COMO
REGIONE
DEI
LAGHI
S. Pellegrino T.
Stresa
Como
Bergamo
Lago d'Iseo
LAGO DI GARDA
Monza
Lago d'Orta
MILANO
Brescia

Dora Baltea
Tunnel du Fréjus
Traforo d. Fréjus
Val di Susa
Susa
Torino
SACRA DI SAN MICHELE
Sáluzzo

Novara
Vigevano
Ticino
CERTOSA DI PAVIA
Pavia
PO
Piacenza
Adda
Cremona
Sabbioneta
Parma
Torrechiara

France
De / En // Es
Fr / It
C. d. Tende
Il Monferrato
Alba
Tanaro
Genova
PROMONTORIO DI PORTOFINO
S. Margherita L.
Cinque Terre
La Spezia
Sarzana
Carrara

FRANCE
RIVIERA DI PONENTE
RIVIERA DI LEVANTE
VIAREGGIO

San Remo
Bordighera
NICE
PISA
Toscana
De/En/Es
Fr/It
Livorno

MARE
LIGURE
Isola d'Elba
Bastia
CORSE

De	in Deutsch
En	in English
Es	en Español
Fr	en Français
It	in Italiano
Ne	in het Nederlands
Po	em Português

The names of towns or sights described in the guide appear in black on the maps; consult the index for the page number.

Seaside resorts ⚏, winter sports resorts ❄ and spas ♨ are classified and graded according to specific criteria

Worth a journey ★★★	⚏⚏⚏	♨♨♨	❄❄❄
Worth a detour ★★	⚏⚏	♨♨	❄❄
Interesting ★	⚏	♨	❄

0   50 km
See Glossary p 5

10

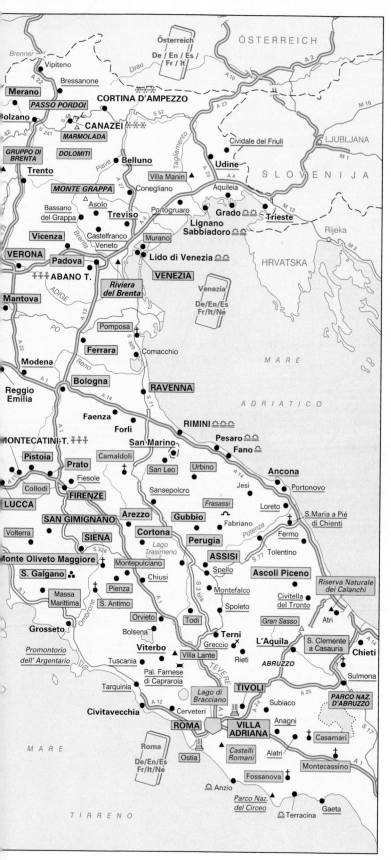

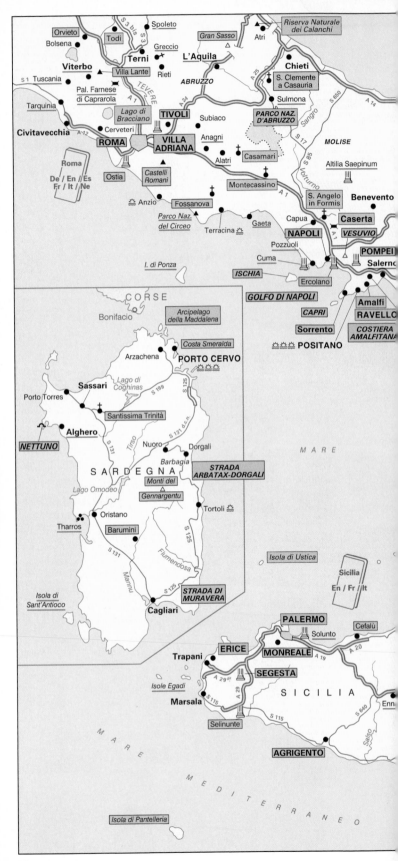

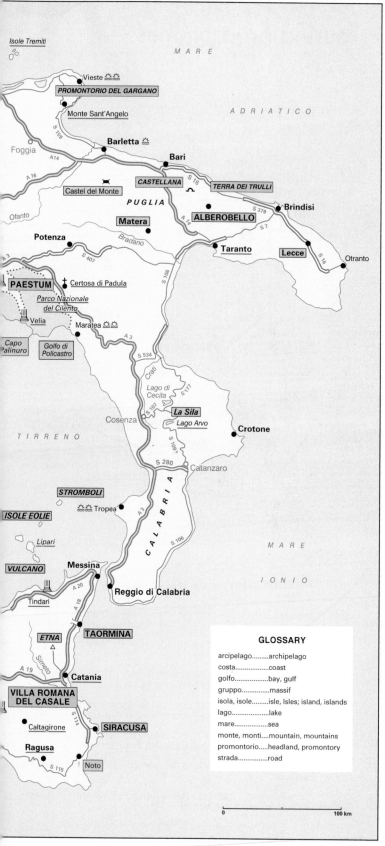

GLOSSARY

arcipelago	archipelago
costa	coast
golfo	bay, gulf
gruppo	massif
isola, isole	isle, Isles; island, islands
lago	lake
mare	sea
monte, monti	mountain, mountains
promontorio	headland, promontory
strada	road

Touring programmes

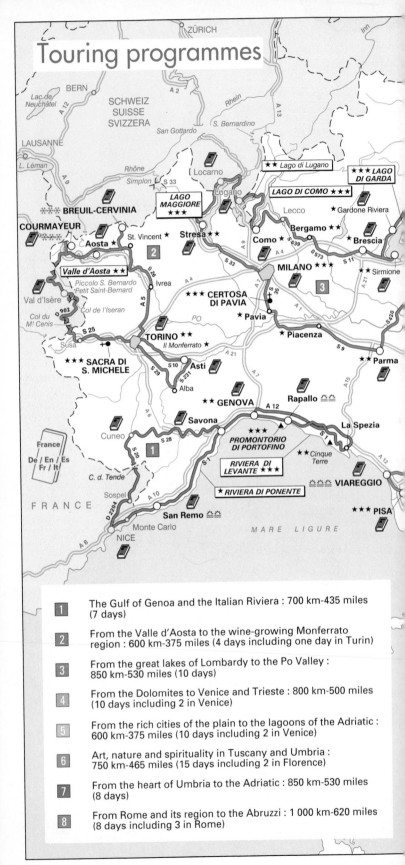

1	The Gulf of Genoa and the Italian Riviera : 700 km-435 miles (7 days)
2	From the Valle d'Aosta to the wine-growing Monferrato region : 600 km-375 miles (4 days including one day in Turin)
3	From the great lakes of Lombardy to the Po Valley : 850 km-530 miles (10 days)
4	From the Dolomites to Venice and Trieste : 800 km-500 miles (10 days including 2 in Venice)
5	From the rich cities of the plain to the lagoons of the Adriatic : 600 km-375 miles (10 days including 2 in Venice)
6	Art, nature and spirituality in Tuscany and Umbria : 750 km-465 miles (15 days including 2 in Florence)
7	From the heart of Umbria to the Adriatic : 850 km-530 miles (8 days)
8	From Rome and its region to the Abruzzi : 1 000 km-620 miles (8 days including 3 in Rome)

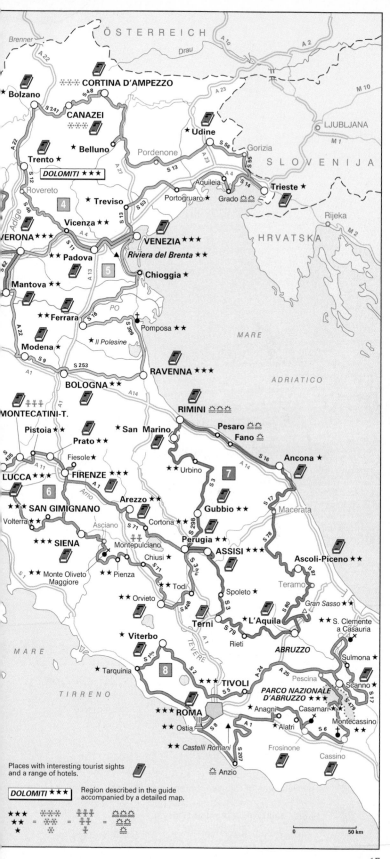

ÖSTERREICH

Brenner
Drau
A 10
A 2
M 10

Bolzano
✶✶✶ CORTINA D'AMPEZZO
CANAZEI ✶✶✶✶
LJUBLJANA

Belluno
★ Udine
M 1

Trento ★
Pordenone
Gorizia
SLOVENIJA

DOLOMITI ★★★
Rovereto
Aquileia
Trieste ★

4
★ Treviso
Portogruaro ★
Grado ♨♨

Vicenza ★★
HRVATSKA

VERONA ★★★
VENEZIA ★★★
Rijeka

★★ Padova
Riviera del Brenta ★★

Mantova ★★
5
Chioggia ★

PO

★★ Ferrara
Pomposa ★★
MARE

Modena ★
★ Il Polesine

RAVENNA ★★★
ADRIATICO

BOLOGNA ★★

✝✝✝
RIMINI ♨♨♨
MONTECATINI-T.

Pistoia ★★
★ San Marino
Pesaro ♨♨
Fano ♨

Prato ★★
Ancona ★

Fiesole ★
★★ Urbino
7

LUCCA ★★★
FIRENZE ★★★

6
Arezzo ★★
Gubbio ★★
Macerata

★★★ SAN GIMIGNANO
Cortona ★★
Perugia ★★
ASSISI ★★★

Volterra ★★
Asciano
Ascoli-Piceno ★★

★★★ SIENA
Montepulciano
Chiusi ★
Teramo

★★ Monte Oliveto Maggiore
★★ Pienza
★ Todi
Spoleto ★
Gran Sasso ★★

★★ Orvieto
L'Aquila ★
★★ S. Clemente a Casauria

Terni
Rieti
ABRUZZO

★ Viterbo
Sulmona ★

Tarquinia
8
Scanno ★

MARE
✶✶✶ TIVOLI
PARCO NAZIONALE D'ABRUZZO ★★★

TIRRENO
Pescina

★★★ ROMA
★ Anagni
Casamari
Montecassino ★★

★★ Ostia
★ Alatri

★★ Castelli Romani
Frosinone
Cassino

♨ Anzio

Places with interesting tourist sights and a range of hotels.

DOLOMITI ★★★   Region described in the guide accompanied by a detailed map.

★★★ = ✶✶✶ = ✝✝✝ = ♨♨♨
★★ = ✶✶ = ✝✝ = ♨♨
★ = ✶ = ✝ = ♨

0   50 km

15

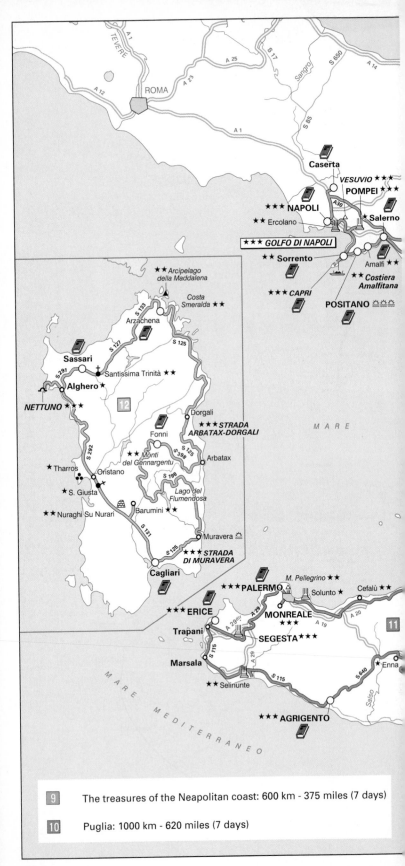

ROMA

A 1

Caserta

VESUVIO ★★★

★★★ NAPOLI

POMPEI ★★★

★★ Ercolano

Salerno

★★★ GOLFO DI NAPOLI

★★ Sorrento

Amalfi ★★

★★★ CAPRI

★★ Costiera Amalfitana

POSITANO 🏛🏛🏛

★★ Arcipelago della Maddalena

Costa Smeralda ★★

Arzachena

Sassari

Santissima Trinità ★★

Alghero ★

NETTUNO ★★★

12

Dorgali

★★★ STRADA ARBATAX-DORGALI

Fonni

★★ Monti del Gennargentu

Arbatax

★ Tharros

Oristano

★ S. Giusta

Lago del Flumendosa

★★ Nuraghi Su Nurari

Barumini ★★

Muravera 🏛

S 131

S 125

★★★ STRADA DI MURAVERA

Cagliari

M. Pellegrino ★★

★★★ PALERMO

Solunto ★

Cefalù ★★

★★★ ERICE

MONREALE ★★★

Trapani

SEGESTA ★★★

11

Marsala

Enna ★

★★ Selinunte

★★★ AGRIGENTO

MARE MEDITERRANEO

9   The treasures of the Neapolitan coast: 600 km - 375 miles (7 days)

10   Puglia: 1000 km - 620 miles (7 days)

16

★★★ *PROMONTORIO DEL GARGANO*

MARE

ADRIATICO

Peschici ☼☼
Vieste ☼☼
S 528

☼ Manfredonia

S 159

A 14

Barletta ☼

S 16

Bari

A 16

★★ Castel
del Monte

★★★ *CASTELLANA*

S 378

TERRA
DEI TRULLI ★★★

★★★ **ALBEROBELLO**

S 172   S 379

Brindisi

PUGLIA

9

★★ **Matera**

A 14

S 7   S 106

Taranto ★

Lecce ★★

S 16

10

S 611

S 407

☼ Porto Cesareo

Gallipoli ☼

S 598

PAESTUM ★★★

A 3

Velia ★

★ Rocca Imperatore

267

Maratea ☼☼

S 18

☼☼ Palinuro

★★ *Golfo di
Policastro*

S 534

S 117

Cosenza

Lago Arvo ★

★★ **La Sila**

TIRRENO

A 3

S 280

S 106

Catanzaro

MARE

S 18

IONIO

Serra S. Bruno

A 3

★ *Costa Viola*

Stilo ★

Messina

CALABRIA

Aspromonte ★

★ Tindari

A 20

Reggio di Calabria

S 113

A 18

★ Pentedattilo

S 114

TAORMINA ★★★

★★★ *ETNA*
△

A 19

Simeto

Catania ★

**VILLA ROMANA
DEL CASALE** ★★★

Caltagirone ★

SIRACUSA ★★★

S 117

★ **Ragusa**

S 115

★★ Noto

0   100 km

11   Sicily and Calabria: 1800 km - 1120 miles (10 days including 7 in Sicily)

12   Sardinia: 1100 km - 685 miles (7 days)

17

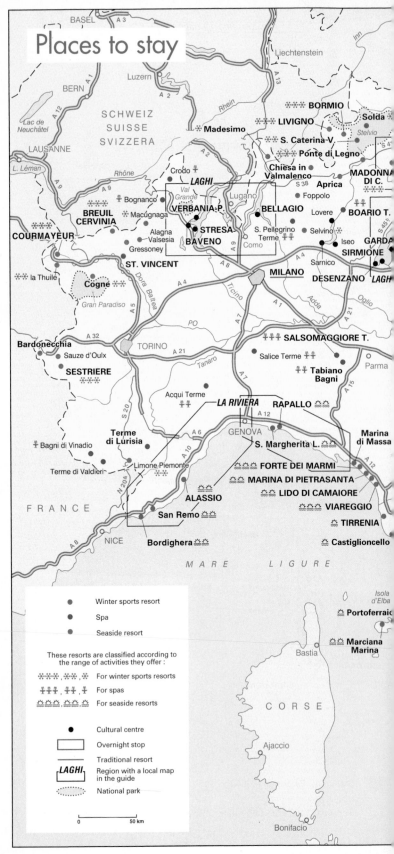

Places to stay

BASEL · A 3
BERN
Luzern
SCHWEIZ
SUISSE
SVIZZERA
Lac de Neuchâtel
LAUSANNE
L. Léman
Liechtenstein
Inn
Rhein
A 13
Rhône
A 2
✳ Madesimo
Crodo ‡
LAGHI
Val Grande
Lugano
Bognanco ‡
✳ Macúgnaga
BREUIL CERVINIA ✳✳✳
Alagna Valsesia
COURMAYEUR
Gressoney
✳✳ la Thuile
Cogne ✳✳
Gran Paradiso
ST. VINCENT
Dora Baltea
Bardonecchia
Sauze d'Oulx
TORINO
SESTRIERE ✳✳✳
A 32
A 21
A 4
Tanaro
Acqui Terme ‡‡
Terme di Lúrisia
‡ Bagni di Vinadio
Terme di Valdieri
Limone Piemonte ✳✳
FRANCE
NICE
A 8
San Remo ☖☖
Bordighera ☖☖
ALASSIO ☖☖
S 20
N 204
LA RIVIERA
A 6
A 10
GENOVA
A 12
RAPALLO ☖☖
S. Margherita L. ☖☖
Terme

✳✳✳ BORMIO
✳✳✳ LIVIGNO
Solda ✳
Stelvio
✳✳ S. Caterina-V.
✳✳ Ponte di Legno
Chiesa in Valmalenco ✳
S 38
Aprica
Foppolo
MADONNA DI C.
VERBANIA-P. ✳
BELLAGIO
Lovere
BOARIO T. ‡‡
STRESA ✳
BAVENO
S. Pellegrino Terme ‡‡
Selvino ✳
Iseo
GARDA
SIRMIONE
Como
A 9
A 8
Sarnico
MILANO
Ticino
Adda
A 4
DESENZANO
LAGHI
Oglio
A 21
A 1
PO
SALSOMAGGIORE T. ‡‡‡
A 7
Salice Terme ‡‡
‡‡ Tabiano Bagni
Parma
A 15
Marina di Massa
A 12
FORTE DEI MARMI ☖☖☖
MARINA DI PIETRASANTA ☖☖
LIDO DI CAMAIORE ☖☖
VIAREGGIO ☖☖☖
TIRRENIA ☖
Castiglioncello ☖

MARE   LIGURE

Isola d'Elba
Portoferraio ☖
Marciana Marina ☖☖
Bastia
CORSE
Ajaccio
Bonifacio

●	Winter sports resort
●	Spa
●	Seaside resort

These resorts are classified according to the range of activities they offer:

✳✳✳, ✳✳, ✳ For winter sports resorts
‡‡‡, ‡‡, ‡ For spas
☖☖☖, ☖☖, ☖ For seaside resorts

●	Cultural centre
▭	Overnight stop
—	Traditional resort
LAGHI	Region with a local map in the guide
⬭	National park

0 ——— 50 km

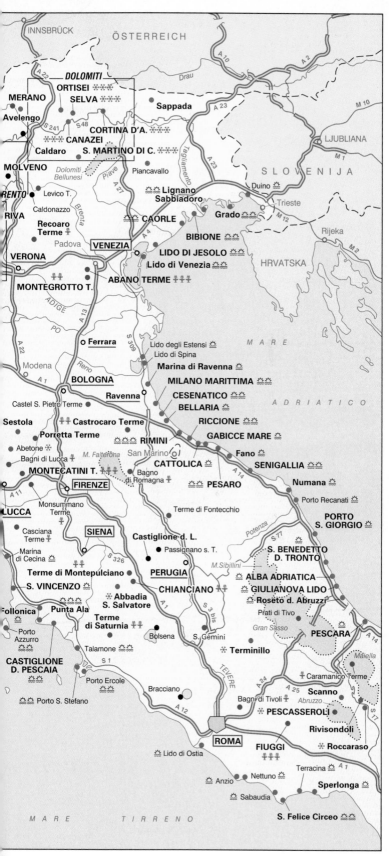

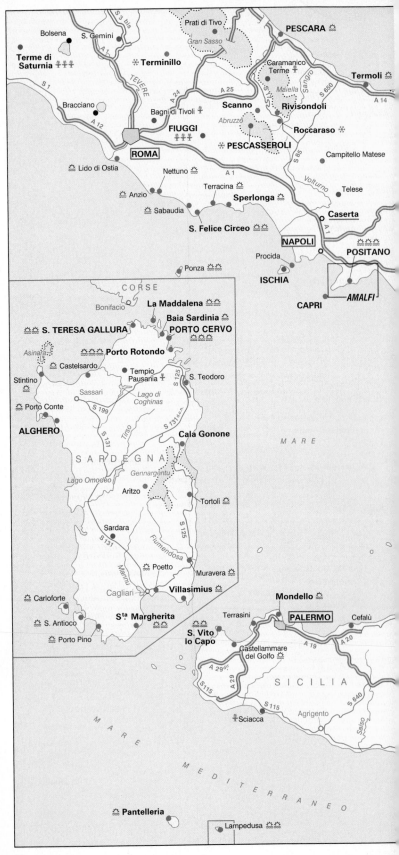

20

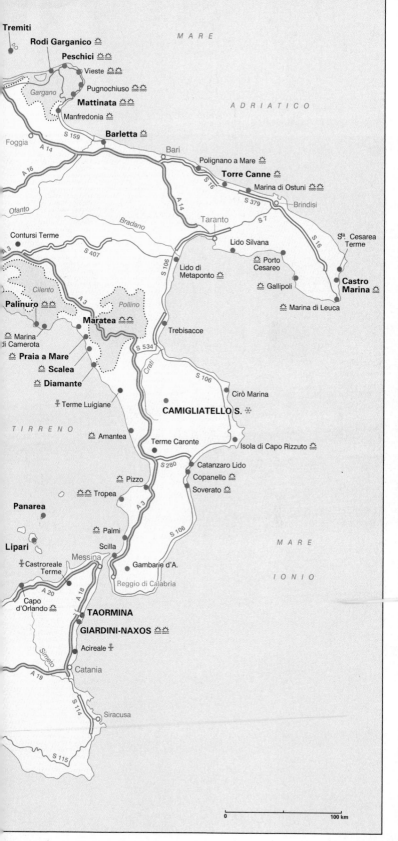

A view of the Odle mountains from Val di Funes

Introduction

Italy Today

LANDSCAPE

The boot of Italy which stretches 1 300km/808mi from north to south, juts into the Mediterranean between Greece and Spain. This peninsula enjoys an extraordinary variety of climate and topography.

Italy's rugged relief rises from great swathes of plain which cover approximately a quarter of its total area of 301 262km²/139 087sq mi. Its coastline (almost 7 500km/4 660mi long) is washed by the waters of four inner seas: the Ligurian, Tyrrhenian, Ionian and Adriatic.

The **Alps**, which were created as the earth's crust folded in the Tertiary Era, form a gigantic barrier with northern Europe and are a formidable source of hydro-electric power. Several passes and tunnels cross the Alps, which reach their highest peak at Mont Blanc (4 810m/15 790ft) to link Italy with France and northern Europe. On the southern side of the Alps between the fertile Po valley and the foothills there are several lakes of glacial origin.

The **Apennines**, a range of limestone hills formed by a more recent Tertiary geological movement, extend from Genoa down into Sicily, dividing the country into two zones. The peaks of this limestone chain are generally lower than those of the Alps. The

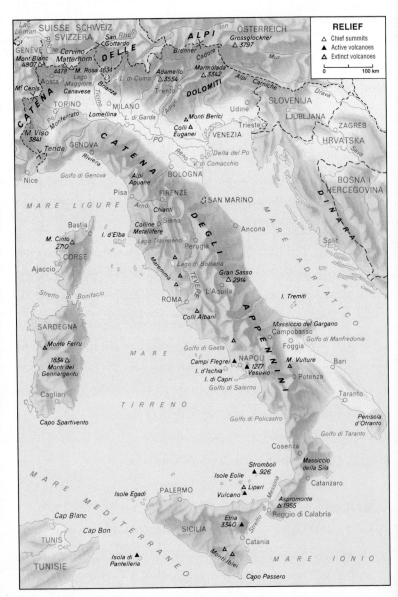

Corno Grande at 2 914m/9 566ft is the highest mountain of the chain's tallest massif, the Gran Sasso. The section between Naples and Sicily is subject to tectonic plate movements resulting in earthquakes, restless volcanoes and marked changes in sea level. Such activity in turn has altered the relief of this southern part of the peninsula.

By the end of 1997 the population of Italy had reached 57 563 344, with an average density of 191 inhabitants/km^2, making it the fourth most densely populated country in Europe after the Benelux countries, the United Kingdom and Germany. Towns are more numerous in northern and central Italy and approximately one third of the population is concentrated in the provincial capitals.

The trend towards a decrease in population is counterbalanced by a substantial influx of immigrants, resulting in a noticeable increase in the number of foreigners resident in Italy in recent years. In order of size, the largest communities are from Morocco, ex-Yugoslavia, Albania, the Philippines, the United States, Tunisia, China, Senegal and Germany.

POLITICAL AND ADMINISTRATIVE ORGANISATION

The referendum of 2 June 1946 set up the Republic and the Constitution of 1 January 1948, a Parliamentary Republic headed by a President who holds office for seven years, with two Houses of Parliament – the Chamber of Deputies and the Senate. Members of both houses are elected by universal suffrage. Since 1994, the electoral system used is mainly based on a majority vote, although 25% of the seats are still assigned by proportional representation.

The Italian State is unusual in that it is neither unitary nor federal. Political power is shared by two autonomous tiers: the State or central government and the regional councils. The latter are also chosen by the people and enjoy some legislative, administrative and financial powers. Their authority must not exceed those

Abruzzo: Abruzzi	**Lazio:** Latium	**Sicilia:** Sicily
Basilicata: Basilicata	**Liguria:** Liguria	**Toscana:** Tuscany
Calabria: Calabria	**Lombardia:** Lombardy	**Trentino-Alto Adige:**
Campania: Campania	**Marche:** Marche	Trentino-Alto
Emilia-Romagna:	**Molise:** Molise	Adige
Emilia-Romagna	**Piemonte:** Piedmont	**Umbria:** Umbria
Friuli Venezia Giulia:	**Puglia:** Puglia	**Valle d'Aosta:** Valle d'Aosta
Friuli-Venezia Giulia	**Sardegna:** Sardinia	**Veneto:** Veneto

prescribed by the laws passed or approved at national level. The 1948 constitution established 20 regions, although it was not enacted until 1970. Five of these (Sicily, Sardinia, Trentino-Alto Adige, Friuli-Venezia Giulia and Valle d'Aosta) have a special statute and enjoy greater administrative autonomy. The regions are subdivided into 95 provinces, which are themselves composed of districts, each headed by a *Sindaco*.

THE REGIONS OF ITALY

Valle d'Aosta – This great deep furrow between the highest mountains in Europe is watered by the Dora Baltea River, whose tributaries run along picturesque lateral valleys: the Valtournenche, Val di Gressoney, Val d'Ayas, Val Grisenche. The **Parco Nazionale del Gran Paradiso** is found in the southwest of the region.

Aosta, well situated in the centre of the valley, is the capital of this region and has enjoyed a degree of administrative autonomy since 1947. In addition to the pastoral activities of the mountain people, the valley's economy depends primarily on tourism which has developed as a result of the Great St Bernard and Mont Blanc tunnels and the hydroelectric and iron and steel industries.

From Pont-St-Martin to Courmayeur the towns and villages have retained French names; many of the local inhabitants still speak French and other varied dialects.

Snow-covered peaks above Courmayeur

Piedmont – Piedmont, at the foot of the mountain range, consists mainly of the extensive Po Plain. Surrounded on three sides by the Alps and the Apennines this fertile area is made up of grassland alternating with fields planted with cereals and rice (three-fifths of the Italian rice production is concentrated in the districts of Vercelli and Novara). The many rivers which cross the region (the Ticino, Sesia, Dora Baltea and Riparia, Tanaro, Bormida and Scrivia) are mainly found in the valley of the river **Po**, which has its source at Pian del Re on Monviso (approximately 100km/62mi southwest of Turin), and which flows for 652km/407mi before joining the Adriatic. Southeast of Turin the gently rolling chalk hills of the **Monferrato** bear the well-known Asti vines and produce the Gorgonzola cheese. Numerous hydroelectric power stations supply electricity to local industry: textile factories in Biella and the metal, engineering and chemical works in Turin. **Turin**, on the Po, is a dynamic and busy town famous for its fashion houses and cars.

Lombardy – Lombardy's emphasis on commercial activity is mainly due to its favourable geographical location in the green Po plain between the Ticino and the Mincio, which together with the Adda supply Lakes Maggiore, Como and Garda. To the north the great lake valleys give access to the Alpine passes. Lombardy, with the mulberry bushes of the **Brianza** district, takes first place in the production of silk. The permanent grazing and grasslands are used by modern dairy farming and processing industries. In the **Lomellina** district, large areas are given over to rice growing.

The many towns, scattered throughout the countryside, were important banking and trading centres in medieval and Renaissance times and spread the name of the Lombards all over Europe. Today Como is the centre of the silk industry, Brescia steel, chemical and engineering industries, Bergamo textile and engineering works, Mantua petrochemicals and plastics, Cremona agriculture and Pavia the seat of an important university.

It is Milan, the economic capital of Italy, that has the highest density of population and businesses. This town with its modern architecture and numerous commercial enterprises and cultural institutions has an outer ring of industrial suburbs which are the home base of textile, oil, chemical, steel and food industries.

Veneto (Venetia) – This comprises mainly the vast alluvial Po Plain and its tributaries which are overlooked in the north by the Venetian Pre-Alps, and further north again in the **Cadore** district by the western massifs of the Dolomites. It is an agricultural region growing wheat, maize, mulberry bushes, olives, fruit trees and vines. The industrial sector includes oil refineries, smelting works and chemical plants which are concentrated in the vicinity of Venice at Mestre-Marghera, as well as a large production of hydro-electric energy in the valleys of the Pre-Alps. The latter supplies the textile industry.

The landscape is punctuated by two small volcanic groups, the **Berici Mountains** south of Vicenza and the **Euganean Hills** near Padua. The slopes of these blackish heights support vines and peach orchards, and there are several hot springs.

In the **Po delta** (Polesina, *see COMACCHIO*) and that of the Adige lie improverished, grandiose and desolate areas, subject to flooding. Following reclamation certain areas are farmed on an industrial scale for wheat and sugar beet. The coastline takes the form of lagoons *(lido)* separated from the sea by spits of sand pierced by gaps *(porti)*. **Venice**, whose industrial sector is continually growing, is built on piles in one of these lagoons.

Trentino-Alto Adige – This is one of five Italian regions to enjoy a special autonomous statute and the people are partly of Germanic culture and German-speaking. The area includes the Adige and Isarco valleys and the surrounding mountains. The Adige Valley, at the southern exit from the Brenner Pass, has always been easy of access and much used by traffic. Though deep, it opens out towards the sunny south and is very fertile. Cereals are grown on the flatter areas of the valley bottom, with vines and fruit trees on the lower slopes and pastures above. Avelengo in the vicinity of Merano is well known for its breed of horses. **Bolzano** and **Trento**, where there is some industrial development, are the regional commercial centres.

The highly-eroded limestone massif of the **Dolomites** extends across the Veneto and Trentino-Alto Adige.

Friuli-Venezia Giulia – This region prolongs the Veneto to the east and it forms the Italian boundary with Austria and Slovenia. The area enjoys a large degree of autonomy in administrative and cultural affairs. In the north is the schistous massif of the **Carnic Alps** with its forests of conifers and alpine pastures. Friuli-Venezia Giulia is an important silkworm breeding and spinning area. Udine is one of the busiest towns. By way of the **Trieste** Riviera you will reach this town which was once the busy port of Austria and now trades with the Far East. Trieste is still subject to a special statute.

Emilia-Romagna – The plain skirting the Apennines derives its name from the Via Emilia, a straight Roman road that crosses it from Piacenza to Rimini. South and east of Bologna the district is known as **Romagna**. Its soil, which is intensively cultivated, is among the best in Italy for wheat and beet. The rhythm of the landscape of extensive fields is punctuated at intervals by rows of mulberries and vines clinging to tall poles, and of maples or elms. Other vines grow on the slopes of the Apennines.

The towns are strung out along the Via Emilia: the most important, **Bologna**, famous for its very old university, is today a communications and industrial (steel, engineering and food) centre and a market for wheat and pigs.

The region to the east of Ferrara through which the Po river runs is devoted to rice growing. To the south is an area of great lagoons, **Valli di Comacchio**, where fishermen catch eels.

Liguria – Liguria, furrowed by deep, narrow valleys at right angles to the coast, had a maritime civilisation before the Roman era. The steep slopes of the inner valleys are dotted with poor hilltop villages, watching over groves of chestnut or olive trees and cultivated terraces. The rocky, indented coastline has few fish to offer but has enjoyed heavy coastal traffic since the time of the Ligurians, facilitated by many small deep-water ports. The Roman Empire gave its present appearance to the country, with olive groves and vineyards, now complemented by vegetables, fruit (melons and peaches) and flowers grown on an industrial scale.

The **Riviera di Ponente** (Western Riviera) west of Genoa, is sunnier and more sheltered than the **Riviera di Levante** (Eastern Riviera), but the latter has a more luxuriant vegetation. The chief towns are Imperia, Savona and **Genoa** (shipyards, steel production, oil terminal and thermal power station) and La Spezia (naval base, commercial port, thermal power station and arms manufacture).

Tuscany – The harmony of the beautiful Tuscan landscape of low-lying hills with graceful curves affording wide views and planted with olive groves, vineyards and cypress trees bathed in the soft, golden light, reflects the great artistic sense of the Tuscan people.

The region has a variety of soils. The Tuscan Archipelago, with the mountainous **Island of Elba** and its rich iron-bearing deposits, faces a shore which is sometimes rocky (south of Livorno), sometimes flat and sandy as in the area around Viareggio, known as **Versilia**. To the north of the Arno the **Apuan Alps** are quarried for marble (Carrara).

In the heart of Tuscany lies the fertile and beautiful **Arno Basin**, an ideal setting for **Florence**. Vines and silvery olives alternate with fields of wheat, tobacco and maize. Peppers, pumpkins and the famous Lucca beans grow among the mulberries. The old farms, with their distinctive grand architectural style, often stand alone on hill tops.

Sienese landscape

Southern Tuscany is a land of hills, soft and vine-clad in the **Chianti** district south of Florence, quiet and pastoral near Siena, dry and desolate round Monte Oliveto Maggiore, and massive and mysterious in the area of the **Colli Metalliferi** (metal-bearing hills) south of Volterra. Bordering Lazio, **Maremma**, with its melancholy beauty, was once a marshy district haunted by bandits and shepherds. Much of the area has now been reclaimed.

Umbria – The land of St Francis is a country of hills, valleys and river basins, where the poplars raise their rustling heads to limpid skies. This is the green Umbria of the Clitumnus Valley **(Valle del Clitunno)**, whose pastures were famous in ancient times. Umbria has two lakes, **Trasimeno** and Piediluco, and many rivers, including the Tiber. Medieval cities which succeeded Etruscan settlements overlook ravines and valleys: grim Gubbio, haughty **Perugia**, the capital of Umbria, Assisi, Spoleto and Spello. Others stand in the centre of a plain, such as Foligno and Terni, the metallurgical centre.

Marches – So called because they were formerly frontier provinces of the Frankish Empire and papal domains, the Marches form a much sub-divided area between San Marino and Ascoli Piceno, where the parallel spurs of the Apennines run down into the Adriatic, forming a series of deep, narrow valleys. There is, however, a flat and rectangular coastal belt dotted with beaches and canal-ports. Apart from the capital, Ancona, a busy port, most of the old towns are built on commanding sites; Urbino (centre of the arts) and Loreto (church) are noteworthy.

Lazio (Latium) – Lying between the Tyrrhenian Sea and the Apennines, from Tuscan Maremma to Gaeta, Latium, the cradle of Roman civilisation, borders a sandy coast whose ancient ports, such as Ostia at the mouth of the Tiber, have silted up. Civitavecchia today is the only modern port on the coastline. In the centre of Lazio, **Rome**, the Italian capital and seat of the Catholic Church, is mainly a residential city and the headquarters of both public and religious organisations. To the east and north, volcanic hills, with lonely lakes in their craters, overlook the famous **Roman Campagna**, beloved by the writers and painters who have often described its great, desolate expanses, dotted with ancient ruins. Today this area, formerly a hotbed of malaria, has regained a degree of activity: the drainage of the Pontine Marches, near Latina, was a spectacular achievement. Cassino is the most important industrial centre.

To the south is the distinctive **Ciociaria**. This area takes its name from the shoes (ciocie), which are part of the traditional costume. They have thick soles and thongs wound round the calf of the leg. The main centres are Frosinone and Casino.

Abruzzi – This is the part of the Apennines which most suggests a country of high mountains, grand and wild, with its **Gran Sasso** and **Maiella Massifs**. The **Parco Nazionale d'Abruzzo**, the doyen of the Italian national parks, was established in the Upper Sangro Valley in 1921. In basins sheltered from the wind are vineyards, almond and olive groves, while industry is concentrated in the Chieti-Pescara zone and other areas such as Vasto (glass making), Sulmona (car factories), L'Aquila (steel works) and Avezzano (textile and food industries). The tourist industry is also important for the coastal regions and the winter resorts of the Gran Sasso massif.

Molise - Molise, with its capital, **Campobasso**, extends south of the Abruzzi, with which it has several common features: a mountainous relief, dark valleys and wild forests which are still haunted by wolves. The region is bordered to the west by the Maiella. The main industry can be found in the Termoli area, although agriculture still forms the basis of the local economy. The main crops are wheat, oats, maize, potatoes and vines.

Campania - Campania forms a fertile crescent around the Bay of Naples, where hemp, tobacco and cereals alternate with olive groves and vineyards. The charm and mystery of the **Bay of Naples**, which once stirred the imagination of the ancients, is dominated by the characteristic silhouette of **Vesuvius**. Although the coast has lost much of its charm owing to building developments, the **Sorrento Peninsula** and the **Island of Capri** are two notable beauty spots.

Puglia (Apulia), Basilicata and Calabria – These three regions cover the foot of the Italian "boot". Puglia, on the east side, facing the Adriatic, has many assets. Cereals are grown in the plain between Foggia and Manfredonia and in the plains of Bari, Taranto, Lecce and Brindisi. Vines flourish almost everywhere and are associated with olives (the Apulian production of olive oil represents 10% of the world total) and almonds on the coast. The elevation of the **Gargano Promontory**, otherwise known as the "boot's spur", is distinctive.
Bari, the capital of Puglia, is a busy port, which still enjoys numerous trading links with the Middle East. Along with Taranto and Brindisi it is one of the three main industrial centres in the region. Basilicata or **Lucania**, and Calabria, comprise very different types of country; the rocky corniche from the Gulf of Policastro to Reggio; the grim, grand mountains of the **Sila Massif** with its extensive mountain pastures and wide horizons; and at the southern extremity of the peninsula between two inner seas, lies the **Aspromonte Massif** clad with pine, beech and chestnut forests.

Sardinia and Sicily - *See SARDINIA and SICILY at the end of the Guide.*

ECONOMY

Far from being hampered by its illustrious past, Italy has transformed its essentially agricultural economy into that of an industrial power which is today one of the most active in Europe and ranks among the seven most industrialised countries in the world. Of the working population, 61.1% are employed in the tertiary sector, 32.1% in industry and only 6.8% in agriculture, compared with 20.1% in 1971.

In addition to the traditional crops and stock raising, Italy has specialised in **rice** growing (Po Plain) and the production of **silk** (Lombardy and Venetia). Lacking in raw materials such as coal and iron ore, the Italian industrial sector has been geared to manufacturing industries where cheap labour is more important than raw materials. Italy has always been an important manufacturer of **motor vehicles** and small machines such as sewing machines, typewriters and other domestic appliances. True to the image of Italy, a major regional industry is the manufacture of **pasta**, the national dish, in all its forms to meet both the home market and export requirements.

The southern part of the peninsula is an exception in that it remains economically underdeveloped. The **Mezzogiorno** (impoverished south) as it is known, extends southwards from a line joining the Gulf of Gaeta to the southern edge of the Abruzzi. The economic backwardness of this area has increased ever since the unification of Italy. In 1950 a special organisation and a fund were created to develop both the agricultural and industrial sectors of this area, which has a particularly small working population. Policies included agrarian reform, with the subdividing of large estates, soil improvement, land reclamation and reafforestation, and also the creation of gigantic industrial complexes - often badly integrated - and public works projects such as the building of dams.

Press - As a general rule the press is decentralised, at least as regards daily newspapers. The Rome *La Repubblica*, the Turin *La Stampa* and the Milan *Il Corriere della Sera* as well as the most important financial daily the Milan *Il Sole 24 ore* are the only papers distributed all over Italy.
The Italian love of sport means that there are three sports dailies: the Milan *La Gazzetta dello Sport* and the Turin *Tuttosport* in the north, and the Rome *Il Corriere dello Sport-Stadio* in the south. In addition the weekly *Guerin Sportivo* has a national circulation.

Fashion - The Italians who are lively and passionate by nature show great fashion flair. Fashion shows are held at yearly intervals in Rome and Florence (Palazzo Pitti) but the fashion capital is undoubtedly Milan where every year the best ready-to-wear collection for women's fashion is awarded the *Occhio d'Oro*. Many great designers have salons in Milan: Armani, Versace, Gianfranco Ferré, Nicola Trussardi, Dolce e Gabbana, Mila Schön, Laura Biagiotti, Romeo Gigli as well as the avant-garde stylists Krizia and Moschino. Valentino and the Fendi sisters have set up their operation in Rome.
Fashion-related professions and products are part of one of the most successful industrial sectors in Italy.
The clothing industry is concentrated mainly in Lombardy, Venetia (Benetton and Stefanel for knitwear), Tuscany and Emilia-Romagna. Como is famous for silk wear, Prato and Biella for wool products, Florence for leather goods (Gucci) and Vicenza for jewellery.

Historical Table and Notes

Ancient Civilisations

Since 2000 BC and throughout antiquity, Italy, the meeting-place of races, has seen the Etruscan, Greek and Latin civilisations flourish on her soil. Two thousand years later, Western civilisation is still impregnated with them. Greeks, Etruscans and Romans were preceded by two peoples who came from the north: the **Ligurians**, who also occupied southern Gaul and the Iberian Peninsula, and the Italics or **Italiots**, who settled in Umbria and Latium and from whom the Latins sprang. The former transmitted their fair hair and blue eyes to some of the present inhabitants of Liguria. The latter built acropolises of which the gigantic foundations still exist in some places, as for instance at Alatri.

Akragas: Agrigento
Caere: Cerveteri
Clusium: Chiusi
Faesulae: Fiesole
Felsina: Bologna
Poseidonia: Paestum
Selinus: Selinunte
Tuder: Todi
Velitrae: Velletri
Veii: Veio
Volsinii: Bolsena
Zancle: Messina

The Greeks

After the **Phoenicians** had settled at Carthage and set up trading posts, the Greeks founded a large number of colonies on the coasts of Sicily and southern Italy (8C BC), known as **Magna Graecia**. It included Ionian, Achaean and Dorian colonies, named after the Greek peoples who had colonised them. The social unit was the "city". The 6C and 5C BC marked the zenith of Greek civilisation in Italy, corresponding to the period of Pericles in Athens. Greek seaborne trade was so successful that Syracuse soon rivalled Athens. Syracuse and Taranto were the two main centres of this refined civilisation. Philosophers, scientists and writers settled in Sicily. Aeschylus lived at Gela. Theocritus defined the rules of bucolic poetry and Archimedes was murdered by a Roman soldier in Syracuse.

But rivalry between these many and varied cities led to warfare, which, with Carthaginian raids, led to decline, culminating in the Roman conquest at the end of the 3C BC.

Greek mythology

The shores of Sicily and southern Italy held a sort of fascination for the ancient Greeks, who regarded them as the limits of the inhabited earth. Many scenes of Greek mythology are set there: the Phlegrean Fields, near Naples, hid the entrance to the Kingdom of Hades; Zeus routed the Titans, with the help of Hercules, on Etna, where the Cyclops lived and Hephaestus, the God of Fire, had his forges; Kore, the daughter of Demeter, was kidnapped by Hades, who had emerged from the River Tartara near Enna. In the *Odyssey*, Homer (9C BC) relates the adventures of Ulysses (Odysseus) after the siege of Troy, sailing between Scylla and Charybdis in the Straits of Messina and resisting the temptations of the Sirens in the Gulf of Sorrento. Pindar (5C BC) describes these mysterious shores, to which Virgil (1C BC) also refers in the *Aeneid*.

The Etruscans

While the Greeks were disseminating their civilisation throughout the south of the peninsula and Sicily, the Etruscans were building up in central Italy, from the 8C BC onwards, a powerful empire whose growth was checked only by that of Rome (3C BC). They are a little-known people whose alphabet along with certain tombstone inscriptions have now been deciphered. Some authorities think they were natives of these parts; others, following the example of Herodotus, say they came from Lydia in Asia Minor. The Etruscans at first occupied the area between the Arno and the Tiber *(see map)* but later spread into Campania and the Po Plain. They reached their zenith in the 6C BC. **Etruria** then comprised a federation of 12 city-states known as *lucumonies*, which included the cities of Tarquinia, Vulci, Vetulonia, Cerveteri, Arezzo, Chiusi, Roselle, Volterra, Cortona, Perugia, Veii and Volsinii (present-day Bolsena). Having grown rich by working iron (Island of Elba), copper and silver mines and by trading in the western Mediterranean, the Etruscans, who were artisans and technicians, had a civilisation derived from a mixture of savagery and refinement.

Auspices and haruspices

The Etruscan gods were the same as those of the Greeks, and included the trinity of Tinia (Zeus), Uni (Hera) and Minerva (Athena), who were later introduced to the Romans by the Etruscan kings. The Etruscans believed in life after death and in divination, and they studied the entrails of animals (for haruspices) and the flight of birds (for auspices), a form of superstition which the Romans adopted and developed.

From the foundation of Rome to the fall of the Roman Empire

BC	From the Origins to the Empire (753-27 BC)
753	Foundation of Rome by Romulus according to legend. (In fact it was born of the union of Latin and Sabine villages in the 8C.)
7C-6C	Royal Dynasty of the Tarquins. Power is divided between the king, the senate, representing the great patrician families, and the *comitia*, representing the rich families.
509	Establishment of the Republic: the king's powers are conferred on two consuls, elected for one year.
451-449	Law of the XII Tables, instituting equality between patricians and plebeians.
390	The Gauls invade Italy and take Rome but are expelled by Camillus.
281-272	War against Pyrrhus, King of Epirus; submission of the southern part of the peninsula to Rome.
264-241	First Punic War: Carthage abandons Sicily to the Romans.
218-201	Second Punic War. **Hannibal** crosses the Alps and defeats the Romans at Lake Trasimeno. Hannibal routs the Romans at Cannae and halts at Capua *(see CAPUA)*. In 210 **Scipio** carries war into Spain, and in 204 he lands in Africa. Hannibal is recalled to Carthage. Scipio defeats Hannibal at Zama in 202.
146	Macedonia and Greece become Roman provinces. Capture and destruction of Carthage.
133	Occupation of all Spain and end of the Mediterranean campaigns.
133-121	Failure of the policy of the Gracchi, who promoted popular agrarian laws.
118	The Romans in Gaul.
112-105	War against Jugurtha, King of Numidia (now Algeria).
102-101	Marius, vanquisher of Jugurtha, stops invasions of Cimbri and Teutons.
88-79	Sulla, the rival of Marius, triumphs over Mithridates and establishes his dictatorship in Rome.
70	Pompey and Crassus, appointed Consuls, become masters of Rome.
63	Plot of Catiline against the Senate exposed by Cicero.
60	The first Triumvirate: **Pompey**, **Crassus**, **Julius Caesar**. Rivalry of the three rulers.
59	Julius Caesar as Consul.
58-51	The Gallic War (52: Surrender of Vercingetorix at Alesia).
49	Caesar crosses the Rubicon and drives Pompey out of Rome.

49-45	Caesar defeats Pompey and his partisans in Spain, Greece and Egypt. He writes his history of the Gallic War.
early 44	Caesar is appointed Dictator for life.
March 15	Caesar is assassinated by Brutus, his adopted son, among others.
43	The second Triumvirate: **Octavius** (nephew and heir of Caesar), **Antony**, Lepidus.
41-30	Struggle between Octavius and Anthony. Defeat (at Actium) and suicide of Anthony.

The Roman consular roads

The **Via Appia**, built in 312 BC, once went from Rome to Brindisi. Now, there is only a short section left in the immediate vicinity of the capital.
The **Via Aurelia** (241 BC) went from Rome via Genoa to Arles in the south of France. It is now the SS1, known as the "Aurelia", and starts at Ventimiglia.
The **Via Cassia**, paved in the 2C BC, crossed Etruria from Rome to Arezzo. It was later extended to Florence and Modena, and west to Luni. The modern SS2, which bears the same name, goes from Rome to Florence.
The **Via Emilia** (187 BC), which went from Rimini to Piacenza, gave its name to the region of Emilia. Under the Empire, it was extended to Aosta and Aquileia. The modern Via Emilia follows the exact route of the original road.
The **Via Flaminia** (220 BC) led from Rome to Rimini. It is now one of the main roads of the Eternal City.

The Early Empire (27 BC to AD 284)

27	Octavius, sole master of the Empire, receives the title of **Augustus Caesar** and plenary powers.
AD	
14	Death of Augustus.
14-37	Reign of Tiberius.
54-68	Reign of Nero, who causes the death of Britannicus, his mother Agrippina and his wives Octavia and Poppaea, and initiates violent persecution of the Christians.
68	End of the **Julio-Claudian dynasty** (Augustus, Tiberius, Caligula, Claudius, Nero).
69-96	**Flavian dynasty**: Vespasian, Titus, Domitian.
96-192	The Century of the **Antonines**, marked by the successful reigns of Nerva, Trajan, Hadrian, Antoninus and Marcus Aurelius, who consolidated the Empire.
193-275	**Severus dynasty**: Septimius Severus, Caracalla, Heliogabalus, Alexander Severus, Decius, Valerian, Aurelian.
235-268	Military anarchy; a troubled period. The legions make and break emperors.
270-275	Aurelius re-establishes the unity of the Empire.

The Later Empire (AD 284-476)

284-305	Reign of **Diocletian**. Institution of **Tetrarchy** or 4-man government.
303	Persecution of the Christians: reign of Diocletian known as "the age of martyrs".
306-337	Reign of **Constantine**. By the **Edict of Milan** (313) Constantine decrees religious freedom. Constantinople becomes the new capital.
379-395	Reign of Theodosius the Great, the Christian Emperor, who establishes Christianity as the state religion in 382. At his death the Empire is divided between his two sons, Arcadius (Eastern Empire) and Honorius (Western Empire) who settled at Ravenna.
5C	The Roman Empire is repeatedly attacked by the Barbarians: in 410, Alaric, King of the Visigoths, captures Rome. Capture and sack of Rome in 455 by the Vandals under Genseric.
476	Deposition by **Odoacer** of the Emperor Romulus Augustus ends the Western Empire.

From the Roman Empire to the Germanic Holy Roman Empire

493	Odoacer is driven out by the Ostrogoths under Theodoric.
535-553	Reconquest of Italy by the Eastern Roman Emperor **Justinian** (527-565).
568	**Lombard** invasion by King Alboin.

Social, political and religious life in ancient Rome

Society in Rome was divided into clans (gentes), or groups of people descended from a common ancestor, and families, each under a pater familias who wielded absolute authority. The **patricians** were the privileged land-owning class participating in the government of the state; the **plebeians**, who had no rights at all, relied on the protection of the patricians and were also known as clientes. The patricians owned a great many slaves, who were the lowest order in the population, but they could be granted their freedom by their masters.

At the time of the kings, the political organisation of Rome comprised two bodies, the Senate and the Comitia, composed of patricians. Under the Republic, the system gradually changed so that wealth became a more important factor than nobility of birth, thus allowing rich plebeians to take part in political life. Executive and military power was given to two consuls, elected for one year and assisted by quaestors in charge of public finance and the criminal police, together with censors of public morals, aediles in charge of the municipal police, and judicial praetors. The Senate had a consultative role and sanctioned laws. Ten Tribunes of the People watched over the rights of the masses. Consuls or praetors administered the provinces.

Generally speaking, the Empire kept the administrative structure of the Republic, but the powers of the consuls were taken by an emperor (Imperator) who was commander-in-chief of the army; he appointed the Senate, and had the right to make peace or war. Under the Later Empire the power of the emperors became absolute.

In religion, Rome drew on all mythological sources for her deities; the main gods and goddesses were the same in number, if not always in name, as their Greek counterparts on Mount Olympus (Greek names are given in italics).

Aesculapius (Asclepius), son of Apollo and the god of medicine, represented by a serpent and a staff.

Apollo (Apollo), god of light and the arts, sings to a lyre accompaniment and is often depicted with laurel, the sun or an arrow.

Ceres (Demeter), protectress of the earth, tillage, corn and fecundity, is represented with a sheaf of corn and a scythe.

Diana (Artemis), Apollo's sister, goddess of hunting, chastity and the moon (she wears a crescent moon on her head). The animal representing Diana is the doe. She often carries a quiver and bow.

Hercules (Herakles), a hero in life and a god after his death, famous for his Twelve Labours. He is represented by a club and shield.

Juno (Hera), the sister and wife of Jupiter, protectress of womanhood and marriage, is shown with a peacock, a pomegranate and a crown.

Jupiter (Zeus), senior god and ruler of the heavens, the elements and light, is often shown with an eagle, holding a thunderbolt and carrying a sceptre.

Mars (Aries), god of war, is identified by his weapons and his helmet.

Mercury (Hermes), protector of commerce and travel, wears winged sandals and carries a caduceus (a staff entwined with two serpents) in his hand. He is the messenger of the gods and accompanies souls to the underworld.

Minerva (Athena), goddess of wisdom, justice and the arts, is represented by an owl. She is the third member of the Capitoline Triad together with Juno and Jupiter, her father, from whose head she sprang fully armed; she is often shown with a shield and a helmet.

Neptune (Poseidon), brother of Jupiter and god of the sea, who rides a chariot and is armed with a trident.

Phoebus (Helios), god of the sun, rides a chariot and is symbolised by the rays of the sun.

Pluto (Hades), brother of Jupiter and bearded god of the underworld, often seated on a throne.

Proserpina (Persephone), daughter of Ceres and wife of Pluto, who symbolises the changing seasons.

Venus (Aphrodite), goddess of love and goodness, is represented by a dove. Born out of the foam of the sea, she is often represented standing in a shell or surrounded by sea deities.

Vesta (Estia), goddess of the hearth, carries a simple flame as a symbol of fire in the home.

Vulcan (Hephaistos), the husband of Venus and god of fire, works in a forge with an anvil and hammer.

Public religion took place in the temples. In private homes, a small oratory called the lararium enshrined the household gods, Lares and Penates, before whom a sacred flame burned always. The souls of the dead, known as manes, were also venerated.

590-604	Papacy of **Gregory the Great**, responsible for the evangelization of the Germans and Anglo-Saxons.
752	Threatened by the Lombards, the Pope appeals to Pepin the Short, King of the Franks.
756	Donation of Querzy-sur-Oise. Pepin the Short returns the Byzantine territories conquered by the Lombards to Pope Stephen II, leading to the birth of the *Patrimonium Petri*, otherwise known as the Papal States, and the temporal power of the Pope.
774	Pepin's son, **Charlemagne** (Charles the Great), becomes King of the Lombards.
800	Charlemagne is proclaimed Emperor of the **Holy Roman Empire** by Pope Leo III.
9C	The break-up of the Carolingian Empire causes complete anarchy and the formation of many rival States in Italy. This is an unsettled period for the Papacy, which is often weak and dissolute. Widespread corruption among the ecclesiastical hierarchy.
951	Intervention in Italy of **Otto I**, King of Saxony, who becomes King of the Lombards.
962	Otto I, now crowned Emperor, founds the Holy Roman Empire.

The Quarrel of the Church and the Empire

11C	Progressive establishment of the **Normans** in Sicily and southern Italy.
1076	The Gregorian Reform of Pope Gregory VII attempts to re-establish the influence of the Church. The dispute between the Pope and the Emperor Henry IV leads to the **Investiture Controversy**.
1077	Humbling of the Emperor before the Pope at Canossa *(see REGGIO NELL'EMILIA)*.
1155	**Frederick Barbarossa** crowned Emperor. Resumption of the struggle between the Empire and the Papacy, with the **Ghibellines** supporting the Emperor and the **Guelphs** supporting the Pope.
1167	Creation of the **Lombard League**. An association of Lombard cities with Guelph tendencies to counter the Emperor.
1176	Reconciliation between Frederick Barbarossa and Pope Alexander III.
1216	Triumph of the Papacy on the death of Pope Innocent III.
1227-1250	A new phase in the struggle between the Empire (Frederick II) and the Papacy (Gregory IX). New triumph of the Papacy.

French Influence and Decline of Imperial Power

13C	Peak of economic prosperity of the Communes.
1265	Charles of Anjou, brother of St Louis, crowned King of Sicily.
1282	Sicilian Vespers: massacre of French settlers in Sicily.
1300	First Jubilee declared by Pope **Boniface VIII**.
1302	The **Anjou Dynasty** establishes itself in Naples.
1303	Attack of Anagni, instigated by King Philip of France, on Pope Boniface VIII *(see ANAGNI)*.
1309-1377	The popes established at Avignon, France. The Avignon popes included Clement V to Gregory XI who took the papacy back to Rome at the instigation of St Catherine of Siena. This period is referred to as the **Avignon Captivity**.
1328	Failure of the intervention in Italy by the Emperor Ludwig of Bavaria. This is the first sign of the slow erosion of the German Emperors' will to exercise political and economic power over the territories of the old Roman empire.
1378-1418	The **Great Schism of the West** (anti-popes in Pisa and Avignon) is brought to an end by the Council of Constance (1414-18).
1402	Last German intervention in Italy (emperor defeated by Lombard militia).
1442	Alfonso V, King of **Aragon**, becomes King of the Two Sicilies.
1453	Constantinople, capital of the Christian Eastern territories, falls to the Turks.
1492	Death of **Lorenzo de' Medici**, the Magnificent.
	Christopher Columbus discovers America.
1494	Intervention of King Charles VIII of France for Ludovico II Moro.

Economic and Cultural Golden Age (15C, early 16C)

The centre and the north of the country were transformed by the commercial activity of craftsmen and merchants, while the south kept its feudal structures based on land ownership. The economic importance of Italy derived from the large-scale production of consumer goods (cloth, leather, glass, ceramics, arms etc) as well as from trade and wide-ranging banking activities. Merchants and bankers who had settled in countries throughout Europe spread the influence of the Italian civilisation, which flourished at the courts of the Italian rulers. There was great rivalry regarding the patronage of artists and the commissioning of splendid palaces among enlightened patrons of the arts such as the Medici of Florence, the Sforza of Milan, the Montefeltro of Urbino, the Este of Ferrara, the Gonzaga of Mantua and the Popes in Rome (Julius II, Leo X).

SCALA

Lorenzo the Magnificent

Decline set in as trade shifted towards the Atlantic with grave consequences for the maritime republics which had prospered during the Middle Ages. Genoa soon faced ruin, Pisa was taken over by its age-old rival Florence, and Amalfi and Venice were in serious trouble as the Turks advanced westwards. In addition, the political fragmentation of the country made Italy an inevitable target for the more powerful nation-states now emerging within Europe.

From the 16C to the Napoleonic era

16C	France and Spain engage in a struggle for the supremacy of Europe.
1515-1526	François I, victor at Marignano but vanquished at Pavia, is forced to give up the Italian heritage.
1527	Capture and **sack of Rome** by the troops of the Constable of Bourbon, in the service of Charles V.
1545-1563	The Church attempts to re-establish its authority and credibility, much damaged by the Protestant Reformation, with the **Council of Trent**.
1559	Treaty of Cateau-Cambrèsis: Spanish domination over Naples and the district of Milan, Sicily and Sardinia until the early 18C.
17C	Savoy becomes the most powerful State in northern Italy.
1713	Victor-Amadeus II of Savoy acquires Sicily and the title of King. The Duke of Savoy is compelled to exchange Sicily for Sardinia in 1720.
1796	**Napoleon's campaign** in Italy. Creation of the Cispadan Republic.
1797	Battle of Rivoli. Treaty of Campo-Formio. Creation of the Cisalpine and Ligurian Republics.
1798-1799	Proclamation of the Roman and Parthenopaean (Naples) Republics.
1805	Napoleon transforms the Italian Republic into a Kingdom, assumes the iron crown of the Lombard kings and confers the vice-royalty on his stepson, Eugène de Beauharnais.
1808	Rome is occupied by French troops. Murat becomes King of Naples.
1809	The Papal States are attached to the French Empire. Pius VII is taken to France as a prisoner (1812).
1814	Collapse of the Napoleonic regime. Pius VII returns to Rome.

Towards Italian Unity (1815-1870)

Although Machiavelli had already dreamed of a united Italy in the 16C, it was not until after the French Revolution that the question of uniting the various regions under the same political regime was seriously contemplated. After the Congress of Vienna in 1815, a number of revolts by the "Carbonari" patriots who opposed the Austrian occupation were crushed and in 1831 the Young Italy movement was founded by **Giuseppe Mazzini**. This period, known as the **Risorgimento**, provided the initial impetus which resulted in the **First War of Independence** against Austria, led by Charles Albert of Savoy, King of Sardinia. Initial Italian successes were followed by a violent Austrian counter-attack, the abdication of Charles Albert in March 1849 and the accession of **Victor Emmanuel II** to the throne. The skilful campaigning of his minister **Camillo Cavour**, an ardent advocate of Italian liberty, and the participation of Piedmont in the Crimean War as France's ally brought the problem of Italian unity to the forefront of European affairs. The Plombières agreement signed by Cavour and Napoleon III in 1858 led to the outbreak of the **Second War of Independence** in the following year, with combined Franco-Piedmontese

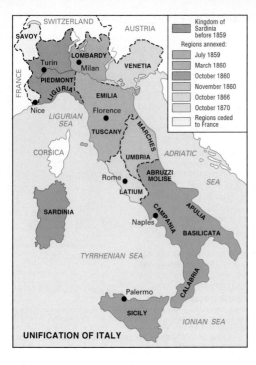

UNIFICATION OF ITALY

Map legend:
- Kingdom of Sardinia before 1859
- Regions annexed:
  - July 1859
  - March 1860
  - October 1860
  - November 1860
  - October 1866
  - October 1870
- Regions ceded to France

victories in Magenta and Solferino. Following popular uprisings in central and northern Italy, Lombardy, Emilia-Romagna and Tuscany were annexed to the Kingdom of Sardinia. In 1860, after **Garibaldi** liberated Sicily and southern Italy from the domination of the Bourbons, southern Italy, the Marches and Umbria were annexed to the emerging Italian State. On 17 March 1861 the inauguration of the Kingdom of Italy was proclaimed with Turin as the capital and Victor Emmanuel as king. In 1866, for political reasons, the capital was moved to Florence.

In the same year, the **Third War of Independence**, with the Prussians as Italy's allies against Austria, led to the annexation of Veneto. Four years later, on 20 September 1870, General Cadorna's troops entered Rome through Porta Pia. Rome was finally annexed to Italy and proclaimed the capital in 1871.

The "Roman Question"

The Papacy became involved in the Risorgimento during the 19C, when it became clear that the Unification of Italy could not take place unless the Pope was willing to relinquish the temporal power that he exercised over part of the country. When the troops of Victor Emmanuel II entered Rome in 1870, Pope Pius IX retired to the Vatican, declaring himself a prisoner of the Italian State. The "Roman Question" was only finally resolved in 1929, under the papacy of Pius XI, with the **Lateran Treaty** drawn up between the Holy See and the Fascist government of Benito Mussolini. These pacts recognised the sovereignty of the Pope within the Vatican City, as well as over certain buildings and organisations in Rome, and granted the Church specific authority regarding education and marriage in Italy. The Lateran Pacts were then included in the new Constitution of the Italian Republic in 1947. They have continued to govern relations between the Italian State and the Church since the end of the Second World War, and were modernised in a new Concordat in 1984.

From 1870 to the Present Day

1882	Italy, Germany and Austria sign the **Triple Alliance**.
1882-1885	The Italians gain a footing in Eritrea and on the Somali Coast.
1900	Assassination of King Umberto I by an anarchist. Accession of Victor Emmanuel III.
1904-1906	Rapprochement of Italy with Britain and France.
1914	Outbreak of the **First World War**. Italy enters the First World War on 24 May 1915 on the side of France, Great Britain and Russia (the Triple Entente) in their struggle against Austria-Hungary, and then against Germany (28 August 1916).
1918	The Battle of Vittorio Veneto marks the end of the First World War for Italy (4 November).
1919	Treaty of St Germain-en-Laye: Istria and the Trentino are attached to Italy.
1921	Social disturbances fermented by the Fascist Party led by **Benito Mussolini**.

1922-1926	The **March on Rome**. Mussolini becomes Prime Minister, then *Duce* (Leader).
1929	**Lateran Treaty** concluded between the Italian Government and the Papacy. This defined the relationship between the Church and State and brought to an end the age-old "Roman Question".
1936	Italian occupation of Ethiopia. Rapprochement with Germany. Rome-Berlin Axis formed.
1939	Outbreak of the **Second World War**.
1940	Italy enters the Second World War, allied with Germany against Britain and France.
1943	10 July: The Allies land in Sicily. 25 July: Overthrow and arrest of Mussolini. 8 September: Armistice. Much of the country is occupied by German troops. 12 September: Mussolini is freed by the Germans and sets up the **Italian Socialist Republic** in the north of the country with Salò as its capital.
1944-1945	The Allies slowly reconquer Italy. The country is liberated (25 April 1945) and the war ends. Mussolini is arrested while trying to flee into Switzerland, is tried and shot.
May 1946	Abdication of Victor Emmanuel III and accession of Umberto II.
June 1946	Proclamation of the Republic after a referendum.

"You are Peter and on this rock I will build my Church" (Matthew 16, 18)

The title of "Pope", derived from the Greek *pápas* meaning father, was originally used for patriarchs and bishops from the orient. From the 5C on, it became widely used in the west, where with the increasing importance of the Roman See, it was eventually reserved for the Bishop of Rome alone. The Bishop of Rome maintained that his See in the traditional capital of the Empire had been founded by the Apostles, Peter and Paul, and therefore claimed first place in the ecclesiastical hierarchy. The Pope was initially chosen by both the people and the clergy, until the Conclave of the Cardinals was established in 1059. Strict regulations regarding this method of election were set out by Gregory X in the 13C. Nowadays the cardinals meet in conclave in the Sistine Chapel and a vote is held twice a day; after

Paul III Farnese and his nephews in a painting by Titian – Museo di Capodimonte, Naples

each inconclusive vote the papers are burned so as to produce dark smoke. A majority of two thirds plus one is required for an election to be valid; then a plume of clear smoke appears above the Vatican. The senior cardinal appears at the window in the façade of St Peter's from which papal blessings are given and announces the election in the Latin formula: *Annuntio vobis gaudium magnum: habemus papam* (I announce to you with great joy: we have a Pope...). Over the centuries the Pope gradually assumed greater political power so that the history of the Papacy is inevitably linked with that of the relationship between the Church and the main political powers of the time. After the Unification of Italy, the Lateran Pacts of 1929 defined the present configuration of the Vatican City, which constitutes a separate State within the Italian State, of which the Pope is the sovereign ruler. The Holy Father is the undisputed leader of the Roman Catholic church and exercises absolute infallibility over all ecclesiastical dogma, as set out in the first Vatican Council in 1870. Through the figure of the Pope, the spiritual influence of the Roman Catholic church can be felt throughout the world.

1947	Treaty of Paris: Italy loses its colonies as well as Albania, Istria, Dalmatia and the Dodecanese. Frontier redefined to the benefit of France.
1948	1 January: The new Constitution comes into effect.
1954	Trieste is attached to Italy.
1957	Treaty of Rome instituting the European Economic Community (now the European Union): Italy is one of the six founding members.
1968	Uprisings against the socio-economic system: *Autunno caldo* (literally, hot autumn).
1970-1980	Riots and terrorism as a result of political unrest.
1970	Institution of the regional system.
1978	Aldo Moro, former Presidente del Consiglio, assassinated.
1981	Attack on Pope John Paul II in St Peter's Square by Turkish terrorist Mehmet Alì Agca.
1982	Prefect of Palermo, Alberto Dalla Chiesa, his wife and one of his entourage killed on 3 September.
1991	Italian Communist Party (PCI), led by Achille Occhetto, splits into two new parties, the Democratic Party of the Left (PDS) and the Communist Refoundation (RC). The first wave of Albanian refugees arrives in Puglia in March.
1992	Operation to fight economic and political corruption in Italy commences, which leads to the collapse of the ruling classes of the Republic. Two judges, Giovanni Falcone and Paolo Borsellino, are assassinated in Sicily.
1994	The centre-right led by Silvio Berlusconi wins the first political elections to take place under the new majority electoral system. Beginning of the Second Republic.
29 January 1996	Teatro La Fenice destroyed by fire in Venice.
21 April 1996	Electoral victory of the Ulivo alliance. The left is in government for the first time in the history of the Republic.
27 March 1998	Italy passes the final test and signs up to the single European currency.
13 May 1999	Carlo Azeglio Ciampi, Governor of the Bank of Italy, becomes the 10th President of the Italian Republic.

Architecture

Ancient art

Peripteral temple

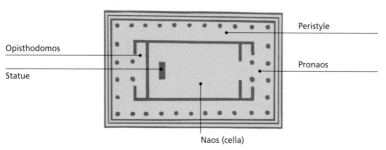

Opisthodomos

Statue

Peristyle

Pronaos

Naos (cella)

Elevation of a Corinthian order temple

The architrave, frieze and cornice are collectively known as the entablature

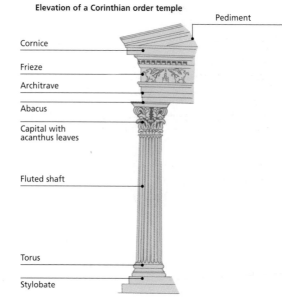

Pediment

Cornice

Frieze

Architrave

Abacus

Capital with acanthus leaves

Fluted shaft

Torus

Stylobate

Orders

Doric

Tuscan

Ionic

Corinthian

Composite

R. Corbel

Baths of the Villa Romana del Casale (3-4C A.D.)

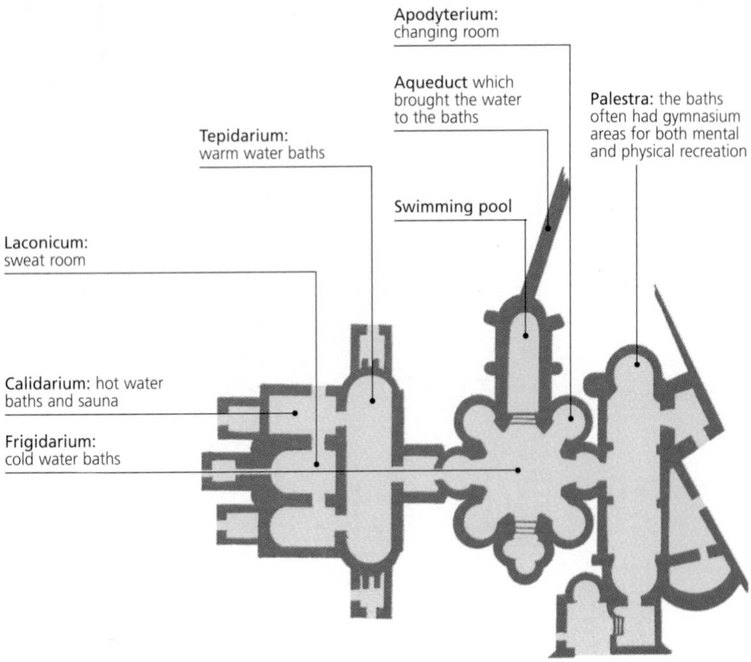

Apodyterium: changing room

Aqueduct which brought the water to the baths

Palestra: the baths often had gymnasium areas for both mental and physical recreation

Tepidarium: warm water baths

Swimming pool

Laconicum: sweat room

Calidarium: hot water baths and sauna

Frigidarium: cold water baths

Colosseum (1C AD)

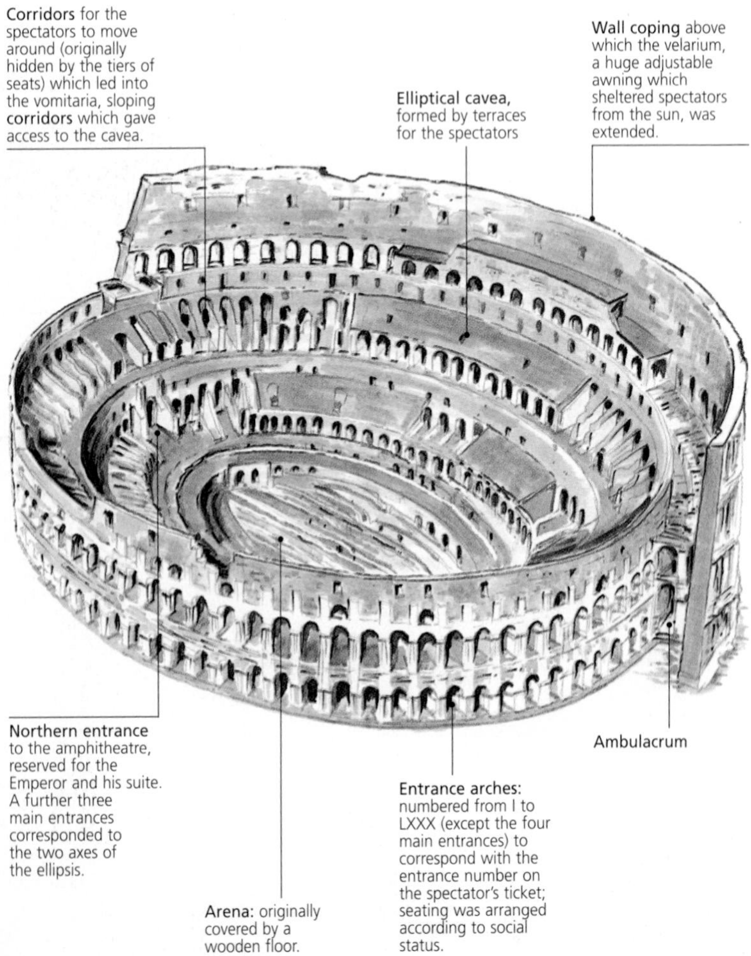

Corridors for the spectators to move around (originally hidden by the tiers of seats) which led into the vomitaria, sloping corridors which gave access to the cavea.

Elliptical cavea, formed by terraces for the spectators

Wall coping above which the velarium, a huge adjustable awning which sheltered spectators from the sun, was extended.

Northern entrance to the amphitheatre, reserved for the Emperor and his suite. A further three main entrances corresponded to the two axes of the ellipsis.

Ambulacrum

Arena: originally covered by a wooden floor.

Entrance arches: numbered from I to LXXX (except the four main entrances) to correspond with the entrance number on the spectator's ticket; seating was arranged according to social status.

R. Corbel

Religious architecture

Plan of Parma cathedral (12-14C)

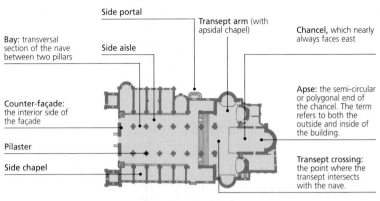

Side portal

Transept arm (with apsidal chapel)

Chancel, which nearly always faces east

Bay: transversal section of the nave between two pillars

Side aisle

Counter-façade: the interior side of the façade

Apse: the semi-circular or polygonal end of the chancel. The term refers to both the outside and inside of the building.

Pilaster

Side chapel

Transept crossing: the point where the transept intersects with the nave.

Cross-section of a church

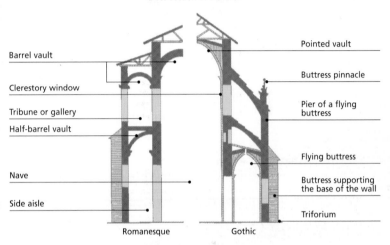

Barrel vault

Pointed vault

Clerestory window

Buttress pinnacle

Tribune or gallery

Pier of a flying buttress

Half-barrel vault

Nave

Flying buttress

Side aisle

Buttress supporting the base of the wall

Triforium

Romanesque

Gothic

ROMANESQUE ARCHITECTURE
Milano – Basilica di Sant' Ambrogio (11-12C)

A masterpiece of harmony and balance, Sant'Ambrogio is striking for the apparent simplicity of its composition and for the careful juxtaposition between the light and the building materials used.

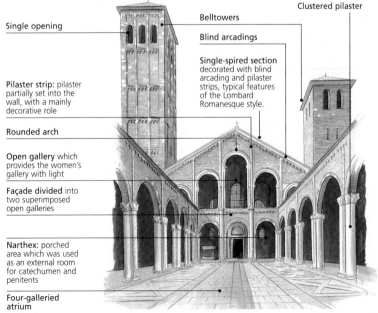

Clustered pilaster

Single opening

Belltowers

Blind arcadings

Single-spired section decorated with blind arcading and pilaster strips, typical features of the Lombard Romanesque style.

Pilaster strip: pilaster partially set into the wall, with a mainly decorative role

Rounded arch

Open gallery which provides the women's gallery with light

Façade divided into two superimposed open galleries

Narthex: porched area which was used as an external room for catechumen and penitents

Four-galleried atrium

H. Choimet

GOTHIC
Milano – Cathedral apse (14-15C)

Milano cathedral is a unique and extraordinary example of the late-Gothic style in Italy. It was started in 1386 and was not finished until the façade was completed in the 19C. The building, commissioned by Gian Galeazzo Visconti, clearly demonstrates a transalpine cultural influence far removed from contemporary Tuscan architecture.

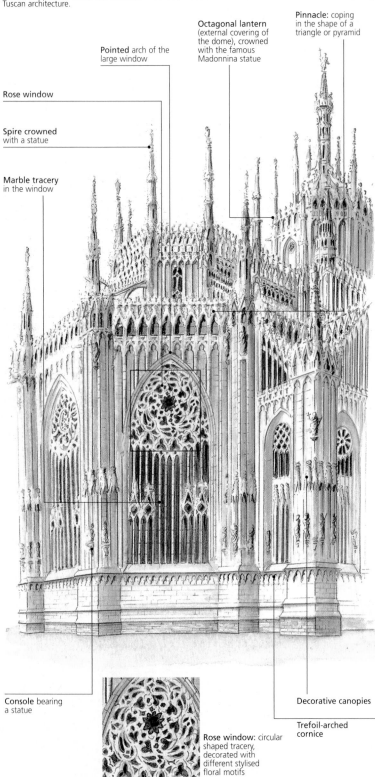

Pointed arch of the large window

Octagonal lantern (external covering of the dome), crowned with the famous Madonnina statue

Pinnacle: coping in the shape of a triangle or pyramid

Rose window

Spire crowned with a statue

Marble tracery in the window

Console bearing a statue

Rose window: circular shaped tracery, decorated with different stylised floral motifs

Decorative canopies

Trefoil-arched cornice

H. Choimet

THE RENAISSANCE
Rimini – Tempio Malatestiano (Leon Battista Alberti, 15C)

Built in honour of Sigismondo Malatesta, this church is a celebration of classical cultures and civilisations, from which many of its structural and decorative features are taken, re-interpreted and adapted to the religious role of the building.

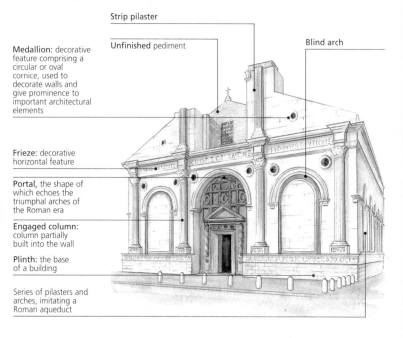

Strip pilaster

Unfinished pediment

Blind arch

Medallion: decorative feature comprising a circular or oval cornice, used to decorate walls and give prominence to important architectural elements

Frieze: decorative horizontal feature

Portal, the shape of which echoes the triumphal arches of the Roman era

Engaged column: column partially built into the wall

Plinth: the base of a building

Series of pilasters and arches, imitating a Roman aqueduct

Firenze – The interior of the Cappella dei Pazzi (Filippo Brunelleschi, 1430-1445)

The harmony of the proportions and the elegant play on colours between the grey of the *pietra serena* stone (which emphasises the architectural features) and the white of the plaster create an atmosphere of dignified and austere simplicity.

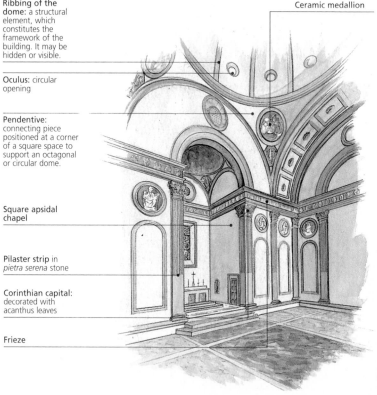

Ribbing of the dome: a structural element, which constitutes the framework of the building. It may be hidden or visible.

Oculus: circular opening

Pendentive: connecting piece positioned at a corner of a square space to support an octagonal or circular dome.

Square apsidal chapel

Pilaster strip in *pietra serena* stone

Corinthian capital: decorated with acanthus leaves

Frieze

Ceramic medallion

H. Choimet

43

BAROQUE
Lecce – Basilica di Santa Croce (15-17C)

The Baroque style of Lecce is influenced both by Roman and Spanish architecture. The exuberant, highly-worked decoration evokes the Spanish Plateresque style (15-16C), in which façades were decorated with the precise detail of a goldsmith (platero in Spanish).

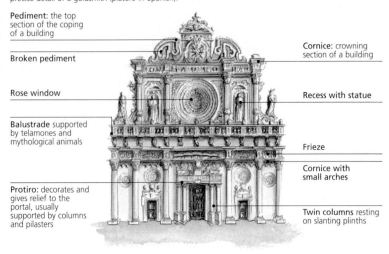

Pediment: the top section of the coping of a building

Broken pediment

Rose window

Balustrade supported by telamones and mythological animals

Protiro: decorates and gives relief to the portal, usually supported by columns and pilasters

Cornice: crowning section of a building

Recess with statue

Frieze

Cornice with small arches

Twin columns resting on slanting plinths

Roma – Interior of St John Lateran (4-17C)

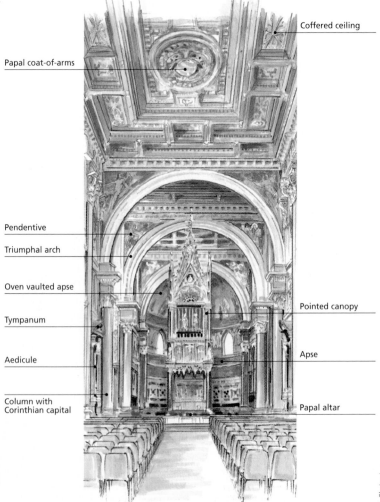

Papal coat-of-arms

Pendentive

Triumphal arch

Oven vaulted apse

Tympanum

Aedicule

Column with Corinthian capital

Coffered ceiling

Pointed canopy

Apse

Papal altar

H. Choimet

Civil architecture

Castel del Monte (13C)

Built by Frederick II, probably as a leisure residence, the castle is dominated by the number eight: the ground plan is octagonal, there are eight octagonal towers and eight rooms on each floor.

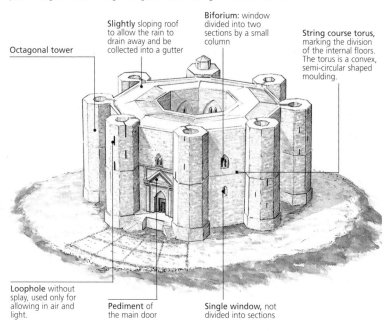

Octagonal tower

Slightly sloping roof to allow the rain to drain away and be collected into a gutter

Biforium: window divided into two sections by a small column

String course torus, marking the division of the internal floors. The torus is a convex, semi-circular shaped moulding.

Loophole without splay, used only for allowing in air and light.

Pediment of the main door

Single window, not divided into sections

Firenze – Palazzo Rucellai (Leon Battista Alberti, 1446-1451)

The palace is composed of three superimposed levels of the three classical orders (Doric, Ionic and Corinthian) and presents a pattern of vertical (the pilasters) and horizontal (the cornices) lines.

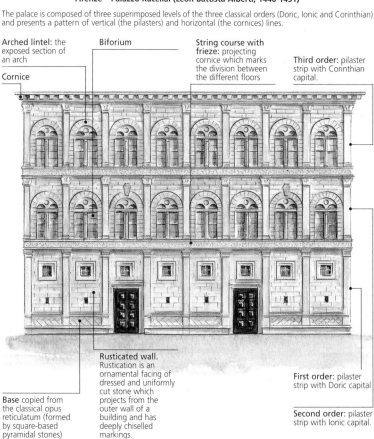

Arched lintel: the exposed section of an arch

Cornice

Biforium

String course with frieze: projecting cornice which marks the division between the different floors

Third order: pilaster strip with Corinthian capital.

First order: pilaster strip with Doric capital

Second order: pilaster strip with Ionic capital.

Rusticated wall. Rustication is an ornamental facing of dressed and uniformly cut stone which projects from the outer wall of a building and has deeply chiselled markings.

Base copied from the classical opus reticulatum (formed by square-based pyramidal stones)

H. Choimet

45

Torino – Palazzo Carignano (Guarino Guarini, 1679-1681)

The façade is striking for the juxtaposition of its straight and curved lines, while the use of brick is a reminder of the Emilian origins of the architect.

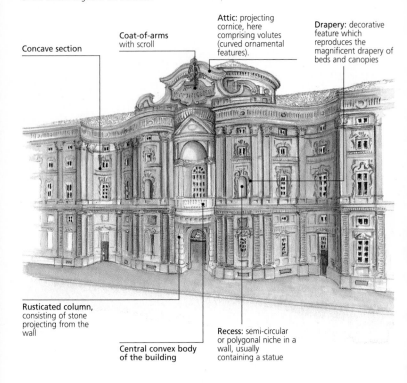

Concave section

Coat-of-arms with scroll

Attic: projecting cornice, here comprising volutes (curved ornamental features).

Drapery: decorative feature which reproduces the magnificent drapery of beds and canopies

Rusticated column, consisting of stone projecting from the wall

Central convex body of the building

Recess: semi-circular or polygonal niche in a wall, usually containing a statue

Milano – Teatro alla Scala (Giuseppe Piermarini, 1776-1778)

The sober and measured simplicity of the façade of this famous Milanese theatre contrasts with the rich decor of the interior. The theatre soon became a model for future neo-Classical theatres.

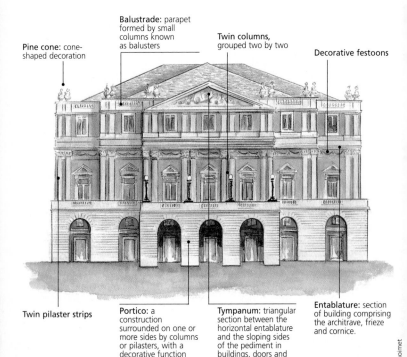

Pine cone: cone-shaped decoration

Balustrade: parapet formed by small columns known as balusters

Twin columns, grouped two by two

Decorative festoons

Twin pilaster strips

Portico: a construction surrounded on one or more sides by columns or pilasters, with a decorative function or as a monumental entrance.

Tympanum: triangular section between the horizontal entablature and the sloping sides of the pediment in buildings, doors and windows.

Entablature: section of building comprising the architrave, frieze and cornice.

H. Choimet

Arches

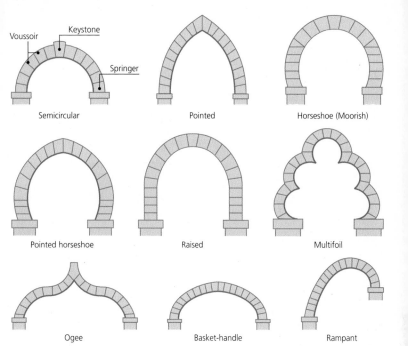

Voussoir · Keystone · Springer

Semicircular

Pointed

Horseshoe (Moorish)

Pointed horseshoe

Raised

Multifoil

Ogee

Basket-handle

Rampant

Vaults

Barrel

Groined vault

Pointed

Fan

Cove

Oven

H. Choimet

Art

ITALIAN ART

To appreciate Italian art in all its diversity and richness from the late Ancient period to the end of the 18C, it is necessary to keep in mind the illustrious historical context. The rightful heir of the Greek, Etruscan and Roman civilisations, Italian art has adopted from each period some of the most essential principles and characteristics. Italy, with its vast geographical area from the Alps in the north down to Sicily, has always been open to diverse foreign influences. Following the fall of the Western Roman Empire, it was Byzantium that held sway and greatly influenced the northern Adriatic shores for several centuries, while a succession of invading peoples, namely the Ostrogoths, Lombards, Franks, Arabs and Normans, left their imprint on the conquered territory in southern Italy.

The extraordinarily malleable Italian character absorbed the various foreign influences and one after another the cities of Florence, Sienna, Verona, Ferrara, Milan, Rome, Venice, Naples, Genoa and many other centres of minor or major importance, became the cradle of a flourishing artistic movement. As early as the 12C, in spite of the regional diversities, Italian artists were already beginning to show certain common characteristics: a shared taste for harmony and solidity of form as well as an innate sense of space inherited from the Classical culture. Italian art is characterised by a sense of harmony and restraint, not present in other artistic traditions, which aims to depict the rational and intelligible order of things.

The Italians rejected the importance accorded to naturalistic art which was so popular with northern schools, and tempered the excessive emphasis placed on intellectual abstraction and decoration by Oriental artists. Slowly the Italian artist evolved a representational technique which reflected his emotions. The Classical preoccupation with idealisation is evident in the emphasis given to human figures whether these be profane or religious in inspiration.

In spite of this scholarly and well-mastered image, Italian art has a strong social component. Parallel to the artist's intellectual attempt to impose order on reality, art gradually developed an openness to naturalism, influenced by the memory of Classical models. A good example of this is the medieval square, the famous **piazza**, containing the main public buildings in the Roman forum: the church, baptistery, town hall or the princely seat. Law courts, a hospital or a fountain were sometimes added. This was the venue for local markets and meetings. Often designed like stage scenery and embellished with ornamentation, the piazza is also the place for business, political decision-making and other important events. It is usually the result of centuries of construction, depicting aesthetic influences and social moods; history can be interpreted by studying how certain elements were reused, ornamental motifs copied and styles mingled or superimposed. This is where the artist who also aspires to be architect, sculptor and painter can best exercise his talents where it may be admired by all.

These excellent town planners, however, retained harmony with nature and the Italian countryside. From Roman times on they embellished the countryside with sumptuous **villas**, splendid terraced gardens with basins, fountains and springs, all landscaped with skill to create shade and please the eye. Follies invited the passer-by to rest, meditate or simply enjoy the beauty of nature. Thus the Italian architects and landscape gardeners, often indifferent to the solemn grandeur of French classicism, have created a great many places where man has established a harmonious relationship with nature: from Hadrian's Villa near Rome to the flower-bedecked terraces of the Borromean Islands, including the Oriental charm of the Villa Rufolo in Ravello, the elegant buildings of the Florentine countryside, the fantastic Mannerist creations of Rome, Tivoli or Bomarzo adorned with grottoes and statues, the urban and regional projects designed by Juvarra in Piedmont, and finally the delightful mansions of the Brenta Riviera; all the work of Palladio.

BYZANTINE INFLUENCE

The Barbarian invasions were to have noticeable consequences for Italian art, bringing about the decline of the late-Roman Imperial tradition and encouraging the popular and narrative early Christian art which later formed the basis of the Romanesque style. Ravenna was chosen by Honorious and his sister Galla Placidia as the capital of the Empire, and after the death of Theodoric and the Gothic invasions, the town came under direct Byzantine rule in the reign of Justinian (527-565 AD). The Byzantine Emperors ruled the region of Ravenna and Venezia Giulia only until the 8C, but they held sway in Sicily and part of southern Italy until the 11C. Byzantine art inherited a certain naturalism and Classical sense of space from the Greek and Latin artistic traditions, and a rich decorative style from its Oriental roots. The capital of Byzantine art in Italy was Ravenna, whose tradition was carried on by Venice, Rome, Sicily and even Lombardy until the early 13C.

SCALA

Peter and Andrew leave their fishing nets to follow Jesus – San Apollinare Nuovo, Ravenna

Architecture and sculpture – Byzantine architecture inherited the vault and dome from the late-Roman period and developed the potential of these structures with often extraordinary results, culminating in the basilica of San Vitale in Ravenna. More simple basilicas were also built, combining plain and sober exteriors with dazzling interior decoration in mosaic and marble. The bas-reliefs on the sides of sarcophagi, chancel parcloses, ambos and pulpits, assume an essentially decorative character: symbolic and stylised figures, animals facing front to front etc.

Mosaics – Byzantine artists excelled in this sumptuous art form. The precious materials used made this the perfect technique for portraying mystical characters from the Bible or striking courtly figures. Mosaics consisted of *tesserae*, fragments of hard stone or glass, glazed and irregularly cut to catch the light. They covered oven-vaults, walls and cupolas, their gold highlights sparkling in the mysterious semi-darkness. Enigmatic, grandiose figures stood out against midnight blue backgrounds and landscapes with trees, plants and animals. The most famous mosaics are those of Ravenna (5C-6C). However, the Byzantine style still prevailed in the 11C-12C at St Mark's in Venice and in Sicily (Cefalù, Palermo, Monreale), and in various forms up to the 13C in Rome.

MIDDLE AGES – ROMANESQUE AND GOTHIC (11C-14C)

As elsewhere in Europe, cathedrals were built all over Italy, but here the Italian predilection for harmony and the Roman tradition of monumental ensembles meant that architecture did not reach the sublime heights of the great Gothic achievements of religious art in France and northern Europe.

Romanesque Period – The development of a new architectural style in the 11C was encouraged by a period of renaissance in the countryside, as well as in the towns and cities. New cathedrals and Benedictine monasteries drew on both the Classical heritage of Carolingian and Ottonian traditions and various regional influences. The main features of Romanesque architecture are alternating columns and pilasters, which provide buildings with rhythm, space and depth, and their continuation into the roof structure, where the square vaults are supported by archivolts and ribs. The structural function of individual architectural features is always visible.

Initially the most flourishing school was in northern Italy, where the master masons were known as the **Maestri Comacini**, who created exceptional buildings in stone in the mountains and in brick in the valleys, and the **Maestri Campionesi**, who came from the Lugano region and the Lombard lakes.

The regions of central Italy were influenced by other cultural models and produced quite different styles. The Classical legacy is strongly felt in Florence, where the highly original medieval Classical style is characterised by a delicate use of colours and a subtle intellectual character, while Rome draws on the early Christian tradition of the magnificent Constantinian basilicas. In Tuscany, especially in Pisa, Lucca and Pistoia, the Romanesque style shows strong Lombard and classical Florentine influences, embellished by detailed decorative work which is perhaps borrowed from Oriental art. Typical features include tiers of arcades with a multitude of small columns on the façades, tall blind arcades on the side walls and east end, decorative lozenges and different coloured marble incrustations.

In Latium in the 12C-13C, the **Maestri Cosmati**, a Roman guild of mosaic and marble workers, held sway. They specialised in assembling fragments of multicoloured marble (pavings, episcopal thrones, ambos or pulpits and candelabra) and the incrustation of columns and friezes in the cloisters with enamel mosaics.

49

Finally, in southern Italy and Sicily, Lombard, Saracen, Byzantine and Norman influences mingled. The result was the monumental and noble **Sicilian-Norman style** *(see SICILY)*, which is oriental in its highly decorative façades and classical in the perfectly poised rhythm of its colonnades.

Sculpture was closely linked with architecture, with a marked use of low-relief, occasionally presented as complex cycles of didactic or symbolic figures, both Biblical and secular. Various influences can be detected in this new, highly expressive artistic style.

Painting was developed alongside mosaics in the large cathedrals, where the vast walls and vaults were literally covered with colour. The bare and often austere walls that can be seen in churches today are almost always the result of the ravages of time or restoration work. Originally the bright and imaginative decoration would have alternated with large frescoes illustrating stories from the Bible, where new experimental artistic forms mingled with old Byzantine influences.

Gothic Period – From a structural viewpoint, Gothic architecture represents the evolution of some of the ideas introduced during the Romanesque period. The development of the use of the pointed arch, the potential of which had not been previously exploited to the full, allowed the height above the transept to be increased by concentrating the weight of the building on tall, spectacular pilasters formed by bands of columns and in so doing, released the walls from their weight-bearing role. As a result, it became possible to replace the opaque mass of the walls with huge glass openings which flooded the church with "divine" light. The buildings reached hitherto unimagined heights, supported externally by a mass of buttresses and flying buttresses, hidden from sight when inside the church, thus accentuating the impression of space and vertical movement. The Cistercians introduced Gothic architecture into Italy, although the style remained close to earlier architectural traditions, with the emphasis purely on a heightened use of light as a structural element. The solid structure of the building and the omnipresent Classical heritage remained of primary importance. The widespread adoption of the Gothic style was due to the many new religious orders, especially the Franciscans and Dominicans, who often used the traditional model of the early Christian basilica, which was practical and economical, and adapted it to current trends.

There was more originality in civil architecture of the Gothic period. Numerous prosperous towns chose to show their civic pride by embellishing their city centres with municipal palaces and loggias. In Venice the ornate Gothic style relieved bare façades with window openings and loggias. Venetian Gothic was to persist until the late 15C.

The **Pisano** family from Pisa gave a decisive impetus to the art of **sculpture** by combining their continued use of ancient traditions seen through the classicism championed by Frederick II (**Nicola**, 1215?-c 1280) and their vigorously expressive realism which was explicitly Gothic in tone (**Giovanni**, 1248-after 1314). These masters and the architect and sculptor **Arnolfo di Cambio** (*c* 1245-1302) introduced new iconography and ambitious projects for pulpits and funerary monuments, all of which exhibited the new humanism.

SCALA

Guidoriccio da Fogliano by Simor

The painted Crucifixes in relief which appeared in the 12C were the first specimens of Italian painting. Gradually the hieratic tradition inherited from Byzantine art lost its extreme rigidity. In the 13C a Roman, **Pietro Cavallini**, (1273-1321) executed frescoes and mosaics with a greater breadth of style reminiscent of antique art. His Florentine contemporary, **Cimabue** (1240-1302), adorned the Upper Basilica of Assisi with frescoes displaying a new sense of pathos which broke away from the Byzantine tradition. This new approach influenced **Giotto** (1266-1337), who revolutionised painting by introducing naturalism into his works: movement, depth and atmosphere were indicated or suggested, and emotion came to light in the frescoes at Assisi, Padua and Florence. All successive painting was influenced in some way by this artist, including Masaccio and Michelangelo, who were directly inspired by his work.

In Siena at the same time **Duccio**'s (c 1255-1318) work still showed a strong Byzantine influence. He founded the Siena school which continued to employ a graceful linear technique and showed a pronounced taste for the decorative use of colour. Some of the most delicate exponents of this school were **Simone Martini** (c 1284-1344) and the brothers **Pietro** (c 1280-1348?) and **Ambrogio Lorenzetti** (1285-1348?).

The masters of the Florentine Trecento period (14C) developed a mystical and realistic style far removed from the harsh and lively work of Giotto, which is characterised by harmonies of line and colour as well as a great refinement in the decorative elements. At the same time the **International Gothic** style developed in the courts of Europe, practised by artists from central and northern Italy and perfected in the frescoes painted by Simone Martini and Matteo Giovannetti (?-1367) in Avignon. Other exponents of this refined, stately and occasionally decadent artistic movement which lasted until the 15C include **Stefano da Zevio** (c 1379-after 1438) from Verona, **Pisanello** (c 1380-1455) a portraitist, animal painter and distinguished medallist (see VERONA) and **Gentile da Fabriano** (c 1370-1427).

QUATTROCENTO (15C)

The early Renaissance was characterised by an abiding passion for antiquity, the well-organised city-states governed by a noble or princely patron, a new vision of man's place at the centre of the universe, and a large number of artists, scholars and poets. The Medici city of Florence united all these conditions and it was an appropriate birthplace for this cultural movement, designated much later as the Renaissance.

Architecture – A new concept of art was introduced by the Florentine sculptor and architect **Filippo Brunelleschi** (1377-1446), who was an enthusiastic admirer of antiquity. His strong personality transformed the practical approach of the medieval master builder into the creative role of the architect who designed new projects on the drawing board. Brunelleschi was both an artist and an intellectual, whose invention of geometrical perspective allowed him to plan harmonious and rationally designed buildings. His intuitive understanding of the reproduction of three-dimensional objects on two-dimensional canvas provided the foundation for all future painting. His intellectual abilities and the abstract character of his architectural creations were imitated and made commonplace by his followers, but were never fully understood. **Leon Battista Alberti** (1406-1472) used his knowledge

...Martini (Palazzo Pubblico, Siena)

of ancient art to give life to a new expressive style, based on a dramatically emotional relationship between objects and space, which is thought to have influenced Bramante.

Sculpture – The magnificent doors of the Baptistery at Florence designed by **Lorenzo Ghiberti** (1378-1455) show the influence of Gothic tradition and ancient art. However, the most powerful sculptor of the period was undoubtedly **Donatello** (1386-1466), who was deeply interested in man and had little inclination for intellectual speculation. He was able to interpret classical forms with a free and innovative spirit, breathing dynamism into his work and bringing it to the height of expressive power. After working in Padua, where he created works that set a standard for all of northern Italy, he returned to Florence and in the changing climate of the second half of the century he gave life to a humanity acquired through suffering, presaging the crisis of the end of the century. His contemporary, **Luca della Robbia** (1400-82), specialised in coloured and glazed terracotta works, while **Agostino di Duccio** (1418-c 1481), **Desiderio da Settignano** (c 1430-c 1464) and **Mino da Fiesole** (1429-84) continued in the Donatello tradition, at the same time moving away from Donatello's intense dramatical style.

Painting – **Masaccio** (1401-28) was with Brunelleschi and Donatello the third major figure of the 15C. He applied Brunelleschi's laws of perspective and added a use of light which gave his figures volume so that for the first time for centuries they cast a shadow, creating an illusion of perspective and the notion of space. His substantial figures thus acquire a certain realism and their solidity lends them a moral dignity. **Paolo Uccello** (c 1397-1475) gave this new concept of space an alternative interpretation, using perspective based on two vanishing points and perhaps demonstrating that more than one method exists for reproducing reality, with the philosophical implications that this entails. At the same time, the Dominican friar, **Fra Angelico** (1387-1435), who remained very attached to Gothic tradition, was attracted to the new theories of the Renaissance, while **Benozzo Gozzoli** (1420-97) adapts his style to the portrayal of brilliant festivities, always purely secular. **Andrea del Castagno** (1423-57) emphasised modelling and monumental qualities *(see FIRENZE)*. **Sandro Botticelli** (1444-1510) produced a miraculous purity of line which gives a graceful and almost unreal fragility to his figures and a deep sense of mystery to his allegorical scenes. At the turn of the century, with the crisis in humanist values, he created dazzling figures of harsh lines and dull colours. **Domenico Ghirlandaio** (1449-94) reveals his gift for narrative painting in monumental frescoes which depicted the ruling class of Florence in an atmosphere of stately serenity.

The work of **Piero della Francesca** (c 1415-92) from Sansepolcro is a supreme example of Tuscan Renaissance art displaying faultless harmony and sure draughtsmanship with his use of form, colour and light *(see AREZZO)*.

SCALA

Spring (detail) by Botticelli
(Galleria degli Uffizi, Florence)

At the Gonzaga court in Mantua, **Mantegna** (1431-1506) painted scenes full of grandeur and rigour, using the ancient models to create paintings of strong and inscrutable heroes. In the esoteric, astrological and alchemical atmosphere of the court of Ferrara, **Cosimo Tura** (1430-1495) created troublingly strange yet original compositions in which men and objects are hurled together in a mix of colours that resemble sharp metals and semiprecious stones.

The second major centre of art at this time was Venice, where **Giovanni Bellini** (1432-1516) created a sense of optical and empirical space in his paintings, emphasising the use of colour and tones in contrast to the geometric, intellectual and anti-naturalist painting of Florence. Bellini was much influenced by the work in the 1470s of **Antonello da Messina** (1430-1479), who had in turn drawn on the work of the Flemish masters and his knowledge of Piero della Francesca.

CINQUECENTO (16C)

The 16C saw the development of human sensibility which had already marked the previous century. Artists were attracted more and more by antiquity, mythology and the discovery of man.

The artistic centre of the Renaissance moved from Florence to Rome where the popes rivalled one another to embellish palaces and churches. The artist became more independent and acquired a certain prestige.

By the end of the century, the canons of Renaissance art were already being exported and put into practice elsewhere in Europe. However, this golden age of poets and humanists was destined to come to an end before reaching its zenith as a result of the political upheavals in Europe and the conflict brought about by the new Lutheran ideas of the time.

Architecture – The century begins with the return of **Bramante** (1444-1514) from Milan to Rome, where he laid the foundations for the new basilica of St Peter's, later to be completed by Michelangelo. Despite appearances, Bramante's architectural style was not completely classical in tone; he made use of *trompe l'œil* effects (such as the false chancel created in San Satiro church in Milan) which feigned a depth that did not exist. As a result, architecture becomes more than just a rational representation of what actually exists, a development that would find perfect expression in the

Accademia, Venezia/SCALA

The Tempest, by Giorgione (Gallerie dell'Accademia, Venice)

53

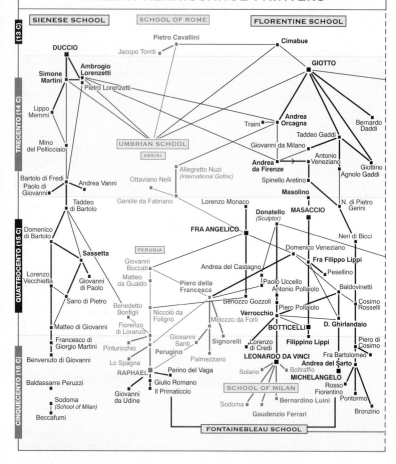

ITALIAN RENAISSANCE PAINTERS

later Baroque style. **Michelangelo**, partly inspired by Bramante's ideas, thought of architecture as a form of sculpture and attempted to give moulded form to large architectural structures. **Vignola** (1507-73) also worked in Rome, while **Palladio** (1508-80) designed a number of buildings in Vicenza *(see VICENZA)*. In his important works on architecture he advocated the Classicism of ancient art and was himself responsible for many churches, palaces and luxury villas in Venetia.

Sculpture – **Michelangelo** (1475-1564) did most of his life's work in either Florence or Rome and was the most outstanding character of the century owing to his creative, idealist and even troubled genius which found its expression in masterpieces of unsurpassed vitality. His art explored questions such as divine revelation, the human longing for something beyond its dissatisfying earthly existence, the soul struggling to release itself from the prison of the body, and the struggle between faith and the intellect. He draws inspiration from ancient art and the work of Donatello, which he reinterprets with impressive moral tension. In his later works this leads to a representation of the disintegration of matter, symbolising the human body, and the immateriality of light, symbolising the spirit, thus shattering the optimisim of Humanist Classicism. Michelangelo towered above his contemporaries, including the elegant and refined **Benvenuto Cellini** (1500-71), a skilled goldsmith and able sculptor known for his Perseus now in Florence, and the powerful sculptor **Giambologna** or **Giovanni Bologna** (1529-1608) of Flemish origin and author of numerous group sculptures, who, together with other contemporaries, followed the dictates of a stately and courtly art.

Painting – The 16C is an important period for painting with numerous outstanding artists producing works in the new humanist vein, and with Rome and later Venice replacing Florence as artistic centres. The century began with exceptional but complementary masters. The fascinating **Leonardo da Vinci** (1452-1519) was the archetype of the enquiring mind of the new humanists. He is famous in painting for his *sfumato* (literally mist), a sort of impalpable, luminous veil which created an impression of distance between persons and things. His insatiable desire for knowledge and interest in the mechanics of how things actually worked, and his attempt to form his observations into a coherent system make him a precursor of

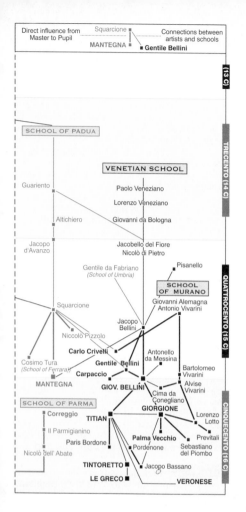

modern science. His reflections on the workings of the soul and his interpretation of such reflections in paintings such as *The Last Supper* in Milan were to have a lasting effect on future painters. **Raphael** (1483-1520) was not only a prodigious portraitist and painter of gently drawn madonnas, but also a highly inventive decorator with an exceptional mastery of composition which was given free rein in the Stanze of the Vatican. His style is classical in the fullest sense of the term and he is able to communicate the most intellectual and sophisticated ideas in logical, fascinating and deceptively simple paintings.

Michelangelo (1475-1564), the last of the three great men, although he was really a sculptor, took on the formidable task of decorating the ceiling of the Sistine Chapel where his skill with relief and his power are triumphant. His paintings portray a magnificent and heroic humanity, which appears devastated by the message of God. The bright optimism of contemporary Classicism is thus shattered and future artists were forced to choose between the art of the divine Raphael or that of the terrifying Michelangelo.

The 16C Venetian school produced many great colourists. **Giorgione** (1478-1510) explores the relationship between man and nature by creating a wonderful sense of landscape and atmosphere. **Titian** (c 1490-1576), a disciple of Bellini, was as a youth influenced by Giorgione and imbued with his skill for both mythological and religious compositions. He was also a fine portraitist and was commissioned by numerous Italian princes and European sovereigns. His later work, characterised by bold compositions and densely coloured brushwork, is the impressive and personal document of one of the greatest artists of the century. **Tintoretto** (1518-94) added a tormented violence to the luminosity of his predecessors, and ably exploited this in his dramatic religious compositions. **Veronese** (1528-88) was first and foremost a decorator in love with luxury and sumptuous schemes who delighted in crowd scenes with grandiose architectural backgrounds. As for the very endearing **Jacopo Bassano** (1518-92), he handled rustic and nocturnal scenes, imbued with a new sense of reality, with a freedom of touch and composition.

THE UNSETTLED YEARS

The crisis at the end of the 15C, the invasion of Italy by foreign armies, with the resulting loss of liberty for many states, the increase in religious tensions, which led to the Lutheran Protestant movement, the sack of Rome and the Counter-Reformation had a dramatic effect on the artists of the time. In northern Italy, **Lorenzo Lotto** (1480-1556) interpreted with sharp psychological insight the spiritual and moral anxieties of the provincial aristocracy and bourgeoisie. In Brescia, following the work of Foppa, artists paid particular attention to reality and morality. Various painters portrayed the distressing reality of their time: the work of **Romanino** (1484-1559) is characterised by a northern and anti-classical expressive violence, **Savoldo** (c 1480-1548) demonstrates a deep, lyrical intensity, while the paintings of **Moretto** (1498-1554) are humble in their touching spirit of faith. But the most obvious examples of the anti-classical crisis were in Florence, where **Pontormo** (1494-1556) was the typical incarnation of a genial but tormented and neurotic artist, a visionary given to bouts of insanity. His paintings were influenced by the works of Raphael and Michelangelo and disturbed the harmony of the Renaissance with their troubled tension, sharp colours and unreal sense of space.

MANNERISM

The art of the Counter-Reformation, with its continued use of Renaissance canon often in an exaggerated or mannered way, marked the transition between Renaissance and Baroque and attempted to give intellectual voice to the preoccupations of the previous generation. It could be described as a stately and refined art, which addressed the cultured public of the Italian and European courts and which pursued ideals of supreme and artificial beauty by copying the stylistic solutions of Raphael and Michelangelo, whose tragic sense would however be crystalised in mannered solutions which rendered the meaning ambiguous. A typical exponent of this style was **Giorgio Vasari** (1511-1574), author of the *Lives of the Artists*, who has had a strong influence on historical and critical judgement up to the present day. While Mannerism was widely adopted throughout Europe, it was countered in Italy by the opposition of the Roman Catholic Church which, following the Council of Trent, proposed that religious art be subjected to greater doctrinal clarity.

The numerous fountains and gardens where the natural and artificial were found side by side are also expressions of the Mannerist taste for festivities and frivolities.

17C – NATURALISM, CLASSICISM AND BAROQUE

Painting – In reaction against Mannerism, a group of Bolognese artists founded the **Accademia degli Incamminati** (Academy of the Eclectic), under the leadership of the **Carracci** family (Annibale, the most original, Lodovico and Agostino). They proposed a less artificial style of art which was truer to nature and which paved the way for future artistic trends. Classicism evolved firstly in Bologna and Rome, and later throughout Italy, following the premises laid down by the Carracci. One of the basic concepts of this style is that certain classical artistic forms, used in ancient art and by Raphael, constitute models of perfection and should be used as a paradigm for any type of creation of high spiritual content. The vault of Palazzo Farnese in Rome, painted by Annibale Carracci, presages the Baroque style with its overwhelming dynamics and its use of *trompe l'œil*. Baroque painting and architecture are characterised by a sense of movement, by broken perspectives, by scrolls and a taste for false reliefs. Painting is used in conjunction with architecture to give life to disturbing visions of impressive verisimilitude. A good example is the ceiling of the Chiesa del Gesù in Rome, where **Baciccia** (1639-1709) created a credible illusion of the sky in the physical architectural space of the ceiling.

It was the work of **Caravaggio** (1573-1610) which revolutionised several centuries of Italian idealism. His intense and often cruel realism, inspired by the artistic traditions of Lombardy and Brescia, drew its inspiration from everyday life in Rome. His unusual use of contrasting light gave a dramatic visual impact to his work and was

Basket of Fruit by Caravaggio (Pinacoteca Ambrosiana, Milan)

Bernini's baldaquin (St Peter's basilica, Rome)

often employed to highlight the moral reasons behind human actions and senti-
ments. He was widely imitated both in Italy, France and the Netherlands and was
without doubt the most influential artist in 17C Europe.

Architecture and sculpture – The main differences between Mannerist architecture,
which is developed on a single level and is therefore intellectual and static in style,
and Baroque, is the use of spatial dynamism, the continual intermingling between
the exterior and interior, the use of curved and broken lines, the use of light as a
vehicle of divine intervention, the combining of different artistic styles, and the use
of scenic devices to amaze and confuse the spectator, persuading the latter of the
existence of what he sees. The true Baroque style, which is structural and found
mainly in Rome, is often the creation of artists who worked as architects, painters,
sculptors and scenographers. The transformation of St Peter's basilica by **Bernini**
(1598-1680) offers typical examples: the famous colonnade solves the problem of
the unharmonious extension of the church and of the monumental but static façade,
making the façade the background of the dynamic piazza, which turns towards the
city of Rome and open its arms to welcome the faithful.

Inside the cathedral, the light flooding into the building and the immense bulk of the
baldaquin compensate for the loss of centrality due to the extension of the nave,
which is transformed into an extraordinary tunnel of perspective of increasing
tension. However, the architecture of **Borromini** (1599-1667) shows the tensions,
contrasts and resolutions of a troubled and tormented spirit, more inclined to find
inspiration in the dilemmas and contradictions of modern spiritual suffering than in
praising the representatives of the Almighty on earth. An interesting variation of
Baroque architecture can be seen in Apulia (especially Lecce) and in Sicily, where
buildings of ornate and imaginative decoration clearly show the influence of the
Spanish Plateresque style.

SETTECENTO (18C)

The deep cultural changes of the new century, with its emphasis on rational and
enlightened thinking, were reflected in art where the Baroque style, exhausted of
its most intimate religious content, became even more secular and decorative in
tone. Art was beginning to free itself from symbolic significance and becoming
more autonomous with its own aims and more inclined to entertain rather than

to educate. This trend began in France, where the style was known as *rocaille*. Italy had by now relinquished its leading role in art, although the peninsula still produced some important artistic figures, especially in Piedmont. The most extraordinary project of the time was the urban and architectural revival of Turin, raising the city to the status of European capital. **Filippo Juvarra** (1678-1736) moved beyond the tension and drama of the 17C Baroque architecture of his predecessor **Guarino Guarini** (1624-1683), designing an urban architecture and town plan (10km-long tree-lined avenues surrounding the buildings) of grandiose theatricality which provided the perfect backdrop for the fine costumes of the Court of Savoy. Art takes another important step away from a mere representation of physical objects with the work of the Venetian **Giovan Battista Tiepolo** (1696-1770), whose luminous painting produced *trompe l'oeil* perspectives created for pure visual pleasure with no real regard for verisimilitude or the content of the stories represented: art was now being valued for its artistic qualities alone.

OTTOCENTO (19C)

In the late 18C and early 19C the vogue for all things Classical spread throughout Italy and all over Europe, following the excavations of Herculaneum and Pompeii. The sober, simple and harmonious lines of this style, which is modelled on the immortal examples of Antiquity, provide a stark contrast to the exuberant irregular lines of Baroque. The Italian neo-Classical style is exemplified by the sculptor **Antonio Canova** (1757-1822), whose works seem to adhere perfectly to the "noble simplicity and quiet grandeur" of Greek art as described by Winckelmann (and only really observed through Roman copies). In his most famous sculpture, the Three Graces, the extreme formal perfection is transformed into an ambiguous sensuality, which resonates with nostalgia for a perfect world which has been lost forever, a subtle allusion to the impalpable screen between life and death which characterises all of his work, as well as the Romantic poetry of the period.

The neo-Classical style can also be seen in the field of architecture, alongside the eclectic style, influenced by so many sources and which was to last throughout the century, with often very erratic results. An exception is **Alessandro Antonelli** (1798-1888), who enlivened the neo-Classical idiom with new engineering principles, binding the academic tradition to the boldest experiments in Europe.

In painting, the often explicitly academic tone of **Hayez** (1791-1882) demonstrates the Romantic style which existed alongside the neo-Classical tradition. This friend of Canova creates paintings of medieval history which he uses to refer to the contemporary events of the Risorgimento and which are highly sentimental in tone. The **Macchiaioli** group, founded in 1855, started a revolt against academism, which was to last about 20 years. The group, who were also known as the "spotters" and were in some ways the precursors of the Impressionist school, often worked outdoors, using colour and simple lines and drawing inspiration from nature. The main exponents of this movement were **Giovanni Fattori** (1825-1908), **Lega** (1826-1895) and **Signorini** (1835-1901). Some artists worked with the Impressionists in Paris: their influence had an indirect but successful effect on Italian art. At the end of the 19C, in parallel with the growth of a flowing and sketch-like style of painting, **Segantini** (1858-1899), **Pellizza da Volpedo** (1868-1907) and **Previati** (1852-1920) developed the Divisionist school. This art reflected the theories of the French post-Impressionists, on the one hand developing a deeper analysis of reality, with strong connations of a social character, while at the same time lending itself to allegorical and symbolist themes, in line with artistic developments in the rest of Europe. Their solutions were of fundamental importance for the avant-garde trends of the 20C.

NOVECENTO (20C)

The 20C began in an explosive manner with the sensational and anti-aesthetic style of the **Futurists**, who under the leadership of the poet **Marinetti** (1876-1944), the movement's theorist, proclaimed their belief in the age of speed, crowds and machinery. This was an explicit and anarchic reaction to bourgeois traditionalist values, which were attacked in the name of a vehement and sometimes superficial vitality; the movement soon adopted a nationalist tone, which in some cases developed into a sympathy for the fascist movement. The futurists attempted to render the dynamism of the modern world often by fragmented forms similar to the Cubist style. However, they differed from the Cubists in their marked sense of rebellion, which was influenced both by the writing of contemporary philosophers such as Bergson and by the violent and impassioned disharmony of the Expressionist movement.

The members of this avant-garde movement were **Boccioni** (1882-1916), **Balla** (1871-1958), **Severini** (1883-1966), **Carrà** (1881-1966) and the architect **Sant'Elia** (1888-1916). **Giorgio De Chirico** (1888-1978), together with Carrà, created **metaphysical painting**, a disturbing form of art where objects are placed in unlikely but credible positions in an ambiguous and enigmatic atmosphere. **Giorgio Morandi** was inspired by some of the same ideas, although his still-life paintings of everyday objects invite the observer to meditate more deeply on history and the meaning of the painting.

After the First World War, the return to normality brought about an increase in artistic activity both in Italy and abroad. This included the founding of the **Novecento** group which developed naturalistic premises through magic realism, interpreted through a re-reading of metaphysics and of Italian medieval and classical art, with often highly poetic and formal results. Most of the painters, sculptors and architects in Italy either belonged to or were influenced by this group, especially when the political regime declared itself in favour of this

Alinari/GIRAUDON

Brawl in the Galleria by Boccioni (Pinacoteca di Brera, Milano)

stylistic trend in the 1920s, opposing any relationship with contemporary European art. A few isolated voices, often criticised by the authorities, were raised in explicit or tacit opposition to these artistic trends by those who were in favour of a less provincial approach. Some of the most important forces in Italian art during this period were involved in the **Corrente** group from Milan, the **Scuola romana**, and the **Sei di Torino**, which, although following individual paths, shared a common interest in expressionism, which often gave their art a highly dramatic realism, a social tension and a deeply humane content. A good example is the painter **Guttuso** (1912-1987), with his personal interpretation of post-Cubist art which he used in combination with explicitly anti-fascist material; even in the general post-war crisis he nearly always managed to avoid the risks of socialist realism, thanks to his openness to different cultural influences. One of the most important contemporary sculptors was **Manzù** (1908-1991), who succeeded in breathing new life into Christian art. Through the use of a clear and luminous sensitivity, which gives his works, especially the low reliefs, an almost Donatellian vitality, Manzù succeeds in making a sorrowful and humane statement against violence, which is shown to be the inexorable and universal mortification of man.

THE POST-WAR PERIOD

The tragedy of war always makes an indelible impression on art: in such circumstances artists query the significance of artistic creation in a world in which all moral values have been brutally set aside. The phrase "the death of art" was also used in the new consumer society of the 1950s and 1960s. The classical artistic language is no longer understood as a system of signs able to give form to the aesthetic experience of reality. New artistic expression is therefore fundamentally anti-aesthetic in style and develops in accordance with trends which were up to this point unrelated to the world of art. To put it more simply, new trends often shared a lack of interest in or even the destruction of the old physical support, the canvas. This is partly true in the case of **Burri** (1915-1995), who came to painting later in life, avoiding the traditional academic circles. By pasting old torn bags onto his canvas, Burri's intention was not to represent ideas or objects, but to exhibit a fragment of reality, of matter, which only acquired significance because it had been transformed by the artist and therefore became a part of his personal experience. **Fontana** (1899-1968) also stretched the physical limits inherent in the traditional method of creating art and cut his canvas in an attempt to find new solutions to the old problem of space, which can be created but not represented, emphasising the importance of the "gesture" and of the action which puts the here and now in contact with the other world of the canvas, destroying the classical pretence of space. Other artists belonged to the movement known as **arte povera**, which was in explicit opposition to the "rich" world. For these artists the break with the classical method of creating and understanding art is complete, right up to the radical refusal of the artist to develop a role, which he believes to be a hoax, dominated by the system against which he is struggling.

SAINTS IN ITALIAN ART

Much of Italian art is religious in nature. The following list describes the traditional attributes of the most important saints and will help visitors to identify some of the many saints to be found in churches and museums.

SAINT	ATTRIBUTES
St Agatha	Amputated breasts, often placed on a plate; tongs.
St Andrew	A cross and the tools of the fisherman.
St Anthony	Fire, a piglet and a demon.
St Anthony of Padua	A lily, a book and often accompanied by the Infant Jesus.
St Bartholomew	Martyred by flaying, he is often pictured carrying his own skin.
St Bernardine of Siena	Represented as an emaciated monk carrying the monogram of Christ (IHS).
St Catherine	Depicted with a cogged wheel representing her martyrdom and a palm branch.
St Cecilia	Musical instruments.
St Christopher	Always depicted carrying the Infant Jesus on his shoulders.
St Dominic	Wears the white and black vestment of the Dominicans; often accompanied by a dog and a torch.
St Francis of Assisi	Unmistakable by his monk's garments and the stigmata; sometimes represented with a wolf and birds.
St Jerome	Whether he is depicted in his cardinal's robes, semi-naked in the desert or reading books in his study, he is usually accompanied by a lion.
St George	Represented as a warrior killing a dragon.
St James the Great	Dressed as a pilgrim and carrying a scallop shell.
St John the Baptist	Covered with animal skins, carrying a lamb and a banner bearing the words *Ecce agnus dei.*
St John the Evangelist	Often portrayed as a youth, always accompanied by an eagle and sometimes by the gospel.
St Lawrence	Martyred by fire on a gridiron, he is depicted with a representation of the grid and a palm branch.
St Luke the Evangelist	Always accompanied by an ox, and sometimes by the gospel.
St Lucy	Associated with light, and the patron saint of sight, often portrayed carrying her eyes in a dish.
St Mark the Evangelist	Always accompanied by a lion and sometimes by the gospel.
St Mary Magdalene	Recognisable by her flowing hair and jar of ointment.
St Matthew the Evangelist	Always accompanied by an angel and sometimes by the gospel.
St Michael the Archangel	Depicted as a warrior, threatening a dragon or devil with his sword.
St Nicholas	Almost always depicted with three golden balls and a ship.
St Ursula	Surrounded by the women who were martyred with her.
St Paul	Often depicted together with St Peter, usually bald and accompanied by a sword and a book.
St Peter	Always carries keys in his hand; often depicted with a cockerel, chains and a cross.
St Peter the Martyr	Shown with a knife stuck into his head, carrying a palm branch.
St Rocco	Identified by a wound in his leg and a dog carrying bread in its mouth.
St Sebastian	Depicted as a handsome youth wounded by arrows.
St Stephen	Represented with the stones used to stone him.
St Teresa of Avila	Portrayed in a state of ecstatic rapture with an angel and a dove.

ANCIENT CIVILISATIONS

The Greeks

Cities – Territory in the Greek settlements was roughly divided into three different areas from the 8C BC onwards, when the first colonists arrived in Italy: places of worship, public spaces and residential areas. Generally the city was laid out in an octagonal grid – designed by **Hippodamus of Miletus**, a Greek philosopher and town planner who lived in Asia Minor in the 5C BC – organised around two main axes, the cardo (*stenopos* in Greek), which ran from north to south, and the **decumanus** (*plateia* in Greek), running from east to west. The road network was completed with minor cardi and decumani, which formed blocks. A number of public areas and buildings were situated within the town, such as the **agorà**, the main, central square where much of public life took place, the **ekklesiastérion**, a public building used for the meeting of the public assembly (*ekklesìa*), and the **bouleutérion**, which housed meetings of the citizens' council (the *boulé*). The temples, sometimes built outside the city limits, were often surrounded by other sacred buildings, which in the most monumental structures could include porticoes, votive monuments, gymnasia and theatres. The city itself was usually protected by fortifications, outside of which lay the agricultural land, subdivided into family plots, and the area used for burials.

Temples – The focus of the building was the **naos**, also known as the cella, which housed the statue of the god; the temple faced east so that the statue was illuminated by the rising sun, considered to be the source of all life. In front of the *naos* was the **pronaos**, a kind of antechamber, while the back of the temple, the **opistodomos**, acted as a treasury room. The temple was surrounded by columns **(peristyle)** and supported by a base; the columns which supported the entablature rested on the last steps **(stylobate)** of the temple. The building was covered by a two-sided sloping roof.

The dominant style in Magna Graecia and in Sicily is the Doric style, with its imposing and sober columns, which are placed directly on the stylobate without a base. The capital has no sculpted carvings, but consists simply of a round buffer (echinus) placed on a square block (abacus). The Doric entablature comprises a smooth architrave, the upper section of which presents a frieze with alternating metopes (panels of sculpted low reliefs) and triglyphs (panels depicting two deep vertical grooves in the centre and two smaller grooves on each side).

The Doric harmony and elegance of Neptune's Temple in Paestum

The architectural style of the Doric temple has long been considered by many to be a prototype for ideal beauty as a result of its simple structure and perfect harmony of proportions. Architects, who took into account the tendency of the human eye to deform the lines of large buildings, were able to make a few optical corrections to the conventional structure. The entablatures, the upper section of which seemed to lean forward slightly, were raised to the centre, thus acquiring an imperceptible arched shape. To create an impression of perfect equilibrium, the columns situated to the sides of the temple façade were bent slightly towards the inside of the building, in order to avoid the effect of divergence. Finally, in very large buildings (such as the

Temple of Concord in Agrigento and the Basilica in Paestum) where the columns seemed to contract towards the top of the temple, this optical illusion was addressed by increasing the size of the shaft by two-thirds of the height.

The temples were often decorated with groups of sculptures and low reliefs and were usually painted in red, blue and white in order to provide the sculptures and columns with maximum relief.

When compared with the architecture of mainland Greece, the temples of Magna Graecia and Sicily are more monumental, pay more attention to spacial effect and show a particular taste for abundant decoration.

Sculpture – The scarcity of marble and the particular Italian taste for pictorial and chiaroscuro effects resulted in the predominant use of limestone and sandstone as raw materials. Clay was widely used in the pediments and acroter of the temples, as well as for votive statues. The Ionic style was employed in the colonies from the end of the 6C BC and was characterised by a greater individualisation of features, an increasingly dramatic sense of pathos and the use of softer shapes. The main artistic centres of the period were Taranto, Naples, Paestum, Agrigento and Siracusa.

Painting and ceramics – Painting was considered by the Greeks to be the most noble and eloquent form of art; unfortunately the perishable nature of the pigments used means that little remains of this art. The only examples of Greek painting to have survived are to be found inside tombs or on the façades of hypogea. Large easel paintings, extolled by original sources, cloud be partially reconstructed from vase paintings, which often took the former as their model.

Vases with black figures painted against a red or yellow background date from the Archaic and beginning of the Classical periods. The detail on the figures was obtained by simply engraving the black varnish with a steel tip. Mythological subjects or scenes depicting daily life were the most common designs used. Red figure vases appeared in southern Italy towards the end of the 5C BC. The black varnish, previously used only for figures, was now used for the background, with the figures drawn in a brick red colour with touches of black and white. This reversal, which gave artists a greater freedom of expression, constituted a revolutionary discovery and allowed artists to produce more subtle designs. The themes used remained much the same. From the 3C BC Italian and Magno-Greek art became more decorative in style.

The Etruscans

The Etruscan towns, built on elevated sites with walls of huge stones, show an advanced sense of town planning, often based on Greek models. Near the towns are vast burial grounds with underground chambers or hypogea filled with objects revealing the customs and art of the Etruscan people. Etruscan art is primitive in character, though strongly influenced by the Orient and especially by Greece from the 6C BC onwards. It has a marked individuality sustained by realism and expressive movement. The discovery in the 19C of masterpieces like the Apollo and Hermes of Veii and the systematic study of artefacts in the 20C have given this vigorous and refined art the place it deserved.

The figurative arts – Since architectural specimens are lacking, **sculpture** appears to us as the artists' favourite medium. The great period is the 6C BC, when large groups of

statuary adorned the pediments of temples: the famous Apollo of Veii (in the Villa Giulia museum in Rome) of obvious Greek influence, belongs to this period. Some portrait busts are more original in their striking realism, intensity of expression and stylised features: their large prominent eyes and enigmatic smiles are characteristic of the Etruscan style. The same applies to the famous groups of semi-recumbent figures on the sarcophagi, many of which are portraits. The Etruscans also excelled in bronze sculpture, as demonstrated by the magnificent Chimera from Arezzo (in the Archeological Museum of Florence).

The only surviving **paintings** are in the burial chambers of the cemeteries (Cerveteri, Veii and especially Tarquinia), where they were supposed to remind the dead of the pleasures of life: banquets, games and plays, music and dancing, hunting etc. These colourful and delicate wall paintings show amazing powers of observation and form an excellent record of Etruscan habits and customs.

SCALA

The Chimera from Arezzo –
Florence, Archeological Museum

Pottery and goldsmiths' work – The Etruscans were artisans of genius. In pottery they used the little known **bucchero** technique, producing black earthenware with figures in relief. Initially decorated with motifs in *pointillé*, the vases developed more elaborate shapes with a more complicated ornamentation, although in general these were not of the same quality as the earlier work. In the 7C BC they modelled beautiful burial urns, *canopae*, in animal or human shape. In the domain of goldsmiths' work, both men and women wore heavy often solid gold ornaments of remarkable workmanship, showing the skill of Etruscan goldsmiths particularly in the filigrane and granulation techniques. Engraved mirrors, cists (cylindrical vessels which usually served as marriage coffers), scent-burners and bronze candelabra of great decorative elegance also show the artisans' skill.

The Romans

A Roman town – Newly-founded Roman towns often have a military origin or were planned as an extension to the *castrum*, the military camp. The new towns built in this way, which had been surrounded with walls during troubled periods, were generally divided into four quarters by two main streets, the *decumanus* and the *cardo*, intersecting at right angles and ending in gateways. Other streets parallel to these two gave the town a grid plan.

The **streets** were edged with footpaths, sometimes 50cm/18in high, and lined with porticoes to shelter pedestrians. The roadway, paved with large flagstones which fitted together perfectly, was crossed at intervals by stepping-stones laid at the same level as the pavements but between which horses and cart-wheels could pass.

A Roman house – Excavations at Herculaneum, Pompeii and especially Ostia have uncovered two main types of Roman house: the *insulae*, dwellings of several storeys divided into apartments, often with shops open to the street and the *domus*, large, luxurious mansions for single families with an atrium, which had evolved from the earlier Greek model.

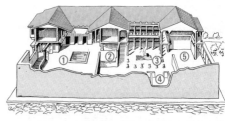

A Roman house

These last had a modest external appearance owing to their bare walls and few windows. But the interiors, adorned with mosaics, statues, paintings and marbles and sometimes including private baths and a fish pond, revealed the riches of their owners. A vestibule overlooked by the porter's lodge led to the *atrium*.

The **atrium** ①, originally the heart of the *domus*, later came to refer to the internal courtyard built around the *impluvium*, a basin under the open section which caught rainwater. The bedrooms (*cubiculae*) opened off the atrium, which was the only part of the house to which strangers were usually admitted. At the far end was the **tablinum** ② or the living and dining room. The atrium and adjoining rooms constituted the oldest form of the Roman house, later inhabited only by less wealthy citizens. High officials, rich colonials and prosperous tradesmen often added a second house, of the more refined Hellenistic type, joined onto the *tablinum*. The **peristyle** ③, a court surrounded by a portico in the centre of the part of the house reserved for the family, was generally made into a garden with basins lined with mosaics, fountains and statues. The living quarters opened on to it. The *cubiculae* were simple sleeping chambers, containing a stone platform built against the wall or a movable bed. There were mattresses, cushions and blankets but no sheets. The dining-room or **triclinium** ④ takes its name from the three couches for the guests, who, adopting a custom that originated in Greece, adopted a reclining pose for eating, stretched out on cushions and leaning on one elbow. In the centre was a table at which the slaves busied themselves. Lastly, there was the great hall or **œcus** ⑤ which was sometimes embellished with a colonnade. The outbuildings included the kitchen with a sink and drain, a built-in stove and oven; baths, which were like the public baths on a smaller scale, and the slaves' quarters, barns, cellars, stables etc. The latrines were usually in a corner of the kitchen in order to make use of the same drainage system.

The forum – The forum was a large square, often surrounded by a portico during the Imperial period. Originally it was a market, usually at the crossing of the two main streets, as well as the centre of the public and commercial life of Roman towns. Men came to read public notices, listen to political speakers, stroll and talk. The women did their shopping, either in shops around the square or from hawkers and artisans who set up their stalls under the porticos. Government offices surrounded the forum. These included the *curia* or headquarters of local government; the voting hall for elections; the public tribune from which candidates for office harangued the crowd;

the Temple of Money or exchange (argentaria); the municipal treasury; the public granaries; the Temple of Justice or law courts; the prison; temples and many commemorative monuments.

The tombs - Roman cemeteries were placed along the roads, at some distance from the towns. The tombs were marked by a simple stele, by an altar or, for the most important families, by a mausoleum. The remains of less affluent families were placed in a *columbarium*, a vault containing a series of niches in the wall for funerary urns. The most famous Roman cemetery is that on the Via Appia Antica, south of Rome. Directly after death the body of the deceased was exposed on a funeral couch surrounded with candlesticks and wreaths of flowers. Then it was buried or cremated by the family. The deceased was provided with objects for use in the after-life: clothes, arms and tools for men, toys for children, and jewellery and toilet articles for women.

Architecture - The Romans borrowed certain elements from Greek architecture, yet Roman architecture differs from Greek in its basic "plastic" and organic vocation, the strict relationship between the external shape and the internal space, and in the important technical innovations which allowed the use of softer, more flexible curved shapes, such as the arch, dome and vault. The column, which was the foundation of the Greek trilithic system (based on two columns and the architrave) was replaced by the wall and the pilaster. The use of **concrete**, thrown into moulds, allowed huge covered spaces to be built. Also noteworthy were the many public civil engineering projects carried out by the Romans, as testified by the huge constructions they have left behind, such as bridges, aqueducts, roads, tunnels, sewerage systems, baths, theatres and amphitheatres, stadia and circuses, basilicas and nymphaea, gymnasia and colonnades, triumphal arches and the many public and private monuments (the private often rivalling the public in terms of size and splendour).

Temples - The temples were dedicated to the worship of gods or emperors, raised to divine status from the time of Augustus. The Roman temple, inspired by the Greek model, consists of a closed chamber, the *cella*, containing the image of the god, and an open vestibule. The building is surrounded, partly or completely, by a colonnade and is built on a podium.

SCALA

Trajan's Arch, Benevento

Triumphal arches - In Rome these commemorated the "triumphs" of generals or conquering emperors. The low reliefs on the arches recorded their feats of arms. In the provinces, such as Aosta, Benevento and Ancona, there are municipal arches commemorating important events or erected in honour of some member of the Imperial family.

The baths - The Roman baths, which were public and free, were not only baths but also physical fitness centres, casinos, clubs, recreation centres, libraries, lecture halls and meeting-places, which explains the amount of time people spent there. Decoration in these great buildings was lavish: mosaic ornaments, coloured marble facings, columns and statues. The bather followed a medically approved circuit. From the gymnasium (palestra) he entered a lukewarm room (tepidarium) to prepare for the high temperature of the hot baths (caldarium); he then returned to a lukewarm room before taking a cold plunge (frigidarium) to tone up the skin. To heat air and water a number of underground furnaces (hypocausts) were used. The hot air was circulated to heat the rooms from below and from the sides.

The amphitheatre - This typically Roman structure, several storeys high, encircles the elliptical arena and was destined to seat the spectators. Posts were fixed to the upper part of the external wall to carry a huge adjustable awning, the *velarium*, which sheltered the spectators from the sun and rain. Inside, enclosing the arena, a wall protected the spectators in the front rows from the wild animals in the ring. A complex of circular galleries, staircases and corridors enabled all the spectators to reach their seats quickly without crowding through the *vomitaria* or passageways.

Always very popular, the performances were announced in advance by painted posters, giving the names of the performers and details of the programme which included fighting of three kinds: between animals, between gladiators and animals, and between gladiators. In principle, a duel between gladiators always ended in the death of one of the opponents. The public could ask for a gladiator's life to be spared and the President of the Games would indicate a reprieve by turning up his thumb. The victorious gladiator received a sum of money if he was a professional, or he was freed if he was a slave or a prisoner.

In some amphitheatres the stage could be flooded for naval battles (naumachia), in which special flat-bottomed boats were used.

The circus – The circus, which was usually connected to the Imperial palace and was used for horse and chariot races, was long and narrow, with a short curved side and a straight side, where the races started. Spectators were seated on the terraces, while the competitors raced around the track. In the later Roman Empire many different types of games took place here. The circus was very similar in shape to the smaller **stadium**, which was copied from the Greek model and which was originally used for athletic competitions.

The theatre – Theatres had rows of seats, usually ending in colonnades, a central area or **orchestra** occupied by distinguished spectators or used for acting, and a raised **stage**. The actors performed in front of a wall which was the finest part of the building and which imitated the façade of a palace in style: its decoration included several tiers of columns, niches containing statues, marble facings and mosaics. The perfect acoustics were generally due to a combination of sophisticated devices. The scenery was either fixed or mobile and there was an ingenious array of machinery either in the wings or below stage, as well as an impressive range of special effects (smoke, lightning, thunder, and the appearance of gods – the famous deus ex machina – or heroes).

The chief function of the theatre was the performance of comedies and tragedies; however, Roman theatres were also used for competitions, lottery draws and the distribution of bread or money.

Until the end of the 2C BC all actors wore wigs of different shapes and colours according to the nature of the character they represented. After that date they adopted pasteboard masks and again each character had a distinctive mask. Tragic actors, to make themselves more impressive, wore buskins or sandals with thick cork soles.

Literature

Birth and splendour of Italian literature – The Italian language acquired a literary form in the 13C. At Assisi **St Francis** (1182-1226) wrote his moving Canticle of the Creatures in the vernacular instead of the traditional Latin, so that the people could read the word of God. The 13C also gave rise to the **Sicilian School** which, at the court of Frederick II, developed a language of love inspired by traditional ballads from Provence.

The most famous of the 13C poetical trends was, however, that of the **dolce stil nuovo** ("sweet new style"): followers included Guinezzelli and Cavalcanti. The term was appropriated by **Dante Alighieri** (1265-1321), author of La vita nuova (The New Life), Convivio (The Banquet) and De vulgari eloquentia (Concerning Vernacular Eloquence), to indicate the lyrical quality of this poetry which would celebrate a spiritual and edifying love for an angel-like woman in verse. It was with this new tool that he wrote one of the most powerful masterpieces of Italian literature: the Divine Comedy is the account of a lively, enquiring and impassioned visitor to Inferno, Purgatorio and Paradiso. It is also an epic account of the Christianised Western world and the height of spiritual knowledge of the period. During the 14C **Petrarch** (1304-1375), the precursor of humanism and the greatest Italian lyrical poet (see PADOVA), and his friend **Boccaccio** (1313-1375), the astonishing storyteller who seems almost modern at times (see SAN GIMIGNANO: Certaldo), continued in the tradition of Dante. Each enriched the Italian language in his own way.

Petrarch in the Sonnets of the Canzoniere brought a fluidity and depth of psychological interrogation inspired by his love for Laura, while Boccaccio in his Decameron added a liveliness of narration and accuracy of description to the 100 tales inspired by the ideals of the emerging bourgeoisie.

Humanism and Renaissance – Florentine humanism reinterpreted the ancient heritage and invented a scholarly poetry in which the tension of the words and images reflected the aspiration of the soul to attain an ideal. Politian, **Lorenzo de' Medici** (1449-1492) and especially **Michelangelo** were exponents of the Neo-Platonic notion of ideal poetry. However the Florentine Renaissance also favoured the development of

Dante explaining the Divine Comedy to the city of Florence (Florence, Duomo)

SCALA

other quite different lines of thought: scientific with Leonardo da Vinci, theorist with Leon Battista Alberti, philosophical with Marsile Fincin and encyclopaedic with the fascinating personality of Pico della Mirandola. Later Giorgio Vasari *(see FIRENZE)* became the first-ever art historian.

In the 16C writers and poets perfected the Italian language to a height of refinement and elegance rarely attained, and all this in the service of princes whom they counselled or entertained. The most famous was **Machiavelli** (1469-1527) *(see Index)*, the statesman and political theorist whose name now symbolises cunning and duplicity. In his work entitled **The Prince** he defined with clarity and intelligence the processes which control the society of man, and the moral and political consequences of these relationships.

At the court in Ferrara, **Boiardo** (1441-94) fused the epic poetry of the Carolingian cycles with the courtly poetry of the Breton cycles in the poem celebrating chivalry, *Orlando Inamorato (Roland in love)*. **Ludovico Ariosto** (1475-1533) and **Tasso** (1544-95) provided an element of intellectual brilliance. The former wrote *Orlando Furioso (Roland the Mad)*, an epic poem in episodes which enjoyed an extraordinary vogue, and Tasso, his successor at court in this genre, published his *Jerusalem Delivered (Gerusalemme Liberata)*.

At Urbino, **Baldassare Castiglione** (1478-1529) was the author of one of the great works of the period *The Courtier (Il cortegiano)* which was read throughout Europe. In Venice, **Aretino** (1492-1556) sketched the implacable portrait of his contemporaries *(Letters)* while in Padua, **Ruzzante** (1502-42) favoured realism in the local dialect.

The Counter-Reformation and the Baroque period – After the discovery of America in 1492, an event which affected the Mediterranean economy adversely, and the spread of Lutheran Protestantism, the 17C to the early 18C marked a period of decadence for Italian literature. The exception was **Galileo** (1564-1642), a scientist, who, taking Archimedes as his point of reference rather than Aristotle, made a distinction between scientific methods and those applicable to theology and philosophy. He was implacably opposed by the Church in an attempt to reassert its influence under the onslaught of the Reformation. The fear of the Inquisition hampered original thought and favoured the development of Baroque poetical concepts in a quest for fantasy.

The Age of Enlightenment and Romanticism – The early 18C was marked by Arcadia, a literary academy which preached "good taste" inspired by the purity of classical bucolic poetry, in opposition to the "bad taste" of the Baroque period.

The philosopher **Giambattista Vico** (1668-1744) elaborated the theory of the ebb and flow of history based on three stages (sense, imagination and reason). The dramatist **Metastasio** (1698-1783) was also a leading figure of the period whose biting yet well-thought out vision advanced scientific and philosophical thought.

In Venice, the 18C was dominated by the dramatist **Carlo Goldoni** (1707-93), known as the Italian Molière, who peopled his plays in an amusing, alert and subtle manner with the stock characters and situations of the *Commedia dell'Arte (see BERGAMO)*, an art form which was then highly popular in Venice.

From the end of the 18C writers began to express a new national spirit (consciousness which developed until the upheaval of the Risorgimento). **Giuseppe Parini** (1729-99), a didactic writer, and **Vittorio Alfieri** (1749-1803) who became known for his tragedies on the themes of liberty and opposition to tyranny, were the precursors of the violent and tormented **Ugo Foscolo** (1778-1827) whose patriotic pride is given full vent in *Of the Sepulchres*. In his later works Foscolo adopted the literary genre of Richardson, Rousseau, Goethe and Gray.

It was **Giacomo Leopardi** (1798-1837) who in some of the finest poems of his verse collection *Canzoni* expresses with a certain lucidity and lyrical purity the growing gulf between the old faith and a fear of the unknown future. He was the main exponent of Italian romanticism and of the theory of historical pessimism based on the contrast between a happy natural state and Reason (or civilisation) which brings unhappiness. This was followed by cosmic pessimism which posits the condemnation of Nature and unhappiness as an intrinsic human condition.

The Milanese author, **Alessandro Manzoni** (1785-1873), wrote one of the most important novels of 19C Italian literature, *The Betrothed (I promessi sposi)*, a grandiose epic of ordinary folk based on the notion of providence in human existence.

Realism and Decadence – The Sicilian **Giovanni Verga** (1840-1922) assured the transition between the 19C and 20C with his novels. He was one of the most important members of the Italian realist *(verismo)* school of novelists which took its inspiration from the French naturalist movement. In his extravagant fiction series entitled *Vinti* he presents his pessimistic vision of the world and his compassion for the disinherited.

In the field of lyrical poetry in the second half of the 19C **Giosuè Carducci** (1835-1907), a Nobel prize winner in 1906, drew inspiration from Classical poetry. He was a melancholy figure who criticised the sentimentality of the romantic movement. **Gabriele d'Annunzio** (1863-1938) adopted a refined and precious style to express his sensual love of language. The complex and anxious voice of the poet **Giovanni Pascoli** (1855-1912) filled the early years of the century. His nostalgic poetry recalls the age of innocence and a sense of wonder.

Modern and contemporary authors – In the early 20C, magazines devoted to political, cultural, moral and literary themes were published. Giuseppe Prezzolini (1882-1982) and Giovanni Papini (1881-1956) were among the contributors.

Futurism, which influenced other forms of artistic expression, was the most important of the contemporary literary movements. In his *Manifesto* (1909) **Filippo Tommaso Marinetti** (1876-1944), the leader and theoretician of the movement, exalted the attractions of speed, machines, war and "feverish insomnia", ideas which were echoed by the disjointed syntax, punctuation and words employed in this literary style.

In line with the European sensibility expressed by Musil, Proust and Joyce, Italian letters favoured the theme of discovery which was influenced by studies on repression and the unconscious in the early years of psychoanalysis. In *Zeno's Conscience*, **Italo Svevo** (1861-1928) examines the alienation of the main protagonist as past and present unfold in a long internal monologue. The Sicilian dramatist **Luigi Pirandello** (1867-1936) also analyses man's tragic solitude and the way in which the identity of the individual is eclipsed by the perceptions of the different persons with whom he associates. The only escape is madness.

Luigi Pirandello

Traces of realism and the influence of D'Annunzio can be detected in the work of **Grazia Deledda** (1871-1936), who shrouds her portrayals of Sardinian society in mythology. Her tales are dominated by passionate emotions and a deep religious sense of life and death.

The **Hermetic Movement**, which developed after the First World War, celebrated the essential nature of words, liberated from the burden of a grandiloquent and commemorative tradition. The poetry of **Giuseppe Ungaretti** (1888-1970) is evocative and intense, while another leading figure of this movement, **Salvatore Quasimodo** (1901-68), produced successful translations of Greek and Latin classical literature and of Shakespeare.

The poetry of **Eugenio Montale** (1896-1981) relates with sharp and incisive eloquence the anguish which afflicts human nature. **Umberto Saba** (1883-1957), whose native Trieste was strongly marked by Central European culture, uses both noble language and everyday vocabulary in his intensely lyrical and autobiographical work.

After the Second World War, **Neo-Realism** – which was ideally suited to the cinema with its popular appeal – gave a graphic account of the life and misery of the working class, of peasants and street children.

The recurring themes in the works of **Cesare Pavese** (1908-1950) are the loneliness and difficulty of existing, described with anguish in his diary which was published posthumously with the title *This Business of Living*.

During recent decades the Italian novel has shown a strong vitality with such diverse personalities as Pratolini *(A Tale of Poor Lovers)*, Guido Piovene *(Pietà contro pietà)*, Ignazio Silone *(Fontarama)*, Mario Soldati *(A cena col commendatore)*, Carlo Levi *(Christ stopped at Eboli)* and Elsa Morante *(Arthur's Island)*.

In recent years, a handful of Italian authors have achieved international fame: **Alberto Moravia** (1907-1990) is regarded as a significant narrator of contemporary Italy identifying the importance of such issues as sex and money. His book, *The Time of Indifference*, recounts the decline and forbearance of a bourgeois Roman family. Another well-known neo-realist author was **Italo Calvino** (1923-1985) who experimented with the mechanisms of language and who wrote short stories tinged with subtle irony.

Leonardo Sciascia (1921-1989) concentrated on revealing some of the ills of Italian society, such as the Mafia. He wrote essays, detective stories, historical memoirs and romantic surveys. **Carlo Emilio Gadda**, known as the "engineer", experiments with language in his works and succeeds in portraying the hypocrisy, follies and obscure ills of contemporary society. **Pier Paolo Pasolini** (1922-1975) provoked and contested the received ideas of his time, contrasting Marxist ideology with Christian spirituality and peasant values.

Dino Buzzati (1906-72), an original figure, was a poet, writer, illustrator and journalist. His penchant for fantasy and surrealism is tinged with scepticism and is reminiscent of Kafka and Poe.

The 1980s saw the huge success of *The Name of the Rose* (1980), a Gothic thriller written by the semeiologist and essayist **Umberto Eco** (1932). The century came to a triumphant close with the awarding of the 1997 Nobel Prize for literature to the playwright and actor **Dario Fo** (1926), a kind of medieval court jester who in his plays attacks the powerful and defends the oppressed.

To plan a special itinerary:

– consult the Map of Touring Programmes which indicates the recommended routes, the tourist regions, the principal towns and main sights;

– read the descriptions in the Sights section which include Excursions from the main tourist centres.

Michelin Maps nos 988 (Italia) and regional maps nos 428,429, 430, 431, 432 and 433 indicate scenic routes, interesting sights, viewpoints, rivers, forests...

The Atlas Italia is a practical spiral-bound atlas with an alphabetical index.

Music

Italy has played a significant role in the evolution of music with the invention of the musical scale and the development of the violin. It is the birthplace of Vivaldi, who inspired Bach and who was surprisingly neglected until the beginning of the 20C, and of Verdi who created operatic works to celebrate the Risorgimento in the 19C.

Great composers and musical composition – As early as the end of the 10C, a Benedictine monk, **Guido** of Arezzo (997-c 1050), invented the scale naming the notes with the initial syllables of the first six lines of John the Baptist's hymn *"Ut queant laxis / Resonare fibris / Mira gestorum / Famuli tuorum / Solve polluti / Labii reatum Sancte Johannes"*. The "Si" formed by the initials of *Sancte Johannes* was added to these and the *Ut* was changed to *Do* in the 17C.

In the 16C, the golden age of vocal polyphony which was then very popular was marked by **Giovanni Pierluigi da Palestrina** (c 1525-1594), a prolific composer of essentially religious music (105 masses). During that period, **Andrea Gabrielli** (c 1510-86) and his nephew **Giovanni** (c 1557-1612) who were the organists at St Mark's in Venice were masters of sacred and secular polyphonic music. The latter composed the first violin sonatas.

Instrumental music from the Baroque period to the 18C – It was only in the 17C and 18C that a proper musical school (for operatic as well as instrumental works) was born in Italy which was characterised by charm and freshness of inspiration and melodic talent. The old and new musical forms evolved with the expressive and stylistic innovations of **Girolamo Frescobaldi** (1583-1643) for the organ and harpsichord, **Corelli** (1653-1713) for the violin and **Domenico Scarlatti** (1685-1757) for the harpsichord. The talented Venetian, **Antonio Vivaldi** (1675-1741), composed a wealth of lively music greatly admired by Bach, particularly his concertos divided into three parts, *allegro/adagio/allegro* and with descriptive interludes as in the *Four Seasons*. **Baldassare Galuppi** (1706-85), a

Vivaldi

native of Burano near Venice composed the music for the librettos of Goldoni as well as sonatas for harpsichord with a lively tempo. Although Venice was in its final period of glory, her musical reputation grew with the **Marcello** brothers, **Benedetto** (1686-1739) and **Alessandro** (1684-1750). The latter composed a famous concerto for oboe, stringed instruments and organ with a splendid adagio. The instrumental compositions of **Tomaso Albinoni** (1671-1750) are reminiscent of Vivaldi's masterpieces.

In the 18C important Italian composers worked outside Italy. In the field of chamber music, **Luigi Boccherini** (1743-1805), a native of Lucca working in Spain, was famous for his melodies and minuets. He also wrote a powerful symphony, *The House of the Devil*.

Antonio Salieri (1750-1825) from the Veneto was an active composer and a famous tutor who taught Beethoven, Schubert and Liszt. Towards the end of his life, he became mentally disturbed and blamed himself for Mozart's death. This episode is the theme of the film *Amadeus* by Milos Forman (1984). The Piedmontese **Giovanni Battista Viotti** (1755-1824), Salieri's contemporary, enriched the violin repertory with 29 fine violin concertos. He lived in Paris and London and died after the failure of his wine business.

Although not a musician, **Lorenzo Da Ponte** deserves a mention for his poetic contribution to great musical works. His love of adventure took him not only to New York where he died but also to Vienna, Europe's musical capital at that time. He collaborated with Mozart and wrote librettos for *The Marriage of Figaro*, *Don Giovanni* and *Così fan tutte* which won him great fame.

La Scala c 1830

This great period ended with the Romantic movement which is wonderfully celebrated by the great violinist **Niccolò Paganini** (1782-1840) although by that time the piano had become more popular than the violin. His adventurous life, genius of interpretation and legendary virtuosity as well as his slim, tall build turned him into a demonic figure. His most famous works include 24 **Capricci** and six concertos; the finale of the second concerto is the well-known *Campanella*.

Opera – Modern opera originated with **Claudio Monteverdi** (1567-1643) from Cremona whose masterpiece was *Orfeo*. Monteverdi heralded this musical idiom combining words and music, which was immediately very successful and became a popular pursuit influencing the whole cultural scene in Italy.

At the end of the 17C, Neapolitan opera with **Alessandro Scarlatti** established the distinction between arias which highlight virtuoso singing and recitatives which are essential for the development of the action. In the 18C, **Giovan Battista Pergolese**, **Domenico Cimarosa** and **Giovanni Paisiello** were the leading composers of comic opera (*opera buffa*), which is in a lighter vein and entirely sung.

In the 19C there were few great composers of instrumental music apart from Paganini, as lyrical art was made to reflect the intense passions of the Risorgimento. **Gioacchino Rossini** (1782-1868) marked the transition from the classical to the romantic period (*Othello, William Tell* and the comic operas *The Italian Girl in Algiers*, *The Thieving Magpie* and *The Barber of Seville*). **Vincenzo Bellini** (1801-35) composed rather average orchestral music but admirable melodies which are successful as such (*La Somnambula, Norma*). His rival **Gaetano Donizetti** (1797-1848) wrote several melodramas (*Lucia di Lammermoor*) where the action takes second place to the

---

The Violin

The violin was created as a new and improved model of the viola. Nowadays its fame is so closely linked to that of the old stringed instrument workshops (second half of the 16C- beginning of the 18C), almost all of which were based in Cremona, that the manufacturer's name (Gasparo da Salò, Amati, Guarneri, Stradivari etc) is almost synonomous with that of the instrument and is often mentioned on concert programmes. The most important composers for the violin include **Arcangelo Corelli** (1653-1713), who wrote a number of sonatas for the violin and basso continuo (the bass part over which the solo instrument plays the melody), including the well-known *Follia*; **Giuseppe Torelli** (1658-1709), the composer of many *Concerti grossi* (compositions for an orchestra and a group of soloists); **Giuseppe Tartini** (1692-1770), who wrote the anguished sonates *The Devil's Trill* (the devil appears to have been the inspiration for many musical pieces, especially those composed for the violin) and *Dido Abandoned*; **Pietro Locatelli** (1695-1764), who perfected violin techniques in his *Capricci* and *Sonate*; Giovan Battista Viotti (see above), and the incomparable Niccolò Paganini (see below).

singing, as well as some charming comic operas: *L'Elisir d'Amore, Don Pasquale.* **Amilcare Ponchielli** (1834-1886) is remembered mainly for his successful opera *La Giocanda.*

The greatest composer of the genre during the troubled period of the fight for independence from Austria was **Guiseppe Verdi** (1813-1901) with his dramatic yet romantic works: *Nabucco, Rigoletto, Il Trovatore, La Traviata, Aida* etc; he also wrote an admirable *Requiem.* The realist movement *(verismo)* then became popular, with Mascagni *(Cavalleria Rusticana),* Leoncavallo *(I Pagliaci),* and especially **Giacomo Puccini** (1858-1924) whose *Tosca, Madame Butterfly, La Bohème* and other works crowned this lyrical era.

The Piano

The piano was invented by **Bartolomeo Cristofori** (1655-1732), who modified the harpischord by replacing the plectra, which "plucked" the strings, with hammers which struck them. The first Italian to introduce this new instrument to the rest of Europe was **Muzio Clementi** (1752-1832), a rival of Mozart. He wrote a hundred studies for the piano, including *Gradus ad Parnassum,* and *Six Sonatas,* which were influenced both by the work of Mozart and Beethoven. The piano's wide range of tones and notes made it the ideal instrument for the Romantics, who composed a number of melancholic and passionate pieces for it. In more recent times some of Bach's compositions were adapted for the piano by **Ferruccio Busoni** (1866-1924).

Modern music – In reaction, the next generation concentrated on orchestral music, like **Ottorino Respighi** (1879-1937) who composed symphonic poems *(The Fountains of Rome, The Pines of Rome, Roman festivals).* 20C composers include Petrassi who explored all musical forms and **Dallapiccola** (1904-75), the leader of the dodecaphonic movement (the 12 notes of the scale are used) in Italy. The sensitive and passionate **Luigi Nono** (1924-90) is an exponent of serial music to express his political and liberating message; he wrote instrumental, orchestral, vocal and choral works.

Venues and artists – The recent unification of the country accounts for the numerous and famous opera houses and concert halls: the prestigious Scala in Milan, for which Visconti created marvellous sets, the Rome Opera House, the San Carlo theatre in Naples, the Poncielli in Cremona, the Politeama in Palermo, the Fenice in Venice (destroyed by fire in January 1996), the Carlo Fenice in Genoa and the Regio and the modern Lingotto in Turin. In spring Florence hosts a renowned music festival, and in summer splendid performances are held in the amphitheatre at Verona and in Caracalla's Baths in Rome.

Among the great orchestras and chamber music groups, the Orchestra of the Accademia di Santa Cecilia in Rome, the Filarmonica of La Scala in Milan, the Solisti Veniti and the Orchestra of Padua and the Veneto are noteworthy.

Among the great Italian conductors, Arturo Toscanini was renowned for the verve and originality of his interpretations. Other famous names include De Sabata and nowadays, Claudio Abbado, Gian Carlo Giulini, Riccardo Muti, Guiseppe Sinopoli who perform all over the world. Artists of international reputation include the violinists Accardo and Ughi, the pianists Campanella, Ciccolini, Lucchesini and Maria Tipo, the cellists Brunello and Filippini and the ballet dancers Carla Fracci, Luciana Savignano and Alessandra Ferri.

The famous singers Cecilia Bartoli, Renato Bruson, Fiorenza Cossotto, Cecilia Gasdia, Katia Ricciarelli, Renata Scotto, Lucia Valentini Terrani as well as Ruggiero Raimondi and Luciano Pavarotti are worthy successors to La Malibran, Renata Tebaldi, Maria Callas, Caruso and Beniamino Gigli.

MICHELIN GREEN TOURIST GUIDES
Landscapes
Monuments
Scenic routes, touring programmes
Geography
History, Art
Places to stay
Town and site plans
Practical information
A collection of guides for your travels in Italy, around Europe and the world.

Cinema

Early years – The Italian cinema industry was born in Turin at the beginning of the 20C and grew rapidly (50 production companies in 1914) with great successes on the international scene. Film makers specialised first in historical epics, in the 1910s they turned to adventure films and in the 1930s to propaganda and escapist films subsidised by the State, which distracted spectators temporarily from the reality of the Fascist State.

Neo-Realism – In 1935 the Cinecittà studios and the experimental cinematographic centre which numbered Rossellini and De Santis among its pupils were founded in Rome.

During the years of Fascist rule the cinema had become divorced from real life and to bridge the gap film directors advocated a return to realism and close observation of daily life. The first major theme of **neo-realism** was the war and its aftermath. **Rossellini** denounced Nazi and Fascist oppression in *Rome Open City* and *Germany Year Zero*. **Vittorio de Sica**'s *Sciuscia* (1946) and *Bicycle Thieves* (1948) depicted the unemployment and misery of the post-war years. In *Bitter Rice* (1949) and *Bloody Easter* (1950) **De Santis** portrays the working class divided between the prevailing ideology and revolutionary ambitions.

Neo-realism ended in the early 1950s as it no longer satisfied the public who wanted to forget this bleak period, but its influence was still felt by future generations of film makers.

1960s to the present day – In the 60s Italian cinema flourished and a large number of films (over 200 a year), generally of very high quality, was made with the support of a strong industrial infrastructure. Three great directors dominated this period. **Fellini** (1920-1993) shot the hugely successful *La Strada (The Street)* in 1954 and *La Dolce Vita* in 1960. His fantasy world is reflected in the original camera work.

Antonioni (1912) made his debut in 1959 with *L'Avventura*, and his work (*The Red Desert*, 1960 and *Blow Up*, 1967) underlines the ultimate isolation of the individual.

Visconti (1906-1976) made *Rocco and his brothers* in 1960 and *The Leopard* in 1963. His films which are characterised by splendour and beauty examine closely the themes of impermanence, degradation and death.

During the same period a new generation of film makers made a political and social statement: Pasolini, Olmi, Rosi, Bertolucci and the Taviani brothers.

Italian cinema won great international success with several masterpieces until the mid- 1970s: *Death in Venice* (1970) and *Ludwig* (1972) by Visconti; *Casanova* (1976) by Fellini, *The Passenger* (1974) by Antonioni; *L'Affare Mattei* (1971) by Rosi etc. Since the late 1970s the industry has been in a state of crisis, as it faces competition from television and the collapse of the market. However, some films made by famous directors have won acclaim: *The Night of San Lorenzo* (1982) by the **Taviani brothers**, *The Ball* (1983) by **Ettore Scola**, *The Last Emperor* (1987) by **Bertolucci**, *Cinema Paradiso* (1989) by **Tornatore**.

Cahiers du cinéma

Claudia Cardinale in Visconti's *The Leopard*

An introduction to Italian cinema would be incomplete without mentioning the famous "Italian comedies", which include masterpieces such as *Guardie e ladri* (1951), *I soliti ignoti* (1958), *La grande guerra* (1959), *L'Armata Brancaleone* (1966) and *Amici miei* (1975) by **Mario Monicelli** and *Divorzio all'Italiana* (1962) by **Pietro Germi**.

The younger generation of film makers embraced realism and their protagonists are engaged in the social struggle. The most interesting films include *Bianca* (1984), *La messa è finita* (1985) and *Caro Diario* (1993) by **Nanni Moretti**; *Il portaborse* (1990) and *La Scuola* (1995) by **Daniele Luchetti**; *Regalo di Natale* (1986) by **Pupi Avati**; *Mery per sempre* (1989), *Ragazzi fuori* (1989) and *Il muro di gomma* (1991) by **Marco Risi** and *Notte italiana* (1987) and *Vesna va veloce* (1996) by **Carlo Mazzacurati**.

Different strands of comedy can also be seen in many Italian films made during the last twenty years. A number of talented actor-writers have succeeded in exporting some of these Italian films abroad. Examples include *Ricomincio da tre* (1981), *Non ci resta che piangere* (1984), *Le vie del Signore sono finite* and *The Postman* (1994) by **Troisi**; *Un sacco bello* (1980), *Compagni di scuola* (1988) and *Maledetto il giorno che ti ho incontrato* (1992) by **Carlo Verdone**; *Il ciclone* (1996) by **Leonardo Pieraccioni**, and *Il piccolo diavolo* (1988), *Johnny Stecchino* (1991) and *Il mostro* (1994) by **Roberto Benigni**, who also produced the 1999 Oscar-winning masterpiece *Life is beautiful* (1997).

The success of Italian cinema is above all due to its famous stars, such as Vittorio Gasmann, Gina Lollobrigida, Sophia Loren, Anna Magnani, Giulietta Masina, Marcello Mastroianni, Alberto Sordi, Ugo Tognazzi, Totò and many others.

AWARDS AND OSCARS

Oscar Academy Awards

Life is beautiful by Roberto Benigni – 3 Oscars, including Best Foreign Film 1999
Mediterraneo by Gabriele Salvatores – Best Foreign Film 1992
Cinema Paradiso by Giuseppe Tornatore – Best Foreign Film 1990
The Last Emperor by Bernardo Bertolucci – 9 Oscars, including Best Film and Best Director 1988
Amarcord by Federico Fellini – Best Foreign Film 1975
Il Giardino dei Finzi-Contini by Vittorio De Sica – Best Foreign Film 1972
Indagine di un cittadino al di sopra di ogni sospetto by Elio Petri – Best Foreign Film 1971
Ieri, oggi, domani by Vittorio De Sica – Best Foreign Film 1965
8 1/2 by Federico Fellini – Best Foreign Film 1964
Le notti di Cabiria by Federico Fellini – Best Foreign Film 1958
La strada by Federico Fellini – Best Foreign Film 1957

Cannes Film Festival

L'albero degli zoccoli (The Tree of Wooden Clogs) by Ermanno Olmi, 1978
Padre padrone by Paolo and Vittorio Taviani, 1977
Il Caso Mattei by Francesco Rosi and *La classe operaia va in Paradiso* by Elio Petri, 1972
Signore e signori by Pietro Germi, 1966
Il Gattopardo (The Leopard) by Luchino Visconti, 1963
La dolce vita by Federico Fellini, 1960
Due soldi di speranza by Renato Castellani, 1952
Miracolo a Milano by Vittorio De Sica, 1951

Venice Film Festival

Così ridevano by Gianni Amelio, 1998
La leggenda del santo bevitore by Ermanno Olmi, 1988
La Battaglia di Algeri by Gillo Pontecorvo, 1966
Vaghe stelle dell'orsa by Luchino Visconti, 1965
Deserto rosso by Michelangelo Antonioni, 1964
Le mani sulla città by Francesco Rosi, 1963
Il generale Della Rovere by Roberto Rossellini and *La grande guerra* by Mario Monicelli, 1959
Giulietta e Romeo by Renato Castellani, 1954

Berlin Film Festival

La casa del sorriso by Marco Ferreri, 1991
The Canterbury Tales by Pier Paolo Pasolini, 1972
Il giardino dei Finzi-Contini by Vittorio De Sica, 1971
Il diavolo by Luigi Polidoro, 1963
La notte by Michelangelo Antonioni, 1961

*Read your **Michelin Map** carefully*
to discover useful and interesting information:
a castle on a lake,
a forest road with picnic grounds,
a panorama, a historic marker.
Italy is a land of endless discovery.

Arts and Crafts

There are approximately 1 400 000 small companies (with a maximum of 20 staff) in Italy which together employ around 5 000 000 people and contribute approximately 20% of the country's gross domestic product. Only a small percentage of these companies are involved in the production of traditional arts and crafts.

The clothing and textile industries are mainly concentrated in northern and central Italy: Milan is the fashion capital of Italy, Carpi (Emilia-Romagna) specialises in knitwear and the Como region is renowned for its silk production. Since the end of the 1950s the fabric industry of Prato has been involved in the collection of scraps of material, which are then recycled.

Another sector found in the northern-central regions of Italy is the furniture industry based in Milan, Brianza, Forlì and Pesaro.

Two of the most famous centres for the production of artistic ceramics (Faenza and Deruta) are found in central Italy, while Florence is famous for its leather products. In Castelfidardo, near Ancona in the Marche region, the tradition of making accordions has expanded over the years to include a range of musical instruments. However, Cremona remains the most famous centre for the manufacture of string instruments.

Gold-working is concentrated in Valenza Po, which is also a centre for semiprecious stones and precious metals, Arezzo (metal-working only), and Sardinia, which specialises in filigree work in both gold and silver.

The following list gives an idea of the traditional arts and crafts found in the different regions of Italy.

Valle d'Aosta: rustic furniture, wooden objects (sculptures, games) and wrought iron, earthenware pots, pillow lace (especially in Cogne) and *drap* (brightly coloured fabrics) from Valgrisenche.

Lombardia: good quality silk (Como), string instruments (Cremona), furniture (Brianza).

Trentino Alto Adige: Tyrolean-style clothing, wooden sculpture (Val Gardena), pewter, copper, brass and wrought iron objects.

Friuli Venezia Giulia: wood (furniture, sculptures, masks), iron, brass, ceramics and mosaics (Spilimbergo).

Veneto: glass (Murano), lace (Burano) and ceramics (Bassano).

Liguria: *mezzari* (frames made from Oriental canvas) can be found in Genoa; slate is worked along the Riviera di Levante (Chiavari and Lavagna).

Tuscany: leather, paper and embroidery, ceramics and terracotta.

Umbria: majolica (Deruta) and lace (Assisi and Orvieto).

Marche: brasswork, pillow lace, musical instruments.

The term "ceramic" comes from the Greek κεραμος (keramos), which means clay

Emilia Romagna: majolica from Faenza.

Lazio: umbrellas from Carpineto Romano, leather articles from Tolfa and *zampogna* bagpipes from Villa Latina.

Campania: coral from Torre del Greco, majolica from Vietri, crèche figurines from Naples.

Abruzzo: woollen articles, wood and wrought iron objects.

Puglia: terracotta whistles from Rutigliano, papier-mâché from Lecce.

Basilicata: terracotta whistles, jars, amphorae and ceramics.

Sicily: puppets, crèche figurines, wrought iron, ceramics (Caltagirone and San Stefano di Camastra) and coral.

Sardinia: woollen tapestries using traditional geometric and simple designs, woven straw baskets (Castelsardo), cork, coral and the Sardinian wedding ring, traditionally made from silver.

Food and Wine

Italy is rich in tasty products and its cooking is among the best known in the world. A traditional meal consists of an **antipasto** or hors d'œuvre (raw vegetable salads with a dressing, fine pork-butchers' meats, pickled vegetables), **primo** (*primo piatto:* first course) rice or *pasta* in its numerous forms, plain or combined with various sauces and trimmings; **secondo** (meat or fish course) often accompanied by a **contorno** (vegetable or green salad). After the cheese (**formaggio**) fruit (**frutta**) is served as well as a choice of numerous other desserts: cakes, pastries and sweets (**dolci**), ices (**gelati**) or frozen cakes (**semi-freddo**). A young wine is usually served in 1/4 (*quarto*), half (*mezzo*) or one litre (*litro*) carafes (*sfuso*). Ask for a wine list if you prefer better quality wines. There is a wide choice of mineral waters available. Traditionally the meal ends with a strong, black espresso coffee. The frothy **cappuccino** dusted with cocoa is also delectable.

SOME REGIONAL SPECIALITIES

Piedmont – Cooking here is done with butter. A popular dish is **fonduta**, a melted cheese dip of milk, eggs and white truffles (*tartufi bianchi*). *Cardi* (chards) are prepared *alla bagna cauda*, i.e. with a hot sauce containing oil, anchovies, garlic and truffles. Other dishes include **agnolotti** (a kind of ravioli), braised beef in red Barolo wine, boiled meat, **fritto misto alla Piemontese** and **bonet** dessert (a type of chocolate pudding). Monferrato and the Langhe is also famous for its excellent cheese, such as **robiola**, **castelmagno** and **bra**, and delicious wines: **Barolo** (used for braising), Barbaresco, **Barbera**, Grignolino, red Freisas, white Gavi and dessert wines such as **Asti**, still or sparkling (*spumante*) and Moscato.

Lombardy – Milan, where cooking is done with butter, gives its name to several dishes; *minestrone alla milanese*, a soup of green vegetables, rice and bacon; *risotto alla milanese*, rice cooked with saffron; **cos-toletta** *alla milanese*, a fillet of veal fried in egg and breadcrumbs with cheese; **osso buco**, a knuckle of veal with the marrow-bone. **Polenta**, maize semolina, is a staple food in traditional country cooking. Also worth trying are the **tortelli di zucca** (pumpkin fritters) from Mantua. The most popular cheeses are the creamy **Gorgonzola**, the hard **Grana Padana** and **Taleggio**. **Panettone** is a large fruit cake containing raisins and candied lemon peel and **torrone** is a speciality of Cremona. Wines produced include Franciacorta (red, white and sparkling) and the red wines of the Valtellina and Pavia districts. The Valtellina is also renowned for its **pizzoccheri** (a type of large tagliatelle made from buck wheat) and its **bitto** cheese.

Veneto – As in the Po Plain, the people eat **polenta**, **bigoli** (a type of spaghetti), **risi e bisi** (rice and peas), **risotto** with chicory and **fegato alla veneziana** (calf's

Polenta is a typical dish of northern Italy

F. Vasseur/VISA

liver fried with onions). The excellent fish dishes include shellfish, eels, dried cod (*baccalà*) and **sardelle in saor** (sardines in brine). Black spaghetti made with squid ink is a popular Venetian dish. The most renowned cheese of the region is **asiago**. Pandoro, a star-shaped cake delicately flavoured with orange-flower, is a speciality of Verona. The best wines come from the district of Verona: **Valpolicella** and **Bardolino**, *rosé* or red, perfumed and slightly sparkling, and **Soave**, which is white and strong.

Trentino-Alto Adige and Friuli-Venetia Giulia – In Alto-Adige, **canederli** is a type of gnocchi (dumplings) made with bread and flour served separately or in a broth. Other specialities include **gröstl** (potato and meat pie) and smoked pork served with sauerkraut. There are delicious pastries, in particular the **Strüdel** cake. Friuli is famous for **cialzons** (a type of ravioli), **jota** (meat soup), pork-butchers' specialities (ham – **prosciutto di San Daniele**), fish dishes (**scampi, grancevole** – spider crabs), **frico** (fried cheese) and montasio cheese. Trentino-Alto Adige is an important wine-producing region: white wines include Chardonnay, Pinot Bianco, Muller-Thurgau and Riesling, while Pinot and Cabernet are two of the best-known red wines. Friuli produces white Sauvignon, Pinot and Tocai and red Cabernet and Merlot wines.

Liguria – The chief speciality of Genoa is **pesto**, a sauce made with olive oil, basil, pine-kernels, garlic and ewes' cheese. It is served with **trenette** (long, thin noodles) and lasagne (flat pasta leaves). Other dishes include **cima** (stuffed meat parcels) and the excellent **pansotti** (a type of ravioli) served with a walnut sauce. The delicious sea-food includes **buridda** (fish soup), **cappon magro** (fish and vegetable salad) and **zuppa di datteri**, a shellfish soup from La Spezia, with which the Ligurians drink Vermentino or Pigato, strong white wines. Sciacchetrà is an excellent dessert wine from the region.

Emilia-Romagna – The region has a fine gastronomic reputation; its pork-butchers' meat is the most famous in Italy: Bologna **salami** and **mortadella**, Modena **zamponi** (pigs' trotters), Parma **prosciutto** (ham). *Pasta* is varied and tasty when served *alla bolognese* – that is, with a meat and tomato sauce. **Parmesan cheese** (*parmigiano*), hard and pale yellow, is strong yet delicate in flavour. Emilia produces **Lambrusco**, a fruity, sparkling red wine, and white Albano.

Tuscany – This is where Italian cooking was born, at the court of the Medici. The most typical first courses of the region are minestrones and soups, including the famous **ribollita**, and **pappardelle**, a type of lasagna. Florence also offers its

Chianti Rufina wine

alla fiorentina specialities: dried cod (**baccalà**) with oil, garlic and pepper, **bistecca**, grilled steak fillets with oil, salt and pepper, **fagioli all'ucelletto** (beans with quails), or fagioli "al fiasco" with oil, onions and herbs cooked in a round bottle (*fiasco*) on a coal fire. Livorno produces **triglie** (red mullet) and **cacciucco** (fish soup) and Siena offers **panforte**, a cake containing almonds, honey and candied melon, orange and lemon. Tuscan cheeses include **pecorino** and **caciotta**. Chianti (both red and white) is the most popular wine but there are other notable red (**Brunello di Montalcino, Nobile di Montepulciano**) and white (**Vernaccia di San Gimignano, Vin Santo**) wines.

Umbria and Marches – Norcia is the capital of Italian cuisine with the black truffles (**tartufo nero**) and pork dishes. The regional dish is the **porchetta**, a whole sucking pig roasted on the spit. Specialities from the Marches include *vincigrassi* (pasta cooked in the oven with a meat and cream sauce), **stringozzi** (a type of hollow spaghetti), stuffed olives, **brodetto** (a fish soup), and **stocco all'anconetana** (dried cod). The region produces both white wine (the famous **Orvieto** and Verdicchio) and red (Rosso Conero and Rosso Piceno).

Lazio – There are many Roman specialities: **fettucine** or flat strips of pasta, **spaghetti all'amatriciana** (with a spicy sauce) or **alla carbonara** (with a creamy sauce), **gnocchi** alla Romana, **saltimbocca** (a fillet of veal rolled in ham and flavoured with sage, fried in butter and served with a Marsala sauce), and **abbacchio al forno** or roast lamb or *alla cacciatora* (with an anchovy sauce). Vegetables include *carciofi alla Giudia*, artichokes cooked in oil with garlic and parsley, which take their name from their origins in the Jewish quarter of Rome. **Pecorino** (ewes' milk cheese), **caciotta**, **ricotta** and the famous white wines of Montefiascone and the **Castelli** (Frascati) will satisfy the most discerning gourmet.

Abruzzi and Molise – Among the *pasta* note **maccheroni alla chitarra**, made by hand and cut into strips. **Latticini** (fresh mountain cheeses) are popular.

Campania – Naples is the home of **spaghetti**, which is often prepared with shellfish *(alle vongole)*. *Trattorie* and *pizzerie* serve *costata alla pizzaiola*, a fillet steak with tomatoes, garlic and wild marjoram, **mozzarella** *in carrozza* (cheese savoury) and especially **pizza** and **calzone** (a folded pizza), topped with cheese *(mozzarella)*, tomato and anchovy and flavoured with capers and wild marjoram. The local **mozzarella di bufala** (buffalo mozzarella cheese) is especially delicious. Other specialities include cakes and pastries, often made with ricotta cheese and candied fruit. Wines from volcanic soil have a delicate, slightly sulphurous taste: red and white Capri, white Ischia, **Lacryma Christi**, Fiano di Avellino and Greco di Tufo and red Gragnano and Taurasi.

Apulia, Basilicata and Calabria – Orecchiette con cime di rapa (pasta with turnip tops), rice with mussels *(cozze)*, stuffed cuttlefish *(seppia)*, the delicious oysters *(ostriche)* of Taranto and **capretto ripieno al forno** (roast kid stuffed with herbs) are among the typical dishes of the Apulia region. Wines include the white Locorotondo and San Severo and the rosé Castel del Monte. Basilicata's specialities include **pasta alla potentina** and a range of lamb and mutton dishes, as well as a good selection of cheeses (caciocavallo, scamorza and ricotta), while Calabria is famous for its stuffed macaroni, pork and roast kid cooked on a spit. Red Cirò is the most popular local wine.

Sicily – Sicilian specialities include **pasta con le sarde** (with sardines) and **alla Norma** (with aubergines, tomatoes and ricotta cheese), swordfish dishes, and, in the Trapani region, **cuscusu** (couscous), a dish inherited from the Arabs and served with a type of fish soup. The island is rich in fruit (lemons, oranges, mandarins, olives, almonds), pastries and ices. The real Sicilian **cassata** is a partly-iced cream cake containing chocolate cream and candied fruits. Other traditional sweets and pastries include **cannoli** (filled with ricotta and candied fruit), almond cakes and marzipan. The best-known wine is **Marsala**, which is dark and strong, but **Malvasia** and the white wines of Etna and Lipari are also delicious.

Spaghetti alla Norma (tomatoes, aubergines and Ricotta cheese)

Sardinia – The island of Sardinia is famous for **malloreddus** (pasta shells with sausage and tomato), delicious lobster soup and pork cooked on a spit. Meals are accompanied by **carasau**, the local soft-doughed bread (known as *carta da musica* in the rest of Italy). The many cheeses include goats' cheese, Sardinian **fiore** and Sardinian **pecorino**. **Sebadas** are round doughnuts which are fried and covered with honey. The best-known local wines are the red **Cannonau** and the white Vermentino. *See SARDINIA.*

The evocative atmosphere of Rocca di Gradara by night

Sights

ABRUZZO★★★

Abruzzi

Michelin map 430 N-R 21-26

The harsh geography of the Apennine range has had a profound effect on the character of this land. For the last 2 000 years sheep breeding, traditionally the stronghold of local economy, has been characterised by the winter journey of flocks along grass and stone cattle-tracks leading to the pastures of Puglia and Lazio. The Abruzzi region is startling in the grandeur and variety of its landscapes: karst formations, forests, desolate plateaux and fertile pastures all enclosed in three Italian national parks which are tourist attractions both for summer holidays as well as for winter sports: the Parco Nazionale d'Abruzzo, pioneer of Italian parks; the Parco Nazionale del Gran Sasso and the Parco Nazionale della Maiella.

HISTORY AND ART

Various Italic populations dominated the region until the 3C BC when Rome took over the territory definitively. After the fall of the Roman Empire the region became a Lombard territory before being taken over by the Franks. In the 12C it became part of the Kingdom of Naples and remained so until the Unification of Italy.

In the Middle Ages the diffusion of Benedictine rule from the neighbouring abbey at Montecassino led to the construction of cathedrals, abbeys and churches whose beautifully ornate ciboria and pulpits constitute the definitive glory of Abruzzi art.

In the 15C-16C the finest examples of Renaissance art were to be found in the work of the painter and architect, **Cola dell'Amatrice**, the painter **Andrea de Litio**, the sculptor **Silvestro dell'Aquila** and in the refined work of the goldsmith **Nicola da Guardiagrele**.

Notable figures of the Abruzzi region include Publio Ovidio Nasone (43 BC-17 AD), Gabriele D'Annunzio (1863-1938), Benedetto Croce (1866-1952) and Ignazio Silone (1900-1978).

★★ GRAN SASSO

From L'Aquila to Castelli

159km/99mi – allow half a day, not including l'Aquila and excursions.

This is the highest massif in the Abruzzi and its main peak is **Corno Grande** (alt 2 912m – 9 560ft). On the northern side spines with many gullies slope away gently, while on the southern face Gran Sasso drops abruptly to the great glacial plateaux edged by deep valleys. The lush pastures and tree-covered slopes to the north contrast with the desolate and grandiose expanses to the south.

★ **L'Aquila** – *See L'AQUILA.*

★★ **Campo Imperatore** ⊘ – It passes through splendid mountain country grazed by large flocks of sheep or hordes of wild horses. It was from here that Mussolini escaped on 12 September 1943, in a daring raid by German airmen whose plane landed and took off near the hotel in which the Duce had been interned.

Return to Fonte Cereto, follow directions for the Valico delle Capannelle road (closed from December to April) and then take the S 80 in the direction of Montorio al Vomano.

The road then skirts the lower slopes of the Gran Sasso, as it follows the long green valley, **Valle del Vomano★★**, before entering the magnificent gorges which have striking stratified rock walls.

On leaving Montorio, take the S491 to the right, the road to Isola del Gran Sasso. At Isola del Gran Sasso follow directions for Castelli.

★ **Castelli** – This town, which stands on a wooded promontory at the foot of Monte Camicia, has been famous since the 13C for its ceramics of which the 17C **ceiling**★ in the **chiesa di S. Donato** is a fine example. Just outside the town, the ex-Franciscan convent (17C) houses the **Museo delle Ceramiche** ⊙, which relates the history of Castelli ceramic production from the 15C to the 19C through the display of works of its leading exponents.

GREAT PLATEAUX

Round tour leaving from Sulmona
138km/86mi – allow at least 1 day excluding tour of Sulmona.

★ **Sulmona** – *See SULMONA.*

Piano delle Cinquemiglia – Beyond, the road sometimes runs along a corniche which affords good view of the Sulmona valley, and eventually reaches the **Piano delle Cinquemiglia**, largest of the Great Plateaux situated between Sulmona and Castel di Sangro. With an average altitude of more than 1 200m/3937ft, the plateau, 5 Romanmi long (8km/5mi), was once the obligatory route for stage-coaches journeying to Naples and was much feared for its harsh winter climate and highway robbers.

Near the village of Rivisondoli, take the S84 to the left.

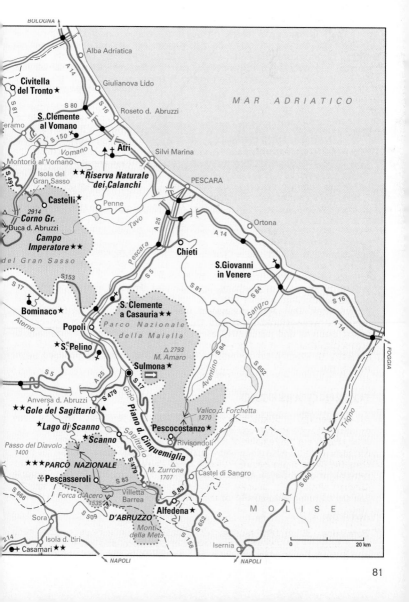

* **Pescocostanzo** – This attractive village with its paved streets and old houses is a flourishing craft centre specialising in wrought-iron work, copper, gold and woodwork as well as lace-making.

  The Collegiate Church of **Santa Maria del Colle** ⊙ although built to a Renaissance plan has several Romanesque features and baroque additions (organ loft, ceiling and grille of the north aisle).

* **Alfedena** – The houses of this small town are grouped about the ruined castle. Paths lead northwards to the ancient city of Alfedena with its cyclopean walls and necropolis.

* **Scanno** – From its high mountain site, Scanno overlooks the lovely Lake Scanno **(Lago di Scanno★)** formed by a landslide which blocked the bed of the river Sagittario. The steep and narrow streets of this attractive holiday resort are lined with old houses and churches.

  Continuing towards Anversa degli Abruzzi, the road hollowed out of the rock skirts the series of deep, wild gorges **(Gole del Sagittario★★)** which afford 10km(6mi) of spectacularly wild and majestic nature.

★★★ PARCO NAZIONALE D'ABRUZZO

A nature reserve was founded in 1923 in the very heart of the massif to protect the fauna, flora and outstanding landscapes of the region. The park extends over an area of approximately 40 000ha/98 838 acres, not including the 4 500ha/11 119 acres of the Mainarde territory (in the Molise region), and is surrounded by an external protected area of 60 000ha/148 257 acres. Two-thirds of the park is made up of forests (mainly beech, maple, oak and black pine) and it offers the ultimate refuge for animals that once lived on the entire Apennine range: brown bears, Apennine wolves, Abruzzi chamois, wild cats, otters, martens and royal eagles. **Pescasseroli**⁑, situated in the small valley whose borders are covered with beech and pine forests, is the principal town in the Sangro valley and headquarters of the park.

A stylish stopover

Villino Mon Repos – Viale Colli dell'Oro, 67032 Pescasseroli, ☎ 0863 91 28 58, fax 0863 91 29 18. This early 20C restored villa, set in a splendid park of age-old trees, used to be the summer residence of Benedetto Croce. 17 comfortable and elegant rooms priced accordingly.

Access and sightseeing ⊙ – By car the main access routes are Bisegna in the north, Barrea to the east and Forca d'Acero in the west. For information on park activities contact the Centro Parchi Internazionale in Rome or local offices at Pescasseroli, Villetta Barrea, Civitella Alfedena, Villavallelonga and Campoli Appennino, open 9am to 12pm and from 3pm to 7pm. The Ufficio Operativo del Parco is in Pescasseroli, Viale S. Lucia, ☎ 08 63 91 07 15, the main office is in Rome, Viale Tito Livio 12, ☎ 06 35 40 33 31.

Within the confines of the park there are four different protection zones in operation allowing various types of activities, depending on conservation programmes. The visitor is however free to visit a large area of the park using the well-surfaced roads and tracks, and facilities include observation posts, camping and picnic sites as well as visitor centres. The only way to appreciate local fauna or flora is on foot or on horseback in some cases. It is advisable to keep to the signposted footpaths and to be accompanied by an official guide.

TOURING ABRUZZO

Alba Fucens ⊙ – *50km/30mi south of l'Aquila on the A24.* These are the **excavations** ⊙ of a Roman colony founded in 303BC. Amidst the foundations (of Italic origin) are the remains of a basilica, the forum, baths, the covered market complete with paved streets, wells, latrines and an **amphitheatre**. Above the ruins rises the **Chiesa di San Pietro** ⊙ (Church of St Peter), erected in the 12C on the remains of a temple of Apollo of the 3C BC. The **interior** houses two notable Cosmati work pieces, unusual in Romanesque Abruzzi production: the **ambo★★** and the stunning **iconostasis★★** of the 13C.

Atri – *See ATRI.*

* **Bominaco** – *30km/18mi southeast of L'Aquila.* Two Romanesque churches stand about 500m - 1 640ft above the hamlet of Bominaco, and are all that remain of a Benedictine monastery which was destroyed in the 15C. The Church of

San Pellegrino★ ⊘ is a 13C oratory decorated with contemporary **frescoes★**, portraying in a rather naive but detailed way the Life of Christ and St Pellegrino. Two elegant 10C plutei demarcate the chancel whose central wall is decorated with the delightful *Calendario bominacense*, depicting courtly scenes which are influenced by the French tradition. The Church of **S. Maria Assunta★** ⊘ (11C and 12C), with its beautifully ornamented apses, is one of the most significant examples of Romanesque architecture in Abruzzi. The elegantly simple interior, with its distinctly Benedictine imprint, has a graceful Romanesque colonnade which makes skilful use of light and volume. Note the striking 12C **ambo★**.

Chieti – *See CHIETI*

★ **Civitella del Tronto** – *See ASCOLI PICENO*

★★ **S. Clemente a Causaria** – *See CHIETI*

S. Giovanni in Venere ⊘ – *36km/22mi southeast of Pescara on the S16.* This abbey, founded in the 8C on the site of a temple dedicated to Venus and remodelled in the 13C, is situated in a panoramic **setting★** on the Adriatic Sea. On the façade note the 13C **Portale della Luna★** (Moon Doorway) adorned with low reliefs depicting sacred and profane subject matter. The austere Cistercian interior has a nave and two aisles with a raised chancel: the crypt rests on bare Roman columns and has 12C-15C frescoes.

AMALFI★★

Campania
Population 5 568
Michelin map 431 F 25

Amalfi, which has given its name to the beautiful Amalfi Coast *(see below)*, is a rather Spanish-looking little town with its tall white houses built on slopes facing the sea in a wonderful **setting★★★**. Amalfi enjoys a very mild climate, making it a popular holiday resort.

The Maritime Republic of Amalfi – This is Italy's oldest republic founded in 840; by the end of the 9C it came under the rule of a doge. It enjoyed its greatest prosperity in the 11C, when shipping in the Mediterranean was regulated by the *Tavole Amalfitane* (Amalfi Navigation Tables), the oldest maritime code in the world. Amalfi traded regularly with the Orient, in particular Constantinople, and the Republic had an **arsenal** *(to the left of Porta della Marina)* where many large galleys were built. This fleet of galleys played a large part in carrying Crusaders to the Levant.

SIGHTS

★ **Duomo di S. Andrea** ⊘ – Founded in the 9C, enlarged in the 10C and 13C and subsequently altered numerous times, the cathedral is a good example of the Oriental splendour favoured by maritime cities. The crypt enshrines relics of St Andrew (Sant'Andrea) which had been removed from Patras to Constantinople, from whence they were transferred in 1206 to Amalfi.

The façade, rebuilt in the 19C on the original model, has a great deal of character: it is the focal point at the top of a stairway and its varied geometrical designs in multicoloured stone are striking. The campanile, on the left, is all that remains of the original church. A beautiful 11C bronze **door★**, cast in Constantinople, opens onto the vast atrium which precedes the church.

The interior of the cathedral is in the baroque style. Two antique columns, two candelabra decorated with mosaics and two 12C ambos are of special interest.

The atrium leads into the Cloisters of Paradise (**Chiostro del Paradiso★★** ⊘) which date from 1268. The architecture combines Romanesque austerity and Arab fantasy. The arcades shelter some sarcophagi. The Museo Diocesano is housed in the **Basilica del Crocefisso**, which used to be the site of the old 9C cathedral. Previously incorporated into the main building and transformed into the Baroque style, it has now reassumed its original

Candied fruit or marzipan?

These are excellent at the **Pasticceria Pansa**, in Piazza Duomo 40.

Romanesque form (note the decorative mullioned triforium and the chapels with fresco remains). From the Basilica make for the crypt which holds the relics of St Andrew Apostle, brought over to Amalfi from Constantinople in 1206.

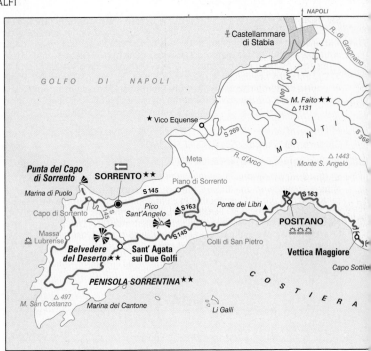

* **Historic centre** – Starting at Piazza Duomo, Via Genova, Via Capuano (its continuation) and Via dei Mercanti (parallel on the right) make up the historic and business heart of the city with its picturesque variety of façades, flowering balconies and niches. The Islamic layout of the town is characterised by winding alleyways, staircases and vaulted passages.

★★★ COSTIERA AMALFITANA (AMALFI COAST) 79km/49mi - allow 1 day

The corniche road follows the indentations of the rocky coast between Sorrento and Salerno which is Italy's finest coastline, namely the Amalfi Coast. The artistic and natural beauty of this area earned it a place in UNESCO's 1997 World Heritage List. For over 30km/19mi its innumerable bends afford constantly changing views of enchanting landscapes, wild, fantastically-shaped rocks plunging vertically into a crystal-clear sea, deep gorges spanned by dizzy bridges and Saracen towers perched on jagged rock stacks. The Amalfi Coast, with its wild and rugged landscape, is formed by the jagged fringe of the Lattari Mountains, a deeply-eroded limestone range. Contrasting with these awe-inspiring scenes are the more charming views of fishing villages and the luxuriant vegetation, a mixture of orange, lemon, olive and almond trees, vines and all the Mediterranean flora. The region is very popular with foreigners and artists. A significant part of the attraction is the local cuisine with abundant seafood (fish, crustaceans and shellfish), and the local *mozzarella* cheese washed down with the red Gragnano or white Ravello and Positano wines.

Boat trips – In the summertime there are hovercraft and motorboat crossings to Capri, Ischia, Sorrento, Salerno and Naples as well as excursions to the Grotta dello Smeraldo and the tiny Li Galli island.

Sightseeing – The local map above locates the towns and sites described in the guide, and also indicates other beauty spots in small black type.

★★ Sorrento and the Sorrento Peninsula – *See SORRENTO.*

Positano – The white cubic houses of this old fishing village reveal a strong Moorish influence; lush gardens dotted on terraced slopes go down to the sea. Positano is "the only place in the world designed on a vertical axis" (Paul Klee). Much loved and frequented in the past by artists and intellectuals (Picasso, Cocteau, Steinbeck, MoraVia and Nureyev who bought Li Galli island) and by the trend-setters of the *Dolce Vita* who used to meet up at the *Buca di Bacco* nightclub, today Positano is one of the most popular resorts of the Amalfi Coast. "Positano fashion" was born here in the fifties, with its brightly coloured materials and equally famous sandals that were desperately sought after by women of the jet set during their trips here.

Vettica Maggiore – Its houses are scattered over the slopes. From the esplanade there is a fine **view**★★ of the coast and sea.

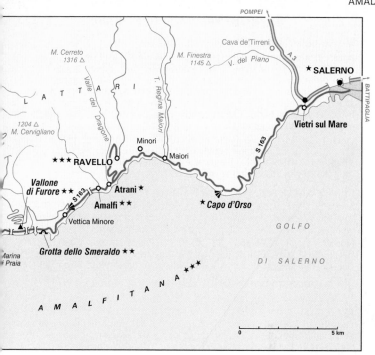

★★ Vallone di Furore – The Furore Valley, between two road tunnels, is the most impressive section of the coast owing to the dark depths of its steep, rocky walls and, in stormy weather, the thunder of wild, rough seas. A fishermen's village has, nevertheless, been built where a small torrent gushes into the sea. The houses clinging to the slopes and vividly coloured boats drawn up on the shore are an unexpected feature in this bleak landscape. Anna Magnani, who came to Furore in 1948 with Roberto Rossellini to shoot *L'Amore*, fell under its spell and wanted to buy a fisherman's house. Those who wish to explore the spot on foot should take the path that goes along one side of the gorge. Note the "**Art walls**", outdoor contemporary paintings and sculptures which relate local history.

★★ Grotta dello Smeraldo ⊙ – The exceptionally clear water of this marine cave is illuminated indirectly by rays of light which give it a beautiful emerald *(smeraldo)* colour. The bottom looks quite near, though the water is 10m - 33ft deep, but it was not always covered by the sea. Fine stalactites add to the interest of the trip. The cave became submerged as a result of variations in ground level caused by the volcanic activity which affects the whole region.

★ Atrani – This pleasant fishermen's village at the mouth of the Dragon Valley (Valle del Dragone) has two old churches: Santa Maria Maddalena and San Salvatore. The latter was founded in the 10C and has a fine bronze door which is very similar to the one in Amalfi Cathedral. An excellent winding road leads to Ravello.

Ph. Roy/Explorer

The Amalfi Coast

AS NIGHT FALLS ON THE COAST...

IF YOU DON'T WANT TO SPEND MUCH

Hostel Brikette – Via G. Marconi 358, 84017 Positano, ☎ and fax 089 87 58 57. It is well a well known fact that staying in Positano is a luxury that few can afford. This pretty hostel, housed in a typical Positano-style building, provides an opportunity to stay in this enchanting place without spending a fortune: 8 rooms, of which 1 single, 1 double, the others have 4/6 beds (all without bath). Terraces with fantastic views. 40 000L a night per person including breakfast.

Hostaria di Bacco – Via Lama 9, 84010 Furore, ☎ 089 83 03 60, fax 086 83 03 52. A simple but pleasant and well kept hotel with good views. 15 rooms all with bath. Excellent value for money makes up for the 10km/6mi road journey to and from the coast road.

COMFORTABLE AND PRICED ACCORDINGLY

Aurora – Piazza dei Protontini 7, 84011 Amalfi, ☎ 089 87 12 09, fax 089 87 29 80. An agreeable hotel with 29 rooms (the front rooms have wonderful views). The small, pretty garden looks out onto the port of Amalfi.

Savoia – Via Colombo 73, 84017 Positano, ☎ 089 87 50 03, fax 089 81 18 44. Housed in a typical Positano-style building with vaulted ceilings and ceramic floors, this is a family run hotel with 38 rooms.

IF YOU WANT TO DAYDREAM... AND MONEY IS NO OBJECT!

If you want to indulge yourself this is the place to stay:

Palazzo Sasso – Via S. Giovanni del Toro 28, 84010 Ravello, ☎ 089 81 81 81, fax 089 85 89 900. Housed in a stunning 12C building with unequalled views of the gulf, this hotel is the epitome of luxury and refinement and even offers limousine and helicopter service. Rooms with a mountain view are "cheaper" than those with sea views. Needless to say they include every possible amenity.

★★★ **Ravello** – See RAVELLO.

★ **Capo d'Orso** – The cape with its jagged rocks affords an interesting view of Maiori Bay.

Vietri sul Mare – At the eastern end of this stretch of coastline, the houses of Vietri sul Mare are terraced up the slope. The town is known for its ceramic ware. It affords magnificent **views**★★ of the Amalfi Coast.

★ **Salerno** – See SALERNO.

ANAGNI★

Lazio

Population 19 901

Michelin map 430 Q 21

Anagni is a small medieval town, built on a rocky spur, overlooking the Sacco Valley. This was the birthplace of several popes, including Boniface VIII (1235-1303) who was famously "slapped" here. In 1303, after years of conflict, the French King, Philip the Fair, who had been excommunicated by the pope, sent a delegation to Anagni to assess its administration and to evaluate accusations of heresy and corruption. The pope was ignobly humiliated and this is what gave birth to the legend of the slap given by the pope which became known as the "Slap (or Outrage) of Anagni".

★★ **Cattedrale** – The town's most important building stands on the site of the former acropolis. This Romanesque cathedral was built in the 11C and 12C and remodelled in the 13C with Gothic additions. Walk round the outside to admire the three Romanesque apses with Lombard mouldings and arcades, the 14C statue of Boniface VIII over the loggia on the north side and the detached massive Romanesque campanile. The interior comprises a nave and two aisles; the 13C **paving**★ was the work of the Cosmati (see Introduction). The high altar is surmounted by a **Romanesque ciborium** or canopy. The **paschal candelabrum** with a spiral column is adorned with multicoloured incrustations; it rests on two sphinxes and is crowned by an infant holding a cup. The work, like the nearby **episcopal throne**, is by Pietro Vassaleto and bears strong similarities with the style of the Cosmati. The **crypt**★★★ ⊙ with its beautiful pavement by the Cosmati also has magnificent 13C **frescoes** depicting the story of the Old Testament, scenes from the lives of the saints and men of science such as Galen and Hippocrates. The **treasury** contains some fine liturgical items, notably Boniface VIII's cope of embroidered red silk.

* **Medieval Quarter** – This quarter consists almost entirely of 13C buildings and is particularly evocative. The façade of **Boniface VIII's Palace** has two pierced galleries one above the other. One has wide round-headed arches while the other consists of attractive twinned windows with small columns. In the Piazza Cavour is the 12C-13C **Palazzo Comunale** with a great **vault** ★ at ground level. The rear façade is in the Cistercian style.

ANCONA ★

Marches

Population 99 074
Michelin map 430 L 22
Town plan in the Michelin Atlas Italy

Ancona, the chief town in the Marches, an Adriatic region of Italy, is built in the form of an amphitheatre on the slopes of a rocky promontory, forming an acute angle from which the name of the town is derived (Greek *ankon* – elbow). It was founded in the 4C BC and became an independent maritime republic in the Middle Ages. It is today a busy port and the main embarkation point for Croatia (Zara, Split, and Dubrovnik) and Greece (Corfu, Igoumenitsa, Patrasso and Cephalonia). The town specialises in the production of accordions, electronic organs and guitars.

SIGHTS

* **Duomo** ⊙ – The cathedral was dedicated to St Cyriacus, 4C martyr and patron saint of Ancona. The Romanesque building combines Byzantine (the Greek cross plan) and Lombard (mouldings and arcades on the outside walls) architectural features. The façade is preceded by a majestic Gothic **porch** in pink stone supported by two lions. The interior is articulated by monolithic marble columns with Romanesque-Byzantine **capitals**. Under the dome, note the clever transition from the square base to the 12-sided drum supporting the dome. The tomb (1509) of Cardinal Giannelli in the chancel is the work of the Dalmatian sculptor Giovanni da Traù.

* **Loggia dei Mercanti** – This 15C hall for merchants' meetings has a Venetian Gothic façade which was the work of another Dalmatian, Giorgio Orsini.

* **S. Maria della Piazza** – This small 10C Romanesque church has a charming façade (1210) adorned with amusing popular figures. It was built over the site of two earlier (5C and 6C) **churches** which retain fragments of mosaic pavements.

Museo Archeologico Nazionale delle Marche ⊙ – *At the southern end of Piazza del Senato.*
The museum, installed in the Palazzo Ferretti, has interesting prehistoric and archaeological collections on view.

Galleria Comunale Francesco Podesti ⊙ – *Via Ciriaco Pizzecolli.* The public gallery displays works by Crivelli, Titian, Lorenzo Lotto, C. Maratta and Guercino. The gallery of modern art has canvases by Luigi Bartolini, Massimo Campigli, Bruno Cassinari and Tamburini.

S. Francesco delle Scale – *Via Ciriaco Pizzecolli, not far from the Galleria Comunale.* This 15C church has a splendid Venetian Gothic doorway by Giorgio Orsini.

Arco di Traiano – The arch was erected at the northern end of Lungomare Vanvitelli in honour of the Emperor Trajan who built the port in AD 115.

EXCURSIONS

* **Portonovo** – *12km/8mi southeast.* Portonovo lies in a picturesque setting formed by the rocky coastline of the **Conero Massif.** A private path leads through woodland to the charming 11C Church of **Santa Maria** ★ ⊙, built on a square plan inspired by Norman churches.

ANZIO ≜

Lazio

Population 413 436
Michelin map 430 R 19

Anzio backs against a promontory facing out to sea and forms with **Nettuno** ≜ a pleasant modern seaside resort. It has a popular yachting harbour.
Anzio is the Antium of antiquity, a Volscian city where Coriolanus took refuge, having abandoned his original intention of engaging in a fratricidal struggle with Rome. Antium was also the birthplace of Nero, in whose villa were found the statues of the Apollo Belvedere, the Fanciulla (young girl) of Anzio and the Borghese Gladiator, now respectively in the Vatican, the National Roman Museum in Rome and the Louvre in Paris.

The name of Anzio is also remembered for the Anglo-American landing of 22 January 1944, which, after a long struggle, ended in the taking of Rome on 4 June 1944. Several military cemeteries, monuments, memorials and museums recall those who gave their lives during this operation.

EXCURSION

★ **Isola di Ponza** – *Access from* **Anzio** *or* **Formia** *(ferry 2hr 30min, motorboat 1hr) and from* **Terracina** *(ferry 2hr).* This volcanic island, lying beyond the Gulf of Gaeta, has a verdant ridge and white or blue-grey cliffs, which are either bordered by narrow beaches or drop abruptly into the sea. At the southeast end of the island is the village of **Ponza** ☆☆ with its serried ranks of cubic and gaily painted houses in a semicircle around a small harbour. The latter is busy with fishing boats, coasting vessels, pleasure craft and the ferries which ply back and forth to the mainland. The island is popular with underwater fishermen.

AOSTA★

Valle d'Aosta

Population 34 989
Michelin map 428 E 3-4
Town plan in the Michelin Atlas Italy

Aosta stands in the valley of the same name and is the capital of the region. It has retained the geometric plan of a military camp *(castrum)* and some interesting monuments from the Roman period. Aosta, an active religious centre in the Middle Ages, was the birthplace of the theologian St Anselm, who became Archbishop of Canterbury where he died in 1109. Today it is an active industrial town and, since the opening of the Mont Blanc Tunnel in 1965, an important tourist centre, at the junction of the transalpine routes to France and Switzerland Via the St Bernard Tunnel.

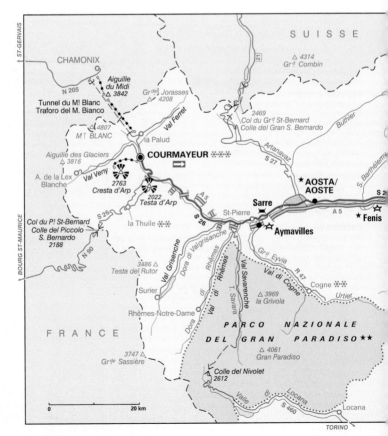

RELAXING FOR A FEW DAYS

Listed below are some hotels that will allow you to enjoy the park in a peaceful setting. They all offer double rooms for under 150 000L.

La Barme – ☎ 0165 74 91 77, fax 0165 74 92 13. This quiet little hotel (14 rooms) situated in Valnontey, 3km/2mi southwest of Cogne, has splendid views of the Gran Paradiso Park.

Granta Parey – ☎ 0165 93 61 04, fax 0165 93 61 44. Situated in Chanavey, 1.5km/1mi north of Rhêmes-Notre-Dame, this is a relaxing hotel that has wonderful views of the Val di Rhêmes.

A l'Hostellerie du Paradis – Eau Rousse, ☎ 0165 90 59 72, fax 0165 90 59 71. Book well in advance to stay in this enchanting mountain hamlet which has been turned into a hotel. 3km/2mi south of Valsavarenche.

* **Roman buildings** – These are grouped in the centre of Aosta and include a gateway **(Porta Pretoria)**, a majestic arch **(Arco di Augusto)**, both dating from the 1C BC, a **Roman bridge**, a **theatre** and the ruins of an **amphitheatre**.

Collegiata di S. Orso ⊙ – The church, dedicated to St Orso, has some lovely carved 15C **stalls** and a baroque rood screen. Beside the 11C **crypt** a doorway opens onto charming little Romanesque **cloisters★** with historiated **capitals★★** illustrating Biblical and secular scenes. The **Priorato di S. Orso** is a Renaissance-style priory with elegant **windows★**.

Cattedrale – The cathedral was built in the 12C and has been remodelled several times; it now boasts a neo-classical façade (1848). The chancel has 12C mosaic paving, 15C Gothic stalls and the 14C tomb of Thomas II of Savoy. The sacristy contains a rich **treasure** ⊙. The cloisters are 15C.

★★ VALLE D'AOSTA

This region comprising the Dora Baltea and adjacent valleys is surrounded by high peaks of both the French and Swiss Alps: Mont Blanc, the Matterhorn (Cervino), Monte Rosa, Grand Combin, Dent d'Hérens, Gran Paradiso and Grande Sassière. Owing to its marvellous situation there are some splendid **viewpoints★★★**. With its secluded valleys, numerous castles, villages with balconied houses roofed with flat stone slabs (lauzes), as well as numerous excursions and scenic routes leading up to glaciers, the Valle d'Aosta is one of the most attractive tourist areas in Italy.

The Valle d'Aosta is also a ski-lover's paradise (resorts at Breuil-Cervinia★★★, Courmayeur★★★, La Thuile★★, Gressoney, Champoluc). The slopes wind down through breathtaking landscapes comprised of woods, forests and glaciers, such as the stunning one at Monte Rosa. Ski-lovers can immerse themselves in the heart of the Parco Nazionale del Gran Paradiso (Cogne★).

Since 1948 the Valle d'Aosta has been, for administrative purposes, an autonomous region: inhabitants still speak a Franco-Provençal dialect and public deeds are published both in Italian and French. Economic activities in the region include cattle breeding and crafts such as woodcarving. Furniture (chests, benches), objects (such as the typical grolle), sculpture and toys (particularly animals such as stylised cows and donkeys) can also be found.

Sightseeing – The local map locates the towns and sites described in the guide, and also indicates other beauty spots in small black type.

★★ **Parco Nazionale del Gran Paradiso** ⊘ – This national park covering an area of almost 70 000ha – 270sqmi includes an area previously preserved as a royal hunting ground. It can be reached by the Rhêmes, Savarenche, Cogne and Locana valleys or the Nivolet Pass road. The park is rich in wildlife and is important as a reserve for endangered species, such as the ibex, and some of the rarest specimens of Alpine flora.

FROM COURMAYEUR TO IVREA *162km/101mi – allow 1 day*

✳✳✳ **Courmayeur** – *Plans of the town and surrounding areas in the Michelin Atlas Italy.* This well-known mountaineering and winter sports resort is a good excursion centre. Take a cable-car to the Cresta d'Arp and to cross the Mont Blanc Massif and make a short detour into France *(for the area beyond La Palud see the Michelin Green Guide Alpes du Nord, in French).* By car explore one of the following valleys: Veny, Ferret or Testa d'Arpi and the road to the Little St Bernard Pass, one of the busiest transalpine routes which was used by the Romans in ancient times.

In Courmayeur, Via Roma 51, **Caffè della Posta** will offer some respite from the rigours of the climate. The huge fireplace has provided warmth for customers since 1911.

The route follows the Dora Baltea Valley. Once through St-Pierre and past the road south up the Cogne valley, on the left stands **Castello di Sarre**, the former summer residence of the Counts of Savoy. Further on, to the right, is the 14C **Fortezza d'Aymavilles**, impressively quartered with great round crenellated towers.

★ **Aosta** – *See beginning of chapter.*

★ **Castello di Fénis** ⊘ – This imposing fortress contains fine carved furniture in the local style. The inner courtyard has remarkable frescoes portraying the Golden Legend.

✳✳✳ **Breuil-Cervinia** – This winter sports resort is admirably situated at 2 050m – 6 822ft. Cable-cars ⊘ climb up to the Rosa Plateau (Plan Rosa) and the Furggen Pass at 3 491m – 11 453ft.

★ **St-Vincent** – The Casino de la Vallée in its fine park is very popular.
The road passes two castles: Castello di Montjovet and the 14C **Castello di Verrès** which curiously enough has no keep or corner towers.

★ **Castello d'Issogne** ⊘ – The castle was built at the end of the 15C by Georges de Challant. It has a fine courtyard with a fountain surmounted by a wrought-iron pomegranate tree. The arcaded gallery is painted with 15C frescoes and inside the furniture is typical of the Val d'Aosta area.

★ **Fortezza di Bard** – The colossal fortress, dismantled on the orders of Napoleon in 1800 and rebuilt during the 19C, commands the upper Dora Baltea Valley.

Pont St-Martin – This village is named after the Roman bridge which was guarded by a chapel dedicated to St John Nepomucene.

Ivrea – This busy industrial town stands at the mouth of the Valle d'Aosta. To the east of Ivrea is the largest moraine in Europe, the Serra d'Ivrea.

AQUILEIA

Friuli-Venezia Giulia
Population 3 279
Michelin map 429 E 22

While the plan of the town was being outlined (181 BC) with a plough, according to Roman custom, an eagle *(aquila)* hovered overhead: hence its name. Aquileia was a flourishing market under the Roman Empire and was used as general headquarters by Augustus during his conquest of the Germanic tribes. The town then became one of Italy's most important patriarchates (554-1751) ruled by bishops.

★★ **Basilica** – The Romanesque church was built in the 11C on the foundations of a 4C building and restored in the 14C. It is preceded by a porch and flanked by a campanile.
The interior with its nave and two aisles is in the form of a Latin cross. The splendid 4C mosaic **paving**★★, which is one of the largest and richest in western Christendom, depicts religious scenes. The timber ceiling and the arcades are both 14C, the capitals are Romanesque and the decoration of the transept Renaissance. The 9C Carolingian crypt **(Cripta degli affreschi)** ⊘ is decorated with fine Romanesque **frescoes**★★.

The **Cripta degli Scavi** ⊙ is reached from the north aisle. Finds from the excavations are assembled here, notably admirable 4C mosaic **paving★★**.

★ **Roman Ruins** ⊙ – Excavations have uncovered the remains of Roman Aquileia: behind the basilica, the Via Sacra leading to the river port, houses and the forum. The Archeological and Paleo-Christian Museums **(Musei Archeologico e Paleocristiano)** ⊙ contain an important collection of finds from local excavations. The remarkable series of portraits, including those of Tiberius and of Augustus as a youth, in the archeological museum is noteworthy.

AREZZO★★

Tuscany
Population 90 907
Michelin map 430 L 17
See Michelin Green Guide Tuscany

After being first an important Etruscan city and then a rich Roman one, Arezzo became an independent commune in the 11C and was annexed by Florence in 1384, following a protracted struggle. The town has many reminders of its past and was the birthplace of several famous men: Guido d'Arezzo (997-1050) the inventor of the musical scale, Petrarch the poet (1304-74), Aretino the author (1492-1566), Giorgio Vasari and probably Maecenas (70-8 BC), the legendary patron of art and letters.

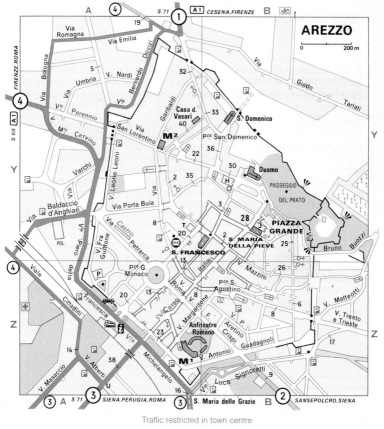

Traffic restricted in town centre

Cavour (Via)	ABY	2	Maginardo (Viale)	AZ	14	Pileati (Via dei)	BY	28
Cesalpino (Via)	BY	3	Mecenate (Viale)	AZ	16	Ricasoli (Via)	BY	30
Chimera (Via della)	AY	5	Mino da Poppi (Via)	BZ	17	S. Clemente (Via)	AY	32
Fontanella (Via)	BZ	6	Mochi (Via F.)	AY	19	S. Domenico (Via)	BY	33
Garibaldi (Via)	ABYZ	8	Monaco (Via G.)	AYZ	20	Saracino (Via del)	AY	35
Giotto (Viale)	BZ	9	Murello (Piagga del)	AY	22	Sasso Verde (Via)	BY	36
Grande (Piazza)	BY		Niccolò Aretino (Via)	AZ	23	Vittorio Veneto		
Italia (Corso)	ABYZ		Pellicceria (Via)	BY	25	(Via)	AZ	38
Madonna del Prato (V.)	AYZ	13	Pescioni (Via)	BZ	26	20 Settembre (Via)	AY	40

Museo Archeologico	AZ	**M¹**	Museo d'Arte Medievale e Moderna	AY **M²**

SIGHTS

S. Francesco – This large aisleless church was designed for preaching; it was built for the Franciscans in the 14C in the Gothic style and remodelled in the 17C and 18C.

★★★ **Frescoes of Piero della Francesca** – The frescoes depicting the Legend of the Holy Cross were executed from 1452 to 1466 on the walls of the apse. This fresco cycle is undoubtedly a milestone in the history of art. Scenes include the death and burial of Adam, Solomon and the Queen of Sheba, the dream of Constantine, the victory of Constantine over Maxentius, the invention of the Cross, the victorious Heraclius overcoming Chosroes and the announcement of Christ's death to Mary. Piero della Francesca, a pupil of the Florentine school, wrote two treatises on perspective and geometry in later life, and the cycle is the result of his wide-ranging experimentation with two-dimensional space and volume; the poses and expressions of the figures are treated with great realism in a strict composition and reflect the Renaissance ideals of serenity and timelessness. The subtle light suffusing the scenes reveals the influence of Domenico Veneziano, who was the artist's master.

★ **S. Maria della Pieve** – This lovely 12C Romanesque church is flanked by a powerful campanile. The Pisan Romanesque-style **faça de**★★ is articulated by three tiers of small columns, adorned with various motifs, whose ranks become closer as the height increases. On the high altar is a 14C polyptych by the Sienese, Pietro Lorenzetti.

★ **Piazza Grande** – This square, behind the above church, is surrounded by medieval houses, Renaissance palaces and the Logge or galleries designed by Vasari (16C). The square is the setting for the **Saracen's Tournament**, when costumed horsemen attack a dummy figure, the Saracen, with lances (see the Calendar of Events at the end of the guide).

Duomo – The cathedral was built from the 13C onwards on the town's highest point. Inside are some fine **works of art**★: stained glass by the French artist Guillaume de Marcillat (1467-1529), a fresco of Mary Magdalene by Piero della Francesca and the tomb of St Donatus (13C).

S. Domenico – This 13C church, dedicated to St Dominic, has frescoes by the Duccio school and an admirable painted **crucifix**★★ (c 1260) attributed to Cimabue.

Casa del Vasari ☉ (**AY**) – The house was sumptuously decorated by **Giorgio Vasari** (1511-74), painter, sculptor, architect and early art historian. Also exhibited are works by Tuscan Mannerists.

★ **Museo statale d'arte medievale e moderna** ☉ (**AY M²**) – The medieval and modern art collections are housed in the Renaissance Palazzo Bruni-Ciocchi and include sculpture, furniture, gold and silver objects, paintings from the Middle Ages to the 19C; **maiolica**★ from Umbria; arms and coins.

Museo archeologico ☉ (**AZ M¹**) – The archeological museum overlooks the 1C-2C **Roman amphitheatre** (**ABZ**). There is a remarkable collection of 6C BC-3C AD Etruscan and Roman bronzes, as well as ceramics from the Hellenistic and Roman periods. The Attic vases (**Euphronius vase**) and red vases made in Arezzo are of special interest.

S. Maria delle Grazie – 1km/0.6mi to the south Via viale Mecenate (**AZ**). In front of the church rises a graceful **portico**★ by the Florentine, Benedetto da Maiano (15C). Inside is a marble **altarpiece**★ by Andrea della Robbia.

Promontorio dell'ARGENTARIO★

Tuscany

Michelin map 430 O 15
Also see Michelin Green Guide Tuscany

This ancient promontory, now linked to the mainland by strips of coastline formed by a build-up of sand (tomboli), consists of the small limestone hill called **Monte Argentario** which rises to a height of 635m and is skirted by a road which affords attractive views. Its name, originally Promontorio Cosano from the nearby town of Cosa, may be a reference to the shiny, silvery appearance of its rocks or to the bankers (argentarii) who once owned it.

Orbetello – Built on the central dike in the lagoon, it is situated at the end of the main access road to the peninsula (SS 440). The town was originally called Urbis Tellus, literally the territory of the city i.e. Rome, probably because it was given in AD 805 to the Abbazia delle Tre Fontane in Rome by Charlemagne. The **fortifications** are a reminder of the influence of the Sienese and, later, the Spaniards (16C - 17C) who made the town the capital of a small state. The **cathedral** was built in the late 14C on the site of an older building and was enlarged by the Spaniards in the 17C. The facade dates from the Gothic period.

DOUBLE'S

Porto Ercole

⌂⌂ **Porto Santo Stefano** – It is the main town in the peninsula, and the embarkation point for trips to the island of Giglio. Its houses are built up the hillside on each side of a 17C Aragon-style fort from which there is a superb **view**★ over the harbour and the Talamone Gulf.

⌂⌂ **Porto Ercole** – This seaside resort has a tiny old urban district beyond a medieval gateway with hoardings and machicolations that is linked to the fortress above the town by two parallel crenelated walls. From the Piazza Santa Barbara lined by the arcading of the former Palazzo del Governatore (Governor's Palace, 16C), there is a view over the harbour, the bay and the two old Spanish forts perched on Monte Filippo.

★ **Ancient town of Cosa** – On the mainland (near Ansedonia), at the far end of the southernmost bar, Tombolo di Feniglia, the ancient **archeological site** ⊙ crowns a promontory affording fine views of the Orbetello lagoon and Monte Argentario. This ancient Roman colony, surrounded by walls made of huge blocks of stone, flourished from the 3C BC to the 4C AD. Near the shore is a tower in which Giacomo Puccini composed part of his opera, *Tosca*.

ASCOLI PICENO★★

Marches
Population 53 505
Michelin map 430 N 22

A city of travertine and a hundred towers which is known as *"piccola Siena"* (little Siena) for the harmony and elegance of its medieval and Renaissance buildings, Ascoli is situated in a valley where the Tronto and Castellano rivers meet.

Several traces of the thriving Roman town of *Asculum* remain, although these are often incorporated into an urban structure of a later date. In the Middle ages and the Renaissance the city was the setting for bitter conflicts between opposing factions; in spite of this the town flourished and a proliferation of civic and religious buildings was constructed. The Renaissance art of **Cola dell'Amatrice** was significant, but the economic and artistic vigour of the town also attracted important figures from other parts of Italy. Among these it is worth noting the Venetian painter **Carlo Crivelli** (1430-1494) who elected to settle in Ascoli permanently. Initially influenced by Mantegna and Bellini, Crivelli developed a highly original style which fused the solidity of Renaissance geometry with late Gothic decorative opulence and had a profound effect on local painters as well as bringing about a flourishing of the arts in the entire region.

On the first Sunday in August the city re-enacts its past in the famed **Torneo Cavalleresco della Quintana**, a pageant whose formation was established in the Ascoli Statutes of 1377.

★★ **Piazza del Popolo** – The main square, elongated and well-proportioned, is the public drawing room of the city. Paved with large flagstones, it is surrounded by imposing Gothic and Renaissance buildings and sheltered by elegant arcades.

The arcades of Piazza del Popolo house the famous **Caffè Meletti**, a jewel of Art Nouveau architecture which was founded in 1904 and made famous by its *"anisetta"* drink and by the film *I delfini* (1960) by Citto Maselli.

The People's Captains' Palace (**Palazzo dei Capitani del Popolo★**), erected in the 13C, owes its current appearance to additions made in the 16C by Cola dell'Amatrice, among others, who also designed the austere rear façade. Inside there is an attractive arcaded courtyard (16C).

The **chiesa di S. Francesco★** (St Francis' church, 13C-16C) has several Lombard features. On the south side there is a fine 16C portal above which stands a monument to Julius II and the Merchants' Loggia (**Loggia dei Mercanti★**), a graceful early-16C building showing Tuscan influence, particularly in the capitals. On the left hand side there are cloisters: the principal **Chiostro Maggiore**, 16C-17C, which shelters a colourful fruit and vegetable market, and the more intimate 14C **Chiostro minore** (*access from Via Ceci*). There is an elegant structure of double bell-towers in the apse.

Duomo ☉ – The grandiose Renaissance façade of this 12C cathedral was the work of Cola dell'Amatrice. On the north side stands the **Porta della Musa**, a fine late Renaissance construction. Inside, in the Cappella del Sacramento (Eucharist Chapel – *south aisle*) there is a superb **polyptych★** by Carlo Crivelli in which the late Gothic grace of the *Madonna and Child* contrasts with the dramatic *Pietà* which derives from Mantegna.

To the left of the Duomo stands the 11C **Baptistry★**, a fine square structure crowned by an octagonal lantern with graceful trefoil openings.

★ **Pinacoteca** ☉ – The picture gallery is housed on the main floor of the town hall (Palazzo Comunale) and has a notable collection of figurative arts from the 16C-19C (Guido Reni, Titian, Luca Giordano, Carlo Maratta). Most notable among the paintings of the Marches region are works by **Carlo Crivelli, Cola dell'Amatrice** and, of Crivelli's circle, **Pietro Alamanno**. A precious, delicately-worked 13C English relic (**piViale★**), the cope donated in 1288 by Nicholas IV to the cathedral chapter, is a prized exhibit.

Opposite the town hall, in Palazzo Panichi, the **Museo Archeologico** ☉ displays ancient works of the Piceno age (9 BC-6 BC) and Roman mosaics from the 1C AD.

On the nearby Via Bonaparte, at no 24, **Palazzo Bonaparte** is one of the best examples of domestic Renaissance architecture.

A STROLL IN THE HISTORIC CENTRE

★ **Corso Mazzini** – This is the grand street of the city and is lined with old palaces of varying epochs embellished by Latin and Italian inscriptions. At no 224 the 16C **Malaspina Palace** has an original loggia with columns shaped like tree trunks. At the beginning of Via delle Torri is the Renaissance St Augustine's church (**grechiesa di S. Agostino** ☉) which has a fresco of Christ by Cola dell'Amatrice and a *Madonna dell'Umiltà* of the Fabriano school (14C).

Via delle Torri – This street owes its name to the many towers that once stood here; of these two 12C **twin towers** remain. At the end of the street stands the 14C Church of St Peter the Martyr (**S. Pietro Martire**).

★ **S. S. Vincenzo e Anastasio** ☉ – This church of paleo-Christian origin is a fine example of Romanesque architecture. Its 14C **façade★** is divided into 64 sections which were originally covered in frescoes. The strikingly simple interior houses a crypt of the 6C with remains of 14C frescoes.

★ **Ponte romano di Solestà** ☉ – Heralded by a 14C gateway, this bridge is a bold construction of the Augustan Age supported by only one arch of 25m – 82ft in height. From the far end there is an attractive view of the 16C **lavatoio pubblico** (public wash-tub).

Via dei Soderini – This street was once the main artery of the medieval city; this can be seen in its numerous mansions, feudal towers and picturesque side streets. The most interesting building is the **Palazzetto Longobardo** (11C-12C) Lombard mansion which is flanked by the elegant Ercolani Tower **(Torre Ercolani)**, more than 40m high. A typical Ascoli architrave stands above its doorway.

EXCURSION

* **Civitella del Tronto** – *24km/15mi southeast.* This charming village perched on a travertine mountain 645m – 2116ft above sea-level enjoys a splendid **setting★★**. Its picturesque winding streets are lined with fine religious and civic architecture of the 16C-17C. The imposing structure of the 16C **Fortress★** ⊙, which dominates the entire village, was the last Bourbon stronghold to surrender to the Sardinian-Piedmontese armies in 1861.

ASSISI★★★

Umbria

Population 25 472
Michelin map 430 M 19

The walled city of Assisi is prettily spread across the slopes of Monte Subasio and retains its medieval character. It is closely associated with **St Francis**, as related in the numerous accounts of his life and work. Under the influence of the Franciscan Order of Minors founded by St Francis, a new, essentially religious, artistic movement developed which marked a turning-point in Italian art.

The son of the rich Assisi draper preached poverty, humility and mysticism, and his teachings gave rise to a new artistic vision which found its expression in the purity and elegance of Gothic art.

During the 13C the stark, austere churches which were designed for preaching, were embellished with a new splendour to reflect the tender and profound love of St Francis for nature and its creatures, as described in the tales of St Bonaventure. From the end of the 14C famous masters came from Rome and Venice to Assisi to work on the Basilica of St Francis. These artists abandoned for ever the rigid traditions of Byzantine art in favour of a more dramatic art imbued with a spiritual atmosphere. Cimabue and later Giotto were its most powerful exponents.

St Francis Preaching to the Birds by an unknown 13C master, Maestro di S. Francesco, Basilica inferiore

★★★ BASILICA DI S. FRANCESCO (ST FRANCIS' BASILICA) (A) *1hr30min*

From the green esplanade or from the road that winds up to Assisi from the flat countryside, the basilica is an imposing and striking vision at all hours of the day. The simple façade has a Cosmati work rose window.

The group of buildings consists of two superimposed churches, resting on a series of immense arches. The whole building, erected after the death of St Francis to the plans of Brother Elias, was consecrated in 1253. It was this monk who influenced the Franciscans to use more splendour and decoration.

Basilica inferiore – Beyond the long narthex, the walls of the dark, sombre four-bay nave are covered with 13C and 14C **frescoes★★★**. From the nave, enter the first chapel on the left with **frescoes★★** by Simone Martini (*c*1284-1344) illustrating the life of St Martin. These are remarkable for their delicate drawing, graceful composition and bright colours. Further along, above the pulpit is a fresco of the *Coronation of the Virgin* attributed to Maso, a pupil of Giotto (14C). The choir **vaulting★★** is painted with scenes symbolising the Triumph of St Francis and the virtues practised by him. They are the work of one of Giotto's pupils.

Francis

The son of a draper, St Francis of Assisi (1182-1226) had a privileged upbringing informed by courtly ideals, a period which he describes in his spiritual *Testamento* stating, "when I was in sin". His conversion took place in 1206 when the Crucifix of St Damian said to him: "Francis, go and repair my house which is falling into ruins". Having literally stripped himself of his family clothes and riches, Francis founded the Order of Minors, inspired by a spirit of **brotherhood** between all God's creatures, **minority**, in the sense of service to all, and of **absolute poverty**. He went on to dedicate himself to contemplation and to serving his neighbour, whom he would greet with the words *Signore ti dia pace* ("May God give you peace"), which was erroneously diffused as *pace e bene* ("peace and good").

The simplicity of his life was transmitted to even the most humble both through the use of the Umbrian dialect in which he wrote *Cantico delle Creature* (Canticle of the Creatures), one of the first and finest works of Italian literature, and through the joy he derived in coming up with new and effective ways of finding salvation for people. The Franciscans made popular several devotional practices in the Roman Catholic church, including the representation of the Christmas Manger – *presepio* – which is still strongly associated with the spiritual life of Assisi, where Francis is venerated as the patron saint.

The north transept is decorated with **frescoes★★** of the Passion. Those on the ceiling, attributed to pupils of Pietro Lorenzetti, are valued for their narrative design and charm of detail; those on the walls, probably by Lorenzetti himself, are striking for their dramatic expression *(Descent from the Cross)*. In the south transept is the majestic work by Cimabue, a *Madonna with Four Angels and St Francis★★*.

From the Sixtus IV cloisters make for the **treasury★★** ⊘ with its many valuable pieces and the **Perkins collection** ⊘ of 14C to 16C paintings.

At the bottom of the steps, beneath the centre of the transept crossing, is **St Francis' Tomb** which is both spare and evocative.

Basilica superiore – *The 1997 earthquake caused considerable damage to the Basilica superiore. On 26 September the central vault collapsed killing four people. At the time of going to print this part of the church is still closed.* This accomplished Gothic work with its tall and graceful nave, bathed in light, contrasts with the lower church. The apse and transept were decorated with frescoes (many have since been damaged) by Cimabue and his school. In the north transept Cimabue painted an intensely dramatic *Crucifixion★★★*.

Between 1296 and 1304 **Giotto** and his assistants depicted the life of St Francis in a famous cycle of **frescoes★★★**. There are 28 clearly defined scenes, each showing a greater search for realism. They mark a new dawning in the figurative traditions of Italian art, which was to reach its apogee during the Renaissance.

IN THE HEART OF THE CITY

★★ Rocca Maggiore ⊘ – The medieval castle is a good example of 14C military architecture. From the top of the keep there is a splendid **view★★★** of the town of Assisi and the surrounding countryside bathed in golden light.

★★ S. Chiara – From the terrace in front of the Church of St Clare there is a pretty view of the Umbrian countryside. The church was built from 1257 to 1265 and closely resembles the Gothic Upper Basilica of St Francis. Inside there are numerous works of art including 14C frescoes depicting the life of St Clare; these were influenced by Giotto.

The Byzantine Crucifix brought here from St Damian's Monastery *(below)*, which is said to have spoken to St Francis and caused his conversion to the Christian faith, can be seen in the small Church of St George, which adjoins the south aisle. The crypt enshrines the remains of St Clare.

★ **Duomo S. Rufino** – The cathedral was built in the 12C and its Romanesque **façade★★** is one of the finest in Umbria, with a harmonious arrangement of its openings and ornamentation.
The interior, on a basilical plan, was rebuilt in 1571. To the right at the entrance is the baptismal font used for the baptism of St Francis, St Clare and Frederick II.

★ **Piazza del Comune (B 3)** – This square occupies the site of the forum: note the **Tempio di Minerva★** (1 BC), a temple converted into a church, and, to the left, the People's Captains' Palace (13C).

★ **Via di S. Francesco (AB)** – This picturesque street is lined by medieval and Renaissance houses. At no 13A the Pilgrims' Chapel (**Oratorio dei Pellegrini** – ⊙ B **B**) is decorated inside with 15C frescoes, notably by Matteo da Gualdo.

★ **S. Pietro** – A Romanesque church, dedicated to St Peter, built by the Benedictines from 1029 to 1268.

EXCURSIONS

★★ **Eremo delle Carceri** ⊙ – *4km/2mi east.* The hermitage stands in a beautiful site at the heart of a forest of age-old green oaks. It is said that, having been blessed by St Francis, a huge flock of birds flew out of one of the trees, symbolising the spread of the Franciscan Order throughout the world. The hermitage was founded here by St Bernardino of Siena (1380-1444). The spot derives its name from the fact that Francis and his followers liked to retire from the world here as if they had been put into prison (*carcere* in Italian) in order, according to one of his biographers, to chase out "from the soul the tiniest speck of dust left in it by contact with mankind". Narrow passageways clearly indicating the structure of the monastery (built around the outline of the rock) lead to St Francis' Cave and the old refectory with its 15C tables.

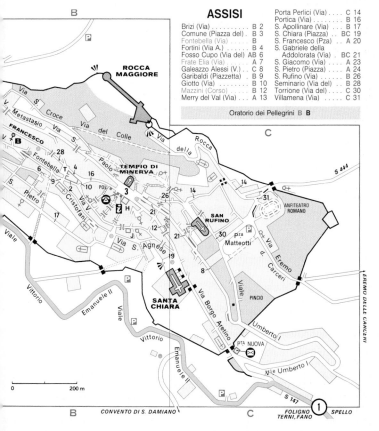

ASSISI

Brizi (Via) . . . . B 2
Comune (Piazza del) . . B 3
Fontebella (Via) . . . . . B
Fortini (Via A.) . . . . . . B 4
Fosso Cupo (Via del) AB 6
Frate Elia (Via) . . . . . . A 7
Galeazzo Alessi (V.) . . C 8
Garibaldi (Piazzetta) . B 9
Giotto (Via) . . . . B 10
Mazzini (Corso) . . . . B 12
Merry del Val (Via) . . . A 13
Porta Perlici (Via) . . . . C 14
Portica (Via) . . . . B 16
S. Apollinare (Via) . . . B 17
S. Chiara (Piazza) . . BC 19
S. Francesco (Pza) . . A 20
S. Gabriele della
  Addolorata (Via) . . BC 21
S. Giacomo (Via) . . . . A 23
S. Pietro (Piazza) . . . A 24
S. Rufino (Via) . . . . . . B 26
Seminario (Via del) . . . B 28
Torrione (Via del) . . . . C 30
Villamena (Via) . . . . . C 31

Oratorio dei Pellegrini B **B**

★ Convento di S. Damiano ⊘ - *2km/1 mile south of the gateway, Porta Nuova.* St Damian's Monastery and a small adjoining church stand alone amidst olive and cypress trees and are closely associated with St Francis, who received his calling here and composed his *Canticle of the Creatures*, and also with St Clare who died here in 1253. The humble and austere interior is a moving example of a 13C Franciscan monastery.

★ Basilica di S. Maria degli Angeli ⊘ - *5km/3mi southwest.* The basilica of St Mary of the Angels was built in the 16C around the **Porziuncola**, a small chapel named after the small plot (*piccola porzione* in Italian) of land on which it was built before the year 1 000 AD. It was in the Porziuncola that St Francis named Clare the "Bride of Christ". It contains a **fresco★** (1393) representing episodes from the history of the Franciscan Order *(above the altar).* It was in the adjacent chapel, Cappella del Transito, that Francis died on 3 October 1226. The St Mary Major Crypt contains an enamelled terracotta **polyptych★** by Andrea della Robbia (*c*1490). Near the church is the rose bush said to have lost its thorns when the saint threw himself onto it to escape temptation, and the cave in which he used to pray. In the corridor leading to the rose bush is a statue of the saint holding a nest where doves roost.

★ Spello - *12km/8mi southeast.* A quiet, picturesque little town in which the bastions and gateways bear witness to its past as a Roman settlement. The Church of St Mary Major (Santa Maria Maggiore) contains **frescoes★★** *(chapel on the left)* by Pinturicchio depicting the Annunciation, the Nativity, the Preaching in the Temple *(on the walls)* and the Sibyls *(on the vaulting).* To each side of the high altar are frescoes by Perugino. Nearby, in St Andrew's Church (**S. 'Andrea**), which was built in 1025, is a painting by Pinturicchio and a Crucifix attributed to Giotto. The village is also famous for its Flower Festival *(Le infiorate del Corpus Domini)* held on the Feast of Corpus Christi.

Foligno - *18km/11mi to the southeast.* Piazza della Repubblica is overlooked by the 14C Palazzo Trinci, built by the local overlords, and the cathedral (**Duomo**) with its magnificent doorway decorated with Lombard-style geometric decoration.

Palazzo Trinci ⊘ - The focal point in this palazzo are the **frescoes★**, executed with an almost perfect technical grasp of perspective. The frescoes in the Loggia depict the legend of Romulus and Remus and seem to almost stand out. In the Studio (referred to as the "Rose room" as roses were presented to apostolical vicars such as the Trinci) there are depictions of the Trivium arts (Grammar, Rhetoric, Dialect) and the Quadrivium arts (Arithmetic, Geometry, Music, Astronomy). Hours of the day are portrayed in relation to the ages of man and the planets. The Gothic thrones would suggest a northern attribution to these frescoes.

The frescoes and decorations along the corridor that leads to the cathedral represent great figures of antiquity on one wall, and the seven ages of man on the other.

Only the frescoes in the chapel, relating the life of Mary, are signed. They were completed by OttaViano Nelli in 1424.

Game of the Quintana

Foligno is passionate about its role in the **Giostra della Quintana** in which horsemen in 17C costumes representing the ten different quarters of the town must carry away, with the points of their spears, a ring which is hung from the outstretched hand of the Quintana, an early-17C wooden statue. On the day before this tournament there is a procession with over 1 000 participants also in 17C costumes.

ATRI

Abruzzo
Population 11 430
Michelin map 430 O 23

The ancient settlement of *Hatria-Picena*, founded by an Italic people and later becoming a Roman colony, has a beautiful hillside setting and overlooks the Adriatic sea. The historic centre of the city has splendid Medieval, Renaissance and Baroque buildings as well as scenic vistas.

★ Cattedrale ⊘ - Built in the 13C-14C on the foundations of a Roman edifice, the cathedral is a good example of the transitional Romanesque-Gothic style, with a series of sculpted **doorways★** which became a model on which later production in the Abruzzi region was based. The lower part of the Romanesque campanile is square but becomes polygonal in its upper part which is of Lombard design. The **interior** has tall Gothic arches and, in the apse, **frescoes★★** by the Abruzzi artist,

Andrea de Litio (1450-73). These depict scenes from the life of Joachim and Mary and fuse Gothic formal opulence with the solid geometry and realism of the Tuscans. Under the presbytery are remains of Roman baths and 3C AD mosaic floors.

The adjoining cloisters lead to the **Roman cistern** and the **Chapter Museum** with its fine collection of ceramics from the Abruzzi region.

In Piazza Duomo traces of the ancient Roman city are still visible.

EXCURSIONS

★★ **Riserva Naturale dei Calanchi** - *2km/1.2mi northwest on the SS 353. Calanchi,* known locally as *"scrimoini"* (streaks) refer to the natural phenomenon that occurred in the Tertiary Age when a plateau was eroded over the ages by water. Comparable to scenes from Dante's *Inferno* this landscape is characterised by precipices descending for hundreds of metres, sparse vegetation and white sediment which gives it an almost lunar appearance.

S. Clemente al Vomano ⊗ - *15km/9mi northwest.* This church was founded in the 9C although it has undergone reconstruction several times since then. The fine Classical door (12C) gives access to the strikingly simple interior whose **ciborium★** (12C) stands out above all else. This ritual object is richly decorated with elegant fretwork and animal and vegetable motifs. The altarpiece underneath is embellished with oriental patterns and inlaid terracotta. Parts of the original edifice can be seen through glass panes on the floor.

BARI

Puglia

Population 333 550
Michelin map 431 D 32

Bari, the capital of Apulia and an agricultural and industrial centre, is first and foremost a port with shipping connections with both Croatia (Split and Dubrovnik), and Greece (Corfu, Igoumenitsa, Patrass and Cephalonia). The Levantine Fair *(Fiera del Levante)*, held in September, is an important trade fair which was inaugurated in 1930 to encourage trade with other Mediterranean countries.

Bari comprises the old town, clustered on its promontory, and the modern town with wide avenues, laid out on a grid plan in the 19C. Bari was the capital of Byzantium's possessions in Italy and a very prosperous city in the Middle Ages due partly to its role as a pilgrimage centre to St Nicholas' shrine and as a port of embarkation for the Crusades. It declined under the Sforza of Milan and Spanish rule in the 16C.

★ CITTÀ VECCHIA *1hr30min*

★★ **Basilica di San Nicola** - The basilica in the heart of the old town *(città vecchia),* also known as Nicholas' stronghold, was begun in 1087 and consecrated in 1197 to St Nicholas, Bishop of Myra in Asia Minor, who achieved fame by resurrecting three children, whom a butcher had cut up and put in brine. St Nicholas' relics were brought home by sailors from Bari and it was decided to build a church to him. The building is one of the most remarkable examples of Romanesque architecture and it was the model for many churches built locally. The plain but powerful façade, flanked by two towers, is relieved by several twinned openings and a sculptured doorway with bulls supporting the flanking columns. On the north side there is the richly decorated 12C Lions' Doorway.

Inside, the nave and two aisles with a triforium were reroofed in the 17C with a fine coffered ceiling. A large 12C ciborium (canopy) surmounts the high altar behind which is an unusual 11C **episcopal throne★** in white marble. In the north apse hangs a painting of the *Virgin and Saints* by the Venetian, Bartolomeo Vivarini, and opposite *St Jerome* by Costantino da Monopoli. The tomb of St Nicholas lies in the crypt. The marble columns are crowned by richly decorated capitals.

★ **Cattedrale** (DY B) - This 11C-12C Romanesque cathedral was added to and then altered at a later date. Inside, the nave and two aisles have oven-vaulted apses and there is a false triforium above the arches. The works of art include a pulpit made up of 11C and 12C fragments, and a baldachin rebuilt from 13C fragments.

In the north aisle is displayed a copy of the *Exultet* (the original is kept in the sacristy just outside the church), a precious 11C Byzantine parchment scroll in Beneventan script, typical of medieval southern Italy. The illustrations are on the reverse side so that the congregation could see them as the parchment was unrolled for the choristers.

★ **Castello** ⊗ - The Emperor Frederick II of Hohenstaufen built the castle in 1233 over the foundations of earlier Byzantine and Norman buildings. The irregular but four-sided courtyard and two of the original towers date from the Swabian period. The castle's defences were strengthened in the 16C.

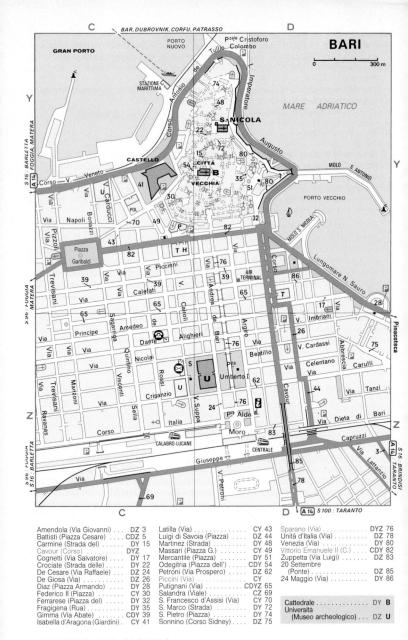

Amendola (Via Giovanni)	DZ 3	Latilla (Via)	CY 43	Sparano (Via)	DYZ 76
Battisti (Piazza Cesare)	CDZ 5	Luigi di Savoia (Piazza)	DZ 44	Unità d'Italia (Via)	DZ 78
Carmine (Strada del)	DY 15	Martinez (Strada)	DY 48	Venezia (Via)	DY 80
Cavour (Corso)	DYZ	Massari (Piazza G.)	CY 49	Vittorio Emanuele II (C.)	CDY 82
Cognetti (Via Salvatore)	DY 17	Mercantile (Piazza)	DY 51	Zuppetta (Via Luigi)	DZ 83
Crociate (Strada delle)	DY 22	Odegitria (Piazza dell')	CDY 54	20 Settembre	
De Cesare (Via Raffaele)	DZ 24	Petroni (Via Prospero)	DZ 62	(Ponte)	DZ 85
De Giosa (Via)	DZ 26	Piccini (Via)	CY	24 Maggio (Via)	DY 86
Diaz (Piazza Armando)	DY 28	Putignani (Via)	CDYZ 65		
Federico II (Piazza)	CY 30	Salandra (Viale)	CZ 69		
Ferrarese (Piazza del)	DY 32	S. Francesco d'Assisi (Via)	CY 70	Cattedrale	DY B
Fragigena (Rua)	DY 35	S. Marco (Strada)	DY 72	Università	
Gimma (Via Abate)	CDY 39	S. Pietro (Piazza)	DY 74	(Museo archeologico)	DZ U
Isabella d'Aragona (Giardini)	CY 41	Sonnino (Corso Sidney)	DZ 75		

ADDITIONAL SIGHTS

Pinacoteca ⊙ – *On Lungomare Nazario Sauro* (DY) *beyond Piazza A. Diaz.* The gallery, on the fourth floor (lift) of the Palazzo della Provincia, comprises Byzantine works of art (sculpture and paintings), a 12C-13C painted wood statue of **Christ★**, *The Martyrdom of St Peter* by Giovanni Bellini and canvases by the 17C-18C Neapolitan school.

Museo archeologico ⊙ (DZ **U**) – *First floor of the university.* The archeological museum displays Greco-Roman collections from excavations made throughout Apulia.

EXCURSION

The road from Bari to Barletta passes through many small but attractive coastal towns which were fortified against invasion by the Saracens during the Middle Ages and the Turks at the end of the 15C. These include **Giovinazzo** with its small 12C cathedral dominating the fishing harbour; **Molfetta** pinpointed by the square towers of its Apulian Romanesque cathedral in white limestone; and **Bisceglie**, a picturesque fishing village, with its cathedral finished in the 13C. The main doorway is flanked by two lions.

BARLETTA ☺

Puglia
Population 91 236
Michelin map 431 D 30

In the 12C and 13C the town of Barletta was an embarkation port for the Crusades and many military or hospitaller Orders chose this as the site for an institution.

Now a commercial and agricultural centre, the town has a fine historic nucleus comprising several medieval religious and secular buildings.

The symbol of the town is a statue dating back to the Roman era. The Colossus (**Colosso**★★ or Statua di Eraclio) is a gigantic statue over 4.5m/15ft tall of a Byzantine emperor whose identity is uncertain (Valentinian I?). Probably 4C, this work is of interest as it marks the transition from decadent Roman to early Christian art. The stiffness of the figure is offset by the intense expression.

The statue stands in front of the Basilica of the Holy Sepulchre **(San Sepolcro)** which dates from the 12C-14C and possesses a fine **reliquary**★, with Limoges enamels on the base.

The castle (**Castello**★) is an imposing fortress built by the Emperor Frederick II of Hohenstaufen and later remodelled especially by Charles V in the 16C. The latter is responsible for its curious plan with four pointed corner bastions; inside are two large superimposed semi-circular blockhouses. The castle houses a gallery (**pinacoteca** ⊙) exhibiting a fine **collection**★ of paintings by the local artist, Giuseppe de Nittis (1846-84) who worked mainly in Paris.

In via Cialdini, on the ground floor of the 14C Palazzo di Don Diego de Mendoza is the **cellar** where the famous Barletta challenge **(la disfida di Barletta)** was issued.

Further along is the 17C **palazzo della Marra**; its façade is richly decorated in the Baroque style.

The Barletta challenge

In 1503 the town which was held by the Spanish was besieged by French troops. The Italians accused of cowardice by a French prisoner issued a challenge, following which 13 Italian knights led by Ettore Fieramosca met and defeated 13 French knights in single combat.

In the 19C this deed was deemed a fine example of patriotism and Ettore Fieramosca became a heroic figure. In 1833 the author Massimo d'Azeglio based a novel on this event (*Ettore Fieramosca o la disfida di Barletta*).

EXCURSION

Canne della Battaglia - *12km/8mi southeast*. The strategic importance of the site in late Antiquity is evidenced by a famous battle in AD 216 when the Carthaginians led by Hannibal won a decisive victory over the Roman army under the leadership of Scipio. There are ruins of a medieval necropolis and of an Apulian village; and on the opposite slope, a stronghold where the main Roman axis, the *decumanus*, intersected by streets (*cardi*) is still visible, as well as the remains of a medieval basilica and of a Norman castle.

BASSANO DEL GRAPPA ★

Veneto – Population 39 625
Michelin map 429 E 17

Bassano del Grappa, a pottery town which also produces brandy (*grappa*), is built on the banks of the Brenta River. The town is attractive with narrow streets lined by painted houses and the squares bordered by arcades. In the centre, Piazza Garibaldi is dominated by the 13C square tower, Torre di Ezzelino, and overlooked by the Church of St Francis **(S. Francesco)**. The church, which dates from the 12C-14C, has an elegant porch (1306). Inside, the 14C Christ is by Guariento. The covered bridge **(Ponte Coperto)** is well known in Italy. Originally built in the 13C, it has been rebuilt many times since.

★ **Museo Civico** ⊙ – The municipal museum is housed in the monastery next to the church of St Francis. The **picture gallery**, on the first floor, has several works by the local da Ponte family. Jacopo da Ponte, otherwise called **Jacopo Bassano** (1510-92), was the best-known member. His works were marked by a picturesque realism and contrasts of light and shade. *St Valentine baptising St Lucia* is his masterpiece. Other Venetian painters include Guariento, Vivarini, Giambono (14C and 15C), Pietro Longhi, Tiepolo and Marco Ricci (18C). There are also two lovely canvases by the Genoese painter Magnasco (18C) and a gallery devoted to the sculptor Canova.

EXCURSIONS

*** **Monte Grappa** – (alt. 1 775m/5 823ft) *32km/20mi north*. The road up passes through fine forests and bare mountain pastures, before reaching the summit, from where there is a magnificent **panorama** reaching as far as Venice and Trieste. The monument is a First World War ossuary.

* **Asolo** – *14km/9mi east*. The streets of this attractive little town, dominated by its castle, are lined with palaces painted with frescoes.
The town is closely associated with Robert Browning and Duse, the famous Italian tragic actress who interpreted the works of Gabriele D'Annunzio. Duse is buried in the peaceful cemetery of Sant'Anna.

Marostica – *7km/4mi west*. The main square (**Piazza Castello★**) of this charming small medieval city serves as a giant chessboard for a highly original game of chess (**partita a scacchi**) with costumed people as the chessmen *(see the table of Principal Festivals at the end of the guide)*.

Cittadella – *13km/8mi south*. This stronghold was built by the Paduans in 1220 to counter the Trevisans' construction of Castelfranco. Cittadella is encircled by fine brick **walls★**.

Possagno – *8km/11mi northwest*. This was the birthplace of the sculptor **Antonio Canova** (1757-1822), known for his neo-classical works. The **house** ⊙ where he was born and a sculpture gallery (**Gipsoteca**) ⊙ nearby are open to the public. The temple (**Tempio di Canova**) ⊙ designed by the master himself, crowns an eminence. Inside are the sculptor's tomb and his last sculpture, a *Descent from the Cross★*.

The chapter on Practical Information at the end of the guide lists:
local or national organisations providing additional information,
recreational sports,
thematic tours,
suggested reading,
events of interest to the tourist,
admission times and charges.

BELLUNO★

Veneto

Population 35 230
Michelin map 429 D 18

This pleasant town stands on a spur at the confluence of the Piave and the Ardo rivers and is surrounded by high mountains. To the north are the Dolomites with the Belluno Pre-Alps in the south. An independent commune in the Middle Ages, Belluno came under the aegis of the Venetian Republic from 1404.

Walk along via Rialto through the 13C gateway, Porta Dojona (remodelled in the 16C), across the **Piazza del Mercato★**, bordered with arcaded Renaissance houses and adorned with a 1409 fountain, along via Mezzaterra and Via Santa Croce to the gateway, Porta Rugo. Via del Piave offers an extensive **view★** of the Piave Valley and the surrounding mountains. The **Piazza del Duomo★** is surrounded by the late-15C Venetian-style Rectors' Palace (**palazzo dei Rettori★**), the Episcopal Palace (**palazzo dei Vescovi**) and the cathedral (Duomo), dating from the 16C with its baroque campanile by Juvara. Inside, there are several good pictures by the Venetian school, notably by Jacopo Bassano and, in the crypt, a 15C **polyptych★** by the Rimini school. The Jurists' Palace (Palazzo dei Giuristi) houses the municipal museum (**Museo civico**) ⊙ with an art gallery (local and Venetian works), a rich coin collection and documents on the *Risorgimento*.

EXCURSION

Feltre – *31km/19mi southwest*. Feltre, grouped around its castle, has kept part of its ramparts and in **Via Mezzaterra★**, old houses, adorned with frescoes in the Venetian manner. **Piazza Maggiore★** is a beautiful square with its noble buildings, arcades, stairways and balustrades. The municipal museum (**Museo civico** ⊙), *23 Via Lorenzo Luzzo, near the Porta Oria*) displays works by Lorenzo Luzzo, a local artist, Marescalchi, Bellini, Cima da Conegliano, Ricci and Jan Massys. The museum also includes a historical section on Feltre and an archeological collection.

BENEVENTO

Campania
Population 63 527
Michelin map 431 D 26

This was the ancient capital of the Samnites, who hindered the Roman expansion for some considerable time. In 321 BC they trapped the Roman army in a defile known as the Caudine Forks (Forche Caudine) between Capua and ancient Beneventum. The Romans occupied the town following the defeat in 275 BC of Pyrrhus (it was on this occasion that the victors transformed the old name *Maleventum* into *Beneventum*) and his Samnite allies. During the reign of Trajan, the town knew a period of glory and it was designated as the starting-point for the Appian Trajan Way (Via Appia Traiana) leading to Brindisi. Under Lombard rule it became the seat of a duchy in 571 and later a powerful principality. Following the Battle of Benevento in 1266, Charles of Anjou who had defeated Manfred, the then king of Naples and Sicily, supported by Pope Urban IV, claimed the kingship.

Teatro Romano ⊙ – *Access from via Port'Arsa,to the left of S. Maria della Verità church.* This is one of the largest Roman theatres still in existence; it was built in the 2C by the Emperor Hadrian and enlarged by the Emperor Caracalla. In the summer it is the arena for theatre, dance and opera performances.

From piazza Duomo, dominated by the imposing cathedral which suffered heavy damages from bombardments in 1943 (of the original structure, only the façade and the substantial campanile remain, both 13C), turn into **corso Garibaldi** which is lined with the most significant buildings of the city's history. Note the **Egyptian obelisk** from Isis' Temple (AD 88).

The witches of Egypt!

In the 1C AD Benevento was one of the principal centres of the cult of Isis which flourished until the 6C. With the advent of the Lombards the practice of magic and mystic rites was considered incompatible with Christianity. It is said that believers continued to conduct rites outside the city walls, near a walnut tree in the valley of the Sabato river. This gave rise to the myth of witches' Sabbaths and the witches of Benevento. According to legend St Barbato put an end to these activities in the 7C by cutting down the walnut tree. The memory of this legend is kept alive, however, by the famous liqueur *Strega* (witch) which was created in 1861 by Giuseppe Alberti who also financed the prestigious literary prize bearing his name.

★★ **Arco di Traiano** – *From corso Garibaldi turn left onto Via Traiano.* The "Porta Aurea", erected in AD 114 to commemorate the emperor who had turned Benevento into an obligatory stopover on the journey to Apulia, is Italy's best-preserved triumphal arch. The low reliefs dedicated to the glory of the Emperor Trajan depicting scenes of peace on the side facing the city and scenes of war and life in the provinces facing the countryside, are of an exceptionally high standard.

S. Sofia ⊙ – *Piazza Matteotti.* An 8C building which was rebuilt in the 17C. The interior has a bold and unusual layout consisting of a central hexagon enclosed by a decagonal structure. In the apses there are remains of 8C frescoes. Adjacent to the 12C **cloisters★** whose splendid columns support Moorish style arches, the **Museo del Sannio★** ⊙ houses an important archeological collection and some fine Neapolitan paintings of the 17C and 18C.

At the end of corso Garibaldi *(piazza IV Novembre)* stands the **Rocca dei Rettori**, a fortress built in the 14C on the remains of a Lombard castle.

BERGAMO★★

Lombardy
Population 117 619
Michelin map 428 E 10-11

Bergamo, one of the principal towns of Lombardy, is situated on the northern edge of the Lombardy plain at the confluence of the Brembana and Seriana valleys. It is an art centre as well as a busy business and industrial centre.

The modern **lower town** is pleasant while the old **upper town** is quiet, picturesque and evocative of the past. It also has many delightful, old cakeshops whose windows are filled with the small yellow cakes that are a local speciality, the *"polenta e osei"*.

From Roman city to Venetian rule – Around 1200 BC the Ligurians occupied the site of the upper town. The Gauls seized the settlement in c AD 550 and called it Berghem. It was renamed Bergomum by the Romans when they took over in 196 BC. The city was destroyed by the Barbarians before enjoying a period of peace under the Lombards and in particular in the reign of Queen Theodolinda. An independent

BERGAMO

Belotti (Largo Bortolo) . . . .   BZ 3
Borgo Palazzo (Via) . . . . .   CZ 6
Botta (Via Carlo) . . . .   BZ 7
Camozzi (Via) . . . .   BCZ
Cesare (Viale Giulio) . . . . .   CY 13
Colleoni (Via B.) . . . .   AY
Conca d'Oro (Galleria) . . . .   AY 16
Dante (Piazza) . . . .   BZ 17

Donizetti (Via G.) . . . .   AY 19
Fantoni (Via A.) . . . .   CZ 23
Giovanni XXIII
   (Viale) . . . .   BZ 24
Gombito (Via) . . . .   AY 27
Lazzaretto (Via) . . . .   CY 28
Libertà
   (Piazza della) . . . .   BZ 30
Lupi (Via Brigata) . . . .   BZ 32
Mercato delle
   Scarpe (Piazza) . . . .   BY 38

Monte
   Ortigara (Via) . . . .   BY 42
Mura di S. Agostino
   (Viale delle) . . . .   BY 45
Mura di S. Grata . . . .   AY 47
Muraine (Viale) . . . .   CY 49
Orelli (Via) . . . .   AZ 53
Partigiani (Via dei) . . . . . .   BZ 56
Petrarca (Via) . . . .   BZ 57
Pradello (Via) . . . .   BZ 60
Previtali (Via Andrea) . . . . .   AZ 62

"Città Alta": traffic restrictions

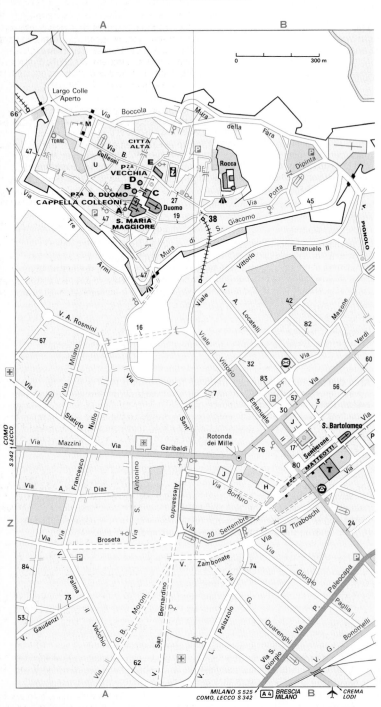

Tempietto di Santa Croce . . . .   AY A
Battistero . . . .   AY B
Palazzo della Ragione . . . .   AY C
Torre . . . .   AY D

S. Alessandro (Via) . . . . AZ
S. Vigilio (Via) . . . . AY 66
S. Lucia (Via) . . . . AY 67
Sauro (Via N.) . . . . CY 69
Scuri (Via E.) . . . . AZ 73
Spaventa (Via S.) . . . . BZ 74
Tasca (Via) . . . . AZ 76
Tasso (Via T.) . . . . BCZ
Vittorio Veneto (Piazza) . . . . BZ 80
Zambianchi (Via E.) . . . . BY 82
Zelasco (Via G. e R.) . . . . BZ 83
Zendrini (Via B.) . . . . AZ 84
20 Settembre (Via) . . . . BZ

commune from the 11C to the 13C, it then joined the Lombard League in its struggle against the Emperor Frederick Barbarossa. The town suffered during the struggles between the Guelphs (followers of the pope) and the Ghibellines (followers of the emperor). Under the rule of **Bartolomeo Colleoni** (1400-75), the town fell first to the Visconti family from Milan and then to the Republic of Venice which the famous mercenary leader served successively. Bergamo came under Austrian rule in 1814 and was liberated by Garibaldi in 1859.

Bergamo and its artists – In addition to a large group of local artists, namely Previtali, Moroni, Cariani, Baschenis and Fra Galgario, numerous others worked in the town, including **Lorenzo Lotto**, Giovanni da Campione and Amadeo.

Masks and Bergamasques – The **Commedia dell'Arte** originated at Bergamo in the 16C. The comedy consists of an improvisation (*imbroglio*) based on a pre-arranged theme (*scenario*), with gags (*lazzi*) uttered by masked actors representing stock characters: the valet (Harlequin), a stubborn but wily peasant from the Brembana Valley, the braggart (Pulcinella) the lady's maid (Columbine), the lover (Pierrot), the knave (Scapino), the old fox (Scaramouch), the clown (Pantaloon) and the musician (Mezzetino). Its element of caricature sometimes springs from triViality. This form of theatre was popular in France in the 17C and 18C. Bergamo is also the home of the composer Donizetti (1797-1848). The vivacity of the people is displayed in the local musical folklore: the Bergamasque, a lively dance, is accompanied by pipers playing their *pifferi*.

★★★ CITTÀ ALTA (UPPER TOWN) (ABY)

No cars allowed in this part of the town – 3 hours

When going by car, park outside the walls or take the funicular (*station in Viale Vittorio Emanuele II*) which ends in **Piazza del Mercato delle Scarpe** (Square of the Shoe Market) (**BY 38**).
The Upper Town, with its 16C Venetian perimeter wall, its strategically-placed castle, and its winding alleyways lined with old houses, boasts Bergamo's finest buildings.

★ **Piazza Vecchia** (**AY**) – This is the historic centre of the town. The **Palazzo della Ragione** (**C**), the oldest town hall in Italy, dates from 1199 but was rebuilt in the 16C. It has graceful arcades and trefoil openings and a central balcony surmounted by the Lion of St Mark symbolising Venetian rule. A 14C covered stairway leads to the majestic 12C **tower** ⊙ (**D**) with its 15C clock.
The **Palazzo Scamozziano** (**E**) opposite is in the Palladian style. The fountain in the centre was offered to Genoa in 1780 by the Doge of Venice, Alvise Contarini.

Through the arcades of Palazzo della Ragione make for **Piazza del Duomo**★★ (**AY**) which is bordered by the chief monuments of the upper town.

Palazzo Scamozziano . . AY **E**
Teatro Donizetti . . . . . . BZ **T**

| Scapino | Pantaloon | Capitan Fracassa | Pulcinella | Scaramouch | Mezzetino |

★★ **Capella Colleoni** ⊙ – The architect of the Carthusian monastery at PaVia, **Amadeo**, designed the chapel (1470-76), a jewel of Lombard-Renaissance architecture, as a mausoleum for Bartolomeo Colleoni, who directed that it should be built on the site of the sacristy of the basilica of St Mary Major. The funerary chapel opens into and is embedded in the north side of the basilica. The domed main structure is adjacent to the north porch which is skilfully used to counterbalance the recess.

The elegant **façade** is faced with precious multicoloured marble and lavishly decorated with delicate sculptures: figures of children (putti), fluted and wreathed columns, sculptured pilasters, vases and candelabra, medallions and low reliefs combining sacred and secular elements after the contemporary fashion (allegories, scenes from the Old Testament, mythological figures including scenes from the life of Hercules with whom Colleoni identified himself).

The interior is sumptuously decorated with low reliefs of extraordinary delicacy, frescoes by Tiepolo and Renaissance **stalls** with intarsia work. The **Colleoni monument**, also by Amadeo, is surmounted by an equestrian statue of the leader in gilded wood and is delicately carved. The low reliefs of the sarcophagi represent scenes from the New Testament separated by niches housing statues of the Virtues. Between the two sarcophagi are portraits of the leader's children. His favourite daughter, Medea, who died at the age of 15, lies near him (to the left), in a tomb by Amadeo which is a marvel of delicacy and purity.

★ **Basilica di Santa Maria Maggiore** ⊙ – This church, dedicated to St Mary Major, is 12C but the two lovely north and south **porches** with loggias and supported by lions in the Lombard Romanesque style were added in the 14C by Giovanni da Campione. The interior, remodelled in the baroque style (late 16C-early 17C), is richly decorated with stucco and gilding. The walls of the aisles and the chancel are hung with nine splendid Florentine **tapestries**★★ (1580-1586), beautifully designed after cartoons by Alessandro Allori which relate the Life of the Virgin. On the west wall of the nave hangs the sumptuous Flemish tapestry depicting the **Crucifixion**★★. It was woven in Antwerp between 1696 and 1698 after cartoons by L Van Schoor. This part of the church also contains Donizetti's tomb (1797-1848). Note also the curious 18C baroque confessional in the north aisle and the interesting 14C frescoes in the transept. Incorporated in the chancel screen are four superb **panels of intarsia work**★★ depicting scenes from the Old Testament. They were made in the 16C after the designs of Lorenzo Lotto.

Leave by the door giving onto Piazza di Santa Maria Maggiore to admire the 14C south porch, as well as the charming **Tempietto Santa Croce** (A) which was built c1000 on the quatrefoil plan in the early-Romanesque style. To return to the Piazza del Duomo walk round the basilica's **east end**★ with its radiating chapels decorated with graceful arcading.

★ **Battistero** (B) – This charming octagonal baptistery is encircled by a red Verona marble gallery with graceful, slender columns and 14C statues representing the Virtues. It is a reconstruction of Giovanni da Campione's original work dating from 1340. It originally graced the east end of the nave of St Mary Major but was deemed too cumbersome and was demolished in 1660 and rebuilt on its present site in 1898.

Duomo – The cathedral has a richly decorated interior (18C). The very lovely baroque stalls were carved by the Sanzi.

Via Bartolomeo Colleoni ⊙ (AY) – This street is lined with old mansions including the Colleoni Mansion, at Nos 9 and 11, which contains frescoes to the glory of the mercenary leader.

Rocca (BY) – Built in the 14C the fortress (rocca) was remodelled by the Venetians. There are interesting **views**★ of the upper and lower towns.

★ CITTÀ BASSA 1 1/2 hours.

The Carrara Academy is in the heart of a district of attractive alleyways, while Piazza Matteotti is at the centre of the present-day business and shopping district in the lower town (città bassa).

★★ **Accademia Carrara** ⊘ (CY) – This collection of 15C-18C Italian and foreign paintings is housed in a neo-classical palace.

Beyond the early-15C works, which still recall the International Gothic style, hang two important portraits of **Giuliano de'Medici** by Botticelli and the elegant and refined one of **Lionello d'Este** by Pisanello. These are followed by works of the Venetian school: by the Vivarini family, Carlo Crivelli, Giovanni Bellini (gentle Madonnas with dreamy expressions which are similar to those of his brother-in-law, Mantegna), Gentile Bellini (delicate but penetrating portraits), Carpaccio (Portrait of the Doge Leonardo Loredan) and by Lorenzo Lotto. Next come the late-15C and early-16C works represented by Cosimo Tura, master of the Ferrarese school (a very realistic Virgin and Child showing the influence of Flemish art), by the Lombard, Bergognone (soft light), and by the Bergamask, Previtali.

The 16C covers works by the Venetian Lorenzo Lotto (including a splendid **Holy Family with St Catherine**), the fine Bergamask portraitist Cariani, and the Venetian masters, Titian and Tintoretto. The colours and delicate draughtsmanship of Raphael greatly influenced Garofalo (Benvenuto Tisi) who was nicknamed the Ferrara Raphael, while the Piedmontese Gaudenzio Ferrari and Bernardino Luini, the main exponents of the Renaissance in Lombardy, were inspired by Leonardo da Vinci. The 16C **portraits** are a particularly rich group, with the Ferrarese school which specialised in this art and the Bergamask, Moroni (1523-78). Foreign artists include Clouet (Portrait of Louis de Clèves) and Dürer.

The 17C-18C Bergamo school is represented by Baschenis (1617-77) and excellent portraits by Fra Galgario (1655-1743). The 17C Flemish and Dutch section (Rubens, Van Dyck, Brueghel...) is dominated by a delightful Van Goyen seascape.

The museum also exhibits 18C Venetian painting: scenes of domestic interiors by Pietro Longhi, topographical views by Carlevarijs, Bernardo Bellotto, Canaletto and Francesco Guardi.

★ **Old quarter** – The main street of this quarter is **Via Pignolo★** (BCYZ) which winds among old palaces, mostly 16C and 18C and churches containing numerous works of art. Among these are: The Church of **San Bernardino** (CY) which has in the chancel a **Virgin Enthroned and Saints★** (1521) by Lorenzo Lotto (note the expressive use of colour with the deep red of the Virgin's robe contrasting with the intense green of the drape held up by the angels) and **Santo Spirito** (CZ) which contains a St John the Baptist surrounded by saints and a polyptych by Previtali, a polyptych portraying the Virgin by Bergognone and a Virgin and Child by Lorenzo Lotto.

★ **Piazza Matteotti** (BZ) – This immense square is in the centre of the modern town. It is flanked by the **Sentierone**, the favourite promenade of the citizens of Bergamo. In the square stand the **Donizetti Theatre** (T) and the **Church of San Bartolomeo** which houses the superb **Martinengo Altarpiece** by Lorenzo Lotto depicting the enthroned Virgin surrounded by saints.

EXCURSIONS

★ **Museo del Presepio** ⊘ – Brembo di Dalmine, 8km/5mi southwest. 4km from the Dalmine motorway exit. Follow directions for the museum.

An outstanding collection of some 800 nativity scenes (presepi) which come from many different places and range in size from one set out in a hazelnut shell to the enormous 18C Neapolitan creche featuring some delightful street scenes. Note too the electronic nativity scene which, in just 15min, presents a diorama of Biblical events that took place on or around Christmas Eve, with background music. The varied materials include card, papier-maché, ceramic, plaster, wood, stone, and even the modest but highly colourful and striking tinfoil of the Polish nativity scenes. Sometimes the little figures have been made using the most unlikely materials such as pins, matches and even the tiny hinges which fix the material to the ribs in an umbrella. Apart from the scenes themselves the interiors of the houses in the various exhibits reveal the great care and attention paid to the realistic depiction of the various countries.

★ **Val Brembana** – 25km/16mi north. For the Brembana Valley leave Bergamo by the S 470 which follows an industrial development zone. Note the curious two-toned limestone strata of the valley. The important thermal spa of **San Pellegrino Terme** ‡‡ lies in a lovely mountain setting.

BOLOGNA★★

Emilia-Romagna

Population 383 761

Michelin 429 and 430 I 15-16 (with plans of the conurbation)

Bologna, portrayed in traditional iconography as being learned, self-indulgent and "red", is by nature anti-aristocratic and democratic. During the course of its illustrious history it has asserted itself as one entity rather than through the expression of power of the individual. This can most especially be seen in the admirably homogeneous design of its historic centre in which all buildings seem to merge into one harmonious monument.

Bologna is without question learned (or better still wise) thanks to its university which, together with the University of Paris, is the oldest university in Europe. It differentiated itself from the University of Paris (a "University of masters") by becoming a "University of scholars" (administrated directly by students). If Paris was the cradle of Medieval theological learning, Bologna became the centre of the great school of law which cast itself as judge in the controversial power struggle over mandates between the Papacy and the Empire.

The self-indulgence associated with Bologna (in Italian it is known as Bologna the Fat) refers to the agricultural abundance of the city and its gastronomic opulence which has enshrined it as the food capital of Italy.

Its "redness", which over time has acquired political connotations, refers to the colour of its buildings, towers and 37km/23mi of arcades which shelter the active but not frenzied pace of a city that in the year 2000 will become Cultural Capital of Europe.

BOLOGNA

Archiginnasio (Via dell')	EU 4	
Bassi (Via Ugo)	DT	
Carbonesi (Via)	DU 17	
Indipendenza (Via dell')	ET	
Manzoni (Via)	DT 46	
Marconi (Via G.)	DT	
Porta Nuova (Via)	DT 73	
Rizzoli (Via)	ET 79	
Roosevelt (Pza F.D.)	DT 80	
Val d'Aposa (Via)	DU 85	
4 Novembre (Via)	DT 99	

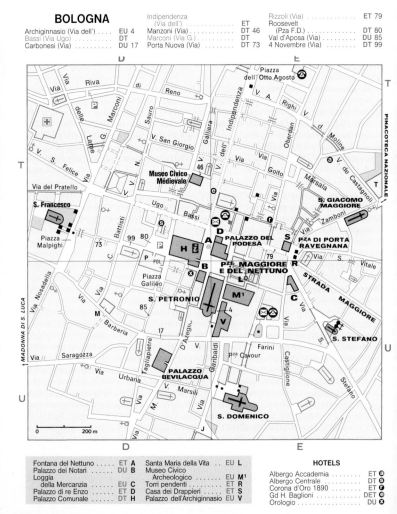

Fontana del Nettuno	ET A	Santa Maria della Vita ..	EU L			
Palazzo dei Notari	DU B	Museo Civico		**HOTELS**		
Loggia della Mercanzia	EU C	Archeologico	EU M¹	Albergo Accademia	ET ❶	
Palazzo di re Enzo	ET D	Torri pendenti	ET R	Albergo Centrale	DT ❺	
Palazzo Comunale	DT H	Casa dei Drappieri	ET S	Corona d'Oro 1890	ET ❼	
		Palazzo dell'Archiginnasio ..	EU V	Gd H. Baglioni	DET ❾	
				Orologio	DU ❿	

STAYING IN BOLOGNA

Wheels, railway tracks or wings?

Well situated on both the national rail and road networks Bologna is easily reached by car, train or plane.

By car – Situated 100km/62mi from Florence, 200km/125mi from Milan and 150km/93mi from Venice, Bologna is at a key intersection of a busy motorway network. For those intending to stay in the city for a while, it is advisable to leave your car in a lot and use public transportation to get around.

By train – The railway station is in Piazza Medaglie d'Oro, at the end of Via dell'Indipendenza, for information ring ☎ 147 88 80 88 (from 7am to 9pm). The Airbus (Aerobus, see below) has connections from the station to Guglielmo Marconi aiport, buses nos 17, 25, 30 and 37 go to Piazza Maggiore.

By plane – Guglielmo Marconi aiport is situated 6km/4mi northwest of the city in Borgo Panigale, ☎ 051 64 79 615. It is served by major national and international airline companies which connect it to major Italian and European cities, inlcuding Amsterdam, Barcelona, Brussels, Frankfurt, Lisbon, London, Paris, Prague,Vienna and Zurich.

The Aerobus – The Airbus offers a fast connection between the airport and major points of the city, the railway station and the exhibition hall (fiera) district. It runs from 6.30am to 7pm every 30min, 7 000L including luggage transport for a full journey, 3 500L for intermediate stops. Journey time between the railway station and airport 20/25min. Tickets can be purchased at ATC ticket offices, automated ticket machines or on board. For information contact ☎ 051 29 02 90.

Public transport – Bologna has a wide network of public transport. For information call ☎ 051 29 02 90. Tickets can be bought at ATC ticket offices, authorised vendors and automated ticket machines. It is advisable to have a supply of tickets in the evening, on public holidays and in the summer as many vendors are closed at these times. There are various types of tickets: the City pass (10 000L) provides 7 journeys, no more than 60min long in the daytime, no more than 70min from 8.30pm to 6.30am, and can be used by one or more people at the same time (passengers must validate their tickets by stamping them in a machine); one-day tickets (6 000L) are valid for 24hr from the moment they are validated; one-hour tickets (1 800L) are valid for 60min in the daytime and for 70min between 8.30pm and 6.30am.

Taxis – CO.TA.BO. (Cooperativa Taxisti Bolognesi) radiotaxi ☎ 051 37 27 27 and C.A.T. (Consorzio Autonomo Taxisti) radiotaxi ☎ 051 53 41 41.

Useful information

Telephone numbers

First aid service (Guardia medica) ☎ 051 33 33 33
Italian Red Cross ☎ 051 23 45 67
Carabinieri police ☎ 051 20 21 11
Traffic police ☎ 051 52 69 11

Car rental

AVIS ☎ 051 25 50 24
HERTZ ☎ 051 25 48 30 and ☎ 051 25 48 52
MAGGIORE ☎ 051 25 25 25

Night chemists

Comunale, Piazza Maggiore 6 , ☎ 051 23 85 09

Night bookshop – RIZZOLI, Via dei Mille 10, ☎ 051 24 03 02 (open until 3am).

Night newspaper stand – Via Marconi 1 (open until 2am) and Via Riva Reno 100 (open until 2am).

Where to sleep?

For a full selection of hotels in Bologna consult this year's Michelin Red Guide Italia. Listed below are some addresses chosen on the basis of good value for money, location and charm. Hotels are divided into three categories based on the price of a double room *(for more information see p. 433)* and are listed in alphabetical order *(to locate them see map)*. Note that most hotels have higher tariffs when exhibitions are being held at the fiera (exhibition hall). It is advisable to check prices by telephone beforehand and to book well in advance, particularly in more reasonably priced hotels which tend to have fewer rooms.

BUDGET...

Some hotels listed in this section have rooms without bath in which case expect to pay about 20-30% less.

Albergo Accademia – Via delle Belle Arti 6. ☎ 051 23 23 18, fax 051 56 35 90. No credit cards. 28 modern and functional rooms with satellite TV and telephone, some without bath. Prices are a little high for this category but include breakfast. The hotel also has a garage (at a charge) which is a rare treat in the historic centre of Bologna.

Albergo Centrale – Via della Zecca 2. ☎ 051 22 51 14, fax 051 23 51 62. Credit cards accepted. On the third floor of a fine old building this is a cosy and airy hotel on two floors, no lift. 20 spacious and pleasantly simple rooms, all with TV and telephone, almost all with bath and some with air conditioning. Room 9 has preserved its original Art Deco furnishings.

Albergo San Vitale – Via San Vitale 94 (EU *off the map*). ☎ 051 22 59 66, fax 051 23 93 96. Credit cards accepted (if a little unwillingly). This pleasant, well-kept hotel was originally an old convent (of which the garden remains, with one room overlooking it). The 17 rooms, spread out over 3 floors (no lift) are simple but comfortable, all with bath, TV and telephone. Excellent value for money.

Albergo Villa Azzurra – Viale Felsina 49 (*off the map, 5 km/3mi east of the historic centre, take Strada Maggiore –* EU). ☎ 051 53 54 60, fax 051 53 13 46. No credit cards. Very convenient for those arriving in Bologna by car (exit at *tangenziale* 11 and 11 bis) who don't require accommodation in the city centre. This is a peaceful hotel located in an attractive old villa with a pretty garden. 15 large, tastefully decorated rooms with bath, TV and telephone. Rooms on the second floor have sloping attic ceilings and are air-conditioned. Free parking. Bus nos 37 and 25 will get you to the city centre in 20min.

OUR SELECTION

Orologio – Via IV Novembre 10. ☎ 051 23 12 53, fax 011 26 05 52. Credit cards accepted. Situated in the heart of the historic centre this hotel has splendid views of the old buildings and monuments of the city. About 30 comfortable, well-kept rooms with air conditioning.

TREAT YOURSELF!

Gd H. Baglioni – Via dell'Indipendenza 8. ☎ 051 22 54 45, fax 051 23 48 40. Credit cards accepted. This beautifully refined hotel combines modern comfort and fine antique furnishings. Its 125 rooms (all air conditioned) are the epitome of luxury.

Corona d'Oro 1890 – Via Oberdan 12. ☎ 051 23 64 56, fax 051 26 26 79. Credit cards accepted. This elegant hotel has been in existence since 1890, although the building itself is much older. Guests will be treated to a 14C structure decorated with terracotta, 15C-16C frescoed ceilings and a stunning Art Nouveau reception hall. Breakfast is served in a charming conservatory. 35 air-conditioned rooms.

Restaurants and excursions

AROUND 50 000L

L'Anatra e l'Arancia (EU, *near S. Domenico*) – Via Rolandino 1/2, ☎ 051 22 55 05. Bistro-restaurant which serves one-course meals at lunchtime.

Da Bertino (DT) – Via delle Lame 55, ☎ 051 52 22 30. Closed at Christmas, New Year's, from 4 to 31 August, Saturdays and Sundays from 20 June to July and Monday evenings in other months. An old trattoria with typical Bolognese dishes.

Gigina (*off the map, 4 km/2.5mi north of the city centre*) – Via Stendhal 1, ☎ 051 32 21 32. Closed Saturdays and from 1-22 August. Famous trattoria outside the city which serves traditional food in a homely setting. Booking advisable. It can also be reached by bus no 27.

Teresina (ET) – Via Oberdan 4, ☎ 051 22 89 85. Closed Sundays and from 5 to 23 August. A menu which allows one to taste a little of everything. Alfresco dining in the summer. Booking recommended.

IF YOU LIKE WINE BARS...

These are two wine bars *(enoteche)* which also serve tasty snacks: **Cantina Bentivoglio**, Via Mascarella 4 b (ET, *Via delle Moline forks into Via delle Belle Arti on the right and Via Mascarella on the left*), ☎ 051 26 54 16 (closed at lunchtime, Mondays and 15 August) and **Bottega del Vino Olindo Faccioli**, Via Altabella 15 b (ET, *parallel to Via Rizzoli*), ☎ 051 22 31 71 (closed at lunchtime, Sundays and in August).

FOR GOURMETS WHO LONG FOR THE BELLE ÉPOQUE

Paolo Atti & Figli – Via Caprarie 7 (ETU, *parallel to Via Rizzoli*). Famous Art Nouveau style patisserie founded in 1880 that has numbered Giosuè Carducci and the painter Morandi among its frequenters.

Zanarini – Piazza Galvani 1 (DEU, *opposite palazzo dell'Archiginnasio*). Another historic Bolognese monument, this café was founded in 1919 and frequented by artists and writers. It has retained all of its original charm.

HISTORICAL AND ARTISTIC NOTES

The Etruscan settlement of Felsina was conquered in the 4C BC by the Boïan Gauls, who were driven out in their turn by the Romans in 190 BC. Roman *Bononia* fell under the sway of the Barbarians and did not recover until the 12C. In the subsequent century the city enjoyed the status of an independent commune and developed rapidly. A fortified city wall, towers, palaces and churches were built and the university flourished and acquired an excellent reputation for its teaching of Roman law. In the struggle which confronted the Ghibellines, supporting the emperor, and the Guelphs, partisans of communal independence, it was the latter who prevailed when in 1249 they defeated the Imperial Army of Frederick II at Fossalta. The emperor's son, Enzo, was taken prisoner and remained at Bologna until his death 23 years later.

In the 15C, following a period of violent struggles between rival families, the city was ruled by the **Bentivoglio** family. Bologna was greatly influenced by the Tuscan Renaissance during the reign of Giovanni II Bentivoglio. The Bentivoglio family was in its turn vanquished in 1506 by **Pope Julius II** and the city remained under papal control until the arrival of Napoleon Bonaparte in 1797. In the early 19C several insurrections were severely repressed by the Austrians and in 1860 Bologna was united with Piedmont.

Famous citizens include the Popes, Gregory XIII, who established our present Gregorian calendar (1582), Gregory XV (17C) and Benedict XIV (18C). In 1530, following the defeat of François I at PaVia and the sack of Rome, the Emperor Charles V obliged Pope Clement VII to crown him in the Basilica of St Petronius in Bologna.

Bologna School of Painting – This term covers the artistic movement founded by the brothers Agostino (1557-1602) and Annibale (1560-1609) and their cousin Ludovico (1555-1619) **Carracci**, who reacted against Mannerism with more "classical" composition and a more naturalistic art which aimed at expressing a simple and intimate spirituality. Numerous artists, in particular the Bolognese painters **Francesco Albani**, **Guercino**, **Domenichino** and **Guido Reni**, followed this movement known as the **Accademia degli Incamminati** (Academy of the Eclectic), whose main teaching precept was the study of nature. In 1595 Annibale Carracci moved to Rome to execute a commission for the Farnese family. His frescoes at Palazzo Farnese veer towards a sense of dynamism and illusionism which herald Baroque art.

★★★ CITY CENTRE *1 day*

The two adjoining squares, **Piazza Maggiore** and **Piazza del Nettuno★★★**, together with **Piazza di Porta Ravegnana★★**, the heart of Bologna, form a harmonious ensemble.

★★ **Fontana del Nettuno** (DT **A**) – The fountain is the work of the Flemish sculptor known as Giambologna or Giovanni Bologna. The gigantic muscular bronze Neptune (Nettuno), is surrounded by four sirens spouting water from their breasts. The group has a rather rough vigour in tune with the town's character.

★ **Palazzo Comunale** ⊘ (DT **H**) – The façade of the Town Hall is composed of buildings of different periods: 13C to the left, 15C on the right; in the centre the main doorway is 16C (the lower section is by Alessi) and is surmounted by a statue of Pope Gregory XIII. Above and to the left of the doorway is a statue of the *Virgin and Child* (1478) in terracotta by Niccolò dell'Arca. At the far end of the courtyard,

> Ochre, blue, white, ivory, brown and grey...the paintings of Giorgio Morandi (1890-1964) re-invented the chromatic spectrum to describe a rigorous world, characterised by the absence of the human figure and a restrained intensity. Bottles, vases, carafes, fruit bowls, all skilfully composed and re-composed in a myriad of variations, make up pictograms, weightless images, whereas the geometric, subtle landscapes show the influence of Cézanne.

under a gallery on the left, rises a great ramp, the so-called *Scala dei cavalli* (at one time climbed by horse-drawn carriages) leading to the richly decorated first-floor rooms, then up again to the second floor.

Opening off the vast Farnese Gallery with 17C frescoes are the splendid rooms, at one time Cardinal Legato's rooms, which now display the town's art collections **(Collezioni comunali d'arte)** ⊙ with sections on furniture, the decorative arts and a selection of Emilian **paintings★** (14C-19C). They also house a museum **(Museo Morandi)** ⊙ which boasts the largest collection of works by the painter and engraver from Bologna including paintings, drawings, watercolours and etchings as well as a reconstruction of the artist's studio with its collection of antiquities.

To the left of the Palazzo Comunale stands the severe 14C-15C Notaries' Palace **(Palazzo dei Notari) (DU B)**.

★ **Palazzo del Podestà** ⊙ – The Renaissance façade of the Governor's Palace facing piazza Maggiore has arcades separated by Corinthian columns on the ground floor and is surmounted by a balustrade. The upper storey is punctuated by flat columns and is crowned by an attic pierced by oculi or round windows.

The 13C King Enzo's Palace **(Palazzo di Re Enzo) (ET D)** stands next to the Governor's Palace. It has a fine inner courtyard and a magnificent staircase leading up to a gallery, to the left of which is a courtyard overlooked by the Arengo Tower and the magnificent Podestà Chamber, to the left.

★★ **Basilica di San Petronio** – Building on the basilica, dedicated to St Petronius, began in 1390 to the plans of Antonio di Vincenzo (1340-1402) and was fully completed only in the 17C when the vaulting was finished. The façade, the upper part of which lacks its marble facing, is remarkable chiefly for the main **doorway★★** on which the Sienese Jacopo della Quercia worked from 1425 to 1438. The lintel, uprights and embrasures are adorned with highly expressive low reliefs.

The immense **interior** has many **works of art★** including frescoes by Giovanni da Modena (15C) in the first and the fourth chapels off the north aisle. Particularly striking is the fourth chapel, the right wall of which depicts *the Journey of the Kings* and the left wall an impressive *Inferno* and *Paradise*. Additional works include a *Martyrdom of St Sebastian* by the late-15C Ferrara school in the fifth chapel; a *Madonna* (1492) by Lorenzo Costa and the tomb of Elisa Baciocchi, Napoleon's sister, in the seventh chapel; and at the high altar a canopy (baldachin) by Vignola (16C). The 15C organ on the right is one of the oldest in Italy.

★★ **Museo Civico Archeologico** ⊙ **(EU M¹)** – The atrium and inner courtyard of the municipal museum house an archaeological collection and the adjacent wing houses the plaster casts gallery. On the first floor is an extensive collection of funerary artefacts (7C BC) from the tombs in the graveyard in Verucchio (near Rimini), one of the major centres of VillanoVian culture in Emilia. Also representative of this civilisation is the **askos Benacci**, thought to be an unguent and perfume jar. The museum also has prehistoric, Egyptian, Greek and Roman (fine Roman copy of the **head of Athena Lemnia**, the bronze statue by Phidias) and Etruscan-Italian sections.

Near the museum is the 16C Bishop's Palace **(Palazzo dell'Archiginnasio)** ⊙ **(EU V)**, the home of an extensive library (10 000 manuscripts) and the 17C-18C Anatomy Theatre **(Teatro Anatomico)**.

In the nearby church of **S. Maria della Vita (EU L)**, note the dramatic **Mourning of Christ★**, a terracotta sculpture by Nicolò dell'Arca (15C).

★★ **Torri pendenti (ET R)** – There are two tall leaning towers which belonged to noble families in the attractive Piazza di Porta Ravegnana. They are symbols of the continual conflict between the rival Guelphs and Ghibellines in the Middle Ages. The taller, **Torre degli Asinelli** ⊙, nearly 100m – 328ft high, dates from 1109. 486 steps lead to the top from where there is an admirable **panorama★★** of the city. The second, known as **Torre Garisenda**, is 50m – 164ft high and has a tilt of over 3m – 10ft. No 1 in the square is the Renaissance Linen Drapers' Hall **(Casa dei Drappieri) (ET S)**.

The 14C **Mercanzia★ (EU C)** or Merchants' House, in the next square, bears the coats of arms of the various guilds and several small statues.

JUST OUTSIDE THE HISTORIC CENTRE

★ **S. Giacomo Maggiore** (ET) – The church, dedicated to St James Major, was founded in 1267. On the north side is a fine Renaissance portico. Inside is the magnificent chapel (**Cappella Bentivoglio★**) whose frescoes depicting *The Triumph of Fame and Death* and the beautiful *Madonna Enthroned with the Bentivoglio Family* were executed by the Ferrarese painter Lorenzo Costa. The chapel also houses a masterpiece of Francesco Francia, the *Madonna Enthroned and Saints* (*c*1494) which is imbued with an elegiac melancholy. Opposite the chapel, in the ambulatory, stands the **tomb★** (*c*1433) of the jurist, Antonio Bentivoglio, by Jacopo della Quercia.

St Cecilia's Chapel *(entrance on Via Zamboni 15)* is a small church, founded in the 13C with additions made in the 15C. Inside there are remarkable **frescoes★** ⊘ depicting St Cecilia (1506) by F. Francia, L. Costa and A. Aspertini.

★★ **Pinacoteca Nazionale** ⊘ – *Via Belle Arti 56, entrance on Via Zamboni* (ET, off the map). An important collection of painting, predominantly of the Bolognese school from the 13C to the 18C. Among the Bolognese works of the 14C-15C, the paintings of **Vitale da Bologna** (first half of the 14C) stand out with their delicate balance of Gothic opulence and a more forceful realism. Among his masterpieces are the energetic *St George and the Dragon★* and the **frescoes★** from the church of St Apollonia at Mezzaratta. The gallery also houses the *Madonna Enthroned and Child* polyptych, the only one of Giotto's works created during his time in Bologna to have survived to the present day and some lovely paintings by Simone de'Crocifissi and Giovanni da Modena. The section on Renaissance painting opens with works from the Venetian school (Vivarini, Cima da Conegliano) followed by some fine examples of **Emilian art★**: the dramatic fragment depicting Mary Magdalene by Ercole de'Roberti, Francesco del Cossa's metallic *Mercanti Altarpiece*, Lorenzo Costa, Amico Aspertini, the delicate Francesco Francia, Garofalo and Parmigianino with his elegant *Virgin and Child with Saints*. Works from other schools include Perugino's **Virgin and Child★**, which had a profound influence on the Bolognese school, *St Cecilia★★* by Raphael, who portrays the theme of renunciation with symbolic instruments abandoned on the ground, the *Visitation* by Tintoretto and the *Crucifixion* by Titian. The **Carracci Room★★** contains numerous masterpieces by Ludovico, one of the great interpreters of the new spirituality of the Counter Reformation with his blend of quiet intimacy and high emotion: the graceful *Annunciation*, the *Bargellini Madonna* (note the view of Bologna), the *Madonna degli Scalzi* and the dramatic *Conversion of St Paul* which heralds Baroque painting. Of Agostino Carracci note the *Communion of St Jerome* and of Annibale Carracci's work, the *Assumption of the Virgin*, a masterpiece that can already be considered an example of Baroque painting. The **Guido Reni Room★★** houses some stunning work by this painter who, after an initial adherence to the work of the Carracci, leant towards a classicism that had its roots in Raphael and Classical art. In the famous **Massacre of the Innocents** the eternal moment is captured in a skilful composition and in the careful balance of architecture and figures who form a reversed triangle. The intense *Portrait of a Widow*, generally thought to be a portrait of the artist's mother, with its blend of keen psychological insight and balanced use of colour, is considered one of the finest portraits of Italian 17C painting. The **Baroque corridor** displays works by artists associated with the Accademia degli Incamminati (Domenichino, Tiarini, Albani) as well as works by Guercino who added an expressive use of colour reminiscent of Titian to the lessons he had learnt from the Carracci (*St William★*, an early masterpiece of Baroque art). Of 18C painting note the works by Giuseppe Maria Crespi, one of the major painters of 18C Italy: the sombre *Self Portrait*, the **Courtyard Scene★**, the *Portrait of a Hunter* and the charming *Girl with a Rose and Cat*.

★ **Strada Maggiore** – Along this elegant street, lined with some fine palaces (note **Casa Isolani** at no 19, a rare example of 13C architecture with a wooden portico) is the **Museo d'Arte industriale e Galleria DaVia Bargellini** ⊘, housed in an attractive palace dating from 1658 *(at no 44)*, which has collections of "industrial art" (applied and decorative arts) and paintings from the 14C-18C.

A little further down, on the right, is the church of **Santa Maria dei Servi** (founded in the 14C) which is heralded by a Renaissance quadrisection **portico★** and is finished off by a beautiful construction in the apse. Inside, on the third chapel on the right, there is a splendid **Maestà★★** (Virgin in Majesty) by Cimabue.

★ **Basilica di S. Stefano** ⊘ – The basilica comprises a group of buildings (originally seven) overlooking the square with its Renaissance mansions. Entrance is through the Church of the Crucifix (**Crocifisso**), an old Lombard cathedral initially restored in the 11C and heavily remodelled in the 19C. Turning left make for the atmospheric 12C Church of the Holy Sepulchre (**Santo Sepolcro**) with its polygonal plan and the shrine of Bologna's patron saint, St Petronius. The black cipolin marble columns were originally part of the ancient Temple of Isis (AD 100) which was turned into a baptistery and later into a church.

The font, originally consecrated with water from the Nile, was re-consecrated with water from the Jordan River. To the left make for the church of **S.S. Vitale e Agricola** (8C-11C) with its plain, robust structure. Go through the Church of the Holy Sepulchre to reach the charming **Court of Pilate** (11C-12C) and, from there, through to the Church of the Trinity, **(Trinità)** 13C, the old *Martyrium* (4C-5C) where the bodies of martyrs were brought. To the right of the Court of Pilate are the Romanesque cloisters where there is access to the small museum (paintings, statues and liturgical objects).

✱ S. Domenico – The church, dedicated to St Dominic, was built at the beginning of the 13C and remodelled in the 18C. It houses the famous and beautiful **tomb★★★** (arca): the fine sarcophagus is by Nicola Pisano (1267) while the arch with statues (1468-1473) crowning it was executed by Niccolò da Bari, who was afterwards known as Niccolò dell'Arca, and completed by Michelangelo in 1494 with the two missing saints (Saints Procolo and Petronius) and the angel on the right. The low reliefs by Nicola Pisano depict the life and miracles of St Dominic while the finial by Niccolò represents the celebration of creation symbol-

> ### The Lord's dogs
>
> During her pregnancy, the future saint's mother had a vision of a dog bearing a torch, symbolising fidelity and the flame of faith. The name of the order which was founded in 1216 by the Spaniard Domenico Guzman refers to the Latin form of this legend (*Domini canes*, the Lord's dogs), which was commemorated by the dog and torch which sometimes appear in representations of St Dominic.

ised by *putti* (the sky), garlands (the earth) and dolphins (the sea).

The chapel to the right of the presbytery has a fine painting by Filippino Lippi, the **Mystic Marriage of St Catherine** (1501). The choir has preserved its choir stalls executed by the monk Domenico da Bergamo in 1541.

Nearby, in Via D'Azeglio, is Palazzo Bevilacqua, an admirable Renaissance, Florentine-style palace.

★S. Francesco – This church was erected in the middle of the 13C and constitutes one of the first examples of Gothic architecture in Italy. From Piazza Malpighi note the three tombs of the glossarists (legal annotators) executed in the 13C. In the background rises the **apse structure★**, characterised by imposing flying buttresses of French influence. Inside, at the high altar, is a magnificent marble **altarpiece★** (1392), by the Venetian sculptor Paolo dalle Masegne.

A door on the right opens on to the Renaissance Chiostro dei Morti (cloisters) which afford a good view of the side of the church and the two bell towers.

Museo Civico Medievale ⊘ (DT) – The Medieval Civic Museum is housed in the fine **palazzo Fava-Ghisilardi★** (late 15C) which stands on the site of the Imperial Roman palace. The collections relate the development of art in Bologna from the Middle Ages to the Renaissance. Among the exhibited works note the University glossarists' tombs, the statue of Boniface VIII by Manno Bandini (1301), a beautiful English cope of the 13C and the fine memorial stone of Domenico Garganelli, made by Francesco del Cossa in about 1478.

EXCURSION

Madonna di S. Luca – *5km/3mi southwest. Leave the city centre by Via Saragozza* (DU). The 18C church is linked to the city by a **portico★** (4km/2.5mi long) of 666 arches. In the chancel is the *Madonna of St Luke*, a painting in the 12C Byzantine style. There is a lovely **view★** of Bologna and the Apennines.

*Read your **Michelin Map** carefully*
to discover useful and interesting information:
a castle on a lake,
a forest road with picnic grounds,
a panorama, a historic marker.
Italy is a land of endless discovery.

BOLSENA

Lazio
Population 4 170
Michelin map 430 O 17

Bolsena, the ancient Etruscan city of Volsinii, stands on the banks of Italy's largest lake of volcanic origin; its level is continually changing owing to earth tremors. Its shady shores welcome many visitors attracted by a gentle and limpid light. In the old part of the town its sombre-coloured houses cluster upon a small hill; there is a good view from the state S2 road, the Viterbo-Siena road.

The Miracle of Bolsena – A Bohemian priest had doubts about the Transubstantiation, that is, the incarnation of Christ in the Host. According to legend, as he was celebrating mass in St Christina's Church, the Host began to bleed profusely at the moment of Consecration. The priest no longer doubted the mystery and the Feast of Corpus Christi was instituted.

★ **S. Cristina** ⊙ – The 3C Saint Christina is said to have belonged to the Bolsena region. She was a victim of the persecutions of Diocletian. Although the church is 11C the façade, articulated by gracefully carved pilasters, is Renaissance. The columns inside are Roman. The north aisle leads to the **Chapel of the Miracle**, where the pavement stained by the blood of the Host is revered, and then to the Grotto of St Christina. In the latter is the Altar of the Miracle and a reclining statue of the saint attributed to the Della Robbia.

Michelin's famous star ratings are allocated for various categories:
regions of scenic beauty with dramatic natural features
cities with an exceptional cultural heritage
elegant resorts and charming villages
ancient monuments and fine architecture
museums and galleries.

BOLZANO★

Bozen – Trentino-Alto Adige
Population 97 073
Michelin map 429 C 15-16
Town plan in the Michelin Atlas Italia
Local map see DOLOMITI

Bolzano, the capital of the Alto Adige, lies on the Brenner transalpine route at the confluence of the Isarco and the Adige. The surrounding slopes are covered with orchards and vineyards. The architecture of the town shows a marked Tyrolean or Austrian influence which was exercised between the 16C and 1918. This industrial and commercial town is now also a busy tourist centre owing to its proximity to the Dolomites. There are some lovely houses in the town centre from **Piazza Walther** to **Via dei Portici**★.

★ **Duomo** – The cathedral is built of pink sandstone and roofed with multicoloured glazed tiles. Construction work was carried out during various periods including the early Christian Era (5C – 6C), the Carolingian Era (8C – 9C), the Romanesque (late 12C) and the Gothic periods (13C). The campanile (1501-1519) rises to a height of 62m/203ft and includes late Gothic bays. On the north side is the "Small Wine Portal" *(porticina del vino)* on which all the decorative features have a connection with vines and grape harvesting. It indicates the privilege enjoyed by this particular church – an exclusive right to sell wine at this doorway. Inside, there are traces of 14C and 15C frescoes and a fine Late Gothic, carved sandstone pulpit★ (1514).

★ **Museo Archeologico dell'Alto Adige** ⊙. **"The Ötzi Museum"** – This archeological museum, spread out over three floors, chronologically illustrates the history of the Alto-Adige region from the end of the last Ice Age (15 000 BC) to the Carolingian age (AD 800).
The first floor houses the "Iceman", more commonly known as "Ötzi", whose remains were found by a couple of German mountain climbers near the Similaun glacier, in the Ötzi Apls, in 1991. Ötzi lived in the Copper Age and is 5 300 years old. He died at about 45 years of age and was trapped in the ice which assured his preservation. He is now kept in refrigerated cells which maintain the mummy's temperature at −6°C/21°F with a level of humidity of about 100%. It is both touching and fascinating to see Ötzi on the other side of the glass with his various belongings such as a cape and an axe. Films and audio guides make the visit come alive for both adults and children.

Chiesa dei Domenicani ⊙ - *Piazza Domenicani.* The Dominican Church was built in the early 14C in the Gothic style with a deep presbytery that is separated from the nave by a rood screen. The church was later altered and was subsequently damaged after the secularisation of 1785. To the right beyond the rood screen is St John's Chapel **(San Giovanni)** which is covered in frescoes from the Giotto School and is reminiscent of the Scrovegni Chapel in Padua. The frescoes depict scenes from the lives of the Blessed Virgin Mary, St John the Baptist, St Nicholas and St John the Evangelist. Another set of frescoes, by Friedrich Pacher (15C), can be seen in the cloisters **(chiostro)** to the right of the church.

Chiesa dei Francescani ⊙ - *1, Piazza Francescani.* Burnt down in 1291, the Franciscan Church was rebuilt in the 14C and the gothic vaulting added in the 15C. The **Nativity altar★** is a remarkable wooden altarpiece carved by Hans Klocker (16C). The delightful little cloisters have elegant fan-vaulting decorated with frescoes by the Giotto School.

Antica parrochiale di Gries - *Access Piazza the Corso Libertà beyond Sant'Agostino.* The original Romanesque building was replaced by a 15C Gothic parish church containing a Romanesque wooden Crucifix (opposite the door) and, to the right of the high altar, a side altar with an **altarpiece★** carved by Michael Pacher (*c* 1430-1498), an Austrian painter and sculptor from the Tyrol. It depicts the Crowning of the Virgin between Archangel Gabriel who is about to strike the devil and St Erasmus who is holding out the winch that kills him by tearing out his guts. The back features the work of a Bavarian artist (1488). A particularly curious detail is the pair of glasses worn by the person at the bottom of the painting to the right.

THE RENON PLATEAU

The Renon (Ritten in German) is the plateau which dominates the Isarco Valley (Eisacktal) between Bolzano and Ponte Gardena.
It can be easily reached (by car from Bolzano north or with the funicular at Soprabolzano in Bolzano) and it can even be romantically explored on the electric train which goes from Maria Assunta (Maria Himmelfahrt) to Collalbo (Klobenstein).
The intense green of the plateau is interrupted only by wooden fences and little churches which appear as if from nowhere in their isolated setting, such as the church of Santa Verena, between Longostagno and Sant'Ingenuino.
The Renon overlooks the Dolomites which are best seen from the funicular that goes to Corno del Renon. The plateau is full of tiny charming villages, one of which, Barbiano, has a pretty leaning tower.
Some of the underlying earth is prone to erosion caused by a strange natural phenomenon called **"earth pyramids"**.
Water erodes the moraine earth "loitering" solely around the rocks thus protecting the underlying terrain. This forms columns surmounted by rocks which last for as long as they can stand the weight of the large stones. When the water makes them too fine, the rocks fall and the unprotected pinnacles crumble.
There are three groups of "pyramids" on the Renon: at Soprabolzano, visible from the funicular, at Monte di Mezzo which can be reached by path no 24 from Longomoso and at Auna di Sotto.

Riviera del BRENTA★★

Veneto

Michelin map 429 F 18 - 35km - 22 miles east of Padua
See Michelin Green Guide Venice

Standing alongside the Brenta Canal between Strà and Fusina are numerous lovely classical **villas★** by Palladio *(see Index).* These were the summer residences of the Venetian nobility who used to lay on sumptuous night-time festivities to music by Vivaldi, Pergolesi or Cimarosa.

Sightseeing - Boat trips **(burchiello** ⊙ boats) leave from both Venice and Padua. By car take the road which follows the Brenta passing through Strà, Dolo, Mira and Malcontenta.

Strà - The **Villa Pisani★** ⊙ has a majestic garden with a delightful vista and basin. The spacious **apartments★** of this 18C palace were decorated by various artists including Giovanni Battista Tiepolo who painted his masterpiece, *The Apotheosis of the Pisani Family*★★.

Villa Pisani, the residence of the doge Alvise Pisani

Mira – The **Palazzo Foscarini** and **Villa Widmann-Foscari** ⊙ are both 18C. The **ballroom**★ of the latter is entirely decorated with frescoes.

Malcontenta - Palladio built the **Villa Foscari**★ ⊙ in 1574. G. B. Zelotti and B. Franco were responsible for the frescoes.
The villa was named after the wife of a Foscari who was ill-pleased (*malcontenta*) at being consigned to the villa.

A new concept in travel planning.

When you want to calculate a trip distance or visualise a detailed itinerary;
when you need information on hotels,
restaurants or campsites, consult Michelin on the Internet.

Visit our Web site to discover our full range of services for travellers:

www.michelin-travel.com

BRESCIA★

Lombardy
Population 190 518
Michelin map 428 and 429 F 12

The important industrial town of Brescia lies at the foot of the Lombard Pre-Alps. It has retained the regular street plan of the Roman camp (*castrum*) of Brixia. The town is dominated to the north by a medieval castle (Castello) and its bustling centre has many fine buildings from all periods: Roman, Romanesque, Renaissance and Baroque.

HISTORICAL NOTES

Brixia flourished under the Empire and the remains of Roman monuments include the Capitoline Temple and the forum.
In the 8C Brescia became a Lombard duchy and then in the 12C and 13C a free commune and member of the Lombard League.
The town was one of the most prosperous in Italy, owing to the manufacture of arms and armour. Brescia supplied all Europe until the 18C. From 1426 to 1797 Brescia was under Venetian rule and acquired numerous secular and religious buildings. A group of artists formed the Brescia school and the most important members were, in the 15C, Vincenzo Foppa and in the 16C, Romanino and Moretto, Savoldo and Civerchio.

★ **Piazza della Loggia (BY 9)** - The **Loggia (BY H)**, now the town hall, was built from the end of the 15C to the beginning of the 16C. Sansovino and Palladio were amongst those involved in the building of the upper storey. The **Clock Tower** opposite the Loggia is topped by two clockwork figures (Jacks) that strike the hours. On the south side of the square stand the graceful palaces, **Monte di pietà vecchio** (1484) and **Monte di pietà nuovo** (1497) (**BY B**). To the north of the square is a picturesque popular quarter with arcades and old houses.

Piazza Paolo VI (**BY 16**) – The 17C New Cathedral (**Duomo Nuovo**) in white marble seems to crush the Old Cathedral (**Duomo Vecchio★**), a late 11C Romanesque building which succeeded an earlier sanctuary known as the rotunda after its shape.

Inside, there is a magnificent sarcophagus in rose-coloured marble surmounted by the recumbent figure of a bishop, and in the chancel paintings by local artists, Moretto and Romanino. The organ was built in 1536 by Antegnati. To the left of the Duomo Nuovo, the **Broletto** (**P**) is an austere Romanesque building dominated by a massive square tower. Proclamations were made from the balcony on the façade.

★ **Pinacoteca Tosio Martinengo** ⊘ (**CZ**) – The art gallery displays works of the **Brescia school**, characterised by richness of colour and well-balanced composition: religious scenes and portraits by Moretto, more sumptuous religious scenes in the Venetian manner by Romanino and other works, as well as canvases by Vincenzo Foppa and Savoldo. The works of Clouet, Raphael, the Master of Utrecht, Lorenzo Lotto and Tintoretto are also on view.

★ **Via dei Musei** (**CY**) – This picturesque street has some interesting sites: the ruins of the **Capitoline Temple★** (AD 73), with the remains of the cells, the tribunal and the adjacent Roman theatre (**Teatro Romano★**). Beyond the remains of the forum is the monastery of **San Salvatore and Santa Giulia★** founded in AD 753 by Ansa, the wife of the last King of the Lombards, Desiderio. Tradition has it that Desiderio's daughter, Ermengarda, wife of Charlemagne, who later repudiated her, died here. The 9C San Salvatore Basilica still has its original decoration of frescoes and

Castellini (Via N.) . . . . CZ 3
Fratelli Porcellaga
  (Via) . . . . BY 7
Loggia (Piazza della) . . . . BY 9
Martiri della
  Libertà (Corso) . . . . AZ 13
Mercato (Piazza del) . . . . BY 15

stucco work; the Church of Santa Giulia, has a dome decorated with a fresco of God the Father giving His blessing against a star-studded sky. Inside the group of buildings a Museum of the City (**Museo della città** ⊘) has been contrived. Its displays relate the history of the city from the Bronze Age to the present day. **Desiderio's Cross★★** (8C-9C), richly decorated with precious stones, cameos, and coloured glass as well as a portrait thought to be that of Galla Placidia and his sons (3C-4C) is to be found in the church of S. Maria in Solario.

Castello (**CY**) – Built in 1343 for the Visconti over the remains of a Roman temple, the castle was given additional bastions in the 16C and its entrance is decorated with the lion representing St Mark. It now houses the **Museo delle armi Luigi Marzoli** ⊘, an interesting collection of arms and armour from the 14C to 18C. Roman remains can be seen inside the museum.

Churches – Brescia boasts several Romanesque, Renaissance and baroque churches and nearly all contain paintings of the Brescia school. The 13C **chiesa di S. Francesco★** (**AY**) has a 14C *Pietà* by Giotto's followers, *Three saints* by Moretto and a *Virgin and Saints* altarpiece by Romanino. The 15C and 16C **S. Maria dei Miracoli** (**AYZ A**) features a lovely marble façade★. **S.S. Nazaro e San Celso** (**AZ**) contains Moretto's masterpiece, the *Coronation of the Virgin★* and a polyptych by Titian. **Sant'Alessandro** (**BZ**) displays a 15C *Annunciation★* by Jacopo Bellini and a *Descent from the Cross★* by Civerchio. **Sant'Agata** (**BY**) with its rich **interior★** adorned with a

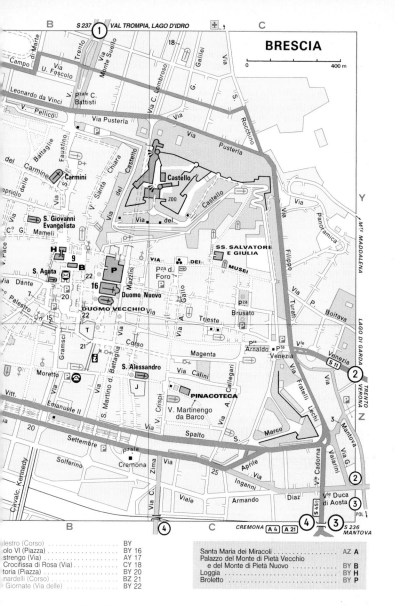

lestro (Corso)	BY
olo VI (Piazza)	BY 16
strengo (Via)	AY 17
Crocifissa di Rosa (Via)	CY 18
toria (Piazza)	BY 20
nardelli (Corso)	BZ 21
Giornate (Via delle)	BY 22

Santa Maria dei Miracoli	AZ **A**
Palazzo del Monte di Pietà Vecchio	
e del Monte di Pietà Nuovo	BY **B**
Loggia	BY **H**
Broletto	BY **P**

polyptych of the *Virgin of Pity*★ by the 16C Brescia school, as well as a *Virgin with Coral*★, a charming 16C fresco. **San Giovanni Evangelista** (BY) is known for its works by Moretto and Romanino, **Madonna delle Grazie** (AY) for its baroque interior and the **Madonna del Carmini** (BY) for its oriental silhouette.

BRESSANONE★

Brixen – Trentino-Alto Adige

Population 17 972

Michelin map 429 B 16 – Local map see DOLOMITI

Set at the confluence of the rivers Rienza and Isarco, Bressanone is an elegant, typically Tyrolean little town that enjoys a dry, invigorating climate with an exceptionally high number of hours of sunshine. There are many reminders of its eventful past. It was conquered by the Romans in 15 BC, was the seat of a Prince-Bishop from 1027 to 1803, became Bavarian for seven years from 1806 to 1813, and then belonged to Austria until 1919 when it became an Italian town.

Duomo – This baroque cathedral which was orginally a Romanesque construction, has a neo-classical west front designed by Jakob Pirchstaller (1783) flanked by two bell-towers. The luminous interior is decorated with marble, stucco work and frescoes by Paul Troger which are more striking for the gold leaf. The fine Romanesque **cloisters★** feature 14C ribbed vaulting and interesting 14C and 15C frescoes. Access to the 11C church of S. Giovanni Battista *(closed to visitors)* is Via the cloisters. The church has 13C Romanesque and 14C Gothic frescoes.

Palazzo Vescovile – *Entrance from the via Vescovado*. Commissioned by Prince-Bishop Bruno de Kirchberg after 1250, the palace underwent numerous alterations in later years but retained its superb **courtyard★** surrounded by three storeys of arcades. This was the Prince-Bishop's residence and the seat of the bishopric. It now houses the vast **Museo diocesano★** ◷ containing a wonderful set of polychrome **wood carvings★★** (Romanesque and Gothic Tyrolean art), a number of **altarpieces★** carved in the round dating from the Renaissance, the cathedral **treasure★** and **Nativity scenes★** dating from the 18C to 20C.

EXCURSIONS

Convento di Sabiona – *10km south. Leave the car in the car park north of Chiusa. To get to the convent from the village, go on foot (30min).* This convent of Benedictine nuns in its attractive setting dates back to the 17C. It was built on the rock where the bishop's palace had stood, the palace having burnt down after being struck by lightning in 1535.

★★★ **Plose** ◷ – Alt 2 446m/8 031ft. *To the southeast.* The cable-car from Valcroce and then another from Plose enable visitors to enjoy a wonderful **panorama★★★** of the Dolomites to the south and the Austrian mountains to the north.

★★ **Abbazia di Novacella** ◷ – *3km/2mi north.* The abbey was founded in 1142 by Bishop Artmanno of Bressanone and run by monks of the Augustinian Order. The courtyard contains the **Well of Wonders** decorated with "eight" wonders of the world, one of which is the abbey itself. The **church** built in the Bavarian baroque style is surprising for the ornateness and brilliance of the interior. Some of the detail in the painting, such as the leg of one of the characters which literally extends out of the fresco, is also striking. The **cloisters**, which were originally Romanesque, are covered with frescoes from a later period and whitewashed over after the plague in the 17C. The memorial stones date back to the 18C. Only in this century were attempts made to recover the original frescoes. The magnificent Rococo **library** contains 76 000 rare books, and illuminated manuscripts.

BRINDISI

Puglia
Population 94 429
Michelin map 431 F 35
Town plan in the Michelin Atlas Italy

This important naval and trading port, on the Adriatic side of the "boot's heel", has a daily shipping connection with Greece. Ever since antiquity the town has played the important role of trading-post with the rest of the Mediterranean basin. Its name probably derives from the Greek *Brenteséion* (stag head), which evokes the shape of the old city which was enclosed by two "breasts of water" surrounding it from east and west. It was Trajan who replaced the old Appian Way beyond Benevento with the new Via Traiana which increased the importance of Brindisi from AD 109 onwards. After the Norman conquest the town became a port of embarkation for the Crusades to the Holy Land, and in particular saw the departure of the Sixth Crusade (1228). Along with Taranto and Bari, Brindisi makes up the triangle delimiting the Mezzogiorno, an area of industrial redevelopment.

The city centre contains the most interesting monuments. Principal access to the old city was through **Porta Mesagne** which was opened in the 13C. Guarding the Seno di Ponente stands the **Swabian Castle** (Castello Svevo) which was built on the initiative of Frederick II in 1227 and today houses the Navy. On the cape, near the port, stand two marble **Roman columns** which probably denoted the end of the Appian Way.

Piazza Duomo – The square is overlooked by the **Balsamo Loggia** (at the corner of Tarantini) which dates from the 14C, the Portico of the **Knights Templar** (14C) and the Romanesque cathedral (duomo) which was rebuilt in the 18C. Inside, at the end of the north aisle and around the high altar are remains of the old mosaic flooring. The Piazza also houses the **Museo Archeologico F. Ribezzo** ⊘ which contains many artefacts from excavations. Note in particular the collection of Apulian, Messapici and Attic vases.

Churches – The historic centre contains numerous churches. **S. Giovanni al Sepolcro**, a Templar church erected in the 11C whose doorway is heralded by a porch held up by columns with stylised lion bases. The church of St Benedict (**S. Benedetto**, 11C) has a very simple interior consisting of a nave and two aisles divided by columns with Corinthian capitals and one column adorned with animal decorations (ox, lion, ram). The ceiling has ribbed vaulting. The adjacent cloisters are enclosed by a portico with polygonal columns with stylised capitals.

The small Romanesque church of **S. Lucia** has 13C fresco remains in its interior (unfortunately these are very patchy). Underneath the church stands the old Basilian structure with its vaulted ceiling held up by columns with Corinthian capitals. The walls are covered with fine **frescoes** (12C), some of which are well preserved such as the Virgin and Child and, on the right, the *Maddalena Mirrofora* (Magdalene bearing Myrrh) holding a casket with two phials.

EXCURSIONS

* **S. Maria del Casale** – *5km/3mi north, near the airport.* This is a splendid Romanesque-Gothic building built on the initiative of Philip d'Anjou and his wife Catherine of Flanders in the 14C. The façade, enlivened by two-coloured geometric patterns, is characterised by a porch crowned by an embellishment consisting of Lombard arches which mirror the motif of the eaves on the façade.

The interior has an interesting cycle of frescoes from the same period in the Byzantine style of which the *Day of Judgement* and the *Tree of the Cross* stand out.

CALABRIA★

Michelin map 431 G-N 28-33

Calabria is in the extreme south of the Italian peninsula, covering the narrow stretch of earth between the Gulf of Policastro and the Gulf of Taranto, a curve in the sea which nearly touches Sicily.

The colour of the sea, which is sometimes purple as suggested by the name of the coast between Gioia Tauro and Villa San Giovanni, can sometimes distract attention from the land itself which is half covered by mountains. From north to south the backbone of Calabria is formed by the **Pollino Massif** (Pollino Mountain has an altitude of 2248m/7375ft), which is a national park, and by the **Sila** and **Aspromonte** massifs.

Different landscapes give rise to varied climates: it is hot in the summer, mild in the winter along the Tyrrhenian coast, alpine in the mountains and very hot on the Ionian coast which sees little rain.

It is enough to drive around Calabria to get an idea of its principal agricultural activities: **olive groves** produce excellent oil – Rossano oil has a very low level of acidity – and **citrus groves** produce clementines and blond and bergamot oranges.

Greeks, Byzantines, Basilian monks (St Basil, father of the Greek Church, lived from *c* AD 300-379) shaped the art and history of this region – the first colonies were founded by the Greeks in the 8C BC on the Ionian coast. It was only in the 3C BC that Rome undertook the conquest of southern Italy, without however establishing a complete and peaceful domination until Silla reorganised the administration of these provinces in the 1C BC. After the fall of the Roman Empire, Calabria and the neighbouring regions fell under the sway of the Lombards, Saracens and Byzantines before being reunited with the Norman kingdom of the Two Sicilies and finally becoming part of a unified Italy in 1860.

Natural disasters, such as the powerful earthquakes which struck in 1783 and 1908, famine, poverty, brigandage, social and emigration problems have plagued Calabria which, thanks to agrarian reform and commitment to tourist and cultural activities, finally has occasion for real hope of a rebirth.

★★ **Massiccio della Sila** – Sila has an ancient name which signifies "primordial forest": the Greek version of the word is *hyla*, the Latin *silva*. The name Sila is accompanied by three adjectives: Great, Small and Greek. It is a plateau measuring 1 700km²/656 sqmi whose forests of **larch pine** and beech trees alternate with prairies. Average altitude is 1 200m/3937ft.

On the Sila Grande are the two towns of Camigliatello and Lorica. About ten kilometres away from Camigliatello the visitors' centre of the **Parco Nazionale della Calabria** offers the chance of taking walks along the fauna enclosures where deer and wolves can be seen in their natural habitat from wooden constructions with mirrored windows. The Centre also offers botanical and geological walks.

The wooden houses which dot the landscape contribute to the illusory sensation of being in a northern country; this is the case particularly along the banks of lakes Cecita, **Arvo**★ and Ampolino.

A tour of the lakes can come to an end at **San Giovanni in Fiore** where Joachim of Fiore (c 1130-1202) founded a hermitage and his new religious order *(ordine florense)* whose rule is similar to that of the Cistercians but stricter.

★ **Aspromonte** – The Aspromonte Massif forms the southern tip of Calabria and culminates in a peak of 2 000m/6 561ft. The face overlooking the Tyrrhenian coast drops in terraces to the shore while the slope on the Ionian coast descends more gently down to the sea. The forest cover includes chestnut trees, oaks and beeches. The massif serves as a catchment area from which radiate deep valleys eroded by fast-flowing torrents *(fiumare)*. The wide river beds are dry in summer but may fill up rapidly and the waters become destructive. The S 183 between the S 112 and Melito di Porto Salvo runs through attractive scenery and affords numerous and often quite spectacular **panoramas**★★★.

Palmi – This small town perched high above the sea has a small fishing harbour and a lovely sandy beach.

The **Museo comunale** ⊙ *(Casa della Cultura, Via San Giorgio)* has an **ethnographic section**★ evoking the life and traditions of Calabria: local costumes, handicrafts, ceramics etc.

★ **Scilla** – The waters around Scilla, like the waters of Bagnara Calabra, contain swordfish.

Scilla's name is mythological: Scilla was a woman who was forced to live the life of a sea monster. She was surrounded by dogs who devoured any passing creature. This was what happened to six of Ulysses' companions.

Opposite Scilla, near Messina, lurks Charybdis whom Zeus turned into a sea monster in punishment for her voracity. But even in the guise of a sea monster Charybdis did not lose her fame: three times a day she engulfs the surrounding waves thereby swallowing everything in the sea around her. Subsequently she spurts the water out thus creating a strong current. Ulysses narrowly escaped her clutches by grabbing a fig tree situated at the entrance of the monster's grotto.

The fisherman's district, the Chinalèa, is comprised of an intricate maze of houses and alleys going down to the water's edge. Higher up, Ruffo Castle (1255) extends its noble and reassuring gaze over the town.

Villa San Giovanni – This is the car-ferry *(traghetti)* terminal for Sicily.

★ **Rocca Imperiale** – *25km/16mi north of Trebisacce*. This picturesque village has grown up around an imposing castle built by the Emperor Frederick II.

⌂⌂ **Tropea** – Tropea is built on a sandy clifftop. Opposite stands the solitary church of Santa Maria dell'Isola which clings to a rock. The most evocative reference to the past is to be found in the Romanesque-Norman cathedral which has its original façade. The Swabian portico which is grafted onto the façade links the church to the bishop's residence.

What has Calabria got to do with *sukkot?*

Sukkot is the Jewish festival of tents, celebrated to commemorate the Exodus when Jews slept in tents. According to *Leviticus 23, 39-40*:

On the fifteenth day of the seventh month, when you have gathered up the produce of the land, you shall keep the festival of the Lord, lasting seven days; a complete rest on the first day, and a complete rest on the eighth day. On the first day you shall take the fruit of majestic trees, branches of palm trees, boughs of leafy trees, and willows of the brook: and you shall rejoice before the Lord your God for seven days.

The fruit traditionally used for this feast (which has to be chosen with painstaking care) is the citron. Thus every summer rabbis come to Santa Maria del Cedro (which has ideal growing conditions for this fruit), in the province of Cosenza, to select citrons for their communities all over the world.

Altomonte – *30km/19mi south of Castrovillari.* The large market town is dominated by an imposing 14C Angevin cathedral dedicated to **Santa Maria della Consolazione**. The façade is embellished with a doorway and an elegant rose window. Inside there are no aisles and the east end is flat. The fine **tomb★** is that of Filippo Sangineto. The small museum **(museo civico)** ⊙ beside the church has several precious works of art in addition to a statue of *St Ladislas★* attributed to Simone Martini.

Cosenza – *Town plan in the Michelin Atlas Italy.*
The modern town is overlooked by the old town where streets and palaces recall the prosperity of the Angevin and Aragonese periods. Cosenza was then considered the artistic and religious capital of Calabria. The 12C-13C **cathedral** (Duomo) has recently been restored to its original aspect. Inside is the **mausoleum★** containing the heart of Isabella of Aragon, the wife of Philip III, King of France and son of Louis IX (St Louis who died in Tunis). She died in 1271 outside Cosenza on the way back from Tunis with the sainted king's body and was buried in St-Denis Basilica in France.

Crotone – *See CROTONE.*

Gerace – *Northwest of Locri on the S 111.* Gerace rises up on a hill with an altitude of 480m/1575ft. The town's symbol is a hawk which is reflected in its Greek name, *hierax*. For a long time Gerace preserved Greek culture and liturgy; for a time it was cohabited by Byzantines and Normans and it was subjected to invasions by the Swabians, French and Aragonese. It was also an illustrious episcopal seat. At one time Gerace possessed so many churches that it was known as "the city of a hundred bells". Its 11C **cathedral** has vast dimensions: 73m/240ft x 26m/85ft. The three aisles are divided by 20 Greek and Roman columns.
In the Largo delle Tre Chiese (square of three churches) stands the **Church of St Francis** (San Francesco), which has an Arab-Gothic doorway and a **high altar★** in polychrome marble.

Locri – Locri was founded by the Greeks in the 7C BC. The town was ruled by the severe laws decreed by Zeleucos, the first legislator of *Magna Graecia*, and was one of the rival cities of Crotone which she defeated during the battle of Sagra. After having sided with Hannibal, along with the other towns on the Ionian coast during the Second Punic War, it declined in importance and was destroyed by the Saracens in the 9C AD. Most of the town's antiquities can be seen in the museum in Reggio di Calabria. There is an interesting excavation site *(Locri Epizefiri)* to the south of the town.

Paola – St Francis of Paola was born here around 1416. A monastery **(santuario)** ⊙ visited by numerous pilgrims stands 2km/1mi away up the hillside. This large group of buildings includes the basilica with a lovely baroque façade which enshrines the relics of the saint, cloisters and a hermitage hewn out of the rock which contains striking votive offerings.

★ **Pentedattilo** – *10km/6mi northwest of Melito di Porto Salvo.* Pentedattilo is a striking ghost town, totally abandoned by its inhabitants. Legend has it that the menacing rock resembling a hand above it (in Greek *pentedàktylos* signifies "five fingers") put an end to Man's violence. There is some truth to this: no voices have echoed in the narrow alleyways of the town since the mid-sixties as it was deemed unsafe due to the danger of collapse.

Reggio di Calabria – *See REGGIO DI CALABRIA.*

Rossano – *96km/60mi northwest of Crotone.* The town spreads over a hillside clad with olive groves. In the Middle Ages it was the capital of Greek monasticism in the west, where expelled or persecuted Basilian monks came for refuge, living in the cells which can still be seen today. The perfect little Byzantine church **San Marco** dates from this period. The flat east end has three projecting semicircular apses with graceful openings. To the right of the cathedral, a museum **(Museo Diocesano)** ⊙ in the former archbishop's residence has a valuable *Purpureus Codex★*, a 6C evangelistary with brightly-coloured illuminations.
20km/12mi to the west of the town is a small church, **Santa Maria del Patire**, the only remaining building of a large Basilian monastery. The church has a nave and two apses ornamented with blind arcading and inside, mosaics portraying various animals.

Serra San Bruno – Between the Sila and Aspromonte Massifs, amidst the Calabrian mountains covered with oak and pinewood **forests★**, this small market town grew up around a **hermitage** founded by St Bruno. The 12C charterhouse *(1km/0.6 mile from the town)* and the cave which served as hermitage *(4km/2.4mi southwest of the latter)* recall the memory of St Bruno who died in 1101.

The Cattolica church in Stilo,
a delicate expression of 10C Greek-Byzantine art

Sibari – *15km/9mi south of Trebisacce.* The town was founded in the 8C BC in a very fertile plain which was the source of the exceptional prosperity of the ancient city of **Sybaris**. It was razed in 510 BC by the neighbouring city of Crotone. There is a small archeological museum (**Museo Archeologico**) ⓥ and an excavation site (**Parco Archeologico della Sibaritide**) ⓥ to the south of the town.

Stilo – *15km/9mi west of Monasterace Marina.* The native town of **Tommaso Campanella** (1568-1639), filled with hermitages and Basilian monasteries, clings to the slopes of a mountain at an altitude of 400m/1312ft. Further up, almost camouflaged, is the Byzantine jewel of a church, **La Cattolica**★ ⓥ. This 10C structure has a square plan and is roofed with five cylindrical domes. The elegant external decoration consists of brickwork, a traced central dome and roof tiles. Inside the Greek cross is composed of nine domed and barrel vaulted sections each held up by four marble columns. Unfortunately one cannot savour the pleasure of admiring the mosaics which are very damaged.

Val CAMONICA

Lombardy

Michelin map 428 and 429 E-D

The valley, which stretches from Lovere to Edolo, is industrial in its lower reaches and becomes more picturesque towards its head with several ruined castles guarding its slopes. Many rock engravings dating from prehistory to the Roman era have been discovered in an area 60km/37 miles long. These have been included in the UNESCO World Heritage List.

★★ **Rock engravings** – The rock faces of Camonica Valley, smoothed by glacial erosion 10 000 years ago, present an even surface ideally suited to decoration. The engravings, made by pitting or scratching the stone, reveal scenes of the daily life of the peoples who lived on the site: in the Paleolithic Era (about 8000 to 5000 BC) they lived solely from the hunt, then took up agriculture in the Neolithic period, and later metalworking in the Bronze Age (from 1800 BC) and the Iron Age (900 BC). There are mainly four types of scenes: the hunt (stags); ox-teams and ploughs; arms and warriors; religious scenes (praying figures, symbols and idols).
The rock engravings are readily accessible in the **Parco Nazionale delle Incisioni Rupestri di Naquane** ⓥ *(2hr – access from Capo di Ponte)* and in the **Riserva Naturale Regionale di Ceto, Cimbergo e Paspardo** ⓥ; for access apply to the **museum** ⓥ at Nadro in Ceto which is devoted to the rock engravings.

Breno – The main town of the valley has a 10C castle and two interesting churches: the 14C-15C Sant'Antonio and San Salvatore.

Palazzo Farnese di CAPRAROLA★

Lazio

Michelin map 430 P 18 – 19km – 12 miles southeast of Viterbo

The **palace** was built from 1559 to 1575 for Cardinal Alessandro Farnese to the designs of Vignola, and is a good example of the late-16C Mannerist style.

Palazzo ⓥ – The five storey-tall building is arranged around a delightful circular inner courtyard. To the left of the entrance hall is Vignola's **spiral staircase**★★ which rises majestically through tiers of 30 paired Doric columns, and is decorated with grotesques and landscapes by Antonio Tempesta.
The paintings which adorn several rooms are by the Zuccaro brothers, Taddeo (1529-66) and Federico (*c*1540-1609) as well as Bertoja (1544-74). These are typical of the refined and sophisticated Mannerist style of the late Italian Renaissance period.

Park – This 18ha/44 acre park with its terraces and monumental fountains, is embellished by a charming **palazzina** also designed by Vignola.

Isola di CAPRI★★★

Campania
Population 7 235
Michelin map 431 F 24

Capri, the Island of Dreams, has always been an enchanting place, with its ideal situation off the Sorrento Peninsula *(see local map on p. 242)*, its beautiful rugged landscape, mild climate and luxuriant vegetation.

Capri captivated two Roman emperors: Augustus moved from Ischia to Capri, and Tiberius spent the latter part of his life here. Since the late 19C the island has attracted numerous celebrities: artists, writers, musicians and actors, in all seasons. Capri is one of the high spots of international tourism.

HOW TO GET THERE

From **Naples** there are daily ferry crossings (1hr15min) operated by **Caremar**-Travel and Holidays, Molo Beverello, ☎ 081 55 13 882, fax 081 55 22 011 and hovercraft and motorboat crossings (45-50min) operated by **Caremar**, by **Alilauro**, Via Caracciolo 11, ☎ 081 76 11 004, fax 081 76 14 250, by **Linee Lauro**, Molo Beverello, ☎ 081 55 22 838, fax 081 55 13 26, by **Aliscafi SNAV**, Via Caracciolo 10, ☎ 081 76 12 348, fax 081 76 12 141 and by **Navigazione Libera del Golfo**, Molo Beverello, ☎ 081 55 20 763, fax 081 55 25 589.

From **Sorrento** there are daily ferry crossings (45min) operated by **Caremar**-Agenzia Morelli, Piazza Marinai d'Italia, ☎ 081 80 73 077, fax 081 80 72 479 or hovercraft and motorboat crossings (20-50min) operated by **Alilauro** (at the port), ☎ 081 87 81 430, fax 081 80 71 221 and by **Navigazione Libera del Golfo** (at the port), ☎ 081 80 71 812, fax 081 87 81 861.

From **Ischia** there are daily hovercraft crossings (40min) from April to October operated by **Alilauro** (at the port), ☎ 081 99 18 88, fax 081 99 17 81.

★MARINA GRANDE

This is the main port where boats arrive on the northern side of the isle. The houses, some white, some in varied hues, nestle around the bay framed by spectacular cliffs. *A **funicular** railway connects Marina Grande to Capri (Piazza Umberto I), where there is a bus service to Anacapri.*

The unmistakable Faraglioni, Capri

BOAT TRIPS

★★ **Grotta Azzurra** ⊘ – *Boats leave from Marina Grande. It is also possible to go by road (8km – 5 miles from Capri).* The Blue Grotto is the most famous among the many marine caves on the island. The light enters, not directly, but by refraction through the water, giving it a beautiful blue colour.

★★★ **Tour of the isle** ⊘ – *Leave from Marina Grande.* Visitors will discover a rugged coastline, pierced with caves and small peaceful creeks, fringed with fantastically shaped reefs and lined with sheer cliffs dipping vertically into the sea.

The island is quite small: barely 6km – 4 miles long and 3km – 2 miles wide. The particularly mild climate favours the growth of a varied flora: pine, lentisk, juniper, arbutus, asphodel, myrtle and acanthus.

The boats go in a clockwise direction and the first sight is the Sea Ox Cave **(Grotta del Bove Marino)**, which derives its name from the roar of the sea rushing into the cave in stormy weather. Beyond is the headland (Punta del Capo) dominated by Mount Tiberius **(Monte Tiberio)**. Once past the impressive cliff known as Tiberius' Leap (see below), the headland to the south, Punta di Tragara, is fringed by the famous **Faraglioni**, rocky islets eroded into fantastic shapes by the waves. The **Grotta dell'Arsenale** (Arsenal Cave) was used as a nymphaeum during the reign of Tiberius. Continue past the small port of Marina Piccola *(see below)* to reach the more gentle west coast. The last part of the trip covers the north coast and includes the visit to the Blue Grotto *(see above)*.

★★★ CAPRI

Capri is like a stage setting for an operetta with its small squares, little white houses and its quite Moorish-looking alleyways. Another of its charms is that wild and lonely spots can still be found near crowded and lively scenes.

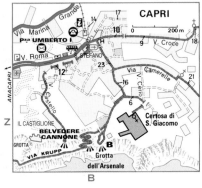

* **Piazza Umberto I** – This famous piazzetta is the centre of town and the spot where fashionable crowds gather. The busy narrow side streets, such as **Via Le Botteghe★ (BZ 10)**, are lined with souvenir shops and smart boutiques selling luxury goods.

★★ **Belvedere Cannone** – To reach the belvedere take the **Via Madre Serafina★ (BZ 12)**, which is almost entirely vaulted. The belvedere presents the peaceful and mysterious aspect of Capri with its covered and winding stepped alleys.

★★ **Belvedere Tragara** – *Access by via Camerelle and via Tragara.* There is a magnificent view of the Faraglioni.

★★ **Villa Jovis** ⓥ – Jupiter's Villa was the residence of the Emperor Tiberius. Excavations have uncovered servants' quarters,

Camerelle (Via)	BZ	Sopramonte (Via) . .	BZ 17
Certosa (Via)	BZ 6	Tiberio (Via)	BZ 18
Croce (Via)	BZ	Tragara (Via)	BZ 21
Fenicia (Scala)	BY 8	Umberto I (Pza) . . .	BZ
Fuorlovado (Via) . . .	BZ 9	Vittorio Emanuele	
Le Botteghe (Via) . .	BZ 10	(Via)	BZ 23
Madre Serafina			
(Via)	BZ 12		
S. Francesco (Via) . .	BZ 14	Giardini d'Augusto **B**	
Serena (Via)	BZ 16		

the cisterns that supplied the baths, and the Imperial apartments with a loggia overlooking the sea.

From the esplanade overlooked by the church, there is a lovely **panorama★★** of the whole island.

Take the stairway behind the church to enjoy a view of Tiberius' Leap **(Salto di Tiberio★)**, the impressive cliff from which the emperor is said to have had his victims thrown.

* **Arco Naturale** – The sea has created this gigantic natural rock arch which rises well above sea level. Lower down is the **Grotta di Matromania**, a cave where the Romans venerated the goddess Cybele.

Certosa di S. Giacomo ⓥ and **Giardini d'Augusto (BZ B)** – This 14C Carthusian Monastery of St James has two cloisters. In the smallest are displayed Roman statues taken from the nymphaeum of the Blue Grotto.

From Augustus' Gardens there is a beautiful **view★★** of Punta di Tragara and the Faraglioni *(see above)*. Lower down, **Via Krupp★**, clinging to the rock face, leads to Marina Piccola.

* **Marina Piccola** – There are beautiful small beaches and a haven for fishing boats.

★★★ ANACAPRI

Take the via Roma and a beautiful corniche road to reach Anacapri, a delightful village with shady streets, which is much less crowded than Capri.

* **Villa S. Michele** ⓥ – *Access from piazza della Vittoria.*

The villa was built at the end of the 19C for the Swedish doctor-writer, Axel Munthe (d 1949), who lived here up to 1910 and described the atmosphere of the island in his *Story of San Michele*. The house contains 17C and 18C furniture,

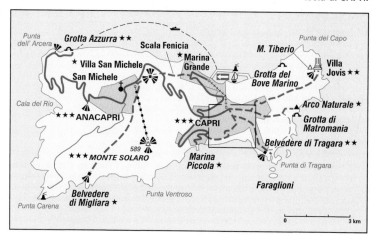

copies of antique works and some original Roman sculptures. The pergola at the end of the beautiful **garden** giddily overhangs the sea and provides a splendid **panorama**★★★ of Capri, Marina Grande, Mount Tiberius and the Faraglioni.
Just below the villa is a stairway, **Scala Fenicia**, which numbers nearly 800 steps and leads down to the harbour. It was for a long time the only link between the town and its port. This is where Axel Munthe met the old Maria "Porta-Lettere" who delivered the mail although she could not read, and who is depicted in his novel.

S. Michele – From the organ gallery note the fine majolica **floor**★ (1761) after a cartoon by Solimena which represents the Garden of Eden.

★★★ **Monte Solaro** ⊙ – The chairlift swings pleasantly above gardens and terraces brimming over with a luxuriant vegetation. From the summit there is an unforgettable **panorama**★★★ of the whole island and the Bay of Naples as far as the island of Ponza, the Apennines and the mountains of Calabria to the south.

★ **Belvedere di Migliara** – *1hr on foot there and back. Pass under the chairlift to take via Caposcuro.* There is a remarkable **view**★ of the lighthouse on the headland, Punta Carena, and of the sheer cliffs.

CAPUA

Campania

Population 18 844

Michelin map 431 D 24

This walled city, founded by the Lombards, is the native town of Pier della Vigna, chancellor to Frederick II and Ettore Fieramosca, Captain of the 13 Italian knights who vanquished the French in the Defeat of Barletta (1503).

Piazza dei Giudici – A harmonious group of buildings including the Baroque Church of S. Eligio, a Gothic arch surmounted by a Loggia and the 16C town hall. The nearby **chiesa dell'Annunziata** (16C) has a lovely drum dome and, inside, a finely crafted wooden chancel and ceiling.

Duomo ⊙ – The cathedral, which dates from the 9C, has been destroyed and rebuilt several times since. The Lombard-style campanile incorporates some ancient fragments at its base. The columns of the atrium have lovely 3C **Corinthian capitals**, while the interior houses a 13C paschal candelabrum, an *Assumption* by F. Solimena and, in the crypt, a *Dead Christ*, a fine sculpture of the 18C.

★ **Museo campano** ⊙ – *At the corner of Via Duomo and Via Roma.*
This museum is housed in a 15C building with a fine lava stone Catalan **doorway**. The archeological section has an astonishing collection of 6C to 1C BC **Matutae**, Italic earth goddesses holding their newborn children and a charming **mosaic**. The medieval section groups some lovely sculptures from remains of the imposing gateway built by the Emperor Frederick II of Hohenstaufen around 1239. Note the head of a woman known as *Capua Fidelis*.

Southeast of the museum there is an area with an interesting series of Lombard churches (S. Giovanni a Corte, S. Salvatore Maggiore a Corte, S. Michele a Corte, S. Marcello).

EXCURSIONS

★★ **Basilica di S. Angelo in Formia** ⓥ - *5km/3mi northeast.* One of the most beautiful medieval buildings in Campania. Erected in the 11C on the initiative of Desiderio, Abbot of Montecassino, the basilica combines a somewhat rudimentary architectural structure with one of the richest Romanesque cycle of frescoes. The interior, divided into a nave and two aisles, is covered in **frescoes**: the Last Judgement (east wall), the Life of Christ (nave), the Old Testament (north and south aisle) and Maestà (apse). Although of local production, these frescoes have a strong Byzantine influence (owing to the intervention of Greek painters who had worked at Montecassino), tempered by local culture as can be seen in the slightly crude use of colour and the brightness of some images. In the apse there is a representation of the Abbot Desiderio offering the church to God (the unusually square halo indicates that the Abbot was still alive when the fresco was painted).

Santa Maria Capua Vetere - This is the famous Roman Capua where the downfall of Hannibal was brought about by the temptations that were cast his way. Famous for the production of bronze and black ceramic vases, Capua was considered one of the most opulent cities of the Roman Empire. After Saracen attacks in the 9C, the inhabitants of the city moved to the banks of the Volturno river where they founded the present Capua. The **anfiteatro campano**★ ⓥ, restored in the 2C AD, is the largest Roman amphitheatre after the Coliseum. It was the seat of the famous gladiator school in which the revolt headed by Spartacus erupted in 73 BC. The **Mitreo** ⓥ (2C AD) is an underground rectangular chamber adorned with a rare **fresco**★ of the Persian god Mithra sacrificing a bull.

The pleasant **Museo Archeologico dell'Antica Capua** ⓥ *(via R. d'Angiò)* has interesting artefacts relating Samaritan history from the Bronze Age to the Imperial Age. These include some fine painted architectural terracotta pieces and three *Matres Matutæ*.

CARRARA

Tuscany
Population 65 871
Michelin map 429 or 430 J 12
See Michelin Green Guide Tuscany

Lying in a fertile basin on the edge of the limestone massif of the Apuan Alps, Carrara owes its fame to the white **marble** which has been quarried here since ancient times. Michelangelo used to come in person to choose blocks from which he carved his masterpieces.

Duomo - The façade is in the Romanesque-Gothic style, adorned with a delicately carved marble rose window and flanked by an elegant 13C campanile. Inside, there are interesting 14C statues.

The slightly glacial appearance of a marble quarry

Cave di marmo – The wild countryside and the gigantic nature of the quarrying operations afford a spectacular sight. The impressive quarries, **Cave dei Fantis-critti**★★ *(5km/3mi northeast)* in a wild site, and the **Cave di Colonnata**★ *(8.5km/5mi east)* in a greener setting, are both actively worked and regularly despatch quantities of marble *(marmo)*. **Marina di Carrara** *(7km/4mi southwest)* is the main port, where marble blocks are stacked high.

EXCURSION

★ **Sarzana** – *16km/10mi north.* The busy town of Sarzana was once an advanced base of the Republic of Genoa, a rival of Pisa, and its numerous historic buildings bear witness to its past importance. The **cathedral** *(Cattedrale)* has a marble **altarpiece**★ (1432) delicately carved by Riccomani. In a chapel to the right of the chancel is a phial which is said to have contained the Blood of Christ. In the chapel to the left is a *Crucifixion*★ (1138), a Romanesque masterpiece of the artist, Guglielmo, probably from Lucca.

The **Fortezza di Sarzanello**★ ⓥ (1322) is a fortress built on a height to the northeast of the town, by the *condottiere* (leader of a mercenary army) from Lucca, Castruccio Castracani. It is a curious example of military architecture with deep moats and massive curtain walls guarded at intervals by round towers. From the top of the keep there is a magnificent **panorama**★★ of the town and the Apennine foothills.

Abbazia di CASAMARI

Lazio

Michelin map 430 Q 22

Casamari Abbey ⓥ standing in a lonely site was originally a Benedictine foundation and was consecrated in 1217 by Pope Honorius III. It was later taken over by the Cistercians who rebuilt the abbey, modelling it on the abbey at Fossanova *(see Abbazia di FOSSANOVA)* and in accordance with the rules of austerity and self-sufficiency laid down by St Bernard, the founder of the Cistercian Order.

This is a lovely example of early Italian Gothic architecture. Above the entrance porch of the abbey church is a gallery of twinned openings, which served as the abbots' lodging during the Renaissance. The simplicity of the façade is typically Burgundian with a round-headed doorway, the rose window, and rising above all the typically Cistercian transept tower.

The interior is spacious, austere and solemn. Built to a Latin cruciform plan, it has a nave and two aisles separated by massive cruciform piers with engaged columns supporting the lofty pointed vaulting. The later canopy seems out of place in the shallow chancel. The apse and arms of the transept are lit by windows with a wheel window above.

On the south side of the church are the cloisters with their twin columns, a well and a lovely flower garden. On the east side, in its traditional position, is the remarkable chapterhouse with delicate ribbed, pointed vaulting supported by clustered columns.

EXCURSIONS

★ **Alatri** – *22km/14mi northwest on the S 214 and the S 155.* This important city, which was built in the 6C BC, retains several of its cyclopean walls (4C BC). The **acropolis**★ which can be reached on foot from the grandiose Porta di Cività is laid out on a trapezoidal plan and is one of the best preserved examples in Italy. It affords a very fine **view**★★ of Alatri and the Frosinone Valley.

A maze of steep stairways and alleyways is lined with Gothic houses. The **Palazzo Gottifredi** *(Largo Luigi di Persiis)* is 13C and the Church of St Mary Major **(S. Maria Maggiore**★**)** in the transitional Romanesque-Gothic style has a façade with three porches. Inside there is interesting 12C-15C **carved woodwork**★. On the by-pass is the 13C Church of St Sylvester **(San Silvestro)** which is built using the dry-stone technique and contains frescoes dating from the 13C to the 16C.

Constantly revised Michelin Maps, at a scale of 1: 200 000, provide much useful information:

   – latest motorway developments and changes;
   – vital data (width, alignment, camber, surface) of motorways or tracks;
   – the location of emergency telephones

Keep current **Michelin Maps** *in the car at all times*

Reggia di CASERTA★★

Campania

Michelin map 431 D 25

In 1752 Charles III of Bourbon commissioned the architect **Luigi Vanvitelli** to erect a royal palace (reggia) that could compete with other courts of Europe, far from the vulnerable Neapolitan coast. Compared to the grand royal residences of the period, Caserta is characterised by a more geometric, severe layout which reflects the personality of the architect. If its purity of line seems almost to anticipate the neo-Classical style, the theatrical design of its interior is still typically rococo.

The Royal Palace of Caserta, together with Vanvitelli's Aqueduct and the S. Leucio buildings (which housed the silk factory founded in 1789 by Ferdinand IV of Bourbon), have been included in UNESCO's World Heritage List.

★★ **Palazzo** ⊙ – The building consists of a vast rectangle (249m/273yds long and 190m/208yds wide) containing four internal courtyards which are interconnected by a magnificent **entrance hall★**. The façade first seen by the visitor is adorned by a projecting colonnade and a double row of windows supported by a rusticated base: the principal façade, facing the garden, reproduces this motif but embellishes it with the use of pilaster strips bordering each window. The sumptuous grand staircase (**scalone d'onore★★**), a masterpiece of Vanvitelli, leads to the Palatine Chapel (not open to visitors) and to the luxurious royal apartments decorated in the neo-Classical style. The Eighteenth Century Apartment (**Appartamento Settecentesco**) is particularly interesting with its vaulted frescoed ceilings depicting the seasons and some wonderful views of ports by J.P. Hackert. The pretty Queen's apartment (**Apartamento della Regina**) is decorated in a rather frivolous rocaille style: some curious pieces include a chandelier adorned with little tomatoes and a cage containing a clock and a stuffed bird. In the Sala Ellittica (the Elliptical Room) there is an attractive 18C Neapolitan crib (**presepe★**).

Park ⊙ – This park epitomises the ideal grand Baroque garden. Its seemingly infinite expanse is arranged around a central axis consisting of a canal. The fountains and fish-ponds are powered by the Aqueduct, a monumentally ambitious work by Vanvitelli which spans five mountains and three valleys with a total length of 40km/25mi. Of the mythological sculptures adorning the park the most notable is the group of **Diana and Actaeon** which stands at the foot of the great **cascade★★** (78m/256ft high) and depicts the striking scene of a pack of hounds attacking a stag.

To the right of the cascade there is a picturesque English garden (**giardino inglese★★** ⊙) created for Maria-Carolina of Austria.

EXCURSIONS

★ **Caserta Vecchia** – 10km/6mi north. This small town is dominated by the ruins of its 9C castle. The town has a certain charm with its almost deserted narrow alleyways lined by old buildings with their brown tufa walls. The fine 12C **Cathedral** ⊙ combines Sicilian-Arab, Apulian and Lombard motifs. Inside there is an attractive 13C pulpit.

Capua – 11km/7mi northwest. See CAPUA.

CASTELFRANCO VENETO★

Veneto

Population 30 562

Michelin map 429 E 17

Castelfranco is a pleasant citadel surrounded by moats. It has a few pretty arcaded houses and is the birthplace of the artist Giorgione. The cathedral (**Duomo**) contains his masterpiece, the **Madonna and Child with Saints★★**.

Born c 1477, **Giorgione** died young at the age of 32, probably of the Black Death. His 20 or so masterpieces influenced not only Venetian artists (Titian, who was his pupil and probably completed several of the master's canvases, Giovanni Bellini in his later works, Sebastiano del Piombo, Palma Vecchio, Savoldo, Dosso Dossi etc) but also all of European art, with his masterful handling of light.

Giorgione accomplished in his short lifetime an admirable synthesis of the human figure and nature with his flowing draughtsmanship and his skilful use of colour. The cathedral's work is among his earlier achievements and it already shows a preoccupation with achieving this fusion, as the figures are set on two different planes: the two saints in the shadow of the paved room while the Virgin enthroned on high stands out from the landscape background.

The artist's birthplace, (**Casa natale di Giorgione**) ⊙ (Piazza del Duomo) is now arranged as a museum.

CASTELLAMMARE DI STABIA‡

Campania

Population 66 345

Michelin map 431 E 25 – Local map under Golfo di NAPOLI

This was an ancient Roman spa town. Occupied successively by the Oscans, the Etruscans, the Samnites and finally the Romans in the 4C, *Stabiae* rebelled against Rome but was destroyed by Silla in the 1C BC. The town was rebuilt in the form of small clusters of houses, while luxury villas for rich patricians spread over the high ground. In the AD 79 eruption of Vesuvius the new town was wiped out along with Herculaneum and Pompeii. The naturalist Pliny the Elder who came by boat to observe the phenomenon at close range perished by asphyxiation.

In the 18C the Bourbons undertook excavations, repaired the port, and built shipyards which are still in use.

* **Antiquarium** ⊙ – *2 Via Marco Mario*. The finds from the excavations are displayed here and include a magnificent series of **mural paintings** from the villas and some very fine stucco **low reliefs**.

Roman villas ⊙ – *2km/1mi to the east. Arriving from the north take the S 145, follow directions for Agerola-Amalfi, take the flyover and after the tunnel turn left to reach the excavation site.*

Ariadne's Villa **(Villa di Arianna)** ⊙ was one of the luxurious villas facing the sea with an incomparable view of the bay and of Vesuvius.

The architectural refinement of **Villa S. Marco** ⊙ with its two storeys was enhanced by gardens and swimming pools. It was probably a sumptuous country residence.

CASTELLI ROMANI★★

Lazio

Michelin map 430 Q 19-20
See Michelin Green Guide Rome

Castelli Romani, or Roman Castles, is the name given to the region of the Alban Hills (Colli Albani), which are of volcanic origin and lie to the southeast of Rome. In the Middle Ages, while anarchy reigned in Rome, the noble families sought refuge in the outlying villages which they fortified. Each of these villages was strategically set on the outer rim of an immense crater, itself pitted with small secondary craters, some of which now contain lakes (Albano and Nemi). Pastures and chestnut groves cover the upper slopes while lower down there are olive groves and vineyards, which produce an excellent wine.

Nowadays the Romans readily leave the capital in summer for the "Castelli" where they find peace, fresh air, good walking country and pleasant country inns.

ROUND TOUR STARTING FROM ROME *122km/76mi – allow a whole day*

Leave Rome by the Via Appia in the direction of **Castel Gandolfo★★**, now the Pope's summer residence. It is thought that Castel Gandolfo was built on the site of ancient Alba Longa, the traditional and powerful rival of Rome. Their rivalry led to the famous combat of the Horatios for Rome and the Curiaces for Alba, as recounted by the Roman historian Livy. **Albano Laziale** was built on the site of Domitian's villa. Today the town boasts an attractive church, **Santa Maria della Rotonda★**, built in the villa's nymphaeum, which has a massive Romanesque campanile, and public gardens **(Villa Comunale★)** which house a villa that belonged to Pompeo (106-48 BC). Not far from Borgo Garibaldi is the so-called **tomb of the Horatios and the Curiaces★**.

Ariccia has a lovely square designed by Bernini, a palace which belonged to the Chigi banking family, and the Church of the Assumption.

Velletri is a prosperous town lying south of the Alban Hills in the heart of a wine-producing region.

Take Via dei Laghi out of Velletri.

This scenic road winds through groves of chestnut and oak trees to reach **Nemi**, a small village in a charming **setting★★** on the slopes of the lake of the same name. The road then climbs to **Monte Cavo** (alt 949m/3 124ft) which was crowned by the Temple of Jupiter. First a monastery and now a hotel have occupied the buildings. From the esplanade there is a fine **view★** of the Castelli region with Rome on the horizon. Beyond the attractively-set **Rocca di Papa**, facing the Alban lakes, the road passes through **Grottaferrata** with its **abbey★** which was founded in the 11C by Greek monks. **Tusculo** was the fief of the powerful Counts of Tusculum who governed the Castelli region. Next comes **Frascati★** pleasantly situated on the slopes facing Rome. It is known for its wines and its 16C and 17C villas, particularly the **Villa Aldobrandini★** ⊙ set above its terraced gardens.

The road back to Rome passes **Cinecittà**, the Italian Hollywood.

CERVETERI

Lazio
Population 20 614
Michelin map 430 Q 18

The ancient Caere was a powerful Etruscan centre, which stood on an eminence to the east of the present town of Cerveteri. Caere attained great prosperity in the 7C and 6C BC and was renowned as an important cultural and religious centre. In the 4C BC Caere began to decline. It was only at the beginning of the 20C that excavation work began on this site. Most of the finds are now displayed in the Villa Giulia in Rome. *(see The Green Guide to Rome).*

★★ **Necropoli della Banditaccia** ◷ – The admirable necropolis which is to be found 2km/1mi to the north of Cerveteri is an important testimonial of Etruscan burial cults. It is laid out like a city with numerous tumuli lining a main street. The site is pervaded by a great sense of peace. The tombs generally dating from the 7C BC add a strange note to the scene. These conical earth mounds, often grass-covered, rest on a stone base, which is sometimes decorated with mouldings, with the burial chambers underneath. Other tombs consist of underground burial chambers reached through simply-decorated doors. A vestibule leads into the burial chambers which often contain two funeral beds placed side by side: one is adorned with a small column if the deceased was a man (the breadwinner) and the other with a small canopy in the case of a woman (guardian of the home).
One of the tombs without a tumulus is the **Tomba delle Rilievi**★★ with its painted low-relief stuccoes giving a realistic picture of everyday Etruscan life.

★★ TOUR AROUND LAKE BRACCIANO *36km/22mi.*

From Cerveteri go 18km/11mi north to Bracciano (see The Green Guide to Rome).

Originally a volcanic island at 164m/538ft above sea-level, Lake Bracciano extends over an area of 57.5km²/36 squaremi (making it the eighth largest Italian lake) with a maximum depth of 160m/525ft. *Lacus Sabatini* has played an important role in supplying water to Rome: Trajan, for example, erected a 30km/18 mile long aqueduct which brought water to Trastevere and survived until the 17C.

★ **Bracciano** – The town of Bracciano is dominated by the splendid **Castello Orsini-Odescalchi**★★★ ◷ (14C-15C) outlined by six imposing cylindrical towers and two castle walls. **The interior** has lovely frescoed rooms, 15C ceilings and furnishings from subsequent periods. There are stunning view of the lake and town from the castle but the real jewel of this place is the enchanting **Central Courtyard**★, a real time machine that magically transports one to the period of the legendary feats of knights and heroes.

★ **Anguillara Sabazia** – This charming medieval village that clings to the promontory offers magnificent views of the lake which is reached by enchanting little streets.

Trevignano Romano – A typical medieval village with its fisherman's houses near the lake arranged in a herring bone pattern.

CHIAVENNA

Lombardy
Population 7 352
Michelin map 428 D 10

Ancient Chiavenna owes its name to its key (*clavis* in Latin) position in the Splügen and Maloja transalpine passes between Italy and Switzerland.

The Collegiate Church of St Lawrence (**Collegiata di San Lorenzo** ◷), built during the Romanesque period and reconstructed in the 16C after a fire, contains two paintings, one by Pietro Ligari (1738) *(2nd chapel on the right)* and one by Giuseppe Nuvoloni (1657) *(1st chapel on the left).*
The **Baptistery** ◷ has a Romanesque **font**★ (1156) in *ollare* stone: the name of the stone being a reference to it being used to make *olle* (urns and vases). The low reliefs illustrate a baptismal scene depicting various social classes (nobleman hunting with his falcon, soldier and craftsman), a child with his godfather, a priest and acolyte, and members of the clergy. The inscription reveals the identity of the sponsors of the work.

The **treasury** ⊙ houses a wonderful 12C **binding for an evangelistary**.

Nearby, above the Palazzo Balbini (15C) is **Il Paradiso**, a rock that was once a fortified site and is now set out as a pleasant garden, the **Giardino botanico e archeologico** ⊙.

See also the strange frescoes decorating the exterior of the Palazzo Pretorio and the entrances in the Via Dolzino on which the inscriptions date back to the days of the Reformation.

Chiavenna is also famous for its **"crotti"**, restaurants housed in natural caves and serving local specialities (found only in Valtellina) such as *pizzoccheri* (buckwheat pasta served with melted cheese) and *bresaola* (dried meat).

EXCURSION

★★ **Strada del Passo dello Spluga** – *30km/19mi from Chiavenna to the pass*. The Splügen Pass Road is one of the boldest and most spectacular in the Alps. The **Campodolcino-Pianazzo section**★★★ is grandiose as it climbs the sheer mountainside in tight hairpin bends.

CHIETI

Abruzzi

Population 57 094
Michelin map 430 ⊙ 24

Chieti is built on the summit of a hill planted with olive trees and enclosed by imposing mountains. Due to its panoramic position it is known as "Abruzzi's balcony". Corso Marrucino, bordered by elegant arcades, is the town's principal street.

★★ **Museo Archeologico degli Abruzzi** ⊙ – The archeological museum is housed in the neo-Classical town hall **(Villa Comunale)** set in lovely **gardens**★, and possesses the most important collection of artefacts excavated in the Abruzzi region. The ground floor has displays from Roman Abruzzi. Statues and portraits (note the *Seated Hercules* discovered at Alba Fucens) relate local history and customs. An interesting coin display, the collection formed by the Sulmonese **Giovanni Pansa** (ex-votos, domestic objects and bronze figures such as the *Venafro Hercules*) and the stunning bone **bier**★ (1C BC-1C AD) complete the section. The first floor is dedicated to funerary cults of pre-Roman Abruzzi with displays of burial accoutrements from the most important necropoleis in Abruzzi (10C-6C BC). The famous *Warrior of Capestrano*★★ (6C BC) has come to symbolise the Abruzzi region and is the most significant artefact of Picenum civilisation. Both disturbing and magical it was used to protect royal tombs as can be seen in the inscription on the right pilaster: "Me, beautiful image, made by Aninis for King Nevio Pompule-donio".

Roman remains – Three 1C AD small **temples** (tempietti) were discovered in 1935 near Corso Marrucino. Nearby there are remains of a **theatre** (1C AD) which was able to house 5 000 spectators. The **baths** (1C AD) are in the eastern part of the town, outside the ancient city centre. Powered by a nine-chamber cistern dug out of the hill, the baths were heated by series of double-walls and interconnecting furnaces.

EXCURSIONS

★★ **S. Clemente a Casauria** ⊙ – *30km/18mi southwest on the SS 5*. This imposing abbey, founded in 871 for Emperor Ludovic II, was reborn in the 12C after devastating Saracen attacks thanks to the Cistercian monks. The **church** was rebuilt in a style that was a crossover between Romanesque and Gothic. Note the **façade** with its portico consisting of three arches supported by fine capitals: the principal **doorway** is embellished by an exceptional sculptural decoration and a bronze door, dated 1191, whose borders depict the castles belonging to the abbey. The **interior** has the atmosphere of mystic sobriety so beloved by St Bernard and the Cistercians. Note the monumental **paschal candelabrum**★ and the splendid **pulpit**★★★ (12C); these are two of the finest examples of the Romanesque style in Abruzzi. The high altar consists of a paleo-Christian sarcophagus dating from the 5C surmounted by a finely sculpted Romanesque **ciborium**★★★. The 9C crypt, with its cross vaulting supported by ancient columns, is one of the few remains of the original abbey.

Discover the suggested Touring Programmes at the beginning of the guide
Plan a trip with the help of the Map of Principal Sights.

CHIUSI*

Tuscany

Population 8 802
Michelin map 430 M 17
See Michelin Green Guide Tuscany

Standing on a hill covered with olive groves, Chiusi is today a quiet and hospitable little town. It was once one of the 12 sovereign cities of Etruria.

* **Museo Archeologico** ⊙ – *Via Porsenna*. The museum presents the various finds from the burial grounds in the neighbourhood: sarcophagi, rounded tombstones *(cippi)*, alabaster and stone funerary urns, burial urns *(canopae)* in the shape of heads, clay ex-votos as well as a variety of utensils, vases, lamps and jewellery. The objects all display the Etruscan taste for fantasy and realism.
Visitors with a car can visit some of the **Etruscan tombs** 3km/2mi out of town, as long as they are accompanied by a museum warden.

Cattedrale di San Secondiano – The cathedral was rebuilt in the 12C over the ruins of a 6C Paleo-Christian basilica. The nave and side aisles are separated by 18 ancient columns taken from a number of Roman buildings.

Museo della cattedrale ⊙ – The cathedral museum houses Etruscan, Roman and Paleo-Christian remains discovered beneath the cathedral and in its vicinity. Fine collection of illuminated religious books dating from the 15C and 16C and brought here from the Abbey of Monte Oliveto Maggiore. The collection includes gold artefacts, reliquaries, religious objects etc.

Parco Nazionale del Cilento*

Campania

Michelin Map 431 F-G 26-28

The Cilento nature reserve was founded in 1991 and in 1997 was included in UNESCO's World Nature Reserve List. For thousands of years a crossroads of the most diverse cultural influences, from the basin of the Mediterranean to the Apennines, this Mediterranean park par excellence constitutes a perfect blend of nature and civilisation. Its territory extends from the Tyrrhenian coast to the Diano Valley (a Pleistocene lake which was engulfed by the Tanagro River) and is bordered to the north by the Alburni Massif and to the south by the Gulf of Policastro. The vast variety of landscapes is the result of the twofold nature of the rocks: the *flysch* variety of the Cilento is to be found in the western part of the park and along the coast (Stella and Gelbison mountains) with its gentle landscape and Mediterranean vegetation, and the calcareous rock of the interior (Alburni mountains and Mount Cerviati) and the southern coast (from Cape Palinuro to Scario) which has a more barren landscape with beech forests and spectacular karst formations, such as the numerous marine and earth caves. The most interesting floral species is the Palinuro primrose, symbol of the park, while typical fauna includes otters, wolves, foxes, hares and royal eagles.

Sights are listed based on an ideal itinerary which from Velia descends towards the coast and then makes its way up to the northwest. Allow at least 1 day.

Velia – *40km/25mi southeast of Paestum on the S 18 and the S 267*. This colony was founded in 535 BC by Phocean Greek refugees who had been expelled by the Persians. An active and prosperous port, Velia (known as Elea to the Greeks) became a Roman territory in 88 BC without, however, losing its cultural and linguistic Greek roots. The city was famous for its Eleatic school of philosophy which flourished in the 6C-5C BC and counted Parmenides and his pupil Zeno among its followers.

Roman ruins ⊙ – *Pass under the railway line to reach this area*. From the entrance there is an interesting view of the archeological site of the **città bassa** (lower town) with its lighthouse, 4C BC city wall, the south sea-gateway and Roman baths from the Imperial era (mosaic and marble floor remains). From the baths via di Porta Rosa borders the marketplace and climbs up to the ancient gateway (6C BC) and the **Porta Rosa**★ (4C BC), a fine example of a cuneiform arch and the most important Greek civic monument in *Magna Graecia*.
The **acropolis** on the promontory above the lower town has remains of the medieval castle erected on the foundations of a Greek temple and the Palatine Chapel which houses epigraphic material. Slightly lower down are the remains of the Greek theatre which was remodelled in the Roman era. Halfway down, towards the lower town, a Hellenistic villa with fresco remains has been discovered.

★★ **Capo Palinuro** – *28km/17mi southeast of Velia on the S 447*. The name Palinuro refers to Aeneas' mythical steersman who was killed and buried at sea here. From the port of Palinuro there are **boat trips** ⊙ to the **Grotta Azzurra**★ and other caves that are scattered over the imposing promontory where in springtime the Palinuro primroses are in bloom.

From the S 562 make for the **natural arch** at the mouth of the Mingardo River and the beautiful beaches on the coast. *(See Gulf of POLICASTRO).*

★ **Certosa di Padula** ⊙ – *11km/7mi southeast of Sala Consilina on the S 19.* The charterhouse of S. Lorenzo, founded in 1306, is one of the largest architectural compounds in southern Italy. Given its vast dimensions, work on the buildings went on for centuries and for the most part its present day appearance is Baroque. From the chiostro della Foresteria (cloisters) a splendid 14C cedarwood doorway leads to the sumptuous Baroque **church** which houses the fine 16C Conversi and **Padri**★ chancels and the notable ceramic high altar. The vast **Great Cloisters** (104x149m/341x488ft) are surrounded by monks' cells. The left arcade leads to the dramatic 18C **staircase**★ inspired by the architecture of Vanvitelli.

Grotte di Pertosa ⊙ – *32km/20mi northwest of Padula on the S 19.* These caves, which extend over an area of about 2.5km/1.5mi, are to be found in the evocative setting of the natural amphitheatre of the Alburni mountains and are reached via a small lake formed by an underground river. Inhabited since Neolithic times, the caves have fine concretions, mainly of sodium carbonate; the most interesting area is the so-called Sponge Room **(Sala delle Spugne)**.

The S 166 leads up to the Sentinella Pass (932m/3057ft) crossing some enchanting **landscapes**★ dotted with yellow broom shrubs.

Persano WWF Oasis ⊙ – *35km/21mi northeast of Pertosa on the S 19.* The land extends over 110ha/271 acres of alluvial planes formed by the River Sele between the Alburni and Picentini mountains. The most interesting flora can be found in the marsh and rain forest, one of the last refuges of the otter, symbol of the oasis. Other fauna in the area include numerous aquatic birds, foxes, boars, badgers and weasels.

CINQUE TERRE★★

Liguria

Michelin map 428 J 11 – Local map see The RIVIERA

Lying northwest of the Gulf of La Spezia, the Cinque Terre (Five Lands) is, even today, an isolated region, best reached by train or boat (parking difficult). This rugged coast is wild but hospitable, with its vineyards and fishing villages where the people remain strongly attached to their old customs and traditions. In 1997 Cinque Terre, together with Portovenere and the Palmaria, Tino and Tinetto islands, was included in UNESCO's World Heritage List.

★★ **Vernazza** – This is the most attractive village with its tall colourful houses and its church clustered together at the head of a well-sheltered cove.

Natural terraces descending towards the sea, Manarola

* **Manarola** – This fishing village with its small 14C church is set in a landscape of terraced vineyards. Starting from the station there is a splendid **walk**★★ *(15min on foot)* which offers lovely views of the coast and the other villages.

* **Riomaggiore** – *Take the branch road off the La Spezia-Manarola road.* The old houses of this medieval village lie in a narrow valley. This tiny fishing harbour backs against the strange black rock strata, typical of the region. A **coastal path** linking all five villages: Riomaggiore, Manarola, **Corniglia**, Vernazza and **Monterosso** affords fine views *(progressively more demanding west of Riomaggiore)*.

CIVIDALE DEL FRIULI★

Friuli – Venezia Giulia
Population 11 413
Michelin map 429 D 22

This is the ancient Forum Julii, which gave the town situated high above the Natisone river its modern name. The Lombards, who came from Scandinavia, settled here in the 6C and founded the first of their many duchies in northern Italy. The town later became the residence of the Patriarchs of Aquileia. From the 15C onward it belonged to Venice. Since the 1976 earthquake, Cividale has been rebuilt.

Duomo – It was extensively rebuilt in the 16C in the Renaissance style by Piero Lombardo (1435-1515) but retains some Gothic features on the façade and in the interior. The high altar has a 12C Veneto-Byzantine silver-gilt altarpiece. The small **Museo christiano** ⊙, a museum of Lombard art *(opening off the south aisle)*, contains numerous valuable items: the octagonal baptismal font of the Patriarch Callisto, rebuilt in the 8C using Byzantine fragments, and the 8C "altar" of Duke Ratchis in marble with carved sides depicting scenes from the Life of Christ.

★★ **Museo archeologico nazionale** ⊙ – *To the left of the cathedral.* Housed in a superb late-16C palace said to have been designed by Palladio, the museum displays on the second floor the numerous items discovered in Lombard graveyards in Cividale and the surrounding area. They include women's and men's jewellery (including some gold and silver items), weaponry and everyday objects that provide an excellent insight into Lombard culture and art in the 6C, during the Carolingian era. Note the Roman sarcophagus which was re-used at a later date, and the objects taken from the grave of Duke Gisulfo (7C). On the ground floor are archeological exhibits, mainly from the Roman and Lombard periods.

★★ **Tempietto** ⊙ – *Near the Piazza San Biagio.* This elegant 8C Lombard building is a square chamber with quadripartite vaulting and an admirable Lombard **decoration** of friezes and stylised stuccos. It is a unique example of the architecture of this period.

CIVITAVECCHIA

Lazio
Population 51 596
Michelin map 430 P 17

Civitavecchia, the Roman Centumcellae, has been the port of Rome since the reign of Trajan and now handles maritime traffic with Sardinia. The port is guarded by the Fort of Michelangelo, a massive Renaissance construction which was begun by Bramante, continued by Sangallo the Younger and Bernini, and completed by Michelangelo in 1557. Henri Beyle, known under the pen-name Stendhal (1783-1842), was appointed French Consul at Civitavecchia in 1831. In his leisure time Stendhal wrote numerous works, including *The Charterhouse of Parma* (1839).

Museo nazionale archeologico ⊙ – *2A, Largo Plebiscito.* The museum has Etruscan and Roman collections composed of finds from local sites. There is an amazing collection of Roman anchors.

Terme di Traiano ⊙ or **Terme Taurine** – *3km/2mi northeast.* There are two groups of baths *(terme)*: the first (to the west) dates from the Republican period and the second, the better preserved, was built by Trajan's successor, the Emperor Hadrian.

COMACCHIO

Emilia-Romagna
Population 21 807
Michelin map 429 H 18

Comacchio is built on sand and water and in many ways it resembles Chioggia. The main activity of the townspeople is eel fishing. Its brightly-coloured fishermen's houses, its canals spanned by some curious bridges, including an unusual triple bridge, and the fishing boats all lend it a special charm.

* **Polesine** – This area around the Po delta was once a malaria-infested marshy district. Land reclamation and drainage have since turned it into a fertile agricultural area. The Chioggia to Ravenna road *(90km – 56 miles)* traverses these flat expanses stretching away to the horizon and interrupted only by large solitary farms. Clumps of poplars and umbrella pines add touches of colour, especially in spring, to the monotony of this countryside where eel fishing is still common on the numerous canals which crisscross the area. At **Mesola** *(28km/17mi north of Comacchio)* there is a massive brick castle dating from 1583 which once belonged to the Este family. In the southern part of the area the **Valli di Comacchio**, Italy's most important zone of lagoons, has its own special melancholy beauty.

COMO ★

Lombardy
Population 83 637
Michelin map 428 E 9 – Town plan in the Michelin Atlas Italy
Local map see Regione dei LAGHI

The city was already prosperous under the Romans but reached its zenith in the 11C. It was destroyed by the Milanese in 1127, rebuilt by the Emperor Frederick Barbarossa and from 1355 onwards shared the fortunes of Milan.
The **"maestri comacini"** known as early as the 7C, were masons, builders and sculptors who spread the Lombard style *(see ART)* throughout Italy and Europe.

★★ **Duomo** – Begun in the late 14C the cathedral was completed during the Renaissance and crowned in the 18C with an elegant dome by the architect, Juvarra. It has a remarkable **façade★★** which was richly decorated from 1484 onwards by the **Rodari brothers**, who also worked on the **north door**, known as the Porta della Rana because of the frog *(rana)* carving on one of the pillars. They were also responsible for the exquisitely-delicate **south door**.
The **interior★**, full of solemn splendour, combines Gothic architecture and Renaissance decoration. In addition to the curious banners, hung between the pillars, and the magnificent 16C-17C **tapestries★**, there are canvases by B Luini *(Adoration of the Magi Virgin and Child with Saints★)*, and G Ferrari *(Flight into Egypt)*, in the south aisle as well as a *Descent from the Cross★* (1489) carved by Tommaso Rodari in the north aisle. Note also the organ in five parts, comprising 96 registers and 6 000 pipes. Various 17C artists were involved in its construction although its current form is the work of the organ-makers Balbiani and Vegezzi-Bossi.
Adjoining the façade is the **Broletto★★**, or 13C town hall, with an arcade at street level and a lovely storey of triple-arched windows above.

* **San Fedele** – In the heart of the picturesque old quarter, this church is in the Romanesque Lombard style. The nave and two aisles are terminated by a splendid polygonal Romanesque **chancel★** with radiating chapels. The whole east end is graced by two storeys of arcading.

* **Basilica di Sant'Abbondio** – This masterpiece of Romanesque Lombard architecture was consecrated in 1093. The noble but severe **façade★** has a lovely doorway. The nave and four aisles are separated by columns. The remarkable 14C **frescoes★** evoke the Life of Christ.

Villa Olmo ⊘ – *3km/2mi north by the S 35 and then the S 340 to the right*. This is a large neo-classical building dating from the late 18C, with a small theatre and gardens, from which there is a lovely **view★** of Como in its lakeside setting.

CONEGLIANO

Veneto
Population 35 021
Michelin map 429 E 18

Conegliano is surrounded by pleasant hills clad with orchards and vineyards, which produce an excellent white wine. This was the birthplace of **Cima da Conegliano** (1459-1518), an admirer of Giovanni Bellini, and a superb colourist who introduced idealised landscapes bathed in a crystal-clear light. The cathedral **(Duomo)** ⊘ has a fine *Sacra Conversazione★* by this artist. The **castello** ⊘ houses two small **museums** and affords a lovely **panorama★** of the town and its setting. Next to the cathedral the walls of the **Scuola dei Battuti** are decorated with 15C and 16C **frescoes★** in both the Venetian and Lombard styles.

CORTINA D'AMPEZZO✱✱✱

Veneto
Population 6 624
Michelin map 429 C 18 Town plan in the current Michelin Atlas Italy
Local map see DOLOMITI

Cortina, the capital of the Dolomites (see DOLOMITI), is a winter sports and summer resort with a worldwide reputation. Set in the heart of the Dolomites, Cortina makes a good excursion centre for discovering the magnificent **mountain scenery✱✱✱**.

✱✱✱ **Tondi di Faloria** ⊙ – From the summit a grand panorama may be enjoyed. There are excellent ski slopes.

✱✱✱ **Tofana di Mezzo** ⊙ – A cable-car climbs to 3 244m/10 743ft, from where there is a superb panorama over the surrounding mountains.

✱✱ **Belvedere Pocol** ⊙ – Lying to the southwest, this viewpoint affords a lovely view of Cortina which is best at sunset.

CORTONA✱✱

Tuscany
Population 22 459
Michelin map 430 M 17
See Michelin Green Guide Tuscany

The quiet town of Cortona with its medieval ramparts clings to the steep slopes of a hill clad with olive groves. It affords good views as far as Lake Trasimeno.

As early as the 14C Cortona attracted artists including the Sienese, Fra Angelico. Cortona was the birthplace of **Luca Signorelli** (1450-1523), who with his dramatic temperament and sculptural modelling, was the precursor of Michelangelo; he died as a result of a fall from scaffolding when he was decorating the Villa Passerini to the east of Cortona. In the 16C Cortona gave France an architect, Domenico Bernabei, known as **Il Boccadoro** (Mouth of Gold) who designed the Hôtel de Ville in Paris for François I. **Pietro da Cortona** (1596-1669), painter and architect with a lively imagination, was one of the masters of Roman baroque and a talented decorative painter. The latest famous artist was the painter **Severini** (1883-1966) who was linked to the Futurist movement.

SIGHTS

Piazza del Duomo, close up against the ramparts, affords a lovely view over the valley. The Romanesque cathedral (**Duomo**), remodelled at the Renaissance, contains some works of art.

✱✱ **Museo diocesano** ⊙ – Opposite the cathedral. This former church houses a remarkable collection of paintings: a beautiful Annunciation and Madonna and Saints by Fra Angelico; works from the Sienese school by Duccio, Pietro Lorenzetti and Sassetta; an excellent group of works by **Signorelli**; and a remarkable Ecstasy of St Margaret by the Bolognese artist, G M Crespi (1665-1747). Note also the fine 2C Roman sarcophagus (Battle of Lapiths and Centaurs).

✱ **Palazzo Pretorio** – The Praetorian Palace was built in the 13C but altered during a later period. Its **façade✱** is original and is decorated with coats-of-arms while the façade overlooking the Piazza Signorelli, which is preceded by a grand staircase, dates from the 17C. Inside, the **Museo dell'Accademia Etrusca✱** ⊙ displays Etruscan exhibits as well as Roman, Egyptian, medieval and Renaissance items. Among the Etruscan objects is a strange 5C BC bronze **oil lamp✱✱** with 16 burners shaped like human figures. The museum also displays works and memorabilia relating to Severini, bequeathed by the artist to his native town.

Santuario di S. Margherita – This enshrines the fine Gothic **tomb✱** (1362) of St Margaret. The Via Santa Margherita leads off to the south of the church. Severini decorated the street with mosaics representing the **Stations of the Cross**.

San Domenico – Largo Beato Angelico. The church is dedicated to St Dominic. In the south apse is a Madonna with angels and saints by Luca Signorelli, a polyptych by Lorenzo di Niccolò at the high altar and a fresco by Fra Angelico.

✱ **Santa Maria del Calcinaio** – 3km/2mi west. Santa Maria, built from 1485 to 1513 by Francesco di Giorgio Martini, strongly resembles the work of Brunelleschi. The church is remarkable for the grace and harmony of its design and its well-balanced proportions. The domed church is built on the Latin cross plan and the lofty interior is well lit.

In the oculus of the façade is a remarkable stained-glass **window** (1516) designed by a French artist, **Guillaume de Marcillat** (1467-1529).

CREMONA★

Lombardy
Population 72 129
Michelin map 428 or 429 G 11-12

Cremona is an important agricultural market town in the heart of a fertile agricultural region. Town life centres on Piazza Roma. The original Gallic settlement became a Latin city before emerging as an independent commune in the Middle Ages. It suffered from the Guelph and Ghibelline troubles of the period.

In 1334 the town came under Visconti rule and was united with the Duchy of Milan in the 15C. At the Renaissance the town was the centre of a brilliant artistic movement. In the 18C and 19C the French and Austrians fought for supremacy over Cremona until the Risorgimento.

From the late 16C the stringed-instrument makers of Cremona gained a reputation as violin and cello makers. The International School of Violin Making carries on this tradition. The Cremonese composer **Claudio Monteverdi** (1567-1643) created modern opera with his *Orfeo* and *The Coronation of Poppea*.

★★ PIAZZA DEL COMUNE (BZ 7) 1hr

★★★ **Torrazzo** ⊙ – The remarkable late-13C campanile is linked to the cathedral by a Renaissance gallery. Its massive form is elegantly crowned by an octagonal 14C storey. From the top (112m/367ft) there is a lovely view★ over the town. The astronomical clock, which dates from 1471, has undergone a number of alterations in its history, the last being in the 1970s. It is notable for its illustrations of the stars and the constellations of the zodiac.

★★ **Duomo** – This magnificent Lombard cathedral was begun in the Romanesque and completed in the Gothic style (1107 to 1332). The richly-decorated white marble façade is preceded by a porch. Numerous decorative features were later additions, namely the frieze by the followers of Antelami, the large 13C rose window and the four statue-columns of the central doorway.

CREMONA

Boccaccino (Via)	BZ 3	Libertà (Piazza della)	BY 14	Risorgimento (Piazza)	AY 29
Cadorna (Piazza L.)	AZ 4	Mantova (Via)	BY 17	S. Maria in Betlem (Via)	BZ 32
Campi (Corso)	BZ 5	Manzoni (Via)	BY 18	S. Rocco (Via)	BZ 33
Cavour (Corso)	BZ 6	Marconi (Piazza)	BZ 19	Spalato (Via)	AY 35
Comune (Piazza del)	BZ 7	Marmolada (Via)	BZ 22	Stradivari (Piazza)	BZ 37
Garibaldi (Corso)	AYZ	Mazzini (Corso)	BZ 23	Tofane (Via)	BZ 39
Geromini (Via Felice)	BY 9	Matteotti (Corso)	BYZ	Ugolani Dati (Via)	BY 40
Ghinaglia (Via F.)	AY 12	Melone (Via Altobello)	BZ 24	Vacchelli (Corso)	BZ 42
Ghisleri (Via A.)	BY 13	Mercatello (Via)	BZ 25	Verdi (Via)	BZ 43
		Monteverdi		Vittorio Emanuele II (Corso)	Z 45
		(Via Claudio)	BZ 27	4 Novembre (Piazza)	BZ 46
		Novati (Via)	BZ 28	20 Settembre (Corso)	BZ 48

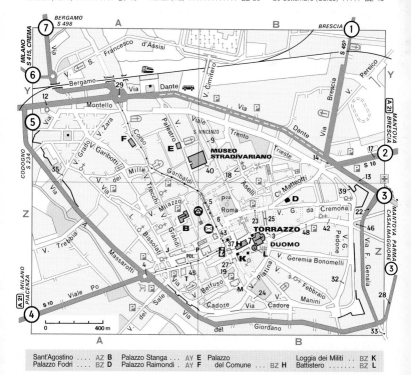

Sant'Agostino	AZ **B**	Palazzo Stanga	AY **E**	Palazzo			Loggia dei Militi	BZ **K**
Palazzo Fodri	BZ **D**	Palazzo Raimondi	AY **F**	del Comune	BZ **H**		Battistero	BZ **L**

The violin town

Cremona was the birthplace of the greatest violin-makers of all time and their instruments are still highly sought after by famous violinists today. The first of the famous violin-makers of Cremona was **Andrea Amati**, from whom King Charles IX of France commissioned instruments in the 16C. His work was continued by his sons and his nephew, Nicolò, master of Andrea Guarneri and the most famous of all of them, **Antonio Stradivarius** (c1644-1737), who made more than 1000 instruments. **Andrea Guarneri** was the first of another renowned dynasty in which the most skilled violin-maker of them all was Giuseppe Guarneri (1698-1744), better known as Giuseppe del Gesù because of the three letters IHS (Jesus, Saviour of Mankind) inscribed on all his violins. Knowledgeable music lovers will find it easy to distinguish between the crystal-clear tones of a Stradivarius and the deeper, powerful tones of a Guarneri de Gesù.

The spacious **interior** is decorated with **frescoes**★ by the Cremona school (B. Boccaccino, the Campi, the Bembo, Romanino da Brescia, Pordenone and Gatti). Also of interest, at the entrance to the chancel, are the **high reliefs**★★ by Amadeo, the architect-sculptor of the Carthusian Monastery at Pavia.

★ **Battistero** (**L**) – This harmonious octagonal baptistery, preceded by a Lombard porch and decorated with a gallery, was remodelled during the Renaissance.

Palazzo comunale ⊙ (**H**) – This 13C palace was remodelled at a later date. Inside are displayed the most famous violins in the world: the *Charles IX of France* (Amati), the *Hammerle* (Amati), the *Quarestani* (Guarneri), the *Cremonese* 1715 (Antonio Stradivarius) and the *Stauffer* (Guarneri del Gesu).
To the left of the palace is the lovely 13C **Loggia dei Militi** (**K**).

ADDITIONAL SIGHTS

Museo Civico Ala Ponzone ⊙ – Installed in a 16C palace this municipal museum has a **picture gallery** with works of the Cremona school Note the dramatic *St Frances in Meditation* by **Caravaggio**, the *Vegetable Gardner* by **Arcimboldo** and a section on **decorative arts** (French ivories).

Stradivarius museum ⊙ – This museum has displays of wooden models and tools belonging to Stradivarius, as well as stringed instruments from the 17-20C).

Renaissance Architecture – The town is embellished with numerous Renaissance palaces including the **Palazzo Fodri**★ (**BZ D**), the **Palazzo Stanga** (**AY E**) and the **Palazzo Raimondi** (**AY F**), as well as churches like **Sant'Agostino** (**AZ B**) rich in works of art: **portraits**★ of Francesco Sforza and his wife by Bonifacio Bembo and an **altarpiece**★ by Perugino.
On the Casalmaggiore road *(2km/1mi out of town by no ③ on the town plan)* is the church of **San Sigismondo** with its lavishly-decorated **interior**★. The frescoes are by the 16C Cremona school (Campi, Gatti, Boccaccino).

CROTONE

Calabria
Population 59 879
Michelin map 431 J 33

The ancient town of Croton was an Achaean colony of Magna Graecia, founded in 710 BC and celebrated in antiquity for its riches, the beauty of its women and the prowess of its athletes, such as Milo of Croton, so admired by Virgil. Around 532 BC Pythagoras founded several religious communities which devoted themselves to the study of mathematics and which once they had become too powerful were expelled northwards towards Metapontum (present-day Metaponto). The rival city of Locari defeated Croton in the mid- 6C BC, which in turn defeated its other rival Sybaris. The city welcomed Hannibal during the Second Punic War before being conquered by Rome. Crotone is today a prosperous seaport and industrial centre as well as a popular holiday resort.

Museo archeologico ⊙ – *Via Risorgimento.*
The archeological collections include local finds from other colonies of Magna Graecia: displays of ceramics, terracottas, coins and sculpture. There are also the remains of the Temple of Hera Lacinia.

EXCURSIONS

Capo Colonna - *11km/7mi southeast.*
This cape was once called Capo Lacinio. From the last decades of the 8C BC one of the most famous temples of Magna Graecia stood here, the temple of Hera Lacinia. It had a golden age in the 5C BC but began to decline in 173 BC when the Counsel Fulvio Flacco removed part of the marble roof which he was subsequently unable to repair due to the complexity of the original design. It was then plundered by pirates and became a quarry from which the Aragonese extracted material used for construction of the foundations of Crotone in the 16C. The temple was finally destroyed by an earthquake in 1683. Now only 48 columns remain of this Doric temple which was dedicated to the most important goddess of the Olympus.

Did you know...? In 1964 Pier Paolo Pasolini shot some scenes of his film The Gospel according to St Matthew here.

★ **Santa Severina** - *34km/21mi northwest.* The 13C cathedral has a remarkable 8C circular **baptistery**★ which shows a strong Byzantine influence. The Norman Castle is also of interest.

CUMA★

CUMAE – Campania
Michelin map 431 E 24
Local map see Golfo di NAPOLI

Cumae, one of the oldest Greek colonies, was founded in the 8C BC. The city soon dominated the whole Phlegrean area *(see Golfo di NAPOLI)* including Naples, leaving an important Hellenic heritage. Its splendour was at its height under the tyrant Aristodemus. After its capture by the Romans in 334 BC, decline set in and continued until AD 915 when it was pillaged by the Saracens.

The ancient city of Cumae stands in a serene and solemn setting near the sea. Visitors have access to the ruins of the Acropolis, the upper town where most of the temples stood. In the lower town, excavations have revealed the remains of an amphitheatre, a temple dedicated to the Capitoline Triad (Jupiter, Juno and Minerva) and baths.

★★ **Acropoli** ⊘ – The acropolis is built on a hill of volcanic material (lava and tufa) in a lonely site and is reached by an alley lined with laurels. After the vaulted passageway, the path to the left leads to the Sibyl's Cave **(Antro della Sibilla★)**, one of the most venerated places of Antiquity. Here the Sibyl delivered her oracles. The cave was hollowed out of the rock by the Greeks in the 6C or 5C BC and it is rectangular in shape with three small niches.

Take the stairway up to the sacred way (Via Sacra). From the belvedere there is a good **view**★ of the sea. Some finds from the excavations are on display. On the right are the remains of the Temple of Apollo **(Tempio di Apollo)** which was later transformed into a Christian church. Further on is the Temple of Jupiter **(Tempio di Giove)** which was also converted by the early Christians. In the centre stands a large font and there are several Christian tombs near the sanctuary.

★ **Arco Felice** – The minor road in the direction of Naples leads to this triumphal arch which was erected on the Via Domitiana; there are still traces of the paved Roman way.

The Cumaean Sibyl

In Antiquity the Sibyls were virgin priestesses dedicated to the cult of Apollo and deemed to be semi-divine creatures with powers of divination. According to tradition they went into a trance conducive to delivering their prophesies with the help of Apollo. The oracles were couched in obscure terms which could have different interpretations, hence the adjective sibylline in reference to words with a mysterious or hidden meaning.

The Sibyl from Cumae (one of the main centres of Greek civilisation in Italy) was a famous prophetess. She is reputed to have sold the Sibylline Books, collections of the Sibyls' prophesies, to the Etruscan King of Rome, Tarquin the Elder or Tarquin the Superb (6C BC). The oracles were later used by the rulers to answer their subjects' petitions and expectations. One of the best known depictions of the Cumaean Sibyl by Michelangelo adorns the ceiling of the Sistine Chapel in the Vatican *(see ROME)*.

DOLOMITI ★★★

The DOLOMITES

Michelin map 429 C 16-19

This fan of rocky "Pale Mountains" *(Monti Pallidi)* which take on red tints at sunset that suddenly vanish when the sun disappears, are situated in the Veneto and Trentino-Alto Adige. Their harsh contours embrace crystalline lakes and mysteries which have become the very stuff of numerous poetic legends.

Monti Pallidi and the colour of a rose garden

Legend has it that a prince who lived at the foot of the Alps married the daughter of the King of the Moon. The young girl loved flowers and meadows but was disturbed by the dark colour of the rocks. She so desperately missed the pale mountains of her home that she felt compelled to return to the Moon. Some dwarfs came to the disconsolate prince's aid and made some skeins of thread from the moon's rays, weaving them into nets which they placed on the mountains. The princess was thus able to return and the dwarfs were allowed to live in the kingdom.

At sunset, however, the Monti Pallidi assumed fiery hues, probably caused by the beautiful rose garden situated on one of the mountains where the King of the Dwarfs lived. One day, attracted by the rose garden, some foreign warriors arrived in the kingdom and imprisoned the king who cursed the plant and ordered that roses would never be seen again, by day or night. The curse did not, however, mention sunset, a moment suspended between day and night. Thus for those few minutes the Catinaccio mountain, which the Germans refer to as *Rosengarten* (rose garden), is still inflamed and throws light onto every rock of the Dolomites.

THE DOLOMITES

The Dolomites are made of a white calcareous rock, dolomia, which takes its name from the French geologist Deodat de Dolomieu who studied its composition in the 18C.

150 million years ago this land was submerged by the Tetide sea. On its sandy depths coral reefs and limestone began to shape the "Pale Mountains".

About 70 million years ago, during the Alpine orogenis (the corrugation of the earth's crust) the layers were violently compressed and forced to the surface. Thus the Dolomites were born out of the sea. Today visitors can still see fossils of marine life. The Dolomites were nearly completed in the Quaternary (about 2 million years ago) when glaciers softened and hollowed out the valleys. Only flora and fauna were missing at this stage; these began to inhabit the Dolomites when the glaciers retreated.

The massifs – To the southeast rise the Pelmo (3 168m/10 393ft) and the Civetta (3 220m/10 564ft). To the south, near the peak of the Vezzana, the Pale di San Martino, streaked by fissures, divide into three chains separated by a plateau. The Latemar (2 842m/9 324ft) and the Catinaccio (2 981m/9780ft), together with the Torri del Vaiolet (Towers of Vaiolet), frame the Costalunga Pass. To the north of the pass rise the Sasso Lungo and the vast Sella Massif (Gruppo di Sella), skirted by a road.

To the east, the chief summits in the Cortina Dolomites are the Tofane, the Sorapis and the Cristallo. Finally, in the heart of the range, stands the **Marmolada Massif** (Gruppo della Marmolada, 3 342m/10 964ft), which dominates the Monti Pallidi. Between Cortina and the Piave Valley the wooded region of **Cadore** boasts the Antelao (3 263m/10 705ft) and the triple peak Tre Cime di Lavaredo (Drei Zinnen) which it shares with the Parco delle Dolomiti di Sesto in Alto Adige.

Flora and fauna – The Dolomite landscape is coloured by coniferous forests, crocuses, alpine gentians, edelweiss, rhododendron, lilies and alpine bluebells.

Although tourists cause animals to flee, the Dolomites are still a refuge for chamois, marmots, royal eagles and woodcock.

★★★ DOLOMITE ROAD

From Bolzano to Cortina *210km/131mi - allow 2 days*

The main touring route in the Dolomites is the great Dolomite Road, which is a wonderful and world-famous example of road engineering. The road was already used during the Renaissance by merchants travelling between Venice and Germany and it was also used during the First World War.

★ **Bolzano** – *See BOLZANO.*

★ **Gola della Val d'Ega** – This narrow gorge, the Ega Valley, with pink sandstone walls, is guarded by the **Castello di Cornedo**.

Tre Cime di Lavaredo

★ **Nova Levante** – The Catinaccio Massif rises up behind this attractive village with its bulbous belfry and pretty houses.

★ **Lago di Carezza** – This tiny lake is set in a dark expanse of fir trees with the jagged peaks of the Latemar and the Catinaccio Massifs in the background.

★ **Passo di Costalunga** – From this pass on the Dolomite Road there is a view★ over the Catinaccio on one side and the Latemar on the other

⁂ **Vigo di Fassa** – This resort, in a picturesque site★ in the famous Val di Farsa, is a mountaineering and excursion centre in the Catinaccio Massif (cable-car).

⁂⁂ **Canazei** – Canazei lies deep in the heart of the massif, framed between the Catinaccio, the Towers of Vaiolet (Torri del Vaiolet), the Sella Massif and the Marmolada. This is the usual base for most excursions and climbs in the Marmolada range. The church has a bulbous belfry and a façade with a painted image of St Christopher.

At Canazei turn right into the S 641.

This road affords very fine views★★ of the Marmolada range and its glacier. As one comes out of a long tunnel a lake, **Lago di Fedaia★**, suddenly appears.

★★★ **Marmolada** – This is the highest massif in the Dolomites famous for its glacier and very fast ski-runs. The cable-car from Malga Ciapela goes up to 3 265m/10 712ft offering admirable panoramas★★★ of the Cortina peaks (Tofana

---

MOUNTAIN FOOTPATHS

The Dolomites have a dense network of footpaths. Whether you are an expert climber or simply want to take a peaceful walk, there is a vast choice of routes for those wishing to get a better look at the Monti Pallidi. Maps and guides listing paths, mountain huts and bivouacs are on sale just about everywhere.

Some mountain pathways include:

No 2 (Bressanone-Feltre): This path crosses the Plose, the Puez Group, the Gardenaccia, the Sella and the Marmolada massif;

No 3 (Villabassa-Longarone):This path winds its way through Val Pusteria, the Croda Rossa, Misurina, the Cristallo, the Sorapis and the Antelao;

No 4 (San Candido)-Pieve di Cadore): This track goes through the Sesto Dolomites, the Cadini di Misurina and the Marmarole.

To be fully prepared for a mountain excursion it is advisable to contact: **AZIENDA DI PROMOZIONE TURISTICA DOLOMITI**, piazzetta S. Francesco 8, 32043 Cortina d'Ampezzo (BL), ☎ 0436 3231. Web site: www.sunrise.it/dolomiti.

ALTO ADIGE PROMOZIONE TURISMO, piazza Parrocchia 11, 39100 Bolzano, ☎ 0471 99 38 08. Web site www.provincia.bz.it

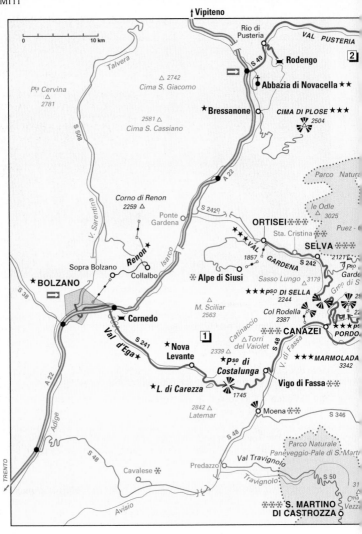

Italian and German place-names:

Adige/Etsch
Alpe di Siusi/Seiseralm
Badia/Abtei
Badia (Val)/Gadertal
Bolzano/Bozen
Braies (Lago di)/Pragser Wildsee
Bressanone/Brixen
Brunico/Bruneck
Campo Fiscalino/Fischleinboden
Carezza (Lago di)/Karersee
Catinaccio/Rosengarten

Cervina (Punta)/Hirzerspitze
Chiusa/Klausen
Cornedo/Karneid
Corvara in Badia/Kurfar
Costalunga (Passo di)/Karerpaß
Croda Rossa/ Hohe Geisel
Dobbiaco/Toblach
Ega (Val d')/Eggental
Gadera/Gaderbach
Gardena (Passo)/Grödnerjoch
Gardena (Val)/Grödnertal

and Cristallo), the Sasso Lungo, the enormous tabular mass of the Sella Massif and in the background the summits of the Austrian Alps including the Grossglockner.

Return to Canazei then after 5.5km/3mi turn left.

★★★ **Passo di Sella** – Linking the Val di Fassa and Val Gardena this pass offers one of the most extensive **panoramas**★★★ in the Dolomites, including the Sella, Sasso Lungo and Marmolada Massifs.

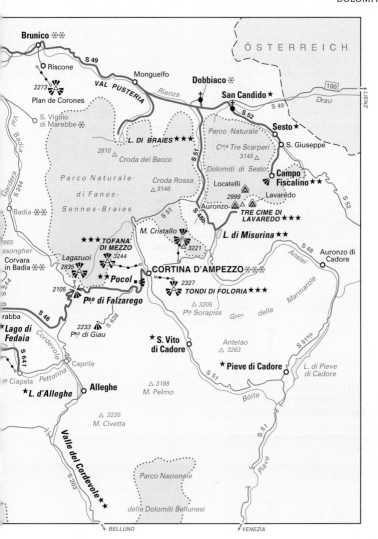

Isarco/Eisack
Lavaredo (Tre Cime di)/Drei Zinnen
Nova Levante/Welschnofen
Odie (le)/Geislerspitze
Ortisei/St-Ulrich
Plan de Corones/Kronplatz
Plose (Cima d.)/Plose Bühel
Rienza/Rienz
Riscon/Reischach
San Candido/Innichen
San Cassiano (Cima)/Kassianspitze

San Giacomo (Cima)/Jakobspitze
San Vigilio di M./St. Vigil
S.-Cristina/St-Christina
Sarentina (Valle)/Sarntal
Sasso Lungo/Langkofel
Sella (Passo)/Sellajoch
Selva in Val Gardena/Wolkenstein im Grödnerta
Sesto (Val di)/Sextental
Talvera/Talfer
Tre Scarperi (Cima)/Dreischusterspitze
Vipiteno/Sterzing

★★★ **Val Gardena** – One of the most famous valleys in the Dolomites both for its beauty and crowds of tourists. The inhabitants still speak a language which was born during the Roman occupation: the Ladin dialect which nowadays can only be heard in some valleys of the Dolomites, the Grigioni mountains and the Carniche Alps. There are some skilful wood-workers as can be seen in some fine shops that are to be found in Selva (Wolkenstein), Santa Cristina and Ortisei (St Ulrich).

★★★ **Selva di Val Gardena** – This resort is situated at the foot of the Sella Massif. It is an active craft centre: wooden objects, pewterware and ceramics.

✳✳✳ **Ortisei** – From Ortisei a cable-car climbs up to **Alpe di Siusi** ✳ (Seiser Alm), a 60km² – 23sq mi plateau in a delightful **setting★★** overlooking the Sasso Lungo and the Sciliar. This is a base for excursions to suit all tastes and abilities.

Return to the Dolomite Road.

★★★ **Passo Pordoi** – The highest pass (2 239m/7 346ft) on the Dolomite Road lies between huge blocks of rock with sheer sides and shorn-off tops.

Passo di Falzarego – Nearing Cortina the scenery becomes more beautiful. The pass goes through the Tofane and skirts the barren landscape of the Cinque Torri which was a source of inspiration for Tolkein when he wrote *The Lord of the Rings*.

✳✳✳ **Cortina d'Ampezzo** – *See CORTINA D'AMPEZZO.*

VAL PUSTERIA AND EXCURSIONS

Val Pusteria, or Pustertal, is bordered to the south by the Dolomites and by the central Alps to the north. From the end of the 13C until the 16C it belonged to the County of Gorizia and formed part of the Strada d'Alemagna, a road which linked Venice and Germany.

The first village encountered arriving on the state road which forks off the motorway is Rio di Pusteria. A few minutes away stands the **Castello di Rodengo** ⊘, decorated with the oldest cycle of Romanesque frescoes (13C) with a profane theme: the epic poem *Iwein* by Hartmann von Aue.

✳✳ **Brunico** – This is the main town in the Pusteria Valley. There is an interesting **Ethnography Museum★** ⊘ in **Teodone** covering an area of 3ha/7 acres) and including various types of rural building: country manor, hayloft, farm, grain store, oven, mill. They provide an effective illustration of the lifestyles and activities of peasants and noblemen in bygone days.

From Brunico go in the direction of Dobbiaco. After Monguelfo turn right where Lago di Braies is signposted.

★★★ **Lago di Braies** – Alt 1 495m/4 905ft. This shimmering lake (called Pragser Wildsee in German) is encircled by the Croda del Becco mountains and can be circumnavigated in one hour. Boat trips can be made and it is also the starting point of some rather arduous mountain footpaths.

*Proceed through the Pusteria Valley. Turn right before Dubbiaco in the direction of Cortina which is signposted. Follow directions for Misurina and then for Tre Cime di Lavaredo. The last stretch of the route is a **toll-road** ⊘.*

★★★ **Tre Cime di Lavaredo** – From the refuge at Auronza the Lavaredo shelter is reached in half an hour. From there the Locatelli shelter is reached in an hour. This last stretch of the path offers spectacular views of the Tre Cime range which forms part of the Parco Naturale delle Dolomiti di Sesto. The Tre Cime can also be reached from Sesto, along path no 102 which leads to Locatelli in two and a half hours.

On the way back from Tre Cime a stop at Lago di Misurino is recommended.

★★ **Lago di Misurina** – Alt 1 759m/5 770ft. This lake is set among a plantation of fir trees and is an excellent starting point for excursions to the surrounding mountains, from the Tre Cime di Lavaredo to the Cristallo.

✳ **Dobbiaco** – Dobbiaco (Toblach in German) was an important town in the Middle Ages as it was at a crossroads with the Strada dell'Alemagna. In the centre of this village there is a Late Baroque church dating from the second half of the 18C.

★ **San Candido** – This pretty village, known as Innichen in German, has the most important Romanesque church in the Alto Adige. The **collegiata★** dates from the 13C, the campanile from the 14C. Above the south doorway there are frescoes by the painter and sculptor Michael Pacher (c 1430-1498). The most striking piece however is the *Crucifixion*, an evocative wood sculptural group of the 13C with Christ's feet resting on Adam's head.

At San Candido turn right for Sesto leaving the Pusteria which eventually leads to Austria.

★ **Sesto** – Sesto overlooks the Dolomites and offers a huge variety of walks, footpaths and alpine excursions which allow one to become better acquainted with this stunning landscape. The Monte Elmo funicular makes distances shorter. Those in search of a peaceful walk should consider path 4D which crosses the forest and high pastures and affords views of the Meridiana del Sesto (from Cima Nove to Cima Uno). This path is known as the "route of biblical meditation" owing to the fact that it is articulated by 14 wood sculptures based on the sciptures. At San Giuseppe (Moos) the Val Fiscalino leads to **Campo Fiscalino★★** which affords truly stunning views of the Meridiana di Sesto and the Cima dei Tre Scarperi.

OTHER TOWNS AND VALLEYS

The Dolomites south of Cortina offer other views of the Dolomites.

★★ **Valle del Cordevole** – The road from Caprile to Belluno is an extremely picturesque one with its hilltop villages and impressive gorges. **Alleghe** on the bank of a **lake**★ is a good excursion centre.

❋❋❋ **San Martino di Castrozza** – An excellent starting point for numerous excursions.

★ **Pieve di Cadore** – This town is pleasantly set at the head of a reservoir. It was the birthplace of the great artist, **Titian**. One of his works is to be found in the church, and the house where he was born is now a **museum** ⊙.

★ **San Vito di Cadore** – This attractive village with its shingle-roofed churches nestles at the foot of the Antelao.

Isola d'ELBA

Tuscany

Population 29 019
Michelin Map 430 N 12-13
See Michelin Green Guide Tuscany

With its beaches, solitary places, peacefulness and mild, dry climate, the Isle of Elba is a good place for a stay rather than an excursion. In the distant geological past Elba was part of the vanished continent of Tyrrhenia. This, the largest island in the Tuscan Archipelago, like Corsica, Sardinia, the Balearics and the Maures and Estérel Massifs on the French Riviera coast, has an indented coastline with small creeks, caves and beaches. The vegetation is typically Mediterranean with palms, eucalyptus, cedars, magnolias and, in great quantity, olives and vines. The wines produced (white Moscato and red Aleatico) are heady with a strong bouquet. The granitic relief culminates in Monte Capane. East of the island the iron mines worked by the Etruscans are no longer exploited.

Elba is closely associated with Napoleon who was exiled here following his abdication. Between 3 May 1814 and 26 February 1815 the fallen emperor ruled over his small court and the island, which was garrisoned by about 1 000 soldiers.

Sightseeing – Start from Portoferraio and follow one of the two itineraries indicated on the map below: **western Elba** *(about 70km/44mi, about 5hr)* and **eastern Elba** *(68km/42mi, about 3hr).*

⌖ **Portoferraio** – This island's capital, guarded by ruined walls and two forts, lies at the head of a beautiful bay. In the upper part of the town is the Napoleonic Museum (**Museo Napoleonico** ⊙) housed in the Villa dei Mulini, a simple house, with a terraced garden, which Napoleon sometimes occupied. His personal library and various mementoes are kept here.

Beyond the great sandy beach at **Biodola**, the road goes towards **Marciana Marina**, a small port protected by two piers, one of which is dominated by a round tower, and climbs the wooded slopes of Monte Capanne

★★ **Monte Capanne** ⊙ – Alt. 1018m/3 339ft. *Cable-cars leave from Marciana.* From the summit not far from the terminus there is a splendid **panorama**★★ of Elba, the Tuscan coast to the east and the coast of Corsica to the west.

Marciana – From this attractive village there is a lovely **view**★ of **Poggio**, perched on its rocky spur, Marciana Marina and the Bay of Procchio. There is a small museum (**Museo Archeologico** ⊙) with displays of prehistoric artefacts and Greek vases.

Getting to Elba

By train – The Genova-Rome train branches of at the Campiglia di Marittima station where there are direct trains to the Port of Piombino (14km/9mi).

By car – Take the S. Vincenzo or Venturina exits off the Livorno-Grosseto dual carriageway. These are well signposted.

From the port – At Piombino there are plenty of boats with connections to Elba. There are several daily crossings to Portoferraio (crossing time approximately 1hr30min by hovercraft) and about 10 crossings (more in high season) to Rio Marina and Porto Azzurro. Once a week there is a crossing from Livorno.

Information – Contact the following shipping companies: Navarma, piazzale Premuda 13, ☎ 0565 22 12 12; Elba Ferries, piazzale Premuda, ☎ 0565 22 09 56, fax 0565 22 09 96; Toremar, piazzale Premuda 13/14, ☎ 0565 31 100, fax 0565 35 294.

Gulf of Stella

Madonna del Monte – Take the road up to the castle which dominates Marciana and from there a rocky path leads up to this sanctuary, built on the northern slope of Monte Giove. Beside the 16C chapel there is a curious semicircular fountain dated 1698 and a "hermitage" where Napoleon and Maria Walewska spent a few days in the summer of 1814.

Marina di Campo – This small fishing port with its popular beach lies at the head of a lovely bay backed by a hinterland plain of olive groves and vineyards.

★ **Villa Napoleone di San Martino** ⊘ – In a setting of silent hills, planted with groves of evergreen oaks and vineyards, this modest house was the ex-emperor's summer residence. There is a lovely view of the Bay of Portoferraio.

Lower down there is a neo-Classical style villa, constructed by Prince Demidoff, son-in-law of King Jerome.

Capoliveri – Nearby this village there is a **panorama**★★ of three bays: Portoferraio, Porto Azzurro and Golfo Stella.

⌂⌂ **Porto Azzurro** – This pretty port is overlooked by a fort which now serves as a prison.

Rio Marina – A pleasant port and mining village protected by a crenellated tower. Beyond **Cavo**, a small port sheltered by the Castello headland, the return journey to Portoferraio is by a high altitude **road**★★ affording remarkable views of the ruins of Volterraio, the Bay of Portoferraio and the sea.

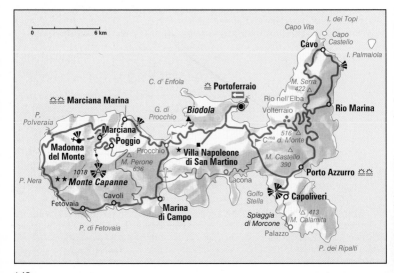

ERCOLANO★★

HERCULANEUM

Campania – Population 58 752
Michelin map 431 E 25 – Local map see Golfo di NAPOLI

Herculaneum was founded, according to tradition, by Hercules. Like Pompeii the Roman town was overwhelmed during the AD 79 eruption of Vesuvius.

It was a more peaceful town than Pompeii. Its port was frequented by fishing boats, there were numerous craftsmen and many rich and cultured patricians were drawn to the resort of Herculaneum because of its beautiful setting, overlooking the Bay of Naples. The five quarters of the town were divided by three main streets (*decumani*). The town has various examples of different types of dwellings, all of which were overwhelmed by the sea of mud which seeped into every nook. The particular interest of a visit to Herculaneum is that all timber structures (frameworks, beams, doors, stairs and partitions) were preserved by a hard shell of solidified mud, whereas at Pompeii they were consumed by fire. The houses were empty, but death caught up with the inhabitants as they tried to flee the city or make for the sea.

In 1997 Herculaneum was included in UNESCO's World Heritage List.

EXCAVATIONS ⏱ 2hr

N.B. Some of the houses listed below may be temporarily closed for maintenance and restoration.

From the access road (*go on foot*) there is a good view of the luxurious villas overlooking the sea.

Casa dell' Albergo – This vast patrician villa was about to be converted into apartments for letting, hence its name. It was one of the most badly damaged by the eruption.

★★ **Casa dell' Atrio a mosaico** – The atrium of this villa is paved with a chequered mosaic. The garden on the right is surrounded by a peristyle. On the left are the bedrooms and at the far end, a pleasant *triclinium* (dining-room). The terrace, flanked by two small rest rooms, offers an attractive view of the sea.

★★ **Casa a Graticcio** – The house gets its name from the wooden trellis frame work (*graticcio*) of the walls. It is a unique example of this type of house from antiquity.

★ **Casa del Tramezzo carbonizzato** – The façade is remarkably well preserved. This is a good example of a patrician dwelling which housed several families. The atrium is separated from the *tablinium* (living-room) by a wooden partition (*tramezzo*). Only the sides of the partition remain standing.

Next door is the dyer's shop (**A**) containing an interesting wooden clothespress.

★★ **Casa Sannitica** – The house was built on the very simple plan typical of the Samnites (an Italic people of the Sabine race). The splendid **atrium** is surrounded by a gallery with Ionic columns. The rooms are decorated with frescoes.

★★★ **Terme** – The baths of Herculaneum which are in excellent condition were built at the time of Augustus. They are not sumptuous but

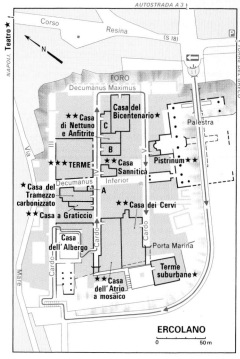

Casa: *House*	**Teatro:** *Theatre*
Foro: *Forum*	**Terme:** *Baths*
Porta: *Gate*	**Palestra:** *Palestra*

Men's Baths
Women's Baths

they show a remarkable degree of practical planning. In the **men's baths** visit the *palestra*, the cloakroom (**a**), the *frigidarium* (**b**) with frescoes on the ceiling, the *tepidarium* (**c**) and the *calidarium* (**d**). The **women's baths** include the waiting-room (**e**), the cloakroom (*apodyterium* – **f**), adorned with a mosaic pavement depicting Triton, the *tepidarium* (**g**) with a fine floor mosaic representing a labyrinth, and the *caldarium* (**k**).

★ **Casa del Mobilio carbonizzato** (**B**). – This small but rather elegant house has the remains of a charred (*carbonizzato*) bed in one room.

★★ **Casa del Mosaico di Nettuno e Anfitrite** – This house is equipped with a **shop**★; its counter opened onto the street. Mosaics depicting Neptune and Amphitrite adorn the nymphaeum.

★ **Casa del Bel Cortile** (**C**). – This is one of the most original houses in Herculaneum with its courtyard (*cortile*), stone staircase and balcony.

★ **Casa del Bicentenario** – This house was laid bare in 1938, two hundred years after digging officially started.
The house has fresco decorations and a small cross incorporated in a stucco panel. This is one of the oldest Christian relics which has been brought to light in the Roman Empire.

★★ **Pistrinum** – An inscription states that this bakery belonged to Sextus Patulus Felix. In the shop and back room may be seen flour mills, storage jars and a large oven.

★★ **Casa dei Cervi** – This rich patrician mansion, probably the most beautiful among those overlooking the bay, is adorned with numerous frescoes and works of art, including an admirable sculptured group of stags (*cervi*) being attacked by dogs.

★ **Terme Suburbane** – These baths, situated near the Sea Gate, are elegantly decorated.

★ **Teatro** – *Corso Resina*. The theatre could accommodate at least 2 000 spectators.

FABRIANO

Marches
Population 29 382
Michelin Map 430 L 20

The town of Fabriano has been famous since the 13C for its manufacture of paper. It was the birthplace of two delightful artists, **Allegretto Nuzi** (1320-73), the main exponent of the Fabriano School who was very much influenced by the Tuscans, and **Gentile da Fabriano** (c 1370-1427), one of the principal exponents of the International Gothic style and a point of reference for artists such as Pisanello and Jacopo Bellini. Unfortunately the town does not house any of his work.

★ **Piazza del Comune** – Characterised by its odd trapezoidal shape, the square is overlooked by the grim 13C Governor's Residence (**Palazzo del Podestà**), one of the finest examples of Medieval civic architecture in the Marches, the Bishop's Palace (Palazzo Vescovile) and by the town hall (Palazzo Comunale) with its adjacent Loggia of St Francis. At the centre of the square stands the *Sturinalto*, a fine Gothic fountain somewhat similar to the Fontana Maggiore in Perugia.

Piazza del Duomo – This peaceful and enchanting square is overlooked by the **Cathedral** dedicated to St Venanzo and decorated with frescoes by Allegretto Nuzi inside. Opposite stands the 15C ex-hospital Madonna del Buon Gesù which now houses an art gallery (**Pinacoteca Civica** ⊙). The gallery illustrates the evolution of painting in Fabriano from the 13C to 15C. There are two fine **wood sculptures**★ from the second half of the 14C, the *Adoration of the Magi* and the *Holy Representation* as well as a collection of tapestries.

★★ **Museo della Carta e della Filigrana** ⊙ – *Largo F.lli Spacca*. Housed in the ex-Convent of St Damian (15C) this is a lively museum which illustrates the manufacture of paper through the reconstruction of a fully operative Medieval workshop. The museum also has displays of antique Fabriano paper and an international collection of watermarked paper.

EXCURSIONS

★★ **Grotte di Frasassi** ⊙ – *15km/9mi northeast*. A tributary of the River Sentino has formed a vast network of underground caves (*grotte*). The largest, the **Grotta del Vento**, is composed of seven chambers where the visitor may admire stalagmites, stalactites and other diverse forms in a variety of colours.

FAENZA

Emilia-Romagna
Population 53 410
Michelin map 429, 430 J 17

Faenza has given its name to the ceramics known as **faïence**, which have been produced locally since the 15C. In Italy faïence is also known as majolica, because during the Renaissance Faenza potters were inspired by ceramics which were imported from Majorca in the Balearic Isles. Faenza ceramics feature fine clay, remarkable glaze, brilliant colours and a great variety of decoration.

An international competition and an international biennial of art ceramics bear witness to a vocation that is still strongly felt by artists and artisans.

A Late 15C plate
– Museo Internazionale delle Ceramiche

Museo Internazionale delle Ceramiche, Faenza

★★ Museo internazionale delle Ceramiche ⓥ – These vast collections present the development of ceramic-making throughout the world. On the first floor is a very fine collection of Italian Renaissance majolica, examples of the local ware, popular Italian pieces and an oriental section. On the ground floor, as well as the contemporary Italian collection, there are fine pieces by Matisse, Picasso, Chagall, Léger, Lurçat and the Vallauris school.

★ Pinacoteca comunale ⓥ – This important collection includes works by Giovanni da Rimini, Palmezzano, Dosso Dossi, Rossellino, and other canvases from foreign schools (portraits by Pourbus).

Cattedrale – The 15C cathedral was built by Florentine architect Giuliano da Maiano but the façade is unfinished. It contains the tomb (1471) of Bishop St Savinus by Benedetto da Maiano. In Piazza della Libertà stands a charming 17C baroque fountain.

Piazza del Popolo – The unusual elongated square has arcades surmounted by galleries. Around it are the 12C governor's house, Palazzo del Podestà and the 13C-15C Palazzo del Municipio.

FANO ⚏

Marches
Population 55 233
Michelin map 430 K 21

This town, now a favourite seaside resort, was ruled by the Malatesta family from Rimini in the 13C-15C.

★ Corte Malatestiana – This 15C Renaissance ensemble includes a courtyard-garden and palace, and it would make an ideal theatrical set. The palace houses a museum, **Museo civico** ⓥ with sections on archeology, coins and medals and 14C-18C sculpture and painting. The latter includes Guercino's well-known work, the *Guardian Angel* (1641).

S. Maria Nuova – 16C-18C. This contains **works★** by Perugino, which are admired for their fine draughtsmanship and their delicate colours: an exquisite *Madonna and Child* (1497) (third altar on the right) and a graceful *Annunciation* (1498) (second altar on the left).

Fontana della Fortuna – This fountain in Piazza XX Settembre presents the protecting goddess, Fortune, perched on a pivoting globe, with her billowing cloak acting as a weathervane.

Arco d'Augusto – *At the far end of the street of the same name.* This 1C arch has a main opening and two side ones for pedestrians. A low relief on the façade of the church of St Michael (San Michele) nearby portrays the arch in its original form. To the left of the arch are the remains of the Roman wall.

FERMO*

Marches

Population 35 466
Michelin map 430 M 23

Situated in a beautiful **setting★** at the foot of a hill looking out onto the surrounding countryside and sea, Fermo, a flourishing colony in Roman times, reached a peak of prosperity in the Middle Ages and Renaissance when it was enriched by the construction of numerous civic and religious monuments.

Currently Fermo's chief enterprise is shoemaking which has developed from a traditional craft into a fully fledged industry.

★ **Piazza del Popolo** – This square in the centre of town is surrounded by arcades and elegant 16C porticoes. It is bordered by numerous palaces including the 15C-16C **Palazzo dei Priori** (Prior's Palace) with a statue of Sixtus V (once the Bishop of Fermo) on its façade, the Palazzo degli Studi, at one time the university and now the municipal library, and opposite, Palazzo Apostolico.

Pinacoteca Civica ⊘ – The municipal art gallery is housed on the first floor of the Palazzo dei Priori and boasts a fine collection, mainly of art from the Veneto and Marches. The most notable works include *Lu Margutta* (16C), a Saracen wood sculpture used as a target in knights' tournaments, the elegant Late Gothic *Scenes from the Life of Saint Lucy*★ by Jacopello del Fiore (fl 1394-1439) and the *Adoration of the Shepherds*★★ by Rubens (1577-1640), probably one of the finest works produced by the artist during his sojourn in Italy. In the Map Room there is a fine **terraqueous globe** from the 18C.

Roman Cisterns ⊘ – *Via degli Aceti.* An imposing construction dating from the 1C AD comprised of 30 interconnecting chambers making up a total surface area of more than 2 000m² – 21 528 sq ft. These cisterns were used as a reservoir of water both for the city and the port.

Corso Cefalonia – The main street of the historic centre is lined with fine Renaissance buildings (Palazzo Azzolino, Palazzi Vitali Rosati) and by the 13C Matteucci Tower.

★ **Piazza del Duomo** – From this esplanade in front of the cathedral there are splendid **views★★** of the Ascoli area, the Apennines, the Adriatic and Conero Peninsula.

Duomo ⊘ – The Romanesque-Gothic cathedral (1227), built by *maestri comacini* has a majestic **façade★** in white Istrian stone. A delicately-carved doorway shows Christ with the Apostles on the lintel, and symbolic scenes or figures on the uprights. In the atrium, part of the old church, note the sarcophagus of Giovanni Visconti, Lord of the city in the 14C. The 18C **interior** has a fine Byzantine **icon** and a 5C AD **mosaic★** in which a peacock drinking from a vase symbolises the resurrection of Christ.

EXCURSION

Montefiore dell'Aso – *20km/12mi south.* The **collegiata** ⊘ in this pretty town possesses a masterpiece of Carlo Crivelli, a **polyptych★★**, which although incomplete, is finely chiselled and highlighted with gold representing six saints. The depiction of Mary Magdalene represents a high point in the career of this artist. The saint, richly apparelled in gold and silk brocade with a scarlet mantle symbolising the passion of Christ, moves gracefully holding the vessel of ointment,

Santa Maria a piè di Chienti ⊘ – *24km/15mi northwest.* This important Romanesque monument was founded in the 12C and subsequently remodelled on more than one occasion. The atmospheric **interior**, illuminated by the golden light of the alabaster windows, is divided into three aisles which open into an ambulatory with surrounding chapels of Cluniac influence. At the end of the 15C the raising of the presbytery created a second church whose apse is decorated with frescoes of the same period.

FERRARA★★

Emilia-Romagna
Population 133 270
Michelin map 429 H 16

In the heart of the fertile Po Plain, Ferrara is a tranquil town which is best explored in a leisurely manner, on foot or by bicycle. The streets are lined with red-brick houses, austere palaces and charming squares; their secret, melancholy atmosphere was a source of inspiration to the 20C metaphysical painters, De Chirico and Carrà. Ferrara, which was a splendid cultural centre during the Renaissance, remains one of the major artistic and cultural centres in Italy. In August the city hosts the **Buskers Festival**, during which street musicians and performers fill the town with a wide variety of entertainment.

A dynasty of patrons of the arts – Initially an independent commune, Ferrara belonged to the **Estensi** from 1208 to 1598, and despite numerous family dramas, often bloodthirsty, the Estes embellished their native city with fine buildings and patronised both men of letters and artists. **Niccolò III** (1393-1441) murdered his wife Parisina and her lover but he begat **Lionello** and **Borso**, moulding them into efficient administrators and enlightened patrons. **Ercole I** (1431-1505), who was responsible for his nephew's murder encouraged artists, as did his two famous daughters, Beatrice and Isabella d'Este. **Alfonso I** (1475 – 1534), the son of Ercole, became the third husband of Lucrezia Borgia, and Ercole II (1508-59) married Renée of France, the protector of the Calvinists.

After the demise of **Alfonso II** (1533-97) who left no heirs, Ferrara came under the rule of the Papacy and the Estes retired to the Duchy of Modena. Owing to the secular university (founded in 1391) and the patronage of the Este dynasty, the town witnessed a prodigious literary and artistic flowering. Three artists benefitted from the Estes' largesse: **Matteo Maria Boiardo** (1441-94), who wrote *Orlando Innamorata (Roland in love)*, **Ludovico Ariosto** (1474-1533) and **Torquato Tasso** (1544-95). **Ariosto** (1474-1533), who spent his lifetime in the service of the Estes, in particular with Alfonso I, produced one of the greatest masterpieces of Italian literature, *Orlando Furioso* (Roland the Mad). In relating the adventures of the knight Orlando and Angelica, the poet gives free reign to his imagination. **Tasso** (1544-95), a native of Sorrento, made several visits to Ferrara. During the first he wrote his epic poem *Gerusalemme Liberata* (Jerusalem Delivered) recounting the capture of Jerusalem by the Christians, enlivened by the love-story of Rinaldo and Armida.

The Ferrarese worshop – The leader of the Ferrarese school of painting (*officina ferrarese*) was **Cosmé Tura** (c 1430-95) with his strong personality, and its main characteristic was a meticulous realism, borrowed from the Northern schools. It was combined with a rather grim expressionism which derived from Mantegna, and powerful modelling reminiscent of Donatello. The main members were **Francesco del Cossa** (1435-77), who tempered the severity and the metallic sense of form of Tura and whose free and luminous style is evocative of Piero della Francesca; **Ercole de' Roberti** (1450-96), who conversely adopted Tura's strong modelling tradition; and **Lorenzo Costa** (1460-1535) who moved his studio to Bologna where prevailed the dark tones of the Umbrian and Tuscan schools. In the 16C the colourist **Dosso Dossi** and **Garofalo** favoured a greater harmony of colour in line with the Venetian style and allied to the classical tradition of Raphael and the Roman school.

OLD TOWN

★ **Castello Estense** ⊙ (BY **B**) – This massive castle, guarded by moats and four fortified gateways with drawbridges, was the seat of the Estes. The ground floor houses the spartan prison where Parisina and her lover were locked away. On the *piano nobile*, where the orangery is, visitors may view the Ducal Chapel collection and the apartments decorated with frescoes by the Filippi, active in Ferrara in the second half of the 16C.

★★ **Duomo** (BYZ) – The cathedral was built in the 12C in the Romanesque-Gothic Lombard style and presents a triple **façade★★** with a splendid **porch**. On the tympanum is depicted the *Last Judgement* recalling the decoration of French Gothic cathedrals and the lunette above the central door, the sculpture of St George, is by Nicholaus, an artist of the school led by the Romanesque master, Wiligelmo, who was responsible for the carved decoration of Modena cathedral. On the south side there are two tiers of galleries on the upper section; below is the Loggia dei Merciai, a portico oc-

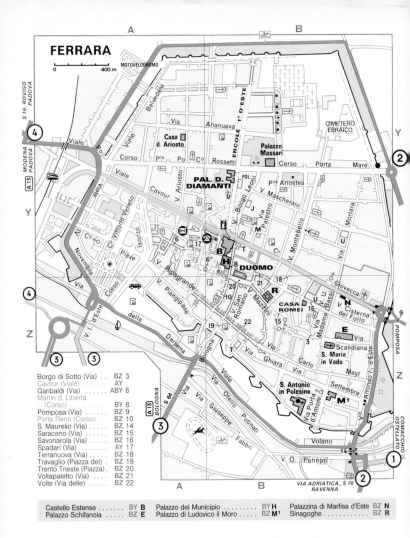

Borgo di Sotto (Via) . .	BZ 3
Cavour (Viale)	AY
Garibaldi (Via)	ABY 6
Martiri d. Libertà	
(Corso)	BY 8
Pomposa (Via)	BZ 9
Porta Reno (Corso) . .	BZ 10
S. Maurelio (Via)	BZ 14
Saraceno (Via)	BZ 15
Savonarola (Via)	BZ 16
Spadari (Via)	AY 17
Terranuova (Via)	BZ 18
Travaglio (Piazza del) .	BZ 19
Trento Trieste (Piazza) .	BZ 20
Voltapaletto (Via)	BZ 21
Volte (Via delle)	BZ 22

Castello Estense	BY B	Palazzo del Municipio	BY H	Palazzina di Marfisa d'Este	BZ N
Palazzo Schifanoia	BZ E	Palazzo di Ludovico il Moro	BZ M¹	Sinagoghe	BZ R

cupied by shops in the 15C. Here stood the Portal of the Months; the panels are kept in the cathedral museum. The bell-tower which was never completed was designed by Leon Battista Alberti. The semi-circular apse with its decorative brickwork is by Biagio Rossetti.

The interior, which was rebuilt in the 18C, contains a number of works of art. In the south arm of the transept note *The Martyrdom of St* Lawrence by Guercino and two 15C bronze statues (Saints Maurelius and George) and *The Last Judgement* by Bastianino on the vaulting in the apse.

The **Museo del Duomo**★ ☉ contains two statues by Jacopo della Quercia, the **panels**★★ of an organ painted by **Cosmé Tura** representing *St George slaying the Dragon* and *The Annunciation* and the admirable 12C **sculptures**★ from the Portal of the Month, admirable in their immediacy and close observation of reality (the finest example is the month of September).

The 13C town hall, **Palazzo del Municipio** (BY H), facing the cathedral, was once the ducal palace.

Medieval streets – Via San Romano (BZ), which is still a commercial artery, linked the market square (Piazza Trento e Trieste) and the port (now via Ripagrande). It is lined with several houses with porticoes, an unusual feature in Ferrara. **Via delle Volte** (BZ 22), which has a distinctive character, has become one of the symbols of the town. Covered alleyways *(volte)* linked the houses of the merchants and their warehouses, thus making more habitable space available.

Sinagoghe ☉ – The synagogue was a gift of the Roman banker, Ser Samuel Mele, in 1481 to the Jewish community. The building comprises three temples for different rites: the Italian and German tradition and that from Fano in the Marches.

★ **Palazzo Schifanoia** ☉ (BZ E) – This 14C palace is where the Estes used to come to relax (*schifanoia* means carefree). It now houses the municipal museum (**Museo Civico**). There are interesting archeological and Renaissance exhibits and splendid

The Jewish community of Ferrara

The Jewish community flourished in the 14C and 15C owing to the policy of the Estes, who welcomed Jews from Rome, Spain and Germany. The ghetto was instituted under Papal rule in 1624: five gates closed at dusk sealing off the area bounded by Via Mazzini, Vignatagliata e Vittoria. The gates were taken down under the new Italian Kingdom in 1859.

The Jewish community of Ferrara is portrayed in the novel, *The Garden of the Finzi-Contini*, by Giorgio Bassani, which was turned into an award-winning film in 1970 by Vittorio De Sica.

frescoes in the Room of the Months (**Salone dei Mesi★★**). This complex cycle to the glory of Borso d'Este unfortunately retains only some of the 12 months. The three levels illustrate three different themes, notably everyday life at court, astrology and mythology. Several artists, including Francesco del Cossa (March, April, May) and Ercole de' Roberti (September), worked under Cosimo Tura. The frescoes, which demonstrate an extraordinary delicacy when portraying detail and a marvellous vivacity in both the use of colour and draughtsmanship, attest to Ferrara's great cultural achievements during the Renaissance.

The palace houses a museum, the **Museo Civico di Arte Antica**, which displays archeological collections, medals, bronzes, marquetry and ivories. The museum is part of the **Lapidario** situated near a former church Santa Libera.

The 15C-16C church, **Santa Maria in Vado**, near the palace, is decorated inside with frescoes and paintings.

★ **Palazzina di Marfisa d'Este** ⊘ (BZ **N**) – This elegant single-storey residence (1559), formerly surrounded by loggias, pavilions and gardens, is where Marfisa d'Este entertained her friends, among whom was the poet Tasso. The interior is remarkable for the ornate ceiling decoration including grotesques, and elegant 16C-17C furniture. Pass into the garden to visit the Orangery (Loggia degli Aranci); the vault features a mock pergola complete with vine shoots and animals.

★ **Casa Romei** ⊘ (BZ) – This is a rare example of a 15C bourgeois residence combining late-Gothic features such as the decoration of the rooms on the ground floor (**Room of the Sibyls**, Room of the Prophets) and Renaissance elements like the portico of the **main courtyard**.

★ **Palazzo di Ludovico il Moro** ⊘ (BZ **M¹**) – The plans for this palace were designed at the end of the 15C by Biagio Rossetti but building was not completed. There is a fine arcaded courtyard and a **grand staircase** with interesting marble decorations. The first floor houses an **archeological museum** with an important collection of 5C-4C BC **Attic vases★** and burial accoutrements found at Spina, at one time one of the most important commercial ports in the Mediterranean. Spina was only brought to light in the 20C after an archeological "mystery" that lasted over 2 000 years and fascinated Boccaccio among others.

Sant'Antonio in Polesine ⊘ (BZ) – The convent founded in 1257 by Beatrice II d'Este, who joined the Benedictine order, stands in an isolated and peaceful setting.

The **church** has three chapels decorated with fine 14C-16C **frescoes★** by the Giotto and Emilian schools.

THE RENAISSANCE TOWN

In 1490 Ercole I d'Este commissioned **Biagio Rossetti** to extend the town to the north. The extension (**Addizione Erculea**) built around two main axes – Corso Ercole I d'Este and Corso Porta Pia, Bragio Rossetti and Porta Mare – is a great Renaissance town featuring parks and gardens. With this grandiose town-planning scheme Ferrara became the first modern city in Europe, according to the art historian, Jacob Burckhardt and in 1995 was included in UNESCO's World Heritage List.

★ **Corso Ercole I° d'Este** (BY) – The street lined with splendid Renaissance palaces but lacking any shops retains its original residential aspect. The focal point is the **Quadrivio degli Angeli** at the intersection with the other main axis, emphasised by three palaces with a rich angular decoration, including the Palazzo dei Diamanti.

★★ **Palazzo dei Diamanti** – The palace takes its name from the marble façade of 12 500 diamond bosses; the angle of the facets varies thus creating a distinctive picture. The palace was designed for a diagonal view: the central feature is therefore the corner embellished with **pilasters** and a balcony.

On the first floor is a gallery, the **Pinacoteca Nazionale★** ⊘, displaying paintings showing the development of the Ferrarese, Emilian and Venetian Schools from the 13C to 18C. Among the masterpieces are two **tondi** dedicated to San Maurelio by Cosmé Tura, a *Death of the Virgin* by the Venetian Carpaccio, a *Descent from the Cross* by Ortolano, an **altarpiece** by Garofalo and **frescoes** from churches in Ferrara. The Sacrati

FERRARA

Strozzi Collection includes paintings of the Muses **Erato** and **Urania** from Leonello d'Este's Studiolo in Palazzo di Belfiore which was situated near the present Corso Ercole I d'Este and was later dismantled when the town was under Papal rule.
At no 17 in Corso Ercole I d'Este a museum (Museo Michelangelo Antonioni) presents the pictorial and photographic work of the great Ferrarese film-director.

Palazzo Massari – This superb late-16C palace now houses the **Museo Boldini** ⓥ containing oils, pastels and drawings that are representative of the artist's development (1842-1931) during the time he spent in Ferrara, Florence and Paris. There are a few works by other artists from Ferrara, including Previati.

Casa dell'Ariosto ⓥ – *Via Ariosto no 67*. Ariosto's house is now a library but it still has the garden where the poet tended his roses and jasmine.

FIESOLE★

Tuscany
Population 14 959
Michelin map 430 K 15
See The Green Guide to Tuscany

The road from Florence winds uphill to Fiesole through olive-clad slopes, past luxuriant gardens and long lines of cypress trees, and affords views of this incomparable **countryside★★★**, so often depicted by the masters of the Italian Renaissance. The Etruscans founded this city in the 7C or 6C BC, strategically built high in the hills with a healthy climate. Fiesole was the most important city in northern Etruria and it dominated its neighbour and rival Florence until the 12C.

★ **Convento di S. Francesco** ⓥ – The climb up to the convent which starts in front of the Duomo offers a splendid **view★★** over Florence (from a small terrace about half-way up). This humble Franciscan convent, with its charming small cloisters, is admirably set on the hilltop.

★ **Duomo** – Founded in the 11C and enlarged in the 13C and 14C, the cathedral was extensively restored in the late 19C. The austere **interior★**, on a basilical plan with raised chancel, has columns supporting antique capitals. There are two handsome **works★** by the sculptor Mino da Fiesole.

Zona archeologica ⓥ – This archeological site, in its enchanting **setting★**, comprises a **Roman theatre★ (K)** (c 80 BC), which is still used for performances, a small **Etruscan temple (L)** and the remains of **baths (N)** built in the 1C BC by the Romans. The museum (**museo archeologico★** ⓥ) **(D)** exhibits finds dating from the Etruscan to the medieval period.

Antiquarium Costantini ⓥ **(A)** – Entrance near the archeological site. Fine collection of Greek and Etruscan vases. In the basement are the results of the archeological digs carried out on the museum site (Roman murals).

Museo Bandini ⓥ – *Opposite the entrance to the archeological site*. The museum houses a collection of 14C and 15C Tuscan paintings. Note, on the first floor, Petrarch's masterpiece *Triumphs* illustrated by Jacopo del Sellaio.

S. Domenico di Fiesole – *2.5km/1.5mi southwest. See the plan of the built-up area of Florence on Michelin map.430*. It was in this 15C church, remodelled in the 17C, that Fra Angelico took his vows. In the first chapel on the north side is a **Madonna and Saints★** by the artist. In the second chapel on the south is a **Baptism of Christ** by Lorenzo di Credi.

Badia Fiesolana – *3km/ 2mi southwest. See the plan of the built-up area of Florence on Michelin map 430*. This former Benedictine convent was partially rebuilt in the 15C thanks to the generosity of Cosimo the Elder who often stayed here. The Romanesque **façade★** of the original church, with its decorative green and white marble geometrical motifs, was incorporated in the new building, left unfinished on the death of Cosimo the Elder. The interior and cloisters are typical of Brunelleschi's style.

Antiquarium Costantini	A	Teatro romano	K
Museo archeologico	D	Tempietto etrusco	L
Palazzo Pretorio (Municipio)	H	Terme	N

156

FIRENZE★★★

FLORENCE – Tuscany
Population 379 687
Michelin map 430 K 15 (with plans of the conurbation)
See Michelin Green Guide Tuscany

Florence is without doubt the city where the Italian genius has flourished with the greatest display of brilliance and purity. For three centuries from the 13C to the 16C, the city was the cradle of an exceptional artistic and intellectual activity from which evolved the precepts which were to dictate the appearance of Italy at that time and also the aspect of modern civilisation throughout Europe. The main characteristics of this movement, which was later to be known as the **Renaissance**, were partly a receptivity to the outside world, a dynamic open-minded attitude which encouraged inventors and men of science to base their research on the reinterpretation of the achievements of ancient Rome, and on the expanding of the known horizons. The desire to achieve universality resulted in a multiplication of the fields of interest.

Dante was not only a great poet but also a grammarian and historian who did much research on the origins and versatility of his own language. He was one of Florence's most active polemicists. **Giotto** was not only a painter but also an architect. **Lorenzo the Magnificent** was the prince who best incarnated the spirit of the Renaissance. An able diplomat, a realistic politician, a patron of the arts as well as a poet himself, he regularly attended the Platonic Academy in the Medici villa at Careggi, where philosophers such as Marsilio Ficino and Pico della Mirandola and men of letters like Politian and others established the principles of a new humanism. This quest to achieve a balance between nature and order had its most brilliant exponent in **Michelangelo**, painter, architect, sculptor and scholar whose work typifies a purely Florentine preoccupation.

Florence is set in the heart of a serenely beautiful **countryside**★★★ which is bathed by a soft, amber light. The low surrounding hills are clad with olive groves, vineyards and cypresses which appear to have been harmoniously landscaped to please the human eye. Florentine architects and artists have variously striven to recreate this natural harmony in their works, whether it be the campanile of La Badia by Arnolfo di Cambio, or that of the cathedral by Giotto, the façade of Santa Maria Novella by Alberti or the dome of Santa Maria del Fiore by Brunelleschi. The pure and elegant lines of all these works of art would seem to be a response to the beauty of the landscape and the intensity of the light. The Florentine preoccupation with perspective throughout the Quattrocento (15C) is in part the result of this fascination for the countryside and that other great concern of the period, the desire faithfully to recreate what the eye could see.

This communion of great minds, with their varied facets and fields of interest, expressed a common desire to push their knowledge to the limits, and found in the flourishing city of Florence an ideal centre for their artistic and intellectual development. The city's artists, merchants, able administrators and its princely patrons of the arts all contributed to the creation of just the right conditions for nurturing such an intellectual and artistic community, which for centuries was to influence human creativity.

SOME TIPS FOR YOUR TRIP AND STAY

Getting there: train, car or plane?

By plane – Florence is served by Amerigo Vespucci airport (☏ 055 37 34 98).The city centre can be reached in about 20min by bus or taxi.

By car – Florence can be easily reached by car as it is a meeting point of several major roads: the A1 (Milan-Naples), the A11 (Florence-sea) and the fast Florence-Pisa-Livorno road.

By train – S. Maria Novella station is within easy walking distance of the historic centre. Taxis and public transport are available.

When you get to the city...

Getting around Florence – Walking is by far the best solution. Florence has an ancient urban structure with narrow streets full of innumerable scooters and cars driven by Florentines who are rather fast drivers. The one-way systems can be daunting if one doesn't know the city, traffic is often restricted to residents only and some car-parks are also open to residents only. It's therefore a good idea to leave your car at the car-parks (2 000L to 3 000L an hour) at Fortezza da Basso or S. Maria Novella station and then walk or take a bus .

Talking of buses... – A guideline of the main routes:
line 13 is the circular line for the Colli and piazzale Michelangiolo,
line 7 goes from the station to Fiesole.
line 10 goes from the station to Settignano.
line17B goes from the station to the youth hostel.
Tickets with one hour validity cost 1 500L, tickets valid for two hours cost
2 000L, a booklet of four tickets valid for one hour costs 5 800L, a tourist
ticket, valid for 24 hours, costs 6 500L.

To call a taxi... – You can dial ☎ 055 4242, 055 4390, or 055 4798.

Car rental – Cars can be rented at the airport or at offices in the city:
AVIS, borgo Ognissanti 128r, ☎ 055 21 36 29, 055 23 98 826.
ITALY BY CAR THRIFTY, borgo Ognissanti 134r, ☎ 055 28 71 61,
055 29 30 21.
EUROPCAR, borgo Ognissanti 53r, ☎ 055 23 60 072/3.
HERTZ, via Maso Finiguerra 23r, ☎ 055 23 98 205, 055 28 22 60.

Accommodation in Florence

Florence is not Venice, but they are similar when it comes to looking for
accommodation. Prices are an age-old problem in both cities and the relationship between quality and price often proves unfavourable for the visitor.
There are, however, alternatives for all tastes and budgets, although some are
recommended for the young and the flexible only. Listed below are some
suggestions, divided into different price ranges for further information, see
page 433 which refer to double rooms in hotels. It is advisable to find out about
current prices beforehand and to book as early as possible.
See map for hotel locations.

BUDGET

Youth hostels – There are three youth hostels: **Ostello Archi Rossi**, via Faenza
94r, ☎ 055 29 08 04, fax 055 23 02 601, **Ostello Villa Camerata**, viale Righi
2/4, ☎ 055 60 14 51, fax 055 61 03 00, **Ostello Santa Monaca**, via Santa
Monaca 6, ☎ 055 26 83 38, fax 055 28 01 85.

Camping – **Campeggio Italiani e Stranieri**, viale Michelangelo 80,
☎ 055 68 11 977, open from April to October, and **Campeggio Villa Camerata**,
viale A. Righi 2/4, ☎ 055 60 03 15.

Convents and monasteries – Several religious orders offer accommodation.
Prices are reasonable and the atmosphere serene. Find out when doors are
closed; understandably this is usually rather early.
Alfa Nuova-Missionari del Sacro Cuore – Via E. Poggi 6, ☎ 055 47 28 83.
Casa Madonna del Rosario-Suore Francescane dell'Immacolata – Via Capodimondo 44,
☎ 055 67 96 21.
Casa Regina del S. Rosario-Suore S. Filippo Neri – Via G. Giusti 35, ☎ 055 24 77 650,
055 29 89 18.
Casa SS. Nome di Gesù-Suore Francescane Missionarie – Piazza del Carmine 21,
☎ 055 21 38 56, 055 21 48 66.
Casa del SS. Rosario-Suore Domenicane – Via Guido Monaco 4, ☎ 055 32 11 71.
Istituto Gould-Tavola Valdese – Via dei Serragli 49, ☎ 055 21 25 76.
Istituto Oblate dell'Assunzione – Borgo Pinti 15, ☎ 055 24 80 582/3.
Istituto Pio X-Artigianelli – Via dei Serragli 106, ☎ 055 22 50 44, 055 22 50 08.
Istituto del Sacro Cuore-Religiose del Sacro Cuore – Viale Michelangelo 27,
☎ 055 68 11 872.
Istituto Salesiano dell'Immacolata – Via del Ghirlandaio 40, ☎ 055 66 34 33,
055 66 61 16.
Istituto San Francesco di Sales Conventino – Viale Ariosto 13, ☎ 055 22 41 90,
055 22 41 17.
Istituto San Giovanni Battista-Suore di San Giovanni Battista – Villa Merlo Bianco, via di
Ripoli 82, ☎ 055 68 02 394.
Istituto San Gregorio-Suore Mantellate Serve di Maria – Via Bonaini 9,
☎ 055 49 08 91.
Istituto Santa Caterina-Suore della Carità – Via Santa Caterina d'Alessandria 15,
☎ 055 49 53 41, 055 47 20 53.
Istituto Santa Chiara-Suore Terziarie Francescane – Borgognissanti 56,
☎ 055 21 59 15.
Istituto Sant'Angela-Suore Orsoline della Sacra Famiglia – Via Fra' Bartolomeo 56,
☎ 055 57 22 32.
Istituto Sant'Anna-Suore Figlie di San Francesco – Via Lanzi 41/43, ☎ 055 48 64 02.
Istituto Sant'Elisabetta-Suore di Sant'Elisabetta – Viale Michelangelo 46,
☎ 055 68 11 884.

Oasi del Sacro Cuore-Congregazione Figlie del Sacro Cuore – Via della Piazzola 4, ☎ 055 57 75 88.

Pensionato San Filippo Neri-Padri Filippini – Via dell'Anguillara 25, ☎ 055 21 13 31, 055 29 09 80.

Scolopium/Via Venezia 18b, ☎ 055 57 52 43.

Suore Oblate dello Spirito Santo – Via Nazionale 8, ☎ 055 23 98 202.

Villa Agape-Suore Stabilite della Carità – Via Torre del Gallo 8, ☎ 055 22 00 44.

Villa I Cancelli-Suore Orsoline – Via Incontri 21, ☎ 055 42 26 001.

Villa SS. Maria Assunta-Suore della Redenzione – Via delle Forbici 38, ☎ 055 57 76 90.

HOTELS

Alternatives in this price range are rather scarce. The following are recommended:

Residenza Hannah e Johanna - Via Bonifacio Lupi 14, ☎ 055 48 18 96, fax 055 48 27 21, 11 rooms. No credit cards accepted.

A pleasant hotel where great attention is paid to detail, to the extent that in some rooms there are niches full of books and magazines. Here, as in its "sister" residence, Residenza Johanna, breakfast is served on a tray in your room. This is an excellent address for its location (near Piazza S.Marco), atmosphere and reasonable prices.

Residenza Johanna *(off the map)* – Via delle Cinque Giornate 12, ☎ and fax 055 47 33 77, 6 rooms with air conditioning. No credit cards accepted. This small hotel, suitably for Florence, is both restrained and welcoming. It is clean and in a pleasantly secluded position, if a little far from the city centre (half an hour on foot). There is also the advantage of a gravel courtyard where you can park your car (a real privilege in Florence!). Breakfast is served in a do-it-yourself formula: everything you need is set out on a tray in your room.

OUR SELECTION

Villa Azalee - Viale Fratelli Rosselli 44, ☎ 055 21 42 42,055 28 43 31, fax 055 26 82 64, 24 rooms with air conditioning.

A patrician villa dating from 1860 converted into a hotel. Each room is decorated differently, but all are in the Florentine style. Guests will appreciate the garden and the drawing room with fireplace.

Hotel Villa Liberty - Viale Michelangelo 40, ☎ 055 68 10 581, 055 68 38 19, fax 055 68 12 595, e-mail: hotel.villa.liberty@dada.it 14 rooms and two suites with air conditioning.

A beautiful turn of the century house, set in the shade of Viale Michelangelo. This hotel will be enjoyed by guests who enjoy a *belle époque* atmosphere and prefer to stay at the gates of the city. There are echoes of the Art Nouveau style in the frescoes, the ceilings, the bedsteads, the *appliques* and the elegant stylised iris which is the leitmotif of the style from which the hotel takes its name ("Liberty" being the Italian equivalent of Art Nouveau).

TREAT YOURSELF

J and J – Via di Mezzo 20, ☎ 055 23 45 005, fax 055 24 02 82, e-mail: jandj@dada.it 14 rooms and 5 suites. with air conditioning. Credit cards accepted.

A hotel in a 17C building which has traces of frescoes on the walls. The decor reflects the age of the house and differs from room to room. There is a pretty courtyard where you can savour your breakfast.

In search of an authentic meal

TUSCAN TRATTORIE

For those who like a rustic atmosphere and genuine Tuscan food, l'**Acquacotta**, via dei Pilastri 51r, is homely and inexpensive.

Acqua al 2, in via della Vigna Vecchia, 40r (at the corner of via dell'Acqua).has a young crowd and a wide selection of first courses. It's always packed so remember to book!

Another address for typical Tuscan food is **Il Latini**, via dei Palchetti 6r.

For some wine tasting **Le volpi e l'uva** wine bar on the other side of the Arno, in Piazza De' Rossi, is also open for lunch.

The **Palle d'oro** trattoria, via Sant'Antonino, 43-45r, has good, reasonably priced food in pleasant surroundings and is much frequented by Florentines.

KOSHER FOOD

For those who adhere to a kosher diet, or simply to find out more about vegetarian kosher food (with klezmer music in the background), **Ruth's**, via Farini 2/A, is an agreeable restaurant in every sense (including the prices which are very reasonable). Booking is highly recommended.

LOOKING FOR A BOOK WHILE HAVING A SNACK

At the café-bookshop CIMA, in Borgo degli Albizi 37r, between the Bargello and the Duomo.

General information...

Tourist Offices – The Azienda di Promozione Turistica is in via Manzoni 16, fax 055 23 46 286 (information available only in writing), but information can also be obtained from the tourist offices in via Cavour 1r, ☎ 055 29 08 32, piazza Stazione, ☎ 055 21 22 45, Borgo Santa Croce 29r, ☎ 055 23 40 444.
APT on the Internet: http://www.firenze.turismo.toscana.it, e-mail: firenze@mail.turismo.toscana.it

24 hour pharmacies – These can be found at the railway station, ☎ 055 21 67 61, 055 28 94 35, in via dei Calzaiuoli 7r, ☎ 055 21 54 72, 055 28 94 90 and at the Santa Maria Nuova hospital.

Post and telephone – In via Pellicceria 3, a stone's throw away from piazza della Repubblica, telephone calls can be made paying for the cost of the units used after the call has been made. Another branch of the Poste is in via Pietrapiana 53/55.

Lost property – Go to via Circondaria 19 from 9am to 12pm except Sundays and public holidays, ☎ 055 32 83 942.

To immerse oneself in the Florentine way of life

GETTING AROUND BY BICYCLE

This is by far the best way of getting around Florence which is always beleaguered by traffic.
Some hotels rent out bicycles but to meet the needs of all cyclists there is an association in via S. Zanobi 120r/122r,called **Florence by bike**, Internet site: www.florencebybike.it Various types of bicycles can be rented and organised tours of the city by bike, with commentary on the sights by a tour leader, are also available.

WHAT THE FLORENTINES READ

The daily newspaper of Florence is *La Nazione*, which includes details of performances and events in the city.
For more information on what city life has to offer the *Firenze avvenimenti* guide, published monthly, is available at the information office in via Cavour 1r.

EATING OUT

Authentic Tuscan food and atmosphere can be found in *buche*, typical Tuscan restaurants which have been converted from existing cellars.

CAFÉS

In piazza della Repubblica, built at the end of the 19C in the area of the ancient forum, are *Le Giubbe Rosse*, which has been a literary café since 1890, and, opposite, *Paszkowski*, founded by a Polish general in 1846, which has a small live orchestra on the terrace, and, full of atmosphere, *Gilli*, dating from 1733.
In piazza della Signoria *Rivoire* is famous for its hot chocolate and has a beautiful 18C style interior, although it actually dates from 1882.
Giacosa, in via de' Tornabuoni 87r dates from 1800.

AN EVENING AT THE THEATRE

Florence is an art and music lover's city even at night, when plays and concerts animate its theatres. To find out what's on look in *La Nazione* and the pages on Florence in national daily newspapers or contact the theatres directly:
Comunale, corso Italia 12, ☎ 055 27 791
Della Pergola, via della Pergola 102/31, ☎ 055 247 96 51
Verdi, via Ghibellina 101, ☎ 055 21 23 20

HISTORICAL NOTES

The colony of Florentia was founded in the 1C BC by Julius Caesar on the north bank of the Arno at a spot level with the Ponte Vecchio. The veteran soldiers who garrisoned the colony controlled the Via Flaminia linking Rome to northern Italy and Gaul.

The Middle Ages – It was only in the early 11C that the city became an important Tuscan centre when Count Ugo, Marquis of Tuscany, took up residence here, and again towards the end of the same century when the Countess Matilda affirmed its independence. During the 12C Florence prospered under the influence of the new class of merchants who built such fine buildings as the baptistery and San Miniato. This period saw the rise of trades organised in powerful guilds *(arti)*, which soon became the ruling class when Florence became an independent commune. In the 13C one third of Florence's population was engaged in either the wool or the silk trades, both of which exported their products to the four corners of Europe and were responsible for a period of extraordinary prosperity. These tradesmen were ably supported by the Florentine moneyhouses which succeeded the Lombard and Jewish institutions, and themselves acquired a great reputation by issuing the first-ever bills of exchange and the famous florin, struck with the Florentine coat of arms. The latter was replaced in the late-15C by the Venetian ducat. The main banking families were the Bardi-Peruzzi who advanced huge sums to England at the beginning of the Hundred Years War; they were soon to be joined in the forefront by the Pitti, Strozzi, Pazzi and of course the Medici.

The Guelph cause – Despite its prosperity, Florence did not escape the internal strife between the Ghibellines who were partisans of the Holy Roman Emperor and the Guelphs who supported the Pope. The Guelphs at first had the advantage; but the Ghibellines on being driven out of Florence, having allied themselves with other enemies of Florence, notably Siena, regained power after the Battle of Montaperti in 1260. The Guelphs counter-attacked and retook Florence in 1266. Under their rule the physical aspect of the city changed considerably, notably with the destruction of the fortified tower houses built by the Ghibelline nobility. They created a republic and established government by a single individual or family; lordship *(signoria)* and committees which in Florence were known as *priori*. There then occurred a split between the Black Guelphs and the White Guelphs who opposed the Papacy. During this latter tragedy Dante, who supported the White Guelphs, was exiled for good in 1302. In 1348 the Black Death killed more than half the population and put an end to the period of internal strife.

A glorious era (15C) – Among the numerous wealthy families in Florence, it was the **Medici** who gave the city several leaders who exercised their patronage both in the sphere of fine arts and finance. The founder of this illustrious dynasty was Giovanni di Bicci, a prosperous banker who left his fortune in 1429 to his son **Cosimo the Elder**, who in turn transformed his heritage into the city's most flourishing business. He discreetly exercised his personal power through intermediaries, and astutely juggled his own personal interests with those of the city, which assured Florence a kind of peaceful hegemony. His chief quality was his ability to gather around him both scholars and artists, whom he commissioned for numerous projects.

Cosimo the Elder was a passionate builder and Florence owes many of her great monuments to this "Father of the Land". His son, Piero II Gottoso (the gouty) survived him by five years only and he in turn bequeathed all to his son **Lorenzo the Magnificent** (1449-92). Having escaped the Pazzi Conspiracy Lorenzo reigned like a true Renaissance prince, although it was always unofficially. He distinguished himself by his skilful politics and managed to retain the prestige of Florence amongst its contemporaries while ruining the Medici financial empire. This humanist and man of great sensitivity was a great patron of the arts, and he gathered around him poets and philosophers, who all contributed to make Florence the capital of the early Renaissance.

A turbulent period – On Lorenzo's death, which had repercussions throughout Europe, the Dominican monk **Savonarola**, taking advantage of a period of confusion, provoked the fall of the Medici. This fanatical and ascetic monk, who became the Prior of the Monastery of St Mark, preached against the pleasures of the senses and of the arts, and drove the citizens of Florence to make a "bonfire of vanities" in 1497 in Piazza della Signoria, on which musical instruments, paintings, books of poetry etc were burnt. A year later Savonarola himself was burnt at the stake on the same spot.

The Medici family returned to power with the help of the Emperor Charles V and they reigned until the mid-18C. **Cosimo I** (1519-74) brought back to Florence some of the splendour which she had lost, conquered Siena and he himself became Grand Duke of Tuscany. He continued the tradition of patron of the arts protecting numerous artists.

S. Chirol

Rooftops in Florence, surrounded by the tower of Palazzo Vecchio and Brunelleschi's reassuring dome

Francesco I (1541-87), whose daughter Maria was to marry Henri IV King of France, took as his second wife the beautiful Venetian Bianca Cappello. The last prominent Medici was Ferdinand I (1549-1609) who married a French princess, Christine de Lorraine.

After the Medici, the Grand Duchy passed to the House of Lorraine, then to Napoleon Bonaparte until 1814, before returning to the House of Lorraine until 1859. When it became part of the Italian Kingdom, Florence was capital from 1865 to 1870.

FLORENCE, CAPITAL OF THE ARTS

The relatively late emergence of Florence in the 11C as a cultural centre and its insignificant Roman heritage no doubt contributed to the growth of an independent art movement, which developed vigorously for several centuries. One of its principal characteristics was its preoccupation with clarity and harmony which influenced writers as well as architects, painters and sculptors.

Dante Alighieri (1265-1321) established the use of the Italian vernacular in several of his works, thus superseding Latin as the literary language. He made an admirable demonstration with his *New Life (Vita Nuova)*, recounting his meeting with a young girl Beatrice Portinari who was to be the inspiration for his **Divine Comedy** *(Divina Commedia)*, in which Dante, led by Virgil and then by Beatrice, visits the Inferno, Purgatory and Paradise. Dante's description of these infernal circles where the damned are chastised, of the mountain of Purgatory where great crowds await redemption, and finally the dazzling vision of the divine splendour of Paradise, have inspired for generations not only Italian writers but men of letters everywhere. In the 14C Dante was responsible for creating an exceptionally versatile literary language to which Petrarch *(see Index)* added his sense of lyricism and Boccaccio *(see Index)* the art of irony.

Machiavelli (1469-1527), born in Florence, was the statesman on whose account Machiavellism became a synonym for cunning; he recounted his experiences as a statesman in a noble and vigorous prose. He was the author of **The Prince** (Il Principe – 1513), an essay on political science and government dedicated to Lorenzo II in which he counselled that in politics the end justifies the means. **Francesco Guicciardini** (1483-1540) wrote an important history of Florence and Italy, while **Giorgio Vasari** (1511-74), much later, with his work *The Lives of the Most Eminent Italian Architects, Painters and Sculptors,* was the first real art historian. He studied and classified local schools of painting, tracing their development from the 13C with the work of Cimabue, whom even Dante had praised in his *Divine Comedy*.

The Florentine school had its origins in the work of **Cimabue** (1240-1302) and slowly it freed itself from the Byzantine tradition with its decorative convolutions, while **Giotto** (1266-1337) in his search for truth gave priority to movement and expression. Later **Masaccio** (1401-28) studied spatial dimension and modelling. From then on perspective became the principal preoccupation of Florentine painters, sculptors, architects and theorists who continually tried to perfect this technique.

The Quattrocento (15C) saw the emergence of a group of artists like **Paolo Uccello** (1397-1475), **Andrea del Castagno** (1423-57), **Piero della Francesca** *(see Index)* a native of the Marches, who were all ardent exponents in the matters of foreshortening and the strictly geometrical construction of space; while others such as **Fra Angelico** (1387-1455), and later **Filippo Lippi** (1406-69) and **Benozzo Gozzoli** (1420-97) were imbued with the traditions of International Gothic *(see ART: GOTHIC PERIOD)* and were more concerned with the visual effects of arabesques and the appeal of luminous colours. These opposing tendencies were reconciled in the harmonious balance of the work of **Sandro Botticelli** (1444-1510), whom Florence is proud to claim as a son. He took his subjects from antiquity as the humanists in the court of Lorenzo de' Medici recommended, and he invented fables peopled by enigmatic figures with subtle linear forms, which created an impression of tension. At times a certain melancholy seems to arrest the movement and dim the luminosity of the colours. Alongside Botticelli the **Pollaiuolo** brothers, **Ghirlandaio** (1449-94) and **Filippino Lippi** (1457-1504) ensure the continuity and diversity of Florentine art.

The High Renaissance with its main centres in Rome and other northern towns reached Florence in the 16C. **Leonardo da Vinci** *(see Index)*, **Michelangelo** *(see Index)* and **Raphael** *(see Index)*, all made their debut at Florence, and inspired younger Mannerist

The Procession of the Magi by Benozzo Gozzoli
(detail showing Lorenzo the Magnificent),
Palazzo Medici Riccardi

artists such as **Pontormo, Rosso Fiorentino, Andrea del Sarto** (1486-1530) and the curious portraitist of the Medici, **Bronzino** (1503-72).

The emergence of a Florentine school of painting is, however, indissociable from the contemporary movement of the architects who were creating a style, also inspired by antiquity, which united the classical traditions of rhythm, a respect for proportion and geometric decoration. The constant preoccupation was with perspective in the arrangement of interiors and the design of façades. **Leon Battista Alberti** (1404-72) was the theorist and grand master of such a movement. However it was **Filippo Brunelleschi** (1377-1446) who best represented the Florentine spirit, and he gave the city buildings which combined both rigour and grace, as in the magnificent dome of Santa Maria del Fiore which has become the symbol of Florence.

Throughout the Quattrocento (15C), buildings were embellished with admirable sculptures which became a harmonious part of the architectural whole. The doors of the baptistery were the object of a competition in which the very best took part. If **Ghiberti** (1378-1455) was finally victorious, **Donatello** (1386-1466) was later to provide ample demonstration of the genius of his art, so full of realism and style, as did **Luca della Robbia** (1400-82) and his dynasty who specialised in glazed terracotta decoration, **Verrocchio** (1435-88) and numerous other artists who adorned the ecclesiastical and secular buildings of Florence. In the 16C **Michelangelo**, who was part of this tradition, confirmed his origins with his New Sacristy (1520-55) of San Lorenzo, which he both designed and decorated with sculpture. Later **Benvenuto Cellini** (1500-71), Giambologna or **Giovanni Bologna** (1529-1608) and **Bartolomeo Ammannati** (1511-92) maintained this unity of style which was responsible for the exceptional beauty of the city of Florence.

SIGHTSEEING

Florence is such an important art centre that it takes at least four days to see the main sights. These are, however, situated fairly closely together in the city centre which is not adapted to heavy traffic. It is therefore advisable to do the sightseeing on foot and establish a visiting programme which takes into account the opening times.

★★★ PIAZZA DEL DUOMO (EU) *1/2 day*

In the city centre, the cathedral along with the campanile and baptistery, form an admirable group of white, green and pink marble monuments, which demonstrate the traditions of Florentine art from the Middle Ages to the Renaissance.

★★ Duomo (S. Maria del Fiore) ⊙ – One of the largest cathedrals in the Christian world, the Duomo is a symbol of the city's power and wealth in the 13C and 14C. It was begun in 1296 by Arnolfo di Cambio and was consecrated in 1436.

This essentially Gothic cathedral is an outstanding example of the Florentine variant of this style, with its sheer size, the predominance of horizontal lines and its polychrome decoration.

Exterior – Walk round the cathedral starting from the south side to admire the marble mosaic decoration and the sheer size of the **east end★★★**. The harmonious **dome★★★** by Brunelleschi took 14 years to build. To counteract the excessive thrust he built two concentric domes which were linked by props. The façade dates from the late 19C.

Interior – The bareness of the interior contrasts sharply with the sumptuous decoration of the exterior. Enormous piers support sturdy arches which themselves uphold the lofty Gothic vaulting. The great octagonal **chancel★★** under the dome is surrounded by a delicate 16C marble balustrade. The dome is painted with a huge **fresco** of the Last Judgement. It is possible to go up to the inner gallery which offers an impressive view of the nave, and then climb to the **top of the dome** ⊙ (464 steps) for a magnificent **panorama★★** of Florence.

The sacristy doors on either side of the high altar have tympana adorned with pale blue terracottas by Luca della Robbia representing the Resurrection and the Ascension. In the new sacristy (left), there are inlaid armorial bearings by the Maiano brothers (15C).

A dramatic episode of the **Pazzi Conspiracy** took place in the chancel. The Pazzi, who were rivals of the Medici, tried to assassinate Lorenzo the Magnificent on 26 April 1478, during the Elevation of the Host. Lorenzo, though wounded by two monks, managed to take refuge in a sacristy, but his brother Giuliano fell to their daggers. The axial chapel contains a masterpiece by Ghiberti, the sarcophagus of St Zanobi, the first Bishop of Florence. One of the low reliefs shows the saint resurrecting a child. The frescoes in the north aisle include: in the first bay near the choir, one showing Dante explaining the *Divine Comedy* to the city of Florence (1465); further along to the right, two equestrian portraits of leaders of mercenary armies *(condottieri)* by Paolo Ucello (1436) and Andrea del Castagno (1456).

A stairway on the other side of the nave, between the first and second pillars, leads to the **Crypt of Santa Reparata**, the only remaining part of a Romanesque basilica which was demolished when the present cathedral was built. The basilica itself was formerly an early Christian church (5C-6C). Excavations have revealed traces of mosaic paving belonging to the original building and Brunelleschi's tomb (behind the railing-enclosed chamber, at the bottom of the stairs, on the left).

★★★ Campanile ⊙ (EU B) – The tower is tall (82m/269ft) and slender and is the perfect complement to Brunelleschi's dome, the straight lines of the former balancing the curves of the latter. Giotto drew the plans for it and began building in 1334, but died in 1337.

The Gothic campanile was completed at the end of the 14C; its geometric decoration with its emphasis on horizontal lines is unusual. The admirable low reliefs at the base of the campanile have been replaced by copies. Those on the lower band were executed by Andrea Pisano and Luca della Robbia and those on the upper band by pupils of Andrea Pisano, but the overall design was by Giotto. The original low reliefs are in the Cathedral Museum.

From the top of the campanile (414 steps) there is a fine **panorama★★** of the cathedral and town.

★★★ Battistero ⊙ (EU A) – The baptistery is faced in white and green marble in a sober and well-balanced Romanesque style. The **bronze doors★★★** are world-famous.

The south door *(entrance)* by Andrea Pisano (1330) is Gothic and portrays scenes from the life of St John the Baptist *(above)*, as well as the Theological Virtues (Faith, Hope, Charity) and the Cardinal Virtues *(below)*. The door-frames which show great skill are by Vittorio Ghiberti, son of the designer of the other doors. The north door (1403-24) was the first done by Lorenzo Ghiberti. He was the winner of a competition in which Brunelleschi, Donatello and Jacopo della Quercia also took part. Scenes from the Life of Christ are evoked with extraordinary nobility and harmony of composition.

The east door (1425-52), facing the cathedral, is the one that Michelangelo declared worthy to be the **Gate of Paradise**. In it Ghiberti recalled the Old Testament; prophets and sibyls adorn the niches. The artist portrayed himself, bald and malicious, in one of the medallions.

Interior – With its 25m/82ft diameter, its green and white marble and its paving decorated with oriental motifs, the interior is grand and majestic. The dome is covered with magnificent **mosaics★★★** of the 13C. The Last Judgement is depicted on either side of a large picture of Christ the King; on the five concentric bands that cover the other five panels of the dome, starting from the top towards the base, are the Heavenly Hierarchies, Genesis, the Life of Joseph, scenes from the Life of the Virgin and of Christ, and the Life of St John the Baptist.

On the right of the apse is the tomb of the Antipope John XXIII, friend of Cosimo the Elder, a remarkable work executed in 1427 by Donatello assisted by Michelozzo.

Under the 14C Gothic **Loggia del Bigallo** (**EU G**) to the south of the baptistery, lost or abandoned children were exhibited.

★★ **Museo dell'Opera del Duomo** ⊘ (**EU M⁵**) – The museum contains items from the cathedral, campanile and baptistery; note models of Brunelleschi's dome on the ground floor. On the mezzanine is the famous **Pietà★★** which Michelangelo left unfinished. In the large room on the first floor are two famous statues by **Donatello** – an impressive repentant **Magdalene★** carved in wood, and the prophets Jeremiah and Habakkuk, the latter being nicknamed *Zuccone* (vegetable marrow) because of the shape of his head.

In the same room are the famous **Cantorie★★**, choristers' tribunes from the cathedral, by Luca della Robbia and Donatello. The museum also houses the famous silver **altarpiece★★** depicting the life of St John the Baptist, a 14C-15C masterpiece and the admirable **low reliefs★★** from the campanile: those by Andrea Pisano and Luca della Robbia depict scenes from the Book of Genesis and various human activities.

★★ **PIAZZA DELLA SIGNORIA**
1 day

★★ **Piazza** – This was, and still is, the political stage of Florence, with a wonderful backcloth formed by the Palazzo Vecchio, the Loggia della Signoria and in the wings the Uffizi Museum. The many statues make it virtually an open-air museum of sculpture: near the centre of the square, the equestrian statue of Cosimo I, after Giovanni Bologna, and at the corner of the Palazzo Vecchio, the Fountain of Neptune (1576) by Ammannati. In front of the Palazzo Vecchio are copies of the proud *Marzocco* or *Lion of Florence* by Donatello and Michelangelo's *David*.

A copy of Michelangelo's *David*, Piazza della Signoria

R. Leslie

★★ **Loggia della Signoria** (**EU K**) – The Loggia, built at the end of the 14C, was the assembly hall and later the guardroom of the Lanzi (foot soldiers) of Cosimo I. It contains ancient (Classical) and Renaissance statues: the *Rape of a Sabine* (1583), *Hercules and the centaur Nessus* by Giovanni Bologna and the wonderful **Perseus★★★** holding up the severed head of Medusa, a masterpiece executed by Benvenuto Cellini from 1545 to 1553.

★★★ **Palazzo Vecchio** ⊘ (**EU H**) – The Old Palace's powerful mass is dominated by a lofty bell-tower, 94m/308ft high. Built from 1299 to 1314 probably to plans by Arnolfo di Cambio, it is in a severe Gothic style without any openings at ground level, a series of twinned windows above and battlements, parapet walk and crenellations on top with the tower.

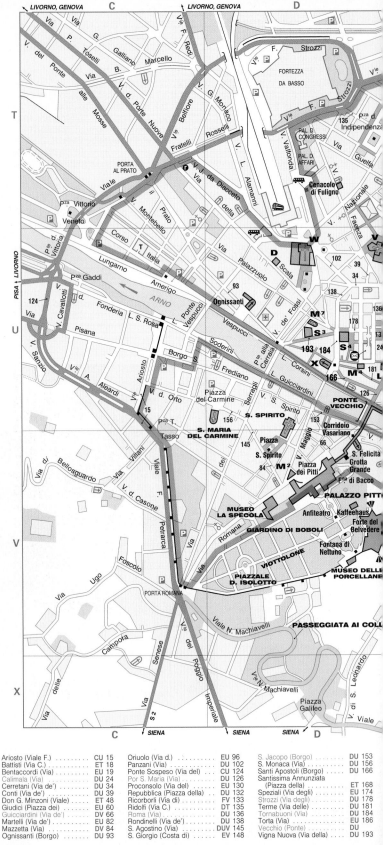

Ariosto (Viale F.)	. . . .	CU 15
Battisti (Via C.)	. . . .	ET 18
Bentaccordi (Via)	. . . .	EU 19
Calimala (Via)	. . . .	DU 24
Cerretani (Via de')	. . . . . .	DU 34
Conti (Via de')	. . . .	DU 39
Don G. Minzoni (Viale)	. . . .	ET 48
Giudici (Piazza dei)	. . . . .	EU 60
Guicciardini (Via de')	. . . . .	DV 66
Martelli (Via de')	. . . .	EU 82
Mazzetta (Via)	. . . .	DV 84
Ognissanti (Borgo)	. . . . . .	DU 93

Oriuolo (Via d.)	. :	EU 96
Panzani (Via)	. . . .	DU 102
Ponte Sospeso (Via del)	. . .	CU 124
Por S. Maria (Via)	. . . .	DU 126
Proconsolo (Via del)	. . . . .	EU 130
Repubblica (Piazza della)	. . .	DU 132
Ricorborli (Via di)	. . . .	FV 133
Ridolfi (Via C.)	. . . .	DT 135
Roma (Via)	. . . .	DU 136
Rondinelli (Via de')	. . . . . .	DU 138
S. Agostino (Via)	. . . .	DUV 145
S. Giorgio (Costa di)	. . . . .	EV 148

S. Jacopo (Borgo)	. . . .	DU 153
S. Monaca (Via)	. . . .	DU 156
Santi Apostoli (Borgo)	. . . . .	DU 166
Santissima Annunziata		
(Piazza della)	. . . .	ET 168
Speziali (Via degli)	. . . .	EU 174
Strozzi (Via degli)	. . . .	DU 178
Terme (Via delle)	. . . .	DU 181
Tornabuoni (Via)	. . . .	DU 184
Torta (Via)	. . . .	EU 186
Vecchio (Ponte)	. . . .	DU
Vigna Nuova (Via della)	. . . .	DU 193

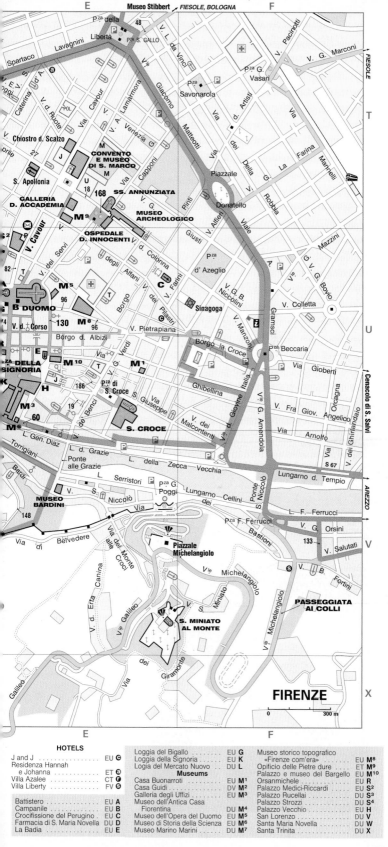

FIRENZE

HOTELS

J and J	EU ⓖ
Residenza Hannah e Johanna	ET ❾
Villa Azalee	CT ❼
Villa Liberty	FV ❺

Battistero	EU A
Campanile	EU B
Crocifissione del Perugino	EU C
Farmacia di S. Maria Novella	DU D
La Badia	EU E

Loggia del Bigallo	EU G
Loggia della Signoria	EU K
Logia del Mercato Nuovo	DU L
Museums	
Casa Buonarroti	EU M¹
Casa Guidi	DV M²
Galleria degli Uffizi	EU M³
Museo dell'Antica Casa Fiorentina	DU M⁴
Museo dell'Opera del Duomo	EU M⁵
Museo di Storia della Scienza	EU M⁶
Museo Marino Marini	DU M⁷

Museo storico topografico «Firenze com'era»	EU M⁸
Opificio delle Pietre dure	ET M⁹
Palazzo e museo del Bargello	EU M¹⁰
Orsanmichele	EU R
Palazzo Medici-Riccardi	EU S²
Palazzo Rucellai	DU S³
Palazzo Strozzi	DU S⁴
Palazzo Vecchio	EU H
San Lorenzo	DU V
Santa Maria Novella	DU W
Santa Trinita	DU X

The refinement and splendour of the Renaissance interior is a complete contrast. The **courtyard**★ was restored by Michelozzo in the 15C and decorated in the following century by Vasari. The 16C fountain is surmounted by a delightful winged goblin, a copy of a work by Verrocchio (the original is housed in the palace). Initially the seat of government (Palazzo della Signoria), the palace was then taken over in the 16C by Cosimo I as his private residence, as it was better suited to accommodating his large court. Most of the redecoration work done by Giorgio Vasari dates from this period. When Cosimo I abandoned the palace in favour of the Pitti Palace it was renamed Palazzo Vecchio. The apartments were lavishly decorated with sculptures by Benedetto and Giuliano da Maiano (15C) and with paintings by Vasari and Bronzino (16C) to the glory of Florence and the Medici.

On the first floor the great Sala dei Cinquecento, painted with frescoes by several artists including Vasari, contains a group carved by Michelangelo, *The Genius of Victory*. The walls of the magnificent **studiolo**★★ or study of Francesco de' Medici, which was designed by Vasari, were painted by Bronzino, who was responsible for the medallion portraits of *Cosimo I* and *Eleanora of Toledo*. Leo X's apartment was decorated by Vasari and his assistants with scenes illustrating episodes of the Medici history.

On the second floor, Cosimo I's apartments are open to the public. They are known as the Apartment of the Elements because of the allegories decorating the first chamber. The decoration was designed by Vasari around the theme of ancient mythology.

Beyond these chambers are Eleonora of Toledo's apartments, again designed by Vasari with the exception of the chapel which is decorated with frescoes by Bronzino. Finally, in the apartments of the Priors of the Arts, the best-known chamber is the Chamber of Lilies **(Sala degli Gigli★)** which has a magnificent coffered **ceiling** by Guiliano da Maiano and the dressing-room **(Sala del Guardaroba★)** lined with 16C maps.

★★★ GALLERIA DEGLI UFFIZI ◷ (EU M³)

This is one of the finest art museums in the world. These collections were assembled by several generations of Medici and the visitor can follow the evolution of Italian art from its beginnings to the 17C.

The early nucleus was gathered together by Francesco I (1541-87) to which were added the collections of the Grand Dukes Ferdinand I, II and Cosimo III. In 1737 the last member of the Medici dynasty, Anna Maria Luisa, Electress Palatine, bequeathed the Medici collection to her native city of Florence.

The Uffizi Museum was then housed in the Renaissance palace, designed by Vasari in 1560, which contained the offices *(uffizi)* of the Medici administration.

Pallas, possibly symbolising Lorenzo il Magnifico, *tames the Centaur*, by Botticelli

The rich collections of drawings and paintings are on the first floor; paintings and sculpture are exhibited in 45 rooms which are linked by two galleries on the second floor.

Galleries – The first gallery *(east)* is essentially dedicated to Florentine and Tuscan artists: there are works by Cimabue, Giotto, Duccio, Simone Martini (the **Annunciation**, a masterpiece of Gothic art), Paolo Uccello **(Battle of San Romano)** and Filippo Lippi. The **Botticelli Room**★★★ houses the artist's major works: the allegories of the **Birth of Venus** and **Spring** and the **Madonna with Pomegranate**. Other exhibits in the gallery include the **Adoration of the Magi** and the **Annunciation** by Leonardo da Vinci and a series of Italian and foreign paintings from the 15C and 16C (Perugino, Cranach, Dürer, Bellini, Giorgione, Correggio etc).

The first 11 rooms of the second gallery *(west)* contain works from the Italian Cinquecento (16C): **Tondo Doni** by Michelangelo, *Madonna and the Goldfinch* and **Leo X** by Raphael, **Madonna and the Harpies** by Andrea del Sarto, **Urbino Venus** by Titian and **Leda and the Swan** by Tintoretto. The other rooms are dedicated to both Italian and foreign paintings from the 17C and 18C: included in the collection are **Isabella Brandt** by Rubens, Caravaggio's **Adolescent Bacchus** and works by **Claude Lorrain** and **Rembrandt**.

★★ PONTE VECCHIO (DU)

As its name suggests, this is the oldest bridge in Florence. It has been rebuilt several times and spans the narrowest point of the Arno. Its orginal design includes a line of jewellers' shops and the **Corridoio Vasariano**, a passageway which was built by Vasari to link the Palazzo Vecchio to the Pitti Palace and passes overhead.

ALTITUDE

The Ponte Vecchio: shop windows and the Corridoio Vasariano overlook the Arno

★★ PALAZZO PITTI (DV)

This 15C Renaissance building, of rugged but imposing appearance, with pronounced rustication and many windows, was built to the plans of Brunelleschi for the Pitti family, the rivals of the Medici. It was Cosimo I's wife, Eleanora di Toledo, who enlarged the palace by the addition of two wings. The court moved to the palace in 1560.

★★★ Galleria Palatina ⊙ – *First floor*. This gallery houses a marvellous collection of paintings: **groups★★★** of works by Raphael (*Portrait of a Lady* or **La Velata**, **Madonna del Granduca** and **Madonna della Seggiola**) and Titian (portraits of **La Bella**, **The Aretino**, **The Concert** and the **Grey-eyed Nobleman**).

On the first floor are the State Apartments (**Appartamenti reali★** ⊙) The building also houses a modern art gallery (**Galleria d'Arte Moderna★** ⊙) which mainly displays Tuscan works from the 19C and 20C. The section devoted to the **Macchiaioli** movement *(see INDEX)* is represented by an exceptional **series★★** by Fattori, Lega, Signorini, Cecioni. This wing also houses a Costume Museum (**Galleria del Costume**) ⊙ *(access by lift located near the ticket office)* which displays Italian costumes dating from the 18C to the present day. In the other wing is the Silver Museum (**Museo degli Argenti★★** ⊙) presenting items largely from the Medici collections.

★ GIARDINO DI BOBOLI ⊙ (DV)

This Italian-style terraced garden, behind the Pitti Palace, was designed in 1549 by Tribolo and is ornamented with antique and Renaissance statues. At one end of an avenue to the left of the palace is the **grotta grande**, a grotto created in the main by Buontalenti (1587-97). Cross the amphitheatre to reach the highest point of the garden from which, on the right, the **Viottolone★**, an avenue of pines and cypresses, runs down to **Piazzale dell'Isolotto★**, a circular pool with a small island, planted with citrus trees and adorned with a fountain by Giovanni Bologna. A pavilion houses a Porcelain Museum (**Museo delle Porcelane★** ⊙). A fort (**Forte del Belvedere**), at the top of the hill, affords a splendid **panorama★★** of Florence and the celebrated Florentine countryside. The elegant villa which dominates the bastion was designed by Buontalenti.

SCALA

Michelangelo: the vestibule of the Biblioteca Laurenziana

★★★ PALAZZO E MUSEO NAZIONALE DEL BARGELLO ⊙ (EU M¹⁰)

This austere palace was formerly the residence of the governing magistrate *(podestà)* and then became police headquarters *(bargello)*. It is a fine example of 13C-14C medieval architecture planned round a majestic **courtyard★★** with a portico and loggia. The Volognona tower (57m/188ft) soars above the building. The palace is now a museum of sculpture and decorative arts with particularly good sections on Italian and Florentine Renaissance sculpture.

The rooms on the ground floor are devoted to the works of 16C Florentine sculptors: *Brutus* and the *Pitti Tondo* (a marble medallion depicting the Virgin and Child with St John) by Michelangelo; **low reliefs** from the pedestal of the Perseus bronze by Benvenuto Cellini.

There is an exceptional collection *(first floor)* of **sculpture★★★** by **Donatello** which includes his *Marzocco* (the Florentine heraldic lion), the bronze *David*, as well as the low relief of *St George* from Orsanmichele.

The rooms on the second floor display terracottas by Giovanni and Andrea della Robbia and works by **Verrocchio**, including the famous bronze statue of *David*.

★★★ S. LORENZO (DU V)

This was the Medici family parish church near the Medici Palace, and it was here that most of the family was buried. The **church★★** was begun by Brunelleschi c 1420. The interior is a perfect example of the sobriety of style introduced by **Brunelleschi** and typical of his thoughtful, measured, rigorous architectural style and its human dimension.

His great achievement is the **Old Sacristy★★** *(at the far end of the north transept)*. Donatello was responsible for part of the decoration of the latter and also the two **pulpits★★** in the nave with bronze panels, which are works of admirable virtuosity and full of a great sense of drama.

★★ Biblioteca Medicea Laurenziana – Cosimo the Elder's library was added to by Lorenzo the Magnificent. Access is from the north aisle of the church or through the charming 15C **cloisters★** ⊙ *(entrance to the left of the church)*. The vestibule was designed as an exterior and is occupied by a magnificent **staircase★★**, supremely elegant as the curved steps of the central flight lead up to the library proper. The staircase was built by Ammannati to Michelangelo's designs. The **library**, also by Michelangelo, displays in rotation some of the 10 000 manuscripts.

★★ Cappelle Medicee ⊙ – *Entrance on Piazza Madonna degli Aldobrandini.* The Medici Chapels include the Princes' Chapel and New Sacristy.

The **Princes' Chapel** (17C-18C), grandiose but gloomy, is faced with semi-precious stones and marbles and is the funerary chapel for Cosimo I and his descendants. The **New Sacristy** was Michelangelo's first architectural work and despite its name was always intended as a funerary chapel. Begun in 1520, it was left unfinished

Cellini:
Cosimo I de' Medici
(Bargello)

Luca Della Robbia:
Madonna col Bambino
(Bargello)

Donatello: *David* (Bargello)

Michelangelo: Sacrestia Nuova di S. Lorenzo, tomba di Lorenzo de' Medici, duca di Urbino

SCALA

when the artist left Florence in 1534. Michelangelo achieved a great sense of rhythm and solemnity by using contrasting materials, dark grey sandstone (*pietra serena*) and the white of the walls and marbles.

The famous **Medici tombs**★★★ were also the work of Michelangelo. Giuliano, Duke of Nemours (d 1516), is portrayed as Action, surrounded by allegorical figures of Day and Night; and Lorenzo II, Duke of Urbino (d 1519), as a Thinker with Dawn and Dusk at his feet.

Of the plans for Lorenzo the Magnificent's tomb only the admirable group of the Madonna and Child flanked by saints was completed. In the plain tomb underneath lie Lorenzo the Magnificent and his brother Giuliano.

★★ PALAZZO MEDICI-RICCARDI ⓥ (EU S²)

This noble but austere building is typical of the Florentine Renaissance with its mathematical plan and rustication, massive at ground level and lighter on the upper level. The palace which has a square arcaded courtyard was begun in 1444 by Michelozzo on the orders of his friend Cosimo the Elder.

From 1459 to 1540 it was a Medici residence, and Lorenzo the Magnificent held court here, attended by poets, philosophers and artists alike. In the second half of the 17C the palace passed to the Riccardi who made extensive alterations to the building.

★★★ **Chapel** – *First floor: entrance by the first stairway on the right in the courtyard.* This tiny chapel was decorated with admirable **frescoes** (1459) by Benozzo Gozzoli. *The Procession of the magi* is a vivid picture of Florentine life with portraits of the Medici and of famous dignitaries from the East who had assembled for the Council of Florence in 1439.

★★ **Luca Giordano Gallery** – *First floor: entrance by the second stairway on the right in the courtyard.* The entire roof of this gallery built by the Riccardi at the end of the 17C and splendidly decorated with gold stucco, carved panels and great painted mirrors, is covered by a brightly-coloured baroque fresco of the Apotheosis of the second Medici dynasty, masterfully painted by Luca Giordano in 1683.

★★ S. MARCO ⓥ (ET)

The museum in a former Dominican monastery, rebuilt c 1436 in a very plain style by Michelozzo, is virtually the **Fra Angelico Museum**★★★. Fra Angelico took orders in Fiesole before coming to St Mark's, where he decorated the walls of the monks' cells with edifying scenes. Humility, gentleness and mysticism were the qualities expressed by this artistic monk in a technique influenced by the Gothic tradition. His refined use of colour, delicate draughtsmanship and timid handling of the subject-matter imbued these frescoes with a pacifying power, particularly appropriate for this oasis of calm and place of meditation.

The former guest hall, opening off the cloisters on the right, contain many of the artist's works on wood, especially the triptych depicting the *Descent from the Cross*, the famous *Last Judgement* and other religious scenes. The chapter-house has a severe *Crucifixion* while the refectory contains an admirable *Last Supper*★ by Ghirlandaio.

The staircase leading to the first floor is dominated by his well-balanced and sober masterpiece, the *Annunciation*. The monks' cells open off three corridors, with lovely timber ceilings. Along the corridor to the left of the stairs are the *Apparition of Christ to the Penitent Magdalene (1st cell on the left)*, the *Transfiguration (6th cell on the left)* and the *Coronation of the Virgin (9th cell on the left)*.

At the far end of the next corridor are the cells of Savonarola, who was prior of St Mark's. Off the corridor on the right is the library★, one of Michelozzo's finest achievements.

★★ GALLERIA DELL'ACCADEMIA ⓥ (ET)

The museum gives the visitor some idea of the extraordinary personality of Michelangelo and the conflict between the nature of his raw materials and his idealistic vision. The **main gallery**★★★ contains the powerful figures of *Four Slaves* (1513-20) and *St Matthew* (all unfinished) who would seem to be trying to struggle free from the marble. At the far end of the gallery, in a specially designed apse (1873), is the monumental figure of *David* (1501-04), the symbol of youthful but well-mastered force and a perfect example of the sculptor's humanism. The **picture gallery**★ has works by 13C-15C Tuscan masters, including a painted chest by Adimari and two Botticellis.

★★ S. MARIA NOVELLA ⓥ (DU W)

The Church of Santa Maria Novella and the adjoining monastery were founded in the 13C by the Dominicans. The church overlooks an elongated square which was originally the setting for chariot races.

The **church**★★, begun in 1279, was completed only in 1360, except for the façade, with harmonious lines and geometric patterns in white and green marble, which was designed by Alberti (upper section) in the 15C.

It is a large church (100m/328ft) designed for preaching. On the wall of the third bay in the north aisle is a famous **fresco**★★ of the Trinity with the Virgin, St John and the donors in which Masaccio, adopting the new Renaissance theories, shows great mastery of perspective. At the far end of the north transept, the Strozzi di Mantora Chapel (raised) is decorated with **frescoes**★ (1357) by the Florentine Nardo di Cione depicting the Last Judgement on a grand scale. The **polyptych**★ on the altar is by Nardo's brother, Orcagna di Cione. The sacristy contains a fine **Crucifix**★ *(above the entrance)* by Giotto and a delicate glazed terracotta **niche**★ by Giovanni della Robbia.

In the Gondi Chapel *(first on the left of the high altar)* is displayed the famous **Crucifix**★★ by Brunelleschi, which so struck Donatello that he is said, on first seeing it, to have dropped the basket of eggs he was carrying.

The chancel is ornamented with admirable **frescoes**★★★ by **Domenico Ghirlandaio** who, on the theme of the Lives of the Virgin and of St John the Baptist, painted a dazzling picture of Florentine life in the Renaissance era.

The church is flanked by two cloisters. The finest are the Green Cloisters (**Chiostro Verde**★ ⊘), so-called after the dominant colour of the frescoes painted by Paolo Uccello and his school (scenes from the Old Testament). Opening off these to the north is the Spaniards' Chapel (**Cappellone degli Spagnoli**) with late-14C **frescoes**★★ by **Andrea di Bonaiuto** (also known as Andrea da Firenze). With an intricate symbolism the frescoes depict the Church Triumphant and the glorification of the action of the Dominicans. To the east is the refectory which houses the church's treasure.

★★ S. CROCE ⊘ (EU) *1hr*

The church and cloisters of Santa Croce give onto one of the town's oldest squares. This is the church of the Franciscans. It was started in 1294 and completed in the second half of the 14C. The façade and the campanile date from the 19C.

The **interior** is vast (140m by 40m/460ft x 130ft) as the church was designed for preaching and consists of a single spacious nave and slender apse with fine 15C stained glass windows. The church is paved with 276 tombstones and along the walls are ornate tombs.

South aisle: By the first pillar, a *Virgin and Child* by A Rossellino (15C); opposite, the tomb of Michelangelo (d 1564) by Vasari; opposite the second pillar, the funerary monument (19C) to Dante (d 1321, buried at Ravenna); by the third pillar, a fine **pulpit**★ (1476) by Benedetto da Maiano and facing it the monument to V. Alfieri (d 1803) by Canova; opposite the fourth pillar, the 18C monument to Machiavelli (d 1527); facing the fifth pillar, an elegant low relief of the *Annunciation*★★ carved in stone and embellished with gold by Donatello; opposite the sixth pillar, the **tomb of Leonardo Bruni**★★ (humanist and chancellor of the Republic, d 1444) by B. Rossellino, and next to it the tomb of Rossini (d 1868).

South transept: At the far end, the Baroncelli Chapel with **frescoes**★ (1338) depicting the Life of the Virgin by Taddeo Gaddi and at the altar the **polyptych**★ of the Coronation of the Virgin from Giotto's studio.

★ Sacristy ⊘ *(access by the corridor on the right of the chancel):* This dates from the 14C and is adorned with **frescoes**★ including a Crucifixion by Taddeo Gaddi and, in the fine Rinuccini Chapel, with scenes from the Life of the Virgin and of Mary Magdalene by Giovanni da Milano (14C). At the far end of the corridor is the harmonious Medici Chapel (1434) built by Michelozzo, with a fine **altarpiece**★ in glazed terracotta by Andrea della Robbia.

Chancel: The first chapel to the right of the altar contains evocative **frescoes**★★ (c1320) by Giotto depicting the life of St Francis; in the third chapel is the tomb of Julie Clary, the wife of Joseph Bonaparte. The chancel proper is covered with **frescoes**★ (1380) by Agnolo Gaddi relating the legend of the Holy Cross.

North transept: At the far end is a famous *Crucifixion*★★ by Donatello, which Brunelleschi tried to surpass at Santa Maria Novella.

North aisle *(coming back):* Beyond the second pillar, a fine **monument to Carlo Marsuppini**★ by Desiderio da Settignano (15C); facing the fourth pillar the tombstone of L. Ghiberti (d 1455); the last tomb (18C) is that of Galileo (d 1642).

★★ Cappella dei Pazzi ⊘ – *At the far end of the first cloisters; entrance to the right of the church.* This chapel by Brunelleschi is entered through a domed portico, and is a masterpiece of the Florentine Renaissance remarkable for its original conception, its pure, rigid lines, its skilful proportions and the harmony of its decoration (glazed terracotta from the Della Robbia workshop).

Great cloisters – *Entrance at the far end of the first cloisters, on the right.* These very elegant cloisters were designed by Brunelleschi shortly before his death (1446) and were completed only in 1453.

Museo dell'Opera di Santa Croce ⊘ – The museum is installed in the buildings around the first cloister and in particular in the former refectory. The museum contains a famous *Crucifixion*★ by Cimabue which was seriously damaged by the 1966 floods which particularly affected Santa Croce.

★★ PASSEGGIATA AI COLLI
2 hours on foot or 1 hour by car.

For a drive to the hills take the road to the east along the south bank of the Arno to the medieval tower in Piazza Giuseppe Poggi. Poggi laid this fine road to the hills from 1865 to 1870. Take the winding pedestrian street to Piazzale Michelangiolo for a splendid **view★★★** of the whole city.

Not far from here, in a splendid **setting★★** overlooking the town, the Church of **S. Miniato al Monte★★**, built from the 11C to 13C, is one of the most remarkable examples of Florentine Romanesque architecture. Its very elegant façade is decorated with geometric designs in green and white marble, not unlike those of the baptistery. The harmonious interior also ornamented with multicoloured marble contains a 13C pavement. The **Chapel of Cardinal James of Portugal★** opening out of the north aisle is a fine Renaissance structure. In the centre of the nave is a Chapel of the Crucifix by Michelozzo. The pulpit and chancel screen *(transenna)* form a remarkable **ensemble★★** beautifully inlaid with marble (early 13C). In the apse is a mosaic depicting Christ giving His Blessing. The **frescoes★** (1387) in the **sacristy** are by Spinello Aretino. The 11C **crypt** has delicate columns with antique capitals.

IF YOU STILL HAVE TIME...

★★ Frescoes of S. Maria del Carmine (DU) – In the **Cappella Brancacci** ⊘ is a fresco cycle (1427) by **Masaccio** depicting Original Sin and the Life of St Peter. It was finished by Filippino Lippi.

La Badia (EU E) – 10C church of a former abbey *(badia)* with an elegant **campanile★**. The interior has a sumptuous coffered **ceiling★★** and houses several works of art including Filippino Lippi's *Virgin appearing to St Bernard★*, a delicate **relief★★** sculpture in marble by Mino da Fiesole and the **tombs★** carved by the same artist.

★ Casa Buonarroti ⊘ (EU M¹) – Michelangelo Buonarroti owned this house although he never lived here. There are several of the sculptor's works on display inside (*Battle of the Centaurs* and *Madonna della Scala*).

Cenacolo di S. Apollonia ⊘ (ET) – In the former refectory hangs a *Last Supper★* by **Andrea del Castagno**.

★ Cenacolo di San Salvi ⊘ – *east of Florence* FU. The former refectory of the abbey contains a splendid **fresco★★** of the Last Supper (1520) by **Andrea del Sarto**.

Ognissanti (DU) – This church was built in the 13C and remodelled in the 17C. Inside are fine frescoes by Botticelli *(St Augustine)* and Ghirlandaio *(St Jerome)*. The latter is also responsible for the *Last Supper★* in the refectory adjacent to the church.

★ S. Spirito (DUV) – The church was built from 1444 onwards to plans by Brunelleschi. It contains fine **works of art★**.

S. Trinita (DU X) – The **Cappella dell'Annunziazione★** in this church is decorated with frescoes by Lorenzo Monaco *(Life of the Virgin)*; those in the **Capella Sassetti★★** are by Ghirlandaio *(Life of St Francis)*.

★ Loggia del Mercato Nuovo (DU L) – This gallery (loggia) with its elegant Renaissance arcades was built in the 16C in the heart of the commercial district. It now serves as a market for Florentine crafts.

★★ Museo Archeologico ⊘ (ETU) – The museum has an important collection of Egyptian, Greek (**François vase★★**, found in an Etruscan tomb but of ancient origin), Etruscan (**Arezzo Chimera★★**, a 5C BC masterpiece) and Roman art.

★★ Museo della Casa Fiorentina Antica ⊘ (DU M⁴) – Artefacts and furniture evoke the life of a rich Florentine family of the period. The museum is housed in **Palazzo Davanzati**, a tall medieval-style 14C building with an inner courtyard.

Museo Marino Marini ⊘ (DU M⁷) – Displayed in this museum are works of the famous Florentine sculptor and painter who died in 1980.

★ Museo di Storia della Scienza ⊘ (EU M⁶) – Presentation of a rich collection of scientific instruments including the lens used by the mathematician and astronomer Galileo.

★ Opificio delle Pietre dure ⊘ (ET M⁹) – Lorenzo the Magnificent was responsible for reviving the ancient tradition of decorating with semi-precious stones in the form of mosaics *(pietre dure)*. This workshop now specialises in restoration work and there is a small **museum**.

★ Orsanmichele (EU R) – Originally a grain storehouse, Orsanmichele was rebuilt in the 14C. There are works by Donatello, Ghiberti, Verrocchio etc. Inside, there is a splendid Gothic **tabernacle★★** by Orcagna.

★★ **Palazzo Rucellai** (DU S³) – The palace was designed by Leon Battista Alberti and built in the 15C. The façade is the first cohesive example of the three ancient orders placed one on top of the other.

★★ **Palazzo Strozzi** (DU S⁴) – The building dates from the end of the 15C and is one of the finest palaces in Florence with its rusticated stonework, cornice and arcaded courtyard.

★ **Piazza della SS. Annunziata** (ET **168**) – This fine piazza is enhanced by Giambologna's equestrian statue of Ferdinando I de'Medici and two baroque fountains.

SS. Annunziata – The church dates from the 15C. In the chancel are some fine **frescoes**★ by Rosso Fiorentino and Pontormo which were completed by Francia-bigio. The interior is in the Baroque style; the north arm of the transept gives access to the Renaissance Cloister of the Dead **(Chiostro dei Morti)**. The vault by the door is adorned with the *Madonna with the Sack*★ by Andrea del Sarto (16C).

★ **Ospedale degli Innocenti** – Brunelleschi's **portico**★★ is decorated by terracotta **medallions**★★ by Andrea della Robbia. The Foundlings' Hospital houses a **gallery** ⊙ displaying Florentine works.

EXCURSIONS

See the plan of the conurbation on Michelin Map 430.

★ **Ville Medicee** – In the 15C and 16C, the Medici built several elegant villas throughout the Florentine countryside.

★ **Villa La Petraia** ⊙ – *3km/2mi north.* In 1576 Cardinal Ferdinand de' Medici commissioned the architect Buontalenti to convert this former castle into a villa. In the 16C **garden**, there is a remarkable fountain by N. Tribolo with a bronze statue of Venus by Giovanni Bologna.

★ **Villa di Castello** ⊙ – *5km/3mi north in Castello.* This villa was embellished by Lorenzo the Magnificent and restored in the 18C. It has a very fine garden adorned with statues and fountains.

★★ **Villa di Poggio a Caiano** ⊙ – *17km/11mi north by the Pistoia road, the S 66.* Sangallo designed this villa for Lorenzo the Magnificent. The loggia is decorated by the Della Robbia. The magnificent drawing-room has a coffered ceiling and **frescoes** by Pontormo representing Vertumnus and Pomona, gods of orchards and fruit.

★★ **Villa La Ferdinanda** – *26km/16mi west in Artimino.* This villa was commissioned from Buontalenti by Grand Duke Ferdinand I at the end of the 16C. Its many chimneys, its double spiral stairway and its magnificent setting overlooking the Arno valley give it a striking appearance. It houses a **museum of Etruscan archaeology** ⊙.

★★ **Certosa del Galluzzo** ⊙ – *6km/4mi south by the Siena road.* The grandiose Carthusian monastery was founded in the 14C and underwent successive alterations until the 17C. The adjoining palace contains frescoes by Pontormo. The monks' cells are grouped around the Renaissance **cloisters**.

The great centres of Renaissance art: Florence, Rome, Siena, Padua, Venice, Milan, Parma, Perugia.

FORLÌ

Emilia-Romagna
Population 107 461
Michelin map 429 or 430 J 18
Town plan in the Michelin Atlas Italy

Forlì is set on the Via Emilia and it was an independent commune ruled by an overlord in the 13C and 14C. The citadel was heroically defended in 1500 by Caterina Sforza against Cesare Borgia.

Basilica di S. Mercuriale – *Piazza Aurelio Saffi.* The basilica is dominated by an imposing Romanesque campanile. The lunette of the doorway is adorned with a 13C **low relief**. The numerous works of art inside include several paintings by Marco Palmezzano and the tomb of Barbara Manfredi by Francesco di Simone Ferrucci.

Pinacoteca ⊙ – *72 Corso della Repubblica.* The art gallery includes works by local 13C-15C artists. There is a delicate *Portrait of a Young Girl* by Lorenzo di Credi.

EXCURSIONS

Cesena - *19km/12mi southeast by the Via Emilia.* The town lies at the foot of a hill on which stands the great 15C castle of the Malatestas. It contains the Renaissance library, **Biblioteca Malatestiana**★ ⊙ *(Piazza Bufalini).* The interior of the library comprises three long aisles with vaulting supported on fluted columns capped with fine capitals. On display are valuable manuscripts, including some from the famous school of miniaturists at Ferrara, as well as the Missorium, a great silver-gilt plate probably dating from the 4C.

Bertinoro - *14km/9mi southeast.* This small town is famous for its panorama and its yellow wine (Albana). In the middle of the town is a "hospitality column" fitted with rings, each corresponding with a local home. The ring to which the traveller tethered his horse would determine which family should be his hosts. From the nearby terrace there is a wide **view**★ of Romagna.

Abbazia di FOSSANOVA★★

FOSSANOVA Abbey – Lazio
Michelin map 430 R 21

Standing, as the rule prescribes, in a lonely site, the Cistercian abbey of Fossanova is the oldest of the Order in Italy. Monks from Cîteaux in France settled here in 1133. In 1163 they began to build their abbey church, which was to serve as a model for many Italian churches (Casamari for instance). Although rather heavily restored, Fossanova has kept its original architecture and plan intact. It was designed in accordance with the rules of austerity laid down by St Bernard. The buildings are laid out to suit the activities of the monks and lay-brothers.

Church ⊙ – The church (consecrated in 1208) is in the Burgundian style but such decoration as there is recalls the Lombard tradition with traces of the Moorish style. As regards the exterior, the Latin cross plan with flat east end, the octagonal transept crossing tower, the rose windows and the triple-bayed window of the east end are typically Cistercian. The well-lit and lofty interior has a central nave balanced by aisles with groined vaulting.

Cloisters - These are picturesque with three Romanesque sides and the fourth or south side in the late-13C pre-Gothic style (transitional Romanesque Gothic style). The small columns are Lombard in form and decoration. The fine Gothic chapterhouse opens into the cloisters through wide twin bays. It was in the guest house, which stands apart, that the teacher and scholar St Thomas Aquinas died on 7 March 1274.

GAETA★

Lazio
Population 22 911
Michelin map 430 S 22

This former fortress, still partly walled, is admirably sited on the point of a promontory bounding a beautiful **bay**★. The coastal road round the bay affords magnificent views. Gaeta has a pleasant beach of fine sand, Serapo Beach, facing south.

Duomo – The cathedral is interesting, especially for its 10C and 15C Romanesque Moorish campanile adorned with glazed earthenware and resembling the Sicilian or Amalfi bell-towers. Inside, the late-13C **paschal candelabrum**★ is remarkable for its size and for its 48 low reliefs depicting scenes from the Lives of Christ and St Erasmus, the protector of sailors.
A picturesque medieval quarter lies near the cathedral.

Castello – The castle, dating from the 8C, has been altered many times. The lower castle was built by the Angevins, while the upper one was the work of the Aragonese.

Monte Orlando ⊙ – Standing on the summit is the tomb of the Roman Consul Munatius Plancus (Mausoleo di Lucio Muniazio Planco), a friend of Caesar who founded the colonies of Lugdunum (Lyons) and Augusta Raurica (Augst near Basle).

EXCURSION

⌂ **Sperlonga** - *16km/10mi northwest.* The village stands on a rocky spur, pitted with many caves, up in the Aurunci mountains.

Grotta di Tiberio e Museo Archeologico. ⊙ - The cave *(grotta)* lies below the Gaeta-Terracina road *(left after the last tunnel).* It was in this cave that the Emperor Tiberius narrowly escaped death when part of the roof fell in.
In the **museum**, by the roadside, there are 4C-2C BC statues, outstanding heads and busts and some realistic theatrical masks. There is also a reconstruction of a colossal group depicting the punishment meted out to the Cyclops Polyphemus by Ulysses.
At the Gaeta end of the tunnel are the charred ruins of Tiberius' Villa.

Promontorio del GARGANO★★★

GARGANO Promontory – Puglia

Michelin map 431 B-C 28-30

The Gargano Promontory, shining white under a blue sky, projects like a spur from the "boot" of Italy. It is one of the most attractive natural regions of Italy with its wide horizons, its deep and mysterious forests and its lonely, rugged coastline. This paradise for amateurs of sun and sea is marred by one drawback: most of the beaches and bays are private as they belong to camping sites and hotels and are not easily accessible.

Geologically, Gargano is quite independent from the Apennine Mountains; it is a limestone plateau fissured with crevices into which water runs. Originally an island, Gargarno was connected to the mainland by an accumulation of deposits brought down by the rivers from the Apennines. Today the massif is riven by high-altitude valleys, with fertile valley floors, and is heavily afforested in the east. The scanty pastures and moors on the plateaux support flocks of sheep and goats and herds of black pigs. The picturesque islands, the **Isole Tremiti** *(see Isole TREMITI)* belong to the same geological formation.

TOUR

Leave from Monte Sant'Angelo and follow the itinerary indicated on the local map (146km/91mi – allow 1 day).

★ **Monte Sant'Angelo** – *See MONTE SANT'ANGELO.*

★★ **Foresta Umbra** – Forests are rare in Apulia and this vast expanse of venerable beeches, elders, pines, oaks, chestnuts, linden trees as well as ancient yews, covers over 11 000ha/24 958 acres of undulating countryside. Visitors are welcome and the forest is well equipped with recreational facilities. Shortly after the turning to Vieste there is a forestry lodge (Casa Forestale) which now serves as a **visitor centre**.

⌂⌂ **Peschici** – Well-situated on a rocky spur jutting out into the sea, this fishing town is now a seaside resort.

⌂⌂ **Vieste** – In a similar setting to Peschici, this small but ancient town, crowded on the clifftop, is dominated by its 13C cathedral. In the town centre there is an interesting Shell Museum (**Museo Malacologico**) ⊙ displaying a large collection of shell from all over the world. To the south is a vast sandy beach with a limestone sea-stack, **Faraglione di Pizzomunno**, standing offshore. Between Vieste and Mattinata there is a very fine **scenic stretch★★** of corniche road, overlooking the indented coastline. After 8km/5mi the square tower in **Testa del Gargano** marks the easternmost extremity of the massif: fine **view★** of the inlet, **Cala di San Felice**, which is spanned by a natural arch at the seaward end. Beyond the popular holiday resort of **Pugnochiuso**⌂⌂, there is another beauty spot, the Bay of Zagare (**Baia delle Zagare★**).

⌂⌂ **Mattinata** – From the road running down towards Mattinata there is a fine **view★★** of this agricultural market town, a white mass amid a sea of olive groves encircled by a rim of mountains.

The chapter on art and architecture in this guide gives an outline of artistic creation in Italy, providing the context of the buildings and works of art described in the Sights section.

This chapter may also provide ideas for touring.

It is advisable to read it at leisure/before setting out.

GENOVA★★

GENOA – Liguria
Population 659 754
Michelin map 428 I 8 (with plans of the conurbation)
See La RIVIERA local map

Genoa the superb, the greatest seaport in Italy, spreads over a mountain amphitheatre. It is a city of surprises and contrasts, where the most splendid palaces stand side by side with the humblest alleyways, known as *carruggi*.

HISTORICAL NOTES

Genoese expansion was based on a strong fleet, which already in the 11C ruled supreme over the Tyrrhenian Sea, having vanquished the Saracens. By 1104 the fleet already comprised 70 ships, all built in the famous dockyards, making it a formidable power much coveted by foreign rulers such as the French Kings, Philip the Fair and Philip of Valois.

The Crusaders offered the Genoese an opportunity of establishing trading posts on the shores of the Eastern Mediterranean. Following the creation of the Republic of St George in 1100, seamen, merchants, bankers and money lenders united their efforts to establish the maritime supremacy of Genoa.

Initially Genoa allied itself with Pisa in the struggle against the Saracens (11C) and then became her enemy in a conflict concerning Corsica (13C). Finally it became the most persistent rival of that other great maritime republic, Venice (14C), disputing with her the trading rights for the Mediterranean. Genoa had colonies as far afield as the Black Sea.

In the 14C the Genoese merchant seamen controlled the trade in precious cargoes from the Orient; in particular they had the monopoly in the trading of alum used in the dyeing trade to fix colours.

Limited partnership companies flourished. Founded in 1408 the famous Bank of St George, grouping the maritime state's lending houses, administered the finances of the trading posts. The merchants became ingenious money lenders and instituted such modern methods as bills of credit, cheques and insurance to increase their profits.

Following continual struggles between the rival families of Genoa the decision was taken in 1339 to elect a doge for life and to seek, essentially in the 15C, foreign protection.

In 1528 the great admiral **Andrea Doria** (1466-1560) gave Genoa its aristocratic constitution which gave it the status of a mercantile republic. The enterprising and independent Andrea was one of Genoa's most famous sons: he was an admiral, a legislator and an intrepid and wise leader who distinguished himself against the Turks in 1519 and, while serving François I, by covering the French retreat after their defeat at Pavia (1525). In 1528, indignant at François I's unjust treatment of him, he entered the service of Charles V, who plied him with honours and favours. Following his death and the development of ports on the Atlantic coast, Genoa declined as a port and it was Louis XIV who destroyed the harbour in 1684. In 1768 by the Treaty of Versailles Genoa surrendered Corsica to France. Later, under the leadership of Giuseppe Mazzini, it became in 1848 one of the cradles of the Risorgimento (*see Index*).

Fine Arts in Genoa – As in many countries, the decline of commercial prosperity in the 16C and 17C coincided with intense artistic activity, evidenced in the building of innumerable palaces and the arrival at Genoa of foreign artists, especially the Flemish. In 1607 Rubens published a work on the *Palazzi di Genova* (Palaces of Genoa) and from 1621 to 1627 Van Dyck painted the Genoese nobility. Puget lived at Genoa from 1661 to 1667, working for patrician families such as the Dorias and the Spinolas.

The art of the Genoese school, characterised by dramatic intensity and the use of muted colours, is represented by Luca Cambiaso (16C), Bernardo Strozzi (1581-1644), the fine engraver Castiglione, and especially **Alessandro Magnasco** (1667-1749) whose sharp and colourful brushwork marks him out as a precursor of modern art.

GIRAUDON

Andrea Doria by Sebastiano del Piombo

In the field of architecture, Galeazzo Alessi (1512-72), when at his best, was the equal of Sansovino and Palladio in the nobility and ingenuity of his designs when integrating isolated buildings in the existing urban landscape.

STAYING IN GENOVA

Art bus (linea 10) – To discover Genova by bus, AMT has provided this route that takes in the most interesting parts of the city. Departure from piazza Caricamento. Regular ticket (valid 90 min) or one-day tourist ticket (5 000L). ☎ 010 59 82 414.

Where to sleep?

For a full selection of hotels in Genova consult this year's Michelin Red Guide Italia. Listed below are some addresses chosen on the basis of good value for money, location and *charm*. To locate an address on the city map see map coordinates in brackets. Hotels are divided into three categories based on the price of a double room *(for more information see p. 433)* and are listed in alphabetical order *(to locate them see map)*. For about ten days in October, when the **Salone Nautico Internazionale** exhibition is on, maximum tariffs are applied.

It is advisable to check prices by telephone and to book well in advance, especially in more reasonably priced hotels which tend to have fewer rooms.

BUGDET

Albergo Cairoli – Via Cairoli, 14/4. ☎ 010 24 61 454, fax 010 24 67 512. 12 rooms. Credit cards accepted. A small, very simply decorated hotel on the third floor (with lift) of a building in the historic centre near via Garibaldi.

OUR SELECTION

Hotel Europa – Via Monachette 8 *(take via Balbi -* EX*)*. ☎ 010 24 63 537, fax 010 26 10 47. 38 rooms with air conditioning. Credit cards accepted. Parking. Situated in a tiny side street off Via Balbi, this hotel is a few metres away from the Genova Principe railway station.

Hotel Galles – Via Bersaglieri d'Italia 13 *(take via A. Gramsci or via Balbi -* EX*)* ☎ 010 24 62 820, fax 010 24 62 822. 20 rooms with air conditioning. Credit cards accepted. Close to the Genova Principe railway station, this is an excellent solution if you are arriving in Genova by train and want to stay in the city centre.

TREAT YOURSELF!

Hotel Bristol – Via XX settembre 35. ☎ 010 59 25 41, fax 010 56 17 56. 128 rooms, 5 suites, air conditioning. Credit cards accepted. Situated in a patrician late 19C *palazzo* this hotel is furnished with antiques.

Restaurants and excursions

UNDER 50 000L

Cantine Squarciafico (FY) – Piazza Ivrea 3 R *(near the church of S. Lorenzo)*. ☎ 010 24 70 823. Situated near the cisterns of the 16C *palazzo* of the same name, this restaurant serves typical Genoese dishes.

GOOD FOOD BETWEEN 50 000L AND 100 000L

Antica Osteria del Bai *(off the map)* – Via Quarto 12, Quarto dei Mille *(7 km east towards Nervi)*, ☎ 010 38 74 78, closed on Monday, 10-20 January and 1-20 August. This historic restaurant is housed in an old watchtower which stands above the beach where Garibaldi's Thousand set sail. The kitchen serves seafood in an elegant setting.

Trattoria Pintori (FY) – Via S. Bernardo 68. ☎ 010 27 57 507. Situated in an old *palazzo* in the historic centre, this is an excellent place in which to taste traditional Ligurian dishes. There is a very good wine list.

TO SATISFY THE EYE AND TASTEBUDS

Mangini (GY) – Piazza Corvetto 3 R. Founded in1876, this café-patisserie which was a meeting point for literary figures of the 19C still retains all its charm.

Romanengo (FY) – Via Soziglia 74/76 R *(the continuation towards the city centre of via Luccoli)*. This confectioner's was founded in 1780 and is one of the most famous in Italy. There is an endless selection of sweets, candies, pralines, pastries and chocolates.

★★ OLD TOWN *allow 1 day*

A picturesque maze of narrow streets extends east of the old port to Via Garibaldi and Piazza De Ferrari.

★★ **Port** ◷ (EXY) – From the raised road (*Strada Sopraelevata* – EXYZ) which skirts the port, there are good views of Italy's principal port. To the east the old port (Porto Vecchio) includes a pleasure boat harbour, shipyards, and quays for ferries leaving for the islands or Africa. It is dominated by the *Bigo, a metallic structure resembling a crane, designed by Renzo Piano* and has a lift which affords an excellent bird's eye **view★** of the *campanile* of the cathedral, the massive structure of Santa Maria di Carignano and Genova's lighthouse, *la Lanterna, symbol of the city*. To the west the modern port (Porto Nuovo) is fringed by an industrial zone with steel and chemical plants as well as oil refineries. This busy port handles imported raw materials (oil and petrol, coal, minerals, cereals, metal and wood) and exports manufactured goods such as machines, vehicles and textiles.

★ **Acquario** ◷ (EY) – The aquarium has a modern, instructive layout. Illuminated panels describe (in Italian and English) the species and explain the varied habitats recreated in the tanks.

The visit begins with a film that provides an introduction to the underwater world. Then, a computerised system offers an opportunity for a "hands-on" experience and various observation points give visitors the impression that they are in amidst the fish and marine mammals. There are also reconstructions of the underwater environments of the Mediterranean, the Red Sea, Madagascar, a tropical forest and a coral reef. Of particular interest are the seals, reptiles with striking camouflage, dolphins, sharks, penguins, muraena and the tank filled with species that can be touched.

Antichi Magazzini del Cotone – Built in the 19C and restored by Renzo Piano to mark the celebrations honouring Christopher Columbus On the first floor is the **Città dei Bambini★** ◷, a space designed in collaboration with the Cité des Enfants at Villette (Paris), devoted to children between the ages of 3 and 14. Through a series of interactive games, young visitors are encouraged to explore their senses, the natural world, basic technological and scientific principles and to develop their social skills and the concepts of respect, tolerance and diversity. The third floor is occupied by the **Padiglione del Mare e della Navigazione★** ◷, an interesting museum which gives an overview of the maritime tradition of the city through the display of instruments and the reconstruction of an arsenal, a business man's library, a 19C *carruggio* complete with shops (a sail-maker, a seascape painter, a figure-head carver), a shipyard and a steamship.

★ **Sailors' Quarter** (FY) – At the centre of this district is the 13C Palazzo San Giorgio which was the headquarters of the famous Bank of St George. The building was remodelled in the 16C.

Behind the palace on Piazza Banchi (of the banks) is the Loggia dei Mercanti which is now a fruit and vegetable market.

★ **Piazza San Matteo** (FY) – In the city centre, this small but harmonious square is lined with 13C-15C palaces that belonged to the Doria family. No 17 is a Renaissance building presented to Andrea Doria by a grateful republic.

The **Chiesa di San Matteo** has a Genoese-style façade with alternating courses of black and white stone. The tomb of Andrea Doria is in the crypt.

★ **Cattedrale di S. Lorenzo** (FY) – The cathedral, originally built in the 12C, with additions made through to the 16C, has a splendid Gothic **façade★★**, typical of the Genoese style. French influence appears in the placing of the 13C doorways and the large rose window.

The carving on the central doorway represents a Tree of Jesse and scenes from the Life of Christ *(on the piers)* and the Martyrdom of St Lawrence and Christ between the Symbols of the Evangelists *(on the tympanum)*. The early-13C knifegrinder, at the right corner of the façade, resembles the angel of the sundial at Chartres and performs the same function. The transept crossing is crowned with a dome designed by Alessi.

The severe and majestic **interior★** has marble columns in the nave and a false gallery above The **Chapel of St John the Baptist★** (at the end of the north aisle) contains the bones of St John.

The **treasury★** ◷ includes the famous **Sacro Catino**, a hexagonal cup in emerald green blown glass, which, according to legend, is said to be the Holy Grail, the tomb with St John the Baptist's ashes(14C) in the international gothic style, and a precious chalcedony plate (whose colour changes according to the light) of the 1C AD with the head of St John the Baptist in the centre (added in the 15C).

Continuing along via S.Lorenzo is piazza G.Matteotti, dominated by the monumental facade of the **Palazzo Ducale** (1778) whose south side looks out onto **piazza De Ferrari** with its prestigious **Teatro Carlo Felice** (partly destroyed in 1944, but rebuilt and opened to the public in 1993) and several other palaces.

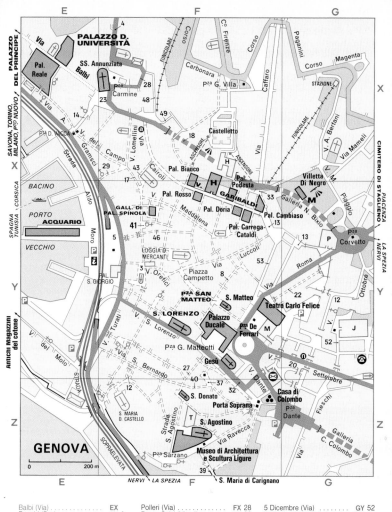

GENOVA

0   200 m

Balbi (Via)	EX	Polleri (Via)	FX 28	5 Dicembre (Via)	GY 52
Banchi (Pza)	FY 3	Ponte Calvi (Via al)	FX 29	20 Settembre (Via)	FGY
Brignole de Ferrari (Via)	FX 4	Porta Soprana (Via)	FZ 32	25 Aprile (Via)	FY 53
Cairoli (Via)	FX	Portello (Pza del)	FY 33		
Caricamento (Pza)	FY 5	Prione (Salita del)	FZ 37		
Chiossone (Via)	FY 8	Ravasco (Via)	FZ 39		
Embriaci (Pza)	FZ 12	Roma (Via)	GY	Palazzo Municipale	FXY H
Fontane Marose (Pza)	FGY 13	S. Donato (Via)	FZ 40	Museo Chiossone	GY M
Fontane (Via delle)	EX 14	S. Lorenzo (Via)	FY		
Fossatello (Via e Pza di)	FXY 17	S. Luca (Via)	FY 41		
Garibaldi (Galleria)	FX 18	S. Siro (Via)	FY 43		
Mazzini (Galleria)	GY 22	Spinola (Vico)	FY 46	HOTELS	
Nunziata (Pza della)	FX 23	Targa (Via C.)	FX 48	Albergo Cairoli	FX ❷
Pollaiuoli (Salita)	FY 27	Zecca (Largo della)	FX 49	Bristol	GY ❶

The **Chiesa del Gesù (FY)**, erected by Tibaldi in 1597, houses in its sumptuous interior the *Assumption* by Guido Reni and two paintings by Rubens: *The Circumsision* and *The Healing by St Ignatius*.

The continuation of via S. Lorenzo leads to **Porta Soprana**, one of the oldest entrances to the city (12C), characterised by two elegant twin towers. Just beyond Porta Soprana are the ruins of the so-called **Casa di Colombo**, with the elegant cloister of S. Andrea(12C) adjacent to it.

S. Donato (FZ) – Built in the 12C and 13C, this church has its original doorway and a delightful Romanesque octagonal **campanile★**. The Romanesque interior is also alluring: it worth noting the Madonna and Child (1401) in the south apse and the sumptuous **Adorazione dei Maghi★★** polyptych by Joos Van Cleve.

Complesso di S. Agostino – This convent building complex, with its adjacent 13C church (today an auditorium), houses the **Museo di Architettura e Scultura Ligure** ⊙ with its collection of fragments and sculptures salvaged from destroyed churches and private houses. Of particular interest are the 13C tombstone of Simonetta Percivalle Lercari which almost has the appearance of a stone illuminated manuscript, the *Monumento a Margherita di Brabante* by Giovanni Pisano (14C) and, on the second floor, sculptures by Pierre Puget *(Rape of Helen)* and Antonio Canova *(Penitent Magdalen)*.

181

* **Via Garibaldi** (FY) – This street of palaces, once known as Via Aurea, was built to designs by Alessi in the 16C. It is one of the loveliest streets in Italy. Alessi was also responsible for the designs of many of the actual palaces amongst which: at No 1 **Palazzo Cambiaso** (1565); at No 4 the **Palazzo Carrega-Cataldi** ⊙ (1588-61) which has preserved a delightful entrance hall decorated with grotesques. This leads into a large reception room that used to open onto the garden which was sacrificed to create more space for the building itself. In this new wing, on an upper floor, is a dazzling gilded **gallery★** in the rococo style. Both No 6, **Palazzo Doria**, and No 7, **Palazzo Podestà** (1565-67), with its fine nymphaeum are by the same architect, G. B. Castello. The **Palazzo Municipale** (Town Hall) ⊙ (**H**), the former Palazzo Doria Tursi, at No 9, has a lovely arcaded courtyard. The collections include manuscripts by Christopher Columbus (normally not on view) and the violin of Paganini *(to view ask at the mayor's office on the first floor)*. No 11, **Palazzo Bianco** ⊙, houses a very fine **art gallery★**. The exquisite *Altarpiece with Scenes from the Lives of Saints Lawrence, Sixtus and Hippolitus* (13C), a gift from the Byzantine Emperor to the Genoese Republic to commemorate a treaty made in 1261, opens the collection. Numerous Flemish and Dutch paintings from the 15C to the 17C bear witness to the close commercial ties that linked Genova to the Low Countries. Amongst these are a *Crucifixion* by Gerard David, highly dramatic in its use of dark colours and the restraint of its composition, the intense **Christ Blessing★** by Hans Memling, works by Jan Matsys, Van Dyck *(Christ of the Coin)* and Rubens *(Venus and Mars)*. Genova also welcomed and appreciated Italian artists such as Veronese *(Crucifixion)* and Palma il Giovane *(Christ and the Samaritan Woman)*. Finally, there are works by Spanish (Murillo, 17C) and Genoese painters, amongst whom B. Strozzi (1581-1644), D. Piola (1627-1703) with *Charity* and G. De Ferrari (1647-1726).

  The **Palazzo Rosso** ⊙ at No 18 also houses a **picture gallery★** with works by Palma il Vecchio, Guido Reni, Guercino *(The Eternal Father with an Angel)*, 1620, Mattia Preti and paintings of the Genoese school such as Guidobono. On the second floor (note the frescoed ceilings by the Genoese painters De Ferrari, Piola and Viviano) are some remarkable **portraits★** by Van Dyck. In addition there are sections on wood baroque sculpture.

* **Galleria Nazionale di Palazzo Spinola** ⊙ (FY) – This palace, built at the end of the 16C by the Grimaldi family and then acquired by the Spinola family, has preserved its original interior decoration. The paintings and period furniture make for an atmospheric setting. The two principal floors are fine examples of 17C (first floor) and 18C (second floor) interior styles. It is thus possible to identify the evolution of fashions not just in furnishings but also in fresco painting of **ceilings★**. Tavarone's ceiling (17C) is richly baroque, while those by L. Ferrari and S Galeotti (18C) are more light and airy. The kitchen between the first and second floors can also be viewed.

  The **art collection★** comprises works by painters of the Italian and Flemish Renaissance amongst which an enchanting **Portrait of Ansaldo Pallavicino** by Van Dyck, a *Portrait of a Nun* by the Genoese painter Strozzi, *Sacred and Profane Love* by Guido Reni and, on the third floor, (which houses the gallery proper) a moving **Ecce Homo★** by Antonello da Messina.

  Chiesa della Santissima Annunziata (EFX) – This 17C church is one of the most splendid in Genoa. The sumptuous decoration inside is a happy mixture of gilding, stucco and frescoes and is a good example of the Genoese baroque style.

  Via Balbi (EX) – This street is joined to Via Garibaldi by Via Cairoli and is lined with palaces. The Royal Palace **(Palazzo Reale)** ⊙, formerly the Balbi Durazzo, at No 10, dates from 1650 and the principal floor has period furnishings of the 18C and 19C. There are frescoes on the ceiling by Domenico Parodi (1668-1740) who also designed the stunning **Mirrored Gallery★** styled on the Gallery in the Doria Pamphili palace in Rome and the more famous one at Versailles. Beyond the sumptuous Throne room, in the Audience room is the *Portrait of Caterina Balbi Durazzo* by Van Dyck. The imposing 17C University building **(Palazzo dell'Universita★)** at No 5 has a court and a majestic staircase. The 17C Palazzo Durazzo Pallavicini is at No 1.

ADDITIONAL SIGHTS

* **Palazzo del Principe** ⊙ – This is the 16C residence of Andrea Doria who was granted the title of prince in 1531. **Perin del Vaga**, a pupil of Raphael in Rome, was responsible for the **frescoes★** in the entrance hall, the Loggia degli Eroi and the symmetrical apartments of the prince and his wife, accessible from the loggia The fresco in the Salone della Caduta dei Giganti (which takes its name from the subject) is particularly well preserved and contains a **Portrait of Andrea Doria★** by **Sebastiano del Piombo** (1526) and another portrait of Doria at the age of 91.

S. Maria di Carignano – *Take Via Ravasco* (FZ **39**). This vast church was built in the 16C to plans by Alessi. Inside, there is a fine statue of **St Sebastian★** by Puget.

Villetta Di Negro (GXY) – On higher ground to the northwest of Piazza Corvetto, this is a sort of belvedere-labyrinth with palm trees, cascades and artificial grottoes.
From the terrace there a lovely **view★** over the town and the sea. Standing on the summit is the **Museo Chiossone★** ⊙ (**M**), which houses the collection of the Genoese engraver Chiossone who was passionate about oriental art after living in Japan for 23 years. The collection includes sculptures, buddhas, objets d'art armoury and a remarkable assortment of prints, ivories and lacquerwork.

Castelletto (FX) – From the terrace *(reached by lift)* there is a fine **view★** of the town.

★ **Cimitero di Staglieno** – *1.5km – 1 mile north. Leave from Piazza Corvetto* (GY), *see the town plan on Michelin map 428.* In this curious cemetery there are ornate tombs and simple clay tumuli.

The palaces of the former maritime republics of Genoa and Venice reflect their past glory and opulence.

GRADO ≙≙

Friuli-Venezia Giulia
Population 9 026
Michelin map 429 E 22

At the time of the Barbarian invasions the inhabitants of Aquileia founded Grado which was from the 5C to the 9C the residence of the Patriarchs of Aquileia. Today Grado is a busy little fishing port and seaside resort with a growing reputation. The town situated in the middle of the lagoon is an imposing sight.

★ **Old Quarter** – This is a picturesque district with a network of narrow alleys *(calli)* running between the canal-port and the cathedral. The cathedral, Duomo di Santa Eufemia, is on the basilical plan and dates from the 6C. It has marble columns with Byzantine capitals, a 6C mosaic pavement, a 10C ambo and a valuable silver-gilt **altarpiece★**, a Venetian work of the 14C. Beside the cathedral a row of sarcophagi and tombs leads up to the 6C Basilica of St Mary of Grace (Santa Maria delle Grazie) which has some original mosaics and fine capitals.

GROSSETO

Tuscany
Population 72 453
Michelin map 430 N 15
See Michelin Green Guide Tuscany

This modern-looking provincial capital is situated in the fertile Ombrone Plain. The old town is encircled with late-16C ramparts and their powerful bastions built by the Medici.

S. Francesco – *Piazza dell'Indipendenza.* This 13C abbey church contains small frescoes by the 14C Sienese school and a lovely painted 13C crucifix.

EXCURSION

Scavi di Roselle ⊙ – *12km/8mi northeast. Leave Grosseto by the Siena road and after 10km6mi turn right into an unsurfaced road.* Important excavation work at this archaeological site has uncovered the Etruscan city of Roselle which was conquered by Rome in the 3C.

Every year,
the **The Red Guide Italia**
is updated for those who appreciate fine dining, selected restaurants, local wines and specialities.
The guide lists a range of establishments from the simplest to the most elegant, those with local flavour and the best value for the cost.
Plan better and save money by investing in this year's guide.

GUBBIO★★

Umbria –

Population 31 342
Michelin map 430 L 19

The small town of Gubbio, spread out over the steep slopes of Monte Ingino, has preserved almost intact its rich cultural and artistic heritage. Encircling ramparts, buildings of warm yellow stone roofed with Roman tiles, and distinctive towers and palaces outlined against a burnt and austere landscape make it one of the Italian towns in which the harsh atmosphere of the Middle Ages is most easily imagined. In the 11C and 12C the free commune of Gubbio, a strong supporter of the Ghibelline cause, enjoyed a period of expansion before being governed by the Montefeltro family in the 15C and then by the Della Roveres. The town came under papal rule from 1624.

Since medieval times the artisans of Gubbio have specialised in ceramics. In the early 16C Mastro Giorgio produced the famous iridescent red lustre – the secret of which was never discovered by nearby towns.

The town is also famous for the wolf which ravaged the country at a time (early 13C) when St Francis lived in Gubbio. The saint set off and reproached the wolf for its misdeeds, whereupon the repentant wild animal laid its paw in St Francis' hand and swore that it would do no more harm. The people then adopted and fed their friend, the wolf, to the end of its life.

Gubbio has its traditional festivals; the most spectacular is the **Candle Race**. Three "candles", or *ceri*, strange wooden poles 4m/13ft tall, each topped with the statue of a saint (including St Ubald, patron saint of the town), are carried through the crowded streets in a frenzied race covering a distance of 5km/3mi, from the historical town centre to the basilica of Sant'Ubaldo situated at an altitude of 820m/2 665ft. During the race the "candle"-carriers, dressed in ancient costumes, demonstrate their skill by attempting not to drop their "candles" and carrying St Ubald into the church first, before the doors are slammed shut after the other two statues have arrived. These three strange *ceri*, whose origins date back to the pre-Christian era, grace Umbria's coat-of-arms.

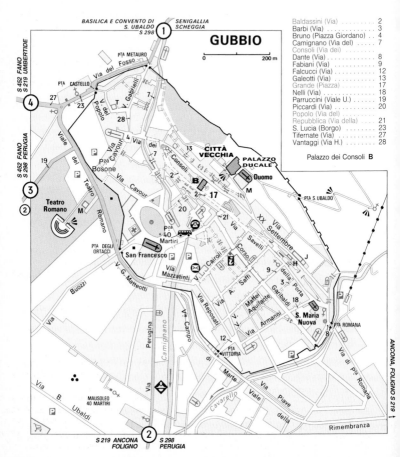

Baldassini (Via)	2
Barbi (Via)	3
Bruno (Piazza Giordano)	4
Camignano (Via del)	7
Consoli (Via dei)	
Dante (Via)	8
Fabiani (Via)	9
Falcucci (Via)	12
Galeotti (Via)	13
Grande (Piazza)	17
Nelli (Via)	18
Parruccini (Viale U.)	19
Piccardi (Via)	20
Popolo (Via del)	
Repubblica (Via della)	21
S. Lucia (Borgo)	23
Tifernate (Via)	27
Vantaggi (Via H.)	28

Palazzo dei Consoli **B**

A STROLL AROUND GUBBIO

★★ **Città vecchia** – Piazza Grande stands at the heart of this charming but austere area of the old town with its steep, narrow streets, sometimes stepped, spanned by arches converted into living quarters. The houses, flanked by palaces and towers of nobility, are often used as ceramic artists' workshops. The façade, often built of a mixture of brick, rubblework and dressed stone, sometimes has two doors; one narrower than the main door is known as the Door of Death through which coffins were brought out.

The most picturesque streets are Via Piccardi, Baldassini, dei Consoli, 20 Settembre, Galeotti and the embankments along the River Camignano leading to Piazza 40 Martiri.

★★ **Palazzo dei Consoli** ⊘ **(B)** – Overlooking Piazza Grande, this imposing Gothic building, supported by great arches rising above Via Baldassini, has a majestic façade which reflects the palace's internal plan. The stairway leads up to the vast hall *(Salone)* where popular assemblies were held and which contains collections of statues and stonework.

Next is a museum, Museo Civico, where the **Tavole eugubine** have pride of place. The bronze tablets (2C-1C BC) are inscribed in the ancient language of Umbria. This document is unique in the fields of linguistics and epigraphy. The tablets record the political organisation and religious practices of the region in Antiquity.

★ **Palazzo Ducale** ⊘ – The Ducal Palace, which dominates the town, was built from 1470 onwards for Frederico de Montefeltre. The design is attributed to Laurana, although it was probably finished by Francesco di Giorgio Martini, who was inspired by the ducal palace at Urbino. The elegant courtyard is delicately decorated. The rooms are adorned with frescoes and lovely chimmeypieces; the Salone is particularly interesting.

Teatro romano – This fairly well-preserved Roman theatre dates from the reign of Augustus.

S. Francesco – The inside walls of the north apse are covered with remarkable early-15C **frescoes★** by the local painter, Ottaviano Nelli. The church is dedicated to St Francis.

Duomo – The plain façade of the cathedral is adorned with low reliefs showing the Symbols of the Evangelists. The interior consists of a single nave. The **Episcopal Chapel** ⊘ opens to the right. It is a luxurious sitting-room decorated in the 17C, from which the bishop could follow the services.

S. Maria Nuova – The church contains a charming **fresco★** by Ottaviano Nelli.

Isola d'ISCHIA★★★

Campania

Population 47 485

Michelin map 431 E 23 – Local map see Golfo di NAPOLI

Ischia, known as the Emerald Island because of its luxuriant vegetation, is the largest island in the Bay of Naples and one of its major attractions. A clear, sparkling light plays over a varied landscape: a coast covered with pinewoods, indented with bays and creeks sheltering villages with their colourful cubic houses; the slopes covered with olive trees and vineyards (producing the white or red Epomeo wine); and an occasional village with its quaint white houses. The cottages, sometimes roofed with a dome and with an outside staircase, often have walls covered with vines.

The island rose out of the sea during the Tertiary era at the time of a volcanic eruption, and has many hot springs with various medicinal properties. The soil is volcanic in origin.

GETTING THERE

From **Naples** there are daily ferry crossings (1hr 25min) run by **Caremar** Travel and Holidays, Molo Beverello, ☎ 081 55 13 882, fax 081 55 22 011 and by **Linee Lauro**, Molo Beverello, ☎ 081 55 22 838, fax 081 55 13 236. Hovercraft (30 min) and motorboat (45 min) crossings are run by **Caremar**, by **Alilauro**, via Caracciolo 11, ☎ 081 76 11 004, fax 081 76 14 250, by **Linee Lauro** and by **Aliscafi SNAV**, via Caracciolo 10, ☎ 081 76 12 348, fax 081 76 12 141.

From **Capri** there are daily hovercraft crossings (40 min) from April to October run by **Alilauro**, Marina Grande 2/4, ☎ 081 83 79 995, fax 081 83 76 995.

From **Pozzuoli** there are daily ferry crossings (1hr) run by **Caremar**-Agenzia Ser.Mar. e Travel, Banchina Emporio, ☎ 081 52 62 711, fax 081 52 61 335 and by **Linee Lauro** (at the port), ☎ 081 52 67 736, fax 081 52 68 411.

There are also ferry (30 min) and motorboat (15 min) crossings from **Procida** run by **Caremar**-Agenzia Lubrano (at the port), ☎ and fax 081 89 67 280.

TOUR

The map below locates the towns and sights described in the guide, and also indicates other beauty spots in small black type.

A tour of the island, which is fairly small, can be done in a matter of hours *(40km/25mi: follow the itinerary on the map)*. The narrow road, as it winds between rows of vines, offers numerous fine viewpoints of the coast and the sea.

★ **Ischia** – The capital is divided into two settlements, **Ischia Porto** and **Ischia Ponte**. The Corso Vittoria Colona, an avenue lined with cafés and smart shops, links the port, in a former crater, and Ischia Ponte. The latter owes its name to the dyke built by the Aragonese to link the coast with the rocky islet on the summit of which

stands the **Castello Aragonese★★**, a beautiful group of buildings comprising a castle and several churches. There is an enchanting **view★★** from the terrace of the bar of the same name. On the outskirts are a large pinewood and a fine sandy beach.

★★★ **Monte Epomeo** – *Access is by a path which branches off in a bend of the road once level with the public gardens. 1hr30 min on foot there and back.* From the summit of this tufa peak there is a vast **panorama** of the entire island and the Bay of Naples.

Serrara Fontana – Not far from this settlement a belvedere offers a plunging **view★★** of the site of Sant'Angelo with its beach and peninsula.

★ **Sant'Angelo** – The houses of this peaceful fishing village cluster round the small harbour. Nearby is the vast Maronti Beach **(Marina dei Maronti)** which has been transformed by the opening of many thermal establishments *(access by a footpath)*.

★ **Spiaggia di Citara** – This fine beach is sheltered by the majestic headland, Punta Imperatore. Another thermal establishment, Giardini di Poseidone, is laid out with numerous warm-water swimming pools amidst flowers and statues.

Forio – The town centre is Piazza Municipio, a tropical garden overlooked by old buildings.

Lacco Ameno – This was the first Greek colony on the island and was called Pithecusa (meaning lots of monkeys) by the Greeks. It is now a holiday resort. The Church of Santa Restituta *(Piazza Santa Restituta)* was built on the remains of an early-Christian basilica and a necropolis. There is a small archeological museum. The tour of the island ends with the important thermal spa of **Casamicciola Terme.**

★Isola di PROCIDA

Procida is formed by craters levelled by erosion and has remained the wildest island in the Bay of Naples. The fishermen, gardeners and winegrowers live in a picturesque setting of colourful houses with domes, arcades and terraces.

GETTING TO PROCIDA

There are daily ferry (1hr) and motorboat (35min) crossings from **Naples** run by **Caremar** Travel and Holidays, Molo Beverello, ☎ 081 55 13 882, fax 081 55 22 011. Daily hovercraft crossings are operated by **Aliscafi SNAV**, Via Caracciolo 10, ☎ 081 76 12 348, fax 081 76 12 141.
From **Ischia** there are ferry crossings (25min) run by **Caremar**-Agenzia Travel and Holidays, Banchina del Redentore, ☎ 081 98 48 18, fax 081 55 22 011 and hovercraft crossings (15 min) run by **Caremar** and by **Aliscafi SNAV**-Ufficio Turistico Romano, via Porto 5/9, ☎ 081 99 12 15, fax 081 99 11 67.
From **Pozzuoli** there are daily ferry crossings (30min) and motorboat crossings (15 min) run by **Caremar**-Agenzia Ser.Mar.e Travel, Banchina Emporio, ☎ 081 52 62 711, fax 081 52 61 335 and by **Linee Lauro** (at the port), ☎ 081 52 67 736, fax 081 52 68 41

JESI

Marches
Population 39 208
Michelin map 430 L 21

The ancient Roman settlement of *Aesis* became a prosperous free Commune in the 12C favoured by Frederick II of Hohenstaufen who was born in Jesi in 1194. The city subsequently became part of the Pontifical states and remained so until the unification of Italy. From its past Jesi retains an urban nucleus, mainly Medieval and Renaissance, surrounded by splendid city **walls★** (13C-16C) interspaced with gates and towers. The municipal theatre (18C) is dedicated to the celebrated composer of Jesi, Giovan Battista Pergolesi. **Corso Matteotti**, the main artery of the city, is bordered by fine palaces and churches.

★ **Pinacoteca comunale** ⊙ – The municipal picture gallery is housed in Palazzo Pianetti. On the first floor there is an admirable rococo **gallery★** with an abundance of symbols and allegories. The collection includes a considerable body of work by the Venetian artist **Lorenzo Lotto** *(see LORETO)*. The *Pala di S. Lucia* is one this artist's masterpieces.

★ **Palazzo della Signoria** – This palazzo was built to designs by the Sienese architect Francesco di Giorgio Martini, a pupil of Brunelleschi. Its imposing square structure has an elegant facade adorned by a stone tabernacle.

Regione dei LAGHI★★★

The Lake District extends from Piedmont to Veneto and from Switzerland to Trentino in the north. Narrow and long, these lakes are all of glacial origin and their banks are covered with a varied and luxuriant vegetation which flourishes in the particularly mild climate.

This fairyland of blue waters at the foot of shapely mountains has always been a favourite haunt of artists and travellers. The charm and originality of these Pre-Alpine lakes are due to the juxtaposition of Alpine and southern scenery, the numerous villas with attractive gardens on the lakesides, the great variety of flowers throughout the year, the small sailing villages with their flotilla of boats where fresh fish is the speciality. Each lake has its own specific character, making it quite different from its neighbour.

Sightseeing ⊙ – The maps below locate the towns and sites described in the guide, and also indicate other beauty spots, in smaller black type. *For places in Switzerland see The Green Guide to Switzerland.*

The atmosphere of bygone ages on the Isola dei Pescatori

★★★ LAGO MAGGIORE ⊙

Lake Maggiore is the most famous of the Italian lakes, in part for its legendary beauty at times both majestic and wild, and also for the Borromean Islands. It is fed by the Ticino River, which rises in Switzerland, and its waters change from a jade green in the north to a deep blue in the south. The mountains of the Alps and Pre-Alps shelter the lake which enjoys a constantly mild climate in which a luxuriant and exotic vegetation flourishes.

★ **Angera** – This wonderful holiday resort stands in the shadow of the **Rocca Borromeo** ⊙. There is a vast panoramic view from a tower, the **Torre Castellana**. Known since the days of the Lombards (8C), the Rocca still has Law Courts decorated with admirable 14C **frescoes**★★ depicting the life of Archbishop Ottone Visconti. The fortress also houses the Doll Museum (**Museo della bambola** ★) with an extensive collection of exhibits showing the development of the doll (*bambola*) since the early 19C.

Arona – The chief town on Lago Maggiore is overlooked by the gigantic statue, **Colosso di San Carlone**★ ⊙, of St Charles Borromeo, the Cardinal Archbishop of Milan who distinguished himself by the authority he showed in re-establishing discipline and morals in the Church and by his heroic conduct during the plague of 1576. The statue is 24m high with a 12m/39ft base.

At the summit of the old town the church of St Mary (**S. Maria**) contains a lovely **polyptych**★ (1511) by Gaudenzio Ferrari.

From the ruined castle (**Rocca**) there is a **view**★ of Lake Maggiore, Angera and its mountain setting.

★ **Baveno** – This quiet holiday resort, once visited by Queen Victoria, has a Romanesque church and an octagonal Renaissance baptistery.

★★★ **Isole Borromee** ⊙ – *Town plan in the Michelin Atlas Italy, under Stresa.* A large area of the lake was given to the princely Borromeo family in the 15C but only gradually did they purchase all the islands in the tiny archipelago. In the 17C, Charles III established a residence on **Isola Bella**★★★ ⊙, named after his wife, Isabella. The palace, built in the Lombard Baroque style, has several state rooms – medals room, state hall, music room, Napoleon's room, ballroom and Hall of Mirrors.

The most unusual feature is the caves where those living in the palace could find cooler air on very hot days. The decoration of light and dark coloured stones and shells is designed to represent an underwater world. The gardens, filled with a variety of exotic plants, form an amazing baroque composition, a truncated pyramid of ten terraces ornamented with statues, basins, fountains and architectural perspectives simulating stage sets. At the top of the garden is the shell-shaped "amphitheatre" providing an extraordinary scenic effect.

Boat trips are available to the **Isola dei Pescatori**★★★ with has retained its original charm and the **Isola Madre**★★★ ⊙, an island totally covered with a splendid garden of flowers and rare or exotic plants. In the palazzo, note the Puppet Theatre that once belonged to the House of Borromeo.

★★ **Cannero Riviera** – The houses of this resort rise in tiers above the lake amid olive trees, vineyards, orange and lemon groves.

★ **Cannobio** – Cannobio is a small resort near the Swiss border. In addition to the Renaissance Church of the Madonna della Pietà there are several other fine old houses. 3km/2mi out of town *(on the Malesco road)* is the **Orrido di S. Anna**★, a precipice formed by the torrent.

★ **Cerro** – This peaceful village on a well-shaded part of the lakeside has a tiny fishing port and an interesting **ceramics museum** ⊙.

Laveno Mombello ⊙ – From here a cable-car climbs up to the summit of **Sasso del Ferro**★★ ⊙ from where there is a vast **panorama** over the entire Lake District.

★★ **Pallanza** – Everywhere flowers deck and scent this wonderful resort. Its **quays**★★, sheltered by magnolias and oleanders, offer lovely views of the lake. On the outskirts of the town on the Intra road is the **Villa Taranto**★★ with its famous **gardens** ⊙ featuring azaleas, heathers, rhododendrons, camelias, dahlias, maples etc.

Santa Caterina del Sasso ⊙ – *About 500m/547yds from Leggiuno.* This hermitage was founded in the 13C by an anchorite, Alberto Besozzo. In a picturesque setting, the building clings to a rock overlooking the lake.

★★ **Stresa** – *Town plan in the Michelin Atlas Italy.* This pleasant resort, which attracts many artists and writers, enjoys a magnificent situation on the west bank of Lago Maggiore facing the Borromean Islands, and is a delightful place with all the amenities of both a holiday resort in spring, summer and autumn and a winter sports resort.

The ski slopes are on **Mottarone**★★★ ⊙ *(take the Armeno road: 29km/18mi; the scenic toll-road from Alpino: 18km/11mi; or the cable-car)* which from its summit provides a magnificent **panorama** of the lake, the Alps and the Monte Rosa massif. Standing on the outskirts of the town, off the Arona road, is the **Villa Pallavicino**★ ⊙ with its wildlife park.

From Stresa, follow the Vezzo Gignese direction. At **Gignese** (8km/5mi southwest) there is a small, interesting museum **(Museo dell'Ombrello e del Parasole)** ⊙ which illustrates the history, from 1850 to the present day, of the umbrella and sunshade, particularly in the context of Lago Maggiore which has a celebrated umbrella making tradition.

★★ LAGO D'ORTA

Lake Orta ⊙, one of the smallest Italian lakes, is separated from Lake Maggiore by the peak, Il Mottarone rising to the northeast. It is perhaps the most delightful and the most gracious of all the lakes with its setting of wooded hills and the tiny islet, Isola San Giulio.

The lakesides have been inhabited since earliest times and in the 4C the people were converted to Christianity by St Julius.

★★ **Madonna dal Sasso** – *5km/3mi from Alzo.* From the church terrace there is a magnificent view of the lake in its verdant mountain setting.

★★ **Orta San Giulio** – This small resort has a delightful site on the tip of a peninsula. The alleyways are lined with old houses adorned with elegant wrought-iron balconies. The **Palazzotto**★ or 16C town hall is decorated with frescoes.

★ **Sacro Monte d'Orta** – *1.5km/1mi from Orta.* This sanctuary dedicated to St Francis of Assisi and set on a hilltop comprises 20 chapels. These are decorated in the Baroque style and the frescoes serve as background to groups of lifelike terracotta statues.

★★ **Isola di San Giulio** – *Boats leave from Orta.* On this jewel of an island, 300m/328yds long and 160m/175yds wide, stands the **Basilica di S. Giulio** ⊙ which is said to date from the 4C, when St Julius came to the island.

Inside there is a lovely 12C **ambo**★ of the 12C decorated with frescoes by the school of Gaudenzio Ferrari (16C). Note also, in the crypt, the shrine containing the relics of St Julius.

Varallo – *About 20km/12mi west.* This industrial and commercial town in the Val Sesia is famous for its pilgrimage to the **Sacro Monte**★★ with its 43 chapels. Again these are decorated with frescoes and groups of life-size terracotta figures (16C-18C) which illustrate the Fall and scenes from the Life of Christ. They were the work of several artists including Gaudenzio Ferrari (1480-1546), a local painter who was a pupil of Leonardo da Vinci. Ferrari showed definite originality and picturesque realism in his work.

★★ LAGO DI LUGANO

Most of **Lake Lugano** ⊘, also known as Lake Ceresio by the Italians, is in Swiss territory. Lugano is wilder than Lakes Maggiore and Como and with its irregular outline has none of the grandeur or majesty of the others. Its mild climate and its steep mountain countryside make it an ideal place for a holiday.

★ **Campione d'Italia** – An Italian enclave in Switzerland, Campione is a colourful, smiling village which is highly popular on account of its casino. A chapel, Oratorio di S. Pietro, is a graceful building dating from 1326. It was the work of the famous maestri campionesi *(see p. 49)*, who vied with the maestri comacini in spreading the Lombard style throughout Italy.

★ **Lanzo d'Intelvi** – Set in the heart of a pine and larch forest, this resort (alt 907m/2 976ft) is also a ski centre in winter. 6km/4mi away is the **belvedere di Sighignola**★★★, also known as the "balcony of Italy" because of its extensive view of Lugano, the Alps as far as Monte Rosa and on a clear day Mont Blanc.

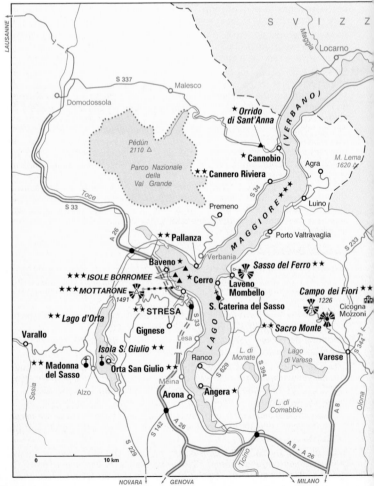

Varese – *13km/8mi southwest of Porto Ceresio. Town plan in the Michelin Atlas Italy*. This busy but pleasant modern town stands not far from the lake of the same name. One of its advantages is a mild and sunny climate due to its proximity to the Italian lakes.

8km/5mi to the northwest rises the hilltop, **Sacro Monte★★**, with its important pilgrimage church dedicated to the Virgin. The road up to the basilica is lined with 14 chapels decorated with frescoes in *trompe-l'œil* and groups of life-size terracotta figures. From the summit there is a magnificent **view★★** of the lakes and surrounding mountains.

10km/6mi to the northwest is the long mountainous ridge, **Campo dei Fiori★★**, which raises its forest-clad slopes above the plain. There is a vast **panorama★★** of the Lake District.

Villa Cicogna Mozzoni, Bisuschio Ⓥ – *8km/5mi northeast of Varese on the road to Porto Ceresio*. The villa, set in fine Italian terraced gardens, was originally a hunting lodge in the 15C which was extended in the 16C with the addition of a residence. In the first floor rooms, complete with furnishings, the upper part of the walls and the ceilings are adorned with fine frescoes in the Renaissance style.

★★★ LAGO DI COMO

Set entirely within Lombardy, Lake Como Ⓥ, of all the Italian lakes, has the most variety. Pretty villages, tiny ports, villas in shady exotic gardens succeed one another along the banks of this Pre-Alpine lake. Bellagio stands on a promontory at the confluence of its three arms.

★★★ **Bellagio** – Bellagio occupies a magnificent site on a promontory dividing Lake Lecco from the southern arm of Lake Como. It has a worldwide reputation for the friendliness of its people and its excellent amenities. The splendid lakeside

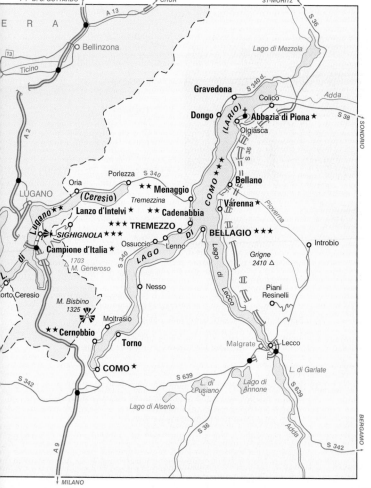

gardens★★ of **Villa Serbelloni** ⊙ and **Villa Melzi** ⊙ with their fragrant and luxuriant vegetation are the main sights in Bellagio. It is pleasant to stroll up and down the pretty, steep little streets on the hillside.

Bellano – This small industrial town stands on the Pioverna River at the mouth of the valley (Valsassina), with the great mass of the Grigne towering behind. The attractive 14C **church** with a façade by Giovanni da Campione is in the Lombard Gothic style.

★★ **Cadenabbia** – This delightful resort occupies an admirable site opposite Bellagio. A splendid avenue of plane trees, Via del Paradiso, links the resort with the Villa Carlotta and Tremezzo.
From a chapel, **Capella di San Martino** *(1hr30min on foot there and back)* there is a good **view**★★ of Bellagio on its promontory, Lakes Como and Lecco and of the Grigne.

★★ **Cernobbio** – This splendid location is famous for the **Villa d'Este**, the opulent 16C residence now transformed into a hotel and surrounded by fine parkland *(access to both the villa and the park is limited to hotel guests)*. The best view of the villa (from the ground) is from Piazza del Risorgimento, near the landing stage with the liberty-style roof.

★ **Como** – *See COMO.*

Dongo – It was in this village that Mussolini and his mistress, Clara Petacci, were captured on 27 April 1945.

Gravedona – This fishing village has an attractive Romanesque Church, **S. Maria del Tiglio**★. The 5C baptistery was remodelled in the Lombard style in the 12C.

S. Chirol

The enchanting Villa Carlotta, Tramezzo

★★ **Menaggio** – Favoured by a cool summer breeze, this is one of the lake's smart resorts.

★ **Abbazia di Piona** – *2km/1 mile from Olgiasca.* This graceful monastery, which was founded in 11C by Cluniac monks, and which adopted Cistercian rule a century later under St Bernard of Clairvaux (1090-1153), has pretty Lombard Romanesque **cloisters**★ (1252).

Torno – On the outskirts of this attractive port, the 14C Church of **S. Giovanni** has a fine Lombard Renaissance **doorway**★.

★★★ **Tremezzo** – A mild climate and a beautiful site combine to make Tremezzo a favourite place for a stay. The terraced gardens, **Parco comunale**★, are a haven of peace.
The 18C **Villa Carlotta**★★★ ⊙ *(entrance beside the Grand Hotel Tremezzo)* occupies an admirable site facing the Grigne Massif.
The numerous statues include a copy by Tadolini of the famous group of Love and Psyche by Canova. The main attraction is, however, the beautiful terraced **gardens**.

★ **Varenna** – This delightful town with its many gardens and cypresses stands on a small promontory. The 16C **Villa Monastero** ⊙ has beautiful **gardens**★★.

★ LAGO D'ISEO

Though **Lake Iseo** ⊙ is not very well known, its wild scenery, its high mountain fringe, its banks sometimes steep and often indented and its peaceful villages, all lend a certain charm to this small lake. From the midst of the deep blue waters emerges the island of Monte Isola (alt 600m/1 969ft).

★ **Iseo** – The church, Pieve di Sant'Andrea, with its 13C campanile faces a charming square.

Lovere – In this small industrial town the **Galleria Tadini** ⊙ has a collection of arms, paintings (Bellini and Parmigianino), porcelain and sculpture by Canova.

★★ **Monte Isola** ⓥ – From the Chiesa della Madonna della Ceriola, crowning the summit of this green island, there is a vast **panorama★★** of the lake and the Alps near Bergamo.

★ **Pisogne** – This small port has an attractive lakeside setting. The church, **Santa Maria della Neve**, is adorned with 16C **frescoes★** by Romanino du Brescia.

★★★ LAGO DI GARDA

Lake Garda ⓥ, the largest lake, is also considered one of the most beautiful. Its many assets include low-lying banks which are alluvial in the south, steep slopes on the west bank, and the mountain chain of Monte Baldo to the east.

The Dolomites to the north shelter the lake from the cold north winds, creating a very mild climate which already earned it the name of "beneficent" lake (Il Benaco) in ancient times. It had both strategic and commercial importance and throughout history has been coveted by neighbouring powers.

Artistically, both as regards painting and architecture, the region was greatly influenced by the Venetian Republic which ruled the region from the 15C to the 18C.

Even in Roman times the banks of the lake were appreciated as a place to stay and today's travellers have a large number of resorts from which to choose.

Bardolino – This village famous for its red wine has an elegant Romanesque **church★** dating from the 11C, which is dedicated to St Severinus.

Campione del Garda – The Bishops of Trento, Brescia and Verona met here to bless the lake.

Desenzano del Garda – The old port, the picturesque Piazza Malvezzi and the neighbouring old quarter are all good places to stroll through. The 16C parish church (**Parrocchiale Santa Maria Maddalena**) has a very intense **Last Supper★** by Tiepolo. To the north of the town in Via Scavi Romani, the **Villa Romana** ⓥ boasts remarkable multicoloured **mosaics★** dating from the Roman period.

★ **Garda** – This popular resort which gave its name to the lake shows a strong Venetian influence. Both the Palazzo dei Capitani and the Palazzo Fregoso are 15C.

★★ **Gardone Riviera** – This small resort enjoys many hours of sunshine and offers the tourist a wide choice of hotels. 1km/0.6mi from the town is the **Vittoriale★** ⓥ estate which belonged to the poet **Gabriele D'Annunzio** (1863-1938) who is buried here. The neo-Classical villa, **La Priora** ⓥ, is full of the solemn atmosphere which this writer-aesthete so cultivated. The museum and park display mementoes of his turbulent life.

Gargnano – This charming resort is surrounded by great expanses of glasshouses for the growing of lemon and citron trees.

The church of **S. Francesco** has lovely 15C cloisters with curious Moorish-style galleries featuring capitals carved with oranges and lemons, recalling the fact that it was probably the Franciscan monks who introduced citrus fruits to the area.

The lakeside promenade leads to the neo-Classical **Villa Feltrinelli** *(not open)* which served as Mussolini's headquarters during the Fascist Republic (1943-45).

★ **Limone sul Garda** – This is one of the lake's most attractive villages. Terraced lemon groves often under glass stretch along the lake shores. From Limone a **panoramic route★★** climbs up to the Tremosine plateau before descending to Tignale. It offers superb **views★★★** of the lake and its mountainous setting.

★ **Malcesine** – This attractive town stands on a promontory at the foot of Monte Baldo and is dominated by the crenellated outline of the **Castello Scaligero★**. This 13C-14C castle belonged to the Scaligers of Verona.
The 15C Palazzo dei Capitani in the Venetian style stands on the edge of the lake. From the summit of **Monte Baldo** ⊙ (cable-car) there is a splendid **panorama★★★** of the lake and to the north the Brenta and Adamello Massifs.

★★ **Punta di San Vigilio** – This headland is in a romantic setting. The 16C **Villa Guarienti** *(not open)* was built to the plans of Sanmicheli for the Veronese humanist, Agostino Brenzoni.

★ **Riva del Garda** – This small resort is dominated to the west by a rocky escarpment. Already in ancient times it was an important trading and communication centre set on the route between Verona and the Alps. Today the picturesque **old town★** is a maze of narrow shopping streets.
The castle **(Rocca)** houses a museum **(Museo civico** ⊙) with its archeological and historical collections.

★ **Salò** – This was the seat of the Venetian Captain under the Venetian Empire and from this period of splendour it has retained its 15C cathedral **(Duomo)**. Inside are a large gilt **polyptych★** (1510) in wood and several works by Moretto da Brescia and Romanino.

San Martino della Battaglia ⊙ – An **ossuary-chapel**, a **museum** and a tall **tower** commemorate the battle of 24 June 1859 at Solferino *(see Solferino)*, and the wars of the Risorgimento *(see Historical Table and Notes)* waged by the Italians to win their independence from Austria.

★★ **Sirmione** – This important resort has been well known since the beginning of the century as a spa. It is said to be particularly effective in the treatment of respiratory disorders. The houses cluster around the 13C castle, **Rocca Scaligera★** ⊙, at the tip of the narrow Sirmione peninsula, as it stretches out into the lake. The small 15C Church of Santa Maria Maggiore has interesting 15C-16C frescoes.
On the rocky tip of the peninsula are the remains of a vast Roman villa which belonged to the poet Catullus. The excavation site is known as the **Grotte di Catullo** ⊙ and it is possible to distinguish the remains of buildings in this attractive **site★★**.

Solferino – A chapel **(capella ossario)** and a museum **(museo)** ⊙ recall the battle of 24 June 1859 (the field of battle extended as far as San Martino, *see above*) when the French and Piedmontese troops defeated the Austrians and brought about Italy's independence *(see Historical Table and Notes)*. The heavy casualties (11 000 dead and 23 000 wounded) led to the founding of the **Red Cross** by Henri Dunant. A **monument** on the site marks the event.

Torbole – This pleasant resort was the venue for a most unusual event in 1439. Venice, in an attempt to rescue the town of Brescia, under siege by the Visconti of Milan, armed a fleet which sailed up the Adige and crossed the mountains towards Torbole on Lake Garda. From there the fleet set sail to occupy Maderno on the west bank. The following year Venice was able to capture Riva and finally achieve suzerainty over the lake.

Valeggio sul Mincio – *Exit the Milan-Venice motorway at Peschiera. Follow signs for Parco Giardino Sigurtà which is 10km/6mi south of Peschiera.* Having been granted the right to pump up spring water from the Mincio, Carlo Sigurtà (1898-1983), an industrial pharmacist who spent 40 years of his life working on the properties of thermal springs, completely transformed the 17C villa used by Napoleon III as his headquarters in 1859. Now, the beautifully maintained park (50ha/123 acres), **Parco Giardino Sigurtà★★** ⊙, can only be visited by car. Thirteen car parks have been set out along the 7km/4 mile route. They mark the start of interesting footpaths. In addition to its magnificent location on the Mincio, the park has a wonderful range of Mediterranean flora, vast grassy swards, architectural and natural features and, in certain areas, the gentle sound of classical music.

Fine gardens: Villa d'Este (Tivoli), Hanbury Gardens (Ventimiglia), Boboli Gardens (Florence), Villa Nazionale (Strà).

L'AQUILA ★

Abruzzi

Population 69 516
Michelin map 430 0 22
Town plan in the Michelin Atlas Italy
Local map under ABRUZZO

According to legend L'Aquila was founded in the 13C when the inhabitants of 99 castles in the valley at the foot of the Gran Sasso joined forces to form a city in which each castle had a corresponding church, square and fountain. Beset by the vicissitudes of the Kingdom of Naples, L'Aquila was besieged, destroyed and rebuilt several times until it became the second most important city of the Kingdom in the 15C. Rich in splendid monuments, it also had a resurgence thanks to the commerce all over Europe of saffron, "red gold", which grows on the plateaux of Navelli. This was the period in which St Bernardino of Siena (who died in L'Aquila in 1444) resided in the city; his initials IHS (*Iesus Hominum Salvator* – Jesus Saviour of Mankind) marked on several doorways, bear witness to his presence.

★★ **S. Maria di Collemaggio** ⊙ – For both its historical and architectural value this is the most celebrated basilica in the Abruzzi region. It was begun in 1287 in the Romanesque style on the initiative of Pietro da Morone, the future Pope **Celestine V**, who was crowned there in 1294. The ample, horizontally crenellated **façade★★**, beautifully adorned with geometrical patterns in white and pink stone, is pierced with rose windows and doorways added in the 15C. To the right, a low octagonal tower functioned as the base of the steeple which was demolished in 1880. On the left side of the basilica stands the **Porta Santa**, a beautiful richly decorated Romanesque doorway. The interior contains the 16C Lombard Renaissance style tomb of S. Pietro Celestino.

> **Colui che fece per viltade il gran rifiuto...** *Him who made the Great Refusal, impelled by cowardice...* (Dante, *Inferno*, Canto III, 59-60)
>
> Pietro da Morrone (1215-1296), hermit and founder of the Celestine order of the Morronese Abbey near Sulmona, was unexpectedly elected pope in September of 1294. Overwhelmed by the intrigues and plots of the pontifical court, Morrone abdicated after only a few months and was banished to the castle of Fumone by his successor, Boniface VIII. He died there shortly afterwards and in 1313 was canonised by Pope Clement V.

★★ **S. Bernardino** ⊙ – This superb church, a masterpiece of Cola dell'Amatrice (1527), has a majestic and rich **façade★★** which is articulated by entablatures that give definition to the three orders of double columns (Ionic, Doric and Corinthian). The spacious and well-lit interior, in the form of a Latin cross, is roofed with a lovely baroque wooden ceiling and contains the **mausoleum of St Bernardino★** adorned with figures by the local sculptor, Silvestro dell'Aquila, as is the elegant **tomb★** of Maria Pereira.

★ **Castello** – Built in the 16C to by Pirro Luigi Escribà who also designed Castel S. Elmo in Naples, this square castle, reinforced with powerful bastions, is a good example of 16C military architecture. The great rooms now house a museum, the **Museo Nazionale d'Abruzzo★★** ⊙. On display on the ground floor are the *Archidiskodon Meridionalis Vestinus*, a fossil of an ancestor of the elephant that lived about one million years ago, and some interesting exhibits from Abruzzi in Roman times such as the *Calendario Amiterno*. On the first floor the section on **Sacred Art** (12C-17C) constitutes the core of the museum and displays some significant examples of painting, sculpture and decorative arts of the Abruzzi region. Among these it is worth noting the polychrome wooden sculptures, the *Croce processionale★* by Nicola di Guardiagrele, a masterpiece of workmanship in gold, and the wooden statue depicting *St Sebastian* by Silvestro d'Aquila. There is also a coin collection, a section on sacred goldwork, a gallery with paintings of the Abruzzi school from the 15C to 18C and a section on contemporary art.

★ **Fontane delle 99 cannelle** – This imposing fountain which was begun in 1272 commemorates the legendary founding of L'Aquila with its 99 castles. It is made of pink and white stone in a trapezoidal form and is adorned with 99 gargoyles, each different from the other.

The length of time given in this guide
– for touring allows time to enjoy the views and the scenery;
– for sightseeing is the average time required for a visit.

LECCE★★

Puglia
Population 99 372
Michelin map 431 F 36

Set in the very heart of the Salento region, Lecce was in Roman times the prosperous town of Lupiae. The Norsemen greatly favoured the town and made it the capital of the region known as Terra d'Otranto.

From the 16C to the 18C, Lecce knew a period of great splendour during which it was embellished with Renaissance, Rococo and Baroque monuments. The local finely-grained limestone was particularly easy to work, and the town's numerous Baroque buildings are remarkable for the abundance of decorative work which has earned the city the nickname of "the Baroque Florence". When seen at night the whole decked in lights resembles a sumptuous theatrical set.

The most inventive artists came from the **Zimbalo** family: their work is to be found in both churches and palaces and is widespread throughout the Salentina Peninsula.

★★ BAROQUE LECCE

The historic centre, once surrounded by ramparts (16C), of which only traces remain, and a **castle** (built by Charles V on an existing Anjou fort), is now delineated by a ring of avenues. The heart of the city is the lively **piazza S. Oronzo** which is dominated by a statue of the patron saint on top of one of the two columns that mark the end of the Appian way, the other being in Brindisi *(see BRINDISI)*.

To the south side of the square parts of a **Roman amphitheatre** (2C), originally double tiered, have been unearthed. Also in the piazza are the small church of **St Mark**, attributed to Gabriele Riccardi and built by the Venetian colony, and the very old **palazzo del Seggio** which temporarily houses a paper maché statue of S. Giuseppe Patriarca (19C).

LECCE

Aragona (Via F. d')	YZ 3	Imperatore Augusto (V.)	Y 15	Realino (Via Bernardino)	Z 29
Caracciolo		Jacobis (V. Agostino de)	Z 17	Rubichi (Via Francesco)	Y 32
(Via Roberto)	Z 7	Ludovico (Via)	Y 21	S. Oronzo (Piazza)	Y
Cavallotti (Viale F.)	Y 8	Marche (Viale)	Z 22	Taranto (Via)	Y 38
Fazzi (Via Vito)	Y 12	Orsini del Balzo (Via)	Z 25	Trinchese (Via Salvatore)	Y
Imperatore Adriano (V.)	Y 14	Palazzo dei Conti		Vitt. Emanuele (Cso)	Y 42
		di Lecce (Via del)	Z 26	Vitt. Emanuele (Pza)	Y 43
		Pietro (Via M. de)	Y 28	25 Luglio (Via)	Y 44

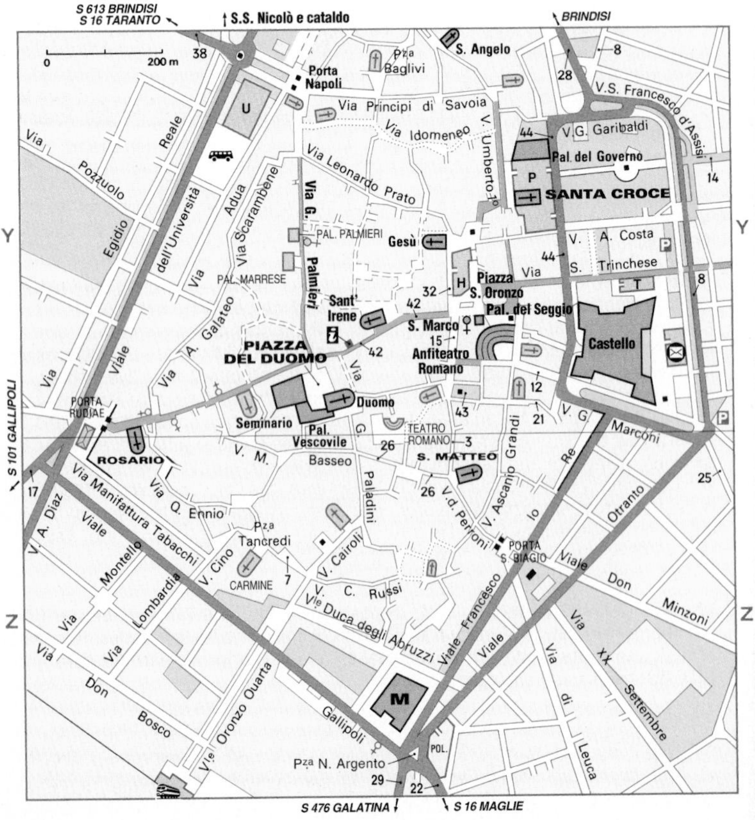

★★ S. Croce (Y) – Several architects worked on this basilica in the 16C and 17C and it constitutes the best example of the Baroque style of Lecce. The façade is sumptuously decorated without being overbearing (the lower part is Renaissance in structure). The upper story is almost without doubt the work of Zimbalo and is richly ornamented. The two stories are linked by a long balcony held up by animal atlantes and caryatids while the parapet is adorned with cherubs holding mitres and books. The central rose window above seems as if it were fashioned by an expert lacemaker.

The delicate Baroque modelling on the façade of Santa Croce

The interior is light and airy and the plainer architectural style is reminiscent of the Florentine Renaissance idiom. There is also an abundant Baroque decoration of great delicacy. The side chapel at the end of the north aisle contains a fine **high altar** with sculptured low reliefs by Francesco Antonio Zimbalo and depicts scenes from the life of S. Francesco da Paola.

Palazzo del Governo (Y) – Adjoining the basilica the Governor's residence, a former Celestine monastery, has a rusticated façade with a frieze above and intricately decorated window surrounds, especially at first-floor level, designed by Zimbalo (ground floor) and G. Cino.

Chiesa del Gesù (o del **Buon Consiglio**) (Y) – The austere style of this church, built by the Jesuits (1575-1579), makes a stark contrast to the other churches in Lecce. Inside there is an ornate **Baroque altar★**.

S. Irene (Y) – Built by Francesco Grimaldi for the monks of the Theatine order, this church has lavish **Baroque altars** attributed to Francesco A. Zimbalo.

★★ Piazza del Duomo (Y) – Completely enclosed in a homogeneous body of Baroque buildings and heralded by an arch facing Corso Vittorio Emanuele, this is one of the most remarkable squares in southern Italy. To the left, the **campanile** (1661-82) and the adjacent cathedral (**Duomo**) (1659-82) are by Giuseppe Zimbalo, the 17C **Palazzo Vescovile** and the **Seminario**, dating from 1709, by Giuseppe Cino.
In the courtyard of the latter there is an ornately-decorated **well★** by the same sculptor.

Duomo – The first sighting of the Duomo is in fact of the north side. It is the most ornate façade of the church with its imposing entrance and arcade with a statue of St Oronzo. The main façade *(visible from the square)* is more restrained. Inside, the crypt, rebuilt in the 16C on an existing medieval structure, is held up by 92 columns with capitals adorned by figures of animals.

★ Chiesa del Rosario (or **San Giovanni Battista**, YZ) – This church was Giuseppe Zimbalo's last work and the façade features an abundance of decoration which is both intricately detailed and yet gracious.
The **interior★** is adorned with Baroque altars and some fine 17C altarpieces.

Via Palmieri (Y) – Several elegant buildings border this street; particularly noteworthy are the ones at Piazza Falconieri, Palazzo Marrese and Palazzo Palmieri (18C). At the end of the street, **Porta Napoli** (or Arco di Trionfo) was built in the 16C in honour of Charles V.

Sant'Angelo (Y) – Although unfinished, this façade is typical of Zimbalo's style (1663) and is decorated with garlands, cherubs, angels etc.

★ San Matteo (Z) – This church with its harmonious façade by Achille Carducci (1667-1700) shows the distinct influence of Borromini and his Roman work, the Church of San Carlo alle Quattro Fontane.

★ Museo Provinciale Sigismondo Castromediano ⊘ (ZM) – Housed in a modern building, the museum has a rich archeological section *(ground floor)* and a very important **ceramics collection★★** *(first floor)*. Of particular interest are the Attic vases decorated with red figures. There is also a collection of epigraphs of various origins and two beautiful bronze statues (a figure of a woman and a priest). There is an art gallery on the third floor.

LECCE

ADDITIONAL SIGHTS

S.S. Nicolò e Cataldo – *North of the town near the cemetery.* The church was built in 1180 by the Norman Tancred of Lecce and rebuilt in 1716, probably by Giuseppe Cino who retained intact the central part of the Romanesque façade with its small rose window and Norman doorway. There is an attractive Baroque structure in the 16C cloisters.

EXCURSION

S. Maria di Cerrate – *14km/9mi north on the road to Brindisi, then turn right (follow directions).* This enchanting Benedictine abbey, in its isolated country setting, dates back to the 12C. The **church★**, closed on the north side by a fine portico with capitals embellished with figurative scenes (13C), has an elegant doorway whose vault is decorated with scenes from the New Testament. The interior retains part of the frescoes that probably once covered its entire surface. Some fresco fragments are conserved in the **Museo delle Tradizioni Popolari** ⊘ which is housed in monastery rooms. The museum also has displays of traditional wares such as oil-presses (the abbey has a hypogeum olive-press).

Michelin spiral bound atlas to Italy
with place name index and 70 city and town plans.

LIGNANO ≙≙

Friuli-Venezia Giulia –
Population 6 331
Michelin map 429 E-F 21

Lignano, the largest seaside resort on the coastline of Friuli, lies on a long, sandy peninsula covered with pine woods. Stretching east from the mouth of the Tagliamento, it closes off part of the Marano Lagoon, an angling reserve. Its **beach★★**, facing Grado, the Trieste Gulf and the coastline of Istria (which is often visible), is popular for its 8km/5mi of fine, golden sand that slopes very gently into the sea; it is a safe holiday resort for families with children.
The resort comprises three areas. At the tip of the peninsula is **Lignano Sabbiadoro**, the oldest part of the town and a convivial place with old houses, shopping streets and a large yachting marina (the *darsena*). Separated from Sabbiadoro by a large expanse of pine wood that belongs to the Vatican and is reserved for children's holiday camps is **Lignano Pineta**, an elegant, modern part of the town laid out like a spiral and divided off by streets radiating out from the central square. **Lignano Riviera** gets its name from the nearby Tagliamento. The water offshore from its beach is slightly colder but the vegetation is thicker here. Inland, holidaymakers can enjoy the 18-hole golf course and visit the zoo, the **Parco zoo Punta Verde** ⊘, which presents animals from all over the world.

LIVORNO

LEGHORN – Tuscany
Population 163 073
Michelin map 428 or 430 L 12 – Town plan in the Michelin Atlas Italy
See Michelin Green Guide Tuscany

The important seaport of Leghorn deals mainly in timber, marble, alabaster, cars and craftwork from Florence. Cosimo I de' Medici started rebuilding the harbour to replace the silted-up Porto Pisano, and it was finished in 1620 under Cosimo II. The main streets are Via Grande lined with arcaded buildings, Via Cairoli and Via Ricasoli. In the Piazza Micheli, from which the Fortezza Vecchia (Old Fortress) can be seen, stands the **monument★** to the last prominent Medici, the Grand Duke Ferdinand. The four bronze Moors (1624) were the work of Pietro Tacca.

EXCURSION

Montenero – *9km/6mi south.* The 18C pilgrimage church dedicated to Our Lady of Grace consists of a richly decorated Baroque church, a monastery and behind railings the *famedio*, a series of chapels reserved for the burial of distinguished citizens of Livorno.

LORETO ★

Marches

Population 11 317

Michelin map 430 L 22

The small city of Loreto is grouped around its well-known church which is the scene of a famous pilgrimage to the "House of Mary". The old quarter is partially encircled by massive brick ramparts dating from the 16C. It is said that the Santa Casa (Holy House) or House of Mary was miraculously carried from Nazareth in several stages by angels and set down in a wood of laurels (*lauretum* in Latin), which gave its name to Loreto. In fact three walls of the House of Mary were transported in 1294 by the Angeli (angels in Italian), a noble family which ruled over Epiros where Nazareth is located. The most popular pilgrimages take place on the Feast of the Virgin, the Nativity (8 September) and the Translation of the Santa Casa (10 December) (*see the Calendar of Events at the end of the guide*).

The Venetian painter **Lorenzo Lotto** (1486-1556), lived at Loreto from 1535 until his death. Towards the end of his life he became an Oblate in the Santa Casa. This moody and sensitive artist rejected the sensuality of Venetian colour in favour of a cold light that bathes his animated compositions which are emotionally charged and characterised by a keen psychological insight.

★★ SANTUARIO DELLA SANTA CASA ⊙ *1hr*

Many famous architects, painters and sculptors contributed to the building and decoration of this church, the Sanctuary of the Holy House. Construction started in 1468 and was only completely finished in the 18C. The architects included firstly Giuliano da Sangallo, then Bramante who built the side chapels, and finally Vanvitelli who designed the bulbous campanile. Go round the outside of the church to admire the lovely triple **apse**★★ and Sangallo's elegant dome. The sober and harmonious façade with its double buttresses surmounted by clocks at the corners is typical of the late Renaissance.

The three **bronze doors**★★ are adorned with fine late-16C and early-17C statues. The interior has a nave and two aisles. At the end of the south aisle the **Sacristy of St Mark**★ (San Marco) is crowned by a dome painted with frescoes (1477) by Melozzo da Forli with an exceptional sense of foreshortening, showing angels carrying the Instruments of the Passion. In the **Sacristy of St John**★ (San Giovanni) is a lavabo designed by Benedetto da Maiano under a vault painted with frescoes by Luca Signorelli. Standing at the transept crossing is the **Santa Casa**★★ which was sumptuously faced with marble carved in the 16C by Antonio Sansovino and other sculptors. The north transept leads to a room decorated by Pomarancio (1605-10).

Piazza della Madonna★, in front of the basilica, is lined by the unfinished portico of the Palazzo Apostolico, which now houses a picture gallery (**pinacoteca**) ⊙. This contains a remarkable collection of **works**★ by Lorenzo Lotto, paintings by Simon Vouet and Pomarancio. The Flemish tapestries were woven to designs by Raphael and there is a superb collection of Urbino faïence vessels.

EXCURSION

Recanati – *7km/4mi southwest*. This little town, perched on a hill, was the birthplace of the poet **Giacomo Leopardi**, the most perceptive but melancholy of men whose work was very melodious. The **Palazzo Leopardi** ⊙ contains mementoes of the writer. The **Pinacoteca Civica** ⊙, housed in the Villa Colloredo Mels complex (*via Gregorio XII*) , has several important works by Lorenzo Lotto, including an Annunciation.

Michelin on the Net: www.michelin-travel.com.

Our route planning service covers all of Europe – twenty-one countries and one million kilometres of highways and byways – enabling you to plot many different itineraries from wherever you are. The itinerary options allow you to choose a preferred route – for example, quickest, shortest, or Michelin recommended.

The network is updated three times weekly, integrating ongoing road works, detours, new motorways, and snowbound mountain passes.

The description of the itinerary includes the distances and travelling times between towns, selected hotels and restaurants.

LUCCA★★★

Tuscany
Population 85 657
Michelin map 428, 429 or 430 K 13
See Michelin Green Guide Tuscany

Situated in the centre of a fertile plain, Lucca has preserved within its girdle of ramparts, often tree-topped, a rich heritage of churches, palaces, squares and streets which gives the town a charming air, unscathed by contemporary developments.

HISTORICAL NOTES

Lucca was colonised by the Romans in the 2C BC and it has retained the plan of a Roman military camp, with the two principal streets perpendicular to one another. During the Middle Ages a complicated system of narrow alleys and oddly-shaped squares was added to the original network. The town became an independent commune at the beginning of the 12C and flourished until the mid-14C with the silk trade as its main activity. In the early 14C the town enjoyed a great period of prosperity and prestige under the control of the mercenary leader Castruccio Castracani (d 1328). Lucca's finest religious and secular buildings date from this period. Luccan architects adopted the Pisan style to which they added their own characteristic refinement and fantasy.

From 1550 onwards the town became an important agricultural centre and with this new prosperity came a renewed interest in building. The countryside was dotted with villas, the town encircled by ramparts and most of the houses were either rebuilt or remodelled.

In the early 19C, Elisa Bonaparte ruled the city for a brief period from 1805 to 1813. Following Napoleon's Italian campaigns he bestowed the titles of Princess of Lucca and Piombino on his sister. She showed a remarkable aptitude for public affairs and ruled her fief with wisdom and intelligence, encouraging the development of the town and the arts.

The Legend of the Holy Cross – The **Volto Santo** (Holy Visage) is a miraculous Crucifix kept in the cathedral. It is said that after Christ had been taken down from the Cross, Nicodemus saw the image of his face on it. The Italian Bishop Gualfredo, when on pilgrimage in the Holy Land, succeeded in tracing the Volto Santo and embarked in a boat without a crew or sails which drifted ashore on the beach at Luni, near La Spezia. As the worshippers at Luni and Lucca disputed possession of the Holy Image, the Bishop of Lucca had it placed on a cart drawn by two oxen; they immediately set off towards Lucca.

The fame of the Volto Santo, spread by merchants from Lucca, gained ground throughout Europe. A most unusual commemorative procession, **Luminara di Santa Croce**, passes through the illuminated town after dark (see the Calendar of Events at the end of the guide).

A Bird's eye view of the Piazza dell'Anfiteatro and San Frediano

THE IMPORTANT CHURCHES *3hr*

From the great **Piazza Napoleone** *(car park)* make for the Piazza San Giovanni, overlooked by the church of the same name, and then the Piazza San Martino, bordered on the left side by the 16C Palazzo Micheletti designed by Ammannati with pretty terraced gardens.

★★ **Duomo** (C) – The cathedral, dedicated to St Martin, was rebuilt in the 11C. The exterior was remodelled almost entirely in the 13C, as was the interior in the 14C and 15C. The strength and balance of the green and white marble **façade★★**, designed by the architect Guidetto da Como, are striking despite its asymmetry. The upper section with its three superimposed galleries is the first example of the Pisan Romanesque style *(see PISA)* as it developed in Lucca; the idiom is characterised by lighter, less rigid lines and by inventive ornamentation. The ornate sculpture and marble-inlaid designs are of great interest.

The slim and powerful campanile harmoniously combines the use of brick and marble, and the number of openings increases with the height.

The sculptural decoration of the porch is extremely rich: pillars with naïvely-carved columns, arcading, friezes and a variety of scenes (barking dogs, Roland sounding his horn, a man wrestling with a bear and another stroking his beard).

The Gothic **interior** has elevations where the round-headed main arches with their robust piers contrast with the delicacy of the elegant triforium. On the west wall is an unusual Romanesque sculpture of St Martin dividing his cloak. The classical and sober lines of this sculpture herald the style of Nicola Pisano. In the north aisle is the lovely shrine *(tempietto)* built by the local artisan Matteo Civitali (1436-1501) to house the Volto Santo. The great 12C figure of **Christ★** in wood blackened through time shows a distinctly Oriental influence because of its hieratic aspect. It is said to be a copy of the legendary one.

In the sacristy is one of the masterpieces of Italian funerary sculpture by the Sienese artist, Jacopo della Quercia (1406): the **tomb of Ilaria del Carretto★★**, wife of Paolo Guinigi, lord of Lucca in the early 15C. The recumbent figure wears a long, delicately-draped robe and at her feet lies a small dog, a symbol of fidelity.

Other works of art include a *Presentation of the Virgin in the Temple* by Bronzino *(north aisle)* and the large-scale **Last Supper★** with its subtle lighting by Tintoretto *(south aisle)*.

★★ **San Michele in Foro** (B) – The white mass of the 12C-14C church on the site of the Roman forum dominates the adjoining square which is lined by old mansions and the Palazzo Pretorio.

The exceptionally tall **façade★★** (the nave itself was to have been taller) is a good example of the Lucca-Pisan style, despite the fact that the lower part was remodelled last century. The four superimposed galleries surmount blind arcading and are decorated with varied motifs. At the top, two instrument-playing angels flank a statue of the Archangel Michael slaying the dragon.

The simplicity of the Romanesque **interior** is a direct contrast to the ornate exterior. On the first altar of the south aisle is a **Madonna★** by Andrea della Robbia. The south transept is adorned with a lovely **painting★** with brilliant colours by Filippino Lippi.

★ **S. Frediano** (B) – This great church, dedicated to St Frigidian, was rebuilt in the original Lucca-Romanesque style in the 12C before the influence of the Pisan school was felt. The sober façade is faced with white marble from the Roman

The delicately chiselled façade
of San Michele in Foro, 13C

S. Chirol

amphitheatre. The upper middle section, remodelled in the 13C, is dominated by a Byzantine-style mosaic depicting the Ascension by local artists.

The interior comprises a nave and two aisles with wooden ceilings (flanked by Renaissance and Baroque side chapels) on the plan of the early-Christian basilicas: the nave which ends in a semicircular apse is articulated by antique columns crowned with fine capitals.

To the right on entering is a curious Romanesque **font★** (12C) with low reliefs depicting the story of Moses. The Chapel of Sant'Agostino is decorated with frescoes by the Ferraran painter Amico Aspertini: one of these depicts the translation of the Volto Santo from Luni to Lucca.

ADDITIONAL SIGHTS

★ **Città Vecchia** (BC) – The streets and squares of old Lucca are full of atmosphere with their Gothic and Renaissance palaces, their towers of nobility, old shops, sculptured doorways and coats of arms, elegant wrought-iron railings and balconies. Starting from Piazza San Michele, follow Via Roma and Villa Fillungo to Piazza del Anfiteatro situated inside the Roman amphitheatre. From here go towards Piazza San Pietro (12C-13C church) and then take Via Guinigi where at No 29 stands **Casa dei Guinigi** ⊘ (C) with its tower (**panorama★** of town from the top) crowned with trees which rises above the great façade with Gothic windows. The houses opposite at Nos 20 and 22 also belonged to the Guinigi family. Continue to the Romanesque Church of **Santa Maria Forisportam** (CW), so-called because it stood outside the Roman walls.

Via Santa Croce, Piazza dei Servi and Piazza dei Bernardini, where the 16C palace of the same name stands (C **N**), lead back to Piazza San Michele.

★ **Passeggiata delle Mura** – A walk is laid out along the ramparts (4km/3mi long) which give the town a special charm. They were built in the 16C and 17C and include 11 bastions, linked by curtain walls, and four gateways.

Traffic

Anfiteatro (Pza dell')	C 2
Angeli (Via degli)	B 3
Antelminelli (Pza)	C 4
Asili (Via degli)	B 5
Bacchettoni (V. dei)	D
Barsanti (Viale)	B
Batoni (V. P.)	C
Battisti (Via C.)	B 7
Beccheria (Via)	B 8
Bernardini (Pza dei)	C 9
Boccherini (Pza L.)	A 10
Cadorna (Viale)	D 12
Calderia (Via)	B 13
Cantore (V.)	D
Carducci (Viale Giosuè)	A
Castracani (Viale)	D
Catalani (Via)	A 15
Cavalletti (V.)	A

Battistero e chiesa dei Santi Giovanni e Reparata	B **B**
Casa d. Guinigi	C
Casa natale di Puccini	B **G**
Città Vecchia	BC

Museo Nazionale di Palazzo Mansi ⊘ (A) – The **apartments** of this 17C palace have a remarkable interior **decoration★** (17C-18C). The **Pinacoteca** includes works by 17C Italian artists (Salimbeni and Barocci) and foreign paintings.

Museo Nazionale di Villa Guinigi ⊘ (D) – *Via della Quarquonia. Closed for restoration.* The villa which once belonged to Paolo Guinigi now contains archeological, sculpture (Romanesque, Gothic and Renaissance) and painting (Lucca and Tuscan) sections. There are some remarkable panels of intarsia work.

EXCURSIONS

Villa Reale di Marlia ⊘ – *8km/5mi north. Leave by* ① *on the town plan.* The Villa Reale is surrounded by magnificent 17C **gardens★★** modified by Elisa Bonaparte. Unusual features include a lemon grove, a 17C nymphaeum and an open-air theatre.

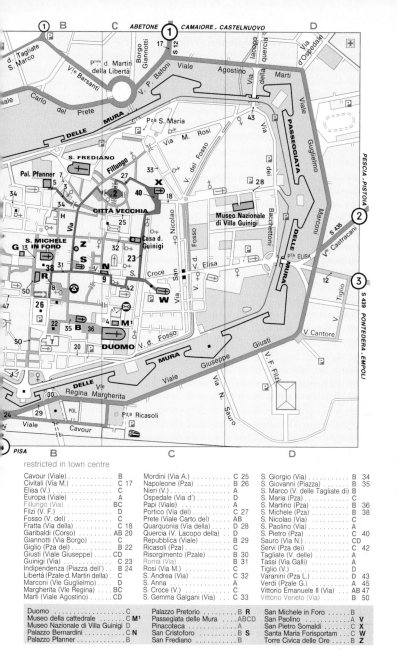

restricted in town centre

Cavour (Viale)	B	Mordini (Via A.)	C 25	S. Giorgio (Via)	B 34
Civitali (Via M.)	C 17	Napoleone (Pza)	B 26	S. Giovanni (Piazza)	B 35
Elisa (V.)	C	Nieri (V.)	A	S. Marco (V. delle Tagliate di)	B
Europa (Viale)	A	Ospedale (Via d')	D	S. Maria (Pza)	C
Fillungo (Via)	BC	Papi (Viale)	A	S. Martino (Pza)	B 36
Filzi (V. F.)	D	Portico (Via del)	C 27	S. Michele (Pza)	B 38
Fosso (V. del)	C	Prete (Viale Carto del)	AB	S. Nicolao (Via)	C
Fratta (Via della)	C 18	Quercia (V. Lacopo della)	D	S. Paolino (Via)	A
Garibaldi (Corso)	AB 20	Quarquonia (Via della)	D 28	S. Pietro (Pza)	C 40
Giannotti (Via Borgo)	C	Repubblica (Viale)	B 29	Sauro (Via N.)	CD
Giglio (Pza del)	B 22	Ricasoli (Pza)	B	Servi (Pza dei)	C 42
Giusti (Viale Giuseppe)	CD	Risorgimento (Pzale)	B 30	Tagliate (V. delle)	A
Guinigi (Via)	C 23	Rosi (Via M.)	C	Tassi (Via Galli)	A
Indipendenza (Piazza dell')	B 24	S. Andrea (Via)	C 32	Tiglio (V.)	D
Libertà (Pzale d. Martiri della)	C	S. Anna	A	Varanini (Pza L.)	D 43
Marconi (Vle Guglielmo)	D	S. Croce (V.)	C	Verdi (Pzale G.)	A 45
Margherita (Vle Regina)	C	S. Gemma Galgani (Via)	C 33	Vittorio Emanuele II (Via)	AB 47
Marti (Viale Agostino)	CD			Vittorio Veneto (Via)	B 50

Duomo	C	Palazzo Pretorio	B R	San Michele in Foro	B
Museo della cattedrale	C M¹	Passegiata delle Mura	ABCD	San Paolino	A V
Museo Nazionale di Villa Guinigi	D	Pinacoteca	A	San Pietro Somaldi	C X
Palazzo Bernardini	C N	Roma (Via)	B	Santa Maria Forisportam	C W
Palazzo Pfanner	B	San Cristoforo	B S	Torre Civica delle Ore	B Z
		San Frediano	B		

Villa Mansi ⊘ – *Segramigno, 11km/7mi north. Leave by ① on the town plan.* This 16C villa, transformed in the 18C, has a façade covered with statues and a vast shady **park★** where statue-lined alleys lead to a lovely pool.

Villa Torrigiani ⊘ (or **Camigliano**) – *12km/8mi northeast. Leave by ① on the town plan.* This 16C villa was converted in the 17C into an elegant summer residence by Marques Nicolao Santini, ambassador of the Lucca republic to the Papal Court and to the Court of Louis XIV. The gardens designed by Le Nôtre, are adorned with fountains, grottoes and nymphaea. The villa, which has a delightful rococo façade, contains rooms adorned with frescoes.

Michelin on-line gives motorists the freedom to create their own itineraries, to stop and discover tourist attractions. At any time, you can print out your complete route map, as well as the information from the Red Guides and the cost of tolls on the selected itinerary.

Log in at www.michelin-travel.com

MANTOVA★★

MANTUA – Lombardy
Population 49 064
Michelin map 428 or 429 G 14

Mantua is set in the heart of a flat fertile plain which was formerly marshland on the southeastern border of Lombardy. It is encircled to the north by three lakes formed by the slow-flowing Mincio. This active and prosperous town has important mechanical and petrochemical industries. The region is also the first producer of hosiery worldwide.

HISTORICAL NOTES

Although, according to a legend quoted by Virgil, Mantua was founded by Monto, daughter of the divine Tiresias, its origins would seem to be Etruscan dating back to the 6C or 5C BC. It passed to the Gauls before becoming Roman in the 3C BC. In 70BC **Virgil** (Publius Virgilius Maro), the great poet, was born in the Mantua area. Author of the *Aeneid* in which he recounts the wanderings of Aeneas, the exiled Trojan prince, and the foundation of the earliest settlement, from which Rome was to spring, Virgil describes his beloved Mantuan countryside, with its soft misty light, and the pleasures of rural life in his own harmonious but melancholy style in the *Eclogues* or *Bucolica* and in the *Georgics*.

In the Middle Ages Mantua was the theatre for numerous struggles between rival factions which successively sacked the town, before it became an independent commune in the 13C and finally the domain of Luigi Gonzaga, nominated Captain General of the People. Under the **Gonzaga** family, who were enlightened rulers and patrons of the arts and letters, Mantua became an important intellectual and artistic centre in northern Italy of the 15C and 16C. Thus Gian Francesco Gonzaga (ruled 1407-44) placed his children in the charge of the famous humanist Vittorio da Feltre (1379-1446) and commissioned the Veronese artist **Pisanello** (1395-1455) to decorate his ducal palace.

His son Ludovico III (1444-78), a mercenary army leader by profession, was a typical Renaissance patron: he gave land to the poor, built bridges and favoured artists. The Sienese humanist Politian (1454-94), the Florentine architect Leon Battista Alberti (1404-72) and the Paduan painter **Andrea Mantegna** (1431-1506) all belonged to his court. Francesco II (1484-1519) married Isabella d'Este, a beautiful and wise woman who contributed to the fame of Mantua. Their son Federico II was made duke by the Emperor Charles V in 1530 and he commissioned the architect and artist **Giulio Romano** (1499-1546), Raphael's pupil, to embellish his native town; the artist worked on the ducal palace and cathedral and the Palazzo del Te.

In 1627 Vicenzo II died without heirs and the succession passed to the Gonzaga-Nevers family, the cadet line, but the Habsburg Emperor Ferdinand II opposed the French succession, and in 1630 sent an army which sacked the town and deserted it following a plague which decimated Milan and Lombardy (the background to these dramatic events is described in the novel *I Promessi Sposi* by Manzoni). The Gonzaga–Nevers, however, restored the fortunes of the town until 1707 when they were deposed and Mantua became part of the Austrian Empire which ruled until 1866, except for a period under Napoleonic rule (1787-1814), when it joined the Kingdom of Italy.

Gastronomy in Mantua

The rich Mantuan cuisine boasts many specialities including the delicious tortelli pasta stuffed with pumpkin, macaroons, mustard and nuts, and *Sbrisolona*, a famous cake which owes its curious name to the fact that it is practically impossible to eat it without getting covered in crumbs.

★★★ PALAZZO DUCALE ⊙ 1hr30min

The imposing Ducal Palace comprises buildings from various periods: the Magna Domus and the Palazzo del Capitano erected in the late 13C by the Bonacolsi, Lords of Mantua from 1272 to 1328; the Castello di San Giorgio, a 14C fortress, and other inner sections built by the Gonzaga in the 15C-16C, including the 15C Palatine chapel of Santa Barbara.

★★★ **Apartments** – Start from the 17C Ducal Stairway which gives access to the first floor. One of the first rooms displays *The Expulsion of the Bonacolsi and the Triumph of the Gonzaga on 16 August 1328* by Domenico Morone (1442-1517). The painting shows the medieval aspect of Piazza Sordello with the old façade of the cathedral. The **Pisanello rooms** on the first floor have fragments of frescoes and remarkable **sinopie**★★ (preparatory sketches using an red earth pigment), which were discovered in 1969 and are a good example of the refined and penetrating work of Pisanello. These lyrical scenes draw inspiration from the feats of the

Knights of the Round Table and the fantastic and timeless world of medieval chivalry. The **Tapestry Room** (Appartamento degli Arazzi), formerly known as the **Green Apartment** (Appartamento Verde), in the neo-Classical style, is hung with nine splendid Brussels tapestries after Raphael. The **Room of the Zodiac** (Camera dello Zodiaco) leads to the **Moors Room** (Stanzino dei Mori), in the Venetian style, and to the **Hall of the Rivers** (Sala dei Fiumi) which overlooks the **Hanging Garden** (Giardino Pensile). The giants depicted on the walls represents the rivers of Mantua. The **Moors Corridor** (Corridoio dei Mori) leads into the famous **Hall of Mirrors** (Sala degli Specchi) used for dance and music. In the elegant **Archers' Room** (Sala degli Arcieri), the antechamber to the ducal apartments, hang paintings by Rubens and Domenico Fetti. The **Ducal Apartments** (Appartamento Ducale) comprise a suite of rooms remodelled for Vincenzi I in the early 17C by Antonio Maria Viani, and including the Paradise Room (Appartamento del Paradiso) and the tiny Dwarfs' Room (Appartamento dei Nani). The building known as the **Rustica** and the **Equestrian Court** (Cortile della Cavallerizza) are by Giulio Romano; the courtyard is lined by a **gallery**, Galleria della Mostra, built in the late 16C by Antonio Maria Viani to house Vicenzo I's art collection, and by the **Hall of the Months** (Galleria dei Mesi) erected by Giulio Romano.

In the Palazzo Ducale plump cherubs gaze from the ceiling of the Camera degli Sposi

Nimatallah/ARTEPHOT

In the **Castello di S. Giorgio** may be viewed the celebrated **Camera degli Sposi★★★** (Room of the Spouses) – so-called because this is where marriages were recorded – executed from 1465 to 1474 by **Andrea Mantegna**. The walls are covered with a cycle of frescoes which glorify the superb and refined world of the Gonzaga court. Mantegna creates an illusion of space with his knowledge of foreshortening and perspective and his skilful use of volume and materials. The painted *trompe-l'œil* and carved stucco decorations and garlands of foliage and fruits are also admirable. On the north wall look for Ludovico II turned towards his secretary, and his wife Barbara seated full-face. The children cluster round their parents, as do other members of the court including an enigmatic dwarf.

On the west wall the fresco presents Ludovico with his son, Cardinal Francesco, against the background of a town with splendid monuments, which could well be Rome as imagined by Mantegna who had not yet visited the city. Mantegna has portrayed himself as the figure in purple which can be glimpsed on the right of the dedication. His great mastery of *trompe-l'œil* culminates in the ceiling oculus from which gaze cupids and servants. This invention was highly successful and introduces a note of wry humour and even oddness to this otherwise rather solemn ensemble.

The lagoon of Mantua

From the Middle Lake and the Lower Lake, near Castel San Giorgio, motorboats leave daily for wonderful trips along the lower course of the Mincio. Visitors who plan a stay in Mantua from mid-July to late August, should not miss the opportunity of an enchanting excursion in a small boat on the river decked with pink and white lotus blooms. *It is advisable to book in advance by contacting the park authorities.* ☎ *0376 22 57 24.*

MANTOVA

Accademia (Via)		BY 2
Acerbi (Via)		AZ 3
Broletto (Via e Piazza)		BZ 4
Canossa (Piazza)		AY 5
Don Leoni (Piazza)		AZ 6
Don Tazzoli (Via Enrico)		BZ 7

Erbe (Piazza delle)		BZ 8
Fratelli Cairoli (Via)		BY 10
Libertà (Corso)		AZ 12
Mantegna (Piazza Andrea)		BZ 13
Marconi (Piazza)		ABZ 15
Martiri di Belfiore (Piazza)		AZ 16

Matteotti (Via)		AZ 17
Roma (Via)		AZ
S. Giorgio (Via)		BY 20
Sordello (Piazza)		BY 21
Umberto (Corso)		AZ
Verdi (Via Giuseppe)		AZ 24
Virgilio (Via)		AY 25
20 Settembre (Via)		BZ 27

«Rotonda» di San Lorenzo . BZ **B**   Palazzo di Giustizia . . . . AZ **J**   Teatro Accademico . . . . . . BZ **T¹**

HISTORIC CENTRE

★ **Piazza Sordello** – This square, which was the centre of old Mantua, has retained its medieval aspect. To the west is the 13C Palazzo Bonacolsi – the tall Torre della Gabbia (Tower of the Cage) still bears on its façade the cage (gabbia) in which wrongdoers were exhibited – and the 18C Palazzo Vescovile where telamones adorn the 18C façade. To the east are the oldest buildings of the Palazzo Ducale: the Magna Domus and the crenellated Palazzo del Capitano.
On the north side stands the Cathedral (Duomo) which features varied elements and styles: the neo-Classical façade, the late-Gothic right wing and a Romanesque campanile. The 16C interior was designed by Giulio Romano.

Piazza Broletto (BZ 4) – This was the centre of public life at the time of the commune (13C) when was built the Palazzo Broletto, a 13C communal palace, partly remodelled in the 15C. On its façade it has a seated statue of Virgil (1225). At the right corner rises the Torre Comunale, a tower later converted into a prison.

★ **Piazza delle Erbe** (BZ 8) – The Square of Herbs derives its name from a fruit and vegetable market. It is lined to the north by the rear façade of the Palazzo Broletto and to the east by the 13C Palazzo della Ragione, flanked by the 15C Clock Tower and the Romanesque church, **Rotonda di San Lorenzo**★ ⊘ (**B**). Sober and elegant, this circular building has a colonnaded ambulatory with a loggia above, and a dome crowning all.

★ **Basilica di S. Andrea** – The basilica dedicated to St Andrew, built in the 15C to the plans of Alberti, is a masterpiece of the Italian Renaissance. The façade retains Classical architectural features: the tympanum, the triumphal arch, the niches between the pilasters. The interior has a single nave. The barrel-vaulting and walls are painted in trompe-l'œil. The first chapel on the left contains the tomb of

Mantegna. The transept crossing is crowned by a dome built from 1732 to 1765 by Filippo Juvarra. In the crypt two urns housed in a reliquary contain a relic of the Blood of Christ brought to Mantua by the Roman soldier Longinus.

Teatro Accademico ⊙ (BZ T') – This small, pretty 18C theatre by Bibiena has a stage set in imitation marble with four orders in pasteboard and a monochrome decor. The theatre which welcomed the 13-year old Mozart on 13 December 1769, is still used for concerts.

Palazzo d'Arco ⊙ – *Piazza d'Arco.* This neo-Classical palace in the Palladian tradition *(see VICENZA)* contains interesting collections of 18C furniture, paintings and ceramics.

FROM THE HISTORIC CENTRE TO PALAZZO TE

Palazzo di Giustizia (AZ J) – The monumental façade of the Law Courts with caryatids is early 17C. At No 18 in the same street is Romano's house built in 1544 to his own designs.

Casa del Mantegna (AZ) – *47 Via Acerbi.* This rather severe looking brick building was in all probability built to designs by Mantegna himself in 1476. It has a delightful courtyard.

★★ **Palazzo Te** ⊙ (AZ) – This large country mansion was built on the plan of a Roman house by Giulio Romano for Federico II from 1525 to 1535. It combines Classical features and melodramatic invention, such as the amazing "broken" entablature in the main courtyard, and is a major achievement of the Mannerist style. The **interior** was ornately decorated by Giulio Romano and his pupils. In the **Horses' Room** (Salone dei Cavalli), used for receptions, some of the finest horses from the Gonzaga stables are depicted. In the **Room of Psyche** (Sala di Psiche), used for banquets, the sensual and lively style of Guilio Romano is the best illustration of the hedonistic character of the palace. The frescoes in the **Giants' Room** (Sala dei Giganti), the most celebrated room of the palace, depict the wrath of Jupiter against the Titans. The overall decoration which covers the walls and vaulted ceiling creates an indefinite spatial illusion and the dome above gives a sense of artificiality in sharp contrast to the effect sought by Mantegna in the Camera degli Sposi in the Palazzo Ducale.

MASSA MARITTIMA★★

Tuscany
Population 9 024
Michelin map 430 M 14
See Michelin Green Guide Tuscany

The name *Massa*, which is of Latin origin, has been linked to *Marittima*, the meaning of which is probably associated with the coastal area and hinterland. It may also be a reference to the nearby *Maremma* region. The town, in a pleasant setting, has a rich historic past and was particularly important during the Middle Ages.

★★ **Piazza Garibaldi** – This lovely square is lined by some fine medieval buildings, three of which are of Romanesque origin – Palazzo del Podestà with its many double-windowed bays, the crenellated Palazzo Comunale and the cathedral.

★★ **Duomo** – The cathedral was probably built in the early 11C. In addition to the Romanesque style, Gothic-style features were added in 1287 by **Giovanni Pisano**. The majestic building is adorned with blind arcades in the lower part and dominated by a fine campanile, at one time crenellated but now surmounted by a spire with four bellcotes, pierced with windows which increase in number with the height.
The interior, in the form of a Latin cross, comprises three aisles which are divided by two rows of columns crowned with capitals of different styles. The inside wall of the façade is decorated with striking pre-Romanesque low reliefs revealing the Byzantine influence (10C). There is an unusual baptismal font (1267). In the chapel to the left of the choir stalls is the panel of the *Virgin of the Graces* which has been attributed to **Duccio di Buoninsegna** and the remains of the *Presentation of Christ at the Temple* by Sano di Pietro (1406-81). In the chapel to the right of the choir stalls is the *Crucifixion* by Segna di Bonaventura (recorded from 1298 to 1327).

Palazzo del Podestà – The palace, which dates back to 1225-30, was the residence of the town's most eminent magistrate *(podestà)*. The façade is decorated with the coat of arms of the *podestà*. The building now houses the **Museo archeologico** ⊙: exhibits include an interesting stele by Vado dell'Arancio and the splendid *Virgin in Majesty* by Ambrogio Lorenzetti (1285-c 1348).

* **Fortezze dei Senesi** ⊙ and **Torre del Candeliere** – The Sienese fortress was built in 1335. The nearby tower, Torre del Candeliere, is all that remains of the fortress built in 1228. The tower is linked to the fortress by an arch 22m across.

S. Agostino – The Church of St Augustine, which dates from the early 14C, has a Romanesque façade, a lovely Gothic apse and a 17C crenellated campanile added in the 17C. To the left are the remaining two wings of the Romanesque cloisters.

Museo della miniera ⊙ – The museum, which is situated near Piazza Garibaldi, evokes the mining activities in the 700m/770yds of tunnels in the surrounding area; note the supporting timberwork and extraction techniques.

EXCURSION

** **Abbazia and eremo di S. Galgano** – *32km/20mi northeast.* This ruined, but still impressive, Gothic Cistercian Abbey, the first gothic church in Tuscany, was built by monks from 1224 to 1288, and dedicated to St Galgan (1148-81). The remains of the old monastery include the cloisters, the chapter house and the scriptorium.
The hermitage, a circular Romanesque construction, overlooks the abbey from 200m/220yds away. The splendid **cupola** (1181-85) was inspired by the Etruscan-Roman tombs and is an ideal point of reference between the ancient and Renaissance worlds. The church was erected to house the rock where in 1180 Galgano Guidotti plunged the sword turning it into the symbol of the cross. There are frescoes by Ambrogio Lorenzetti in the chapel to the left of the altar.

MATERA★★

Basilicata
Population 56 387
Michelin map 431 E 31

Matera overlooks a ravine separating it from the Murge Hills in Puglia. This provincial capital stands in the heart of a region dissected by deeply eroded gorges - a desolate landscape with wide horizons. Modern Matera, the town's centre of activity, is laid out on a plateau overlooking the lower town with its many rock dwellings *(sassi)*, now mostly abandoned. In the town and surrounding area there are some 130 churches hewn out of the rock. These date back to the 8C BC and the arrival of oriental (non-Latin) monastic communities who settled locally and in Puglia. They were adept in this form of underground architecture which shows a Byzantine influence.

** **The Sassi** - The two main troglodyte quarters are on either side of the rock crowned by the cathedral. The roofs on some houses serve as walkways while the lower storeys are hewn out of the rock. Little white-ashed houses and stairways overlap and overhang one another in a labyrinth which is difficult to unravel.

** **Strada dei Sassi** - This panoramic street skirts the wild gorge and runs round the cathedral rock. The natural rock walls are riddled with both natural and man-made caves.

* **Duomo** - The cathedral was built in the 13C Apulian-Romanesque style; the façade has a lovely rose window and a projecting gallery above the single doorway. The walls are embellished with blind arcades. On the south side are two richly-sculpted doorways. The interior was remodelled in the 17C and 18C. The Byzantine fresco portraying the Madonna dates from the 12C-13C, the Neapolitan crib is 16C and the lovely carved stalls of the choir are 15C. The **Chapel of the Annunciation★** *(the last one on the south side)* has a beautiful Renaissance decoration.

San Pietro Caveoso ⊙ - This Baroque church stands at the foot of Monte Errone, which has several churches hewn out of the rock and decorated with frescoes, namely Santa Lucia alle Malve, Santa Maria de Idris and San Giovanni in Monterrone.

Musio Nazionale Ridola ⊙ - This museum in a former monastery has an interesting collection of archeological finds, which were discovered locally.

** **Views of Matera** - *4km/2.4mi by the Altamura road, then take the Taratnto road and finally make a right turn to follow the signpost "chiese rupestri" (rock churches).* The road leads to two belvederes affording splendid views of Matera. On the left below the parking area are several churches hollowed out of the rock face.

MERANO ★★

MERAN – Trentino-Alto Adige
Population 33 947
Michelin map 429 B 15

Merano, lying at the start of the wider upper valley of the Adige, known as the Val Venosta, is an important tourist centre and spa. It is blessed with a mild climate. There are numerous cable-cars and chairlifts up to **Merano 2000**, a good winter sports centre also popular in summer for excursions into the mountains.

★★ **Passeggiate d'Inverno e d'Estate** – These winter and summer promenades run along the Passirio River. The winter one, facing south, is shady and flower-decked and attractively lined with shops, cafés and terraces and is by far the busier. It is prolonged by the Passeggiata Gilf which ends near a powerful waterfall. The summer promenade, on the opposite bank, meanders through a lovely park planted with pines and palm trees.

★★ **Passeggiata Tappeiner** – This magnificent promenade (4km/2.4mi long) winds high above Merano affording remarkable viewpoints as far as the Tyrol.

Duomo di S. Nicolò – This Gothic cathedral has a huge belfry and a west front with a crenellated gable. The right-hand side is decorated with a 14C statue of St Nicholas and a gigantic statue of St Christopher that was repainted in the 19C. The interior, roofed with beautiful ribbed **Gothic vaulting★**, includes two 15C stained glass windows and two painted wooden **Gothic polyptychs★** (16C) by Knoller, a native of the Tyrol. In the neighbouring **Cappella di Santa Barbara** standing at the start of the old footpath leading to Tirolo is a 16C high relief of the *Last Supper*.

★ **Via Portici (Laubengasse)** – This arcade-lined street is overlooked by houses with painted façades and oriel windows. The shops have curiously-sculpted façades.

★ **Castello Principesco** ⊘ – Built in the 14C and extended in the 15C, this castle has crenellated gables and a tower with a pepper-pot roof. It was used by the Princes of Tyrol as their residence when they stayed in the town. It has some fine apartments that are stylishly if austerely furnished.

EXCURSIONS

★ **Avelengo (Hafling)** – *10km/6mi to the southeast*. A scenic road leads to the plateau of Avelengo which dominates the Merano valley.

★ **Merano 2000** ⊘ – *Access by cable-car from Val di Nova, 3km/1.9mi east*. This conifer-clad plateau is a winter sports centre. It also makes a good base for excursions into the mountains in summer.

★ **Tirolo** – *4km/2mi north. It can also be reached by skilift from Merano*. This charming Tyrolean village in the middle of vineyards and orchards is dominated by its castle (**Castel Tirolo**) ⊘ built in the 12C by the Counts of Val Venosta. **Castel Fontana** (also known as the **Brunnenburg**) is a strange set of 13C fortifications rebuilt at a later date. The American poet Ezra Pound worked on his *Cantos* here from 1958, when the accusation of collaboration with the Nazi regime based on his radio programmes was lifted.

★ **Val Passiria** – *50km/31mi to the Rombo Pass; 40km/25mi to the Monte Giovo Pass*. The road follows the Passiria Valley as far as the attractive Tyrolean village of **San Leonardo**, which clusters round its church. The **Rombo Pass Road★** (Timmelsjoch), steep and often cut out of the living rock, offers impressive views of the mountain peaks on the frontier. The **Monte Giovo Pass Road★** (Jaufenpass) climbs amidst conifers. On the way down, there are splendid **views★★** of the snow-capped summits of Austria.

To plan a special itinerary:

– consult the Map of Touring Programmes which indicates the recommended routes, the tourist regions, the principal towns and main sights;

– read the descriptions in the Sights section which include Excursions from the main tourist centres.

Michelin Maps nos 988 (Italia) and regional maps nos 428, 429, 430, 431, 432 and 433 indicate scenic routes, interesting sights, viewpoints, rivers, forests...

The Atlas Italia is a practical spiral-bound atlas with an alphabetical index.

MILANO★★★

MILAN – Lombardy
Population 1 302 808
Michelin map 428 F 9 (with plans of the conurbation) and
Michelin City Map 46 of Milan

Milan, the lively capital of Lombardy, is the second city in Italy as regards population, politics and cultural affairs, and first in the field of commerce, industry and banking. Set in the heart of northern Italy at the foot of the Alps, the enterprising spirit of its people has combined with certain historic circumstances to make Milan one of the country's most dynamic towns which is even today in full expansion.

The town is bounded by two concentric boulevards: the shorter, enclosing the medieval centre, has replaced the 14C ramparts, of which traces remain, among them the Porta Ticinese (**JY**) and the Porto Nuovo (**KU**). The outer wall marks the town's expansion during the Renaissance. After 1870 Milan expanded rapidly beyond its fortifications, particularly along the main communication axes.

S. Chirol

Books, records, sandwiches, ice-cream... just about anything can be found under
the arcades of the Galleria Vittorio Emanuele

HISTORICAL NOTES

Milan is probably Gallic (Celtic) in origin, but it was the Romans who subdued the city of Mediolanum in 222 BC and ensured its expansion. At the end of the 3C Diocletian made Milan the seat of the rulers of the Western Empire, and in 313 Constantine published the **Edict of Milan** which gave freedom of worship to the Christians. In 375 **St Ambrose** (340-396), a Doctor of the Church known for his eloquence, became bishop of the town, thus adding to its prestige.

The Barbarian invasions of the 5C and 6C were followed by the creation of a Lombard Kingdom with Pavia as capital. In 756 Pepin, King of the Franks, conquered the area, and his son Charlemagne was to wear the Iron Crown of the Kings of Lombardy from 774. In 962 Milan once again became capital of Italy.

In the 12C Milan allied itself to other cities to form the Lombard League (1167) to thwart the attempts of the Emperor Frederick Barbarossa to conquer the region. With the decisive victory at **Legnano** the cities of the league achieved their independence. In the 13C the **Visconti**, Ghibellines and leaders of the local aristocracy, seized power. The most famous member was **Gian Galeazzo** (1347-1402), an able war leader, man of letters, assassin and pious builder of Milan's Cathedral and the Carthusian Monastery of Pavia. His daughter, Valentina, married Louis, Duke of Orleans, the grandfather of Louis XII of France. This family connection was the reason for the later French expeditions into Italy.

After the death of the last Visconti, Filippo-Maria (d 1447), and three years of the Ambrosian Republic, the Sforza took over the rule of Milan, thanks to Francesco, the son of a simple peasant and son-in-law of Filippo-Maria Visconti. The most famous figure in the **Sforza** family, **Ludovico il Moro** (1452-1508) made Milan a new Athens by attracting to his court the geniuses of the time, Leonardo da Vinci and Bramante. However, Louis XII of France proclaimed himself the legitimate heir to

STAYING IN MILAN

Getting to the city

By car and train – Setting aside traffic problems, getting to Milan by car isn't too difficult as there is a good network of motorways serving the city (A4 Turin-Venice, A8/A9 Milan-Lakes, A7 Milan-Genova, A1 Autostrada del Sole which heads south). Getting to Milan by train is even simpler: the main railway station, the Stazione Centrale, is very close to the city centre and is connected to the underground system.

By plane – For flights arriving at Malpensa airport there is a train, leaving every half hour, that goes to Cadorna station (journey time 30min) which in turn is connected to the underground. Tickets cost 20 000L, 13 000L for children.
There are also buses from the airport which leave approximately every 20 minutes (journey time 45 min/1hr depending on traffic) and stop at both the Stazione Centrale and the Stazione Cadorna (in this case the bus serves as a substitute when the train doesn't run: before 6.50am and after 8.20pm). Tickets cost 13 000L.
Note that taxis are rather expensive as the airport is about 40km/25mi away from the city.
For flights landing at Linate airport there are buses which go to San Babila (line 73). Tickets cost 1 500L.

Getting around town

By public transport – It is highly advisable to use public transport: in general it is punctual and quick (especially the three underground lines). It also avoids problems like getting stuck in heavy traffic, losing one's way (particularly in the city centre with its obligatory traffic systems that frequently result in leading you far away from your required destination) and wandering around looking for parking spaces which often seem like mirages.

By car – If you do use a car bear in mind that parking in the city centre and the fiera (exhibition centre) district is by payment only and subject to regulations. Yellow lines indicate parking for residents only, blue lines allow parking for up to 2 hours as long as pre-paid cards, purchased from parking attendants or at tobacconist's, are displayed (1hr 2 500L, 2hr 5 000). It is advisable to park in garages (look out for blue signposts) or just outside the central zone of the city, but only where blue lines are displayed. Prices here are slightly lower than in the city centre and sometimes flat rates are charged (before you leave your car find out from the parking attendant what the charges are).

Accommodation in Milan

There is certainly no shortage of hotels in Milan but high prices make recommendations difficult. Suggestions below are divided into price ranges (for further information, see page 433), which, for hotels, refer to the price of a double room). It is important to check prices beforehand and to book as early as possible.

BUDGET

Youth hostel – Ideal for young people: **Ostello per la Gioventù A.I.G. Piero Rotta**, viale Salmoiraghi 1, Metrò: QT8 or Lotto. ☎ 02 39 26 70 95.

HOTELS
See map for hotel locations.
Città studi – Via Saldini 24, ☎ 02 74 46 66, fax 02 71 31 22. 45 rooms with air. conditioning. Credit cards accepted.
Simple, quiet and reasonably priced.
Garden – Via Rutilia 6, ☎ 02 55 21 28 38, fax 02 57 30 06 78. 23 rooms. Credit cards accepted. Closed in August.
Simple, but good value for money.

OUR SELECTION
Gala – Viale Zara 89, ☎ 02 66 80 08 91, fax 02 66 80 04 63. 23 rooms with air conditioning. Credit cards accepted. Closed in August.
This is a cosy hotel housed in a 19C villa with a garden.

TREAT YOURSELF!
Four Seasons – Via Gesù 8. ☎ 02 77 088, fax 02 77 08 50 00. 82 rooms with air conditioning, 16 suites. Credit cards accepted.
Originally a convent in the 15C, this is now one of the most luxurious hotels in Milan boasting cloisters and frescoes, impeccable service and every amenity including 2 restaurants and a fitness centre.

Spadari al Duomo – Via Spadari 11. ☎ 02 72 00 23 71, fax 02 86 11 84. 40 rooms with air conditioning. Credit cards accepted.

A collection of contemporary art adds to the pleasure of staying in this elegant hotel.

Enjoying Milan

While there are beautiful works of art to be found int he city, they tend to reveal themselves subtly and only to those with a sharp eye. If you are in a hurry (most people in Milan are) or are here on business, it is advisable to stick to those areas that best divulge the true character of this city which cannot be over-simplified with the usual criticisms about its hectic way of life, heavy traffic and stressful working conditions.

In the hope of contradicting sceptics, we recommend that you start the day with a cappuccino and brioche, have a drink accompanied by something to nibble on, listen to some music, have something tasty to eat, perhaps in an ethnic restaurant, or sip some thick, dark hot chocolate.

N.B. – The free magazine "**Zer02**", distributed in numerous bars and clubs, gives a good survey of what's on in the city – clubs, concerts and other events.

CAPPUCCINO, BRIOCHE, CHOCOLATE AND MORE

Bar Bianco – In the Palestro park, a stone's throw away from Porta Venezia. Also has the entire range of the Dairy Board.

Gattullo – Piazzale Porta Lodovica 2, Genova-Ticinese district. For straight-out-of-the-oven brioches and good cappuccino.

Taveggia – Via Visconti di Modrone 2, city centre. One of the best places in Milan for hot chocolate which is thick and dark.

SANDWICHES, SNACKS, ICE CREAM AND MILKSHAKES

Bar Basso – Via Plinio 39, in the Città Studi area. This is where the "wrong" Negroni cocktail was invented, using champagne instead of gin.

Bar della Crocetta – Corso di Porta Romana 67. The perfect place if you love sandwiches which come with a myriad of fillings and are enormous. An excellent address if you go to the Carcano Theatre which is literally next door.

Bar Magenta – Via Carducci 13, near S. Ambrogio. This is one of the most famous bars in Milan, frequented by people of different generations and ideological extraction, according to the fashion of the moment. It is worth tasting the very rich *aperitivo* while taking a look around: the counter is typical of the decor of this Art Nouveau style bar.

Crota piemunteisa – Piazza C. Beccaria 10. This tiny space behind the Duomo is just big enough to hold tables and wooden stools, a juke-box, two counters (one for beer, one for sandwiches – be sure to try the excellent frankfurters and sauerkraut): this is enough to have attracted over decades students old and new and a mixed bag of people who seem to have no common denominator.

Gelateria Marghera – Via Marghera 33, not far from the Teatro Nazionale and the fiera district. Excellent selection of creamy ice-creams.

Moscatelli – Corso Garibaldi 93, in the city centre. The perfect place to taste Italian wines accompanied by something to nibble on.

Victoria – Via Clerici 1, in the city centre. A classic bar that has a bit of everything including pizza.

Viel – Foro Bonaparte 71 and corso Buenos Aires 15. Famous for its milkshakes, this bar has been a student hang-out for decades.

BRUNCH?

Gran Burrone – Via P. Paoli 2. This bar-restaurant on the canal front, with its simple yet distinct personality, serves American style brunches (fruit juices, filter coffee, pancakes, hash browns, sausages, hamburgers, yoghurt) on Sundays from 10.30 am to 5pm. Expect to pay about 30 000L. Booking recommended. ☎ 02 58 10 02 16.

Il Melograno – Via V. Monti 16,not far from S. Maria delle Grazie and S. Ambrogio. The first of its kind in Milan. A pleasant restaurant that also has outdoor tables. Expect to pay about 20 000L. Booking recommended. ☎ 02 48 19 54 68.

PIZZA?

Geppo – Via G. B. Morgagni 37, in the Buenos Aires district. Practically a broom cupboard that serves delicious, large but thin pizza. Booking is recommended as everyone knows about this place! ☎ 02 29 51 48 62.

La Pizzaccia – Via Don Bosco 11, close to corso Lodi. An excellent address for pizza and other unusual dishes, as well as for the congenial atmosphere. Booking is advisable. ☎ 02 56 92 094.

Premiata Pizzeria – Alzaia Naviglio Grande 2. Tasty pizza in a setting where everything from the sign-board to the covered courtyard is pleasant. Very crowded (on arrival leave your name and you will be told how long you will have to wait, then go and have a walk in the neighbouring vicolo dei Lavandai until your table is ready). ☎ 02 89 40 06 48.

Rino Vecchia Napoli – Via G. Chavez 4, in the Loreto district. Excellent pizzas that deserve manifold awards. Go there armed with patience (it's always very crowded) and be prepared to make way for the next customers. Needless to say service is speedy. Don't forget to book! ☎ 02 26 19 056.

TRATTORIE AND MORE

La Bettola di Piero – Via Orti 17, a stone's throw away from Porta Romana. A simple establishment that reflects the agreeable nature of the family that runs it. Home cooking, mainly from the Lombardy region. Expect to pay about 35 000L. ☎ 02 55 18 49 47.

Le Scimmie – Via A. Sforza 49, in the canal district. A very dark trattoria with live music (mostly jazz). Opposite there is large boat on the canal that often has paintings on exhibit. ☎ 02 89 40 28 74.

Trattoria Madonnina – Via Gentilino 6, in the Genova-Ticinese district. A simple, pleasant trattoria with typical red and white checked tablecloths, even the window is welcoming. Home cooking and good desserts. Expect to pay about 40 000L. Remember to book. Open for lunch only except for Fridays and Saturdays. ☎ 02 89 40 90 89.

ETHNIC RESTAURANTS

These restaurants are reasonably priced. Expect to pay about 35/40 000L.

Bodeguita del Medio – Via Col di Lana 3, in the Genova-Ticinese district. If you like Cuban food.

Dixieland Cafè – Piazzale Aquileia 12, not from from corso Vercelli, ☎ 02 43 69 15, and via M. Quadrio, near the Cimitero Monumentale (cemetery). ☎ 902 659 85 13. Tex-mex food.

Fondaco dei Mori – Via Solferino 33, in the Brera district ☎ 02 65 37 11. For lovers of couscous and Arab food.

Mykonos – Via Tofane 5, in the viale Monza district, along the Martesana canal. A pretty, typical Greek restaurant. Booking essential. ☎ 02 26 10 209.

Shri Ganesh – Via Lombardini 8, in the canal district. A good Indian restaurant. ☎ 02 58 11 09 33.

the Duchy of Milan and set out to conquer the territory in 1500. His successor François I renewed the offensive but was thwarted at Pavia by the troops of the Emperor Charles V. From 1535 to 1713 Milan was under Spanish rule. During the plague, which ravaged the town from 1576 to 1630, members of the Borromeo family, St Charles (1538-84) and Cardinal Federico (1564-1631) distinguished themselves by their religious and humanitarian work.

Under Napoleon, Milan became the capital of the Cisalpine Republic (1797) and later of the Kingdom of Italy (1805). In 1815 Milan assumed the role of capital of the Venetian-Lombard Kingdom.

LIFE IN MILAN

The most frequented parts of Milan are around Piazza del Duomo (MZ), Via Dante (JX) and Via Manzoni (KV). At the **Galleria Vittorio Emanuele II**★ (MZ), which was laid out in 1877 to the plans of Giuseppe Mengoni, the Milanese come to talk, read their *Corriere della Sera* or drink coffee side by side with the tourists. For visitors looking for luxury items or just wanting to stroll through the most fashionable districts in the city, the Corso Vittorio Emanuele II (NZ), the Piazza San Babila (NZ), the Corso Venezia (LV), and the Via Monte Napoleone (NZ 171) and Via della Spiga (KV) – where the couture houses are – are pleasant areas to explore. The picturesque Brera District (KV), which is popular with artists and full of art galleries, is particularly busy in the evening. The Corso Magenta (HJX) and the streets around Sant'Ambrogio (HJX) have retained all the charm of the Milan of another age with old houses and winding, narrow streets lined with old cafes and antique shops.

Further artistic attractions include the excellent concerts and recitals at **La Scala** and the Conservatory (**Conservatorio** NZ T²). There are also numerous theatres (**Piccolo** JX T¹, Lirico, Manzoni, Carcano).

Milanese cooking is famous for its fillets of veal in breadcrumbs (*scaloppina alla milanese*), marrow bone (shin of veal) with its meat (*osso buco*), saffron-tinted *risotto* and vegetable and pork soup (*minestrone*). The perfect accompaniment is the Valtellina wines or those from the Pavia region.

FINE ARTS

The Cathedral (Duomo) marks the climax of architecture of the Gothic period. Prominent architects during the Renaissance were the Florentine, Michelozzo (1396-1472) and especially **Donato Bramante** (1444-1514), favourite master mason of Ludovico il Moro before he left for Rome. An admirer of Classical art, he was both a classicist and a man of great imagination who invented the **rhythmic articulation** (a façade with alternating bays, pilasters and niches) which imparted much of their harmony to many Renaissance façades.

The Lombard school of painting sought beauty and grace above all else. Its principal exponents were Vincenzo Foppa (1427-1515), Bergognone (1450-1523) and Bramantino (between 1450 and 1465-1536). The works of Andrea Solario (1473-c 1520), Boltraffio (1467-1516) and especially the delicate canvases of **Bernardino Luini** (c 1480-1532) attest to the influence of **Leonardo da Vinci** who stayed in Milan for some time.

Today Milan is the capital of Italy's publishing business and is an important centre, with its numerous art galleries, for contemporary art.

★★★ DUOMO (CATHEDRAL) ⊙ (MZ) **AND PRECINCTS** *1 1/2 hours*

★★★ **Exterior** – This Gothic marvel of white marble, both colossal and ethereal, bristling with belfries, gables, pinnacles and statues, stands at one end of a great paved esplanade teeming with people and pigeons. Whilst they are part of the setting, the pigeons are largely responsible for the building's deterioration. Its recent restoration was a lengthy and highly technical process. It should be seen late in the afternoon in the light of the setting sun. Building began with the chevet in 1386 on the orders of Gian Galeazzo Visconti, and continued in the 15C and 16C under the direction of Italian, French and German master masons. The façade was finished only between 1805 and 1809, on the orders of Napoleon.

MILANO

Albricci (Via A.)	MZ 3	Manzoni (Via A.)	MZ 140	Torino (Via)	MZ	
Arcivescovado (Via)	MNZ 10	Marconi (Via)	MZ 144	Unione (Via)	MZ 264	
Augusto (Largo)	NZ 12	Marino (Piazza)	MZ 147	Verdi (Via)	MZ 269	
Baracchini (Via)	MZ 17	Mengoni (Via)	MZ 153	Verziere (Via)	NZ 270	
Bergamini (Via)	NZ 27	Mercanti (Piazza e Via)	MZ 155	Visconti di Modrone (Via)	NZ 275	
Borgogna (Via)	NZ 36	Missori (Piazza)	MZ 162	Vittorio		
Cantù (Via C.)	MZ 48	Monforte (Corso)	NZ 168	Emanuele II (Corso)	NZ	
Cordusio (Piazza)	MZ 72	Monte Napoleone (Via)	NZ 171			
Edison (Piazza)	MZ 83	Morone (Via)	MNZ 176			
Festa del Perdono (Via)	NZ 93	Orefici (Via)	MZ 188	Palazzo dei Giureconsulti	MZ C	
Gonzaga (Via)	MZ 105	Pattari (Via)	MZ 197	Palazzo della Ragione	MZ D	
Laghetto (Via)	NZ 120	S. Clemente (Via)	NZ 231	Museo del Duomo	MZ M¹	
		S. Radegonda (Via)	MZ 237	Casa di Manzoni	MZ M⁷	
		S. Stefano (Via Piazza)	NZ 240	Conservatorio	NZ T²	
		Sforza (Via Francesco)	NZ 248			

Traffic is restricted in the central zone divided into sectors outlined in green
To pass from one sector to another return to the perimeter road

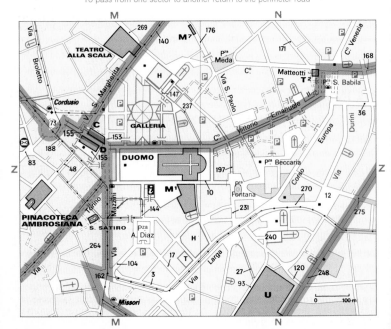

Walk round the cathedral to view the **east end** with three vast bays of curved and counter-curved tracery and wonderful rose windows. The overall design is the work of a French architect, Nicolas de Bonaventure, and of a Modenese architect, Filippino degli Organi.

From the 7th floor of the Rinascente store in Corso Vittorio Emanuele there is an interesting close-up view of the architectural and sculptural features of the roofs.

The saints keep a vigilant eye over Milan from the cathedral spires

S. Chirol

★★★ **Interior** – In contrast with the exterior this is bare, severe and imposing, an impression further strengthened by the dim light. The nave and four aisles are separated by 52 pillars of tremendous height (148m/486ft). The width across the transepts is 91m/299ft. The windows of the nave, aisles and transept have fine stained glass, which dates in part back to the 15C and 16C.

The mausoleum of Gian Giacomo Medici in the south arm of the transept is a fine work by Leoni (16C). In the north arm is the curious statue of St Bartholomew (who was flayed alive), by the sculptor Marco d'Agrate. Pass under the dome and in front of the monumental chancel (1570-90) with the high altar by Pellegrino Tibaldi. The magnificent bronze candelabrum in the north transept is a French work of the 13C. In the crypt **(cripta)** and treasury **(tesoro)** ⊘, visitors can see the silver urn containing the remains of St Charles Borromeo, Bishop of Milan, who died in 1584, as well as ivories and gold and silver church plate. On the way out, you can see the entrance to the Paleo-Christian baptistery **(battistero)** ⊘ and the 4C basilica of Santa Tecla whose outline has been marked out on the parvis.

★★★ **Visita ai Terrazzi** ⊘ – Take a walk on the roof to view the 135 pinnacles, numerous white marble statues (2 245 in all!), full of grace and elegance, and the Tiburio or central tower (108m/354ft), surmounted by a small gilt statue, the Madonnina (1774).

★★ **Museo del Duomo** ⊘ (MZ **M¹**) – Housed in the royal palace built in the 18C by Piermarini, the cathedral museum shows the various stages in the building and restoration of the cathedral, and houses sculptures, tapestries and old stained glass windows. Also of note are the splendid **Aribert Crucifix★** (1040), the original support for the Madonnina (1772-73), and the large wooden **model★** (modellone) of the cathedral made to a scale of 1:20 in the 16C-19C.

★ **Via and Piazza Mercanti** (MZ **155**) – In Via Mercanti stands the Palace of Jurisconsults (Palazzo dei Giureconsulti **C**), built in 1564 with a statue of St Ambrose teaching on the façade. The Piazza Mercanti is quiet and picturesque. The charming Loggia degli Osii (1316) is decorated with heraldic shields, statues of saints and the balcony from which penal sentences were proclaimed. To the right of the loggia is the Baroque palace of the Palatine schools, with statues of the poet Ausonius and St Augustine in the niches. Opposite is the town hall, the **Palazzo della Ragione** or Broletto Nuovo (**D**) which was built in the 13C and extended in the 18C. The **equestrian statue** on the façade is of the governing magistrate (podestà) Oldrado da Tresseno. It is a Romanesque work by Antelami.

MILANO

Aurispa (Via)	JY 14	Circo (Via)	JX 63	Giardini (Via dei)	KV
Battisti (Via C.)	KLX 20	Coldi Lana (Viale)	JY 65	Guastalla (Via)	KX
Bocchetto (Via)	JX 30	Col Moschin (Via)	JY 66	Maffei (Via A.)	LY
Borgogna (Via)	KX 36	Conca del Naviglio (Via)	JY 69	Manzoni (Via A.)	KV
Borgonuovo (Via)	KV 38	Cordusio (Piazza)	KX 73	Melzo (Via)	LU
Calatafimi (Via)	JY 45	Curie (Viale P.N.)	HV 77	Mercato (Via)	JV
Caradosso (Via)	HX 49	Dugnani (Via)	JX	Modestino (Via)	HY
Ceresio	JU 59	Dugnani (Via)	HY 80	Molière (Viale E.)	HY
		Fatebenefratelli (Via)	KV 92	Monte Napoleone (Via)	KV
		Ghisleri (Via A.)	HY 101	Muratori (Via L.)	LY

Traffic is restricted in the central zone divided into sectors outlined in green

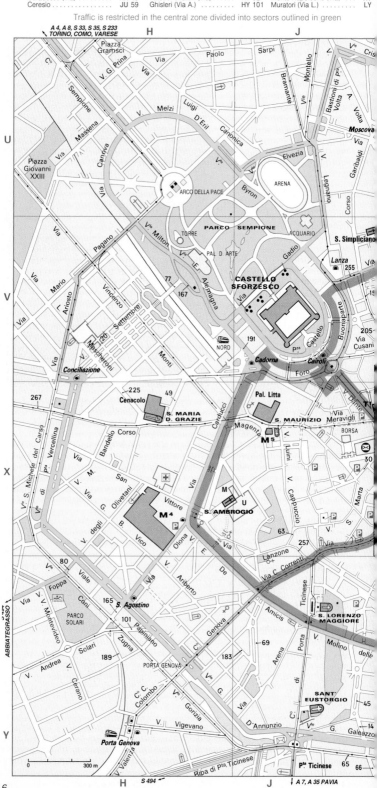

216

Oggiono (Via M. d')	.....	HJY 183
Orseolo (Via)	....	HY 189
Paleocapa (Via)	....	JV 191
Ponte Vetero (Via)	....	JV 205
Ruffini (Via Flli)	....	HX 225
S. Babila (Piazza)	....	KX 228
S. Calimero (Via)	....	KY 230
Savoia (Viale F. di)	....	KU 243
Tivoli (Via)	....	HV 255
Torchio (Via)	....	JX 257
Torriani (Via N.)	....	LU 258
Vercelli (Corso)	....	HX 267
Verdi (Via)	....	KV 269
Vittorio Veneto (Viale)	....	KLU 278
Zezon (Via)	....	LU 281

HOTELS

Spadari al Duomo	....	KX ⓒ
Four Seasons	....	KV ⓓ
Pal. Bagatti Valsecchi	....	KV L
Museo Poldi Pezzoli	.....	KV M²
Galleria d'Arte Moderna	..	LV M³
Museo Nazionale della Scienza e della Tecnica L. da Vinci		HX M⁴
Museo Civico di Archeologia		JX M⁵
Museo Civico di Storia Naturale		LV M⁶
Piccolo Teatro		JX T¹

To pass from one sector to another return to the perimeter road

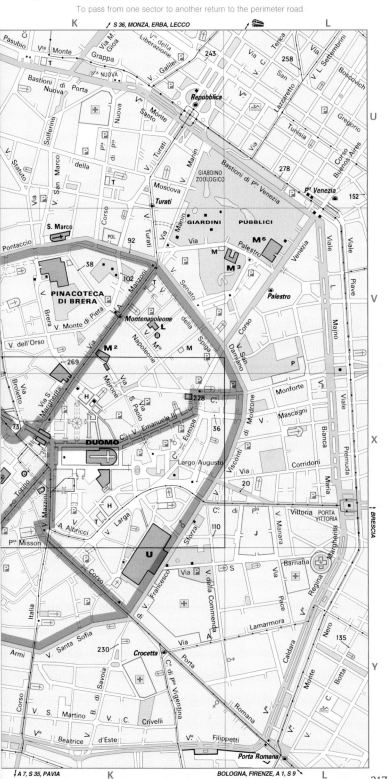

★★ **Teatro alla Scala** (MZ) – Traditionally recognised as being the most famous opera in the world, La Scala surprises people seeing it for the first time because of the simplicity of its exterior, which gives no hint of the magnificence of its auditorium. Built from 1776 to 1778 with six levels of boxes, it can seat an audience of 2 000 people.

The **Museo teatrale alla Scala**★ ⊘ presents memorabilia relating to Toscanini and Verdi, including busts, portraits and stage costumes. From the museum, you can go into one of the boxes and see the auditorium.

★★★ MUSEUMS

★★★ **Pinacoteca di Brera** ⊘ (KV) – The Brera Art Gallery forms part of series of institutes – the Accademia di Belle Arti (Fine Arts Academy), the Biblioteca (library), the Osservatorio Astronomico (observatory) and the Istituto Lombardo di Scienze, Lettere ed Arti (The Lombardy Institute of Science, Arts and Letters) – all of which are housed in a fine 17C building. In the courtyard looms a statue of Napoleon (1809) depicted as a victorious Roman emperor by Canova.

The tour of the gallery starts with the Jesi collection which introduces the main artistic movements of the first-half of the 20C: note the sense of movement and dynamism of the futurist painters (Boccioni's *La Rissa in galleria*) and the clean geometry of the metaphysical works by Carrà *(The metaphysical muse)* and Morandi *(Still Life)*. The sculpture collection is dominated by three artists: Medardo Rosso, Arturo Marini and Marino Marini. Along the passage to the left, it is possible to admire the Maria Theresa Room and the library, Biblioteca Braidense.

The Cappella Mocchirolo gives a brief review of Italian painting from the 13C to 15C (*Polyptych of Valle Romita* by Gentile da Fabriano).

The Brera holding of **Venetian paintings** is the largest and most important one outside Venice. Masterpieces include the *Pietà*★★ by Giovanni Bellini, in which the tragic event is echoed by the deserted landscape and metallic sky, and the famous *Dead Christ*★★★ by Mantegna, an admirable meditation on death with a realism given added pathos by the artist's skill in foreshortening. In the Napoleon Rooms hang major works by Tintoretto **(Miracle of St Mark★)**, Veronese *(Dinner at the house of Simon)* and Giovanni and Gentile Bellini *(St Mark preaching at Alexandria in Egypt)*.

The **Lombard school** is well represented and pride of place is given to a *polyptych with Madonna and Saints*★ by Vicenzo Foppa, whose work shows the influence of the Paduan school and Mantegna in particular, and the lovely, Leonardesque *Madonna of the rose garden*★★★ by Bernardino Luini.

In another room are the *Montefeltro altarpiece*★★★ by Piero della Francesca, in which the ostrich egg symbolises both the immaculate conception and the abstract and geometrical perfection of form sought by the artist, and the *Marriage of the Virgin*★★★ by Raphaël, in which the graceful, delicate figures merge in the background with the circular Bramante-style building. Further along, Caravaggio's magnificent *Meal at Emmaus*★★★ is a fine example of the artist's use of strong contrast between light and shade and of his realism.

In the Room of 18C Venetian painting *Rebecca at the Well*★★ by Piazzetta is an exquisite portrayal of the girl's gaze, with expressions of both astonishment and innocence, even though the portrait is in profile.

The last rooms are dedicated to 19C-20C painting. Paintings on display include the *Carro rosso* by Fattori and *(The Kiss)* by Hayez. Amongst the foreign artists are Ribera, Van Dyck, Rubens and Reynolds.

★★★ **Castello Sforzesco** ⊘ (JV) – This huge brick quadrilateral building was the seat of the Sforza, Dukes of Milan. The **municipal art collections** are now on display in the castle.

★★ **Museo di Scultura** – *Ground floor.* The minimalist approach of the museum's layout is particularly effective. Romanesque, Gothic and Renaissance works are mainly by Lombard sculptors. Interesting works include the **tomb of Bernabò Visconti**★★ (14C) surmounted by his equestrian statue from the Romanesque period; and the **reclining figure of Gaston de Foix** with accompanying **statues**★★ (1523) by Bambaia in his usual classical and harmonious style, as well as the unfinished *Rondanini Pietà*★★★ by Michelangelo, both from the Renaissance.

★ **Pinacoteca** – *1st floor.* The gallery displays works by Mantegna, Giovanni Bellini, Crivelli, Bergognone, Luini, Moretto, Moroni, Magnasco, Tiepolo, Guardi, Lotto etc.

★ **Museo degli strumenti musicali** – An extensive collection of stringed instruments, some of which are made to resonate by the use of a bow and others which are plucked, wind instruments and keyboards.

Museo archeologico – *In the vault under the Rochetta courtyard*. The museum includes a prehistory collection, Egyptian art and a lapidary exhibition. Another section of the museum is housed in the monastery of San Maurizio (*see below*).

★★ **Pinacoteca Ambrosiana** ⊙ (MZ) – This palace, erected in 1609 for Cardinal Federico Borromeo, was originally one of the first libraries open to the public. A few years later the gallery was added and housed the collection donated by the cardinal.

This is one of the richest libraries in the world and boasts a fine collection of drawings including Leonardo's **Codice Atlantico** series.

The gallery is housed on the first floor and opens with the original body of work donated by the cardinal, as well as subsequent acquisitions of the same period (15C and 16C). Note the *Portrait of a Lady* by De Predis and the delightful *Infant Jesus and the Lamb*★★ by Bernardino Luini, imbued with the warm intimacy that the artist expresses to bring alive a tender moment. One of the most notable paintings of the Lombard School is the *Sacra Conversazione* by Bergognone (1453-1523), with its Madonna dominating the composition whose use of perspective is still very much anchored in the Middle Ages. The *Musician*★★ by Leonardo da Vinci has an unusually dark background for the artist who tended to create a strong relationship between the dominant figures and their surrounding space. In Room 3 the *Madonna Enthroned with Saints*★ by Bramantino is striking for the huge toad at the feet of St Michael (symbolising the dragon slain by the saint) contrasting with the grotesque swollen figure of Arius (a reference to the defeat of Arian heresy led by St Ambrose). Note also the slightly masculine appearance of the Madonna's face which seems to be veiled by the hint of a beard. The delicate *Nativity*, a copy from Barocci, is pervaded by a glowing light which irradiates from the child, illuminating the Virgin's tender face. The splendid preparatory **cartoons**★★★ for Raphael'a School of Athens (the fresco was painted in the Vatican *Stanze* in Rome) are the only surviving example of large Renaissance cartoons. Caravaggio's *Basket of Fruit*★★★ made still-lives the central subject matter in painting. On a monochrome background shrivelled leaves and almost rotten fruit render the idea of death and the transitory nature of life. The cardinal's collection also includes a series of fine Flemish paintings by Paul Bril and Jan Brueghel's remarkable *Mouse with a Rose*★ painted on copper. Other rooms are mainly devoted to Italian art from the 16C-19C and focus on painting from Lombardy. Of particular note are four stunning **portraits**★ by Francesco Hayez.

★★ **Museo Poldi Pezzoli** ⊙ (KV M²) – Attractively set out in an old mansion, the museum displays collections of weapons, fabrics, paintings, **clocks**★, and small bronzes. Among the paintings on the 1st floor (at the top of an old staircase built into an irregular, octagonal-shaped stairwell) are works by the Lombard School (Bergognone, Luini, Foppa, Solario, Boltraffio), **portraits**★★ of Luther and his wife by Lucas Cranach and, in the Golden Hall decorated with a **Persian carpet**, the famous *Portrait of a Woman*★★★ by Piero del Pollaiolo, a *Descent from the Cross* and a *Madonna and Child*★★ by Botticelli, and a *Dead Christ*★ full of pathos by Giovanni Bellini. The other rooms are hung with works by Pinturicchio, Palma il Vecchio (*Portrait of a Courtesan*), Francesco Guardi, Canaletto, Tiepolo, Perugino, and Lotto.

Galleria d'Arte Moderna ⊙ (LV M³) – *16 Via Palestro*. The Modern Art Gallery has been set out in the Villa Reale built in 1790 which also houses the Marino Marini Museum and the Grassi Collection. It includes *The Fourth Estate* by Pelliza da Volpedo, works by Giovanni Segantini (*The Two Mothers, The Angel of Life*), a famous *Portrait of Alexander Manzoni* by Francesco Hayez, and sculptures by the Milanese sculptor, Medardo Rosso (1858-1928). The **Carlo Grassi Collection** comprises works by Gaspare Van Wittel, Pietro Longhi, Cézanne, Van Gogh, Manet, Gauguin, Sisley, Corot, Toulouse-Lautrec, Boccioni and Balla. The **Marino Marini Museum** displays sculptures and paintings by the artist. The **Contemporary Art Pavilion** (PAC) (*14 Via Palestro*) has been designed for temporary exhibitions (*additional charge*).

★ **Casa del Manzoni** ⊙ (MZ M⁷) – *1 Via G. Morone*. It was in this luxurious mansion that Manzoni lived for 60 years. On the ground floor, visitors can see the library with the writer's books and desk. On the first floor are memorabilia, photographs, portraits, letters and illustrations of his most famous novel, *The Betrothed*. The bedroom where he died still has its original furniture.

★ **Museo Civico du Storia Naturale** ⊙ (LV M⁴) – *55 Corso Venezia*. The Natural History Museum contains interesting geological, paleontological and zoological collections. The instructive layout with numerous dioramas is particularly suitable for children.

★★ **Palazzo Bagatti Valsecchi** ⊘ (**KV L**) – The façade of the palace is divided into two parts: they are connected by a loggia *(1st floor)* surmounted by a balcony. All that can be seen of the present residence *(opposite)* of the Bagatti Valsecchi family is the beautiful internal courtyard.

Museum/ At the top of the flight of steps embellished with a wrought iron railing is the piano nobile of the residence of Fausto and Giuseppe Bagatti Valsecchi, who, at the end of the 19C, decided to furnish their house in the Renaissance style, as was customary at the time. They used authentic pieces and faithful reproductions, adding their own personal touch. The two private apartments, belonging to Fausto and Giuseppe, are open to the public as well as the reception rooms.

Fausto's rooms comprise: the **Fresco Room** (depicting the *Madonna of Mercy* (1496)), the **library** decorated with two splendid 16C leather globes (the blue one is a particularly fine example) and various objects including a 17C German roulette set and the **Bedroom** which is dominated by a magnificent bed carved with *Christ's Ascent to Calvary* and various battle scenes. The bathroom is particularly charming: the bath is set in a Renaissance-style niche. The **Labyrinth Passage**, which is aptly named after the ceiling decoration, leads to the **Domed Gallery**, an area that serves to link the various rooms on the floor. The **room** containing a stove from Valtellina (sala della stufa valtellinese) gives access to Giuseppe's apartment: the warm atmosphere is due to the fine wood panelling embellished with a sculpted frieze with human figures, animals and floral patterns. The **Red Room**, used by Giuseppe and Carolina Borromeo, his wife, contains children's furniture including a baby walker, commode and two cradles as well as a 17C Sicilian bed; Giuseppe's room, all in green, has a fine sculpted ceiling.

Access to the formal rooms is via the domed gallery: the huge **reception hall**, heated by an impressive chimney, the **Arms Room** with its fine collection of bayonets and the **Dining Room** decorated with 14C Flemish tapestries, paintings and 17C ceramics.

★ **Museo Nazionale della Scienza e della Tecnica Leonardo da Vinci** ⊘ (**HX M⁴**) – This vast museum exhibits interesting scientific documents. In the **Leonardo da Vinci Gallery**, visitors can see models of the Tuscan artist's inventions. The other sections of the museum deal with acoustics, chemistry, telecommunications, and astronomy. Large pavilions are given over to displays relating to the railways, aircraft and shipping.

HISTORIC MILAN

★ **Santa Maria delle Grazie** (**HX**) – This Renaissance church erected by the Dominicans from 1465 to 1490 was finished by Bramante. The interior (restored), is adorned with frescoes by Gaudenzio Ferrari in the fourth chapel on the right, and the impressive **dome**★, gallery and cloisters all by Bramante. The best view of the **east end**★ is to be had from Via Caradosso (**HX 49**).

Cenacolo ⊘ – In the former refectory *(cenacolo)* of the monastery is the famous portrayal of *The Last Supper*★★★ by **Leonardo da Vinci**, painted between 1495 and 1497 at the request of Ludovico il Moro. It is a dramatic and skilful composition that creates the illusion that the painted space is a continuation of the room itself. Christ is depicted at the moment of the institution of the Eucharist: His half-open mouth suggests that he has just finished speaking. Around Him there is a tangible sense of shock and premonition of imminent disaster with its intimation of Judas' betrayal.

The technique used (Leonardo chose egg tempera, possibly mixed with oil and placed the image on the coldest wall in the room), dust, the ravages caused by a bombardment on the refectory in 1943 and, more recently, smog have all contributed to the necessity of considerable restoration work (it has been documented that the painting has undergone restoration 10 times). In fact the condition of the painting was already compromised in 1517 and in 1901 Gabriele D'Annunzio wrote an ode with an explicit title: *On the Death of a Masterpiece*. In May 1999, after 21 years of restoration work, the Cenacolo was finally unveiled and its original colours and use of *chiaroscuro* admired.

Opposite the fresco is a superb *Crucifixion*★ (1495) by Montorfano, unfortunately somewhat overshadowed by *The Last Supper*.

★★ **Basilica di Sant'Ambrogio** (**HX**) – The basilica was founded at the end of the 4C by St Ambrose and it is a magnificent example of the 11C-12C Lombard-Romanesque style with its pure lines and fine **atrium**★ adorned with capitals. The façade pierced by arcading

---

The seating of the Apostles

From left to right: Bartholomew, James the Great, Andrew, Judas Iscariot, Peter and John.

To the right of the figure of Christ, from left to right: Thomas, James the Less, Philip, Matthew, Judas Thaddeus and Simon the Zealot.

> **The curious story of a Milanese born in Treviri who became a bishop before being baptised, baptised St Augustine, changed the liturgical calendar and the rite of the Milanese Church and then became Patron**
>
> ### Saint of Milan
>
> Ambrose (c 337/339-397), an Imperial civil servant born in Treviri, was one of the key figures of the Roman Empire. He brought peace to the Christians of Milan who were disunited following the death of the Arian bishop Aussenzio (Arianism was a heresy which denied the divine nature of Christ) and by public acclaim was declared Bishop of Milan before having even been baptised.
>
> He was authoritative with emperors and even imposed a public penitence on Emperor Theodosius who had been responsible for the massacre of Thessalonicans.
>
> The power of his sermons proved crucial in the conversion of St Augustine whom he baptised in 387.
>
> Ambrose also renewed the liturgy and calendar of the Milanese Church which even today follows the "Ambrosian" rite.

is flanked by a 9C campanile to the right and a 12C one to the left. The doorway was renewed in the 18C and has 9C bronze panels. In the crypt, behind the chancel, lie the remains of St Ambrose, St Gervase and St Protase.

Inside the basilica there is a magnificent Byzantine-Romanesque **ambo★** (12C) to the left of the nave, and at the high altar a precious gold-plated **altar front★★** which is a masterpiece of the Carolingian period (9C). In the chapel of San Vittore in Ciel d'Oro *(at the end of the south transept)* there are remarkable 5C **mosaics★**. From the far end of the north transept one can gain access to Bramante's portico.

★ **S. Eustorgio** (JY) – The Romanesque basilica, dedicated to St Eustorgius, was founded in the 9C and belonged to the Dominicans. The side chapels were added in the 15C. Behind the choir is a chapel, the **Cappella Portinari★★**, a jewel of the Renaissance style by the Florentine, Michelozzo. The architecture, frescoes illustrating the life and martyrdom of St Peter by Vincenzo Foppa, and sculpture (richly carved marble tomb, 1339) by Giovanni di Balduccio, are all in complete harmony.

★ **Basilica di S. Satiro** (MZ) – With the exception of the 9C square campanile and the west front, which dates from 1871, the basilica, like the baptistery, was designed by Bramante. The architect adopted a totally Classical idiom to solve the problem posed by lack of space, skilfully integrating gilded stucco and *trompe-l'œil* work to create the impression of a chancel. The **dome★** is also remarkable. The basilica also includes a small Oriental-style chapel on the plan of a Greek Cross, decorated with a 15C painted terracotta statue of the *Descent from the Cross* and fragments of 9C-12C frescoes.

★ **Ca'Granda-Ex Ospedale Maggiore** (NZ) – The hospital, founded by Francesco Sforza in 1456, was completed in the 17C and is at present occupied by various University faculties. It is composed of three different ranges and five courtyards; the loggias of the façades are decorated with the busts of famous men.

In the Brera district, the **Church of San Marco** (KV) is also open to the public. It was rebuilt in 1286 over much older foundations. It houses an interesting black and white fresco painted by the Leonardo da Vinci School *(north aisle)* representing a *Madonna and Child with St John the Baptist*. It was discovered in 1975.

Not far away is the **Basilica di San Simpliciano** (JV), built in 385 AD on the orders of St Ambrose, Bishop of Milan. A few extensions were made to the Paleo-Christian basilica during the Early Middle Ages and the Romanesque period. On the vaulting in the apse is a *Coronation of the Virgin* by Bergognone (1481-1522).

Both these churches host excellent concerts.

★★ **San Maurizio** (or **Monastero Maggiore**) (JX) – This is a monastery church built in the Lombard-Renaissance style (early 16C). The bare façade, which often goes unnoticed on Corso Magenta despite the narrowness of the pavement, conceals an interior divided into two, well-lit sections and entirely decorated with **frescoes★** by Bernardino Luini. To reach the chancel (where concerts are held), take the passageway situated to the left at the back of the church.

Opposite is the **Palazzo Litta** with its 18C façade.

Museo Civico di Archeologia ⊙ (JX **M⁵**) – *Corso Magenta 15*. The museum housed in the extant buildings of the great Benedictine monastery is divided into five sections: Roman and Barbarian art on the ground floor and Greek, Etruscan and Indian (Gandhara) art in the basement. The most outstanding Roman exhibits are the 4C **Trivulzio cup★** with fine openwork cut from a single piece of glass, and the large **silver platter from Parabiago★** (4C) featuring the festival of the goddess Cybele.

There are interesting remains of the 3C Roman wall in the garden.

Opposite the museum stands Palazzo Litta with its 18C façade.

* **Basilica di San Lorenzo Maggiore** (JY) – The basilica was founded in the 4C and rebuilt in the 12C and 16C. It has kept its original octagonal plan. In front of the façade is a majestic **portico*** of 16 Roman columns, all that remains of the Roman town of Mediolanum. The majestic interior is in the Byzantine-Romanesque style and has galleries exclusively reserved for women, a vast dome and spacious ambulatory. From the south side of the chancel pass through the atrium and then a 1C Roman doorway to a chapel, the **Cappella di Sant'Aquilino*** ⊙ dating from the 4C. It has retained its original plan and the paleo-Christian mosaics.

Further on, the **Porta Ticinese** (JY), a vestige of the 14C ramparts, leads to the attractive quarter (Naviglio Grande), where the artists gather.

EXCURSION

* **Abbazia di Chiaravalle** ⊙ – *7km/4mi southeast. Leave by Porta Romana* (LY) *then consult the plan of the built-up area on Michelin Map 428.*

The abbey, founded by St Bernard of Clairvaux (hence Chiaravalle) in 1135, is dominated by an elegant polygonal **bell tower***. It is an early example of Gothic architecture in Italy. Brick and white stone are combined in the typical Cistercian style. The porch was a 17C addition. Inside, there are a nave and two aisles and 14C frescoes on the dome. Another fresco in the south transept represents the Tree of the Benedictine Saints. The small cloisters are delightful.

MODENA*

Emilia-Romagna

Population 175 013

Michelin map 428, 429 or 430 I 14

Town plan in the Michelin Atlas Italy

Modena, situated between the Secchia and Panaro Rivers, at the junction of the Via Emilia and the Brenner Autostrada, is an active commercial and industrial centre (manufacture of shoes and cars and railway engineering) and one of the most important towns in Emilia-Romagna. However, Modena with its archbishopric and university, remains a quiet town whose old quarter in the vicinity of the cathedral is adorned by several spacious squares lined with arcades. It is in this part of the town that one finds such gastronomic specialities as *zamponi* (stuffed pigs' trotters) and Lambrusco, a sparkling red wine which is produced locally.

The original Roman colony of Mutina then became independent before becoming part of the Lombard League, falling under the domination of the **Este** from Ferrara to avoid being ruled by Bologna. In 1453 the duchy of Modena was created for Borso d'Este. In 1598 they were expelled from Ferrara by the pope and they took refuge at Modena which reached the peak of its prosperity during the 17C.

In 1997 the Duomo, Torre Civica and Piazza Grande were included in UNESCO's World Heritage List.

SIGHTS

*** **Duomo** – The cathedral is dedicated to St Geminian and is one of the best examples of Romanesque architecture in Italy. Here the Lombard architect, Lanfranco, gave vent to his sense of rhythm and proportion. The *maestri campionesi (see p. 49)* put the finishing touches to his work. Most of the sculptural decoration is due to Wiligelmo, a 12C Lombard sculptor.

The façade is divided into three parts and is crowned by the Angel of Death carrying a fleur-de-lys, a work carried out by the "*campionesi*" masters. The central portal is enhanced by a porch supported by two lions by Wiligelmo whose name can be seen on one of the stones to the left of the portal. The doorway also includes the date 1099, the year in which the church was founded. The low reliefs above the side doors and to each side of the central portal depict episodes from the Book of Genesis.

The south side overlooking the square is remarkable for its architectural rhythm. From left to right, are the Prince's Doorway carved by Wiligelmo, the Royal Entrance, a gem carved by the *campionesi* masters in the 13C and a 16C pulpit decorated with the symbols of the four Evangelists.

To reach the other side of the church, walk under the Gothic arches linking the cathedral to the huge Romanesque campanile built of white marble (88m/286ft) known as *Ghirlandina* because of the bronze garland on its weather-vane. On the north side is the Fishmarket Door, so-called because it used to lie near the fish market at the bishop's palace; it was carved by the Wiligelmo School. The recessed orders of the arches are decorated with episodes from the Breton cycle, one of the first examples of this subject matter in Italy.

The interior of the cathedral reveals the ebullience of Gothic churches and the simplicity of Romanesque architecture. It has ogival vaulting. The great arches are supported on alternating mighty brick pillars and on more slender pillars which support the triforium. In the north aisle beyond the Statuine Altar (with small statues), rises a 14C pulpit and, opposite this, a rough wooden seat traditionally said to have been used by the public executioner.

The choir stalls in the presbytery, the work of Lendinara, date from the 15C. The **rood screen**★★★, a Romanesque masterpiece, is supported by Lombardy lions and telamones and is the work of *"campionesi"* masters dating from 12C-13C. The parapet is decorated with scenes from Christ's Passion.

The atmospheric crypt has a large number of slender columns. It contains a terracotta sculpture group of the *Holy*★ *Family* (15C) by Guido Mazzoni and St Geminiano's tomb. In the south aisle of the church is an exquisite 16C terracotta Nativity scene.

A museum **(museo del Duomo)** ⊙ contains the famous 12C **metopes**★★, low reliefs which used to surmount the flying buttresses. They represent wandering players or symbols incomprehensible today, but whose modelling, balance and style have an almost classical air.

Palazzo dei Musei – This 18C palace contains the two most important art collections gathered by the Este family.

★ **Biblioteca Estense** ⊙ – *1st floor, staircase on the right*. This is one of the richest libraries in Italy, containing 600 000 books and 15 000 manuscripts, the most interesting of which are on display. The prize exhibit is the **Bible of Borso d'Este**★★. It has 1 020 pages illuminated by a team of 15C Ferrara artists, including Taddeo Crivelli.

★★ **Galleria Estense** ⊙ – This gallery opens with the **Marble bust of Francesco I d'Este**, a masterpiece of Gian Lorenzo Bernini. The 15C Modena School is well represented (Bonascia, Francesco Bianchi Ferrari); it owes much to the Ferrarese School which is represented by the powerfully modelled *St Anthony*★ by Cosmè Tura. There is also a fine collection of Venetian masters (Cima da Conegliano, Veronese, Tintoretto, Bassano), 16C Ferrarese painting (Dosso Dossi, Garofalo) and works linked to the Accademia degli Incamminati in Bologna (the Carracci, Guido Reni, Guercino). The foreign schools are also well represented; note the **Portrait of Francesco I d'Este** by Velasquez.

As well as paintings the gallery also has some fine terracotta figures, typical works by Modenese sculptors from the 15C-16C. (Nicolò dell'Arca, Guido Mazzoni, Antonio Begarelli). There are also collections of ceramics and musical intruments; note the splendid **Este harp** (1581).

★ **Palazzo Ducale** – This noble and majestic building, the ducal palace, was begun in 1634 for Francesco I d'Este and has an elaborately elegant design. Today it is occupied by the Infantry and Cavalry schools.

EXCURSIONS

Abbazia di Nonantola ⊙ – *11km/7mi north*. The abbey was founded in the 8C and flourished during the Middle Ages. The 12C abbey church has some remarkable **Romanesque sculpture**★ carved by Wiligelmo's assistants in 1121.

Carpi – *18km/11mi north*. This attractive small town has a 16C Renaissance cathedral by Peruzzi, overlooking **Piazza dei Martiri**★. The **Castello dei Pio**★ ⊙, an imposing building bristling with towers, includes a courtyard by Bramante and contains a small museum. The 12C-16C Church of Sagra has a tall Romanesque campanile, **Torre della Sagra**.

MOLISE

Michelin Map 431 A-C 24-27

An ancient land of thoroughfares for passing herds, armies and travellers, Molise is shaped like a wedge inserted between the Apennines and the sea. Mountains dominate the territory and inhabitants of the region have always looked to them as a natural defence and refuge: strongholds, fortified castles and villages nestling on hillsides characterise its landscape.

Sights are listed in alphabetical order.

Agnone – *42km/26mi northeast of Isernia*. This old village owes its fame to the **Fonderia pontificia Marinelli** ⊙, the oldest bell factory in the world, founded in the 10C. The central street via Vittorio Emanuele is bordered by the Church of St Emidius (15C) and the Italo-Argentinian theatre which was founded in the last century with funds raised from immigrants in South America. **Via Garibaldi**, lined with houses embellished by lions which bear witness to the community of Venetian merchants, leads to the **Ripa**★, a garden with a fine view over the Verrino Valley.

★ Altilia Sæpinum ⊘ – *25km/15mi south of Campobasso on the S 87*. The ruins of *Sæpinum* rise in the middle of an attractive town on which construction began in the 17C using plundered stone. The Samnites founded the city which was subsequently occupied by the Romans who made it a municipality and in the Augustan Age built a city wall measuring 1 250m/4 101ft with four fortified doors and articulated by 25 towers.

Sightseeing – Access is through the Porta di Terravecchia gateway at the extreme south of the *cardo*, the city's principal street. At the crossroads of the *cardo* and the *decumano* streets the remains of the **basilica** (with Ionic columns on its peristyle) to the left and, to the right, the **forum**, a huge paved rectangular area. Turning right on the *decumano* note the remains of the senate house *(curia)*, the temple dedicated to Jupiter, Juno and Minerva, some remains of mosaic flooring, a semicircular recess belonging to the "house of oil-presses" with four brick oil containers and the impluvium of a Samnite house. To the extreme east of the *decumano*, beyond the **Porta di Benevento** gateway, lies the **Mausoleum of Ennius Marsus**, a fine semicircular crenellated building standing on a square plinth.

Returning to the main crossroads and continuing up the *decumano* cross the old residential and commercial quarters with remains of workshops and the *macellum* (market). At the eastern end of the street rises the **Porta di Boiano★**. From the top there is a good view of the western part of the fortifications and the ruins of the well-preserved central part of the city. Outside the fortifications turn right and make for the **Mausoleum of Numisius Ligus**. This square tomb is crowned by four acroteria and has a simple elegance.

Against the inner face of the wall, the intimate **theatre★** has preserved its monumental entrance of white stone. The pretty adjacent buildings house a **museum** which has displays of material pertaining to *Sæpinum*.

Pietrabbondante – *28km/17mi northeast of Isernia*. In an evocative natural setting stands the **Italic Sanctuary of Pietrabbondante★** ⊘. This was a sacred site for the Samnites who turned it into a political as well as religious centre and thus a symbol of anti-Roman resistance. All that remains of the sanctuary are the foundations of the **high temple**, remains of the minor temple and the fine **theatre** which stands on the slopes of the hill.

Santa Maria di Canneto – *36km/22mi southeast of Vasto*. This monastery, erected in the 8C, is a fine expression of Lombard-Cassinese culture. The **church** has two admirable sculptural works: the **pulpit★** (8C) and the **altarpiece★** portraying the refectory (10C). Adjacent to the church remains of a Roman villa have been discovered, with traces of mosaic flooring (3C-4C AD).

San Vincenzo al Volturno ⊘ – *28km/17mi northwest of Isernia*. In an enchanting natural setting with the backdrop of the Mainarde mountains and striking hilltop towns, stands this Benedictine monastery which was founded in the 8C and repeatedly destroyed by Saracen attacks. The **church**, rebuilt in around 1950 using remains from previous constructions, is heralded by a **sequence of arches** of the 13C. The **excavations** currently being carried out beyond Volturno have brought to light some priceless remains of the original abbey.

Termoli – Termoli is the only port in Molise and the departure point for the Tremiti islands. It has a fine **castle** (13C) which forms part of the fortifications ordered by Emperor Frederick II to defend the port. The narrow alleyways wind their way up to the **Cathedral★★** (12C), one of the most significant examples of Romanesque architecture in Molise. The façade is enlivened by lesenes and blind twin arches. The motif of the arches continues on the left side and on the apse which dates from the 13C. Inside the crypt has mosaic flooring from the 10C-11C.

Abbazia di MONTECASSINO★★

MONTE CASSINO ABBEY – Lazio

Michelin map 430 R 23

The access road to one of the holy places of Roman Catholicism climbs in hairpin bends, affording remarkable views of the valley. The monastery of Monte Cassino, the mother house of the Benedictines, was founded in 529 by St Benedict (d 547). It was here that the saint drew up a complete and precise set of rules combining intellectual study and manual labour with the virtues of chastity, obedience and poverty. In the 11C under Abbot Didier the abbey's influence was at its height. The monks were skilled in the arts of miniatures, frescoes and mosaics and their work greatly influenced Cluniac art.

The abbey has been destroyed several times since its foundation and was most severely damaged at the **Battle of Cassino** (May 1944). After the Allies had taken Naples, the Germans made Cassino the key stronghold in the system of defences guarding the approaches to Rome. On 17 May the Allies launched their final assault, with the Polish corps as the spearhead. After a raging battle, the Germans abandoned Cassino on the following day, allowing the Allies to join forces and leaving open the road to Rome.

The abbey has been rebuilt to the original plans as a truncated square building with massive underpinnings, and once again crowns the summit of Monte Cassino.

★★ **Abbey** ⊙ – It is preceded by a suitably solemn suite of four communicating cloisters. The bare façade of the basilica quite belies the sumptuousness of the **interior**★★ where marble, stucco, mosaics and gilding create a dazzling if somewhat austere ensemble in the 17C-18C style. The chancel has lovely 17C walnut stalls and the marble tomb enshrining the remains of St Benedict.

★★ **Museo** ⊙ – The museum presents documents on the abbey's history and works of art which survived the 1944 bombing.

On the way down to Cassino are a museum, the **Museo archeologico nazionale** ⊙, and the neighbouring excavation site (amphitheatre, theatre and tomb of Umidia Quadratilla).

The length of time given in this guide
– for touring allows time to enjoy the views and the scenery;
– for sightseeing is the average time required for a visit.

MONTECATINI TERME✝✝✝

Tuscany
Population 20 650
Michelin map 428, 429 or 430 K 14
See Michelin Green Guide Tuscany

Montecatini is one of Italy's most frequented and most fashionable thermal spas and specialises in treating stomach, intestinal and liver ailments. There is an interesting museum of modern art **(Museo dell'Accademia d'Arte)** ⊙ which has works by Italian artists (Guttaso, Primo Conti, Messina) and some of the personal belongings of Verdi and Puccini.

EXCURSION

★★ **Collodi** – *15km/9mi west.* Collodi was the pen-name adopted by Carlo Lorenzini, the author of *Pinocchio*, whose mother was born in the village. A park, **Parco di Pinocchio**★ ⊙, in the form of a maze is laid out on the banks of the Pescia River.

★★ **Villa Garzoni** ⊙ – The villa is an amazing building dating from the Baroque period and the 17C. In the **gardens**★★★ are vistas, pools, clipped trees, grottoes, sculpture and mazes creating a charming and imaginative spectacle.

LARA PESSINA

The spas

MONTEFALCO★

Umbria
Population 5 609
Michelin map 430 N 19

14C ramparts still girdle this charming little town, which lies among vineyards and olive groves. It is perched – as its name suggests – like a falcon on its nest and has been called the Balcony of Umbria. Montefalco, won over to Christianity in 390 by St Fortunatus, has its own saint, Clara, not to be confused with the companion of St Francis of Assisi.

Torre Comunale ⓥ – From the top (110 steps) of the Communal Tower there is a beautiful **panorama**★★★ of nearly the whole of Umbria.

Museo di S. Francesco ⓥ – This historic Franciscan church, now deconsecrated, provides an enchanting setting for the museum which contains mid-15C **frescoes**★★ depicting scenes from the life of St Francis and St Jerome by Benozzo Gozzoli, a *Nativity* by Perugino and an awe inspiring *Crucifix* by the Expressionist Master of Santa Chiara (active in Umbria from the end of the 13C to the beginning of the 14C), who possibly collaborated with Giotto in the Basilica of Assisi. The museum also houses a gallery displaying works by Francesco Melanzio (c 1487-1526), a native of Montefalco.

S. Illuminata – The church is Renaissance in style. The tympanum of the main doorway and several niches in the nave were painted by Francesco Melanzio.

S. Agostino – *Corso G. Mameli*. The church, dedicated to St Augustine, is Gothic with frescoes by Umbrian painters of the 14C, 15C and 16C.

San Fortunato – *1km/0.6mi south*. The church is preceded by a small 14C cloister. On the tympanum of the doorway Benozzo Gozzoli painted a **fresco**★ showing the Madonna between St Francis and St Bernardino. Inside, the south altar is adorned with a fresco of St Fortunatus, also by Gozzoli.

Abbazia di MONTE OLIVETO MAGGIORE★★

MONTE OLIVETO MAGGIORE ABBEY – Tuscany
Michelin map 430 M 16 – 36km – 22 miles southeast of Siena
See Michelin Green Guide Tuscany

The extensive rose-coloured brick buildings of this famous **abbey** ⓥ lie hidden among cypresses, in a countryside of eroded hillsides. Monte Oliveto is the Mother House of the Olivetans, a congregation of the Benedictine Order which was founded in 1313 by Blessed Bernard Tolomei of Siena.

Chiostro Grande – The great cloisters are decorated with a superb cycle of 36 **frescoes**★★ depicting the life of St Benedict by **Luca Signorelli** from 1498 and by **Il Sodoma** from 1505 to 1508. The frescoes begin on the right by the west door at the great arch, with two of Sodoma's masterpieces: Christ of the Column and Christ bearing His Cross. The majority of the frescoes are by Il Sodoma, a refined artist, who was influenced by Leonardo da Vinci and Perugino (*see Index*) and shows great interest in the flattering representation of different human types, landscapes and picturesque details, as illustrated in the following frescoes: no 4 depicting St Benedict receiving his hermit's robe; no 12 the saint greeting two young men in a crowd – the people are shown in different poses; no 19 voluptuous courtesans have been sent to seduce the monks (splendid architectural elements open onto a long perspective). Signorelli (*see Index*), who completed only eight frescoes, is more concerned with the powerful, sculptural nature of the figures and the dramatic effect of the compositions where landscape is only secondary: in no 24 St Benedict resuscitates a monk who has fallen off a wall.
The cloisters lead to the refectory (15C), the library and the pharmacy.

Chiesa abbaziale – The interior of the abbey church was remodelled in the Baroque style in the 18C. The nave is encircled by inlaid **stalls**★★ (1505) by Fra Giovanni da Verona. Access to the crib is to the right of the chancel.

Help us in our constant task of keeping up-to-date.
Send us your comments and suggestions to

Michelin Travel Publications
38 Clarendon Road – WATFORD Herts WD1 1SX
Tel: (01923) 415000

thegreenguide-uk@uk.michelin.com

MONTEPULCIANO★★

Tuscany

Population 13 846
Michelin map 430 M 17
See Michelin Green Guide Tuscany

Montepulciano, perched on the crest of a hill of volcanic rock, with impressive **views**★★ in between valleys, has numerous religious and secular buildings influenced by the Florentine Renaissance. Inhabitants of Chiusi, fleeing from the Barbarian invasion, founded the town in the 6C. This was the birthplace of **Politian** (1454-94), one of the most exquisite Renaissance poets. The poet was a great friend of Lorenzo de' Medici, whom he called Lauro (Laurel) and whom he saved from assassination during the Pazzi Conspiracy (see Duomo in FIRENZE). The *Stanzas*, Politian's masterpiece, describe a sort of Garden of Delight haunted by attractive women. Politian's verse matches the painting of his friend Botticelli.

★ **Città antica** – Beyond the gateway, Porta al Prato, the high street, the first part of which bears the name Via Roma, loops through the monumental area in the old town. At no 91 Via Roma stands the 16C **Palazzo Avignonesi** attributed to Vignola; no 73, the palace of the antiquarian Bucelli, is decorated with stone from Etruscan and Roman buildings; further along, the **Renaissance façade**★ of the church of **S. Agostino** was designed by Michelozzo (15C); a tower opposite has a Pulcinello as Jack. At the Logge del Mercato (Grain Exchange) bear left into Via di Voltaia nel Corso: Palazzo Cervini (no 21) is a fine example of Florentine Renaissance architecture with its rusticated stonework and curvilinear and triangular pediments designed by Antonio da Sangallo, a member of an illustrious family of architect-sculptors, who designed some of the most famous buildings in Montepulciano. Continue along Via dell'Opio nel Corso and Via Poliziano (no 1 is the poet's birthplace).

★★ **Piazza Grande** – Forming the centre of the city, this square with its irregular plan and varying styles avoids architectural monotony while blending into a harmonious whole. The Town Hall **(Palazzo Comunale★)** is a Gothic building which was remodelled in the 15C by Michelozzo. From the top of the square tower **(torre)** ⊙ there is an immense **panorama★★★** of the town and its environs. The majestic Renaissance **Palazzo Nobili-Tarugi★** facing the cathedral is attributed to Antonio da Sangallo the Elder. The palace has a portico and great doorway with semicircular arches; six Ionic columns, standing on a lofty base, support the pilasters of the upper storey. The square also has an attractive **well★** adorned with an admirable sculpture of lion supporters holding aloft the Medici coat of arms. Inside the 16C-17C cathedral **(Duomo)** to the left of the west door lies the recumbent figure of Bartolomeo Aragazzi, secretary to Pope Martin V; the statue was part of a monument by Michelozzo (15C), as were the low reliefs of the two first pillars and the statues flanking the high altar. The monumental **altarpiece★** (1401) above the high altar is by the Sienese artist, Taddeo di Bartolo.

Museo civico-Pinacoteca Crociani ⊙ – *Via Ricci*. There is a fine collection of glazed terracotta by Andrea della Robbia; Etruscan remains and paintings dating from the 13C to 18C.

Continue along the high street to Piazza San Francesco for a fine **view** of the surrounding countryside and of the church of San Biagio. Walk down Via del Poggiolo and turn right into Via dell'Erbe to return to the Logge del Mercato.

★★ **Madonna di San Biagio** – *1km/0.6mi. Leave by the Porta al Prato and then take the Chianciano road before turning right*. This splendid church built in pale-coloured stone and consecrated in 1529 is an architectural masterpiece by **Antonio da Sangallo**. The building, which was greatly influenced by Bramante's design for St Peter's in Rome, is a useful example of Bramante's concepts. San Biagio's design is simpler although it is planned in the shape of a Greek cross and is crowned by a dome. Two campaniles flank the main façade; one is unfinished and the other includes the three architectural orders (Doric, Ionic and Corinthian). The south transept is prolonged by a semicircular sacristy. The interior gives the same impression of majesty and nobility. To the left of the west door is a 14C Annunciation. The 16C marble high altar is imposing.

Opposite the church stands the Canonica (canonry), an elegant porticoed building.

EXCURSION

‡‡ **Chianciano Terme** – *10km/6mi southeast*. This fashionable thermal spa is pleasantly situated. The healing properties of its waters (which can relieve kidney and liver disorders) were known to the Etruscans and the Romans. There are some fine parks and plenty of sophisticated hotels and spas.

MONTE SANT'ANGELO★

Puglia

Population 14 027

Michelin map 431 B 29 – Local map Promontorio del GARGANO

Monte Sant'Angelo stands in a wonderful site★★. The town is built on a spur (803m/2 634ft) dominated by the massive form of its castle and overlooks both the Gargano Promontory and the sea. It was in a nearby cave between 490 and 493 that the Archangel Michael, chief of the Heavenly Host, appeared three times to the bishop of Siponto. After a further apparition in the 8C it was decided to found an abbey. During the Middle Ages all the Crusaders came to pray to the Archangel Michael, the saintly warrior, before embarking at Manfredonia.

On 29 September the annual feast day includes the procession of the Archangel's Sword.

★ **Santuario di San Michele** – The church dedicated to St Michael, designed in the transitional Romanesque-Gothic style, is flanked by a detached octagonal campanile dating from the late 13C. Opposite the entrance a long covered stairway leads down to the very beautiful and richly worked bronze door★ which is of Byzantine origin and dates from 1076. It gives access to both the nave with pointed vaulting which opens onto the cave (to the right) in which St Michael is said to have made his apparition. The marble statue of the saint is by Andrea Sansovino (16C) and the 11C episcopal throne is decorated in a style characteristic of Puglia.

★ **Tomba di Rotari** ⊙ – *Go down the stairs opposite the campanile.* The tomb is to the left of the apse of the ruined Church of St Peter's. Above the entrance are scenes from the Life of Christ. Inside, the tower rises in stages through a square, an octagon and finally a triangle to the dome. The tomb was supposed to contain the remains of Rotharis, a 7C King of the Lombards, but is really a 12C baptistery.

Chiesa di S. Maria Maggiore – *Left of Tomba di Rotari.* The church built in the Apulian Romanesque style boasts a fine doorway. Inside there are traces of the Byzantine frescoes which covered the walls. Note the figure of St Michael in the south aisle.

EXCURSION

San Giovanni Rotondo – *24km/15mi west on the S 272.* This is a site of pilgrimage dear to myriad devotees of **Padre Pio** (1887-1968). The Capuchin monk from **Pietrelcina**, near Benevento, was ordained and lived here. In 1918 stigmata appeared on his body which disappeared on his death. He was sanctified in 1999.

MONZA

Lombardy

Population 118 928

Michelin map 428 F 9

Monza is quite an attractive industrial town specialising mainly in textiles. It stands on the edge of the Brianza, a lovely green hilly area dotted with lakes, attractive towns and villas set in lovely gardens.

★ **Duomo** – This cathedral was built in the 13C-14C and has an attractive Lombard façade★★ (1390-96) in alternating white, green and black marble, which is remarkable for its harmonious proportions and variety of openings. It was the work of Matteo da Campione, one of the famous *maestri campionesi (see p. 49)*, who spread the Lombard style throughout Italy.

The interior★ was remodelled in the 17C. The splendid silver gilt altar front★ dates from the 14C. To the left of the chancel is the Chapel of the Queen of the Longobards, Theodolinda (6C-7C), with its fascinating 15C frescoes★ depicting scenes in the life of this pious sovereign.

The treasury (tesoro★) ⊙ has the famous 5C-9C Iron Crown★★ of the Kings of Lombardy, which was offered by Pope Gregory I the Great to the queen. In addition there are fine pieces of 6C to 9C plate, 17C reliquaries and 16C tapestries.

★★ **Parco di Villa Reale** – The majestic neo-Classical royal villa was the residence of Eugène de Beauharnais and Umberto I of Italy, who was assassinated at Monza by an anarchist in 1900. This vast park is landscaped in the English manner.

In the northern part of the park there are several sporting facilities and the Monza racing circuit which is the venue for the annual Grand Prix Formula One race.

NAPOLI★★★

NAPLES – Campania
Population 1 035 835
Michelin map 431 E 24 (with plans of the conurbation)
Local map see Golfo di NAPOLI

The beauties and surprises of Naples have been praised by innumerable poets and writers. Even UNESCO's committee fell under her spell, to the extent that in 1995 they included the historic centre of the city in their World Heritage List. The lovely bay, with its horizon bounded by Posillipo, the islands, the Sorrento Peninsula and lofty Vesuvius, is one of the most beautiful in the world. Its fame has also been enhanced by the area's attractive climate and the special atmosphere evoked by the streetlife, a world of fantasy and superstition, magic and fate. This is why it is important to experience the everyday life of the Neapolitans (so vital, vivacious yet fatalistic and sad) as well as the sights of historical interest. It is Naples' streetlife which gives this town its theatrical character.

Even if the chaotic traffic and the industrial quarters to the East might be disappointing, it is a city rich with artistic interest waiting to be explored and it is well worth persevering. As in every big city sightseeing in poorer areas, often the most picturesque and interesting (Spaccanapoli or via Tribunale), requires some caution to avoid spoiling an otherwise pleasant holiday. It is therefore advisable to leave valuables at the hotel and not carry around large sums of cash, important documents (passports, driving licences) and large bags. If you are travelling by car in Naples (not recommended) avoid leaving luggage or flashy belongings in the car. Finally, avoid the area around via Forcella and the Sanità district, even in the daytime.

HISTORICAL NOTES

According to legend, the siren Parthenope gave her name to a town which had sprung up round her tomb, which is why Naples is called the Parthenopaean City. In fact, Naples originated as a Greek colony named Neapolis, conquered by the Romans in the 4C BC. Rich inhabitants of Rome like Virgil, Augustus, Tiberius, Nero etc used to spend the winter there, but the Neapolitans themselves retained the Greek language and customs until the decline of the Empire.

Since the 12C seven princely families have reigned over Naples: the Normans, Hohenstaufens, Angevins, Aragonese, Spanish and Bourbons. The French Revolution of 1789 brought in French troops, and in 1799 a **Parthenopaean Republic** was set up, followed by a French kingdom (1806-15) under Joseph Bonaparte (Napoleon's brother) and afterwards Joachim Murat (Napoleon's brother-in-law), both of whom promoted excellent reforms. From 1815 to 1860 the restored Bourbons remained in power in spite of the 1820 and 1848 revolts.

Ferdinand of Aragon's fleet in Naples harbour (15C)

229

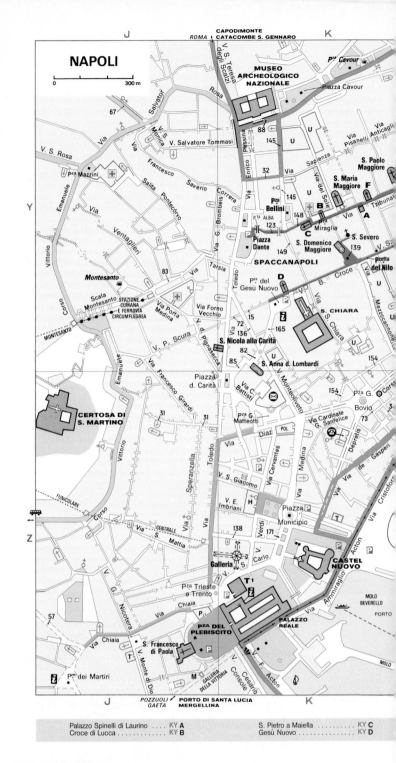

NAPOLI

| Palazzo Spinelli di Laurino .... | KY A | S. Pietro a Maiella .... | KY C |
| Croce di Lucca .... | KY B | Gesù Nuovo .... | KY D |

ART IN NAPLES

A royal patron of the arts – Under the princes of the House of Anjou, Naples was endowed with many ecclesiastical buildings, which were greatly influenced by the French Gothic style. **"Good King Robert" of Anjou** (1309-43) attracted poets, scholars and artists from various regions of Italy to his court in Naples. Boccaccio spent part of his youth in Naples where he fell in love with Fiammetta, whom some believe to have been the king's own daughter. His friend Petrarch also spent some time in this city. In 1324 Robert the Wise brought the Sienese sculptor **Tino di Camaino** to adorn many

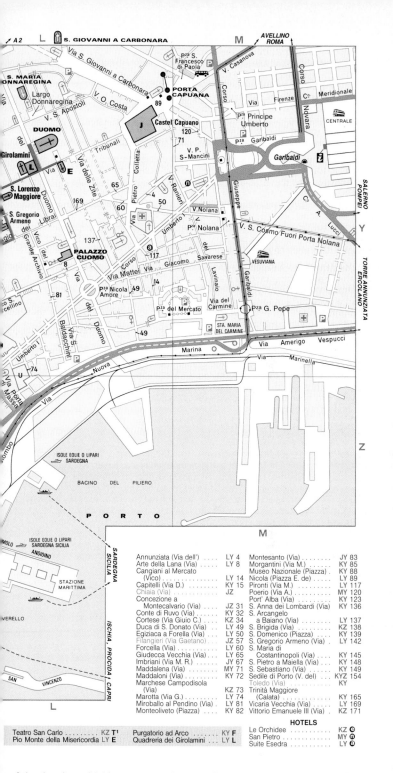

Annunziata (Via dell')	LY 4	Montesanto (Via)	JY 83
Arte della Lana (Via)	LY 8	Morgantini (Via M.)	KY 85
Cangiani al Mercato		Museo Nazionale (Piazza)	KY 88
(Vico)	LY 14	Nicola (Piazza E. de)	LY 89
Capitelli (Via D.)	KY 15	Pironti (Via M.)	LY 117
Chiaia (Via)	JZ	Poerio (Via A.)	MY 120
Concezione a		Port' Alba (Via)	KY 123
Montecalvario (Via)	JZ 31	S. Anna dei Lombardi (Via)	KY 136
Conte di Ruvo (Via)	KY 32	S. Arcangelo	
Cortese (Via Giuio C.)	KZ 34	a Baiano (Via)	LY 137
Duca di S. Donato (Via)	LY 49	S. Brigida (Via)	KZ 138
Egiziaca a Forella (Via)	LY 50	S. Domenico (Piazza)	KY 139
Filangieri (Via Gaetano)	JZ 57	S. Gregorio Armeno (Via)	LY 142
Forcella (Via)	LY 60	S. Maria di	
Giudecca Vecchia (Via)	LY 65	Costantinopoli (Via)	KY 145
Imbriani (Via M. R.)	JY 67	S. Pietro a Maiella (Via)	KY 148
Maddalena (Via)	MY 71	S. Sebastiano (Via)	KY 149
Maddaloni (Via)	KY 72	Sedile di Porto (V. del)	KYZ 154
Marchese Campodisola		Toledo (Via)	KY
(Via)	KZ 73	Trinità Maggiore	
Marotta (Via G.)	LY 74	(Calata)	KY 165
Miroballo al Pendino (Via)	LY 81	Vicaria Vecchia (Via)	LY 169
Monteoliveto (Piazza)	KY 82	Vittorio Emanuele III (Via)	KZ 171

HOTELS

Teatro San Carlo	KZ T¹	Purgatorio ad Arco	KY F	Le Orchidee	KZ ◯
Pio Monte della Misericordia	LY E	Quadreria dei Girolamini	LY L	San Pietro	MY ⓜ
				Suite Esedra	LY ⓢ

of the churches with his monumental tombs. Other churches were embellished with frescoes by the Roman artist Pietro Cavallini, slightly later by Giotto whose works have unfortunately disappeared, and by Simone Martini.

The Neapolitan School of Painting (17C - early 18C) – The busiest period in Neapolitan painting was the 17C which began with the arrival in Naples in 1607 of the great innovator in painting, **Caravaggio**. The master's style was bold and realistic: he often used real people as models for his crowd scenes. He used chiaroscuro with dramatic effect with light playing a fundamental part. So a new school of painting flourished, its members greatly inspired by the master. The principal followers were Artemisia Gentileschi, the Spaniard **Jusepe de Ribera** alias Spagnoletto, **Caracciolo** and the Calabrian Mattia Preti. One pupil who differed greatly from the others was **Luca Giordano** whose spirited compositions were full of light. His decorative work heralds the painting of the 18C. **Francesco Solimena** perpetuated the former's style but he was also influenced by the more sombre style of Mattia Preti and by Classicism drawing inspiration from Arcadia. His paintings are characterised by chiaroscuro effects which lend solidity to shapes and a strong balance to the use of space. There are examples of this artist's works in several churches in Naples including the Church of San Nicola alla Carità (**KY**).

The Baroque period – Numerous were the architects who built fine Baroque buildings in Naples and the surrounding area. **Ferdinando Sanfelice** (1675-1748) had a highly inventive and theatrical approach to staircases, which he placed at the far end of the courtyard where they became the palace's most important decorative feature. It was, however, **Luigi Vanvitelli** (1700-73) who was the great Neapolitan architect of the 18C. The Bourbon King, Charles III, entrusted Vanvitelli with the project to build another Versailles at Caserta (see CASERTA).
It was in the 17C that Naples began to specialise in the marvellous **Christmas Mangers** (presepi) which were to become very famous.

Music and theatre – Neapolitans have always shown a great love of music, be it for **opera**, where great importance is placed on the virtuosity of the singer, or for more **popular music**, sometimes joyful, sometimes melancholy, practised to the accompaniment of a guitar or a mandolin. Naples gave the character Scaramouch (old fox) to the Commedia dell' Arte (see BERGAMO) as well as Pulcinella which is the true Neapolitan face. The great theatrical tradition has continued to the present day with such prodigious exponents as the **De Filippo** brothers, particularly **Eduardo** (1900-1984).

Religious festivals – In Naples these are sumptuous and the best known are the Festivals of Madonna di Piedigrotta, Santa Maria del Carmine and especially the Feast of the Miracle of St Januarius. Between Christmas and Epiphany (Twelfth Night) the local churches are adorned with splendid cribs. See the Calendar of Events at the end of the guide.

★★ CITY CENTRE 2hr30min

★★ **Castel Nuovo** ⊙ (or **Maschio Angiono**) (**KZ**) – This imposing castle, surrounded by deep moats, was built in 1282 by Pierre de Chaulnes and Pierre d'Agincourt, the architects of Charles I of Anjou. It was modelled on the castle in Angers. A remarkable **triumphal arch**★★ embellishes the entrance on the town side. This masterpiece bearing sculptures to the glory of the House of Aragon, was built to designs by Francesco Laurana in 1467. Access to the **Sala dei Baroni** is via the staircase in the inner courtyard (at the far end on the left). The fine vaulting is star shaped, formed by the tufa groins intersecting with other architectural features. The **Cappella Palatina** (14C) features an elegant Renaissance doorway which was previously surmounted by Laurana's splendid **Virgin** now kept, along with other works by the same artist in the sacristy.

★ **Teatro San Carlo** ⊙ (**KZ T¹**) – The theatre was built under Charles of Bourbon in 1737 and rebuilt in 1816 in the neo-Classical style. The opera house is an important institution in the Italian world of music.
The splendid auditorium, with boxes on six levels and a large stage, is built entirely of wood and stucco to achieve perfect acoustics.

★ **Piazza del Plebiscito** (**JKZ**) – This noble semicircular "square" (19C) is enclosed on one side by the royal palace, on the other by the neo-Classical façade of the Church of St Francis of Paola (**San Francesco di Paola**), built on the model of the Pantheon in Rome and prolonged by a curving colonnade. The equestrian statues of Ferdinand I and Charles III of Bourbon are by Canova.

★ **Palazzo Reale** ⊙ (**KZ**) – The royal palace was built at the beginning of the 17C by the architect Domenico Fontana and has been remodelled several times. The façade retains more or less its original appearance. Since the late 19C the niches on the façade contain eight statues of the most famous Kings of Naples. A huge **staircase** with twin ramps and crowned by a coffered dome leads to the **apartments**★ and the sumptuously decorated **royal chapel**. It was only after 1734 that royalty lived in the apartments. The richly ornamented rooms have retained their numerous works of art, tapestries, paintings, period furniture and fine porcelain. Of particular interest are the splendid **door knockers**★ made of wood: putti, nymphs and animals are set off against a gilded background in a floral pattern.

★★ **Porto di Santa Lucia** – See plan of the built up area on Michelin Map 431. Santa Lucia is the name of the small suburb that juts out towards the sea. It is best known as the name of a tiny port, immortalised by a famous Neapolitan song, nestling between a rocky islet and the jetty linking it to the shore. **Castel dell'Ovo** is a severe edifice built by the Normans and remodelled by the Angevins in 1274. Legend has it that Virgil hid a magic egg *(uovo)* within its walls and that the destruction of the egg would result in a similar fate for the castle.

From the jetty there is a splendid **view★★** of Vesuvius on the one hand and of the western side of the bay on the other. In the evening, go further along to Piazza Vittoria which offers a **view★★★** of the residential suburbs on the Vomero and Posillipo hillsides, brightly lit up by a myriad of twinkling lights.

Legend and mystery around Castel dell'Ovo

B. Morand/DIAF

★★ SPACCANAPOLI AND DECUMANUS MAXIMUS

4hr on foot

This is the heart of old Naples. With its numerous churches, dilapidated palaces, small crafts and businesses, and its ancient streets where swarms a lively populace, it is undoubtedly the most engaging part of the town. Its main axis, formed by the Via S. Benedetto Croce, S. Biagio dei Librai and Vicaria Vecchia is nicknamed Spaccanapoli, meaning the street which bisects Naples. It follows the course of one of the main roads through ancient Naples, the Decumanus Maximus which now more or less forms the Via Tribunali (**KLY**). Strolling through these streets is to witness Naples' evolution through the centuries, beginning with the Greeks and the Romans.

In Piazza del Gesù Nuovo, which is dominated by the impressive Baroque monument of the Virgin, is the **Church of Gesù Nuovo** ⊘ (**KY D**) with its fine façade and diamond pointed facing, a unique testimony to the 15C Palazzo Sanseverino nearby. The inside of the façade is decorated with Solimena's *Chasing Heliodorus from the Temple.*

Enter Via Benedetto Croce.

★ **Santa Chiara** ⊘ (**KY**) – Sancia of Majorca, the wife of Robert the Wise of Anjou, had this Church of the Poor Clares built in the Provençal-Gothic style. The simple façade is preceded by a porch in peperine, the grey colour of which is in pleasant contrast to the yellow tufa. The interior, having been restored with Baroque features, was destroyed in the 1943 bombing and then rebuilt in its original form. A bare, lofty nave, lit by tall, narrow twin windows, opens onto 9 chapels. At the end, in place of an apse, a long wall is lined with memorials to the Anjou dynasty: including the **tomb★★** of Robert the Wise, the work of Florentine sculptors, and on the right the tomb of Charles of Anjou, attributed to Tino di Camaino who is also responsible for the **tomb★** of Marie de Valois *(near the south wall).* To the right of the presbytery a vestibule leads to the 14C **chancel★** which is accessed via a fine marble doorway: on the walls there are remains of frescoes by Giotto's followers.

★★ **Cloisters** – The current lay-out is the work of Domenico Antonio Vaccaro who, in the 18C, transformed the interior of the cloisters into a garden. It was divided into four parts with two covered avenues that intersect at the centre to form a cross. He was also responsible for embellishing the wall of the portico, the seats and the columns lining the avenues with fine **majolica decoration★** which features floral motifs, landscapes, pastoral scenes and mythological subjects.

LIFE IN NAPLES

Getting there – It is preferable to get to Naples by train or plane as traffic in the city is chaotic and few hotels have garages. Capodichino Airport, ☎ 081 78 96 111 or 147-86 56 641 (for ALITALIA flights), is 6km/4mi away from the city. Bus no 14 connects to Naples, the terminus is in piazza Garibaldi where the railway station is.

Getting around the city – In general Naples has a good network of public transport although overground transport does fall prey to traffic which can be chock-a-block. *Information listed is intended as a guideline only, for details check transport maps available from Tourist Offices.*

Trains – The **Cumana** and **Circumflegrea** trains (terminus in piazza Montesanto) connect Naples to Bagnoli and the Campi Flegrei district. The **Circumvesuviana** train (terminus in corso Garibaldi) has swift connections to Herculaneum, Pompei, Castellammare, Vico Equense and Sorrento.

Underground – The **Metropolitana FS** crosses the city vertically from piazza Garibaldi down to Pozzuoli, while the **metropolitana collinare** from piazza Vanvitelli goes back up to Piscinola/Secondigliano.

Funicular railway – Three routes offer swift connections to the Vomero: the **Funicolare centrale** (via Toledo-piazza Fuga), the **Funicolare di Chiaia** (via del Parco Margherita-via Cimarosa) and the **Funicolare di Montesanto** (piazza Montesanto-via Morghen). The **Funicolare di Mergellina** links via Mergellina to via Manzoni.

Tickets – "GiraNapoli" tickets allow travel on buses, trams, the funicular railway and the underground (both the Metropolitana FS and the Metropolitana collinare). There are two types of ticket: 90min tickets and 1-day tickets. Monthly passes are also available.

Radiotaxi – There are 4 radio taxi companies in operation: **Cotana** ☎ 081 57 07 070, **Free** ☎ 081 55 15 151, **Napoli** ☎ 081 55 64 444 and **Partenope** ☎ 081 55 60 202.

Sea connections – Ferry and hovercraft crossings to Capri, Ischia, Procida and Sorrento leave from molo Beverello and Mergellina port.

City quarters – City life is very much centred around **piazza del Plebiscito** and **Galleria Umberto I** (**JKZ**). Working-class quarters, with their narrow streets adorned with hanging washing, are to be found in the **Spaccanapoli** area and in the area to the west of via Toledo (**KY**), the Spanish quarter **(Quartieri spagnoli)** with its steep narrow streets. To the west of the city lie the residential areas spread over the hillsides of **Vomero** and **Posillipo** which look out on to the sea.

Useful telephone numbers

Carabinieri Police ☎ 081 54 81 111
State Police ☎ 081 79 41 111
Road Police ☎ 081 59 54 111
City Police ☎ 081 75 13 177
Emergency Ambulance ☎ 081 75 28 282 o 081 75 20 696
Railway information ☎ 147-88 80 88

The elegant iron and glass structure of Galleria Umberto I

Where to sleep?

For complete listings of hotels in Naples consult the current Michelin Red Guide Italy. Addresses listed below are chosen on the basis of good value for money, location or particular charm. Hotels are divided into three categories; prices refer to double rooms (for more information see p. 433) and are listed in alphabetical order (to locate them see map).

It is advisable to check prices by telephone and to book well in advance, particularly in more reasonably priced hotels which usually have fewer rooms.

BUDGET

Some hotels listed have rooms without bath and therefore cost 20-30% less.

Ausonia – Via Caracciolo 11 (in Mergellina, off the map), ☎ 081 68 22 78. 24. Credit cards accepted. This hotel is situated in the internal courtyard of a building which overlooks the port of Mergellina. There is a peaceful atmosphere and 20 rooms pleasantly decorated in a marine style.

Le fontane al mare – Via Tommaseo 14 (in Santa Lucia, off the map), ☎ 081 76 43 470 o 081 76 43 811. Credit cards accepted. The 20 rooms situated on the fourth floor of the building (200L for use of the lift) are somewhat modest but almost all afford excellent sea views.

Le orchidee – Corso Umberto I 7, ☎ and fax 081 55 10 721. No credit cards. This hotel is housed on the fifth floor (50L for use of lift) of an old building and is very central. The eight spacious and pleasant rooms have good views of the city.

San Pietro – Via San Pietro ad Aram 18, ☎ 081 28 60 40, fax 081 55 35 914. Credit cards accepted. This slightly anonymous but decent hotel is well located and within walking distance of the railway station. 50 rooms.

OUR SELECTION

Suite Esedra – Via Cantani 12 (corso Umberto I), ☎ 081 55 37 087, fax 081 55 37 087. Credit cards accepted. Located in a restored old building this hotel, which also boasts a small library, has 17 small rooms which are, however, pleasantly decorated with natural materials and have air conditioning.

Villa Capodimonte – Via Moiariello, 66 (Capodimonte hill, off the map, take via Santa Teresa degli Scalzi – JY), ☎ 081 45 90 00, fax 081 29 93 44. Credit cards accepted. This hotel is located about 1km/0.6mi from exit no 5 "Capodimonte" of the ring road. Ideally located for those travelling by road who want be "far from the madding crowd", it is well-kept and has a pleasant atmosphere. 49 air-conditioned rooms. Amenities include parking, a garden and a restaurant.

TREAT YOURSELF!

Grand Hotel Parker's – Corso Vittorio Emanuele, 135 (to the west, off the map - JZ), ☎ 081 76 12 474, fax 081 66 35 27. Credit cards accepted. The perfect combination of refined elegance and modern comfort, this hotel affords unparalleled views of the Bay of Naples. 70 rooms with air conditioning. Garage parking at a charge.

Grande Albergo Vesuvio – Via Partenope, 45 (in Santa Lucia, off the map), ☎ 081 76 40 044, fax 081 58 90 380. Credit cards accepted. Founded in 1882 this prestigious hotel is a local institution and has stunning views of Castel dell'Ovo and the little port of di Santa Lucia. 165 rooms with air conditioning. Garage parking at a charge.

Restaurants and excursions

NEAPOLITAN CULINARY DELIGHTS

Pasta, pizza, ricotta, tasty mozzarella (buffalo milk cheese), fish and shellfish are ingredients which are commonly found in Neapolitan cooking. Spaghetti served al dente (lightly cooked) with clams (vongole), thin, crusty pizza, deep-fried fish or a plate of sea-food such as clams and mussels accompanied by a glass of the local Greco di Tufo wine can all be enjoyed in restaurants which stay open late into the night. The more gluttonous can finish off their meal with a slice of the famous Neapolitan pastry (pastiera napoletana) eaten at Christmas and Easter with a filling of candied peel and ricotta, polished off with a glass of Lacrima Christi (tears of Christ), a sweet wine.

The local vines are grown in volcanic soil and the wines include Falerno, red and white wines from Capri, as well as the white from Ischia.

SOME ADDRESSES...

The Michelin Red Guide has a full selection of the city's best restaurants. Restaurants listed below have typical cuisine in a homely atmosphere at reasonable prices.

Europeo – Via Campodisola 4 (KZ **73**), ☎ 081 55 21 323. Closed on Sundays, in the evening (except Friday, Saturday and days preceding public holidays) and from 15 to 31 August. A simple cosy restaurant, over a hundred years old. The kitchen serves Neapolitan specialities and pizza. Expect to pay about 45 000L.

La Chiacchierata (JZ, *behind Galleria Umberto I, on a side street off via Toledo*) – Piazzetta Matilde Serao, 37, ☎ 081 41 14 65. Closed in August, in the evening (except Friday), Sundays and from June to September on Friday evening and Saturday. A cosy restaurant which serves Neapolitan specialities. Expect to pay about 40 000L.

Marino – Via Santa Lucia, 118 (*Santa Lucia, off the map*), ☎ 081 77 40 280. Closed Mondays and in the month of August. A traditional *trattoria* which serves seafood and the inevitable pizza. Expect to pay about 30 000L.

Osteria della Mattonella (JZ) – Via G. Nicotera, 13, ☎ 081 41 65 41. Closed on Sunday evenings. A small pizzeria, founded over a hundred years ago, which serves traditional Neapolitan dishes. Expect to pay about 25 000L.

PIZZERIE

It goes without saying that in Naples pizza is a veritable institution but certain peculiarities of Neapolitan pizzerie should be pointed out. Only more traditional pizzas are served and service is geared towards serving as many customers as possible in the shortest possible time. Thus there is little time for lingering conversation at the table and it is best to free the table as soon as possible; as the evening goes on the queues outside become interminable. Listed below are some of the more classic pizzerie:

Bellini – Via S. Maria di Costantinopoli 80 (KY **145**, *behind the Museo Archeologico*), ☎ 081 45 97 74.

Brandi (JZ) – Salita S. Anna di Palazzo 1 (*at the corner of via Chiaia, behind Piazza Trento e Trieste*), ☎ 081 41 69 28. This is where the mythical Margherita pizza was born in 1889, so-called in honour of Queen Margherita.

Da Michele (LY) – Via C. Sersale, 1 (*not far from Hotel Suite Esedra*), ☎ 081 55 39 204.

Lombardi a S. Chiara (KY) – Via B. Croce, 59, ☎ 081 55 20 780.

Trianon (LY) – Via P. Colletta 46 (*not far from Hotel Suite Esedra*), ☎ 081 55 39 426.

IF YOU HAVE A SWEET TOOTH...

Those in search of coffee and a pastry should try **Caflish** on via Chiaia 143, **La caffettiera** in piazza dei Martiri, **Motta** on via Toledo 152 and of course the famous **Gran Caffè Gambrinus**, in piazza Trieste e Trento, whose sumptuously decorated rooms have witnessed 150 years of the most important events of Neapolitan history.

For those strolling around Spaccanapoli a visit to **Scaturchio** (piazza S. Domenico Maggiore) is essential. Try the *sfogliatella riccia*, a flaky pastry straight out of the oven or a baba, a sweet of foreign origin but very much appreciated in the Kingdom of Naples.

A WELL DESERVED REST...

...from the fatigues of being a tourist can be savoured at the **Caffè Letterario Intra Moenia**, in piazza Bellini.

San Domenico Maggiore ⊘ (KY) – The church apse gives onto a square ornamented with a small Baroque votive monument (*guglia*) to St Dominic. The interior of the church has both Gothic (**caryatids** by Tino di Camaino support a huge paschal candelabrum) and Baroque features. In the side aisle to the right, the second chapel is decorated with frescoes by Pietro Cavallini (1309). The 18C sacristy lined with panelling contains numerous coffins of members of the court of Aragon (*in the balustrade*).

Cappella Sansevero ⊘ (KY) – This 16C chapel was completely restored in the 18C by Raimondo de Sangro, an eccentric whose passion for alchemy and scientific study gave rise to a certain notoriety. There are even two skeletons complete with "petrified" circulatory system (*in an underground chamber, access from the south aisle*).

In the chapel there are fine marble **sculptures★**: on either side of the choir are *Chastity* (the veiled woman) and *Despair* (the latter being symbolised by a man struggling with a net); the central one depicts the splendid **Christ covered by a shroud★**, a masterpiece by Giuseppe Sammartino. The folds of a thin shroud are draped on the peaceful recumbent figure.

Just before Via S. Biagio dei Librai, is the charming **Piazzetta del Nilo** which derives its name from a statue of the Nile found in the square. A little further along, to the left, is the attractive Via S. Gregorio Armeno. It is lined with small shops and workshops where the small figurines for the Nativity scenes *(presepio)* are produced. The skills required have been handed down from father to son since the 19C. These days the statuettes include modern figures. The area is particularly charming around Christmas time. At the end of the street, at the bend, rises the campanile of the church of San Gregorio Armeno.

San Gregorio Armeno ⊘ (LY) – This church is dedicated to St Gregory. A spacious atrium leads onto the **interior★** of the church which is opulently Baroque in style. The frescoes along the nave and in the cupola are the work of Luca Giordano. At the end of the nave are two huge Baroque **organs**. Of particular interest in the presbytery is the high altar with intarsia work in polychrome marble and, to the right, the *comunichino*, a brass screen from behind which the nuns followed mass. The beautiful ceiling, in gilded wood, features medallions decorated by Teodoro di Enrico.

The **cloisters** *(access via the steps in the monastery)* have a splendid fountain *(centre)* decorated with statues of Christ and the Samaritan (late 18C).

At the end of Via S. Gregorio Armeno is Via dei Tribunali which runs into the Decumamo Maggiore that dates back to ancient Rome.

San Lorenzo Maggiore ⊘ (LY) – The Church of St Lawrence was built in the 14C over an early Christian church, the remains of which include the perimeter walls and the columns from the nave. Restored in the Baroque style, it was eventually returned to its original appearance after recent restoration work.

It is built on the plan of a Latin cross with an elegant **arch★** that spans the transept crossing. The nave, a simple, austere rectangular space (except for a chapel on the west wall which has kept its splendid Baroque additions) is a testament to the Franciscan influence. The **polygonal apse★** is an interesting specimen of French Gothic architecture in southern Italy. It is surmounted by elegant arches crowned by twin bays and terminates in an ambulatory onto which open chapels with frescoes by disciples of Giotto. The north transept houses a large chapel dedicated to St Anthony and, on the altar, a painting of the saint surrounded by angels (1438), on a gold background. To the right of the high altar is the remarkable **tomb★** of Catherine of Austria, attributed to Tino di Camaino.

From the cloisters of the church make for the **chapter-house**, with its frescoed walls and vault, which houses a unique "illustrated bible" – terracotta figurines placed inside nutshells which date from the 1950s. Access to the **ruins** ⊘ is also from the cloisters. The ruins reveal a crucial part of Naples' Greco-Roman history: along with the forum there are traces of the treasury, bakery and *macellum* (large covered market).

★★ **Decumanus Maximus** ⊘ (KLY) – Turn right to get to the 17C **Pio Monte della Misericordia** (LY E) which houses six panels; the themes are linked to the charitable works carried out by the institute. Of particular interest are *St Peter freed from Prison* by Caracciolo and the fine **The Seven Works of Mercy★★★** by **Caravaggio**.

Turn back and at the junction of via Duomo turn right.

★ **Duomo** (LY) – Built in the 14C, the cathedral was considerably altered at a later date. Held in great veneration by the people, the Chapel of St Januarius **(Tesoro di San Gennaro★)** ⊘, in a rich baroque style, is preceded by a remarkable 17C bronze grille: behind the high altar are two glass phials containing the saint's blood which is supposed to liquefy, failing which disaster will befall the town. The Feast of the **Miracle of St Januarius** is held twice annually on the first Sunday in May and on 19 September. The dome is decorated with a Lanfranco fresco showing an admirable sense of movement.

The south transept houses an *Assumption* by Perugino and the Gothic **Minutolo Chapel** which has a beautiful 13C mosaic floor and frescoed walls. The **succorpo** (crypt) is an elegant Renaissance structure.

A door in the middle of the north aisle gives access to the 4C **Basilica di Santa Restituta** ⊘, which was transformed in the Gothic period and again in the 17C. At the far end of the nave, the 5C Baptistery of St John (**San Giovanni**) is a fine structure containing **mosaics★★** of the same period. From the north apse make for the **archeological displays** which afford some evocative time travel through Greek, Roman and Medieval Naples.

Quadreria dei Girolamini ⊘ (LY L) – *Entrance on via Duomo 142).* Housed on the first floor of a convent, this collection has a considerable body of work from the Neapolitan, Roman and Florentine schools of the 16C-18C. These include paintings by Luca Giordano, G. B. Caracciolo, Jusepe de Ribera (*Apostles*), Guido Reni and Francesco Solimena (*Prophets*). The convent also houses a **Library** ☉ with a splendid **18C room★**.

The **chiesa dei Girolamini** (*entrance on via dei Tribunali*) has works of art by Pietro Bernini (father of Lorenzo), Pietro da Cortona, Luca Giordano and Francesco Solimena.

A little further on is the Church of **San Paolo Maggiore★** (KY). In front is a splendid flight of steps; the interior is Baroque and very ornate: note the polychrome altar. The sacristy houses fine **frescoes★** by **Solimena**: *The Fall of Simon Magus* and the *Conversion of St Paul (side walls)* are amongst this artist's masterpieces.

Further along, to the right, is the Church of **Purgatorio ad Arco** (KY F) with its tiny underground cemetery (cimitero sotterraneo) where, until recently, the unique practice of cleaning the bones was carried out for the purposes of receiving grace, a widespread practice in Naples.

At no 362 is **Palazzo Spinelli di Laurino** (KY A) with a curious elliptical courtyard embellished by one of Sanfelice's staircases.

On the parvis of the Church of **Santa Maria Maggiore** (KY), also known as Pietrasanta, with its beautiful flooring in brick and majolica (1764) rise, to the left, the Renaissance chapel, Cappella Pontano, and, to the right, a fine campanile which dates back to the original church (11C).

Beyond **Croce di Lucca** ((KY B), a 17C church with coffered ceiling of gilded wood, is the Church of **San Pietro a Majella** ((KY C). It has Gothic overtones but was restored in the 17C. Features include the fine carved choir stalls and the frescoes in the apse.

The tour ends in Piazza Bellini which is a pleasant place to spend the evening. In the centre are the ruined Greek walls. A little further on is **Piazza Dante** (KY), overlooked by a semicircular range of buildings, the work of Vanvitelli.

★★★ MUSEO ARCHEOLOGICO NAZIONALE ☉ (KY) 2hr

The National Archeological Museum occupies a group of 16C buildings which were originally intended to house the royal cavalry, and then became the seat of the university from 1610 to 1777. The collections comprise mainly works of art belonging to the Farnese family and treasures discovered at Pompeii and Herculaneum. It is one of the richest museums in the world for Greco-Roman antiquities.

Ground floor

★★★ Greco-Roman sculpture – The large atrium displays sculptures from Pompei and Herculaneum. At the front of the room a staircase on the right leads to the section in the basement dedicated to the **epigraphy section** (ancient inscriptions) and the **Egyptian collection**.

Galleria dei Tirannicidi – *Turn right on entering the Atrium*. The Tyrant-Slayers' Gallery is devoted to Archaic art. The **Aphrodite Sosandra** with a fine, proud face and elegantly-draped robe is a splendid copy of a Greek bronze (5C BC), while the powerful marble group of the **Tyrant-Slayers**, a copy of a Greek bronze, represents Harmodios and Aristogiton who delivered Athens from the tyrant, Hipparchus, in the 6C BC.

Galleria dei Grandi Maestri – *Access from the Galleria dei Tirannicidi*. The Great Masters' Gallery contains the majestic statue of the Farnese Pallas (Athena), Orpheus and Eurydice bidding each other farewell, a low relief of touching simplicity copied from an original by Phidias (5C BC) and the **Doryphorus**, the spear-bearer, a copy of the famous bronze by Polyclitus.

At the end of the Galleria dei Tirannicidi, to the left, is a gallery displaying the famous **Callipygian Aphrodite** (Callipige signifies "with lovely buttocks", 1C), two copies of **Aphrodite crouching** by Doidalsas (3C) and the lovely. statue of **Artemis of Ephesus** (2C) in alabaster and bronze, representing the deity venerated at the famous temple by the Aegean Sea. She is sometimes considered as a nature goddess in the oriental tradition and is represented with numerous breasts symbolising her motherly nature.

Galleria del Toro Farnese – *Access from the preceding gallery*. This gallery houses the monumental sculptural groups found at the Baths of Caracalla in Rome in the 16C. In the centre is the colossal *Flora farnese*. The **Warrior and Child** on the left is admirable, and in front a fine *Nike (Victory)* or statue of a woman in basalt. In the last room is the impressive sculptured group called the **Farnese Bull** depicting the death of Dirce, a legendary queen of Thebes. It was carved from a single block of marble. It is a 2C Roman copy, which like many works in the Farnese collection has undergone much restoration, thereby altering its original characteristics. In the right wing is the **Farnese Hercules**, resting after his famous labours.

From this gallery make for the section dedicated to **engraved gemstones** which includes one of the greatest masterpieces of the museum, the celebrated **Tazza Farnese**, an enormous cameo in the shape of a cup made in Alexandria in the 2C BC.

★★ **Mosaics** – *To the left on the mezzanine.* Although most of these come from Pompeii, Herculaneum and Stabia they offer a wide variety of styles and subject matter. There are two small works (*Visit to a Fortune-Teller* and *Roving Musicians*) by Dioscurides of Samos along with the *Actors on stage* found in Room of the Tragic Poet (*Room LIX*). Mosaics including a *frieze with festoons and masks* and the splendid mosaic of the **Battle of Alexander and Darius** (*Room LXI*) which paved the floor of the House of the Faun at Pompeii, are housed in Rooms LX and LXI. The latter reveals a remarkable sense of depth (rear view of a horse in the foreground) and movement (the horses champing at the bit, the lances crossed and the Persian king prostrate in front of Alexander). The collection also includes some fine examples of *opus sectile*

First floor

★★★ **Works from Villa di Pisone or dei Papiri** – *At the beginning of the Salone della meridiana, on the right.* The villa, which was discovered at Herculaneum in the 18C but was later reburied, is thought to have belonged to L Calpurnius Pison who was Julius Caesar's father-in-law. The owner had turned the house into a museum. The documents and splendid works of art from his collections are priceless. The Sala dei Papiri Room (CXIV) contains photographs of some of the 800 papyri from the library. In Room CXVI are exhibited **bronze statues** that adorned the peristyle of the villa: the **Drunken Faun** lost in euphoria, a **Sleeping Satyr** with a beautiful face in repose; the two lifelike **Wrestlers** are inspired from Lysippus (4C BC); the famous **Dancers from Herculaneum** are probably in fact water-carriers; the famous **Hermes at Rest**, with a tall strong figure, reflects Lysippus' ideal.

In Room CXVII, in addition to the **portrait** mistakenly identified as that of **Seneca** and one of the most remarkably expressive works handed down from antiquity, are exhibited an "Ideal Head" identified as Artemis, and the majestic statue of Athena Promachos (1C BC).

★★ **Silver, ivory, terracotta and glass gallery** – *At the beginning of the Salone della Meridiana, on the left.* These rooms are mostly devoted to finds brought back from Pompeii and Herculaneum. Exhibits include silver found in the House of Menander in Pompei, ivory ornaments, Greek and Italic arms, glass objects, among which note the stunning **Blue vase**★★ decorated with *putti* and harvest scenes.

From this section make for the room displaying the cork **model of Pompei** made in the 19C.

★★★ **Sale del Tempio di Iside** – *After the room above.* The room features objects and pictures from the Temple of Isis discovered behind the Great Theatre at Pompeii. Three areas have been partially reconstructed to evoke the original structure: the portico, the *ekklesiasterion* (the assembly room where the worshippers of Isis met) and the *sacrarium* (sanctuary). The frescoes on the walls illustrate a still life (figs, grapes, geese and doves are all elements linked to the worship of this Egyptian goddess and were part of the Isis cult). Of particular interest are the beautiful large panels which are well preserved and depict sacred rights and scenes illustrating the myths surrounding Io (Isis).

★★★ **Sala degli affreschi** – *At the far end of the Salone della meridiana, on the left, or after the Sale del tempio di Iside.* The collection includes some splendid frescoes from Pompeii, Herculaneum and Stabia in particular. The diversity of style and colour is a testament to the richness of this form of decorative art practised by the Romans (*see POMPEI*). Exhibits include beautiful paintings with mythological subjects such as Heracles and Ariadne, the tragic Medea and Iphigenia, and epic poems including episodes from the Trojan war which are often inserted in architectural perspectives, friezes of cupids, satyrs and maenads. The female figures found at Stabia which represent *Leda, Medea, Flora* and *Artemis* are notable for their grace and gentleness. The medallions depicting Campanian landscapes were originally in a villa at Boscotrecase.

At the far end of the Salone della meridiana, to the right, a **Topographical section** is in the process of being set up. It will display artefacts from Campania dating from prehistory to the Roman age.

OTHER PLACES OF INTEREST IN THE HISTORIC CENTRE

★ **Porta Capuana** (LMY) – This is one of the fortified gateways in the walls built in 1484 to the plans of Giuliano da Maiano. The Capuan Castle **(Castel Capuano)** (LY) nearby was the former residence of the Norman princes and the Hohenstaufens.

★ **San Giovanni a Carbonara** (LY) – An 18C stairway leads to the elegant Gothic doorway of this 14C church. Inside are the tomb of Ladislas of Anjou (15C) and many works of art in two chapels, the Carracciolo del Sole behind the choir and the Carracciolo del Vico, to the left of the previous one.

★ **Santa Maria Donnaregina** (LY) – Go through the cloisters adorned with 18C faïence. A Baroque church of the same name precedes the small 14C Gothic church which shows a French influence. Inside is the **tomb★** of the founder, Mary of Hungary, widow of Charles II of Anjou, by Tino di Camaino. The walls of the nuns' chancel are decorated with 14C **frescoes★**.

★ **Palazzo Como** (LY) – This majestic late-15C palace, with its rusticated stonework, is a reminder of the Florentine Renaissance. It contains the **Museo Civico Filangieri** ⊘ which displays collections of arms and armour, ceramics and porcelain, furniture and paintings by Ribera, Carracciolo, Mattia Preti etc.

Sant'Anna dei Lombardi ⊘ (KYZ) – This Renaissance church, dedicated to St Anne of the Lombards, is rich in contemporary Florentine **sculpture★**. Inside is the tomb of Mary of Aragon *(1st chapel on the left)* by Antonio Rossellino and an *Annunciation (1st chapel on the right)* by Benedetto da Maiano. In the oratory to the right of the choir is a *Descent from the Cross*, a late-15C terracotta by Guido Mazzoni who introduced this style of rather theatrical realism to Naples which was to become very popular in southern Italy. The former sacristy has lovely stalls which are attributed to Fra Giovanni da Verona (1457-1525).

★★ CERTOSA DI SAN MARTINO ⊘ (JZ) *1hr*

This immense Carthusian Monastery of St Martin is beautifully situated on a spur of the Vomero hill. The **Castel Sant'Elmo**, a massive structure with bastions, overlooks the monastery to the west; it was rebuilt by the Spaniards in the 16C and was for a long time used as a prison. From the drill square *(access on foot or by lift)* there is a wonderful view over the city and the bay. The monastery was founded by the Anjou dynasty in the 14C and was almost completely remodelled in the 16C and 17C. The monastic buildings can be visited, as well as the museum which is arranged in the buildings overlooking the Procurators' Cloisters.

Church – The **interior★★** is lavishly Baroque and is adorned with paintings by Caracciolo, Guido Reni and Simon Vouet. To the left of the choir, beyond the sacristy with its superb furnishings embellished with inlay, is the treasury decorated with frescoes by Luca Giordano and a painting by Ribera, *La Pietà*.

Great Cloisters – This harmonious ensemble is the work of the architect-sculptor Cosimo Fanzago.

★ **Museum/The section devoted to festivals and costumes contains an exceptional collection of figurines and Neapolitan cribs★★** *(presepi)* in poly-chrome terracotta from the 18C and 19C. The collection is a wealth of objects (from baskets of fruit and vegetables in wax to animals and utensils) widely used in Neapolitan cribs: the four cribs on display are fine examples. The tour concludes with a large, impressive crib from the late 19C (some of the figures date back to the 18C).To the left of the cloisters there is also an interesting **sculpture** section including works by Tino di Camaino.

★★ PALAZZO AND GALLERIA NAZIONALE DI CAPODIMONTE ⊘ *2hr*

The Capodimonte Palace and Art Gallery are on the northern outskirts of Naples and can be reached by bus no 24 which from piazza Municipio (KZ) goes along via Medina, via Monteoliveto and via S. Teresa degli Scalzi (JKY).

This former **royal estate★** extends over high ground to the north of the city. The whole includes a massive and austere palace which was built from 1738 to 1838, an extensive park, and the remains of the famous 18C porcelain factory. The palace itself has an art gallery in addition to the royal apartments.

Gallery – The nucleus of the holding is the Farnese collection, inherited by the Bourbons and enriched over the years. The works are presented mostly in chronological order and trace the main trends in the evolution of Italian painting; there are also important works by foreign artists.
The collections open with the Farnese Gallery which displays famous portraits of the most important members of the Farnese family. Note the portrait of *Paolo III with his nephews***★★**, a masterpiece of Titian showing all his penetrating psychological insight.
In the intense *Crucifixion***★★★** by Masaccio, the figure of Mary Magdalene in a bright red dress with arms dramatically stretched towards the cross is a fine example of perspective that made Masaccio such a key figure in the revolution that was the Renaissance. The hunched figure of Christ is not an error but results from the fact that originally the painting was placed above another polyptych and therefore had to be looked at from below. Renaissance painting is represented by the works of Botticelli (*Madonna and Child with Saints*), Filippino Lippi and Raphael. A fine example of the Venetian school is the *Transfiguration***★★** by Giovanni Bellini; the soft colours and light convey a sense of serenity which suffuses the landscape.

In the Venetian section note the celebrated *Portrait of Fra Luca Pacioli*. Among the main exponents of Mannerism are Sebastiano del Piombo *(Portrait of Clement VII*★)*, Pontormo and Rosso Fiorentino. Titian's study of light is exemplified in the sensual *Danae* and in the works of his pupil El Greco: light is an important feature in the *Boy lighting a candle with a firebrand*. Serenity and tenderness are evoked in a small canvas, *The Mystic Marriage of St Catherine*, by Correggio and in the *Holy Family* by Parmigianino, which stresses the essential role of the mother: the child is only partly shown. By the same artist note the *Lucrezia* and the elegant *Antea*★. The section devoted to Flemish artists includes two fine works by the Flemish master, Peter Breugel the Elder (*The Misanthrope* and *The Parable of the Blind*★★). The second floor houses the "Neapolitan Gallery", a collection formed by Gioacchino Marat of works acquired from suppressed monastic orders. Masterpieces on display include *St Ludovic of Toulouse* by Simone Martini, the celebrated *St Jerome in his studio* by Colantonio and the *Flagellation*★★ by Caravaggio. There are also works by Caracciolo, Ribera, Mattia Preti, Luca Giordano and Francesco Solimena.

The third floor is devoted to collections of contemporary art.

Royal apartments – *1st floor*. The rooms have fine furnishings. Of particular note is the **room**★ with walls faced in porcelain and decorated with chinoiserie flowers and scenes. Also on view are a fine porcelain collection including the elegant *Procession of Aurora* in biscuit porcelain dating from the 19C, and an especially rich collection of royal armoury.

ADDITIONAL SIGHTS

The following sights are off the town plan, see plan of the built up area on Michelin Map 431.

★ **Villa Floridiana** – *To the west of Naples*. This graceful small white palace (*palazzina*) in the neo-Classical style stands high up on the Vomero hillside and is surrounded by a fine park. The façade overlooks the gardens which afford a splendid **panorama**★.

★ **Museo Nazionale di Ceramica Duca di Martina** ⊙ – An interesting museum, housed inside the villa, displays a collection of enamels, ivories, faïence and especially porcelain.

★★ **Catacombe di San Gennaro** ⊙ – *North of Naples*. The catacombs dug in the volcanic rock extend over two floors and consists of vast galleries illuminated by a gentle light. The galleries open out to form a "baptistery" in the lower section and a spacious basilica with three aisles (4C-6C) in the upper section. The tomb of St Januarius, whose remains were transferred here in the 6C, is decorated with frescoes of the saint. There are beautiful paintings in the niches (3C-10C). In the upper section, the vault of the atrium is adorned with early Christian work and portraits of the dead adorning the family tombs. The Bishops' Crypt above the tomb of St Januarius, contains fine mosaics depicting the bishops.

Villa Comunale – Vanvitelli laid out these public gardens along the waterfront in 1780. They are very popular with the Neapolitans for the evening walk. At the centre of the gardens is the **Aquarium** ⊙ which presents a large variety of sea creatures to be found in the Bay of Naples.

Museo Principe di Aragona Pignetelli Cortes ⊙ – *Riviera di Chiaia, opposite the Villa Comunale*. The ground floor of the summer residence of the Princess Pignatelli (she lived here until the 1950s) is open to visitors. Furnishings date back to the 19C. In the garden, the old stables house an interesting collection of carriages from the same period. The vehicles which have been very well preserved are of English, French and Italian origin.

★ **Mergellina** – Mergellina, at the foot of the Posillipo hillside with the small port of Sannazzaro, is one of the few places in Naples ideal for a stroll. It affords a splendid **view**★★ of the bay: the Vomero hillside, crowned by Castel Sant'Elmo, slopes down gently towards the Santa Lucia headland and Castel dell'Ovo beyond, with Vesuvius in the distance.

Michelin Route Planning on Internet www.michelin-travel.com

Michelin, your companion on the road, invites you to visit our Web site and discover European route planning on the Internet.

Whether you just want to know the distance between two points, or need a detailed itinerary, for a holiday or on business, we provide all the information necessary for accurate travel planning.

Golfo di NAPOLI ★★★

Bay of NAPLES – Campania
Michelin map 431 E-F 24-26

The Bay of Naples, extending from Cumae to Sorrento, has a rich history and is one of the most beautiful Italian gulfs. It is an area of striking contrasts where one may find in close proximity isolated areas conducive to meditation, such as the archeological sites, the bare slopes of Vesuvius, the Sibyl's Cave or Lake Averno, and others bustling with activity, noisy, crowded with traffic, all of which are enlivened by the exuberance of the population itself. Its legendary beauty is somewhat marred by the uncontrolled sprawl of industrial development which has reached the outskirts of Naples. However, its islands, capes and mountains offer unforgettable excursions.

Sightseeing – Follow the itineraries indicated on the local map.

★★ ① FROM NAPLES TO CUMAE

Campi Flegrei *45km/28mi – about 6hr*

This volcanic area, the Phlegrean Fields, which received its name from the ancients ("phlegrean" is derived from a Greek word meaning "to blaze"), extends in an arc along the Gulf of Pozzuoli. Hot springs, steam-jets and sulphurous gases rise from

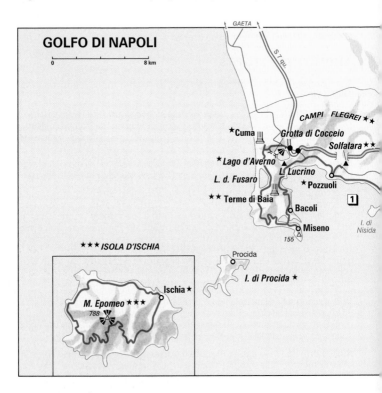

the ground and from the sea, and are proof of an intense underground activity. Lakes have formed in the craters of extinct volcanoes. This stretch of coastline is subject to variations in ground level due to volcanic activity.

★★★ **Naples** – *See NAPOLI.*

★ **Posillipo** – This famous hill forms a promontory and separates the Bay of Naples from Pozzuoli Bay. Posillipo, dotted with villas and their lovely gardens and modern buildings, is Naples' main residential area. It affords splendid views of the bay.

★ **Marechiaro** – This small fishermen's village built high above the sea was made famous by a Neapolitan song *Marechiare*.

Parco Virgiliano (or **Parco della Rimembranza**) – From the Garden of Remembrance there are splendid **views**★★ over the Bay of Naples, from Cape Miseno to the Sorrento Peninsula, as well as the islands of Procida, Ischia and Capri.

★ **Pozzuoli** – *See POZZUOLI.*

★★ **Solfatara** – *See POZZUOLI: Solfatara.*

Lago Lucrino – In antiquity, oyster farming was practised here on the lake and the banks were lined with elegant villas. One of these belonged to Cicero and another was the scene of Agrippina's murder, on the orders of her son Nero.

242

★★ Terme di Baia ⊘ – This Greek colony was in Roman times a fashionable beach resort, as well as a thermal spa *(terme)* with the most complete equipment in the world for hydrotherapy. The Roman emperors and patricians had immense villas, all of which disappeared under the sea after a change in ground level. However, ruins of the famous baths remain on the hilltop overlooking the sea. Facing the hill, these include from left to right the baths of Venus, Sosandra and Mercury.

Bacoli – On the high ground in the old town rises the **Cento Camerelle★** ⊘ *(Via Cento Camerelle, to the right of the church)*. This huge reservoir, which belonged to a private villa, is built on two levels: the grandiose upper level built in the 1 C AD has four sections and immense arches; the lower part, built much earlier, has a network of narrow galleries forming a cross, that emerge high above sea level. The famous **Piscina Mirabile★** ⊘ *(at the church take the road to the left, Via Ambrogio Greco, and then Via Piscina Mirabile to the right)* was an immense cistern designed to supply water to the Roman fleet in the port of Miseno. It is 70m long, 25m wide and nearly 15m high (230ft×82ft×49ft) and is divided into five sections with 48 pillars supporting the roof. There are remarkable light effects.

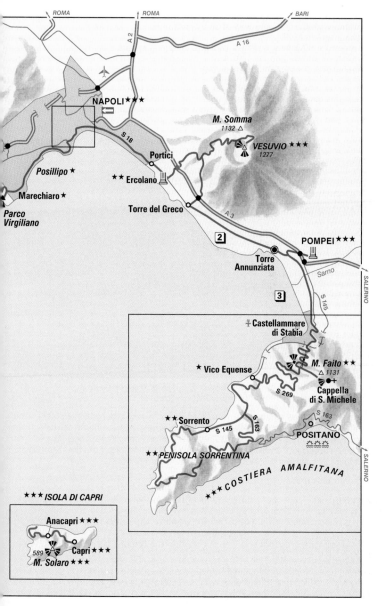

Miseno – This name is given to a lake, a port, a promontory, a cape and a village. Lake Miseno, a former volcanic crater, was believed by the ancients to be the Styx, across which Charon ferried the souls of the dead. Under the Emperor Augustus it was linked by a canal to the port of Miseno, which was the base of the Roman fleet. The village of Miseno is dominated by Monte Miseno, on which Misenus, the companion of Aeneas, is said to have been buried. The slopes of the promontory were studded with luxurious villas, including the one where in AD 37 the Emperor Tiberius choked to death.

Lago del Fusaro – A lagoon with a small island on which Vanvitelli built a hunting lodge for King Ferdinand IV of Bourbon in 1782.

★ **Cumae** – *See CUMAE.*

★ **Lago d'Averno** – *The lake lies below the Cumae-Naples road: belvedere on the right approximately 1km/0.6mi beyond Arco Felice.* This lake within a crater is dark, still and silent and wrapped in an atmosphere of mystery, which was all the more intense in antiquity as birds flying overhead were overcome by fumes and dropped into the lake to be swallowed up. Virgil regarded it as the entrance to the Underworld. Under the Roman Empire, Agrippa, a captain in the service of the Emperor Augustus, developed it as a naval base and linked it by canal with Lake Lucrino *(see above)*, which in turn was linked to the open sea. An underground gallery 1km/0.6mi long, known as Cocceio's Cave **(Grotta di Cocceio)**, connected Avernus with Cumae, and was used by chariots.

★★★ ② FROM NAPLES TO TORRE ANNUNZIATA

Vesuvius *44km/27mi – allow 1 day*

The coast road relieves the Salerno motorway across a densely-populated industrial zone, once a favoured resort of the Neapolitan aristocracy (18-19C). There are two important sites located a short distance from the road.

The Bay of Naples with the characteristic profile of Vesuvius

Portici – The road crosses the courtyard of the **royal palace** built in 1738 for the Bourbon King Charles III. Today the palace buildings are the home of the Naples Faculty of Agronomy. In his opera *The Mute Girl of Portici (Muette de Portici)*, the French composer, Auber, features the 17C revolt against the Spaniards, instigated by **Masaniello**, a young fisherman from Portici.

★★ **Herculaneum/** *See ERCOLANO.*

★★★ **Vesuvio** – The outline of Vesuvius, one of the few still active volcanoes in Europe, is an intrinsic feature of the Neapolitan landscape. It has two summits: to the north **Monte Somma** (alt 1 132m/3 714ft) and to the south Vesuvius proper (alt 1 277m/4 190ft). In time the volcanic materials on the lower slopes have become fertile soil with orchards and vines producing the famous *Lacryma Christi* wine.

The eruptions of Vesuvius – Until the earthquake of AD 62 and the eruption of AD 79 which buried Herculaneum and Pompeii, Vesuvius seemed extinct; its slopes were clothed with famous vines and woods. By 1139, seven eruptions had been recorded. Then came a period of calm during which the slopes of the mountains were cultivated. On 16 December 1631 Vesuvius had a terrible awakening, destroying all the settlements at its foot: 3 000 people perished. The eruption of 1794 devastated Torre del Greco. The volcano had minor eruptions in 1858, 1871, 1872, from 1895 to 1899, 1900, 1903, 1904, a major eruption in 1906, 1929, and one in 1944 altering the shape of the crater. Since then, apart from brief activity linked with the 1980 earthquake, Vesuvius has emitted only a plume of smoke.

Ascent ⊙ – *From Herculaneum and via Torre del Greco: 27km/17mi plus 45min on foot there and back. Wear good walking shoes.* A good road leads to a junction in the midst of lava flows. Take the left fork *(car park a few km further on)*. The path is an easy but most impressive climb up the volcano, scattered with cinders and lapilli.

From the summit there is an immense **panorama★★★** over the Bay of Naples with the Sorrento Peninsula in the south and Cape Miseno in the north. Beyond is the Gulf of Gaeta.

The crater affords an unforgettable sight for its sheer size and the sense of desolation on the slopes of the jagged walls, for the great yawning crater, which takes on a pink colour in the sun, and the spouting steamjets.

Torre del Greco – This town which has been repeatedly destroyed by the eruptions of Vesuvius, is well known for its ornaments made of coral and volcanic stone, and cameos.

Torre Annunziata – This town is the centre of the famous Neapolitan pasta industry. It has been buried under the lava of Vesuvius seven times. Here is the sumptuous Villa di Oplontis which is open to the public and in 1997 was included in UNESCO's World Heritage List.

★★ **Villa di Oplontis** ⊙ – This fine example of a Roman suburban villa is thought to have belonged to Poppea, wife of Nero. The vast building, in which can be identified the slaves' quarters (to the east) and the area given over to the imperial apartments (to the west), has many well-preserved examples of beautiful original **wall paintings**. In particular, there are landscape scenes featuring architectural elements, portrait medallions and still-lifes, including a basket of figs and details of fruit (in the two recesses or *triclinia* to the east and west of the atrium respectively). Of the various animals depicted, the peacock appears so frequently as to have supported the theory that the name of the villa was derived from it. Within the villa, the kitchens are easily identified (with ovens and sink), as are the latrines which represent an advanced drainage system. The area to the west of the piscina, perhaps used as a conservatory, has fine wall paintings with foreshortened flowers and fountains.

★★★ ③ **FROM TORRE ANNUNZIATA TO SORRENTO**

69km/43mi – allow 1 day

Torre Annunziata - *See above.*

★★★ **Pompeii** - *See POMPEI.*

★ **Castellammare di Stabia** - *See CASTELLAMMARE DI STABIA.*

★★ **Monte Faito** - *Access is from Vico Equense via a scenic route; alternatively there is a* **cable-car** ⊙ *which departs from piazza Circumvesuviana in Castellammare di Stabia* Monte Faito is part of the **Lattari range**, a headland which separates the Bay of Naples from the Gulf of Salerno and forms the Sorrento Peninsula. Its name is derived from the beech trees (*fagus* in Latin) which offer shade in summer. From Belvedere dei Capi there is a splendid **panorama★★★** of the Bay of Naples. From there the road continues up to a chapel, **Cappella San Michele**, which affords another enchanting **panorama★★★** – the wild landscape of the Lattari mountains contrasts strongly with the smiling scenery of the Bay of Naples and the Sarno plain.

★ **Vico Equense** - A small health and seaside resort on a picturesque rocky site.

★★ **Sorrento and Sorrento Peninsula** - *See SORRENTO.*

★★★ **ISLANDS**

★★★ **Capri** - *See Isola di CAPRI.*

★★★ **Ischia** - *See Isola d'ISCHIA.*

★ **Procida** - *See Isola d'ISCHIA: Procida.*

In this guide town plans show the main streets and the way to the sights;
local maps show the main roads and the roads o the recommended tour.

NOVARA

Piedmont

Population 102 404
Michelin map 428 F 7
Town plan in the Michelin Atlas Italy

Novara is situated on the borders of Piedmont and Lombardy to the north of the Lomellina *(see PAVIA)*, a vast rice-growing area. It is a busy commercial and industrial town as well as an important road junction in the road network of northern Italy.

★ **Basilica di San Gaudenzio** – Built from 1577 to 1659 to the designs of the Lombard architect, Pellegrino Tibaldi, it was crowned with a tall slender **dome**★★ (1844-78), an audacious addition by a local architect, A. Antonelli. Inside are several interesting works of art, including paintings by Morazzone (17C) and Gaudenzio Ferrari (16C) and the silver **sarcophagus**★ of the city's patron saint (St Gaudentius).

Cortile del Broletto – This lovely courtyard has several interesting buildings including the 15C Palazzo Podestà, the 13C Broletto (Town Hall) and the Palazzo degli Paratici, now the **Museo Civico** (art gallery and archeological section).

Duomo – This neo-Classical cathedral by Antonelli has a 6C-7C paleo-Christian baptistery. The chancel is adorned with a black and white Byzantine-style mosaic **floor**★.

ORVIETO★★

Umbria

Population 20 813
Michelin map 430 N 18

This important Etruscan centre later became a papal stronghold and it was here that Clement VII took refuge in 1527 when Rome was sacked by the troops of the French King, Charles V.

Orvieto is a pleasant city with its wealth of historic buildings and it enjoys a particularly remarkable **site**★★★ on the top of a plug of volcanic rock. Those arriving by the Bolsena or Montefiascone roads have particularly good views of this site. The region produces a pleasant, white wine, the cool and fragrant Orvieto.

★★★ DUOMO *1hr*

In the heart of the town the quiet Piazza del Duomo, of majestic proportions, is lined with several interesting buildings. The cathedral, a perfect example of the transitional Romanesque-Gothic style, was begun in 1290 to enshrine the relics of the Miracle of Bolsena. Over 100 architects, sculptors, painters and mosaicists took part in the build-ing of the cathedral which was completed only in 1600. The austere Palace of the Popes (**Palazzo dei Papi**★ ⊙) (**M²**) now houses the Cathe-dral Museum, **Museo dell'Opera**.

★★★ **Façade** – This is the boldest structure and the richest in colour among Italian Gothic buildings. The vertical lines are accentuated by the slender gables and especially by the soar-ing buttresses, which are clad with small panels of coloured marble, elongated in shape and further prolonged by pinnacles. The sumptuous decora-tive effect is obtained by the use of sculptures lower down with multi-coloured marbles and mosaics above.

Marble, mosaics and intricate stone patterns enliven the façade of the Duomo

J. Ciganovic/EXPLORER

The original design, elaborated (c 1310-30) by the Sienese, Lorenzo Maitani, was further developed by Andrea Pisano, Andrea Orcagna and Sanmicheli. Maitani was also responsible for the astonishing **low reliefs★★** adorning the pillars which, reading from left to right, portray: *Genesis, Jesse's Tree, Scenes from the New Testament*, and the *Last Judgement*.

Orcagna was the designer of the rose window, fitted into a square frame and surrounded by statues of the Apostles and the Prophets. The mosaics on the spire depict the *Coronation of the Virgin* and date from the end of the eighteenth century.

Interior – A nave and two aisles built in alternating courses of black and white stone rest on semicircular arches supported by lovely bracketed capitals. A moulding projects above the arches. The nave and aisles are roofed with a timber ceiling, while Gothic vaulting covers the transepts and the chancel. The paving slopes up towards the chancel, reducing the perspective. Alabaster window-panes let in plenty of light. At the entrance stand the 15C stoup and the Gothic font. A fresco of the *Virgin and Child* (1425) in the north aisle is by Gentile da Fabriano. In the north transept under the 16C monumental organ is the entrance to a chapel, the **Cappella del Corporale**, which enshrines the relics of the Miracle of Bolsena and notably the linen cloth (corporal) in which the bleeding Host was wrapped. A tabernacle encloses the **Reliquary★★** of the Corporal, a masterpiece of medieval goldsmiths' work (1338) encrusted with enamels and precious stones. In the chapel on the right is a *Madonna of Pity* (1320) by the Sienese painter, Lippo Memmi.

A fine Gothic stained glass **window★** in the chancel illustrates the Gospel with recognisable figures of theologians and prophets.

The south transept gives access, beyond a wrought-iron grille (1516), to the famous chapel, **Cappella della Madonna di San Brizio** ⊙, painted with admirable **frescoes★★**. These were begun in 1447 by Fra Angelico who began by decorating the vaulting. He left them unfinished and the work was taken up in 1490 by **Luca Signorelli** (c 1445-1523). As the human figure was his main interest, while landscape and colour remained secondary considerations, the theme of the frescoes enabled him to perfect his talent. Although he lacked the spiritual depth of Michelangelo, he can be considered the latter's predecessor in terms of an almost sculptural approach to painting, the careful portrayal of human anatomy, dramatic compositions and the sense of pathos he confers on his figures.

A few minutes in front of Luca Signorelli's frescoes

The atmosphere which permeates the Chapel of San Brizio is even more disturbing if one considers the images as the anticipation of an apocalyptic day which could strike at any time. Monsters, the torture of the damned and the corpse-like colour of the demons all contribute to a sense of anguish. Every detail is imbued with a monstrous quality, even the grotesques.

The frescoes should be read starting from the north wall. The first is a portrayal of the *Preaching of the Antichrist*; the Antichrist, who has the devil as his adviser, has taken on the appearance of Christ. Signorelli has portrayed himself in the noble dark figure on the extreme left. This image is followed by the *Calling of the Elect to Heaven*.

On the wall of the altar, on the left: the *Angels leading the Elect to Paradise*; on the right: *Angels chasing out the Reprobates* with scenes of hell.

On the right wall: *The Damned in Hell* and the *Resurrection of the Dead*.

On the west wall, in the *End of the World*, the sun and moon have lost all traces of familiarity, the earth is in the throes of an earthquake. A sibyl, a prophet and demons are all represented in this scene.

ADDITIONAL SIGHTS

Underground Orvieto ⊙ – Orvieto lies on a bed of volcanic earth. To understand the history and structure of the city it is worth visiting its "cellars". The majority of the underground chambers (already present in Etruscan times) which have been dug out of the hill are in fact cellars. A visit to these caves (of which more than 1 000 are officially listed) will reveal Medieval niches for funerary urns, the foundations of a 14C oil mill and the 6C BC base of a well with steps to enable ascent and descent.

★★ **Pozzo di San Patrizio** ⊙ – St Patrick's Well was dug in the volcanic rock by order of Pope Clement VII de' Medici to supply the town with water in case of siege. Sangallo the Younger was entrusted with the work. Two spiral staircases, lit by 72 windows, wind up and down without meeting. The well is over 62m/203ft deep and its water cold and pure.

Traffic restricted in the town centre

Alberici (Via degli)	2	Garibaldi (Via)	10	Pza del Popolo (Via di) 17
Cava (via della)	5	Maitani (Via)	12	Repubblica (Pza della) 19
Cavallotti (Via Felice)	6	Malabranca (Via)	13	
Cavour (Corso)		Nebbia (Via)	14	Museo Archeologico Faina . . . M¹
Duomo (Pza del)	7	Orvieto (Via A. da)	15	Palazzo dei Papi . . . . M²
Duomo (Via del)	9	Popolo (Piazza del)	16	

★ **Palazzo del Popolo** – The town hall is built of volcanic rock in the Romanesque-Gothic style. The façade has a majestic balcony, elegant windows and curious fluted merlons.

★ **Quartiere Vecchio** – This quiet, unfrequented quarter has retained its old houses, medieval towers and churches. At the western extremity stands the Church of **San Giovenale**; the Gothic apse is decorated with 13C-15C frescoes.

Museo archeologico Faina ⊘ (**M¹**) – This important **Etruscan Collection**★ includes splendid painted vases, carved terracotta funerary urns and a rare 4C sarcophagus.

San Bernardino – A charming Baroque church dedicated to St Bernard with the refined decoration of a theatre. The oval interior is delightfully decorated and has an organ carved with figures.

Piazza della Repubblica – It stands on the site of the ancient forum, dominated by the Church of Sant'Andrea, dedicated to St Andrew, with its lovely 12-sided Romanesque tower.

The length of time given in this guide
– for touring allows time to enjoy the views and the scenery;
– for sightseeing is the average time required for a visit.

OSTIA ANTICA★★

Lazio
Michelin map 430 Q 18 – 24km/15mi southwest of Rome
See The Green Guide to Rome

Ostia, at the mouth of the Tiber, takes its name from the Latin word *ostium* meaning mouth. According to Virgil, Aeneas landed here but its foundation dates in reality back to the 4C BC when Rome embarked on her conquest of the Mediterranean. From that time on, Ostia's development has reflected that of Rome: a military port during the period of expansion, a commercial port once Rome had established an organised system of trade. At first there was simply a castle to protect the port from pirates but by 1BC Ostia had become a real town around which Sulla built ramparts in 79BC. Like Rome, Ostia began to decline in the 4C.
Slowly the harbour silted up and malaria decimated the population. Ostia was soon covered by alluvium deposited by the Tiber. It was 1909 before Ostia was discovered and regular excavations began.

On this extensive site the visitor can discover a variety of interesting remains: warehouses (*horrea*); baths; sanctuaries; the substantial dwelling-house, the *domus* built around its atrium or courtyard; and the more usual block of flats, several storeys high (*insula*). They were nearly all built of brick and unrendered (*for a description of Roman houses also see p. 63*). Some had elegant entrances framed by a triangular pediment resting on two pillars. Here and there a porch or a balcony added interest to the street front.

In addition there are the numerous meeting-places for both business and pleasure, and the forum which was the hub of both political and social life. During the empire Ostia was a town with a population of 100 000 which included a large number of foreigners.

P. Roy/EXPLORER

Nowadays it is hard to imagine the fervent activity that surrounded the forum and Capitol

TOUR OF THE EXCAVATIONS ⊘ *3hr*

Follow the itinerary outlined on the map which includes many other places of interest in addition to the ones described. *For a more detailed description consult the current Michelin Red Guide Rome.*

Once past the **Via delle Tombe**, just outside the **Porta Romana** (the main entrance to the town coming from Rome) is the **Decumanus Maximus**, the east-west axis of all Roman towns; in Ostia it was paved with large slabs and lined with porticoed houses and shops.

On the right are the **Terme di Nettuno**. This 2C building has a terrace with a view of the fine **mosaics★★** which depict the marriage of Neptune and Amphitrite. A little further on, on the opposite side is the **Horrea di Hortensius★**, grand 1C warehouses built round a pillared courtyard which is lined with shops. The theatre has been much restored but is nevertheless very evocative of life in a Roman city.

★★★ **Piazzale delle Corporazioni** – Under the portico in the square were the offices of the 70 trading corporations which represented the trading links with the Roman world. The mosaic pavement portrays their emblems, which in turn indicate the commodity they traded in and the country of origin. The temple in the centre of the square is sometimes attributed to Ceres, goddess of corn and the harvest.

On the right is the Casa di Apuleio and then the Mitreum **(Mitreo)**, a temple to Mithras and one of the best preserved in Ostia.

★★ **Thermopolium** – This bar with a marble counter served hot drinks (hence its name).

★ **Casa di Diana** – This is a striking example of an *insula* (block of flats) with rooms and passages arranged around an inner courtyard.

★ **Museo** ⊘ – The museum displays objects found in Ostia: crafts, oriental religious cults (numerous in Ostia), sculptures and **portraits★**, and examples of the rich interior decoration found in Ostia.

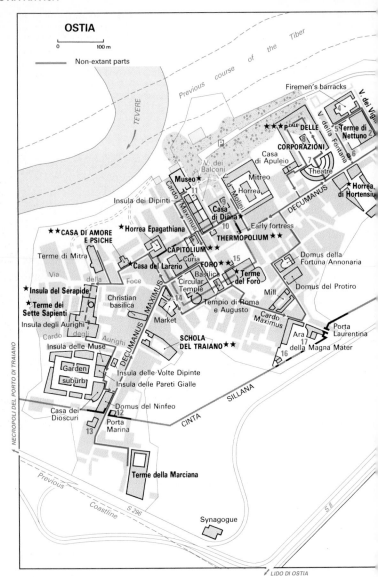

OSTIA

0   100 m

——— Non-extant parts

TEVERE

Previous course of the Tiber

Firemen's barracks

V. dei Vigili

★★★ P.ZALE DELLE
CORPORAZIONI

★Terme di Nettuno

V. della Fontana

Casa di Apuleio

N. dei Balconi

Mitreo

Theatre

Museo★

Horrea

DECUMANUS

★Horrea di Hortensiu

Insula dei Dipinti

Cardo Maximus

Casa di Diana★

Early fortress

★★CASA DI AMORE E PSICHE

★Horrea Epagathiana

THERMOPOLIUM ★★

Domus della Fortuna Annonaria

Terme di Mitra

CAPITOLIUM ★★

★Casa del Larario

Curia

FORO ★★

★Terme del Foro

Domus del Protiro

Via

della

Foce

Basilica

Circular Temple

Mill

★Insula del Serapide

Christian basilica

DECUMANUS MAXIMUS

CARDO MAXIMUS

Tempio di Roma e Augusto

Cardo Maximus

★Terme dei Sette Sapienti

Insula degli Aurighi

Market

Ara della Magna Mater

Porta Laurentina

Cardo degli Aurighi

Insula delle Muse

SCHOLA DEL TRAIANO ★★

Garden suburb

Insula delle Volte Dipinte

Insula delle Pareti Gialle

SILLANA

Casa dei Dioscuri

Domus del Ninfeo

Porta Marina

CINTA

NECROPOLI DEL PORTO DI TRAIANO

Previous

Coastline

S 296

Terme della Marciana

Synagogue

S.8

LIDO DI OSTIA

★★ **Capitolium** and **Foro** – The **Capitol** was the largest temple in Ostia, built in the 2C and dedicated to the Capitoline triad: Jupiter, Juno and Minerva. Some of the pillars of the surrounding portico in the **forum** (extended in the 2C) are still standing. At the far end stands the 1C Temple of Rome and Augustus (Tempio di Roma e Augusto), faced with marble.

Beyond the **Casa del Larario★** so-called because of the red and ochre brick decoration is the **Horrea Epagathiana★**, a warehouse with a fine doorway featuring columns and frontispiece.

★★ **Casa di Amore e Psiche** – This 4C building, facing the seashore, has interesting remains of mosaic and marble floors and a lovely nymphaeum.

Terme – There is a series of baths (terme) starting with the **Terme di Mitra** with traces of the steps and frigidarium. Further along are the **Insula del Serapide★** and the **Terme dei Sette Sapienti★** – there is a handsome mosaic floor in the large circular room. Beyond the walls are the **Terme della Marciana** with a beautiful **mosaic★** in the frigidarium.

★★ **Schola del Traiano** – This impressive 2C to 3C building was the headquarters of a guild of merchants. Inside can be seen several porticoed courtyards and a rectangular basin.

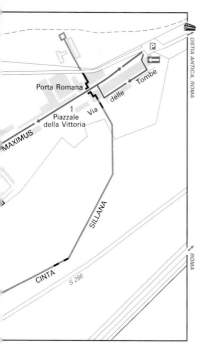

1	Statue of Minerva Victoria
2	Mosaic *(Marriage of Neptune and Amphitrite)*
3	Mosaic *(The Winds and Four Roman Province)*
4	Augusteum
5	Public fountain
6	Fortunatus' tavern
7	Masks
8	Temple
9	Mill stones
10	Piazza dei Lari
11	Oil store
12	Tavern
13	Tomb
14	Fishmongers' shops
15	Public lavatory
16	Temple of Cybele
17	Sanctuary of Attis

Antico corso del Tevere:	*Previous cours of the Tiber*
Antico limite del mare:	*Previous sea shore*
Basilica cristiana:	*Christian basilica*
Casa:	*House*
Caserma del Vigili:	*Firemen's barracks*
Cinta Sillana:	*Sulla's Wall*
Città giardina:	*Garden Suburb*
Curia:	*Curia*
Foro:	*Forum*
Fortezza primitiva:	*Early fortress*
Mercato:	*Market*
Mulino:	*Mill*
Museo:	*Museum*
Necropoli del Porto: di Traiano:	*Necropolis of Trajan's Port*
Porta:	*Gate*
Sinagoga:	*Synagogue*
Teatro:	*Theater*
Templo Rotondo:	*Circular temple*
Terme:	*Baths*

Make for the **Basilica cristiana**, a 4C Christian basilica; a row of columns separates the aisles which end in apses. An inscription on the architrave of a colonnade marks the entrance to what has been identified as the baptistery.

A little further on are the **Terme del Foro★** which are the largest baths in Ostia. Along one side is a good example of a public lavatory. In the rectangular enclosure of the **Campo della Magna Mater** are the remains of a temple dedicated to Cybele (or the Magna Mater, the Great Mother).

OTRANTO

Puglia

Population 5 279

Michelin map 431 G 37

Otranto lies on the Adriatic coast of the "heel" of the peninsula. This fishing port was once capital of "Terra d'Otranto", the last remaining Byzantine stronghold, and resisted the Lombards and then the Normans for some considerable time. In the 15C when the town was besieged by the troops of Mohammed II the townspeople took refuge in the cathedral where they were massacred. Survivors were taken prisoner and killed on the summit of a hill, Colle della Minerva, where a sanctuary was built to the memory of the martyrs. Greek influence has been so strong in the Terra d'Otranto" that even today inhabitants speak a dialect which is very similar to Greek.

Città vecchia – There is a good view of the old town from the northeast pier; to the left is the 15C **Castello Aragonese**, trapezoidal in form and flanked by massive cylindrical towers. To reach this stronghold perched on the clifftop pass through the gateways Porta di Terra and the 15C Porta Alfonsina.

★ **Cattedrale** – This 12C cathedral was altered in the late 15C. The interior, with antique columns separating the nave from the two aisles, is remarkable for its astonishing mosaic **floor★★★** which was executed between 1163 and 1165 by Pantaleone, a priest. The decoration has simple, almost primitive patterns but the vivacity of the figures' poses and attitudes, the freshness of the colours and variety of symbols make this a fascinating illustrated story. The central nave portrays the Tree of Life which is held up by two Indian elephants. The tree's outstretched branches embrace biblical scenes, Medieval beasts, heroes of courtly poems, mythological images and the cycle of months and astrological signs. This pattern is taken up at the end of the two aisles with two other trees and representations of Paradise and Hell on the left and biblical and mythological figures on the right. Equally interesting is the vast **crypt** which is divided into five aisles and sustained by a veritable forest of ancient capitals (Classical, Byzantine and Romanesque).

Chiesetta di S. Pietro – Erected between the 9C and 10C this Byzantine style church (built in the form of a Greek cross within a square and with a central dome on pendetives) has fine frescoes of the same period; unfortunately these are in very poor condition.

EXCURSION

* **The coast to the south** – Between Otranto and **Santa Maria di Leuca** *(51km/32mi)* the road offers fine views of this wild and indented coastline. At the head of an inlet is the cave, **Grotta Zinzulusa** ⊙, with concretions and two lakes, one salt water and the other fresh, which are inhabited by rare marine species.

PADOVA★★

PADUA – Veneto
Population 211 985
Michelin map 429 F 17

There are few traces of ancient Patavium which was one of the most prosperous Roman cities in the Veneto during the 1C BC owing to its fluvial trade, its agriculture and the sale of horses.

In the 7C Padua was destroyed by the Lombards, and from the 11C to 13C it became an independent city-state. This was the period when numerous churches and palaces were built. The city underwent its greatest period of economic and cultural prosperity under the enlightened rule of the lords of Carrara (1337-1405). In 1405 Padua came under the sway of the Venetian Republic and remained a loyal subject until 1797 when the Venetian Constitution was abolished by Napoleon.

The historic centre of Padua, a busy town and an art and pilgrimage centre, is **Piazza Cavour** (DY **15**), with the neo-Classical **Caffè Pedrocchi**, which was a meeting-place of the liberal élite in the Romantic period.

The city of St Anthony the Hermit – The saint is venerated in Padua. He was born in Lisbon in 1195 and died at the age of 36 in the environs of Padua. This Franciscan monk was a forceful preacher. His help was invoked by the shipwrecked and those in prison and he is generally represented holding a book and a lily.

A famous university – The University of Padua founded in 1222 is the second oldest in Italy after Bologna. It expanded rapidly and attracted students from the whole of Europe. Galileo was a professor and among its students were the Renaissance scholar Pico della Mirandola, the astronomer Copernicus and the poet Tasso.

Art in Padua – In 1304, **Giotto** came to Padua from Florence to decorate the Scrovegni Chapel. He painted a cycle of frescoes which is one of the masterpieces of Italian art. In the 15C the Renaissance in Padua was marked by Donatello, another Florentine, who stayed in the city from 1444 to 1453.

Also in the 15C Paduan art flourished under the guiding influence of the Paduan artist, **Andrea Mantegna** (1431-1506). A painter of powerful originality, he was fascinated by anatomy and archeology and was also a technical innovator in the field of perspective.

ARTISTIC CENTRE 2hr30min

*** **Frescoes by Giotto** – The cycle of 39 frescoes was painted c 1305-10 by Giotto on the walls of the **Cappella degli Scrovegni** ⊙ (DY). The chapel, built in 1303, illustrates the lives of Joachim and Anna, Mary and Jesus: the *Flight into Egypt*, *Judas' Kiss* and the *Entombment* are among the most famous. On the lower register, the powerful monochrome figures depict the Vices *(left)* and Virtues *(right)*. The *Last Judgement* on the west wall completes the cycle.

This work shows an exceptional unity and is Giotto's masterpiece, displaying great dramatic power, harmonious composition and intense spirituality. On the altar stands a *Virgin*★ by the Tuscan sculptor Giovanni Pisano.

** **Frescoes in the Chiesa degli Eremitani** (DY) – The 13C Church of the Hermits was badly damaged by bombing in 1944 but has been rebuilt in the original Romanesque style. In the Cappella Ovetari *(the second on the right of the Cappella Maggiore)* are fragments of frescoes by **Mantegna**. The various scenes (*Martyrdom of St James* on the north wall, *Assumption* in the apse and *Martyrdom of St Christoper* on the south wall) display his powerful visionary talent and his careful attention to perspective and architectural detail. The Lady Chapel (Cappella Maggiore) has splendid frescoes by **Guariento**, Giotto's Venetian pupil.

★ **Museo Civico agli Eremitani** ⊘ (**DY M**) – The municipal museum in the Hermitage of St Augustine (Sant'Agostino) comprises several collections: archeology (Egyptian, Etruscan, Roman and Pre-Roman), coins (Bottacin Bequest) and 15C-18C Venetian and Flemish paintings (Emo Capodilista collection).

The museum also contains the extensive collection from the former Art Gallery including not only furniture, ceramics and sculptures but also **paintings★★**, most of them from the Venetian School (14C-18C). In particular, note works by Giotto, Guariento, Giovanni Bellini, Veronese, and Tintoretto and the splendid 15C tapestry entitled *The Expedition of Uri*.

PILGRIMAGE CENTRE *1hr30min*

★★ **Basilica del Santo** ⊘ (**DZ**) – This important pilgrimage church dedicated to St Anthony overlooks the square in which Donatello erected an **equestrian statue★★** of the Venetian mercenary leader **Gattamelata** (nickname of Erasmo di Nardi who died in Padua in 1443) (**A**). This bronze was the first of its size to be cast in Italy.

The basilica with its eight-tiered bulbous domes was built from 1232 to 1300 in the transitional Romanesque-Gothic style and brings to mind St Mark's in Venice. The imposing **interior★★** contains numerous works of art: off the north aisle is the **Cappella del Santo★★**, a Renaissance masterpiece, which contains the tomb-cum-altar of St Anthony (Arca di Sant'Antonio) by Tiziano Aspetti (1594); on the walls are magnificent 16C **high reliefs★★** by several artists. In the chancel the **high altar★★** is adorned with bronze panels (1450) by Donatello. The third chapel, off the south aisle, has **frescoes★** by Altichiero (14C), an artist from Verona.

There is a fine **overall view★** of the building from the cloisters to the south of the basilica.

★ **Oratorio di S. Giorgio e Scuola di S. Antonio** ⊘ (**DZ B**) – St George's Oratory was built as a funerary chapel and is decorated with 21 **frescoes★** (1377) by Altichiero and his pupils, depicting various religious scenes.

In the adjacent Scuola di Sant'Antonio, a room on the first floor contains 18 16C **frescoes★** relating the life of St Anthony. Four of these are by Titian.

IF YOU STILL HAVE TIME...

★ **Palazzo della Ragione** ⊘ (**DZ J**) – The Law Courts, standing between two attractive **squares★**, the Piazza della Frutta (**DZ 25**) and the Piazza delle Erbe (**DZ 20**), are remarkable for their loggias and roof in the form of an upturned ship's keel. The first-floor **salone★★** is adorned with a 15C cycle of frescoes depicting the *Labours of the Months*, the *Liberal Arts*, the *Trades* and the *Signs of the Zodiac*.

Piazza dei Signori (**CYZ**) – This square is lined by the 14C-15C Palazzo del Capitano (**E**), one-time residence of the Venetian Governors, the Clock Tower (**Torre dell'Orologio★**) with its arcade, and the graceful Renaissance gallery, Loggia del Consiglio.

Università ⊘ (**DZ U**) – The University is housed in a palace known as the "Bo" from the name of an inn with an ox as its sign which once stood on the site. It has retained a lovely 16C courtyard and an anatomy theatre, **Teatro Anatomico** (1594) ⊘. University life is very animated here. One of the most attractive spectacles is graduation day when the students are celebrating, dressed up in their pointed hats.

Caffè Pedrocchi (**DZ N**) – This neo-Classical building, erected in 1831, is a café with white, red and green rooms. It was here that the student rebellion against the Austrians was played out in 1848. On the upper storey are meeting rooms and concert halls **(sale)** ⊘ built in a range of different styles.

Battistero (**CZ D**) – The baptistery adjoining the Duomo (Cathedral) has interesting frescoes and a polyptych by Menabuoi (14C).

Santa Giustina (**DZ**) – This 16C domed Classical church, dedicated to St Justina, is reminiscent of the Saint's Basilica. At the far end of the chancel is an **altarpiece★** by Veronese.

Orto Botanico ⊘ (**DZ**) – The botanical gardens are among the oldest of their kind in Europe. They were laid out in 1545 and contain many exotic species including the palm tree which inspired Goethe in his reflections on the development of plants.

Prato della Valle (**DZ**) – This 17C oval garden is planted with plane trees and encircled by the still waters of a canal, lined with statues of famous men.

EXCURSIONS

★ **Montagnana** – *47km/29mi southwest.* This small town is girt with impressive 14C **ramparts**★★ reinforced with 24 polygonal towers and four gateways. The cathedral **(Duomo)**, attributed to Sansovino, contains a *Transfiguration* by Veronese at the high altar, 16C frescoes and stalls. The Church of **San Francesco**, dedicated to St Francis, with its lovely Gothic belfry abuts the town wall.

PADOVA

Altinate (Via)	DYZ	Frutta (Piazza della)	DZ 25	Roma (Via)	DZ
Carmine (Via del)	DY 10	Garibaldi (Corso)	DY 27	S. Canziano (Via)	DZ 57
Cavour (Piazza e via)	DY 15	Garibaldi (Piazza)	DY 28	S. Fermo (Via)	DY
Cesarotti (Via M.)	DZ 17	Gasometro (Via dell' ex)	DY 29	S. Lucia (Via)	DY 59
Dante (Via)	CY	Guariento (Via)	DY 35	Vandelli	
Erbe (Piazza delle)	DZ 20	Insurrezione (Piazza)	DY 39	(Via D.)	CZ 66
Eremitani (Piazza)	DY 21	Monte di Pietà (Via del)	CZ 45	Verdi (Via G.)	CY 67
Filiberto (Via E.)	DY 24	Petrarca (Via)	CY 50	Vittorio Emanuele II	
		Ponte Molino (Vicolo)	CY 52	(Corso)	CZ 70
		Ponti Romani		8 Febbraio (Via)	DZ 74
		(Riviera dei)	DYZ 53	58 Fanteria (Via)	DZ 75

Statua equestre del Gattamelata	DZ **A**	Battistero	CZ **D**	Museo civico agli Eremitani	DY **M**
Oratorio di San Giorgio		Palazzo del Capitano	CZ **E**	Caffè Pedrocchi	DZ **N**
e Scuola di Sant'Antonio	DZ **B**	Palazzo della Ragione	DZ **J**	Università	DZ **U**

* **Colli Euganei** – The Euganean hills to the south of Padua are of volcanic origin. This pleasant hilly area is planted with orchards and vineyards and was already appreciated in Roman times for its numerous hot springs and its wines.

✝✝✝ **Abano Terme** – This modern and elegant thermal spa well-shaded by pines is one of Italy's most famous spa towns.

✝✝ **Montegrotto Terme** – Although less important than Abano it is rapidly growing in importance. This was the ancient *Mons Aegrotorum* (mountain of the sick).

* **Monselice** – This town, whose Latin name *Mons Silicis* bears witness to its importance as a mining community during Roman times, has retained a large section of its walls and is dominated by the ruins of a castle. From Piazza Mazzini, go up the picturesque Via del Santuario to reach the 13C-14C castle, the Romanesque cathedral (Duomo), the early-17C Sanctuary of the Seven Churches and the Villa Balbi with its Italian garden. The upper terrace affords a lovely **view**★ of the region.

* **Arquà Petrarca** – *6.5km/4mi northwest of Monselice*. It was here, in these tranquil, medieval surroundings, that **Petrarch** (1304-1374) died. He was born in Arezzo in 1304 but his stormy life took him to various places in Italy and abroad. In a church in Avignon, he met Laura, the woman with whom he fell in love for all time and whom he immortalised in his collection of sonnets entitled the *Canzoniere*. His works became a reference throughout Europe for lyric poetry and, during the Renaissance, they gave rise to attempts at imitation after the poet had become virtually a cult figure.

The house (**casa**★ ⊘) where he lived and died is open to the public. It has 16C frescoes and the original coffered ceiling. Exhibits include memorabilia of the poet and autographs of famous visitors such as Carducci or Byron. His pink marble tomb was erected on the church square in 1380.

Este – Cradle of the Este family, rulers of Ferrara, the town still has an attractive section of **town wall**★ to the north. The **Museo Nazionale Atestino**★ ⊘, housed in the 16C Mocenigo Palace, has an extensive archeological collection relating to local farming from the Paleolithic to the Roman eras. The collection is displayed chronologically. *Ateste* was the name of the town during Roman times. The Duomo (cathedral), on an elliptical plan, contains a large canvas (1759) by Tiepolo.

* **Riviera del Brenta** – *See Riviera del BRENTA.*

Michelin on the Net: www.michelin-travel.com.

Our route planning service covers all of Europe – twenty-one countries and one million kilometres of highways and byways – enabling you to plot many different itineraries from wherever you are. The itinerary options allow you to choose a preferred route – for example, quickest, shortest, or Michelin recommended.

The network is updated three times weekly, integrating ongoing road works, detours, new motorways, and snowbound mountain passes.

The description of the itinerary includes the distances and travelling times between towns, selected hotels and restaurants.

PAESTUM★★★

Campania

Michelin map 431 F 26-27

One of Italy's most important archeological sites, Paestum was discovered by chance around 1750, when the Bourbons started to build the road which crosses the area today. The initial settlement was an ancient Greek colony founded around 600 BC under the name of Poseidonia by colonists from Sybaris. Around the year 400 BC the city fell to a local tribe, the Lucanians. It became Roman in the year 273 BC but began to decline towards the end of the Empire because of the malaria which finally drove out its inhabitants.

TOUR ⊘ 2hr

The suggested itinerary proceeds from south to north. Those wishing to visit the museum first should start from the north.

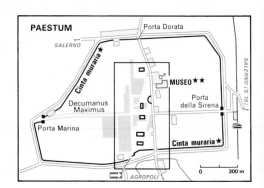

The temples, built of a fine yellow limestone, stand amidst the ruins (rovine) of dwellings sheltered by cypresses and oleanders. Take the Porta della Giustizia through the 5km/3 mile-long city wall **(Cinta muraria★)** and follow the **Via Sacra**, the principal street of the Greek and Roman city.

★★ **Basilica** – The rear of the "Basilica", so-called by 18C archeologists, stands to the right of the Via Sacra. This mid-6C BC temple, the oldest in the city, was dedicated to Hera, sister and bride of Zeus. The great age of the monument is attested to by the pronounced swelling at the centre of the columns (entasis) and the squashed echini of the columns. These deformations convey the way in which architectural structures were considered living entities which swell and squash when submitted to undue pressure. The porch (pronaos) leads into the central chamber divided into two aisles, probably indicating that two cults were practised here.

★★★ **Tempio di Nettuno** – When Paestum was first discovered this well-preserved temple was thought to have been dedicated to Neptune (or Poseidon in Greek, hence the town's name Poseidonia). It has

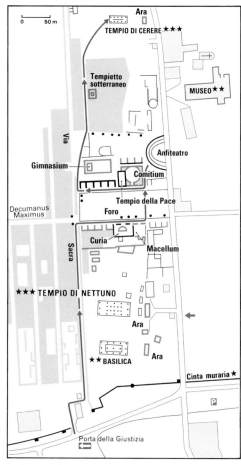

Anfiteatro:	*Anphiteatre*	**Museo:**	*Museum*
Ara:	*Altar*	**Tempietto**	*Underground*
Cinta muraria:	*Wall*	**sotterraneo:**	*temple*
Foro:	*Forum*	**Tempio:**	*Temple*

since been proved that it was dedicated to Hera and more recent hypotheses suggest that it may have been dedicated to Zeus or Apollo. Dating from the mid- 5C BC it is in an admirably harmonious Doric style. One of the most impressive structural devices is the slight convexity (2cm) of the horizontal lines which makes the numerous columns look straight. For this same reason the fluting on the corner columns veer slightly inwards.

In the centre of the city stands the forum **(foro)**, surrounded by a portico and shops, and overlooked by the **curia**, the adjacent *macellum* (covered market) and the *comitium* (c 3C BC), the most important public building where magistrates were elected. To the left of the *comitium* stands the **temple of peace** (2C-1C BC) constructed on a north-south plan according to Italic custom.

To the east of the forum stands the **amphitheatre**, constructed between the Republican and Imperial ages and divided by the main road. Unusually it is not located outside the city centre, a measure that was adopted to enable an easy flow of people to and from the amphitheatre.

The *gimnasium* (c 3C BC) was probably a sanctuary with a pool. During ritualistic celebrations the statue of the divinity was immersed in the pool and then placed on a platform on the west side. The pool was buried in the 1C AD and the structure subsequently housed the gymnasium.

The **Tempietto Sotterraneo** (small underground temple, 6C BC) has been interpreted as being a *heroon*, a kind of cenotaph devoted to the cult of the city's founder who was made a hero after his death. Some bronze vases with traces of honey were also found here; these are housed at the museum.

★★★ **Tempio di Cerere** – Originally erected in the late 6C BC in honour of Athena, the Temple of Ceres combines an interesting mix of styles: the Doric colonnade is solid and massive whereas the internal Ionic columns are more graceful and decorative. Near the entrance of the temple, on the east side, is the sacrificial altar **(ara)**.

★★ **Museo** ⊘ – The masterpieces in this museum include the famous **metopes**★★, 6C BC low reliefs in the Doric style which adorned both the *Thesaurós*, or temple of Hera (scenes from the life of Heracles and the Trojan Wars), and the High Temple (Dancing Girls) of the Sanctuary of Hera at Sele *(10km/6mi north near the mouth of the Sele River)* as well as the Tomb of the Diver **(Tomba del Tuffatore**★★**)**. The tomb constitutes a rare example of Greek funerary painting with lively banquet scenes and the famous dive, symbol of the passage from life to death, which is directed beyond the columns of Hercules, the frontier of the known world. The museum also houses the stunning **vases**★ (6C BC) from the underground temple, a true masterpiece of bronze sculpture, the painted Lucanian tombs (4C BC) and the representations, executed in a style which is typical of Paestum art, of Hera Argiva with a pomegranate (symbol of fertility) and the flower-woman in terracotta, used as an incense burner.

PARMA★★

Emilia-Romagna
Population 167 165
Michelin map 428 or 429 H 12-13

Parma, at the junction of the Via Emilia and the Mantua-La Spezia road, is an important market town and industrial centre with a rich heritage. The town has a certain refined charm and is often bathed in a diaphanous light. Piazza Garibaldi (**BZ 9**) is a popular meeting-place for the townspeople. The famous 20C conductor Arturo Toscanini was born in Parma.

HISTORICAL NOTES

A settlement was founded on this site by the Etruscans in 525 BC and it became a Roman station on the Via Emilia in 183 BC. It declined but revived in the 6C under the Ostrogoth King, Theodoric. After having been an independent commune from the 11C-13C, it became a member of the Lombard League *(see Index)*. After the fall of the commune's government in 1335, Parma was governed in turn by the Visconti, the Sforza and, later, the French before being annexed by the papacy in 1513. In 1545 Pope Paul III Farnese gave two papal territories, Parma and Piacenza, having made them a duchy, to his son Pier Luigi Farnese, who was assassinated in 1547. However, the **Farnese** dynasty continued to reign until 1731 and several members of the house were patrons of the arts and letters, collectors and great builders.

When it passed to the Bourbons, its first sovereign was Charles, successively King of Naples then King of Spain. When Don Philip, the son of Philip V of Spain and Elizabeth Farnese, married Louise Elizabeth, the favourite daughter of Louis XV, the town underwent a period (1748-1801) of great French influence in several domains (customs, administration and the arts).

Numerous Frenchmen came to work in Parma while others like Stendhal chose to live here; he made Parma the setting of his well-known novel, *The Charterhouse of Parma*. The Bourbon of Parma had their Versailles at Colorno, north of the town.

The Parma School – The school is represented by two main artists, Correggio and Il Parmigianino, whose works formed the transition between the Renaissance and Baroque art. Antonio Allegri (1489-1534), known as **Correggio**, was a master of light and chiaroscuro; his work shows a gracefully sensual and optimistic vision which seemed to herald 18C French art. Francesco Mazzola (1503-40), or **Il Parmigianino** (The Parmesan) as he was commonly known, was a more troubling and melancholy personality. His elongated forms and cold colours were characteristic of Mannerism. His canon of feminine beauty influenced the Fontainebleau school and all the other European Mannerists of the 16C, through the intermediary of Niccolò dell'Abbate and Il Primaticcio.

★★★ CITY CENTRE *half a day*

This historic core of the city comprises the Romanesque **Episcopal Centre★★★** (CYZ) including the cathedral and baptistery, the Baroque Church of St John and the surrounding palaces as well as the Palazzo della Pilotta (16C-17C) and Correggio's Room.

★★ **Duomo** (CY) – The cathedral is in the Romanesque style and is flanked by an elegant Gothic campanile. The façade includes a Lombard porch supported by lions and surmounted by a loggia and three tiers of galleries with little columns. Inside, the dome is decorated with the famous **frescoes** painted by Correggio from 1522 to 1530. The ascending rhythm of the *Assumption of the Virgin* with the central figure amidst a swirling group of cherubim is remarkable. The artist's mastery of perspective and movement is expressed in an original and exuberant style virtually Baroque in spirit. In the south transept the ***Descent from the Cross*** (1178) by the sculptor Antelami clearly shows the influence of the Provençal School, despite the solemnity of the figures. In the nave, the frescoes are by Gambara (1530-1574); on the vaulting they were painted by Bedoli (16C). The gilded copper *Angel* (1284) which crowned the spire of the bell-tower is now on the third pillar to the left of the nave.

★★★ **Battistero** (CY **A**) – This is Italy's most harmonious medieval monument. The octagonal baptistery in Verona rose-coloured marble was started in 1196 and the architecture and carved decoration, which show great unity of style, date from the 13C. The baptistery is attributed to the sculptor Antelami who was also responsible for the sculptures; his signature appears on the lintel of the north door, dedicated to the Virgin. Inside (the interior is a 16-sided polygon), the admirable 13C **frescoes** of Byzantine inspiration depict scenes from the *Life of Christ* and the *Golden Legend*.

San Giovanni Evangelista (CYZ) – This Renaissance church, dedicated to St John the Evangelist, has a Baroque façade. Inside, the **frescoes on the dome★★**, painted by Correggio (1520-24), depict the *Vision of St John at Patmos* and the *Translation of St John the Evangelist*. Those on the arches of the chapels to the north (1st, 2nd and 4th) were executed by Parmigianino.
In the convent next door are the Renaissance **cloisters** ⊙.

Antica spezeria di S. Giovanni Evangelista ⊙ (CY **N**) – *1 Borgo Pipa*. This 13C pharmacy was started by the Benedictine monks. The furnishings date from the 16C.

Palazzo della Pilotta (BY) – The palace was so-called because the game of fives (*pilotta*) was played in its courtyards. This rather austere building, erected by order of the Farnese from 1583 to 1622, now houses two museums, the Palatine Library and the Farnese Theatre.

★ **Museo Archeologico Nazionale** ⊙ – The National Museum of Antiquities displays pre-Roman and Roman artefacts including the finds made in the excavation of Velleia to the west of Parma.

★★ **Galleria Nazionale** ⊙ – The well-laid out gallery exhibits Emilian, Tuscan and Venetian paintings of the 14C, 15C and 16C by: Fra Angelico, Dosso Dossi, El Greco, Canaletto, Bellotto, Piazzetta and Tiepolo. Il Parmigianino is represented by his astonishing portrait **Turkish Slave**, which is of considerable elegance, and Correggio by one of his masterpieces, **The Virgin with St Jerome** (1528), as well as other works. The gallery also houses a sketch by Leonardo da Vinici, *(La Scapigliata)*.

★★ **Teatro Farnese** ⊙ – This imposing theatre was built in wood in 1619 by G. B. Aleotti, following the model of Palladio's Olympic Theatre in Vicenza *(see VICENZA)*. Inaugurated for the marriage of Margaret de' Medici and Odoardo Farnese, the theatre was almost totally destroyed in 1944 and was rebuilt exactly as before in the 1950s.

PARMA

Basetti (Viale) . . . . BZ 2
Cavour (Strada) . . . . BY 3
Duomo (Strada al) . . . . . . CY 8
Farini (Strada) . . . . BZ

Garibaldi (Piazza) . . . . BZ 9
Garibaldi
   (Strada) . . . . BCY
Mazzini (Strada) . . . . BZ 13
Pace (Piazza della) . . . . . . BY 15
Pilotta (Piazza) . . . . BY 17
Ponte Caprazucca . . . . . . BZ 19

Ponte di Mezzo . . . . BZ 21
Ponte Verdi . . . . BY 22
Regale (Borgo) . . . . CZ 25
Repubblica
   (Strada della) . . . . . . CZ
Studi (Borgo degli) . . . . . . CY 27
Toscanini (Viale) . . . . BZ 28

Battistero . . . . CY A
Madonna della Steccata . . . . BZ E
Museo Glauco-Lombardi . . . . BY M¹

Casa Toscanini . . . . BY M²
Antica spezieria di San Giovanni Evangelista . . CY N
Teatro Regio . . . . BY T¹

★ **Camera del Correggio o di S. Paolo** ⊘ (CY) – Correggio's Room was the dining-room of the Abbess of St Paul's Convent. The ceiling frescoes depicting mythological scenes with a luminous quality are Correggio's first major work (1519-20). The garlands of flowers and trelliswork and the reliefs and architectural detail at the base of the vault reveal the influence of Mantegna, whom he met in his youth in Mantua (*see MANTOVA*). The next room was decorated by Araldi (1504).

ADDITIONAL SIGHTS

★ **Fondazione-Museo Glauco-Lombardi** ⊘ (BY M¹) – The Glauco-Lombardi museum is chiefly devoted to life in the Duchy of Parma Piacenza in the 18C and 19C. It contains paintings and mementoes of the former Empress Marie-Louise who governed the duchy. There are numerous works by French artists: Nattier, Mignard, Chardin, Watteau, Fragonard, Greuze, La Tour, Hubert Robert, Vigée-Lebrun, David and Millet.

S. Maria della Steccata ⊘ (BZ E) – This 16C church, designed by the architects Bernardino and Zaccagni, contains fine **frescoes**★ by Il Parmigianino representing *the Foolish and the Wise Virgins*, between Adam and Moses, and Eve and Aaron. The mausoleum of Neipperg, husband of the former French Empress Marie-Louise who became Duchess of Parma, is on the left, and the tombs of the Farnese family and the Bourbon-Parma are in the crypt.

Teatro Regio (BY T¹) – The Royal Theatre, built between 1821 and 1829 at the request of Marie-Louise of Habsburg, has a Classical frontage. The inaugural performance was of Bellini's opera, *Zaira.* The acoustics are excellent.

Palazzo del Giardino (BY) – The ducal garden (**parco ducale**★) was landscaped by the French architect Petitot and adorned with statues by another Frenchman, Boudard.

Casa Toscanini ⊘ (BY M²) – The birthplace of the famous conductor (1867-1957) houses interesting documents for anybody with a love of music: distinctions and decorations granted to the musician, sculptures and objects connected with the Toscanini family, Verdi and Wagner, letters from Mazzini, Garibaldi, D'Annunzio and Einstein, and numerous reminders of the master's work in America. There is also an audiovisual presentation of the conductor's career.

EXCURSIONS

★ **Castello di Torrechiara** ⊘ – *17km/11mi south by the Langhirano road.* This 15C fortress, built on a hilltop, is powerfully fortified by double ramparts, massive corner towers, a keep and machicolated curtain walls. The upper rooms (the Gaming and Gold Rooms) have remarkable **frescoes**★. From the terrace there is a superb **view**★ which reaches as far as the Apennines.

Fidenza – *23km/14mi west. Leave Parma by Via Massimo D'Azeglio* (**AY**). This attractive agricultural town has a remarkable 11C cathedral (**Duomo**★) which was completed in the Gothic style in the 13C. The lovely sculptured decoration of the **central porch**★★ is most likely the work of the Parmesan sculptor, Antelami. The three fine **Romanesque doors** are adorned with lions, a typically Emilian feature (see Reggio, Modena, Ferrara, Parma).

Fontanellato – *19km/12mi to the northwest by the Fidenza road and then the road to Soragna, to the right.* The vast moat-encircled castle, **Rocca Sanvitale** ⊘, stands in the centre of town. The ceiling of one of the rooms is decorated with a **fresco**★ depicting Diana and Actaeon by Il Parmigianino. The fine furnishings date from the 17C.

PAVIA★

Lombardy

Population 74 065
Michelin map 428 G 9

This proud city on the banks of the Ticino River is rich in buildings from the Romanesque and Renaissance periods. The many old feudal towers dotted around the city were built by the noble families of Pavia, often as a public sign of their wealth – the taller the tower, the richer the family.

This important military camp under the Romans then became, successively, the capital of the Lombard Kings, rival of Milan in the 11C, famous intellectual and artistic centre during the 14C under the Visconti, a fortified town in the 16C and one of the most active centres of the 19C independence movements. The university, one of the oldest and most famous in Europe, was founded in the 11C and its students included Petrarch, Leonardo da Vinci and the poet Ugo Foscolo (*The Last Letters of Jacopo Ortiz*).

The dreams of conquest of the French kings ended at Pavia when, after his victory at Marignano (1515), François I was defeated and taken prisoner by the Emperor Charles V at the Battle of Pavia on 24 February 1525.

★ **Castello Visconteo** ⊘ – This impressive brick building was built by the Visconti. It now houses the **Musei Civici**★, the municipal collections, which are rich in archeological finds, medieval and Renaissance sculpture and particularly paintings. The picture gallery (**pinacoteca**★), on the first floor, has numerous masterpieces including a lovely altarpiece by the Brescian artist Vincenzo Foppa, a *Virgin and Child* by Giovanni Bellini and a very expressive *Christ bearing the Cross* by the Lombard artist, Bergognone. The last room contains a 16C model of the cathedral by Fugazza after plans by Bramante.

★ **Duomo** – This vast cathedral, surmounted by one of Italy's largest domes, was begun in 1488: both Bramante and Leonardo da Vinci are said to have worked on the plan. The façade is 19C. To the left of the façade stood an 11C municipal tower, which fell down in March 1989, while opposite is the 16C Bishop's Palace. The adjoining Piazza Vittoria is overlooked by the 12C **Broletto** or town hall. The square affords an interesting view of the cathedral's chevet.

★ **S. Michele** – This lovely Romanesque church, dedicated to St Michael, has a pale-coloured sandstone **façade**★ which is quite remarkable for the balance and variety of its sculptural ornamentation. An impressive Romanesque doorway on the south side has a lintel on which Christ is seen giving a papyrus volume to St Paul and the Keys of the Church to St Peter. Inside, there are interesting architectural features (dome on squinches, the friezes and modillions beneath the galleries, the elevated chancel, mosaics, capitals etc). The apse is decorated with a lovely 15C **fresco**★ portraying the *Coronation of the Virgin*.

S. Pietro in Ciel d'Oro – This Lombard-Romanesque church, dedicated to St Peter, which was consecrated in 1132, has a richly decorated west **door**★. In the chancel is the **Arca di Sant'Agostino**★ (the tomb of St Augustine – 354-430), the work of the *maestri campionesi* (see Index).

San Lanfranco – *2 km/1mi west.* In the chancel of this church, a **cenotaph**★ (late 15C) by Amadeo commemorates Lanfranc, who was born in Pavia and became Archbishop of Canterbury, where he is buried (d 1098).

EXCURSION

La Lomellina – This region lying between the Ticino and the Po is the great rice-growing area of Italy and a landscape of vast stretches of flooded land divided by long rows of willows and poplars. The chief towns of architectural interest are: **Lomello** *(32km/20mi southwest of Pavia)*, whose 11C Church of Santa Maria and 8C baptistery form a particularly harmonious ensemble; **Mortara** *(15km/9mi north of Lomello on the S 211)* with its 14C Church of San Lorenzo (paintings by G. Ferrari) and finally **Vigevano** *(12km/7mi northeast of Mortara on the S 494)* with its outstanding elliptical **Piazza Ducale**★★. The square (possibly designed by Leonardo da Vinci) lies at the foot of the Sforza castle and is dominated by Bramante's imposing tower.

Certosa di PAVIA★★★

PAVIA CARTHUSIAN MONASTERY – Lombardy
Michelin map 428 G 9 – 9km/6mi north of Pavia

The *"Gratiarum Cartusia"* (Charterhouse of the Graces), is one of the most remarkable and characteristic examples of Lombard art as well as being home to a small community of **Cistercian** monks. It was founded as a family mausoleum in 1396 by Gian Galeazzo Visconti of Milan. Most of the monastery was built in the 15C and 16C to the plans of successive architects. The former palace of the Dukes of Milan (1625) is on the right of the courtyard, and on the left are the studios of the sculptors in charge of the decoration.

★★★ **Façade** – The façade is an elaborate, richly detailed work whose underlying structure is, however, characterised by a restrained elegance. The more ornate lower part (1473-99) was the work of the Mantegazza brothers, the famous architect and sculptor Amadeo, who worked also in Bergamo, and his pupil, Briosco. The upper part was completed in 1560 by another architect and sculptor, Cristoforo Lombardo.

The façade is adorned with multicoloured sculptures in marble, with medallions at the base, statues of saints in the niches and an endless variety of foliage, garlands and ornaments. Round Amadeo's famous windows are scenes from the Bible, the Life of Christ and the life of Gian Galeazzo Visconti. The low reliefs round the central doorway by Briosco depict events in the history of the Carthusians. Before entering the church, walk round to the left for a general view of the late Lombard-Gothic style, with its galleries of superimposed arcades.

★★★ **Interior** ⓥ – The interior has a certain solemn grandeur and, although it is essentially Gothic, the beginnings of the Renaissance can be detected in the transept and the chancel.

The Certosa is a harmonious blend of Late Lombard Renaissance,
Gothic and monastic spirituality

R. Bouquet/DIAF

Upon entering, look up: above the south chapels a painted Carthusian monk peeks out at visitors from a window with twin openings. From higher up, visitors are observed by stars which emblazon the intense blue of the vaulting.

The south arm of the transept is decorated with a *Virgin and Child* (1481-1522) by **Bergognone** who was also responsible for the *Madonna del tappeto* above the entrance of the **small cloisters**, with its Lombard terracottas.

Adjacent to the small cloisters, the ceiling of the **refectory** is decorated with the *Madonna del Latte*, also by Bergognone.

The atmospheric **large cloisters** occupy a vast space; above its arcades note the roofs and chimneys of the 24 monks' cells which until 1968 were inhabited by **Carthusians**. Enter one of the cells and observe the surprising interior: although spartan in the extreme, each cell is a veritable apartment which looks out on the garden.

Back in the church, on the vaulting of the right altar of the transept, note the *Virgin Enthroned* receiving the charterhouse from Gian Galeazzo Visconti. The latter's tomb dates from the late 15C.

In the lavatorium **(lavabo)** note the *Madonna del Garofano* (Virgin with Carnation) by Bernardino Luini (*c* 1480-1532).

The sad story (with a happy ending) of a masterpiece

In 1984 the *Tryptych* was stolen. The prior had a heart attack resulting from the suffering for this great loss.

To raise the ransom money a concert was organised and a great flautist was invited to perform in the church: Severino Gazzelloni (1919-1992).

The happy ending is attested to by the presence of the *Tryptych* in the monastery: some stolen parts of the painting which had been sold were discovered and this eventually led to the apprehension of the thieves.

The transept is separated from the chancel by a marble partition wall. The inlay work of the choir stalls was executed to plans by Bergognone.

The **old sacristy** houses a **Tryptych** by Baldassare degli Embriachi (late 14C), made from ivory and hippopotamus teeth, with scenes from the lives of the Virgin and Christ. In the middle of the sacristy note the *Virgin and Child*, a recurring theme in the monastery which attests to the profound gratitude felt by Gian Galeazzo's wife Catherine to the Virgin.

The north arm of the transept contains another work by Bergognone: the *Ecce Homo* as well as the cenotaph of Ludovico il Moro and Beatrice d'Este, by Cristoforo Solari (1497).

Proceeding towards the exit, in the second chapel on the north side note the *Eternal Father* by Perugino (*c* 1445-1523).

Carthusians and Cistercians: who exactly are they? The Carthusians, the first monks to occupy the monastery, belong to the order of St Bruno of Cologne (925-965). The Cistercians belong to the order founded in 1098 by Robert of Molesme. The term "Cistercian" derives from Cîteaux, in Burgundy, where the order's first monastery was located.

PERUGIA★★

Umbria

Population 154 566
Michelin map 430 M 19

Perugia was one of the 12 Etruscan city-states known as *lucumonies* which comprised the federation of Etruria in the 7C and 6C BC. The massive Etruscan wall with its gateways gives some idea of the splendour of that age. The town also has numerous ecclesiastical and secular buildings from the Middle Ages. Today the capital of Umbria is an industrial and commercial centre and a university town.

Umbrian Painting – In harmony with their peaceful countryside, the Umbrian painters had gentle, mystic souls. They loved landscapes with pure lines, punctuated with trees; and in their stylised compositions, the women are depicted with a tender gracefulness, sometimes too mannered. Their technique is characterised by extremely delicate draughtsmanship and soft colours. The masters were Giovanni Boccati (1410-*c* 1485), Fiorenzo di Lorenzo (d 1520) and especially Pietro Vannucci alias **Perugino** (1445-1523), the teacher of Raphael. His favourite subjects were religious; in them he showed his sense of space, atmosphere and landscape, marred only by a touch of mannerism. The historical artist **Pinturicchio** (1454-1518) was influenced by Perugino but his charmingly realistic scenes were painted more naïvely than those of his predecessor.

★★ PIAZZA IV NOVEMBRE (BY) 2hr

This square in the heart of Perugia is one of the grandest in Italy. Here are grouped the chief buildings of the glorious period as an independent commune: the Priors' Palace, the Great Fountain and the Cathedral. Leading off from the far end of the square is the picturesque **Via Maestà delle Volte★** (ABY **29**) with its medieval houses and vaulted passageways.

★★ **Fontana Maggiore** – The Great Fountain was built to the designs of Fra Bevignate (1278) and is admirably proportioned. The sculpted panels are the work of Nicola Pisano (lower basin) and his son Giovanni (upper basin). Copies replace some of the originals, which are on display in the National Gallery of Umbria.

★★ **Palazzo dei Priori** (BY **D**) – The Priors' Palace was begun in the 13C and enlarged in the following centuries. It forms an ensemble of impressive grandeur. The façade overlooking the square has a majestic outside staircase leading up to a marble pulpit from which the priors harangued the people. The corso Vannucci (BY **51**) façade boasts a fine 14C doorway. Inside, the palace rooms are decorated with either 14C frescoes or beautifully carved 15C panelling in the Notaries' Chamber and college of the Mercanzia.

★★ **Galleria Nazionale dell'Umbria** ⊘ – The National Gallery of Umbria, housed on the top floor of the Priors' Palace, presents a large selection of Umbrian art showing its development from the 13C to the late 18C.
On display are: a *Madonna* by Duccio, a *Crucifix* by the unknown master, Maestro di San Francesco, a *polyptych of St Anthony* by Piero della Francesca and works by Fra Angelico, Boccati and Fiorenzo di Lorenzo.
Masterpieces by Pinturicchio and Perugino include a *Dead Christ* with its black background and an admirable *Madonna of Consolation*. Note also the marble statuettes by Nicola and Giovanni Pisano from the Great Fountain, and other works by Arnolfo di Cambio. The 17C is represented by Federico Barocci, Pietro da Cortona and Orazio Gentileschi.
The 15C Priors' Chapel is dedicated to the city's patron saints: St Herculanus and St Louis of Toulouse, whose story is told by Benedetto Bonfigli (d 1496) in a remarkable cycle of **frescoes**. The museum also has some lovely 13C and 14C French enamels and ivories.

★ **Cattedrale** (BY **F**) – The cathedral is Gothic, but the Piazza Dante façade was completed with a Baroque doorway.
The south chapel contains an interesting *Descent from the Cross* by Barocci, which inspired Rubens in his *Antwerp Descent*. In the north chapel is a ring said to be the Virgin's wedding ring. In both these chapels, note the superb **stalls** with 16C marquetry work.

ADDITIONAL SIGHTS

★★ **San Pietro** (BZ) – To reach the church, dedicated to St Peter, go through the **Porta San Pietro★** (BZ), a majestic but unfinished work of the Florentine Agostino di Duccio. The church was built at the end of the 10C and remodelled at the Renaissance. Inside are 11 excellent canvases by Vassilacchi, alias Aliense, a Greek contemporary of El Greco. Also of note are: the **carved tabernacle** by Mino da Fiesole and the marvellous 16C **stalls★★**.

★ **San Domenico** (BZ) – An imposing Gothic church dedicated to St Dominic. The interior was altered in the 17C. To the right of the chancel is the 14C **funerary monument** of Benedict XI.

★★ **Museo Archeologico Nazionale dell'Umbria** ⊘ (BZ **M¹**) – The National Archeological Museum comprises prehistoric, Etruscan and Umbrian sections. The remarkable collections include funerary urns, sarcophagi and Etruscan bronzes.

★ **Collegio del Cambio** ⊘ (BY **E**) – The Exchange was built in the 15C for the money-changers. In the Audience Room are the famous **frescoes★★** of Perugino and his pupils. These frescoes display the humanist spirit of the age, which sought to combine ancient culture and Christian doctrine. The statue of Justice is by Benedetto da Maiano (15C).

★★ **Oratorio di San Bernardino** (AY) – To reach the church of St Bernardine, walk along the picturesque **Via dei Priori★**. This Renaissance jewel (1461) by Agostino di Duccio is exquisite in its harmonious lines, the delicacy of its multicoloured marbles and its sculptures. The low reliefs on the façade depict St Bernardine in glory on the tympanum, the life of the saint on the lintel and delightful angel musicians on the shafts. Inside the church, the altar consists of a 4C Paleo-Christian sarcophagus.

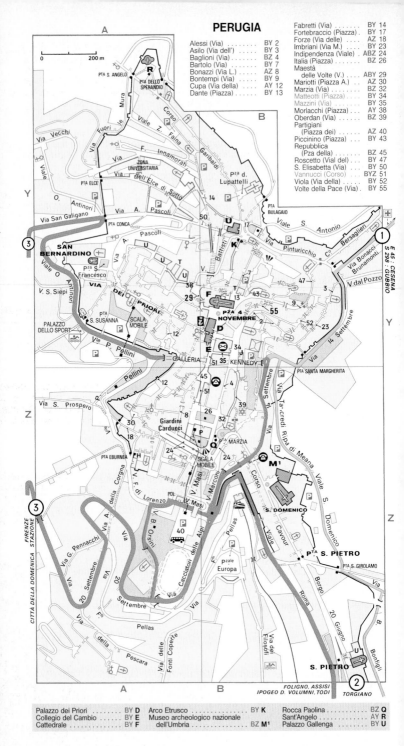

PERUGIA

Alessi (Via)	BY	2
Asilo (Via dell')	BY	3
Baglioni (Via)	BZ	4
Bartolo (Via)	BY	7
Bonazzi (Via L.)	AZ	8
Bontempi (Via)	BY	9
Cupa (Via della)	AY	12
Dante (Piazza)	BY	13
Fabretti (Via)	BY	14
Fortebraccio (Piazza)	BY	17
Forze (Via delle)	AZ	18
Imbriani (Via M.)	BY	23
Indipendenza (Viale)	ABZ	24
Italia (Piazza)	BZ	26
Maestà delle Volte (V.)	ABY	29
Mariotti (Piazza A.)	AZ	30
Marzia (Via)	BZ	32
Matteotti (Piazza)	BY	34
Mazzini (Via)	BY	35
Morlacchi (Piazza)	AY	38
Oberdan (Via)	BZ	39
Partigiani (Piazza dei)	AZ	40
Piccinino (Piazza)	AY	43
Repubblica (Pza della)	BZ	45
Roscetto (Vial del)	BY	47
S. Elisabetta (Via)	BZ	50
Vannucci (Corso)	BYZ	51
Viola (Via)	BY	52
Volte della Pace (Via)	BY	55

Palazzo dei Priori	BY D	Arco Etrusco	BY K	Rocca Paolina	BZ Q
Collegio del Cambio	BY E	Museo archeologico nazionale		Sant'Angelo	AY R
Cattedrale	BY F	dell'Umbria	BZ M¹	Palazzo Gallenga	BY U

★ **Via delle Volte della Pace** (BY 55) – The picturesque medieval street is formed by a long 14C Gothic portico as it follows the Etruscan town wall.

★ **Sant'Angelo** (AY R) – This small church is circular in plan and dates from the 5C-6C. The interior includes 16 ancient columns.

★ **Rocca Paolina** (BZ Q) – *Access via Porta Marzia*. These are the remains of a fortress built in 1540 on the orders of Pope Paul III; hence the name "Pauline". The impressive interior still has huge walls, streets and wells dating from the 11C to 16C. Escalators have been built to facilitate access within the fortress.

★ **Arco Etrusco (BY K)** – This imposing Etruscan Arch is built of huge blocks of stone. A 16C loggia surmounts the tower on the left.
Alongside, the majestic 18C **Palazzo Gallenga (U)** serves as a summer school for foreign students.

Giardini Carducci (AZ) – There is a superb view★★ from the Carducci Gardens, dominating the San Pietro quarter, over the Tiber Valley.

EXCURSIONS

★ **Ipogeo dei Volumni** ⊙ – *6km/4mi southeast. Leave by ② on the town plan.* This vast Etruscan hypogeum hewn out of the rock, comprises an atrium and nine burial chambers. The Volumnian tomb is the largest; it contains six rounded tombstones *(cippi)*, the biggest being that of the head of the family (2C BC).

Torgiano – *16km/10mi southeast. Leave by ② on the town plan.* This village dominating the Tiber Valley, has an interesting wine museum (**museo del vino★** ⊙) (Lungarotti Foundation) describing wine-growing traditions in Umbria and Italy since the days of the Etruscans: excellent historical and photographic documents.

Panicale – *32km/20mi southwest. Take the S 220, turn right after Tavernelle and follow directions.* Panicale is a medieval town perched on a hillside overlooking Lake Trasimeno.
St Sebastian's Church houses a *Martyrdom of St Sebastian* by Perugino.

Città della Pieve – *42km/26mi southwest on the S 220.* This warm ochre-coloured town, founded in about AD 7-8 and originally called *Castrum Plebis*, was the birthplace of Pietro Vannucci, better known as **Perugino**. Some of his works are housed in the cathedral *(Baptism of Christ. Virgin with Saints Peter, Paul, Gervase and Protasius)*, in the Oratorio di Santa Maria dei Bianchi (*Adoration of the Magi*, an elegant composition balanced by the portrayal of the gentle Umbrian countryside) and in Santa Maria dei Servi *(Descent from the Cross)*.
In the Oratorio of St Bartholomew there are mid-14C frescoes by the Sienese artist, Jacopo di Mino del Pellicciaio *(Weeping of the Angels)*.
Among the numerous monuments in the city, which date from the Middle Ages to the 18C, note the Palazzo della Corgna, built in the middle of the 16C by the Perugian architect Galeazzo Alessi and frescoed by Niccolò Pomarancio and Salvio Savini.

PESARO ♨♨

Marches
Population 88 210
Michelin map 430 K 20
Town plan in the Michelin Atlas Italy

Pesaro is on the Adriatic coast at the mouth of the smiling Foglia Valley, which is terraced with vineyards, orchards and Italian poplars. The town was the birthplace of the composer **Gioacchino Rossini** (1792-1868), whose house (**casa natale** ⊙ no 34 Via Rossini) is now a museum.

Gioacchino Rossini (Pesaro 1792-Passy 1868)

Rossini's career was characterised by a "crescendo" which catapulted him from Pesaro into a realm of the most prestigious recognition, first from the important Italian cities and later from the principal European courts. He is often hastily labelled as a "light" composer but in reality his work contains a kind of aloof sense of irony about the worries of the world, in the context of a typically theatrical humour, and ultimately attains a pessimistic view similar to that of Leopardi, who was also from the Marches. Aged 37, at the peak of his career, Rossini stopped composing and retired from public life.
Among his most celebrated works are *L'Italiana in Algeri*, *The Barber of Seville*, *Cinderella* and *William Tell*.

★ **Musei Civici** ⊙ – The **picture gallery** in the Municipal Museum contains several works by the Venetian Giovanni Bellini. The famous **Pala di Pesaro** (1475) is an immense altarpiece representing the Virgin being crowned on the central panel, and numerous other scenes on the predella.
In the **ceramics section★★**, the Umbrian potteries are well represented but there are also examples of work from the Marches region.

Palazzo Ducale – The great mass of the Ducal Palace, built for a member of the Sforza family in the 15C, overlooks the Piazza del Popolo with its fountain adorned with tritons and sea horses. The crenellated façade has an arcaded portico with, above, windows adorned with festoons and cherubs.

Museo Oliveriano ⊘ – *97 Via Mazza*. There is an interesting collection of archeological items of varied origins: Italic, Greek, Etruscan and Roman.

Antica Chiesa di San Domenico – *In Via Branca behind the post office*. All that remains of the church, dedicated to St Dominic, is the 14C façade with a lovely pointed doorway flanked by spiral columns and sculpture.

EXCURSION

Gradara – *15km/9mi northwest*. Gradara is a medieval town, almost intact, surrounded by walls and battlemented gateways. The **Rocca★** ⊘, built on a square plan with corner towers, is a well-preserved example of military architecture in the 13C and 14C. It is here that Gianni Malatesta is said to have come upon and then murdered his wife, Francesca da Rimini, and her lover, Paolo Malatesta, who were in the throes of passion while reading a courtly romance. Dante portrayed the inseparable couple in his *Divine Comedy:*

"When we read how that smile, so much desired,
was kissed by such a lover, in the book,
He, who will never be divided from me,
kissed my mouth, he was trembling as he did so;
The book, the writer played the part of Galahalt;
That day we got no further with our reading"
(Dante, Inferno, Canto V, 133-138)

PIACENZA★

Emilia-Romagna
Population 99 078
Michelin map 428 G 11
Town plan in the Michelin Atlas Italy

Piacenza was originally built by the Romans at the end of the Via Emilia on the south bank of the Po. It flourished in the Middle Ages and is now a member of the Lombard League. In 1545 Pope Paul III, Alessandro Farnese, gave Piacenza and its neighbour Parma to his natural son Pier Luigi along with a dukedom. After this the Farnese ruled Piacenza until 1731 when the dukedom passed to the Bourbons *(see PARMA)*.
A somewhat reserved but hospitable city, Piacenza is not inclined towards ostentation but offers visitors numerous art treasures that attest to its illustrious past.

Piazza Cavalli – The old political and economical centre of the city, this square derives its name from the **equestrian statues★★** of Dukes Alessandro and Ranuccio I Farnese, a Baroque masterpiece by Francesco Mochi (1580-1654).
The square is very much dominated by the imposing **"Gotico"★★**, the old town hall, a masterpiece of 13C Lombard-Gothic architecture. The building is both severe and harmonious and displays a notable contrast between the marble lower part and the brick upper storeys, the great openings and the elegantly decorated windows.
To the left of the square is the façade of the 13C **Church of St Francis**, an interesting example of Franciscan Gothic architecture, embellished by a fine splayed doorway.

★ **Duomo** ⊘ – This remarkable Lombard-Romanesque cathedral dates from the 12C-13C. The façade is adorned with a rose-window and a porch with three notable doorways. The two lateral doorways are influenced by the sculptural styles at Modena and Nonantola. The **interior** on the plan of a Latin cross is simple but enriched by the sweeping frescoes (Guercino, Morazzone, 17C) which adorn the dome, and by the canvases in the chancel (C. Procaccini and L. Carracci).

S. Antonino – *Piazza Sant'Antonino*. This former paleo-Christian basilica dedicated to St Anthony was remodelled in the 11C and has interesting features: an octagonal tower (40m/131ft high) and the north "Paradise" vestibule (1350) in the Gothic style.

Galleria d'Arte Moderna Ricci Oddi ⊘ – *via S. Siro 13*. The modern art collections include Italian paintings from various regions ranging from the Romantic period to the 20C: works by the landscape painter Antonio Fontanesi, the Macchiaioli (Fattori), artists influenced by the Impressionist school (Boldini, Zandomeneghi), works in an oriental and figurative idiom (De Pisis), Futurist (Boccioni) and metaphysical (De Chirico, Carrà) paintings. There are also sculptures (Medardo Rosso) and works by foreign artists such as Klimt who influenced Italian art.

San Savino ⓥ – *Near the junction of Via G. Alberoni with Via Roma.* This 12C church, with its very pure architectural lines, contains priceless traces of the original construction, such as the fine capitals and the **mosaic flooring**★ in the chancel and in the crypt.

Palazzo Farnese ⓥ – This imposing late-Renaissance palace, built to designs by Vignola but never completed, now houses a museum (**Museo Civico**★ ⓥ). On the ground floor the sumptuous *Fasti farnesiani*★ cycle of frescoes by Draghi and Ricci is richly framed in stucco-work. The images portray stories of Alessandro Farnese and Pope Paul III. There are also collections of ceramics and glass, frescoes from local churches (14C-15C) and a series of Romanesque sculptures of the "Piacenza School" which combine influences both from the contemporary French school and Wiligelmo (*The Prophets David and Ezechiel*, 12C). Note also the bronze **Etruscan divining liver**★★, a soothsayer's device dating from the 2C-1C BC. The first floor, with its richly decorated ceiling, houses collections of paintings from the 16C-19C Emilian, Lombard and Ligurian schools, a *Virgin and Child with St John* by Botticelli and the *Fasti Farnesiani* dedicated to Elisabetta Farnese. There is also a **Carriage Museum** and a **Risorgimento Musem**.
In the adjacent fortress, erected by the Visconti in the 14C, an archeological section is currently being set up.

San Sisto ⓥ – *At the northern end of Via S. Sisto.* This rather curious 16C building was designed by Alessio Tramello, an architect from Piacenza. The façade is preceded by a doorway, dated 1622, which opens onto a 16C atrium. The **interior** has an interesting Renaissance decoration and a splendid 16C **wood chancel**. Raphael painted the famous *Sistine Madonna* for this church, now replaced by a copy.

★ **Madonna di Campagna** ⓥ – *Via Campagna.* This beautiful church, in the form of a Greek cross and built in the idiom of Bramante, constitutes one of the most important Renaissance buildings in Italy. The interior contains splendid **frescoes**★ by Pordenone (1484-1539), an exponent of the Mannerist style who painting was characterised by a vivid use of colour and sculptural forms.

Galleria Alberoni ⓥ – *Via Emilia Parmense 77, 2.5km/1.5mi southeast.* The gallery is situated within the precincts of a college founded in the 18C by Cardinal Alberoni, and comprises a fine collection of 16C-17C Flemish and Italian **tapestries** as well as a rich collection of 15C-19C Italian (Guido Reni, Baciccia, Luca Giordano) and Flemish (Jan Provost) paintings. The jewel of the collection is the moving *Ecce Homo* by Antonello da Messina. The gallery also has war relics and furnishings owned by the cardinal from Piacenza who was Philip V of Spain's Prime Minister.

PIENZA★★

Tuscany
Population 2 281
Michelin map 430 M 17
See Michelin Green Guide Tuscany

The former town of Corsignano was renamed in honour of its most famous son, the diplomat and humanist poet, Eneo Silvio Piccolomini (1405-64), who became Pope Pius II in 1458. He commissioned the Florentine architect, **Bernardo Rossellino** (1409-82), a pupil of Alberti, to build in his native village a square which would be the focal point of an **ideal city** and would bring together the civil and religious authorities. The architectural unity of the square, which was the first example of Renaissance town planning, was intended to reflect the city's harmony. The principal monuments line the town's main axis: the town hall opposite the cathedral has a ground-floor loggia. The other sides of the square are framed by the Bishop's Palace (simply restored in the 15C) and the Palazzo Piccolomini; a pretty well in front of the latter enhances the overall plan.
There is a fine **view**★ over Orcia Valley from behind the cathedral.

★ **Cattedrale** – The cathedral, which was completed in 1462, has a Renaissance façade. The interior (restored) shows Gothic influences and contains several paintings by the Sienese school, including an *Assumption*★★, a masterpiece by Vecchietta.

Museo Diocesano ⓥ – The Cathedral Museum contains pictures of the 14C and 15C Sienese school and a remarkable 14C historiated cope made in England.

★ **Palazzo Piccolomini** ⓥ – Rossellino's masterpiece was greatly influenced by the Palazzo Rucellai in Florence (*see FIRENZE*). The three sides facing the town are similar; the fourth overlooking Orcia Valley has three tiers of loggias and gives onto hanging gardens which are among the earliest to have been created. The elegant inner courtyard features slim Corinthian columns. The palace still has its armoury, and the incunabula and a Baroque bed from the papal bedchamber.

EXCURSIONS

R. Leslie

In the Monastery of Sant'Antimo silence is transformed into music
as the small community sings Gregorian chants

★ **Montalcino** – *24km/15mi west.* In addition to part of its 13C walls, this small hillside town still has a magnificent fortress (**fortezza**★★ ⊘) built in 1361, a consummate example of defensive forts at that time. It is shaped like a pentagon and its tall walls, with machicolations and parapet walk, are punctuated by five towers. One of them was used as officers' quarters and, in case of siege, could be used by the nobility. The ordinary people would seek shelter within the outer walls. It was here that the government of Siena took refuge when the town was captured by Holy Roman Emperor Charles V in 1555.

Montalcino is also famous for its **Brunello**, a red wine of excellent quality produced in a small vineyard. The town is a picturesque labyrinth of medieval streets leading to a Romanesque and Gothic church, to the 13C town hall (**Palazzo Comunale**★) flanked by a loggia and topped by a tall tower, or to the small museum (**Museo Civico e Diocesano**) ⊘ – paintings and sculptures from the 14C-15C Siena School, ceramics from Montalcino, and antique remains.

★★ **Abbazia di Sant'Antimo** ⊘ – *35km/22mi southwest.* The abbey, which was founded in the 9C, stands in an isolated hill **site**★ amid cypress and olive groves. Its prosperity was at its peak in the 12C when the **church** was built. It is a fine example of Cistercian Romanesque architecture with Burgundian (ambulatory and apsidal chapels) and Lombard (porch, belltower with Lombard bands and façades) influences. The interior is spacious and austere. Columns topped by fine alabaster capitals divide the nave with its wooden roof from the aisles which have groined vaulting. Only some of the monastic buildings remain standing.

Consult the Places to Stay map at the beginning of this guide to select the a stopover or holiday destination. The map offers the following categories:
>   *Short holidays*
>   *Weekend breaks*
>   *Overnight stops*
>   *Resorts*

Depending on the region, this map also shows marinas, ski areas, spas, centres for mountain expeditions, etc.

PISA★★★

Tuscany
Population 93 133
Michelin map 428, 429 or 430 K 13
See The Green Guide to Tuscany

This calm and pleasant town, near the sea, has splendid buildings recalling the past grandeur of the Pisan Republic.

HISTORICAL NOTES

Sheltered from raiding pirates, Pisa was a Roman naval base and commercial port until the end of the Empire (5C). It became an independent maritime republic at the end of the 9C and continued to benefit from its geographical location. Pisa became the rival of Genoa and Venice, and the Pisans waged war against the Saracens in the Mediterranean basin. It was in the 12C and the beginning of the 13C that Pisa reached the peak of its power and prosperity. This period was marked by the construction of some fine buildings and the foundation of the university.

During the 13C struggles between the Emperor and the Pope, Pisa supported the Ghibellines *(see Index)* and thus opposed Genoa on the seas and Lucca and Florence on land. In 1284 the Pisan fleet was defeated at the **naval battle of Meloria**. Ruined and wracked by internal strife, Pisa's maritime empire foundered; Corsica and Sardinia which she had ruled since the 11C were ceded to Genoa. Pisa herself passed under Florentine rule and the Medici took a special interest in the city, especially in the world of science. Its most famous son was the astronomer and physicist **Galileo** (1564-1642). His patron was Cosimo II, Grand Duke of Tuscany. Nevertheless Galileo, aged 70, had to defend his theory of the rotation of the earth before the Inquisition and in fact renounced it.

PISAN ART

The economic prosperity of the powerful maritime Pisan Republic from the 11C to the 13C fostered the development of a new art style which is particularly evident in the fields of architecture and sculpture. The **Pisan-Romanesque style**, with the cathedral as the most rigorous example, is characterised by external decoration: the alternate use of different coloured marbles to create geometric patterns, a play of light and shade due to the tiers of loggias with small columns on the upper parts of the façade, and intarsia decoration showing the strong influence of the Islamic world and of Christian countries of the Near East which had relations with the maritime republic. Alongside architects such as Buscheto, Rainaldo and Diotisalvi there were numerous sculptors to embellish the exteriors. Pisa became an important centre for Gothic sculpture in Italy, thanks to the work of **Nicola Pisano** (1220-*c* 80), originally from Puglia, and his son **Giovanni Pisano** (1250-*c* 1315). Their work included carved pulpits with two good examples in the Baptistery and the Cathedral, which greatly influenced the early Tuscan Renaissance.

Piazza dei Miracoli, a suitable name for this magical masterpiece

PUBLI AFER FOTO

★★★ PIAZZA DEL DUOMO ⊘ (AY) *3hr*

In and around this famous square, also known as **Campo dei Miracoli**, are four buildings which form one of the finest architectural complexes in the world. It is advisable to approach on foot from the west through the **Porta Santa Maria (AY)** to enjoy the best view of the leaning tower.

★★ **Duomo** ⊘ (AY) – This splendid cathedral was built with the fantastic spoils captured during the expeditions against the Muslims. Building started in 1063 under Buscheto and was continued by Rainaldo, who designed the façade.
The **west front**★★★ is light and graceful with four tiers of small marble columns and a decorative facing of alternating light – and dark-coloured marble. The church itself is built on the plan of a Latin cross. The original doors were replaced by **bronze doors**★ cast in 1602 to designs by Giovanni Bologna. The south transept door has very fine Romanesque bronze **panels**★★ (late 12C) by Bonanno Pisano, depicting the Life of Christ in a naïve but free creative style.
The **interior**★★, with its nave and four aisles, is impressive for its length (100m/328ft), its deep apse, its three-aisled transept and the forest of piers which offer an astonishing variety of perspectives. Note in particular the beautiful **pulpit**★★★ of **Giovanni Pisano** on which he worked from 1302 to 1311. It is supported by six porphyry columns and five pillars decorated with religious and allegorical statues. The eight panels of the pulpit evoke the Life of Christ and group a multitude of personages with dramatic expressions. Near the pulpit is Galileo's lamp, which gave the scholar his original idea for his theory concerning the movement of the pendulum.

★★★ **Torre pendente** (AY) – The **Leaning Tower of Pisa** is both a bell-tower and belfry. This white marble tower (58m/189ft high) was begun in 1173 in a pure Romanesque style by Bonanno Pisano and completed in 1350. Built, like the towers of Byzantium, as a cylinder, the tower has six storeys of galleries with columns which seem to wind round in a spiral because of the slope of the building. On the lower level is the blind arcading decorated with lozenges that is specific to the architecture of Pisa. The tower slowly began leaning in 1178 and it has continued to do so ever since at a rate of between 1 and 2 millimeters a year. It is caused by the alluvial soil on which the tower is built, soil that is insufficiently resistant to bear the weight of the building. Over the years, architects have tried in vain to correct the unfortunate "lean". After the tower was closed to the public in 1990, it was surrounded by two stainless steel cables at first floor level and, in 1993, the base was strengthened by a reinforced concrete "corset", which included 670 tonnes of lead to counterbalance the lean.

★★★ **Battistero** ⊘ (AY) – Work on the Baptistery began in 1153 and the two lower storeys are in the Romanesque Pisan style, while the frontons and pinnacles above the first-floor arcades are Gothic. The building is roofed with an unusual dome and has four doorways with fine carving. The majestic interior is full of light and has a diameter of 35m/115ft. The sober decoration consists of light– and dark-coloured marble; in the centre is a lovely octagonal **font**★ (1246) by an artist from Como, Guido Bigarelli. The masterpiece of the baptistery is the admirable **pulpit**★★ (1260) by Nicola Pisano. It is less ornate than the one done by his son for the cathedral and stands on simple columns. The five panels of the pulpit depict the Life of Christ: its noble, Classical sculptures are no doubt inspired by Roman art and the sarcophagi to be found in the neighbouring Composanto.

★★ **Camposanto** ⊘ (AY) – This burial ground was begun in 1277 by Giovanni di Simone, one of the architects of the leaning tower. Work was interrupted by the naval Battle of Meloria (*see above*) and completed only in the 15C. The large rectangular area is bounded on the outside by a blind portico. Inside, the majestic semicircular arcading includes four delicate lancet windows with Gothic tracery. The soil in the Camposanto (Sacred Field) proper, in the centre, is said to have been brought back from the Hill of Calvary by the Crusaders. There are Greco-Roman sarcophagi in the galleries, which are paved with about 600 tombstones. The majority of the wall frescoes have been destroyed in a fire caused by artillery shelling in 1944. One of the most famous cycles comprising **The Triumph of Death**★★★ and the **Last Judgement**★★ and **Hell**★ by a 14C artist was saved and is displayed in the north gallery. The transience and vanity of wordly pleasures are illustrated with great realism.

★★ **Museo dell'Opera del Duomo** ⊘ (AY M¹) – The Cathedral Museum contains works of art from the monuments in Piazza del Duomo: 12C-16C sculptures (Romanesque period influenced by Islamic and Burgundian art, Gothic and Renaissance); cathedral treasure (ivory **Madonna and Child** by Giovanni Pisano) and silver ware. On the first floor are displayed 15C-18C paintings and sculpture; fragments of Renaissance stalls and 12C-13C illuminated manuscripts; episcopal vestments and ornaments; archeological artefacts found in the early 19C in the cemetery by Carlo Lasinio, who made a series of engravings of the Camposanto frescoes.

★ **Museo delle Sinopie** ⊘ (AY M²) – This museum contains the sketches or *sinopie* (sketches in a reddish-brown pigment, sinopia, which came from Sinope on the Black Sea) which were under the frescoes and were brought to light by a fire following the 1944 bombing. They have been well restored and give a good idea of the vitality and free draughtsmanship of these 13C-15C painters.

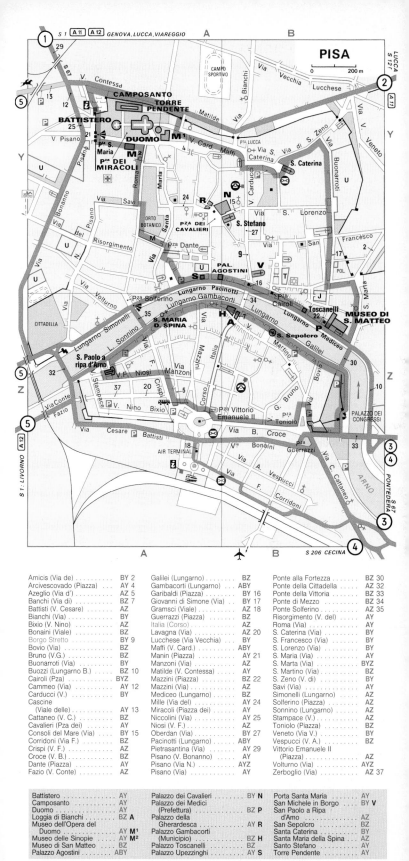

PISA

Amicis (Via de)	BY 2	Galilei (Lungarno)	BZ	Ponte alla Fortezza	BZ 30
Arcivescovado (Piazza)	AY 4	Gambacorti (Lungarno)	ABY	Ponte della Cittadella	AZ 32
Azeglio (Via d')	AZ 5	Garibaldi (Piazza)	BY 16	Ponte della Vittoria	BZ 33
Banchi (Via di)	BZ 7	Giovanni di Simone (Via)	BY 17	Ponte di Mezzo	BZ 34
Battisti (V. Cesare)	AZ	Gramsci (Viale)	AZ 18	Ponte Solferino	AZ 35
Bianchi (Via)	BY	Guerrazzi (Piazza)	BZ	Risorgimento (V. del)	AY
Bixio (V. Nino)	AZ	Italia (Corso)	AZ	Roma (Via)	AY
Bonaini (Viale)	BZ	Lavagna (Via)	AZ 20	S. Caterina (Via)	BY
Borgo Stretto	BY 9	Lucchese (Via Vecchia)	BY	S. Francesco (Via)	BY
Bovio (Via)	BZ	Maffi (V. Card.)	ABY	S. Lorenzo (Via)	BY
Bruno (V.G.)	BZ	Manin (Piazza)	AY 21	S. Maria (Via)	AY
Buonarroti (Via)	BY	Manzoni (Via)	AZ	S. Marta (Via)	BYZ
Buozzi (Lungarno B.)	BZ 10	Matilde (V. Contessa)	AY	S. Martino (Via)	BZ
Cairoli (Pza)	BYZ	Mazzini (Piazza)	BZ 22	S. Zeno (V. di)	BY
Cammeo (Via)	AY 12	Mazzini (Via)	AZ	Savi (Via)	AY
Carducci (V.)	BY	Mediceo (Lungarno)	BZ	Simonelli (Lungarno)	AZ
Cascine		Mille (Via del)	AY 24	Solferino (Piazza)	AZ
(Viale delle)	AY 13	Miracoli (Piazza dei)	AY	Sonnino (Lungarno)	AZ
Cattaneo (V. C.)	BZ	Niccolini (Via)	AY 25	Stampace (V.)	AZ
Cavalieri (Pza dei)	AY	Niosi (V. F.)	AZ	Toniolo (Piazza)	BZ
Consoli del Mare (Via)	AY 15	Oberdan (Via)	BY 27	Veneto (Via)	BY
Corridoni (Via F.)	BZ	Pacinotti (Lungarno)	ABY	Vespucci (V. A.)	BZ
Crispi (V. F.)	AZ	Pietrasantina (Via)	AY 29	Vittorio Emanuele II	
Croce (V. B.)	BZ	Pisano (V. Bonanno)	AY	(Piazza)	AZ
Dante (Piazza)	AY	Pisano (Via N.)	AYZ	Volturno (Via)	AYZ
Fazio (V. Conte)	AZ	Pisano (Via)	AY	Zerboglio (Via)	AZ 37

Battistero	AY	Palazzo dei Cavalieri	BY N	Porta Santa Maria	AY
Camposanto	AY	Palazzo dei Medici		San Michele in Borgo	BY V
Duomo	AY	(Prefettura)	BZ P	San Paolo a Ripa	
Loggia di Bianchi	BZ A	Palazzo della		d'Arno	AZ
Museo dell'Opera del		Gherardesca	AY R	San Sepolcro	BZ
Duomo	AY M¹	Palazzo Gambacorti		Santa Caterina	BY
Museo delle Sinopie	AY M²	(Municipio)	BZ H	Santa Maria della Spina	AZ
Museo di San Matteo	BZ	Palazzo Toscanelli	BZ	Santo Stefano	AY
Palazzo Agostini	ABY	Palazzo Upezzinghi	AY S	Torre Pendente	AY

ADDITIONAL SIGHTS

* **Piazza dei Cavalieri** (AY) – This, the historic centre of Pisa, gets its name from the Cavalieri di Santo Stefano (Knights of St Stephen), a military order which specialised in the struggle against the infidels. Around the square are: the **Palazzo dei Cavalieri** (BY N) with a façade★ decorated by Vasari; the **Chiesa di S. Stefano** (AY) built in 1569 with its white, green and pink marble façade and dedicated to St Stephen; and the **Palazzo Gherardesca** (AY R) designed in 1607 by Vasari to stand on the site of a former prison, Torre della Fame, where Count Ugolino della Gherardesca and his children were condemned to die by starvation, having been accused of treason after the naval defeat at Meloria.

S. Caterina (BY) – The Church of St Catherine has a graceful Pisan-Gothic façade★. Inside there are statues by Nino Pisano, in particular an *Annunciation* (on either side of the chancel).

S. Michele in Borgo (BY V) – The façade★ of the church of St Michael is an excellent example of the transitional Pisan Romanesque-Gothic style.

The quays – Prestigious palaces line the quays, **Lungarno Pacinotti** (ABY) and **Lungarno Mediceo** (BZ), notably **Palazzo Upezzinghi** (AY S), a 17C building now occupied by the university; **Palazzo Agostini★** (ABY), a 15C mansion with a highly-decorated entrance front (the Caffè dell'Ussero was the haunt of the Risorgimento poets), and on the opposite bank the Palazzo Gambacorti (BZ H), a late-14C building; **Palazzo Toscanelli** (BZ) where Byron wrote *Don Juan*; and the **Palazzo Medici** (BZ P), a 13C-14C palace.

★★ **Museo Nazionale di S. Matteo** ⊙ (BZ) – The National Museum houses works created in Pisa between the 13C and 15C, showing the town's importance as an artistic centre at the end of the Middle Ages. There is a small section of ceramics, but the museum concentrates mainly on sculpture and painting with works by great sculptors such as Andrea Pisano *(Virgin of the Annunciation)* and Nino Pisano *(Virgin Mary Nursing)* and by early Pisan painters or Florentines who came to work in the town in the 14C when work was in progress on the cemetery (Camposanto). Note the **polyptych** by Simone Martini and Masaccio's *St Paul*.

S. Sepolcro (BZ) – This 12C Church of the Holy Sepulchre in the form of a pyramid was built by Diotisalvi. Inside, the nobly-proportioned **chancel★** is roofed with a tall dome. There is also the tomb of Maria Mancini, Louis XIV's mistress and Mazarin's niece who came to Pisa to die in 1715.

★★ **S. Maria della Spina** (AZ) – This early-14C church, dedicated to St Mary of the Thorn, resembles a finely-worked reliquary shrine with all its gables, pinnacles, statues and statuettes by the Pisano, their assistants and followers. Some of the originals have been replaced by replicas.

S. Paolo a Ripa d'Arno (AZ) – The Church of St Paul which stands on the bank of the Arno boasts a lovely Pisan-Romanesque façade★.

EXCURSIONS

* **Basilica di San Piero a Grado** – *6km/4mi southwest. Leave by ⑤, the Via Conte Fazio.* This Romanesque church stands on the spot on which St Peter is said to have landed when he came from Antioch. The apse with its three apsidal chapels is remarkable.

⌂⌂ **Viareggio** – *20km/12mi northwest. Leave by ① on the town plan.* This fashionable seaside resort, on the Tyrrhenian Coast, has some lovely beaches and plenty of amenities for holidaymakers. At **Torre del Lago Puccini** *(5km/3mi to the southeast)* the composer Puccini wrote the majority of his operas. The **Villa Puccini** ⊙ contains the tomb and other mementoes of Puccini.

PISTOIA★★

Tuscany
Population 86 118
Michelin map 428, 429 or 430 K 14
See Michelin Green Guide Tuscany

This industrial town has a rich historic centre which is evidence of its importance in the 12C-14C. Both Lucca and Florence coveted Pistoia, but it was Florence and the Medici who annexed it for good in 1530.

★★ PIAZZA DEL DUOMO *1hr*

This is a most attractive and well-proportioned square lined with elegant secular and religious buildings.

* **Duomo** – Rebuilt in the 12C and 13C, the cathedral's **façade★** is a harmonious blend of the Pisan-Romanesque style (tiers of colonnaded galleries) and the Florentine-Renaissance style (porch with slender columns added in the 14C). The

lower part of the campanile is quite massive but it becomes more graceful towards the top with three tiers of colonnaded galleries. The interior was remodelled in the 17C. Inside is the famous **altar of St James**★★★ ⊘, a masterpiece of silversmith work dating from the 13C, which was modified and extended in the following centuries. The saints surround the apostle seated in a niche, with Christ in Glory above. Scenes from the Old and New Testaments complete the composition. In the chapel to the left of the chancel is a lovely *Madonna in Majesty*★ (c 1480) by Lorenzo di Credi.

* **Battistero** ⊘ – This Gothic octagonal baptistery with polychrome marble facing dates from the 14C. The tympanum of the central doorway bears a statue of the *Virgin and Child* between St Peter and St John the Baptist, attributed to Nino and Tommaso Pisano.

Palazzo Pretorio – This palace was built in the 14C as the residence of the governing magistrate *(podestà)* and remodelled in the 19C.

Palazzo del Comune – The Town Hall was built from 1294 to 1385 and has a graceful arcaded façade with elegant paired windows or triple bays. The palace houses the **Museo Civico** ⊘ with a collection of paintings and sculptures from the 13C-20C Tuscan school.

ADDITIONAL SIGHTS

Palazzo del Tau – *Corso Silvano Fedi*. This former monastery of the Order of the Monks Hospitaller of St Anthony was built in the 14C. It owes its name to the blue enamel "T" that used to adorn the monks' habits. It is now an **Information Centre** ⊘ on the work of the sculptor **Marino Marini** (1901-1980).

Ospedale del Ceppo – The portico on the hospital façade has a magnificent **frieze**★★ in terracotta (1530) by Giovanni della Robbia showing the Seven Works of Mercy.

* **S. Andrea** – This church dedicated to St Andrew is in the pure Pisan-Romanesque style and has a famous **pulpit**★★ executed (1298-1308) by Giovanni Pisano in his dramatic but intensely lively manner: the panels represent five scenes from the Life of Christ. The lovely **crucifix**★ in gilded wood is by Giovanni Pisano *(in a niche beyond the first altar on the right)*.

S. Giovanni Forcivitas – The Church of St John outside the City, built from the 12C to the 14C, has a long and spectacular **north façade**★ in the Pisan-Romanesque style. Inside, there is a **pulpit**★ (1270) by Fra Guglielmo from Pisa, a polyptych by Taddeo Gaddi *(to the left of the altar)* and an admirable glazed terracotta of the *Visitation*★★ by Luca della Robbia.

EXCURSION

* **Vinci** – *24km/15mi south*. The great Leonardo da Vinci was born not far from this town. The **Museo Leonardiano** ⊘ is housed in the castle in honour of its famous son. The birthplace **(casa natale)** ⊘ of the artist lies 2km/1.2mi to the north amidst olive trees, bathed in a pellucid light.

Admission times and charges for the sights described are listed at the end of the guide. Every sight for which there are times and charges is identified by the symbol ⊘ in the Sights section of the guide.

Golfo di POLICASTRO★★

Gulf of POLICASTRO – Campania – Basilicata – Calabria
Michelin map 988 or 431 G 28

This magnificent gulf extending from the tip of Infreschi to Praia a Mare is backed by high mountains whose sharp, needle-like peaks soar skywards.
The lower slopes are planted with cereals and olive groves with clumps of chestnut trees above. Between Sapri and Praia a Mare the corniche road overlooks the green waters which lap the charming creeks. A series of small villages succeed one another along this enchanting coast.

⌂⌂ **Maratea** – This seaside resort has many beaches and creeks and its hotels and villas are hidden behind a screen of luxuriant vegetation. The village itself is spread over the slopes of Monte Biagio, on the summit of which stands the Basilica of San Biagio and the great white figure of the Statue of the Redeemer (22m/72ft tall), the work of Innocenti (1965). Nearby there is a superb **panorama**★★ of the Gulf of Policastro and the Calabrian coast.

POMPEI★★★

POMPEII – Campania

Population 26 121
Michelin map 431 E 25

Pom peii, the opulent town which was buried in AD 79 in one of the most disastrous volcanic eruptions in history, provides important evidence of the ancient way of life. The extensive and varied ruins of the dead city, in its attractive setting, movingly evoke on a grand scale a Roman city at the time of the Empire.

In 1997 Pompei was included in UNESCO's World Heritage List.

HISTORICAL NOTES

Pompeii was founded in the 8C BC by the Oscans, but by the 6C BC a Greek influence was already prevalent in the city from its neighbour Cumae, which was then a powerful Greek colony. From the end of the 5C BC, when it came under Samnite rule, to the beginning of the 1C AD the city knew great prosperity; town planning and art flourished. In the year 80 BC, the town fell under Roman domination and then it became a favourite resort of rich Romans. Roman families settled there. Pompeii adopted Roman organisation, language, lifestyle, building methods and decoration. When the eruption of Vesuvius struck, Pompeii was a booming town with a population of about 25 000. The town was situated in a fertile region, trade flourished and there was even some industrial activity; it also had a port. The numerous shops and workshops which have been uncovered, its wide streets and the deep ruts made in the cobblestones by chariot wheels are evidence of the intense activity that went on in the town.

The people had a lively interest in spectacles, games and active politics, as can be seen in a fresco housed at the Archeosical Museum in Naples. In 59 BC, after a bloodthirsty fight between rival supporters, the amphitheatre was closed for 10 years and only re-opened after Nero's wife Poppea interceded. In the year AD 62, an earthquake extensively damaged the town but before all could be put to rights, Vesuvius erupted (August AD 79) and also destroyed Herculaneum and Stabiae. In the space of two days Pompeii was buried under a layer of cinders 6m to 7m/20ft to 23ft deep. Bulwer-Lytton describes these events in *The Last Days of Pompeii*.

It was only in the 18C, under the reign of Charles of Bourbon, that systematic excavations began. The finds had a tremendous effect in Europe, creating a revival of antique art and the development of a so-called Pompeiian style.

ARCHITECTURE AND DECORATION

Building methods – Pompeii was destroyed before a degree of uniformity in building methods had been achieved and it presents examples of the diverse methods and materials used: **opus quadratum** (large blocks of freestone piled on top of one another, without mortar of any kind); **opus incertum** (irregularly-shaped blocks of tufa or lava bonded with mortar); **opus reticulatum** (small square blocks of limestone or tufa arranged diagonally to form a decorative pattern); **opus testaceum** (walls are faced with triangular bricks laid flat with the pointed end turned inwards). Sometimes the walls were faced with plaster or marble. There are several types of dwelling in Pompeii: the sober and austere house of the Samnites, which became larger and more richly decorated through Greek influence. With the arrival of the Romans and the problems arising from a growing population, a new kind of house evolved in which limited space is compensated for by richness of decoration.

Pompeiian painting – A large number of paintings which adorned the walls of the dwellings have been transferred to the Archeological Museum in Naples. However, a visit to the dead city gives a good idea of the pictorial decoration of the period. There are four different **styles**. The 1st style by means of relief and light touches of colour imitates marble. The 2nd style is by far the most attractive: walls are divided into large panels by false pillars surmounted by pediments or crowned by a small shrine, with false doors all designed to create an illusion of perspective.

The artists show a partiality for the famous Pompeiian red, cinnabar obtained from mercury sulphide, and a dazzling black, both of which make for a very striking style. The 3rd style abandoned false relief in favour of scenes and landscapes altogether more ethereal and painted in pastel colours. Most of the frescoes uncovered at Pompeii belong to the 4th style. It combines elements from the 2nd style with others from the 3rd style to produce ornate compositions.

SIGHTSEEING ⊙

allow 1 day

N.B. some of the houses listed may occasionally be closed for cleaning and maintenance.

Porta Marina – This was the gateway through which the road passed to go down to the sea. There were separate gates for animals and for pedestrians.

Streets – The streets are straight and intersect at right angles. They are sunk between raised pavements and are interrupted at intervals by blocks of stone to enable pedestrians to cross without getting down from the pavement. This was particularly useful on rainy days when the roadway was awash; these stepping-stones were positioned so as to leave enough space for chariots. Fountains, of simple design, were set in square basins.

★★★ **Foro** – The forum was the centre of the town and the setting for most of the large buildings. In this area, religious ceremonies were held, trade was carried out and justice was dispensed. The immense square, closed to traffic, was paved with broad marble flagstones and adorned with statues of past emperors. A portico surmounted by a terrace enclosed it on three sides.

The **Basilica**★★ is the largest building (67m by 25m/220ft by 82ft) in Pompeii where judicial affairs and business were conducted.

The **Tempio di Apollo**★★ is a temple dedicated to Apollo which was built before the Roman occupation and stood against the majestic background of Vesuvius. The altar was placed in front of the steps leading to the shrine (*cella*). Facing each other are copies of the statues of Apollo and Diana found on the spot (the originals are in the Naples Museum).

The **Tempio di Giove**★★, in keeping with tradition, has pride of place. The temple dedicated to the Capitoline Triad (Jupiter, Juno and Minerva) is flanked by two triumphal arches, formerly faced with marble.

The **Macellum** was a large covered market lined with shops. In the centre, a kiosk surrounded by pillars and crowned by a dome contained a basin used for cleaning fish.

The **Tempio di Vespasiano**, dedicated to Vespasian, contained a marble altar adorned with a sacrificial scene.

A fine **doorway**★ with a marble frame decorated with carvings of plants gives access to the **Edificio di Eumachia** (Building of Eumachia), built by the priestess for the powerful guild of the *fullones (see below)* of which she was the patron.

★ **Foro Triangolare** – There are several Ionic columns of a majestic propylaeum which preceded the Triangular Forum. A few vestiges of its small **Doric temple** provide rare evidence of the town's existence in the 6C BC.

★ **Teatro Grande** – The Great Theatre was built in the 5C BC, remodelled in the Hellenistic period (200-150 BC) and again by the Romans in the 1C AD. It was an open-air theatre which could be covered by a canopy on sunny days and could hold 5 000 spectators.

Caserma dei Gladiatori – The barracks for the gladiators has a large esplanade bounded by a gateway, originally used as a foyer for the theatres.

★★ **Odeion** – Odeions, or covered theatres, were used for concerts, oratorical displays and ballets. This held only 800 spectators. It had a wooden roof and it dates from the early days of the Roman colonisation.

★ **Tempio d'Iside** – The cult of this Egyptian goddess spread in the Hellenistic Age thanks to contact with the Orient and Egypt. The small building stands on a podium in the middle of an arcaded courtyard. To the left of the temple is the *purgatorium*, a site set aside for purification cerimonies which contained water from the Nile. The pictorial decorations of the temple are housed in the Archeological Museum in Naples.

Casa di L. Ceius Secundus – This is an interesting house (*casa*) with its façade faced with stucco in imitation of stone as in the 1st style, and with its pretty little *atrium*.

★★ **Casa di Menandro** – This large patrician villa named after Menander, was richly decorated with paintings (4th style) and mosaics and had its own baths. Part of the building was reserved for the servants' quarters. There is a Tuscan *atrium (see page 63)* with a *lararium* arranged as a small shrine in one corner. It has a remarkable peristyle with Doric columns faced with stucco, between which stands a low wall adorned with plants and animals.

The house opens onto **Via dell'Abbondanza**★★, a commercial street which is now most evocative with its shops and houses.

Casa del Criptoportico – *No 2, Via dell'Abbondanza.* After passing through the peristyle (note the painting in the *lararium*: Mercury with a peacock, snakes and foliage), go down to the Cryptoporticus, a wide underground passage surmounted by a fine barrel vault and lit by small windows. This type of corridor, which was very popular in Roman villas during the Empire, was used as a passage and for exercise as it was sheltered from the sun as well as from bad weather.

★★ **Fullonica Stephani** – *No 7, Via dell'Abbondanza.* This is an example of a dwelling-house converted into workshops. The clothing industry flourished in Roman times as the full, draped costume required a lot of material. In the *fullonicae*, new fabrics were finished and clothes were laundered. Several of these workshops have been uncovered in Pompeii. The *fullones* (fullers) cleaned the cloths by trampling them underfoot in vats filled with a mixture of water and soda or urine.

Termopolio di Asellina – This was a bar which also sold pre-cooked dishes (*thermopolium*). A stone counter giving directly onto the street formed the shop front; jars embedded in the counter contained the food for sale.

★ **Termopolio Grande** – This bar, which is similar to the previous one, has a painted *lararium*.

Casa di Trebius Valens – The inscriptions on the wall are electoral slogans. At the far end of the peristyle the polychrome fresco is in imitation of a stone wall.

★ **Casa di Loreius Tiburtinus** – This was a rich dwelling, judging from the fine marble *impluvium*, the *triclinium* adorned with frescoes and the **decoration**★ against a white background of one of the rooms, which is among the best examples of the 4th Pompeiian style. But its most luxurious feature was the splendid **garden**★ which was laid out for water displays.

★ **Villa di Giulia Felice** – Built just within the town boundary, it has three main parts: the dwelling, the baths which the owner opened to the public, and a section for letting, including an inn and shops. The large garden is bounded by a fine **portico**★ and embellished by a fine series of basins.

★ **Anfiteatro** – This is the oldest Roman amphitheatre known (80 BC). It was built away from the city centre to enable easy access. On particularly hot days spectators were protected from the heat by a linen drape held up by wooden poles. Alongside is the great **palestra** used as a training ground by athletes.

★ **Necropoli at the Porta di Nocera** – According to custom, tombs line one of the roads leading out of town, via the Nocera Gate.
   Take the Via di Porta Nocera to return to the Via dell' Abbondanza, then turn left.

Anfiteatro:	Amphitheatre	Edificio:	Building	Necropoli:	Necrop
Casa:	House	Foro:	Forum	Porta:	Gate

★★★ **Terme Stabiane** – *See details of Roman baths on page 64.*
These baths, the oldest in Pompeii (2C BC), are divided into sections for men and women. The entrance is through the gymnasium, *palestra* for athletic games, to the left of which are changing-rooms, *spogliatoio*, and a swimming pool, *piscina*. The **women's baths** begin at the far end on the right, with changing-rooms (**e**) fitted with lockers, a *tepidarium* (lukewarm, **f**) and a *caldarium* (hot, **g**). The central heating apparatus (**D**) is between the men's and women's baths. The **men's baths** have large, well preserved changing-rooms (**h**), a *frigidarium* (cold, **k**), a *tepidarium* (**l**) and a *caldarium* (**m**). There is a fine stucco decoration on the coffered ceiling.

Lupanare – The official brothel of Pompei is decorated with licentious subject matter, aimed at illustrating the "specialities" of the prostitutes. Graffiti on the walls describes the customers' opinions on services received.

Pistrinum/Note the baker's oven and flourmills.

★★★ **Casa dei Vettii** – The Vettii brothers were rich merchants. Their dwelling, the most lavishly decorated in the town, is the finest example of a house and garden that have been faithfully restored. The reroofed *atrium* opens directly onto the peristyle surrounding a delightful garden with statues, basins and fountains.

The **frescoes** in the *triclinium*, on the right of the peristyle, depict mythological scenes and friezes of cupids, and are among the finest from antiquity.

★ **Casa degli Amorini Dorati** – This house shows the refinement of the owner, who probably lived during the reign of Nero, and his taste for the theatre. The glass and gilt medallions depicting cupids *(amorini)* have deteriorated. But the building as a whole, with its remarkable peristyle with one wing raised like a stage, is well preserved. There is an obsidian mirror set in the wall near the passage between the peristyle and *atrium*.

Casa dell'Ara Massima – There are well-preserved **paintings★** (one in *trompe-l'œil*).

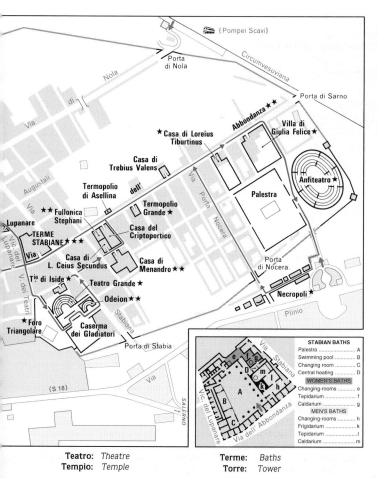

Teatro: *Theatre*	**Terme:** *Baths*
Tempio: *Temple*	**Torre:** *Tower*

Casa del Labirinto – One of the rooms opening onto the peristyle has a mosaic of the labyrinth with Theseus killing the Minotaur.

★★ **Casa del Fauno** – This vast, luxurious house had two atriums, two peristyles and dining-rooms for all seasons. The bronze original of the famous statuette of the faun that adorned one of the impluviums is in the Naples Museum. The rooms contained admirable mosaics including the famous *Battle of Alexander and Darius* (Naples Museum) which covered the area between the two peristyles.

Casa della Fontana Grande – Its main feature is the large **fountain**★ (fontana) shaped as a niche decorated with mosaics and fragments of coloured glass in the Egyptian style.

★ **Torre di Mercurio** – A tower on the town wall, dedicated to the god Mercury, now affords an interesting **view**★★ of the excavations.

★ **Casa del Poeta Tragico** – This house takes its name from a mosaic now in the Naples Museum. A mosaic of a watchdog at the threshold bears the inscription *Cave Canem* (Beware of the dog).

Casa di Pansa – A very spacious house partly converted for letting.

★★ **Porta Ercolano** – The Herculaneum Gate was the main gateway of Pompeii, with two gates for pedestrians and one for vehicles.

★★ **Via delle Tombe** – A great melancholy feeling pervades this street lined with mounumental tombs and cypresses. There are examples of all forms of Greco-Roman funerary architecture: tombs with niches, small round or square temples, altars resting on a plinth, drum-shaped mausoleums, simple semicircular seats or exedrae.

Villa di Diomede – This important dwelling dedicated to Diomedes has a loggia overlooking the garden and the swimming pool.

★★★ **Villa dei Misteri** – Located outside the city centre this ancient patrician villa is comprised of two areas: a luxurious residential part (west) and the eastern half reserved for domestic and agricultural work and the servants' quarters. In the area inhabited by the owners, the dining room *(from the apsed room in the west of the villa, enter the tablinium, turn right into the cubiculum and right again into a room which leads into the triclimium)* contains the splendid **fresco** from which the villa derives its renown as well as its name. This vast composition, which fills the whole room, depicts against a Pompeian red background the initiation of a young bride to the mysteries *(misteri)* of the cult of Dionysus (from the left: Child reading the rites; scenes of offerings, sacrifices and Dionysian rites; flagellation of a girl; dancing Bacchante; dressing of the bride). The mistress of this house was probably a priestess of the cult of Dionysus, which was then very popular in southern Italy. There is a fine peristyle and an underground passage *(criptoportico)*.

Abbazia di POMPOSA★★

POMPOSA ABBEY – Emilia-Romagna
Michelin map 429 H 18
49km/30mi east of Ferrara

This Benedictine **abbey** ⊙ was founded in the 6C and enjoyed great fame in the Middle Ages, especially from the 10C to 12C when it was distinguished by its abbot, St Guy (Guido) of Ravenna, and by another monk, **Guido d'Arezzo**, the inventor of the musical scale and note system. In July and August the abbey hosts classical music concerts *(for information and bookings contact the Tourist Office,* ☎ *0533 71 91 10)*.

The fine pre-Romanesque **church**★★ in the style typical of Ravenna is preceded by a narthex whose decoration exemplifies the Byzantine style. To the left, an admirable Romanesque campanile (1063) is remarkable for the progression in the number and size of its windows and the elegant simplicity of the Lombard bands and arches adorning its nine storeys; and finally, the variety of geometric decoration obtained with the use of bricks.

The nave has some magnificent **mosaic flooring** and two Romanesque stoups, one in the Romanesque style and the other in the Byzantine style. The walls bear an exceptional cycle of 14C **frescoes** based on the illuminator's art. From right to left the upper band is devoted to the Old Testament while the lower band has scenes from the Life of Christ; the corner pieces of the arches depict the *Apocalypse*. On the west wall are a *Last Judgement* and in the apsidal chapel *Christ in Majesty*. Opposite the church stands the Palazzo della Ragione, where the abbot dispensed justice.

Promontorio di PORTOFINO ★★

PORTOFINO PENINSULA – Liguria
Michelin map 428 J 9

This rocky, rugged promontory offers one of the most attractive landscapes on the Italian Riviera. The coastline is dotted with small villages in sheltered bays. Part of the peninsula has been designated as a nature reserve **(Parco Naturale)** to protect the fauna and flora. By taking the corniche roads and the numerous footpaths the visitor can discover the secret charms of this region.

★★★PORTOFINO

To reach the port which gave the peninsula its name, take the road that passes via **Santa Margherita Ligure**▲▲ *(5km/3mi)*, a fashionable seaside resort, and then the **corniche road**★★ (Strada Panoramica) which affords lovely views of the rocky coast. This small fishing village with its gaily-coloured houses lies at the head of a sheltered creek. The **walk to the lighthouse**★★★ *(1hr on foot there and back)* is beautiful, especially in the evening, when the setting sun shines on the Gulf of Rapallo. Wonderful views unfold between the olive trees, yews and sea pines. From the castle **(castello)**Ⓥ – formerly Castello San Giorgio *(take the stairway which starts near the harbour and the Church of San Giorgio)* – there are splendid **views**★★★ of Portofino and the Gulf of Rapallo. Continue along the pathway to the lighthouse, from where the view extends right round the coast as far as La Spezia.

EXCURSIONS

San Lorenzo della Costa - *10km/6mi north.* At Santa Margherita Ligure take the **scenic road**★★ which offers a succession of lovely views over the Gulf of Rapallo. The Church of **San Lorenzo** contains a **triptych**★ (1499) by an artist from Bruges. It may have been the work of Gerard David (Gheeraert Davit) who spent some time in Genoa.

★★ **Portofino Vetta**Ⓥ – *14km/9mi.* From this elevated site (450m/ 1 476ft) there is a lovely view of the peninsula and the Ligurian coast.

★★ **San Fruttuoso** – **On foot:** *take the signposted footpath starting in Portofino (4hr30min there and back) or another from Portofino Vetta, but the final stages are difficult (3hr there and back).* **By boat:** Ⓥ *services operate from Rapallo, Santa Margherita Ligure, Portofino and Camogli.* This small village stands at the head of a narrow cove in the shadow of Monte Portofino. There is a beautiful abbey, **Abbazia di S. Fruttuoso**, built from the 13C to 14 century.

★★ **Belvedere di S. Rocco** – *13km/8mi northwest.* From the terrace beside the church there is a view of Camogli and the western coast from the headland, Punta della Chiappa, right round to Genoa. A path leads to **Punta della Chiappa**★★★ *(2hr 30min there and back by a stepped footpath which starts to the right of the church).* There are unforgettable views of the peninsula and, from the chapel, of the Genoa Coast.

★★ **Camogli** – *15km/9mi northwest.* Tall houses crowd round a small harbour.

THE GREEN GUIDE covers the world's great cities:

New York, London, Paris, Rome, Brussels, Berlin, Vienna, Washington DC, San Francisco, Chicago, Venice, Amsterdam

POTENZA

Basilicata
Population 69 695
Michelin map 431 F 29
Town plan in the Michelin Atlas Italy

Potenza overlooks the upper Basento Valley with wide mountain views. The ancient town, founded by the Romans, flourished during the Empire. Today it is an active town, the growth of which was favoured by the development of the road and rail networks in the region. Its tall, modern buildings, curiously terraced, make an unusual sight which is quite dazzling by night. The old town suffered extensive damage in the 1980 earthquake. The 13C Church of **San Francesco**, with its lovely Renaissance **doorway**★ carved in wood, contains a marble Renaissance tomb and a 13C Madonna.

Potenza is situated in **Lucania**, an indescribably wild region ravaged by erosion.

POZZUOLI★

Campania
Population 81 526
Michelin map 431 E 24
Local map see Golfo di NAPOLI

Pozzuoli, which is of Greek origin, became an active trading port under the Romans. As the town is at the centre of the volcanic area known as the Phlegrean Fields and is constantly affected by changes in the ground level which occur in this region, the town centre has been evacuated.

The town has given its name to *pozzolana*, a volcanic ash with a high silica content which is used in the production of certain kinds of cement.

★★ **Anfiteatro Flavio** ⊙ – *Corso Terracciano*. This amphitheatre is one of the largest in Italy and dates from the reign of Vespasian, the founder of the Flavian dynasty. It could accommodate 40 000 spectators. Built of brick and stone, it is relatively well preserved: note the outer walls, the entrances and the particularly well-preserved **basements**★★.

★ **Tempio di Serapide** – *Set back from Via Roma*. The temple, dedicated to Serapis, which is situated near the sea, was really the ancient market place and was lined with shops. There is a sort of apse in the end wall which contained the statue of Serapis, the protecting god of traders. The central edifice shows the effects of variations in ground level: the columns reveal signs of marine erosion.

★ **Tempio di Augusto** – The temple, dedicated to Augustus, dated from the early days of the Empire and was converted into a Christian church in the 11C. A recent fire has revealed a grandiose marble colonnade with its entablature.

★★ **Solfatara** ⊙ – *2km/1mi northeast by the Naples road*. Although extinct, this crater still has some of the features of an active volcano such as jets of steam charged with sulphurous fumes, strong-smelling and with traces of yellow, miniature volcanoes spitting hot mud and bubbling jets of sand. The ground gives a hollow sound and the surface is hot. The sulphurous vapours have been used for medicinal purposes since Roman times.

PRATO★★

Tuscany
Population 169 927
Michelin map 429 or 430 K 15
See The Green Guide to Tuscany

In spite of the peaceful and provincial air of its old quarter, Prato is a bustling and important town which has developed with the textile industry since its early beginnings in the 13C. For a long time Prato was in conflict with Florence, but in 1351 she fell under the sway of her illustrious neighbour and remained thus until the 18C. In the 14C a fortified wall in the form of a hexagon was erected around the old town.

★ **Duomo** – The cathedral, built in the 12C and 13C and extended in later centuries, presents a harmonious blend of the Romanesque and Gothic styles. The façade, with its partial facing of white stone and green marble, owes its elegance to its lofty central part, its finely carved decoration and the graceful circular pulpit with a canopy (15C) by Michelozzo. The south side has blind arcading in the true Pisan tradition. The campanile has a Gothic upper storey.

The interior of the church, sober in style, has massive columns of green marble and numerous works of art: the Chapel of the Holy Girdle **(Capella del Sacro Cingolo)** contains the precious relic which, legend has it, the Virgin had given to Thomas as proof of her Assumption. The girdle was brought from Jerusalem by a citizen of Prato in the 12C. The chapel is enclosed by two delicately-worked bronze **screens★** and decorated with frescoes (1392-95) by Agnolo Gaddi and his pupils. The *Virgin and Child★* (1317) is by the sculptor Giovanni Pisano.

The **frescoes★★** by **Filippo Lippi** in the axial chapel form a striking picture of the lives of St Stephen and St John the Baptist. From 1452 to 1465 this artistic monk, renowned for his libertine ways, painted this masterpiece with its pleasantly fresh colours and spontaneous attitudes; the graceful melancholy of the feminine figures in two scenes, the *Banquet of Herod★★★* and *Salome's Dance*, are more typical of the work of one of his pupils, Botticelli. On the walls of the chapel to the right are **frescoes★** started by Paolo Uccello and completed by Andrea di Giusto. Note also the marble **pulpit★** with the original shape of a chalice, and in a niche a moving *Virgin with an Olive★*, a terracotta statue (1480) by Benedetto da Maiano.

Michelozzo's pulpit (15C)

LARA PESSINA

Museo dell'Opera del Duomo ⊙ – The Cathedral museum is housed in several rooms overlooking a delightful courtyard. Amongst the exhibits are the seven **panels★** carved from 1428 to 1438 by Donatello for the pulpit from which the Holy Girdle used to be displayed. The pulpit was set on the corner of the cathedral's west front. Also on display are pieces of ecclesiastical plate and paintings by Filippino Lippi (1457-1504), the son of Filippo, and by Carlo Dolci (1616-1686).

★ Palazzo Pretorio – This austere and massive building, a curious mixture of the Romanesque and Gothic styles, overlooks a charming small square, **Piazza del Comune**, with a gracious bronze fountain (1659) by Tacca. Three floors of the building are occupied by the Municipal Gallery **(Galleria Comunale)** which presents works by the 14C and 15C Tuscan school and notably an important collection of **polyptychs★** by Bernardo Daddi, Lorenzo Monaco, Filippo Lippi etc. There are also works by the Neapolitan Caracciolo (17C) and the Dutchman Van Wittel the Elder.

Castello dell'Imperatore – This is one of the rare existing examples in northern and central Italy of a castle built by the Emperor (Imperatore) Frederick II of Hohenstaufen. This imposing structure, on a square plan around a central courtyard, has massive walls with very few openings and enormous projecting towers. The castle is modelled on Castel del Monte *(see Index)* in the south. With its cleft Ghibelline crenellations, this fortified stronghold guarded the route between the Emperor's northern empire and his Kingdom of Sicily in the south.

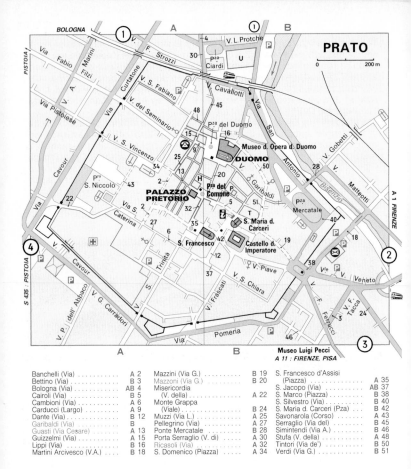

Banchelli (Via)	A 2	Mazzini (Via G.)	B 19	S. Francesco d'Assisi		
Bettino (Via)	B 3	Mazzoni (Via G.)	B 20	(Piazza)	A 35
Bologna (Via)	AB 4	Misericordia		S. Jacopo (Via)	AB 37
Cairoli (Via)	B 5	(V. della)	A 22	S. Marco (Piazza)	B 38
Cambioni (Via)	A 6	Monte Grappa		S. Silvestro (Via)	B 40
Carducci (Largo)	A 9	(Viale)	B 24	S. Maria d. Carceri (Pza)	B 42
Dante (Via)	B 12	Muzzi (Via L.)	A 25	Savonarola (Corso)	A 43
Garibaldi (Via)	B	Pellegrino (Via)	A 27	Serraglio (Via del)	B 45
Guasti (Via Cesare)	A 13	Ponte Mercatale	B 28	Simintendi (Via A.)	B 46
Guizzelmi (Via)	A 15	Porta Serraglio (V. di)	A 30	Stufa (V. della)	A 48
Lippi (Via)	B 16	Ricasoli (Via)	A 32	Tintori (Via de')	B 50
Martini Arcivesco (V.A.)	B 18	S. Domenico (Piazza)	A 34	Verdi (Via G.)	B 51

S. Maria delle Carceri - This attractive late-15C building was designed by Giuliano da Sangallo. The **interior** displays both a severity and a nobility typical of Florentine architecture as influenced by Brunelleschi.

S. Francesco - This church, dedicated to St Francis, was built from the 13C to the 15C. The chapterhouse has **frescoes**★ by Nicolo di Pietro Gerini, a Florentine artist who was influenced by Giotto.

This guide, which is revised regularly, incorporates tourist information provided at the time of going to press. Changes are however inevitable owing to improved facilities and fluctuations in the cost of living.

PUGLIA★

Michelin map 988 D-H 29-37

This region takes its name from the ancient Roman province of Apulia. It extends from the spur of the Italian "boot" right down to the heel, all along the Adriatic coast in the south of the country. With the exception of the Gargano Promontory and the limestone Murge Hills which rise behind Bari, it is a flat plain planted with cereals, olive trees, vines or in pasture.

Away from the main tourist haunts, Puglia offers the visitor its beautiful yet severe scenery, quiet beaches and some marvellous architectural gems, both religious and military.

HISTORICAL NOTES

As early as the late 8C BC Greeks from Laconia and Sparta founded the towns of Gallipoli, Otranto and most significantly Taranto on the Apulian coast. In the 5C and 4C BC Taranto was the most prosperous town in Magna Graecia. The local tribe, the Lapyges, tenaciously resisted Greek colonisation; in the 3C BC the Greek cities and the Italiots both came under Roman domination.

Taranto declined as Brindisi, a trading-post facing the eastern part of the Mediter-ranean, flourished. The latter was linked to Rome when Trajan prolonged the Appian Way. The Roman colonisation greatly benefited this area by introducing improved communications and political organisation. Christianity was first introduced to the area in the 3C and was strengthened in the 5C with the appearances of the Archangel Michael at Monte Sant'Angelo.

The area was occupied successively by the Byzantines, Lombards and Arabs before Puglia sought help in the 11C from the Normans who then dominated the entire area. Puglia greatly increased its trade and its architectural heritage during both the early Crusades, most of which embarked from the Apulian ports, and the reign of Roger II of Sicily (1095-1154).

It was under the Emperor Frederick II of Hohenstaufen, an unusual, authoritarian and cruel character, an atheist but a cultured and highly intelligent person, that the region knew a period of splendour in the first-half of the 13C. The King was captivated by the country and chose to reside here. This favoured trade, the unification of the country and the establishment of an efficient administration. His son Manfred continued his work but had to submit to Charles of Anjou in 1266. The French lost interest in the region and it began to lose its vitality and prestige. Puglia then passed to the Aragon dynasty who, by isolating the region, greatly contributed to its decline.

After a period of Austrian domination, the Bourbons of Naples improved to some small extent the misery and stagnation to which the country had been reduced by the Spanish. The brief Napoleonic period followed a similar policy. In 1860 Puglia was united with the rest of unified Italy.

During the 20C Apulia has progressively emerged from the difficult position of inferiority which was prevalent throughout the rest of the Italian south or Mezzo-giorno. The region has achieved a certain independence and vigour and now claims two thriving industrial towns, Taranto and Lecce, a Trade Fair in Bari and several newly-founded universities.

TOWNS AND SIGHTS *(in alphabetical order)*

Altamura – This large market town in the Murge Hills also has its old quarter on a hilltop. The 13C cathedral **(Duomo)** in the transitional Romanesque-Gothic style forms the focal point at the upper end of the main street. The façade is crowned with two bulbous bell-towers, 16C additions, and pierced by a delicately decorated 13C **rose window★** and a richly-sculptured 14C-15C **doorway★**.

Bari – *See BARI.*

⌂ **Barletta** – *See BARLETTA.*

Bitonto – *17km/11mi southwest of Bari.* Set amidst a sea of olive groves this small town has a fine cathedral **(Duomo★)** which strongly resembles those in Trani and Bari. The three-part façade is enlivened by large, richly-sculptured openings. On the south side an elegant gallery with small columns surmounts the ground-floor arcade. Inside, columns with fine capitals support a gallery with triple openings. The fine pulpit dates from 1229.

Brindisi – *See BRINDISI.*

Canosa di Puglia – *23km/14mi southwest of Barletta.* The inhabitants of this Greek, then Roman, city were known for their ceramic vases *(askoi)*. The 11C Romanesque cathedral **(Duomo)** which shows a certain Byzantine influence, was remodelled in the 17C following an earthquake. The façade is 19C. Inside note the 11C episcopal throne and the **tomb★** of Bohemond, Prince of Antioch (d 1111), the son of Robert Guiscard (1015-85), a Norman adventurer who campaigned in southern Italy. This curious mausoleum is in the form of a domed cube. In the Via Cadorna there are three 4C BC hypogea **(Ipogei Lagrasta)** ⊘ and to the right of the Andria road stand the remains of a Paleo-Christian basilica **(San Leucio)** which was itself built on the site of a Roman temple.

★★ **Castel del Monte** ⊘ – *29km/18mi southeast of Barletta.* The Emperor Frederick II of Hohenstaufen built this powerful castle c 1240. It stands, proud and solitary, on the summit of one of the Murge Hills. With its octagonal plan the Castel del Monte is the sole exception in a series of 200 quadrilateral fortresses built by this sovereign on his return from the Crusades. The octagonal plan of the fortress, built in a pale-coloured stone, is strengthened at each of its angles by an octagonal tower (24m/79ft tall). The overall plan combines balance, logic and strict planning with delicate decoration.

The superb Gothic gateway takes the form of an ancient triumphal arch and opens into the inner courtyard. Arranged around this at ground-floor level are eight vast trapezoidal chambers with pointed vaulting. Above, the eight identical rooms are lit by delicately-ornamented windows. The arrangement of the water conduits is quite ingenious: water runs from the rooftops into the cisterns of the towers and is then piped into the different rooms.

Frederick's castles

A cultivated and eclectic man, Frederick II of Hohenstaufen (1194-1250) had numerous castles and fortresses built in Puglia, and was closely involved in their construction. Their basic plan is the square, deriving from the Roman *castrum* as well as symbolising the number four, which was considered a magical number in the Middle Ages. The square and the circle were considered symbols of the earth and the sky, Man and God. This magical and practical synthesis reached a peak in the octagonal plan of Castel del Monte. The octagon was considered a perfect balance between the circle and the square, the form that blended and united the human and the divine. Eight is the number which comes up almost obsessively in this building: the castle is eight-sided, there are eight towers and each floor has eight rooms.

Among Frederick's memorable castles in Puglia are those in Bari, Barleta, Brindisi, Castel del Monte, Gioia del Colle, Lagopesole, Manfredonia (erected by Frederick's son Manfred) and Trani.

*** **Grotte di Castellana** ⊘ – *40km/25mi southeast of Bari, at Castellana-Grotte.* This network of caves was created by the underground rivers which filter down through the limestone soil of the Murge Hills. The vast chambers were discovered in 1938 and has an infinite variety of magnificent concretions: curtains, richly-coloured stalactites and stalagmites. This grand spectacle reaches a climax at the White Cave **(Grotta Bianca)** which glistens with calcite crystals.

Foggia – *Town plan in the Michelin Atlas Italy.*
Foggia is set in the heart of a vast cereal-growing plain, the Tavoliere. This trading and industrial centre was founded in c 1050 by the Norman, Robert Guiscard. In 1223 the Emperor Frederick II of Hohenstaufen built a castle which has now disappeared.
The present cathedral **(Duomo)** incorporates parts of an earlier building (13C), notably the lower walls with some blind arcading and a sculptured cornice above, and the crypt. This earlier structure, which was destroyed by the 1731 earthquake, has been rebuilt.

Galatina – This craft and wine-making centre stands on the flat and stony Salento Peninsula. The cathedral with its Baroque façade recalls the gracious style of Lecce. The 14C Church of **Santa Caterina di Alessandria★**, commissioned by Raimondello del Balzo Orsini, is decorated with a marvellous cycle of **frescoes★** by several 15C artists. Many of the women depicted in the frescoes bear the features of Maria d'Enghien, Raimondello's wife. In the nave: Scenes of the Apocalypse (first segment); Genesis (2nd); scenes from the life of Christ (3rd). In the south aisle: the Life of the Virgin. In the chancel: Scenes from the life of St Catherine. The octagonal apse with its ribbed vaulting dates from 1455-60.

Galatone – *24km/15mi southwest of Lecce.* The **Chiesa del Crocifisso della Pietà** has a lovely **façade★** embellished in the Baroque style typical of the Lecce area. The sumptuous interior decoration includes gilding and stucco ornamentation.

⌂ **Gallipoli** – The old town with its attractive small port is set on an island and linked to the modern town by a bridge. Note the imposing castle, rebuilt in the 16C on the site of an Angevin fortress, and the cathedral with a baroque façade which recalls Lecce (the interior contains many paintings of the 17C and 18C). Along the *Riviera*, which follows the outline of the old city wall, stands the church **(chiesa della Purità)**; the **interior★** is sumptuously decorated with ornate stucco-work, some fine 18C paintings and a remarkable ceramic floor.

*** **Gargano Promontory** – *See Promontorio del GARGANO*

Gioia del Colle – In the centre of the town stands the massive **Norman castle** ⊘ built on the site of a Byzantine fortress and very much echoing the lines of the castles erected by Frederick II of Hohenstaufen in Puglia. From the square courtyard there is access to the ground floor rooms which house the Archeological Museum (note the fine 4C BC Apulian red-figure bowl depicting a burial temple at the centre), as well as the old bakery and prison. On the upper storey the **Throne room**, illuminated by a mullioned opening, is notable for its large round arch.

** **Lecce** – *See LECCE.*

Locorotondo – *See Terra dei TRULLI.*

Lucera – Already important in Roman times, Lucera was ceded by the Emperor Frederick II of Hohenstaufen to the Saracens of Sicily, who in turn were expelled by Charles II of Anjou. Lucera has an imposing 13C fortress **(fortezza★)** built by the Angevins, which affords a fine **panorama★** of the Tavoliere Plain. The historic centre is dominated by a 14C cathedral **(Duomo)** which overlooks a fine square, the focal point of the town. Nearby stands another imposing Romanesque church with sober architectural lines which is dedicated to St Francis of Assisi but is linked with San Francesco Fasani who lived in the area in the 18C and restored the building. Further along, a fine palace, unfortunately in poor condition, houses a museum **(Museo Civico G. Fiorelli)** ⊘ which displays a marble *Venus★*, a Roman replica of a model by the school of Praxiteles. A short distance from the centre stands a well-preserved Roman amphitheatre **(anfiteatro romano★)** built during Augustus' reign.

⌂ **Manfredonia** – Manfred, the son of the Emperor Frederick II of Hohenstaufen, founded the port in the 13C. It is guarded by a fine 13C castle **(castello)** and a bastion pierced with pointed openings. The Church of **Santa Maria di Siponto★** *(3km/2mi south by the S 89)* is an elegant 11C building in the Romanesque style which shows influences both oriental (square plan and terraced roof hiding the dome), and Pisan (blind arcades with columns enclosing lozenges).
The late-11C Church of **San Leonardo** *(beyond the Church of Santa Maria, take the Foggia road to the right)* has a fine delicately-sculptured **doorway★** dating from the early 13C.

★ **Martina Franca** – *See Terra dei TRULLI.*

★ **Monte Sant'Angelo** – *See MONTE SANT'ANGELO.*

★ **Ostuni** – *35km/22mi west of Brindisi.* This large market town now spreads over several hillsides. At the centre of the old town with its white alleyways and Aragonese ramparts stands the late-15C cathedral **(Cattedrale)** which has both Romanesque and Gothic elements. The **façade★** is crowned by an unusual pattern of concave (central section) and convex (side sections) lines enhanced by an arched decoration. In the centre there is a beautiful **rose window★** with complex symbolism relating to the passage of time: 24 external arcades, standing for the hours in a day, 12 internal ones standing for the months of the year, while Christ, in the centre, is surrounded by seven angels' heads which stand for the days of the week. Nearby the Church of S. Vito (or Santa Maria Maddalena dei Pazzi) houses a small **Archeological museum** ⊘ with displays the plaster cast of **Delia**, a young woman who lived about 25 000 years ago and died shortly before childbirth (her skeleton shows the foetus' tiny bones).

Otranto – *See OTRANTO.*

Ruvo di Puglia – *34km/21mi west of Bari.* On the edge of the Murge Hills, Ruvo has an Apulian-style Romanesque cathedral **(Duomo★)** with a sober façade embellished by a rose window, a twin opening, a sculptured doorway and at the very top a frieze of arches. Inside the lofty nave, tall arches carry a deep cornice supported by sculptured corbels. The **Museo Archeologico Jatta** ⊘ has a fine collection

> ### A "historical" night
>
> At the port of Ostuni, the **Hotel Novecento**, Contrada Ramunno, ☎ 0831 30 56 66, has preserved all of its *belle époque* charm.

of Attic, Italic and Apulian vases. Of these the superb **Crater of Talos★★**, a red-figured vase with a black background, is particularly notable.
Take Via De Gaspari, with its 16C Clock Tower (Torre dell'Orologio) – opposite is the Renaissance Palazzo Caputi – to reach Piazza Matteotti which is flanked by fine palaces and the ruins of a medieval castle.

Trani – This wine-growing town has an ancient port surrounded by old houses. The 11C-13C Romanesque cathedral **(Duomo★★)** is one of the finest in Puglia and is dedicated to St Nicholas the Pilgrim, a humble Greek shepherd who arrived in Trani on the back of a dolphin.
Blind arcades encircle the building and there is a fine **bronze door★** which was cast in 1180. Beyond the lofty transept the chancel has a delicately-decorated window. To the south rises the bell-tower. Inside, one detects a strong Norman influence. The nave and aisles are slightly raised as they are built over two immense crypts, the lower of which is literally a forest of ancient columns. The upper church is well lit but severe with slender twin columns carrying the main arches and an elegant gallery with triple openings.

From the public gardens (**giardino pubblico★**) to the east of the port there is an attractive view of the old town and its tall cathedral. The castle (**castello** – restored) on the seashore was built by Frederick II.

Troia – *17km/11mi southwest of Foggia.* This agricultural market town is well situated on a hilltop overlooking the Tavoliere plain. The Romanesque **cathedral** in the Apulian style was begun in the 11C and completed two centuries later. The façade is embellished with blind arcading and a lovely **rose window★**. A fine 12C **bronze door★** in the Byzantine tradition opens into the nave and two aisles separated by columns with finely-worked capitals. The north doorway has a sculptured **tympanum** depicting Christ flanked by two angels.

★ Taranto – *See TARANTO.*

★ Tremiti Islands – *See Isole TREMITI.*

★★★ Trulli Region and Alberobello – *See Terra dei TRULLI.*

RAVELLO★★★

Campania

Population 2 544

Michelin map 431 F 25 – Local map see AMALFI

Ravello with its alleys, stairways and roofed passages clings to the steep slopes of the Dragon Hill. The **site★★★**, suspended between sea and sky, is unforgettable. The road from Amalfi climbs in hairpin bends up the narrow Dragon Valley, planted with vines and olive groves. The aristocratic restraint of Ravello has, over the centuries, beguiled artists, musicians and writers such as members of the Bloomsbury Group of Virginia and Leonard Woolf *(see Villa Cimbrone below)*, D. H. Lawrence, Graham Greene, Gore Vidal, Hans Escher and Joan Mirò.

★★★ Villa Rufolo ⊘ – *Like the cathedral it overlooks Piazza Vescovado.* The villa was built in the 13C by the rich Rufolo family of Ravello (cited in Boccaccio's *Decameron*) and was the residence of several popes, Charles of Anjou and more recently, in 1880, of Richard Wagner. When the German composer, in search of inspiration for *Parsifal*, laid eyes on the villa's splendid garden he exclaimed, "the garden of Klingsor is found". A well-shaded avenue leads to a Gothic entrance tower. Beyond is a Moorish-style courtyard with typical sharply-pointed arches in the Sicilian-Norman style and interlacing above. This was originally the cloisters in the 11C. A massive 11C tower overlooks the well-tended gardens and the elegant villa.

From the terraces there is a splendid **panorama★★★** of the jagged peaks as far as Cape Orso, the Bay of Maiori and the Gulf of Salerno. In the summer there are concerts in the gardens with an unequalled backdrop of trees, flowers and the sea. *For information contact the Società dei Concerti di Ravello,* ☎ *089 85 81 49, fax 089 85 82 249, or the Tourist Office.*

Duomo – The cathedral, founded in 1086, was remodelled in the 18C. The campanile is 13C. The splendid **bronze door★** with its panels of reliefs was cast in 1179 by Barisanus da Trani. In the nave the antique columns have been uncovered and there is a magnificent mosaic-covered **pulpit★★** with a remarkable variety of motifs and fantastic animals (1272). On the left is an elegant 12C **ambo** adorned with green mosaics representing Jonah and the Whale. The small museum **(museo)** ⊘ in the crypt has sculptural fragments, mosaics, a silver **head-reliquary** with the relics of St Barbara.

To the left of the Duomo, the Cameo Factory houses a tiny **Coral museum** which displays some highly prized pieces. Of particular note is the snuff-box encrusted with cameos.

San Giovanni del Toro ⊘ – Via S. Giovanni del Toro, with its stunning **belvedere★**, leads to this beautiful 11C church with three apses. Inside, antique columns support the arches. There is a richly-decorated 11C **pulpit★**, a Roman sarcophagus (south aisle) and 14C frescoes in the apses and the crypt.

★★★ Villa Cimbrone ⊘ – A charming **alley★** leads from Piazza Vescovado to the villa, passing on the way through the Gothic porch of the convent of St Francis. The villa was built at the beginning of the 19C by Lord William Bechett in an eclectic style with references to Villa Rufolo and San Francesco. Villa Cimbrone is a homage to the history of Ravello and a point of reference for the **Bloomsbury Group** for whom the garden embodied the ideal aesthetic of clarity, order and harmony. On entering the grounds note the charming cloisters on the left and the lovely hall with ogival vaulting. A wide alley leads through the splendid garden to the belvedere, adorned with marble busts. There is an immense **panorama★★★** over the cultivated, terraced hillsides, Maiori, Cape Orso and the Gulf of Salerno.

RAVENNA ★★★

Emilia-Romagna
Population 137 721
Michelin map 429 or 430 I 18

In the peaceful provincial-looking town of Ravenna, the sober exteriors of its buildings belie the wealth of riches accumulated initially when Ravenna was the capital of the Western Empire and later when it was an Exarchate of Byzantium. The mosaics which adorn the city's ecclesiastical buildings are breathtakingly beautiful for the brightness of their colours, richness of decoration and powerful symbolism which evoke a sense of great spirituality.

After the division of the Empire in 395 by Theodosius, Rome, already in decline, was abandoned in AD404 by Honorius who made Ravenna the capital of the Roman Empire. Honorius' sister, **Galla Placidia**, lavishly governed the Western Empire before the Barbarian invasions brought the Ostrogoth Kings Odoacer (476-493) and **Theodoric** (493-526) to Ravenna; they also embellished Ravenna in their turn. The strategic location of Ravenna's port, Classis, on the Adriatic sea facing the Greek world, inevitably led to trading with Byzantium which had become capital in 476. Ravenna came under Byzantine rule in 540 in the reign of the Emperor Justinian (482-565), and was administered by Exarchs. From then on Ravenna exercised considerable influence over a large part of the Italian peninsula.

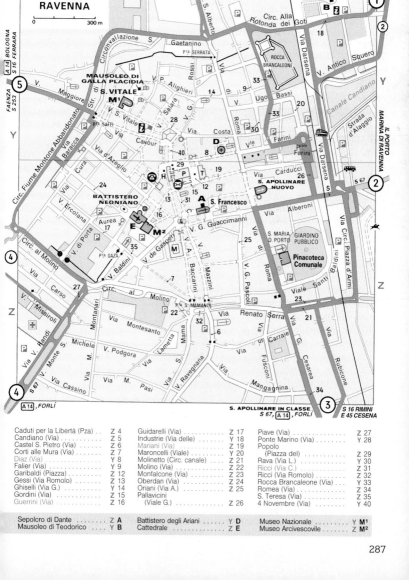

Caduti per la Libertà (Pza)	Z 4	Guidarelli (Via)	Z 17	Piave (Via)	Z 27
Candiano (Via)	Z 5	Industrie (Via delle)	Y 18	Ponte Marino (Via)	Y 28
Castel S. Pietro (Via)	Z 6	Mariani (Via)	Z 19	Popolo	
Corti alle Mura (Via)	Z 7	Maroncelli (Viale)	Y 20	(Piazza del)	Z 29
Diaz (Via)	Y 8	Molinetto (Circ. canale)	Z 21	Rava (Via L.)	Y 30
Falier (Via)	Y 9	Molino (Via)	Z 22	Ricci (Via C.)	Z 31
Garibaldi (Piazza)	Z 12	Monfalcone (Via)	Z 23	Ricci (Via Romolo)	Z 32
Gessi (Via Romolo)	Z 13	Oberdan (Via)	Z 24	Rocca Brancaleone (Via)	Y 33
Ghiselli (Via G.)	Y 14	Oriani (Via A.)	Z 25	Romea (Via)	Z 34
Gordini (Via)	Z 15	Pallavicini		S. Teresa (Via)	Z 35
Guerrini (Via)	Z 16	(Viale G.)	Z 26	4 Novembre (Via)	Y 40

Sepolcro di Dante	Z A	Battistero degli Ariani	Y D	Museo Nazionale	Y M¹
Mausoleo di Teodorico	Y B	Cattedrale	Z E	Museo Arcivescovile	Z M²

The mosaics – The oldest mosaics are in the Neoni Baptistery and the Galla Placidia Tomb (5C). Next in chronological order are those adorning the Arians' Baptistery, St Apollinaris the New, St Vitalis, and finally St Apollinaris in Classe (6C). The mosaic heritage of the city combines the two great schools of the ancient world: The Hellenic-Roman School, characterised by a realistic rendition of figure and landscape, and the Byzantine School whose rarefied and stylised figures seem to be fixed on their gold background. In 1996 these early Christian monuments of Ravenna were included in UNESCO's World Heritage List.

DISCOVERING RAVENNA

★★ **Basilica di San Vitale** ⊘ (Y) – Access to the basilica affords a view of the fine recomposed **fresco** by Pietro da Rimini (c 1320), originally in the Church of Santa Chiara. Consecrated in 547 by Archbishop Maximian, the basilica is an architectural masterpiece; the splendour, originality and light effects are typical features of the later period of ancient art. The church, dedicated to St Vitalis, has an octagonal plan, two storeys of concave exedrae encircled by an ambulatory and a deep apse. The richly-decorated interior is dazzling: precious marbles, splendidly carved Byzantine capitals, frescoes and especially the **mosaics** of the apse with their brilliant colours. The chancel is adorned with sacrificial scenes from the Old Testament; on the side walls of the apse are wonderful groups representing the **Empress Theodora** with her retinue and the **Emperor Justinian** attended by his court. These works display the splendour, hieratic power and strong outlines which are typical of Byzantine art. On the ceiling *Christ in Majesty* is enthroned between St Vitalis and Bishop Ecclesio (on the right), the founder of the church.

★★ **Mausoleo di Galla Placidia** ⊘ (Y) – This mid-5C mausoleum in the form of a Latin cross has a great architectural harmony and is embellished by wonderful mosaics. The vaulting, shining with stellar and floral motifs, and the dome are painted a deep blue whose magic is enhanced by the shadowy light created by the alabaster windows. On the tympanum and pendentives the symbolic scenes are full of serenity, in particular the idyllic Good Shepherd, on the west wall. The sarcophagi in the projecting arms of the mausoleum were made to house Galla Placidia and her family.

GIRAUDON

Empress Theodora, severe and opulent
in her self-possession

The Benedictine monastery adjacent to the basilica houses a museum (**Museo Nazionale**) ⊘ (Y **M¹**) with displays of Late-Roman and paleo-Christian artefacts, textiles, ivories, Cretan-Venetian icons and mosaics.

★ **Battistero Neoniano (or degli Ortodossi)** ⊘ (Z) – The baptistery, erected in the 5C by Bishop Neoni, is also known as the Orthodox Baptistery in contrast to the Arian baptistery erected by the Goth Theodoric. It has an octagonal plan and comprises two orders of arcades supporting the vault which is covered in splendid mosaics: in the dome there is a portrayal of the *Baptism of Christ* accompanied by the Apostles; the lower section portrays eight small temples with altars and thrones surmounted by the cross, an eastern iconography which refers to the preparation of the Almighty's throne for the last judgement. Around the side windows there are Byzantine low relief sculptures depicting the prophets.

The 18C **cathedral** (Z **E**), adjacent to the baptistery, is dominated by a 10C-11C round campanile. The 6C marble ambo is adorned with symbolic animals.

Museo Arcivescovile ⊘ (Z **M²**) – The Episcopal Palace museum displays a small lapidary collection and Archbishop Maximian's **throne**★★ (6C), a masterpiece in carved ivory. St Andrew's Chapel (**Sant'Andrea**★★) contains remarkable mosaics.

Sepolcro di Dante (Z A) – Dante was exiled from Florence and took refuge first at Verona and then at Ravenna, where he died in 1321. The classical building in which the tomb now stands was erected in 1780.

> ### A snack and a glass of romagna wine
>
> Ca' de ven (via Ricci 24, ☎ 0544 30 163, closed on Mondays, open 11am-2pm and from 5.30pm to 10.15pm) is a trattoria-wine bar housed in an atmospheric "medieval inn" in the heart of the historic centre.

San Francesco – This 10C Romanesque church, dedicated to St Francis, is flanked by a campanile of the same period. Remodelled after the Second World War, it still retains some fine Greek marble columns, a 5C high altar and a 10C crypt.

Battistero degli Ariani (Y D) – The **Arians' Baptistery** ⊘ was built by the Goth Theodoric in the 6C. The dome is decorated with fine **mosaics** which make use of the same iconography, if a little less elegantly, as the Neoniano Baptistery.

> ### What is Arianism?
>
> The spread of Arianism began in the 4C following the preaching of the Alexandrian priest Arius (280-336). The Arian heresy maintained that Christ was not fully divine. Condemned by the Council of Nicaea in 325, Arianism flourished in the East in the 4C and among Goths, Vandals and Lombards until the 6C.

* **Basilica di Sant'Apollinare Nuovo** ⊘ (Z) – Erected between 493 and 526 by Theodoric, probably as a Palatine church, St Apollinaris is divided into a nave and two aisles articulated by beautifully crafted columns in Greek marble with Corinthian capitals. The north and south walls are decorated with a series of **mosaics** on a gold background distributed over three sections: the upper sections date from Theodoric's reign while the lower section was remodelled under Justinian who eliminated any reference to Arianism. On both sides the upper registry portrays Scenes from the Life of Christ, inserted into a "naturalistic" background which still shows a Graeco-Roman influence. In the middle section between the large windows are representations of saints and prophets. The lower registry on the south side shows a **Procession of martyrs** leaving Theodoric's palace lead by St Martin making their way towards Christ the King. The drapes of the sumptuous palace replace the previous portrayals of Theodoric's dignitaries; of these only the spectral hands on the columns remain. The opposite side shows a **Procession of virgins** lead by the Magi leaving the city of Ravenna and the port of Classis with its three anchored ships. Their colourful, dynamic appearance makes a notable contrast with the measured, hieratic procession of martyrs. Around the figure of Christ observe the tender portrayal of the Virgin and Child surrounded by angels.

> ### To all young women searching for a husband...
>
> It might be cheering to know that according to legend, women who kiss Guido Guidarelli will marry within the year. It is advisable not to wait until the last days of December.

Pinacoteca Comunale ⊘ (Z) – The ex-monastery of the Lateran Canons, whose façade facing the Public Gardens has a **Lombard loggia** (16C), houses the municipal picture gallery. Collections include works from most of the Italian schools (in particular the Emilian and Romagna schools) from the 14C to the 20C. The **recumbent figure★** (1525) of a young knight, Guidarello Guidarelli, by Tullio Lombardo, is the jewel of the museum.

OUTSIDE THE HISTORIC CENTRE

* **Mausoleo di Teodorico** ⊘ (Y B) – This curious mausoleum, erected by Theodoric around 520, is built of huge blocks of freestone assembled without mortar. The two-storey building is covered by a remarkable monolithic dome 11m/36ft in diameter in Istrian stone. Inside, the decoration is sober and austere. A Romanesque porphyry basin has been transformed into a sarcophagus.

★★ **Basilica di Sant'Apollinare in Classe** ⊙ – *5km/3mi south. Leave Ravenna by* ④ *on the plan, the S 67. For those without a car there are buses (nos 4 or 44) which leave from Piazza Caduti, the railway station and Via Roma (15/20min).* The basilica stands in open country not far from the sea. The basilica was begun in 534 and consecrated in 549; a cylindrical campanile was added in the 11C.

The majestic interior is composed of a nave and two aisles separated by arches on marble columns with splendid Corinthian capitals. In the aisles lie superb Christian sarcophagi (5C-8C). The triumphal arch and apse feature magnificent 6C-7C mosaics with a marked freedom and simplicity of composition and a lovely harmony of colour. The triumphal arch shows Christ the Saviour surrounded by symbols representing the Evangelists; underneath there are two groups of six lambs (the Apostles) leaving two towered cities (Bethlehem and Jerusalem). The vaulting of the apse shows the Transfiguration: dominated by the hand of God, the cross bearing an image of Christ stands out, with its surrounding starry sky. At the ends of the arms the Greek letters alpha and omega indicate that Christ is the beginning and the end. There are depictions of the prophets Moses and Elijah; the three sheep represent Saints Peter, James and John, witnesses of the Transfiguration. Below there is a charming portrayal of a meadow with the figure of Apollinaris surrounded by his sheep (the flock of the faithful).

REGGIO di CALABRIA

Calabria
Population 180 158
Michelin map 431 M 28
Town plan in the Michelin Atlas Italy

Reggio, which backs against the Aspromonte Massif, is a pleasant town of modern appearance, rebuilt after the earthquake of 1908 along the Straits of Messina. Reggio is surrounded by rich groves of olives, vines, orange and lemon trees, and fields of flowers used for making perfume. Half the world production of bergamot (a citrus fruit) comes from Reggio. There are daily boat and car ferry services to Sicily.

* **Lungomare** – This long and elegant sea-front promenade lined with palm trees and magnolias affords views of the Sicilian coastline and Etna.

★★ **Museo Nazionale Archeologico** ⊙ – Although most visitors come to this museum wanting to look at the mysterious bronze warriors, it would be a pity not to have a look at other, smaller historic mementoes housed here. Stop and look at the *pinakes*★, terracotta low reliefs that were used in Locri as ex-votos in the 5C BC. They were dedicated to Persephone, bride of Hades who carried her off to the Underworld while she was picking flowers. There is also an intimate and familiar scene portrayed in the *Woman putting a peplum into a decorated chest*.

The lower floor is "home" to the two **Riace Warriors**★★★, found in the sea of Riace in 1972.

A few minutes in front of the Riace Warriors

Made in Greece in the 5C BC, the statues are 1.98m/6.5ft and 2m/6.6ft tall respectively. Cleaned of marine sediment and hollow inside, they each weigh 250kg - 550lb. Their names – A and B – are clinical in the extreme but their expressions are anything but anonymous. Their eyes (B is missing one) have ivory and limestone corneas, pupils made from a vitreous paste, silver eyelashes and teeth, which are revealed only through the lips of A. Both hold, on their folded left arms, the slings of shields and in their right hands a lance. But each warrior seems troubled by different thoughts and feelings: A seems aggressive and indomitable and has been captured while thrusting his left leg forward. He has just turned his head and seems about to speak. B has a frightened and tentative expression, the position of his shoulders suggest that he is reluctant to advance forward.

EXCURSION

* **Aspromonte** – *From its junction (bivio Brandano) with the S 112 to Melito di Porto Salvo on the south coast, the S 183 crosses the Aspromonte Massif from north to south, allowing the visitor to discover its many varied aspects. See CALABRIA.*

REGGIO EMILIA

Emilia-Romagna
Population 139 200
Michelin map 428 or 429 H 13
Town plan in the Michelin Atlas Italy

This rich industrial and commercial centre, set on the Via Emilia, was the birthplace of Ariosto and the landscape painter Antonio Fontanesi (1818-1882). Like Modena and Ferrara, it belonged to the Este family from 1409 to 1776.

The historic centre – **Piazza Prampolini**, the political, religious and economic centre of the town, is overlooked by the cathedral which was remodelled in the 15C but dates back further, the Romanesque Baptistery and the Town Hall with its 16C Bordello tower.

To the right of the cathedral is the picturesque and lively **Via Broletto** which leads into Piazza San Prospero. This square is dominated by the 18C façade and unfinished campanile of the **Church of San Prospero** ⊙ which has a fine cycle of frescoes in the apse by C. Procaccini and B. Campi as well as a fine wooden chancel.

Nearby *(take via S. Carlo)* lies the atmospheric Piazza Fontanesi which is bordered by antique shops and art galleries.

Musei Civivi ⊙ – *Via Spallanzani 1*. The municipal museums include the Spallanzani Museum of Natural History, an anthropological section with artefacts from the area around Reggio, Roman and Medieval mosaics, marbles, paintings of the local school (15C-20C) among which *Solitude*★ by Antonio Fontanesi and a section dedicated to M. Mazzacurati (1908-1969).

★ **Galleria Parmeggiani** ⊙ – *2 Corso Cairoli*. An early 20C palace in the eclectic style, with a 15C Hispano-Moresque doorway, the gallery houses a rich collection of French goldwork, textiles, costumes, weaponry, furniture, Flemish and Spanish painting (works attributed to El Greco and Ribera) and pictures by Italian Mannerists.

Madonna della Ghiara ⊙ – *Corso Garibaldi*. This is a beautiful church, erected at the beginning of the 17C following a miracle. The **interior** contains splendid frescoes, altarpieces and paintings which constitute a fine anthology of 17C Emilian painting. One of the most significant paintings is the dramatic *Crucifix* by Guercino.

EXCURSIONS

Brescello – *28km/17mi northwest*. The town owes its name (Brixellum) to the Celts who settled in the Po Plain and who, as they had moved along the plain, had already founded the settlements of Bressanone (Brixen) and Brescia (Brixia).

In spite of its ancient origins, Brescello nowadays is famous for being the setting of the films of **Don Camillo** and **Peppone**. The museum **(museo)** ⊙ contains memorabilia and posters relating to the films and as well as objects used during the filming such as bicycles, a motorcycle and sidecar and even a tank.

> **Giovanni Guareschi** (1908-1968), a journalist and novelist who liberally dipped his pen in humour, together with Giovanni Mosca (1908-1983) founded a newspaper (the **Candido**) and wrote *Small world: Don Camillo* which was made into a famous film starring Fernandel and Gino Cervi.

Castello di Canossa – *32km/20mi southwest*. Only the romantic ruins, perched on a rock, remain of the imposing stronghold which belonged to the great Countess of Tuscany, Matilda (1046-1115), who supported the pope against the emperor for 30 years during the quarrel over the investiture of bishops and abbots. The Emperor Heinrich IV of Germany came barefoot and in his shirtsleeves through the snow, to make amends to Pope Gregory VII in 1077. He had to wait three days for his absolution. This is the origin of the expression "to go to Canossa"; that is, to humble oneself after a quarrel.

RIETI

Lazio

Population 45 830
Michelin map 430 O 20

Rieti lies at the junction of several valleys in the heart of a fertile plain and is the geographical centre of Italy. It is also a good excursion centre from which to follow in the footsteps of St Francis of Assisi, who preached locally.

Piazza Cesare Battisti – This is the centre of the town, where the most important buildings are to be found. Take the gateway to the right of the 16C-17C Palazzo del Governo with its elegant loggia to reach the pleasant **public garden★**, from where there is a lovely view of the town and its surroundings.

Duomo – This cathedral has a 15C porch and a lovely Romanesque campanile dating from 1252. Inside, the fresco of the Madonna dates from 1494 while the **crypt** is 12C.

Palazzo Episcopale – *Behind the cathedral.* This 13C episcopal building has heavily-ribbed **vaulting★** over the two vast naves.

EXCURSIONS

Convento di Fonte Colombo ◯ – *5km/3mi southwest. Take the Contigliano road and after 3km/2mi turn left.* It was in the old monastery that St Francis underwent an eye operation. He dictated the Franciscan Rule in the grotto after having fasted for 40 days. Visitors will see the 12C Chapel of St Mary Magdalene adorned with frescoes depicting the "T", the emblem of the Cross designed by St Francis; the St Michael Chapel and the grotto where he fasted; the tree-trunk in which Jesus appeared to him; the old monastery and the 15C church.

★ **Convento di Greccio** ◯ – *15km/9mi northwest. Take the road via Contigliano to Greccio and continue for 2km/1.2mi. Leave the car on the esplanade at the foot of the monastery.*
This 13C monastery clings to a rocky overhang at an altitude of 638m/2 093ft. It was here that St Francis celebrated Christmas in 1223 and said mass at a manger *(presepio)* between an ox and an ass, thus starting the custom of Christmas Nativity scenes.
Visitors have access to the Chapel of the Crib (Cappella del Presepio – frescoes by the school of Giotto) and the areas where St Francis and his companions lived. On the upper floor is the church of 1228 with its original furnishings.

Convento di Poggio Bustone ◯ – *10km/6mi north by the Terni road.* Perched at an altitude of 818m/2 684ft in a lovely green setting, the monastery consists of a 14C church, much altered, with its 15C to 17C frescoes, charming 15C-16C cloisters, a 14C refectory, and two caves in which St Francis is said to have lived.

Convento La Foresta ◯ – *5km/3mi north.* It was in this mountain retreat that St Francis wrote his *Canticle of the Creatures* and performed the miracle of the vine. In the wine cellar is the vat which was filled by the miraculous grape. The cave where St Francis stayed is also open to visitors.

RIMINI ☆☆☆

Emilia-Romagna

Population 130 074
Michelin map 429 or 430 J 19
Town plan in the Michelin Atlas Italy

Once the destination for élite tourism (even King Umberto I came here), today Rimini is an internationally known seaside resort with modern hotels, a marina, an airport and a great beach of fine sand.
But Rimini is not just a summer hotspot; it has an illustrious past, well documented in its historic centre.
This Umbrian and Gallic colony, with its strategic situation at the junction of the Via Emilia and the Via Flaminia, flourished during the Empire.
In the 13C the town grew to fame with the notoriety of its ruling house, the Malatesta. Dante immortalised the fate of the tragic lovers, Paolo Malatesta and Francesca da Rimini, who were murdered by Gianni Malatesta (see also p. 266, the brother of Paolo and the husband of Francesca. Later Sigismondo I Malatesta (1417-1468) combined open-minded political action with a patronage of the arts that summoned Piero della Francesca and Leon Battista Alberti to his court. In the 16C Rimini became a papal town.
In the arts Giotto's work in the church of St Francis (now the Tempio Malatestiano) engendered the development of a Riminese school in the 14C which is similar to Giotto's style but sharper and more dramatic.
More recently, the city has achieved international fame as the birthplace of the film director, Federico Fellini (1920-1993) who paid homage to his roots in cinematic masterpieces such as I vitelloni and Amarcord.

★★ Tempio Malatestiano – The church was built in the 13C by the Franciscans and became the Malatesta mausoleum in the 14C. It was remodelled from 1447 by **Leon Battista Alberti** on Sigismondo I's orders. Based on the principal that the church was to glorify Sigismondo and his beloved wife Isotta by housing their tombs, Alberti decided to adopt the Classical model of a triumphal arch (inspired by the nearby Arch of Augustus) and a whole series of Classical elements. Although unfinished Rimini's "temple" was the first of a new kind of religious building and a point of reference a few decades later for the church of Sant'Andrea in Mantua.

The **interior** includes an allegorical decoration exquisitely and subtlety crafted by Agostino di Duccio who composed a kind of Medieval encyclopaedia updated with pagan and classical elements (note the enchanting *Childhood games* in the second chapel on the right). The south aisle houses Sigismondo's tomb and the reliquary chapel *(if closed contact the sacristy)* with the famous portrait *Sigismondo Malatesta and St Sigismondo*★★ by Piero della Francesca. In the adjacent chapel Isotta's tomb rests on elephants (her husband's favourite animal) who hold up Sigismondo's crest (SI). In the third chapel on the right the signs of the zodiac and the planets (note the view of Rimini in Cancer, the city's sign) celebrate the divine creation contrasting with human activity which is represented by the liberal arts in the opposite chapel in the north aisle. Behind the altar is Giotto's **painted 14C crucifix**★★.

Arco d'Augusto – *Piazzale Giulio Cesare.* The arch of Augustus was built in 27 BC and has a majestic appearance, with fine fluted columns and Corinthian capitals.

The historic centre – Piazza Cavour is bordered by the Town Hall (Palazzo Comunale), Palazzo dell'Arengo and the Palazzo del Podestà, all dating from the 13C-14C but considerably remodelled since then. Going through the arcades of the fish market and turning right onto Via Cairoli make for the **Church of St Augustine** which has interesting examples of 14C Riminese painting. In the nearby Piazza Malatesta stands the imposing **Castel Sigismonso**, an austere building erected by Sigismono 1 who consulted Brunelleschi with regard to its design.

Museo della Città ⊘ – *Via Troini 1.* The museum has collections of archeological artefacts pertaining to Roman Rimini *(Ariminum)* as well as works dating from the 14C-19C. Of particular note are the Riminese paintings and crucifixes, the delicate *Pietà* by Giovanni Bellini, the **S. Vincenzo Ferrer Altarpiece** by Domenico Ghirlandaio and, in the 17C section, paintings by Guercino and Guido Cagnacci.

Ponte di Tiberio – The bridge was begun under Augustus and completed under Tiberius in AD 21. The building material is massive blocks of Istrian limestone.

La RIVIERA LIGURE★★

Liguria
Michelin map 428 I-K 4-12

From Ventimiglia to the Gulf of La Spezia, the coast describes a curve backed by the slopes of the Alps and the Ligurian Apennines, with Genoa in the middle.

The enchanting Italian or Ligurian Riviera is like the French Riviera, a tourist paradise. The mild climate makes it particularly popular in winter. The coast is dotted with popular resorts with good amenities and a wide range of hotels. The hinterland provides a large choice of walks for those who prefer solitude.

Sightseeing – The map below locates the towns and sites described in the guide, and also indicates other beauty spots in small black type.

★ ① RIVIERA DI PONENTE (WESTERN RIVIERA)

From Ventimiglia to Genoa *175km/109mi – allow a day*

The main road of the Riviera, the Via Aurelia, is of Roman origin. It is difficult, as it is winding and narrow, and carries heavy traffic. Nevertheless, there are remarkable viewpoints from the stretches of corniche road or when the road runs close to the blue waters of the Ligurian Sea. Slightly inland the A10 motorway with its many tunnels and viaducts runs parallel. The road passes through a succession of resorts with villas often screened by luxuriant and varied vegetation, or crosses a stretch of coastal plain traversed by mountain torrents. With its exceptionally good exposure the Riviera specialises in the growing of flowers, often under glass, throughout the year.

The hinterland provides a sharp contrast, with the tranquility of its wild forested landscapes.

Ventimiglia – Not far from the French border, Ventimiglia has an old quarter (Città Vecchia) crisscrossed by narrow alleyways, an 11C-12C cathedral (Duomo), an 11C octagonal baptistery, an 11C-12C Church of San Michele and the 17C Neri Oratory. The Hanbury Gardens (**Giardini Hanbury★★** ⊙) in **Mortola Inferiore** *(6km/ 4mi*

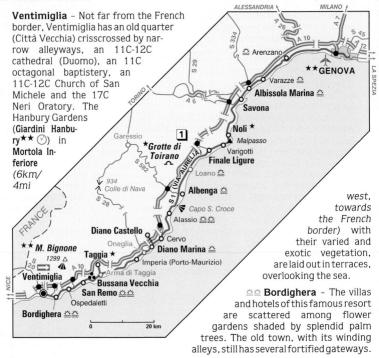

west, towards the French border) with their varied and exotic vegetation, are laid out in terraces, overlooking the sea.

⌂⌂ **Bordighera** – The villas and hotels of this famous resort are scattered among flower gardens shaded by splendid palm trees. The old town, with its winding alleys, still has several fortified gateways.

⌂⌂ **San Remo** – *See SAN REMO.*

★ **Taggia** – Taggia, set amidst vineyards, orchards and olive groves, commands the Argentina Valley. In the 15C and 16C Taggia was an important art centre frequented by Louis Bréa from Nice, the Piedmontese Canavese, and the Genoese Perino del Vaga and Luca Cambiaso.
The Church of **San Domenico**, dedicated to St Dominic, has a fine collection of **works★** by Louis Bréa (*Virgin of Pity* and the *Baptism of Christ*).

⌂ **Diano Marina** – From here it is possible to visit the fortified village of **Diano Castello** and its 12C Chapel of the Knights of Malta (Cappella dei Cavalieri di Malta) with its multicoloured wooden roof.

⌂ **Albenga** – Albenga lies a short distance inland, in an alluvial plain with rich market gardens. The medieval **old town★** is clustered round the cathedral **(Cattedrale)** with its imposing late-14C campanile. The vaulting of the nave is covered with *trompe-l'œil* frescoes. The octagonal 5C baptistery has a baptismal font and a charming Paleo-Christian mosaic in the style typical of Ravenna.

Grotte di Toirano ⊙ – The caves were inhabited in the late-Neolithic period. There are traces of human footprints, torch marks, bear remains and prints, and mud balls used as missiles. The caves open into a series of chambers bristling with stalagmites and stalactites. The last section is the most interesting: a cave once filled with water, which has hollowed it out and given it its round shape.

Finale Ligure – **Finale Marina** has a basilica with a fanciful baroque façade. In **Finale Pia** the abbey church is graced with an elegant late-13C campanile. The old town of **Finale Borgo★**, 2km/1mi inland, still has its town walls and its Collegiate Church of San Biagio with its elegant 13C polygonal campanile. Inside are a polyptych of St Catherine (1533) and a 16C painting of St Blaise surrounded by saints.
From **Castel San Giovanni** *(1hr on foot there and back; start from Via del Municipio)* there is a **view★** of Finale Ligure, the sea and the hinterland. Higher up, **Castel Gavone** retains a 15C round tower with diamond-shaped rustication.

★ **Noli** – This fishing village still has ancient houses, 13C towers and a Romanesque church with a huge wooden statue of Christ, also of the Romanesque period.

Savona – Italy's seventh port, Savona handles crude oil, coal, cellulose and Italian cars for export to Britain and the United States. The old town has several Renaissance palaces, a 16C cathedral (Duomo) and on the sea-front a 16C fortress, **Fortezza Priamar**, where the Italian patriot Mazzini was imprisoned in 1830.

⌂ **Albisola Marina** – This town is known for its production of ceramics, which carries on a 13C tradition. At the end of the 16C a Duke of Nevers, a member of the

> Don't miss a stop at **Caffè Defilà**, corso Garibaldi 4, Chiavari. For over a century this has been a social and cultural meeting place for intellectuals and artists.

Italian Gonzaga family, summoned the Conrade brothers from Albisola to Nevers to found a faïence factory. The 18C **Villa Faraggiana** ⊙ with its exotic **park★**, now houses the Ligurian Ceramics Centre. The exhibits include: the rich Empire furnishings, ceramic pavements and flooring, and the superb **ballroom★** with its stucco and fresco decoration.

★★★ 2 RIVIERA DI LEVANTE (EASTERN RIVIERA)

From Genoa to La Spezia 173km/108mi – allow 1 day

This stretch of coast has more character and is wilder than the Riviera di Ponente. Sharp promontories, little sheltered coves, tiny fishing villages, wide sandy bays, cliffs, the pinewoods and olive groves of the hinterland, all lend it charm. The road is often winding and hilly but there are fewer stretches of corniche road and the road often runs much further from the coast.

★★ **Genoa** – See GENOVA.

★★★ **Portofino** – See Promontorio di PORTOFINO.

⌂⌂ **Rapallo** – This sophisticated seaside resort is admirably situated at the head of a bay to the east of the Portofino peninsula. The Lungomare Vittorio Veneto is a lovely palm-shaded **promenade★** along the sea-front.

⌂ **Chiavari** – This seaside resort has a vast beach and a pleasure-boat harbour. In San Salvatore 2km/1.2mi to the northeast is the small 13C **Basilica dei Fieschi★** with its alternating courses of black and white marble. The vaulting is pointed. Opposite stands the Palazzo Fieschi, a graceful 13C Genoese Gothic building.

★★ **Cinque Terre** – See CINQUE TERRE.

La Spezia – Town plan in the Michelin Atlas Italy. This naval base and important port comprises Italy's largest naval dockyard and specialises in the manufacture of arms. The **museo navale** ⊙ displays souvenirs, arms and models. The Lia Museum can also be visited.

★★ **Museo Lia** ⊙ – Housed in a completely restored 17C monastery, this collection was accumulated by Amedeo Lia who amassed (and then donated to the city) 1 110 works of art in his lifetime, dating from Roman times to the 18C. The museum has important sections on ivory, enamels, crosses and devotional objects, a beautiful series of illuminated manuscripts, paintings, glass and rock crystal. Listed here are some of the most significant pieces (numbers used are those used in the museum). Room 1: the collection opens with an Umbrian *Virgin and Child* in polychrome wood (13C). To the right of the entrance, in a glass case devoted to Roman art, is an **amethyst head**, probably a portrait of one of Caligula's sisters. To the left are some ivories (note the sumptuous German Baroque Cup with Alboin and Rosamund – A20), enamels (St George and the Dragon in enamel and gold) and a gold and enamel medallion portraying the Adoration of the Magi (565). At the end of the room note the crosses, in particular the 13C Limoges cross (516). Room II: This room displays illuminated manuscripts with three complete antiphonaries and numerous illuminated

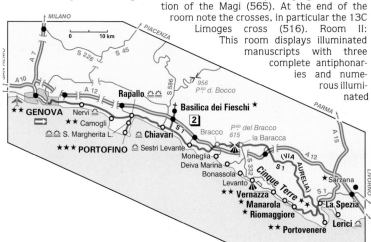

pages, mostly Italian (14C-16C). The paintings (13C-18C) begin in Room IV and are displayed in chronological order. Among the numerous artists it is worth noting the followers of Giotto, Bernardo Daddi and Pietro Lorenzetti *(St John the Evangelist)* and Alvise Vivarini *(St Jerome)*. 16C painters include Giampietrino *(Madonna and Child with St John)*, Bellini and a self-portrait by **Pontormo**. The 17C and 18C are represented respectively by followers of Caravaggio and Venetian landscapes and portraits (Longhi, Guardi). Rooms XI and XII have displays of bronze figures, rock crystal and Roman glass – note the bottle with gilded bands dating from the 1C B. The last room has a collection of mainly 17C still-lives.

★★ **Portovenere** – This small, severe-looking town is dominated by a 12C-16C citadel. Some of the houses date as far back as the 12C and were in fact once fortified by the Genoese.

The Church of San Lorenzo dates from the 12C, while the Church of San Pietro incorporates parts dating from the 6C. From the terrace there is a very fine view of the Gulf of La Spezia and the Cinque Terre region.

⌂ **Lerici** – At the head of a well-sheltered cove Lerici has an important 13C castle (castello) which was rebuilt in the 16C by the Genoese.

ROMA★★★

ROME – Lazio
Population 2 653 245
Michelin map 430 Q 19 (with plans of the conurbation)
See The Green Guide to Rome

The capital of the Roman Empire to which it owes its name, and the centre of Christendom since the fall of the Empire, Rome is rich in monuments of its ancient history which justify its renown as the Eternal City.

Today Rome is no longer the marble city left behind by Augustus and the Emperors, nor is it the opulent court of the Papal era: since 1870, the year in which it was proclaimed capital of Italy, Rome has seen a widespread and, especially after the Second World War, uncontrolled urban expansion.

The surrounding countryside has been more fortunate, so that even today those landscapes dotted with pine trees and cypresses, under a pure blue sky and bathed in a golden light, form an unforgettable panorama.

HISTORY AND LEGEND

The legendary origins of Rome were perpetuated by both Roman historians and poets, such as Livy, in the more than 100 volumes of his monumental opus, *Roman History*, and Virgil in the *Aeneid*. Both claimed that Aeneas, son of the goddess Aphrodite, fled from Troy when it was captured, and landed at the mouth of the Tiber. Having defeated the local tribes he founded Lavinium. His son Ascanius (or Iulus) founded Alba Longa. It was here that Rhea Silvia the Vestal, following her union with the god Mars, gave birth to the twins Romulus and Remus, who were abandoned on the Tiber. The twins, transported by the current of the river, came to rest at the foot of the Palatine where they were nursed by a wolf. Later Romulus marked a furrow round the sacred area on which the new city was to be built. Jesting, Remus stepped over the line; Romulus killed him for violating the sacred precinct. Romulus populated his village with outlaws who settled on the Capitol and married women who had been seized from the Sabines. An alliance grew up between the two peoples who were ruled by a succession of kings, alternately Sabine and Latin, until the Etruscans arrived.

But beyond legend modern historians emphasise the strategic location of Rome's seven hills especially that of the Palatine, which was a staging-post on the salt road (Via Salaria). This no doubt led to the development of settlements around the Palatine in the 8C BC.

Two centuries later the Etruscans had transformed these villages of shacks into a well-organised town, with a citadel on the Capitol. The last Etruscan king, Tarquin the Superb, was thrown out in 509 BC and the Consulate was instituted.

The Republican era was an ambitious one of territorial expansion. During the 2C and 1C BC the Republican regime tore itself to pieces in a civil war. To restore order disrupted by the rival political factions and rule the newly-conquered territories, it required a clever man of very determined character. **Julius Caesar** (101-44 BC) emerged from amidst the contenders by reason of his audacious strategies (he conquered the whole of Gaul in 51), his grasp of political affairs, his talents as an orator and his unbounded ambition. Appointed consul and dictator for life, he was assassinated on the Ides of March, 15 March 44 BC. He was succeeded by his nephew, **Octavian**, a young man who was of delicate health and had won no military glory. Octavian was to demonstrate tenacity of purpose and political genius and ably rid his path of possible rivals. In 27 BC the Senate granted Octavian the title **Augustus**, which invested him with an aura of holiness. He soon became the first Roman emperor. His achievements were considerable: he extended Roman government and restored peace to the whole of the Mediterranean basin.

Among Augustus' successors there were those who were driven by madness and cruelty (Caligula, Nero and Domitian); and others who continued the good work of Roman civilisation: the good administrator, Vespasian; Titus who was known as the love and delight of the human race; Trajan, the "best of Emperors" and great builder; and Hadrian, an indefatigable traveller and passionate Hellenist.

Christianity – As the old order passed away, undermined from within by economic misery and the concentration of authority in the hands of one man, and from without by Barbarian attacks, a new force – Christianity – began to emerge. It had first reached Rome in the reign of Augustus. The religion of Jesus of Nazareth originated in Palestine and Syria, and was spread throughout the pagan world by his disciples, eventually reaching Rome. During the last years of the 1C and the early years of the 2C the Christian Church became organised, but transgressed the law from the beginning because the Emperor embodied religious power. It was not until the Edict of Milan (313), which allowed Christians to practise their religion openly, and the conversion of **Constantine** (314) that the Church could come out into the open.

S. Chirol

After nearly 2 000 years the coliseum has lost none of its imposing allure

From the first days of Christianity, the bishop was Christ's representative on earth. The bishop of Rome, capital of the Empire, claimed primacy. Gradually the name **"Pope"**, which had been used for all bishops, was reserved for the Bishop of Rome alone. For 19 centuries the popes at the head of the Roman church have influenced the history of Christianity and given the Eternal City its particular character. In the 11C **Gregory VII** restored order to the Christian church, which had by then an appalling reputation. He dealt with two scourges: the buying and selling of church property, and the marriage of the clergy. In so doing he started the **Investiture Controversy**, which opposed the Sovereign Pontiff and the Emperor.

During the Renaissance numerous popes distinguished themselves as ambitious patrons of the arts, bringing to their court such artists as Raphael and Michelangelo whose genius contributed to the embellishment of the capital. They included Pius II, Sixtus IV (who built the Sistine Chapel, Santa Maria della Pace and Santa Maria del Popolo), Julius II (who commissioned Michelangelo to decorate the ceiling of the Sistine Chapel), Leo X (who had a great personal fortune and nominated Raphael as intendant of the arts), Clement VII, Sixtus V (a great builder) and Paul III who built the Farnese Palace.

LIFE IN ROME

Getting to Rome

Information – Information offices of the E.P.T. (Ente provinciale del Turismo, main office in Via Parigi 11) distribute information leaflets (*Qui Roma* among others) and maps of the city. Offices can be found at the following addresses:
- Fiumicino Airport ☎ 06 65 95 60 74.
- Termini Railway Station, platform no 4 ☎ 06 48 71 270
- Via Parigi 5 ☎06 48 89 92 53.

By train – National trains arrive at Termini and Tiburtina and are connected to the city centre by underground lines A and B. Some towns north of Rome, such as Viterbo, are connected to the capital by the Roma Nord line which arrives at the station in Piazzale Flaminio.
Useful telephone numbers – **Ferrovie dello Stato (National Railways):** information ☎ 1478-88 088. **Termini station,** Piazza dei Cinquecento, ☎ 06 48 84 466; **Ostiense station,** piazza Partigiani, ☎ 06 57 50 732; **S. Pietro station,** via Stazione S. Pietro, ☎ 06 63 13 91; **Tiburtina station,** circonvallazione Nomentana, ☎ 06 44 04 856; **Trastevere,** piazzale Biondo, ☎ 06 58 16 076; **Club Euro Star Italia,** ☎ 06 47 42 155.

By plane – The principal airport is Leonardo da Vinci in Fiumicino, 26 km/16mi from Rome. There are connections to the city centre operated by two railway lines:
- the direct train **Roma Termini-Fiumicino** (30min) leaves every hr at non-peak times, and every half hr at peak time. Tickets cost 15 000L.
- FM1 line **Fiumicino-Fara Sabina** departs every 20min. Tickets cost 7 000L. Departures: from Fiumicino 6.30am – 11.30pm (from 8.15pm trains stop at Roma Tiburtina station); from Tiburtina 5.00am – around 10.30pm. On Sundays and public holidays trains leave every hr.
There is also a night bus service from Tiburtina station to the airport (and vice versa). Journey time 45min. Tickets cost 7 000L.
Useful telephone numbers – **Leonardo da Vinci Airport – Fiumicino,** ☎ 06 65 951; **Ciampino,** ☎ 06 79 49 41. **Bookings for national flights:** ☎ 06 65 641. **Flight information:** ☎ 06 65 95 36 40 e 06 65 95 44 55.

By car – Most city traffic makes use of two ring roads: the outer ring road (Grande Raccordo Anulare), lies on the outskirts of the city at a junction of main national roads as well as the A 1, A 2, A 24, A 18 motorways; the second ring-road is the Tangenziale Est which forms part of the traffic network within the city. It connects the Olympic stadium to Piazza San Giovanni in Laterano, passing through the eastern quarters of the city (Nomentano, Tiburtino, Prenestino...).

Getting around the city

Taxis – Radiotaxi telephone numbers are: ☎ 06 3570, 06 4994, 06 6645, 06 4157.

Buses, trams, underground – Public transport maps are on sale at newspaper stands and bookshops. A.T.A.C. maps (Azienda Tramvie e Autobus del Comune di Roma, ☎ 06 46 951) are available at their information stands in Piazza dei Cinquecento. Tickets must be purchased before boarding.

... by car – Access to the city centre by car is problematic. Many streets are open only to pedestrians, residents, taxis and buses. The historic centre forms part of the so-called *fascia blu*, an area closed to non-commercial traffic from 6am to 7.30pm (on Fridays and Saturdays also from 10pm to 2am). There are two large underground car parks in the centre of Rome: one underneath the gardens of Villa Borghese, near Porta Pinciana; the other is the Parking Ludovisi on Via Ludovisi, 60.

Useful information

Emergency telephone numbers
Central police station, via S. Vitale, 15: ☎ 06 46 86
Foreign Office, via Genova, 2: ☎ 06 46 29 87
Traffic police (emergency service): ☎ 06 67 691
Lost property office, via N. Bettoni 1: ☎ 06 58 16 040
Emergency ambulance – Red cross: ☎ 06 55 10
24-hr First aid: ☎ 06 58 20 10 30
S. Paolo 24hr pharmacy, via Ostiense, 168 ☎ 06 57 50 143

Banks – Open from 8.30am to 1.30pm and from 2.30pm 4pm Monday to Friday. On Saturdays only a few branches in the historic centre and commercial districts are open.

Pharmacies – 24hr pharmacies in the city centre can be found at: Piazza dei Cinquecento 49/50/51 (Termini station), via Cola di Rienzo 213, corso Vittorio Emanuele 343/343A, Corso Rinascimento 50, piazza Barberini 49, via Arenula 73, piazza della Repubblica 67 and via Nazionale 228.

Sightseeing

The city of Rome has information booths located at strategic points of the city centre. These offer information on all cultural and tourist events in the capital. Open Tuesday to Saturday from 10am to 6pm and on Sundays from 10am to 1pm, up-to-the-minute information is provided to tourists in Italian and English.
Internet fans can visit the web site: http://www.comune.roma.it

Disabled visitors – To find out which monuments are accessible to the disabled and for information on guided tours contact **CO.IN** (Consorzio Cooperative Integrate), via Enrico Giglioli, 54/a; ☎ (also fax) 06 23 26 75 04/5. Offices are open from Monday to Friday from 9am to 5pm.

Accommodation

Rome offers a large choice of accommodation but in practically every season is visited by crowds of tourists and pilgrims. It is predicted that the city will be literally invaded for the Jubilee in 2000. To be sure of securing accommodation and to avoid disappointment it is advisable to book well in advance.
Listed below are some addresses chosen on the basis of good value for money, location and charm. Hotels are divided into three categories based on the price of a double room *(for more information see p. 433)* and are listed in alphabetical order. It is advisable to check prices by telephone beforehand, especially in the Jubilee year when tariffs could increase considerably. For more complete listings of hotels consult the lastest editions of either the Michelin Red Guide to Italy or the The Michelin Red Guide to Rome.

Hotel booking service – To make a hotel reservation call **Hotel Reservation**, ☎ 06 69 91 000, lines open from 7am to 10pm. This service, completely free of charge, has a choice of about 200 hotels in Rome.

BUDGET

Some of the listed hotels have rooms without bath and therefore cost 20-30% less.

Pensione Barrett BY s – Largo Torre Argentina 47. ☎ 06 68 68 481. TORRE ARGENTINA quarter. This simple but well kept hotel is run by someone who takes hospitality very seriously indeed. The rooms have thoughtful little touches that would be hard to find elsewhere, such as foot-baths. 20 rooms.

Hotel Campo dei Fiori BY o – Piazza del Biscione 6. ☎ 06 68 80 68 65. CAMPO DEI FIORI district. Housed in a six-storey building (no lift) this hotel has a nice terrace overlooking Campo de' Fiori. The 27 rooms (nine with bath) are small but cosy. Credit cards accepted.

Hotel Casa tra Noi AY n – Via Monte del Gallo 113. ☎ 06 39 38 73 55. VATICAN-ST PETER'S district. A simple and peaceful hotel at the top of a street which affords a view of the dome of St Peter's. Suitable for large groups, the hotel has 110 rooms and two suites for three or four people. Half or full board offer good value for money. Credit cards accepted.

Albergo del Sole BY r – Via del Biscione 76. ☎ 06 68 80 68 73. CAMPO DEI FIORI quarter. A stone's throw away from the lively Campo de' Fiori, the oldest hotel in Rome is built on the foundations of the theatre of Pompeo. There is a nice terrace with good views and a garage (at a charge). 40 rooms with bath, 20 rooms without.

OUR SELECTION

Hotel Coronet BX u – Piazza Grazioli 5. ☎ 06 67 92 341. PANTHEON QUARTER. Housed in Palazzo Doria Pamphilj this is a comfortable hotel with spacious rooms on the third floor (with lift). 13 double rooms of which 10 with ensuite bath and 3 with private bath in the corridor. Credit cards accepted.

Hotel Invictus DX a – Via Quintino Sella 15. ☎ 06 42 01 14 33. PORTA PIA quarter. This hotel is under the same management as the Solis Invictus *(see below)*. Cosy and comfortable, it has just been remodelled and is situated on the first floor (with lift) of a building near the forum.

Hotel Parlamento BX c – Via delle Convertite 5. ☎ 06 69 92 10 00. PIAZZA DI SPAGNA quarter. A very pleasant hotel situated on the third and fourth floor (with lift). There are 23 rooms of which 16 with air conditioning. In the summer breakfast is served on a pretty terrace which overlooks Piazza San Silvestro. Credit cards accepted.

Hotel Solis Invictus CY x – Via Cavour 305. ☎ 06 69 92 05 87. FORUM quarter. This small, family-run hotel is cosy and comfortable. It is situated on the first floor (with lift) of a building only minutes away from the Fori Imperiali. 10 rooms. Credit cards accepted.

TREAT YOURSELF!

Hotel Hassler Villa Medici CX e – Piazza Trinità dei Monti 6. ☎ 06 69 93 40. PIAZZA DI SPAGNA QUARTER. A classic and prestigious hotel stunningly located at the top of Trinità dei Monti. 85 rooms and 15 suites. Credit cards accepted.

Hotel Eden CX i – Via Ludovisi 49. ☎ 06 47 81 21. PIAZZA DI SPAGNA/VIA VENETO quarter. Situated in a late 19C building and recently restored with elegance, this restaurant houses the famous **La Terrazza** restaurant which, as its name suggests, has tables on the roof garden which affords a beautiful view of Rome. 101 rooms and 11 suites. Credit cards accepted.

Hotel Lord Byron *not shown on the map* – Via De Notaris 5. ☎ 06 32 20 404. VILLA BORGHESE district. This elegant hotel is a real gem. Situated in a pleasant residential area, its **Relais Le Jardin** restaurant offers a refined and beautifully presented cuisine. 28 rooms and 9 suites. Credit cards accepted.

OTHER TYPES OF ACCOMMODATION

Youth hostels and youth organisations – The **Associazione Italiana Alberghi per la Gioventù** -AIG- is in via Cavour 44 ☎ 06 48 71 152. The Comitato regionale Lazio has its central office in viale delle Olimpiadi, 61, which is also the address of the **Foro Italico hostel**, ☎ 06 32 36 267.

Convents and religious houses – These have very reasonably priced rooms but inconveniently close at night (usually at around 10.30pm). A list of convents offering rooms is available at the centro Peregrinatio ad Petri Sedem, piazza Pio XII 4 (Vatican city), ☎ 06 69 88 48 96, fax: 06 69 88 56 17. This organisation takes care of bookings but only for large groups.

Food!

Listed below are simple trattorie as well as more elegant restaurants which offer typical Roman cuisine.
The **GOURMET** section lists some of the best restaurants in the city with prices to match.

UNDER 50 000 L

Da Betto e Mary – Via dei Savorgnan 99. ☎ 06 24 30 53 39. PRENESTINO QUARTER. Open evenings only except Sundays and closed on Thursdays. An "authentic" Roman trattoria which serves traditional dishes such as ravioli with sweetbreads. The barbecued meat, particularly horsemeat steaks, is also recommended.

Trattoria dal Cav. Gino – Vicolo Rosini 4. ☎ 06 68 73 434. MONTECITORIO quarter. A good address for real home cooking. Booking is advisable as the restaurant is small and much frequented by *habitués*.

FROM 50 000L TO 100 000 L

Paris – Piazza S. Callisto 7a. ☎ 06 58 15 378. TRASTEVERE quarter. In the heart of Trastevere this restaurant is housed in a Baroque room and has tables outside in the summer. The cuisine is essentially Jewish-Roman. Recommended dishes include tagliolini pasta with fish sauce, fish "all'acqua pazza" (boiled with tomato, garlic and parsley), Jewish-style artichokes (carciofi alla giudìa), deep fried vegetables and, to end the meal, the delicious ricotta dumplings.

Sora Lella – Via di Ponte Quattro Capi 16. ☎ 06 68 61 601. ISOLA TIBERINA quarter. This famous restaurant was once run by Lella Fabrizi, sister of the actor Aldo Fabrizi. Today it is managed by her son who has added new recipes to traditional family dishes. Don't miss the cheeses with jam and the home made desserts.

GOURMET COOKING

Agata e Romeo – Via Carlo Alberto 45. ☎ 06 44 66 115. S. MARIA MAGGIORE quarter. This restaurant offers excellent traditional food with a twist and has an incredibly rich, well-chosen wine list.

La Terrazza – Via Ludovisi 49. ☎ 06 47 81 21. PIAZZA DI SPAGNA/VIA VENETO quarter. This hotel is housed on the roof garden of the Hotel Eden (*see above*), which affords a breathtaking view of Rome. Modern, creative cuisine.

If you want some excellent fish...

La Rosetta – Via della Rosetta, 9. ☎ 06 68 61 002. PANTHEON quarter. This restaurant is famous for its high quality seafood.

FOR SOMETHING A LITTLE DIFFERENT

L'Asino cotto – Via dei Vascellari 48. ☎ 06 58 98 985. TRASTEVERE quarter. Web site: http://www.giulianobrenna.com. Closed Mondays. A warm, cosy atmosphere and reasonably priced, refined cuisine (40 000L a head). An excellent address.

L'EAU Vive – Via Monterone 85. ☎ 06 68 80 10 95. PANTHEON quarter. This restaurant, run by French missionary nuns, is housed on the first floor of the 16C Palazzo Lante in a frescoed room. French cuisine. 60 000L.

Il Pulcino Ballerino – Via degli Equi 66. ☎ 06 49 41 255. S. LORENZO FUORI LE MURA quarter. The distinguishing feature of this pleasant, informal restaurant is the stone cooking pot placed on each table allowing guests to cook their own vegetables, meat and cheese. Expect to pay about 35 000 L.

IF YOU JUST WANT A SNACK

In the last few years Rome has witnessed the birth of many American-style fast food chains which have not however succeeded in pushing out the traditional and inviting pizza-slice takeaways These are present in almost every quarter and sometimes have a counter and a few stools so that you can sit down and enjoy your pizza. For those who love fine wine, wine bars (which began to appear in the 1970's in Rome) are very popular. In these bars wine is often accompanied by tasty, traditional snacks. Here are a few addresses:

Bookowsky – Via Pomponio Leto 1. ☎ 06 68 33 844. Closed on Sundays. This small bar in the PRATI district has taken inspiration from literary bistros that are to be found in major European capitals. There are various books to leaf through while enjoying a glass of wine as well as *bruschette* and other hot and cold snacks.

La Bottega del Vino da Anacleto Bleve – Via S. Maria del Pianto 9A. ☎ 06 68 65 970. ISOLA TIBERINA quarter. Closed on Sundays, open at lunchtime only on Mondays, Tuesdays and Saturdays. This wine bar in the heart of the Jewish ghetto has a window displaying delicate flans and carpaccios made by the owner, salads and cheeses (the mozzarella is excellent) which can be selected before sitting down at your table. The lemon and coffee creams are delicious. A homely atmosphere with good service.

Trimani il Wine Bar – Via Cernaia 37B. ☎ 06 44 69 630. PORTA PIA quarter. Closed on Sundays (expect to pay about 45 000L excluding wine). Run by the oldest family of vintners in Rome, this bar with a gazebo outside has delicious specialities such as smoked fish, vegetable tarts, Italian and foreign cheeses as well as a vast choice of wines. New dishes include swordfish with orange, Camembert with truffles and Tarte Tatin (apple tart) with dried fruit.

FAMOUS CAFÉS

Caffè della Pace – Piazza della Pace 4. ☎ 06 68 61 216. PIAZZA NAVONA quarter. Situated in a beautiful small square near Piazza Navona this café attracts a show business clientele, particularly in the evening at the outdoor tables. The two indoor rooms are permeated by a Central European atmosphere with their comfortable sofas, dim lighting and smoky mirrors.

Caffè Greco – Via dei Condotti 86. ☎ 06 67 82 554. PIAZZA DI SPAGNA quarter. Situated near the Piazza di Spagna, this is one of the oldest literary cafés in Rome and has preserved all of its historic atmosphere.

Doney – Via V. Veneto 145. ☎ 06 48 21 790. VIA VENETO quarter. This elegant café with a piano bar has an air of nostalgia and is one of the most legendary cafés on the Via Veneto.

S. Eustachio – Piazza S. Eustachio 82. ☎ 06 68 61 309. PANTHEON quarter. This is the place to taste the aromatic, creamy "gran caffè speciale", whose secret is closely guarded by its creator. Those who prefer their coffee without sugar should inform the waiters as coffee is served already sweetened.

Tre Scalin – Piazza Navona 28. ☎ 06 68 80 19 96. PIAZZA NAVONA quarter. This café, situated in one of the most beautiful squares in Rome, is also renowned for its excellent truffles.

ROME TODAY

No other city in the world has managed to combine so successfully such a diverse heritage of Classical antiquities, medieval buildings, Renaissance palaces and Baroque churches. Far from being discordant they constitute a logical continuity where revivals, influences and contrasts are evidence of the ingenuity of Roman architects and builders. Of course, the ruins no longer present the splendour they displayed under the Empire, when they were faced with marble, and only a few of the palaces have retained the painted decoration of their façades. And even the city more recently acclaimed by Goethe and Stendhal has changed, owing to the damage caused by heavy traffic and the developments resulting from the modernisation of a busy capital city.

However, today's visitor cannot fail to be impressed by the immensity of the great centre of ancient civilisation and lively modern activity that is Rome.

The best overall views of this urban complex sprawling over the seven hills are from the belvederes on the Janiculum (Gianicolo AY), the Aventine (Aventino CZ) and the Pincio (BV). At dusk the visitor will discover a city bathed in a golden light, the green masses of the gardens, the silhouettes of umbrella pines shading the areas of ruins, as well as the numerous domes and bell-towers rising above the pink-tiled roofscape. Rome with some 300 churches is the city of churches, where it is not uncommon to find two side by side. It is often impossible to stand back and admire their façades but the richness of the decoration and the ingenious use of trompe-l'œil tend to compensate for this drawback. Often the interiors are astonishing for their silence and light and the inventiveness and audacity of the ultimate design.

In the older districts of Rome (Vecchia Roma) around the Pantheon (BX), the Piazza Navona (BX) and the Campo dei Fiori (BY), there is a wealth of fine palaces. Those who wander through these districts will often catch a glimpse between ochre-coloured façades of a small square with all the bustle of a market, or several flights of stairways descending to a fountain. In the evening these areas are lit by tall street lights and are bathed in a soft glow which gives them a certain charm, a pleasant change from the bustling main arteries.

Luxury shops are to be found around the Piazza del Popolo (BV), Via del Corso (BCX), Piazza di Spagna (CX) and the streets which open off them. Via Veneto (CX) lined with cafés and luxurious hotels is a fashionable tourist centre. Piazza Navona is another fashionable meeting-place while the Trastevere (BY), which has never lost its popular character, has a variety of restaurants. Antique and second-hand shops line Via dei Coronari (BX 25).

DISCOVERING THE ETERNAL CITY

For a detailed visit of the city consult the The Green Guide to Rome.

A minimum stay of two or three days is recommended. The following paragraphs give general information on some 20 of the best-known sights, listed in alphabetical order. The section entitled "Additional Sights" lists by type other interesting buildings, beauty spots or museums highlighting the city's outstanding wealth of places to visit.

★★★ CAMPIDOGLIO (CAPITOL – CY)

On the hill which symbolised the power of ancient Rome, there now stand the city's administrative offices, the Church of Santa Maria d'Aracoeli, Piazza del Campidoglio and its palaces, and pleasant gardens.

★★ **Santa Maria d'Aracoeli** (CY D²) – The church has a lovely staircase built as a votive offering after the plague of 1346, and a beautiful, austere façade. It was built in 1250 on the spot where the Sibyl of Tibur (Tivoli) announced the coming of Christ to Augustus. In the first chapel on the right are frescoes★ painted by Pinturicchio in about 1485.

★★★ **Piazza del Campidoglio** (CY 17) – Capitol Square was designed and partly laid out by Michelangelo from 1536 onwards. It is framed by three palaces and a balustrade with statues of the Heavenly Twins or Dioscuri. In the centre stood the equestrian statue of Marcus Aurelius installed by Michelangelo and now housed in the Capitoline Museums (below).

The **Palazzo dei Conservatori**★★★ ⏱ (CY M⁴), built in the 15C and remodelled in 1568 by Giacomo della Porta, houses a **museum**★★★ of antique art which includes the *She-Wolf*★★★ (6C-5C BC), the *Boy Extracting a Thorn*★★, a Greek original or a very good copy dating back to the 1C BC, and a **Bust of** *Junius Brutus*★★, a remarkable head dating from the 3C BC placed on a bust in the Renaissance period. The picture gallery (**pinacoteca**★ *2nd floor*) contains mainly 14C to 17C paintings (Titian, Caravaggio, Rubens, Guercino, Reni).

ROMA

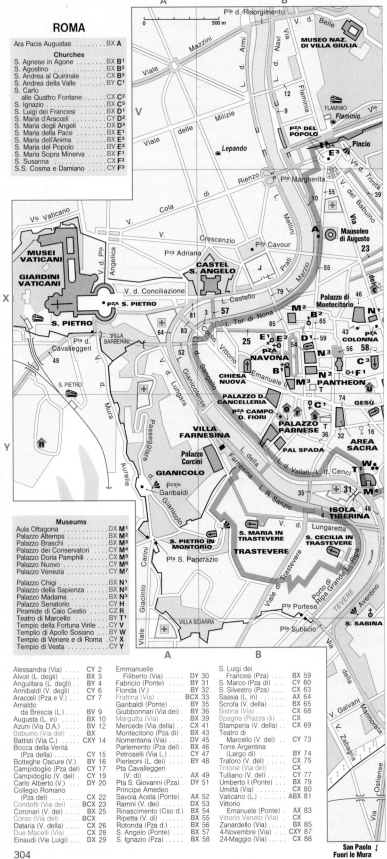

Ara Pacis Augustae . . . . BX **A**

Churches
S. Agnese in Agone . . . . BX **B¹**
S. Agostino . . . . BX **B²**
S. Andrea al Quirinale . . . . . CX **B³**
S. Andrea della Valle . . . . . . BY **C¹**
S. Carlo
  alle Quattro Fontane . . . . CX **C²**
S. Ignazio . . . . BX **C³**
S. Luigi dei Francesi . . . . . . BX **D¹**
S. Maria d'Aracœli . . . . CY **D²**
S. Maria degli Angeli . . . . . DX **D³**
S. Maria della Pace . . . . BX **E¹**
S. Maria dell'Anima . . . . . . BX **E²**
S. Maria del Popolo . . . . . . BV **E³**
S. Maria Sopra Minerva . . . BX **F¹**
S. Susanna . . . . CX **F²**
S.S. Cosma e Damiano . . . . CY **F³**

Museums
Aula Ottagona . . . . DX **M¹**
Palazzo Altemps . . . . BX **M²**
Palazzo Braschi . . . . BX **M³**
Palazzo dei Conservatori . . CY **M⁴**
Palazzo Doria Pamphili . . . CX **M⁵**
Palazzo Nuovo . . . . CY **M⁶**
Palazzo Venezia . . . . CY **M⁷**
Palazzo Chigi . . . . BX **N¹**
Palazzo della Sapienza . . . . BX **N²**
Palazzo Madama . . . . BX **N³**
Palazzo Senatorio . . . . CY **H**
Piramide di Caio Cestio . . . CZ **R**
Teatro di Marcello . . . . BY **T¹**
Tempio della Fortuna Virile . CY **V**
Templio di Apollo Sosiano . BY **W**
Tempio di Venere e di Roma . CY **X**
Tempio di Vesta . . . . CY **Y**

Alessandra (Via) . . . . CY 2
Alvoti (L. degli) . . . . . BX 3
Anguillara (L. degli) . . BY 4
Annibaldi (V. degli) . . CY 6
Aracœli (Pza e V.) . . . CY 7
Arnaldo
  da Brescia (L.) . . . . BV 9
Augusta (L. in) . . . . . BX 10
Azuni (Via D.A.) . . . . BV 12
Babuino (Via del) . . . . BX
Battisti (Via C.) . . . . CXY 14
Bocca della Verità
  (Pza della) . . . . . . CY 15
Botteghe Oscure (V.) . BY 16
Campidoglio (Pza del) CY 17
Campidoglio (V. del) . CY 19
Carlo Alberto (V.) . . . DY 20
Collegio Romano
  (Pza del) . . . . CX 22
Condotti (Via dei) . . . BCX 23
Coronari (V. dei) . . . . BX 25
Corso (Via del) . . . . . BCX
Dataria (V. della) . . . . CX 26
Due Macelli (Via) . . . . CX 28
Einaudi (Vie Luigi) . . . DX 29

Emmanuele
  Filiberto (Via) . . . . DY 30
Fabricio (Ponte) . . . . BY 31
Florida (V.) . . . . BY 32
Frattina (Via) . . . . BCX 33
Garibaldi (Ponte) . . . BY 35
Giubbonnari (Via dei) . BY 36
Margutta (Via) . . . . . . BX 39
Mercede (Via della) . . CX 41
Montecitorio (Pza di) . BX 43
Nomentana (Via) . . . . DV 45
Parlemento (Pza del) . BX 46
Petroselli (Via L.) . . . . CY 47
Pierleoni (L. dei) . . . . BY 48
Pta Cavalleggeri . . . . AX 49
Pta S. Giovanni (Pza) . DY 51
Principe Amedeo
  Savoia Aosta (Ponte) . AX 52
Ramni (V. dei) . . . . . . DX 53
Rinascimento (Cso d') . BX 54
Ripetta (V. di) . . . . . . BX 55
Rotonda (Pza d.) . . . . BX 56
S. Angelo (Ponte) . . . BX 57
S. Ignazio (Pza) . . . . . BX 58

S. Luigi dei
  Francesi (Pza) . . . . BX 59
S. Marco (Pza di) . . . . CY 60
S. Silvestro (Pza) . . . . CX 63
Sassia (L. in) . . . . AX 64
Scrofa (V. della) . . . . BX 65
Sistina (Via) . . . . CX 68
Spagna (Piazza di) . . . CX
Stamperia (V. della) . . CX 69
Teatro di
  Marcello (V. del) . . CY 73
Torre Argentina
  (Largo di) . . . . BY 74
Traforo (V. del) . . . . . CX 75
Tritone (Via del) CX
Tulliano (V. del) . . . . . CY 77
Umberto I (Ponte) . . . BX 79
Umiltà (Via) . . . . CX 80
Vaticano (L.) . . . . ABX 81
Vittorio
  Emanuele (Ponte) . AX 83
Vittorio Veneto (Via) . CX
Zanardelli (Via) . . . . . BX 85
4-Novembre (Via) . . . CXY 87
24-Maggio (Via) . . . . CX 88

304

San Paolo
Fuori le Mura

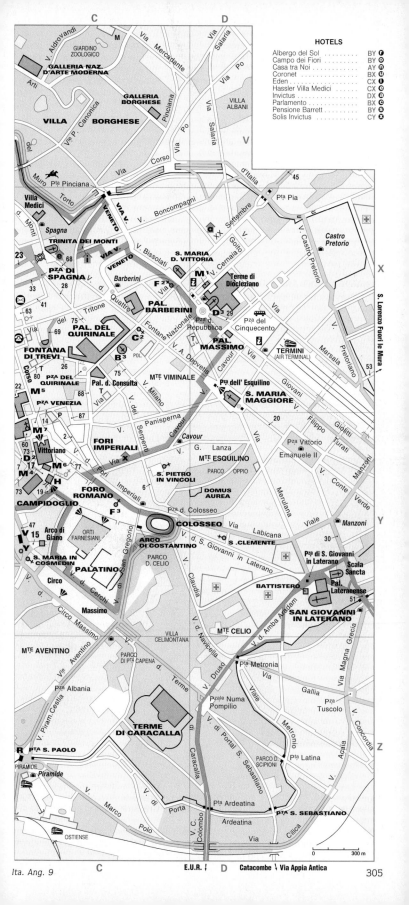

The **Palazzo Nuovo** (New Palace) (**CY M⁶**), built in 1655 by Girolamo Rainaldi, houses the **Museo Capitolino**★★ ⏱ which contains: the **equestrian statue of** *Marcus Aurelius*★★ (late 2C); the *Dying Gaul*★★★, a Roman sculpture based on a bronze of the Pergamum school (3C-2C BC) ; the Emperors' Room **(Sala degli Imperatori**★★**)** with portraits of all the emperors; the *Capitoline Venus*★★, a Roman work inspired by the Venus of Cnidus by Praxiteles; and the **Mosaic of the Doves**★★ from Hadrian's Villa at Tivoli.

The **Palazzo Senatorio**★★★ (**CY H**) is a 12C building, remodelled between 1582 and 1602 by Giacomo della Porta and Girolamo Rainaldi.

From Via del Campidoglio (**CY 19**) there is a beautiful **view**★★★ of the ruins.

★★★ Terme di CARACALLA ⏱ (CZ)

These baths built by Caracalla in AD 212 extend over more than 11 ha/27 acres and could take 1 600 bathers at a time. The main rooms (*caldarium, tepidarium* and *frigidarium*) occupy the middle part of the central section; the secondary rooms (vestibule, palestra and *laconicum*) are symetrically positioned at the sides. The ruined caldarium for the very hot bath, a circular room (34m/112ft in diameter), is the setting for operatic performances in summer.

★★★ CASTEL SANT'ANGELO ⏱ (ABX)

The imposing fortress was built in AD 135 as a mausoleum for the Emperor Hadrian and his family. In the 6C, Gregory the Great erected a chapel on top of the mausoleum to commemorate the apparition of an angel who, by putting his sword back into its sheath, announced the end of a plague. In the 15C Nicholas V added a brick storey to the ancient building and corner towers to the surrounding wall. Alexander VI (1492-1503) added octagonal bastions.

Castel Sant'Angelo

In 1527, during the sack of Rome, Clement VII took refuge in the castle and installed an apartment which was later embellished by Paul III; the **Popes' Apartment**★ stands isolated at the summit of the fortress and testifies to the graciousness of the popes' life style.

A long passageway (Il Passetto) links the fortress to the Vatican palaces. A fine spiral ramp dating from antiquity leads to the castle. From a terrace at the summit there is a splendid **panorama**★★★ of the whole town.

The Castel Sant'Angelo is linked to the left bank of the Tiber by the graceful **Ponte Sant'Angelo★** (BX 57), which is adorned with baroque angels carved by Bernini and with statues of Sts Peter and Paul (16C).

★★★ CATACOMBE (CATACOMBS)

There are numerous underground Christian cemeteries alongside the Via **Appia Antica**. In use from the 2C they were rediscovered in the 16C and 19C. They consist of long galleries radiating from an underground burial chamber *(hypogeum)* which belonged to a noble Roman family of the Christian faith. They permitted fellow Christians to use the galleries.

The decorations of the catacombs (carvings or paintings of symbolic motifs) are precious examples of early Christian art.

The visitor with little time to spare should visit the following ones:

Catacombe di San Callisto★★★ ⊙ along the Appian Way, famous for its exceptional collection of paintings.

Catacombe di San Sebastiano★★★ ⊙ along the Appian Way.

Catacombe di Domitilla★★★ ⊙ *entrance at no 282 Via delle Sette Chiese.*

★★★ COLOSSEO (COLISEUM ⊙ - CY)

This amphitheatre, inaugurated in AD 80, is also known as the Flavian Amphitheatre after its initiator, Vespasian, first of the Flavian emperors. With its three superimposed Classical orders (Doric, Ionic and Corinthian), it is a masterpiece of classical architecture. Fights between men and beasts, gladiatorial contests, races and mock naval battles took place in the arena.

Now an integral part of the Coliseum, the **arco di Constantino★★★** is an arch erected to commemorate Constantine's victory over Maxentius in AD 315. Some of the low reliefs were removed from other 2C monuments.

★★★ FORI IMPERIALI (IMPERIAL FORUMS - CY)

These were built by Caesar, Augustus, Trajan, Nerva and Vespasian. There are hardly any remains of the latter two. The Via dei Fori Imperiali, laid out in 1932 by Mussolini, divides the imperial forums.

Of Caesar's Forum (**Foro di Cesare★★** - *view from Via del Tulliano*) (CY 77) there remain three lovely columns from the Temple of Venus Genitrix. Of the Augustan Forum (**Foro di Augusto★★** - *view from Via Alessandrina*) (CY 2) there remain a few columns of the Temple of Mars the Avenger, vestiges of the stairway and of the wall enclosing the forum (behind the temple).

The forum is dominated by the House of the Knights of Rhodes (Casa dei Cavalieri di Rodi), built in the Middle Ages and rebuilt in the 15C amidst the ancient ruins.

All that remains of the largest and finest, Trajan's Forum (**Foro di Traiano★★★**), is Trajan's column (**Colonna Traiana★★★**) which depicts, in over 100 scenes, episodes of the war waged by Trajan against the Dacians. It is an unrivalled masterpiece. The markets (**Mercati Traianei★★★** ⊙ - *entrance in Via 4 Novembre* - CXY 87), which have kept their semicircular façade, were a distribution and supply centre. They comprised about 150 shops which were also retail outlets. The Tower of the Militia (**Torre delle Milizie★**) is part of a 13C fortress. It leans slightly as the result of an earthquake in the 14C.

★★★ FORO ROMANO (ROMAN FORUM ⊙ - CY)

The remains of the Roman Forum, the religious, political and commercial centre of ancient Rome, reflect the 12 centuries of history which created Roman civilisation. The forum was excavated in the 19C and 20C.

Take the Sacred Way, **Via Sacra★**, along which victorious generals marched in triumph to the **Curia★★**, rebuilt in the 3C by Diocletian. Senate meetings were held here; nowadays it houses Trajan's low reliefs (**Plutei di Traiano★★**), sculpted panels depicting scenes from the life of the Emperor, and sacrificial animals.

Nearby rises an imposing Triumphal Arch, **Arco di Settimio Severo★★**, built in AD 203 to commemorate the Emperor's victories over the Parthians. At the foot of the Capitol stood some remarkable monuments: the late 1C Temple of Vespasian (**Tempio di Vespasiano★★**) of which only three elegant Corinthian columns remain; the Temple of Saturn (**Tempio du Saturno★★★**) which retains eight 4C columns; and the **Portico of the Di Consentes★**, a colonnade of pillars with Corinthian columns dating back to restoration work of AD 367 - the portico was dedicated to the 12 principal Roman deities.

The Column of Phocas (**Colonna di Foca★**) was erected in AD 608 in honour of the Byzantine Emperor Phocas who presented the Pantheon to Boniface IV. The **Basilica Giulia★★**, which has five aisles, was built by Julius Caesar and completed by Augustus. It served as a law court and exchange.

PICTOR

The majestic ruins of the Forum seen from the Palatine Hill

Three beautiful columns with Corinthian capitals remain of the Temple of Castor and Pollux **(Tempio di Castore e Polluce★★★)**. The circular Temple of Vesta **(Tempio di Vesta★★★)** stands near the House of the Vestal Virgins **(Casa delle Vestali★★★)**. The Temple of Antoninus and Faustina **(Tempio di Antonino e Faustina★★)** was dedicated to the Emperor Antoninus Pius and his wife (note the fresco of grotesques and candelabra). The temple now houses the Church of San Lorenzo in Miranda rebuilt in the 17C.

The grandiose Basilica of Maxentius **(Basilica di Massenzio★★★)** was completed by the Emperor Constantine. The Triumphal Arch of Titus **(Arco di Tito★★)**, erected in 81, commemorates the capture of Jerusalem by this emperor, who only reigned for only two years.

★★★ PALATINO ⊙ (CY)

The Palatine Hill, where Romulus and Remus were discovered, was chosen by Domitian as the site for the Imperial Palace. The building included three main areas: the **Domus Flavia★** or official state apartments, the **Domus Augustana★★** or private imperial apartments, and the **Stadium★**. The House of Livia **(Casa di Livia★★)** probably belonged to Augustus (fine vestiges of paintings). The Farnese Gardens **(Orti Farnesiani)**, laid out in the 16C on the site of Tiberius' palace, afford **views★★** of the Forum and town.

Leave the Palatine by an exit alongside the Arch of Titus.

★ **Tempio di Venere e di Roma** (CY X) – The Temple of Venus and Rome built between 121 and 136 by Hadrian was the largest in the city (110m/361ft by 53m/174ft). It was unique in that it comprised two *cellae* with apses back to back. One was dedicated to the goddess of Rome and faced the Forum; the other was dedicated to Venus and faced the Coliseum.

★★★ Chiesa del GESÙ (BY)

The mother-church of the Jesuits in Rome, built by Vignola in 1568, is a typical building of the Counter-Reformation. On the outside, the engaged pillars replace the flat pilasters of the Renaissance, with light and shade effects and recesses. The interior, spacious and ideal for preaching, was lavishly decorated in the baroque style: on the dome, the **Baciccia frescoes★★** illustrate the *Triumph of the Name of Jesus* (1679); the **Cappella di Sant'Ignazio★★★** *(north transept)*, a chapel where the remains of St Ignatius Loyola rest, is the work (1696-1700) of the Jesuit Brother Andrea Pozzo and is sumptuously decorated.

★★★ PANTHEON ⏱ (BX)

The Pantheon, an ancient building perfectly preserved, founded by Agrippa in 27 BC and rebuilt by Hadrian (117-125), was a temple which was converted into a church in the 7C.

Access is through a porch supported by 16 single granite columns, all ancient except for three on the left. The doors are the original ones. The **interior★★★**, a masterpiece of harmony and majesty, is dominated by the **antique dome★★★**, the diameter of which is equal to its height. The side chapels, adorned with alternately curved and triangular pediments, contain the tombs of the kings of Italy and that of Raphael *(on the left)*.

The shadows and silence of the Pantheon contain centuries of history

★★ PIAZZA DEL POPOLO (BV)

The **Piazza del Popolo** was designed by Giuseppe Valadier (1762-1839). The **Porta del Popolo★** was pierced in the Aurelian wall in the 3C, and adorned with an external façade in the 16C and with an inner façade designed by Bernini in the 17C.

The Renaissance Church of **Santa Maria del Popolo★★** (BV E³) was remodelled in the Baroque period. It contains 15C **frescoes★** by Pinturicchio *(first chapel on the right)*; two **tombs★** by Andrea Sansovino *(in the chancel)*; two **paintings★★★** by **Caravaggio**: the *Crucifixion of St Peter* and the *Conversion of St Paul (first chapel to the left of the chancel)*; and the **Cappella Chigi★** *(2nd on the left)*, a chapel designed by Raphael. The Egyptian obelisk, which was brought to Rome in the reign of Augustus, was erected in the centre in the 16C by Pope Sixtus V.

Leading off the Piazza del Popolo is the main street of central Rome, **Via del Corso★★** (BCX), lined with handsome Renaissance palaces and fashionable shops.

Pincio (**BV**) – This fine public park was laid out in the 19C by Giuseppe Valadier. It affords a magnificent **view★★★** particularly at dusk when the golden glow so typical of Rome is at its mellow best.

Viale della Trinità dei Monti (**BCVX**) leads southwards and is overlooked by the **Villa Medici** (**CX**), now the home of the French Academy.

★★★ PIAZZA DI SPAGNA (CX)

This square, a popular tourist attraction, was so named in the 17C after the Spanish Embassy occupied the Palazzo di Spagna. It is dominated by the majestic Spanish Steps (**Scalinata della Trinità dei Monti★★★**) built in the 18C by the architects de Sanctis and Specchi, who adopted the baroque style of perspective and *trompe-l'œil*. At the foot of the stairway are the Boat Fountain (**Fontana della Barcaccia★**) by Bernini's father, Pietro (17C), and Keats' House where the poet died in 1821.

At the top of the stairs, Holy Trinity on the Hill (**chiesa della Trinità dei Monti★**) (**CX**) is the French church built in the 16C and restored in the 19C. It contains a *Deposition from the Cross★ (2nd chapel on the left)* dating from 1541 by Daniele da Volterra, a great admirer of Michelangelo.

Leading off from this square is **Via dei Condotti** (**BCX 23**) lined with elegant shops. It is also renowned for the Caffè Greco, a famous establishment which was opened in 1760 and frequented by celebrities (Goethe, Berlioz, Wagner, Stendhal etc).

★★★ PIAZZA NAVONA (BX)

The square built on the site of Domitian's stadium retains its shape. A pleasant and lively pedestrian precinct, it is adorned at the centre with Bernini's Baroque masterpiece, the Fountain of the Four Rivers (**Fontana dei Fiumi★★★**), completed in 1651. The statues represent the four rivers – Danube, Ganges, Rio de la Plata and Nile – symbolising the four corners of the earth.

Among the churches and palaces lining the square are **Sant'Agnese in Agone★★** (**BX B'**) with a baroque façade by Borromini (attractive **interior★** on the plan of a Greek cross), and the adjoining 17C **Palazzo Pamphili**.

★ PIAZZA VENEZIA (CY)

The Piazza in the centre of Rome is lined with palaces: Palazzo Venezia, Palazzo Bonaparte, where Napoleon's mother died in 1836, and the early 20C Palazzo delle Assicurazioni Generali di Venezia.

★ Palazzo Venezia ⊘ (**CY M'**) – This palace, built by Pope Paul II (1464-71), is one of the first Renaissance buildings. A **museum** ⊘, on the first floor, presents collections of medieval art (ivories, Byzantine and Limousin enamels, Italian Primitive paintings on wood, gold and silver work, ceramics and small bronzes (15C-17C).

The Basilica of St Mark (**Basilica di San Marco**), which was incorporated within the palace in the 15C, has a fine Renaissance **façade★** overlooking Piazza di San Marco (**CY 60**).

Monumento a Vittorio Emanuele II (Il Vittoriano) (**CY**) – This huge memorial by Giuseppe Sacconi, begun in 1885 in honour of the first king of a united Italy, Victor Emanuel II, overshadows the other monuments of Rome by its sheer size and dazzling white colour. It affords a **view★★** of the Eternal City.

★★★ SAN GIOVANNI IN LATERANO ⊘ (DY)

St John Lateran, the cathedral of Rome, is among the four major basilicas in Rome. The first basilica was founded by Constantine prior to St Peter's in the Vatican. It was rebuilt in the Baroque era by Borromini and again in the 18C.

The main façade by Alessandro Galilei dates from the 18C and the central door has bronze panels that originally belonged to the Curia of the Roman Forum (modified in the 17C). The vast and grandiose interior has a 16C **ceiling★★** which was restored in the 18C. In the nave the **Statues of the Apostles★** by pupils of Bernini stand in niches built by Borromini. The elegant **Cappella Corsini★** *(first in the north aisle)* was designed by Alessandro Galilei. The transept **ceiling★★** dates from the end of the 16C.

The Chapel of the Blessed Sacrament (**Cappella del SS Sacramento** – *north transept*) has fine ancient **columns★** in gilded bronze. The pretty cloisters (**chiostro★**) are the work of the Vassalletto (13C), marble-masons who were associates of the Cosmati *(see page 49)*. The baptistery (**Battistero★**), built in the 4C, is decorated with beautiful 5C and 7C mosaics.

In **Piazza di San Giovanni in Laterano** rises a 15C BC Egyptian obelisk, the tallest in Rome.

The Lateran Palace (**Palazzo Lateranense**), rebuilt in 1586, was the papal palace until the papal court returned from Avignon. The staircase, **Scala Sancta**, is a precious vestige from the medieval papal palace and is traditionally identified as the one Christ used in the palace of Pontius Pilate. Worshippers climb the stairs on their knees. At the top is the papal chapel (Sancta Sanctorum) with its many precious relics.

★★★ SANTA MARIA MAGGIORE ⊙ (DX)

It is one of the four major basilicas in Rome. It was built by Sixtus III (AD 432-440) and is dedicated to St Mary Major. It has since undergone extensive restoration. The campanile, erected in 1377, is the highest in Rome. The façade is the work of Ferdinando Fuga (1743-1750). The adjoining **loggia** ⊙ is decorated with **mosaics★** by Filippo Rusuti (end 13C), much restored in the 19C.

The impressive **interior★★★** contains remarkable **mosaics★★★**: in the nave, those above the entablature are among the most ancient Christian mosaics in Rome (5C) and depict scenes from the Old Testament; on the 5C trimphal arch are scenes from the New Testament; in the apse, the mosaics are composed of 5C elements but were completely redone in the 13C.

The coffered **ceiling★** is said to have been gilded with the first gold brought from Peru. The floor, the work of Cosmati (12C) was subject to much restoration in the 18C. The **Cappella di Sisto V** (south aisle) and the **Cappella Paolina** (north aisle) were both built in the form of a Greek cross and surmounted by a cupola. Another chapel was added at the end of the 16C and one in the 17C: they were richly decorated in the Baroque style. Sistus V, Pius V of Clemente and Paul V are buried here.

Leave the church by the door at the far end of the south aisle.

From **Piazza dell'Esquilino**, with its Egyptian obelisk, there is a **view★★** of the imposing 17C chevet.

★★★ SAN PAOLO FUORI LE MURA ⊙ (BZ)

Leave by Via Ostiense. Plan of the built-up area in the current Michelin Red Guide Italia.

One of the four major basilicas. It was built by Constantine in the 4C on the site of St Paul's tomb. It was rebuilt in the 19C, after it had been wholly destroyed by fire in 1823, on the original basilical plan of early Christian churches.

The impressive **interior★★★** contains: an 11C bronze door cast in Constantinople *(at the entrance of the first south aisle)*; and a Gothic **ciborium★★★** (1285) by Arnolfo di Cambio, placed on the high altar which stands above a marble plaque inscribed with the name Paul and dated 4C. In the Chapel of the Blessed Sacrament **(Cappella del SS. Sacramento★)** *(left of the chancel)* are: a 14C wooden figure of Christ attributed to Pietro Cavallini; a statue of St Brigitta kneeling, by Stefano Maderno (17C); a 14C or 15C statue of St Paul; and the **paschal candelabrum★★**, a 12C Romanesque work of art by the Vassalletto.

The cloisters **(chiostro★)** are also attributed, at least in part, to this same family of artists.

★★★ Fontana di TREVI (TREVI FOUNTAIN – CX)

This late-Baroque creation was commissioned from Nicola Salvi in 1762 by Pope Clement XIII. The central figure, the Ocean, rides in a chariot drawn by two sea-horses and two tritons.

Tourists continue the tradition of throwing two coins over their shoulders into the fountain – one coin to ensure their return to Rome and the other for the fulfilment of a wish.

VATICANO (VATICAN ⊙ – AX)

The Vatican City is bounded by a wall, overlooking Viale Vaticano, and to the east by the colonnade of St Peter's Square. This makes up the greater part of the Vatican state as laid down in 1929 in the Lateran Treaty. The Vatican City, now reduced to only 44 ha/109 acres and with less than a thousand inhabitants, stems from the Papal States, a donation made in the 8C by Pepin the Short to Pope Stephen II, and lost in 1870 when Italy was united into one Kingdom with Rome as its capital. The Vatican State, with the Pope as ruler, has its own flag and anthem; it prints stamps and mints its own coinage which is legal tender throughout Italy. In 1970, Pope Paul VI dissolved the armed forces, retaining only the Swiss Guard who wear a colourful uniform said to have been designed by Michelangelo.

The Pope, who is the Head of State, is also the Supreme Head of the Universal Church, and from this very small state, the spiritual influence of the church radiates throughout the world through the person of the Sovereign Pontiff. When the Pope is in residence, he grants public audiences **(udienza pubblica)** ⊙ on Wednesdays.

★★★ Giardini Vaticani ⊙ (AX) – The vast, magnificent gardens are adorned with fountains and statues, gifts from various countries. Of particular interest is the Casina of Pius IV, a fine 16C building decorated with stucco work and paintings. From the gardens are glorious views of the cupola.

★★★ PIAZZA DI SAN PIETRO (ST PETER'S SQUARE – AX)

This architectural masterpiece was begun in 1656 by Bernini, master of the Baroque. The two semicircles of the colonnade which adorn the square and frame the façade of the basilica form an ensemble of remarkable sobriety and majesty. At the centre of the square stands a 1C BC obelisk brought from Heliopolis in Egypt to Rome in AD 37 by order of Caligula. It was erected here in 1585 on the initiative of Sixtus V by Domenico Fontana. At the top is a relic of the Holy Cross.

★★★ Basilica di SAN PIETRO (ST PETER'S BASILICA ⊘ – AX)

Constantine, the first Christian Emperor, decided in AD 324 to build a basilica on the site where St Peter was buried after he had been martyred in Nero's circus. In the 15C it proved necessary to rebuild.

For two centuries, the plan of the new basilica was constantly revised. The plan, of a Greek cross surmounted by a dome designed by Bramante and adopted by Michelangelo, was altered to a Latin cross at the behest of Paul V in 1606, when he instructed Carlo Maderna to add two bays and a façade to Michelangelo's square plan. From 1629 onwards, the basilica was decorated in a sumptuous Baroque style by Bernini.

The façade (115m/377ft long and 45m/151ft high) was completed in 1614 by Carlo Maderna; it is surmounted by colossal figures, and masks the dome. In the centre is the balcony from which the Sovereign Pontiff gives his benediction *Urbi et Orbi* (to the City and the World).

Under the **porch**, the first door on the left has bronze panels carved by Giacomo Manzù (1964); the bronze central door dates from the Renaissance (1455); the door on the right or Holy Door is opened and closed by the Pope to mark the beginning and end of a Jubilee Year.

Inside, it is customary to approach the stoups in the nave which at first glance appear of normal size but are in fact huge. Such size emphasises the gigantic dimensions of the basilica, otherwise not apparent because of the harmony of its proportions. The length of St Peter's can be compared to that of other great basilicas throughout the world by means of markers inlaid in the pavement of the nave.

The first chapel on the right contains the *Pietà*★★★, the moving and powerful masterpiece carved by Michelangelo in 1499-1500, which shows his creative genius.

Basilica di San Pietro

In the right aisle, adjoining the Cappella del SS Sacramento, **Gregory XIII's Monument**★ is adorned with low reliefs illustrating the institution of the Gregorian calendar devised by that pope. Immediately beyond the right transept, **Clement XIII's Monument**★★★ is a fine neo-Classical design by Canova dating from 1792. The apse is dominated by St Peter's Throne **(Cattedra di San Pietro**★★★) by Bernini (1666), a great carved throne in bronze encasing a 4C episcopal chair but symbolically attributed to St Peter, and surmounted by a glory in gilded stucco.

In the chancel of the right is **Urban VIII's Monument**★★★, again by Bernini (1647), a masterpiece of funerary art. On the left stands **Paul III's Monument**★★★ by Guglielmo della Porta (16C), a disciple of Michelangelo.

St Leo the Great's Altar (chapel to the left of the chancel) has a fine Baroque **altarpiece**★ carved in high relief by Algardi. Nearby, **Alexander VII's Monument**★, characterised by extreme exuberance, is a late work by Bernini (1678) assisted by his pupils. The **baldaquin**★★★ which crowns the pontifical altar and is 29m/95ft tall (the height of the Farnese Palace) was strongly criticised: partly because the bronze had been taken from the Pantheon and partly because it was thought to be too theatrical and in bad taste. It does, however, fit in well with the overall architectural plan.

The **dome**★★★ designed by Michelangelo, which he himself built as far as the lantern, was completed in 1593 by Giacomo della Porta and Domenico Fontana. From the **summit** ⓥ (leave the basilica by the right aisle for access) there is a **view**★★★ of St Peter's Square, the Vatican City and Rome from the Janiculum to Monte Mario.

The 13C bronze **Statue of St Peter**★★ overlooking the nave is attributed to Arnolfo di Cambio and is greatly venerated by pilgrims, who come to kiss its feet.

Innocent VIII's Monument★★★ (between the second and third bays in the left aisle) is a Renaissance work (1498) by Antonio del Pollaiuolo. The **Stuart Monument** (between the first and second bays in the left aisle) carved by Canova is adorned with beautiful **angels**★ in low relief.

The Historical Museum **(Museo Storico**★ ⓥ) (entrance in the left aisle, opposite the Stuart Monument) has many treasured items including **Sixtus IV's tomb**★★★ (1493) by Pollaiuolo.

★★★ MUSEI VATICANI (VATICAN MUSEUMS ⊘ – AX)

Entrance: Viale Vaticano.

The museums of the Vatican occupy part of the palaces built by the popes from the 13C onwards, which have been extended and embellished to the present day.

These include on the first floor the **Museo Pio-Clementino★★★** (Greek and Roman antiquities) with its masterpieces: the ***Belvedere Torso★★★*** (1C BC), greatly admired by Michelangelo; the ***Venus of Cnidus★★***, a Roman copy of Praxiteles' Venus; the ***Laocoon Group★★★***, a 1C BC Hellenistic work; the ***Apollo Belvedere★★★***, a 2C Roman copy; ***Perseus★★***, a neo-Classical work by Canova, which was purchased by Pius VII; ***Hermes★★★***, a 2C Roman work inspired by the work of Praxiteles; and the ***Apoxyomenos★★★***, the athlete scraping his skin with a strigil after taking exercise, a 1C Roman copy of the Greek original by Lysippus.

The **Museo Etrusco★**, on the second floor, has a remarkable 7C BC gold **fibula★★** adorned with lions and ducklings in high relief *(Room II)* and the ***Mars★★*** found at Todi, a rare example of a large bronze statue from the 5C BC *(Room III)*.

The **Sala della Biga** derives its name from the **two-horse chariot** *(biga)*, a 1C Roman work reassembled in the 18C.

The four Raphael Rooms **(Stanze di Rafaello★★★)**, the private apartments of Julius II, were decorated by Raphael and his pupils from 1508 to 1517. The result is a pure Renaissance masterpiece. The frescoes are remarkable: the *Borgo Fire*, the *School of Athens*, *Parnassus*, the *Expulsion of Heliodorus from the Temple*, the *Miracle of the Bolsena Mass* and *St Peter delivered from prison*. The **Collezione d'Arte Moderna Religiosa★★** assembled by Pope Paul VI, is displayed in the apartment of Pope Alexander VI.

On the first floor the Sistine Chapel **(Cappella Sistina★★★)** is open to the public; its splendid vault, painted by Michelangelo from 1508 to 1512, illustrates the Bible, the Creation, the Flood and above the altar the Last Judgement which was added by the artist in 1534. The lowest sections of the side walls were decorated by Perugino, Pinturicchio and Botticelli. The Picture Gallery **(Pinacoteca★★★)** also contains some first-class works: three **compositions★★★** by **Raphael** (*The Coronation of the Virgin, The Madonna of Foligno* and *The Transfiguration* – Room VIII); ***St Jerome★★*** by Leonardo da Vinci *(Room IX)* and a **Descent from the Cross★★** by Caravaggio *(Room XII)*.

ADDITIONAL SIGHTS

Churches

★ **Chiesa Nuova (BX)** – This church dates from the Counter-Reformation. Alongside is the **Oratorio dei Filippini** with an elegant **façade★** by Borromini.

★★ **Sant'Andrea al Quirinale (CX B³)** – This masterpiece by Bernini has an elliptical **interior★★**.

★ **Sant'Andrea della Valle (BY C¹)** – This early-17C church has a **façade★★** by Rainaldi (17C) and a lovely **dome★★** by Carlo Maderna, painted by Lanfranco. Domenichino decorated the **apse★**.

★ **Sant'Agnese fuori le Mura** – *Take Via Nomentana* (DV).
A **mosaic★** adorns the apse. The Church of **Santa Costanza★**, originally a 4C mausoleum, also boasts a fine **mosaic★**.

★ **Sant'Agostino (BX B²)** – The church of St Augustine contains Jacopo Sansovino's **Madonna del Parto★**, Raphael's fresco of the **Prophet Isaiah★** and Caravaggio's **Madonna of the Pilgrims★★★**.

★★ **San Carlo alle Quattro Fontane (CX C²)** – Borromini's masterpiece with an intricate façade which reveals the torment of the architect, and an **interior★★** on an elliptical plan.

★ **Santa Cecilia in Trastevere** ⊘ **(BY)** – A much-altered 9C building. The statue of **St Cecilia★** (1599) is by Stefano Maderno and the **Last Judgement★★★** ⊘ (c 1293) is the work of Pietro Cavallini.

★★ **San Clemente (DY)** – The basilica is arranged over several levels. There are 12C **mosaics★★★** in the apse and **frescoes★** by Masolino.

★★ **Sant'Ignazio (BX C³)** – The façade and central ceiling **frescoes★★** are by the Jesuit, Andrea Pozzo.

★★ **San Lorenzo fuori Le Mura** – *Take Via dei Ramni* (DX **53**).
The basilica of St Lawrence Without the Walls dates from the 6C and the 13C: 5C-6C **harvest sarcophagus**, 13C **ambos★** and a 13C **papal throne★**.

** **San Luigi dei Francesi** (BX D¹) – This is the French church in Rome. It contains **frescoes**★ by Dominichino and **paintings**★★★ by Caravaggio.

** **Santa Maria degli Angeli** (DX D³) – This prestigious church was built amidst the ruins of Diocletian's baths. The **transept**★ gives a good idea of the solemn magnitude of the ancient building.

Santa Maria dell'Anima (BX E²) – One of Rome's rare Gothic interiors.

** **Santa Maria in Cosmedin** (CY) – Elegant 12C **campanile**★. In the porch is the **Bocca della Verità** (Mouth of Truth).

** **Santa Maria Sopra Minerva** (BX F¹) – The church has numerous works of art: **frescoes**★ by Filippino Lippi and both Gothic and Baroque **tombs**★.

* **Santa Maria della Pace** (BX E¹) – The four **Sibyls**★ are by Raphael.

** **Santa Maria in Trastevere** (BY) – 12C basilica with 12C-13C **mosaics**★★★ in the chancel.

Who will dare place a hand in the notorious Bocca della Verità?

** **Santa Maria della Vittoria** (CX) – This is Carlo Maderna's masterpiece. The sumptuous **interior**★★★ provides the setting for Bernini's *Ecstasy of St Theresa of Avila*★★★ (1652).

One of the greatest masterpieces of Baroque art:
The Ecstasy of St Theresa by Bernini

* **San Pietro in Montorio** (BY) – This 15C church has Sebastiano del Piombo's *Flagellation*★ and Bramante's **Tempietto**★ in the courtyard. **View**★★★ of Rome from the esplanade.

* **San Pietro in Vincoli** (CY) – The church of St Peter in chains contains Julius II's mausoleum and *Moses*★★★ by Michelangelo.

** **Santa Sabina** (BY) – This 5C building is one of Rome's oldest basilicas. Beautiful cypress wood **door**★★ (5C). The **interior**★★ is well proportioned and full of light.

** **Santa Susanna** (CX F²) – The 9C-16C church has a beautiful **façade**★★★ by **Carlo Maderna**.

Santi Cosma e Damiano (CY F³) – 5C church with a beautiful 16C coffered **ceiling**★ and 6C and 7C **mosaics**★.

Monuments from antiquity

★★ **Ara Pacis Augustae** (BX A) – The altar is the major work of the Augustan "golden age" and is decorated with magnificent **low-relief carvings**.

Arco di Giano (CY) – Through this public gateway, the Arch of Janus, passed some of Rome's busiest roads.

★★ **Area Sacra del Largo Argentina** (BY) – These ruins of four temples date from the days of the ancient Roman Republic.

Circo Massimo (CY) – This was the largest circus in Rome and was used exclusively for chariot races.

★★ **Domus Aurea** ⊘ – (in the grounds of Parco Oppio, CDY) – This was the luxurious residence erected by Nero after the fire of AD 64. The grotto-like underground rooms are decorated with geometric designs, grapes, faces and animals. These "grotesques" were a great source of inspiration to Renaissance artists.

Mausoleo di Augusto – Augustus' mausoleum takes the form of an Etruscan tumulus tomb.

★ **Piramide di Caio Cestio** (CZ R) – Rome's most original mausoleum was erected in the 12C BC by a rich citizen, Caius Cestius.

★★ **Teatro di Marcello** (BY T¹) – One of Rome's largest theatres, it was inaugurated by Augustus in the 11C BC.

★★ **Tempio di Apollo Sosiano** (BY W) – The temple was dedicated to Apollo medicus and retains three elegant fluted **columns**★★.

★ **Tempio della Fortuna Virile** (CY V) – This rectangular and austere temple dates from the late 2C BC.

★ **Tempio di Vesta** (CY Y) – An elegant circular construction dating from the Augustan period.

★ **Tomba di Cecilia Metella** (off the map, take the Via Appia Antica) (DZ) – A fine example of a noble woman's tomb.

Museums and palaces

★ **Galleria Nazionale d'Arte Moderna** ⊘ (CV) – The National Gallery of Modern Art contains Italian painting and sculpture from the 19C to the present day.

★★★ **Galleria Borghese** ⊘ (CV) – Sculptures by Canova and Bernini and paintings by Raphael, Correggio, Titian and Caravaggio.

★★★ **Museo Nazionale Romano** (DX) – The collections of this museum are currently housed in four separate locations: decorative arts from the Late-Republican and Imperial eras are in **Palazzo Massimo alle Terme**★★★ ⊘ (DX, behind Piazza del Cinquecento, entrance on Largo di Villa Peretti 1); the Boncompagni Ludovisi collection is housed in **Palazzo Altemps**★★★ ⊘ (BX M²) (to the right of Via Zanardello BX 85, entrance on Piazza S. Apollinare 44); the oldest part of the collection will be re-exhibited in the **Terme di Diocleziano**, (DX, in the group of buildings around the church of Santa Maria degli Angeli); the **Aula Ottagona**★★★ ⊘ (DX M¹) (entrance on Via G. Romita 8) is already open to the public.

★★★ **Museo Nazionale di Villa Giulia** ⊘ (BV) – Exceptional collection of antiquities relating to the Etruscan civilisation. The setting is Julius III's elegant country villa.

★★ **Palazzo Barberini** ⊘ (CX)

– This Baroque palace now houses a remarkable Art Gallery (**Galleria Nazionale di Arte Antica**★★) – paintings by Tintoretto, Caravaggio, Raphael, Titian, Quentin Metsys, Holbein etc.

★ **Palazzo Braschi** ⊘ (BX M³) – A late-18C papal family palace now housing a museum (**Museo di Roma**★) tracing the city's history from the Middle Ages to the present day.

★★ **Palazzo della Cancelleria** (BXY) – An elegant palace built from 1483 to 1513 with a harmonious inner courtyard.

Palazzo Chigi (BX N¹) – This 16C palace now belongs to the Presidency of the Council of Ministers.

Palazzo della Consulta (CX) – This palace with its **façade**★ by Ferdinando Fuga (18C) is now the seat of the Constitutional Court.

Palazzo Corsini ⊘ (ABY) – A 15C palace rebuilt in the 18C. A picture Gallery (**Galleria Nazionale di Pittura**) has paintings by Fra Angelico and Caravaggio among others.

★ **Palazzo Doria Pamphili** ⊘ (CX M⁵) – A handsome 16C palace with a **collection**★★ of paintings by Caravaggio, Velasquez, the Carracci etc.

★★ **Palazzo Farnese** (BY) – *(Not open to the public).* Now the French Embassy, Palazzo Farnese was built from 1515 by several architects: Antonio da Sangallo the Younger, Michelangelo (who designed the upper cornice of the façade, the Farnese coat of arms above the central balcony and the second floor of the inner court), Vignola who collaborated on the inner court and built the palace's rear façade, and Giacomo della Porta who designed the loggia of the same façade.

Palazzo Madama (BX N³) – A 16C palace now the seat of the Senate.

Palazzo di Montecitorio (BX) – This 17C palace houses the Chamber of Deputies.

★★ **Palazzo del Quirinale** (CX) – This handsome 16C palace was designed as a summer residence for the popes and is now the official residence of the President of the Republic.

Palazzo della Sapienza (BX N²) – A 16C palace with Borromini's masterpiece, the Church of **Sant'Ivo**★ with its bell-tower, in the inner courtyard.

★ **Palazzo Spada** ⊘ (BY) – The **Galleria di Pittura**★ presents the private collection of the 17C churchman, Cardinal Spada.

★★ **Villa Farnesina** ⊘ (ABY) – This villa was built from 1508 to 1511 for Agostino Chigi who commissioned Raphael and his pupils to decorate the interior.

Squares, streets, sites, parks and gardens

★ **Piazza Bocca della Verità** (CY 15) – A combination of ancient (Arco di Giano, Tempio della Fortuna Virilis and Tempio Totondo known as the Tempio di Vesta), medieval (Santa Maria in Cosmedin) and Baroque buildings, makes a typical Roman scene.

★ **Campo dei Fiori** (BY) – This well-known square and one of the most popular in Rome is the site of a picturesque food market held every morning.

★ **Piazza Colonna** (BX) – At the centre of this busy square stands the 2C **column**★ in honour of Marcus Aurelius.

★★ **Piazza del Quirinale** (CX) – This elegant and gently-sloping square is adorned with a fountain, an obelisk, statues of the Dioscuri and is overlooked by the Palazzo del Quirinale and Palazzo della Consulta *(above).*

★ **Piazza Sant'Ignazio** (BX 58) – This charming square was designed in imitation of a theatre stage.

★ **Porta San Paolo** (CZ) – This gate opens onto Via Ostiense which led to St Paul's Basilica, from which the gate took its present name.

★ **Porta San Sebastiano** (DZ) – This is Rome's most spectacular gate, in honour of St Sebastian (3C).

★ **Via dei Coronari** (BX 25) – This attractive street known for its second-hand and antique shops is lined with palaces glowing in ochre and stone.

★★ **EUR** – *Take Via Cristoforo Colombo* (DZ) *Town plan on Michelin map 430.* This new district (1939) to the south of Rome with its colossal modern architecture is the site of the Museum of Roman Civilisation (**Museo della Civiltà Romana**★★ ⊘).

★ **Isola Tiberina** (BY) – This peaceful spot, the Tiber Island, is linked to the bank by the Fabrician Bridge (**Ponte Fabricio**) (BY 31), the only Roman bridge to survive intact.

Gianicolo (AY) – This attractive promenade affords extensive **views**★★★ over the city.

★★ **Villa Borghese** (CV) – This is Rome's largest public park.

Roman historians generally counted the years as from the foundation of Rome (Ab Urbe Condita). The system of counting from the birth of Christ (AD) was introduced in the 6C by Dionysius Exiguus, a Scythian monk.

SABBIONETA ★

Lombardy
Population 4 438
Michelin map 428 or 429 H 13

The town was built from 1558 by Vespasiano Gonzaga (1531-91), a mercenary leader in the service of Philip II of Spain who conferred on his loyal servants the glorious order of the Golden Fleece. The order was created in 1429 by Philip the Good, Duke of Burgundy. Vespasiano was a cultured man and he wanted to take charge of the building of his ideal town.

★ **Town** ⊘ – Its hexagonal walls, star plan and monuments make Sabbioneta a jewel of Italian Mannerism.
The Garden Palace (**Palazzo del Giardino**) was designed for festivities and its walls and ceilings were richly painted with frescoes by Bernardino Campi and his school. The great **Galleria** (96m/315ft long) is one of the longest Renaissance galleries.

The Olympic Theatre (Teatro Olimpico★), a masterpiece by Vicentino Scamozzi (1552-1616), was built from 1588 to 1590 and is one of the oldest covered theatres in Europe. The interior is decorated with frescoes by the school of Veronese and there is a ducal box adorned with colonnades and statues of the gods.

The Ducal Palace (Palazzo Ducale), has finely-carved wooden and coffered ceilings. There are interesting equestrian statues of the Gonzaga family. The Galleria degli Antenati is also noteworthy.

Vespasiano Gonzaga is buried in the Chiesa dell'Incoronata with its octagonal plan and dome. Vespasiano's mausoleum is adorned with a bronze statue by Leone Leoni (1509-90); he is depicted as Marcus Aurelius.

The Museo d'Arte Sacra displays the Golden Fleece discovered in 1988 in Vespasiano's tomb (see above) in the church.

The 19C Synagogue (Sinagoga) traces the story of the town's Jewish community whose great legacy was the elegant printworks also used by Vespasiano.

SALERNO★

Campania
Population 142 658
Michelin map 431 E-F 26
Local map see AMALFI

Salerno was at first Etruscan, then Roman and became a principality under the Lombards. The Norman Robert Guiscard made it his capital in 1077. A rich trading city, Salerno became famous for its university, which attracted some of the greatest scholars of the time, and in particular its school of medicine (also open to women) which flourished from the 11C to 13C. The town acquired the nickname of City of Socrates. With the arrival of the Kings of Anjou the city declined and witnessed the rise of its neighbour and rival, Naples. It was just south of Salerno that the 5th US Army landed on 9 September 1943.

Traffic restricted in town centre

Abate Coforti (Largo)	AB 2	Paglia (Via M.)	B 13	Sedile di Pta Nuova (Pza)	B 24
Alfano I (Piazza)	B 3	Plebiscito (Largo)	B 14	Sorgente (Via Camillo)	B 25
Cavaliero (Via L.)	B 4	Portacatena (Via)	A 15	Velia (Via)	B 26
Cilento (Via A.)	B 6	Porta di Mare (Via)	A 16	Vittorio Emanuele (Corso)	B
Dogana Vecchia (Via)	A 7	Sabatini (Via A.)	A 19	24 Maggio (Piazza)	B 27
Duomo (Via)	B 8	S. Eremita (Via)	B 20		
Indipendenza (Via)	A 9	S. Tommaso d'Aquino			
Lista (Via Stanislas)	A 10	(Largo)	B 22	Arco di Arechi	A A
Luciani (Piazza M.)	A 12	Sedile del Campo		Museo Archeologico	B M¹
Mercanti (Via)	AB	(Largo)	A 23		

Salerno, lying along the graceful curve of its gulf, has retained a medieval quarter on the slopes of a hill crowned by a castle. From the **Lungomare Trieste★** promenade, planted with palm trees and tamarinds, there is a wide view of the Gulf of Salerno.

★★ Duomo ⊘ (**B**) – The cathedral is dedicated to St Matthew the Evangelist, who is buried in the crypt. It was built on the orders of Robert Guiscard and consecrated by Pope Gregory VII in 1085. The Norman-style building was remodelled in the 18C and suffered considerable damage in the 1980 earthquake. The church is preceded by a delightful arcaded **atrium** built of multicoloured stone with ancient columns. The square tower to the right is 12C. The central doorway has 11C **bronze doors★** cast in Constantinople.

The interior is of impressive dimensions. The two **ambos★★** encrusted with decorative mosaics and resting on slender columns with marvellously-carved capitals, along with the **paschal candelabrum** and the elegant iconostasis which encloses the chancel, form an outstanding 12C-13C group. The Crusaders' Chapel at the far end of the south aisle is where the Crusaders had their arms blessed. Under the altar is the tomb of Pope Gregory VII who died in exile at Salerno (1085).

In the north aisle stands the tomb of Margaret of Durazzo, the wife of Charles III of Anjou.

Museo Archeologico ⊘ (**BM¹**) – Housed in the attractive St Benedict monastery complex, the museum has artefacts dating from pre-history to the Late Imperial Era. Of particular note is the bronze **Head of Apollo★** (1C BC) and a fine collection of pre-Roman amber.

★ Via Mercanti – This street is one of the most picturesque with its shops, old houses and oratories. At its west end stands an arch, **Arco di Arechi** (**A A**) built by the Lombards in the 8C.

SALUZZO

Piedmont

Population 15 680
Michelin map 428 I4

This pretty town, situated on the slopes of a hill, has an imposing castle at the heart of its Medieval buildings. From the 12C-16C Saluzzo was the seat of a powerful marquisate making it a prosperous centre of art and culture.

Take a pleasant stroll around the narrow streets with their stone stairways or have a glance at the shops selling antiques, woodwork and wrought iron.

Saluzzo was the birthplace of the patriot and writer **Silvio Pellico** (1789-1854), author of *My Prisons (a museum in currently being set up in the house where Pellico was born)* and General Alberto Dalla Chiesa (1920-1982).

★ Casa Cavassa ⊘ – The fine Renaissance portal of this elegant 15C house is surmounted by the motto *"droit quoy qu'il soit"* (forward at all costs) and by the emblem of the Cavassa family, a fish swimming upstream (in the dialect of Lyon, fish is *chavasse*). The gallery of the beautiful panoramic loggia is adorned with a *grisaille* decoration depicting the *Labours of Hercules* by the Flemish-Burgundian artist Hans Clemer. The various rooms which open on to the loggia have all preserved their original Renaissance furnishings and a splendid altarpiece, *Madonna della Misericordia★*, also by Hans Clemer, which is surrounded by fine 15C choir stalls.

S. Giovanni ⊘ – The austere façade of this 14C church conceals a rich interior. In the north aisle there is a fine cycle of 15C **frescoes★** with scenes from the life of Christ framed by views of the city and lively groups of figures. The masterpiece of the church is the extraordinary **apse★★**, a jewel of Burgundian Gothic art, "embroidered" in green Sampeyre stone. The niche on the left houses the **Tomb of Ludovic II**, by Benedetto Briosco (master builder of the Charterhouse of Pavia after Amedeo). The niche on the right was to have housed the tomb of Ludovic's wife, Margherita di Foix, who was ultimately buried in Spain (note the corbel in the left hand corner with the strange figure of a prophet wearing glasses). From the north aisle make for the cloisters and the chapter-house with the **Mausoleum of Galeazzo Cavassa**.

Near the church, on the other side of the square, stands the **Torre Civica** ⊘, erected by Marquess Ludovic I in the 15C. The effort required to reach the top of the tower is made up for by the fine **view★** at the top.

EXCURSIONS

★ **Abbazia di Staffarda** ⊙ – *10km/6mi north on the S 589*. This imposing monastery was erected by Cistercian monks in the 12C-13C in the Romanesque-Gothic style and constituted an important economic centre that hosted fairs and markets. The guest rooms on the right after the entrance have a fine Gothic refectory and a little beyond, to the left, is the 13C Loggia del Mercato. Opposite, from the long building which housed the lay brothers, make for the **cloisters**. At the end of the monastery buildings, on the right, stands the **church**, preceded by a portico. The solemn austerity of the interior, whose only decorative motif consists of the contrast formed between the red bricks and the white stone, is given movement by an asymmetry which seems to allude to the imperfection of Man. In the apse you may feel you are being watched by the slightly perplexed gaze of the sun's face on the vaulting (15C).

On the street leading up to the abbey note the fine **apse complex**.

Castello della Manta ⊙ – *4km/2.5mi south on the S 589*. This 12C stronghold was turned into an aristocratic residence in the 15C by Valerano, son of Tommaso III, Marquess of Saluzzo. The splendid **frescoes★★★** in the Baronial Room (first half of the 15C), with all the taste and decorative elegance of the International Gothic Style, depict the *Procession of Heroes and Heroines*. The characters portrayed derive from the courtly poem *The Wandering Knight*, written by Tommaso III. There is also a lively representation of the allegory of the Fountain of Youth.

On the return journey a short detour to **Savigliano** (*13km/20mi east of Saluzzo on the P 7*) is recommended. Note the atmospheric **Piazza Santarosa★**, bordered by Renaissance and Medieval buildings.

THE LANGHE

From Bra to Alba, a 90km/56-mile itinerary.

The Tanaro and Bormida di Spigno rivers mark the borders of this region of limestone hills, notable for its pointed peaks and deep valleys which have been carved out by torrents. The hill peaks are covered in vineyards which produce prized wines such as Barolo and Nebbiolo. Other typical products include the famous white truffles from Alba and hazelnuts. Specialities of this region can be tasted in the numerous wine bars (*enoteche*). This route starts from Bra and, passing through La Morra, Monforte, Dogliani, Belvedere Langhe, Bossolasco, Serralunga d'Alba and Grinzane Cavour, finally reaches Alba. The landscape is dominated by castles and vineyards and affords splendid panoramic **views★**. The castle at Grinzane Cavour has hosted the literary prize of the same name since 1982.

Alba – Alba was the ancient Roman city of Alba Pompeia, the birthplace of the Roman Emperor Pertinax (AD 126-193). It is a gourmet centre famous for its delicious **tartufi bianchi** or white truffles (annual truffle fair in autumn) and its wines.

Priceless mushrooms

White truffles are an underground mushroom tuber which grow in symbiosis with the roots of oaks, willows or poplars in damp, clay soil which has little exposure to the sun. They are mainly composed of water and mineral salts which are absorbed through the roots of the trees. They are hunted out by "trifolai" (from "trifola", a dialect word for truffle), accompanied by highly trained dogs who have to find the truffles without damaging them.

The town boasts several **feudal towers**, churches and medieval houses. Inside the Gothic cathedral dedicated to St Lawrence **(Duomo)** are Renaissance choir stalls inlaid with intarsia work of very delicate craftsmanship.

THE GREEN GUIDE covers the world's great cities:

New York, London, Paris, Rome, Brussels, Berlin, Vienna, Washington DC, San Francisco, Chicago, Venice, Amsterdam

SAN GIMIGNANO★★★

Tuscany
Population 7 042
Michelin map 430 L 15
See The Green Guide to Tuscany

San Gimignano with its many medieval towers stands on a hilltop in the rolling Tuscan countryside where vineyards and olive groves flourish. Its numerous Medieval towers have earned it the nickname of San Gimignano dalle belle torri (of the Fine Towers).

In the 12C the town was an independent commune and it prospered during the next 200 years. The towers of nobility were thought for a long time to have been built for defensive purposes, and as a sign of the power of the noble families who were split in the internecine fighting between the Ghibellines and the Guelphs. The former supported the emperor and the latter the pope.

The holes in the walls served to fix gangways between the towers of allied nobles, enabling them to meet quickly in times of danger. A simpler explanation may be that the towers were linked to the town's past economic success. In the Middle Ages it was an important textile centre which guarded the secret of yellow saffron dye, and to protect the precious cloth (the length determined the value) from the sun and dust, the wealthy manufacturers were forced to build the tall towers as they had no room to spread it out on a flat surface, owing to the town plan. The stairways were fixed on the outside, in holes which are still to be seen, so as not to waste any space inside.

★★ **Piazza della Cisterna** – The square is paved with bricks laid on their edges in a herring-bone pattern and it derives its name from a 13C cistern or well (cisterna). It is one of the most evocative squares in Italy with its tall towers and austere 13C-14C mansions all around.

★★ **Piazza del Duomo** – The Collegiate Church, palaces and seven towers of nobility line this majestic square.

Collegiata di Santa Maria Assunta ⊙ – This 12C Romanesque Church was extended in the 15C by Giuliano da Maiano. The façade was restored in the 19C. Inside are a *Martyrdom of St Sebastian* (1465) by Benozzo Gozzoli and an *Annunciation* in wood by Jacopo della Quercia *(west wall)*.

The walls of the left aisle are adorned with **frescoes★** evoking scenes from the Old Testament by Bartolo di Fredi (14C), while the **frescoes★★** (c 1350) of the right aisle are by Barna da Siena and depict scenes from the Life of Christ *(start at the top)*. They display an elegant draughtsmanship and delicate colours. In the **Cappella di Santa Fina** ⊙ (railings) designed by Giuliano da Maiano, the harmonious **altar★** is by his nephew Benedetto da Maiano and the **frescoes★** (1475) by Domenico Ghirlandaio.

Along the left side aisle of the collegiate church is the charming little **Piazza Pecori**. Beneath a portico is a lovely statue of the *Annunciation* by Ghirlandaio.

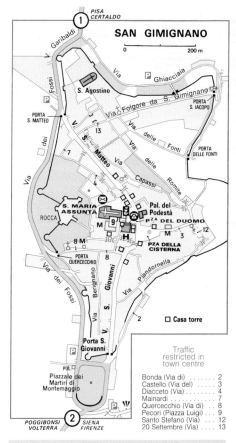

Casa torre

Traffic restricted in town centre

Bonda (Via di) 2
Castello (Via del) 3
Diacceto (Via) 4
Mainardi 7
Quercecchio (Via di) . . 8
Pecori (Piazza Luigi) . . . 9
Santo Stefano (Via) . . . 12
20 Settembre (Via) 13

Palazzo del Popolo (Municipio) **H**

321

Palazzo del Popolo ⏱ **(H)** – The 13C-14C Town Hall is dominated by a tall **tower**, from the top of which unfolds an unusual **view**★★ over the brown roofs and towers of the town. The Council Chamber has a remarkable *Maestà*★ (Madonna and Child enthroned in Majesty) (1317) by Lippo Memmi, which was restored c 1467 by Benozzo Gozzoli. A museum **(Museo Civico**★**)** on the second floor presents paintings from the 12C to 15C Florentine and Sienese schools.

Palazzo del Podestà – This 13C Governor's Palace has a vast porch on the ground floor. It also comprises an impressive tower (51m/167ft high) known as the Torre Rognosa. Close by stands the 13C Palazzo Chigi.

Sant'Agostino – This 13C church has in its chancel a cycle of 17 **frescoes**★★ painted from 1463 to 1467 by Benozzo Gozzoli. The life of the famous theologian St Augustine is depicted with the fresh colour, sense of perspective and love of detail typical of this artist. Near the west door stands the **tomb**★ of St Bartolo by Benedetto da Maiano (15C).

San Gimignano wears a "crown of towers"

EXCURSIONS

★★ **Volterra** – *29km/18mi southeast. See VOLTERRA.*

★ **San Vivaldo** ⏱ – *17km/10mi northwest. Leave by* ①. In 1500 Franciscan monks settled here to honour the body of St Vivaldo who died here in 1320. During the next 15 years they built a monastery and a series of chapels (17 are still extant) recreating the holy places of Jerusalem in miniature. The chapels of the **sacro monte** contain painted terracottas which depict nearly-to-scale scenes ranging from the Passion to Whitsuntide.

Certaldo – *13km/8mi north.* It was in this village, in the wooded Elsa Valley, that **Giovanni Boccaccio** (1312-75) spent the last years of his life. Along with Dante and Petrarch, he was one of the three great Italian writers.
In the upper town are the **Casa del Boccaccio** ⏱, now converted into a museum, the Church of San Jacopo where the writer is buried and the **Palazzo Pretorio** ⏱, which was rebuilt in the 16C.

Consult the Places to Stay map at the beginning of this guide to select the a stopover or holiday destination. The map offers the following categories:
Short holidays
Weekend breaks
Overnight stops
Resorts
Depending on the region, this map also shows marinas, ski areas, spas, centres for mountain expeditions, etc.

Repubblica di SAN MARINO ★

SAN MARINO REPUBLIC

Population 25 515
Michelin map 429 or 430 K 19
Town plan in the Michelin Atlas Italy

One of the smallest states in the world (61km²/23sqmi), San Marino stands in an admirable **site★★★** on the slopes of the jagged sandstone ridge of Monte Titano. This ancient republic strikes its own coinage, issues its own postage stamps and has its own army and police force.

San Marino is believed to have been founded in the 4C by a pious mason, Marinus, who was fleeing from the persecutions of the Emperor Diocletian. The system of government has changed little in nine centuries, and the leading figures are still the two Captains Regent, who are chosen from among the 60 members of the Grand Council and installed every six months during a colourful ceremony (see the Calendar of Events at the end of the guide). The economy is based on tourism, trade, the sale of postage stamps, craft industries and agriculture. San Marino produces a very pleasant wine, Moscato.

Palazzo Pubblico Ⓥ – *Piazza della Libertà*. Government House was rebuilt in the Gothic style in the late 19C. The Great Council Chamber is open to visitors.

Basilica di S. Marino – *Piazzale Domus Plebis*. The basilica contains the relics of St Marinus.

In the nearby Church of San Pietro there are two niches hewn in the rock, in which St Marinus and his companion St Leo are said to have slept.

Rocca Guaita; Rocca Cesta or della Fratta; Rocca Montale – These three peaks are crowned with three towers *(torri)* which are linked by a watchpath. From the towers there are splendid **views★★★** of the Apennines, the plain, Rimini and the sea as far as the Dalmatian coast. In the Torre Cesta there is a museum, **Museo delle Armi Antiche** Ⓥ, with a collection of 12C to late-medieval arms. It also features gunpowder firearms, as well as guns and rifles dating from the 16C, 17C and 18C.

Museo-Pinacoteca di San Francesco Ⓥ – 12C to 17C and modern paintings (20C) as well as Etruscan pottery and funerary objects.

Museo Filatelico e Numismatico Ⓥ – *At Borgo Maggiore*. Collection of stamps and coins issued by the Republic since the mid-19C.

EXCURSION

★★ **San Leo** – *16km/10mi southwest. Leave to the north then take the road to the left leading down to the Marecchia Valley. Just before Pietracuta and the S 258 bear left.*

A steep winding road climbs to the summit of the huge limestone rock (alt 639m/2 096ft) in an impressive **setting★★**, made famous by Dante in his *Divine Comedy*, with the historic village of San Leo and its 15C fortress **(Forte★)**, designed by Francesco di Giorgio Martini, where the charlatan Count Cagliostro (18C) was imprisoned and died. From the fortress, which houses a **museum** Ⓥ, there is an immense **panorama★★★** of the Marecchia Valley, Montefeltro and San Marino.

The cathedral, which is in the Lombard-Romanesque style (1173), and the pre-Romanesque parish church (restored) are noteworthy. The 16C Palazzo Mediceo (*Piazza Dante Alighieri 14*) houses the **Museo di Arte Sacra** Ⓥ, with works from the 14C-18C.

SAN REMO ♨♨

Liguria

Population 56 168
Michelin map 428 K 5 – Town plan in the Michelin Atlas Italy
Local map see La RIVIERA

San Remo curves round its wide bay protected by two headlands, and is backed by a rim of mountains. The luxurious capital of the Riviera di Ponente enjoys a pleasantly warm temperature all the year round and the highest number of sunshine hours on the Ligurian coast. In addition to these advantages San Remo boasts a wide choice of hotels, thermal establishments, a pleasure boat harbour, casino, racecourse, lively festivals and other cultural and sporting events.

San Remo is the main Italian flower market and millions of roses, carnations and mimosa are exported worldwide. The flower market takes place from October to June from 6 to 8am.

Corso Imperatrice – It is Liguria's most elegant seafront promenade and it is particularly known for its Canary palms.

★ **La Pigna** – This is the name given to the old town, because of its pointed shape (*pigna* meaning beak). It has a medieval aspect with its winding alleys lined with tall and narrow houses. From Piazza Castello climb up to the baroque Church of Madonna della Costa, from where there is an attractive **view★** of the town and bay.

EXCURSIONS

★★ **Monte Bignone** – Alt 1 299m/4 262ft. *13km/8mi to the north.*
From the summit of this pine-covered peak there is a splendid **panorama**★★ which
extends as far as Cannes in France.

Bussana Vecchia – *Take the road to Arma di Taggia and turn into a road just
beyond San Remo.* The medieval fortified village was destroyed by an earthquake
in 1887 and was deserted until the 1960s, when some artists, mostly foreigners,
set about restoring the houses and moved in. At first somewhat reserved and
solitary, they eventually opened up shops selling their work and crafts.

SANSEPOLCRO★

Tuscany
Population 15 664
Michelin map 430 L 18
See The Green Guide to Tuscany

This small industrial town (famous for its pasta) still has its old town walls and
numerous **old houses**★ dating from the Middle Ages up to the 18C, a reminder of its
early, but long-lasting, prosperity. The finest streets are the **via XX Settembre** and the
via Matteotti where there is also an austere Romanesque-Gothic cathedral. However,
Sansepolcro's main claim to fame is the birth here in c 1415 of the most important
artist of the Italian Quattrocento (15C), **Piero della Francesca**. *See the Calendar of Events
at the end of the guide.*

★★ **Museo Civico** ⊙ – *65 via Aggiunti.* The most interesting exhibits in the
municipal museum are the admirable **paintings**★★★ by **Piero della Francesca**: his
Resurrection (an impressive example of a mature style of art), the beautiful
polyptych of the *Virgin of Mercy* and two fragments of frescoes, one of *St Julian*
and the other of *St Ludovic.* The museum also has works by Bassano, Signorelli,
and the Della Robbia School, as well as etchings and a few pieces of church
plate. From the upper floor, there is a beautiful view of the via Matteotti and
fragments of frescoes and sinopies (red chalk drawings) (14C). The basement
contains sculptures and architectural ornamentation dating from the 13C to the
18C.

San Lorenzo – The church, dedicated to St Lawrence, contains a superb *Descent
from the Cross*★ by the Mannerist artist Rosso Fiorentino.

S. Chirol

The castle of Poppi

EXCURSIONS

★★ **Camaldoli** – *76km/47mi northwest.* Camaldoli, situated in a great forest in the heart of the mountains, was the cradle of the Camaldulian Order, founded in the 11C by St Romuald. The monastery, standing at the head of an austere valley, was rebuilt in the 13C. Higher up in a grim, isolated site is the Hermitage (**Eremo★**), a cluster of buildings encircled by ramparts. These include St Romuald's cell and a fine 18C church.

★ **Convento della Verna** – *36km/22mi northwest.* The monastery, pleasantly situated, was founded in 1213 and it was here that St Francis of Assisi received the Stigmata. The visitor can see the Chapel of the Stigmata, St Francis' sleeping place and the enormous projecting rock under which he used to pray. The basilica and the small church of Santa Maria degli Angeli are adorned with terracottas by Andrea della Robbia.

★ **Poppi** – *61km/38mi northwest.* This proud and attractive city, formerly the capital of the Casentino, overlooks the Arno Valley. The city itself is crowned by its proud-looking castle (**castello★** ⊙), former seat of the Counts of Guidi. This 13C Gothic palace has a curious **courtyard★** decorated with coats of arms.

Monterchi – *17km/11mi south.* The cemetery chapel has a strange but compelling work by Piero della Francesca, the *Madonna del Parto★*, which has been detached and placed above the altar. This is a rare depiction of the pregnant Virgin in Italian art.

SIENA★★★

Tuscany
Population 54 668
Michelin map 430 M 15-16
See The Green Guide to Tuscany

Siena "the Beloved" is a mystical, gentle, passionate and generous art centre. Siena invites the visitor to stroll through its narrow Gothic streets, lined with palaces and patrician mansions, which converge on the famous Piazza del Campo. It is encircled by massive ramparts.
More than anywhere else Siena conveys the aspect of a medieval city. Its plan extends over three converging red clay hills (from which the colour "burnt sienna" is named) at the very heart of the high Tuscan plateau.
For those wishing to visit the town in more detail, we recommend **The Green Guide** to **Tuscany**.

HISTORICAL NOTES

Siena's greatest period of prosperity was the 13C-14C, when it was an independent republic with a well-organised administration of its own. It flourished essentially on trade and banking. During the Guelphs versus Ghibellines conflict, Siena was opposed to its powerful neighbour Florence. One of the most memorable episodes of this long struggle was the Battle of Montaperti (1260), when the Sienese Ghibellines resoundingly defeated the Florentine Guelphs. During this troubled time Siena acquired her most prestigious buildings, and a local school of painting evolved which played a notable part in the development of Italian art.
In 1348 the plague decimated Siena's population and the city began to decline as dissension continued to reign among the rival factions. By the early 15C Siena's golden era was over.
The mystical city of Siena was the birthplace in 1347 of **St Catherine**. By the age of seven, it seems, she had decided on her spiritual marriage with Christ. She entered the Dominican Order aged 16 and had many visions and trances throughout her life. She is said to have received the Stigmata at Pisa. In 1377 she helped to bring the popes back from Avignon to Rome, which they had left in 1309. **St Bernardine** (1380-1444) is also greatly venerated in Siena. He gave up his studies to help the victims of the plague in the city. At the age of 22, he entered the Franciscan order and was a leader of the Observants, who favoured a stricter observance of the rule of St Francis. A great preacher, he spent much of his time travelling throughout Italy.

SIENESE ART

It was not only in political matters that Siena opposed Florence. In this, Dante's city, Cimabue and Giotto were innovators, but were greatly influenced by the Roman traditions of balance and realism which led to the development of Renaissance art in all its glory. Siena, on the other hand, remained attached to the Greek or Byzantine traditions, in which the graceful line and the refinement of colour gave a certain dazzling elegance to the composition, which was one of the chief attractions of Gothic painting.

Duccio di Buoninsegna (c 1255-1318/19) was the first to experiment with this new combination of inner spirituality and increased attention to space and composition as well as the splendour of the colours.

Simone Martini (c 1284-d 1344 in Avignon) followed in Duccio's footsteps but imitated nature more closely with his exquisite harmonies of colour and taste for detail. He had a considerable reputation in Europe and worked at the Papal Court in Avignon. His contemporaries **Pietro** and **Ambrogio Lorenzetti** introduced an even greater realism with minute delicate details, while at the same time remaining true to the sense of line of their predecessors. One of the favourite themes of the Sienese school was the Virgin and Child.

The Sienese artists of the Quattrocento (15C) continued in the spirit of the Gothic masters. While Florence concentrated on rediscovering antiquity and its myths, minor masters such as **Lorenzo Monaco, Giovanni di Paolo** and **Sassetta** continued to emphasise affectation in figure design, flexibility of line and subtlety of colour which made Siena an ideal refuge for Gothic sensibilities.

In the field of secular architecture, the Gothic style gave Siena its own special character with the use of elements which made for a more graceful aspect. Brick and stone were often associated on the lower storeys, while windows became more numerous, especially in the Sienese style with a depressed triple arch supporting a pointed one.

Building activity was concentrated on the cathedral where construction work and transformations lasted over two centuries. There again the façade is in a unique Gothic style where one can detect the transition from the Romanesque to the Flamboyant Gothic in an interpretation full of affectation.

Sculpture, also influenced by the building of the cathedral, was enriched by the output of two Pisan artists, Nicola and Giovanni Pisano (see Index). The latter decorated the cathedral façade with a series of highly expressive figures and his work influenced **Tino di Camaino**, born in Siena in 1280 but who spent the last years of his life at the Angevin Court in Naples. However, the important figure in Sienese sculpture is **Jacopo della Quercia** (1371-1438), who successfully combined Gothic traditions with the Florentine Renaissance style.

★★★ PIAZZA DEL CAMPO (BX) *1hr15min*

This piazza forms a monumental ensemble of almost matchless harmony. It is shaped like a scallop or a fan and is paved with brick and encircled by a ring of stone slabs. The piazza slopes down to the long brick and stone façade of the Palazzo Pubblico. Eight white lines radiate outwards dividing the area into nine segments, each symbolising one of the forms of government that ruled Siena. This consisted of nine members representing trade and banking who ruled the city during its greatest period of prosperity from the late–13C to the mid–14C.

At the upper end is the **Fonte Gaia** (Fountain of Joy) so-called because of the festivities which followed its inauguration in 1348. Fountains were at that time a symbol of the city's power. It was embellished with panels sculpted by Jacopo della Quercia but these, now badly deteriorated, have been replaced by replicas.

The Piazza del Campo is the venue twice annually (see the Calendar of Events at the end of the guide) for the popular festival **Palio delle Contrade**. The whole town participates in the preparation of this event for weeks beforehand and it recalls the medieval administrative organisation of Siena with its three main quarters, themselves subdivided into parishes (contrade). Stands are put up for spectators around the piazza, and the surrounding houses are decked with pennants. The festivities begin with a procession of the contrade in costume, who then compete in a dangerous horserace round the square. There is much betting on the outcome. The palio, a standard bearing the effigy of the Virgin, the city's protectress, is awarded to the winner.

★★★ **Palazzo Pubblico** ☉ (BX H) – The Town Hall, built between the late-13C and mid 14C in the Gothic style, is of a rare elegance with its numerous triple bays under supporting arches, which adorn the gently-curved façade. High up

Piazza del Campo

on the central part is a circular bronze panel inscribed with the monogram IHS (*Iesus Hominum Salvator* Jesus Men's Saviour) used as a badge by St Bernardine. From one end of the façade rises the slim form of the **Torre del Mangia**, a tower (88m/289ft high) designed by Lippo Memmi. At the foot of the tower, **Cappella di Piazza** is a chapel in the form of a loggia dating from 1352, built to mark the end of the plague. It was remodelled in the Renaissance style a century later.

This palace was the seat of Siena's successive governments and most of the great artists of the Sienese school contributed to its decoration.

Sala dei Priori – In the Priors' Room, frescoes (1407) by Spinello Aretino recount the struggles between Pope Alexander III and the Emperor Frederick Barbarossa.

★ **Cappella** – The chapel contains frescoes by Taddeo di Bartolo portraying the Life of the Virgin, a very lovely **railing**★ and its magnificent early-15C **stalls**★★ with intarsia work illustrating the Creed, and on the high altar a Holy Family by Sodoma.

★★ **Sala del Mappamondo** – In the Globe Room the admirable *Maestà*★★ (1315) is Simone Martini's earliest known work, and opposite is the famous *equestrian portrait*★★ of the Sienese general, Guidoriccio da Fogliano, by the same artist. Note the curious contrast between the realism with which the figure is portrayed and the unreality of the background landscape.

★★ **Sala della Pace** – In the Peace Room are the famous frescoes, although badly damaged (1335-40), of Ambrogio Lorenzetti, entitled *Effects of Good and Bad Government*★★, where the artist has achieved a happy combination of a scholarly and noble allegorical approach with that of meticulous narrative detail.

★★ **Torre** ⊘ – From the top of the tower there is a superb **panorama**★★ of Siena's chaotic rooftops and of the gently-rolling Sienese countryside beyond.

★★★ DUOMO (CATHEDRAL AND PRECINCTS) *1hr30min*

★★★ **Duomo** ⊘ (**AX**) – The richly-decorated façade of the cathedral was begun in the 13C by Giovanni Pisano who added some remarkably expressive statues. The upper part was modelled on Orvieto Cathedral. The sober Romanesque campanile dates from 1313.

The walls of the **interior** are faced with alternating bands of black and white marble. The profusion of pillars provides a multitude of perspectives as one moves about. The 15C-16C **paving**★★★ is unique. About 40 artists including **Beccafumi** worked on

S. Chirol

327

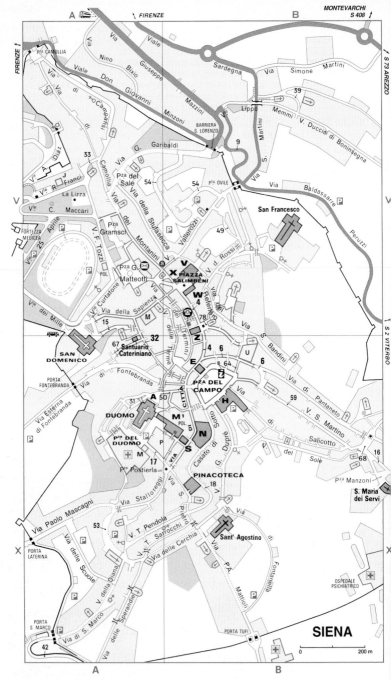

Traffic restricted in town centre

Banchi di Sopra (Via)	BVX 4	Fusari (Via)	AX 31	Pian dei Mantellini	AX 53
Banchi di Sotto (Via)	BX 6	Galluzza (Via della)	AX 32	Pian d'Ovile	ABV 54
Beccafumi (Via D.)	BV 9	Gazzani (Via)	AV 33	Porrione (Via del)	BX 59
Camporegio (Via)	AV 15	Maitani (Via L.)	BV 39	Rinaldini (Via)	BV 64
Cantine (Via delle)	BX 16	Massetana (Strada)	AX 42	S. Caterina (Via di)	AX 67
Capitano		Montanini (Via dei)	AV	S. Girolamo (Via)	BX 68
(Via del)	AX 17	Montluc (Via Biagio di)	BV 45	Tolomei (Piazza)	BV 78
Casato di Sopra	BX 18	Orti (Via degli)	BV 49	Vittorio Emanuele II
Città (Via di)	BX	Pellegrini (Via dei)	BX 50	(Viale)	AV 85

Battistero S. Giovanni	AX **A**	Palazzo Piccolomini	BX **S**	Pinacoteca	BX
Duomo	AX	Palazzo Pubblico	BX **H**	San Domenico	AX
Loggia dei Mercanti	BX **E**	Palazzo Salimbeni	BV **V**	San Francesco	BV
Museo dell'Opera		Palazzo Spannocchi	BV **W**	Sant' Agostino	BX
Metropolitana	BX **M¹**	Palazzo Tantucci	BV **X**	Santa Maria dei Servi	BX
Palazzo Chigi-Saracini	BX **N**	Palazzo Tolomei	BV **Z**	Santuario Cateriniano	AX

the 56 marble panels which portray, either in graffiti or intarsia work, mythological figures such as Sibyls, Virtues and Allegories and scenes from the Old Testament in a lively and delicate manner.

In the chancel is a 15C bronze tabernacle by Vecchietta and richly decorated 14C-16C **stalls**★★. At the entrance to the north transept stands the famous **pulpit**★★★ carved from 1266 to 1268 by **Nicola Pisano**, who relates the Life of Christ in seven panels in a grandiose and exceptionally-dramatic style.

From the north aisle a charming doorway leads to the famous library, **Libreria Piccolomini**, built in 1495 by Cardinal Francesco Piccolomini, the future Pius III, to house his uncle's books. The Umbrian painter **Pinturicchio** adorned it with **frescoes**★★ (1502-09) depicting episodes in the life of Aeneas Silvius Piccolomini (Pius II). The delicate draughtsmanship is typical of miniatures, while the brilliant colours are more typical of illuminations. In the centre stands the famous marble statue of the *Three Graces*, a 3C Roman sculpture (damaged) showing Hellenistic influence.

★★ **Museo dell'Opera Metropolitana** ⊘ (BX **M¹**) – The museum is in the extant part of the vast building started in 1339. The present cathedral was to have been its transept. The project was abandoned owing to technical problems and especially the terrible plague of 1348. The museum contains Giovanni Pisano's statues which originally adorned the cathedral façade, a low relief by Jacopo della Quercia and the famous *Maestà* (Virgin in Majesty) by **Duccio**. This altarpiece was originally painted on both sides (now separated). The panels of the reverse side depict scenes from the Passion of Christ, with a wealth of intimate details.

★ **Battistero di San Giovanni** ⊘ (AX **A**) – The baptistery, dedicated to St John, lies below the cathedral, under an extension of the chancel, and dates from the 14C. The façade started in the Gothic style was never completed.

The interior is decorated with 15C frescoes. The **font**★★ is adorned with panels designed by Jacopo della Quercia. The bronze panels were by several Tuscan masters such as Lorenzo Ghiberti and Donatello. Of note is the latter's *Feast of Herod*.

IF YOU STILL HAVE TIME...

★★ **Pinacoteca Nazionale** ⊘ (BX) – The extensive collection of 13C-16C Sienese paintings is displayed in the 15C **Palazzo Buonsignori**★.

On the second floor is the rich section of the **Primitives**. Beyond the late-12C to early-13C painted Crucifixes and the works of a local artist, Guido da Siena, are the masterpieces of the Sienese school such as Duccio, with the **Madonna of the Francisans**. The *Virgin and Child* is by Simone Martini. There are also numerous works by the Lorenzetti brothers including the **Pala del Carmine**. Note the *Virgin of Humility* by Giovanni di Paolo.

On the first floor note Pinturicchio's works, a *Birth of the Virgin Mary* by Beccafumi and *Christ on the Pillar* by Sodoma.

★ **Via di Città** (BX), **Via Banchi di Sopra** (BVX) – These narrow, flagstoned streets bordered by remarkable **palaces**★ bustle with life.

Coming from Via San Pietro the visitor will see in the Via di Città, on the left the 15C **Palazzo Piccolomini** or Palazzo delle Papesse (**S**) with the lower part of its façade rusticated in the Florentine manner. Practically opposite stands the long curving Gothic façade of the **Palazzo Chigi-Saracini** (**N**), now the home of the Academy of Music. Farther along, on the right, the **Loggia dei Mercanti** (BX **E**) or Merchants' Loggia, in the transitional Gothic-Renaissance style with a 17C top storey, is the seat of the Commercial Courts.

Beyond on the left is the 13C **Palazzo Tolomei** (**Z**), an austere but elegant building. Robert of Anjou, King of Naples, stayed here in 1310. The **Piazza Salimbeni**★ (BV **V**) is enclosed on three sides by buildings with different architectural styles: at the far end the 14C **Palazzo Salimbeni** (**V**) is Gothic; on the left the 15C **Palazzo Spannocchi** (**W**) is Renaissance; while the 16C **Palazzo Tantucci** (**X**) on the left is Baroque.

★ **Basilica di San Domenico** (AX) – St Catherine had her trances in this 13C-15C Gothic conventual church. Inside, there is an authentic portrait of the saint by her contemporary Andrea Vanni.

In the Cappella di S. Caterina (*halfway down the south aisle*) is a lovely Renaissance **tabernacle**★ carved in marble by Giovanni di Stefano which contains the head of the saint. The **frescoes**★ by Sodoma on the walls depict scenes from the life of the saint.

Casa di S. Caterina (AX) - *Entrance in Via Santa Caterina*. St Catherine's house has been transformed into a series of superimposed oratories. In the basement is the cell where St Catherine lived. Above is the 13C painted crucifix in front of which the saint is said to have received the Stigmata.

Sant'Agostino (BX) – This 13C church, dedicated to St Augustine, has a baroque interior. There is a remarkable *Adoration of the Crucifix*★ by Perugino, and the Cappella del Santo Sacramento contains **works**★ by Ambrogio Lorenzetti, Matteo di Giovanni and Sodoma.

SORRENTO ★★

Campania
Population 17 371
Michelin map 431 F 25
Local map see AMALFI

This important Italian resort, known for its many beautiful gardens, overlooks the gulf of the same name. Orange and lemon groves are to be found in the surrounding countryside and even encroaching on the town. Local craftsmen produce various marquetry objects. The poet **Torquato Tasso** was born in Sorrento in 1544.

★ **Museo Correale di Terranova** ⊙ – Housed in an 18C palace, the museum has some splendid examples of local intarsia work (*secretaire*, 1910), a small archeological section and, on the first floor, a collection of 17C and 18C furniture as well as an interesting collection of 17C-18C Neapolitan paintings. Two rooms are devoted to the landscape painters of the **Posillipo School** which flourished in the 1830's, including the main exponent of this school, **Giacinto Gigante** (1806-1876). On the second floor there is a fine collection of porcelain and ceramics. From the terrace, beyond the orange grove, there is a very fine **view**★★ over the Gulf of Sorrento.

The historic centre – Via S. Cesareo, the *decumanus* of the Roman city, leads to the **Sedile Dominova**, seat of city administration in the Angevin period. It consists of a loggia decorated with frescoes surmounted by a 17C ceramic dome. The perpendicular street, Via San Giuliani, leads to the Chiesa di S. Francesco. This Baroque church has a bulbous campanile and is flanked by delightful 13C **cloisters**★ whose vegetable-motif capitals sustain interlaced arcades in the Sicilian-Arab style.
The nearby public gardens, **Villa Comunale**, offer a good **view**★★ of the Bay of Naples.

★★ PENISOLA SORRENTINA *33km/21mi. See local map under AMALFI*

Leave Sorrento to the west by the S 145 and at the junction take the road to the right to Massa Lubrense. This winding road skirts the Sorrento Peninsula and affords fine views of the hillsides covered with olive groves, orange and lemon trees and vines. The last cling to the trelliswork which supports rush matting in winter to protect the citrus from the cold. From the headland **(Punta del Capo di Sorrento)** *(footpath: from the church in the village of Capo di Sorrento take the road to the right and after the college the paved path, 1hr there and back)* there is a superb **view**★★ of Sorrento. At **Sant'Agata sui Due Golfi**, perched on a crest which dominates both the Gulf of Salerno and the Bay of Naples, the **Belvedere del Deserto** ⊙ (a Benedictine monastery situated 1.5km/1mi west of the town) affords a splendid **panorama**★★.
Beyond Sant'Agata, the road which descends steeply to Colli di San Pietro is spectacular. The return to Sorrento by the S 163 offers on the way down some superb **views**★★ over the Bay of Naples.

SPOLETO ★

Umbria
Population 37 622
Michelin map 430 N 20

This former Roman municipium became the capital of an important Lombard duchy from the 6C to the 8C. The town covers the slopes of a hill crowned by the Rocca dei Papi. The city was dear to St Francis, who loved its austere character, tempered by the grace of the narrow winding alleys, the palaces and numerous medieval buildings. Each summer the town hosts an international arts festival, the **Spoleto Festival** (*see Calendar of Events at the end of the guide*).

★★ **Duomo** – Flanked by a baptistery, the cathedral provides the focal point of **Piazza del Duomo**★. The façade is fronted by a fine Renaissance porch and adorned above by a rose window and 13C mosaic. Inside note the altar-cross painted on parchment applied to wood by Alberto Sozio (1187), frescoes (*first chapel on the south side*) by Pinturicchio, Fra Filippo Lippi's burial monument (*south transept*) and in the apse **frescoes** depicting the life of the Virgin by Fra Filippo Lippi and his assistants. In the episode depicting the Virgin sleeping, note the self-portrait of Lippi dressed in Dominican vestments.

★★ **Ponte delle Torri** – A pleasant walk leads to the Bridge of Towers (80m/262ft high with a length of 230m/755ft), built in the 13C over a Roman aqueduct which was used as a foundation. The bridge with its ten Gothic arches is guarded by a small fortified gatehouse at one end.

★ **Basilica di S. Salvatore** – St Saviour's Basilica, one of the first Christian churches in Italy, was built by Oriental monks in the 4C and modified in the 9C. Roman materials were re-used in the building of the later edifice.

★ **San Gregorio Maggiore** – This 12C Romanesque church, dedicated to St Gregory Major, was modified in the 14C. The 14C baptistery to the left of the entrance porch has walls covered with frescoes *(Massacre of the Innocents)*. The campanile is built of stone from ancient buildings.

The dark, bare nave and aisles rest on massive columns with roughly-hewn capitals. In the chancel note the 15C fresco and a carved stone cupboard of the same period.

Arco di Druso – This arch was built in AD 23 in honour of Tiberius' son, Drusus.

Chiesa di S. Domenico – This lovely 13C church, dedicated to St Dominic, is built of alternating courses of white and pink stone. The nave is decorated with 14C and 15C frescoes and the south transept contains a canvas by Lanfranco.

EXCURSIONS

★ **Monteluco Road** – *8km/5mi east.* An attractively-winding road leads up to **Monteluco**. On the way up, the Church of St Peter **(San Pietro)** has a lovely 13C Romanesque **façade★** with relief sculptures. On the summit, **Monteluco★** was once the seat of an ancient cult, but is now a health resort. The monastery founded by St Francis still exists.

★ **Fonti del Clitunno** – *13km/8mi north.* These crystal-clear waters which surge amid aquatic plants were sacred to the Romans. They plunged animals into the water for purification prior to sacrifice. 1km/0.6mi below stands a temple **(tempietto★** ⊘) of Clitumnus, a minuscule early-Christian building dating from the 5C. It boasts columns and a carved pediment.

SUBIACO

Lazio
Population 8 999
Michelin map 430 Q 21

St Benedict, founder of the Benedictine Order, and his twin sister Scolastica retired to this spot at the end of the 5C and built 12 little monasteries before moving to Monte Cassino.

To reach the monasteries of Santa Scolastica and San Benedetto (3km/2mi) take the Frosinone road and shortly before the Aniene Bridge turn left.

Monastero di Santa Scolastica ⊘ – Standing in the fine site overlooking the Aniene Gorges the monastery has preserved a majestic 11C campanile, its church which was remodelled in the 18C, and three cloisters. The third, the work of the Cosmati, is admirable in its simplicity.

★ **Monastero di San Benedetto** ⊘ – This monastery, dedicated to St Benedict, stands above the previous one clinging to the rock face in a wild site, overhanging the gorge. The buildings date from the 13C and 14C.

The church has two storeys. The **upper church** has walls painted with frescoes of the 14C Sienese school and the 15C Umbrian school. The **lower church**, itself with two storeys, is covered with frescoes by Magister Consolus, an artist of the 13C Roman school.

Visitors are admitted to the Sacred Cave **(Sacro Speco)** where St Benedict lived a hermit's existence for three years. A spiral staircase then leads up to a chapel which contains the earliest portrait of St Francis (without Stigmata or halo), painted to commemorate the saint's visit to the sanctuary. The Holy Staircase **(Scala Santa)** leads down to the Chapel of the Virgin (frescoes by the Sienese school) and the Shepherd's Cave. From there the visitor can enter the rose garden where St Benedict threw himself into brambles to resist temptation.

SULMONA★

Abruzzi
Population 25 656
Michelin map 430 P 23
Local map see ABRUZZO

Sulmona, which lies at the head of a fertile basin framed by majestic mountains, was the birthplace of the Roman poet **Ovid**, who immortalised his origins in the verse "Sulmo mihi patria est" (hence the acronym SMPE of the town's emblem). Sulmona was and still is a lively economic and craft town, known especially for its gold work.

★ **Porta Napoli** – *Southern town gateway.* This Gothic gate has historiated capitals (14C). The exterior has an unusual decoration of gilded bosses, Angevin coats of arms and Roman low reliefs. The elegant **Corso Ovidio**, which cuts through the Medieval heart of the city, commences here.

Piazza Garibaldi – This square is the scene on Wednesdays and Saturdays of a large and highly-colourful market. The square is bordered by the pointed arches of the 13C **aqueduct★**, the Baroque corner of Santa Chiara and the Gothic doorway

---

Colourful little delicacies

From the windows of Corso Ovidio colourful and unusual bunches of flowers peep out: these are the famous Sulmona sweets which were created at the end of the 15C. A taste of these little sweets will hold some pleasant surprises in store: a glacé of pure sugar hides Sicilian almonds, hazelnuts, chocolate, candied fruit and rosolio. To find out more, go to the small museum, **Museo dell'Arte e della Tecnologia confettiera** ⊘, at the Pelino factory in Via Introdacqua 55.

---

of San Filippo. At the corner of the aqueduct by Corso Ovidio stands the Renaissance fountain, **Fontana del Vecchio** which derives its name from the inscription under the bearded head above the curved gable.

On Easter Sunday, the **feast of the "Madonna che scappa in piazza"** is celebrated in Piazza Garibaldi: the statue of the Virgin is borne to a meeting with the Risen Christ; as she comes within sight of Him, she sheds her mourning clothes and appears in a resplendent green robe.

S. Francesco della Scarpa – This church was erected in the 13C by Franciscan monks who had shoes and didn't limp (hence its name, *scarpa* being the Italian for "shoe"). It has a fine Romanesque **doorway★** on Corso Ovidio flanked by a campanile and the remains of the apse.

★★ **Palazzo dell'Annunziata** – This monumental construction documents four centuries of Sulmonese art. Built by a Brotherhood of Penitents from 1415, the palace constitutes a synthesis of Gothic (the rich Gothic doorway with statues of the Virgin and St Michael, the ornate **trefoil★** openings and statues of four Doctors of the Church), Renaissance (the elegant middle doorway, the right portal and the two twin openings) and Baroque art (the theatrical façade of the adjacent church). There is an astonishingly carved **frieze** halfway up the façade depicting hunts and love scenes. Inside, the palace houses the **Museo Civivo** ⊘.

EXCURSIONS

★ **Basilica di S. Pelino** ⊘ – *13km/8mi northwest, near the village of Corfinio.* This bishop's seat was erected in the 11C and 12C. The rear of the basilica offers a good view of the **apse complex★** and the adjacent Oratory of St Alexander. The **interior** houses a fine 12C **ambo**.

Popoli – *17km/10mi northwest.* This pretty town is clustered around Piazza Matteotti. The square is bordered to the left by the Church of St Francis, with its Gothic façade and Baroque crenellations, and to the right by the theatrical staircase which leads up to the 18C church of SS. Trinità. Next to the square stands the **Taverna Ducale★**, an elegant 14C Gothic building adorned with coats of arms and low reliefs which in the past was used a storeroom for tithes

TARANTO★

Puglia
Population 210 536
Michelin map 431 F 33
Town plan in the Michelin Atlas Italy

Taranto is a well-protected naval base at the end of a great roadstead, closed at the seaward end by two fortified islands. Taranto was founded in the 7C BC and became one of the most important colonies of Magna Graecia.

During Holy Week many impressive ceremonies take place in the town, including several processions between Thursday and Saturday, one lasting 12 hours and another 14 hours, which go from church to church at a very slow pace *(see the Calendar of Events at the end of the guide).*

★★ **Museo Nazionale** ⊘ – *The museum is currently undergoing improvements so not all pieces may be exhibited.* The National Museum has a good collection of local archeological finds which illustrate the history of Magna Graecia. Among the statues it is worth mentioning the figure of **Poseidon★★** which was brought to light at Ugento. This bronze statue, probably of local manufacture and dating from the 6C BC, most likely depicts the god of the sea or possibly **Zeus** holding a thunderbolt and a bird (both lost). The museum also houses a notable **collection of ceramics★★★** with elegantly decorated vases in the Corinthian, Attic, proto-Italiot and Apulian styles and an astonishing collection of Hellenic **gold jewelry** (4C and 3C BC) which was found in local tombs. These pieces are composed of filigree and lamina which are sometimes enriched by stones and enamels.

★ **Giardini Comunali** – From the municipal gardens, a haven of exotic and luxuriant vegetation, there is a magnificent view over the harbour's inner basin, the Mare Piccolo.

★★ **Lungomare Vittorio Emanuele** – A long promenade planted with palm trees and oleanders.

The old city – This island is connected to the mainland by two bridges, one of which is a revolving bridge. At the eastern extremity of the island stands the **Aragonese Castle** which today is the seat of the Navy.

Duomo – The 11C-12C cathedral with a Baroque façade has been greatly remodelled. The nave and two aisles are separated by ancient columns with Romanesque or Byzantine capitals and the ceiling is 17C. The Chapel of **San Cataldo**★ was faced with polychrome marble and embellished with statues in the 18C.

San Domenico Maggiore – This 14C church was considerably remodelled in the Baroque era. There is a fine, if rather damaged, façade with an ogival portal surmounted by a rose-window.

TARQUINIA★

Lazio
Population 14 868
Michelin map 430 P 17

The town of Tarquinia crowns a rocky platform, facing the sea, in a barley- and corn-growing region interspersed with olive groves. Tarquinia is famous for the Etruscan burial ground which lies quite near. According to legend, the town was founded in the 12C or 13C BC. Archeologists have found 9C BC vestiges of the Villanovian civilisation which derived its name from the village of Villanova near Bologna, and developed around the year 1000 BC in the Po Plain, in Tuscany and in the northern part of Latium, where the Etruscans later settled. Standing on the banks of the Marta River, Tarquinia was a busy port and in the 6C BC ruled the coast of Etruria. Under Roman rule, Tarquinia was decimated by malaria in the 4C BC and was sacked by the Lombards in the 7C. The inhabitants then moved to the present site about a mile to the northeast of the original position.

★★ **Necropoli Etrusca** ⊘ - *4km/2.5mi southeast.* The burial ground is on a bare, windswept ridge parallel with that on which the former Etruscan city stood. The necropolis extends over an area 5km/3mi long and 1km/0.6 mile wide and contains around 600 tombs dating from the 6C-1C BC. As at Cerveteri there are no visible remains at ground level but there are remarkable **paintings**★★★ on the walls of the underground burial chambers. These colourful and lively paintings are of the utmost importance for the light they shed on the Etruscan civilisation. The most important tombs include: the tomb of the Baron **(tomba del Barone)**, dating from the 6C BC; the 5C BC tomb of the Leopards **(tomba del Leopardi)**, one of the finest, in which are depicted leopards as well as scenes of a banquet and dancing; the 6C BC tomb of the Bulls **(tomba dei Tori)** with its erotic paintings; the tomb of the Lionesses **(tomba delle Leonesse)** dating from around 530-520 BC; the 4C BC Giglioli tomb **(tomba Gigliogi)** decorated with *trompe-l'œil* paintings of costumes and arms; and the late-6C BC tomb with Hunting and Fishing Scenes **(tomba delle Caccia e della Pesca)**, which consists of two chambers displaying the return from the hunt, a banquet and the art of fishing.

★ **Museo Nazionale Tarquinie-se** ⊘ – The National Museum is housed in the **Palazzo Vitelleschi**★ built in 1439 and has a most remarkable collection of Etruscan antiquities originating from the excavations in the necropo-

The Winged Horses, Museo Nazionale

Ross/RAPHO

lis. Artefacts include sarcophagi, pottery, ivories, votive offerings and 6C BC Attic kraters and amphorae. The following exhibits are of great interest: two admirable **winged horses★★★** in terracotta and on the second floor several reconstructed tombs, notably the tomb with the Funeral Bed **(tomba del Letto Funebre)** (460 BC) and the tomb of the Triclinium **(tomba del Triclinio)** (480-470 BC), one of the finest in the necropolis.

★ **Santa Maria in Castello** ⊘ – *Take the Via Mazzini, then the Via di Porta Castello beyond the wall.* This Romanesque church (1121-1208), dedicated to St Mary, stands near a tall tower built in the Middle Ages and was part of the fortified citadel guarding the town. It has an elegant doorway decorated with Cosmati work and an imposing interior.

TERNI

Umbria

Population 108 108

Michelin map 430 O 19

Terni, an important industrial centre, has an old town with several fine palaces, the Church of St Francis with its 15C belltower, and St Saviour's Church, which has early-Christian (5C) origins. The bustling town centre comprises Piazza della Repubblica and Via Roma.

EXCURSIONS

★★ **Cascata delle Marmore** ⊘ – *Take the Macerata road the S 209 (7km/4mi east of Terni) or the Rieti road, the S 79 (9km/6mi to the east plus 30min there and back on foot).*
This artificial waterfall created by the Romans falls in three successive drops down sheer walls of marble *(marmore)* to disappear at the bottom of a wooded ravine.

Carsulae: Roman Ruins – *16km/10mi northwest. Go via S. Gemini and S. Gemini Fonte.* These are the remains of a Roman town destroyed in the 9C.

Ferentillo – *18km/11mi northeast.* This picturesque village is dominated by two ruined castles. From here *(5km/3mi north, then 2km/1.2mi further by a poor road)* it is possible to reach the solitary **Abbazia di San Pietro in Valle** ⊘, an abbey which was founded in the 7C and rebuilt in the 12C. The cloisters are decorated with 12C frescoes and there are Roman sarcophagi.

TERRACINA 🏛

Lazio

Population 38 366

Michelin map 430 S 21

Terracina stands in an attractive setting at the head of a bay and is backed by a limestone cliff. In the Roman era it was already a fashionable country resort. Terracina has retained part of its medieval wall and some Roman remains.

Duomo – The cathedral overlooks the attractive **Piazza del Municipio** which still has the paving of the Roman forum. It was consecrated in 1075 and is fronted by a portico on ancient columns which support a 12C mosaic frieze. The campanile with its small columns is in the transitional Romanesque-Gothic style.
Inside, the **pulpit** and **paschal candelabrum★**, a lovely 13C work by the Cosmati, are of special interest.

★ **Tempio di Giove Anxur** – *4km/2.5mi plus 15min on foot there and back by Via San Francesco Nuovo.* Although there are few remains other than the foundations, a vaulted gallery and an underground passage *(cryptoporticus)*, it is worth visiting the site of the Temple of Jupiter for its beauty alone and for the extensive **panorama★★** of the town, the canals and port, Monte Circeo and the Pontine marshes, the plain of Fondi with its lakes, and the coast as far as Gaeta.

EXCURSION

* **Parco Nazionale del Circeo** – Designated in 1934 this park covers a narrow coastal strip between Anzio and Terracina and includes part of the former Pontine marshes. Some of the most attractive beauty spots are: **Monte Circeo**, the refuge of the wicked witch Circe who transformed Ulysses and his companions into a herd of pigs; **Lago di Sabaudia**, a lake which can be reached by a bridge leading to the town of **Sabaudia**⌂, a pleasant country resort; the **scenic route** *(5km/3mi from the San Felice – Torre Cervia road)* is lined with luxury villas and brightened by typically-Mediterranean plants and flowers. The park is one of UNESCO's protected nature reserves.

Santuario della Madonna di TIRANO

Lombardy

Michelin map 428 or 429 D 12

The Church of **Madonna di Tirano** was built from 1505 onwards on the spot where the Virgin Mary had appeared in a vision. It has a nave and side aisles. The west front dates from 1676 and is enhanced with highly-ornate Baroque decoration including frescoes by Cipriano Valorsa di Grosio (1575-1578), nicknamed the "Raphael of La Valtellina" *(nave)*, a fresco of the Apparition dating from 1513 *(left, above the confessional)*, paintings by a pupil of Morazzone *(chancel)* and a highly-ornate, grandiose 17C **organ**. The loft was made by Giuseppe Bulgarini and the panels on the gallery representing the *Birth of the Infant Jesus*, *The Adoration of the Magi* and *The Circumcision* were painted by G B Salmoiraghi (1638).

TIVOLI★★★

Lazio

Population 52 735

Michelin map 430 Q 20

See The Green Guide to Rome

Tivoli is a small town on the lower slopes of the Apennines where the river Aniene plunges in cascades into the Roman plain.
The villas testify to Tivoli's importance as a holiday resort from the Roman period through to the Renaissance. Tivoli or Tibur in antiquity came under Roman control in the 4C BC and it was there that a Sibyl prophesied the coming of Jesus Christ to the Emperor Augustus.

★★★ VILLA D'ESTE ⊙ 2hr

See the detailed town plan in The Green Guide to Rome.

In 1550 Cardinal Ippolito II d'Este, who had been raised to great honours by François I of France but had fallen into disgrace when the king's son Henri II succeeded to the throne, decided to retire to Tivoli, where he immediately began to convert the former Benedictine convent into a pleasant country seat. The Neapolitan architect, Pirro Ligorio, was invited to prepare plans. The simple architecture of the villa contrasts with the elaborate terraced gardens. The statues, pools and fountains enhance the natural beauty with all the grace of the Mannerist style.
To the left of the main entrance stands the old abbey church of St Mary Major **(Santa Maria Maggiore)** with its attractive Gothic façade and a 17C bell-tower. Inside, in the chancel, are two 15C triptychs: above the one on the left is a painting of the Virgin by Jacopo Torriti, who also worked in mosaic at the end of the 13C.

★★★ **Palace and gardens** – From the former convent cloisters go down through the elaborately-decorated Old Apartments. From the ground-floor level there is a pleasant **view**★ of the gardens and Tivoli itself. A double flight of stairs leads to the upper garden walk. A fountain with a shell-shaped basin, **Fontana del Bicchierone**, is attributed to Bernini. To the left the **Fontana Rometta**, or "Mini Rome", reproduces some of the well-known monuments of Classical Rome. From here a splendid avenue lined with fountains, **Viale delle Cento Fontane★★★**, leads to the Oval Fountain **(Fontana dell'Ovato★★★)** dominated by a statue of the Sibyl. At a lower level the Fishpond Esplanade **(le Peschiere)** is overlooked at one end by the Organ Fountain

One of the splendid fountains at Villa d'Este

(Fontana dell' Organo★★★) in which a concealed water-powered organ once played music. Right at the very bottom of the garden is the Nature Fountain (Fontana della Natura) with a statue of Diana of Ephesus. Return by the central avenue to admire the Dragon Fountain (Fontana dei Draghi), built in 1572 in honour of Pope Gregory XIII, then turn right to pass the Bird Fountain (Fontana della Civetta) which used to produce bird song, and finally the modernised Fountain of Proserpina (Fontana di Proserpina).

★★★ VILLA ADRIANA ⊙ 2hr30min

6km/4mi southwest by the Rome road, the S 5, and then a local road to the left, 4.5km/3mi from Tivoli.

This was probably the richest building project in antiquity and was designed entirely by **Hadrian** (AD 76-138), who had visited every part of the Roman Empire. He had a passion for both art and architecture and he wished to recreate the monuments and sites he had visited during his travels. In AD 134 the villa was almost finished, but the 58 year-old Hadrian, ill and grief-stricken by the death of his young favourite Antinoüs, was to die four years later. Although later emperors probably continued to visit Tivoli, the villa was soon forgotten and fell into ruin. The site was explored from the 15C to the 19C and the recovered works were dispersed to various museums and private collections. It was only in 1870 that the Italian government organised the excavation of Tivoli, thus revealing this magnificent complex.

Before exploring the site it is advisable to study a model of the villa displayed in a room next to the bar. *Follow the itinerary shown on the accompanying plan.*

★★ **Pecile** – The water-filled Pecile takes its name from a portico in Athens. It was built in the shape of a large rectangle with slightly curved ends and is lined with a portico; it was oriented so that one side was always in the shade.

The apsidal chamber called the philosophers' room (**Sala dei Filosofi – 1**) was perhaps a reading room.

★★★ **Teatro Marittimo** – The circular construction consists of a portico and a central building surrounded by a canal. It provided an ideal retreat for the misanthropic Hadrian. Bear south to pass the remains of a nymphaeum (**ninfeo**) and the great columns which belonged to a building comprising three semi-circular rooms round a courtyard (cortile – **2**).

★★ **Terme** – The lay-out of the baths shows the high architectural standards attained in the villa. First come the Small Baths and then the Great Baths with an apse and splendid vaulting.

The tall building, called the Praetorium (**Pretorio**), was probably a storehouse.

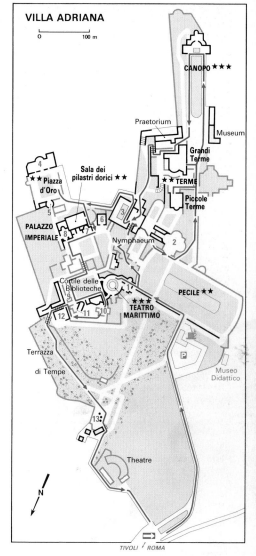

Museo:	Museum	Pretorio:	Law Courts
Ninfeo:	Nymphaeum	Teatro:	Theatre
Palazzo:	Palace	Terme:	Baths

★★★ **Canopo** – Beyond the museum (**museo**) which contains the finds from the most recent excavations is a complex which evokes the Egyptian town of Canope with its famous Temple of Serapis. The route to Canope from Alexandria consisted of a canal lined with temples and gardens. At the southern end of this site is a copy of the Temple of Serapis.

Having reached the ruins overlooking the nymphaeum, turn right before skirting the large **fishpond** (**3**) surrounded by a portico.

Palazzo Imperiale – The palace complex extended from Piazza d'Oro to the Libraries.

★★ **Piazza d'Oro** – The rectangular piazza was surrounded by a double portico and was an esthetic indulgence serving no useful purpose. On the far side are traces of an octagonal chamber (**4**) and a domed chamber (**5**) opposite.

★★ **Sala dei Pilastri Dorici** – The hall takes its name from the surrounding portico which was composed of pilasters with Doric bases and capitals.

Also visible are the firemen's barracks (**Caserma dei Vigili – 6**), remains of a summer dining-room (**7**) and a nymphaeum (**8**). These buildings overlook a courtyard which is separated from the **library court** by a cryptoporticus, part of a network of underground passages which ran from one villa to another without emerging above ground.

The suite of ten rooms along one side of the library court was an infirmary (**9**). Note the fine mosaic **paving**★. According to custom the **library** was divided in two for a Greek section (**10**) and a Latin section (**11**).

The route to the **Terrazza di Tempe** goes past rooms paved with mosaic which belonged to a dining-room (**12**).

The path runs through the trees on the slope above the valley past a **round temple** (**13**) attributed to the goddess Venus, and skirts the site of a **theatre**, on the left, before ending at the entrance.

★ VILLA GREGORIANA ⊘

This wooded park has a tangle of paths which wind down the steeply-wooded slopes to the river Aniene where it cascades through the ravine. The waters of the Aniene plunge down at the Great Cascade (**Grande Cascata**★★), disappear out of sight at the Siren's Cave (**Grotta della Sirena**) and burst from the rock-face in Neptune's Cave (**Grotta di Nettuno**). Climb the slope overlooking the ravine to leave the Villa Gregoriana and visit Sibyl's Temple (**Tempio della Sibilla**), also known as the Temple of Vesta. This elegant Corinthian-style structure dates from the end of the Republic. An Ionic temple stands alongside.

EXCURSIONS

★ **Palestrina** – *23km/14mi southeast.* With its panoramic position overlooking the Prenestini mountains, an old historic centre and the remains of the celebrated Temple of Fortuna Primigenia, Palestrina makes for an extremely pleasant excursion. This splendid town flourished from the 8C to 7C BC; after various vicissitudes it submitted to Roman domination. The Romans turned it into a holiday resort for Emperors and nobles. The cult of the goddess Fortune prospered until the 4C AD when the sanctuary was abandoned and the Medieval city born on its remains.

Tempio della Fortuna Primigenia – This magnificent sanctuary, one of the finest examples of Hellenic architecture in Italy, dates from the 2C-1C BC and originally comprised a series of descending esplanades. In the Lower Sanctuary the Basilical room remains as well as two side buildings, a natural grotto and the Apse room from where the celebrated Nile fresco was taken *(see below)*. The Upper Sanctuary was built on the fourth esplanade of the temple (now Piazza della Cortina). In the 11C Palazzo Colonna, later Barberini, now the archeological museum, was built here. From the terrace there is a fine view of the **town**★ and the valley.

Museo archeologico prenestino ⊘ – The museum has artefacts from several necropoleis as well as objects from the Barberini collection. The museum's masterpiece is the magnificent **Nile mosaic**★★ which portrays Egypt with the Nile flooding.

TODI★★

Umbria
Population 16 899
Michelin map 430 N 19

Todi, a charming old town perched on an attractive **site**, has retained three sets of walls dating from the Etruscan (Marzia Gateway), Roman and medieval periods.

★★ **Piazza del Popolo** – This square in the centre of Todi is surrounded by buildings which are evidence of the town's flourishing commercial life in the Middle Ages. The 13C Gothic **Palazzo dei Priori**★ was formerly the seat of the governor *(podestà)*. Its windows were remodelled at the Renaissance and it is dominated by a curious 14C tower on a trapezoidal plan.

The 13C **Palazzo del Capitano**★ ⊘ has attractive windows in groups of three flanked by small columns. Both this and the neighbouring building have arcades with round-headed arches and massive pillars at ground level. The adjoining **Palazzo del Popolo**★ ⊘, one of the oldest communal palaces in Italy (1213), houses a lapidary museum, a picture gallery and a museum of Etruscan and Roman antiquities.

★★ **San Fortunato** – *Piazza della Repubblica.* Building on the church, dedicated to St Fortunatus, lasted from 1292 to 1460; the structure combines Gothic and Renaissance features. The **central doorway**★★ catches the eye with the richness and delicacy of its decoration. The well-lit and lofty interior has **frescoes** (1432) by Masolino (fourth chapel to the south) and the tomb of **Jacopone da Todi** (1230-1307), a Franciscan monk, a poet and author of the *Stabat Mater*.

* **Duomo** – This great early-12C Romanesque building is preceded by a majestic staircase leading up to its harmonious façade, all in pink and white marble, with a great rose window pierced and fretted in the Umbrian manner. Walk round the building to admire the Romanesque apse. Inside note the Gothic capitals, the Renaissance font and the lovely stalls with intarsia work dating from 1530.

Piazza Garibaldi – This square adjoining the Piazza del Popolo is graced with a monument to Garibaldi. From the terrace, there is a pretty **view**★★ of the valley and distant rounded hills.

Rocca – Pass to the right of St Fortunatus and walk up to the ruins of the 14C castle. There is a well-shaded and pleasant public garden.

* **Santa Maria della Consolazione** – *1km/0.6mi west on the Orvieto road.* This Renaissance church was built of pale stone from 1508 to 1609 by several architects who drew inspiration from the designs of Bramante. The plan is that of a Greek cross; four polygonal apses are reinforced by pilasters with composite capitals. The dome, whose drum is designed in accordance with Bramante's rhythmic principles *(see pages 53 and 211)*, rises roundly from the flat terrace roof. The interior is austere and well lit. The dome was decorated in the 16C and the 12 statues of the Apostles are by Scalza (16C).

TOLENTINO

Marches
Population 18 657
Michelin map 430 M 21

This small town in the Marches region was where Napoleon Bonaparte and Pope Pius VI signed the Treaty of Tolentino ratifying the surrendering of Avignon to France. In 1961 a group of artists from Tolentino founded the **Biennale Internazionale dell'Umorismo nell'arte** (The International Biennial of humour in art). The growing success of this exhibition led to the creation of the **Museo della Caricatura** (Caricature Museum) ⊙, housed in Palazzo Sangallo *(Piazza della Libertà)*.

★★ **Basilica di S. Nicola** ⊙ – The basilica is dedicated to the Augustine monk who was venerated for his magic powers. St Nicholas died in Tolentino in 1305 and was buried in the basilica's crypt. Building lasted from 1305 to the 18C and the exterior reflects the different construction periods. The façade, remodelled in the 17C in the Baroque style, has an elegant late-Gothic doorway by the Florentine sculptor Nino di Bartolo (15C), a pupil of Donatello.

The **interior** is striking for the opulence of its marble, gold and stucco decoration and the magnificent coffered ceiling (1628). In the first chapel on the south side is the *Vision of St Anne* by Guercino (1591-1666).

Il Cappellone di S. Nicola – The chapel serves as south transept and is the most famous part of this pilgrimage church, owing to its cycle of 14C **frescoes**★★ by an unknown master of the Rimini school. The images on the vaulting portray the Evangelists and the Doctors of the Church while the walls recount episodes from the Lives of the Virgin and Christ (upper and central frescoes) and scenes from the life of St Nicholas of Tolentino (lower frescoes).

Museums ⊙ – These include the **Museo delle Ceramiche** (Ceramics museum), the **Museo dell'Opera**, which has a fine 14C wood **nativity** and the **Galleria degli ex voto** (Gallery of ex-votos), which is striking for the ingenuous and spontaneous devotion reflected in the votive offerings.

EXCURSIONS

San Severino Marche – *11km/7mi northwest.* The Medieval and Renaissance heart of this town clusters around the elliptical-shaped **Piazza del Popolo**. There is a delightful **view**★ of the town and surrounding mountains from the hill where the cathedral stands *(go up Via della Pitturetta)*.

Pinacoteca Civica ⊙ – *Palazzo Tacchi-Venturi, via Salimbeni 39.* This picture gallery has a fine collection of interesting local paintings: **Lorenzo Salimbeni** and his brother **Jacopo** revolutionised the idiom of 15C painting by adding a vivid realism to the International Gothic Style. The collection also includes an opulent **polyptych** by Vittore Crivelli and the delicate *Madonna della Pace* by Pinturicchio (1454-1513).

Nearby *(turn left at the end of Via Salimbeni)* is the church of **San Lorenzo in Doliolo** ⊙ (11C) which is architecturally very interesting and has a beautiful **crypt**★ covered in frescoes attributed to the Salimbeni brothers and their school.

TORINO★★

TURIN – Piedmont
Population 914 818
Michelin map 428 G 4-5
Plans of the conurbation in the Michelin Atlas Italy

Turin is unwilling to reveal its true character to the rushed visitor who will almost certainly fail to capture the profound contrasts which comprise the soul and charm of this city. On two occasions Turin has had to reinvent itself as a capital; first of the newly created Kingdom of Italy and more recently of the automobile industry. Now the city is attempting to shake off the role of "factory-city" and become an important cultural centre for the new millennium. Technology has always been its economic and cultural motor although Turin has never lost a rather conservative spirit which has always had trouble in adjusting to those historic and social changes in which it has played an active role. The military tradition of the ruling Savoy dynasty has given Turin a rather severe imprint which is reflected in its splendid but restrained, balanced Baroque architecture, a far cry from the opulence of Rome. For centuries the city has jealously guarded the Turin shroud without renouncing a vocation for the esoteric which has attracted personalities such as Paracelsus, Nostradamus and Cagliostro. Nietzsche lived his last lucid years in Turin where he wrote his major works. He claimed that "Turin is the first place where I am possible".

HISTORICAL NOTES

During the 1C the capital of the Celtic tribe, the Taurini, was transformed by the Romans into a military colony and given the name of Augusta Taurinorum. Converted to Christianity, it became the seat of a bishopric in the early 5C and then a century later a Lombard duchy before passing under Frankish rule. From the 11C onwards and for nearly nine centuries the destiny of Turin was linked to that of the **House of Savoy**. This dynasty descended from Umberto the Whitehanded (d 1056), reigned over Savoy, Piedmont, Sardinia and finally all of Italy. It was Italy's reigning royal family from 1861 to 1946. They were skilful rulers, often siding with the pope rather than the emperor, and playing France off against the Dukes of Milan. They slowly extended their rule over the area. It was in the early 18C that Charles Emmanuel II and Victor Amadeus II embellished their adopted city with splendid buildings by Guarini and Juvarra.

Charles Emmanuel III increased the importance of Turin during his long reign (1732-73) by reorganising the kingdom's administration and by establishing in his capital a court with very formal etiquette, similar to the one at Versailles. In 1798 Charles Emmanuel IV was expelled from Turin by French troops who wanted to impose a regime based on the revolutionary principles of 1789. On the fall of Napoleon Bonaparte, Victor Emmanuel I was restored without difficulty to his kingdom and promoted a policy against any foreign interference in Piedmontese affairs. Turin then became the centre of the struggle against the Austrians and for the unification of Italy.

The elegance and clean lines of Juvarra's Stupinigi Hunting Lodge

Following the reorganisation of the Piedmont by the statesman Camillo Cavour, the Franco-Piedmontese alliance against Austria, the victories at Solferino and Magenta (1859), Victor Emmanuel II was proclaimed the first King of Italy and Turin became the seat of the Italian government, to be replaced by Florence in 1865. The House of Savoy reigned over Italy until the proclamation of an Italian Republic in 1946.

ECONOMY

The intense activity of its suburban industries has made Turin the capital of Italian engineering. It was in the Piedmontese capital that the **Italian motor industry** was born with FIAT, founded in 1899 by Giovanni Agnelli, and Lancia, created in 1906 by Vincenzo Lancia and eventually taken over by the FIAT group in 1969. The **Lingotto**, the famous FIAT factory which was built in 1920 with such avant-garde technical features as the spectacular test ramp on the roof, was defined by Le Corbousier as "one of the most striking spectacles provided by industry". When production ceased the building was transformed by **Renzo Piano** into a highly modern conference and exhibition centre with an auditorium and a commercial area. Important tyre manufacturers and well-known coachbuilders (one of the most famous was the great Pinin Farina) have contributed to the prosperity of the motor industry of Turin itself.

Not just Fiat...

For many Turin is synonymous with Fiat but numerous companies known all over the world were born here or have their central offices in or around the city. Among these are: Lavazza, Cinzano, Martini & Rossi, Gancia, Caffarel and Peyrano in the food and drink sector; the textile group GFT, producers of the Armani, Valentino, Cerruti and Ungaro brands; the Istituto Bancario San Paolo and the Cassa di Risparmio di Torino (the second largest bank in Italy) in the banking sector; SAI, Toro and Reale Mutua Assicurazioni in the insurance sector; STET-Telecom Italia in the telecommunications sector; Robe di Kappa, Superga and Invicta in the sports clothing sector and De Fonseca in the shoe manufacture industry. Without forgetting Michelin naturally, who opened their first factory outside France in 1906 in the famous building on Via Livorno.

But Turin boasts other very solid traditions. There are numerous publishing companies such as Bollati Boringhieri, Einaudi, Lattes, Loescher, Paravia, S.E.I. and U.T.E.T. as well as one of the major national newspapers, La Stampa, founded in 1895. Music also thrives in Turin thanks to the presence of the R.A.I. National Symphony Orchestra and the prestigious *Teatro Regio*.

These diverse traditions are all displayed in the numerous fairs and exhibitions hosted by the city: the *Salone dell'Automobile* (every two years), the *Salone del Libro* (Book Fair), the *Salone della Musica* and the *Settembre Musica* festival which also encompasses the prestigious *Cinema Giovani* (Young cinema) festival, a homage to the "tenth art" in a city which until the First World War was the Italian capital of cinema.

LIFE IN TURIN

🚹 **Turismo Torino** – Information centres in **piazza Castello 161**, ☎ 011 53 51 81 or 011 53 59 01, and at the station, **Stazione di Porta Nuova**, ☎ 011 53 13 27 are open daily from 8.30am to 7.30pm, the centre at **Caselle Airport**, ☎ 011 56 78 124, is open daily from 8.30am to 11.30pm. Web site http://www.turismotorino.ogr; e-mail info@turismotorino.org

Wheels, tracks or wings?

By car – In spite of its decentralised position (the city is only about 100km/62mi from the French border) there is a good network of motorways linking Turin to various cities (A4 for Milan, 140 km/87mi; A21 and A26 for Genoa, 170 km/106mi; A21 and A1 for Bologna 325 km/203mi, A5 for Aosta 115 km/72mi). Furthermore, thanks to its famous octagonal plan and wide 19C avenues, traffic, although heavy at times, is manageable and it is easier to travel in and around Turin by car than it is in many other Italian cities.

Bus – The terminus is in corso Inghilterra at the corner of corso Vittorio Emanuele II, ☎ 011 43 32 525.

By train – The main railway stations in the city are:
Porta Nuova, corso Vittorio Emanuele II 53, ☎ 011 66 92 825 (ticket office) and 011 53 24 27 (reservations);
Porta Susa, piazza XVIII Dicembre 8, ☎ 011 53 85 13.

By plane – Turin's international airport is situated 11 km/7mi north of the city in Caselle, ☎ 011 56 76 361, fax 011 56 76 420, web site http://www.turin-airport.com. It is served by major national and international airline companies and has flights to principal Italian and European cities such as Amsterdam, Barcelona, Brussels, Frankfurt, Lisbon, London, Madrid, Paris, Vienna and Zurich.

Taxi journeys to the city centre (about 30min) vary from 45 000 L (daytime) to 75 000 L (evenings). Airport taxi service ☎ 011 99 14 419.

Buses operated by Sadem ensure connections to the city every 45min, from 5.15am to 10.30pm (departs from Porta Nuova – corso Vittorio Emanuele II at the corner of via Sacchi – and Porta Susa – corso San Martino at the corner of piazza XVIII Dicembre) and from 6.30am to 11.30pm (departs from the airport, arrivals floor, opposite the national flights exit). Tickets cost 6000L and can be purchased from ticket counters adjacent to the terminals or on the vehicle when leaving from Turin and from the newspaper stand in the departure lounge, the automated ticket machine or the ticket office in the National Arrival lounge when departing from the airport.

Car rental at the airport:

AVIS ☎ 011 47 01 528
Eurodollar ☎ 011 47 02 381
Europcar ☎ 011 56 78 048
Hertz ☎ 011 56 78 166
Italy by Car/Thrifty ☎ 011 56 78 096
Maggiore/Budget ☎ 011 47 01 929

Useful addresses and telephone numbers

Camping – Villa Rey, Strada Superiore Val San Martino 27, ☎ 011 81 90 117
Public telephones: Porta Nuova and Porta Susa railway stations and via Roma 18
Central post-office: Via Alfieri 10, ☎ 011 54 68 00
Police station: Piazza Castello 201, ☎ 011 55 891
City police: Corso XI Febbraio 22, ☎ 011 26 091
National rail information: ☎ 1478-88 088 (toll-free number)
Information on tunnels, mountain passes and tolls: ☎ 194
Motorway information: ☎ 02 35 201

Enjoying Turin by day...

Walking – The best way of discovering the city is on foot. Although Turin is a large city the historic centre is rather compact and can be pleasantly covered on foot; pedestrians are protected from inclement weather by the elegant arcades lining the main streets.

Public transport – ATM (City transport company) has its head office in corso Turati 19/6, ☎ 011 57 641 and 167-01 91 152 (toll-free number), web site http://www.comune.torino.it/-atm. Tickets can be purchased at tobacconists, newspaper stands and authorised bars. There are various types of tickets: the biglietto ordinario urbano (1400L) is valid for 70 min, a biglietto giornaliero (one-day ticket – 4200L) allows unlimited travel all day, the Shopping ticket (2400L) is valid for four hours from when it is stamped, from 9am to 8pm, the Shopping insieme ticket (4500L) is valid only on Saturdays and allows unlimited travel for three people from 2.30pm to 8pm.

Taxis – Central Taxi Radio ☎ 011 57 44 or 011 57 48, Centrale Radio ☎ 011 57 37, Radio Taxi ☎ 011 57 30.

Some suggestions for discovering the city

Boat trips on the Po – Boat trips of varying lengths are operated along the Po (Departure from the river bank at Lungopo Diaz). For information ☎ 011 57 64 590 and 011 88 80 10 (further information can be obtained at Turismo Torino).

Touristbus – This service operates tours of the city, the hills and the Savoy residences. For booking and information contact Turismo Torino ☎ 011 53 51 81 e 011 53 59 01.

Sassi superga rack tram-line – A tram with old-fashioned carriages departs from Sassi station (to get to the station from the city centre take tram line no 14) and after a 3km/1.8mi journey through the countryside, arrives at the Basilica of Superga. Departures every hour in autumn and winter from 10am to 4pm (from 9am to 8pm Saturdays, Sundays and public holidays) and from 9am to 8pm in the spring and summer. For information call ☎ 011 57 64 590.

Take a nice bicycle ride... – through the magnificent Mandria a Venaria Reale Park (1340 ha/3311 acres of parkland 15 km/9mi northwest of the city centre), where bicycles can be rented. The park also offers excursions on horseback and nature walks. For information call ☎ 011 49 93 311.
It is also possible to rent bicycles in other parks in the city, for information call ☎ 1670-18 235 (toll-free number).

... and by night

Music lovers – There are several prestigious concert halls in Turin such as the **Auditorium Giovanni Agnelli** del Lingotto, via Nizza 262/43, ☎ 011 66 44 551 (classical music), the **Auditorium RAI**, piazza Rossini at the corner of via Rossini, ☎ 011 81 04 653 (classical and chamber music) and the **Conservatorio Giuseppe Verdi**, via Mazzini 11, ☎ 011 81 21 268. Without forgetting the **Teatro Regio**, in piazza Castello 215, ☎ 011 88 15 241, where with a bit of luck an opera or ballet can be enjoyed.

Some addresses in the heart of the old city

After years of decay the area between Via Garibaldi and Piazza Emanuele Filiberto is finally experiencing a rebirth thanks to architectural restoration and the improvement of social conditions. As a result this fascinating quarter has undergone a complete metamorphosis and now attracts a fashionable bohemian crowd.

Hafa Café – Via Sant'Agostino 23/C (*a cross street of via Garibaldi near piazza Palazzo di Città* CV), ☎ 011 43 67 091. Open from 11.30am to 1am and connected to the shop of the same name which sells ethnic furniture and objects (closing time 9pm), this Moroccan café is decorated with exquisite taste. North African specialities are served with music in the background.

La Nottola (CV) – Via Sant'Agostino 17/C, ☎ 011 52 16 285, closed Sundays. A literary café which hosts debates, lectures, exhibitions and jazz concerts.

Taqueria Las Rosas (CV) – Via Bellezia 15/F, ☎ 011 52 13 907, closed Sundays at lunch. As its name suggests tacos and tapas are served here washed down with sangria and Mexican cocktails.

Tre Galli (CV) – Via Sant'Agostino 25, ☎ 011 52 16 027. Closed on Sundays. A pleasant wine bar-restaurant with a rustic-minimalist atmosphere. Tables outside in the summer. Open from 12.30pm to 2.30pm and from 6pm to 2am, this is a good after-theatre address.

Shopping in the city

There are 18km/11mi of arcades in the historic centre. On Via Roma (CXY), which the architect Piacentini modernised in the 1930s, particularly in the first stretch (*coming from Porta Nuova station*), there are luxurious shops and the elegant San Federico gallery.

Art and antique lovers should head for the nearby Via Cavour (CDY), Via Maria Vittoria (CDXY) and Via San Tommaso (CX) in search of furniture, ceramics and Art Nouveau objets d'art. Most antiquarian bookshops are concentrated around Via Po, Via Accademia Albertina and Piazza San Carlo, while Via Lagrange is a gourmet's paradise. Turin specialities include agnolotti pasta, *bagna cauda*, the famous grissini breadsticks and naturally chocolate (chocolates with fillings, hazelnut-chocolate *gianduiotti*, *bonet*). All of which can be accompanied by prized local wines and vermouth which was created in Turin at the end of the 18C.

Two streets lead off Piazza Castello: the famous Via Po *(see below)* and the lively shopping street Via Garibaldi (CVX), one of the longest pedestrian streets in Europe, characterised by a young informal style. On the second Sunday of the month an unmissable appointment is the **Balôn** in Porta Palazzo, Turin's traditional flea market which has been in existence since 1856.

Where to sleep?

For a full selection of hotels in Turin consult this year's Michelin Red Guide Italia. Listed below are some addresses chosen on the basis of good value for money, location and charm. Hotels are divided into three categories based on the price of a double room *(for more information see p. 433)* and are listed in alphabetical order *(to locate them see map)*. Note that some hotels offer discounts at weekends and in the winter.

It is advisable to check prices by telephone beforehand and to book well in advance, particularly in more reasonably priced hotels which tend to have fewer rooms.

BUDGET

Some of the hotels listed have rooms without bath in which case expect a discount of 20-30%.

Hotel Artuà – Via Brofferio 1. ☎ 011 51 75 301, fax 011 51 75 141. Credit cards accepted. This hotel is situated on the fourth floor of an old building in a quiet, peaceful neighbourhood. There are ten simple but comfortable rooms with bath, satellite TV, telephone and air conditioning. This is an excellent address for the thoughtful management, pleasant communal areas overlooking Piazza Solferino and very reasonable prices offered on winter weekends. Covered parking lot.

HotelCentrale – Via Mazzini 13. ☎ 011 81 24 182, fax 011 88 33 59. Credit cards not accepted. This hotel is currently being remodelled. It has 12 brand new rooms on the first floor, all with modern and functional decor, telephone and bath. Some singles have shower but no WC. Excellent value for money.

Hotel Magenta – Corso Vittorio Emanuele II 67. ☎ 011 54 26 49, fax 011 54 47 55. Credit cards accepted. Housed in a beautiful old building near Porta Nuova station, this hotel has 18 simple but decent rooms, all with TV and telephone, some with bath (about half).

Hotel Roma e Rocca Cavour – Piazza Carlo Felice 60. ☎ 011 56 12 772, fax 011 56 28 137. Credit cards accepted. This elegant hotel, overlooking the square opposite the station, has been run with true passion by the same family for over a hundred years. The 90 rooms (all with bath and some in the process of being remodelled) are beautifully kept and decorated with old-fashioned good taste: antique furniture, magnificent wood or marble floors, carpets, Murano glass chandeliers. Trying asking for the suite with a fireplace on the third floor, it is unlikely that it will be free but it is worth trying. The hotel offers excellent discounts on weekends, in the month of August and during the Easter and Christmas holidays. In August 1950 Cesare Pavese put an end to his tormented life in room 346.

Hotel Solferino – Via Brofferio 3. ☎ 011 56 13 444, fax 011 56 22 241. Credit cards accepted. This hotel is under the same management as the Hotel Artuà, prices are the same and it is situated in the adjacent building. 10 rooms with air conditioning. Covered parking lot.

Vinzaglio – (off the map, take via Cernaia, CX) Corso Vinzaglio 12. ☎ 011 56 13 793. Credit cards not accepted. This simple but peaceful hotel is situated on the third floor of an old building. The 14 rooms, some without bath, are plain but clean and have TV and telephone. The best address in its category for good value for money.

OUR SELECTION

Hotel Dogana Vecchia – Via Corte d'Appello 4. ☎ 011 43 66 752, fax 011 43 67 194. Credit cards accepted. The inn of the old customs-house, built at the end of the 18C and situated in the heart of the historic centre, was a stopping place for travellers, some of the most illustrious of which include Mozart, Napoleon and Verdi. Of the 70 rooms the prettiest are those decorated with antique furnishings, but there are a few modern, functional rooms for the more practical-minded. Parking.

Hotel Liberty – Via Pietro Micca 15. ☎ 011 56 28 801, fax 011 56 28 163. Credit cards accepted. This hotel, founded at the end of the 19C, has preserved all of its fin de siècle atmosphere, both in the splendid exedra on to which the communal areas open and in the old-fashioned rooms on the third and fourth floors. Those who prefer more modern, functional decor, should ask for a room on the fifth floor. Fine views of the elegant Via Pietro Micca.

Hotel Victoria – Via Nino Costa 4. ☎ 011 56 11 909, fax 011 56 11 806. Credit cards accepted. A small, charming hotel, a real haven of peace and elegance. 90 rooms with all amenities (including air-conditioning), some of which are particularly special and decorated with a theme.

TREAT YOURSELF!

Turin Palace Hotel – Via Sacchi 8. ☎ 011 56 25 511, fax 011 56 12 187. Credit cards accepted. A classic hotel, founded in 1872, which is characterised by a refined elegance. Rooms are luxuriously decorated.

Relais Villa Sassi – Strada al Traforo di Pino 47 (off the map, take corso Moncalieri, DY). ☎ 011 89 80 556, fax 011 89 80 095. Credit cards accepted. This 17C villa is surrounded by a beautiful park (over 20 000 m² – 5 acres) with century-old trees situated at the foot of the Turin hill, 4 km/2.5mi from the historic centre. Beautiful rooms and a good restaurant with splendid views of the park.

Restaurants and Excursions

AVOIDING ANONYMOUS SANDWICHES...

Listed below are bars and restaurants and bars in the historic centre which offer one-course meals or so-called "light lunches" for little more than the price of a sandwich and a beer.

Arcadia (CX) – Galleria Subalpina 16, ☎ 011 56 13 898, closed on Sundays. This refined restaurant, also a sushi bar, is located in the attractive setting of the Subalpina gallery (piazza Castello) and serves one-course meals.

Brek – Piazza Carlo Felice 22 (CY 16), ☎ 011 53 45 56 and via Santa Teresa 23 at the corner of piazza Solferino (CX 75), ☎ 011 53 54 24. A pleasant self-service restaurant with a wide choices of dishes, some of which are made to order.

Caffè Baratti e Milano (CX) – Piazza Castello 29, ☎ 011 56 13 060. This famous café is next door to Arcadia and serves one-course meals and light dishes in a charming room.

Mamma Licia (DZ) – Via Mazzini 50 (parallel street north of corso Vittorio Emanuele), ☎ 011 88 89 42, closed on Mondays. A homely trattoria with a cosy atmosphere, decorated with travel mementoes and paintings donated by its habitués.

Olsen (CX) – Via dei Mercanti 4B (a cross street of via Pietro Micca), ☎ 011 43 61 573, closed on Sundays and Mondays. A cake and tea-room, open from 11am to 11pm, serving organic food.

Porto di Savona (DY) – Piazza Vittorio Veneto 2, ☎ 011 81 73 500, closed all day on Mondays and on Tuesdays at lunchtime. A typical trattoria adorned with old photographs of the city and famous customers.

THE INEVITABLE PIZZA

Turin lies in the shadow of the Mole rather than Vesuvius but good pizzas can be enjoyed anywhere. Booking is recommended.

Da Gennaro Esposito (CV) – Via Passalacqua 9 (near piazza Statuto), ☎ 011 53 59 05, closed on Saturday mornings and Sundays.

Da Michele (DY) – Piazza Vittorio Veneto 4, ☎ 011 88 88 36, closed on Tuesdays.

Fratelli La Cozza (off the map) – Corso Regio Parco 39, ☎ 011 85 99 00. This pizzeria merits a brief description. Opened by the Italian comedian Piero Chiambretti in a converted farm, it is decorated with Neapolitan kitsch and naturally the dominant leitmotif is the mussel (cozza). To find out more see the web site: http://www.lacozza.com

La Focacceria (CV) – Via Porta Palatina 4. Take-away pizza and focaccia.

Il Rospetto (CZ) – Piazza Madama Cristina 5 (take via Madama Cristina). ☎ 011 66 98 221.

La Spaccanapoli (CY) – Via Mazzini 19 (parallel street north of corso Vittorio Emanuele). ☎ 011 81 26 694.

La Stua (DZ) – Via Mazzini 46, ☎ 011 81 78 339.

GOURMET FOOD

Ristorante del Cambio – Piazza Carignano 2 (CX 12). ☎ 011 54 37 60, fax 011 53 52 82. Founded in the mid-18C this is one of the most famous restaurants in Italy and "the" restaurant of Turin. Velvet textiles, Baroque mirrors and gilded decorations all make for a very refined ambience where time seems to have stood still. It is possible to dine at Count Cavour's table and admire the magnificent Palazzo Carignano. Expect to pay about 100 000L a head.

CAFÉS (IN THE COMPANY OF CAVOUR AND AVA GARDNER)

Aristocrats, politicians, intellectuals and artists have frequented cafés in Turin since the 18C. These elegant establishments serve ice-creams, sweets and chocolates as well as bicerin (little glass), a delicious drink made of coffee, chocolate and whipped cream of which Alexander Dumas wrote, "I shall never forget the bicerin, an excellent drink which is served in all cafés". Here is a list of famous cafés which must be seen to experience the combination of the refined atmosphere of the past and the glorious Turin pastries.

Al Bicerin – Piazza della Consolata 5 (take via della Consolata, CV 27). This café was founded in 1763. Cavour came here to take refuge from the troubles of politics.

Baratti & Milano (CX) – Piazza Castello 29. Founded in 1875, this was originally a confectionery shop. With its elegant Art Nouveau rooms it was a favourite with the ladies of Turin's high society.

Fiorio (DX) – Via Po 8. Founded in 1780, this was the traditional meeting place for aristocrats and conservative intellectuals. Its ice-cream is one of the glories of Turin.

Mulassano (CX) – Piazza Castello 15. Founded in 1907, this charming and intimate café, decorated in marble, bronze, wood and leather, was frequented by members of the Savoia family and performers from the nearby Teatro Regio. It counted the comedian Macario and the poet Guido Gozzano among its habitués.

Platti (CY) – Corso Vittorio Emanuele II 72. Founded in 1870, this was originally a shop selling liqueurs and later became an Art Nouveau café. It was frequented predominantly by intellectuals and writers such as Cesare Pavese.

San Carlo (CX) – Piazza San Carlo 156. This opulent café, founded in 1822, was a patriotic stronghold during the Risorgimento and later became a salon frequented by artists, literary personalities and statesmen.

Torino (CY) – Piazza San Carlo 204. Founded in 1903, this Art Nouveau café is adorned with gilded friezes, huge chandeliers and marble and wood fireplaces. It was frequented by members of the royal family, intellectuals and actors such as James Stewart, Ava Gardner and Brigitte Bardot.

IF YOU HAVE A SWEET TOOTH...

Avvignano – Piazza Carlo Felice 50 (CY **16**). This confectioner's was founded in 1926.

Peyrano Pfatisch (CY) – Corso Vittorio Emanuele II 76. This is the definitive chocolate house of Turin.

Stratta (CY) – Piazza San Carlo 191. Confectioner's founded in 1836.

CITY CENTRE

★★ **Piazza San Carlo** (CXY) – This is a graceful example of town planning. The Churches of **San Carlo** and **Santa Cristina**, symmetrically placed on the south side, frame the Via Roma. The curious façade of Santa Cristina (on the left), surmounted by candelabra, was designed by the famous Sicilian-Turinese architect Juvarra, who was responsible for many of Turin's lovely buildings. On the east side is the 17C palace which was the French Ambassador's residence from 1771 to 1789. In the centre of the square stands the famous "bronze horse" by C. Marocchetti (1838), an equestrian monument to Emanuele Filiberto of Savoy who, after defeating the French at the battle of San Quintino in 1557, salvaged his states after 25 years of French occupation (Treaty of Cateau-Cambrésis).

Palazzo dell'Accademia delle Scienze (CX **M¹**) – This 17C palace by Guarini now houses two major Italian museums.

★★★ **Museo Egizio** ⊘ – Ground and first floors. The Egyptian Museum is one of the richest collections of Egyptian antiquities in the world. The basement houses the finds from the excavations carried out in 1911 by the two Italian archeologists, Schiaparelli and Farina.

On the ground floor is the section on **statuary art** with 20 seated or standing figures of the lion-headed goddess Sekhmet from Karnak, and an important series of **statues of Pharaohs** of the New Kingdom (1580-1100 BC), Egypt's Golden Age. The **Rock Temple of Thutmose III** (c 1450 BC), a gift from the United Arab Republic, originated from Ellessya 200km/124mi to the south of Aswan.

The collections on the first floor evoke all aspects of Egyptian civilisation, in particular: the **sarcophagi** – simple examples dating from the Middle Kingdom (2100-1580 BC) and sculpted ones during the New Kingdom; a collection of **canopic urns**; and an important number of mummies and copies of funerary papyri rolls known as the **Book of the Dead**. In addition to the recreated **funeral chambers** (mastabas) (Giza 2500 BC), there is an exceptional collection of **funerary steles** dating from the Middle and New Kingdoms. Jewellery and pottery from the pre-dynastic civilisations, known as Nagadian, date from the 4000-3000 BC. The influence of the Greek world made itself felt from the 4C BC following the conquest by Alexander the Great (masks and statuettes), followed by the Romans from 30BC (bronze vases). Another room is devoted to **inscriptions**; the hieroglyphs (deciphered by Champollion in 1824), and texts in hieratic script using cursive on papyrus, limestone flakes and fragments of pottery.

★★ **Galleria Sabauda** ⊘ – 2nd and 3rd floors. The gallery houses the collections of the House of Savoy and is divided into various thematic and chronological sections.

On the second floor the section on **14C to 16C Piedmontese painting**★ has works by Martino Spanzotti (1455-1528), the principal exponent of the Late Gothic Piedmontese school, his pupil Defendente Ferrari (1510-1531), Macrino d'Alba (1495-1528) and Gaudenzio Ferrari (1475-1546), an artist profoundly linked to the Milanese school. One of his masterpieces is the *Crucifixion*★. The section on **14C to 16C Italian painting** includes works by Fra Angelico, Antonio and Piero Pollaiolo (Tuscan school), Bergognone (Lombard school), Bartolomeo Vivarini and Giovanni Bellini (Venetian school). The **Prince Eugene Collection** has both Italian and European painting including a collection of **Dutch and Flemish painting**★★. One of the richest in Italy, it includes the *Stigmata of St Francis* by Van Eyck

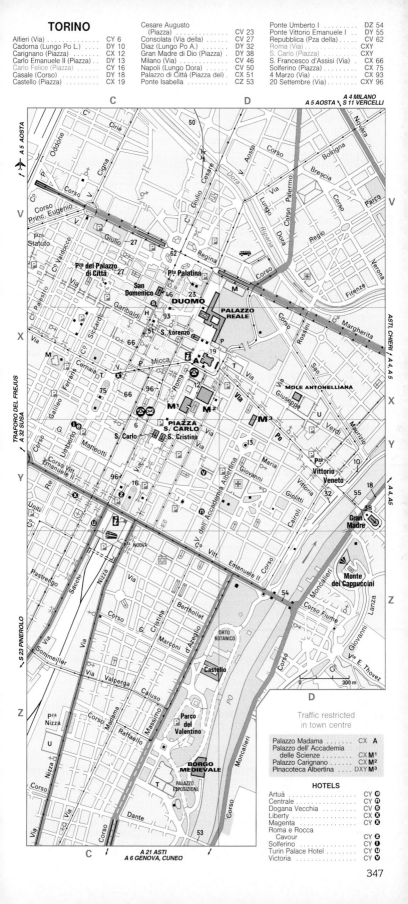

TORINO

Alfieri (Via)	CY	6
Cadorna (Lungo Po L.)	DY	10
Carignano (Piazza)	CX	12
Carlo Emanuele II (Piazza)	DY	13
Carlo Felice (Piazza)	CY	16
Casale (Corso)	DY	18
Castello (Piazza)	CX	19
Cesare Augusto (Piazza)	CV	23
Consolata (Via della)	CV	27
Diaz (Lungo Po A.)	DY	32
Gran Madre di Dio (Piazza)	DY	38
Milano (Via)	CV	46
Napoli (Lungo Dora)	CV	50
Palazzo di Città (Piazza del)	CX	51
Ponte Isabella	CZ	53
Ponte Umberto I	DZ	54
Ponte Vittorio Emanuele I	DY	55
Repubblica (Pza della)	CV	62
Roma (Via)	CXY	
S. Carlo (Piazza)	CXY	
S. Francesco d'Assisi (Via)	CX	66
Solferino (Piazza)	CX	75
4 Marzo (Via)	CX	93
20 Settembre (Via)	CXY	96

Traffic restricted in town centre

Palazzo Madama	CX	A
Palazzo dell' Accademia delle Scienze	CX	M¹
Palazzo Carignano	CX	M²
Pinacoteca Albertina	DXY	M³

HOTELS

Artuà	CY	
Centrale	CY	
Dogana Vecchia	CV	
Liberty	CX	
Magenta	CX	
Roma e Rocca Cavour	CY	
Solferino	CY	
Turin Palace Hotel	CY	
Victoria	CY	

347

(1390-1441), *Scenes from the Passion of Christ* by Hans Memling (ca1435-1494), the *Old Man Sleeping* by Rembrandt (1606-1669) and enchanting landscapes by Jan Brueghel (1568-1625).

On the third floor the **Dynastic Collections**, divided into three sections presented in chronological order, include fine examples of Italian and European painting from the 15C to 18C. Some of the most notable works include the *Visitation*★ by the Flemish artist Van der Weyden (1400-1464), *The Meal at the House of Simon*★, an early work of Veronese (1528-1588), the *Trinity* by Tintoretto (1519-1594), the great canvasses by the **Bassano** family (16C) whose dynamic use of light heralds the work of Caravaggio, the *Assumption*★★ by Orazio Gentileschi (1563-1639), one of the artist's masterpieces characterised by a violent realism, the *Sons of Charles I of England*★, a fine portrait by Van Dyck (1599-1641), *The Four Elements* by the Bolognese painter F. Albani (1578-1660) whose classicism derives from the work of the Carracci and Guido Reni, the portrait of *Philip IV of Spain* by Velasquez (1599-1660), *The Triumph of Aurelius* by Tiepolo (1696-1770) and the beautiful views★ by the Venetian painter Bellotto (1720-1780), a nephew of Canaletto. The fine **Gualino Collection** includes works from the fine and decorative arts of various periods and nationalities, among which some very fine Chinese sculpture.

★★ **Palazzo Carignano** (CX M²) – Victor Emmanuel II (1820-1878), responsible for the Unification of Italy and the country's first king (1861), was born in this beautiful Baroque palace by **Guarini**. It houses the **Museo del Risorgimento Italiano**★★ ⊘, a rich collection of documentation pertaining to the history of Italy from the end of the 18C to the Second World War with particular reference to the Risorgimento. The museum includes a visit to the **Sala del Parlamento Subalpino**★, where from 1848-1860 speakers included Cavour, Garibaldi, Verdi and Manzoni. It is also possible to visit the **Aula del Parlamento Italiano**, built to accommodate the growing number of members of parliament but never actually used as during its construction Florence was made the capital of Italy.

Piazza Castello – The political and religious heart of the city, this square was designed by the architect Ascanio Vitozzi (1539-1615). The main city streets lead off this square and it is bordered by the Royal Palace and the arcades of the **Teatro Regio**, inaugurated in 1740. Severely damaged by bombardments in the Second World War, it was rebuilt and opened to the public in 1973. In the theatre's atrium there is a gateway designed by the artist Umberto Matroianni entitled *Musical Odyssey* In the centre of the square stands the imposing castle from which it derives its name. The castle was later named Palazzo Madama.

★ **Palazzo Madama** ⊘ (CX A) – The palace derives its name from the two "Madame Reali" who stayed here in the 17C-18C: Maria Cristina of France, widow of Victor Amadeus I and Giovanna of Savoia-Nemours, widow of Charles Emmanuel II. The castle was erected in the 14C and 15C on the remains of the Roman gateway, Porta Pretoria which formed part of the Augustan ramparts, while the west façade was designed in the 18C by Juvarra. Part of a more ambitious project which was brought to a halt by the death of Giovanna of Nemours, the classically elegant façade and the grand staircase are based on French and Roman models although tempered by the restraint of Turin Baroque.

There is a Museum of Ancient Art **(Museo d'Arte Antica**★ ⊘) on the ground floor. The exhibits include Gothic carvings, 15C choir stalls, canvases of the 15C-16C Piedmontese school (Gian Martino Spanzotti, Macrino d'Alba, Defendente and Gaudenzio Ferrari), a *Portrait of a Man* (1475) by Antonello da Messina and a 14C *Madonna* by Barnaba da Modena. The decorative arts section comprises Greek, Roman and Barbarian gold work, enamels, ivories, wooden caskets, ceramic ware, a large collection of engraved glass, and 15C furniture.

★ **Palazzo Reale** (CDVX) – The princes of the House of Savoy lived in this plain building until 1865. The façade was designed by Amedeo di Castellamonte in the 17C. The sumptuous apartments **(appartementi)** ⊘ are accessed by the fine staircase *(Scala delle Forbici)* designed by Filippo Juvarra and are decorated in the Baroque, rococo and neo-Classical styles.

The Royal Armoury **(Armeria Reale**★ ⊘) contains a splendid collection of arms and armour and interesting military memorabilia dating from the 13C to 20C.

To the left of the palace stands the **Church of San Lorenzo** (CX) to which the architect Guarini added a dome and rather daring crenellations.

★ **Duomo** ⊘ (CX) – This Renaissance cathedral, dedicated to St John, Turin's patron saint, was built at the end of the 15C for Cardinal Della Rovere. The façade has three finely-carved doorways; the crown of the brick campanile was designed by Juvarra.

Inside, behind the high altar surmounted by a dome, a Baroque masterpiece by Guarini, is the Chapel of the Holy Shroud **(Cappella della Santa Sindone)** which enshrined the precious but much-contested **Holy Shroud**★★★ in which Christ is said to have been wrapped after the Descent from the Cross. In 1997 a raging fire caused grave damage to Guarini's dome (temporarily replaced by a *trompe-l'oeil*) but fortunately the urn containing the precious relic was saved.

There are some interesting Roman remains near the cathedral: remains of a 2C AD theatre and the **Porta Palatina** (1C AD), a fine example of a Roman city gateway.

Via IV Marzo crosses the oldest part of the city and leads to the harmonious, elegant **Piazza del Palazzo di Città**, dominated by the Town Hall which was erected in the 17C by Francesco Lanfranchi.
Nearby (*turn right onto Via Milano*, CV) stands **San Domenico** ⊙ (14C), the only Gothic church in the city which inside has works by Ferrari and Spanzotti and a beautiful cycle of 14C frescoes.

FROM PIAZZA CASTELLO TO THE PO

★ **Via Po** – Created between the 17C and 18C to connect the historic centre to the Po river and bordered by harmoniously arranged palaces and arcades, this is one of the most beautiful streets in Turin.
Nearby stands the **Pinacoteca Albertina** ⊙ (DXY **M³**), a picture gallery which has collection of Piedmontese, Lombard and Venetian painting, a section on Flemish and Dutch painting as well as a fine group of **cartoons**★ by Gaudenzio Ferrari and his school.

★ **Mole Antonelliana** ⊙ (DX) – This unusual structure, towering 167m/548ft up into the air, is the symbol of Turin. Its daring design was the work of the architect Alessandro Antonelli (1798-1888). Originally destined to be a temple for the Jewish community (1863), it was ceded to the city in 1877. The summit affords a vast **panorama**★★ of Turin. Inside is the **Museum of Cinema**.

Piazza Vittorio Veneto (DY) – This large 19C square affords a wonderful **view**★ of the hills and dips down towards the river which can be reached by going down to the **Murazzi** (Lungopo Diaz), ramparts erected in the 19C. Beyond the Victor Emmanuel I bridge, erected by Napoleon, stands the imposing neo-Classical church, **Chiesa della Gran Madre**.

To the right of the church, **Monte dei Cappuccini** (DZ, alt. 284m/932ft) affords an exceptional **panorama**★★★ of the city.

Parco del Valentino (CDZ) – This wooded park extends along the Po for about 1.5km/1mi and affords a pleasant walk along the river. To the north stands the **Castello del Valentino**, erected in the first half of the 17C for Duchess Marie Christine of France. There is also the Palazzo delle Esposizioni (Exhibition Hall), the Teatro Nuovo (T) and the **Borgo Medievale**★ ⊙, an interesting reconstruction of a Medieval town and Fénis Castle.

ADDITIONAL SIGHTS

★★ **Galleria Civica di Arte Moderna e Contemporanea** ⊙ – *Via Magenta 31.* This ample collection of fine art gives a good overview of Italian art and its main exponents, focusing on the 19C and 20C Piedmontese schools. The second floor, devoted to 19C art, has the largest body of work by the Reggio artist **Antonio Fontanesi** (1818-1882), whose landscapes are notable for their solemn compositions, veiled light and dense, rich colours. The first floor, devoted to the 20C, shows the development of Italian and European art through the work of the more significant artists and movements: Balla, Casorati, Martini, the Milanese Novecento group, the Ferrara metaphysical paintings (Carlo Carrà, Giorgio de Chirico), the Roman school (Scipione, Mafai), Turin's "Gruppo dei Sei" (J. Boswell, G. Chessa, N. Galante, C. Levi, F. Menzio and E. Paolucci), examples of Informal Art and "Arte Povera" from the 1960s. The ground floor has collections of international art of the last 30 years.

★★ **Museo dell'Automobile Carlo Biscaretti di Ruffia** ⊙ – *South of the town. Take Corso Massimo d'Azeglio (CZ) and then follow the plan of the built-up area in the Michelin Atlas Italy. The address is No 40 Corso Unità d'Italia.*
A vast modern building houses an extensive collection of cars, chassis and engines as well as graphic documents outlining the history of the automobile from its beginnings to the last 20 years. Another room devoted to tyre manufacture traces the tremendous development of materials, structure, technology and research, famous car races, types of vehicle (cycles to planes etc). The museum also includes a library and archives *(open by appointment only)*.

A much-deserved homage to Turin's motor industry:
the Museo dell'Automobile Carlo Biscaretti di Ruffia

EXCURSIONS

Plan of the built-up area in the Michelin Atlas Italy.

★ **Basilica di Superga** – *10km/6mi east.* This masterpiece was built by Juvarra from 1717 to 1731 on a hill (670m/2 198ft high). The basilica is circular in plan and roofed with a dome and its most remarkable feature is its monumental façade with its imposing columns and pilasters. The chapel dedicated to the Virgin, in the chancel, is a pilgrimage centre. The basilica is the Pantheon of the Kings of Sardinia. **Tombe dei Reali** ⊘: The royal tombs in the crypt include that of Victor Amadeus II, who built the basilica to fulfil a vow made when his capital was being besieged by a French and Spanish army in 1706. Alongside are the tombs of Charles-Albert and other princes of the House of Savoy. From the esplanade there is a fine **view★★★** of Turin, the Po Plain and the Alps.

---

4 May 1949

Heavy rain and fog over Turin. An aeroplane flies over Superga with its illustrious passengers: 18 players from Grande Torino, the legendary football team who won five championships in a row and provided Italy's national team with ten players. They were on their way back from Lisbon where they had played a friendly and were accompanied by technicians, executives and journalists. With zero visibility, at 5.05pm the plane loses radio contact and plunges down, its left wing hitting the basilica, finally crashing to the ground. The city of Turin is paralysed with grief, the Grande Torino team dies and its memory is imbued with a sense of nostalgia and the desire to make the sport live forever.

★ **Circuito della Maddalena** – *32km/20mi east.* From Superga take the scenic route via Pino Torinese which affords good **views★★** of Turin. From Pino Torinese continue to the hilltop, **Colle della Maddalena**, and the **Parco della Rimembranza**, a very popular large public park which commemorates those who died in the First World War.
On the way down there are more lovely **views★** of Turin. The **Parco Europa** at Cavoretto overlooks the southern part of the town.

★ **Palazzina di caccia di Stupinigi** ⊘ or **Palazzina Mauriziana** – *11km/7mi southwest.* This huge building was a hunting -lodge built by Juvarra for Victor Amadeus II of Savoy. Napoleon stayed here before assuming the crown of Italy. The palace now houses a Fine Arts and Furniture Museum **(Museo d'arte e del mobilio)**. The apartments are richly decorated in the rococo style of the 18C. A magnificent park surrounds the palazzina.

VAL DI SUSA *150km/93mi, allow 1 day.*

From Turin take the west exit in the direction of Corso Francia

Castello di Rivoli ⊘ – *14km/8.5mi west.* Victor Amadeus II commissioned Juvarra to build a grandiose residence (18C) in the Baroque style. Only the left wing (some rooms are decorated) and the lower part of the central range

were built. The château now houses a Museum of Contemporary Art (**Museo d'arte contemporanea**★ ◷) (1960 to the present day as well as temporary exhibitions).
Take the S 25

★ **Abbazia di Sant'Antonio di Ranverso** ◷ – *From the S 25 follow the deviation 6km –4mi after Rivoli.* This abbey was a resting place for pilgrims as well as a centre for the "fire of St Anthony" cure. The church, founded in the 12C, has a fine façade and three 15C doorways adorned with gothic pediments and pinnacles. The interior has beautiful **frescoes**★ by **Giacomo Jaquerio** (1401-1453) who combined the realism of Burgundian art with the refinement of the International Gothic Style. The frescoes in the sacristy are better preserved; the scene portraying two peasants offering two pigs refers to the tradition of curing St Anthony's fire with pork fat. At the high altar there is a fine **polyptych** by Defendente Ferrari (1510-1531).

Avigliana – Until the 15C this town was one of the Savoia's favourite residences. The heart of the historic centre is the pretty square, **Piazza Conte Rosso**, dominated by the ruins of a **Castle** (15C). Nearby stands the Romanesque-Gothic parish church of **St John**. Southeast of the ruins stands the church of St Peter (**San Pietro**★ ◷) (10C-11C) which has a fine cycle of frescoes (mainly 14C-15C).

A scenic road skirts the two **lakes of Avigliana**, originally glaciers, eventually leading up to the Abbey of St Michael. *(13.5km/8mi)*.

★★★ **Sacra di San Michele** ◷ – This Benedictine abbey, perched on a rocky site (alt 962m/3 156ft), was a powerful establishment in the 13C with over 100 monks and 140 sister houses. It was built at the end of the 10C by Hughes de Montboissier from Auvergne and its layout bears a strong resemblance to the abbey at Mont Saint Michel in France. After passing through the iron doors of the entrance gatehouse, climb the great staircase leading to the **Zodiac Door**; its pilasters and capitals were decorated by the famous Master Nicolò (1135). The Romanesque-Gothic **church** built on top of the rocky eminence has 16C frescoes. The early-16C triptych on the high altar is by Defendente Ferrari. The carved capitals are outstanding.
From the esplanade there is a lovely **view**★★★ of the Alps, the Dora Valley, the Po and Turin plains.

★ **Susa** – *30km/19mi from Avigliana on the S 25 or the A 32 through the Fréjus tunnel.* Situated at the foot of an impressive mountain range, of which the Rocciamelone (3 538m/11 608ft) stands out, Susa stands at a junction of two roads which lead to France. This has resulted in its being referred to as "Italy's gateway". Because of its strategic position Susa, which was founded by the Celts and flourished in Roman times, was destroyed on several occasions (by Constantine in 312 and by Barbarossa in 1174).
The symbol of the city is the **Savoy Door**★ which takes its name from the French region and dates from the late-3C-early-4C AD when the ramparts were built. Next to the door stands the **Cathedral**, founded in the years 1027-29 with Gothic additions made in the 14C. To the south side of the church is the small square, Piazza San Giusto which is dominated by the magnificent **Romanesque campanile**★★. In a delightful corner stands the elegant **Arco di Augusto**★, the oldest monument in the city (8C BC). The arch is decorated with low reliefs which depict an alliance between Cozio, Lord of Susa, and Augustus. In front of the arch there are remains of the **Roman Aqueduct** (4C AD); beyond stand the Celtic **rocks** (6C-5C BC), used by Druid priests for sacrificial rites.
To the south, in a typically decentralised position stands the **amphitheatre**, erected in the 1C-2C AD.

Abbazia della Novalesa ◷ – *8km/5mi northeast.* This powerful Benedictine abbey was founded in the 8C and destroyed by Saracens in the 10C. It was later rebuilt but began to decline in the 13C. The real jewel of this abbey are the extraordinary **frescoes**★★ in the chapel (**Cappella S. Eldrado**, 12C) which depict scenes from the lives of Saints Eldrado and Nicola of Bari.

★ **MONFERRATO** *150km/93mi – allow 1 day*

The proposed itinerary takes the visitor through this attractive region of limestone hills, bordered to the north by the Po, to the east by the plains of Alessandria and to the southwest by the Langhe hills. The valley of Villafranca d'Asti and the lower part of the Tanaro river divide the area into Lower and Upper Monferrato (north and south respectively in spite of their names). Defended by numerous strongholds and covered in castles, towers and fortified towns, Monferrato is a generous region which has given Piedmont some of its finest wines: Barbera, Dolcetto and Grignolino among red wines, Cortese and Gavi among white wines and the dessert wines Asti Spumante, Moscato and Brachetto.
Leave Turin to the east by the S 10, 14km/9mi..

Chieri – This town is known for its cuisine. It has some fine Piedmontese Gothic monuments such as the 15C cathedral flanked by the Romanesque-Gothic baptistery and the 13C-15C Church of San Domenico with its fine campanile.

Follow directions for Castelnuovo Don Bosco (4km/2.5mi south of **Colle Don Bosco** stands the house where Giovanni Bosco was born and the sanctuary) and Albugnano.

Abbazia di Vezzolano ⊙ – *17km/10mi northeast of Chieri.* Immersed in a silent green valley this abbey is one of the finest examples of Piedmontese Romanesque-Gothic architecture. Its beautiful terracotta and sandstone façade has a doorway adorned with low reliefs. Beyond stands the real jewel of Vezzolano, the splendid *jubé*★★ (footbridge) dated 1189, whose beautiful polychrome low reliefs depict episodes from the life of the Virgin. These structures served to separate the faithful from those areas reserved for the monks. The interior of the church, with two aisles, has pointed arches and cross vaulting supported by pilasters. At the end of the south aisle there is access to the evocative and elegant **cloisters**★ (which have incorporated one of the church's aisles) with 13C-14C fresco remains.

Asti – *38km/24mi southeast on the S 458.* The home town of the tragic poet, Vittorio Alfieri (1749-1803), is the scene of an annual horse race *(palio)* which is preceded by a procession with over 1 000 participants in 14C and 15C costume *(see the table of Principal Festivals at the end of the guide)*. The 12C baptistery **(Battistero di San Pietro★)**, the 15C Church of San Pietro and the Gothic cloisters form an attractive group. In the heart of the old town the 14C Gothic cathedral **(Cattedrale)** is decorated with Baroque paintings.

Take the E 74 dual-carriageway and then the S 456 for Acqui Terme, 46km/28mi southeast of Asti.

★ **Strada dei Castelli dell'Alto Monferrato** – From Acqui Terme to Gavi *(24km/15mi to Ovada on the S 456 and another 24km/15mi to Gavi on minor roads)* this scenic route, also known as the wine route, follows the crest of the hillsides covered with vineyards. **Acqui Terme** ‡‡, famous in Roman times for its healing mud and spa water, is a pleasant town with remains of Roman and Medieval architecture. Along the road there is a series of hilltop villages, each one guarded by a castle. Among these are Visone, Morsasco, Cremolino, Molare, Tagliolo, Lerma, Casaleggio, Mornese and, making a short detour to the northeast, Montaldeo, Castelletto d'Orba and Silvano d'Orba.

Isole TREMITI★

TREMITI ISLANDS – Puglia
Population 374
Michelin map 431 A 28

This tiny archipelago, the only one on the Adriatic coast, lies offshore from the Gargano Promontory and belongs to the same geological formation. There are two main islands, San Nicola and San Domino as well as two uninhabited isles, Capraia and Pianosa; the latter is much further out in the Adriatic.

The boat trip out from Manfredonia offers unforgettable **views**★★★ of the Gargano coastline with its dazzling white limestone cliffs. As the boat rounds the promontory there are also good views of the coastal towns of Vieste, Peschici and Rodi Garganico set on their precipitous sites. On the points of the rocky headlands there are typical platforms *(trabocco)* equipped with square fishing nets.

GETTING THERE

From June to September there are daily ferry crossings (1hr40min) from **Termoli** operated by **Navigazione Libera del Golfo** (at the port), ☎ 0875 70 39 37, fax 0875 70 48 59. Daily hovercraft crossings (40min-1hr) are operated by **Navigazione Libera del Golfo** and **Adriatica di Navigazione** – Agenzia Intercontinental Viaggi, corso Umberto 1 93, ☎ 0875 70 53 41, fax 0875 70 64 29.

From June to September **Adriatica di Navigazione** also operates daily motorboat crossings (2hr) from **Ortona**, Agenzia Fratino, via Porto 34, ☎ 085 90 63 855, fax 085 90 64 186; from **Vieste** (1hr by motorboat), Agenzia Gargano Viaggi, piazza Roma 7, ☎ 0884 70 85 01, fax 0884 70 73 93 and from Punta Penna in **Vasto** (1hr by motorboat), Agenzia Massacesi, piazza Diomede 3, ☎ 0873 36 71 74, fax 0873 69 380.

* **San Nicola** – High on the clifftop stands the **Abbazia di Santa Maria al Mare** ⊙, an abbey originally founded by the Benedictines in the 9C. A fortified ramp leads up to the abbey. Of particular interest are the remains of an 11C mosaic pavement, a 15C Gothic polyptych and a 13C Byzantine crucifix. From the cloisters there are good glimpses of the second island, San Domino.

* **San Domino** ⊙ – Take a boat trip round this island and discover the wild beauty of its very indented and rugged coasts covered in pine forests.

TRENTO ★

TRENT – Trentino-Alto Adige
Population 103 668
Michelin map 429 D 15
Town plan in the Michelin Atlas Italy

Trent (or Trento), capital of Trentino, stands on the Adige not far from the Brenta Massif and is encircled by rocky peaks and valleys. Austrian and Italian influences meet here. This agricultural and industrial centre stands at an important crossroads with the converging of routes from the Brenner Pass, Brescia and Venice.

HISTORICAL NOTES

This Roman colony under the Empire became an episcopal See in the 4C, was occupied successively by the Ostrogoths under Theodoric, and by the Lombards in the 6C before being united to the Holy Roman Empire in the late 10C. From 1004 to 1801 the town was governed by a succession of Prince-Bishops.
The **Council of Trent** (1545-63), called by Pope Paul III to study methods of combating Protestantism, met in the town. These important deliberations marked the beginning of the Counter-Reformation and the findings were to change the character of the Church. The main decisions which aimed at the re-establishment of ecclesiastical credibility and authority, concerned compulsory residence for bishops and the abolition of the sale of indulgences.
After a period of Napoleonic rule in the 19C, Trento was ceded to the Austrians in 1814.
In 1918, the town was liberated, after a long hard struggle, by Italian troops.

★ CITY OF THE PRINCE-BISHOPS 2hr

* **Piazza del Duomo** – This cobbled square is the town centre. All around stand the cathedral, the Palazzo Pretorio (13C, restored), the belfry and the Rella houses painted with 16C frescoes.

  Duomo – The majestic 12C-13C cathedral is in the Lombard-Romanesque style. The façade of the north transept is pierced with a window forming a Wheel of Fortune which determines man's destiny: Christ stands at the summit, the Symbols of the Evangelists rise towards him.
  Inside, note the unusual sweep of the stairway leading to the towers. To the right, in the 17C Chapel of the Crucifix (Cappella del Crocifisso), is a large wooden Christ in front of which the decrees of the Council of Trent were proclaimed. In the south transept is the tomb of the Venetian mercenary leader Sanseverino who was killed in 1486.
  The remains of a 5C early-Christian basilica **(Basilica paleocristiana)** ⊙ lie beneath the chancel.

* **Museo Diocesano** ⊙ – The Diocesan Museum installed in the Palazzo Pretorio displays the most important items from the cathedral's treasure, paintings, carved **wooden panels★**, **altarpiece★** and eight early-16C **tapestries★** which were woven in Brussels by Pieter Van Aelst.

  Via Belenzani – This street is lined with palaces in the Venetian style. Opposite the 16C town hall (Palazzo Comunale) stand houses with walls painted with frescoes.

  Via Manci – The Venetian (loggias and frescoes) and mountain (overhanging roofs) styles are intermingled all along the street. No 63, the Palazzo Galazzo with its embossed stonework and huge pilasters is 17C.

★★ **Castello del Buon Consiglio** ⊙ – From the 13C to the dawn of the 14C this castle was the residence of Trento's prince-bishops. Castelvecchio (Old Castle), as its name implies, is the oldest part of the castle and incorporates the **Torre Aquila** *(there are excellent guided tours of the tower: contact the guard at the Loggia del Romanino)*, which an artist of Bohemian origin decorated with frescoes depicting the months in a fine expression of the International Gothic Style. Everyone will have a favourite: the month of January portrays the inhabitants of the castle throwing snowballs; the month of May depicts the season of love and the month of December shows the gathering of fire-burning wood for the winter months. The prince-bishop who most influenced life in Trento in the 16C was Bernardo Cles who enlarged the castle adding the Magno Palazzo. Cles was a true Renaissance prince, calling renowned artists to decorate his residence. The Ferrarese painters Dosso and Battista Dossi adorned the most important rooms, such as the Sala Grande. The frescoes on the vaulting and lunettes of the **loggia** depict biblical and mythological scenes and are by the Brescian artist Gerolamo Romanino.

The castle also houses collections of paintings, coins and archeological artefacts as well as a Risorgimento Museum.

ADDITIONAL SIGHTS

* **Palazzo Tabarelli** – A remarkable building in the Venetian-Renaissance style with pilasters, pink marble columns and medallions.

Santa Maria Maggiore – Numerous meetings of the Council of Trent were held in this Renaissance church, dedicated to St Mary Major, with a Romanesque campanile. The elegant marble organ loft (1534) in the chancel is by Vincenzo and Girolamo Grandi. At the second altar on the right, in the nave, is a 16C altarpiece of the Madonna and saints by Moroni.

Sant'Apollinare – This small Romanesque church on the west bank of the Adige has a curious pointed roof covering two Gothic domical vaults. It is dedicated to St Apollinaris.

*** GRUPPO DEL BRENTA

Round tour starting from Trento *233km/145mi – allow two days*

The wild limestone Brenta Massif prolongs the Dolomites beyond the Adige Valley. Its characteristic features are deep valleys, solitary lakes and erosion-worn rocks.

Sightseeing – The map below locates the towns and sites described in the guide and also indicates other beauty spots in small black type.

Take the S 45b in the direction of Vezzano.

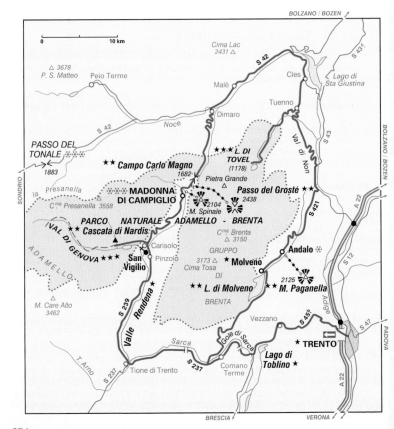

* **Lago di Toblino** – This charming lake fringed with tall rushes, stands against a background of rocky walls. An attractive little castle, once the summer residence of the Bishops of Trent, stands on a small peninsula.

* **Val Rendena** – This wide valley clad with firs and larches has charming villages with churches covered with frescoes, protected by overhanging roofs.
  The Church of **San Vigilio** near Pinzolo has a remarkable *Dance of Death* (1539) by Simone Baschenis.

*** **Val di Genova** – The valley crosses the granite Adamello Massif and is known for its wild grandeur. The road follows a fast-flowing river as it tumbles and foams along the rock-strewn bed to reach a waterfall **(Cascata di Nardis★★)** where the waters drop over 100m/328ft.

*** **Madonna di Campiglio** – This pleasant resort and winter sports centre has many hotels and numerous possibilities for excursions.

** **Campo Carlo Magno** – A supposed visit by Charlemagne gave this place its name. It has become a winter sports centre.
  From a pass **(Passo del Grosté** ⊙**)** – *cable-car and then on foot* – there is a fine **panorama★★** of the Brenta Massif.
  Continue to Dimaro and Malè and at Cles turn right towards Tuenno.

*** **Lago di Tovel** – Pass through wild gorges to reach this lovely lake fringed by wooded slopes. In hot weather the waters of the lake take on a reddish tinge due to the presence of microscopic algae.

⁜ **Andalo** – This small holiday resort is set in majestic scenery amidst a great pine forest and overlooked by the crests of the Brenta Massif.
  From the summit of **Monte Paganella** ⊙ *(cable-car)* at 2 125m/6 972ft there is a splendid **panorama★★** of the whole region, and in clear weather as far as Lake Garda.

* **Molveno** – This choice resort is situated amid gently-sloping meadows at the north end of a **lake★★** which lies on the floor of a cirque.

TREVISO★

Veneto

Population 81 328
Michelin map 428 E-F 18
Town plan in the Michelin Atlas Italy

Treviso, situated in the rich Venetian plain, is an important agricultural and industrial centre but has retained its old walled town. Ever since the 14C its fortunes have been linked with those of Venice.

* **Piazza dei Signori** – This forms the historic centre of Treviso and is bordered by impressive monuments: the Palazzo del Podestà with its tall municipal bell-tower, the **Palazzo dei Trecento★** (1207) and the Renaissance Palazzo Pretorio. Lower down in Piazza del Monte di Pietà is the former pawn shop **(Monte di Pietà)** ⊙ with the Chapel of the Rectors (Cappella dei Reggitori).
  In Piazza San Vito there are two adjoining churches: **San Vito** and **Santa Lucia** which is adorned with remarkable **frescoes★** by Tommaso da Modena, one of the finest 14C artists after Giotto.

* **San Nicolò** – This large Romanesque-Gothic church, dedicated to St Nicholas, contains interesting frescoes, especially those on the columns which are by Tommaso da Modena. In the Onigo Chapel there are portraits of people from Treviso by Lorenzo Lotto (16C). The *Virgin in Majesty* at the far end of the chancel is by Savoldo (16C). In the adjoining monastery the chapter-house has portraits of famous Dominicans by Tommaso da Modena.

* **Museo Civico Bailo** ⊙ – *22 Borgo Cavour*. In the municipal museum are works by Tommaso da Modena, Girolamo da Treviso (15C) and others of the Venetian school such as Cima da Conegliano, Giovanni Bellini, Titian, Paris Bordone, Jacopo Bassano and Lorenzo Lotto.

Duomo – The 15C and 16C cathedral has seven domes, a neo-Classical façade and a Romanesque crypt. Left of the cathedral stands an 11C-12C baptistery. In the Chapel of the Annunciation (Cappella dell'Annunziata), to the right of the chancel, there are frescoes in the Mannerist style by Pordenone and on the altarpiece an *Annunciation* by Titian.

San Francesco – *Viale Sant' Antonio da Padova*. This church in the transitional Romanesque-Gothic style has a fine wooden ceiling, the tombstone of Petrarch's daughter and the tomb of one of Dante's sons, as well as frescoes by Tommaso da Modena in the first chapel to the left of the chancel. The church is dedicated to St Francis.

EXCURSIONS

Maser ⓥ - *29km/18mi northwest by the S 348*. This small agricultural town is known for its famous **villa★★★** built in 1560 by Palladio for the Barbaro brothers: Daniele, patriarch of Aquileia and Marcantonio, ambassador of the Venetian Republic. The interior was decorated from 1566 to 1568 with a splendid cycle of **frescoes★★★** by Veronese. It is one of his best decorative schemes and he used all his amazing knowledge of perspective, *trompe-l'œil*, foreshortening and his sense of movement and colour. Not far from the villa is a **Tempietto**, a graceful circular chapel with a dome which was also the work of Palladio.

Vittorio Veneto - *41km/26mi north*. The name of this town recalls the great victory of the Italians over the Austrians in 1918. In Ceneda to the south of the town, a museum **(Museo della Battaglia)** ⓥ which presents documents on this victory is installed in a 16C loggia (Loggia Cenedese) with a frescoed portico by Sansovino. The suburb of Serravalle in the north has retained a certain charm. The Church of **San Giovanni** *(take Via Roma and then Via Mazzini)* has interesting **frescoes★** attributed to Jacobello del Fiore and Gentile da Fabriano (15C).

★ **Portogruaro** - *56km/35mi east*. The town grew up from the 11C onwards along the banks of the river Lemene, a trade route that brought the town its wealth. Two fine main streets lined with attractive porticoes flank the river banks and there are numerous palaces built in a style that is typically Venetian, dating from the late Middle Ages and the Renaissance (14C-16C). On the **Corso Martiri della Liberta★★** (the busiest of the shopping streets) not far from the 19C cathedral and its leaning Romanesque campanile is the strange **Palazzo Municipale★** built in a late-Gothic style (14C) on which the façade is crowned with Ghibelline merlons. Behind the palace is the river: note, to the right, the two 15C watermills (now restored) and a small 17C fishermen's chapel (Oratorio del Pesce) with its own landing-stage. In the Via del Seminario (the main street on the opposite bank) stands a museum **(Museo Nazionale Concordiese** ⓥ - *no 22)* which has Roman exhibits (small bronze of Diane the Huntress) and Paleo-Christian artefacts from Concordia Sagittaria *(3km/2mi south)*, a Roman colony founded in 40 BC.

TRIESTE★

Friuli-Venezia Giulia –

Population 230 644

Michelin map 988 fold 6 or 429 F 23

Plan of the conurbation in the current Michelin Red Guide Italia

Trieste is a modern town which stands at the head of a bay of the same name and at the foot of the Carso Plateau. The edge of the latter forms a steep coast with magnificent white cliffs as far as Duino in the north. Trieste is the largest seaport on the Adriatic. Its extensive port (12km/8mi of quays stretch as far as the Slovenian border) handles more goods from abroad than from Italy. An oil pipeline links Trieste to refineries in Austria and Bavaria. The vast shipyards, specialising in the building of large vessels, are important to the local economy.

HISTORICAL NOTES

Trieste is of very ancient origin; the Celts and Illyrians fought over the town before the Romans made it their great trading centre of Tergeste, which had the important role of defending the eastern frontiers of the Empire. In the Middle Ages it came under the sway of the Patriarch of Aquileia and then, in 1202, under Venice. In 1382 Trieste rebelled and placed itself under the protection of Austria and it played the role of mediator between the two powers until the 15C. In 1719 Charles VI declared it a free port and established the headquarters of the French Trading Company (Compagnie d'Orient et du Levant) in the city. Trieste then enjoyed a second period of prosperity and was embellished by numerous fine buildings. Many political exiles sought refuge in Trieste. It was only in 1919 after fierce fighting that Trieste was united with the Kingdom of Italy.

At the beginning of the 20C Trieste boasted an active literary group under the leading influence of the novelist Italo Svevo and the poet Umberto Saba. James Joyce lived in the town for some years until 1914.

★★ COLLE DI SAN GIUSTO *1hr*

This hilltop was the site of the ancient city and today the **Piazza della Cattedrale★** **(BY)** is lined with the ruins of a Roman basilica, a 15C-16C castle, a 1560 Venetian column, the altar of the Third Army (1929) and the Basilica of St Justus.

★ **Basilica di San Giusto (BY)** - It was founded in the 5C on the site of a Roman building, but the present buildings date in large part from the 14C. The façade is pierced with a fine Gothic rose window and decorated with a low relief and bronze

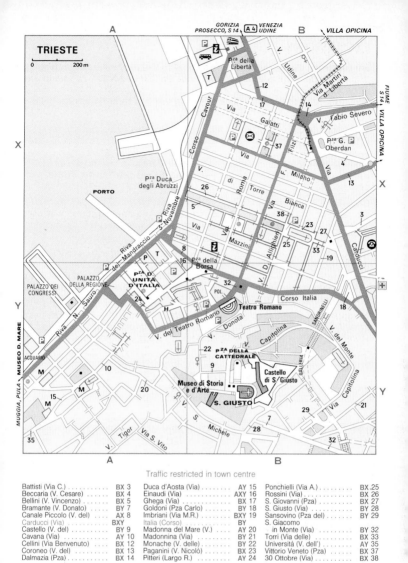

Battisti (Via C.)	BX 3	Duca d'Aosta (Via)	AY 15	Ponchielli (Via A.)	BX 25
Beccaria (V. Cesare)	BX 4	Einaudi (Via)	AXY 16	Rossini (Via)	BX 26
Bellini (V. Vincenzo)	BX 5	Ghega (Via)	BX 17	S. Giovanni (Pza)	BX 27
Bramante (V. Donato)	BY 7	Goldoni (Pza Carlo)	BY 18	S. Giusto (Via)	BX 28
Canale Piccolo (V. del)	AX 8	Imbriani (Via M.R.)	BXY 19	Sansovino (Pza del)	BY 29
Carducci (Via)	BXY	Italia (Corso)	BY	S. Giacomo
Castello (V. del)	BY 9	Madonna del Mare (V.)	AY 20	in Monte (Via)	BY 32
Cavana (Via)	AY 10	Madonnina (Via)	BY 21	Torri (Via delle)	BX 33
Cellini (Via Benvenuto)	BX 12	Monache (V. delle)	BY 22	Università (V. dell')	AY 35
Coroneo (V. del)	BX 13	Paganini (V. Nicolò)	BX 23	Vittorio Veneto (Pza)	BX 37
Dalmazia (Pza)	BX 14	Pitteri (Largo R.)	AY 24	30 Ottobre (Via)	BX 38

busts. The massive campanile has fragments of Roman columns built into its lowest storey and bears a 14C statue of St Justus. From the top there is an attractive view★ of Trieste.

The **interior**★ comprises a nave and four aisles. The side aisles belonged to two separate basilicas which were joined together in the 14C by the building of the nave. In the south aisle there are: a lovely 13C mosaic and 11C frescoes depicting the life of St Justus. A magnificent 12C **mosaic**★★ in the north apse shows the Virgin in Majesty between the Archangels Michael and Gabriel, and the Apostles.

Castello di San Giusto ⊙ (BY) – The castle houses a **museum** of furniture and a fine collection of **arms**★.

Museo di Storia e d'Arte ⊙ (BY) – The Museum of History and Art contains a remarkable collection of red-figured **Greek vases**★ and charming **small bronzes**★ dating from the Roman Archaic period.

Teatro Romano (BY) – The remains of an early-2C Roman theatre lie at the foot of the Hill of St Justus.

LOWER TOWN *1hr*

★ **Piazza dell'Unità d'Italia** (AY) – Three early 20C palaces line this square, namely the Palazzo del Governo (Government Palace), Palazzo del Comune (Town Hall) and the offices of Lloyd Trieste.

★ **Museo del Mare** ⊙ – *Via A. Ottaviano. Take Riva Nazario Sauro* (AY). The history of seafaring is traced from its beginnings to the 18C. The **fishing section**★ is of special interest.

357

EXCURSIONS

Santuario del Monte Grisa - *10km/6mi north. Leave by Piazza della Libertà* (BX) *in the direction of Prosecco and then Villa Opicina and follow the signposts to "Monte Grisa".*
This modern sanctuary is dedicated to the Virgin. From the terrace there is a splendid **panorama**★★ of Trieste and its bay.

Villa Opicina ⊙ - *9km/6mi north. Leave by Via Fabio Severo* (BX). *After 4.5km/3mi turn left off the S 14 to take the S 58. It is also possible to take the funicular which leaves from Piazza Oberdan.*
Villa Opicina stands on the edge of the Carso Plateau (alt 348m/1 142ft). From the belvedere with its obelisk there is a magnificent **view**★★ over Trieste and its bay.

★ **Castello di Miramare** ⊙ - *8km/5mi northwest by the coast road.* Standing on the point of a headland, this castle with its lovely terraced **gardens**★ was built in 1860 for Archduke Maximilian of Austria, who was executed by shooting in Mexico in 1867, and his wife, Princess Charlotte, who died insane.

★ **Grotta Gigante** ⊙ - *13km/8mi north. Follow the above directions to Villa Opicina and then turn left in the direction of Borgo Grotta Gigante.*
An impressive stairway leads down to this chamber of amazing size where one can walk among the splendid concretions. There is a speleological museum **(Museo di Speleologia)** at the entrance to the cave.

Muggia - *14km/9mi south. Leave by Riva Nazario Sauro* (AY). Facing Trieste, this small Venetian-looking town boasts a 15C Gothic cathedral (Duomo) with an attractive pointed campanile and an elegant façade in Istrian limestone.

Terra dei TRULLI★★★

Puglia

Michelin map 431 E 33

This region extending between Fassano, Ostuni, Martina Franca and Alberobello takes its name from the very curious buildings, the *trulli*, which are to be found almost everywhere. These square structures have conical roofs covered with *chiancarelle*, local grey limestone roof slabs. Originally built without using mortar, the walls and the edges of the roof are whitewashed. They are crowned by differently shaped pinnacles, each with a magic significance. Each dome corresponds to a room and each abode usually comprises three of four *trulli*. A tall chimney crowns the side of the building. The external staircase leads to the attic. The doorway stands in a recessed arch surmounted by a triangular gable. Inside, the rooms are domed.

Trulli in Alberobello

★★★ Alberobello – This small town has an entire district of *trulli* (about 1 400) which often abut one another. They spread over the hillside to the south of the town (ZonaMonumentale, Rioni Monti and Aia Piccola). On the hilltop stands the Church of **Sant'Antonio** also in the form of a *trullo (take Via Monte Sant'Angelo)*. Inside, the transept crossing is covered with a dome, similar to those in the *trulli*.

It is possible to visit some of these strange dwellings: from the rooftops there is often a good view of the site. A good example can be visited at the **Museo del Territorio** (in the new quarter, Piazza XXVII Maggio) ⊙, a large 18C *trullo* which is now used for exhibitions. The **Trullo Sovrano★** ⊙, a two-storeyed *trullo*, the largest in Alberobello, stands near the principal church on Piazza Sacramento. Built in the mid-18C it has a total of twelve cones and has preserved enough of its furnishings to be able to make out what the various rooms were used for.

Locorotondo – *36km/22mi north of Taranto*. This town takes its name from the layout of its alleyways which wind in concentric circles (*loco rotondo:* round place) around the hill on which it is set. Building of note in the **historic centre★** include the neo-Classical church of St George and the church of Santa Maria la Greca whose façade is adorned with a fine Gothic rose-window.

The road from Locorotondo to Martina Franca follows the **Valle d'Itria★★**, a vast and fertile plain planted with vines and olive trees and dotted with *trulli*.

★ Martina Franca – This white city rises on a hilltop in the Murge Hills. The architecture of the old town, girdled by its ramparts, is an attractive combination of the Baroque and rococo styles.

The pleasant **Piazza Roma** is bordered by the former ducal palace (**Palazzo Ducale** ⊙, 1668) whose principal floor is enriched by beautiful 18C frescoes. Make for Corso Vittorio Emanuele which leads to Piazza del Plebiscito, dominated by the white façade of the Collegiate Church, **Collegiata San Martino**. The saint's image is depicted in the high reliefs above the doorway. Inside, the high altar (1773) is flanked by two fine marble statues portraying Hope and Charity. The adjacent square, Piazza Maria Immacolata, has attractive arcades and leads into **Via Cavour★** which is lined by numerous Baroque palaces. Nearby, in Via Principe Umberto, the church of St Dominic has a lovely Baroque façade.

The chapter on art and architecture in this guide gives an outline of artistic creation in Italy, providing the context of the buildings and works of art described in the Sights section.

This chapter may also provide ideas for touring.

It is advisable to read it at leisure/before setting out.

TUSCANIA ★

Lazio
Population 7 900
Michelin map 430 O 17

Tuscania was a powerful Etruscan town, a Roman municipium and an important medieval centre. The town retains fragments of its walls and two superb churches, a little way out of town. Tuscania's artistic heritage was considerably damaged by the earthquake of February 1971.

★★ San Pietro – The golden-hued façade of St Peter's stands at the far end of an empty square on the site of the Etruscan acropolis. To the left are two medieval towers and to the right the former bishop's palace. The harmonious façade dates from the early 13C. The symbols of the Evangelists surround a rose window, probably of the Umbrian school. Lower down an atlante (or a dancer?) and a man (Laocöon?) being crushed by a snake probably came from Etruscan buildings.

The interior was built by Lombard masons in the 11C. Massive columns with beautiful capitals support curious denticulated arches. The nave retains its original and highly decorative paving. The frescoes in the apse are 12C. The crypt (**cripta★★** ⊙) is a forest of small columns, all different and of various periods – Roman, Pre-Romanesque and Romanesque – supporting groined vaulting.

★ Santa Maria Maggiore – This late-12C church, dedicated to St Mary Major, is modelled on St Peter's. The 13C Romanesque **doorways★★** are decorated with masterly sculptures.

Inside is an ambo rebuilt with 8C, 9C and 12C fragments. Above the triumphal arch there is a realistic 14C fresco of the *Last Judgement*.

UDINE★

Friuli-Venezia Giulia

Population 94 823

Michelin map 988 fold 6 or 429 D 21

Town plan in the current Michelin Red Guide Italia

This charming town was the seat of the Patriarchs of Aquilea from 1238 to 1420 when it passed under Venetian rule. Udine nestles round a hill encircled by the picturesque lane, Vicolo Sottomonte, with a castle on its summit. The charm of Udine lies in its Gothic and Renaissance monuments, its secluded squares and narrow streets, often lined with arcades. The town was badly damaged, like most of Friuli, by the 1976 earthquake.

★★ **Piazza della Libertà** – This very harmonious square has kept its Renaissance character and is bordered by several public buildings. The former town hall is also known as the **Loggia del Lionello** (1457), from the name of its architect. Its Venetian-Gothic style is characterised by the elegant arcades and its white and rose-coloured stonework. Opposite on a slightly higher level is the 16C **Loggia di San Giovanni**, a Renaissance portico surmounted by a 16C clock tower, with Moorish jacks *(Mori)* similar to the ones in Venice. A 16C fountain plays in the centre of the square, not far from statues of Hercules and Cacus and the columns of Justice and St Mark.

Castello ⊙ – This imposing early-16C castle is preceded by an esplanade from which there is a good view of Udine and the surrounding Friuli countryside. This was the seat of the representatives of the Most Serene Republic (Venice).
Alongside is the 13C Church of **Santa Maria del Castello** with a 16C façade and campanile which bears a statue of the Archangel Gabriel at its summit. Inside, there is a 13C fresco of the *Descent from the Cross.*

Duomo ⊙ – This 14C Gothic cathedral remodelled in the 18C has a lovely Flamboyant-Gothic doorway. The massive campanile has, on one of its faces, statues of the Angel of the Annunciation and of Archangel Gabriel (14C). Inside, there is attractive **Baroque decoration★**: organ loft, pulpit, tombs, altarpieces and historiated stalls. Tiepolo painted the remarkable *trompe-l'œil* frescoes in the Chapel of the Holy Sacrament (Cappella del Santo Sacramento).
The Oratory of Purity **(Oratorio della Purità)**, to the right of the cathedral, has a ceiling decorated with a remarkable *Assumption* (1757) by Tiepolo.

Palazzo Arcivescovile ⊙ – The 16C-18C Archbishop's Palace boasts **frescoes★** by Tiepolo. The ceiling of its grand staircase depicts the *Fall of the Rebel Angels*, while the apartments are decorated with scenes from the Old Testament.

Piazza Matteotti – This lovely square bordered by arcaded houses is the site of a lively open-air market. Also of interest are: the elegant 16C Baroque Church of San Giacomo, a 16C fountain and a 15C column of the Virgin. It is pleasant to stroll in Via Mercato Vecchio and Via Vittorio Veneto with their shops beneath the arcades.

EXCURSION

★★ **Villa Manin** ⊙ – *30km/18mi southwest, in Passariano.* Having lived in the Friuli area (territory under Venetian control) since the 13C, the Manins occupied very high-ranking positions in the service of the Republic. The villa was a summer residence, the counterpart of their palace on the Grand Canal. The 16C villa was rebuilt in the 17C and rapidly completed with two wings set at right angles to the main part of the building, recalling the grandeur of Versailles. Finally, it was extended by semi-circular outbuildings based, in design, on St Peter's Square in Rome. This grandiose building was requisitioned by Napoleon Bonaparte when preparing the Treaty of Campoformio *(8km/5mi southwest of Udine)* which, by a quirk of history, was signed (without being renamed despite the fact that it marked the end of the Republic of Venice) in the palace of the last Doge, Ludovico Manin.
In the right wing of the villa, visitors can see the magnificent chapel and its sacristy, the stables with their 18C and 19C coaches and carriages, and the weapons room (15C-18C arms). The villa itself houses temporary exhibitions every summer, and they provide an opportunity to admire the luxurious decoration and frescoes in its vast chambers. The superb grounds are decorated with statues.

Help us in our constant task of keeping up-to-date.
Send us your comments and suggestions to

Michelin Travel Publications
38 Clarendon Road – WATFORD Herts WD1 1SX
Tel: (01923) 415000

thegreenguide-uk@uk.michelin.com

URBINO★★

Marches

Population 15 143
Michelin map 430 K 19

The walled town of Urbino, with its rose-coloured brick houses, is built on two hills overlooking the undulating countryside bathed in a glorious golden light. Urbino was ruled by the Montefeltro family from the 12C onwards and reached its peak in the reign (1444-82) of Duke **Federico da Montefeltro**, a wise leader, man of letters, collector and patron of the arts. Urbino was the birthplace of **Raphael** (Raffaello Sanzio) (1483-1520). In 1998 Urbino's evocative historic centre was added to UNESCO's World Heritage List.

★★★ PALAZZO DUCALE (DUCAL PALACE) *1hr30min*

The palace (1444-72), started by order of Duke Federico by the Dalmatian architect Luciano Laurana and completed by the Sienese Francesco di Giorgio Martini, is a masterpiece of harmony and elegance. The design hinges on the panorama to the west of the old town, and the original façade overlooking the valley is pierced by superimposed loggias and flanked by two tall round towers. The severe east wing facing Piazza Rinascimento has irregularly-spaced windows, while the austerely majestic north façade is punctuated by three great doors at ground level and four rectangular windows on the first floor.

The inner courtyard, inspired by earlier Florentine models, is a classic example of Renaissance harmony with its pure, delicate lines, serene architectural rhythm and subtle combination of rose-coloured brick and white marble.

On the ground floor are a museum (**Museo Archeologico** – lapidary fragments: inscriptions, steles, architectural remains etc), a library (**Biblioteca del Duca**) and cellars (**cantine**).

★★ **Galleria Nazionale delle Marche** ⊘ – The palace's first-floor rooms with their original decoration are the setting for the National Gallery of the Marches which contains several great **masterpieces**★★★: a predella of the *Profanation of the Host* (1465-9) by Paolo Uccello, a *Madonna* di Senigallia and a curious *Flagellation of Christ* by Piero della Francesca *(see Index)*, the *Ideal City (see Pienza)* by Laurana and the famous portrait of a woman, known as ***The Mute***, by Raphael. Duke Federico's **studiolo**★★★ is decorated with magnificent intarsia panelling.

A collection of 16C-17C Italian paintings and 17C-18C maiolica is displayed on the second floor.

To the north of the palace stands the early-19C cathedral built by Valadier.

ADDITIONAL SIGHTS

★ **Casa di Raffaello** ⊘ – *57 Via Raffaello*. Raphael lived here up to the age of 14. This typical 15C house belonged to the boy's father, Giovanni Sanzio or Santi, and contains mementoes and period furniture.

Chiesa Oratorio di San Giovanni Battista e San Giuseppe ⊘ – *Via Barocci*. Of these two adjacent churches, the first is 14C and contains curious **frescoes**★ by the Salimbene brothers depicting the life of St John the Baptist. The second, dating from the 16C, has in the nave a colossal statue of St Joseph (18C) painted in grisaille, and a very lovely stucco **crib**★, a life-size work by Federico Brandani (1522-75).

★★ **Strada Panoramica** – Starting from Piazza Roma, this scenic road skirts a hillside and affords admirable **views**★★ of the town walls, the lower town, Ducal Palace and cathedral: a wonderful scene in various hues of pink brick.

VELIA★

Campania

Michelin map 988 fold 38 or 431 G 27 – 14km/9mi northwest of Pisciotta

The extensive ruins ⊘ of the ancient city of Velia (**Elea**) are situated in the vicinity of Castellammare di Velia in the region of Cilento. Excavations have uncovered only part of the site. This colony was founded in 535 BC by Phocean Greek refugees who had been expelled by the Persians. Before settling in Massalia (Marseilles) they lived in the Corsican settlement of Alalia (Aleria), where they were victorious in a naval battle (*c*538) against the combined Carthaginian and Etruscan fleets. The busy and prosperous port of Velia – known for a long time as Elea – is famous for its school of the Eleatic philosophers (5C). Two of the better-known philosophers were Parmenides and his pupil Zeno.

Lower town – *Pass under the railway line to reach this quarter.* From the entrance there is an interesting view of the ruins which include the former lighthouse, 4C BC town wall, the baths, the south sea-gateway and the 4C BC gateway, **Porta Rosa**★.

Acropolis – A medieval castle abuts the remains of a 5C BC Greek temple. Laid out below are the ruins of the amphitheatre. A small **museum** houses statues of Parmenides, Zeno and Aesculapius which were found amidst the ruins.

VENEZIA★★★

VENICE – Veneto
Population 293 731
Michelin map 429 F 18-19
See The Green Guide to Venice

Venice is a legendary city. She chose the waters of the lagoon for her queen-like existence that has lasted over a thousand years, the same water that has saved her from the clutches of time and yet threatens her very being.

She is a city of a multitude of moods and faces: lively and embracing to the inhabitants that fill her streets with their chatter; on the verge of a painful goodbye for those who prefer her in the tragic guise of *Death in Venice*. Venice offers each of her visitors their own highly personal impression of her essence.

VARIOUS ASPECTS OF VENICE

Venice is built on 117 islands; it has 150 canals and 400 bridges. A canal is called a *rio*, a square a *campo*, a street a *calle* or *salizzada*, a quay a *riva* or *fondamenta*, a filled-in canal *rio Terrà*, a passageway under a house *sottoportego*, a courtyard a *corte* and a small square a *campiello*.

The squares are charming, with their well-curbs often sculpted *(vera da pozzo)*.

The hub of public life is the Piazza San Marco *(see below)* where tourists and citizens sit on the terraces of the famous Florian and Quadri cafés. The Florian is the best-known café; founded in 1720 it has received Byron, Goethe, George Sand, Musset and Wagner within its mirrored and allegory-painted walls.

The shops in St Mark's have sumptuous window displays of lace, jewellery, mirrors and the famous glassware from Murano. The **Mercerie** (**EU**), shopping streets, lead to the Rialto Bridge.

On the far side of this are the displays of greengrocers' *(erberie)* and fishmongers' shops *(pescherie)*.

In addition to these well-known and busy areas there are the **Frari Quarter** (**BU**) and that of **Santa Maria Formosa** (**FTU**), which have a certain peaceful charm with their brick façades and silent canals. Visitors can also discover the Venice of the Venetians by moving out of the crowds that congregate in and around San Marco or the Rialto.

Meals in the restaurants *(trattorie)* are among the attractions of Venice. The fare consists chiefly of sea-food, squid *(calamaretti)*, cuttlefish, eels and mussels in the Venetian manner but also calf's liver cooked in the Venetian way, with onions. These dishes should be accompanied by the pleasant local wines: Valpolicella, Bardolino and Amarone for red wines, and Soave and Prosecco for the whites.

The Grand Canal winds through Venice

Y. Arthus Bertrand/ALTITUDE

Gondolas – For centuries gondolas have been the traditional means of transport in Venice. The gondola is an austere and sober craft except for its typical iron hook, which acts as a counterweight to the gondolier. The curved fin is said to echo the dogal *corno* (horn-shaped hat) and the prongs to represent the *sestieri* or districts of the city. The prong on the back of the stern symbolises the Giudecca.

The Venetians – The Venetians are both proud and fiercely traditional, known for their commercial and practical skills. The "**bautta**" (black velvet mask) and **domino** (a wide hooded cape), once very popular with the locals and still worn in Venice at Carnival time, add to their elusiveness. Skilled courtesans, diplomats and spies have given Venice a reputation for intrigue and manoeuvring in love and politics. Venetian is a very lively dialect which is used in place of Italian, even in place names.

The Marriage of Venice and the Sea – A sumptuous ceremony that, since the year 1000 (with a few interruptions) has celebrated the capture of the towns of Istria and Dalmatia from the pirates. It is an admirable expression of the link between Venice and the sea, the element that made the city great for many centuries and the one that still gives it its beauty to this day.
In memory of this historic past, every year on the Feast of the Ascension, or "**Sensa**" in Venetian, the Doge, dressed in cloth of gold, would board *Bucentaur*, his golden state barge, and throw a ring into the sea with the words, "We wed you, o Sea, as a sign of true and perpetual dominion".

HISTORICAL NOTES

Venice was founded in AD 811 by the inhabitants of Malamocco, near the Lido, fleeing from the Franks. They settled on the Rivo Alto, known today as the Rialto. In that year the first Doge – a name derived from the Latin *dux* (leader) – Agnello Partecipazio, was elected and thus started the adventures of the Venetian Republic, La Serenissima, which lasted 1 000 years. In 828 the relics of St Mark the Evangelist were brought from Alexandria; he became the protector of the town.

The Venetian Empire – From the 9C to the 13C Venice grew steadily richer as it exploited its position between East and West. With its maritime and commercial power it conquered important markets in Istria and Dalmatia. The guile of Doge Dandolo and the assistance of the Crusaders helped the Venetians capture Constantinople in 1204. The spoils from its sack flowed to Venice, while trade in spices, fabrics and precious stones from markets established in the east grew apace.
Marco Polo (1254-1324) returned from China with fabulous riches. He related his amazing adventures in French in his *Book of the Wonders of the World* and won great fame throughout Europe.
The 14C war with its rival Genoa ended in victory for the Venetians in 1381.

Glory – The first-half of the 15C saw Venetian power at its peak: the Turks were defeated at Gallipoli in 1416 and the Venetians held the kingdoms of Morea, Cyprus and Candia (Crete) in the Levant.
In mainland Italy, from 1414 to 1428, they captured Verona, Vicenza, Padua, Udine, and then Brescia and Bergamo. The Adriatic became the Venetian Sea from Corfu to the Po.

Decline – The capture of Constantinople by the Turks in 1453 started the decadence. The discovery of America caused a shift in the patterns of trade and Venice had to keep up an exhausting struggle with the Turks who were defeated in 1571 in the naval battle of **Lepanto**, in which the Venetians played an important part. Their decline, however, was confirmed in the 17C when the Turks captured Candia (Crete) after a 25-year siege.
The "Most Serene Republic" came to an end in 1797. Napoleon Bonaparte entered Venice and abolished a thousand year-old constitution. Then, by the **Treaty of Campoformio**, he ceded the city to Austria. Venice and the Veneto were united with Italy in 1866.

The long-lasting oligarchy – The government of the Republic was from its earliest days organised to avoid the rise to power of any one man. The role of doge was supervised by several councils: the Grand Council drew up the laws; the Senate was responsible for foreign affairs, military and economic matters; the Council of Ten, responsible for security, kept a network of secret police and informers which created an atmosphere of mistrust but ensured control of all aspects of city life.

VENETIAN PAINTING

The Venetian school of painting with its marked sensuality is characterised by the predominance of colour over draughtsmanship, and by an innate sense of light in hazy landscapes with blurred outlines. Art historians have often noted the contrast between the scholarly and idealistic art of the Florentines and the freer, more spontaneous work of the Venetians, which later influenced the Impressionists.
The real beginnings of Venetian painting are exemplified by the **Bellini** family: Jacopo, the father, and Gentile (1429-1507) and **Giovanni** (or **Giambellino**, 1430-1516), his

sons. The latter, who was the younger son, was a profoundly spiritual artist and one of the first Renaissance artists to integrate landscape and figure compositions harmoniously. In parallel, their pupil **Carpaccio** (1455-1525) recorded Venetian life with his usual imagination and care for detail while **Giorgione** remained a major influence. His pupil, **Lorenzo Lotto**, was also influenced by the realism of Northern artists.

The Renaissance came to a glorious conclusion with three great artists: **Titian** (c 1490-1576) who painted dramatic scenes where dynamic movement is offset by light effects; **Veronese** (1528-88), whose sumptuous ornamentation and rich colours reflected the splendor of the Most Serene Republic; and **Tintoretto** (1518-94), a visionary whose dramatic technique reflects an inner anxiety.

The artists of the 18C captured Venice and its peculiar light, grey-blue, iridescent and slightly misty: **Canaletto** (1697-1768) whose works won favour with English Grand Tourists, and his pupil Bellotto (1720-80), were both inspired by townscapes; Francesco **Guardi** (1712-93) who painted in luminous touches; Pietro **Longhi** (1702-58), the author of intimate scenes; Giovanni Battista **Tiepolo** (1696-1770), a master decorator who painted frescoes with sacred and secular scenes full of light and movement. His son, Gian Domenico (1727-1804), adopted a similar style.

Spontaneity and colour are also found in the musicians of Venice, of whom the best known is **Antonio Vivaldi** (1678-1743), who was master of violin and viola at a hospice, Ospedale della Pietà, for many years. (Hospices were charity institutions and orphanages but were also academies of music and drama.)

VENICE: ON THE WATER'S EDGE, SQUARES AND STREETS

A vaporetto, a gondola or... a boat

It goes without saying that in Venice public transport uses only liquid roads. It is important to bear in mind that heavy traffic on the Grand Canal and the fact that stops do not always take one "door to door" mean that walking can sometimes be quicker. However, on arrival in the city, the very vision of the first bridge (Ponte degli Scalzi, opposite the station, is particularly steep) can be tiring for visitors carrying heavy luggage. Likewise, walking up and down bridges all day can put even the most energetic walker to the test.

Visitors will find that they will happily make use of the famous Venetian ferry-boats, **vaporettos**.

Listed below are the most convenient routes with their corresponding numbers:

- 1:   stops at all stops along the Grand Canal. Terminates at the Lido after stopping at piazzale Roma, the station and San Marco.
- 82:   faster than Line 1 as it makes fewer stops. Stops at Tronchetto, Piazzale Roma, the Giudecca, San Giorgio, San Marco and the Lido.
- 52 e 52:   these are useful routes that run along two canals that penetrate interesting, less well-known areas of Venice (the Cannaregio canal and the Arsenale canal) before making their way to the island of Murano.
- 12 e 14:   both lines go to the islands of Burano and Torcello, no 14 also goes to Punta Sabbioni.

One-way tickets cost 6000L, return journeys 10 000L. 24 hr(18 000L) and 72hr (35 000L) tickets can also be purchased, these need be stamped only on the initial journey. Weekly passes cost 60 000L.

Visitors who opt to walk will be relieved to learn that as well as a choice of three bridges crossing the Grand Canal (Scalzi, Rialto, Accademia) they can be "ferried" across the canal in a gondola. This service is available at seven points along the Grand Canal (Station, S. Marcuola, S. Sofia, al Carbon, S. Tomà, S. Samuele, S. Maria del Giglio): it is a very rapid journey and costs only 700 L (except when exhibitions are on at Palazzo Grassi, in which case the S. Samuele crossing costs 1000L. Be careful to keep your balance!

Visitors who want to enjoy the full experience of a **gondola** ride must be prepared to spend considerably more: a 50 minute journey through canals costs 120 000L (official starting price which does not include musical accompaniment). This price can be divided among six people who can be accommodated in a gondola. Each 25min after the initial 50min costs 60 000L. A tour in a gondola by night is an unforgettable experience but incurs considerable costs: from 8pm to 8am a 50min journey costs 150 000L, each 25min thereafter costs 75 000L. For more information contact the Istituzi-one per la Conservazione della Gondola e la Tutela del Gondoliere, ☎ 041 528 50 75.

Visitors wanting to tour the lagoon by water in peace can rent a **boat**. For information contact Brussa, Cannaregio 331, ☎ 041 71 57 87, 720 550.

Information

Upon arrival by rail visitors can contact the information office in the station. The main tourist office is a stone's throw away from St Mark's square, in the gardens along the quay near Harry's Bar (☎ 041 522 63 56). The information point at the station can be contacted at (☎ 041 529 87 27). Visitors staying at the Lido can contact ☎ 041 526 57 21.

For something a little different

For those who have experience in art restoration the **Centro europeo di formazione degli artigiani per la conservazione del patrimonio architettonico** runs courses on restoration techniques on the island of San Servolo. For information contact the centre at Isola di San Servolo, casella Postale 676, 30100 Venezia, ☎ 041 526 85 46/7, fax 041 27 60 211.

For those in search of peace and quiet, why not contact the Franciscan monks at San Francesco del Deserto? The monks themselves will pick visitors up at Burano in their boat to take them for a spiritual retreat on their own island. ☎ 041 528 68 63.

For young visitors

For those who are lucky enough to be aged between 14 and 29, the *Rolling Venice* card (cost 5000L) offers a range of discounts on youth hostels, hotels, camping sites, public transport, university canteens, restaurants, museums, the Biennale and various shops taking part in this scheme. Cards can be purchased with proof of identity at the following addresses:

at Santa Lucia station at the Agenzia Transalpino, ☎ 041 52 41 334 (Monday to Friday, from 8.30am to 12.30pm and from 3pm to 7pm; open mornings only on Saturday), or, from July to September, at the *Rolling Venice* booth, opposite the station (open every day from 8am to 8pm);

at San Marco, corte Contarina 1529 at the offices of the Assessorato alle politiche giovanili, ☎ 041 27 47 645 (Monday to Friday morning from 9.30am to 1pm; Tuesdays and Thursdays from 3pm to 5pm);

in Dorsoduro, 3252, at the CTS, Centro Turistico Studentesco e Giovanile, ☎ 041 520 56 60 (Monday to Friday from 9.30am to 1.30pm and from 3pm to 7pm);

in Santa Croce, corte Canal 659, at the Agenzia Arte e Storia, ☎ 041 52 49 232 (Monday to Friday morning from 9am to 1pm and from 3.30pm to 7pm);

in San Polo, calle del Castelforte San Rocco 3101, at the Associazione Italiana Alberghi per la Gioventù, ☎ 041 52 04 414 (Monday to Saturday from 8am to 2pm).

An additional fee of 10 000L provides a guided tour of Venice and a book of useful information. 15 000L will get you a pass, a guide, an information booklet and/or a *Rolling Venice* t-shirt.

What to read in Venice

The *Gazzettino* newspaper has a mine of information on the city as well as articles on famous people, book reviews, tourist information and theatre and music programmes.

Theatres

Music and theatre have always formed an intrinsic part of the spirit of Venice. As well as the three major theatres, concerts and plays are also held in numerous churches such as the Pietà, the Frari, S. Stefano, all ideal concert halls. See the *Gazzettino* for all information on concerts and shows in the city.

Gran Teatro La Fenice – It is not true that the Fenice no longer exists: to find out what's on (concerts are temporarily being held at the PalaFenice, on the island of Tronchetto) look at the relevant posters on view all over the city. For further information call ☎ 041 786 537 from 8am to 2pm.

Teatro Goldoni – Situated on the *calle* (street) of the theatre. Offers a rich season of plays and concerts.

Teatro a l'Avogaria – Situated in calle Avogaria, 1617 in the Dorsoduro quarter. ☎ 041 520 61 30.

Teatro Fondamenta Nuove – Situated on the fondamenta Nuove, near the Sacca della Misericordia (Cannaregio 5013). Plays, concerts and dance. For information call ☎ 041 522 44 98.

Accommodation in Venice

Finding a hotel in Venice can be surprisingly easy just as it can prove to be an arduous enterprise. The list of hotels and rooms for rent listed below is long but prices are always a (justified) source of worry for visitors to the city. Expressions like "high" and "low" season seem to lose all meaning in Venice which people want to visit every month of the year (paradoxically the summer months are less desirable as heat and humidity make getting about tiring rather than pleasant). **Remember to book well in advance.**

Suggestions listed below try to cater to the most varied tastes. These hotels are scattered about in different quarters and are listed in groups according to price, which refers to **double rooms**. It is advisable to check prices beforehand as tariffs **vary considerably throughout the year**. In most cases the price of a room includes breakfast.

See map to locate hotels.

BUDGET

It Is worth bearing in mind that rooms for rent are available from various religious orders. Prices are very reasonable, the only drawback being that doors close at about 10.30pm.

Istituto S. Giuseppe – A stone's throw away from St Mark's, at S. Marco 5402, ☎ 041 52 25 352.

Ostello della Giudecca (Youth hostel) – Giudecca 86, ☎ 041 52 38 211.

OUR SELECTION

Pensione La Calcina – Zattere 780, vaporetto stop Zattere, ☎ 041 52 06 466, fax 041 52 27 045, 29 rooms with air-conditioning. Credit cards accepted.
Only a photograph remains in the hallway of the "La Calcina" inn where Ruskin stayed in 1876, but this hotel, completely remodelled, stands on that very site. And it is as pleasant now as it was then; in the breakfast room as in the bedrooms, on the roof terrace as on the waterside terrace. The fine location on the Grand Canal adds to its charm as does the light which floods in, a rarity in Venice's narrow streets.

Hotel Falier – Salizzada S. Pantalon 130, vaporetto stop San Tomà, ☎ 041 71 08 82, fax 041 52 06 554, 19 rooms. Credit cards accepted.
A good address (near the Frari church)for those in search of a peaceful, quiet hotel in a quarter off the beaten track. The hotel has a small garden.

Hotel Paganelli – Riva degli Schiavoni 4182, vaporetto stop San Zaccaria, ☎ 041 52 24 324, fax 041 52 39 267, 22 rooms, air conditioning. Credit cards accepted.
This family-run hotel overlooks the basin of St Mark. Some rooms (all decorated in the Venetian style) enjoy this view, others (in an adjoining building) look out onto campo S. Zaccaria.

Hotel Serenissima – Calle Goldoni 4486, vaporetto stop Rialto or San Marco, ☎ 041 52 00 011, fax 041 52 23 292, 34 rooms with air conditioning. Credit cards accepted. Restaurant.
A stone's throw away from St Mark's, this is a simple, pleasant hotel (the walls are hung with paintings by modern artists).

TREAT YOURSELF!

Hotel Abbazia – Calle Priuli 68, vaporetto stop Ferrovia, ☎ 041 71 73 33, fax 041 71 79 49, 39 rooms with air-conditioning. Credit cards accepted.
This is perfect for those wishing to be near the station but the real attraction of this elegantly restrained hotel is its setting: the interior of the Discalced Carmelite Monks monastery. The bar is in fact the refectory, replete with choir stalls and a pulpit. Walking down the endless corridors one can almost hear the monk's footsteps.

Hotel Cipriani – Giudecca, ☎ 041 52 07 744, fax 041 52 03 930, 12 suites (7 in Palazzo Vendramin) with air-conditioning. Credit cards accepted. Garden and pool. Restaurant.
The epitome of tasteful elegance. The position alone, secluded and peaceful, sums up the refined style of the hotel. The main suite in Palazzo Vendramin overlooks St Mark's square.

Hotel Danieli – Riva degli Schiavoni 4196, vaporetto stop San Zaccaria, ☎ 041 52 26 480, fax 041 52 00 208, 221 rooms, 9 suites with air-conditioning. Credit cards accepted. Restaurant.
For many the image conjured up by Venice is that of palaces in the mist, decadent shapes and colours blurred in the mind's eye with cinematic and literary associations.

Walking into Palazzo Dandolo, the Hotel Danieli since 1822, is like walking into that imaginary portrait. The columns, staircase, open gallery and architectural embroidery are reminiscent of the decorative richness of Ludwig's castle at Neuschwanstein.

It goes without saying that the Danieli has been frequented by illustrious writers and musicians: Dickens, Wagner, Balzac, Proust, George Sand and Alfred de Musset.

Hotel Des Bains – Lido, Lungomare Marconi 17, ☎ 041 52 65 921, fax 041 52 60 113, 190 rooms with air-conditioning. Credit cards accepted. Swimming pool. Restaurant.

This hotel evokes the *belle époque* ambience of the cinematic version of *Death in Venice*. The veranda, the park and the huge private beach, the airy neo-Classical dining room and the Art Nouveau salon all conjure up the atmosphere described in Thomas Mann's novel.

Hotel Flora – Calle larga XXII Marzo 2283/A, vaporetto stop San Marco or Santa Maria del Giglio, ☎ 041 52 05 844, fax 041 52 28 217, 44 rooms with air conditioning. Credit cards accepted.

This hotel is redolent with the atmosphere of the *belle époque*. Art is very much at home here and is reflected in the carefully decorated rooms, the 1920s staircase and the pleasant, secluded garden.

Hotel Gritti Palace – Campo S. Maria del Giglio 2467, vaporetto stop Santa Maria del Giglio, ☎ 041 79 46 11, fax 041 52 00 942, 87 rooms, 6 suites. Credit cards accepted. Restaurant.

"To be treated like a doge" is more than just a saying in this hotel, where the doge Gritti was born five centuries ago.

During the Venice Film Festival stars pose on the terrace which "floats" on the grand canal and affords stunning views of Santa Maria della Salute.

The interior has preserved in every detail the past allure of the Serene Republic.

In search of "bacari", "cicheti", "spriz" and "ombre"

FOUR WORDS IN LOCAL DIALECT TO DISCOVER VENETIAN CUISINE

A *bàcaro* is the Venetian for *osteria*, a typical meeting place to savour a *cicheto* with and *ombra*. These open very early in the morning.

A "cichèto" is a typically Venetian snack that accompanies an "ombra". It might consist of a of bacalà (cod), sarde in saor (fried sardines marinated with onions, vinegar, pine nuts and raisins) or meatballs.

A spriz is the famous Venetian aperitif, made with white whine, amaro and soda water.

An Ombra is a classic and much-loved glass of wine which is drunk at the counter.

FOOD!

Al Mascaròn, calle Lunga S. Maria Formosa, Castello 5525, is a typical *osteria* that serves hot food. Booking is essential! ☎ 041 52 25 995.

Alla Patatina, calle Saoneri, 2741 San Polo, is a lively, crowded restaurant with a vast choice of vegetables at the counter and plenty of other dishes that can be enjoyed sitting down.

Alla Zucca, Santa Croce 1762, offers varied and creative food. The vegetables are highly recommended. Booking is advisable. ☎ 041 52 41 570.

Da Zorzi, calle dei Fuseri, San Marco 4359, has excellent whipped cream (still whipped by hand!).

Gam-Gam, fondamenta Pescaria 1122, at the sotoportego del Gheto Vechio, is a Jewish restaurant with a very pleasant atmosphere.

L'Olandese volante, campo S. Lio 5658, between campo S. Maria Formosa and the Rialto, has a wide choice of beers, aperitifs and some good salads.

Piero e Mauro, calle dei Fabbri 881, very near San Marco, serve sandwiches (tramezzini), and bruschetta accompanied by good beers. The rather cramped room is decorated like the interior of a boat.

Taverna S. Trovaso, along the *rio* of the same name, at 1016 Dorsoduro, near the Accademia, serves various dishes and good pizza. It is always very crowded so remember to book! ☎ 041 520 37 03.

SIGHTSEEING

We recommend The Green Guide to Venice for an extended visit.

Visitors spending one day in Venice should take in Piazza San Marco; those on a two- to three-day tour will have time to visit the Accademia and the Scuole (Schools) and churches which contain many treasures; those who spend a whole week will be captivated by the atmosphere of the alleyways and of the islands in the lagoon.

★★★ PIAZZA SAN MARCO (ST MARK'S SQUARE) (EV)

St Mark's Square is the heart of Venice. All around, the covered galleries of the procuratorships **(Procuratie)** shelter famous cafés (Florian, Quadri), and luxury shops.

The square opens on the Grand Canal through the delightful **Piazzetta**. The two granite columns crowned by "Marco" and "Todaro" were brought from the East in 1172.

A bird's eye view of Piazza San Marco

Y. Arthus Bertrand/ALTITUDE

★★★ Basilica

St Mark's combines the Byzantine and Western styles. Building was carried out throughout the 11C and when the basilica was consecrated in 1094, the body of St Mark had been recovered by a miracle.

Visitors are overcome by a feeling of awe, perhaps owing to the rich decoration of marble and **mosaic**. Built on the plan of a Greek cross, the basilica is crowned by a bulbous dome flanked by four smaller domes of unequal height placed on the arms of the cross.

Façade – This is pierced by five large doorways adorned with variegated marbles and sculptures. The central doorway has three arches adorned with Romanesque-Byzantine low reliefs, and above are copies of the four famous **Bronze Horses** (the originals are in the gallery of the Basilica).

On the first arch on the left is depicted the Translation of the body of St Mark. On the south side near the Doges' Palace stands the porphyry group, known as the **Tetrarchs** (4C). At the corner is the proclamation stone (pietra del bando), where laws were proclaimed. The pretty Piazzetta dei Leoncini (**21**) lies to the north.

Atrium – As an introduction to the narrative told in mosaic inside the basilica, the mosaics in the atrium depict scenes from the Old Testament.

The atrium gives access to the **Galleria e Museo marciano** ⊘ which displays the **gilded bronze horses★★**.

Interior – The dazzling decoration of St Mark's combines the luminous mosaics (1071) by artists from Constantinople and a 12C pavement decorated with animal and geometric motifs – its uneven surface has been caused by subsidence. An iconostasis separates the raised presbytery (sanctuary) from the nave. Beyond, a ciborium raised on **alabaster columns★★** precedes the Golden Altarpiece (**Pala d'Oro★★★** ⊘), a masterpiece of Gothic art dating from the early 10C. The relics of St Mark rest in the main altar.

The mosaic decoration depicts the New Testament, starting with the dome of the apse with Christ as *Pantocrator* and ending with the *Last Judgement* in the area above the atrium. Near the entrance, the Arch of the Apocalypse illustrates the visions described in the gospel of St John. The dome nearest the doorway is dedicated to Pentecost. As one approaches the central dome, the west arch presents a synthesis of the Passion and Death of Christ. The south arch opening onto the south transept depicts the Temptation of Christ and His Entry into Jerusalem, the Last Supper and the Washing of the Feet. In the centre is the Dome of the Ascension depicting the Apostles, the Virgin, the Virtues and the Beatitudes. Christ in Benediction dominates the scene. The Presbytery Dome is dedicated to the Season of Advent. The mosaics on the North Arch giving onto the north transept, are after cartoons by Tintoretto (St Michael, Last Supper and Marriage at Cana) and Veronese (Healing of the Leper). The Dome of St John the Evangelist in the left transept illustrate the Sermon on the Mount and scenes from the Life of St John the Evangelist.

The south transept gives access to the treasury (**tesoro**★ ⊘) which contains a collection of religious objects and ornaments which came into Venice's possession after the conquest of Constantinople.

★★ **Campanile** ⊘ – The bell-tower (99m/325ft high) which dominates the square is the symbol of Venice. It is a careful reconstruction of the 15C campanile which collapsed in 1902. The **panorama**★★ from the top extends from the Guidecca Canal to the Grand Canal across a sea of roofs and beyond, to the islands in the lagoon. At the base of the campanile is the **Loggetta Sansoviniana**; statues of Minerva, Apollo, Mercury and Peace adorn the niches.

The terrace is enclosed by a balustrade punctuated by a 17C gate.

★★ **Palazzo Ducale** ⊘ (**Doge's Palace**) – The palace was a symbol of Venetian power and glory, and was the residence of the doges and the seat of government and the law courts as well as being a prison. It was built in the 12C but was completely transformed between the end of the 13C and the 16C.

A pretty, geometric pattern in white and pink marble lends great charm to the two **façades**. The groups at the corners of the palace represent, from left to right, the *Judgement of Solomon* (probably by Bartolomeo Bon), Adam and Eve, and *Noah's Drunkenness* (14C-15C Gothic sculptures). The small loggia on the first floor is a delicate structure with quatrefoil motifs.

The main entrance is the **Porta della Carta**★★, so called perhaps because of the scribes which worked there or the archives kept inside. It is in the Flamboyant-Gothic style (1442) and has on its tympanum a Lion of St Mark before which kneels Doge Foscari (19C copy). The gateway leads into the Porticato Foscari; directly opposite is the Giants' Staircase (**Scala dei Giganti**) dominated by statues of Mars and Neptune by Sansovino.

Interior – Start at the top of Sansovino's Golden Staircase (**Scala d'Oro**★★★) and pass through a suite of rooms as follows: the Room of the Four Doors (**Sala delle Quattro Porte**) where the ambassadors waited for their audience with the doge; an antechamber (**Sala dell'Antecollegio**) for diplomatic missions and delegations; the College Chamber (**Sala del Collegio**) where the doge presided over meetings; the Senate Chamber or Pregadi Chamber (**Sala del Senato o "dei Pregadi"**) where the members of the Senate submitted their written request to participate in the meetings. The Chamber of the Council of Ten (**Sala del Consiglio dei Dieci**) is where met the powerful magistrates who used the secret police and spies to safeguard the institutions. Beyond the **Sala della Bussola**, the waiting-room for those awaiting interrogation and the armoury (Armeria) is the Grand Council Chamber (**Sala del Maggior Consiglio**). In this vast room (1 300m² – 14 000sq ft) sat the legislative body which appointed all public officials; here also was conducted the constitutional election of the new doge. In the chamber hang paintings and portraits of 76 doges as well as Tintoretto's *Paradise*. Proceed to the Ballot Chamber (**Sala dello Scrutinio**) where the counting of the votes took place; the new prisons (**Prigione Nuove**), the Bridge of Sighs (Ponte dei Sospiri). Further along are the Censors' Chamber (**Sala dei Censori**), the seat of the judiciary body, and the Avogaria Chamber (Sala dell'Avogaria) – the *avogadori* were lawyers appointed by the state whose duty was to ensure that the law was obeyed.

★★ **Ponte dei Sospiri** (**Bridge of Sighs**) – The Bridge of Sighs connects the Doges' Palace with the prisons (Prigioni Nuove). It was built in the 16C-17C and owes its name to romantic literary notions which held that the prisoners would suffer their final torment at the enchanting view of Venice from the window.

Torre dell'Orologio ⊘ (**N**) – At the top of the Clock Tower which dates from the late 15C are the famous Moors (*Mori*), a pair of giant bronze jacks, which strike the hours.

★★ **Museo Correr** ⊘ (**EV**) – Next to the Ara Napoleonica which bounds the square to the west is a museum which traces the 1 000 year-old history of the city: paintings, sculpture and artefacts.

★ **Libreria Sansoviniana** – This noble and harmonious building was designed by Sansovino in 1553. At No 7 is a library (**Biblioteca Nazionale Marciana**, **EV**) where it is possible to view manuscripts, maps and engravings.

★★★ CANAL GRANDE
(GRAND CANAL)

The Grand Canal (3km/2miles long, between 30km and 70km/18-44mi wide and, on average, 5.5m/18ft deep) takes the form of an inverted S and affords the best view of the palazzi.

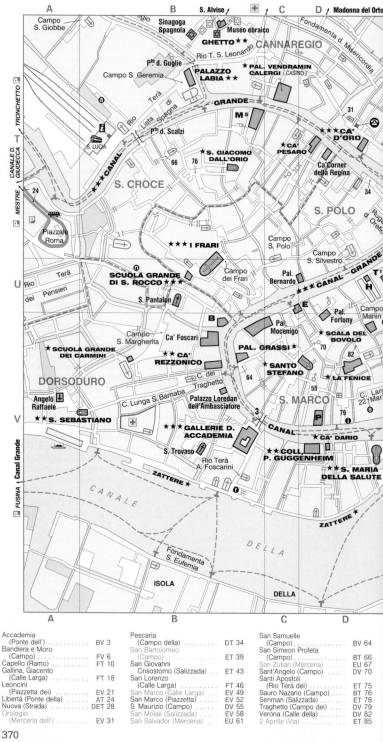

Accademia (Ponte dell')	BV 3	Pescaria (Campo della)	DT 34	San Samuele (Campo)	BV 64
Bandiera e Moro (Campo)	FV 6	San Bartolomeo (Campo)	ET 39	San Simeon Profeta (Campo)	BT 66
Capello (Ramo)	FT 10	San Giovanni Crisostomo (Salizzada)	ET 43	San Zulian (Merceria)	EU 67
Gallina, Giacento (Calle Larga)	FT 18	San Lorenzo (Calle Larga)	FT 46	Sant'Angelo (Campo)	DV 70
Leoncini (Piazzetta dei)	EV 21	San Marco (Calle Larga)	EV 49	Santi Apostoli (Rio Terà dei)	ET 75
Libertà (Ponte della)	AT 24	San Marco (Piazzetta)	EV 52	Sauro Nazario (Campo)	BT 76
Nuova (Strada)	DET 28	S. Maurizio (Campo)	DV 55	Seriman (Salizzada)	ET 78
Orologio (Merceria dell')	EV 31	San Moisè (Salizzada)	EU 58	Traghetto (Campo dei)	DV 79
		San Salvador (Merceria)	EU 61	Verona (Calle della)	DV 82
				2 Aprile (Via)	ET 85

Left Bank

★★ **Palazzo Labia** (BT) – The elegant late-18C residence of the Labia family who were Spanish merchants.

★ **Palazzo Vendramin Calergi** (CT) – An early-16C mansion, the residence of the Codussi, where Wagner lived and died.

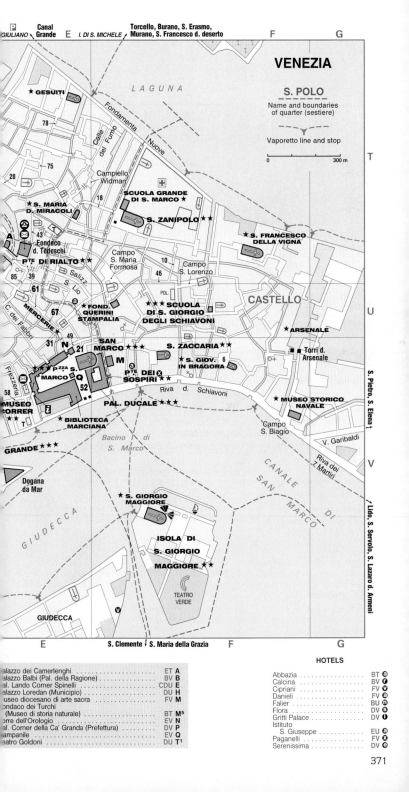

alazzo dei Camerlenghi	ET	A
alazzo Balbi (Pal. della Ragione)	BV	B
al. Lando Corner Spinelli	CDU	E
alazzo Loredan (Municipio)	DU	H
useo diocesano di arte sacra	FV	M
ondaco dei Turchi		
(Museo di storia naturale)	BT	M⁵
orre dell'Orologio	EV	N
al. Corner della Ca' Granda (Prefettura)	DV	P
ampanile	EV	Q
eatro Goldoni	DU	T¹

HOTELS

Abbazia	BT	❸
Calcina	BV	❼
Cipriani	FV	❺
Danieli	FV	❹
Falier	BU	⓫
Flora	DV	❾
Gritti Palace	DV	❶
Istituto S. Giuseppe	EU	❷
Paganelli	FV	❽
Serenissima	DV	❻

The Ca' d'Oro, which once upon a time was blue, black, white and of course gold

OSVALDO BOHM

★★★ **Ca' d'Oro** ⊙ (DT) – Although it has lost the gilded decoration which gave it its name, the mansion retains an elegant façade in the ornate Gothic style. It houses the **Galleria Franchetti** ⊙ which displays a fine *St Sebastian* by Mantegna.

★★ **Ponte di Rialto** (ET) – The Rialto Bridge was built by Antonio da Ponte and was opened in 1591. The present structure is the sixth version but the first one built of stone. It is the main crossing between the two banks. The original 12C bridge was built of wood.

★ **Palazzo Grassi** (BV) – It was built in the 18C by Giorgio Massari and was the last great Venetian palace to be constructed before the fall of the Republic. It is the venue for major exhibitions.

Right Bank

★ **Ca' Pesaro** (DT) – The palace built by Longhena has an unusual ground floor with diamond-pointed rustication. It is the home of the Museum of Oriental Art **(Museo d'arte orientale)** ⊙ and the International Gallery of Modern Art **(Galleria internazionale di arte moderna)** ⊙.

★★ **Ca' Rezzonico** (BV) – This was the last palace designed by Longhena which was completed by Massari. It houses the Museum of 18C Venice **(Museo del Settecento Veneziano)** ⊙.

★ **Ca' Dario** (DV) – The small late-15C palazzo is embellished with polychrome marble decoration. It has gained a sinister reputation owing to the death in suspicious circumstances of several of its owners.

★★★ GALLERIE DELL'ACCADEMIA ⊙ (ACADEMY OF FINE ARTS) (BV)

The Academy presents the most important collection of Venetian art from the 14C to the 18C. Masterpieces include a *Madonna enthroned* and the *Virgin and Child between St Catherine and Mary Magdalene* by Giovanni Bellini; the *Calling of the Sons of Zebedee* by Marco Basaiti; *St George* by Andrea Mantegna; *The Tempest* by Giorgione, the crystallisation of a state of mind rather than the representation of a specific moment; a *Portrait of a young gentleman* in his study by Lorenzo Lotto, which suggests that the sitter is distracted from his book by a thought or memory; an impressive but sinister *Pietà* by Titian; *Christ in the House of Levi* by Veronese; the cycle of luminous paintings of the *Miracles of the Relics of the True Cross* by Gentile Bellini and Carpaccio. The latter also painted the colourful and magical series of canvasses relating the *Story of St Ursula*.

CHURCHES

★★ **Santa Maria della Salute** (DV) – The church, dedicated to St Mary of Salvation, was built in the 17C to fulfil a vow by the Venetians and marking the end of a plague epidemic (1630). The white church designed by Longhena is a distinctive feature with its modillions and concentric volutes (*orrechioni* – big ears). In the sacristy hangs a *Wedding at Cana* by Tintoretto in which the artist has included himself as the first Apostle on the left.

★ **San Giorgio Maggiore** (FV) – The church on the Island of San Giorgio, was designed by Palladio. The top of the tall **campanile** ⊙ affords the finest **vista**★★★ of Venice. In the presbytery (sanctuary) hang two large paintings by Tintoretto, the *Last Supper* and the *Harvest of Manna*.

★★ **San Zanipòlo** (FT) – The square in which stands an **equestrian statue**★★ of the mercenary leader Bartolomeo **Colleoni** by Verrocchio is flanked by the deceptive perspective of St Mark's School **(Scuola Grande di San Marco★)** to one side, and is dominated by the Gothic church of Santi Giovanni e Paolo, dedicated to St John and St Paul (in the Venetian dialect Zanipolo is a contraction of the two names). The grandiose and solemn church is a fitting setting as the burial place for the doges and is lit by the brightly-coloured stained glass windows in the right transept.

★★★ **I Frari** ⊙ (BTU) – This great Franciscan church – its name is derived from the abbreviation of Fra*(ti Mino)*ri – can be compared to San Zanipolo on account of its imposing appearance and its funerary monuments. The focal point of the perspective is an *Assumption of the Virgin* by Titian in the main chapel, Cappella Maggiore.

★★ **San Zaccaria** (FV) – The Renaissance-Gothic Church of St Zachary has a tall white façade with its three tiers of round-headed windows; it is visible from the windows of the Palazzo Ducale. The interior is covered with paintings; the most important is Giovanni Bellini's *Sacra Conversazione*, a work of great sensitivity.

★★ **San Sebastiano** (ABV) – This church has frescoes by Veronese depicting the saint to which it is dedicated.

The Venetian Scuole

Instituted during the Middle Ages, the Scuole (literally meaning schools) were lay guilds drawn from the middle classes which were active in all aspects of life, be it devotional, charitable and professional, until the fall of the Republic. Each school had its own patron saint and Mariegola, a rule book and constitution of the guild.

In the 15C the scuole were housed in magnificent palaces with their interiors decorated by famous artists.

To appreciate the rich artistic heritage of the guild, visit the **Scuola di San Rocco**★★★ ⊙ (BU), decorated with scenes of the Old and New Testaments by Tintoretto, and the **Scuola di San Giorgio degli Schiavoni**★★★ ⊙ (FU), a perfect setting for the exquisite paintings in warm colours by Carpaccio relating the lives of St George, St Tryphon and St Jerome.

OTHER AREAS AND MUSEUMS OF VENICE

Arsenale (FGUV) – There was a dockyard in Venice as early as 1104 when the crusades stimulated shipbuilding activity. The Arsenal is enclosed by a medieval wall punctuated by towers and has two entrances: the land gateway surmounted by lions from Ancient Greece, and the water gate marked by two towers through which passes the *vaporetto*.

★★ **Ghetto** (BT) – The Jewish quarter (ghetto) is a hauntingly beautiful and secret corner of the Canneregio district close to the bustling Strada Nuova. It was the first Jewish quarter to be differentiated as such in Western Europe. In the Venetian dialect the term *geto* referred to a local mortar foundry. The g, normally pronounced soft (as in George) was hardened by the first Jews who came from Germany. The term ghetto now evokes the persecutions endured by the Jewish people. A museum (Museo ebraico) and synagogues **(sinagoghe)** ⊙ are open to visitors.

Giudecca (AV-FV) – Giudecca Island offers visitors a simple, quiet charm as well as a glorious view of Venice. The Palladian Church of the Redeemer **(Il Redentore★)**, *(Fondamenta S. Giacomo)*, was built like Santa Maria della Salute after the 1576 plague. On the third Sunday in July the church celebrates the Feast of the Redeemer which ends with a spectacular fireworks display.

* **Collezione Peggy Guggenheim** ⊘ (DV) – An 18C palazzo where the American Peggy Guggenheim lived from the end of the Second World War until her death, is the setting for an interesting collection of paintings and sculpture by the best 20C artists.

* **Fondazione Querini-Stampalia** ⊘ (FU) – The museum is a must for those interested in the Venice of old. There is a charming series of **panels★★** by Pietro Longhi dedicated to the sacraments and to the hunt.

LAGOON

See the plan of the lagoon in The Green Guide to Venice.

≛≛ **Lido** – Venice's seaside resort on the Adriatic has a slightly decadent air. It has a casino, which is one of the few in Italy, and hosts a Film Festival.

★★ **Murano** – By the end of the 13C, the threat of devastating fire was constant in Venice with its wooden buildings and the Grand Council decided to move the glassworks away from the city to Murano. It became known as the glassmaking island and a museum (**Museo di arte vetraria★** ⊘) displays a unique collection of glassware. The furnaces, the shouts of the vendors coaxing visitors into the glassware shops, should not detract from the artistic atmosphere of the island. The apse of the fine basilica, **Santi Maria e Donato★★**, is a masterpiece of 12C Veneto-Byzantine art and the **mosaic floor★★** recalls that of St Mark's.

★★ **Burano** – This is the most colourful of the islands in the lagoon. At the doors and windows of the brightly painted houses the women are engaged in lace-making.

★★ **Torcello** – It is almost a ghost island where only the stones speak of its glorious past. In 639 The inhabitants of Altinum fleeing from the Lombards settled on the island and built a church. Torcello became a See. The 10C witnessed the glorious ascent of Venice whose power extended over the lagoon; an aura of gloom pervaded the island as malaria decimated the population.
The noble Churches of **Santa Maria Assunta** and **Santa Fosca** and ruined buildings stand in a square overgrown with grass. The deserted air of the island is offset by the bright **mosaics★★** in the **basilica** ⊘: in the *Last Judgement* Torcello seems to be repopulated as the sound of the angels' trumpets summons the dead from the bowels of the sea monsters that devoured them.

* **Brenta Riviera** – *See Riviera del BRENTA.*

Val VENOSTA

VINSCHGAU – Trentino-Alto Adige

Michelin map 429 B-C 13-14

Val Venosta is a long, sunny valley covered in apple orchards which gradually becomes wider and wider to the west as it climbs towards the Resia pass. It can be reached from Merano, just after the attractive Birreria Forst. It is bordered by the Valtellina at the Stelvio Pass, by Switzerland at the Tubre mountain pass and by Austria at the Resia pass.
Val Venosta's history reaches far back into time and is best recounted by its most famous inhabitant, Ötzi, who lived 5 300 years ago and whose body was preserved by the ice in the spot where he died, in Val Senales, a bifurcation of Val Venosta. (*Ötzi is now an important exhibit in the Archeological Museum of Bolzano. See BOLZANO).*

ASCENDING THE ADIGE, FROM MERANO TO THE RESIA PASS

Merano – *See MERANO*

Naturno – From Merano take the road in the direction of the Resia pass for 15km/9mi. After passing the massive Birreria Forst, the road leads to Naturno which stands at a crossroads of the Val Venosta and the Val Senales. This "junction" is dominated by the 13C **Juval Castle** ⊘, now owned by the mountain climber Reinhold Messner who has decorated the castle with priceless souvenirs from his explorations in Tibet.

* **San Procolo** ⊘ – Before entering the town, this slightly hidden church, surrounded by fruit orchards, can be seen. The tiny structure houses the oldest frescoes in the German-speaking part of the Alto Adige (8C). The most notable fresco is the **Saint on a Swing**, a jolly and expressive figure who is thought to portray Procolo, the Bishop of Verona who fled the city. The scene portrays his flight; the saint undulates on the swing watched by the curious gazes of the men watching from the upper "windows" and the six people on the right.

Sluderno – This town is dominated by **Coira Castle** ⊙ which dates from 1253. Its current appearance is Renaissance; the internal loggia (1570) is particularly beautiful and adorned with the family tree of the owners, the Trapp family. The castle is also renowned for its very large and old armoury.

Glorenza – This old city counts less than 1 000 inhabitants. Glorenza was already documented in 1178 and is well worth a visit as it is the only fortified town in the Alto Adige where time has stood still. It is entirely surrounded by ramparts and has the only arcading in the whole valley. The parish church, situated outside the city walls, has a frescoed exterior (1496) depicting *The Last Judgment*.

Malles – Malles is home to a jewel of Romanesque architecture, the Church of **St Benedict** ⊙, dating from the 9C. Note the frescoes depicting a Frank nobleman holding a sword and an ecclesiastic holding a model of the church. Their faces are framed by two square haloes.

Burgusio – Those en route to the Resia pass cannot fail to see the huge white abbey of **Montemaria** ⊙. Even when it is snowing the sloping roof and the bulbous towers and campanile are still visible.
A visit to the **crypt** will reveal extraordinary Romanesque frescoes dating from the 12C when the abbey was founded. The paintings are based on the *Apocalypse* and show a clear Byzantine influence. The pantacrator is depicted in a lozenge bordered by a rainbow, a symbol of peace. On the sides are cherubims and seraphims with their wings fanning out above the heads, lower down the Evangelists are portrayed. The painting on the opposite walls depicts the walls of celestial Jerusalem.

Lago di Resia – A campanile mysteriously appears out of the waters of the lake: originally part of the church of Curono vecchia, it was submerged by water of this artificial basin in 1950.

VERONA★★★

Veneto
Population 254 748
Michelin map 428 or 429 F 14-15
Town plan in the Michelin Atlas Italy

Verona stands on the banks of the Adige in a hilly setting and is, after Venice, the finest art centre in Venetia. The fashionable **Piazza Bra** (**ABVX**) is linked by the Via Mazzini (**BV**) to the heart of the old town. The opera and theatre summer seasons *(see the Calendar of Events at the end of the guide)* both draw large crowds.
This Roman colony under the Empire was coveted by the Ostrogoths, Lombards and Franks. The town reached the peak of its glory under the **Scaliger**, Princes of the Scala, who governed for the emperor from 1260 to 1387. Then it passed to the Visconti of Milan before submitting to Venetian rule from 1405. Verona was occupied by the Austrians in 1814 and united as part of the Veneto with Italy in 1866.

Romeo and Juliet – These two young people, immortalised by Shakespeare, belonged to rival families: Romeo to the Montecchi (Montagues), who were Guelphs and supported the Pope, and Juliet to the Capuleti (Capulets), who were Ghibellines and supported the Emperor. Verona was the setting for this drama which took place in 1302 when conflicts between the two factions raged.

Pisanello and the Veronese School – Artists of this school were influenced by northern art from the Rhine Valley and they developed a Gothic art which combined flowing lines with a meticulous attention to detail.
Pisanello (c 1395-c 1450), a great traveller, active painter, prodigious medal-maker and enthusiastic draughtsman, was the greatest exponent of this school. His painting, with the soft colours, the meticulous details and flowing lines, was reminiscent of the rapidly-disappearing medieval world and heralded the realism typical of the Renaissance.

A WALK AROUND VERONA

★★ **Piazza delle Erbe** – The Square of Herbs was the former Roman forum and it is today attractive and lively, especially on market day.
In line, down the middle of the square, stand the market column; the *capitello* (a rostrum from which decrees and sentences were proclaimed) of the 16C governors *(podesti)*; the fountain known as the Verona Madonna, with a Roman statue symbolising the town; and a Venetian column surmounted by the winged Lion of St Mark (1523).

Palaces and old houses, some with pink marble columns and frescoes, make an attractive framework round the square: on the north side is the Baroque **Palazzo Maffei (B)**.

In the Via Cappello (No 23) is Juliet's House **(Casa di Giulietta)** ⊘; in fact it is a Gothic palace which belonged to the Capulet family; the famous balcony is in the inner courtyard.

★★ **Piazza dei Signori** – Take Via della Costa to reach this elegant square which resembles an open-air drawing-room. On the right is the 12C **Palazzo del Comune** (Town Hall) ⊘ **(D)**, also known as the Palazzo della Ragione dominated by the **Torre dei Lamberti**, a tower built of brick and stone and with an octagonal upper storey. This building is connected by an arch with the **Palazzo dei Tribunali** (Law Courts) **(J¹)**, formerly the Palazzo del Capitano (Governor's Residence) which is also flanked by a massive brick tower, Torrione Scaligero. The **Loggia del Consiglio (E)** on the opposite side is an elegant edifice in the Venetian-Renaissance style.

At the far end of the square the late-13C **Palazzo del Governo (P)** with its machicolations and fine Classical doorway (1533) by Sammicheli was initially a Scaliger residence before it became that of the Venetian Governors.

★★ **Arche Scaligere** – The Scaliger built their tombs between their palace and their church. The sarcophagi bear the arms of the family, with the symbolic ladder *(scala)*.

The elegant Gothic mausolea are surrounded by marble balustrades and wrought-iron rails, and are decorated with carvings of religious scenes and statues of saints in niches.

Over the door of the Romanesque Church of **Santa Maria Antica** is the tomb of the popular Cangrande I (d 1329) with his equestrian statue above *(the original is in the Castelvecchio Museum)*.

★★ **Arena** ⊘ – This amphitheatre, among the largest in the Roman world, could accommodate 25 000 spectators with its 44 tiers of seats. It is built of blocks of pink marble, flint and brick; this indicates that it probably dates from the late 1C. In summer it is the venue for a prestigious opera season. From the topmost row there is a good **panorama★★** of the town in its hilly setting, which on a clear day reaches as far as the Alps.

★★ **Castelvecchio** and **Ponte Scaligero** – This splendid fortified complex was built in 1354 by Cangrande II Scaliger. The castle itself is divided into two parts separated by a passageway guarded by a keep.

The castle contains an Art Museum (**Museo d'Arte★★** ⊘) created by the architect Carlo Scarpa. The **collection** shows the development of Veronese art from the 12C to 16C and its links with Venice and the International Gothic *(see Index)*. There are frescoes by local artists and canvases by Stefano da Verona, Pisanello, Giambono, Carlo Crivelli (splendid *Madonna of the Passion*), Mantegna, Carpaccio as well as the Bellinis.

The rooms on the upper floor contain works from the Renaissance period by Veronese artists: Morone, Liberale da Verona *(Virgin with a Goldfinch)*, Girolamo dai Libri and Veronese. There are also some Venetian works by Tintoretto, Guardi, Tiepolo and Longhi. Also on display are arms, jewellery and sculpture.

★★ **San Zeno Maggiore** – *Access via Largo D. Bosco* (AV **7**). *Plan of the built-up area in the Michelin Atlas Italy.*

St Zeno is one of the finest Romanesque churches in northern Italy. It was built on the basilical plan in the Lombard style in the 12C. The façade is decorated with Lombard bands and arcading; the side walls and campanile have alternate brick and stone courses. In the entrance porch resting on two lions, there are admirable bronze **doors★★★** (11C-12C) with scenes from the Old and New Testaments. On either side are low reliefs by the master sculptors Nicolò and Guglielmo (12C). On the tympanum of the doorway is a statue of St Zeno, patron saint of Verona.

The imposing interior has a lofty, bare nave with a cradle roof flanked by aisles with shallow roofing. On the high altar is a splendid **triptych★★** (1459), a good example of Mantegna's style characterised by precise draughtsmanship and rich ornamentation. There are 14C statues on the chancel screen and a curious polychrome statue of St Zeno laughing in the north apse.

To the north of the church are small Romanesque cloisters.

★ **Sant'Anastasia** ⊘ – This church was begun at the end of the 13C and completed in the 15C. The campanile is remarkable and the façade is pierced with a 14C double doorway adorned with frescoes and sculpture. The lofty interior contains several masterpieces: four **figures of the apostles** by Michele da Verona; Pisanello's famous fresco *(above the Pellegrini Chapel, to the right of the high altar)* of

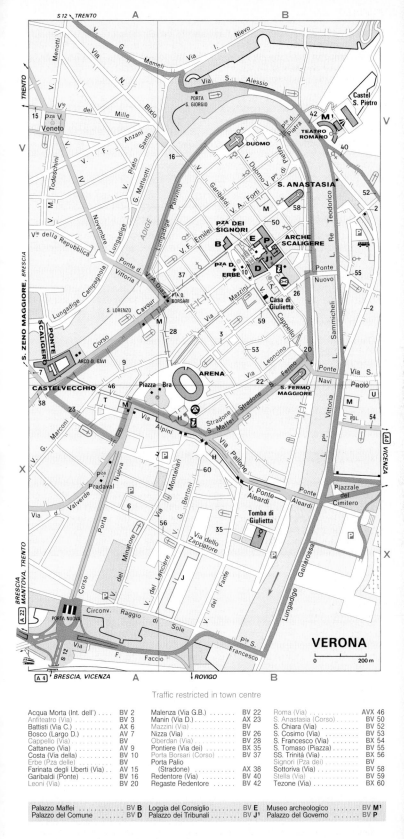

VERONA

Traffic restricted in town centre

Acqua Morta (Int. dell')	BV 2	Malenza (Via G.B.)	BV 22	Roma (Via)	AVX 46
Anfiteatro (Via)	BV 3	Manin (Via D.)	AX 23	S. Anastasia (Corso)	BV 50
Battisti (Via C.)	AX 6	*Mazzini (Via)*	BV	S. Chiara (Via)	BV 52
Bosco (Largo D.)	AV 7	Nizza (Via)	BV 26	S. Cosimo (Via)	BV 53
Cappello (Via)	BV	Oberdan (Via)	BV 28	S. Francesco (Via)	BX 54
Cattaneo (Via)	AV 9	Pontiere (Via dei)	BX 35	S. Tomaso (Piazza)	BV 55
Costa (Via della)	BV 10	Porta Borsari (Corso)	BV 37	SS. Trinità (Via)	BX 56
Erbe (Pza delle)	BV	Porta Palio		*Signori (Pza dei)*	BV
Farinata degli Uberti (Via)	AV 15	(Stradone)	AX 38	Sottoriva (Via)	BV 58
Garibaldi (Ponte)	BV 16	Redentore (Via)	BV 40	*Stella (Via)*	BV 59
Leoni (Via)	BV 20	Regaste Redentore	BV 42	Tezone (Via)	BX 60

Palazzo Maffei	BV B	Loggia del Consiglio	BV E	Museo archeologico	BV M¹
Palazzo del Comune	BV D	Palazzo dei Tribunali	BV J¹	Palazzo del Governo	BV P

Use the Map of Principal Sights to plan an itinerary.

St George delivering the Princess of Trebizond★★ (1436), which has an almost surreal combination of realistic precision and Gothic fantasy; 17 **terracottas**★ by Michele da Firenze in the Cappella Pellegrini and the fresco showing *Knights of the Cavalli family being presented to the Virgin*★ (1380) by the Veronese artist, Altichero (first chapel in the south transept).

★ **Duomo** – The cathedral has a 12C Romanesque chancel, a Gothic nave and a Classical tower. The remarkable main doorway in the Lombard-Romanesque style is adorned with sculptures and low reliefs by Maestro Nicolò. The interior has fine pink marble pillars. The altarpiece *(first altar on the left)* is decorated with an *Assumption* by Titian. The marble chancel screen is by Sammicheli (16C).
The canons' quarters are pleasant to walk through.

★ **Teatro romano** ⊙ – The Roman theatre dates from the time of Augustus but has been heavily restored. Theatrical performances are still given here.
A former monastery, **Convento di San Girolamo** *(access by lift)* has a small museum **(Museo Archeologico)** ⊙ (**M¹**) and there is a lovely **view** over the town.

Castel San Pietro – *Take the stairway which leads off Regaste Redentore* (**BV 42**). St Peter's Castle dates back to the Visconti and the period of Venetian rule. The terraces afford splendid **views**★★ of Verona.

★ **San Fermo Maggiore** – The church, dedicated to St Firmanus Major, was built in the 11C-12C and remodelled at a later date. The façade is in the Romanesque and Gothic styles. The aisleless church is covered by a stepped, keel-shaped roof. On the left by the west door the Brenzoni mausoleum (1430) is framed by a fresco of the *Annunciation*★ by Pisanello.

Tomba di Giulietta ⊙ (**BX**) – *Via del Pontiere*. Juliet's tomb is in the cloisters of the Church of San Francesco al Corso, where, it is said, Romeo and Juliet were married.

VICENZA★★

Veneto
Population 108 947
Michelin map 429 F 16
Town plan in the Michelin Atlas Italia

The proud and noble city of Vicenza lies in a pretty setting at the foot of the Berici Mountains. This busy commercial and industrial centre now has, in addition to its traditional textile industry, mechanical and chemical industries and a reputation as a gold-working centre. Vicenza is strategically set at the crossroads of routes between the Veneto and Trentino.
The gastronomic speciality of Vicenza is *baccalà alla Vicentina*, cod with a sauce served with slices of *polenta* (maize semolina), which is best with wine from the Berici Mountains (Barbarano, Gambellara and Breganze).

HISTORICAL AND ARTISTIC NOTES

The ancient Roman town of Vicetia became an independent city state in the 12C. After several conflicts with the neighbouring cities of Padua and Verona, Vicenza sought Venetian protection at the beginning of the 15C. This was a period of great prosperity, when Vicenza counted many rich and generous art patrons among its citizens and it was embellished with an amazing number of palaces.

Palladio – Vicenza was given the nickname of "Venice on *terra firma*" due to an exceptionally gifted man, Andrea di Pietro, known as Palladio, who spent many years in Vicenza. The last great architect of the Renaissance, Palladio was born at Padua in 1508 and died at Vicenza in 1580. He succeeded in combining, in a supremely harmonious idiom, the precepts of ancient art with the contemporary preoccupations. Encouraged by the humanist Trissino, he made several visits to Rome to study her monuments and the work of Vitruvius, a Roman architect of the time of Augustus. He perfected the Palladian style and in 1570 published his **Treatise on Architecture**, in four volumes, which made his work famous throughout Europe.
The **Palladian style** is characterised by rigorous plans where simple and symmetrical forms predominate and by harmonious façades which combine pediments and porticoes, as at San Giorgio Maggiore in Venice *(see VENEZIA)*. Palladio was often commissioned by wealthy Venetians to build residences in the countryside around Venice. He combined architectural rhythm, noble design and, in the case of the

country mansions, a great sense of situation and decoration with the utmost attention being paid to the base, so that the villas seemed to rise like a series of new temples on the banks of the Brenta *(see Riviera del BRENTA)* or the slopes of the Berici Mountains. His pupil, Vicenzo Scamozzi (1552-1616), completed several of his master's works and carried on his style.

★★ THE PALLADIAN CITY *a half day*

★★ **Piazza dei Signori** – Like St Mark's Square in Venice, it is an open-air meeting-place recalling the forum of antiquity. As in the Piazzetta in Venice, there are two columns bearing effigies of the Lion of St Mark and the Redeemer.

With the lofty **Torre Bissara**★, a 12C belfry, the **Basilica**★★ ⓥ (1549-1617) occupies one whole side of the square. The elevation is one of Palladio's masterpieces, with two superimposed galleries in the Doric and Ionic orders, admirable for their power, proportion and purity of line. The great keel-shaped roof, destroyed by bombing, has been rebuilt. The building was not a church but a meeting-place for the Vicenzan notables. The 15C **Monte di Pietà** (pawn shop) opposite, with buildings framing the Baroque façade of the Church of S. Vincenzo, is adorned with frescoes. The **Loggia del Capitano**★, formerly the residence of the Venetian Governor, which stands to the left, at the corner of the Contrà del Monte, was begun to the plans of Palladio in 1571 and left unfinished. It is characterised by its colossal orders with composite capitals and its statues and stuccoes commemorating the naval victory of Lepanto *(see Index)*.

★★ **Teatro Olimpico** ⓥ – This splendid building in wood and stucco was designed by Palladio in 1580 on the model of the theatres of antiquity. The tiers of seats are laid out in a hemicycle and surmounted by a lovely **colonnade** with a balustrade crowned with statues. The **stage**★★★ is one of the finest in existence with its superimposed niches, columns and statues and its amazing perspectives painted in *trompe-l'œil* by Scamozzi who completed the work.

★ **Corso Andrea Palladio** – This, the main street of Vicenza, and several neighbouring streets are embellished by many palaces designed by Palladio and his pupils. At the beginning is the **Palazzo Chiericati** *(see below)*, an imposing work by Palladio; at No 147 the 15C **Palazzo Da Schio** in the Venetian-Gothic style was formerly known as the Ca d'Oro (Golden House) because it was covered with frescoes with gilded backgrounds. The west front of **Palazzo Thiene** overlooking Contrà S. Gaetano Thiene was by Palladio, while the entrance front at No 12 Contrà Porti is Renaissance dating from the late 15C.

The **Palazzo Porto-Barbaran** opposite is also by Palladio. At No 98 the **Palazzo Trissino** (1592) is one of Scamozzi's most successful works. Next is the Corso Fogazzaro, where the **Palazzo Valamarana** (1566) at No 16 is another work by Palladio.

★ **Museo Civico** ⓥ – The municipal museum is housed on the first floor of Palazzo Chiericati. The collection of paintings includes Venetian Primitives (*The Dormition of the Virgin* by Paolo Veneziano); a *Crucifixion*★★ by Hans Memling; canvases by Bartolomeo Montagna (pupil of Giovanni Bellini), Mantegna and Carpaccio, one of the most active artists in Vicenza. There are Venetian works by Lorenzo Lotto, Veronese, Bassano, Piazzetta, Tiepolo and Tintoretto as well as Flemish works by Velvet Brueghel and Van Dyck.

IF YOU STILL HAVE TIME...

Santa Corona – *Contrà Santa Corona.* The church was built in the 13C in honour of a Holy Thorn presented by St Louis, King Louis IX of France, to the Bishop of Vicenza. The nave and two aisles have pointed vaulting while the chancel is Renaissance. Works of art include: a *Baptism of Christ*★★ by Giovanni Bellini *(fifth altar on the left)* and an *Adoration of the Magi*★★ (1573) by Veronese *(third chapel on the right)*. The fourth chapel on the right has a lovely coffered **ceiling**★, richly painted and adorned with gilded stucco, and a *Mary Magdalene and Saints* by Bartolomeo Montagna.

Duomo – The cathedral, built between the 14C and 16C, has an attractively-colourful Gothic façade and a Renaissance east end. Inside, the lovely **polyptych**★ (1356) is by Lorenzo Veneziano *(fifth chapel on the right)*.

Giardino Salvi – This garden is attractively adorned with statues and fountains. Canals run along two sides of the garden and two lovely Palladian 16C and 17C loggias are reflected in the waters.

EXCURSIONS

★★ **Villa Valmarana ai Nani** ⓥ – *2km/1mi south by the Este road and then the first road to the right*. The villa dates from the 17C and was adorned in 1757 with splendid **frescoes**★★★ by **Gian Domenico Tiepolo**. He portrays with plenty of verve and vigour the different aspects of daily life in the province and in particular, carnival scenes.

★ **La Rotonda** ⓥ – *2km/1mi southeast by the Este road and then the second road to the right*. The Rotonda is one of Palladio's most famous creations and the plan of Chiswick House in London was inspired by it. The gracefully-proportioned square building is roofed with a dome and fronted on each side by a pedimented portico, making it look like an ancient temple.

★ **Monte Berico Basilica** and **Monti Berici** – *2km/1mi south by Viale Venezia and then Viale X Giugno*. As the Viale X Giugno climbs uphill, it is lined with an 18C portico and chapels. On the summit is the baroque basilica roofed with a dome. From the esplanade there is a wide **panorama**★★ of Vicenza, the Venetian plain and the Alps. Inside, there is a *Pietà* (1500) by Bartolomeo Montagna.
From here the road runs southwards to Arcugnano and Barbarano, where one can catch occasional glimpses of former patrician villas now used as farmhouses in this attractive countryside of volcanic hills.

Montecchio Maggiore – *13km/8mi southwest by the S 11*. The ruins of these two castles remind one of Romeo and Juliet. There are good **views**★ of the Po Plain and Vicenza.
On the outskirts of Montecchio on the Tavernelle road the **Villa Cordellina-Lombardi** ⓥ has one room entirely covered with **frescoes**★ by Tiepolo.

Villas and palaces by the 16C architect Palladio are to be found at Malcontenta, Maser and Vicenza.

VIPITENO

STERZING – Trentino-Alto Adige
Population 5 652
Michelin map 429 B 16

Vipiteno's long history began in the Bronze Age. In Roman times there was a road station named *Vipitenum* and in 1180 the town was documented as *Stercengum* (from which Sterzing derives). Vipiteno flourished between the 15C and 16C when silver and lead were mined in nearby valleys (a visit to the mines in the nearby Val Ridanna and Valle Aurina, in Predoi will give an idea of mining activity in the Alto Adige).

A city along a street – Only 15km/9mi from the Austrian border, Vipiteno is a pretty town grouped around one street lined with typical Tyrolean houses (Erker) and arcading. The 15C tower, Torre dei Dodici, cuts the street in half, the more picturesque **Citta Nuova**★ (New City) street lying to the south and the Città Vecchia (Old City) street to the north. On Via Città Nuova stands the 16C town hall.
In the square where the two streets converge stands the Church of the Holy Spirit (Chiesa dello Spirito Santo), richly decorated with 15C frescoes.

EXCURSIONS

Cascate di Stanghe ⓥ – *Take the road in the direction of Racines and then follow directions to Stanghe*. This waterfall descends a narrow gorge that, having been eroded by the water, is coloured white and green. Walking through the winding gorge is facilitated by the presence of long passageways and small wooden bridges attached to the rocks. A walk through the ravine and the wood near the town is pleasant and can be done uphill (obviously more tiring) or downhill. To vary the excursion it is possible to descend via the waterfall (leaving the car at the top where there is a cafeteria and a small chapel) and return up via footpath no 13 which passes through meadows and affords fine views of the pastures. Whether one chooses the waterfall or footpath route, the journey time is roughly the same: about an hour to ascend and three quarters of and hour to descend.

Montecavallo – Along the Brennero road, just after Via Città Vecchia, there is a cable-car to Montecavallo (alt 2 000m/6562ft). On arrival there is a wide choice of footpaths and walks.

VITERBO★

Lazio

Population 60 319

Michelin map 430 ○ 18

Viterbo, still girdled by its walls, has kept its medieval aspect notably in the **San Pellegrino quarter**★★, a working-class area with many craftsmen. Here there are typical vaulted passageways, towers and external staircases.

★★ **Piazza San Lorenzo** – This square, which occupies the site of the former Etruscan acropolis, takes one back to the Middle Ages with a 13C house on Etruscan foundations (now a chemist's), its cathedral dating from 1192 and adorned with a fine Gothic campanile, and its 13C Papal Palace **(Palazzo dei Papi**★★**)** – one of the most interesting examples of medieval secular architecture in Lazio. From the Piazza Martiri d'Ungheria there is a lovely view of the piazza.

Museo Civico ○ – *Piazza F. Crispi.* The municipal museum is housed in the former Monastery of Santa Maria della Verità and contains collections of Etruscan and Roman objects discovered in the area: sarcophagi and grave artefacts from the tombs. The picture gallery, on the first floor, has a terracotta by the Della Robbias as well as works by Salvator Rosa, Sebastiano del Piombo and a local painter, Pastura (15C-16C).

EXCURSIONS

Madonna della Quercia – *3km/2mi northeast.* The church, dedicated to the Madonna of the Oak *(quercia),* is in the Renaissance style with a rusticated façade and tympana by Andrea della Robbia. The cloisters are part Gothic, part Renaissance.

★★ **Villa Lante in Bagnaia** ○ – *5km/3mi northeast.* This elegant 16C villa was built to the designs of Vignola and became the residence of several popes. A lovely Italian terraced garden with geometric motifs and numerous fountains makes an ideal setting for the villa.

★ **Teatro romano di Ferento** ○ – *9km/6mi north.* The 1C BC Roman theatre is quite well preserved and is the most important vestige of the ancient Ferentium, the ruins of which lie scattered over a melancholy plateau. The theatre ruins stand between the road and the Decumanus and consist of a brick back wall as well as a portico of well-dressed blocks without any mortar, and 13 tiers of seats.

Bomarzo – *21km/13mi northeast by the S 204.* Extending below the town is the park **(Parco dei Mostri** ○**)**, a Mannerist creation of Vicino Orsini (16C) adorned with a series of fantastically shaped **sculptures**★.

Montefiascone – *17km/11mi northwest.* Montefiascone stands in the vineyard country which produces the delicious white wine *Est, Est, Est.*
The imposing cathedral **(Duomo)** has a dome designed by Sammicheli, while a curious church, **San Flaviano**★, in the Lombard-Romanesque style is in reality two churches superimposed. In the lower church, frescoes illustrate the *Story of the Three Dead and the Three Living Men* symbolising the brevity and vanity of human life; opposite stands the tombstone of Johann Fugger, the German prelate who died on his way to Rome. As he was fond of good food and wine, he sent one of his servants ahead of him with orders to mark the inns where the wine was the best, with the word *est* ("is" short for *Vinum est bonum* in Latin). When he arrived at Montefiascone the faithful servant found the wine so good that he wrote, in his enthusiasm, "*Est, Est, Est*". And his master, becoming enthusiastic in his turn, drank so much, much, much of it that he died.

★ **Lago di Vico** – *18km/11mi southeast by the Via Santa Maria di Gradi.* This solitary but charming lake occupies a crater with forested slopes (beech, chestnut, oak and on the lake shores, hazel trees).

Civita Castellana – *36km/22mi southeast.* Civita Castellana occupies the site of the Etruscan city Falerii Veteres which was destroyed by the Romans in 241, but rebuilt in the 8C or 9C. The cathedral **(Duomo)** is fronted by an elegant **portico**★ built in 1210 by the Cosmati *(see Index).*
The late-15C castle **(Rocca)** was built by Sangallo the Elder and became the residence of Cesare Borgia.

Michelin Maps, The Red Guide and The Green Guide
are complementary publications
to be used together

VOLTERRA★★

Tuscany
Population 11 993
Michelin map 430 L 14

The Tuscan hills, very different from those around Florence, a commanding position and well-preserved walls make a harmonious setting for the Etruscan, Roman and medieval town of Volterra. The town has numerous alabaster workshops. Large salt pans to the west are used in the manufacture of fine salt and soda.
To the northwest of the town there is a view of the **Balze★**, impressive precipices, which are part of a highly-eroded landscape furrowed by gully erosion.

The furrowed landscape of the Balze

★★ **Piazza dei Priori** – The piazza is surrounded by austere palaces. The 13C Palazzo Pretorio has paired windows and is linked with the Torre del Podestà, also known as Torre del Porcellino because of the wild boar sculpted high up on a bracket. The early-13C Palazzo dei Priori, opposite, is decorated with terracotta, marble and stone shields of the Florentine governors.

★ **Duomo** and **Battistero** – The cathedral in the Pisan-Romanesque style, although it has been remodelled several times, stands in the picturesque Piazza San Giovanni. The interior comprises a nave and two aisles with monolithic columns and 16C capitals. On the second altar in the nave, on the left is a lovely late-15C *Annunciation*. The transept contains, in the north arm, a *Virgin* of the 15C Sienese school, and in the south arm, a 13C painted wooden sculpture, **Descent from the Cross★★**. The nave has a superb 17C pulpit with 12C low reliefs. The octagonal baptistery dates from 1283.
Take the Via Roma and then pass through the Arco Buomparenti.

Via dei Sarti – This street is lined with palaces: No 1, Palazzo Minucci-Solaini attributed to Antonio da Sangallo which now houses the art gallery *(see below)*, and No 37, the **Palazzo Viti** ⊘ **(A)** with its superb Renaissance façade designed by Ammanati. In 1964 Luchino Visconti shot some scenes from his film *Vaghe stelle dll'orsa*. Some beautiful Indian clothes of the alabaster merchant and Emir to Nepal, Giuseppe Viti, are conserved here.

Pinacoteca ⊘ – *1 Via dei Sarti.* The Art Gallery displays numerous works of art by 14C to 17C Tuscan artists, notably a lovely *Annunciation* by Luca Signorelli and a *Descent from the Cross*, a masterpiece of Florentine Mannerism by Rosso Fiorentino.

★ **Museo Etrusco Guarnacci** ⊘ – More than 600 Etruscan funerary urns, made of tufa, alabaster and terracotta, make up the exhibition.

★ **Porta all'Arco** – This Etruscan gateway is built of colossal blocks of stone.

Rovine romane – 1C BC Roman ruins lie to the west of the Porta Fiorentina.

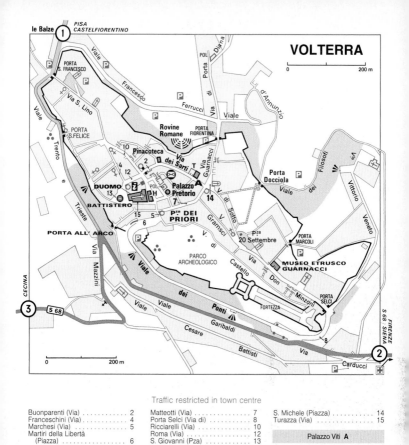

VOLTERRA

Traffic restricted in town centre

Buonparenti (Via) 2	Matteotti (Via) 7	S. Michele (Piazza) 14
Franceschini (Via) 4	Porta Selci (Via di) 8	Turazza (Via) 15
Marchesi (Via) 5	Ricciarelli (Via) 10	
Martiri della Libertà	Roma (Via) 12	Palazzo Viti A
(Piazza) 6	S. Giovanni (Pza) 13	

Porta Docciola - At the end of a very long flight of steps is a fortified gate near which there is a curious medieval washtub.

Viale dei Ponti - The Viale is a favourite walk with Volterrans. It affords splendid views★★ of the Colli Metalliferi (see below). Above stands the Fortezza, now used as a prison, an impressive mass of military architecture formed by the 14C Rocca Vecchia and the Rocca Nuova, built in 1472 with a keep and four corner towers.

EXCURSION

Larderello - 33km/21mi south by ③. Larderello is situated in the heart of the **Colline Metalliferi★** or metal-bearing hills as the name suggests. In the past they were mined for iron ore, copper and pyrites. Larderello is one of Tuscany's more unusual places with its desolate landscapes, the hissing of its volcanic steam jets, belching smoke from the blast furnaces and the rumble of machinery.

The clear blue waters of Maddalena island, Sardinia

The Islands

Sardinia

Sardinia offers an almost primeval landscape of rocks sculpted by the wind and sea, forests of holm and cork oaks, oleander, aromatic plants and shrubs, the clear blue waters of the Mediterranean and the silence of an earlier age broken only by the sounds of nature.

THE ISLAND

Sardinia (Sardegna) is the largest island in the Mediterranean after Sicily. It is surrounded by the Tyrrhenian sea to the east and south, the Sardinian sea to the west and the Bonifacio straits, which divide the island from Corsica, to the north. The island has a number of bays, among them Golfo dell'Asinara in the north, Golfo di Orosei in the east, Golfo di Cagliari in the south and Golfo di Oristano in the west.

A number of smaller islands lie off the Sardinian coast, such as Asinara, Maddalena, Caprera, Tavolara, Sant' Antioco and San Pietro. The Punta la Marmora in the Gennargentu mountains is the highest peak of the island with an altitude of 1 834m/6 017ft.

HISTORICAL NOTES

Earliest inhabitants – Sardinia has traces of human settlement dating back to prehistoric times – *domus de janas*, with their disturbing human-like features, dolmens standing alone in the middle of fields and ancient nuraghi unchanged by the passing centuries.

The Nuraghic civilisation lasted from 1800 to 500 BC; its golden age is considered have lasted from 1200 to 900 BC.

The island has over 7 000 **nuraghi** or fortified tower houses, structures in the form of a truncated covered cone. The name comes from the root *nur*, also found in *nurra*, which means both "mass" and "cavity". The nuraghi were built of huge blocks of stone without any mortar, possibly using an inclined plane along which they would have been pushed or rolled. They were used as dwellings, as watchtowers from which to keep an eye on both livestock and territory and, when built together as a group, as fortresses.

Other structures remain from this prehistoric period, including dolmens, "covered avenues", *allée couverte*, ie funeral monuments comprising a rectangular room covered by stone slabs and a tumulus, and Giants' Tombs *(see ARZACHENA)*.

As water was a rare commodity on the island, it played an important part in the nuraghic religion. The god who lived in the wells and rivers and who had the power to overcome periods of drought was represented by the bull, often pictured throughout the island.

Successive invasions – Sardinia has been subject to a number of invasions throughout history. The first settlers were the Phoenicians in the 8C BC, followed by the Romans in 238 BC, the Vandals in AD 455 and the Byzantines in AD 534.

Travelling to Sardinia

Ferries leave from Civitavecchia, Genoa, La Spezia, Livorno, Palermo and Trapani for the ports of Cagliari, Golfo Aranci, Olbia, Porto Torres and Arbatax *(see Practical Information section at the end of the guide)*. Visitors are advised to book their crossing in advance if travelling in the summer season.

Sardinia can also be reached by **air**, with airports in Alghero, Cagliari, Olbia and Sassari.

Consult the Michelin Red Guide Italia and Michelin map 433 for further information on companies and specific routes.

Travelling in Sardinia

Sardinia offers endless opportunities for visitors with its rugged scenery, views of the sea and megalithic remains. Visitors should allow at least a week in order to explore the island fully.

When exploring the east side of the island it is advisable to leave with a full tank of petrol, as petrol stations are few and far between.

Sights described in this section are marked on the map in bold, while additional itineraries for visitors with more time at their disposal are marked in black. Those who wish to enjoy the landscape at a slower pace may like to take the old steam locomotive known as the **trenino verde**. A number of routes are available (Mandras-Sorgono, Mandras-Arbatax, Macomer-Bosa, Sassari-Tempio Pausania-Palau), but it is also possible to hire the entire train. For information, contact the **Servizio Turistico delle Ferrovie della Sardegna**, which also runs a railway museum: Museo delle Ferrovie, via Pompeo, 09040 Monserrato, ☎ 070 58 02 46.

The Saracens arrived in the 7C and after the year 1000 the island was fought over by the Pisans and Genoese. It then fell to the Spanish in 1295 and later during the War of Succession to the Austrian Empire in 1713. The Kingdom of Sardinia was created in 1718 by Vittorio Amedeo II of Savoy and the island was annexed to the new united Italy in 1861. Sardinia was granted the special status of an autonomous region in 1948.

LOCAL PRODUCTS

Food and drink – The traditional recipes of Sardinia are simple but tasty, flavoured with the many aromatic plants and herbs that grow in profusion on the island.
Bread is often the soft-doughed **carasau**, known as *carta da musica* in the rest of Italy.
Gnocchetti sardi, a type of pasta shell which has nothing to do with the traditional Italian *gnocchi*, are also known as **malloreddus**, and are often served with a sausage and tomato sauce. Meat-lovers should try the suckling pig *(porchetto da latte)* roasted on a spit.
The island has many different varieties of cheese, including goats' cheese, Sardinian **fiore** and Sardinian **pecorino**.
Local desserts include the rhomboid-shaped **papassinos**, which are often covered with icing and sprinkled with small coloured sugar balls, and **sebadas**, round doughnuts which are fried and covered with honey.
The best-known local wines are the **Anghelu Ruju** and **Cannonau; Mirto** is an excellent local liqueur.

Arts and crafts – Sardinia is also well known for its cottage industries, which produce a range of products including goldwork, ceramics, leather, wood and cork, tapestries and basketware.

Constantly revised Michelin Maps, at a scale of 1: 200 000, indicate:
- *difficult or dangerous roads, sharp gradients*
- *car and passenger ferries*
- *bridges with height and weight restrictions*

Keep current Michelin Maps in the car at all times

ALGHERO★

Population 40 477
Michelin map 433 F 6

The early history of this pleasant little walled port set amid olive trees, eucalyptus and parasol pines is unknown. Coral divers operate from the port which is the main town on the Riviera del Corallo. In 1354 Alghero was occupied by the Catalans; the town still has a Catalan-Gothic centre and its inhabitants still speak Catalan. Its Spanish air has earned it the nickname of the Barcelonetta of Sardinia.
The beach extends 5km/3mi to the north of the village.

★ **Città Vecchia** – The fortifications encircle a network of narrow streets in the old town. The cathedral **(Duomo)** *(Via Roma)* has a beautiful doorway and a campanile in the Catalan-Gothic style. The 14C-15C Church of **San Francesco** has a Gothic interior and lovely **cloisters** in golden-coloured tufa.
The fishing harbour stands close against the fortifications in the northern part of the town. The harbour is the embarkation point for the boat trips to Neptune's Cave **(Grotta di Nettuno★★★)**.

EXCURSIONS

★★★ **Grotta di Nettuno** ⊙ – *27km/17mi west; access also possible by boat.* The road out to the headland, **Capo Caccia**, offers splendid **views★★** of the rocky coast. **Neptune's Cave** is on the point. A stairway (654 steps) leads down the cliff face. There are small inner lakes, a forest of columns, and concretions in the form of organ pipes.

★ **Nuraghe Palmavera** ⊙ – *10km/6mi on the Porto Conte road.* This nuraghe is surrounded by the remains of a prehistoric village, formed by approximately 50 individual dwellings crowded closely together. The nuraghe is a particularly fine building in white limestone with two vaulted towers and two separate entrances.

Necropoli di Anghelu Ruju ⊙ – *10km/6mi from Alghero on the Porto Torres road.* This necropolis comprises 38 hypogea (underground chambers) dating from the Neolithic era (c 3000 BC).

ARZACHENA

Population 10 284
Michelin map 433 D 10

SARDINIA

Arzachena, once an agricultural market town, owes its fame to its position in the heart of the Costa Smeralda hinterland at the foot of a curious mushroom-shaped rock (Fungo) and its proximity to important archeological remains.

Megalithic Stones

The remains of a Giants' Tomb **(Tomba dei Giganti di Li Muri)** and a necropolis can be seen not far from Arzachena.

Giants' Tomb

Popular tradition gave the name Giants' tomb to these tombs dating from the nuraghic period. The funeral chambers lined and roofed with megalithic slabs (like a dolmen) were preceded by an arc of standing stones forming the exedra or area of ritual. The front of the structure is formed by a central stele with fascia in relief, which leads to the corridor of stones. This "false door" may have symbolised the connection with the afterlife.

★ **Tomba di Giganti di Li Golghi** – *Follow signs for Luogosanto from Arzachena. Take a right turn after about 7km/4mi. Signposted.*
This megalithic tomb dates from between 1800 and 1200 BC. It would once have been covered by an ellipsoidal tumulus 27m/88ft in length.

Necropoli di Li Muri – *Return to the junction and follow signs to Necropoli di Li Muri. Park by the first or second house (the road after this becomes narrow and bumpy) and continue on foot for the last 500m/0.3mi.*

This circular necropolis dates from 3500-2700 BC. It consists of a central dolmen, the tomb, surrounded by five concentric stone circles which supported a tumulus.

To choose a hotel or a restaurant,
to find an auto mechanic,
consult the current edition of the **The Red Guide Italia.**

BARBAGIA

Michelin map 433 G-H 9-10

This wild region of Sardinia, with its pastoral farming traditions, lies behind the immense Gennargentu massif. The area is full of steep ravines, known only to local shepherds, and has a wide variety of flora (holm oak, chestnut, hazelnut, holly, dwarf juniper, thyme and yew) and fauna (golden and Bonelli eagle, peregrine falcon, golden kite, wild boar, fox and moufflon).
The **Monti del Gennargentu**★★ and **Supramonte**, a limestone plateau in the Orgosolo, Oliena and Dorgali areas, are also situated in this region.

WILD NATURAL LANDSCAPES, HISTORY AND THE SEA

Between Lotzorai and Baunei – The SS 125 road **from Arbatax to Dorgali**★★★ passes through an increasingly atmospheric landscape as it runs further into the Barbagia region.
At Lotzorai, a yellow sign indicates the turn off for the **Domus de janas**. This archeological area contains approximately ten of these unusual stone constructions, which are occasionally built so that the opening in the rock gives the impression of a human face.

Domus de janas

These attractively named hypogei (*domus de janas* means "house of fairies") were built from the beginning of the fourth to the middle of the third millennium.
They are constructed from sandstone, granite, limestone and basaltic rock and some are decorated with drawings of oxen and goats.

It is worth stopping at the highest point of the road (1 000m/3 282ft) to admire the view. In summer the mountains are dotted here and there with patches of sweet-smelling yellow broom.

Dorgali – This town, the main resort in the Barbagia, lies in the bay of Cala Gonone and is the cultural, culinary and craftwork centre of the region. Its main street, via Lamarmora, offers a pleasant stroll past traditional shops selling local rugs made with a distinctive knot, while the archeological remains in the region take the visitor back to prehistoric times. The local *cannonau* grape has been producing excellent wine for the past two thousand years.

The nuraghic village of **Serra Orrios**★ lies not far from Dorgalio on the road leading to the S 129, while the Giants' Tomb **Sa Ena 'e Thomes** is situated on the Lula road. This tomb has the traditional layout of a Giants' Tomb. The funerary chamber, in the form of a passage roofed with large slabs like a dolmen, is preceded by a series of stones forming the arc of a circle. The larger central stone is carved with a moulding and pierced with a small passageway at ground level.

Cala Gonone – A winding road★★ leads to this resort built in an attractive bay with a small harbour. Boat trips leave from the port.

Cala Luna – This attractive white sandy beach is lapped by calm, clear water and backed by oleander plants. There are a number of caves around the bay.

Grotta del Bue Marino ⊘ – The *bue marino* or Sea Ox refers to the monk seal which occupied this cave until the end of the 1970s. The galleried cave has some lovely concretions and a small spring at the back of the area which can be visited.

Dolmen Mottorra – *Head north. After a bend in the road, at the km 207 point on the S 125, a sign marks the path to the dolmen.* The dolmen is situated in the middle of a field which is reached after following the path for approximately five minutes. It consists of an almost-circular slab of schist supported by seven upright stones and dates from the beginning of the third millennium BC.

★★ **Grotta di Ispinigòli** ⊘ – *The road to the cave is approximately 7km/4mi from Dorgali on the S 125.* On entering the cave, the visitor immediately comes to a large chasm and realises that the cave is formed by an immense cavity and not by a tunnel. The eye is caught by an impressive **stalagmite column** which appears to support the roof. This column (38m/125ft) is the second tallest in the world (the tallest is in New Mexico). The cave is now a fossil, as there is no more water to form new concretions, which are lamellar (in the shape of knives or drapes) or cauliflower (formed under water, like coral) in form.

The dominant colour is red, because the rock strata of the roof is thin. Had it been thicker, water would have filtered through depositing limestone, which would have given the concretions a white colour.

The abundant flow of water in the past quickly built up deposits on the floor of the cave; as a result the stalagmites are much larger than the stalactites.

Phoenician jewellery and human bones have been found in the cave, suggesting that it was perhaps used for sacrificial purposes or as a burial chamber for the nuraghic people.

★ **Su Gologone** – *20 km/12.5mi to the southeast of Nuoro, on the Oliena-Dorgali road.* The large town of **Oliena** stands at the foot of a particularly steep slope of the Sopramonte.

Just beyond Oliena take a local road to the right for about 6km/4mi.

The lovely spring at Su Gologone gushes from a rocky face (300 litres per second) in a picturesque green setting.

Not far from Supramonte di Dorgali a cave open to the sky hides the **nuraghic village of Tiscali.**

Orgosolo – *20km/12mi south.* This market town with its calm appearance is notorious for being the stronghold of bandits and outlaws (popularised by the Italian film producer Vittorio de Seta in his film *Banditi a Orgosolo* made in 1961). Today it is a pleasant town with bright murals adding a touch of life and colour to its streets.

BARUMINI★★

Population 1 471
Michelin map 433 H 9

The town of Barumini is surrounded by numerous traces of the earliest period of Sardinian history.

★★ **Nuraghe Su Nuraxi** – *2km/1mi west, on the left-hand side of the Tuili road.* The oldest part of Su Nuraxi dates from the 15C BC. The fortress was consolidated as a result of the threat posed by the Phoenician invaders between the 8C and 7C BC and was later taken by the Carthaginians between the 5C and 4C BC. The settlement was gradually enlarged over the centuries until it was abandoned in the 3C with the arrival of the Romans.

★ **Santa Vittoria di Serri** – *38km/24mi east by the Nuoro road and a road to the right in Nurallao.* There are remains of a prehistoric religious centre. On the way out pass through the village of **Isili** with two thriving craft industries (furniture-making and weaving).

S. Chirol

Su Nuraxi nuraghic settlement

CAGLIARI

Population 170 768
Michelin map 433 J 9

Cagliari is the capital of the island. It is a modern-looking town with a busy harbour and an old nucleus surrounded by fortifications, built by the Pisans in the 13C. Before becoming Roman it was a flourishing Carthaginian city called Karalis.

The **Feast of St Efisio** (an officer in Diocletian's army who converted to Christianity and became the patron saint of Sardinia) is undoubtedly one of the most splendid in the whole of Italy *(see the Calendar of Events at the end of the guide).*

The **Terrazza Umberto 1º** affords a fine **view★★** of the town, harbour and bay.

Cattedrale – Built in the 13C Pisan style, the cathedral was remodelled in the 17C. Inside are magnificent **pulpits★★** (1162) by Guglielmo of Pisa with carved panels illustrating the Life of Christ. A little door on the right of the choir leads down to the Sanctuary or **Santuario**, a crypt with 17C decoration, which contains the remains of 292 Christian martyrs in urns placed along the walls.

A door opens on the right into a chapel containing the tomb of Marie-Louise of Savoy, the wife of the future King Louis XVIII of France and sister of the King of Sardinia.

★ **Museo Archeologico Nazionale** ⊘ – The National Archeological Museum has a large collection of arms, pottery and small **bronzes★★★**, grave artefacts from the earliest period of Sardinian history. Phoenician, Punic and Roman art are represented in the other rooms.

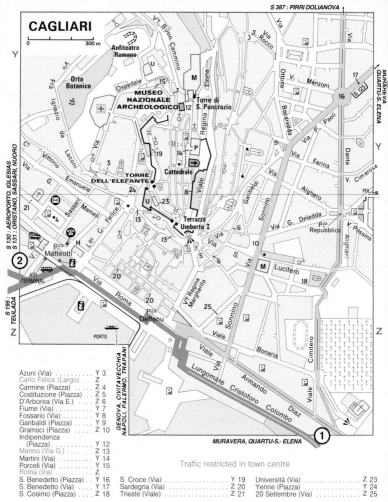

CAGLIARI

0 — 300 m

Azuni (Via)	Y 3	S. Croce (Via)	Y 19	Università (Via)	Z 23
Carlo Felice (Largo)	Z	Sardegna (Via)	Z 20	Yenne (Piazza)	Y 24
Carmine (Piazza)	Z 4	Trieste (Viale)	Z 21	20 Settembre (Via)	Z 25
Costituzione (Piazza)	Z 5				
D'Arborea (Via E.)	Y 6				
Fiume (Via)	Y 7				
Fossario (Via)	Y 8				
Garibaldi (Piazza)	Y 9				
Gramsci (Piazza)	Z 10				
Indipendenza (Piazza)	Y 12				
Manno (Via G.)	Z 13				
Martini (Via)	Y 14				
Porceli (Via)	Y 15				
Roma (Via)	Z				
S. Benedetto (Piazza)	Y 16				
S. Benedetto (Via)	Y 17				
S. Cosimo (Piazza)	Z 18				

Traffic restricted in town centre

Torre dell'Elefante and **Torre San Pancrazio** – The early-14C Elephant and St Pancras towers were part of the Pisan fortifications.

Anfiteatro Romano – This amphitheatre is the most important Roman monument in Sardinia.

Orto Botanico ⊙ – The displays in the botanical garden are of both Mediterranean and tropical vegetation.

EXCURSION

*** **Strada di Muravera** – *Leave by ① on the town plan.* 30km/19mi from Cagliari, the SS 125 road enters wild gorges with reddish-coloured walls of porphyritic granite, dotted with oleander bushes and prickly pear cacti.

Michelin presents **In Your Pocket**

A new pocket-size collection of friendly, easy-to-use guides with the basics on what to see and do in some of the world's most attractive cities and regions. More than 30 destinations are now available:

Algarve – Amsterdam – Barcelona – Berlin – Brittany (France) – Bruges, Ghent, Antwerp Brussels – Budapest Channel Islands Dublin – Florida – Greek Islands – Istanbul – Italian Lakes – Lisbon – London – Loire Valley – Madrid – Malta – Morocco – Munich and the royal castles of Bavaria – Naples, Pompeii, Capri, Sorrento and the Amalfi Coast – New Orleans – New York City – Paris – Prague – Rome – Saint Petersburg – San Francisco – Sicily – South of France: Riviera – Southern Spain – Thailand – Tuscany – Venice – Vienna

COSTA SMERALDA★★

EMERALD COAST
Michelin map 433 D 10

This wild and undulating region has one of the most indented coastlines of the island. It is a succession of pink granite headlands, covered with maquis scrub and overlooking the sea which is a clear emerald green.

Not so long ago the region was one of farmers and shepherds, but in 1962 it was discovered by the international jet-set. The development of the **Emerald Coast** was promoted by a consortium originally presided over by the Aga Khan. This eastern peninsula of the Gallura region now offers a range of tourist facilities and is the perfect spot for those keen on windsurfing, sailing, golf and tennis.

The main resorts are **Porto Cervo**⚑⚑⚑, Cala di Volpe and **Baia Sardinia**⚑.

> ### Gallura
>
> Gallura is the northeastern point of Sardinia. The interior is dominated by Monte Limbara (1 359m/4 461ft) and boasts a dramatic landscape of granite plateaux, cork oaks and caves, while the wild indented coastline offers visitors glimpses of the clear waters of the Mediterranean.

Arcipelago della MADDALENA★★

MADDALENA ARCHIPELAGO
Michelin map 433 D 10

The Maddalena Archipelago consists of the islands of Maddalena, Caprera, Santo Stefano, Spargi, Budelli, Razzoli, Santa Maria and other islets found in the **Straits of Bonifacio**.

These isolated islands, occasionally frequented by Corsican shepherds, were annexed to the Kingdom of Sardinia in 1767. Maddalena then became a military base and has recently been used as such by NATO. The archipelago was made a **national park** in 1996.

★★ **Maddalena** – A lovely scenic route *(20km/ 12 mi)* follows the magnificent coastline of this small island, providing views of small creeks and bays and the clear blue waters of the Mediterranean.

> ### Getting there
>
> Boats leave every 15min from Palau, overlooked by the granite mass of Capo d'Orso. *See the current Michelin Red Guide Italia.*

★ **Caprera** – This island was once the home of Garibaldi and is connected to Maddalena by the Passo della Moneta causeway. It now houses a well-known sailing centre.

★ **Casa di Garibaldi** ⊙ – The tree planted by Garibaldi (1807-1882) on the birth of his daughter Clelia (1867) can still be seen in the garden of his one-time home. Objects and clothes that belonged to the general, his wife and family are exhibited in the museum. There are fine views of Corsica from one of the rooms, where Garibaldi died in 1882. He is buried in the garden with his sons and his last wife.

NUORO

Population 37 955
Michelin map 433 G 9/10

Nuoro lies at the foot of Monte Ortobene, on the borders of the Barbagia region to the north of the Gennargentu Mountains. In this large town of central Sardinia the customs, traditions and folklore have remained unchanged since ancient times.

The **Sagra del Redentore** (Feast of the Redeemer) includes a procession through the town in local costumes and a folk festival *(see the Calendar of Events at the end of the guide)*.

★ **Museo della Vita e delle Tradizioni Popolari Sarde** ⊙ – *55 Via A Mereu*. The museum, evoking the popular traditions of the island, has a fine collection of Sardinian costumes. The author Grazia Deledda, a native of Nuoro, won the Nobel Prize for Literature in 1926 for her description of Sardinian life.

EXCURSIONS

★ **Monte Ortobene** – *9km/6mi east*. This is a popular excursion with local people. The summit affords several good viewpoints.

ORISTANO

Population 33 066
Michelin map 433 H 7

Oristano is the main town on the west coast. Founded in 1070 by the inhabitants of nearby Tharros *(see THARROS)*, Oristano put up a strong fight against the Aragonese in the 14C.

Piazza Roma – The crenellated tower, Torre di San Cristoforo, overlooking this vast esplanade, was originally part of the town wall built in 1291. Opening off Piazza Roma is **Corso Umberto**, the town's main shopping street.

San Francesco – The church, rebuilt in the 19C, has some interesting **works of art**★ including a wooden statue of Christ by the 14C Rhenish school, a fragment of a polyptych *(St Francis receiving the Stigmata)* by Pietro Cavaro, a 16C Sardinian artist, and a statue of *St Basil* by Nino Pisano (14C).

EXCURSIONS

★ **Basilica di Santa Giusta** – *3km/2mi south*. This church, built between 1135 and 1145, stands in the town of the same name, on the banks of a lake.
The sober elegance of Santa Giusta is characteristic of all Sardinian churches where Pisan and Lombard influences mingle. The façade, divided into three sections in the Lombard manner, has an attractively-carved doorway typical of the Pisan style. Inside, the columns are either of marble or of granite and have bases and capitals often taken from Roman and early medieval buildings. The central nave is slighty raised, the roof is trussed and the side aisles are covered by cross vaults. The chapels in the right aisle and the belltower are modern constructions. There is a crypt under the slightly-raised choir.

Arborea – *18km/11mi south*. This charming little town was planned and laid out in 1928 by the Fascist government, following the draining of the marshes and the extermination of the malaria mosquito.

PORTO TORRES

Population 21 999
Michelin map 433 E 7

Situated at the head of a large bay, Porto Torres is the port for Sassari. Founded by Caesar it enjoyed considerable importance in the Roman period, as can be testified by the remains in the vicinity of the station.

★ **San Gavino** – The church was built at the end of the 11C by the Pisans (the long series of blind arcades on the north side are characteristic of the Pisan style) and enlarged shortly afterwards by the Lombard master builders. It is a fine example of medieval Sardinian art. A 15C doorway in the Catalan-Gothic style interrupts the arcades. Inside, piers alternate with groups of four clustered columns giving a harmonious result. A large **crypt** enshrines the relics of St Gavin and a very fine Roman **sarcophagus**★, decorated with sculptures portraying the muses.

Isola di SANT'ANTIOCO ★

SANT'ANTIOCO'S ISLAND
Population 11 938
Michelin map 433 J/K 7

This volcanic island is the largest of the Sulcis Archipelago, lying off the southwest coast of Sardinia. It has a hilly terrain with high cliffs on the west coast.
The chief town, also called Sant'Antioco, is linked to the mainland by a road.
Catacombs, some of which have been transformed from Punic hypogea, can be seen under Sant'Antioco church. They date from the 6C and 7C AD.

★ **Vestigia di Sulcis** ⊙ – The ancient town of Sulci, founded by the Phoenicians in the 8C BC, gave its name to this group of islands.
The archeological site is divided into a number of different areas. The tombs in the **necropolis**, carved out of volcanic tufa, were used by the Carthaginians until the Roman period. The **archeological museum** displays finds from the excavations and includes a fine collection of **steles**★. The archeological area comprises the Punic-Phoenician **tophet**★, once believed to be where the first-born male child was sacrificed, but now understood to be a cemetery for still-born babies or children who died in infancy.

Excursions

Tratalias – *18km/11mi from Sant'Antioco*. The 13C Pisan-Romanesque church of Santa Maria towers above this small village, which has a hint of the Far West about it.

Monte Sirai – *19km/12mi from Sant'Antioco*. Traces of a Punic-Phoenician settlement remain on this hill. The Phoenicians arrived here in 750 BC. Their city was destroyed by the Cathaginians who settled here in 520 BC, building a new fortress. This fortress was in turn destroyed by the Romans in 238 BC, who remained on Monte Sirai until 110 BC, when the site was abandoned.

SASSARI

Population 121 038
Michelin map 433 E 7
Town plan in the current Italy Road Atlas

Sassari is the second largest town in Sardinia. Its spacious, airy modern quarters contrast with its medieval nucleus, nestling round the cathedral. The busiest arteries are the Piazza d'Italia and the Corso Vittorio Emanuele II.

Sassari is known for its festivals. The famous **Cavalcata Sarda** is a colourful procession of people from nearly all the provinces of Sardinia in their beautiful and varied local costumes. The procession ends with a frenetic horse race. The **Festa dei Candelieri** (Feast of Candles), dating from the late 16C, was the result of a vow to the Virgin, made during an epidemic of the Black Death. The different trade guilds each carry huge beribboned wooden candles, gilded or painted silver *(see the Calendar of Events at the end of the guide)*.

* **Museo Nazionale Sanna** ⊙ – The museum contains rich archeological collections, including an interesting section devoted to Sardinian ethnography and a small picture gallery.

Duomo – The cathedral is built in many styles and has a 13C campanile with a 17C upper storey, a late-17C Spanish Baroque **façade**★ and a Gothic interior.

EXCURSION

★★ **Santissima Trinità di Saccargia** – *17km/11mi southeast by the Cagliari road, the S 131, and then the road to Olbia, the S 597.*
This former Camaldulian abbey church, dedicated to the Holy Trinity, was built in the 12C in decorative courses of black and white stone, typical of the Pisan style. The elegant façade includes a porch added in the 13C and is flanked by a slender campanile. Inside, the apse is adorned with fine 13C frescoes showing a strong Byzantine influence and depicting scenes of the Passion, including the Virgin and the Apostles in the upper section and Christ surrounded by angels and archangels on the vault.

THARROS★

Michelin map 433 H 7
1.5km – 1 mile south of San Giovanni di Sinis

The Phoenicians founded Tharros on the Sinis Peninsula north of the Gulf of Oristano in the 8-7C BC. It was an important depot on the Marseilles-Carthage trading route, before it was conquered by the Romans in the 3C BC. The inhabitants left the site for Oristano around the year 1000 before it was buried under wind-blown sand.

Zona archeologica ⊙ – The excavation site lies near a hill crowned by a Spanish tower (Torre di San Giovanni). Here are remains of Punic fortifications, a sewerage system, tanks, baths, a Punic temple with Doric half-columns and, on the hilltop, a tophet *(see SANT'ANTIOCO)*. The two white columns standing alone are reconstructions dating from the 1960s.

TORTOLÌ ⚓

Population 9 693
Michelin map 433 H 10

Tortolì is the main town of **Ogliastra**, a wild region characterised by cone-like rocks known as "*Tacchi*". The land in the interior is used for sheep rearing, while arable farming is practised along the coast.

Tortolì coastline

The sea is calm along this coastline, especially at Gairo, where the pebbles are called "*coccorocci*" (literally coconut rocks). Juniper plants grow at **Orri**.

Arbatax – *5.5km/3mi.* This isolated port is situated in a beautiful mountain setting overlooking the Tortolì sea and is particularly well known for the outcrops of porphyry rock not far from the harbour. A more secluded bay can be found at Cala Moresca *(follow signs)*. The magnificent stretch of **road**★★★ between Arbatax and Dorgali *(70km/43 miles)* skirts impressive gorges.

Sicily

Sicily (Sicilia), the largest of the Mediterranean islands, has an area of 25 709km²/9 927sq miles. It is triangular in shape and was named Trinacria (Greek for "three points") under Greek rule.

Nearly 5 million people live on the island, which is generally mountainous and reaches at its highest point, Mount Etna (an active volcano), an altitude of 3 340m/10 958ft.

Throughout its history Sicily has suffered numerous earthquakes: the earthquake in 1693 damaged most of the towns in the southwest of the island, in 1908 Messina was almost entirely destroyed and the earthquake in 1968 badly affected the western part of the island.

Access – *see PRACTICAL INFORMATION.*

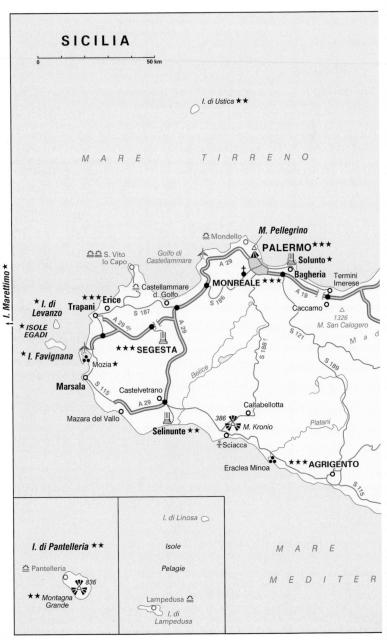

Sightseeing – The island can be visited in a quick tour of 6 to 7 days. The map overleaf locates the towns and sites described in the guide, and also indicates other beauty spots in small black type.

Look in the introduction at the Map of Touring Programmes for the suggested itinerary for Sicily.

More detailed information on Sicily can be found in The Green Guide to Sicily.

HISTORICAL AND ARTISTIC NOTES

Sicily has been a constant pawn for marauding forces in the Mediterranean owing to its strategic location, lying near the peninsula and controlling the Mediterranean. Firstly there were the Greeks in the 8C who discovered an island divided between two ethnic groups: the **Sicani**, the oldest inhabitants, and the **Siculi** (Sicels) who came from the peninsula.

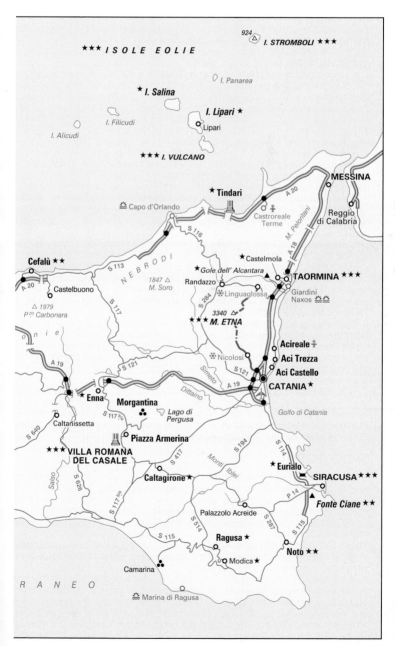

The Carthaginians were for several centuries the main rivals of the Greeks. Although they had colonised the coastal areas, they were finally pushed back to the western part of the island, where they remained until the siege of Mozia by Denys the Elder in 397 BC.

The 5C BC, excluding the rules of the tyrants of Gela and Syracuse *(see SIRACUSA)*, was the apogee of Greek rule in Sicily (Magna Graecia). After erecting some magnificent buildings, they neutralised their enemies and Syracuse grew to become the rival of Athens.

This fragile peace was broken by the arrival of the Romans who coveted the island for the richness of its soil.

By 241 BC, at the end of the First Punic War, the whole of Sicily had been conquered and it became a Roman province, governed by a praetor. The Romans exploited the island's resources to the full with the help of more or less dishonest officials. The island was also a victim of the numerous Barbarian invasions which unfurled on southern Italy.

In 535 the island passed to the Byzantines before experiencing a period of great prosperity under the Aghlabid dynasty (Tunisia), in the 9C. The Saracens were in turn expelled by the Normans (11C).

The son of the Great Count Roger I of Sicily, **Roger II** (1095-1154), created the Norman Kingdom of Sicily. He established his court at Palermo and during his reign the island was to enjoy a prosperous period of considerable political power and cultural influence.

The name of the Hohenstaufen Emperor, **Frederick II**, dominated the reign of this Swabian dynasty. The house of Anjou followed in 1266; however, Charles of Anjou was expelled following the Palermo revolt of 1282 known as the **Sicilian Vespers**. Power passed to the Aragon dynasty and it was Alfonso V the Magnanimous who reunited Naples and Sicily and took the title of King of the Two Sicilies (1442). The island passed to the Bourbons of Naples by marriage until they were overthrown by the Expedition of Garibaldi and the Thousand (1860).

The Second World War left its mark on Sicily; the Anglo-American landings between Licata and Syracuse in 1943 ended in the abandonment of the island by the Germans after more than a month of heavy fighting.

Each period has left its mark on the island's heritage, be it in the field of art or customs and daily life. The Greeks built admirable Doric temples with the mellow local limestone, and also splendid theatres. During the brief period when the Normans dominated the island, Sicily knew an era of economic prosperity and artistic development.

This style was unique for its blending of a variety of different influences. The architectural style was still essentially Norman but the decoration (horseshoe-shaped arches, bulbous belltowers and intricately decorated ceilings) showed a strong Moorish influence, while the decoration of the walls with dazzling mosaics on golden backgrounds was Byzantine.

Known variously as the **Sicilian-Norman** or **Arab-Norman**, this style can be seen at Palermo, Monreale, Cefalu and Messina.

If the Renaissance has left few traces in the island – with some outstanding exceptions by **Antonello da Messina** *(see Index)* who usually worked on the mainland – the Sicilians adopted the Spanish-influenced Baroque style with great fervour in the late 18C. The main exponents were the architects **Rosario Gagliardi** in Noto and Ragusa, **Vaccarini** in Catania, and **Giacomo Serpotta** who embellished numerous oratories in Palermo with his sculpted fantasies.

Sicilian literature is particularly rich, especially in the 19C, with **Giovanni Verga** *(see Index)* who created a new form of Italian novel, and **Luigi Pirandello** *(see Index)*. Noteworthy among the 20C writers to describe contemporary life are **Elio Vittorini** (1908-66) and **Leonardo Sciascia** (1921-89). Other writers include **Gesualdo Bufalino** (1920-96) and the poet **Salvatore Quasimodo** (1901-68).

SICILY TODAY

The long period of foreign domination in Sicily has left its imprint not only on the art, culture and literature of the island but also on its economy. Following the Arab invasions, the island's economy was neglected by its foreign rulers, with the exception of the Normans and Swabians. Vegetation and forests were cleared, the locals exploited, and the island was prevented from developing and making the most of its potential.

Today Sicily survives on an assisted economy in the hope that new development projects will stem the emigration of its young people, increase the wealth of the island and return it to its former glory.

Geographically and economically Sicily can be divided into three regions. The first region comprises the provinces of Catania, Siracusa and the southern part of Messina. Industries established in this area include chemical and petrochemical plants and oil refineries. The agriculture of the region tends to be intensive and of high quality. Palermo, Trapani and the north of Messina make up the second region, in which the tertiary sector and the building industry are highly developed.

Finally, the poorest part of Sicily consists of the provinces of Agrigento, Caltanissetta and Enna. This region is under-developed economically and has poor agricultural land, which has resulted in a flow of emigration.

The fishing industry is still of prime importance to the Sicilian economy; island specialities include tuna from Trapani and swordfish from Messina.

The folk traditions and customs which once animated the streets have almost completely disappeared. It is only on feast days and in the museums that the visitor can now see the famous **Sicilian carts** which were gaily decorated with bright colours and intricate wrought-iron work. These colourful carts were the main method of transport for over a century, until the end of the 1950s. In Palermo the popular puppet (*pupi*) theatres which are mentioned in the 12C *Song of Roland* and Ariosto's *Orlando Furioso (Roland the Mad)* can still be seen.

AGRIGENTO★★★

Population 55 798
Michelin map 432 P 22

Agrigento, the Greek Akragas, is attractively set on a hillside facing out to sea. The Greek poet Pindar referred to Agrigento as "man's finest town". It includes a medieval quarter on the upper slopes above the modern town, and impressive ancient ruins strung out along a ridge below, wrongly called the Valley of the Temples (declared a UNESCO World Heritage Site in 1997).

The town was founded in 580 BC by people from Gela who originated from Rhodes. Of the governing "tyrants", the cruellest in the 6C was **Phalaris**, while **Tero** (7C) was renowned as a great builder. The 5C philosopher **Empedocles** was a native of Agrigento, as was **Luigi Pirandello** (1867-1936), winner of the Nobel Prize for Literature in 1934 and innovator in modern Italian drama (*Six Characters in Search of an Author*), whose plays were woven around the themes of incomprehension and absurdity.

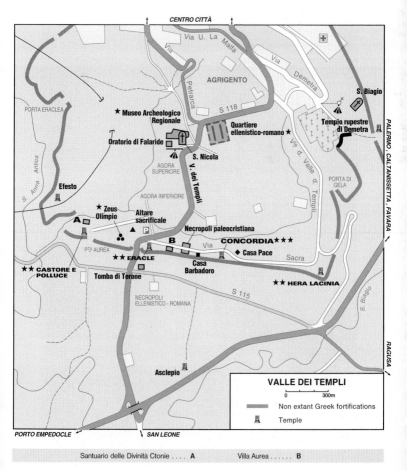

Santuario delle Divinità Ctonie .... **A**   Villa Aurea ...... **B**

SICILY

★★★ VALLE DEI TEMPLI (VALLEY OF THE TEMPLES) ⊘ *allow 3hr*

Of the many temples built in late 6C - late 5C BC, parts of nine are still visible. The destruction of the temples was for long thought to have been caused by earthquakes but is now also attributed to the anti-pagan activities of the early Christians. Only the Temple of Concord was spared when it became a church in the late 6C AD.

★ **Tempio di Zeus Olimpio (Giove)** – Had this now-ruined temple been completed, its size (113m/371ft long by 56m/184ft wide) would have made it one of the largest in the ancient world. The entablature of the Temple of Jupiter was supported by 20m/66ft tall columns, between which stood **telamones** (columns in the form of male figures), colossal statues, one of which, standing 7.5m/25ft high, has been reconstructed and is now on view in the Archeological Museum *(see below)*. A reproduction of the giant, lying on the ground in the centre of the ruins, gives some idea of the immense size of the building.

★★ **Tempio dei Dioscuri (Temple of Castor and Pollux)** – Of this hexastyle temple only four of the columns supporting part of the entablature remain. The small rose at the corner of the entablature is a typical decorative feature.

Alongside is a **sacred area** dedicated to Demeter and Persephone the Chthonic or underground gods: there are two sacrificial altars, one of which is circular, with a holy well in the middle, and the other square.

Return to the square and take Via dei Templi.

★★ **Tempio di Eracle (Ercole)** – Dating from the late 6C the Temple of Hercules is probably the oldest of the Agrigento temples and is built in the ancient Doric style. Eight of its columns have been raised.

Temple of Castor and Pollux

B. Kaufmann

Further on to the left can be seen the deeply-grooved ruts thought to have been made by ancient wheeled vehicles. The deep marking is possibly due to the ruts having been used at a later date as water channels.

★★★ **Tempio della Concordia** – The Temple of Concord is the most massive, majestic and best preserved of the Doric temples in Sicily. It has a peristyle of 34 tufa limestone columns, the original stucco facing having since disappeared.
It is not known to what deity it was dedicated and its present name (Concordia) is taken from a Roman inscription found nearby. The internal arrangement dates from the Christian period (mid-5C).

★★ **Tempio di Hera Lacinia (Giunone)** – Set on the edge of the ridge, this temple, dedicated to Juno, conserves part of its colonnade. On the east side there is a sacrificial altar and behind the temple an ancient cistern.

CITY CENTRE

★ **Museo Archeologico Regionale** ⊙ – *Enter via the cloisters of the Church of St Nicholas (see below).* The museum contains a fine collection of **Greek vases**★ including the *Dionisius Cup* and the *Perseus and Andromeda Cup* on a white background. One room is devoted to the **telamones**★ from the Temple of Jupiter. There are also the 5C BC marble statue of the youth *Ephebus of Agrigento (Room 10)* and the beautiful *Gela Cup*★★ *(Room 15)* which illustrates a centaur in the upper part and the battle between the Greeks and the Amazons in the lower part.

Oratorio di Falaride ⊙ – Legend has it that the palace of Phalaris, the first tyrant of Agrigento, was in the vicinity. The building is in fact a small Roman-Hellenistic temple which was transformed during the Norman period.

San Nicola ⊙ – This sober church, dedicated to St Nicholas, in the transitional Romanesque-Gothic style contains a magnificent **Roman sarcophagus**★ on which the death of Phaedra is portrayed. From the terrace there is a fine **view**★ of the temples.

★ **Quartiere Ellenistico-Romano** ⊙ – In the Greco-Roman quarter, the layout of the main streets lined with houses is a good example of 4C BC town planning.

Town centre – The centre of the town is concentrated around the shady **Piazzale Aldo Moro**, which leads into the attractive **Via Atenea**, a busy shopping street. Crowning the old town with its stepped streets is the cathedral **(Cattedrale)**, a Norman building which was greatly altered in the following centuries. On the way back down to Piazzale A. Moro visit a small abbey church, **Abbaziale di Santo Spirito**★ ⊙, which has four charming **high reliefs**★ in stucco attributed to Giacomo Serpotta.

EXCURSIONS

Tomba di Terone – *Visible from the Caltagirone road.* The tomb (3m/10ft high), said to be that of Tero, Tyrant of Agrigento, in fact dates from the Roman era and is thought to have been erected in honour of soldiers who died during the Second Punic War.

Casa di Pirandello ⊙ – *6km/4mi west by the Porto Empedocle road, the S 115.* Shortly after the Morandi viaduct turn left. This small house surrounded by vineyards was the birthplace of the famous dramatist Luigi Pirandello (1867-1936), who is buried under a nearby pine tree.

CALTAGIRONE★

Population 39 187
Michelin map 432 P 25

Caltagirone is famous for its pottery which is not only displayed in profusion in the local shops (vases, plates, household goods) but also adorns bridges, balustrades, balconies (note the lovely balcony of the 18C **Casa Ventimiglia**), and the façades of palaces lining Via Roma in the town centre.

★ **Villa Comunale** – This beautiful garden was designed in the mid-19C by Basile as an English garden. The side flanking Via Roma is bounded by a balustrade adorned with maiolica vases. On an esplanade stands the delightful Arab-style bandstand **(palchetto della musica)** decorated with ceramics.

Museo della ceramica ⊙ – A curious little 18C theatre **(Teatrino)**, decorated with ceramics houses an interesting museum which traces the history of local ceramics from prehistory to the early 20C. The importance of this craft is illustrated by a fine **cup**★ dating from 5C BC depicting a potter and a youth working at the wheel.

★ **Scala di Santa Maria del Monte** – The stairway built in the 17C to join the old and new town, has 142 steps in volcanic stone; the risers are decorated with polychrome ceramic tiles with geometric, floral and other decorative motifs. On the 24 and 25 July the stairway is covered in lights which form different patterns: the most frequent is the symbol of the town, an eagle with a shield on its breast.

Villa Romana del CASALE★★★

Michelin map 432 O 25

This immense 3C or 4C Roman villa (3 500m²/37 670sq ft) probably belonged to some dignitary and is important for its **mosaic pavements★★★** which cover almost the entire floor-space. These picturesque mosaics, in a wide range of colours, were probably the work of African craftsmen and portray scenes from mythology, daily life, and events such as hunts or circus games.
The Villa Romana del Casale was declared a UNESCO World Heritage Site in 1997.

Tour ⊙ – The most noteworthy mosaics portray **cupids★★** fishing or playing with dolphins, a hunting scene in the **Sala della Piccola Caccia★★★**, the capturing and selling of **wild animals** for circus use in the **Ambulacro della Grande Caccia★★★** and sports practised by young girls who appear to be wearing modern swimwear in the **Sala delle Dieci Ragazze in Bikini★★**. Finally, the mosaics of the **triclinium★★★** portray the *Labours of Hercules*.

Mosaic from the *Sala delle Dieci Ragazze in Bikini*

EXCURSIONS

Piazza Armerina – *5km/3mi southwest*. The interesting **medieval centre★** of Piazza Armerina huddles round its Baroque **cathedral** on the pleasantly green slopes of a valley.

CATANIA★

Population 342 275
Michelin map 432 O 27 (including a plan of the built-up area)

Catania is a busy seaport and industrial town which has developed considerably in recent years, despite being destroyed several times by the eruptions of Mount Etna. This fine city has wide, regular streets overlooked by numerous Baroque buildings by the architect **Vaccarini**, who rebuilt Catania after the 1693 earthquake.
Natives of the town include the musician **Vicenzo Bellini** (1801-35), composer of the opera *Norma*, and the novelist, **Giovanni Verga**.
Catania holds the heat record for the whole of Italy: over 40ºC (104ºF).

★ **Piazza del Duomo** (DZ) – This square is the centre of town and is surrounded by a Baroque ensemble designed by Vaccarini which includes the Elephant Fountain (**Fontana dell'Elefante**) dating from 1735, the **Palazzo Senatorio o degli Elefanti** (town hall) with its well-balanced façade, and the cathedral (**Duomo**)★ dedicated to St Agatha, the town's patron saint. The cathedral, built at the end of the 11C by the Norman, Roger I, was remodelled after the 1693 earthquake and has an elegant **façade★** by Vaccarini. To the left of the cathedral, the beautiful abbey church **Badia di Sant' Agata★** (EZ B) contributes to the harmony of the square.

CATANIA

Angelo Custode (Via)	DZ 3
Benedetto (Piazza A. d.)	DZ 11
Biondi (Via)	EY 12
Bovio (Piazza G.)	EY 15
Carlo Alberto (Piazza)	EY 19
Castello Ursino (Via)	DZ 21
Conte di Torino (Via)	EY 25
Currò (Piazza)	DZ 26
Cutelli (Piazza)	EZ 27
Dante (Piazza)	DY 29
Etnea (Via)	DXY
Giuffrida (Via Vincenzo)	EY 39
Guardie (Piazza delle)	EY 42
Imbriani (Via Matteo Renato)	DEX 43
Landolina (Via)	EZ 45
Lupo (Piazza Pietro)	EY 47
Museo Biscari (Via)	EZ 57
Orlando (V. Vitt. E.)	EX 60
Porticello (Via)	EZ 68
Rabbordone (Via)	EY 69
Rapisardi (Via Michele)	EY 70
Rotunda (Via d.)	DYZ 77
S. Anna (Via)	DZ 79
San Francesco d'Assisi (Piazza)	DZ 80
San Gaetano alle Grotte (Via)	DEY 81
San Giuseppe al Duomo (Via)	DZ 82
Spirito Santo (Piazza)	EY 87
Stesicoro (Piazza)	DY 91
Teatro Massimo (Via)	EYZ 92
Trento (Piazza)	EX 95
Umberto I (Via)	DEX
Università (Piazza dell')	DZ 96
Verga (Piazza)	EX 98
Vittorio Emanuele III (Piazza)	EY 100

Anfiteatro	DY A
Badia di S. Agata	EZ B
Casa di Verga	DZ C
Collegiata	DY D
Museo Belliniano	DZ M¹
Museo Emilio Greco	DZ M¹
Odeon	DZ N
Palazzo Asmundo	DZ R¹
Palazzo Manganelli	EY R²
Palazzo S. Demetrio	DY R³
S. Agata al Carcere	DY S¹
S. Benedetto	DZ S²
S. Francesco	DZ S⁴
S. Francesco Borgia	DYZ S⁵
S. Giuliano	DY S⁶
S. Michele Arcangelo	DY S⁷
S. Nicolò l'Arena	DY S⁸
Teatro Antico	DZ T¹
Teatro Bellini	EY T²
Terme della Rotonda	DZ V

SICILY

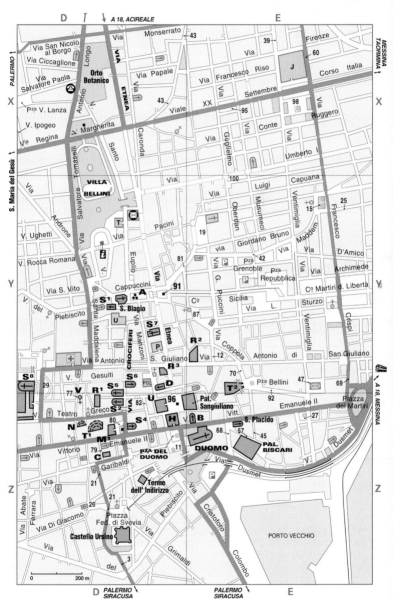

Not far from here, in via Museo Biscari, stands **Palazzo Biscari★** ⊙, one of the most beautiful examples of civil architecture in the city. The south side of the mansion has a highly-decorated **façade★★** of figures, cherubs and scrolls.

★ Via Etnea - The town's main shopping artery is over 3km/2mi long. All the way along it affords a view of Etna. It is bordered by numerous palaces, churches and gardens **(Villa Bellini★)**.

Quartiere Occidentale – This district to the west of the town runs through via Vittorio Emanuele II, along which the old theatre **(Teatro Antico)** ⊙ (DZ T¹) can be seen, and which is crossed by **via Crociferi★**, considered to offer some of the best examples of Baroque architecture in Catania.

★ **Castello Ursino** ⊙ – This bare, grim castle, fortified by four towers, was built in the 13C by the Emperor Frederick II of Hohenstaufen and houses a museum **(Museo Civico)**.

EXCURSION

Acireale – *17km/11mi north*. The itinerary passes through **Aci Castello**, with its **castle★** built from black volcanic rock, and **Aci Trezza**, a small fishing village. Offshore, the Cyclops' Reefs **(Faraglioni dei Ciclopi★)** emerge from the sea. These are supposed to be the rocks hurled by the Cyclops Polyphemus after Ulysses had blinded him by thrusting a blazing stake into his single eye.

The road leads to **Acireale**, a modern town with numerous Baroque buildings which include those of the **Piazzo del Duomo★** with the Basilica of Sts Peter and Paul and the Town Hall, as well as the Church of **San Sebastiano** with its harmonious **façade★** embellished with columns, niches and friezes.

CEFALÙ★★

Population 14 045
Michelin map 432 M 24

Cefalù is a small fishing town in a fine **setting★★**, hemmed in between the sea and a rocky promontory. It boasts a splendid Romanesque cathedral.

★★ **Duomo** ⊙ – Built of a golden-tinted stone which blends in with the cliff behind, this cathedral was erected to fulfil a vow made by the Norman King, Roger II (12C), when in danger of shipwreck. The church (1131-1240) has well-marked Norman features in its tall main apse flanked by two slightly-projecting smaller ones and especially in its façade, abutted by the two square towers. The portico was rebuilt in the 15C by a Lombard master.

The timber ceiling of the two aisles and the transept galleries are also Norman. The columns are crowned with splendid **capitals★★** in the Sicilian-Norman style *(see INTRODUCTION)*.

The presbytery is covered with beautiful **mosaics★★** on a gilded background, displaying a surprising variety of colour and forming an admirable expression of Byzantine art. Above is Christ Pantocrator (Ruler of All) with underneath, on three different levels, the Virgin with four archangels and the 12 apostles. In the choir, the angels on the vaulting and the prophets on the side walls date from the 13C. Note the episcopal throne (south side) and the royal throne (north side), both in marble and mosaic.

Museo Mandralisca ⊙ – The museum, facing the cathedral in the picturesque Via Mandralisca, has a fine *Portrait of an Unknown Man* by Antonello da Messina.

Isole EGADI★

EGADI ISLANDS
Population 4 621
Michelin map 432 M-N 18-19

The three islands ⊙ – Favignana, Levanzo and Marettimo – which make up this small archipelago lie offshore from Trapani. The islands are popular for their wild aspect, clear blue sea and beautiful coastlines. It was here in 241 BC that the treaty ending the First Punic War was concluded, in which Carthage surrendered Sicily to Rome.

★ **Favignana** – The island covers an area of 20km²/8sq miles and is butterfly-shaped. The **Montagna Grossa** culminating at 302m/991ft runs right across the island and ends as an indented coastline. The islanders were masters in the art

---

GETTING TO THE ISLANDS

Ferries (1h-2h 45min) and hydrofoils (15min-1h) leave regularly from **Trapani** and are operated by **Siremar**-Agenzia Mare Viaggi, via Staiti 61/63, (☎ 0923 54 05 15, fax 0932 20 663). During the summer **Ustica Lines** (☎ 081 76 12 515) operates a return hydrofoil service between Trapani-Favignana-Ustica-Naples. The Favignana-Napies crossing takes about 6h.

of tunny fishing which took place for about 50 days between May and June. Having captured the tunny in a series of nets, they would perform a dangerous manoeuvre and pull in the fish towards the shore where they were harpooned. The main town of the group of islands, **Favignana**, is guarded by the fort of Santa Caterina, a former Saracen lookout tower, which was rebuilt by the Norman King, Roger II, and served as a prison under the Bourbons. To the east of the harbour are the former **tufa quarries**★ now drowned by the sea. Boat trips take visitors to the various caves (contact the fishermen at the harbour), including the **Grotta Azzurra**★ which is situated on the west coast.

★ **Levanzo** – This tiny island is only 6km²/2sq miles in size. In 1950 traces of life in prehistoric times were found in the **Grotta del Genovese**★, which is reached on foot or by boat from Cala Dogana.

★ **Marettimo** – Off the beaten tourist track, Marettimo with its attractive **harbour** (*no landing stage, rowing boats take visitors to the quay*) has several restaurants but no hotels. Take a **trip**★★ around the island in a boat (contact the fishermen at the harbour) to discover the numerous caves which riddle the cliff faces.

ENNA★

Population 28
Michelin map 432 O 24

Enna lies in an isolated, sun-scorched landscape at the centre of the island. Its panoramic **site**★★ at an altitude of 942m/3 091ft has earned it the nickname of the Belvedere of Sicily.
According to legend it was on the shores of a lake, **Lago di Pergusa** (*10km/6 mi to the south*), that Pluto carried off the youthful Proserpine, future Queen of the Underworld.

★ **Castello di Lombardia** ⊘ – This medieval castle has six of its original 20 towers. From the top of the tallest there is an exceptional **panorama**★★★ of the hilltop village of Calascibetta, Etna and most of the Sicilian mountain peaks. Beyond the castle, the **belvedere**, once the site of a temple to Demeter, offers a fine **view**★ of Calascibetta and of Enna itself.

Duomo ⊘ – The cathedral was rebuilt in the Baroque style in the 16C and 17C but still has its 14C Gothic apses. Inside the building the finely carved coffered **ceiling**★ is worthy of note, with its strange winged creatures at the end of each beam.

★ **Torre di Federico** – *At the far end of Via Roma facing the castle.* In the past Enna could have been described as the town of towers. The town's strategic, defensive function accounts for the large number of these. The octagonal tower built by Frederick II of Swabia is impressively located at the centre of a small public garden.

Isole EOLIE★★★

ÆOLIAN or LIPARI ISLANDS
Population 12 945
Michelin map 432 L 25-27 and K 27

The **Æolian Islands**, also known as the **Lipari Islands**, are so called because the ancients thought Æolus, the God of the Winds, lived there. The archipelago comprises seven main islands, Lipari, Vulcano, Stromboli, Salina, Filicudi, Alicudi and Panarea⌂, all of exceptional interest for their volcanic nature, their beauty, their light and their climate.
A deep blue, warm, clear sea, ideal for underwater fishing, interesting marine creatures including flying-fish, swordfish, turtles, sea-horses and hammerfish, make the islands a refuge for those who like to live close to nature. Boat trips provide good views of the beautiful indented coastlines and hidden coves and bays. The inhabitants of the islands fish, grow vines and quarry pumice-stone.

★★ **Lipari** – This, the largest island in the archipelago, is formed of volcanic rock dipping vertically into the sea. In ancient times Lipari was a source of obsidian, a glazed black volcanic rock, from which pumice-stone was quarried on the east coast (the industry is now in decline). Today the islanders fish and grow cereals and capers.
Two bays (Marina Lunga with its beach and Marina Corta) frame the town of **Lipari**★, dominated by its old quarter encircled by 13C-14C walls. Inside is the castle rebuilt by the Spaniards in the 16C on the site of a Norman building. The castle houses a museum (**Museo Archeologico Eoliano**★★ ⊘) which exhibits a recreation of Bronze Age necropoli, a lovely collection of **red-figure kraters**★, **amphorae**★ and terracotta **theatrical masks**★★.

GETTING TO THE ISLANDS

Ferries run regularly from **Milazzo** (1h 30min-4h) and are operated by **Siremar**, via dei Mille, ☎ 090 92 83 242, fax 090 92 83 243. The same agency also runs a hydrofoil service (40min-2h 45min), as does **Aliscafi SNAV**, via Rizzo 9/10, ☎ 090 92 87 728, fax 090 92 81 798.

Aliscafi SNAV operates a daily service from **Messina**, via San Raineri 22, ☎ 090 77 75, fax 090 71 73 58, **Reggio Calabria**, Stazione Marittima, ☎ 0965 29 568, **Palermo** (from June to September), piazza Principe di Belmonte 51/55, ☎ 091 58 65 33, fax 091 58 48 30, and **Cefalù** (from June to September only; not daily), corso Ruggero 76, ☎ 0921 42 15 95. Ferries (14h) and hydrofoils (4h, from June to September) also leave from **Naples**. The former are operated by **Siremar**, via Depetris 78, ☎ 081 55 12 112, fax 081 55 12 114, and the latter by **Aliscafi SNAV**, via Caracciolo 10, ☎ 081 76 12 348, fax 081 76 12 141.

There are **boat trips**★★ ⊘ leaving from Marina Corta which take the visitor round the very rugged southwest coast of the island. When making a **tour of the island by car**★★, stop at Canneto and Campo Bianco to visit the pumice-stone **quarries**★. The splendid **view**★ from the **Puntazze** headland includes five of the islands: Alicudi, Filicudi, Salina, Panarea and Stromboli. However, it is the belvedere in **Quattrocchi** which affords one of the finest **panoramas**★★★ of the whole archipelago.

Lava eruption at Stromboli

★★★ **Vulcano** – This 21km²/8sq mile island is in reality four volcanoes. According to mythology it is here that Vulcan, the God of Fire, had his forges – whence the term volcanism. Although there has been no eruption on the island since 1890 there are still important signs of activity: fumaroles (smoke-holes), spouting steam-jets often underwater, hot sulphurous mud-flows greatly appreciated for their therapeutic properties. The island has a wild but forbidding beauty, with its rugged rocky shores, desolate areas and strangely-coloured soils due to the presence of sulphur, iron oxides and alum. The island's main centre, **Porto di Levante**⌂, stands below the great crater. The beach is known for its particularly warm water due to the underwater spouting steam-jets.

Excursions to the **Great Crater**★★★ (about 2hrs on foot rtn) are interesting for the impressive views they afford of the crater and of the archipelago. The headland, **Capo Grillo,** affords a view of several islands.

A tour of the island by boat ⊙ (starting from Porto Ponente) offers the visitor many curious views, especially along the northwestern coast, which is fringed with impressive basalt reefs.

★★★ **Stromboli** – The volcano of Stromboli, with its plume of smoke, has a sombre beauty, and is a wild island with steep slopes. There are very few roads and such soil as can be cultivated is covered with vines yielding a delicious golden-coloured Malvasia wine. The little square, white houses are markedly Moorish in style.

Cafes and restaurants

The **Filippino** restaurant in piazza del Municipio (☎ 090 98 11 002) is a real local institution which has been serving regional dishes for almost a century. Approximately 70 000 L per person.

Cannoli, cassata, ice-cream and other specialities can be sampled at **Pasticceria Subba,** 92, corso Vittorio Emanuele.

The **crater**★★★ ⊙, in the form of a 924m/3 032ft cone, has frequent minor eruptions with noisy explosions and accompanying flows of lava. To see the spectacle climb up to the crater (about 5hrs on foot rtn, difficult climb, visitors are advised to make the ascent in the company of a guide) or watch from a boat the famous flow of lava along the crevasse named Sciara del Fuoco towards the sea. At night the scene becomes both beautiful and awesome.

★ **Salina** – The island is formed by six extinct volcanoes of which two have retained their characteristic outline. The highest crater, **Monte Fossa delle Felci** (962m/3 156ft) dominates the archipelago. There is a pleasant panoramic road round the island. Caper bushes and vines grow on the lower terraced slopes. The latter yield the delicious golden Malvasia wine.

ERICE★★

Population 31 077
Michelin map 432 M 19

This ancient Phoenician and Greek city occupies a unique and beautiful **setting**★★★ almost vertically (750m/2 461ft) above the sea. Erice is clustered within its town walls and is crisscrossed by a labyrinth of quiet alleyways lined with attractive dwellings. In antiquity Erice was a religious centre famous for its temple consecrated to Astarte, then to Aphrodite and finally Venus who was venerated by mariners of old.

Erice presents two faces: during the hot summers it is bright and sunny and the sun-drenched streets of this village, strategically located, offer splendid **views**★★ over the valley, whilst in winter Erice is wreathed in mist and seems a place lost in time.

Castello di Venere – This castle, built by the Normans in the 12C, crowns an isolated rock on Monte Eryx, on the site of the Temple of Venus (Venere). From here and the nearby gardens (Giardino del Balio) there are admirable **views**★★: in clear weather the Tunisian coast can be seen.

★ **Chiesa Matrice** – This church was built in the 14C using stones quarried from the Temple of Venus. The porch was added in the 15C and flanked by the square battlemented bell-tower (13C) with its elegant openings.

The Red Guides (hotels and restaurants)
Benelux – Deutschland – España-Portugal – Europe – France – Great Britain and Ireland – Ireland – Italia – London – Paris et environs – Portugal – Switzerland.

ETNA★★★

Michelin map 432 N 26/27 – Alt approx. 3 340m – 10 958ft

Etna is the highest point in the island and is snow-capped for most of the year. It is still active and it is the largest and one of the most famous volcanoes in Europe.

Etna was born of undersea eruptions which also formed the Plain of Catania, formerly covered by the sea. Its eruptions were frequent in ancient times: 135 are recorded. But the greatest disaster occurred in 1669, when the flow of lava reached the sea, largely devastating Catania as it passed.

The worst eruptions in recent times occurred in 1910, when 23 new craters appeared, 1917, when a jet of lava squirted up to 800m/2 500ft above its base, and 1923, when the lava ejected remained hot 18 months after the eruption. Since then, stirrings of Etna have taken place in 1928, 1954, 1964, 1971, 1974, 1978, 1979, March 1981, March 1983 and 1985; the volcano still smokes and may erupt at any time.

In 1987 the **Parco dell'Etna** was created, covering an area of 59 000ha/145 790 acres; in the centre of the park the mountain has the appearance of a huge, black, distorted cone which can be seen from a distance of 250km/155 miles. On its lower slopes, which are extremely fertile, orange, mandarin, lemon and olive trees flourish as well as vines which produce the delicious Etna wine. Chestnut trees grow above the 500m/1 500ft level and give way higher up to oak, beech, birch and pine. Above 2 100m/6 500ft is the barren zone, where only a few clumps of *Astralagus Siculus* (a kind of vetch) will be seen scattered on the slopes of secondary craters, among the clinker and volcanic rock.

★★★ **Ascent of Etna** ⊘ – By the south face from Catania via Nicolosi, or by the northeast face from Taormina via Linguaglossa. *Wear warm clothing and strong shoes.*

South face – The ascent is made partly by cable-car and partly by four-wheel drive up to almost 3 000m/9 843ft, depending on the conditions on the volcano. This point is close to the grandiose valley, **Valle del Bove**, which is hemmed in by walls of lava (1 200m/3 937ft high) pierced with pot-holes and crevasses belching smoke.

Northeast face – The road goes through Linguaglossa, a lovely pinewood and the winter sports resort of Villaggio Mareneve. The surfaced road ends at Piano Provenzana (1 800m/5 906ft). There is a magnificent **view**★★ from the area around the new observatory. The climb ends amidst an extraordinary landscape of lava, which still smokes at times.

Circumetnea – This road runs around Etna, offering varied views of the volcano and passing through a number of interesting villages.

MARSALA

Population 80 689
Michelin map 432 N 19

Marsala, the ancient Lilybaeum on Capo Lilibeo, the westernmost point of the island, owes its present name to the Saracens, who first destroyed and then rebuilt the city, calling it Marsah el Ali (Port of Allah). It is known for its sweet Marsala wine which an English merchant, John Woodhouse, rediscovered in the 18C.

It was at Marsala in 1860 that Garibaldi landed at the start of the **Expedition of the Thousand**, which freed southern Italy from the sway of the Bourbons.

Piazza della Repubblica is the hub of city life, lined by the cathedral and Palazzo Senatorio.

A former wine cellar, near the sea, now houses a museum, the **Museo Archeologico di Baglio Anselmi** ⊘ (*Via Boeo*): the exhibits include the wreck of a **warship**★ which fought in the Punic War and was found off near Mozia (*see Trapani – Excursions*).

MESSINA

Population 262 172
Michelin map 432 M 28 (including town plan)

Despite having been destroyed numerous times throughout the centuries, Messina or the ancient Zancle of the Greeks, is today an active market town. Messina has suffered repeated earthquakes (especially the 1908 one which destroyed 90% of the town and killed 60 000 in the region), epidemics and bombings.

★ **Museo Regionale** ⊙ – *North of the town at the end of the Viale della Libertà*. The museum comprises an art gallery and a sculpture and decorative arts section. In the sculpture section there is a fine wooden crucifix dating from the early 15C. The painting section displays a *polyptych of St Gregory* (1473) by Antonello da Messina, a remarkable composition which combines the Tuscan idiom with the earliest Flemish influences, a remarkable *Descent from the Cross* by the Flemish artist, Colin van Coter (15C); and two Caravaggios, *Adoration of the Shepherds* and *Resurrection of Lazarus*, both painted towards the end of his life from 1608 to 1610. The *Berlina del Senato*★ painted in 1742 is particularly worthy of note.

Duomo – The cathedral, almost entirely rebuilt after the 1908 earthquake and the bombings of 1943, still displays the main features of its original Norman style (12C). The finely-carved central **doorway**★ dates from the 15C. To the left stands the campanile (60m/196ft tall) with its **astronomical clock**★ which was made in Strasbourg in 1933 and is believed to be the world's largest.

Santi Annunziata dei Catalani – *Take the Via Cesare Battisti from the south side of the cathedral*. The church which was built in 1100 during the Norman reign and altered in the 13C, takes its name from the Catalan merchants who owned it. The **apse**★ is characteristic of the composite Norman style which blends Romanesque (small columns supporting blind arcades), Moorish (geometric motifs and polychrome stonework) and Byzantine (dome on a drum) influences.

Antonello da Messina

The artist was born in 1430 and he studied in Naples where he was influenced by the then popular Flemish art. Later he was to be attracted by the innovations of Tuscan painting which with its increasing use of perspective emphasised volume and architectural details. His works show a complete mastery of his art: forms and colours, skilfully balanced, enhance an inner vision which greatly influenced the Venetian painters of the Renaissance, notably Carpaccio and Giovanni Bellini. Antonello died on his native island around 1479.

MONREALE★★★

Population 29 122
Michelin map 432 M 21 – 8km – 5 miles southwest of Palermo

The town, dominating the green plain known as the Conca d'Oro (Golden Basin) of Palermo, grew up around the famous Benedictine **abbey** founded in the 12C by the Norman King, William II.

★★★ **Duomo** ⊙ – The finely-carved central doorway of the cathedral has beautiful **bronze doors**★★ (1185) embellished with stylised figures, which were carved by Bonanno Pisano. The more Byzantine north **doorway**★ is the work of Barisano da Trani (12C). The decoration of the **chevet**★★ is remarkable for the blending of Moorish and Norman styles.
The cathedral has a basilical plan. The interior is dazzling with multicoloured marbles, paintings, and especially the 12C and 13C **mosaics**★★★ adorning the oven vaults and the walls. They represent the complete cycle of the Old and New Testaments.
A gigantic *Christ Pantocrator* (Ruler of All) is enthroned in the central apse. Above the episcopal throne, in the choir, a mosaic represents King William II offering the cathedral to the Virgin. Another mosaic opposite, over the royal throne, shows the same King William receiving his crown from the hands of Christ.

★★★ **Ascent to the terraces** ⊙ – From the terraces there are magnificent **views**★★ of the cloisters and over the fertile plain of the Conca d'Oro.

★★★ **Chiostro** ⊙ – The cloisters to the right of the church are as famous as the mosaics. They afford views of the abbey church. On the south side there is a fountain that was used as a lavabo by the monks. The galleries, with their sharply-pointed arches, are supported by twin columns with remarkably carved capitals.

Beautiful mosaics in the Duomo

NOTO★

Population 21 818
Michelin map 432 Q 27

Noto, which dates from the time of the Siculi, was completely destroyed by the terrible earthquake of 1693. It was rebuilt on a new site 10km/6 miles distant from the original town. Lining the streets, laid out on a grid plan, are handsome palaces, churches and other Baroque monuments in the local white limestone, which has mellowed with time to a golden hue. Several Sicilian architects worked together on this project. The most inventive was probably **Rosario Gagliardi**.

The Baroque centre – The hub of the town is **Corso Vittorio Emanuele**, which widens into three squares overlooked by the monumental façades of churches designed in an imposing but flexible Baroque style: **San Francesco all'Immacolata** ⊘ and the **cathedral★★** (the cupola and much of the central nave collapsed in 1996) in the attractive **Piazza Municipio★**, and **San Domenico★** ⊘. To the right of San Domenico is **Via Corrado Nicolaci★**, a gently-sloping street which offers an enchanting vista with the Church of Montevergine as focal point. It is lined with palaces sporting splendid balconies; the most notable is **Palazzo Nicolaci di Villadorata** with exuberantly-fanciful **balconies★★**.

PALERMO★★★

Population 688 369

Michelin map 432 M 21-22 (including plan of built-up area)

Palermo, the capital and the chief seaport of Sicily, is built at the head of a wide bay enclosed to the north by Monte Pellegrino and to the south by Capo Zafferano. It lies on the edge of a wonderfully fertile plain bounded by hills and nicknamed the **Conca d'Oro** (Golden Basin), where lemon and orange groves flourish.

HISTORICAL NOTES

Palermo was founded by the Phoenicians, conquered by the Romans and later came under Byzantine rule.

From 831 to 1072 it was under the sway of the Saracens, who gave it the peculiar atmosphere suggested today by the luxuriance of its gardens and the shape of the domes on some buildings.

Conquered by the Normans in 1072, Palermo became the capital under **Roger II**, who took the title of King of Sicily.

This great builder succeeded in blending Norman architectural styles with the decorative traditions of the Saracens and Byzantines: his reign was the golden age of art in Palermo. Later the Hohenstaufen and Angevin kings introduced the Gothic style (13C). After more than three centuries of Spanish rule, the Bourbons of Naples gave Palermo its splendid Baroque finery.

The Sicilian Vespers – Since 1266 the brother of Louis IX of France, Charles I of Anjou, supported by the pope, had held the town. But his rule was unpopular. The Sicilians had nicknamed the French, who spoke Italian badly, the *tartaglioni* or stammerers. On the Monday or Tuesday after Easter 1282, as the bells were ringing for vespers, some Frenchmen insulted a young woman of Palermo in the Church of Santo Spirito. Insurrection broke out, and all Frenchmen who could not pronounce the world *cicero* (chick-pea) correctly were massacred.

PRACTICAL PALERMO

Arriving in Palermo – The easiest and quickest way to get to Palermo is by **air**. The city airport, Punta-Raisi (now also known as Falcone-Borsellino, after the two judges who were murdered in 1992), is situated 20km/12mi north of Palermo. A bus links the airport with the city centre every 30min, stopping in Via le Lazio, Piazza Ruggero Settimo in front of Teatro Politeama, and at the main railway station in front of Hotel Elena (☎ 091 58 04 57).

The island can also be reached by **ferry** from Genoa, Naples, Livorno, Cagliari and a number of the smaller islands (Ustica, Egadi and Eolie), as well as from Malta and Tunis. Contact travel agents for further information.

Getting around – It is best to avoid driving in Palermo because of traffic congestion and the difficulty of finding somewhere to park. Large car parks can be found on the outskirts of the city (marked by a on the map); it is also sometimes possible to park in Via Lincoln, next to the Botanical Gardens, which is a short walk from Piazza della Kalsa.

However, by far the best way to see the city is by public transport and taxi for longer distances and on foot once in the old town.

Taxis – Autoradio Taxi ☎ 091 51 27 27 and Radio Taxi Trinacria ☎ 091 22 54 55.

Markets – The food markets in Palermo are full of life and regional character, with a range of colourful lamp-lit stalls selling fresh fruit, vegetables and local fish. The most famous is without a doubt **Vucciria** market, a vibrant, colourful food market which is held every morning (except Sunday) until 2pm not far from the quayside in Via Cassari-Argenteria and the surrounding area (almost up to Piazza San Domenico). Other lively markets include the **Ballarò** food market in the area around Piazza del Carmine, and **Capo** market, the most interesting part of which sells food (Piazza Beati Paoli) and the second section of which sells a variety of clothing (Via San Agostino and Via Bandiera).

Where to stay

For a more exhaustive list of hotels in Palermo consult the current Michelin Red Guide Italia. We have listed a selection of hotels below, chosen for their value for money, location or character. Hotels are sub-divided into three categories, each based on the price of a double room, and are listed in alphabetical order (for the location of individual hotels see map).

Visitors are advised to check prices before booking and to book ahead of time, especially in the more central hotels which usually have a smaller numbers of rooms available.

BUDGET

Hotel Azzurro di Lampedusa – Via Roma, 111. ☎ 091 61 71 409. Credit cards accepted. This recently restored hotel is situated on the 5th floor of a *palazzo* in the old town (lift). Reasonably priced. 12 rooms.

Hotel Gardenia – Via Marino Stabile, 136. ☎ 091 32 27 61. Credit cards accepted. Small family-run hotel in the old town located on the 7th floor (lift). 10 rooms with air-conditioning. Garage (20 000L).

Hotel Moderno – Via Roma, 276. ☎ 091 58 86 83. Credit cards accepted. On the 3rd and 4th floor of this building (lift), this simple and well-kept hotel has 38 rooms with air-conditioning.

OUR SELECTION

Massimo Plaza Hotel – Via Maqueda, 437. ☎ 091 32 56 57. Credit cards accepted. On the first floor of a building situated opposite Teatro Massimo, this small, elegant hotel has 15 rooms. Rooms with excellent soundproofing and air-conditioning.

TREAT YOURSELF

Centrale Palace Hotel – Corso Vittorio Emanuele, 327. ☎ 091 33 66 66. Credit cards accepted. The elegant, tasteful Centrale Palace is located in an 18C mansion and offers excellent hospitality. This hotel has attractive public areas, including a panoramic restaurant on the top floor. 63 well-appointed rooms.

Eating out

TYPICAL RESTAURANTS

Capricci di Sicilia (BX) – Via Istituto Pignatelli on the corner of Piazza Sturzo, ☎ 091 32 77 77. Closed Mon and in August. Simple surroundings offering excellent food, with the emphasis on regional specialities.

Santandrea (BY) – Piazza S. Andrea 4, ☎ 091 33 49 99. Closed Tues and in January. This restaurant in the heart of the Vuccira district serves traditional Sicilian cuisine.

Tonnara Florio *(off the map)* – Discesa Tonnara, 4, quartiere Arenella. This attractive Liberty-style building, unfortunately in need of restoration, has a beautiful garden and a number of rooms once used for processing tuna and repairing fishing boats. The building now houses a night-club and a pizzeria. Old fishing tools and mementoes belonging to the Florio family can still be seen in the old tuna rooms where the pizzeria is now located.

The **Vecchia Tonnara**, at via Mondello, 76, **Mondello**, is also housed in an old tuna warehouse. This restaurant serves fish and seafood specialities.

SNACKS

Local specilaties include *u sfinciuni* or *sfincione* (pizza topped with tomato, anchovies, onion and bread crumbs), *panino con la milza* (spleen-filled roll) and *panelle* (fried chickpea flour pancakes), which are often sold in the local markets. The **Antica Focacceria San Francesco**, situated in the heart of the old town opposite San Francesco church, serves stuffed focaccia bread, rice croquettes, savoury pies, fried Ricotta cheese and *sfincione* in a beautiful old-style cafe with marble-topped tables and an old cast-iron stove as a counter.

Visitors who find themselves in the Viale della Libertà district should try the rolls at **Di Martino** (Via Mazzini 54).

Pastry shops – Two of the many pastry shops in Palermo are **Oscar** (Via Mariano Migliaccio 39), whose best-known speciality is a Devil's food cake, and **Bar Costa** (Via G. D'Annunzio 15), which specialises in all kinds of cakes and pastries (especially lemon and orange mousses). Also worth a visit are the **Pasticceria Scimone** (Via Miceli 18) and the long-established **Pasticceria Mazzara** (Via Generale Magliocco 15), where the writer Giuseppe Tomasi di Lampedusa used to stop for breakfast.

FROM QUATTRO CANTI TO THE PALAZZO DEI NORMANNI *3hr*

The route begins at two pretty squares which form the busy centre of Palermo and ends at the Palazzo dei Normanni, the focus of Sicilian politics, both past and present.

★ **Quattro Canti** (BY) – Two main streets, Via Vittorio Emanuele and Via Maqueda, intersect to form this busy crossroads with four canted corners (*Quattro Canti*) decorated with statues and fountains. The crossroads form a fine early-17C ensemble in the Spanish Baroque style.

The Church of **San Giuseppe ai Teatini** has an astonishingly decorative **interior**★.

B. Kaufmann

Piazza Pretoria at night

★★ **Piazza Pretoria** – The square has a spectacular **fountain**★★ surmounted by numerous marble statues, the work of a 16C Florentine artist. The town hall (**Palazzo Pretorio** – **BY H**) occupied one side of this square.

★★ **La Martorana** ⊘ (**BY**) – The real name of this church is Santa Maria dell'Ammiraglio (St Mary of the Admiral). It was founded in 1143 by the Admiral of the Fleet to King Roger II and altered in the 16C and 17C by the addition of a Baroque façade on the north side. Pass under the elegant 12C belfry-porch to enter the original church which is decorated with beautiful Byzantine **mosaics**★★ depicting scenes from the New Testament (*Annunciation, Nativity, Death of the Virgin*) and in the cupola, the imposing figure of *Christ Pantocrator* surrounded by angels, the Prophets and Evangelists. At the very end of the two side aisles note the two panels depicting *Roger II crowned by Christ (right)*, and *Admiral George of Antioch kneeling before the Virgin (left)*.

★★ **San Cataldo** ⊘ (**BZ**) – This splendid church, founded in the 12C, recalls Moorish architecture with its severe square shape, its domes, its decorative crenellations and the traceried openings of the façade.

The two churches face each other on the small **Piazza Bellini**★. The Moorish and Norman features of the square are particularly evident in the three rose-coloured cupolas of San Cataldo.

★ **Cattedrale** (**AYZ**) – Founded at the end of the 12C, the cathedral is built in the Sicilian-Norman style *(see Historical and Artistic Notes to Sicily)* but has often been modified and added to (15C south porch and the 18C dome). The **apses**★ of the east end have retained their typically Sicilian-Norman decoration.

In the interior, which was modified in the 18C in the neo-Classical style, note the tombs of the Emperor Frederick II and other members of the Hohenstaufen dynasty as well as other Angevin and Aragonese rulers.

The Treasury (**Tesoro**) ⊘ displays the ornate **imperial crown**★ which belonged to Constance of Aragon.

★★ **Palazzo dei Normanni** ⊘ (**AZ**) – Of the immense royal palace built by the Normans on the site of an earlier Moorish fortress, only the central part and the massive Pisan Tower are of the Norman period. The **Cappella Palatina**★★★ on the first floor was built in the reign of Roger II from 1130 to 1140. It is a wonderful example of Arab-Norman decoration. Ten ancient columns separate the nave and two aisles. The upper walls, the dome and the apses are covered with dazzling **mosaics**★★★ which along with those of Constantinople and Ravenna are the finest in Europe. This splendid decoration is complemented by the carved stalactite ceiling, marble paving, and the ornate pulpit and paschal candelabrum. On the second floor the old royal apartments, **Antichi appartamenti reali**★★, house the 12C King Roger's chamber, **Sala di re Ruggero**★★, which is adorned with mosaics of the chase.

The attractive gardens, **Villa Bonanno**★ (**AZ**), boast superb palm trees.

★★ **San Giovanni degli Eremiti** ⊘ (**AZ**) – Only a stone's throw from the palace, this church, with its surrounding gardens, is a green oasis where even the noise of the traffic is dulled. The church, dedicated to St John of the Hermits, which Arab architects helped to construct, was built in 1132 at the request of King Roger II and is picturesquely crowned with pink domes. Beside it is a garden of tropical plants with pleasant 13C **cloisters** of small twin columns.

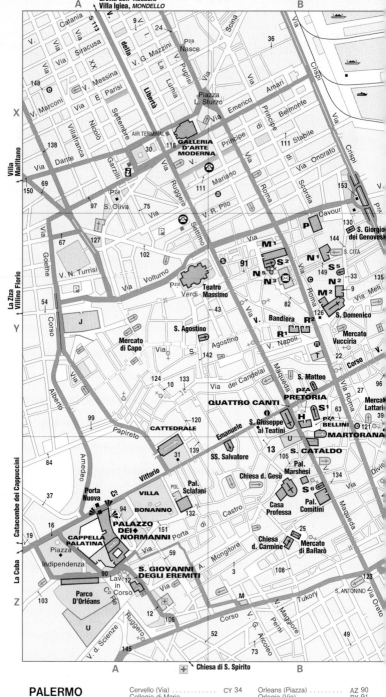

PALERMO

Albergheria (Via) . . . . BZ 3
Aragona (Piazza) . . . . CY 6
Aragona (Via) . . . . CY 7
Archimede (Via) . . . . AX 9
Beati Paoli (Via) . . . . AY 10
Benedettini (Via d.) . . . . . . AZ 12
Bologni (Piazza) . . . . BYZ 13
Calatafimi (Corso) . . . . AZ 16
Cappuccini
  (Via dei) . . . . AZ 19
Caracciolo (Piazza) . . . . . . BY 22
Carini (Via I.) . . . . AX 24
Carmine
  (Piazza d.) . . . . BZ 25
Cassa di Risparmio
  (Piazza) . . . . BY 27
Cassari (Via) . . . . BCY 28
Castelnuovo (Piazza) . . . . . AX 30
Cattedrale (Piazza d.) . . . . . AZ 31
Cavalieri di Malta
  (Largo) . . . . BY 33

Cervello (Via) . . . . CY 34
Collegio di Maria
  (Via) . . . . BX 36
Colonna Rotta (Via) . . . . . . AZ 37
Croce dei Vespri
  (Piazza d.) . . . . BY 39
Donizetti (Via G.) . . . . ABY 43
Errante (Via V.) . . . . BZ 49
Filiciuzza (Via) . . . . ABZ 52
Finocchiaro Aprile (C.) . . . . AY 54
Fonderia (Piazza) . . . . CY 57
Garibaldi (Via) . . . . CZ 58
Generale Cardona
  (Via) . . . . AZ 59
Giudici (Discesa d.) . . . . . . BY 63
Juvara Cluviero (Via) . . . . . AY 67
Latini (Via B.) . . . . AY 69
Marino (Via S.) . . . . BZ 73
Meccio (Via S.) . . . . AX 75
Monteleone (Via) . . . . BY 82
Mosca (Via G.) . . . . AZ 84
Mura del Cattive
  (Salita) . . . . CY 85

Orleans (Piazza) . . . . AZ 90
Orlogio (Via) . . . . BY 91
Paternostro (Via A.) . . . . . . BCY 96
Paternostro (Via P.) . . . . . . AX 97
Peranni
  (Piazza D.) . . . . AY 99
Pignatelli d'Aragona
  (Via) . . . . AY 102
Pisani (Corso P.) . . . . AZ 103
Ponticello (Via) . . . . BZ 105
Porta Montalto (Piazza) . . . . AZ 106
Porta S. Agata (Via) . . . . . . BZ 108
Porto Salvo (Via) . . . . CY 109
Principe Granatelli
  (Via) . . . . ABX 111
Rivoluzione (Piazza) . . . . . . CZ 117
Roma (Via) . . . . BXCZ
Ruggero Settimo
  (Piazza) . . . . AX 118
Ruggero Settimo
  (Via) . . . . AXY
S. Agata (Via) . . . . AY 120
S. Anna (Piazza) . . . . BY 121

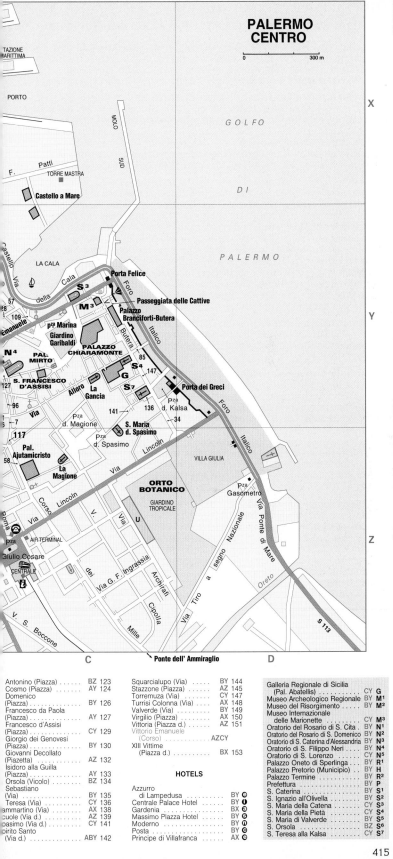

PALERMO
CENTRO

0   300 m

SICILY

GOLFO

DI

PALERMO

TAZIONE
MARITTIMA

PORTO

X

MOLO SUD

F. Patti
TORRE MASTRA

Castello a Mare

Castello Via

LA CALA

Cala della Via

Porta Felice

Foro Italico

S 3

M 3

Passeggiata delle Cattive

Palazzo
Branciforti-Butera

pza Marina
Giardino
Garibaldi

PALAZZO
CHIARAMONTE

N 4

PAL.
MIRTO

S. FRANCESCO
D'ASSISI

Alloro

La
Gancia

G

S 4

147

S 7

Butera

Porta dei Greci

Via

96

141

136

Pza
d. Kalsa

34

Foro Italico

7

Pza
d. Magione

117

Pza
d. Spasimo

S. Maria
d. Spasimo

Pal.
Ajutamicristo

58

La
Magione

Lincoln

VILLA GIULIA

Corso Lincoln Via

Via

ORTO
BOTANICO

GIARDINO
TROPICALE

U

Pza
Gasometro

Roma Via

AIR TERMINAL

Giulio Cesare

CENTRALE

Via G. F. Ingrassia

Via Ponte di Mare

Archirafi

Cipolla

Mille

V. S. Boccone

Via Tiro a segno Nazionale

Oreto

S 113

Ponte dell' Ammiraglio

C   D

Antonino (Piazza) . . . . . . BZ 123
Cosmo (Piazza) . . . . AY 124
Domenico
(Piazza) . . . . BY 126
Francesco da Paola
(Piazza) . . . . AY 127
Francesco d'Assisi
(Piazza) . . . . CY 129
Giorgio dei Genovesi
(Piazza) . . . . BY 130
Giovanni Decollato
(Piazzetta) . . . . AZ 132
Isidoro alla Guilla
(Piazza) . . . . AY 133
Orsola (Vicolo) . . . . BZ 134
Sebastiano
(Via) . . . . BY 135
Teresa (Via) . . . . CY 136
ammartino (Via) . . . . AX 138
cuole (Via d.) . . . . AZ 139
pasimo (Via d.) . . . . CY 141
pirito Santo
(Via d.) . . . . ABY 142

Squarcialupo (Via) . . . . . BY 144
Stazzone (Piazza) . . . . . . AZ 145
Torremuza (Via) . . . . CY 147
Turrisi Colonna (Via) . . . . AX 148
Valverde (Via) . . . . BY 149
Virgilio (Piazza) . . . . AX 150
Vittoria (Piazza d.) . . . . . . AZ 151
Vittorio Emanuele
(Corso) . . . . AZCY
XIII Vittime
(Piazza d.) . . . . BX 153

HOTELS

Azzurro
di Lampedusa . . . . BY ⊙
Centrale Palace Hotel . . . . . . BY ❶
Gardenia . . . . BX ❸
Massimo Plaza Hotel . . . . BY ❾
Moderno . . . . BY ❶
Posta . . . . BY ⊙
Principe di Villafranca . . . . . . AX ⊙

Galleria Regionale di Sicilia
(Pal. Abatellis) . . . . CY G
Museo Archeologico Regionale BY M¹
Museo del Risorgimento . . . . BY M²
Museo Internazionale
delle Marionette . . . . CY M³
Oratorio del Rosario di S. Cita . BY N¹
Oratorio del Rosario di S. Domenico BY N²
Oratorio di S. Caterina d'Alessandria BY N³
Oratorio di S. Filippo Neri . . . . BY N⁴
Oratorio di S. Lorenzo . . . . . . CY N⁵
Palazzo Oneto di Sperlinga . . BY R¹
Palazzo Pretorio (Municipio) . . BY R²
Palazzo Termine . . . . BY P
Prefettura . . . . BY P
S. Caterina . . . . BY S¹
S. Ignazio all'Olivella . . . . BY S²
S. Maria della Catena . . . . . . CY S³
S. Maria della Pietà . . . . CY S⁴
S. Maria di Valverde . . . . BY S⁵
S. Orsola . . . . BZ S⁶
S. Teresa alla Kalsa . . . . CY S⁷

FROM SAN FRANCESCO TO PALAZZO ABATELLIS *2hr*

Via Vittorio Emanuele, the main thoroughfare in the centre of the city, divides Palermo into two parts. Immediately to the north is a lively food market, the **Vucciria** (BY), which is open every morning except Sunday. To the other side is a quieter area where visitors can enjoy exploring the churches and palaces.

★ **San Francesco d'Assisi** (CY) – The church, dedicated to St Francis of Assisi, was built in the 13C. After its destruction during the Second World War it was rebuilt in the original style. Particularly noteworthy are the **portal** (original) and the rose window on the façade. The spacious, simple interior contains statues of allegorical figures by Giovanni Serpotta.

Next to the church is the **Oratorio di San Lorenzo** which has unfortunately been closed for many years. The interior is decorated with curious Baroque plaster mouldings by Giacomo Serpotta.

★ **Palazzo Mirto** ⏲ (CY) – The main residence of the Lanza-Filangieri princes contains its original 18C and 19C furnishings. Outside the palace, the **stables**★ which date back to the 19C, are of interest. The piano nobile *(1st floor)* with its drawing-rooms and formal rooms is open to visitors. The splendid Chinese Room **(Salottino cinese)** has leather flooring and silk wall coverings depicting scenes from everyday life, while the walls in the unusual Smoking Room **(fumoir★)** are decorated with painted and engraved leather. The Pompadour Room **(Salottino Pompadour)** is impressive for the richness of the silk that covers the walls. Exhibits of note include a 19C Neopolitan dinner service depicting figures in traditional costume *(in the passageway facing the Chinese Room)* and the 18C Meissen porcelain decorated with flowers and animals *(in the dining-room)*.

★ **Palazzo Chiaramonte** (CY) – A fine Gothic palace (1307) which served as a model for many buildings in Sicily and southern Italy.

In the gardens, Giardino Garibaldi, opposite there are two spectacular **magnolia-fig trees**★★ (ficus).

★★ **Museo Internazionale delle Marionette** ⏲ (CY M³) – This museum is a testament to the lively tradition of puppet *(marionette)* shows in Sicily. These animated spectacles were an even bigger part of Sicilian life in the past. Shows generally concentrated on chivalric themes, in particular the adventures of two important heros, Rinaldo and Orlando, who personified very different characters and temperaments.

The museum houses a splendid collection of Sicilian puppets. The delicate features of Gaspare Canino's puppets are admirable: these puppets are amongst the oldest in the collection (19C). The second part of the museum is dedicated to European and non-European craftsmanship and features puppets from all over Asia and Africa. The darkness of the room lends an air of mystery to the collection.

★★ **Galleria Regionale di Sicilia** ⏲ (CY G) – This museum and gallery is housed in the attractive 15C **Palazzo Abatellis**★. It includes a medieval art section and a picture gallery featuring works from the 11C to the 18C. The design of the gallery, which was built by Carlo Scarpa in the 1950s, is particularly interesting. The famous architect and designer concentrated on finding the best backdrop for the most important paintings, focusing on the frame and background, the materials and colours in order to maximise the impact of the natural light.

Outstanding works include the dramatic fresco of *Death Triumphant*★★★ from Palazzo Sclafani and a very fine *bust of Eleonora of Aragon*★★ by Francesco Laurana. Paintings of note include the *Annunciation*★★ by Antonello da Messina, with Mary's face exuding both a sense of peace and acceptance, and a triptych, the *Malvagna Altarolo*★★, by the Flemish artist, Mabuse.

THE CALA DISTRICT

The old harbour of the city is known as the *cala*, and was once enclosed by chains kept in the Gothic-Renaissance style church of **Santa Maria alla Catena**★ (CY S³).

★★★ **Oratorio del Rosario di San Domenico** ⏲ (BY N²) – The stucco decor of this church was the work of **Giacomo Serpotta**, an important artist of the Baroque period. The freedom of movement achieved in the cherubim figures is particularly striking.

★★★ **Oratorio del Rosario di Santa Cita** ⏲ (BY N¹) – This church is considered to be the masterpiece of **Giacomo Serpotta**, who worked on it between 1686 and 1718. Panels depicting the Mysteries are framed by a group of rejoicing angels and cherubim.

★ **Museo Archeologico Regionale** ⏲ (BY M¹) – The archeological museum, which is housed in a 16C convent, contains the finds from excavations of the numerous ancient sites in Sicily. On the ground floor are displayed two Phoenician sarcophagi, an Egyptian inscription known as the Palermo Stone, pieces from

Selinunte including a fine series of twin stele and the reconstruction of a temple pediment *(Sala Gabrici)* and especially the remarkable **metopes**★★ from temples (6C and 5C BC). On the first floor are displayed bronzes including *Heracles with stag*★★ and the famous *ram*★★, a Hellenistic work from Syracuse, and marble statues: *Satyr*★, a copy of an original from Praxiteles. On the second floor are two fine mosaics (3C BC), *Orpheus with animals* and the *mosaic of the seasons*.

ADDITIONAL SIGHTS

★★ **Villa Malfitano** Ⓥ – *Off the map. Follow Via Dante* (**AX**). Surrounded by beautiful **gardens**★★, this Liberty-style villa has retained its elegant interior decor, including many Oriental furnishings. Paricularly worthy of note is the **decoration** of the Summer Room **(Sala d'estate)** by Ettore de Maria Bergler; the *trompe-l'œil* effect transforms the room into a cool veranda surrounded by greenery.

★★ **Catacombe dei cappuccini** Ⓥ – *Access by Via dei Cappuccini, at the bottom of Corso Vittorio Emanuele.* (**AZ**). These Capuchin catacombs are an impressive sight. About 8 000 mummies were placed here from the 17C to 19C and have been preserved by the very dry air. They are decked in their finery and are placed in a line.

★ **La Zisa** Ⓥ – *Access by Corso Finocchiaro Aprile* (**AY 54**). This magnificent pleasure palace in the Arab-Norman style was built in the 12C and remodelled in the 17C. The palace (restored) now houses a collection of Egyptian works from the Mameluke and Ottoman periods, which probably complemented the decoration of the palace. The austere exterior is in contrast to the very ornate decoration inside.

★ **Orto Botanico** Ⓥ (**CDZ**) – A quiet and secluded garden with a fine collection of exotic plants and trees, including some magnificent **magnolia-fig trees**★★ (ficus).

Parco della Favorita – *3km/2mi north along Via Diana.* This park was laid out for the Bourbons in the 18C. Beside the Chinese pavilion (Palazzina Cinese) is a museum, the **Museo Etnografico Pitrè** Ⓥ, which displays a number of traditional Sicilian objects.

EXCURSIONS

★★★ **Monreale** – *See MONREALE.*

Monte Pellegrino – *14km/9mi north.* The road out of the city affords splendid **glimpses**★★★ of Palermo and the Conca d'Oro. On the way up, the road passes a 17C sanctuary, **Santuario di Santa Rosalia.**

★ **Rovine di Solunto** – *19km/12mi east.* Soluntum stands in an admirable site on a rocky ledge on the promontory which overlooks a headland, Capo Zafferano. It was a Phoenician city before it fell under the sway of Rome in the 3C BC.
The site **(zona archeologica)** Ⓥ includes ruins of the baths, forum, theatre, streets, houses, drainage system and numerous cisterns. Take Via Ippodamo da Mileto to reach the summit. There is a splendid **view**★★ of the bay of Palermo and Monte Pellegrino.

Bagheria – *16km/10mi east.* Bagheria is known for its Baroque villas and especially for the **Villa Palagonia** Ⓥ, which is decorated with **sculptures**★ of grotesques and monsters.

Isola di PANTELLERIA★★

PANTELLERIA ISLAND – Population 7 442
Michelin map 432 Q 17-18

Situated in the Sicilian Channel, the Island of Pantelleria is only 84km/52miles away from Cape Bon in Tunisia. It is the westernmost island of the Sicilian group and lies on the same latitude as Tunis.
Known as the "Black Pearl of the Mediterranean", the island is full of character with its indented coastline, steep slopes covered with terraces under cultivation, and its Moorish-looking cubic houses *(dammusi)*. The highest point of this volcanic island is **Montagna Grande** (836m/2 743ft). The vineyards produce some pleasant wines such as the sparkling Solimano and the muscat Tanit. Capers are also grown on Pantelleria.
Pantelleria has remains of prehistoric settlements and later suffered invasions like Sicily by the Phoenicians, Carthaginians, Greeks, Romans, Vandals, Byzantines, Moors and Normans who in 1123 united the island with Sicily.

GETTING TO THE ISLAND

The quickest way to reach the island is **by air** with connecting flights operated by Alitalia and Air Sicilia. There are also direct flights from Rome and Milan during the summer months.

Ferries leave from **Trapani** (*about* 5hr) operated by **Siremar**, via Staiti 61/63, ☎ 0923 54 05 15, fax 0932 20 663.

TOUR *3hr*

★★ **Tour of the island by car** – about *40km/25mi*. The very picturesque coastal road gives the visitor a good chance to discover the beauty of the indented coastline, cliffs, inlets, caves, thermal springs and lakes. Driving south from Pantelleria, roadsigns indicate a neolithic village, where the **sese grande★**, a flat, elliptic funerary monument can be seen. Further along the road, the village of **Scauri★** boasts a lovely site. On the south coast towards **Dietro Isola** the corniche road affords beautiful plunging **views★★** of this coastal area. The cape, **Punta dell'Arco★**, is terminated by a splendid natural rock arch in grey volcanic stone known as the **Elephant Arch★** (Arco dell'Elefante). On the northeast coast the inlet, **Cala dei Cinque Denti★**, and the rest of the coastline further north make a lovely volcanic landscape. From here, you can go on to visit the **Specchio di Venere★** (Venus' Mirror), a beautiful green lake.

★★ **Montagna Grande** – *13km/8mi southeast of Pantelleria*. From the summit of this peak there is a splendid **panorama★★** of the island. In clear weather the view extends as far as Sicily and Tunisia.

Every year,
*the **The Red Guide Italia***
is updated for those who appreciate fine dining, selected restaurants, local wines and specialities.
The guide lists a range of establishments from the simplest to the most elegant, those with local flavour and the best value for the cost.
Plan better and save money by investing in this year's guide.

RAGUSA★

Population 69 606
Michelin map 432 Q 26

Ragusa, partly rebuilt following the 1693 earthquake, lies in a typical **setting★** on a plateau between deep ravines. The modern town lies to the west while the old town, Ragusa Ibla, clusters on an outlier of the hills, Monti Iblei to the east. The Syracuse road offers magnificent **views★★** of the old town.

Asphalt and oil are produced or refined locally in large industrial complexes.

★★ **Ragusa Ibla** – The medieval area is a maze of streets, but much of the old town was rebuilt in the Baroque style. Here many of the beautiful buildings are adorned with richly decorated corbels depicting exaggerated figures and masks. The hub of the town is Piazza del Duomo, where the elegant Baroque Church of **San Giorgio★★** ⊙ stands. The church was designed by the architect Rosario Gagliardi who also worked in Noto. The pink stone façade has a convex central section which is flanked by three orders of columns and two wings crowned with scrolls. The nearby church of **San Giuseppe★** ⊙ shares certain similarities with San Giorgio, suggesting that it may be the work of the same architect.

Città nuova – The new town is laid out in a grid pattern around the 18C cathedral of **San Giovanni** ⊙, which is fronted by a wide terrace. Not far away, the **Museo Archeologico Ibleo** ⊙ (*Palazzo Mediterraneo, Via Natalelli*) contains the finds from excavations undertaken locally, notably from the ancient Greek city of Camarina.

Excursion

Modica – *15km/9mi south*. This village, situated in a narrow valley, has retained many of its magnificent Baroque buildings, the most impressive of which is the majestic church of San Giorgio, preceded by a long flight of stairs. The **Museo delle Arti e Tradizioni Popolari** ⊙ offers interesting reconstructions of old workplaces, including workshops and a farm.

SEGESTA ★★★

Michelin map 432 N 20 – 35km – 22 miles southeast of Trapani

Splendidly situated against the hillside, its ochre colours in pleasant contrast to the vast expanse of green, the archeological park is dominated by a fine Doric temple standing in an isolated site. Probably founded, like Erice, by the Elimi Segesta soon became one of the main cities in the Mediterranean basin under Greek influence, rivalling Selinunte in importance. It was probably destroyed by the Vandals.

★★★ **Tempio** ⊙ – The temple of Segesta stands alone, on an eminence encircled by a deep ravine, in a landscape of receding horizons. The Doric building (430 BC), pure and graceful, is girt by a peristyle of 36 columns in golden-coloured limestone. The road leading up to the theatre *(2km/1mi; shuttle bus available)* affords a magnificent **view**★★ of the temple.

The elegant Doric temple at Segesta

★ **Teatro** ⊙ – This Hellenistic theatre (63m/207ft in diameter) is built into the rocky hillside. The tiers of seats are orientated towards the hills, behind which, to the right, is the Gulf of Castellammare.

Antica città di SELINUNTE ★★

SELINUS (Ancient city)

Michelin map 432 O 20

Selinus was founded in the mid-7C by people from the east coast city of Megara Hyblaea and was destroyed twice, in 409 and 250 BC, by the Carthaginians. The huge ruins of its temples with their enormous platforms, probably wrecked by earthquakes, are impressive. The admirable metopes which adorned these temples are in the National Museum at Palermo.

Zona archeologica ⊙ – Visitors to the site first reach an esplanade around which are grouped the remains of three **temples**. The first to appear into view is **Temple E** (5C BC) which was rebuilt in 1958. To the right stands **Temple F**, completely in ruins. The last of the three, **Temple G**, probably dedicated to Apollo, was one of the largest in the ancient world. It was over 100m/328ft long; its columns were built of blocks each weighing several tonnes. The rubble of the fallen stonework gives some indication of its great size.

Cross the depression, Gorgo Cottone, to reach the **acropolis** with its perimeter wall. The site is dominated by the partially rebuilt (1925) columns of **Temple C** (6C BC), the oldest. There are four more ruined temples in the immediate vicinity.

Westwards, on the opposite bank of the Modione stand the remains of a sanctuary to Demeter Malophoros (the dispenser of pomegranates).

The length of time given in this guide
   – for touring allows time to enjoy the views and the scenery;
   – for sightseeing is the average time required for a visit.

SIRACUSA ★★★

SYRACUSE

Population 126 884
Michelin map 432 P 27

Syracuse, superbly situated at the head of a beautiful bay, enjoys a very mild climate. It was one of Sicily's, if not Magna Graecia's, most prestigious cities and at the height of its splendour rivalled Athens. Syracuse was colonised in the mid-8C BC by Greeks from Corinth who settled on the Island of Ortygia. It soon fell under the yoke of the tyrants, and it developed and prospered. In the 5C-4C BC the town had 300 000 inhabitants. Captured by the Romans during the Second Punic War (212 BC), it was occupied successively by the Barbarians, Byzantines (6C), Arabs (9C) and Normans.

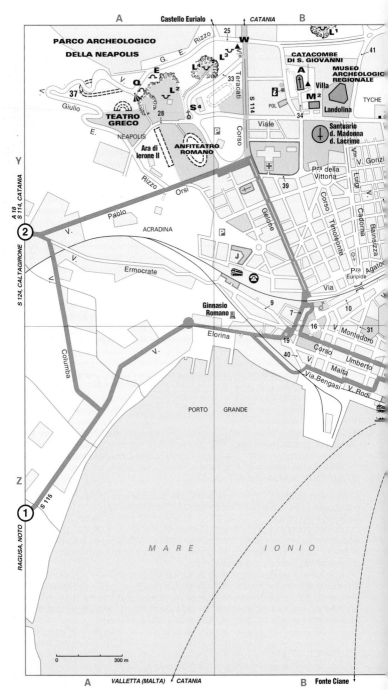

Tyrants and intellectuals – In the Greek world, dictators called tyrants (from the Greek word *turannos*) exercised unlimited power over certain cities, especially Syracuse. Already in 485 BC **Gelon**, the tyrant of Gela, had become master of Syracuse. His brother **Hiero**, an altogether more unpleasant person, nonetheless patronised poets and welcomed to his court both **Pindar** and **Æschylus**, who died in Gela in 456.

Denis the Elder (405-367 BC) was the most famous but even he lived in constant fear. To demonstrate the many dangers which threatened a ruler he had a sword suspended by a horsehair above the head of Damocles, a jealous courtier. He rarely left the safety of his castle on Ortygia, wore a shirt of mail under his clothing and changed his room every night. He had Plato expelled from the city when the philosopher came to study the political habits of the people under his dictatorship.

SIRACUSA

Agrigento (Via) . . . . BCY 2
Archimede (Piazza) . . . . CZ 3
Capodieci (Via) . . . . CZ 4
Castello Maniace (Via) . . . . CZ 6
Catania (Via) . . . . BY 7
Crispi (Via F.) . . . . BY 9
Diaz (Viale A.) . . . . BY 10
Dionisio il Grande (Riviera) . . . . CY 12
Duomo (Piazza) . . . . CZ 13
Foro Siracusano . . . . BYZ 16
Gelone (Corso) . . . . BY
Maestranza (Via d.) . . . . CZ 18
Marconi (Piazzale) . . . . BZ 19
Matteotti (Corso G.) . . . . CZ 21
Mergulensi (Via) . . . . CZ 22
Mirabella (Via) . . . . CZ 24
Necropoli Groticelle (Via d.) . . . BY 25
Pancali (Piazza) . . . . CZ 27
Paradiso (Via) . . . . AY 28
Puglia (Via) . . . . CY 30
Regina Margherita (Viale) . . . . . BYZ 31
Romagnoli (Via) . . . . ABY 33
S. Giovanni (Viale) . . . . BY 34
S. Martino (Via) . . . . CZ 36
Sepolcri (Via d.) . . . . AY 37
Svevia (Piazza F. d.) . . . . CZ 38
Testaferrata (Via G.) . . . . BY 39
Tripoli (Via) . . . . BZ 40
Umberto I (Corso) . . . . BZ
Von Platen (Via A.) . . . . BY 41
XX Settembre (Via) . . . . CZ 42

Basilica di S. Giovanni
   Evangelista . . . . BY A
Chiesa dei Gesuiti . . . . CZ C¹
Chiesa di S. Benedetto . . . . CZ C²
Duomo . . . . CZ D
Galleria Civica d'Arte
   Contemporanea . . . . CZ M¹
Grotta dei Cordari . . . . AY E
Latomia del Casale . . . . BY L¹
Latomia del Paradiso . . . . . . BY L²
Latomia di S. Venera . . . . . . BY L³
Latomia Intagliatella . . . . . . AY L⁴
Museo del Papiro . . . . BY M²
Orecchio di Dionisio . . . . AY Q
Palazzo Beneventano
   del Bosco . . . . CZ R¹
Palazzo del Senato . . . . CZ R²
Palazzo Mergulese-Montalto . CZ R⁴
S. Filippo Neri . . . . CZ S¹
S. Francesco all'Immacolata . CZ S²
S. Lucia . . . . CZ S³
S. Nicolò dei Cordari . . . . . . AY S⁴
Tempio di Apollo . . . . CZ V
Tomba di Archimede . . . . BY W

HOTELS

Domus Mariae . . . . CZ 🅰
Grand Hotel Villa Politi . . . . CY 🅱

Archimedes, the famous geometrician born at Syracuse in 287 BC, was so absent-minded that he would forget to eat and drink. It was in his bath that he discovered his principle: any body immersed in water loses weight equivalent to that of the water it displaces. Delighted, he jumped out of the bath and ran naked through the streets shouting "Eureka" (I have found it!).

When defending Syracuse against the Romans, Archimedes set fire to the enemy fleet by focusing the sun's rays with a system of mirrors and lenses. But when the Romans succeeded in entering the town by surprise, Archimedes, deep in his calculations, did not hear them, and a Roman soldier ran him through with his sword.

★★ L'ORTIGIA (CZ) 45min

The Island of Ortygia boasts numerous medieval and Baroque palaces. The latter are found mainly in **Via della Maestranza** (CZ 18). These narrow streets are shaded in summer and are ideal for a stroll.

The **Piazza Duomo★** is particularly attractive, lined by palaces adorned with wrought-iron balconies and the monumental façade of the cathedral (**Duomo★** ⊙ – CZ D). It was built in the 7C on the foundations of a Doric temple dedicated to Athena, some columns of which were reused in the Christian building (north and interior).

Inside, there are several sculptures (including the *Madonna of the Snow*) which are attributed to the Gagini, a family of artists who settled in Sicily in the 16C.

★ **Fonte Aretusa** – This is the legendary cradle of the city. The nymph Arethusa, pursued by the river-god Alpheus, took refuge on the Island of Ortygia where she was changed into a spring *(fonte)* by Artemis. Though near the sea, the fountain, built into a wall, runs with fresh water.

The **Passaggio Adorno**, a favourite walk for the Syracusans, starts below.

★ **Galleria Regionale di Palazzo Bellomo** ⊙ – The museum is housed in the beautiful 13C palace which was remodelled in the Catalan style in the 15C. The art gallery has an admirable *Annunciation★* (damaged) by Antonello da Messina and *The Burial of St Lucy★* by Caravaggio. There is also a collection of goldsmiths' work, Sicilian cribs, liturgical objects and furniture.

★★★ PARCO ARCHEOLOGICO DELLA NEAPOLIS ⊙ (AY)

2hr on foot. Access by Via Rizzo or Via Paradiso.

★★★ **Teatro Greco** – The Greek theatre dates from the 5C BC and is one of the largest of the ancient world. The tiers of seats are hewn out of the rock. The first performance of *The Persians* of Æschylus was held here.

Behind the theatre stretches the road to the tombs **(Via dei Sepolcri)**, which is hewn out of the rock.

★★★ **Latomia del Paradiso** (AY L²) – This former quarry, now an orange grove, dates from ancient times. Part of its roof fell in during the 1693 earthquake.

The Ear of Denis **(Orecchio di Dionisio★★★** – AY Q)** is an artificial grotto in the form of an earlobe. The grotto was so named in 1608 by the painter Caravaggio as a reminder of the legend recounting how the exceptional echo enabled the tyrant Denis to overhear the talk of the prisoners he confined in a room below.

Ara di Ierone II – This huge altar (c 200m/656ft long), partly hewn out of the rock, was used for public sacrifices.

★ **Anfiteatro Romano** – This Roman amphitheatre dates from the Imperial period and is hewn out of the rock.

★★ MUSEO ARCHEOLOGICO REGIONALE ⊙ (BY) 1hr

In the charming grounds of the **Villa Landolina** stands the museum built in memory of the archeologist Paolo Orsi (1859-1935).

It presents the history of Sicily from prehistoric times up to the Greek colonies of Syracuse (7C BC).

The first section explains the local geology – skeletons of the two dwarf elephants – and prehistory, starting from the Upper Palaeolithic, when man made his first appearance in Sicily.

The second part features the Greek colonisation (from mid-8C BC onwards); many artefacts were salvaged in the Lentinoi excavations (marble kouros) but more importantly at Megara Hyblaea and at Syracuse: chalk statue of the **goddess-mother★**, ceramics, architectural fragments and small-scale replicas of the great sanctuaries of Ortygia, the oldest district in Syracuse. The **Venus Anadiomede★**, a Roman copy of a Greek statue by Praxiteles, is on temporary display just before the section dedicated to Syracuse.

The third part of the museum is devoted to the various Syracuse colonies. The town became very powerful and in 664 BC it founded Akrai (Palazzolo Acreide). Then followed Kasmenai (Monte Casale) in 644 BC and Camarina (598 BC); chalk statues, horsemen used in the ornamentation of temples etc. This part of the building also shows artefacts from the Greek colonies inland (large statue of Demeter or Koré enthroned) and the excavation sites at Gela and Agrigento, which were conducted by Paolo Orsi.

ADDITIONAL SIGHTS

★★ **Catacombe di San Giovanni** ⓥ **(BY)** - After the catacombs in Rome, these are the finest examples in Italy. In contrast to those in Rome that have been dug out of fragile tufa, the catacombs in Syracuse have been excavated from solid rock to create spacious chambers, big enough to hold up to seven tombs. They consist of a main gallery off which branch secondary galleries ending in circular chapels or rotundas; several of the tombs are in the form of arched niches.

EXCURSIONS

★ **Fonte Ciane** ⓥ - *8km/5mi southwest. It is best to visit by boat.* The river, **Fiume Ciane**★★, is lined with papyrus beds, which are unique in Italy. It was here that the nymph Ciane was changed into a spring when she opposed the abduction of Proserpine by Pluto.

★ **Castello Eurialo** ⓥ - *9km/6mi northwest of the plan.* This was one of the greatest fortresses of the Greek period; it was built by Denis the Elder. Fine **panorama**★.

TAORMINA★★★

Population 10 560
Michelin map 432 N 27
Town plan in the current Michelin Italy Atlas

Taormina stands in a wonderful **site**★★★ at an altitude of 250m/820ft and forms a balcony overlooking the sea and facing Etna. It is renowned for its peaceful atmosphere and its beautiful monuments and gardens.

★★★ **Teatro Greco** ⓥ - The Greek theatre dates from the 3C BC but was remodelled by the Romans who used it as an arena for their contests.
Performances of Classical plays are given in summer. From the upper tiers there is an admirable **view**★★★ between the stage columns of the coastline and Etna.

★ **Corso Umberto** - The main street of Taormina has three gateways along its course: Porta Catania; the middle one, Porta di Mezzo, with the Torre dell' Orologio (Clock Tower); and Porta Messina.
The Piazza del Duomo is overlooked by the Gothic façade of the **cathedral** and adorned by an attractive Baroque fountain. Almost halfway along, the **Piazza 9 Aprile**★ forms a terrace which affords a splendid **panorama**★★ of the gulf. The Piazza Vittorio Emanuele was laid out on the site of the forum and is overlooked by the 15C Palazzo Corvaja.

The theatre and Mount Etna, Taormina

Helbig/ZEFA

★★ **Giardino di Villa Comunale** - From these terraced public gardens of flowers and exotic plants there are views of the coast and the sea.

EXCURSIONS

Castello – *4km/2mi northwest by the Castelmola road, and then a road to the right. It is also possible to walk up (1hr rtn).*
The castle was built in the medieval period on the summit of Monte Tauro (390m/1 280ft), on the remains of the former acropolis. There are splendid **views**★ of Taormina.

★ **CastelMola** – *5km/2mi northwest.* This tiny village is strategically located near Taormina and enjoys a splendid **site**★ with panoramic views. The focus of the village is the attractive Piazzetta del Duomo with its fine, intricate paving. From various points there are fine **views**★ of Etna, the north coast and the beaches below Taormina.

★ **Gole dell'Alcantara** ⊙ – *17km/11mi west.* The volcanic walls of these narrow gorges are formed by irregular geometrical shapes, turning the waterfalls which occasionally cascade down the rock into prisms of light. Visitors can hire boots and overhalls at the entrance to the gorge in order to explore the first section of the river bed.

TINDARI★

Michelin map 432 M 27 – 62km – 39 miles west of Messina

The ancient Greek Tyndaris, founded in 396 BC, is perched on the summit of the cape of the same name. At the very point stands a sanctuary **(santuario)** with a Black Virgin which is a place of pilgrimage. The ruins **(rovine)** ⊙ are essentially those of the city **ramparts**, the **theatre** on a site facing the sea, and the so-called **Basilica**, a fine arcaded Roman building (access by the main street, the Decumanus) which preceded the forum.

TRAPANI

Population 69 469
Michelin map 432 M 19

Trapani has a sheltered port within sight of the Egadi Islands.

★ **Santuario dell'Annunziata** ⊙ – Built in the 14C, the church was remodelled and enlarged in the 17C. The campanile is Baroque. On the north side the attractive Renaissance Sailors' Chapel **(Cappella dei Marinai)** is crowned with a dome.
Inside, access to the **Cappella della Madonna**★ is through a Renaissance arch carved in the 16C; the chapel contains the graceful statue of the Virgin (14C) known as the **Madonna di Trapani** and attributed to Nino Pisano.

★ **Museo Pepoli** ⊙ – The Pepoli Museum is located in the former Carmelite convent which adjoins the Annunziata. The works include sculpture (by the Gagini) and paintings, such as the 15C Trapani polyptych, a *Pietà*★ by Roberto di Oderisio and *St Bartholomew* by Ribera. There is also a display of local crafts: coral work and a very delicate crib.

★ **Centro storico** – The old town is built on the promontory that juts into the sea, with the Villa Margherita to the east. It contains a number of beautiful old mansions, especially along Rue Nova (now Via Garibaldi) and Rua Grande (now Corso Vittorio Emanuele).

Market stall

EXCURSIONS

Saline dello Stagnone – The coastal road which leads from Trapani to Marsala is lined with saltpans *(saline)* and fine open **views**★★; the water is divided into a multi-coloured grid by strips of land. In places there are windmills, a reminder of times gone by when they were the main way to pump water and grind the salt. The view is even more evocative in the summer, at harvest time, when the rose-coloured tint of the water in the basins is more intense (the colour changes as the saline content increases) and the shimmering pools of water inland are drying out in the sun. At Nubia there is a small, but interesting salt museum **(Museo del Sale)** ⊙ housed in a 17C saltworks where an exhibition illustrates this ancient craft: tools, display panels. A restored **mill** can be visited not far from Mozia *(see below)*.

★ **Isola di Mozia** ⊙ – *14km/9mi south of Trapani. Leave the car at the jetty. Fishermen provide a ferry service to the island.* This ancient Phoenician colony was founded in the 8C BC on one of the four islands of the **Laguna dello Stagnone**. Visitors can explore the ruins of the Phoenician city by following the path around the island *(about 1hr30min; anti-clockwise direction recommended)*. A small **museum** houses exhibits found on the island, including the magnificent **Ephebe of Mozia**★★, a noble figure of rather haughty bearing clothed in a long, pleated cloak which shows an obvious Greek influence.

USTICA★★

Population 1 370
Michelin map 432 K 21

This small volcanic island boasts an indented coastline which hides magnificent caves, inlets and small bays. It has been a marine reserve since 1987.

Getting to the island

Ferries (c 2hr 30min) and hydrofoils (about 70min) leave from **Palermo** and are operated by **Siremar**, via Crispi 118, ☎ 091 58 26 88. During the summer months, **Ustica Lines**, (☎ 081 76 12 515) runs a return hydrofoil service to Trapani-Favignana-Ustica-Naples. The Naples-Ustica crossing takes approximately 4 hr.

Island – The small village of **Ustica**★ is built overlooking the bay and harbour. An extensive **prehistoric village**★ ⊙ dating from the Bronze Age has been discovered near **Faraglioni** in the Colombaia district. The coastline is dotted with small beaches and rocky inlets, such as the bay known as the natural swimming pool **(piscina naturale**★**)**.

Riserva marina ⊙ – This marine reserve was established in 1987 to preserve and protect the fauna and natural marine environment around Ustica, where the sea is particularly free of pollution (Ustica is located right in the middle of the Atlantic current). The reserve organises guided tours to some of the caves around the island as well as snorkelling trips. Experienced divers can enjoy a spectacular **underwater show**★★ near **Scoglio del Medico**.

Santa Lucia cloisters, Naples

Practical Information

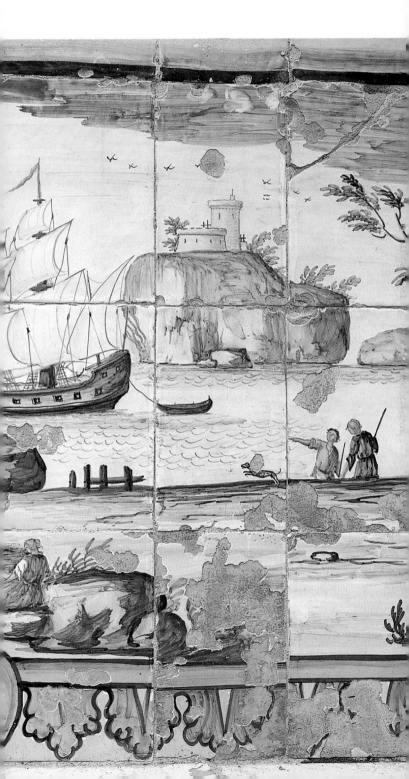

Main tourist routes

This map gives the distances and journey times between some main towns in Italy. It does not aim to show all the fast routes throughout the country but to give an indication of the journey time to be allowed for on a trip.

The Italian road network ranks second in Europe; its bold design has produced some remarkable feats of engineering and brings the landscape into play to spectacular effect.

When planning a trip travellers should also consult:
  the map of Principal Sights
  the map of Touring Programmes
  the Calendar of Events at the end of the guide

Michelin's famous star ratings are allocated for various categories:
regions of scenic beauty with dramatic natural features
cities with an exceptional cultural heritage
elegant resorts and charming villages
ancient monuments and fine architecture
museums and galleries.

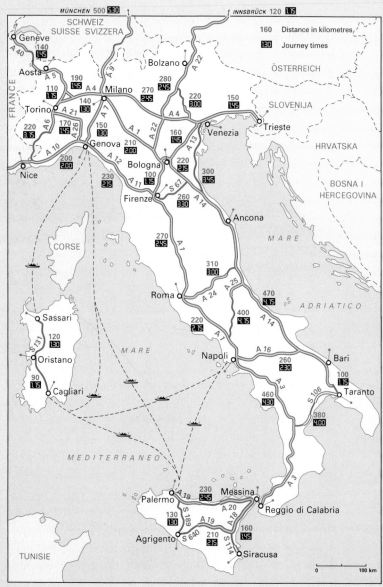

Travelling to Italy

When to visit – The best time of year to visit Italy is during the months of April, May, June, September and October, when the weather is generally pleasant throughout the country and the cities and beaches are not overrun with visitors. June and September are the best months for beach holidays, especially in the south. July and August should be avoided where possible, because of the high temperatures, crowds and increased prices. Flights, ferries, train tickets and hotels should be booked well in advance during these two months.

Passport – Visitors entering Italy must be in possession of a valid national **passport**. Citizens of other European countries need only a national identity card. In case of loss or theft, report to the embassy or consulate and the local police.

Visa – Entry visas are required by Australian, New Zealand, Canadian and US citizens (if their intended stay exceeds three months). Apply to the Italian Consulate (visa issued same day; delay if submitted by mail). US citizens should obtain the booklet *Safe Trip Abroad* ($1), which provides useful information on visa requirements, customs regulations, medical care etc for international travellers. Published by the Government Printing Office, it can be ordered by phone – ☎ (202) 512-1800 – or consulted on-line (www. access.gpo.gov).

Customs – Apply to the Customs Office (UK) for a leaflet on customs regulations and the full range of "duty free" allowances; available from HM Customs and Excise, Dorset House, Stamford Street, London SE1 9PS, ☎ 0171 928 3344. The US Customs Service offers a publication *Know before you go* for US citizens: for the office nearest you, consult the phone book, Federal Government, US Treasury (www.customs.ustreas.gov).
There are no customs formalities for holidaymakers bringing their caravans into the Italy for a stay of less than six months. No customs document is necessary for pleasure boats and outboard motors for a stay of less than six months but the registration certificate should be kept on board.

By air – Many international and other independent airlines operate services to Rome and to the major provincial airports (Milan, Turin, Verona, Genoa, Bologna, Pisa, Naples; Florence often requires a change in Milan, although there are direct trains from Pisa airport to the centre of Florence – transport time about 1 hour). There are several flights per day from London (Heathrow) to Rome and Milan; there are also daily flights from London (Heathrow) to Turin, Verona, Genoa, Bologna, Pisa and Naples, from London (Gatwick) to Rome, Naples and Genoa, and from Manchester or Birmingham to Milan; and a few flights per week from Dublin to Rome. There are package tour flights and Fly-Drive schemes available. Information, brochures and timetables are available from airlines and travel agents.
The domestic network operates frequent services covering the whole country. There are transfer buses to town terminals and railway stations.

It is advisable to book well in advance for the holiday season

By sea – Details of passenger ferry and car ferry services from the UK and Eire to the Channel ports, linking up with the European rail and motorway network can be obtained from travel agents and from the main operators: P & O European ferries, Stena Sealink, Hoverspeed etc. For details of crossing via the **Channel Tunnel** (high-speed undersea rail shuttle link between Folkestone and Calais), telephone Le Shuttle Passenger enquiries: ☎ 0990 353535. Website: http://www. eurotunnel.com

By road – Roads from France into Italy, with the exception of the Menton/-Ventimiglia (Riviera) coast road, are dependent on Alpine passes and tunnels. The main roads go through the Montgenèvre pass near Briançon, the Fréjus tunnel and Mont-Cenis pass near Saint-Jean-de-Maurienne, the Petit-Saint-Bernard pass near Bourg-Saint-Maurice and the the Mont-Blanc tunnel near Chamonix.
Via Switzerland, three main routes are possible – through the tunnel or pass at Grand-Saint-Bernard, through the Simplon pass, and through the St Gottard pass which goes via Ticino and Lugano to the great lakes of Lombardy. Those planning to drive through Switzerland should remember to budget for the Swiss road tax *(vignette)*, which is levied on all motor vehicles and trailers with a maximum weight of 3.5 tonnes, instead of charging tolls on the motorways (the *vignette* costs 40 Swiss francs and can be bought at the border crossings, post offices, petrol stations, garages and cantonal motor registries, or in advance from the Swiss National Tourist Office).
For those driving down through Germany and Austria, there is the Brenner pass south of Innsbruck.
Remember that most of these tunnels or passes levy a **toll**.
Use **Michelin maps 987, 989 and 988** or the **Michelin Road Atlas Europe** to help you plan your route.

Regular **coach services** are operated from London to Rome and to large provincial Italian towns. Details and bookings from: Eurolines (subsidiary of National Express), Luton (Head Office), ☎ 01582 404511. Eurolines serves Rome, Turin, Milan, Bologna and Florence; the Rome service is on Mondays, Wednesdays and Fridays departing at 09.00 from London-Victoria coach station and arriving the following day at 18.00. National Express, Victoria Coach Station, London SW1, ☎ 0990 808080. Website: http://www.nationalexpress.co.uk
Eurolines, 52 Grosvenor Gardens, London SW1W 0AU, ☎ 0171 730 8235. Website: http://eurolines.co.uk

By rail – From London and the Channel ports there are rail services to many Italian towns including many high-speed passenger trains and motorail services. For tourists residing outside Italy, there are rail passes offering unlimited travel, and group travel tickets offering savings for parties on the Italian Railways network. Italian State Railways in the UK: ☎ 0207 724 0011.
Tickets from Wasteels Travel, 121 Wilton Road, London SW1, ☎ 0171 834 7066 (fax 0171 630 7628); and from principal British and American Rail Travel Centres and travel agencies.
All trains for Italy from the UK go via Paris, daily.
Travelling by rail is a particularly good way of getting to Milan, Venice and Florence, as the rail stations here are within easy reach of the centre of town.

Travelling in Italy

By road

Documents – Nationals of EU countries require a valid **national driving licence** with an Italian translation (except in the case of the UK pink licence); nationals of non-EU countries require an **international driving licence** (available in the US from the American Automobile Association for US$10).
For the vehicle, it is necessary to have the car **registration papers**, and a nationality plate of the approved size.

Insurance – Insurance cover is compulsory, and an International Insurance Certificate (Green Card), although no longer a legal requirement, is the most effective proof of insurance cover and is internationally recognised by the police and other authorities. Certain UK motoring organisations (AA; RAC; Routiers, 25 Vanston Place, London SW6, ☎ 0171 385 6644) run accident insurance and breakdown service schemes for their members. Europ-Assistance (252 High St, Croydon CRO 1NF) also has special policies for motorists. Members of the American Automobile Association should obtain the free brochure *Offices to Serve You Abroad*.
The **Italian Automobile Club (ACI)** has its head office at Via Marsala 8, 00185 Roma, ☎ 06 4998. A 24hr car breakdown service (tax levied) is operated by the ACI for foreign motorists; dial 116 for assistance in case of breakdown. The ACI also offers a telephone information service in English (and other languages) for road and weather conditions as well as for tourist events: ☎ 06 4477.

Highway Code – The minimum driving age is 18. Traffic drives on the right. It is compulsory for the driver and front-seat passengers to wear seat belts, and seat belts must be worn in the back where they are fitted. Children under 12 must travel in the back seats, unless the front seat is fitted with a child restraint system. Full or dipped headlights must be switched on in poor visibility and at night; use sidelights only when a stationary vehicle is not clearly visible.
In the event of a breakdown, a red warning triangle must be displayed in the road; these can be hired from the ACI offices at the frontier (deposit refunded).
Drivers should watch out for unfamiliar road signs and take great care on the road (it is not without some justification that people say Italian drivers prefer using their horn to their brakes!). At crossroads drivers coming from the right have priority. Severe penalties are applicable for drink-driving offences.

Speed limits: in built-up areas, 50kph/31mph
on country roads, 90kph/55mph
on motorways, 90kph/55mph for vehicles up to 1000cc and 130kph/80mph for vehicles over 1100cc.

Parking – There are many car parks with attendants, particularly in the Naples area. Obviously, you should check the rates before parking, to avoid any unpleasant surprises as you leave, but it is advisable, particularly in the south, to use these car parks rather than leave vehicles unattended.
In many large towns, the historical town centre is subject to traffic restrictions (authorized vehicles only may enter), indicated by large rectangular signs saying "Zona a traffico limitato riservata ai veicoli autorizzati". In this case, park your vehicle outside the town before proceeding on foot, as the streets are often very narrow and have no pavements (sidewalks).

Petrol – Gasolio = diesel. Super = super leaded (98 octane).
Senza piombo = premium unleaded petrol (95 octane).
Super Plus or Euro Plus = super unleaded petrol (98 octane).
Petrol stations are usually open between 7am to 7pm. Many close at lunch-time (between 12.30pm and 3pm), Sundays and public holidays and many refuse payment by credit card.

Route planning – **Michelin map 988** at a scale of 1:1 000 000 covers the whole country. At 1:400 000, **Michelin map 428** covers the northwest, **429** the northeast, **430** the centre, **431** the south, **432** Sicily and **433** Sardinia; at 1:200 000, **218** covers Bolzano and **219** covers from Aosta to Milan; at 1:100 000, **115** covers the very western stretch of the Italian Riviera. The **Michelin Road Atlas Italia** (1:300 000) contains a complete index of towns, 80 plans of the largest cities and covers all of Italy. Maps **38** (1:10 000) and **46** (1:15 000) cover the cities of Rome and Milan.
Michelin has also created a website to help motorists prepare their journey. The service enables browsers to select their preferred route (fastest, shortest etc) and to calculate distances between towns and cities: **www.michelin-travel.com**
The **Touring Club Italiano (TCI)**, Corso d'Italia 10, 20139 Milano, ☎ 02 85 26 72, publishes a regional map series at 1:200 000.
The Italian road network is excellent, and there are many motorways *(autostrade)*, most of which are **toll-roads**. The toll is calculated according to the distance between the car axles and engine capacity. **Motorway tolls** can be paid with money or with the **Viacard**, a magnetic card with a value of 90 000L or 50 000L which is sold in Italy at the beginning of motorways, in Autogrill restaurants or in the offices of the ACI. See above for details of the ACI breakdown service.

Road signs – Motorways (autostrade – subject to tolls) and dual carriageways (superstrade) are indicated by green signs; ordinary roads by blue signs; tourist sights by yellow signs.

Car Rental – There are car rental agencies at airports, railway stations and in all large towns and resorts throughout Italy. The main agencies are Avis, Hertz, Eurodollar, Europcar and Maggiore Budget. Fly-drive schemes or train-and-car packages are available. European cars usually have manual transmission, but automatic cars are available on demand. An **international driving licence** is required for non-EU nationals.

By rail

Special train tickets can be bought once in Italy. The *biglietto chilometrico* (kilometre ticket) is valid for a distance of 3 000km/1 875mi (for a maximum of 20 journeys) and allows travellers to save approximately 15% off the full price of a ticket. It is valid for two months from the date ofhte first journey and can be bought up to a month prior to travelling. A *carnet* allows the purchase of a minimum of 4 tickets with a 10% (if the distance is between 71km/44mi and 350km/218mi) or 20% (for longer journeys) discount. Other special railcards include the *Carta verde* (for those under 26) and the *Carta d'argento* (for those over 60) which give 20% discounts on all journeys. The **Pendolino** or high speed train runs between Milan-Rome (4hr), Turin-Rome (5hr), Genoa-Rome (4hr), Rome-Venice (4hr) and Rome-Bari (4hr 30min).
Bicycles can be taken on those trains with a guard van (usually all local trains) for a supplement of 5 000L.

By air

The main Italian airline companies are Alitalia, Airone, Meridiana, Avianova, Air Dolomiti, Aliadriatica and TAS. They normally offer special weekend rates, family discounts and reduced prices for young people. For information, contact travel agencies and individual airline offices.

Alitalia: ☎ 0870 544 8259. Website: http://www.alitalia.it

Main Italian airports *(the approximate time and method of transport to the city is given in brackets)*:
Alghero: Fertilia 11km/7mi northwest, ☎ 079 93 50 33 (bus 15min)
Ancona: Falconara 13km/8mi west, ☎ 071 28 271 (bus 30min)
Bari: Palese 9km/6mi northwest, ☎ 080 58 35 204 (bus 30min)
Bergamo: Orio al Serio 3.5km/2mi southeast, ☎ 035 32 61 11 (bus 20min)
Bologna: Guglielmo Marconi 6km/4mi northwest, ☎ 051 64 79 615 (bus 20min)
Bolzano: 4km/2.5mi south, ☎ 0471 25 40 70 (bus 15min)
Brindisi: Papola Casale 6km/4mi north, ☎ 0831 41 88 05
Cagliari: Elmas 6km/4mi west, ☎ 070 24 10 14 (bus 15min)
Catania: Fontanarossa 4km/2.5mi south, ☎ 095 72 39 111 (bus 30min)
Florence: Amerigo Vespucci 4km/2.5mi, ☎ 055 37 34 98 (bus 20min)
Genoa: Cristoforo Colombo 6km/4mi west, ☎ 010 60 151 (bus 30min)
Lamezia Terme: Santa Eufemia ☎ 0968 41 41 11
Lampedusa: ☎ 0922 97 00 06
Milan: Forlanini, 8km/5mi east, ☎ 02 74 85 22 00 and Malpensa, 45km/28mi northwest, ☎ 02 40 09 92 40 (bus 25min from Linate and 1hr from Malpensa; Malpensa Express train from Stazione di Cadorna 35min)

Naples: Capodichino 6km/4mi northeast, ☎ 081 70 91 111 (bus 30min)
Olbia: Costa Smeralda 4km/2.5mi southwest, ☎ 0789 52 634
Palermo: Punta Raisi 30km/19mi west, ☎ 091 70 20 111 (bus 1hr)
Pantelleria: 4km/2.5mi southeast, ☎ 0923 91 13 98
Perugia: Sant' Egidio 17km/10mi southeast, ☎ 075 69 29 447
Pisa: Galileo Galilei 3km/2mi south, ☎ 050 44 325
Reggio Calabria: Ravagnese 4km/2.5mi south, ☎ 0965 64 27 22
Rome: Leonardo da Vinci-Fiumicino 26km/16mi southwest, ☎ 06 65 951 (train 30min)
Turin: Caselle 15km/9mi north, ☎ 011 56 76 749 (bus 30min)
Trieste: Ronchi dei Legionari 32km/20mi northwest, ☎ 0481 77 32 24 (bus 40min)
Venice: Marco Polo 13km/8mi northeast, ☎ 041 26 06 111 (bus 20min)
Verona: Villafranca Veronese 14km/9mi southwest, ☎ 045 80 95 666

By sea

Sicily and Sardinia – These two islands are linked to the mainland by ferries and hydrofoils and are very popular, especially during the summer months. Visitors are therefore advised to book their crossing well in advance, especially if travelling with a car or if a cabin is required. For those for whom comfort is less of a priority, seats are available on deck; although it is preferable to book these ahead of time, they can also be purchased a couple of hours before departure from the ferry terminal.

Crossings to Sicily are operated from the following cities:
Cagliari: Tirrenia Navigazione, Agenzia Agenave, via Campidano 1, ☎ 070 66 60 65, fax 070 66 38 53 (14hr 30min to Palermo, 11hr to Trapani).
Genoa: Grandi Navi Veloci, via Fieschi 17, ☎ 010 58 93 31, fax 010 55 09 225 (20hr to Palermo).
Livorno: Grandi Navi Veloci, varco Galvani Darsena, ☎ 0586 40 98 04, fax 0586 42 97 17 (17hr to Palermo).
Naples: Tirrenia Navigazione, Stazione Marittima, molo Angioino, ☎ 081 25 14 740, fax 081 25 14 767 (11hr to Palermo).
Reggio Calabria: Stazione Ferrovie dello Stato (railway station), ☎ 0965 97 957 (25min to Messina) and Aliscafi SNAV (hydrofoil), Stazione Marittima, ☎ 0965 29 568 (15min to Messina).
Villa San Giovanni: Ferrovie dello Stato, piazza Stazione, ☎ 0965 75 82 41, and Società Caronte Shipping, via Marina 30, ☎ 0965 79 31 31, fax 0965 79 31 28 (20min to Messina).
For connections to the Egadi and Aeolian islands see EGADI and EOLIE.

Crossings to **Sardinia** are operated from the following cities:

Civitavecchia: Sardinia Ferries, Calata Laurenti, ☎ 0766 50 07 14, fax 0766 50 07 18 (7hr to Golfo degli Aranci); Tirrenia Navigazione, Stazione Marittima, ☎ 0766 20 332, fax 0766 28 804 (to Cagliari, Olbia and Arbatax).
Fiumicino: Tirrenia Navigazione, agenzia Vacanzando, viale Traiano 97, ☎ 06 65 23 501 (4hr to Arbatax and Golfo degli Aranci).
Genova: Tirrenia Navigazione, Stazione Marittima, Pontile Colombro, ☎ 010 26 981, fax 010 26 98 241 (21hr to Cagliari, 13hr 30min to Olbia, 19hr to Arbatax and 13hr to Porto Torres); Grandi Navi Veloci, via Fieschi 17, ☎ 010 58 93 31, fax 010 55 09 225 (10hr to Porto Torres).
La Spezia: Tirrenia Navigazione, Agenzia Lardon, via Crispi 39, ☎ 0187 77 02 50, fax 0187 27 223 (5hr 30min to Golfo degli Aranci).
Livorno: Sardinia Ferries, Calata Carrara, ☎ 0586 89 89 79, fax 0586 89 61 03 (9hr to Golfo degli Aranci).
Palermo: Tirrenia Navigazione, Calata Marinai d'Italia, ☎ 091 33 33 00, fax 091 60 21 221 (14hr 30min to Cagliari).
Trapani: Tirrenia Navigazione, Agenzia Salvo, corso Italia 48, ☎ 0923 21 896, fax 0923 29 436 (11hr 30min to Cagliari).

For further details on the different shipping routes (passenger and car ferries) between the Italian peninsula and the various islands, consult the **Michelin map 988** and the **Michelin Red Guide Italia**.

A new concept in travel planning.

When you want to calculate a trip distance or visualise a detailed itinerary; when you need information on hotels,

restaurants or campsites, consult Michelin on the Internet.

Visit our Web site to discover our full range of services for travellers:

www.michelin-travel.com.

Accommodation

Places to Stay - The maps on pages 8-11 indicate the recommended places for overnight stops.

The provincial tourist boards and the local tourist offices of the various cities and resorts publish accommodation lists and leaflets available by writing direct to these offices (addresses from the Italian State Tourist Office and the Michelin Red Guide Italia). The TCI *(see previous page)* publishes a guide to tourist villages which are located in or near popular resorts.

Hotels - The new **Travellers' Addresses** section (pages marked with a blue margin), which has been added to the largest towns and cities in this guide, offers a choice of hotels in three categories to suit all budgets. Prices are based on a double/twin room:
- **Budget:** Under 150 000L.
- **Moderately priced:** Hotels in this category offer rooms between 150 000 and 300 000L.
- **Luxury:** Comfort and charm for a memorable stay - with prices to match!

For a more extensive list of hotels consult the **Michelin Red Guide Italia**, which is revised each year, and which lists a selection of hotels, guest-houses and restaurants together with their type, location, price, amenities and level of comfort.

Visitors are advised to check prices before booking, especially during high season (July and August), when prices may well go up. It is advisable to book rooms in advance at this time of year. Those travelling on a budget with their own transport will generally find that rooms a few miles outside the medieval town centres offer better value for money.

Rural accommodation - In certain regions of Italy, it is often possible to find accommodation in rural areas by staying in farm guesthouses, which offer rooms and often a chance to taste the products made on the farm. Some of these guesthouses are as elegant as the best hotels, with prices to match. The regions with the most choice of this type of accommodation are Tuscnay, Umbria, Alto-Adige, Sicily and Sardinia.

Listings of such accommodation are published in **Vacanze e Natura** (by Associazione Terranostra, ☎ 06 46 821), **Agriturismo e Vacanze Verdi** (by Associazione Agriturist, ☎ 06 68 52 342), **Guida all'Agristurismo** by Demetra and **Vacanze Verdi** by Edagricole, which offers a selection of over 400 addresses. Information is also available from **Turismo Verde**, Via Flaminia 56, Roma, ☎ 06 36 11 051.

Convents and monasteries - A number of religious orders provide rooms for visitors in the major cities. Accommodation is simple, but clean and reasonably priced. The only disadvantage is the curfew; visitors are usually expected to be in by 10.30/11pm. For information, contact tourist offices or the archidioceses.

Bed & Breakfast - The Bed & Breakfast formula is becoming increasingly popular in Italy. For information, contact **Bed & Breakfast Italia**, Palazzo Sforza Cesarini, Corso Vittorio Emanuele II 282, 00186 Rome, ☎ 06 68 78 618, Fax 06 68 78619, Website: http://www.bbitalia.it, e-mail: info@bbitalia.it; or **Dolce Casa**, Via Messina 15, 20154 Milan, ☎ 02 33 11 814, Fax 02 33 13 009, website: http://www.touritel.com/dolcecasa, e-mail: dolcecasa@touritel.com

Youth Hostels - In Italy, these are called *Alberghi per la Gioventù*. Although some accept national cards, it is best to obtain an international youth hostel federation card. A list of youth hostels is available from the International Federation or the **AGI** (Italian Youth Hostels Association), Via Cavour 44, 00184 Roma, ☎ 06 48 71 152.

Youth Hostels Association, Trevelyan House, 8 Stephen's Hill, St Albans, Herts AL1 2DY. Website: http://www.yha.org.uk
American Youth Hostel Inc, National Offices, PO Box 37613, Washington DC 20013-7613. Website: http://www. gatewayhiayh.org

Camping - Italy has over 16 000 officially-graded camp sites with varying ranges of facilities. There are very few possibilities for camping other than on an officially recognised site, and in the summer it is highly recommended that you **reserve a pitch in advance**, as camp sites get extremely crowded in high season.

An International Camping Carnet for caravans is useful, but not compulsory; it can be obtained from the motoring organisations or the Camping and Caravanning Club (Greenfields House, Westwood Way, Coventry CV4 8JH, ☎ 01203 694 995; website: http://www.campingandcaravanning club.co.uk).

The Italian Camping Federation (Federcampeggio, Via Vittorio Emanuele II 11, 50041 Calenzano (Firenze), ☎ 055 88 23 91), Fax 055 88 25 918, publishes a map of camp sites and a list of those which offer special rates to holders of the international camping card. It also publishes an annual guide *Campeggi e Villagi Turistici in Italia* in collaboration with the TCI. Local tourist boards also supply information on camp sites.

Eating Out

Travellers' Addresses – The restaurants listed in this section (marked by a blue margin under the larger cities) have been chosen for their surroundings, ambience, typical dishes or unusual character. For a wider selection of restaurants and more detailed gastronomic information, consult the **Michelin Red Guide Italia**.

General information

Electricity – The electric current is 220 volts AC (50 cycles). Circular 2-pin plugs are standard.

Time – In winter, standard time is Greenwich Mean Time + 1 hour. In summer the clocks go forward an hour to give Italian Summer Time (GMT + 2 hours) from the last weekend in March to the last weekend in September.

Medical treatment – British citizens should apply to the Department of Health and Social Security for **Form E111**, which entitles the holder to urgent treatment for accident or unexpected illness in EU countries.

Nationals of non-EU countries should check that their insurance policy covers them specifically for overseas travel, including doctor's visits, medication and hospitalization in Italy (in most cases you will probably have to take out supplementary medical insurance).

American Express offers its cardholders (only) a service called *Global Assist* to help in financial, legal, medical or personal emergencies. For further information, consult their website: http://www.americanexpress.com

All prescription drugs should be clearly labelled, and it is recommended that you carry a copy of the prescription with you.

A list of chemists open at night or on Sundays may be obtained from chemists shops (*farmacia* – red cross sign). First Aid service *(pronto soccorso)* is available at airports, railway stations and in hospitals.

Currency – In Italy, the currency is the **lira** which is issued in notes (100 000, 50 000, 20 000, 10 000, 5 000, 2 000, 1 000L) and in coins (500, 200, 100, 50L). There are no restrictions on the amount of currency visitors are allowed to take into Italy. If exporting currency in foreign bank notes in excess of the given allocation, visitors are advised to complete a currency declaration form (V2) on arrival.

Banks – Banks are generally open from 8.30am to 1.30pm and from 3pm to 4pm and closed on Saturdays, Sundays and public holidays.

Money can also be changed at the Post Office (except travellers' cheques), in exchange offices and at railway stations and airports. A commission is always charged.

Most banks have cash dispensers which accept international credit and debit cards.

Eurocard – Eurocheques are widely accepted, although the value guaranteed is restricted – it is advisable to check on the rules before departure. Money withdrawn from Bancomat machines with a PIN incurs a lesser commission than a withdrawal transacted over the counter at a bank.

Credit cards – American Express, Visa (Barclaycard), Diners Club and Eurocard (Mastercard/Access) are widely accepted in shops, hotels and restaurants, but not always at petrol stations. Call the Italian tourist board (ENIT) for details of special offers open to Visa card-holders ("Italy welcomes Visa – VIP pass").

Post – Italian post offices are open from 8.30pm to 2pm (12pm on Saturdays and the last day of the month). Stamps are also sold at tobacconists *(tabacchi)* which display a black *valori bollati* sign outside.

Telephone – The telephone service is organised by TELECOM ITALIA (formerly SIP). Some offices have public booths where the customer pays for units used *(scatti)* at the counter after the call.

Public phones: Orange phones in the street or in bars may be operated by phone cards, coins or L 200 brass tokens. To make a call: lift the receiver, insert payment, await dialling signal, punch in the number.

Phone cards: These are sold in denominations of 5 000L, 10 000L, 15 000L (schede da cinque, dieci, quindici mila lire) and are available from CIT offices, post offices, tobacconists and newsagents.

In Italy, phone calls are cheaper after 6.30pm. Lower rates apply from 10pm to 8am, at weekends (from 1.30pm on Saturdays) and public holidays.

The country code for Italy is 39. To make an international call from Italy, dial 00 + country code + area code (minus any preceding zeros) + correspondent's number.

When making a call within Italy, the area code (e.g. 06 for Rome, 055 for Florence, etc.) is always used, both from outside and within the city you are calling.

Useful telephone numbers:
12 directory enquiries
15 assisted operator service – reverse-charge (collect) call
112 *carabinieri* police *(in emergencies only)*
113 police, Red Cross, emergency first aid
115 fire brigade
116 ACI (Italian Automobile Club) vehicle breakdown service
176 information in foreign languages
1412 information on addresses from phone number
1515 forest rangers.

Tobacconists – Besides cigarettes and tobacco, *tabacchi* sell postcards and stamps, confectionery, phonecards, public transport tickets, lottery tickets etc.

Shopping

Opening hours – Most shops open from 8.30-9am to 12.30-1pm and 3.30-4pm to 7.30-8pm, although in the centre of large towns and cities, shops usually remain open at lunchtime. In northern Italy, shops often take a shorter midday break and close earlier. Late-night shopping is frequent in seaside resorts. Many tourist resorts have an open-air market once or twice a week.

Public holidays – **Museums** and other **monuments** are usually closed on Mondays and public holidays. **Churches** often closed at lunchtime and cannot be visited during services. The following are days when museums and other monuments may be closed or vary their hours of admission:
1 January
6 January (Epiphany)
Easter Day and Easter Monday
25 April (anniversary of the 1945 liberation)
1 May
15 August ("Ferragosto")
1 November (All Saints)
8 December
25 and 26 December
Each town also celebrates the feast day of its patron saint (details of local festivals can be obtained from the local tourist offices).
For information on specific opening hours, see the Admission Times and Charges section.

Beaches – In some of the extremely popular parts of Italy – Liguria, the Tuscan Coast, the Adriatic Coast, etc. – private beaches (often very clean and with excellent facilities), for which an entrance fee is charged, alternate with public beaches (free of charge), which are not as well maintained.

Tourist information

Italian State Tourist Office – ENIT (Ente Nazionale Italiano per il Turismo) – For information, brochures, maps and assistance in planning a trip to Italy, apply to the ENIT in your country or consult the ENIT website: http://www.enit.it

Canada 1 Place Ville-Marie, Suite 1914, Montréal, Québec H3B 3M9, ☎ 514 866 7667/8/9

UK 1 Princes Street, London W1R 8AY, ☎ 0171 408 1254, Fax 0171 493 6695 ; 24-hour brochure request line: ☎ 0900 1600 280 (calls charged at 60p/min); e-mail: enitlond.@globalnet.co.uk

USA 630 Fifth Avenue, Suite 1565, New York, NY 10111, ☎ 212 245 4822 12400 Wilshire Boulevard, Suite 550, Los Angeles, CA 90025, ☎ 310 820 0098

Regional and local tourist information centres – In each regional capital there is a regional tourist board **(Assessorato per il Turismo)**. The Michelin Red Guide Italia gives the addresses and telephone numbers of provincial tourist boards (**Ente Provinciale Turismo** or **Azienda di Promozione Turistica**) and local tourist boards (**Azienda Autonoma di Soggiorno, Cura e Turismo – AST)**, for information on particular towns or regions, and also the addresses of the offices of the Italian Automobile Club (ACI). The addresses and telephone numbers of the most important regional tourist offices are given in the Admission Times and Charges section.

Tourism for the Disabled – A number of sights described in this guide are accessible to the disabled. They are indicated by the symbol ♿ in the section entitled *Admission Times and Charges* at the end of the guide. Further information is available from the Associazione Italiana Disabili, via S. Barnaba 29, 20122 Milan, ☎ 02 55 01 75 64. The Michelin Red Guide Italia (hotels and restaurants) indicates hotels with rooms which are easily accessible to the physically handicapped.

Embassies

Australia via Alessandria 215, 00198 Roma, ☎ 06 85 27 21

Canada via Zara 30, 00198 Roma, ☎ 06 44 59 81

Eire piazza di Campitelli 3, 00186 Roma, ☎ 06 69 79 121

UK via XX Settembre 80a, 10122 Roma, ☎ 06 48 25 441/551

USA via Veneto 119a, 00187 Roma, ☎ 06 46 741

Consulates

Australia via Borgogna 2, 20122 Milano, ☎ 02 77 70 41

Canada via Vittor Pisani 19, 20124 Milano, ☎ 02 66 97 451

UK Dorsoduro 1051, 30123 Venezia, ☎ 041 52 27 207 or 52 27 408
Lungarno Corsini 2, 50123 Firenze ☎ 055 28 41 33 or 21 25 94
via Crispi 122, 80122 Napoli, ☎ 081 66 35 11
via S Paolo 7, 20121 Milano, ☎ 02 72 30 01

USA Lungarno A Vespucci 38, 50123 Firenze, ☎ 055 239 82 76
piazza Repubblica 2, 80122 Napoli, ☎ 081 583 81 11
via Principe Amedeo 2/10, 20121 Milano, ☎ 02 29 03 51

Recreation

Sport and Leisure

Useful addresses for outdoor enthusiasts include:

Canoeing – Federazione Italiana Canottaggio, viale Tiziano 70, 00196 Roma, ☎ 06 32 33 770 and the Federazione Italiana Canoa e Kayak, via Flaminia 357, 00196 Roma, ☎ 06 32 42 050.

Cycling – Federazione Ciclistica Italiana, Stadio Olimpico, curva Nord, cancello L, porta 91, 00194 Foro Italico, Roma, ☎ 06 68 57 813.

Fishing – Federazione Italiana Pesca Sportiva e Attività Subacquee, viale Tiziano 70, 00196 Roma, ☎ 06 36 85 85 22.

Golf – Federazione Italiana Golf, viale Tiziano 74, 00196 Roma, ☎ 06 36 85 81 08.

Hunting – Federazione Italiana della Caccia, viale Tiziano 70, 00196 Roma, ☎ 06 32 33 779.

Mountaineering and Rambling – Both the Alps and the Apennines offer a wide range of mountain climbs and footpaths of varying difficulty. Federazione Italiana Escursionismo, via La Spezia 58/r, 16149 Genova, ☎ 010 41 41 94 and Club Alpino Italiano, via Fonseca Pimentel 7, 20121 Milano, ☎ 02 86 46 35 16.

Riding and Pony Trekking – Federazione Italiana di Turismo Equestre, via Ponte di Castel Giubileo 27, 00188 Roma, ☎ 06 33 28 060.

Sailing and Wind surfing – Federazione Italiana Vela, viale Brigata Bisagno 2, 16129 Genova, ☎ 010 58 94 31.

Skiing – The Alps offer excellent facilities for both downhill and cross-country skiing. Major ski resorts are shown on the map of Places to Stay at the beginning of this guide. For detailed information on individual resorts, contact Federazione Italiana Sport Invernali, via Piranesi 44, 20137 Milano, ☎ 02 75 731.

Spas – Italy has been well-known for its spa towns since Etruscan times. A holiday in a spa resort provides visitors with a relaxing break in beautiful surroundings, as well as enabling them to benefit from the therapeutic powers of the waters.
Each spa has its own particular characteristics, suitable for specific ailments. For details, contact the National Italian Tourist Office (ENIT) in Rome, via Marghera 2, 00185 Roma, ☎ 06 49 711 *(or see Tourist Information above for local ENIT addresses)*.

Speleology – Società Speleologica Italiana, via Zamboni 61, 40127 Bologna, ☎ 051 25 00 49.

Water-skiing – Federazione Italiana Sci Nautico, via Piranesi 44, 20137 Milano, ☎ 02 76 11 02 40.

Theme Parks

The following is a list of the main theme parks in Italy, which provide a range of amusements and rides for both young and old:

Edenlandia – Viale Kennedy 76, Napoli, ☎ 081 23 99 693. Take exit 10 or 11 off the Naples by-pass, Open June, Mon to Fri, 4-10pm, Sat and Sun, 10.30am-midnight; July and Aug, 5pm-midnight (Sun 10.30am-midnight); Apr and May, Mon to Fri, noon-8pm, Sat and Sun 10.30am-midnight; Oct to Mar Sat and Sun only, 10.30am-midnight. Open over Christmas holidays (times vary). Admission 4 000L; attractions 16 000L.

Fantasy World Minitalia – Via Vittorio Veneto 52, Capriate, ☎ 02 90 90 169. A4 motorway, exit Capriate. Open in the summer 9.30am-7.30pm (Aug until 11pm); the rest of the year until 6pm; from mid-Nov to mid-Mar open Sat-Sun only. 22 000L; 18 000L for children under 1.4m/4.6ft; free for children under 1m/3.28ft.

Fiabilandia – Loc. Rivazzurra di Rimini, ☎ 0541 37 20 64. A4 motorway, exit Rimini sud. Open mid-June to Sept, 10am-midnight; the rest of the year until 6pm. Closed Nov to Easter. 25 000L; 18 000L from 3 yrs to 1.4m/4.6ft.

Gardaland – Castelnuovo del Garda, loc. Ronchi, ☎ 045 64 49 777. A4 motorway, exit Peschiera del Garda or A22 motorway exit Affi. Open from mid-June to mid-Sept, 9am-midnight; the rest of the year until 6pm; Oct Sat-Sun only, 9.30am-6.30pm. Closed Nov to Mar. 36 000L; 31 000L under 10 yrs.

Italia in Miniatura – Via Popilia 239, Viserba (RN), ☎ 0541 73 20 04. A14 motorway, exit Rimini nord. Open July and Aug, 9am-midnight; the rest of the year 9am-dusk. Last admission 2hrs before closing. The attractions open 1hr after and close 1hr before the park and do not operate from Nov to Mar. 22-24 000L depending on time of year, 17-18 000L under 18 and over 65, free for the disabled and children under 1m/3.28ft.

Mirabilandia – Statale Adriatica 16, km 162, Ravenna, ☎ 0544 56 11 11. A14 motorway, exit Ravenna (from the north) or Rimini nord (from the south). Open July, 10am-11pm; Aug, 10am-midnight; the rest of the year, 10am-6pm; Oct open only the first two weekends of the month. Closed Oct to Mar. 34 000L, 27 000L between 1m/3.28ft and 1.5m/4.9ft.

Nature Parks

National nature parks are the ideal destination for holidaymakers more in search of contact with nature than regular tourist pursuits. An excellent website for further information is http://web.ctsviaggi.com/parchionline (in Italian only).

Parco Nazionale del Gran Paradiso – Extends from the Valle d'Aosta to Piedmont. From Turin follow the SS 460. After Rivarolo Canavese, take the Ceresole Reale road or the A5 motorway and the S 47 to Cogne *(see AOSTA)*.

Parco Nazionale dello Stelvio – This includes the Ortles-Cevedale and Valfurva massifs and the Martello, Ultimo, Solda and Trafoi valleys. The park covers the provinces of Bolzano, Trento, Sondrio and Brescia and can be reached via Lombardy on the SS 38 to Bormio, or via Trentino by taking first the motorway, then the SS 43 to Rabbi. For further information, contact the tourist offices of Solda ☎ 0473 61 30 15 or Malè ☎ 0473 90 12 80, or Associazione Turistica Val Martello ☎ 0473 74 45 98.

Parco Nazionale delle Dolomiti Bellunesi – This park runs along the right bank of the Piave river, between Feltre and Belluno, and covers three main mountain ranges: the Vette Feltrine, Monti del Sole and Schiara massif. The park can be reached by taking the SS 50 from Grappa, or the SS 348 from Treviso as far as Feltre. The park authority office is in Feltre, piazzale Zancanaro 1, ☎ 0439 30 42 33.

Parco Naturale della Maremma – The Monti dell'Uccellina is located in the heart of this park. Take the A 12 motorway to Grosseto. After Grosseto, follow signs to Alberese where the visitor centre is located (the tourist office is open from 7.30am-6pm.

Parco Nazionale dei Monti Sibillini – This park comprises a large limestone massif which stretches from the Marches to Umbria. It can be reached from Macerata on the S 78 to Sarnano and Amandola and from Spoleto the Forca di Cerro pass on the S 209, S 320 and S 396 to Norcia. For information on the park, contact the Marche region tourist office: Servizio Turismo della Regione Marche, via Gentile da Fabriano 9, 60125 Ancona, ☎ 071 80 61.

Parco Nazionale del Gran Sasso – *(See ABRUZZO)*. For information on the park, contact the Aquila region tourist office, ☎ 0862 41 08 08.

Parco Nazionale d'Abruzzo – *(See ABRUZZO)*. For information on the park, contact Ufficio di Zona di Pescasseroli, via Consultore 1, ☎ 0863 91955.

Parco Nazionale della Maiella – This can be reached via the A 5 motorway, exits Sulmona, Bussi, Torre de' Passeri and Scafa. For information, contact the park authorities (Ente Parco) at Presidenza della Regione Abruzzo, viale Bovio 425, 65123 Pescara, ☎ 085 74 463.

Parco Nazionale del Circeo – *(See TERRACINA)*.

Parco Nazionale del Cilento e Vallo di Diano – *(See Parco Nazionale del CILENTO E VALLO DI DIANO)*.

Parco Nazionale del Gargano – This park runs along the promontory of the same name and also includes the Tremiti islands. There are visitor centres at San Marco in Lamis, via della Vittoria 64, ☎ 0882 83 32 82 and at Monte Sant'Angelo, loc. Foresta Umbra, ☎ 0884 56 09 44. Information is also available from the Ente Provinciale per il Turismo di Foggia, via E. Perrone 17, ☎ 0881 23 141.

Parco Nazionale del Pollino – This park covers the area around Monte Pollino (2 248m/7 380ft), which is part of the Calabrian Apennine chain. For information, contact Castrovillari tourist office, ☎ 0981 32 591.

Parco Nazionale della Calabria – Situated in the heart of Calabria, this park covers the wooded massifs of Sila and Aspromonte. For information, contact the Ufficio Parco Nazionale della Calabria, viale della Repubblica 26, Cosenza, ☎ 0984 76 760.

Parco Nazionale del Golfo di Orosei, Gennargentu e Asinara – The best base for trips into the park is Nuoro. For information, contact the Ente Provinciale per il Turismo, piazza Italia 19, Nuoro, ☎ 0784 32 307.

Further reading

We list below only a selection of the many books on Italy. Some, which may be out of print, will be available only from libraries.

History and Art

A Concise Encyclopaedia of the Italian Renaissance by J R Hale *(Thames and Hudson)*
A History of Italian Renaissance Art by F Hartt *(Thames and Hudson)*
Architecture of the Italian Renaissance by Peter Murray *(Thames and Hudson)*
Leonardo da Vinci by Martin Kemp, Jane Roberts and Philip Steadman *(Yale University Press)*
Michelangelo by Howard Hibbard *(Penguin)*
Rise and Fall of the House of Medici by Christopher Hibbert *(Penguin)*
Roman Italy by T W Potter *(British Museum Publications Ltd)*
Siena: A City and its History by Judith Hook *(Hamish Hamilton)*
The Art of the Renaissance by Linda and Peter Murray *(Thames and Hudson)*
The Grandeur that was Rome by J C Stobart *(Sidgwick and Jackson)*
The Italian World by J J Norwich *(Thames and Hudson)*
Venetian Painting: A Concise History by John Steer *(Thames and Hudson)*
Villas of Tuscany by H Acton *(Thames and Hudson)*
A Traveller's History of Italy by Valerio Lintner *(The Windrush Press)*
Italy: The Unfinished Revolution by Matt Frei *(Mandarin)*

Travel

D H Lawrence and Italy *(Penguin)*
Guide to Tuscany by Bently *(Penguin)*
Living in Italy by Y M Menzies *(Hale)*
Mediterranean Island Hopping by Dana Facaros and Michael Pauls *(Gentry Books Ltd)*
The Path to Rome by Hilaire Belloc *(Penguin)*
Stones of Florence and Venice by Mary McCarthy *(Penguin)*
Venetian Evenings by James Lees-Milne *(Collins)*
Venice by John Kent *(Viking)*
Under the Tuscan Sun by Frances Mayes *(Bantam Books)*

Food and Wine

Italy: The Beautiful Cookbook
Life beyond Lambrusco (Understanding Italian Fine Wine) by N Belfrage *(Sidgwick and Jackson)*
Traditional Italian Food by L B Birch *(Fontana)*
The Fratelli Camisa Cookery Book by Elizabeth Camisa *(Penguin)*

Fiction

Italian Short Stories by R Trevelyan *(Penguin Parallel Text)*
A Room with a View by E M Forster *(Penguin)*
Where Angels Fear to Tread by E M Forster *(Penguin)*
Sicilian Carousel by Lawrence Durrell *(Faber)*
The Ant Colony by F King *(Flamingo)*
The Leopard by Giuseppe Tomasi di Lampedusa *(Flamingo)*
The Slow Train to Milan by Lisa St Aubin de Teran *(Penguin)*
The Name of the Rose by Umberto Eco *(Vintage)*

Films

See the chapter on CINEMA in the Introduction.

1935 **The Last Days of Pompeii** by Merian C Cooper

1945 **Roma, Città Aperta** (Rome Open City) by Roberto Rossellini

1948 **Ladri di biciclette** (Bicycle Thieves) by Vittorio de Sica

1950 **Domenica d'Agosto** (Sunday in August) by Luciano Emmer

1950 **Francesco, Giullare di Dio** (Francis, God's Jester) by Roberto Rossellini

1950 **September Affair** by William Dieterle (Capri)

1951 **Quo Vadis** by Mervyn Le Roy

1951 **The Little World of Don Camillo** by Julien Duvivier (in a village in the Po Plain). Followed by three sequels featuring Don Camillo and Peppone.

1953 **Roman Holiday** by William Wyler

1955 **Summertime** (Summer Madness) by David Lean

1957 **Le Notti di Cabiria** by Federico Fellini

1959 **Ben Hur** by William Wyler

1960 **Il Bell'Antonio** by Piero Piccioni (Sicily)

1960 **La Dolce Vita** by Federico Fellini

1960 **L'Avventura** by Michelangelo Antonioni (Lipari Islands and Sicily)

1960 **Spartacus** by Stanley Kubrick

1963 **Il Gattopardo** (The Leopard) by Luchino Visconti

1969 **Il Conformista** (The Conformist) by Bernardo Bertolucci

1971 **Death in Venice** by Luchino Visconti

1975 **Cadaveri eccellenti** (Illustrious corpses) by Francesco Rosi

1976 **Novecento** (1900) by Bernardo Bertolucci (Italy 1900-45)

1977 **Un giornata particolare** by Ettore Scola

1978 **L'albero degli zoccoli** (The Tree of Wooden Clogs) by Ermanno Olmi (19C Lombardy)

1979 **Christ stopped at Eboli** by Francesco Rosi (Campania)

1985 **A Room with a View** by James Ivory (Florence and thereabouts)

1987 **Cronica Di Una Morta Annunciata** (Chronicle of a Death Foretold) by Francesco Rosi

1987 **Oci Ciornie** (Black Eyes) by Nikita Mikhalkov

1987 **The Belly of an Architect** by Peter Greenaway (Rome)

1989 **Cinema Paradiso** by Giuseppe Tornatore

1994 **Caro Diario** (Dear Diary) by Gianni Moretti

1994 **Il Postino** (The Postman) by Michael Radford

1997 **La vita è bella** (Life is Beautiful) by Roberto Benigni

Vocabulary

ON THE ROAD AND IN TOWN

a destra	to the right	lavori in corso	men at work
a sinistra	to the left	neve	snow
aperto	open	passaggio a livello	level crossing
autostrada	motorway	passo	pass
banchina	pavement	pericolo	danger
binario	(railway) platform	piazza, largo	square, place
corso.	boulevard	piazzale	esplanade
discesa	descent	stazione	station
dogana	customs	stretto	narrow
fermata	(bus-) stop	uscita	exit, way out
fiume	river	viale	avenue
ingresso	entrance	vietato	prohibited

PLACES AND THINGS TO SEE

abbazia, convento	abbey, monastery	mercato	market
affreschi	frescoes	mura	walls
arazzi	tapestries	navata	nave
arca	monumental tomb	opere	works
biblioteca	library	pala	panel, altarpiece
cappella	chapel	palazzo	palace
casa	house	paliotto	altar frontal
cascata	waterfall	passeggiata	walks, promenade
castello	castle	piano	floor, storey
Cena	The Last Supper	pinacoteca	picture gallery
chiesa	church	pulpito	pulpit
chiostro	cloisters	quadro	picture
chiuso	closed	rivolgersi a	to apply to
città	town	rocca	feudal castle
cortile	courtyard	rovine, ruderi	ruins
dintorni	environs	sagrestia	sacristy
duomo	cathedral	scala	stairway
facciata	façade	scavi	excavations
funivia	cable-car	seggiovia	chair-lift
giardini	gardens	spiaggia	beach
gole	gorges	tesoro	treasure
lago	lake	torre, torazzo	tower
lungomare	seafront promenade	vista	view

COMMON WORDS

yes, no	si, no	goodbye	arrivederci
Sir	Signore	how much?	quanto?
Madam	Signora	where? when?	dove? quando?
Miss	Signorina	where is?	dov'è?
today	oggi	much, little	molto, poco
yesterday	ieri	more, less	più, meno
tomorrow morning	domani mattina	all	tutto, tutti
morning	mattina	large	grande
evening	sera	small	piccolo
afternoon	pomeriggio	dear	caro
please	per favore	the road to...?	la strada per...?
thank you so much	grazie tante	may one visit?	si può visitare?
excuse me	mi scusi	what time is it?	che ora è?
enough	basta	I don't understand	non capisco
good morning	buon giorno	I would like	desidero

NUMBERS

0	zero	16	sedici
1	uno	17	diciasette
2	due	18	diciotto
3	tre	19	diciannove
4	quattro	20	venti
5	cinque	30	trenta
6	sei	40	quaranta
7	sette	50	cinquanta
8	otto	60	sessanta
9	nove	70	settanta
10	dieci	80	ottanta
11	undici	90	novanta
12	dodici	100	cento
13	tredici	1 000	mille
14	quattordici	5 000	cinquemila
15	quindici	10 000	diecimila

GASTRONOMIC GLOSSARY

Caffè corretto: *espresso* laced with brandy or *grappa*

Caffè decaffeinato (caffè "Hag"): decaffeinated coffee

Caffè latte: mainly hot milk, with a splash of coffee

Caffè lungo: coffee which is not quite as strong as *espresso*

Caffè macchiato: *espresso* with a splash of milk

Cannelloni: large pasta tubes filled with a meat or other sauce

Cappellini: very thin spaghetti

Cappuccino (or *cappuccio*): coffee topped with frothy milk and a dusting of cocoa

Cassata: ice cream containing chopped nuts and mixed dried fruit (similar to tutti-frutti)

Crema: vanilla (ice cream)

Farfalle: pasta bow-ties

Fettuccine: slightly narrower, Roman version of tagliatelle

Fior di latte: very creamy variety of ice cream

Fusilli: small pasta spirals

Gnocchi: tiny potato dumplings

Lasagne: sheets of pasta arranged in layers with tomato and meat sauce (or other) and cheese sauce, topped with Parmesan and baked

Maccheroni: small pasta tubes

Panino: type of sandwich (bread roll)

Panna: cream; similar to *fior di latte*

Prosciutto: cured ham

Ravioli: little pasta cushions, enclosing meat or spinach

Schiacciata: type of sandwich (on a pizza-type base)

Spaghetti: the great classic

Stracciatella: chocolate chip (ice cream)

Tagliatelle: long narrow pasta ribbons

Tiramisù: coffee-flavoured frozen gateau *(semifreddo)*

Tortellini: small crescent-shaped pasta rolls filled with a meat or cheese stuffing, often served in a clear meat broth

Tramezzino: type of sandwich (on slices of bread)

Zabaglione: dessert made from egg yolks and Marsala wine

Zuppa inglese: trifle

G. del Magro/SIPA PRESS

Calendar of Events

30 and 31 January
Aosta .... St Orso Fair: craft fair with sale of articles from the Valle d'Aosta.

First two weeks of February
Agrigento .... Almond in bloom festival.

February (Carnival)
Venice .... Events throughout Venice, theatre and concerts.

Viareggio .... Carnival: masked processions; folklore events.

Ivrea .... Folk festival, including the famous battle of the oranges.

Last Friday of carnival
Verona .... "Venerdì gnocolar" procession.

1 April
San Marino .... Investiture of the town regents.

Holy Week (Maundy Thursday and Good Friday)
Taranto .... Holy Week services: procession of Our Lady of Sorrows and the Mysteries.

Easter Day
Florence .... Scoppio del Carro; in the morning, in the Piazza del Duomo, fireworks display from a decorated float – the fireworks are set off by a dove sliding along a wire from the high altar of the Cathedral to the float. Parade in Renaissance costume.

Sulmona .... Feast of the "Madonna che scappa in Piazza".

Wednesday after Easter to the following Sunday
Loreto .... International sacred music festival.

May and June
Florence .... Florentine May music festival; numerous cultural events.

1 May
Cagliari .... Feast of Sant'Efisio.

First Sunday in May
Naples .... Feast of the Miracle of St Januarius inside the cathedral.

First Thursday after 1 May
Assisi .... Calendimaggio (three days)

7 to 9 May
Bari .... Feast of St Nicholas; 7 May – procession, 8 May – Mass and procession along the shore; the statue of the saint is taken out to sea and worshipped.

15 May
Gubbio .... Ceri race.

Penultimate Sunday in May
Sassari .... Cavalcata Sarda.

Last Sunday in May
Gubbio .... Palio della Balestra in Piazza Grande.

Late May – early June
Taormina .... Festival of Sicilian costume and carts.

June – November, even years
Venice .... Biennial Arts Festival.

442

16 and 17 June
Pisa .... Feast of St Ranieri.

24 June and two other days of the month (varies)
Florence .... Calcio Storico Fiorentino: ball game in Piazza Croce, accompanied by procession in 16C costumes; fireworks in the Piazzale Michelangelo.

Penultimate Sunday in June
Arezzo .... Giostra del Saracino – Saracen's Joust.

Last week in June – 1st fortnight in July
Spoleto .... Spoleto Festival; international drama, music and dance festival.

July – August
Perugia .... Umbria Jazz Festival.

Late July to late August
Verona .... Opera season in the Roman amphitheatre.

2 July
Siena .... Palio delle Contrade.

3rd Saturday in July
Venice .... Feast of the Redeemer, on Saturday night, at the Giudecca. Firework display. On Sunday, religious services and regatta.

Last week in August
Ferrara .... Ferrara Buskers Festival.

1st Sunday in August
Ascoli Piceno .... Festa della Quintana; procession of representatives of the various districts, in 15C costumes; joust.

14 August
Sassari .... Feast of the Candles.

16 August
Siena .... Palio delle Contrade.

29 August and previous Sunday
Nuoro .... Feast of the Redeemer.

Late August to early September
Venice .... International Film Festival at the Lido.

1st Sunday in September
Arezzo .... Giostra del Saracino – Saracen's Joust.
Venice .... Historical Regatta on the Grand Canal.

7 September
Florence .... Feast of the Rificolona (coloured paper lanterns); musical and folklore events in the different districts.

8 September
Loreto .... Feast of the Nativity of the Virgin.

2nd Friday, Saturday and Sunday of September in even years
Marostica .... Partita a scacchi.

2nd Sunday in September
Asti .... Festival of the Sagre (*Festival delle Sagre*).
Sansepolcro .... Palio della Balestra; crossbow competition, in medieval costumes.

13 September
Lucca .... Luminara di Santa Croce.

2nd and 3rd Sundays in September
Foligno .... Quintana Games.

19 September
Naples .... Feast of the Miracle of St Januarius, in the cathedral.

3rd Sunday in September
Asti .... Corsa del Palio.

1 October
San Marino .... Investiture of the town's regents.

Night of the 9 to 10 December
Loreto .... Feast of the Translation of the Santa Casa.

S. Chirol

Saracen's Joust, Arezzo

UNESCO World Heritage List

In 1972, the United Nations Educational, Scientific and Cultural Organization (UNESCO) adopted a Convention for the preservation of cultural and natural sites. To date, more than 150 States Parties have signed this international agreement, which has listed over 500 sites "of outstanding universal value" on the World Heritage List. Each year, a committee of representatives from 21 countries, assisted by technical organizations (ICOMOS – International Council on Monuments and Sites; IUCN – International Union for Conservation of Nature and Natural Resources; ICCROM – International Centre for the Study of the Preservation and Restoration of Cultural Property, the Rome Centre), evaluates the proposals for new sites to be included on the list, which grows longer as new nominations are accepted and more countries sign the Convention. To be considered, a site must be nominated by the country in which it is located.

The protected cultural heritage may be monuments (buildings, sculptures, archeological structures etc) with unique historical, artistic or scientific features; groups of buildings (such as religious communities, ancient cities); or sites (human settlements, examples of exceptional landscapes, cultural landscapes) which are the combined works of man and nature of exceptional beauty. Natural sites may be a testimony to the stages of the earth's geological history or to the development of human cultures and creative genius or represent significant ongoing ecological processes, contain superlative natural phenomena or provide a habitat for threatened species.

Signatories of the Convention pledge to co-operate to preserve and protect these sites around the world as a common heritage to be shared by all humanity.

Some of the most well-known places which the World Heritage Committee has inscribed include: Australia's Great Barrier Reef (1981), the Canadian Rocky Mountain Parks (1984), The Great Wall of China (1987), the Statue of Liberty (1984), the Kremlin (1990), Mont-Saint-Michel and its Bay (France, 1979), Durham Castle and Cathedral (1986).

UNESCO World Heritage sites included in this guide are:

Valcamonica cave paintings
Historic centre of Rome, the Vatican City
and San Paolo fuori le Mura
Santa Maria delle Grazie church
and refectory, Milan
Historic centre of Florence
Venice and the Venetian lagoon
Piazza del Duomo, Pisa
Historic centre of San Gimignano
Rock dwellings, Matera
Vicenza and the Palladian villas
Historic centre of Siena
Historic centre of Naples
Crespi d'Adda
The Renaissance city of Ferrara
Castel del Monte
Trulli dwellings, Puglia
Paleo-Christian monuments, Ravenna
Historic centre of Pienza

La Reggia palace and gardens, Vanvitelli
aquaduct and San Leucio buildings, Caserta
Residence of the House of Savoy, Turin
Botanical gardens, Padua
Portovenere, the Cinque Terre and Palmaria,
Tino and Tinetto islands
The Cathedral, Torre Civica
and Piazza Grande, Modena
Pompeii, Herculaneum
and Torre Annunziata
The Amalfi Coast
Agrigento archeological site
Villa Romana del Casale
Su Nuraxi, Barumini
The Cilento region and Vallo di Diano,
the archeological sites of Paestum and Velia,
and Padula Carthusian monastery
Historical centre of Urbino
Aquileia Basilica and archeological site

Admission Times and Charges

The visiting times marked in the text with the **clock-face** ⊘ symbol indicate the normal hours of opening and closing. These are listed here in the same order as they appear in the main text. Sights which have partial or full access for the disabled are indicated by the symbol ♿. The symbol ⬛ after the name of a town indicates the tourist office. Admission times and charges are liable to alteration without prior notice. Due to fluctuations in the cost of living and the constant change in opening times, the information given here should merely serve as a guideline. Visitors are advised to phone ahead to confirm opening times.

Please note that museums, churches or other monuments may be closed without prior notice or may refuse admittance during private functions, religious services or special occasions; they may also stop issuing tickets up to an hour before the actual closing time.

The **admission prices** indicated are for single adults benefiting from no special concession; reductions for children, students, the over 60s and parties should be requested on site and be endorsed with proof of ID. Special conditions often exist for groups but arrangements should be made in advance.

For nationals of European Union member countries, some museums provide free admission to visitors under 18 and over 60 with proof of identification.

During National Heritage Week (*Settimana dei Beni Culturali*), which takes place at a different time each year, access to a large number of sights is free of charge. Contact the tourist offices for more detailed information.

Churches and chapels are usually open from 8am–noon and from 2pm–dusk. Notices outside a number of churches formally request visitors to dress in a manner deemed appropriate when entering a place of worship – this excludes sleeveless and low-cut tops, short miniskirts or skimpy shorts and bare feet.

Visitors are not admitted during services and so tourists should avoid visiting at that time. Visitors are advised to visit churches in the morning, when the natural light provides better illumination of the works of art; also churches are occasionally forced to close in the afternoons due to lack of staff. Works of art are often illuminated by coin-operated lighting (100L, 200L or 500L). When visits to museums, churches or other sites are accompanied by a custodian, it is customary to leave a donation.

Telephone numbers are given here with the area code (*prefisso*): this prefix must now always be used with the number, whether dialling within the city, outside the province or from abroad. If calling from overseas, dial 00 39 + area code + number.

A

ABRUZZO

Il Gran Sasso

Campo Imperatore – Access by cable-car (7min), Oct to May, 8.30am-4.45pm every 30min (except 1.30pm); in summer, 8.30am-5pm every hour; 20 July to 25 Aug, 8.30am-6pm every 30min. 22 000L return ticket (round trip), Sat-Sun and public holidays; 18 000L return ticket (round trip), Mon to Fri. ☎ 0862 60 61 43 or 0862 40 00 07. Access also by car from Fonte Cerreto on the S 17 bis (closed Dec to Apr).

Castelli: Museo delle Ceramiche – Open June to Sept, daily, 10am-7pm; the rest of the year, daily (except Mon), 10am-1pm (Feb to May, Sun and public holidays also open 3-6pm). Guided tours available (40min) in English and Italian. 5 000L (adult), 3 000L (child aged 6-14). ☎ 0861 69 90 14.

Great Plateaux

Pescocostanzo: Santa Maria del Colle – Usually open 8am-noon and 5-7pm. For further information, contact ☎ 0864 64 14 40.

Touring Abruzzo

Alba Fucens

Excavations – Open 9am –1hr before sunset. Apply to Signor Di Mattia. ☎ 0863 23 561.

San Pietro – Apply in advance to Signor Di Mattia. ☎ 0863 23 561.

Bominaco: Churches – Guided tours only. Apply in advance to custodian Signor Cassiani. Donation welcome. ☎ 0862 93 604.

San Giovanni in Venere – Open daily, 7am-7pm. Donation welcome. ☎ 0872 60 132.

AMALFI
corso delle Repubbliche Marinare, 19/21 - ☎ 089 87 11 07

Duomo di Sant'Andrea: Chiostro del Paradiso and **Museo Diocesano** – Open mid-June to mid-Sept, 9am–9pm; Nov to Feb, 10am–12.45pm and 2.30–5.15pm; rest of the year, 9am–7pm. 3 000L. ☎ 089 87 22 03.

Costiera amalfitana

Grotta dello Smeraldo – Access to cave by lift from street above 10am-4pm. 5 000L (lift and tour included). Visit also possible by boat from Amalfi harbour. 10 000L return ticket (round trip), admission not included.

ANAGNI

Cattedrale: crypt – Guided tours only (15min, also in English and French by appointment), Apr to Oct, 9am-1pm and 4-7pm; Nov to Mar, 9am-1pm and 3-6pm. 3 000L, no charge for children under 12. ☎ 0775 72 83 74. www.axa.it/anagni

ANCONA
via Thaon de Revel 4 - ☎ 071 33 249

Duomo di San Ciriaco – Open in summer, 8am-noon and 3-7pm (rest of the year, 6pm). ☎ 071 52 688.

Museo Archeologico Nazionale delle Marche – ⅙ (partial access). Open 8.30am-1.30pm (last admission 1pm). Longer opening hours in summer. Closed 25 Dec, 1 Jan and 1 May. 8 000L, no charge under 18 and over 60. ☎ 071 20 26 02.

Open all year, daily, 8.30am-1.30pm (Sat also 2.40-7.30pm). Longer opening hours in summer. Closed public holidays. 4 000L. Audio-visual presentation. ☎ (071) 20 75 390, 20 26 02.

Galleria Comunale Podesti – Open daily (except Mon pm), 9am-7pm; Sun 3-7pm. Closed public holidays and 4 May. Bookshop. 5 000L,; no charge for children. ☎ 071 22 25 041. www.comune.ancona.it

Excursions

Portonovo: Chiesa di Santa Maria – For admission times apply to the Sopraintendenza office in Ancona. ☎ 071 22 831.

AOSTA
piazza Chanoux 8 - ☎ 0165 23 66 27

Collegiata di Sant'Orso – Open Apr to Sept, daily (except Sun am), 9am-7pm; Oct to May, daily (except Sun am) 10am-5pm. Last admission 30min before closing time. Closed during services ☎ 0165 23 66 27.

Cattedrale: Treasury – ⅙ Open Apr to Sept, daily, 8-11.30am and 3-5.30pm; Oct to Mar, Sun and public holidays only, 8-9.30am, 10.30-11.30am and 3-5.30pm, Mon to Sat, apply to custodian. Guided tours available (30min). 4 000L (adult), 1 500L (child). ☎ 0165 31 361.

Valle d'Aosta

Parco Nazionale del Gran Paradiso – Guided excursions are organised by the Ente Parco Nazionale del Gran Paradiso. For further information, contact the Centro Visitatori office in Noasca ☎ 0124 90 10 70 or the following guiding associations: Cooperativa Habitat, via Aubert 48, Aosta ☎ 0165 36 38 51; Cooperativa Il Roc, via Umberto I 1, Noasca ☎ 0124 90 11 01; Associazione Guide della Natura, piazza Chamoux 40, 11012 Cogne (AO) ☎ 0165 74 282; Associazione Opuntia, Casella Postale 1280, 10100 Torino ☎ 011 66 95 014.

There are a number of information centres in the Park:

Val d'Aosta side: Rhêmes-Notre-Dame (in Chanavery), open daily in summer; the rest of the year Sat-Sun, Christmas and Easter only. Valsavaranche (in Degioz), open daily July and Aug; in June and Sept, Sat-Sun only; open Christmas and Easter. Giardino Botanico Alpino Paradisia, (in Valnontey, Valle di Cogne), open in summer.

Piedmont side: Ronco Canavese (Valle Soana), piazza del Municipio; Ceresole Reale, (in Pian della Balma, Valle Orco); Locana, in the old church of San Francesco (Valle Orco). Centres are open daily in July and Aug; Sat-Sun only in June and September; open Christmas and Easter.

For further information contact the Segreteria Turistica del Parco, c/o Centro Visitatori, Noasca ☎ 0124 90 10 70.

Castello di Fénis: Open Apr to Sept, 9am-7pm, (audioguide available); Oct to Mar, 10am-5pm (last admission 30min before closing time). Closed Christmas and 1 Jan. Guided tours (30min) available in English, French, Spanish and German. 6 000L (adult), no charge for children. ☎ 0165 23 66 27.

Castello di Issogne: Guided tours only every 30min, Apr to Sept, 9am-6.30pm; Oct to Mar, 10am-5pm. 10 000L, no charge under 18 and over 65. ☎ 0125 92 93 73.

AQUILEIA

Basilica: Crypts - Open Apr to Sept, daily, 8.30am-7pm (7.30pm Sun and public holidays); Oct to Mar, daily, 8.30am-12.30pm and 2.30-5.30pm (6pm Sun and public holidays). 3 000L, no charge for children under 10. ☎ 0431 91 067.

Roman ruins - Open 9am-1hr before sunset. Closed 1 Jan, 1 May and 25 Dec. No charge. ☎ 0431 91 016.

Museo Archeologico - Open all year, 9am-2pm. Closed 1 Jan, 1 May and 25 Dec. 8 000 L, no charge under 18 and over 60. ☎ 0431 91 016.

Museo Paleocristiano - Open all year, 9am-2pm. Closed 1 Jan, 1 May and 25 Dec. No charge. ☎ 0431 91 131.

AREZZO   🛈 piazza della Repubblica 28 - ☎ 0575 37 76 78

Casa del Vasari - Open all year, daily (except Tues), 9am-7pm (last admission 6.30pm); Sun and public holidays, 9am-1pm (last admission 12.30pm). Closed 1 May. No charge. ☎ 0575 40901.

Museo Statale d'Arte Medievale e Moderna - Open all year, daily (except Mon), 9am-6.30pm (12.30pm Sun and public holidays). Closed 1 Jan. 8 000L. Interactive audio-visual/multimedia programme available. ☎ 0575 30 03 01.

Museo Archeologico - ♿ (partial access). Open Mon to Sat, 9am-2pm (last admission 1.30pm); Sun and public holidays, 9am-1pm (last admission 12.30pm) Closed 1 Jan, 25 April, 1 May and 25 Dec. Guided tours (2hr) available by appointment. 8 000L; no charge under 18 and over 60. ☎ 0575 20 882.

Promontorio dell'ARGENTARIO

Archeological site: Cosa - Open May to Sept, daily, 9am-7pm; Oct to Apr, daily, 9am-1.30pm. No charge for archeological site. Museum: 4 000L, no charge under 18 and over 60. ☎ 0564 88 14 21.

ASCOLI PICENO   🛈 piazza del Popolo 17 - ☎ 0736 25 30 45

Duomo - Open daily, 7am-12.30pm and 4-7pm. ☎ 0736 25 97 74.

Pinacoteca - ♿ Open 15 June to 15 Sept, Mon to Fri, 9am-1pm and 3-7.30pm; Sat 9am-1pm and 3-7.30pm; Sun and public holidays, 9am-12.30pm and 3.30-7.30pm; 16 Sept to 14 June, daily 9am-1pm (12.30pm Sun and public holidays). Closed 1 Jan, 1 Nov and 25 Dec. Bookshop. 6 000L, 3 000L under 18 and over 60, no charge for children under 13. ☎ 0736 29 82 82.

Museo Archeologico - ♿ Open daily (except Sun and public holidays), 8.30am-1.30pm. 4 000L, no charge under 18 and over 60. ☎ 0736 25 35 62.

Sant'Agostino - Open daily, 7am-12.30pm and 3.30-8pm. For further information, contact the tourist information centre (APT) ☎ 0736 25 52 50.

Santi Vincenzo ed Anastasio - Apply in advance to the tourist information centre. ☎ 0736 25 52 50.

Ponte romano di Solestà - Guided tour (30min). Apply to the tourist information centre at least two days in advance. ☎ 0736 25 52 50.

Excursions

Civitella del Tronto: Fortress - Open in summer 10am-1pm and 3-8pm (Aug open all day until midnight); Apr to June, 10am-1pm and 3-7pm; rest of the year, 10am-1pm and 2.30-5.30pm. Guided tours available (50min). Bookshop. 5 000L (adult), 1 000L (child under 10). ☎ 0861 91 588 or 0337 66 62 21 (mobile).

ASSISI   🛈 piazza del Comune 12 - ☎ 075 81 25 34

Basilica di San Francesco: Treasury and **Perkins Collection** - ♿ Open daily (except Sun), 9.30am-noon and 2-6pm. Closed 15 Aug, 4 Oct and November to March. Guided tours available (45min). Bookshop. 3 000L (adult), 1 500L (student), no charge for children. ☎ 075 81 90 01.

Rocca Maggiore - Open daily, 10am-sunset. 5 000L (adult), 3 500L (child). Bar. ☎ 075 81 52 92.

Oratorio dei Pellegrini - Closed for restoration at time of going to press. Usually open 9am-noon and 3-6pm. For further information, contact ☎ 075 81 22 67.

Excursions

Eremo delle Carceri - Open daily, 6.30am-7.30pm during the summer; the rest of the year, 6.30am-5pm. Guided tours available ☎ 075 81 23 01.

Convento di San Damiano - Open from Easter to early Oct, daily, 10am-12.30pm and 2-6pm; the rest of the year 10am-12.30pm and 2-4.30pm.

Basilica di Santa Maria degli Angeli - Restoration should be completed in August 1999.

Palazzo Trinci - ♿ Open daily (except Mon), 10am-7pm. Guided tours available (1hr) in English, Italian, French and German. Audio-visual presentation. Closed 1 Jan and 25 Dec. Bookshop. 5 000L (adult), no charge for children under 6. ☎ 0742 35 79 89.

ATRI

Cattedrale - Open April to Sept, 8am-noon and 3-7pm; Oct to Dec, 8am-noon and 3-6pm; rest of the year, 8am-noon and 3-4pm. Closed during services. Donation welcome. ☎ 085 87 286.

Excursions

San Clemente al Vomano - Apply to ☎ 085 89 81 28. Donation welcome.

B

BARI
🛈 piazza Aldo Moro 32/a - ☎ 080 52 42 244

Castello - ♿ (partial access). Open all year, daily (except Mon and Sun pm), 9am-1pm and 3.30-7pm (last admission 30min before closing time). Closed 1 Jan, 1 May and 25 Dec. Guided tours (1hr). 4 000L.; no charge under 18 and over 60. ☎ 080 52 86 200. www.castelli-puglia.org

Pinacoteca - ♿ Open all year, daily (except Mon), 9.30am-1pm and 4-7pm; Sun, 9am-1pm. Closed Mon, weekday public holidays and 8 May. Bar and bookshop. 5 000L, 1 000 (students and over 60). ☎ 080 54 12 423.

Museo Archeologico - Closed for reorganisation.

BARLETTA
🛈 via Ferdinando d'Aragona 95 - ☎ 0883 33 13 31

Pinacoteca - Open May to Sept, daily (except Mon), 9am-1pm and 4-7pm; Oct to Apr, daily (except Mon), 9am-1pm and 3-7pm. Guided tours (1hr, also in English and French). 5 000L (adult), 2 000L (child aged 12-18), no charge under 12 and over 60.

BASSANO DEL GRAPPA
🛈 largo Corona d'Italia 35 - ☎ 0424 52 43 51

Museo Civico - Open daily (except Mon), 9am-6.30pm; Sun and public holidays, 3.30-6.30pm. Guided tours available (1hr 30min) in Italian, by appointment (charge). Bookshop. 8 000L. ☎ 0424 52 22 35; www.x-land.it/MuseoBassano

Excursions

Possagno

Canova's birthplace and Gipsoteca - ♿ (partial access) Open May to Sept, daily (except Mon), 9am-noon and 3-6pm (7pm Sun and public holidays); Oct to Apr, daily (except Mon), 9am-noon and 2-5pm. Open Mon public holidays. Closed 1 Jan, Easter and Christmas. Guided tours available (1hr). 5 000L (adult) 4 000L (child). ☎ 0423 54 43 23.

Tempio di Canova - Open May to Sept, daily (except Mon), 9am-noon and 3-6pm (7pm Sun); Oct to Apr, daily (except Mon), 9am-noon and 2-5pm. Open Mon public holidays. Closed during services. 3 000L admission to the dome. ☎ 0423 54 40 21.

BELLUNO
🛈 piazza dei Martiri 8 - ☎ 0437 90 00 83

Museo Civico - Open from second Tues in Apr to Sept, daily (except Mon), Tues to Sat, 10am-noon and 4-7pm; Sun and public holidays, 10.30am-12.30pm; rest of the year, daily (except Sun and public holidays), 10am-noon and 3-6pm, Mon and Sat, 10am-noon. Closed 1 May, 15 Aug and 11 Nov. 4 000L (adult), 2 000L (child over 6), no charge (child under 6). ☎ 0437 94 48 36.

Excursions

Feltre: Museo Civico - Open daily (except Mon), Apr to Sept, 10am-1pm and 4-7pm; Oct to Mar, daily (except Mon), 10am-1pm and 3-6pm. Closed 1 Jan, Easter, 1 May, 8 Dec and 25 Dec. 8 000L (adult), 3 000L (child aged 9-14), no charge (under 8). ☎ 0439 88 52 42. www.comune.feltre.bl.it

BENEVENTO
🛈 piazza Roma - ☎ 0824 31 99 38

Teatro Romano - Open 9am-1hr before sunset. 4 000L.

BENEVENTO

Santa Sofia – Open year-round, daily, 7.30-11am; also in summer, 5.30-7.30pm; the rest of the year for further information enquire at church ☎ 0824 81 206.

Museo del Sannio – ♿ Open daily (except Mon) 9am-1pm. Closed 1 Jan, Easter, 25 and 26 Dec. Bookshop. 5 000L (adult), 2 000L (under 14 and over 60). ☎ 0824 21 818.

BERGAMO   🖪 vicolo Aquila Nera 2 – ☎ 035 24 22 26

Palazzo della Ragione: Tower – Open May to mid-Sept, daily, 10am-8pm (10pm Sat); mid-Sept to Oct, daily, 9.30am-12.30pm and 2.30-7pm (Sat-Sun 10am-7pm); Nov to Feb, open Sat-Sun and public holidays only, 10.30am-12.30pm and 2-4pm; the rest of the year, daily (except Mon and Tues) 10.30am-12.30pm and 4-6pm. 2 000L (adult), 1 000L (under 18), no charge (under 5 and over 65). ☎ (035) 24 22 26. www.apt.bergamo.it

Cappella Colleoni – Open March to Oct, daily, 9am-12.30pm and 2-6pm; Nov to Feb, daily (except Mon), 9.30am-12.30pm and 2-4.30pm. Closed 1 Jan and 25 Dec. Audio-guided tours available. Bookshop. No charge.

Basilica di Santa Maria Maggiore – Open daily, 9am-12.30pm and 2.30-6.30pm; Sun 9-11am and 3-6pm. ☎ 035 22 33 27.

Via Bartolomeo Colleoni Nos 9 and 11 – Open by appointment only. Apply a few days in advance to ☎ 035 21 71 85.

Accademia Carrara – ♿ Open all year, daily (except Tues), 9.30am-12.30pm and 2.30-5.30pm (last admission 30min before closing time). Closed public holidays. Bookshop. 5 000L, no charge on Sun and for visitors under 18 and over 60. ☎ 035 39 96 43. www.accademiacarrara.bergamo.it

Excursions

Brembo di Dalmine: Museo del Presepio – ♿ Open Dec and Jan, daily, 2-6pm and public holidays, 9am-noon and 2-7pm; the rest of the year, open Sun and public holidays only, 2-6pm by appointment. 6 000L (adult), 4 000L (child). ☎ 035 56 33 83.

BOLOGNA   🖪 piazza Maggiore 6 – ☎ 051 23 96 60

Palazzo Comunale – ♿ Open when rooms are not in use. No charge. For information ☎ 051 20 31 11 or 051 20 30 40.

Collezioni comunali d'arte – ♿ (partial access). Open all year, daily (except Mon), 10am-6pm. Closed 1 Jan and 25 Dec. 8 000L, no charge for child under 14. ☎ 051 20 36 29. www.comune.bologna.it/cultura/museicivici/

Museo Morandi – ♿ Open all year, daily (except Mon), 10am-6pm. 8 000L, 4 000L (under 18 and over 60). Guided tours (1hr 30min) in English, French and Italian; audio-guided tours in English and Italian. ☎ 051 20 36 46. www.comune.bologna.it/bologna1/Cultura/Museicomun/Morandi

Palazzo del Podestà, Palazzo di Re Enzo – The interior is open only during exhibitions and special events. For information, contact ☎ 051 23 96 60.

Museo Civico Archeologico – ♿ Open Tues to Fri, 9am-2pm; Sat-Sun, 9am-1pm and 3.30-7pm. Closed Mon except public holidays and public holidays. 8 000L, no charge for child under 14. Guided tours (1hr 30min) available. ☎ 051 23 38 49. www.comune.bologna.it/bologna/Musei/Archeologico/

Palazzo dell'Archiginnasio (Teatro Anatomico) – ♿ (partial access). Open daily (except Sun), 9am-1pm. Closed public holidays and Aug (not every year). No charge. Audio-visual presentation. ☎ 051 23 64 88.

Torre degli Asinelli – Open daily, 9am-6pm (5pm in winter). 3 000L. ☎ 051 49 10 71.

San Giacomo Maggiore: frescoes – Guided tours daily, 10.30am-noon and 3.30-5pm; Sun and public holidays, 9.45-11am and 3.30-5pm. Donation welcome. ☎ 051 22 59 70.

Pinacoteca Nazionale – Open daily (except Monday), 9am-2pm (1pm Sun). Closed public holidays. 8 000L, no charge (under 18 and over 60). ☎ 051 24 32 22.

Museo d'Arte Industriale e Galleria Davia Bargellini – ♿ (partial access). Open daily (except Mon), 9am-2pm (1pm Sun). Closed public holidays and weekday holidays. No charge. ☎ 051 23 67 08.

Basilica di Santo Stefano – Open 9am-noon (12.45pm Sun) and 3.30-6pm (6.30pm Sun). ☎ 051 22 32 56.

Museo Civico Medievale – ♿ Open Mon to Fri, 9am-2pm, Sat-Sun, 9am-1pm and 3.30-7pm. Closed Tues, 25 Dec and 1 Jan. 8 000L, no charge child under 14. Bookshop. ☎ 051 20 39 30. www.comune.bologna.it/cultura/museicivici/

BOLSENA

Santa Cristina – Open daily, Apr to Oct, 7.15am–12.30pm and 3.30–8pm; Nov to Mar, 7.15am–12.30pm and 3–6pm. 5 000L, 2 500L child. Guided tours of the Grotto only, every 30min from 9.30-11.30am and 3pm-1hr before closing time. Book at least one week ahead. ☎ 0761 79 90 67.

BOLZANO
🛈 piazza Parrochia 11 – ☎ 0471 99 38 08

Museo Archeologico dell'Alto Adige – ♿ Open daily (except Mon), 10am-6pm, (8pm Thurs); last admission 1hr before closing time. Closed 1 Jan, 1 May and 25 Dec. 10 000L (adult), 5 000L (student under 27 and senior over 60), no charge (child under 6). Family pass 20 000L (parents and children under 14). Cafeteria. Bookshop. ☎ 0471 98 20 98 or 0471 98 25 76. www.iceman.it

Chiesa dei Dominicani – Open daily, 9.30am–5.30pm. Donation welcome. ☎ 0471 97 31 33.

Chiesa dei Francescani – Open daily, 10am–noon and 2.30–6pm. Donation welcome. ☎ 0471 97 72 93.

Riviera del BRENTA

Villa boat trip – The "Burchiello" excursion runs from late Mar to late Oct and follows the old 18C transport route along the river.
Departure from Padua (Piazzale Boschetti) on Wed, Fri and Sun at 8.15am and arrival in Venice (Piazza San Marco) in late pm including visits to Villa Pisani, Villa Widmann (also known as Barchessa Valmerana) and Villa Foscari (known as *La Malcontenta*). Departure from Venice (Pontile della Pietà) on Tues, Thur and Sat at 9am; same programme but visits in reverse order. Arrival in Padua in late pm.
120 000L, 70 000L (6–17 years old), no charge (child under 6).
For information, contact New Siamic Express S.r.l. ☎ 049 66 09 44.

Villa Pisani – Open summer, daily, 9am–6pm; winter, daily, 9am-4pm. Closed 1 Jan, 1 May and 25 Dec. 5 000L (park only), 10 000L (park and villa), no charge (under 18 and over 60). ☎ 049 50 20 74.

Villa Widmann Foscari – Open June to Sept, daily (except Mon), 10am-6pm, Sun and public holidays, 10am-7pm; May, 10am-5pm, Sun and public holidays, 10am-6pm; Oct, 10am-5pm, Sun and public holidays, 10am-6pm. ☎ 041 42 41 56 or 041 56 09 350.

Villa Foscari *La Malcontenta* – Open April to mid-Nov, Tues and Sat, 10am-noon. Closed Mon. 12 000L. Other days, book ahead by phone ☎ 041 52 03 966 or fax 041 27 70 204. 15 000L.

BRESCIA
🛈 corso Zanardelli 34 – ☎ 030 43 418

Pinacoteca Tosio Martinengo – ♿ (partial access). Open June to Sept, daily (except Mon), 10am–5pm; Oct to May, daily (except Mon), 9.30am–1pm and 2.30–5pm. 5 000 L, no charge (under 16 and over 65). Guided tours available (30min) in English, French, German and Spanish. Closed 1 Jan, 25 Dec and 31 Dec pm. Audio-visual programme. Bookshop. ☎ 030 29 77 834.

Museo della Città in Santa Giulia – ♿ (partial access) Open in summer, daily (except Mon), 10am-8pm; rest of the year, 10am-6pm. Closed 1 Jan, Tues after Easter Monday, 25 Dec and 31 Dec pm. 10 000 L, no charge under 16 and over 65. Guided tours (30min) in English, French, German and Spanish. Audio-visual presentation. Bar. Bookshop. ☎ 030 29 77 834.

Museo delle Armi Luigi Marzoli – Same admission times and charges as Pinacoteca Tosio Martinengo.

BRESSANONE
🛈 viale Stazione 9 – ☎ 0472 83 64 01

Museo Diocesano – Open daily (except Mon), 10am–5pm. Closed Nov and Feb to mid-Mar. Bookshop. 8 000L, 4 000L child. ☎ 0472 83 05 05.

Excursions

Plose: Panorama of the Dolomites – From the village of Sant'Andrea, southeast of Bressanone, cable-car to Valcroce (operates in winter and July to Sept), then chair-lift to Plose (operates in winter only). For further information, apply to Associazione Turistica di Bressanone. ☎ 0472 83 64 01, or to Società Funivia Plose ☎ 0472 20 04 33.

Abbazia di Novacella – Guided tours only (church, cloisters, pinacoteca and library) at 10am, 11am, 2pm, 3pm and 4pm; Nov to Easter in the morning only. Closed Sun and public holidays. 6 500L. ☎ 0472 83 61 89. www.kloster-neustift.it

BRINDISI
🛈 lungomare Regina Margherita – ☎ 0831 52 30 72

Museo Archeologico F. Ribezzo – Open all year, daily except Sat-Sun, 9.30am–1.30pm; on Tues, also 3.30–6.30pm. No charge. When temporary exhibitions are held, only part of the museum's permanent collections is on view. ☎ 0831 56 54 01.

CALABRIA

Palmi: Museo Comunale – Open Mon to Fri, 8.30am–1.30pm and 3.30–5.30pm. Closed Thurs pm, Sat, Sun and public holidays. Guided tours available (2hr). 3 000L. ☎ 0966 26 22 50.

Altomonte: Museo Civico – ♿ (partial access). Open Apr to Oct, daily, 8am-8pm; Nov to Mar, daily, 10am-1pm and 4-7pm. 3 000L (adult) 1 000L (child). ☎ 0981 94 82 16. www.diemme.it/altomonte

Paola: Santuario – Open Apr to Sept, daily, 6am-1pm and 2-8pm; Oct to Mar, daily, 6am-1pm and 2-5.30pm. Guided tours. No charge. ☎ 0982 58 36 95.

Rossano: Museo Diocesano – Open May to Sept, daily (except Mon), Tues to Sat, 9am-1pm and 4.30-8pm, Sun, 9.30am-1pm and 4.30-7pm; Oct to Apr, daily (except Mon), Tues to Sat, 9.30am-noon and 4-6pm, Sun, 10am-noon and 4.30-6pm. Guided tours available (20min) in English, Italian and French. Audio-visual presentation. 2 000L (with guide 4 000L). ☎ 0983 52 52 63.

Sibari

Museo Archeologico – ♿ Open all year, daily, 9am-7pm (last admission 6.30pm). Closed first and third Monday of every month, 1 Jan, 1 May and 25 Dec. Audio-guided tour available. 4 000L, no charge (child). ☎ 0981 79 392.

Parco Archeologico della Sibaritide – Open all year, daily, 9am-7pm (last admission 6.30). Closed 1 Jan, 1 May and 25 Dec. No charge. ☎ 0981 79 166.

Stilo: La Cattolica – ♿ (partial access). Open all year, daily, 8am-8pm. Guided tours available (30min). Bar. Bookshop. No charge. ☎ 0964 77 50 31. www.calnet.it/territorio/comuni/stilo/welcome.htm

Val CAMONICA

Parco Nazionale delle Incisioni Rupestri di Naquane – ♿ (partial access). Open Tues to Fri, 8.30am-6pm; Sat, 8.30-4pm; Sun and public holidays 9am-5.30pm. 8 000L, no charge (under 18). Guided tours available (2hr) in English, Italian and German. Bookshop. ☎ 0364 42 140.

Riserva Naturale delle Incisioni Rupestri di Ceto, Cimbergo e Paspardo – ♿ (partial access). Open all day. Closed 1 Jan and 25 Dec. 3 000L. Guided tours available (3hr-all day) in English, Italian, German and French. ☎ 0364 43 34 465.

Museo di Nadro – ♿ (partial access). Open daily, 9am-noon and 2-5pm. 3 000L. Guided tours (3hr-all day) in English, Italian, German, French. Closed 1 Jan and 25 Dec. ☎ 0364 43 34 65.

Palazzo Farnese di CAPRAROLA

Open 16 Apr to 15 Sept, Tues to Sun, 9am–7.30pm; Mar to 15 Apr and 16 Sept to end Oct, 9am–5.30pm; Nov to Feb, 9am–4.30pm. Last admission 1hr before closing time. Closed Mon except Easter Mon, 1 Jan, 1 May and 25 Dec. 4 000L, no charge (under 18 and over 60). ☎ 0761 64 60 52.

Isola di CAPRI   🛈 piazza Umberto 1, 19 – ☎ 081 83 70 686

Grotta Azzurra – Boat trip and visit to the cave all year, daily (except at high tide and when the sea is rough), 9am–one hour before sunset. 1hr. 7 500L (small boat), 8 000L (entrance to grotto) Excursion from Marina Grande: 23 500L (including trip by fast boat, small boat and grotto). Prices may be increased by 700L (small boat) and 1 000L (fast boat) on public holidays.

Tour of the Isle – Boat trip all year, daily (except when the sea is rough). Departure from Marina Grande at 9.30am. About 2hr. Mon to Sat, 19 000L (plus 15 500L to visit the Blue Grotto); Sun and public holidays, 20 000L (plus 16 200L to visit the Blue Grotto).

Villa Jovis – Open all year, 9am to one hour before sunset. 4 000L, no charge under 18 and over 60, in May during heritage week and in December during museum week. ☎ 081 83 70 381.

Certosa di San Giacomo – ♿ (partial access). Open all year, Tues to Sun, 9am–2pm. Closed Mon and public holidays. No charge. ☎ 081 83 76 218.

Villa San Michele (Anacapri) – ♿ (partial access). Open May to Sept, 9am–6pm; Mar, 9.30am–4.30pm; Apr and Oct, 9.30am–5pm; Nov to Feb, 10.30am–3.30pm. 6 000L, no charge (child under 10). ☎ 081 83 71 401. www.caprionline.com/axelmunthe

Monte Solaro (Anacapri) – Closed for maintenance. The cable-car usually operates daily (except Tues, Nov to Feb), 9am-1hr before sunset. Children under 11 not admitted. Bar. 7 000L return ticket (round trip). ☎ 081 83 71 428.

CAPUA
🛈 piazza Giudici 4 - ☎ 0823 96 13 22

Duomo – Open daily, 8am-noon and 5-7.30pm, Sunday morning only.

Museo Campano – Open daily (except Mon), 9am-1.30pm (1pm Sun). Closed public holidays. 8 000L, no charge (under 18 and over 60). Guided tours available (1hr 30min). Audio-visual presentation. ☎ 0823 96 14 02.

Excursions

Basilica di Sant'Angelo in Formia – Open daily, 10am- 4pm. If closed, contact the custodian or enquire at ☎ 0823 96 00 69.

Santa Maria Capua Vetere

Anfiteatro Campano – Open daily (except Mon), 9am to 2hrs before sunset. Closed 1 Jan, 1 May and 25 Dec. 4 000L (adult), no charge (under 18 and over 60). ☎ 0823 79 88 64.

Mitreo – For information, contact the amphitheatre. ☎ 0823 79 88 64.

Museo Archeologico dell'Antica Capua – ♿ Open daily (except Mon), 9am-6pm. Closed 1 Jan, 1 May and 25 Dec. 4 000L (adult), no charge (under 18 and over 60). ☎ 0823 84 42 06.

CARRARA

Excursions

Sarzana: Fortezza di Sarzanello – Open Sat-Sun and public holidays, 3-6pm. Guided tours available (1hr) in English, French and German. 4 000L (adult), 3 000L (child). ☎ 0187 61 42 90.

Abbazia di CASAMARI

Guided tours only, daily (except Sun morning), 9am-noon and 3-6pm. Book three days in advance at Abbazia cistercense di Casamari, 03020 Casamari. ☎ 0775 28 23 71.

La Reggia di CASERTA
🛈 corso Trieste 39 (ang. piazza Dante) - ☎ 0823 32 11 37

Palazzo – Open daily (except Mon), 9am-2pm (in summer, also open afternoons and evenings; visitors are advised to phone for information). Closed 1 Jan, 1 May and 25 Dec. 8 000L, no charge (under 18 and over 60). Guided tours available (1hr). ☎ 0823 27 71 11.

Park – ♿ Open daily (except Mon), 9am-1hr before sunset. Closed 1 Jan, 1 May and 25 Dec. 4 000L, no charge (under 18 and over 60). ☎ 0823 27 71 11.

English Garden – Guided tours only every hr from 10.30am-5.30pm. Closed Mon.

Excursions

Caserta vecchia: Cattedrale – Open daily, 9am-1pm and 3.30-6.30pm (summer 7.30pm). ☎ 0823 37 13 18.

CASTELFRANCO VENETO

Casa Natale di Giorgione – ♿ Open daily (except Mon), 9am-noon and 3-6pm. Closed 1 Jan, Easter, 15 Aug, 25 and 26 Dec. 2 500L, 1 500L child. Audio-visual presentation. ☎ 0423 49 12 40.

CASTELLAMMARE DI STABIA
🛈 piazza Matteotti 34/35 - ☎ 081 87 11 334

Antiquarium – Closed for restoration. For information, contact ☎ 081 14 541.

Roman villas – Open all year, daily, 9am-2hrs before sunset. Closed 1 Jan, 1 May and 25 Dec. No charge. ☎ 081 87 14 541.

CASTELLI ROMANI

Villa Aldobrandini – Gardens open daily (except Sat-Sun), in summer, 9am-1pm and 3-6pm; rest of the year, 9am-noon and 3-5pm. Closed public holidays. Book in advance (even on day of visit) at the tourist office, piazza Marconi 1. ☎ 06 94 20 311.

CERVETERI

Necropoli della Banditaccia – Open daily (except Mon), 9am-sunset. Closed 1 Jan, 1 May and 25 Dec. 8 000L, no charge (under 18 and over 60). Guided tours available (2hr). ☎ 06 99 40 001.

Tour around Lake Bracciano

Bracciano: Castello Orsini-Odescalchi – Guided tours only (1hr), Tues to Fri, every hour from 10am-noon and 3-5pm (summer 6pm); Sat-Sun and public holidays, every 30min from 9am-noon (summer 12.30pm) and 3-5pm (summer 6.30pm). Closed Monday (except Aug),1 Jan and 25 Dec. 11 000L. ☎ 06 99 80 43 48.

CHIAVENNA

Collegiata di San Lorenzo: Baptistery and Treasury: ♿ Open Mar to Oct, Tues to Sat, 10am–noon and 3-6pm, Sun and public holidays, 2-6pm; Nov to Feb, Tues to Fri, 2-5pm, Sat, 10am–noon and 2-5pm, Sun and public holidays, 2-6pm. 6 000L, 3 000L (child) Guided tours available (30min) ☎ 0343 37 152.

Giardino botanico e archeologico – Open in summer, daily (except Mon), 2-6pm, Sun, also 10am–noon; in winter, daily (except Mon), 2-5pm, Sun, also 10am–noon. 3 000L, no charge (under 15 and over 65). ☎ 0343 33 795. Guided tours in English, French, Italian and German by appointment with the tourist information centre in Chiavenna. ☎ 0343 33 442.

CHIETI
🛈 via Spaventa 29 (palazzo Inail) – ☎ 0871 63 640

Museo Archeologico Nazionale d'Abruzzo – ♿ Open all year, daily, 9am-7pm (last admission 6.30pm). Closed 1 Jan, 1 May and 25 Dec. 8 000L, no charge (under 18 and over 60). ☎ 0871 33 16 68; www.udanet.abruzzo.it/museo

Excursions

San Clemente a Casauria – Open all year, daily, 8am-6pm. Guided tours available Mon to Fri, 8.30am-1.30pm and 3-5.30pm. ☎ 085 88 85 828.

CHIUSI
🛈 piazza Duomo 1 – ☎ 0578 22 76 67

Museo Archeologico and Etruscan tombs – Open May to Oct, daily, 9am-8pm; Nov to Apr, daily, 9am-2pm (1pm Sun and public holidays). Last admission 30min before closing time. Closed 1 Jan, 1 May and 25 Dec. 8 000L, no charge (under 18 and over 60). Guided tours available in English, Italian, French and German; contact Chiusi tourist office. Audio-visual presentation. ☎ 0578 20 177.

Museo della Cattedrale – Open June to mid-Oct, daily, 9.30am-12.45pm and 4.30-7pm; rest of the year, Mon to Sat, 9.30am-12.45pm, Sun and public holidays 9.30-12.45pm and 4-7pm. Closed Easter and 25 Dec. 3 000L (museum), 4 000L (Etruscan tombs, guided tour only, 45min), no charge (child under 10). Guided tours of the museum in Italian, also in English, French and German by appointment. ☎ 0578 22 64 90.

Parco Nazionale del CILENTO

Velia: Roman ruins – Open all year, daily, 9am to 1hr before sunset. Closed 1 Jan, 1 May and 25 Dec. 4 000L. ☎ 0974 97 23 96.

Capo Palinuro: boat trips – Apr to Oct, daily, 9am-6pm. 2hr. 20 000L (adult), 10 000L (child). ☎ 0974 93 82 94.

Certosa di Padula – Open Apr to Oct, daily, 9am-6.30pm; Nov to Mar, 9am-4.30pm. 4 000L (adult), no charge (under 18 and over 60). ☎ 0975 77 745. www.general.it/arte/certosa.html

Grotte di Pertosa – Guided tour Apr to Sept, daily, every hour from 9am-7pm; Oct to Mar, daily, 9am-4pm. 10 000L (short tour), 15 000L (long tour, recommended). ☎ 0975 39 70 37.

Persano WWF Oasis – ♿ (partial access). June to Sept, guided tours only (2hr), daily at 9am and 5pm; Oct to Mar, at 10am, 11am and 3pm. Book at least one day ahead. Audio-visual presentation. Bar, restaurant. Bookshop. 10 000L (adult), 5 000L (child). ☎ 0828 97 46 84.

CIVIDALE DEL FRIULI
🛈 corso d'Aquileia 10 – ☎ 0432 73 14 61

Duomo: Museo Cristiano – ♿ Open Apr to Oct, daily, 9.30am–noon and 3-7pm (6pm Nov to Mar), public holidays 3-7pm only, (6pm Nov to Mar). No charge. ☎ 0432 73 04 03.

Museo Archeologico Nazionale – ♿ Open in summer, daily, 9am-7pm (1.30pm Mon); in winter, daily, 8.30am-2pm (last admission 1.30pm). Closed 1 Jan, 1 May and 25 Dec. 4 000L, no charge (under 18 and over 60). ☎ 0432 70 07 00.

Tempietto – Open daily, Apr to Oct, 9am-1pm and 3-6.30pm; Nov to Mar, 10am-1pm and 3.30-5.30pm. 4 000L, 2 000L (student and over 60), no charge (under 10). Audio-guided tours available. ☎ 0432 70 08 67.

CIVITAVECCHIA
🛈 viale Garibaldi 42 – ☎ 0766 25 348

Museo Nazionale Archeologico – Open all year, daily (except Mon), 9am-2pm. Closed public holidays. No charge. ☎ 0766 23 604.

Terme di Traiano – Open by appointment only. Apply at least 2 days in advance to the Museo Nazionale Archeologico di Civitavecchia. ☎ 0766 23 604.

COMO
🛈 piazza Cavour 17 – ☎ 031 26 97 12

Villa Olmo: Open all year, daily (except Sun), 9am–noon and 3-6pm. ☎ 031 25 24 43.

CONEGLIANO

via Colombo 45 - ☎ 0438 21 230

Duomo – Open 9am-noon and 3-6pm.

Castello – Open Apr to Sept, Tues to Sun, 10am-12.30pm and 3.30-7pm (in Aug, Fri and Sat also 9-10.30pm); Oct to Mar, Tues to Sun, 10am-12.30pm and 3.30-6pm. Closed Mon (except public holidays), in Nov (except public holidays) and the Tues after a public holiday Mon. 3 000L, 2 000L (child 6-14). ☎ 0438 22 871.

CORTINA D'AMPEZZO

piazzetta S. Francesco 8 - ☎ 0436 32 31

Tondi di Faloria – Cable-car service from Via Ria di Zeto to Faloria. From Faloria to Tondi di Faloria: in winter, "Tondi" ski-lift and "Girilada" chairlift; in summer, a jeep service operates.

Tofana di Mezzo – "Freccia nel Cielo" cable-car 40 000L return ticket (round trip).

Pocol Belvedere – Hourly bus service from Piazza Roma from 1 Dec to Easter and 15 July to 15 Sept.

CORTONA

via Nazionale 42 - ☎ 0575 63 03 52

Museo Diocesano – ♿ (partial access). Open daily (except Mon), Apr to Sept, 9.30am-1pm and 3.30-7pm; Oct to Mar, 10am-1pm and 3-5pm. Closed 1 Jan and 25 Dec. 8 000L, 1 000L (child). Guided tours available through the tourist office.

Museo dell'Accademia Etrusca – Open daily (except Mon), Apr to Sept, 10am-7pm; Oct to Mar, 9am-1pm and 3-5pm (Sat-Sun 7pm). Closed 1 Jan and 25 Dec. 8 000L. Guided tours (1hr) available in English and Italian. Bookshop. ☎ 0575 63 72 35 or 0575 63 04 15; www.accademia-etrusca.net

CREMONA

piazza del Comune 5 - ☎ 0372 23 233

Torrazzo – Open in summer, Mon to Sat, 10.30am-noon and 3-6pm, Sun and public holidays, 10.30am-12.30pm and 3-7pm; in winter by appointment. 6 000 L, 3 000L (child). Bookshop. ☎ 0330 73 58 35.

Palazzo Comunale – ♿ Open all year, Tues to Sat, 8.30am-6pm; Sun and public holidays, 10am-6pm. Closed 1 Jan, 1 May and 25 Dec. 10 000L. Guided tours available (2hr). Bookshop. ☎ 0372 40 72 50.

Museo Civico Ala Ponzone – Open all year, Tues to Sat, 8.30am-6pm; Sun and public holidays, 10am-6pm. Closed 1 Jan, 1 May and 25 Dec. 10 000L. Guided tours available (3hr) in English, Italian, French and German by appointment. Bookshop. ☎ 0372 46 18 85.

Stradivarius museum – ♿ (partial access) Open all year, Tues to Sat, 8.30am-6pm; Sun and public holidays, 10am-6pm. Closed 1 Jan, 1 May and 25 Dec. 10 000L. Guided tours available (2hr) in English, Italian, French and German by appointment. Audio-visual presentation. Bookshop. ☎ 0372 46 18 86.

CROTONE

via Torino 148 - ☎ 0962 23 185

Museo Archeologico – Open all year, daily, 9am-7pm. Closed when preparations for exhibitions are in progress. No charge. ☎ 0962 20 179.

CUMA

Acropoli – Open 9am-2hr before sunset. Closed 1 May. 4 000L, no charge (under 18 or over 60). ☎ 081 85 43 060.

D

DOLOMITI

Val Pusteria: Castello di Rodengo – Guided tours only (1hr) from May to mid-Oct at 11am and 3pm, in summer also at 4pm. 6 000L.

Brunico: Ethnography museum – ♿ (partial access). Open Easter to Oct, daily (except Mon) 9.30am-5.30pm, Sun and public holidays 2-6pm only. Closed from Nov to Easter. 5 000L (adult), no charge (child under 12). Audio-visual presentation. Bar, restaurant and bookshop. ☎ 0474 55 20 87.

Tre Cime di Lavaredo: Toll-road – 30 000L return ticket (round trip) by car.

Pieve di Cadore: Titian museum – Open 20 June to mid-Sept, daily (except Mon), 9.30am-12.30pm and 4-7pm; the rest of the year by appointment. 2 500L (adult), 1 500L (reduction). Apply to Magnifica Comunità del Cadore ☎ 0435 31 644.

E

Isola d'ELBA

calata Italia 26, Portoferraio - ☎ 0565 91 46 71

Portoferraio: Museo Napoleonico – Open daily, in summer, 9am-7.30pm (last admission 7pm); in winter, 9am-4.30pm (last admission 4pm). Closed 1 Jan, Easter and 1 May. 8 000L, no charge (under 18 and over 60). Ticket also valid for Villa Napoleone di San Martino, same admission times and charges. ☎ 0565 91 58 46.

Monte Capanne – Cable-car **(cabinovia)** operates from Easter to Oct, 10am–12.15pm and 2.30–6pm (6.30pm in July, Aug). Closed Nov to Easter. 20 000L, 12 000L (child) return ticket (round trip). ☎ 0565 90 10 20.

Marciana: Museo archeologico – Closed at time of going to press. For information, contact ☎ 0565 90 12 15.

San Martino: Villa Napoleone – Same admission times and charges as Museo Napoleonico. ☎ 0565 91 58 46.

ERCOLANO

Excavations – ♿ (partial access). Open 9am–2hr before sunset. Closed 1 Jan, 1 May and 25 Dec. 12 000L, no charge (under 18 and over 60). ☎ 081 73 90 963.

F

FABRIANO   **🄸** corso della Repubblica 70 – ☎ 0732 53 87

Pinacoteca Civica – Closed following the recent earthquake.

Museo della Carta e della Filigrana – ♿ (partial access). Open all year, daily (except Mon), 10am-6pm, Sun 10-12am and 2-5pm. Closed 1 Jan, Easter, 1 May, 15 Aug and 25 Dec. Guided tours available (1hr) in English, Italian, French, Spanish and German.Audio-visual presentation. Bookshop. 5 500L (adult), no charge (child under 6). ☎ 0732 70 92 97.

Excursions

Grotte di Frasassi – ♿ (partial access). Guided tours only (1hr). Closed 1 Jan, 8-30 Jan, 4 and 25 Dec. 16 000L (adult), 14 000L (child). ☎ 0732 97 211. www.frasassi.com

FAENZA   **🄸** piazza del Popolo 1 – ☎ 0546 25 231

Museo Internazionale delle Ceramiche – ♿ (partial access). Open Apr to Oct, daily (except Mon), 9am–7pm, Sun and holidays, 9.30am–1pm and 3-7pm; Nov to Mar, daily (except Mon), 9am–1.30pm (Sat also 3–6pm), Sun and holidays, 9.30am–1pm and 3–6pm. Closed 1 Jan, 1 May, 15 Aug and 25 Dec. 10 000L, 5 000L (over 65), no charge (child under 11). Guided tours available (1-2hr) in English, French, Italian and German by appointment with the tourist office ☎ 0546 21 240; www.racine.ra.it/micfaenza

Pinacoteca Comunale – Closed for restoration. Occasional guided tours to selected works only. For information, contact ☎ 0546 25 231.

FANO   **🄸** viale Cesare Battisti 10 – ☎ 0721 80 35 34

Museo Civico – ♿ (partial access). Open 15 June to 15 Sept, Tues to Sat, 8am–1pm and 5-7pm, Sun, 8am–1pm; rest of the year, Tues to Sun, 8am–1pm. Closed 10 July and public holidays. 5 000L, 3 000L (over 65). Guided tours available (1hr 30min). ☎ 0721 82 83 62.

FERMO   **🄸** piazza del Popolo 5 – ☎ 0734 22 87 38

Pinacoteca Civica – ♿ Open daily (except Mon) 9.30am-1.30pm. 3 000L (adult) 1 500L (child aged 8-12). ☎ 0734 28 43 49; www.sapienza.it/html-doc/fermo/musei.htm

Roman Cisterns – Same admission times and charges as the Pinacoteca.

Duomo – Open in summer, daily, 10am–1pm and 3-7pm; rest of the year by appointment, ☎ 0734 22 09 214.

Excursions

Montefiore dell'Aso: Collegiata – Usually open daily, 7.30–noon and 3-7.30pm. For further information and guided tours ☎ 0734 93 81 03.

Santa Maria a piè di Chienti – Open Mon to Fri, 8am-6pm, Sat, 8am-5pm, Sun, 8-9am and 11.30am-5pm. For guided tours contact the parish priest in advance at Via Santuario, 1, 62010 Montecosaro Scalo. Donation welcome. ☎ 0733 86 52 41.

FERRARA   **🄸** Castello Estense – ☎ 0532 20 93 70

Castello Estense – Open all year, Tues to Sun, 9.30am–5pm. 8 000L (adult), 6 000L (child). ☎ 0532 29 92 33.

Museo del Duomo – The museum is currently being transferred to the former Chiesa di San Romano, via San Romano. For further information on admission times and charges, contact the tourist office.

Sinagoghe – Guided tours only (1hr) in English and Italian at 10am, 11am and noon. Closed Aug, Fri-Sat and Jewish feasts. 7 000L. Audio-visual presentation. Bookshop.

Palazzo Schifanoia – Open all year, daily, 9am-7pm. Closed public holidays. 8 000L, no charge (under 18 and on the first Mon of each month), 10 000L combined ticket for the Palazzo, Lapidarium and Palazzina di Marfisa d'Este. Audio-visual presentation. Bar. Bookshop. ☎ 0532 64 178; www.comune.fe.it/musei-aa/schifanoia.hmtl

Palazzina di Marfisa d'Este – Open all year, daily, 9.30am-1pm and 3-6pm. Closed public holidays. 4 000L, no charge (under 18 and on 1st Mon of each month), 10 000L combined ticket for the Palazzina and Palazzo Schifanoia. ☎ 0532 20 74 50.

Casa Romei – ♿ (partial access). Open all year, daily, 8.30am-7pm (2pm Mon and Sun). Closed public holidays. 4 000L, no charge (under 18 and over 60). ☎ 0532 24 03 41.

Palazzo di Ludovico il Moro – Open all year, daily (except Mon), 9am-2pm. Closed 1 Jan, 1 May and 25 Dec. 8 000L, no charge (child). Audio-guided tours in English and Italian. Audio-visual presentation. Bookshop. ☎ 0532 66 299.

Sant'Antonio in Polesine – Open all year, Mon to Fri, 9.30-11.30am and 3-5pm. Closed Sat pm and Sun. Donation welcome. ☎ 0532 64 068.

Palazzo dei Diamanti: Pinacoteca Nazionale – Open all year, daily (except Mon), 9am-2pm (1pm Sun). Closed public holidays. 8 000L, no charge (under 18). ☎ 0532 20 58 44.

Museo Boldini – ♿ Open all year, daily, 9am-1pm and 3-6pm. 8 000L, no charge (under 18 and on 1st Mon of each month). Guided tours (1hr) by appointment. Bookshop. ☎ 0532 20 99 88; www.comune.fe.it

Casa dell'Ariosto – Closed for restoration. For information, contact ☎ 0532 23 92 81.

FIESOLE
🛈 piazza Mino da Fiesole 36 – ☎ 055 59 87 20

Convento di San Francesco – Open Apr to Sept, Mon to Fri, 9.30am-12.30pm and 3-7pm, Sat, 10.30am-12.30pm and 3-7pm, Sun and public holidays, 9.30-11am and 3-7pm; Oct to Mar, Mon to Fri, 9.30am-12.30pm and 3-6pm, Sat 10.30am-12.30pm and 3-6pm, Sun and public holidays, 9.30-11am and 3-6pm. Closed during church services. Donation welcome. ☎ 055 59 175.

Zona archeologica and Museo Archeologico – ♿ (partial access). Open daily, 29 March to Sept, 9.30am-7pm; 25 Oct to Feb, 9.30am-5pm; March and 1-24 Oct, 9.30am-6pm (last admission 30min before closing time). Closed 1st Tues of each month, 1 Jan and 25 Dec. 10 000L, 6 000L (reduction), no charge (under 8), 25 000L for family. Combined ticket with the Museo Bandini. Guided tours (1hr) in English, French and German. Bookshop. ☎ 055 59 477.

Antiquarium Costantini – Same admission times and charges as for zona archeologica.

Museo Bandini – Same admission times and charges as for zona archeologica.

FIRENZE
🛈 via Cavour 1r – ☎ 055 29 08 32

Duomo – Open all year, daily, 10am (1pm Sun and public holidays)-5pm, the 1st Sat of the month 10am-3.30pm. ☎ 055 23 02 885.

Top of the dome – Access all year, daily (except Sun), 8.30am-7pm (5pm Sat), last admission 6.20pm, 1st Sat of the month 8.30am-4pm. Closed 1 and 6 Jan, Holy Week, 24 June, 15 Aug, 1 Nov, 8 Dec, 25 and 26 Dec. 10 000L. ☎ 055 23 02 885.

Campanile – Open daily, Apr to Oct, 9am-7.30pm (last admission 6.50pm). Closed 1 Jan, Easter, 8 Sept and 25 Dec. 10 000L. ☎ 055 23 02 885.

Battistero – Open all year, Mon to Sat, noon-6.30pm, Sun and public holidays, 8.30am-1.30pm. Closed 1 Jan, Easter, 24 June and 25 Dec. 5 000L. ☎ 055 23 02 885.

Museo dell'Opera del Duomo – Open Apr to Oct, Mon to Sat, 9am-7.30pm (last admission 6.50pm); Nov to Mar, Mon to Sat, 9am-7pm (last admission 6.20pm). Sun, 6 Jan, 1 Nov, 8 and 26 Dec, 9am-2pm. Closed 1 Jan, Easter and 25 Dec. 10 000L. ☎ 055 23 02 885.

Palazzo Vecchio – ♿ (partial access). Open all year, Mon to Wed, Fri and Sat, 9am-7pm, Sun and public holidays, 8am-1pm. Closed Thur (or open 9am-2pm), 1 Jan, Easter, 1 May, 15 Aug and 25 Dec. 10 000L, no charge (child under 12). Audio-guided tours available in English, Italian and French. Audio-visual presentation. Bar and restaurant. Bookshop. ☎ 055 26 25 961; www.comune.firenze.it

FIRENZE

Galleria degli Uffizi - ♿ (partial access). Open all year, daily (except Mon), 8.30am-6.50pm (usually 1.50pm Sun and public holidays). Closed 1 Jan, 1 May and 25 Dec. 12 000L, no charge (under 18 and over 60). Bar. Bookshop. ☎ 055 23 88 651.
musa.uffizi.firenze.it

Palazzo Pitti:

Galleria Palatina - Open in summer, daily (except Mon), 8.30am-9pm (midnight Sat, 8pm Sun and public holidays); in winter, daily (except Mon), 8.30am-7pm (2pm Sun and public holidays). 12 000L. ☎ 055 23 88 614.

Appartmenti Reali - ♿ Open May to Oct, daily (except Mon), 8.30am-9pm (8pm Sun and public holidays); rest of the year 8.30am-7pm (2pm Sun and public holidays). Jan to Apr by appointment only to Firenze Musei ☎ 055 29 48 83. Closed 1 Jan, 1 May and 25 Dec. 12 000 L, no charge (under 18 and over 60). Guided tours available in English, German, French and Spanish by appointment to Firenze Musei (5 000L). Bar and restaurant. Bookshop. ☎ 055 23 88 614.

Galleria d'Arte Moderna - Open 1st, 3rd and 5th Sun and 2nd and 4th Mon in the month, 8.30am-1.50pm (last admission 30min before closing time). Closed 1 Jan, 1 May and 25 Dec. 8 000L. Bar and restaurant. Bookshop. ☎ 055 23 88 601/616.
www.sbas.firenze.it//galleriad'artemoderna

Museo degli Argenti - ♿ (partial access). Open all year, daily (except 1st, 3rd and 5th Mon and 2nd and 4th Sun in the month), 8.30am-1.50pm. Closed 1 Jan, 1 May, Easter and 25 Dec. 4 000L, no charge (under 18 and during museum week). Bar. Bookshop. ☎ 055 23 88 709.

Giardino di Boboli - Open daily (except 1st and last Mon in the month) June to Aug, 9am-7.30pm; Apr, May and Sept, 9am-6.30pm; Oct and Mar, 9am-5.30pm; Nov to Feb, 9am-4.30pm. Closed 1 Jan, 1 May and 25 Dec. 4 000L. Bar and restaurant. Bookshop. ☎ 055 29 48 83.

Museo delle Porcellane - Open 9am-1.50pm. Closed same dates as Museo degli Argenti. 4 000L, no charge (under 18). ☎ 055 23 88 709.

Palazzo e Museo Nazionale del Bargello - ♿ Open all year, daily (except 1st, 3rd and 5th Sun and 2nd and 4th Mon in the month), 8.30am-1.50pm (last admission 1.20pm). Closed 1 Jan, 1 May and 25 Dec. 8 000L, no charge (under 18 and over 60). Bookshop. ☎ 055 29 48 83; www.sbas.firenze.it

Biblioteca Medicea Laurenziana: Cloisters - ♿ (partial access). Open all year, daily (except Sun), 9am-1pm (last admission 12.40pm). Closed public holidays. No charge. ☎ 055 21 07 60.

Cappelle Medicee - ♿ Open Mar to Dec, daily (except 1st, 3rd, 5th Mon and 2nd and 4th Sun in the month) 8.30am-5pm (1.50pm Sun and public holidays). Closed 1 Jan, 1 May and 25 Dec. Charges being revised at the time of going to press, no charge under 18 and over 60. Bookshop. ☎ 055 23 88 602.

Palazzo Medici Riccardi - Open all year, Mon, Tues, Thur to Sat, 9am-1pm and 3-6pm, Sun and public holidays, 9am-1pm. Closed Wed, 1 May and 25 Dec. 6 000L, 4 000L (child). ☎ 055 27 60 340.

San Marco - ♿ (partial access). Open all year, daily (except 1st, 3rd and 5th Mon and 2nd and 4th Sun in the month), 8.30am-1.50pm (last admission 1.20pm). Closed 1 Jan, 1 May and 25 Dec. 8 000L, no charge (under 18 and over 60). ☎ 055 23 88 608/704; www.sbas.firenze.it

Galleria dell'Accademia - ♿ Open all year, Tues to Sat, 8.30am-6.50pm (last admission 6.20pm); Sun and holidays, 8.30am-1.50pm (last admission 1.20pm). Closed 1 Jan, 1 May and 25 Dec. 12 000L, no charge (under 18). Bookshop. ☎ 055 23 88 609; www.sbas.firenze.it/musei/acca01.htm

Santa Maria Novella - Open all year, Mon to Fri, 7am-noon and 3-6pm, Sat, 7am-noon and 3-5pm, Sun and public holidays, 3-5pm.

Chiostro Verde - ♿ Open all year, Mon to Sat (except Fri), 9am-2pm; Sun and public holidays, 8am-1pm. Closed 1 Jan, Easter, 1 May, 15 Aug and 25 Dec. 5 000L, no charge (child under 12). ☎ 055 26 25 961; www.comune.firenze.it

Santa Croce:

Church and Sacristy - Open Apr to Nov, daily, 8am-5.45pm; rest of the year, 8am-noon and 3-5.45pm. ☎ 055 24 46 19.

Cappella dei Pazzi and **Museo dell'Opera di Santa Croce** - ♿ (partial access). Open Mar to Sept, daily (except Weds), 10am-12.30pm and 2.30-6.30pm; Oct to Feb, 10am-12.30pm and 3-5pm. Closed 1 Jan and 25 Dec. 5 000L, 2 000L (child). Guided tours available (30min). ☎ 055 24 46 19, 23 42 289.

Santa Maria del Carmine: Cappella Brancacci - Open daily (except Tues), 10am-5pm, Sun and holidays 1-5pm. Closed Easter, 1 May, 16 July, 15 Aug and 25 Dec. 5 000L, 25% reduction (under 20), no charge(under 12). ☎ 055 26 25 961.

Casa Buonarroti - Open all year, daily (except Tues), 9.30am-1.30pm. Closed public holidays. 12 000L, 8 000L (reduction). Audio-visual presentation. Bookshop. ☎ 055 24 17 52; www.casabuonarroti.it

Cenacolo di Sant'Apollonia - Open all year, daily (except 2nd and 4th Mon and 1st, 3rd and 5th Sun in the month), 8.30am-1.50pm. Closed 1 Jan, 1 May and 25 Dec. No charge. ☎ 055 23 88 607.

Cenacolo di San Salvi - ♿ (partial access). Open all year, daily (except Mon), 9am-2pm. Closed 1 Jan, 1 May and 25 Dec. No charge. ☎ 055 23 88 603.

Museo Archeologico - Open all year, Tues to Sat, Mon following Sun closing, 9am-2pm; 2nd and 4th Sun in the month, 9am-1pm. Last admission 30min before closing time. 8 000L, no charge (under 18). Bookshop. ☎ 055 23 575.

Museo della Casa Fiorentina Antica (Palazzo Davanzati) - Closed for restoration at time of going to press.

Museo Marino Marini - ♿ Open all year, daily (except Tues), 10am-5pm (11pm Thur from June to Sept, 1pm Sun and public holidays). Closed 1 May, 2 weeks in Aug and 25 Dec. 8 000 L, 4 000L (child). Guided tours available (1hr) in English and Italian. ☎ 055 21 94 32.

Museo di Storia della Scienza - ♿ Open all year, daily (except Sun), 9.30am-1pm, and also 2-5pm on Mon, Wed and Fri. Closed public holidays and 24 June. 10 000L, 5 000L (under 14), no charge during science week. ☎ 055 23 98 876; www.imsS-.firenze.it

Opificio delle Pietre dure - ♿ Open all year, daily (except Sun), 9am-2pm. Closed public holidays. 4 000L, no charge (under 18 and over 60). Bookshop. ☎ 055 26 51 357; www.dada.it/propart/opd.htm

Ospedale degli Innocenti: Gallery - Open daily (except Wed), 8.30am-2pm. Closed public holidays. 5 000L, 3 000L (reduction). Bookshop. ☎ 055 24 91 723.

Excursions

Ville Medicee

Villa della Petraia - Guided tours only (30 min), June to Aug, 9am-7.30pm; Apr, May, Sept and Oct, 9am-6.30pm; Mar, 9am-5.30pm; Nov to Feb, 9am-4.30pm. Closed 2nd and 3rd Mon in the month, 1 Jan, 1 May and 25 Dec. 4 000 L (ticket also valid for Villa di Castello), no charge (child). ☎ 055 45 26 91.

Villa di Castello - Open (park only) daily June to Aug, 9am-7.30pm; Apr, May and Sept, 9am-6.30pm; Mar and Oct, 9am-5.30pm (1hr later during summertime and 1hr earlier during wintertime); Nov to Feb, 9am-4.30pm (last admission 1hr before closing time). Closed 2nd and 3rd Mon in the month. 4 000L (ticket also valid for Villa della Petraia). ☎ 055 45 47 91.

Villa di Poggio a Caiano - ♿ (with assistance). Guided tours every hr, June to Aug, 9am-6.30pm; Apr, May and Sept, 9am-5.30pm; Mar and Oct, 9am-4.30pm; Nov to Feb, 9am-3.30pm. Closed 2nd and 3rd Mon in the month. 4 000L, no charge (under 18 and over 60). ☎ 055 87 70 12.

Villa La Ferdinanda di Artimino: Etruscan museum - ♿ (partial access). Open all year, daily (except Wed), 9am-1pm (12.30pm Sun and public holidays). Closed 14 to 22 Aug, 1 Jan, 4 Apr, 1 May, 1 Nov, 25 and 26 Dec. 5 000L, 2 000L (child and over 60). Guided tours available (40min) in English (by appointment) and Italian. Audio-visual presentation. Bookshop. ☎ 055 87 18 124.

Certosa del Galluzzo - Guided tours only, all year, daily (except Mon), 9am-noon and 3-6pm (5pm in winter). Donation welcome. ☎ 055 20 49 226.

FORLI   🛈 corso della Repubblica 23 - ☎ 0543 71 24 35

Pinacoteca - ♿ (partial access). Open daily (except Mon), 9am-1.30pm (1pm Sun; also 3-5pm Tues and Thur). Closed public holidays and 4 Feb. No charge. ☎ 0543 71 26 06.

Excursions   🛈 piazza del Popolo 11 - ☎ 0547 35 63 27

Cesena

Biblioteca Malatestiana - Guided tours only (45min), Sun, 10am-12.30pm, Mon to Sat, from mid-June to mid-Sept, 9am-12.30pm and 4-7pm; the rest of the year, 9am-12.30pm and 3-6pm. 5 000 L (adult), 3 000 L (over 60). Audio-visual presentation. Bookshop. ☎ 0547 61 08 92.

Abbazia di FOSSANOVA

Guided tours by appointment at least ten days in advance, in summer, Mon to Fri, 7am-noon and 4-7.30pm, Sat at 11am, Sun and public holidays, 7.30am-1pm and 4-7.30pm; in winter, Mon to Fri, 7am-noon and 3-5.30pm, Sat at 11am, Sun and public holidays, 7.30am-1pm and 3-6pm. ☎ 0773 93 061.

G

GÀETA

🛈 piazza XIX Maggio (15 June to 15 Sept) - ☎ 0771 46 11 65

Monte Orlando - Park open daily (access by foot only), in summer, 8am-7pm; rest of the year, 8am-5pm. A shuttle bus operates to the summit from June to mid-Sept, daily, 9am-6.30pm; rest of the year, Sat-Sun only, 10.20am-4.30pm. 2 000L return ticket (round trip). For guided excursions, apply to Cooperativa Elios, ☎ 0338 45 74 621 (mobile).

Excursions

Sperlonga: Museo Archeologico - Open all year, daily, 9am-2hrs before sunset. Closed 1 Jan, 1 May and 25 Dec. 4 000L (adult), no charge (under 18 and over 60). ☎ 0771 54. 028.

Promontorio del GARGANO

🛈 piazza Kennedy - ☎ 0884 70 88 06

Vieste

Museo Malacologico - Open daily, 15 Mar to May and 1-15 Oct, 9am-1pm and 4-9pm; June, 9am-1pm and 4-10pm; July and Aug, 9am-1pm and 5-11pm; Sept, 9am-1pm and 4-10pm. Closed 15 Oct to 15 Mar. No charge. ☎ 0884 70 76 88.

GENOVA

🛈 stazione Principe - ☎ 010 24 62 633
🛈 via al Porto Antico (Palazzina S. Maria) - ☎ 010 24 87 11

Port: Boat trip - Departing from the aquarium and main harbour station "Ponte dei Mille", daily, all day, frequency according to demand. 45min. 10 000L; it is advisable to telephone in advance. ☎ 010 26 57 12.

Mini-cruises are also organised from May to Sept for San Fruttuoso, Portofino, the Cinque Terre and Porto Venere, as well as wildlife excursions organised jointly with the WWF to see marine mammals. Departure 8.30am and 12.30pm, return to Genoa at 7pm. 25 000-55 000L. Book several days ahead. ☎ 010 26 57 12.

Acquario - ♿ (partial access) Open all year, Mon to Fri, 9.30am-7pm (except Mon from Oct to Mar); Sat, Sun and public holidays, 9.30am-8pm (last admission 1hr 30min before closing time). 19 000L (adult), 12 000 L (child aged 3-12). Audio-guided and guided tours (1hr 30min) in English, French and German. ☎ 010 24 81 205; www.acquario.ge.it

Antichi Magazzini del Cotone

Città dei Bambini - Children allowed only if accompanied by an adult. Daily sessions available (except Mon), 10am-6pm, by prior appointment. Closed last week in Sept and first week in Oct. 8 000L. ☎ 010 24 75 702.

Padiglione del Mare e della Navigazione - Open Apr to 15 Sept, Mon to Fri, 10.30am-6pm; Sat-Sun, 10.30am-7pm; rest of the year, Tues to Fri, 10.30am-5.30pm, Sat-Sun, 10.30am-6pm. Closed Mon in winter. 9 000L (adult), 6 000L (child aged 6-12), no charge (under 5). Guided tours available. ☎ 010 24 63 678.

Cattedrale di San Lorenzo: Treasury - Guided tours only, 9am-noon and 3pm-6pm (Sun 3pm-6pm only). 8 000L. ☎ 010 31 12 69.

Museo di Architettura e Scultura Ligure - ♿ Open Tues to Sat, 9am-7pm; Sun, 9am-12.30pm. Closed public holidays. 6 000L, no charge Sun. ☎ 010 25 11 263.

Palazzo Carrega-Cataldi - Open by appointment only (apply in advance to Signora Rosangela Pedemonte ☎ 010 27 04 358), Mon to Fri, 9am-5pm. Closed public holidays. No charge. www.lig.camcom.it/cciaa ge

Palazzo Municipale - Open Mon to Thur, 8am-noon and 1-4.30pm; Fri, 8am-3pm. Closed public holidays. Guided tours available (20min). ☎ 010 55 71 11; www.comune.genova.it

Palazzo Bianco - Open Tues, Thur and Fri, 9am-1pm; Wed, Sat, 9am-7pm; Sun, 10am-6pm. Closed Mon and public holidays. 6 000L, no charge Sun. ☎ 010 24 76 377.

Palazzo Rosso - Open Tues, Thur, Fri, 9am-1pm; Wed, Sat, 9am-7pm; Sun and public holidays, 10am-6pm. Closed Mon. 6 000L, no charge Sun. ☎ 010 24 76 351.

Galleria Nazionale di Palazzo Spinola - ♿ (partial access). Open all year, Tues to Sat, 9am-7pm; Sun and public holidays, 2-7pm. Closed 1 Jan, 1 May and 25 Dec. Audio-visual presentation. 8 000L. ☎ 010 27 05 300.

Palazzo Reale - ♿ (partial access). Open Sun to Tues, 9am-1.45pm; Wed to Sat, 9am-7pm. Closed 1 Jan, 1 May and 25 Dec. 8 000L, no charge (over 60). Guided tours available (1hr) in Italian and French. ☎ 010 27 10 202.

Palazzo del Principe - Open Sat, 3-6pm and Sun, 10am-1pm. Closed Easter, 1 May, August and 25 Dec. ☎ 010 25 55 09.

Villetta Di Negro: Museo Chiossone – Open all year, daily (except Mon and Weds) 9am–1pm. Closed public holidays. 6 000L, no charge Sun. Guided tours available (1hr). ☎ 010 54 22 85.

GROSSETO
🛈 via Fucini 43 – ☎ 0564 41 43 03

Excursion

Scavi di Roselle – Open May to Aug, 9am-7.30pm; Mar, Apr and Sept, 9am-6.30pm; Nov to Feb, 9am-5.30pm. 4 000 L, no charge (under 18 and over 60). ☎ 0564 40 24 03.

GUBBIO
🛈 piazza Oderisi 6 – ☎ 075 92 20 693

Palazzo dei Consoli – Open all year, daily, 10am–1pm and 3–6pm (5pm, Oct to Mar). Closed 14, 15 May and 25 Dec. 7 000L, 4 000L (under 25 and over 60). ☎ 075 92 74 298.

Palazzo Ducale – ♿ Open all year, Mon to Sat, 9am–7pm (1.30pm Sun and public holidays); last admission 30min before closing time. Closed 1st Mon in the month, 1 Jan, 1 May and 25 Dec. 4 000L, no charge (under 18 and over 60). Audio-visual presentation. ☎ 075 92 75 872.

Duomo: Episcopal Chapel – Closed for restoration work at time of going to press.

J – L

JESI

Pinacoteca comunale – Open mid-June to Mid-Sept, daily (except Mon), 10am–1pm and 5–11pm; rest of the year, Tues to Sat, 10am–1pm and 4–7pm, Sun, 10am–1pm and 5–8pm. 4 000L, no charge (under 12). Guided tours available (30min). Audio-visual presentation. ☎ 0731 53 83 43; www.comune.jesi.ancona.it

Regione dei LAGHI

Numerous boat and hydrofoil (aliscafo) trips can be combined for each of the lakes. Look under the name of each lake, where some of the trips, times and prices will be mentioned. For further details apply to the local tourist office.

LAGO MAGGIORE

Boat trips on lake – Main trips: from Arona and/or Angera to Locarno, with the option of lunch on board; from Stresa and/or Laveno to the Isole Borromee and Villa Taranto. Car-ferry between Intra and Laveno and back. Lake passes for unlimited travel are also available for one day. Reduced fares for groups and pensioners. Night cruises in summer. For further information, call toll-free ☎ 800 55 18 01.

Angera: Rocca Borromeo – Open daily 9.30am-12.30pm and 2-6pm; Oct, 9.30am-12.30pm and 2-5pm. Closed Nov to 26 Mar. 10 000L (adult), 6 000L (aged 6-15). Guided tours available (1hr 30min) in English, French, German and Italian. Bar and restaurant. Agricultural tourism. Bookshop. ☎ 0331 93 13 00.

Arona: San Carlone – Open daily mid-Mar to Sept, 8.30am-12.30pm and 2-6.30pm; Oct, 9am-12.30pm and 2-5pm; rest of the year, open Sat, Sun and public holidays only, 9am-12.30pm and 2-5pm. Closed 25 Dec. 5 000 L (adult), 3 000 L (child). Audio-guided tours available. ☎ 0322 24 96 69.

Isole Borromee – One-day pass for unlimited travel to islands, departure from Baveno, Stresa, Pallanza, Intra, Laveno, Arona, Angera, Luino and Cannobbio, 12 000/27 000L (adult) depending on embarkation point, 6 000/13 500L (child). Fares may change. For more information, contact Direzione Navigazione Lago Maggiore ☎ 0322 23 32 00 and toll-free ☎ 800 55 18 01 or Ufficio Informazioni Turistiche in Stresa ☎ 0323 30 416.
Isola Bella: Open daily 27 Mar to 24 Oct, 9am-noon and 1.30-5.30pm (5pm in Oct). Closed 25 Oct to 26 Mar. 14 000L (adult), 6 000L (child under 15). Guided tours available. ☎ 0323 30 556.
Isola Madre: Open daily 27 Mar to 24 Oct, 9am-noon and 1.30-5.30pm (5pm in Oct). Closed 25 Oct to 26 Mar. 13 000 L (adult), 6 000 L (child under 15). Guided tours available. ☎ 0323 31 261.

Cerro: Ceramics museum – Open daily (except Mon) July and Aug, 10am-noon and 3.30-6.30pm; rest of the year, 10am-noon and 2.30-5.30pm (Sept to Dec, closed am). Closed 1 Jan, Easter, 15 Aug and 25 Dec. 4 000 L (adult), 2 000 L (child). Guided tours available (45min). Bookshop. ☎ 0332 66 65 30.

LAGO MAGGIORE

Laveno Mombello: Sasso del Ferro cable-car – Operates Apr to Sept, Mon to Fri, 10am-5.30pm, Sat 9.30am-6pm, Sun and public holidays, 9.30am-7pm; rest of the year, Sat, Sun and public holidays only, 10am-5pm. ☏ 0332 66 80 12.

Pallanza: Villa Taranto gardens – Open daily, Apr to Sept, 8.30am-7.30pm; Oct, 8.30am-5.30pm (last admission 1hr before closing time). Closed 1 Nov to 31 Mar. 11 000L (adult), 10 000L (child). Bar and restaurant. Bookshop. ☏ 0323 40 45 55 or ☏ 0323 55 66 67.

Eremo di Santa Caterina del Sasso – Open daily, from Good Friday to Oct, 8.30am-noon and 2.30-6pm; rest of the year, 8.30am-noon and 2-5pm. No charge. ☏ 0332 64 71 72.

Stresa　　　　　　　　　　　　🄯 via Principe Tomaso 70/72 – ☏ 0323 30 416

Mottarone – Access by toll-road (Strada Borromea). 6 000L, return ticket (round trip); by cable-car from Stresa. ☏ 0323 30 399 or ☏ 0323 55 66 33.

Villa Pallavicino – Open daily, 28 Fev to 1 Nov, 9am-6pm. Closed 2 Nov to 27 Feb. 11 000L (adult), 8 000L (child under 14). Bar and restaurant. ☏ 0323 32 407.

Gignese: Museo dell'Ombrello e del Parasole – Open Apr to Sept, daily, 10am-noon and 3-6pm. Closed the rest of the year and Monday except public holidays (Aug, also open Mon). 2 500L (adult), 1 000L (child). ☏ 0323 20 80 64.

LAGO D'ORTA　　　　　　　🄯 via Bossi 47, Orta San Giulio – ☏ 0322 91 19 37

Boat trips on lake – Departures from Orta San Giulio, Easter to Oct, every 30min; rest of the year, Sun and public holidays only, every 45min, (also Sat in Oct, Nov and Mar). Trips last 5min. Fares vary during season. ☏ 0322 84 48 62. Public boats also operate; 4 000L return ticket (round trip), for further information contact Signor Urani ☏ 0338 30 34 904 (mobile) or Signor Fabris ☏ 0330 87 98 39 (mobile).

Isola di San Giulio: Basilica di San Giulio – Open, summer, Mon to Sat, 9.30am (Mon 11am)-12.15pm and 2-6.45pm, Sun, 9.30-10.45am, 2-4.45pm, 5.45-6-45pm; in winter, Mon to Sat, closes 5.45pm, Sun and public holidays, 9.30-10.45am and 2-5.45pm. No admission during services.

LAGO DI LUGANO

Boat trips on lake – The "Gran Giro del Lago" tour takes place daily, early Apr to mid-Oct, departing from Lugano at 2.40pm, returning at 5.15pm. Commentary in 4 languages; restaurant. Other boat trips, of variable length and price are available both in the Italian and Swiss regions of the lake: contact the Società Navigazione del Lago di Lugano. ☏ 0041 91 97 15 223.

Bisuschio: Villa Cicogna Mozzoni – ♿ (partial access). Guided tours only (45min) in English, Italian and French, Sun and public holidays, 9.30am-noon and 2.30-7pm (last admission 6pm); Aug, open daily, 2.30-7pm. Closed from 1st Sun in Nov to 3rd Sun in March and Easter. Bookshop. 10 000L (adult), 5 000L (child). ☏ 0332 47 11 34.

LAGO DI COMO　　　　　　🄯 piazza Cavour 17, Como – ☏ 031 26 97 12

Boat trips on lake – Boat trips from Como to Colico, Lecco, Tremezzo, Bellagio or Menaggio. From Tremezzo to Dongo, Domaso and Colico. Hydrofoil trips (aliscafo) from Como to Tremezzo, Bellagio and Menaggio. Car-ferries to Bellagio, Varenna, Menaggio and Cadenabbia and back. One-day passes also available for unlimited travel on lake. Night cruises Sat, in summer. Reduced fares for groups and pensioners. For further information, call toll-free ☏ 800 55 18 01.

Bellagio　　　　　　　　　🄯 piazza della Chiesa 14 – ☏ 031 95 02 04

Giardini di Villa Serbelloni – Guided tours only (1hr 30min) daily (except Mon) at 11am and 4pm, in English, Italian and French. Closed Nov to Mar. 6 000L (adult), 4 000L (child). ☏ 031 95 02 O4; www.fromitaly.net/bellaggio/

Giardini di Villa Melzi – ♿ (partial access). Open late Mar to Oct, 9am-6.30pm. 7 000L (adult), no charge (child under 6). ☏ 031 95 02 04.

Tremezzo　　　　　　　　🄯 piazzale Trieste 1 (May to Oct) – ☏ 0344 40 493

Villa Carlotta – Open Apr to Sept, daily, 9am-6pm; Mar to Oct, daily, 9-11.30am and 2-4.30pm. Closed Nov to Feb. 11 000L (adult), 6 000L (over 65), no charge (child under 6). Guided tours available (1hr 30min). ☏ 0344 40 405; www.unicei.it/uni/villacarlotta/

Varenna: Giardini di Villa Monastero – Open Apr, May, Sept and Oct, daily, 9am-6pm; June, July and Aug, daily, 9am-7pm. 3 000L (adult), 2 000L (under 10 and over 60). ☏ 0341 29 54 50.

LAGO D'ISEO

🏛 lungolago Marconi 2/c, Iseo – ☎ 030 98 02 09

Boat trips on lake – In spring and summer: Tour of lake, with morning departure (from Sarnico, Iseo or Lovere) and evening return; about 7 hours; stop at Monte Isola; lunch on board optional. Tour of lake with afternoon departure (from Sarnico, Iseo, Lovere or Monte Isola) and evening return. Afternoon trip to the three islands departing from Iseo; 1hr 30min. For further information, contact Iseo tourist office.

Lovere: Galleria Tadini – Open mid-Apr to mid-Oct, daily, 3-6pm, Sun also open 10am-noon. 7 000L (adult), 4 000L (child). ☎ 035 96 01 32; www.intercam.it/tadini

Monte Isola: access by boat – Daily departures from **Iseo**: in summer and on public holidays in spring, every 30min; rest of the year, every hour. From **Sulsano**, departure every 15min. 4 200 L return ticket (round trip). The island can also be reached from other lakeside towns (Sale Marasino). For further information, contact Iseo tourist office.

LAGO DI GARDA

Boat trips on lake – Departure from Desenzano and/or Peschiera to Riva del Garda, lunch on board optional. Excursions across the lake to Sirmione, Gardone, Salò and Limone. Car-ferry from Maderno to Torri and back. One-day passes are also available for unlimited travel on lake. Reduced fares for groups and pensioners. Night cruises in summer. For further information, call toll-free ☎ 800 55 18 01.

Desenzano

🏛 via Porto Vecchio 34 – ☎ 030 91 41 510

Villa Romana – ♿ Open Mar to 14 Oct, Tues to Sat, 8.30am-7pm, Sun, 9am-6pm; rest of the year, 8.30am (Sun 9am) -4.30pm. Closed Mon (except public holidays, in which case closed Tues), 1 Jan, 1 May and 25 Dec. 4 000L (adult), no charge (under 18 and over 60). ☎ 030 91 43 547.

Gardone Riviera

🏛 corso Repubblica 39 – ☎ 0365 20 347

Vittoriale – Open Apr to Sept, daily, 8.30am-8pm; rest of the year, daily, 9am-5pm (5.30pm Sat-Sun). Closed 24 and 25 Dec. 10 000L (adult), 8 000L (over 60), no charge (child under 6). Bar. Bookshop. ☎ 0365 20 130; www.vittoriale.it

La Priora – Guided tours only (30min) in English, Italian, French and German, Apr to Sept, daily (except Mon), 10am-6pm; rest of the year, daily (except Mon), 9am-1pm and 2pm-5pm (5.30pm Sat-Sun). Closed 24 and 25 Dec. 20 000L (adult), 15 000L (over 60). Audio-visual presentation. Bar. Bookshop. ☎ 0365 20 130; www.vittoriale.it

Malcesine: Monte Baldo – Departures every 30min, daily, 8am-5pm, 6pm or 7pm according to season. Cable-car does not operate in Mar and Nov to mid-Dec. 14 000L one-way, 19 000L return ticket (round trip). ☎ 045 74 00 206 or 045 74 00 044.

Riva del Garda

🏛 Giardini di Porta Orientale 8 – ☎ 0466 55 44 44

Museo Civico – ♿ Open July and Aug, daily (except Mon), 4-10pm; Mar to June, daily (except Mon), 9.30am-12.30pm and 2-6pm; Sept to Dec, daily (except Monday), 9.30am-12.30pm and 2-5.30pm. 8 000L (adult), no charge (child). Bookshop. ☎ 0464 57 38 69.

San Martino della Battaglia: ossuary-chapel, museum and tower – ♿ Open 15 Mar to late Sept, daily (except Tues), 9am-12.30pm and 2-7pm, Sun, 9am-7pm; rest of the year,daily (except Tues), 9am-12.30pm and 2-5pm. Closed 1-15 Dec. 6 000L (adult), 3 000L (child). Guided tours available. ☎ 030 99 10 370.

Sirmione

🏛 viale Marconi 2 – ☎ 030 91 62 45

Rocca Scaligera – Open all year, daily (except Mon), 8.30am-1.30pm. Closed 1 Jan, 1 May and 25 Dec. 8 000L. ☎ 030 91 64 68.

Grotte di Catullo – ♿ (partial access). Open Mar to 14 Oct, Tues to Sat, 8.30am-7pm, Sun and public holidays, 9am-6pm; rest of the year, 8.30am-4.30pm, Sun and public holidays, 9am-4.30pm. Closed Mon (except public holidays, in which case closed Tues), 1 Jan, 1 May and 25 Dec. 8 000L, no charge (under 18 and over 60). Bar. ☎ 030 91 61 57.

Solferino: ossuary-chapel and museum – ♿ (partial access). Open Apr to Sept, daily (except Mon), 9am-12.30pm and 2.30-6.30pm, Sun and public holidays, 9am-12.30pm and 2.30-7pm; rest of the year, 9am-noon and 2-5pm. Closed 1-15 Dec. 3 000L (adult), 1 500L (child). Guided tours (2hrs) available in English, Italian and French. ☎ 0376 85 40 19.

Valeggio sul Mincio: Parco Giardino Sigurtà – ♿ Open Mar to early Nov, daily, 9am-7pm (last admission 6pm). Closed mid-Nov to Feb. 30 000L (car up to 5 persons), 20 000L (motorcycle), 10 000L (bicycle or scooter). ☎ 045 64 71 033; www.sigurta.it

L'AQUILA
🖪 piazza Santa Maria di Paganica 5 - ☎ 0862 41 08 08

Santa Maria di Collemaggio – Open 8am-12.30pm and 3-7pm (6pm in winter). For information or key (when closed) ☎ 0862 26 744 or 0862 28 10 73.

San Bernardino – Open daily, 9.30am-noon (9.45-10.30am Sun) and 4-6pm (5pm in winter). ☎ 0862 22 255.

Castello: Museo Nazionale d'Abruzzo – ♿ Open May to mid-Sept, daily (except Mon), 9am-7pm; rest of the year, daily, 9am-2pm. Closed 1 Jan, 1 May and 25 Dec. 8 000L, no charge (under 18 and over 60) Guided tours available (1hr). Audio-visual presentation. ☎ 0862 63 32 29; www.muvi.org/museonazionaledabruzzo/

LECCE
🖪 corso Vittorio Emanuele 24 - ☎ 0832 24 80 92

Museo Provinciale S. Castromediano – ♿ (partial access). Open all year, Mon to Fri, 9am-1.30pm and 2.30-7.30pm; Sat-Sun, 9am-1.30pm. Closed 1 Jan, 25 Apr, 1 May and 25 Dec. No charge. Bookshop. ☎ 0832 24 70 25.

Excursion

Santa Maria di Cerrate: Museo della Tradizioni Popolari – Same admission times and charges as for Museo S. Castromediano.

LIGNANO
🖪 via Latisana 42 - ☎ 0431 71 821

Parco Zoo Punta Verde – ♿ Open Apr to 1 Nov, daily, 9am-sunset; Mar, Mon to Sat, 10am-3pm (4pm Sat), Sun, 9am-5pm; Feb, Sun only, 10am-4pm. Closed 2 Nov to Jan. 14 000L, 10 000L (child) Bar and restaurant. Bookshop. ☎ 0431 42 87 75; www.lignano.com/parco-zoo

LORETO
🖪 via Solari 3 - ☎ 071 97 02 76

Santuario della Santa Casa – Open Apr to Oct, daily, 7am-8pm (7pm in winter). Santa Casa closed 12.30-2.30pm. Donation welcome. ☎ 071 97 01 04.

Pinacoteca – Open Apr to Oct, daily (except Mon), 9am-1pm and 4-7pm; Nov to Mar, Sat-Sun only, 10am-1pm and 3-6pm. 7 000L, 5 000L (over 65), no charge (child under 12 accompanied by adult and 3rd Sun of each month). ☎ 071 97 77 59.

Excursion

Recanati

Palazzo Leopardi – ♿ (partial access). Guided tours only (20min), mid-June to late Sept, 9am-8pm; in winter, 9.30am-12.30pm and 2.30-6.30pm; rest of the year, 9am-6pm (Sat-Sun 7pm). Closed 1 Jan and 25 Dec. 7 000L adult (12 000L combined ticket for permanent collection and library), 3 500L under 15 and over 65 (6 000 L combined ticket), no charge child under 6 and 1st Mon in the month (except public holiday). ☎ 071 75 73 380.

Pinacoteca Civica – ♿ Open all year, daily (except Mon), 10am-1pm and 4-7pm. Closed 1 and 6 Jan, 25 Dec. 6 000L (adult), 3 000L (child). Guided tours (1hr). Audio-visual presentation. ☎ 071 75 70 410.

LUCCA
🖪 Vecchia Porta San Donato, piazzale Verdi - ☎ 0583 41 96 89

Casa dei Guinigi: Tower – Open daily, Mar to Sept, 9am-7.30pm; Oct, 10am-6pm; Nov to Feb, 10am-4.30pm. Closed 25 Dec. Audio-visual presentation. Bookshop. 4 500L, 3 000L (aged 6-12). ☎ 0583 48 524.

Museo Nazionale di Palazzo Mansi: Pinacoteca – ♿ (partial access). Open all year, daily (except Mon), 9am-7pm (2pm Sun and public holidays). Closed 1 Jan, 1 May and 25 Dec. 4 000L, no charge (under 18). ☎ 0583 49 60 33.

Museo Nazionale di Villa Guinigi – ♿ (partial access). Open all year, daily (except Mon), 9am-7pm, (2pm Sun and public holidays). Closed 1 Jan, 1 May and 25 Dec. 8 000L, no charge (under 18). ☎ 0583 55 570.

Excursions

Villa Reale di Marlia – ♿ (partial access). Guided tours only (1hr), Mar to Nov, at 10am, 11am, 3pm, 4pm, 5pm and 6pm; rest of the year, by appointment only. Closed Mon, except public holidays. 9 000L. ☎ 0583 30 108.

Villa Mansa – Open Mar to Nov, daily (except Mon), 10am-12.30pm and 3pm-sunset; rest of the year, Fri to Sun, 10am-12.30pm and 3-5pm. Closed 25 Dec. 10 000L (adult), 5 000L (child over 6). ☎ 0583 92 00 96; www.ante-primaweb.com/villamansi

Villa Torrigiani – Guided tours only (30min) inside the villa, in English and Italian, mid-June to mid-Sept, daily (except Tues), 10am-1pm and 3-7pm (2.30-7pm Sun and public holidays); Mar to mid-June, daily (except Tues), 10am-12.30pm and 3-6pm (2.30-6pm Sun and public holidays); mid-Sept to mid-Nov, 10am-1pm and 3-6pm (2.30-6pm Sun and public holidays). Closed Nov to Feb. 15 000L (adult), 12 000L (under 18 and over 65), no charge (child under 12). 10 000L (park only). ☎ 0583 92 80 41 or ☎ 0368 32 09 614.

M

MANTOVA
☷ piazza Mantegna 6 - ☎ 0376 32 82 53

Palazzo Ducale – ♿ (partial access). Open daily (except Mon), 9am-7pm (2pm Sun and public holidays); last admission 30min before closing time. Closed 1 Jan, 1 May and 25 Dec. 12 000L. Bar. Bookshop. Audio-guided tours available. ☎ 0376 32 02 83.

Rotonda di San Lorenzo – Open mid-Mar to mid-Nov, daily, 10am-noon and 3-5pm; rest of the year, 11am-noon.

Teatro Accademico – Open all year, daily (except Mon), 9.30am-12.30pm and 3-6pm. Closed 1 Jan, 1 May, 15 Aug and 25 Dec. 4 000L, 2 000L (under 18 and over 60). Phoning ahead is recommended as the theatre is closed during conferences and concerts. ☎ 0376 32 76 53.

Palazzo d'Arco – Guided tours only (45min) in English, Italian, French and German, Mar to Oct, daily (except Mon), 10am-noon and 2.30-5.30pm; Nov to Feb, 10am-noon and 2.30-4.30pm. Closed 1 Jan and 25 Dec. 5 000L. Bookshop. ☎ 0376 32 22 42.

Palazzo Te – ♿ (partial access). Open all year, daily, 9am (1pm Mon)-6pm. Closed 1 Jan, 1 May and 25 Dec. 12 000L, 10 000L and 5 000L (reductions), no charge (child under 11). Bar. Bookshop. ☎ 0376 32 32 66.

MASSA MARITTIMA

Museo Archeologico – Open daily (except Mon), Apr to Oct, 10am-12.30pm and 3.30-7pm; Nov to Mar, 10am-12.30pm and 3-5pm. 5 000L, 2 500L child. Audio-guided tours available. Bookshop. ☎ 0566 90 22 89.

Fortezza dei Senesi and **Torre del Candeliere** – Open daily (except Mon), Apr to Nov, 11am-1pm and 3-6pm (Nov 2.30-4.30pm); Dec-Mar, Sat-Sun only, 10am-1pm and 2.30-4.30pm. 3 000L, 1 500L child. ☎ 0566 90 22 89.

Museo della Miniera – Closed for maintenance at time of going to press. For information, contact ☎ 0566 90 22 89.

MATERA
☷ via De Viti de Marco 9 - ☎ 0835 33 19 83

San Pietro Caveoso – Open all year, Mon to Sat, 9am-noon and 3.30-7pm; Sun, 9.30am-12.30pm and 4-7pm. ☎ 0835 31 15 10.

Museo Nazionale Ridola – ♿ Open all year, daily, 9am-7pm. Closed 1 Jan, 1 May and 25 Dec. 5 000L. ☎ 0835 31 00 58.

MERANO
☷ corso della Libertà 35 - ☎ 0473 23 52 23

Castello Principesco – Open, all year, daily (except Mon), 10am-5pm, Sun and public holidays, 10am-1pm (July-Aug, 4-7pm). Closed 1 Jan, 1 May and 25 Dec. 4 000 L (adult), 3 000 L (child). ☎ 0473 23 60 15.

Excursions

Merano 2000 – Cable-car operates 1 June to 7 Nov and 18 Dec to 10 Apr approx., daily, 9am-5pm. ☎ 0473 23 48 21.

Tirolo: Castel Tirolo – Open late Mar to early Nov, daily (except Mon) 10am-5pm. 7 000 L (adult), no charge (child under 6). Guided tours available (45min) in Italian and German. Bookshop. ☎ 0473 22 02 21.

MILANO
☷ via Marconi, 1(piazza Duomo) - ☎ 02 72 52 43 00

Duomo – **Crypt, Treasury:** Open daily, 9am-noon and 2-6pm. 2 000L. No charge for the crypt.

Baptistery – Open daily, 9.45am-12.45pm and 2-5.45pm. 3 000L. ☎ 02 72 02 26 56.

Visita ai Terrazi – Open daily, mid-Feb to mid-Nov, 9am-5.45pm (4.15pm in winter). Closed 25 Apr, 1 May and 25 Dec. 6 000L (on foot), 9 000L (by lift). ☎ 02 72 02 26 56.

MILANO

Museo del Duomo – ᕹ (partial access). Open daily (except Mon), 9.30am-12.30pm and 3-6pm. Closed Mon (except public holidays), Easter, 25 Apr, 1 May and 25 Dec. 10 000L, 5 000L (student and over 60). Bookshop. ☎ 02 72 02 26 56.

Museo teatrale alla Scala – Open Mon to Sat all year, and Sun (except Nov to Apr), 9am-12.30pm and 2-5.30pm; last admission 30min before closing time. Closed 1 Jan, Easter, 15 Aug and over Christmas. 6 000L. Guided tours available (1hr). Bookshop. ☎ 02 80 53 418; www.museoteatrale.com

Pinacoteca di Brera – ᕹ Open daily (except Mon), 9am-6pm (1pm Sun and public holidays); last admission 45min before closing time. Closed 1 Jan and 1 May. 8 000L, no charge (under 18 and over 60). Guided and audio-guided tours available (1hr). Bookshop.☎ 02 72 26 31.

Castello Sforzesco: Municipal Art Collections – Open daily, 9.30am-5.30pm. Closed 1 Jan, 1 May, 15 Aug and 25 Dec. No charge. Bookshop. ☎ 02 80 46 30 54.

Pinacoteca Ambrosiana – Open daily (except Mon), 10am-5.30pm. Closed 1 Jan, Easter, 1 May and 25 Dec. 12 000L, 6 000L (child). Bookshop. ☎ 02 80 692.

Museo Poldi-Pezzoli – Open daily (except Mon), 10am-6pm. Closed 1 Jan, Easter, Easter Mon, 1 May, 15 Aug, 1 Nov, 25 and 26 Dec and the afternoons of 6 Jan, 25 Apr, 7 and 8 Dec. 10 000L, no charge (child under 10). Guided tours available in English and Italian (by appointment); audio-guided tours also available. Bookshop. ☎ 02 79 48 89 or 02 79 63 34.

Galleria d'Arte Moderna – Open daily (except Mon), 9.30am-5.30pm. Closed 1 Jan, 1 May, 15 Aug and 25 Dec. No charge. ☎ 02 86 46 30 54.

Casa di Manzoni – Open Tues to Fri, 9am-noon and 2-4pm. Closed Sat, Sun, Mon, also during Aug and from 25 Dec to 7 Jan. No charge. ☎ 02 86 46 04 03.

Museo Civico di Storia Naturale – ᕹ (partial access). Open Mon to Fri, 9am-6pm, Sat-Sun 9.30am-6.30pm. Closed 1 Jan, 1 May and 25 Dec. No charge. Guided tours available (1hr 30min) in English, French, German and Portuguese. Bookshop. ☎ 02 78 13 12.

Palazzo Bagatti Valsecchi – Open daily (except Mon), 1-5pm. Closed public holidays and for 2 weeks in Aug. 10 000L (5 000L Wed), 2 500L (aged 6-14). Guided tours available (1hr 30min) in English, Italian, French and German, by apointment. Bookshop. ☎ 02 76 00 61 32; www.museobagattivalsecchi.org

Museo della Scienza e della Tecnica Leonardo da Vinci – ᕹ Open Tues to Fri, 9.30am-5pm; Sat, Sun and public holidays, 9.30am-6.30pm. Closed Mon except holiday Mon, 1 Jan and 25 Dec. 10 000L, 6 000L (child). Bar, restaurant. Bookshop. ☎ 02 48 55 51; www.museoscienza.org

Santa Maria delle Grazie: Cenacolo – By appointment to ☎ 199 199 100 (from Italy, call charged at over 60km long-distance rate) or ☎ 02 894 211 46 (from abroad). Open all year, daily (except Mon), 9am-9pm (midnight Sat, 8pm Sun). 12 000L, plus 2 000L reservation fee, no charge (under 18 and over 60).

Museo Civico di Archeologia – Open daily (except Mon), 9am-5.30pm. Closed 1 Jan, 1 May and 25 Dec. No charge. Audio-visual presentation. Bookshop. ☎ 02 86 45 00 11.

Basilica di San Lorenzo Maggiore: Cappella di Sant'Aquilino – Open all year, daily, 9.30am-6.30pm. 2 000L.

Excursion

Abbazia di Chiaravalle – Open daily (except Mon), 9am-11.45am and 3-5.45pm; Sun and public holidays, 11-11.30am and 3-4.45pm (in summer 5.45pm). Guided tours on Sun at 11am, 3pm and 4pm. Book at least 3 weeks in advance for guided tours Tues to Sat. ☎ 02 57 40 34 04.

MODENA
🛈 piazza Grande 17 – ☎ 059 20 66 60

Museo del Duomo – Closed for restoration.

Biblioteca Estense – ᕹ Open daily (except Sun), 9am-1pm. Closed public holidays and the first two weeks of Sept. No charge. ☎ 059 22 22 48.

Galleria Estense – Open Tues, Fri, Sat, 9am-7pm; Wed, Thur, 9am-2pm; Sun, 9am-1pm. Closed 1 Jan, 1 May and 25 Dec. 8 000L, no charge (under 18 and over 60). ☎ 059 22 21 45.

Excursions

Abbazia di Nonantola – Open daily, 8am-7.30pm; Sun, 8am-12.30pm and 3-7.30pm. ☎ 059 54 90 53.

Carpi: Castello dei Pio – 🔥 (partial access). Open June to Aug, Thur, Sat-Sun, 10am-1pm and 4-7pm; rest of the year, 9.30am-12.30pm and 3.30-6.30pm. Closed Nov to 20 Mar. 3 000L (adult), no charge (child under 14). Guided tours available (2hr 30min) in English, Italian and French. ☎ 059 64 92 98.

MOLISE

Agnone: Fonderia Pontificia Marinelli – 🔥 (with help of local guide). This former bell-foundry now houses the Museo Storico Internazionale della Campana (bell museum). Guided tours only (30min) at 11am and 4pm. Closed 1 Jan, Easter, 15 Aug and 25 Dec. 5 000L. Audio-visual presentation. Bookshop. ☎ 0865 78 235.

Altilia Saepinum – Open daily, 9am-1hr before sunset. No charge. ☎ 0874 79 02 07.

Pietrabbondante: Italic Sanctuary – Open daily, 9am-1hr before sunset. 4 000L, no charge (under 18 and over 60). ☎ 0865 76 129.

San Vincenzo al Volturno – Guided tours (approx 2hrs) of ruins and church led by Associazione Culturale Atena. Book 3-4 days ahead. 5 000L. ☎ 0865 95 10 06 .

Abbazia di MONTECASSINO

Open Apr to Oct, daily, 9am-noon and 3.30-6pm (5pm rest of the year). No charge. ☎ 0776 31 15 29.

Museo Abbaziale – Open Apr to Oct, daily, 9am-noon and 3.30-6pm; Nov to Mar, Sat-Sun only, 9am-noon and 3.30-5pm. 3 000L, 2 000L (under 15). Guided tours available (1hr) in English, Italian, French and German by appointment. ☎ 0776 31 15 29.

Cassino: Museo Archeologico Nazionale – 🔥 (partial access). Open all year, daily, 9am-1hr before sunset. Closed 1 Jan, 1 May and 25 Dec. 4 000L. ☎ 0776 30 11 68.

MONTECATINI TERME   🛈 viale Verdi 66/a – ☎ 0572 77 22 44

Museo dell'Accademia d'Arte – 🔥 (partial access). Open daily (except Sun), Apr to Oct, 9am-12.30pm and 4-7.30pm; Nov to Mar, 9am-noon and 4-7pm (closed Sat afternoons). Closed public holidays. No charge. ☎ 0572 76 63 36.

Excursions

Collodi

Parco di Pinocchio – 🔥 (partial access). Open daily, 8.30am-sunset. 12 000L (adult), 7 000L (child). Bar and restaurant. Bookshop. ☎ 0572 42 93 42; www.pinocchio.it

Castello e Giardino Garzoni – Castle closed for restoration at time of going to press. Gardens can be visited from 15 Mar to 10 Nov, 9am-sunset; rest of the year, 9am-sunset (ring bell to call warden). Guided tours (40min) available in English, French and German by appointment a few days in advance. Bar and restaurant. For information on admission charges contact ☎ 0572 42 95 90.

MONTEFALCO

Torre Comunale – Closed for restoration.

Museo di San Francesco – Open daily, June to Aug, 10.30am-1pm and 3-7pm; Mar to May, Sept, Oct, 10.30am-1pm and 2-6pm; Nov to Feb, daily (except Mon), 10.30am-1pm and 2.30-5pm. Closed 1 Jan and 25 Dec. 5 000L. ☎ 0742 37 95 98.

Abbazia di MONTE OLIVETO MAGGIORE

Open all year, daily, 9.15am-noon and 3.15-6pm (5pm Nov to Mar). No charge. Bookshop. ☎ 0577 70 76 11.

MONTEPULCIANO

Torre del Palazzo Comunale – Open, all year, Mon to Sat, 9am-1pm. Closed Sun and public holidays. No charge. ☎ 0578 71 21.

Museo civico-Pinacoteca Crociani – Closed for restoration at time of going to press. ☎ 0578 71 69 35.

MONTE SANT'ANGELO

Tomba di Rotari – Open Apr to Oct, 9am-1pm and 2.30-7.30pm; Nov to Mar, by appointment only. 1 000L. Contact ☎ 0884 56 18 09.

MONZA

Duomo: Treasury – Open daily, 9am-noon and 3-5.30pm; Sun and public holidays, 9am-12.30pm and 3-6pm. 5 000L. ☎ 039 32 34 04.

7 Palazzo Reale (piazza del Plebiscito) - ☎ 081 41 87 44
7 Piazza del Gesù Nuovo 7 - ☎ 081 55 23 328
7 Piazza dei Martiri 58 - ☎ 081 40 53 11

Castel Nuovo - ♿ (partial access) Open Jan to Sept, Mon to Sat, 9am-7pm; rest of the year, 8.30am-2pm. 10 000L, no charge (under 12 and over 65). ☎ 081 79 52 003.

Teatro San Carlo - Open Sat-Sun, 2-3.30pm. 5 000L. ☎ 081 79 72 331.

Palazzo Reale - ♿ Open June to Oct, daily (except Wed), 9am-8pm (midnight Sat, 9pm Sun); rest of the year, daily (except Wed), 9am-2pm (1pm Sun and public holidays). Closed 1 Jan, 1 May and 25 Dec. 8 000L, no charge (under 18 and over 60). ☎ 081 58 08 111.

Chiesa del Gesù Nuovo - Open all year, daily, 8am-12.30pm and 4-7pm. ☎ 081 55 78 12.

Santa Chiara - Open all year, daily, 7am-1pm and 4-8pm. ☎ 081 79 71 235. **Cloisters and museum**: Open 9.30am-1pm and 2.30-5.30pm (Sun, morning only). 6 000L, no charge (over 65). ☎ 081 55 21 597.

San Domenico Maggiore - Open all year, daily, 9am-12.30pm and 4-6pm. ☎ 081 45 90 03.

Cappella Sansevero - Open all year, daily (except Tues), 10am-4.30pm (6.30pm in July). 8 000L. ☎ 081 55 18 470.

San Gregorio Armeno - Open all year, daily, 9.30am-noon (9am-12.30pm and 4-6pm Sun in May). ☎ 081 55 20 186.

San Lorenzo Maggiore - Open all year, Mon to Sat, 8am-12.30pm and 4.30-6.30pm, Sun 8am-1pm. ☎ 081 45 49 48.
Tour of the archeological excavations, Mon to Sat (except Tues), 9am-1pm and 3.30-5.30pm (4-6.30pm in summer), Sun, 9am-1.30pm. 5 000L, 2 500L (child). Guided tours available (1hr). ☎ 081 45 49 48.

Decumanus Maximus - Visit of all monuments all year, Mon to Sat, 9am-1.30pm.
Pio Monte della Misericordia ☎ 081 44 69 73.
Chiesa dei Girolami ☎ 081 44 91 39.
San Paolo Maggiore: also open Sun mornings ☎ 081 45 40 48.
Purgatorio ad Arco: also open Sun mornings ☎ 081 45 93 12.
Santa Maria Maggiore ☎ 081 45 81 01.
Croce di Lucca ☎ 081 56 65 285.
San Pietro a Maiella: also open Sun mornings ☎ 081 45 90 08.

Duomo

Tesoro di San Gennaro - Open Mon to Sat, 8.30am-12.30pm and 4.30-6.30pm; Sun, 8.30am-12.30pm. ☎ 081 29 47 64.

Basilica di Santa Restituta and archeological displays - Open Mon to Sat, 9am-noon and 4.30-7pm; Sun, 9am-noon. 5 000L for the archeological displays. ☎ 081 44 90 97.

Quadreria dei Girolamini - Open Mon to Sat, 9.30am-1pm (last admission 12.45pm). Closed Aug and public holidays. No charge. ☎ 081 44 91 39.

Library - Closed for restoration. For information, contact ☎ 081 29 44 44.

Museo Archeologico Nazionale - ♿ Open all year, daily (except Tues), 9am-2pm (last admission 1.30pm). Usually longer opening hours in summer. Closed 1 Jan, 1 May and 25 Dec. 12 000L, no charge (under 18 and over 60). ☎ 081 29 28 23.

Museo Civico Filangieri - Open all year, Tues to Sat, 9.30am-1.30pm and 3.30-6.30pm, Sun, 9.30am-1.30pm. Closed public holidays. 5 000L. ☎ 081 20 31 75.

Sant'Anna dei Lombardi - Usually open in the morning.

Certosa di San Martino - Open all year, daily (except Mon), 9am-2pm. Closed public holidays. 9 500L, no charge (under 18). ☎ 081 57 81 769.

Palazzo e Galleria Nazionale di Capodimonte - ♿ Open all year, Tues to Sat, 10am-7pm; Sun, 9am-2pm. Closed public holidays. 12 000L, no charge (under 18). Bar, restaurant. Bookshop. ☎ 081 74 99 111.

Museo Nazionale di Ceramica Duca di Martina - Open all year, daily (except Mon), 9am-2pm. Closed public holidays. 5 000L, no charge (under 18). ☎ 081 57 88 418.

Catacombe di San Gennaro - Guided tours only (40min, at least two persons) daily, 9.30am, 10.15am, 11am and 11.45am. Closed 1 Jan. 5 000L, 3 000L (under 15). Audio-visual presentation. ☎ 081 74 11 071.

Acquarium - ♿ Open Mar to Oct, Tues to Sat, 9am-6pm, Sun, 9.30am-7.30pm; Nov to Feb, Tues to Sat, 9am-5pm, Sun, 9am-2pm. 3 000L, 1 500L (child). Guided tours available in English and French on request and by appointment. ☎ 081 58 33 263.

Museo Principe di Aragona Pignatelli Cortes - ♿ (partial access). Open all year, daily (except Mon), 9am-2pm. Closed public holidays. 4 000L, no charge (child). Guided tours available (1hr) in English, Italian and French. ☎ 081 66 96 75.

Golfo di NAPOLI

Baia: Terme - Open all year, 9am-1hr before sunset. Closed 1 Jan and 1 May. 4 000 L, no charge (under 18 and over 60). ☎ 081 86 87 592; www.campiflegrei.it

Bacoli

🛈 Comune di Bacoli, via Fusaro 104 - ☎ 081 86 87 541

Cento Camerelle - Open 9am-1hr before sunset. Apply to the custodian in via Cento Camerelle. For information contact the Ufficio Beni Culturali in Bacoli. ☎ 081 86 87 541.

Piscina Mirabile - Open 9am-1hr before sunset. No charge, donation welcome. For information contact ☎ 081 52 61 481 or 081 52 65 068.

Vesuvio: Ascent - Paying car park at the end of the road or at Herculaneum; there is a bus service from the railway station - the "Circumvesuviana" line. At the top, visitors wishing to go to the crater edge must be accompanied by a guide (9 000L). Head guide: Signor Pompilio. ☎ 081 73 22 726 or 081 77 75 720. Ufficio Collegio Regionale Guide Alpine, via Panoramica 172, Ercolano, Signor Maddaloni, ☎ 0337 94 249 (mobile).

Torre Annunziata: Villa di Oplontis - Open all year, daily, 9am-2hr before sunset. Closed 1 Jan, 1 May and 25 Dec. 4 000L, no charge (under 18 and over 60). ☎ 081 86 21 755.

Monte Faito: cable-car - Cable-car (10min) operates Apr to Oct, with departures every 20/30min, 9.25am-4.25pm (7.25am-7.15pm mid-June to late Aug). 12 000L. For information contact ☎ 081 87 11 334.

ORVIETO

🛈 piazza Duomo 24 - ☎ 0763 34 17 72

Palazzo dei Papi: Museo dell'Opera del Duomo - Closed for restoration.

Cappella della Madonna di San Brizio - Open Mon to Sat, 7.30am-12.45pm and 2.30-7.15pm (Apr to Sept), 6.30pm (Mar and Oct) and 5.15pm (Nov to Feb); Sun and public holidays, 2.30-5.45pm (6.45pm July to Sept). Closed during church services. 3 000L. ☎ 0763 34 24 77.

Orvieto Underground - Guided tours only (1hr) in English, Italian, French and German. Departures from piazza Duomo 24, daily (except 25 Dec), 11am and 4pm. 10 000L, 6 000L (child). ☎ 0763 34 48 91 or 0347 38 31 472.

Pozzo di San Patrizio - Open daily, Mar to Sept, 10am-6.45pm; Oct to Feb, 10am-5.45pm. 6 000L, 4 000L (child). ☎ 0763 34 37 68.

Museo archeologico Faina - ♿ Open daily, 31 Mar to 28 Sept, 10am-1pm and 2-6pm; rest of the year, daily (except Mon in winter), 10am-1pm and 2.30-5pm. Closed 1 Jan and 25 Dec. 8 000L, 5 000L (child). Guided tours available (1hr) in Italian. Audio-visual presentation. Bookshop. ☎ 0763 34 15 11.

OSTIA ANTICA

Excavation site - Open summer, daily (except Mon), 9am-6pm; rest of the year, daily (except Mon), 9am-2hr before sunset. Closed 1 Jan, 1 May and 25 Dec. 8 000L, no charge (under 18 and over 60). ☎ 06 56 35 80 99; itnw.roma.it/ostia/scavi

Museo - Closed for restoration. Re-opening sometime in 1999. For information, contact ☎ 06 56 35 80 99.

OTRANTO

Excursion

Grotta Zinzulusa - Guided tours only (20min) in Italian (also English and French in summer), 15 July to 15 Sept, 9.30am-7pm; rest of the year, 10am-4pm. No tours when the sea is rough. 4 000-5 000L, 3 000 (child). Bar, restaurant. ☎ 0836 94 38 12 or 0836 94 70 05; www.anet.it/Castro

P

PADOVA

🚉 Stazione - ☎ 049 87 52 077

Cappella degli Scrovegni - Open daily, Feb to Oct, 9am-7pm; Nov to Feb, 9am-6pm. 10 000L. ☎ 049 82 04 550; www.padovanet.it/museicivici

Museo Civico agli Eremitani - Open daily (except Mon), Feb to Oct, 9am-7pm; Nov to Feb, 9am-6pm. Closed 1 Jan, 1 May, 15 Aug, 25 and 26 Dec. 10 000L, 7 000L (aged 11-17), 5 000 (aged 6-10). Bookshop. ☎ 049 82 04 550; www.padovanet.it/museicivici

Basilica del Santo - Open all year, daily (except Sun and public holidays), 6.30am-7.45pm (7pm 25 Oct to 27 Mar). Guided tours by appointment (book a few days in advance), noon-4pm. Donation welcome. ☎ 049 82 42 811, Fax 049 87 63 802; www.mess-s-antonio.it/basilica/index.htm

Oratorio di San Giorgio and **Scuola di Sant'Antonio** - Oratorio is closed for restoration. Scuola di Sant'Antonio is open daily, Mar to Sept, 9am-12.30pm and 2.30-7pm; rest of the year, 9am-12.30pm and 2.30-5pm. Closed 1 Jan and 25 Dec. 3 000L, 2 000L (child). Guided tours available. ☎ 049 87 55 235.

Palazzo della Ragione - Open daily (except Mon), Feb to Oct, 9am-7pm; rest of the year, 9am-6pm. Closed 1 Jan, 1 May, 15 Aug, 25 and 26 Dec. 7 000L, 4 000L (child). Bookshop. ☎ 049 82 05 006; www.padovanet.it/museicivici

Università: Teatro Anatomico - Guided tours only (30/50min) in English, Italian, French, German, Spanish and Japanese, Mar to Oct, Mon, Weds and Fri at 3pm, 4pm and 5pm, Tues, Thur and Sat at 9am, 10am and 11am; rest of the year, Tues and Thurs at 9am, 10am and 11am, and Fri at 3pm, 4pm and 5pm. Closed during university holidays. 5 000L, 2 000L (child). ☎ 049 82 09 711.

Caffè Pedrocchi: sale - Open daily (except Mon unless public holiday), 9.30am-12.30pm and 3.30-6pm. Closed 1 Jan, 1 May, 15 Aug, 25 and 26 Dec. 5 000L, 3 000L (child). ☎ 049 82 05 007 or ☎ 049 87 50 655; www.padova.net.it./cultura

Orto Botanico - ♿ (partial access). Open Apr to Oct, daily, 9am-1pm and 3-6pm; Nov to Mar, Mon to Sat, 9am-1pm. Closed public holidays Nov to Mar. 5 000L, 3 000L (reductions). ☎ 049 65 66 14.

Excursions

Arquà Petrarca: Casa del Petrarca - Open daily (except Mon unless public holiday), Feb to Sept, 9am-noon and 2-6.30pm; Oct to Jan, 9am-noon and 2.30-5pm. Closed 1 Jan, 1 May, 15 Aug, 25 and 26 Dec. 6 000 L, 4 000 L (child). Bookshop. ☎ 0429 71 82 94.

Este: Museo Nazionale Atestino - ♿ Open all year, daily, 9am-7pm. Closed 1 Jan, 1 May and 25 Dec. 4 000 L, no charge (under 18 and over 60). Guided tours (2hr) available by appointment. ☎ 0429 20 85.

PAESTUM

🚉 via Magna Grecia 151/156 (archeological site) - ☎ 0828 72 23 22

Ruins - ♿ (partial access). Open all year, daily, 9am-1hr before sunset. Closed 1 Jan, 1 May, 15 Aug and 25 Dec. 8 000L, no charge (under 18 and over 60, and during museum week). Guided tours (1hr 30min) available in English, French, German and Spanish. ☎ 0828 81 10 16.

Museo - ♿ (partial access). Open all year, daily, 9am-6.30pm. Closed 1st and 3rd Mon in the month, 1 Jan, 1 May, 15 Aug and 25 Dec. 8 000L, no charge (child, and during museum week). Guided tours (1hr) available in English, French, German and Spanish. ☎ 0828 81 10 16.

PARMA

🚉 via Melloni 1/b - ☎ 0521 21 88 89

San Giovanni Evangelista: convent cloisters - Open all year, Mon to Sat, 9am-noon and 3.30-6pm; Sun, 10am-noon and 3.30-6pm. Donation. ☎ 0521 23 55 92.

Antica Spezieria di San Giovanni Evangelista - ♿ Open all year, daily, 9am-2pm. Closed 1 Jan, 1 May and 25 Dec. 4 000L, no charge (under 18 and over 60). ☎ 0521 23 36 17.

Museo Archeologico Nazionale - ♿ (partial access). Open all year, daily (except Mon), 9am-7pm (last admission 6.30pm). Closed public holidays. 4 000L, no charge (child). ☎ 0521 23 37 18.

Galleria Nazionale - ♿ Open all year, daily, 9am-2pm. Closed 1 Jan, 1 May and 25 Dec. 12 000L, no charge (under 18 and over 60). Bookshop. ☎ 0521 23 36 17.

Teatro Farnese - ♿ Open all year, daily, 9am-2pm. Closed 1 Jan, 1 May and 25 Dec. 14 000L, no charge (under 18 and over 60). ☎ 0521 23 36 17.

Camera del Correggio (or **Camera di San Paolo**) - ♿ Open all year, daily, 9am-2pm. Closed 1 Jan, 1 May and 25 Dec. 4 000L, no charge (under 18 and over 60). ☎ 0521 23 36 17.

Fondazione-Museo Glauco-Lombardi - Restoration work is set to finish end 1999. Visitors are advised to phone and check the following information. ♿ Open all year, daily (except Mon), 9am-2pm. Closed public holidays. Bar. Bookshop. For information, contact ☎ 0521 23 37 27.

Santa Maria della Steccata - Open Mon to Sat, 10.45-noon, 3-4pm and 5.30-6.30pm, Sun and public holidays, 8.45-9.30am, 10.15-11am, 3-4pm and 5.30-6.30pm. Donation welcome. ☎ 0521 23 49 37.

Casa Toscanini - Guided tours only (30min) in English, Italian and French, Tues to Sat, 10am-1pm and 3-6pm; Sun, 10am-1pm. 3 000L, 1 000L (child). ☎ 0521 21 85 93.

Excursions

Castello di Torrechiara - ♿ (partial access). Open in summer, Tues to Fri, 9am-2.30pm; Sat-Sun, 9am-7pm; in winter, daily (except Mon), 8.30am-2pm. Closed public holidays. 4 000L, no charge (child under 12). ☎ 0521 35 52 55.

Fontanellato: Rocca San Vitale - ♿ (partial access). Guided tours only (1hr 30min) Apr to Oct, 9.30-12.30am and 3-7pm; Nov to Mar, 9.30-12.30pm and 3-6pm (last admission 1hr before closing time). Closed Mon from Nov to Mar (unless public holiday) and 25 Dec. 7 000L, 4 000L (child). Bookshop. ☎ 0521 82 23 46.

PAVIA
🛈 via Fabio Filzi 2 - ☎ 0382 22 156

Castello Visconteo - Open all year, daily (except Mon), 9am-1.30pm (1pm Sun). In Apr to June, Sept, Oct, occasional afternoon opening on Sat-Sun. Closed public holidays. 8 000L. ☎ 0382 33 853.

Certosa di PAVIA

Open daily (except Mon, unless holiday Mon), May to Sept, 9-11.30am and 2.30-6pm (5.30pm in April); Oct to Mar, 9-11.30am and 2.30-4.30pm. Guided tours available (about 1hr). Donation welcome. ☎ 0382 92 56 13.

PERUGIA
🛈 piazza IV Novembre 3 - ☎ 075 57 23 327

Galleria Nazionale dell'Umbria - ♿ (partial access). Open all year, Mon to Sat, 9am-7pm; Sun and public holidays, 9am-2pm: June to Sept, 9am-7pm and 9pm-midnight; May and Oct, 9am-8pm. Last admission 30min before closing time. Closed 1st Mon in the month, 1 Jan, 1 May and 25 Dec. 8 000L, no charge (child) Guided tours available (1hr 30min). ☎ 075 57 41 257.

Museo Archeologico Nazionale dell'Umbria - ♿ (partial access). Open all year, Mon to Sat, 9am-7pm; Sun and public holidays, 9am-1pm (last admission 1hr before closing time). Closed 1 Jan, 1 May and 25 Dec. 4 000L, no charge (under 18 and over 60). ☎ 075 57 27 141 or 075 57 59 61.

Collegio del Cambio - Open Mar to Oct (and 20 Dec to 6 Jan), daily, 9am-12.30pm and 2.30-5.30pm (closed afternoon on Sun and public holidays); Nov to Feb, daily (except Mon), 8am-2pm (9am-12.30pm Sun and public holidays). Closed 1 Jan, 1 May and 25 Dec. 5 000L. Guided tours available (15min) in Italian. ☎ 075 57 28 599; www.perusia.it/cambio

Excursions

Ipogeo dei Volumni - Open July and Aug, Mon to Sat, 4.30-6.30pm; Sept to June, Mon to Sat, 9.30am-12.30pm and 3-5pm; Sun and public holidays all year, 9.30am-12.30pm. 4 000L, no charge (under 18 and over 60). ☎ 075 39 33 29; www.archeopg.arti.beniculturali.it

Torgiano: Museo del Vino - Open all year, daily, 9am-1pm and 3-7pm (6pm in winter); last admission 30min before closing time. 5 000L, 4 000L (child). Guided tours (1hr) available in English, German, Italian, French and Japanese. Bookshop. ☎ 075 98 80 200.

PESARO
🛈 viale Trieste 164 - ☎ 0721 69 341

Casa Natale di Rossini - Open daily (except Mon), July and Aug, 5-11pm; May and June, 9.30am-12.30pm; Sept to Apr, 8.30am-1.30pm and 4-7pm. 5 000L, 8 000L combined ticket with Museo della Ceramica and Pinacoteca, no charge (under 25 and over 65). ☎ 0721 67 815.

Musei Civici - Same admission times and charges as Casa Rossini.

Museo Oliveriano - ♿ Open July and Aug, Mon to Sat, 4.30-7.30pm; Sept to June, visit by appointment. Closed Sun, public holidays and 24 Sept. No charge. ☎ 0721 33 344.

Excursion

Gradara   🄴 Piazza Paolo e Francesca 1 (mornings only) - ☏ 0541 96 41 15

La Rocca - ♿ (partial access). Open daily (except Mon pm), July to Sept, 9am-7pm (also 8-11pm Thurs to Sat); rest of the year, daily, 9am-2pm. Last admission 30min before closing time. Closed 1 Jan, 1 May and 25 Dec. 8 000L, no charge (under 18 and over 60). Guided tours available (30min); apply a few days in advance.

PIACENZA   🄴 piazza Cittadella (Palazzo Farnese) - ☏ 0523 32 93 24

Duomo - Open all year, daily, 7am-noon and 4-7pm. ☏ 0523 32 20 74; www.agonet.it/piacenza.piacenza.htm

Galleria d'Arte Moderna Ricci Oddi - Closed for restoration, scheduled to re-open end 1999. ☏ 0523 32 07 42.

San Savino - Open all year, daily, 6.45am-noon and 3-4pm (noon Sun). ☏ 0523 32 20 74; www.agonet.it/piacenza.piacenza.htm

Palazzo Farnese: Museo civico - ♿ Guided tours only (1hr 30min), Tues to Fri, 8.30am-1pm (also 3-6.30pm Fri and Sat), Sun 9.30am-1pm and 3-6pm. Closed 4 July and public holidays. 10 000L, 8 000L (under 18). ☏ 0523 32 82 70 or 0523 32 69 81; www.Farnese.net

San Sisto - Open all year, daily, 7-10am and 4.30-6.30pm (3-6pm Sat, 7-noon and 3-5.30pm Sun). ☏ 0523 32 20 74; www.agonet.it/piacenza.piacenza.htm

Madonna di Campagna - Open all year, daily, 8.30am-noon and 3.30-6.30pm. ☏ 0523 32 20 74; www.agonet.it/piacenza.piacenza.htm

Galleria Alberoni - ♿ (partial access). Guided tours only (1hr 30min) in English, French and Italian, Apr to June and Oct, Sun, 3-6pm. 10 000L, 7 000L (child). Bookshop. ☏ 0523 32 20 74.

PIENZA

Museo Diocesano - Open mid-Mar to Oct, daily (except Tues), 10am-1pm and 2-6.30pm; Nov to mid-Mar, Sat, Sun and public holidays only, 10am-1pm and 3-6pm. 8 000L. ☏ 0578 74 99 05.

Palazzo Piccolomini - Guided tours only, in summer, daily (except Mon), 10am-12.30pm and 4-7pm; in winter, 10am-12.30pm and 3-6pm. 5 000L. ☏ 0578 74 85 03.

Excursions

Montalcino

Fortress and parapet walk - Open Apr to Oct, daily, 9am-8pm; Nov to Mar, daily (except Mon), 9am-1pm and 2-6pm. Closed 25 Dec. Bar. Bookshop. 3 500L, no charge (child under 6). ☏ 0577 84 92 11.

Museo Civico e Diocesano - ♿ Open Apr to Oct, daily (except Mon) 10am-6pm; Nov to Mar, daily (except Mon), 10am-1pm and 2-5pm (6pm Nov and Dec). 8 000L, 5 000L (child). Guided tours available (50min) in English and Italian. Audio-visual presentation. Bookshop. ☏ 0577 84 60 14.

Abbazia di Sant'Antimo - Open Mon to Fri, 10.30am-12.30pm and 3-6.30pm; Sun and public holidays, 9.15-10.45am and 3-6pm. Liturgy in Gregorian chant: Mass at 9am weekdays and 11am Sun; Vespers at 7pm weekdays, 6.30 Sun. www.to/antimo

PISA   🄴 piazza del Duomo - ☏ 050 56 04 64

A combined ticket can be purchased for the Duomo, Battistero, Camposanto, Museo dell'Opera del Duomo and Museo delle Sinopie. 18 000L (15 000L in winter when there is no charge for the Duomo).

Duomo - Open daily, 10am-1hr before sunset (1pm Sun and public holidays). 3 000L, no charge Oct to March.

Battistero - Same admission times and charges as for the Museo dell'Opera del Duomo.

Camposanto - Same admission times and charges as for the Museo dell'Opera del Duomo.

Museo dell'Opera del Duomo - Open daily, in summer, 8am-7.20pm; in spring and autumn, 9am-5.20pm; in winter, 9am-4.20pm. 10 000L (ticket valid for two monuments).

Museo delle Sinopie - Same admission times and charges as for the Museo dell'Opera del Duomo.

Museo Nazionale di San Matteo – ♿ (partial access). Open daily (except Mon), 9am-7pm (2pm Sun and public holidays); last admission 30min before closing time. Closed 1 Jan, 1 May and 25 Dec. 8 000L, no charge (under 18 and over 60). ☎ 050 54 18 65.

Excursion

Torre del Lago Puccini: Villa Puccini – Guided tours only (30min) in English, French, German and Italian, all year, daily (except Mon), 10am-12.30pm and 3-6.30pm (6pm Apr and May, 5.30pm Dec to Mar). Closed the month of Nov. 7 000L, 3 000L (aged 7-10). ☎ 0584 34 14 45.

PISTOIA 🚍 piazza del Duomo – ☎ 0573 21 622

Duomo: Altar of St James – For information, contact the sacristan: Mon to Sat, 10am-noon and 4-5.45pm; Sun and public holidays, 11.20-noon and 4-5.30pm. 3 000L, 2 000/1 000L (reductions). ☎ 0573 25 095.

Battistero – ♿ (partial access). Open all year, daily (except Mon), 9.30am-12.30pm and 3-6pm, (12.30pm Sun and public holidays). Audio-guided tours available. ☎ 0573 21 622.

Palazzo Comunale: Museo Civico – Open all year, Tues to Sat, 10am-7pm; Sun and public holidays, 9am-12.30pm. Closed 1 Jan, 1 May and 25 Dec. 6 000L, no charge Sat afternoons. ☎ 0573 37 12 78.

Palazzo del Tau: Marino Marini Information Centre – ♿ (partial access). Open all year, Tues to Sat, 9am-1pm and 3-7pm, Sun and public holidays, 9am-12.30pm. Closed 1 Jan, 1 May and 25 Dec. 6 000L, no charge (under 18 and Sat afternoons). Audio-visual presentation. Bar. Bookshop. ☎ 0573 30 285.

Excursion

Vinci 🚍 via della Torre 11 – ☎ 0571 56 80 12

Museo Leonardiano – Open daily, Mar to Oct, 9.30am-7pm (6pm Nov to Feb). Closed 1 Jan and 25 Dec. 5 000L, 3 000L (child). Guided tours available in English, French, German, Spanish and Italian; book through the tourist office. Audio-visual presentation. Bookshop. ☎ 0571 56 80 12.

Casa di Leonardo – ♿ (partial access). Same admission times as for Museo Leonardiano. No charge. ☎ 0571 56 80 12.

POMPEI 🚍 via Sacra 1 – ☎ 081 85 07 255

Open all year, daily, 9am-2hr before sunset. Closed 1 Jan, 1 May and 25 Dec. Bar and restaurant. Bookshop. 12 000L, no charge (under 18 and over 60). ☎ 081 85 75 111.

Abbazia di POMPOSA

♿ (partial access). Open daily, Apr to Oct, 8.30am-noon and 2.30-7pm; Nov to Mar, 9.30am-4pm. Times may vary; visitors are advised to phone ahead. Closed 1 Jan, 1 May and 25 Dec. Entrance to Museo Pomposiano 4 000L, no charge (under 18 and over 65). ☎ 0533 71 91 10.

Promontorio di PORTOFINO 🚍 via XXV Aprile 2, S. Margherita Ligure – ☎ 0185 28 74 86

Portofino: Castello – Open all year, daily (except Tuesday), 10am-6pm (5pm Oct to Mar). 3 000L, no charge (child under 12). ☎ 0185 26 90 46.

Excursions

Access to Portofino Vetta – Private toll-road: no charge at time of going to press. For information, contact ☎ 0185 77 01 60, Pro Loco Camogli ☎ 0185 77 10 66.

San Fruttuoso: access by boat – From Rapallo, Santa Margherita and Portofino, 13 000L-21 000L return ticket (round trip), Servizio Marittimo del Tigullio, ☎ 0185 28 46 70. From Camogli, 13 000L return ticket (round trip), Servizio Motobarche "Golfo Paradiso". ☎ 0185 77 20 91.

POZZUOLI 🚍 piazza Matteotti 1/A – ☎ 081 52 66 639

Anfiteatro Flavio – Open all year, Apr to Sept, 9am-5pm; Oct to Dec, 9am-2.45pm; Jan to Mar, 9am-3pm. Closed 1 Jan, 1 May and 25 Dec. 4 000L, no charge (under 18 and over 60). ☎ 081 52 66 007.

Solfatara – ♿ Open daily, Apr to Sept, 8.30am-7pm; Oct, 8.30am-6pm; Nov to mid-Mar, 8.30am-4pm. 8 000L, 5 000L (child). Guided tours (45min) in English, French, German and Italian. Bar, restaurant. Bookshop. ☎ 081 52 62 341; www.kenno.com/solfatara

PRATO

Museo dell'Opera del Duomo - ♿ (partial access). Open all year, Mon, Wed to Sat, 9.30am–2.30pm and 3–6.30pm; Sun and public holidays, 9.30am–2.30pm. Closed 1 Jan, Easter, 1 May, 15 Aug and 25 Dec. 8 000L, no charge (child and 26 Dec). ☎ 0574 29 339.

PUGLIA

Canosa di Puglia: Ipogei Lagrasta – Open May to Sept, daily (except Mon), 9am–1pm and 5–7pm; Mar and Apr, daily (except Mon), 9am–1pm and 4–6pm; Oct to Feb, Sun and public holidays, 8am–2pm. No charge. Guided tours available (1hr) in English, French and German. ☎ 0883 66 21 83.

Castel del Monte – Open Apr to Sept, 9am–7pm; Oct to Mar, 9am–1pm. 8 000 L, no charge (under 18 and over 60). Guided tours (45min) in English and Italian. ☎ 080 52 86 238; www.castelli-puglia.org

Grotte di Castellana – Guided tours only in English, Italian, French and German daily, late Mar to early Nov, short tours (1km/0.5mi, about 1hr) every hour 8.30am–1pm and 2.30–7pm. 15 000 L, 12 000 L (child aged 6–14). Longer tour ending at Grotta Bianca (3km/2mi, about 2hr), late Mar to early Nov, every hour 9am–noon and 3–6pm. 25 000 L, 20 000 L child (child aged 6–14). Tour not recommended for visitors with heart problems. For information on visits during the rest of the year, contact ☎ 0800 21 39 76 (toll-free) or ☎ 080 49 98 211.

Gioia del Colle: Norman castle – ♿ (partial access). Open all year, daily, 9am–1pm and 4–7pm. Closed 1 Jan, 1 May and 25 Dec. 4 000L, no charge (child). ☎ 080 34 81 305.

Lucera: Museo Civico G. Fiorelli – Open Apr to Sept, daily (except Mon), 9am–1pm and 4–7pm; Oct to Mar, daily (except Mon), 9am–1pm and 3.30–6.30pm; Sun and public holidays 9am–1pm. Closed weekday public holidays, Easter, Easter Mon, 15 Aug, 25 and 26 Dec. 1 500L, 1 000L (child). Guided tours (45min). ☎ 0881 54 70 41.

Ostuni

Archeological museum – Open Tues to Sat, 8.30am–1pm (Thurs also 3.30–7pm), Sun and public holidays, 10am–12.30pm and 3.30–7pm. 3 000L, 1 500L (child). Guided tours available (40min). Audio-visual presentation. ☎ 0831 33 63 83.

Ruvo di Puglia: Museo Archeologico Jatta – Open all year, daily, 8.30am–1.30pm (also Fri and Sat, 2.30–7.30pm). Closed 1 Jan, 1 May and 25 Dec. Guided tours (1hr 30min). ☎ 080 36 12 848.

R

RAVELLO

Villa Rufolo – ♿ (partial access). Open all year, daily, 9am–8pm (6pm Oct to Mar). Closed 1 Jan and 25 Dec. 5 000L, 3 000L (under 18 and over 60). ☎ 089 85 76 57.

Museo del Duomo – Open Mar to Oct, daily, 9am–1pm and 3–7pm; rest of the year reduced opening times (contact tourist office for further information). 2 000L.

San Giovanni del Toro – For information contact the tourist office.

Villa Cimbrone – Open all year, daily, 9am–sunset. 8 000L. ☎ 089 85 71 38.

RAVENNA

Combined ticket for the Mausoleo di Galla Placidia, Basilica di San Vitale, Battistero Neoniano, Basilica di Sant'Apollinare Nuovo and Museo Arcivescovil: 10 000L; combined ticket for Museo Nazionale, Basilica di Sant'Apollinare in Classe and Mausoleo di Teodorico: 12 000L.

Basilica di San Vitale – Open daily, in summer, 9am–7pm; rest of the year, 9am–4.30pm. Closed 1 Jan and 25 Dec. 6 000L, ticket also valid for Mausoleo di Galla Placidia. ☎ 0554 21 81 58

Mausoleo di Galla Placidia – Open daily, in summer, 9am–7pm; rest of the year, 9am–4.30pm. Closed 1 Jan and 25 Dec. 6 000L, ticket also valid for Basilica di San Vitale, no charge (child under 11). ☎ 0554 21 81 58.

Museo Nazionale – Open all year, daily (except Mon), 8.30am–6.30pm (1pm Sun). Closed public holidays. 8 000L, no charge (under 18 and over 65). ☎ 0544 47 36 43.

Battistero Neoniano – Open daily, in summer, 9.30am–6.30pm; rest of the year, 9.30am–4.30pm. Closed 1 Jan and 25 Dec. 5 000L, ticket also valid for Museo Arcivescovile. ☎ 0544 21 81 58.

Museo Arcivescovile – Open all year, daily, 9.30am–6.30pm (4.30pm in winter). Closed 1 Jan and 25 Dec. 5 000L, ticket also valid for Battistero Neoniano. ☎ 0554 21 81 58.

Battistero degli Ariani – Open all year, daily, 8.30am–7pm (1.30pm mid-Oct to Mar). No charge. ☎ 0544 34 424.

Basilica di Sant'Apollinare Nuovo – Open all year, daily, 9am–6.30pm (4.30pm in winter). Closed 1 Jan and 25 Dec. 5 000L. ☎ 0544 21 81 58.

Pinacoteca Comunale – Open in summer, Mon to Sat, 9am–1pm, (also 4–7pm Tues and Thur), Sun and public holidays, 4–7pm; rest of the year, Mon to Sat, 9am–1pm (also 2.30–5.30pm Tues and Thur), Sun and public holidays, 2.30–5.30pm. Closed 1 Jan, 1 Nov and 25 Dec. 6 000L, 3 000L (under 18 and over 60). ☎ 0544 48 28 74.

Mausoleo di Teodorico – Open daily, Apr to Oct, 8.30am–7pm (1pm mid-Nov to mid-Feb, 6pm rest of the year). Closed 1 Jan, 1 May and 25 Dec. 4 000L, no charge (under 18 and over 65). ☎ 0544 45 16 83.

Basilica di Sant'Apollinare in Classe – Open all year, daily, 9am–7pm (5pm Oct to Mar). Closed 1 Jan, 1 May, 23 July and 25 Dec. 4 000L, no charge (under 18 and over 65). ☎ 0544 47 36 43.

REGGIO CALABRIA   🛈 corso Garibaldi 329 – ☎ 0965 89 20 12

Museo Nazionale – ♿ Open all year, daily, 9am–7pm (last admission 6.30pm). Closed 1st and 3rd Mon in the month, 1 Jan, 1 May and 25 Dec. 8 000L. Audio-visual presentation. Bookshop. ☎ 0965 31 61 11.

REGGIO EMILIA   🛈 piazza Prampolini 5/c – ☎ 0522 45 11 52

San Prospero – ☎ 0522 43 46 67.

Musei Civici – ♿ (partial access). Open daily (except Mon), 9am–noon (also 3–6pm Sat-Sun); 1 July to 15 Aug, open 9pm–midnight only. Closed 1 Jan, 16 to 31 Aug and 25 Dec. No charge. ☎ 0522 45 64 77.

Galleria Parmeggiani – Same admission times and charges as Musei Civici.

Madonna della Ghiara – Open all year, Mon to Sat, 10am–noon and 4–5.30pm, Sun and public holidays, 10.25–10.50am and 3.30–5.30pm. ☎ 0522 43 97 07.

Excursion

Brescello: Museo – Open, Mon to Sat, 9am–noon and 3–6pm (2.30–6.30pm Sat), Sun and public holidays, 9.30am–12.30pm and 2–7pm. For weekday morning visits, apply to Signor Carpi at the town hall. Guided tours (1hr) available in English, Italian, French and German; advance booking. Donation. ☎ 0522 68 75 26 or 0522 96 21 58.

RIETI   🛈 piazza Vittorio Emanuele 17 (Portici del Comune) – ☎ 0746 20 32 20

Excursions

Convento di Fonte Colombo – Open daily, 8am–noon and 3.30–7pm. Guided tours by request. ☎ 0746 21 01 25.

Convento di Greccio – Open daily, 9am (9.30am Sun)–12.30pm and 3–6.30pm (6pm in winter). ☎ 0746 75 01 27.

Convento di Poggio Bustone – Open daily, 9am–noon and 3–6pm. Guided tours (30min) and audio-guided tours available. ☎ 0746 68 89 16.

Convento La Foresta – Guided tours only, all year, daily, 8.30am–noon and 3–7pm. Closed 10–11.15am Sun for mass. ☎ 0746 20 00 85.

RIMINI   🛈 via Dante 86 (railway station) – ☎ 0541 51 331
🛈 piazzale Fellini 3 – ☎ 0541 56 902

Museo della Città – ♿ Open Tues to Sat, 8.30am–12.30pm and 5–7pm, Sun and public holidays, 4–7pm. Guided tours available (2hr). 6 000L, no charge Sun. ☎ 0541 21 482.

La RIVIERA LIGURE

Riviera di Ponente

Mortola Inferiore: Giardini Hanbury – Open mid June to late Sept, daily, 9am–7pm; Oct and Apr to mid-June, daily, 10am–6pm; Nov to Mar, daily (except Wed unless public holiday), 10am–5pm. Last admission 1hr before closing time. 12 500L, 7 000L (under 14). Bar. ☎ 0184 22 95 07.

Grotte di Toirano - Guided tours only (1hr) in English, Italian, French and German, July and Aug, daily, 9am-noon and 2-5.30pm; Apr and May, daily, 9am-12.30pm and 2-5pm; Sept to Mar, daily, 9am-noon and 2-5pm. Closed 25 Nov to 25 Dec. 15 000L, 8 000L (child). ☎ 0182 98 062.

Albissola Marina
🚺 piazza Sisto IV 4 - ☎ 019 40 02 008

Villa Faraggiana - Guided tours only (40min) in Italian and French, Mar to Sept, daily (except Mon), 3-7pm. Closed Easter, Oct to Feb. 8 000 L. ☎ 019 48 06 22.

Riviera di Levante

La Spezia
🚺 via Mazzini 45 - ☎ 0187 77 09 00

Museo Navale - ♿ (partial access). Open all year, Mon and Fri, 2-6pm; Tues, Wed, Thur and Sat, 9am-noon and 2-6pm; Sun, 8.30am-1.15pm. Closed weekday public holidays. 3 000L, no charge on San Giuseppe's Day and on Armed Forces Day. Bookshop. ☎ 0187 77 07 50.

Museo Lia - Open all year, daily (except Mon), 10am-6pm. Closed Mon (except Easter Mon), 1 Jan, 15 Aug and 25 Dec. 12 000L, 8 000L (child aged 14-18), 6 000L (under 14 and over 60). Guided tours available (2hr) in English, Italian, French and Spanish. Bookshop. ☎ 0187 73 11 00; www.castagna.it/mal

ROMA
🚺 via Parigi 5 - ☎ 06 48 89 92 53
🚺 Stazione Termini - ☎ 06 48 71 270
🚺 Fiumicino - ☎ 06 65 95 60 74

Palazzo dei Conservatori: Museum - Major reorganisation in progress, scheduled to re-open autumn 1999. For information, contact ☎ 06 67 10 20 71.

Museo Capitolino - Reorganisation in progress, scheduled to re-open early 2000. ☎ 06 67 10 20 71.

Terme di Caracalla - Open all year, daily, 9am-1hr before sunset (2pm Mon, Sun and public holidays). Last admission 1hr before closing time. Closed 1 Jan, 1 May and 25 Dec. 8 000L, no charge (under 18 and over 60). ☎ 06 57 58 626 or 06 48 15 576 (archeology department).

Castel Sant'Angelo - Open all year, daily, 9am-8pm (last admission 45min before closing time). Closed 1 Jan, 1 May and 25 Dec. 8 000L, no charge (under 18 and over 60). Guided tours available (90min) in English, Italian, French and German. Audio-guided tours available in English, Italian, French, German, Spanish and Japanese. Bar. ☎ 06 68 19 11 65.

Catacombe di San Callisto - Guided tour (45-60min) only in English, Italian, French, German and Spanish, daily (except Wed), 8.30am-12.30 and 2.30-5.30pm (5pm in winter). Closed 1 Jan, Feb, Easter and 25 Dec. 8 000L, no charge (on European Heritage Days and the last Sun in Sept). Bar. ☎ 06 51 30 151.

Catacombe de San Sebastiano - Same opening hours and charges as Catacombe di San Callisto. Closed Sun, 1 Jan, Easter, mid-Nov to mid-Dec and 25 Dec. ☎ 06 78 50 350.

Catacombe di Domitilla - Same opening hours and charges as Catacombe di San Callisto. Closed Tues, 1 Jan, Easter and 25 Dec. ☎ 06 51 10 342; www.catacombe-.domitilla.it

Colosseo - Open all year, daily, 9am-1hr before sunset. Closed 1 Jan, 1 May and 25 Dec. 10 000L, no charge (under 18 and over 60). Guided and audio-guided tours available. ☎ 06 70 04 261 and for guided tours ☎ 06 70 05 469.

Mercati Traianei - ♿ (partial access). Open daily (except Mon), 9am-6.30pm (4.30pm in winter); last admission 30min before closing time. Closed 1 Jan, 1 May and 25 Dec. 3 750L, no charge last Sun in the month. ☎ 06 67 90 048.

Foro Romano and Palatino - Open all year, daily, 9am-1hr before sunset (2pm Sun and public holidays); longer opening hours in summer, visitors are advised to phone for information. Closed 1 Jan, 1 May and 25 Dec. Foro Romano: no charge. Palatino: 12 000L, no charge (under 18 and over 60, and on 21 Apr). Guided and audio-guided tours available. ☎ 06 69 90 110.

Pantheon - Open all year, daily, 9am-6.30pm (1pm Sun). Closed 1 Jan, 1 May and 25 Dec. No charge. ☎ 06 68 30 02 30.

Palazzo Venezia: Museum - ♿ Open daily (except Mon), 9am-2pm. Closed 1 Jan, 1 May and 25 Dec. 8 000L, no charge (under 18 and over 60). The great halls house temporary exhibitions. ☎ 06 69 99 43 19.

San Giovanni in Laterano - Open all year, daily, 7am-7pm (6pm Oct to Mar). ☎ 06 77 20 79 91.

Santa Maria Maggiore - Open all year, daily, 7am-6.30pm (except during religious services). ☎ 06 488 10 94. **Loggia:** open 9.30am-5.30pm. 5 000L. ☎ 06 48 81 094.

San Paolo Fuori le Mura - Open all year, daily, 7am-6.30pm (6pm winter). The cloister is open 9am-1pm and 3-6.30pm. ☎ 06 54 09 374.

Vaticano   🏛 Pilgrim and Tourist Information Office - ☎ 06 69 88 44 66 or 06 69 88 48 66

Giardini Vaticani - Guided tour only (about 2hr), daily (except Wed and Sun) at 10am (Sat only in Jan, Feb, Nov, Dec). Closed same public holidays as for Musei Vaticani. 20 000L. Apply in advance to the tourist office: ☎ 06 69 88 44 66.

Basilica di San Pietro - Open all year, daily, 7am-7pm (6pm in winter) depending on religious services and Jubilee events. ☎ 06 69 88 44 66 (Vatican City Pilgrim and Tourist Information Office).

Ascent of the Dome - Access all year, daily (except Wed), 8am-5.30pm (4.30pm in winter). Lift: 8 000L; on foot, 7 000L.

Museo Storico - ♿ Open all year, daily, 9am-7pm (6pm Oct to Mar); last admission 45min before closing time. Closed Easter and 25 Dec. 8 000L, 5 000L (child under 12). ☎ 06 69 88 18 40.

Musei Vaticani - ♿ Open Mar to Oct, Mon to Fri, 8.45am-4.45pm (1.45pm Sat and last Sun in the month and Oct to mid-Mar). Last admission 1hr before closing time. Closed Sun (except last Sun in month), 1 and 6 Jan, 11 Feb, 19 Mar, Easter Monday, 1 May, Ascension Day, Corpus Domini, 29 June, 15 Aug, 1 Nov, 8, 25, 26 Dec. 18 000L (adult), 12 000L (child under 14 and students under 26 with a student card), no charge (child under 6 and last Sun in the month). Guided tours (4 itineraries, 1hr 30min-5hr). Audio-guided tours in English, French, German, Japanese, Spanish. 4 itineraries for disabled visitors, wheelchairs available. Bar, cafeteria, self-service restaurant. ☎ 06 69 88 33 33.

Additional Sights

Santa Cecilia in Trastevere - Open daily, 8am-6pm. Guided tours available. Crypt: 2 000L. **Cavallini's Last Judgement:** Open Tues and Thur, 10-11.30am. Donation welcome. ☎ 06 58 99 289.

Domus Aurea - Open by appointment only. 10 000L, no charge (under 18 and over 60), 2 000L booking fee. Guided and audio-guided tours available. ☎ 06 39 74 99 07.

Galleria Nazionale d'Arte Moderna - ♿ Open daily (except Mon), 9am-7pm (possibly later in summer). Closed 1 Jan, 1 May and 25 Dec. 12 000L, no charge (under 18 and over 60). Guided tours (1hr) in English, Italian and French (by appointment). Bar, restaurant. ☎ 06 32 29 83 02; www.gnam.arti.beniculturali.it

Galleria Borghese - Open by appointment daily (except Mon), 9am-7pm (1pm Sun). Closed 1 Jan, 1 May and 25 Dec. For advance booking ☎ 06 32 810 (office open Mon to Fri, 9.30am-6pm). 10 000L, no charge (under 18 and over 60), 2 000L booking fee. Bar. ☎ 06 85 48 577.

Museo Nazionale Romano

Palazzo Massimo alle Terme - ♿ Open Tues to Sat, 9am-7pm (2pm Sun and public holidays; 10pm summer, visitors are advised to phone for confirmation of opening times); last admission 1hr before closing time. Closed 1 Jan, 1 May and 25 Dec. 12 000L, no charge (under 18 and over 60). Guided tours only to second floor, by appointment. Guided tours with archeologist available (4 tours daily), 6 000L; audio-guided tours, 7 000L. For information and bookings, contact ☎ 06 48 15 576 or ☎ 06 39 08 07 30.

Palazzo Altemps - Open daily (except Mon), 9am-7pm (2pm Sun and public holidays); last admission 1hr before closing time. Longer opening hours possible in summer, visitors are advised to phone for further information. Closed 1 Jan, 1 May and 25 Dec. 10 000L, no charge (under 18 and over 60). Guided (1hr) and audio-guided tours available in English and Italian ☎ 06 68 33 759, 06 68 33 759 or 06 68 64 682.

Aula Ottagona - Open daily (except Mon), 9am-2pm. Closed 1 Jan, 1 May and 25 Dec. No charge.

Museo Nazionale Villa Guilia - Open daily (except Mon), 9am-7pm (2pm Sun and public holidays). Closed 1 Jan, 1 May and 25 Dec. 8 000L, no charge (under 18 and over 60). Guided tours available in English, Italian and French. Bar, restaurant. ☎ 06 32 26 571.

Palazzo Barberini: Galleria Nazionale di Arte Antica - ♿ Open in summer, daily (except Mon), 9am-8.30pm (7.30pm Sun); in winter, daily (except Mon), 9am-6.30pm (12.30pm Sun). Closed 1 Jan, 1 May and 25 Dec. 12 000L. For information and bookings, contact ☎ 06 32 810.

Palazzo Braschi: Museo di Roma - Closed for restoration, scheduled to re-open mid-2000. For information, contact ☎ 06 68 75 880; braschi1@comune.roma.it

Palazzo Corsini: Galleria Nazionale di Pittura - Open daily (except Mon), 9am-7pm (2pm Sat, 1pm Sun). Closed 1 Jan, 1 May, and 25 Dec. 8 000L, no charge (under 18 and over 60). ☎ 06 68 80 23 23.

Additional Sights

Palazzo Doria Pamphili: Galleria – & Open daily (except Thur), 10am–5pm. Closed 1 Jan, Easter, 1 May, 15 Aug and 25 Dec. 13 000L (includes 1hr audio-guided tour in English, Italian or French). For information and visits outside of opening hours, contact ☎ 06 67 97 323; www.doriapamphilj.it

Palazzo Spada: Galleria di Pittura – Open daily (except Mon), 9am–6.30pm (12.30pm Sun). Closed 1 Jan, 1 May and 25 Dec. 10 000L, no charge (under 18 and over 60). Guided tours (about 1hr) in English, Italian, French and German. ☎ 06 68 61 158.

Villa Farnesina – & Open daily (except Sun), 9am–1pm (last admission 12.40pm). 8 000L. ☎ 06 68 80 17 67; www.lincei.it

E.U.R.: Museo della Civiltà Romana – Open daily (except Mon), 9am–7pm (1.30pm Sun). Closed 1 Jan, 1 May and 25 Dec. 5 000L, no charge on last Sun in the month and for visitors under 18 and over 60. ☎ 06 59 26 135.

S

SABBIONETA
🛈 piazza d'Armi 1 – ☎ 0375 52 039

Guided tours – Organized by the Ufficio del Turismo, Apr to Sept, 9am–12.30pm and 2.30–6pm (7pm Sun); Mar and Oct, 9.30am–12.30pm and 2.30–5.30pm (6.30pm Sun); rest of the year, Mon to Fri, 9am–1pm, Sat-Sun, 9.30am–12.30pm and 2.30–5pm (6pm Sun). Tickets available until 30min before closing time. The Tourist Office is closed Mon except public holidays. 10 000L.

SALERNO
🛈 via Roma 258 – ☎ 089 22 47 44

Duomo – Open all year, daily, 8am–noon and 4-8pm. ☎ 089 23 13 87.

Museo Archeologico – & (partial access). Open daily, 9am–8pm (2pm Sun and public holidays). No charge. Guided tours available in Italian. Bookshop. ☎ 089 23 11 35.

SALUZZO
🛈 via Griselda 6 – ☎ 0175 46 710

Casa Cavassa – Open daily (except Mon), 9am–12.15pm and 3-6.15pm (2.15-5.30pm Oct to Mar); Tues by appointment only. 5 000L, 2 500L (under 18 and over 60), 6 000L combined ticket with Torre Civica. ☎ 0175 41 455.

San Giovanni – Open daily, 9am–noon and 3-6pm.

Torre Civica – Open daily, 9am–noon and 3-6.30pm (5.30pm Oct to Mar); Mon and Tues, mornings only by appointment (contact the Tourist Office). 2 500L, 6 000L combined ticket with Casa Cavassa.

Excursions

Abbazia di Staffarda – Open daily (except Mon), 9am–12.30pm and 2-6pm (5pm Oct to Mar). 8 000L, 4 000L (over 65). ☎ 0175 27 32 15.

Castello della Manta – Open 10am–1pm and 2-6pm (5pm Oct to mid-Dec). Closed Mon (unless public holiday), the last 2 weeks in Dec and the month of Jan. 6 000L, 4 000L (under 11). ☎ 0175 87 822.

SAN GIMIGNANO
🛈 piazza Duomo 1 – ☎ 0577 94 00 08

Collegiata di Santa Maria Assunta and **Cappella di Santa Fina** – Open Apr to Oct, Mon to Sat, 9.30am–7.30pm (5pm Sat), Sun and public holidays 1pm–5pm; Nov to Mar, Mon to Sat, 9.30–5pm, Sun and public holidays, 1–5pm. Closed during mass on Sun. 6 000L, 3 000L (child aged 6-18).

Palazzo del Popolo – Open daily (except Mon), Mar to Oct, 9.30am–7.20pm; Nov to Feb, 9.30am–12.50pm and 2.30-4.50pm (last admission 20min before closing time). Closed all day 1 and 31 Jan, 1 May and 25 Dec; closed afternoons from 24 to 31 Dec. 7 000L, 5 000L (students under 18 and family with child aged 6-18), no charge (child under 6). For further information, contact the tourist office at www.sangimignano.com

Excursions

San Vivaldo: Sacro Monte – Open Mon to Fri, 9-11.30am and 3pm-sunset, Sat, 9-11.30am, Sun and public holidays, 1pm-sunset. Donation welcome. Book at least three days in advance at Convento di San Vivaldo. ☎/Fax 0571 68 01 14.

Certaldo

Casa del Boccaccio – Open all year, daily, 10.30am–12.30pm and 3.30-6.30pm. No charge. Audio-visual presentation. ☎ 0571 66 42 08.

Palazzo Pretorio - Open daily (except Mon), Apr to late Oct, 10am-1pm and 2.30-7.30pm; late Oct to Mar, 10am-12.30pm and 3-6pm. 5 000 L, 2 500 L (under 18 and over 60). Guided tours available in English, French, German and Italian, by appointment. ☎ 0571 66 12 19.

Repubblica di SAN MARINO   🗗 contrada Omagnano 20 - ☎ 0549 88 24 10

Palazzo Pubblico - Open daily, Apr to Sept, 8am-8pm; Oct to Mar, 8.50am-5pm. Closed 1 Jan, 2 Nov (afternoon) and 25 Dec. 4 000L. ☎ 0549 88 27 08.

Museo delle Armi Antiche - Open daily, Apr to Sept, 8am-8pm; Oct to Mar, 8.50am-5pm. Closed 1 Jan, 2 Nov (afternoon) and 25 Dec. 4 000L. Audio-guided tours in English, French, German, Italian and Spanish. ☎ 0549 88 26 70.

Museo-Pinacoteca di San Francesco - Same admission times and charges as for Museo delle Armi Antiche.

Museo Filatelico e Numismatico - Closed for restoration. For information, call ☎ 0549 88 24 00.

San Leo   🗗 piazza Dante Alighieri 14 - ☎ 0541 91 63 06

Museums - Open daily, 9am-6pm (usually 11pm July and Aug). 10 000L (combined tickets for all museums and monuments), 5 000L (child under 14). Guided tours (3hr) by appointment. Free shuttle bus to the fortress. ☎ 0541 91 63 06 or 167 55 38 00 (toll-free).

SANSEPOLCRO

Museo Civico - ♿ (partial access). Open daily, June to Sept, 9am-1.30pm and 2.30-7.30pm; Oct to May, 9.30am-1pm and 2.30-6pm (last admission 30min before closing time). Closed 1 Jan, 15 Aug and 25 Dec. 10 000L, 5 000L (child aged 10-16). Bookshop. ☎ 0575 73 22 18; www.sansepolcro.net

Excursion

Poppi: Castello dei Conti Guidi - Open Apr to mid-Oct, daily (except Mon), 9.30am-12.30pm and 3-6pm; rest of the year, Sat only, 9.30am-12.30pm and 2-5pm. 5 000L, 3 000L (child). Guided tours available (1hr). Audio-visual presentation. Bookshop. ☎ 0575 50 22 20/21; www.casentino.net

SIENA   🗗 piazza del Campo 56 - ☎ 0577 28 05 51

Palazzo Pubblico - Open July and Aug, daily, 10am-11pm; Mar to June and Sept, Oct, daily, 10am-6pm; Jan, Feb, Nov and Dec, Mon to Sat, 10am-4pm, Sun and public holidays, 9.30am-1.30pm. Closed 1 Jan, 1 May, 1 and 25 Dec. 8 000L, 4 000L (student), no charge (child under 11). ☎ 0577 29 22 26.

Torre - Open daily, July and Aug, 10am-11pm (6pm Mar to June and Sept, Oct; 4pm Nov and Dec). Closed 1 Jan, 1 May, 1 and 25 Dec. 7 000L.

Duomo - Open daily, 16 Mar to Oct, 7.30am-7.30pm; Nov to 15 Mar, 7.30am-1pm and 2.30-5pm. ☎ 0577 28 30 48. Libreria Piccolomini: 2 000L.

Museo dell'Opera Metropolitana - Open daily, 16 Mar to Oct, 9am-7.30pm; Nov to 15 Mar, 9am-1.30pm (last admission 30min before closing time). Closed 1 Jan and 25 Dec. 6 000L. Bookshop. ☎ 0577 28 30 48; www.operaduomo.it

Battistero di San Giovanni - Open daily, 16 Mar to Oct, 9am-7.30pm (last admission 7.15pm); Nov to 15 Mar, 10am-1pm and 2.30-5pm. Closed 1 Jan and 25 Dec. 3 000L. ☎ 0577 28 30 48; www.operaduomo.it

Pinacoteca - ♿ (partial access). Open July to Sept, Mon, 8.30am-1.30pm, Tues to Sat, 9am-7pm (also 9pm-midnight Sat), Sun and public holidays, 8am-1pm and 2-8pm; rest of the year, as a guideline only, Mon, 8.30am-1.30pm, Tues to Sat, 8.30am-1.30pm and 2.30-7pm, Sun and public holidays, 8am-1pm. Closed 1 Jan, 1 May and 25 Dec. 8 000L, no charge (under 18 and over 60). ☎ 0577 28 11 61.

SORRENTO   🗗 via de Maio 35 - ☎ 081 80 74 033

Museo Correale di Terranova - Open daily (except Tues), 9am-2pm. Closed last 2 weeks of Jan and public holidays. 8 000L. Guided tours (2hr) available in English and Italian, by appointment. ☎ 081 87 81 846.

La Penisola Sorrentina

Sant'Agata sui Due Golfi: Belvedere del Deserto - Open Sun and public holidays, 8.30-11am; Mon to Sat, Apr to Sept, 4-7.30pm, rest of the year, 2.30-4.30pm. Key available from the nuns. For information, call ☎ 081 80 89 571.

SPOLETO   🗗 piazza Libertà 7 - ☎ 0743 22 03 11

Excursion

Fonti del Clitunno: Tempietto - Open daily (except Mon), Apr to Oct, 9am-8pm; Nov to Mar, 9am-2pm. No charge. ☎ 0743 22 03 11.

SUBIACO

Monastero di Santa Scolastica – Guided tours only every 30min, Mon to Sat, 9am-12.30pm and 3.30-7pm, Sun and public holidays, 9-10am, 11.30am-12.30pm and 3.30-7pm. Donation welcome. ☏ 0774 85 525; www.osb-subiaco-it.org

Monastero di San Benedetto – Open daily 9am-12.30pm and 3-6pm. Book 10-15 days in advance. Donation welcome. ☏ 0774 85 039; www.osb-subiaco-it.org

SULMONA
🚹 corso Ovidio 208 – ☏ 0864 53 276

Museo dell'Arte e della Tecnologia Confettiera – Guided tours only (15-30min), daily (except Sun), in English, French and Italian, 9am-noon and 3.30-6.30pm. Closed public holidays and 2 weekdays around 15 Aug. No charge. ☏ 0864 21 00 47; www.pelino.it

Museo Civico – Open daily (except Mon), 10am-noon and 4-6pm. 1 000L. ☏ 0864 21 02 16.

Excursion

Basilica di San Pelino – Open daily, 8.30am-noon and 2.30-6pm (in winter by appointment). ☏ 0864 72 81 20.

T

TARANTO
🚹 corso Umberto 113 – ☏ 099 45 32 329

Museo Nazionale – Re-organisation work in progress, times may change; visitors are advised to phone ahead. Open all year, Mon to Sat, 8.30am-1.30pm and 2.30-7.30pm, Sun, 8.30am-1.30pm. Closed 1 Jan, 1 May and 25 Dec. 4 000L, no charge (under 18 and over 60). ☏ 099 45 32 112.

TARQUINIA
🚹 piazza Cavour 1 – ☏ 0766 85 63 84

Necropoli Etrusca – Open all year, daily (except Mon), 9am-sunset (7pm in summer). Closed 1 Jan, 1 May and 25 Dec. 8 000L.

Museo Nazionale Tarquiniese – Open all year, daily (except Mon), 9am-7pm. Closed 1 Jan, 1 May and 25 Dec. 8 000L, no charge (under 18 and over 60). Guided tours (2hr) available in English. Bookshop. ☏ 0766 85 60 36.

Santa Maria in Castello – To visit, apply to Signora Bassi at the house behind the tower. Leave a gratuity.

TERNI
🚹 viale Cesare Battisti 7 – ☏ 0744 42 30 47

Excursions

Cascata delle Marmore – July and Aug, Mon to Fri, noon-1pm, 5-6pm, 9-10pm, Sat, 11am-1pm and 3-10pm, Sun and public holidays, 10am-1pm and 3-10pm; June, Mon to Fri, 4-5pm and 9-10pm, Sat, 11am-1pm and 3-10pm, Sun and public holidays, 10am-1pm and 3-10pm; mid-Mar to Apr, Mon to Fri, noon-1pm and 4-5pm, Sat, 11am-1pm and 4-9pm, Sun and public holidays, 10am-1pm and 4-9pm; May, Mon to Fri, noon-1pm and 4-5pm, Sat, 11am-1pm and 4-10pm, Sun and public holidays, 10am-1pm and 3-10pm; Sept, Mon to Fri, noon-1pm, 4-5pm and 9-10pm, Sat, 11am-1pm and 4-9pm, Sun and public holidays, 10am-1pm and 3-9pm; Oct, only Sat, 11am-1pm and 4-8pm, and Sun and public holidays, 10am-1pm and 3-8pm; Nov to mid-March, Sun and public holidays only, 3-4pm.

Ferentillo: Abbazia di San Pietro in Valle – Open all year, daily, 9am-noon and 1-7pm. ☏ 0744 78 03 16.

TIVOLI
🚹 largo Garibaldi – ☏ 0774 31 12 49

Villa d'Este – Open Apr to mid-Sept, daily (except Mon), 9am-6.30pm (4pm Nov to Feb, 5.30pm rest of the year). Closed 1 Jan, 1 May and 25 Dec. 8 000L, no charge (under 18). Bar. ☏ 0774 31 20 70.

Villa Adriana – Open all year, daily, 9am-2hr before sunset. Closed 1 Jan, 1 May and 25 Dec. 8 000L, no charge (under 18 and over 60). Bar. ☏ 0774 53 02 03.

Villa Gregoriana – Open all year, daily, 10am-6.30pm (5pm Mar to May, 4pm Nov to Feb). 3 500L. ☏ 0774 31 12 49.

Excursion

Palestrina: Museo Archeologico Prenestino – ♿ Open daily, 9am-1hr before sunset. Closed 1 Jan, 1 May and 25 Dec. 4 000L, no charge (under 18 and over 60). Guided and audio-guided tours available (1hr). ☏ 06 95 38 100.

TODI
🛈 piazza Umberto I 6 - ☎ 075 89 43 395

Palazzo del Popolo and **Palazzo del Capitano** - Open, daily (except Mon), Apr (daily) to Sept, 10.30am-1pm and 2.30-6pm; Mar, 10.30am-1pm and 2-5pm; Oct to Feb, 10.30am-1pm and 2-4.30pm. Closed 1 Jan and 25 Dec. 6 000L, 4 500/3 000L (reductions). Guided tours (45min) in English and Italian. Audio-visual presentation. ☎ 075 89 44 148.

TOLENTINO
🛈 piazza Libertà 19 - ☎ 0733 97 29 37

Museo della Caricatura - &. Open daily (except Mon), 22 Mar to 22 Sept, 10am-1pm and 4-7pm; rest of the year, 10am-1pm and 3-6pm. Closed 1 Jan, 1 May and 25 Dec. 5 000L, 2 000L (child under 14). Guided tours (30min). ☎ 0733 96 97 97.

Basilica di San Nicola and museums - Open all year, daily, 9.30am-noon and 4-7pm. ☎ 0733 96 99 96; www.sannicola.sinp.net

Excursions

San Severino Marche

Pinacoteca Civica - &. Open July to Sept, Tues to Sat, 9am-1pm and 4.30-6.30pm; Oct to June, 9am-1pm; Sun (alternate weeks) and weekday public holidays, 9am-1pm. Closed 1 Jan, 15 Aug and 25 Dec. 4 000L, no charge (under 16 and over 65). Guided tours (1hr). ☎ 0733 63 80 95.

San Lorenzo in Doliolo - Open daily, 9am-7pm. ☎ 0733 63 83 51

TORINO
🛈 piazza Castello, 161 - ☎ 011 53 51 81 or 011 53 59 01
🛈 Stazione di Porta Nuova - ☎ 011 53 13 27
🛈 Aeroporto di Caselle - ☎ 011 56 78 124

Museo Egizio - &. Open all year, daily (except Mon), 9am-7pm (2pm Sun). Closed 1 Jan, 1 May and 25 Dec. 12 000L, no charge (child and during museum week). Guided tours (1hr 30min) available in English, Italian, French, German, Spanish and Russian. Bookshop. ☎ 011 56 17 776; www.multix.it/museoegizio to/

Galleria Sabauda - &. (partial access). Open all year, Tues to Sat, 9am-2pm (Thur in summer 2-7pm, in winter 10am-7pm). Closed public holidays. Sun, guided tour only to parts of the museum. 8 000L, no charge (under 18 and over 60), 15 000L (combined ticket with Museo Egizio). ☎ 011 54 74 40.

Museo Nazionale del Risorgimento Italiano - Open all year, daily (except Mon), 9am-7pm (1pm Sun and public holidays); last admission 1hr before closing time. Closed 4 Apr, 1 May and 25 and 31 Dec. 8 000L, 3 000L (aged 10-18), no charge (child under 10). Guided tours (1hr 30min) available in English and French. ☎ 011 56 21 147; www.regione.piemonte.it/cultura/risorgimento/

Palazzo Madama: Museo d'Arte Antica - Closed for restoration. For information, call ☎ 011 44 29 911.

Palazzo Reale:

Appartamenti - &. (partial access). Guided tours only (40min) all year, daily (except Mon), 9am-7pm (last tour 6.15pm). Closed 1 Jan, 1 May and 25 Dec. 8 000L, no charge (under 18 and over 60). ☎ 011 43 61 455; www.ambiente.arti.beniculturali.it

Armeria Reale - Open Tues and Thur, 1.30-7pm; Wed, Fri and Sat, 9am-2pm (Wed and Fri usually reserved for groups); for Mon, Sun and public holidays, telephone for opening times. Closed alternating Mon or Sun, 1 Jan, 1 May and 25 Dec. 8 000L, no charge (under 18 and over 60). ☎ 011 51 84 358.

Duomo - &. Open 7am-noon and 3-7pm. ☎ 011 43 60 790 or 011 43 61 594.

San Domenico - Open 7.30am-noon and 4-6.30pm. ☎ 011 43 62 237.

Mole Antonelliana - Closed for restoration to house a new Cinema Museum.

Pinacoteca Albertina - &. Open daily (except Mon), 9am-1pm and 3-7pm. Closed public holidays. 8 000L, 5 000L (under 18 and over 65). Guided tours (1hr 30min) available by appointment. ☎ 011 81 77 862.

Borgo Medievale - &. (partial access). Open all year, daily, 9am-7pm (8pm in summer). No charge. **Castello:** daily (except Mon), 9am-7pm; no access to castle for disabled visitors. Closed 1 Jan, Easter, 1 May and 25 Dec. 5 000L, no charge (child under 10 and first Friday in the month). Audio-guided and guided tours (35min) available. Bar, restaurant. Bookshop. ☎ 011 66 99 372.

Galleria Civica di Arte Moderna e Contemporanea - &. Open daily (except Mon), 9am-7pm. Closed public holidays. 10 000L, no charge (child under 10 and the afternoon of the first Friday in the month). Guided tours (1hr 30min) available in English, Italian and French. Bar. Bookshop. ☎ 011 56 29 911; http://www.comune.torino.it/turismo/musei/galleria/galleria.htm

TORINO

Museo dell'Automobile Carlo Biscaretti di Ruffia – ♿ Open all year, daily (except Mon), 10am-6.30pm (last admission 6pm). 10 000L, 7 000L child. Bar. Bookshop. ☎ 011 67 76 66.

Excursions

Basilica di Superga: royal tombs – Guided tours only, Apr to Sept, daily (except Fri), 9.30am-noon and 3-6pm; Oct to Mar, daily (except Fri), 10am-noon and 3-5pm. Donation. ☎ 011 89 80 083.

Palazzina di caccia di Stupinigi – Guided tours only (40min), all year, daily (except Mon), 10-6pm (5pm in winter); last admission 40min before closing time. Closed 1 Jan, 1 Nov and 25 Dec. 10 000L, 8 000L (child), 5 000L (over 65). ☎ 011 35 81 220.

VAL DI SUSA

Castello di Rivoli: Museo d'Arte Contemporanea – ♿ Open Tues to Sun, 10am-5pm (7pm Sat-Sun). Closed 1 Jan, 1 May and 25 Dec. 12 000L, no charge (child under 10). Guided tours (1hr) at no extra charge, Sat at 3.30pm and Sun at 11am and 3.30pm. Bar and restaurant. Bookshop. ☎ 011 95 65 222; www.regione.piemonte.it/cultura/rivoli/rivoli.html

Abbazia di Sant'Antonio di Ranverso – Open daily (except Mon), 9am-noon and 2.30-5.30pm (4pm in winter). 5 000L, 3 000L (reductions). ☎ 011 93 67 450.

Avigliana
ℼ piazza del Popolo 6 – ☎ 011 93 28 650

San Pietro – Open in summer, Sat-Sun, 9am-noon and 3-6pm; for winter opening times contact the tourist office.

Sacra di San Michele – Open daily (except Mon unless holiday Mon), 16 Mar to 15 Oct, 9.30am-12.30pm (noon Sun) and 3pm (2.40pm Sun)-6pm (5pm the rest of the year). Last admission 30min before closing time. 4 000L, 2 000L (under 14 and over 65), no charge (child under 6). Guided tours every 20min on Sun. ☎ 011 93 91 30.

Abbazia della Novalesa
Guided tours only (45min), July and Aug, Mon to Fri, at 10.30am and 4.30pm, Sat, 9-11.30am and at 4.30pm, Sun at 11.30am; rest of the year, Sat-Sun only, 9-11.30am. Donation welcome. ☎ 0122 65 32 10. The Cappella di Sant'Eldrado is closed in the event of rain or snow in order to protect the fragile frescoes.

Monferrato
Abbazia di Vezzolano – Open daily (except Mon), 9.30am-12.30pm and 2-6.30pm (5pm in winter). ☎ 011 99 20 607.

Isole TREMITI
San Nicola: Abbazia di Santa Maria al Mare – Guided tours only, July and Aug, 9-11.30am and 12.30-6pm (6.30pm Sat); Sept to June, 10am-4pm (6pm Sat). Donation. ☎ 0882 46 31 16.

San Domino: boat trips – To go around the island of San Domino, San Nicola or the archipelago, contact Signor Calabrese, at the Società Cooperativa AMA. ☎ 0360 37 35 27.

TRENTO
ℼ via Alfieri 4 – ☎ 0461 98 38 80

Basilica paleocristiana – Open daily (except Sun), 10am-12.30pm and 2.30-6pm. Closed public holidays. 2 000L; combined ticket with Museo Diocesano 5 000L. Guided tours by appointment. Apply 2 weeks in advance to Signora Domenica Primerano on ☎ 0461 23 44 19.

Museo Diocesano – ♿ Open daily (except Sun), 9.30am-12.30pm and 2.30-6pm. Closed 1 Jan, 26 June, 15 Aug, 1 Nov, 8 and 25 Dec. 5 000L, 1 000L (child aged 12-18), no charge (child under 12). ☎ 0461 23 44 19.

Castel del Buon Consiglio – ♿ (with assistance from museum staff). Open daily (except Mon unless hol Mon), all year, 9am-noon and 2-5.30pm (5pm Oct to Mar); times may vary slightly during temporary exhibitions. Closed 1 Jan, 1 Nov and 25 Dec. 9 000L, 5 000L (under 18 and over 60), no charge (child under 12). Guided tours (1hr 30min) in summer. Bookshop. ☎ 0461 23 37 70.

Gruppo del Brenta
Campo Carlo Magno: Passo del Grostè – The cable-car operates from early July to the 3rd weekend in Sept. ☎ 0465 44 77 44.

Andalo: Monte Paganella – Access by cable-car or chairlift July to mid-Sept and Dec to Apr. Access also by chairlift from Fai della Paganella. Same conditions.

TREVISO
piazza Monte di Pietà 8 - ☎ 0422 54 76 32

Monte di Pietà - ♿ Open daily (except Sat-Sun), 8.15am-1.30pm and 2.30-5pm. Closed public holidays. No charge. Apply for appointment at least one day in advance to Cassamarca, piazza San Leonardo, 1, Treviso ☎ 0422 65 41.

Museo Civico Bailo - ♿ (partial access). Open all year, Tues to Sat, 9am-12.30pm and 2.30-5pm; Sun, 9am-noon. Closed public holidays. 3 000L, no charge on opening day of exhibitions. Bookshop. ☎ 0422 59 13 37.

Excursions

Maser: Villa - Open Mar to Oct, Tues, Sat, Sun and public holidays, 3-6pm; Nov to Feb, Sat, Sun and public holidays, 2.30-5pm. Closed Easter and 24 Dec-6 Jan. 9 500L, 4 500L (child under 15). ☎ 0423 92 30 04.

Vittorio Veneto: Museo della Battaglia - Open daily (except Mon), May to Sept, 10am-noon and 4-6.30pm; Oct to Apr, 10am-noon and 2-5pm. Closed 1 and 16 Jan, Easter and 25 Dec. 5 000L, no charge (under 18 or over 60). Guided tours (1hr) available in Italian. Audio-visual presentation. ☎ 0438 57 695.

Portogruaro: Museo Nazionale Concordiese - Open all year, daily, 9am-7pm. Closed 1 Jan, 1 May and 25 Dec. 4 000L, no charge (under 18 and over 60). ☎ 0421 72 674.

TRIESTE
via S. Nicolo 20 - ☎ 040 67 96 11
Stazione Centrale - ☎ 040 42 01 82

Castello di San Giusto - Open all year, daily, 9am-7pm (5pm Oct to Mar). Closed 1 and 6 Jan, 25 and 26 Dec. 2 000L, no charge (child under 5). ☎ 040 30 86 86.

Museo di Storia e d'Arte - Open all year, daily (except Mon), 9am-1pm (7pm Wed). Closed 1 Jan, Easter, 25 Apr, 1 May, 15 Aug and 25 Dec. 3 000L, 2 000L (reductions), no charge (child under 5). Bookshop. ☎ 040 31 05 00.

Museo del Mare - Open all year, daily (except Mon), 8.30am-1.30pm. Closed public holidays. 5 000L, 3 000L (child, student and over 60). ☎ 040 30 49 87.

Excursions

Villa Opicina - The funicular operates daily, every 20min; from 7am-8pm (departure from Opicina); from 7.11am-8.11pm (departure from Piazza Oberdan). ☎ 1670 16 675 (Mon to Thur, 8.30am-3.30pm, Fri and Sat, 8.30am-1pm).

Castello di Miramare - ♿ (partial access). Open daily, Apr to Sept, 9am-6pm (5pm, Mar and Oct; 4pm, Nov to Feb). 8 000L, no charge (under 18 and over 60). Guided tours (1hr) in English, French, German, Italian, Russian and Slovenian. Bar and restaurant. Bookshop. ☎ 040 22 41 43.

Gardens - ♿ (partial access). Open daily, Apr to Sept, 8am-7pm (6pm, Mar and Oct, 5pm, Nov-Feb). No charge. Guided tours (1hr) in Italian. Bar and restaurant. Bookshop. ☎ 040 22 41 43.

Grotta Gigante - Guided tours, daily (except Mon unless holiday Mon), Apr to Sept, every 30min from 9am-noon and 2-7pm (daily, July and Aug); Mar and Oct, every hour from 9am-noon and 2-5pm; Nov to Feb, 10am, 11am, noon, 2.30pm, 3.30pm and 4.30pm. Closed 1 Jan and 25 Dec. ☎ 040 32 73 12.

Terra dei TRULLI

Alberobello

Museo del Territorio - ♿ Audio-guided tours (20min) in English and Italian, Apr to Oct, 10am-1pm and 4.30-7.30pm; Nov to Mar, 10am-1pm and 4-7pm. Closed 1 Jan and 25 Dec. 2 500L, 1 000L (child). ☎ 0338 73 98 753 (mobile).

Trullo Sovrano - ♿ (partial access). Guided tours only (20min) in English, Italian and French, 1 Aug to 14 Sept, 9.30am-1pm and 3-8pm (9am-9pm Sun); June to Oct, 10am-1pm and 3-7.30pm (8.30pm Sun); rest of the year, Mon to Fri, 10am-1pm and 3.30-7pm, Sat 9.30-1pm and 3-7.30pm, Sun, 9am-1pm and 3-8pm. Closed Nov and Jan, Mon to Fri in Dec, Feb and Mar, 1 Jan and 25 Dec. 2 500L, 1 000L (child).

Martina Franca: Palazzo Ducale - Open Mon to Sat, 8am-8pm, Sun and public holidays, 9am-noon and 4-8pm. No charge. ☎ 080 48 36 255/4.

TUSCANIA

San Pietro: cripta - Open daily, in summer, 9am-1pm and 2-7pm; in winter, 9am-noon and 2-5pm. No charge. ☎ 0761 43 63 71.

U

UDINE
piazza I Maggio 7 - ☎ 0432 29 59 72

Castello - Open daily (except Mon), 9.30am-12.30pm and 3-6pm; Sun and public holidays, 9.30am-12.30pm. Closed 1 and 6 Jan, Easter, 25 Apr, 1 May, 12 July, 15 Aug, 1 Nov and 25 Dec. 4 000L, no charge (child under 10 and on Sun and public holidays). Bookshop. ☎ 0432 50 18 24.

Duomo - Open all year, Mon to Sat, 7.30am-noon and 4-8pm; Sun and public holidays, 7.30am-1pm and 4-8pm. Closed during church services. For guided tours, contact the sacristy. Donation. ☏ 0432 50 68 30.

Palazzo Arcivescovile - Open all year, daily (except Mon, Tues), 10.30am-12.30pm and 3.30-6.30pm. 7 000L, 5 000L (child). Guided tours available (1hr 30min). Bookshop. ☏ 0432 25 003.

Excursion

Passariano: Villa Manin - &. Open all year, daily (except Mon), 9am-12.30pm and 3-6pm. Bar, restaurant. Bookshop. ☏ 0432 90 66 57.

URBINO   🛈 piazza Duca Federico 35 - ☏ 0772 24 41

Galleria Nazionale delle Marche - Open all year, daily, 9am-7pm (2pm Mon and Sun, except special events in summer); last admission 1hr before closing time. Closed 1 Jan, 1 May and 25 Dec. 8 000L, no charge (under 18 and over 60). ☏ 0722 32 90 57 or 0722 27 60.

Casa di Raffaello - Open all year, Sun and public holidays, 10am-1pm; Mon to Sat, 9 Mar to 31 Oct, 9am-1pm and 3-7pm, rest of the year, 9am-2pm. Closed 1 Jan and 25 Dec. 5 000L, no charge (under 14 and 28 Mar to 6 Apr). Guided tours avialable (30min). Bookshop. ☏ 0722 32 01 05.

Chiesa Oratorio di San Giovanni Battista e San Giuseppe - Open Mar to Oct, 10am-12.30pm and 3-5.30pm, Sun and public holidays, 10am-12.30pm; Nov to Jan, 10am-12.30pm, Sat, 10am-noon and 3-4.45pm. Closed Feb to Mar. 3 000L. ☏ 0347 67 11 181 (mobile).

V

VENEZIA   🛈 Palazzetto Selva, Molo di S. Marco 71/c - ☏ 041 52 26 356

Basilica di San Marco:

Galleria e Museo Marciano - Open daily, 16 May to 29 Sept, 9.45am-5pm; 30 Sept to 15 May, 9.45am-4pm. 3 000L, 1 500L child. ☏ 041 52 25 205.

Pala d'Oro - Open 16 May to 29 Sept, daily, 9.45am (2pm Sun and public holidays)-5pm; 30 Sept to 15 May, daily, 9.45am (2pm Sun)-4pm. 3 000L, 1 500L (child). ☏ 041 52 25 205.

Tesoro - Same admission times as Pala d'Oro. 4 000L, 2 000L (child). Audio-guided tour (no charge). ☏ 041 52 22 205.

Campanile - Open daily, Apr to Oct, 9.30am-6pm (4pm Jan to Apr and Oct to Dec). Closed Jan. 8 000L. Bookshop. ☏ 041 52 25 205.

Palazzo Ducale - Open daily, Apr to Oct, 9am-7pm (last admission 5.30pm); Nov to Mar, daily, 9am-5pm (last admission 3.30pm). Closed 1 Jan and 25 Dec. 18 000L, 10 000L (student aged 15-29), 6 000L (child aged 6-14), no charge (child under 6). Audio-guided tours available. Cafeteria. Ticket also entitles holder to entry to the Museo Correr, Museo Archeologico, Biblioteca Nazionale Marciana, Palazzo Mocenigo, Museo Vetrario di Murano and Museo del Merletto di Burano. ☏ 041 52 24 951.
Itinerari segreti guided tour by appointment at 10am and noon in Italian (11am instead of noon in summer) and 10.30am in English. Tours in French on request. 24 000L, 14 000L (student aged 15-29), 8 000L (child aged 6-14).

Torre dell'Orologio - Closed for restoration at time of going to press.

Museo Correr - Same admission times and charges as Palazzo Ducale.

Ca'd'Oro: Galleria Franchetti - Open all year, daily, 9am-2pm (last admission 1.30pm). Closed 1 Jan, 1 May and 25 Dec. Guided tours (1hr) and audio-guided tours available. 6 000L, no charge (under 18 and over 60). ☏ 041 52 22 349.

Ca' Pesaro: Museo d'arte orientale - Open daily (except Mon), 9am-2pm. Closed 1 Jan, 1 May and 25 Dec. 4 000L, no charge (under 18 and over 60). ☏ 041 52 41 173.

Ca' Pesaro: Galleria internazionale d'Arte moderna - Closed for restoration. For latest information on admission times and charges: ☏ 041 72 11 27.

Ca' Rezzonico: Museo del Settecento Veneziano - Closed for restoration at time of going to press. ☏ 041 520 40 36 (Ca'Rezzonico) or 041 522 56 25 (museum administration).

Gallerie dell'Accademia - Open in summer, daily, 9am-9pm (11pm Sat, 8pm Sun and 2pm Mon); in winter, Tues to Sat, 9am-7pm, Sun and Mon, 9am-2pm. Closed 1 Jan, 1 May and 25 Dec. 15 000L, no charge (under 18 or over 60). ☏ 041 52 22 247.

San Giorgio Maggiore: Campanile – The bell-tower is open the same times as the church: in summer, 9am–noon and 2.30–6pm and in winter, 10am–noon and 2.30–4.30pm (as a guideline only). 3 000L (including lift).

I Frari – Open all year, daily, 9am (1pm Sun and public holidays)–6pm. 3 000L. Chorus Associazione Chiese di Venezia ☎ 041 27 50 462.

Scuola Grande di San Rocco – Open 28 Mar to 2 Nov, daily, 9am–5.30pm; Nov, 26 Dec to 6 Jan, Carnival week and Mar, 10am–4pm; Dec to Feb, Mon to Fri, 10am–1pm, Sat–Sun and public holidays, 10am–4pm (last admission 30min before closing time). Closed 1 Jan, Easter and 25 Dec. 9 000L, 6 000L (students aged 18-26), no charge (under 18 accompanied by parents and for all on 16 Aug). Audio-guided tours available. ☎ 041 52 34 864.

Scuola di San Giorgio degli Schiavoni – Open Apr to Oct, Tues to Sat, 9.30am–12.30pm and 3.30–6.30pm, Sun, 9.30am–12.30pm; Nov to Mar, Tues to Sat, 10am–12.30pm and 3–6pm, Sun, 10am–12.30pm. Last admission 20min before closing time. Closed weekday public holidays, 1 Jan, 1 May, 15 Aug and 25 Dec. May also close without prior warning at the request of the local brotherhood. 5 000L, 3 000L (under 18). ☎ 041 52 28 828.

Ghetto: sinagoghe – Guided tours only (45-60min) daily (except Sat and Jewish festivals), in English and Italian (also German, French, Spanish and Hebrew by appointment), June to Sept, 10am–7pm (last admission 5.30pm), Oct to May, 10am–4.30pm (last admission 3.30pm). Closed 1 Jan, 1 May, 25 Dec and Jewish festivals. Possible early Fri closing for religious services when 3.30pm visit may be cancelled or shortened. Bar. 12 000L, 9 000L (child) including entrance to museum. Entrance to museum only, 5 000L, 3 000L (child). ☎ 041 71 53 59.

Collezione Peggy Guggenheim – Open all year, daily (except Tues), 11am–6pm. Closed 25 Dec. 12 000L, 8 000L (student), no charge (child under 10). Audio-guided tours available. Bar. Restaurant. ☎ 041 24 05 411.

Fondazione Querini-Stampalia – Open Tues to Sat, 10am–1pm and 3–6pm (10pm Fri and Sat, concerts from 5-8.30pm); open Sun and public holidays, 10am–1pm and 3–6pm. 12 000L, 8 000L (student and over 60). ☎ 041 27 11 411.

Murano: Museo di arte vetraria – Open daily (except Wed), in summer, 10am–5pm; in winter, 10am–4pm; last admission 30min before closing time. Closed 1 Jan, 1 May and 25 Dec. For admission charges, see Palazzo Ducale. For further information, contact ☎ 041 73 95 86.

Torcello: Basilica – Open Apr to Oct, 10.30am–5.30pm; Nov to Mar, 10am–12.30pm and 2–5.30pm (last admission 30min before closing time). 5 000L. From Apr to Oct, admission includes an audio-guided tour (available in English, Italian, French, German and Spanish). ☎ 041 27 02 464.

Val VENOSTA
🛈 via dei Cappuccini 10, Silandro – ☎ 0473 62 04 80

Naturno
Juval castle – Guided tours only (1hr) in Italian and German, Palm Sunday to 30 June and Sept to late Oct, daily (except Weds), 10am–4pm. Tours in Italian at 11.15am and 3.15pm; also 10.15am and 4.15pm by appointment. 12 000L, 6 000L (child). ☎ 0348 44 33 871 (mobile).

San Procolo – Open daily (except Mon unless public holiday), early Apr to early Nov. Guided tours (20min) available in Italian and German. ☎ 0473 66 73 12.

Sluderno: Coira castle – Guided tours only (1hr) in English, Italian and German, 20 Mar to 1 Nov, daily (except Mon), 10am–noon and 2–4.30pm. 10 000L, 5 000L (child).

Malles: San Benedetto – Open daily (except Sun), 9–11.30am and 1.30–5pm. Key may be obtained from the Weisskopf family at n° 31. 1 000L.

Burgusio: Abbazia di Monte Maria – Guided tours only, July to Oct, Mon to Fri, at 10am, 11am, 3pm and 4pm, Sat at 10am and 11am; Nov to Mar, by appointment only; Apr to June, Mon to Fri, at 10.45am and 3pm, Sat at 10.45am. ☎ 0473 831 306.

VERONA
🛈 piazza delle Erbe 38 – ☎ 045 80 00 065

Casa di Giulietta – Open all year, daily (except Mon), 9am–6.30pm. Closed 1 Jan, 25 and 26 Dec. 6 000L, 2 000L (child/student), no charge (first Sun in the month). Bookshop. ☎ 045 80 34 303.

Palazzo del comune: Torre dei Lamberti – Open all year, daily (except Mon), 9–6pm. Closed 1 Jan, 25 and 26 Dec. 4 000L, 2 000L (child/student), no charge (first Sun in the month). ☎ 045 80 32 726.

Arena – Open daily (except Mon), 9am–6pm; 9am–3.30pm during opera season. Closed 1 Jan, 25 and 26 Dec. 6 000L, 2 000L (child/student), no charge (first Sun in the month). ☎ 045 80 03 204.

VERONA

Castelvecchio: Museo d'Arte - Open all year, daily (except Mon), 9am-6.30pm. Closed 1 Jan, 25 and 26 Dec. 6 000L, 2 000L (child/student), no charge (first Sun in the month). Guided tours (2hr) available in English, French and German. Bookshop. ☎ 045 59 47 34.

Chiesa di Sant'Anastasia - Open Mar to Oct, daily, 9am(1pm Sun and public holidays)-6pm; Nov to Feb, daily (except Mon), 10am-1pm and 1.30-4pm (5pm Sat, 1-5pm only Sun and public holidays). 3 000L. For further information, contact the Associazione Chiese Vive ☎ 045 59 28 13.

Teatro Romano - Same admission times and charges as for Tomba di Giulietta. ☎ 045 80 00 360.

Museo Archeologico - Same admission times and charges as for Teatro Romano.

Tomba di Giulietta - Open all year, daily (except Mon), 9am-6.30pm. Closed 1 Jan, 25 and 26 Dec. 5 000L, 2 000L (child/student), no charge (first Sun in the month). ☎ 045 80 00 361.

VICENZA   🛈 piazza Matteotti 12 - ☎ 0444 32 08 54

Basilica - Open all year, Tues to Sat, 9.30am-noon and 2.15-5pm, Sun and public holidays, 9.30am-12.30pm. ☎ 044 43 23 681.

Teatro Olimpico - Open all year, Tues to Sat, 9am-12.30pm and 2.15-5pm, Sun and public holidays, 9.30am-12.30pm. 5 000L. ☎ 044 43 23 781.

Museo Civico - ♿ (partial access). Open mid-June to late Aug, daily (except Mon), 10am-7pm; rest of the year, daily (except Mon), 9am-5pm (last admission 15min before closing time). Closed 25 and 26 Dec. 12 000L, 6 000L (student). Combined ticket with Teatro Olimpico and Museo Naturalistico Archeologico. ☎ 0444 32 13 48.

Excursions

Villa Valmarana "ai Nani" - Open Wed, Thur, Sat and Sun, 10am-noon; also every afternoon in Mar and Apr, 2.30-5.30pm, May to Sept, 3-6pm, Oct to Nov, 2-5pm. Closed Mon and 6 Nov to 14 Mar. 10 000L. ☎ 044 45 43 976.

La Rotonda - Open 15 Mar to 4 Nov, Tues to Thur, 10am-noon and 3-6pm (villa interior Wed only); Fri to Sun and public holidays, opening times depend on availability of staff. Closed 5 Nov to 14 Mar. 10 000L, 5 000L (garden only). ☎ 044 43 21 793.

Montecchio Maggiore: Villa Cordellina-Lombardi - Open Apr to 15 Oct: Tues to Fri, 9am-1pm; Sat, Sun and public holidays, 9am-noon and 3-6pm. Closed Nov to Mar. 4 000L, 1 500L (students and pensioners). ☎ 044 43 99 111.

VIPITENO   🛈 piazza Città 3 - ☎ 0472 76 53 25

Excursions

Cascate di Stanghe - Open May to Oct, 9.30am-5.30pm. 4 000L, 1 500L (child).

VITERBO   🛈 piazza S. Carluccio - ☎ 0761 30 47 95

Museo Civico - ♿ Open all year, daily (except Mon), 9am-7pm (6pm Nov to Mar). Closed 1 Jan, 1 May and 25 Dec. 6 000L, no charge (under 18 and over 60). Guided tour (2hr) available in English, Italian, French and German. ☎ 0761 34 82 75.

Excursions

Villa Lante in Bagnaia - ♿ Guided tours only (30min) to the Italian garden and the two loggia, daily (except Mon), 16 Apr to 15 Sept, 9am-7.30pm; 1-15 Apr and 16 Sept to 31 Oct, 9am-6.30pm; Mar, 9am-5.30pm; Nov to Feb, 9am-4.30pm. Last admission 1hr before closing time. Closed 1 Jan, 1 May and 25 Dec. 4 000 L, no charge (under 18 and over 60). ☎ 0761 28 80 08.

Ferento: Teatro romano - ♿ Open daily (except Mon), in summer, 9am-1hr before sunset (1.30pm Sun and public holidays); in winter 9am-1.30pm. No charge. ☎ 0761 32 59 29.

Bomarzo: Parco dei Mostri - ♿ Open all year, 8am-sunset. 15 000 L. Audio-visual presentation. Bar. Bookshop. ☎ 0761 92 40 29.

VOLTERRA   🛈 piazza dei Priori 20 - ☎ 0588 87 257

Palazzo Viti - Open Apr to Oct, daily (except Tues), 9am-1pm (also 3-5.30pm Sat-Sun and public holidays). 5 000L. ☎ 0588 84 047.

Pinacoteca and Museo Etrusco Guarnacci - ♿ (partial access). Open daily, mid-Mar to early Nov, 9am-7pm; rest of the year, 9am-2pm. Closed 1 Jan and 25 Dec.

All-inclusive pass for museums and archeological sites 12 000L, 8 000L (student/65 and over), 25 000L (family, max 4 persons). Audio-guided tours. Bookshop. ☎ 0588 86 347; www.volterratur.it

Sardinia

ALGHERO
🚹 piazza Portaterra 9 - ☎ 079 97 90 54

Excursions

Grotta di Nettuno - Guided tours only, every hour, Apr to Sept, 9am-7pm, Jan to Mar and Nov to Dec, 9am-2pm, Oct, 10am-5pm. 13 000L, 6 000L (child aged 3-12). ☎ 079 94 65 40 or 079 97 90 54.

Nuraghe Palmavera - Open Apr to Oct, 9am-7pm, Nov to Mar, 9.30am-4pm. 5 000L including guide (45min), 4 000L without guide, 2 500L (child). Combined ticket for Anghelu Ruju and Palmavera 7 000 without guide (9 000L including guide). ☎ 079 98 07 50.

Necropoli di Anghelu Ruju - Same admission times and charges as Nuraghe Palmavera.

BARBAGIA

Grotta del Bue Marino - Guided tours only (1hr) in Aug at 9am, 10am, 11am, noon, 3pm, 4pm and 5pm; in July at 10am, 11am, noon and 3pm; in Sept at 10am, 11am and 3pm; Apr to June and Oct, Nov at 11am and 3pm. Closed Dec to Mar. 10 000L, 6 000L (child). ☎ 0784 96 243, 0784 93 696 or 0784 93 305.

Grotta di Ispinigòli - Guided tours only, every hour, July and Aug, 9am-1pm and 3-6pm; Apr and May, 9am-noon and 3-5pm; June and Sept, 9am-noon and 3-6pm; Oct and Nov, 9-11am and 3-5pm. Closed Dec to Mar (except over Christmas period, when Oct opening times usually apply) 10 000L, 6 000L (child/student). ☎ 0784 96 243.

CAGLIARI
🚹 piazza Matteotti 9 - ☎ 070 66 92 55

Museo Archeologico Nazionale - ♿ (partial access). Open daily (except Mon), Apr to Sept, 9am-2pm and 3-8pm; Oct to Mar, 9am-7pm. Closed 1 Jan, 1 May and 25 Dec. Audio-visual presentation. 5 000L, no charge (under 18 and over 60). ☎ 070 65 59 11.

Orto Botanico - ♿ (partial access). Open daily, May to Aug, 8am-1.30pm and 3-8pm (6.30pm Apr and Sept to mid-Oct); mid-Oct to Mar, 8am-1.30pm. Closed Easter, Easter Monday, the morning of 1 May, 15 Aug and 25 Dec. Guided tour in Italian (1hr), 2nd and 4th Sun in the month, 11am. 1 000L, no charge (under 6 and over 60). ☎ 070 67 53 501.

Arcipelago della MADDALENA
🚹 Cala Gavetta - ☎ 0789 73 63 21

Isola di Caprera: Casa di Garibaldi - ♿ Guided tours, all year, daily, 9am-1.30pm (also afternoons in July and Aug). Closed 1 Jan, 1 May and 25 Dec. 4 000L. ☎ 0789 72 71 62.

NUORO
🚹 piazza Italia 19 - ☎ 0784 30 083

Museo della Vita e delle Tradizioni popolari Sarde - Open daily, 15 June to Sept, 9am-7pm; Oct to 14 June, 9am-1pm and 3-7pm. 5 000L, 1 000L (under 18 and over 60). Bookshop. ☎ 0784 24 29 00.

Isola di SANT'ANTIOCO

Vestigia di Sulcis - ♿ (partial access). Open all year, daily, 9am-1pm and 3.30-6pm (7pm in summer). Closed 1 Jan, Easter, 8 Dec and 25 Dec. 8 000L, 5 000L (child). Guided tours (2hr) in English and Italian. Bar. Bookshop. ☎ 0781 83 590.

SASSARI
🚹 viale Caprera 36 - ☎ 079 29 95 79

Museo Nazionale Sanna - Open all year, daily (except Mon), 9am-7pm (1.30pm Sun and public holidays). Closed 1 Jan, 1 May and 25 Dec. 4 000L, no charge (under 18 and over 60). ☎ 079 27 22 03.

THARROS

Zona archeologica and **necropoli** - Open daily, Mar to June, 9am-7pm; July to Sept, 9am-8pm; Oct to Feb, 9am-5.30pm. 8 000L, 4 000L (under 14 and over 60).

Sicily

AGRIGENTO
🛈 via Cesare Battisti - ☎ 0922 20 454

Valle dei Templi - Open all year, daily, 8.30am-1hr before sunset (10pm in summer). ☎ 0922 49 72 26. The archeological area (Tempio di Zeus e dei Dioscuri) is open daily, in summer, 8.30am-7pm; in winter, 8.30am-6pm. 4 000L, no charge (under 18 and over 60). ☎ 0922 49 72 21.

Museo Archeologico Regionale - ♿ (partial access). Open all year, daily, 9am-1pm; also Wed to Sat, 2-6pm (5pm in winter). Opening hours subject to change, telephone in advance. 8 000L, no charge (under 18 and over 60). ☎ 0922 49 72 35 or 0922 49 72 04.

Oratorio di Falaride - Open all year, daily, 9am-1.30pm; also Wed to Sat, 2-6.30pm. No charge.

San Nicola - Open all year, daily, 9.30am-noon and 3.30-5.30pm.

Quartiere Ellenistico-Romano - Open all year, daily, 9am-1hr before sunset. No charge. ☎ 0922 40 15 65.

Abbazia di Santo Spirito - Visit: apply at the adjacent monastery.

Excursion

Casa di Pirandello - Open all year, daily, 8am-7.30pm. Audio-visual presentation. 4 000L, no charge (under 18 and over 60). ☎ 0922 44 41 11.

CALTAGIRONE
🛈 Palazzo Libertini di S. Marco - ☎ 0933 53 809

Museo della Ceramica - Open all year, daily, 9am-4.30pm. 8 000L, no charge (under 18 and over 60). Guided tours available; book a couple of days in advance. ☎ 0933 21 680.

Villa Romana del CASALE

Open all year, daily, 9am-2hr before sunset. 4 000 L, no charge (under 18 and over 60). ☎ 0935 68 00 36.

Excursion

Piazza Armerina: Duomo - Open all year, daily, 8am-12.30pm and 3.30-6.30pm. ☎ 0935 68 02 14.

CATANIA
🛈 via Cimarosa 10 - ☎ 095 73 06 211

Palazzo Biscari - Guided tours only (20min), daily (except Sun), 9.30am-12.30pm and 4-7pm. Book in advance. Closed Aug and public holidays. 10 000L, no charge the first Tues in the month. ☎095 32 18 18.

Teatro Antico - Closed for restoration. For further information, contact the tourist office.

Castello Ursino - Interior currently undergoing restoration. For further information, contact either the tourist office or the castle ☎ 095 34 58 30.

CEFALU
🛈 corso Ruggero 77 - ☎ 0921 42 10 50

Duomo - Open all year, daily, 8am-noon and 3.30-6pm (7pm in summer). ☎ 0921 92 20 21.

Museo Mandralisca - Open daily, Apr to Sept, 9am-9pm (midnight in Aug); Oct to Mar, 9am-12.30pm and 3.30-7pm. 6 000L. ☎ 0921 42 15 47.

Isole EGADI
🛈 piazza Madrice 8, Favignana - ☎ 0923 92 16 47

Levanzo: Boat trip to the Grotta del Genovese. Apply to Signor Natale Castiglione, via Calvario 27, Levanzo. ☎ 0360 63 92 61 (mobile).

ENNA
🛈 via Roma 413 - ☎ 0935 52 82 28

Castello di Lombardia - Undergoing restoration at the time of going to press, but partly open to the public. No charge. ☎ 0935 40 347.

Duomo - Open all year, daily, 9am-1pm and 4-7pm. ☎ 0935 50 31 65.

Isole EOLIE
🛈 corso Vittorio Emanuele 202, Lipari - ☎ 090 98 80 095
🛈 Via Levante 4, Vulcano (July to Sept) - ☎ 090 98 52 028

Boat Trips - Trips to all the islands 15 Mar to 15 Oct (from July, 3-4 departures per day). For information, apply to Società VIKING, vico Himera 3, 98055 Lipari, ☎ 090 98 12 584; Compagnia di Navigazione G. LA CAVA, via Vittorio Emanuele 124, ☎ 090 98 11 242; PIGNATARO SHIPPING, via Prof. Carnevale 29, ☎ 090 98 11 417 or 0368 67 59 75.

Lipari: Museo Archeologico Eoliano – Open all year, daily, 9am–2pm and 4–7pm (6pm Oct to May). Last admission 1hr before closing time. 8 000L, no charge (under 18 and over 60). ☎ 090 98 80 174.

Stromboli: Ascent to the crater – Guided tours: apply to the Information Office of the Alpine Guides, Piazzale San Vincenzo, Stromboli. ☎ 090 98 62 11.

ETNA

Ascent of Etna – As the volcano may erupt at any time, tourist facilities (roads, paths, cable-cars and refuge huts) may be closed, moved or withdrawn. Excursions may be cancelled in the case of bad weather (fog) or volcano activity. The best time for the ascent is early morning. Wear warm clothing even in summer (anorak, thick pullover) and walking shoes (no heels – the stony terrain of the paths through the lava can cause injuries particularly to ankles). Wind-cheaters and walking shoes for hire. Wear sunglasses because of the glare.

South face – From 15 Apr to 31 Oct. 3 hours there and back. 65 000L (including insurance and guide). For additional information and details regarding nightime excursions, apply to Gruppo Guide Alpine Etna Sud, via Etna 49, Nicolosi, ☎ 095 79 14 755 or Funavie S.I.T.A.S., piazza Vittorio Emanuele 45, Nocolosi, ☎ 095 91 11 58 or 095 91 41 41.

Northeast face – From mid-May to mid-Oct departing from Piano Provenza. About 2hr 30min there and back. 60 000L (including guide). For additional information and details regarding nightime excursions, apply to S.T.A.R., via G. Marconi 28, Linguaglossa, ☎ 095 64 31 80 or Piano Provenzana, ☎ 095 64 34 30 or Pro Loco (Tourist Office) in Linguaglossa, piazza Annunziata 5, ☎ 095 64 30 94.

MARSALA ▪ via XI Maggio 100 – ☎ 0923 71 40 97

Museo Archeologico di Baglio Anselmi – Open all year, daily, 9am–1.30pm; also Wed and Sat, 4–7pm. 4 000L, no charge (under 18 and over 60). Audio-visual presentation. ☎ 0923 95 25 35.

MESSINA ▪ via Calabria isolato 301 bis – ☎ 090 67 42 36

Museo Regionale – Open all year, Mon to Sat, 9am–2pm; Sun, 9am–1pm; also Tues, Thur and Sat, 4–7pm (3–6pm winter). Last admission 30min before closing. Guided tours available (1hr). 8 000L, no charge (under 18 and over 60). ☎ 090 36 12 92.

MONREALE

Duomo – Open all year, daily, 8am–noon and 3.30–6pm (open all day in summer). Ascent to the terraces 2 000L. ☎ 091 64 04 413.

Chiostro – Open Mon to Sat, 9am–1pm and 3–6.30pm, Sun, 9am–12.30pm. 4 000L. ☎ 091 64 04 403.

NOTO ▪ piazza XVI Maggio 16 – ☎ 0931 83 67 44

San Francesco all'Immacolata – Open 7.30am–noon and 4–8pm. Guided tours available. ☎ 0931 83 50 05.

San Domenico – Currently undergoing restoration. For information, contact the Associazione Allakatalla, ☎ 0931 83 50 05.

PALERMO ▪ piazza Castelnuovo 34 – ☎ 09158 38 47

La Martorana – Open in summer, daily (except Sun afternoons), 8.30am–1pm and 3.30–7pm (5pm in winter). ☎ 091 61 61 692.

San Cataldo – Open all year, daily, 8.30am–3pm (12.30pm Sat-Sun). For information apply to Chiesa della Martorana.

Cattedrale – Open daily, 9.30am–5.30pm. **Tesoro:** Same opening times as for Cattedrale; closed Sun and public holidays. 1 000L.

Palazzo dei Normanni

Cappella Palatina – Open all year, Mon to Fri, 9am–noon and 3–5pm; Sat, 9am–noon; Sun and public holidays, 9–10am and noon–1pm. ☎ 091 70 54 878.

Antichi appartamenti reali – Open Mon, Fri and Sat, 9am–noon; for groups by appointment to the Servizio Questura, fax 091 705 47 37.

San Giovanni degli Eremiti – Open all year, daily, 9am–1pm and 3–6.30pm; Sun and public holidays, 9am–12.30pm. ☎ 091 65 15 019.

San Francesco d'Assisi – Open all year, daily (except Sun), 9am–11.30am and 4.30–6.30pm. ☎ 091 61 62 819.

Palazzo Mirto – Open all year, daily, 9am–1pm and 3–7pm; Sun and public holidays, 9am–12.30pm. Closed afternoons of public holidays. 4 000L, no charge (under 18 and over 60). ☎ 091 61 64 751.

Museo internazionale delle Marionette - Open all year, daily (except Sat and Sun afternoon), 9am-1pm and 4-7pm. Closed public holidays and week of 15 Aug. 5 000L, 3 000L (child/senior citizen). Audio-visual presentation. ☎ 091 32 80 60.

Galleria Regionale della Sicilia - Open all year, Mon to Sat, 9am-1.30pm, also Tues and Thur, 3-7.30pm; Sun, 9am-12.30pm. 8 000L, no charge (under 18 and over 60). ☎ 091 623 00 11.

Oratorio del Rosario di San Domenico - Usually open daily, 10am-noon and 4-6pm (the custodian is not always available at these times).

Oratorio del Rosario di Santa Cita - Open daily (except Sun), 8.30am-1pm and 3-4.30pm. Closed during weddings. Donation. ☎ 091 33 27 79.

Museo Archeologico Regionale - Open all year, Mon to Sat, 9am-1.45pm; also Tues and Fri, 3-6.45pm; Sun and public holidays, 9am-1.15pm (last admission 30min before closing). 8 000L, no charge (under 18 and over 60). Audio-visual presentation. ☎ 091 61 16 805.

Villa Malfitano - Open daily (except Sun), 9am-1pm. Closed public holidays. 5 000L, 3 000L (student). Guided tours available (1hr). ☎ 091 68 16 133.

Catacombe dei Cappucini - Open all year, daily, 9am-noon and 3-5pm. Donation. ☎ 091 21 21 17.

La Zisa - Open all year, Mon to Sat, 9am-1pm and 3-7pm; Sun, 9am-12.30pm. 4 000L, no charge (under 18 and over 60). ☎ 091 65 20 269.

Orto Botanico - Open all year, Mon to Fri, 9am-6pm; Sat-Sun, 8.30am-1.30pm. Closed public holidays. 6 000L, 3 000L (child aged 10-16), no charge (under 10 and over 65). ☎ 091 62 38 241.

Parco della Favorita: Museo Etnografico Pitrè - ♿ (partial access). Open all year, daily (except Fri), 9am-8pm. Closed public holidays. 5 000L, no charge (under 18 and over 60). ☎ 091 74 04 893.

Excursions

Solunto: Zona Archeologica - Open daily, Apr to Sept, 9am-6pm (12.30pm Sun); Nov to Mar, 9am-4pm (12.30pm Sun). 4 000L, no charge (under 18 and over 60). ☎ 091 90 45 57.

Bagheria: Villa Palagonia - Open in summer, daily, 9am-1pm and 4-7pm; in winter, daily, 9am-1pm and 3-5pm. 5 000L, 2 000L (child under 11). ☎ 091 93 20 88.

RAGUSA   🛈 via Capitano Bocchieri 33, Ibla - ☎ 0932 62 14 21

San Giorgio - Open all year, daily, 9am-noon and 4-7pm.

San Giuseppe - Open all year, daily, 7.30am-noon and 3-6pm.

San Giovanni - Open all year, daily, 7am-noon and 4-8pm. ☎ 0932 62 16 58.

Museo Archeologico Ibleo - Open all year, daily, 9am-1.30pm and 4-7.30pm. 4 000L, no charge (under 18 and over 60). ☎ 0932 62 29 63.

Excursion

Modica   🛈 Etnos, via Rollo 106 - ☎ 0932 75 27 47

Museo delle Arti e Tradizioni Popolari - Open in summer, daily, 10am-1pm and 4-7pm; in winter, daily, 10am-1pm abd 3.30-6.30pm. For information, contact Cooperativa Etnos, ☎ 0932 75 27 47.

SEGESTA

Tempio - Open all year, daily, 9am-1hr before sunset. 4 000L, no charge (under 18 and over 60). Shuttle bus to the theatre (teatro): 2 000L. Bar, restaurant. ☎ 0924 95 23 56.

Antica città di SELINUNTE

Open all year, daily, 9am-2hrs before sunset. 4 000L, no charge (under 18 and over 65). ☎ 0924 46 277.

SIRACUSA   🛈 via S. Sebastiano 45 - ☎ 0931 67 710
🛈 Largo Paradiso (zona archeologica) - ☎ 0931 60 510

Duomo - Open daily, 9am-noon and 4-6.30pm.

Galleria Regionale di Palazzo Bellomo - Open all year, daily, 9am-2pm (1pm Sun and public holidays, Wed and Fri, 3-7pm). 8 000L, no charge (under 18 and over 60). ☎ 0931 69 511.

Parco Archeologico della Neapolis - ♿ (partial access). Open daily, 9am-2hrs before sunset. 4 000L, no charge (under 18 and over 60). ☎ 0931 66 206 or 0931 48 11 42.

Museo Archeologico Regionale P. Orsi - ♿ Open daily, 9am-2pm and 3.30-7.30pm; last admission 30min before closing time. Closed Mon morning and some Sun. Telephone in advance to confirm opening times. Audio-visual presentation. 8 000L, no charge (under 18 and over 60). ☎ 0931 46 40 22.

Catacombe di San Giovanni - ♿ Guided tours only (30min), daily (except Tues) 9am-12.30pm and 2.30-5pm. 4 000L, 2 000L (child). ☎ 0931 67 955.

Excursions

Fonte Ciane - Visit: telephone Signori. Vella. ☎ 0931 69 076 or 0368 31 68 199 (mobile).

Castello Eurialo - Open all year, daily, 9am-2hr before sunset. No charge. ☎ 0931 71 17 73.

TAORMINA
🄵 Palazzo Corvaja (Piazza S. Caterina) - ☎ 094223 243

Teatro Greco - ♿ (partial access). Open all year, daily, 9am-2hr before sunset. 4 000L, no charge (under 18 and over 60). ☎ 0942 23 220.

Excursion

Gole dell'Alcantara - Open all year, 7am-8pm (5pm Nov to Apr). Bar and restaurant. Boots and overalls for hire: 13 000L. Entrance 4 000L, 2 000L (child). ☎ 0942 98 50 10.

TINDARI

Rovine - Open all year, daily, 9am-2hr before sunset. 4 000L, no charge (under 18 and over 60). ☎ 0941 36 90 23.

TRAPANI
🄵 via S. Francesco d'Assisi 25 - ☎ 0923 54 55 11

Santuario dell'Annunziata - Open all year daily, 8am-noon and 4-7pm. Guided tours: apply 1 day in advance. ☎ 0923 53 91 84.

Museo Pepoli - Open all year, Mon to Sat, 9am-1.30pm (also 3-6.30pm Tues and Thur); Sun and public holidays, 9am-12.30pm. 8 000L, no charge (under 18 and over 60). Audio-visual presentation. ☎ 0923 55 32 69.

Excursions

Museo del Sale di Nubia - Open daily, in summer, 10am-1pm and 3.30-7pm; in winter, 9am-1pm and 3.30-5.30pm. ☎ 0923 86 71 42.

Isola di Mozia: access and visit - Ferry service operates 9am-1pm and 3-6.30pm (mornings only Sept to Mar). 5 000L (ferry crossing) and 5 000L (museum) ☎ 0923 75 25 98.

USTICA

Prehistoric village - The village is visible through a fence; for an in-depth visit contact the Riserva Naturale Marina, ☎ 091 84 49 456.

Riserva marina - The marine reserve centre *(centro riserva marina)* is situated in the main square of the village. ☎ 091 84 49 456.

Index

Amalfi *Campania* .... Towns, sights and tourist regions followed by the name of the region.

Dante Alighieri .... People, events and artistic styles mentioned in the guide.

Botanical Gardens .... Important sights in a large town.

Isolated sights (castles, ruins, lakes, islands etc.) are listed under their proper name.

A

Abano Terme *Veneto* 255
Abbazia di Chiaravalle
   Lombardy 222
Abruzzi 28, 80
Abruzzo,
   Parco Nazionale d' *Abruzzi* 82
Accademia degli Incamminati 111
Accommodation 433
Acireale *Sicily* 404
Acqui Terme *Piedmont* 352
Agnone *Molise* 223
Agrigento *Sicily* 399
Alatri *Lazio* 129
Alba *Piedmont* 320
Alba Fucens *Abruzzi* 82
Albani, Francesco 111
Albano Laziale *Lazio* 131
Albenga *Liguria* 294
Alberobello *Puglia* 359
Alberti, Leon Battista .. 51, 163, 293
Albinoni, Tomaso 69
Albissola Marina *Liguria* 295
Alcantara gorges *Sicily* 424
Alfedena *Abruzzi* 82
Alfieri, Vittorio 67
Alghero *Sardinia* 388
Alleghe *Trentino-Alto Adige* 147
Alpe di Siusi
   Trentino-Alto Adige 146
Alps 24
Altamura *Puglia* 283
Altilia Sæpinum *Molise* 224
Altomonte *Calabria* 123
Amadeo 106
Amalfi *Campania* 83
Amalfitana, Costiera *Campania* 84
Amatrice, Cola dell' 93
Ambrose, Saint 210
Ammannati, Bartolomeo 163
Anacapri *Campania* 126
Anagni *Lazio* 86
Ancient Civilisations 30
Ancona *Marches* 87
Andalo *Trentino-Alto Adige* 355
Angelico, Fra 163
Angera *Lombardy* 188
Anguillara Sabazia *Lazio* 132
Anjou dynasty 34
Annunzio, Gabriele d' 67
Antonelli, Alessandro 58
Antonines 32
Antonioni 72
Antony, Mark 32
Anzio *Lazio* 87

Aosta *Valle d'Aosta* 26, 88
Apennines 24
Apuan Alps 28
Aquileia *Friuli-Venezia* 90
Arbatax *Sardinia* 395
Arborea *Sardinia* 394
Archimedes 422
Architecture 64
Aretino 66
Arezzo *Tuscany* 91
Arezzo, Guido d' 278
Argentario, Promontorio
   dell' (Promontory) *Tuscany* 92
Ariccia *Lazio* 131
Ariosto, Ludovico 66, 153
Arnolfo di Cambio 50
Arona *Piedmont* 188
Arquà Petrarca *Veneto* 255
Art 48
Arte Povera 59
Arts and Crafts 74
Arzachena *Sardinia* 389
Ascoli Piceno *Marches* 93
Asolo *Veneto* 102
Aspromonte *Calabria* 122
Aspromonte, Massiccio della
   (Massif) *Calabria* 29
Assisi *Umbria* 95
Asti *Piedmont* 352
Atrani *Campania* 85
Atri *Abruzzo* 98
Augustus 32
Avati, Pupi 73
Avelengo *Trentino-Alto Adige* 209
Averno, Lago d' (Lake)
   Campania 244
Avigliana *Piedmont* 351
Aymavilles, Fortezza di
   Valle d'Aosta 90

B

Baciccia 56
Bacoli *Campania* 243
Badia Fiesolana *Tuscany* 156
Bagheria *Sicily* 417
Baia, Terme di (Baths)
   Campania 243
Balla, Giacomo 58
Barbagia *Sardinia* 389
Barbarossa, Frederick 34
Bard, Fortezza di (Fortress)
   Valle d'Aosta 90
Bardolino *Veneto* 193

Bari *Puglia* 99
Barletta *Puglia* 101
Barletta *challenge* 101
Baroque 56
Barumini *Sardinia* 391
Basilicata 29
Bassano del Grappa *Veneto* 101
Bassano, Jacopo 55
Baveno *Piedmont* 188
Bellagio *Lombardy* 191
Bella, Isola (Island) *Piedmont* 189
Bellano *Lombardy* 192
Bellini, The 363
Bellini, Giovanni 53, 265
Bellini, Vincenzo 70
Belluno *Veneto* 102
Belvedere Pocol *Veneto* 138
Benedict, Saint 224
Benevento *Campania* 103
Benigni, Roberto 73
Bentivoglio 111
Bergamo *Lombardy* 103
Bernini, Gian Lorenzo 57
Bertinoro *Emilia-Romagna* 176
Bertolucci, Bernardo 72
Biodola *Tuscany* 147
Bisceglie *Puglia* 100
Bitonto *Puglia* 283
Bloomsbury group 286
Boccaccio, Giovanni 65, 322
Boccioni, Umberto 58
Boiardo 66
Boiardo, Matteo Maria 153
Bologna *Emilia-Romagna* 108
    Carracci Room 113
Bologna, Giovanni 54, 163
Bolsena *Lazio* 115
Bolzano *Trentino-Alto Adige* 115
Bomarzo *Lazio* 381
Bominaco *Abruzzi* 82
Boniface VIII 34, 86
Bordighera *Liguria* 294
Borromee,
    Isole (Islands) *Piedmont* 189
Borromini, Francesco 57
Botticelli, Sandro 52, 163
Bracciano *Lazio* 132
Bracciano, Lago di (Lake) *Lazio* .. 132
Braies, Lago di (Lake)
    Trentino-Alto Adige 146
Bramante, Donato 53, 211
Brembana, Val (Valley)
    Lombardy 107
Breno *Lombardy* 124
Brenta, Gruppo del (Massif)
    Trentino-Alto Adige 354
Brenta, Riviera del *Veneto* 116
Brescello *Emilia-Romagna* 291
Brescia *Lombardy* 117
Bressanone
    Trentino-Alto Adige 119
Breuil-Cervinia *Valle d'Aosta* 90
Brianza *Lombardy* 26
Brindisi *Puglia* 120
Bronzino 163
Brunelleschi, Filippo 51, 163
Brunico *Trentino-Alto Adige* 146
Burgusio *Trentino-Alto Adige* 375
Burri 59
Buskers Festival 153
Busoni, Ferruccio 71
Bussana Vecchia *Liguria* 324
Buzzati, Dino 68
Byzantine Art 48

C

Cadenabbia *Lombardy* 192
Cadore *Veneto* 27, 142
Caesar, Julius 297
Caesar, julius 31
Cagliari *Sardinia* 391
Calabria 29, 121
Cala di San Felice *Puglia* 177
Calanchi,
    Riserva Naturale dei *Abruzzi* 99
Cala Gonone *Sardinia* 390
Caltagirone *Sicily* 401
Calvino, Italo 68
Camaino, Tino di 230, 326
Camaldoli *Tuscany* 325
Camogli *Liguria* 279
Camonica, Val (Valley)
    Lombardy 124
Campanella, Tommaso 124
Campania 29
Campi Flegrei *Campania* 242
Campione del Garda *Lombardy* .. 193
Campione d'Italia *Lombardy* 190
Campo Carlo Magno
    Trentino-Alto Adige 355
Campo Fiscalino
    Trentino-Alto Adige 146
Campo Imperatore *Abruzzi* 80
Canaletto 364
Canazei *Trentino-Alto Adige* 143
Canne della Battaglia *Puglia* 101
Cannero Riviera *Piedmont* 189
Cannobio *Piedmont* 189
Canosa di Puglia *Puglia* 283
Canossa, Castello di (Castle)
    Emilia-Romagna 291
Canova, Antonio 58, 102
Caprera *Sardinia* 393
Capoliveri *Tuscany* 148
Capo Palinuro *Campania* 134
Caprarola,
    Palazzo Farnese di *Lazio* 124
Capri, Isola di (Island)
    Campania 125
Capua *Campania* 127
Caracciolo 232
Caravaggio 56, 231
Carducci, Giosuè 67
Carezza, Lago di (Lake)
    Trentino-Alto Adige 143
Carnic Alps
    Veneto, Friuli-Venezia Giulia 27
Carpaccio 364
Carpi *Emilia-Romagna* 223
Carracci 56
Carrara *Tuscany* 128
Carrà, Carlo 58
Carsulae *Umbria* 334
Casale, Villa romana *Sicily* 402
Casamari,
    Abbazia di (Abbey) *Lazio* 129
Caserta, Reggia di *Campania* 130
Caserta Vecchia *Campania* 130
Cassino, Battle of 224
Castagno, Andrea del 52, 163
Castel del Monte *Puglia* 283
Castelfranco Veneto *Veneto* 130
Castel Gandolfo *Lazio* 131
Castel Gavone *Liguria* 294
Castellammare di Stabia
    Campania 131

Castellana, Grotte di (Caves)
  Puglia 284
Castelli *Abruzzi* 81
Castelli dell'Alto Monferrato,
  Strada dei (Scenic route)
  Piedmont 352
Castelli Romani *Lazio* 131
Castello *Sicily* 424
Castello Eurialo *Sicily* 423
Castelmola *Sicily* 424
Castel San Giovanni *Liguria* 294
Castiglione, Baldassare 66
Catania *Sicily* 402
Cavallini, Pietro 51
Cavour, Camillo 35
Cefalu *Sicily* 404
Celestine V 195
Cellini, Benvenuto 54, 163
Ceramics 62
Cernobbio *Lombardy* 192
Cerro *Lombardy* 189
Certaldo *Tuscany* 322
Cerveteri *Lazio* 132
Cesena *Emilia-Romagna* 176
Champoluc *Valle d'Aosta* 89
Charlemagne 34
Chianciano Terme *Tuscany* 227
Chianti *Tuscany* 28
Chiavari *Liguria* 295
Chiavenna *Lombardy* 132
Chieri *Piedmont* 352
Chieti *Abruzzo* 133
Chirico, Giorgio de 58
Chiusi *Tuscany* 134
Christianity 297
Cimabue 51, 162
Cinema 72
Cinquemiglia, Piano delle
  (Plateau) *Abruzzi* 81
Cinque Terre *Liguria* 135
Ciociaria *Lazio* 28
Circeo, Monte *Lazio* 335
Circeo,
  Parco Nazionale del *Lazio* 335
Cittadella *Veneto* 102
Città della Pieve *Umbria* 265
Cividale del Friuli
  Friuli-Venezia Giulia 136
Civita Castellana *Lazio* 381
Civitavecchia *Lazio* 136
Civitella del Tronto *Marches* 95
Clementi, Muzio 71
Cogne *Valle d'Aosta* 89
Colle Don Bosco *Piedmont* 352
Colleoni, Bartolomeo 105
Colli Euganei *Veneto* 255
Collodi *Tuscany* 225
Colonna, Capo *Calabria* 141
Comacchio *Emilia-Romagna* 137
Comacchio,
  Valli di *Emilia-Romagna* 137
Commedia dell'Arte 105
Como *Lombardy* 137
Como, Lago di (Lake)
  Lombardy 191
Conegliano *Veneto* 137
Conegliano, Cima da 137
Conero Massif *Marches* 87
Constantine 32, 297
Cordevole, Valle del (Valley)
  Trentino-Alto Adige 147

Corelli, Arcangelo 70
Corfinio *Abruzzi* 332
Corniglia *Liguria* 136
Correggio 258
Corrente 59
Cortina d'Ampezzo *Veneto* 138
Cortona *Tuscany* 138
Cortona, Pietro da 138
Cosa, Ancient town of *Tuscany* 93
Cosenza *Calabria* 123
Cosmati, Maestri 311
Cosmati 49, 331, 334, 334
Cossa, Francesco del 153
Costa, Lorenzo 153
Costalunga, Passo di (Pass)
  Trentino-Alto Adige 143
Costa Smeralda *Sardinia* 393
Council of Trent 35
Courmayeur *Valle d'Aosta* 90
Crafts 74
Crassus 31
Cremona *Lombardy* 139
Cristofori, Bartolomeo 71
Crivelli, Carlo 93, 152
Crotone *Calabria* 140
Cuma *Campania* 141

D

Dallapiccola, Luigi 71
D'Annunzio, Gabriele 67, 193
Dante Alighieri 65
Dante Alighieri 162
De Filippo 232
Deledda, Grazia 67
Desenzano del Garda *Lombardy* . 193
Diano Castello *Liguria* 294
Diano Marina *Liguria* 294
Dobbiaco *Trentino-Alto Adige* 146
Dolce stil nuovo 65
Domenichino 111
Donatello 52, 163
Dongo *Lombardy* 192
Donizetti, Gaetano 70
Dorgali *Sardinia* 390
Doria, Andrea 178
Dossi, Dosso 153
Duccio, Agostino di 52
Duccio di Buoninsegna 51, 326

E

Eco, Umberto 68
Egadi, islands *Sicily* 404
Emerald Coast *Sardinia* 393
Emilia-Romagna 27
Enna *Sicily* 405
Eolie, Isole *Sicily* 405
Ercolano *Campania* 149
Erice *Sicily* 407
Este 222
Este *Veneto* 255
Estensi, The 153
Etna *Sicily* 408
Etruria 31
Etruscans 31, 62

F

Fabriano *Marches* 150
Fabriano, Gentile da 51
Faenza *Emilia-Romagna* 151
Faito, Monte (Mount)
   Campania 245
Falzarego, Passo di (Pass)
   Trentino-Alto Adige 146
Fano *Marches* 151
Farnese, The 257
Fashion 29
Fattori, Giovanni 58
Favignana *Sicily* 404
Fedaia, Lago di (Lake)
   Trentino-Alto Adige 143
Fellini, Federico 72
Feltre *Veneto* 102
Fénis, Castello di (Castle)
   Valle d'Aosta 90
Ferentillo *Umbria* 334
Ferento, Teatro Romano di
   (Roman theatre) *Lazio* 381
Fermo *Marches* 152
Ferrara *Emilia-Romagna* 153
Fidenza *Emilia-Romagna* 260
Fiesole *Tuscany* 156
Fiesole, Mino da 52
Finale Borgo *Liguria* 294
Finale Ligure *Liguria* 294
Finale Marina *Liguria* 294
Finale Pia *Liguria* 294
Firenze *Tuscany* 157
   Battistero 164
   Casa Buonarroti 174
   Cenacolo di Sant'Apollonia 174
   Certosa del Galluzzo 175
   Frescoes of Santa Maria
     del Carmine 174
   Galleria degli Uffizi 168
   Galleria dell'Accademia 172
   Giardino di Boboli 169
   La Badia 174
   Loggia del Mercato Nuovo 174
   Museo Archeologico 174
   Museo della Casa
     Fiorentina Antica 174
   Museo dell'Opera del Duomo 165
   Museo di Storia della Scienza 174
   Museo Marino Marini 174
   Ognissanti 174
   Opificio delle Pietre dure 174
   Orsanmichele 174
   Ospedale degli Innocenti 175
   Palazzo e Museo Nazionale
     del Bargello 170
   Palazzo Medici-Riccardi 172
   Palazzo Pitti 169
   Palazzo Rucellai 175
   Palazzo Strozzi 175
   Palazzo Vecchio 165
   Passeggiata ai Colli 174
   Piazza del Duomo 164
   Piazza della Signoria 165
   Ponte Vecchio 169
   San Lorenzo 170
   San Marco 172
   San Miniato al Monte 174
   Santa Croce 173
   Santa Maria Novella 172
   Santa Trinita 174
   Santissima Annunziata 175
   Santo Spirito 174

Villa di Castello 175
Villa di Poggio a Caiano 175
Villa La Ferdinanda 175
Villa La Petraia 175
Flavian dynasty 32
Florence *see Firenze*
Foggia *Puglia* 284
Foligno *Umbria* 98
Fontana 59
Fontanellato *Emilia-Romagna* 260
Fonte Colombo, Convento di
   (Monastery) *Lazio* 292
Fonte Ciane *Sicily* 423
Fonti del Clitunno *Umbria* 331
Food 75
Foresta Umbra *Puglia* 177
Forlì *Emilia-Romagna* 175
Foscolo, Ugo 67
Fossanova,
   Abbazia di (Abbey) *Lazio* 176
Fo, Dario 68
Francesca, Piero della 52
Francis of Assisi, Saint 65, 96
Frasassi,
   Grotte di (Caves) *Marches* 150
Frascati *Lazio* 131
Fra Angelico 52
Frescobaldi, Girolamo 69
Friuli-Venezia Giulia 27
Fusaro, Lago del (Lake)
   Campania 244
Futurists 58, 67

G

Gabrielli, Andrea 69
Gabrielli, Giovanni 69
Gadda, Carlo Emilio 68
Gaeta *Lazio* 176
Galatina *Puglia* 284
Galatone *Puglia* 284
Galileo Galilei 66, 269
Gallura *Sardinia* 393
Galuppi, Baldassare 69
Garda *Veneto* 193
Garda, Lago di (Lake) *Lombardy,*
   Veneto, Trentino-Alto Adige 193
Gardena, Val (Valley)
   Trentino-Alto Adige 145
Gardone Riviera *Lombardy* 193
Gargano, Promontorio del
   (Promontory) *Puglia* 177
Gargnano *Lombardy* 193
Garibaldi, Giuseppe 36
Garofalo 153
Genova *Liguria* 178
   Carruggi 178
Genova, Val di (Valley)
   Trentino-Alto Adige 355
Gerace *Calabria* 123
Germi Pietro 72
Ghibellines 34, 184, 325
Ghiberti, Lorenzo 163, 52
Ghirlandaio, Domenico 163, 52
Gignese *Piedmont* 189
Giordano, Luca 232
Giorgione 55, 130, 364
Giotto 51, 162, 252
Giovinazzo *Puglia* 100
Glorenza *Trentino-Alto Adige* 375
Goldoni, Carlo 66

Gonzaga, The 204
GOODKINGROBERTOFANJOU ... 230
Gothic Art 50
Gozzoli, Benozzo 52, 163
Gradara Marches 266
Grado Friuli-Venezia Giulia 183
Gran Paradiso, Parco Nazionale del
   (National Park) Valle d'Aosta 90
Gran Sasso Abruzzi 80
Gran Paradiso, Parco Nazionale del
   Valle d'Aosta 26
Gravedona Lombardy 192
Great Schism of the West 34
Greccio, Convento di
   (Monastery) Lazio 292
Greeks 30, 61
Greek mythology 30
Gregory VII 298
Gregory the Great 34
Gressoney Valle d'Aosta 89
Grosseto Tuscany 183
Grotta Azzurra (Cave)
   Campania 125
Grottaferrata Lazio 131
Grotta Gigante (Cave)
   Friuli-Venezia Giulia 358
Grotte di Pertosa Campania 135
Guardi 364
Guarini, Guarino 58
Gubbio Umbria 184
Guelphs 34
Guercino 111
Guicciardini, Francesco 162
Guido d'Arezzo 69
Guttuso 59

H

Hadrian 336
Hannibal 31
Hermetic Movement 67
Hippodamus of Miletus 61
Historical Table and Notes 30
Holy Roman Empire 34
Humanism 65
Hayez 58

I

International Gothic style 51
Investiture Controversy 34, 298
Ipogeo dei Volumni Umbria 265
Ischia, Isola di (Island)
   Campania 186
Iseo Lombardy 192
Iseo, Lago di (Lake) Lombardy ... 192
Ispinigoli, Grotta di (cave)
   Sardinia 390
Issogne, Castello d' (Castle)
   Valle d'Aosta 90
Italian Socialist Republic 37
Italiots 30
Italy Today 24
Itria, Valle d' Puglia 359
Ivrea Piedmont 90

J

Jaquerio, Giacomo 351
Jesi Marches 187
Julio-Claudian dynasty 32
Justinian 32
Juvarra, Filippo 58

L

La Foresta,
   Convento di (Monastery)
   Lazio 292
Laghi, Regione dei (Lakes)
   Piedmont, Lombardy, Trentino,
   Veneto 188
Langhe Piedmont 320
Lante, Villa Lazio 381
Lanzo d'Intelvi Lombardy 190
L'Aquila Abruzzi 195
Larderello Tuscany 383
La Spezia Liguria 295
Lateran Treaty 36, 37
La Thuile Valle d'Aosta 89
Laveno Mombello Lombardy 189
Lazio 28
Lecce Puglia 196
Lega 58
Leonardo da Vinci 54, 163
Leopardi, Giacomo 67, 199
Lerici Liguria 296
Levanzo Sicily 405
Lignano Friuli-Venezia Giulia 198
Liguria 27
Ligurians 30
Limone sul Garda Lombardy 194
Lippi, Filippino 163
Lippi, Filippo 163
Literature 65
Livorno Tuscany 198
Locatelli, Pietro 70
Locorotondo Puglia 359
Locri Calabria 123
Lombardy 26
Lombard League 34, 222
Lomellina Lombardy 26
Lomello Lombardy 261
Longhi 364
Lorenzetti, Pietro
   and Ambrogio 326
Lorenzetti, Ambrogio 51
Lorenzetti, Pietro 51
Lorenzo the Magnificent 161
Loreto Marches 199
Lotto,
   Lorenzo .. 55, 105, 187, 199, 364
Lovere Lombardy 192
Lucania 29
Lucca Tuscany 200
Lucera Puglia 285
Luchetti, Daniele 72
Lucrino, Lago (Lake)
   Campania 242
Ludovico il Moro 210
Lugano, Lago di (Lake) Lombardy,
   Switzerland 190

M

Macchiaioli 58
Machiavelli, Niccolò 66, 162
Maddalena, Circuito della (Hill)
  Piedmont 350
Maddalena archipelago
  Sardinia 393
Madonna dal Sasso Piedmont 189
Madonna della Quercia Lazio 381
Madonna del Monte Tuscany 148
Madonna di Campiglio
  Trentino-Alto Adige 355
Madonna di San Luca
  Emilia-Romagna 114
Madre, Isola (Island) Piedmont .. 189
Maestri comacini 137
Maestri Comacini 49
Maestri Campionesi 49, 190
Maggiore, Lago (Lake)
  Piedmont, Lombardy 188
Magnasco, ALessandro 178
Magna Graecia 30
Malatesta 266, 292
Malcesine Veneto 194
Malcontenta Veneto 117
Malles Trentino-Alto Adige 375
Manarola Liguria 136
Manfredonia Puglia 285
Manin, Villa
  Friuli-Venezia Giulia 360
Mannerism 56
Mansi, Villa Tuscany 203
Manta, Castello della
  (Castle) Piedmont 320
Mantegna, Andrea 53, 204
Mantova Lombardy 204
Manzoni, Alessandro 67
Manzù 59
Maratea Basilicata 273
Marcello, Alessandro 69
Marcello, Benedetto 69
Marches 28
March on Rome 37
Marciana Tuscany 147
Marciana Marina Tuscany 147
Marechiaro Campania 242
Maremma Tuscany 28
Marettimo Sicily 405
Marina di Campo Tuscany 148
Marinetti, Filippo Tommaso ... 58, 67
Marlia, Villa Reale di Tuscany 202
Marmolada Trentino-Alto Adige .. 143
Marmolada Massif Veneto 142
Marmore, Cascata delle
  (Waterfall) Umbria 334
Marostica Veneto 102
Marsala Sicily 408
Martina Franca Puglia 359
Martini, Simone 51, 326
Masaccio 52, 162
Masaniello 244
Maser Veneto 356
Massa Marittima Tuscany 207
Matera Basilicata 208
Mattinata Puglia 177
Mazzacurati, Carlo 73
Mazzini, Giuseppe 35
Medici 161
Medici, Lorenzo de' 65
Meloria, Battle of 269
Menaggio Lombardy 192

Merano 2000
  Trentino-Alto Adige 209
Merano Trentino-Alto Adige 209
Mesola Emilia-Romagna 137
Messina Sicily 409
Messina, Antonello da 53
Metalliferi, Colline (Hills) Lazio .. 383
Metastasio, Pietro 66
Mezzogiorno 29
Michelangelo 54, 55, 65, 163
  Basilica di S. Ambrogio 220
  Basilica di S. Lorenzo Maggiore 222
  Basilica di S. Satiro 221
  Basilica di S. Simpliciano 221
  Brera, Pinacoteca di 217
  Ca'Granda-Ex Ospedale Maggiore ... 221
  Casa di Manzoni 219
  Castello Sforzesco 218
  Cenacolo 220
  Church of San Marco 221
  Duomo and Precincts 211
  Galleria d'Arte Moderna 219
  Museo Civico di Archeologia 221
  Museo Civico di Storia Naturale 219
  Museo del Duomo 214
  Museo della Scienza e della
    Tecnica Leonardo da Vinci 220
  Museo Poldi Pezzoli 219
Milano Lombardy 210
  Galleria Vittorio Emanuele II 211
  Museo teatrale alla Scala 214
  Palazzo Bagatti Valsecchi 220
  Palazzo Litta 222
  Pinacoteca Ambrosiana 219
  Porta Ticinese 222
  San Maurizio 221
  Santa Maria delle Grazie 220
  S. Eustorgio 221
  Teatro alla Scala 214
  Via and Piazza Mercanti 214
Milan, Edict of 32, 210, 297
Mira Veneto 117
Miracle of Bolsena, The 115
Miramare, Castello di (Castle)
  Friuli-Venezia Giulia 358
Miseno Campania 244
Misurina, Lago di (Lake)
  Trentino-Alto Adige 146
Modena Emilia-Romagna 222
Modica Sicily 418
Molfetta Puglia 100
Molise 29, 223
Molveno Trentino-Alto Adige 355
Monferrato Piedmont 351
Monicelli, Mario 72
Monreale Sicily 409
Monselice Veneto 255
Montagnana Veneto 254
Montalcino Tuscany 268
Montale, Eugenio 68
Monte Berico Basilica Veneto 380
Monte Bignone Liguria 324
Monte Capanne Toscana 147
Montecassino,
  Abbazia di (Abbey) Lazio 224
Montecatini Terme Tuscany 225
Monte Cavo Lazio 131
Montecchio Maggiore Veneto 380
Montefalco Umbria 226
Montefeltro, Federico da 361
Montefiascone Lazio 381
Montefiore dell'Aso Marches 152
Monte Grappa Veneto 102

Monte Grisa, Santuario del (Sanctuary) *Friuli-Venezia Giulia* 358
Montegrotto Terme *Veneto* 255
Monte Isola (Island) *Lombardy* ... 193
Monteluco *Umbria* 331
Montemaria, Abbazia di (Abbey) *Trentino-Alto Adige* 375
Montenero *Tuscany* 198
Monteoliveto Maggiore, Abbazia di (Abbey) *Tuscany* 226
Monte Paganella (Mount) *Trentino-Alto Adige* 355
Montepulciano *Tuscany* 227
Monterchi *Tuscany* 325
Monterosso *Liguria* 136
Monte Sant'Angelo *Puglia* 228
Monte Somma *Campania* 244
Monteverdi, Claudio 70, 139
Monza *Lombardy* 228
Morandi, Giorgio 58, 112
Moravia, Alberto 68
Moretti, Nanni 72
Moretto 55
Mortara *Lombardy* 261
Mosaics 49
Mottarone *Piedmont* 189
Muggia *Friuli-Venezia Giulia* 358
Music 69
Mussolini, Benito 36

N

Napoli *Campania* 229
  Aquarium 241
  Cappella Sansevero 236
  Castel Capuano 239
  Castel dell'Ovo 232
  Castel Nuovo 232
  Castel Sant'Elmo 240
  Catacombe di S. Gennaro 241
  Certosa di San Martino 240
  Chiesa dei Girolamini 238
  Chiesa del Purgatorio ad Arco ... 238
  Church of Gesù Nuovo 233
  Church of San Pietro a Maiella .. 238
  Croce di Lucca 238
  Decumanus Maximus 237
  Duomo 237
Napoli, Golfo di (Bay) *Campania* 242
  Maschio Angioino 232
  Mergellina 241
  Miracle of St Januarius ... 237, 238
  Museo Civico Filangieri 240
  Museo Nazionale di Ceramica Duca di Martina 241
  Museo Principe di Aragona Pignatelli Cortes 241
  Palazzo Como 240
  Palazzo e Galleria Nazion-ale di Capodimonte 240
  Palazzo Reale 232
  Palazzo Spinelli di Laurino 238
  Piazza Dante 238
  Piazza del Plebiscito 232
  Pio Monte della Misericordia 237
  Porta Capuana 239
  Porto di S. Lucia 232
  Quadreria dei Girolamini 237
  San Domenico Maggiore 236

San Francesco di Paola 232
San Giovanni a Carbonara 239
San Gregorio Armeno 237
San Lorenzo Maggiore 237
San Paolo Maggiore 238
Santa Chiara 233
Santa Maria Donnaregina 240
Santa Maria Maggiore 238
Sant'Anna dei Lombardi 240
Spaccanapoli and Decumanus Maximus 233
Teatro San Carlo 232
Villa Comunale 241
Villa Floridiana 241
Nardis, Cascata di (Waterfall) *Trentino-Alto Adige* 355
Naturno *Trentino-Alto Adige* 374
Nemi *Lazio* 131
Neo-Realism 72, 68
Nettuno *Lazio* 87
Nettuno, Grotto di (cave) *Sardinia* 388
Noli *Liguria* 294
Nonantola, Abbazia di (Abbey) *Emilia-Romagna* 223
Nono, Luigi 71
Normans 34
Noto *Sicily* 410
Novacella, Abbazia di (Abbey) *Trentino Alto-Adige* 120
Novalesa, Abbazia della (Abbey) *Piedmont* 351
Nova Levante *Trentino-Alto Adige* 143
Novaro *Piemonte* 246
Nuoro *Sardinia* 393
Nuraghi 388

O

Octavian 297
Octavius 32
Opera 70
Oplontis, Villa di (Roman villa) *Campania* 245
Orbetello *Tuscany* 92
Orgosolo *Sardinia* 390
Oristano *Sardinia* 394
Orso, Capo d' *Campania* 86
Orta, Lago d' (Lake) *Piedmont* ... 189
Orta San Giulio *Piedmont* 189
Ortisei *Trentino-Alto Adige* 146
Orvieto *Umbria* 246
Ostia Antica *Lazio* 248
Ostuni *Puglia* 285
Otranto *Puglia* 251

P

Padova *Veneto* 252
Padre Pio 228
Padula, Certosa di *Campania* 135
Paestum *Camapania* 256
Paganini, Niccolò 70
Painting 62
Palermo *Sicily* 411
Palestrina *Lazio* 338
Palestrina, Giovanni Pierluigi da ... 69

Palladio 378
Palladio, Andrea 54
Pallavicino, Villa *Piedmont* 189
Palmi *Calabria* 122
Panicale *Umbria* 265
Pantelleria, island *Sicily* 417
Paola *Calabria* 123
Parco Giardino Sigurtà
    Trentino-Alto Adige 194
Parini, Giuseppe 67
Parma *Emilia-Romagna* 257
Parmigianino 258
Parthenopaean Republic 229
Pascoli, Giovanni 67
Pasolini, Pier Paolo 68
Passiria, Val (Valley)
    Trentino-Alto Adige 209
Passo del Grosté (Pass)
    Trentino-Alto Adige 355
Pavese, Cesare 68
Pavia *Lombardy* 260
Pavia, Certosa di (Monastery)
    Lombardy 261
Pellico, Silvio 319
Pelligrino, Monte *Sicily* 417
Pentedattilo *Calabria* 123
Persano, WWF Oasis *Campania* .. 135
Perugia *Umbria* 262
Pesaro *Marches* 265
Pescasseroli *Abruzzi* 82
Pescatori, Isola dei (Island)
    Piedmont 189
Peschici *Puglia* 177
Pescocostanzo *Abruzzi* 82
Petrarch 65, 255
Phoenicians 30
Piacenza *Emilia-Romagna* 266
Piano, Renzo 180, 341
Piazza Armerina *Sicily* 402
Pallanza *Piedmont* 189
Piedmont 26
Pienza *Tuscany* 267
Pieraccioni, Leonardo 73
Piero della Francesca 163, 324
Pietrabbondante *Molise* 224
Pietrelcina *Puglia* 228
Pieve di Cadore
    Trentino Alto-Adige 147
Piombo, Sebastiano del 182
Piona, Abbazia di (Abbey)
    Lombardy 192
Pirandello, Luigi 67, 399
Pisa *Tuscany* 269
Pisanello 375
Pisanello, Antonio 51
Pisano, Nicola 50, 269
Pisano, Giovanni 50
Pisogne *Lombardy* 193
Pistoia *Tuscany* 272
Plose *Trentino-Alto Adige* 120
Poggio *Tuscany* 147
Poggio Bustone, Convento di
    (Monastery) *Lazio* 292
Polesine *Emilia-Romagna* 137
Policastro, Golfo di (Gulf)
    *Campania, Basilicata,
    Calabria* 273
Politian 65, 227
Pollaiolo 163
Pompei *Campania* 274
Pompey 31
Pomposa, Abbazia di (Abbey)
    Emilia-Romagna 278
Ponchielli, Amilcare 71

Ponte, Lorenzo da 69
Pontormo 163
Pontormo, Jacopo 55
Pont- Saint-Martin *Valle d'Aosta* .. 90
Ponza *Lazio* 88
Ponza, Isola di (Island) *Lazio* 88
Popoli *Abruzzi* 332
Poppi *Tuscany* 325
Pordoi, Passo (Pass)
    Trentino-Alto Adige 146
Portici *Campania* 244
Porto Azzurro *Tuscany* 148
Porto Ercole *Tuscany* 93
Portoferraio *Tuscany* 147
Portofino *Liguria* 279
Portofino, Promontorio di
    (Peninsula) *Liguria* 279
Portogruaro *Veneto* 356
Portonovo *Marches* 87
Porto Santo Stefano *Tuscany* 93
Portovenere *Liguria* 296
Porto Torres *Sardinia* 394
Posillipo *Campania* 242
Positano *Campania* 84
Possagno *Veneto* 102
Potenza *Basilicata* 280
Pozzuoli *Campania* 280
Po Delta *Veneto* 27
Prato *Tuscany* 280
Press 29
Previati 58
Puccini, Giacomo 71
Puglia 29, 282
Pugnochiuso *Puglia* 177
Punic Wars 31
Punta del Capo di Sorrento
    (Cape) *Campania* 330
Punta della Chiappa *Liguria* 279
Pusteria,
    Val *Trentino-Alto Adige* 146

Q

Quasimodo, Salvatore 67
Quercia, Jacopo della 326

R

Ragusa *Sicily* 418
Rapallo *Liguria* 295
Raphael 55, 163
Ravello *Campania* 286
Ravenna *Emilia-Romagna* 287
Realism 67
Recanati *Marches* 199
Reggio di Calabria *Calabria* 290
Reggio Emilia *Emilia-Romagna* .. 291
Renaissance 65
Rendena, Val (Valley)
    Trentino-ALto Adige 355
Reni, Guido 111
Resia, Lago di (Lake)
    Trentino-Alto Adige 375
Respighi, Ottorino 71
Riace Warriors 290
Ribera, Jusepe di 232
Rieti *Lazio* 292
Rimini *Emilia-Romagna* 292
Riomaggiore *Liguria* 136

Rio Marina *Tuscany* 148
Risi, Marco 73
Risorgimento 35
Riva del Garda
   Trentino-Alto Adige 194
Riviera di Ponente *Liguria* 293
Riviera Ligure *Liguria* 293
Robbia, Luca della 52, 163
Roberti, Ercole de' 153
Rocca di Papa *Lazio* 131
Rocca Imperiale *Calabria* 122
Rodengo, Castello di (Castle)
   Trentino-Alto Adige 146
Roma *Lazio* 297
   Appia Antica 307
   Ara Pacis Augustae 316
   Arco di Costantino 307
   Arco di Giano 316
   Area Sacra di Largo Argentina 316
   Basilica di San Pietro 312
   Campidoglio 303
   Campo dei Fiori 317
   Castel Sant'Angelo 306
   Catacombe di Domitilla 307
   Catacombe di San Callisto 307
   Catacombe di San Sebastiano 307
   Chiesa del Gesù 308
   Chiesa della Trinità dei Monti 310
   Chiesa Nuova 314
   Circo Massimo 316
   Colonna Traiana 307
   Colosseo 307
   Domus Aurea 316
   EUR 317
   Fontana dei Fiumi 310
   Fontana di Trevi 311
   Fori Imperiali 307
   Foro di Augusto 307
   Foro di Cesare 307
   Foro Romano 307
   Foro di Traiano 307
   Galleria Borghese 316
   Galleria Nazionale
      d'Arte Moderna 316
   Gianicolo 317
   Giardini Vaticani 311
   Isola Tiberina 317
   Mausoleo d'Augusto 316
   Mercati Traianei 307
   Musei Vaticani 314
   Museo Capitolino 306
   Museo della Civiltà Romana 317
   Museo Nazionale di Villa Giulia ... 316
   Museo Nazionale Romano 316
   Palatino 308
   Palazzo Barberini 316
   Palazzo Braschi 316
   Palazzo Chigi 316
   Palazzo Corsini 316
   Palazzo dei Conservatori 303
   Palazzo dei Conservatori Museum .. 303
   Palazzo della Cancelleria 316
   Palazzo della Consulta 316
   Palazzo della Sapienza 317
   Palazzo del Quirinale 317
   Palazzo di Montecitorio 317
   Palazzo Doria Pamphili 316
   Palazzo Farnese 317
   Palazzo Lateranense 310
   Palazzo Madama 317
   Palazzo Nuovo 306
   Palazzo Pamphili 310
   Palazzo Senatorio 306
   Palazzo Spada 317
   Palazzo Venezia 310
   Pantheon 309
   Piazza Bocca della Verità 317
   Piazza Colonna 317
   Piazza del Campidoglio 303
   Piazza dell'Esquilino 311
   Piazza del Popolo 309
   Piazza del Quirinale 317
   Piazza di San Giovanni in Laterano . 310
   Piazza di San Pietro 312
   Piazza di Spagna 310
   Piazza Navona 310
   Piazza Sant'Ignazio 317
   Piazza Venezia 310
   Pincio 310
   Piramide di Caio Cestio 316
   Ponte Fabricio 317
   Ponte Sant'Angelo 307
   Porta San Paolo 317
   Porta San Sebastiano 317
   San Carlo alle Quattro Fontane 314
   San Clemente 314
   San Giovanni in Laterano 310
   San Lorenzo Fuori le Mura 314
   San Luigi dei Francesi 315
   San Paolo fuori le Mura 311
   San Pietro in Montorio 315
   San Pietro in Vincoli 315
   Santa Cecilia in Trastevere 314
   Sant'Agnese Fuori Le Mura 314
   Sant'Agnese in Agone 310
   Sant'Agostino 314
   Santa Maria d'Aracœli 303
   Santa Maria degli Angeli 315
   Santa Maria dell'Anima 315
   Santa Maria della Vittoria 315
   Santa Maria in Cosmedin 315
   Santa Maria in Trastevere 311, 315
   Santa Maria sopra Minerva 315
   Sant'Andrea al Quirinale 314
   Sant'Andrea della Valle 314
   Santa Sabina 315
   Santa Susanna 315
   Santi Cosma e Damiano 315
   Sant'Ignazio 314
   Scalinata della Trinità dei Monti 310
   Teatro di Marcello 316
   Tempio della Fortuna Virile 316
   Tempio di Apollo Sosiano 316
   Tempio di Venere e di Roma 308
   Tempio di Vesta 316
   Terme di Caracalla 306
   Tomba di Cecilia Metella 316
   Vaticano 311
   Via dei Condotti 310
   Via dei Coronari 317
   Villa Borghese 317
   Villa Farnesina 317
   Vittoriano, Il 310
Romanesque Art 49
Romanino 55
Romans 63
Roman gods 33
Roselle, Scavi di
   (Archaeological site) *Tuscany* .. 183
Rossano *Calabria* 123
Rossellini, Roberto 72
Rossellino, Bernardo 267
Rossetti, Biagio 155
Rossini, Gioacchino 70, 265
Rosso Fiorentino 163
Rotonda, La *Veneto* 380
Ruvo di Puglia *Puglia* 285
Ruzzante 66

S

Sabaudia *Lazio* 335
Sabaudia, Lago di (Lake) *Lazio* ... 335
Saba, Umberto 68
Sabbioneta *Lombardy* 317
Sabiona, Convento di
  Trentino-Alto Adige 120
Sack of Rome 35
Sacra di San Michele *Piedmont* .. 351
Sacro Monte de Varallo
  Piedmont 190
Sacro Monte de Varese
  Lombardy 191
Sacro Monte d'Orta *Piedmont* 189
Sagittario, Gole del (Gorges)
  Abruzzi 82
Saints 60
Saint-Vincent *Valle d'Aosta* 90
Salerno *Campania* 318
Salieri, Antonio 69
Salimbeni, Lorenzo and Jacopo ... 339
Salina *Sicily* 407
Salò *Lombardy* 194
Saluzzo *Piedmont* 319
San Candido
  Trentino-Alto Adige 146
San Clemente a Casauria
  (Abbey) *Abruzzo* 133
San Clemente al Vomano
  (Church) *Abruzzi* 99
San Domenico *Puglia* 353
San Domenico di Fiesole
  Tuscany 156
Sanfelice, Ferdinando 232
San Fruttuoso *Liguria* 279
San Galgano, Abbazia di (Abbey)
  Tuscany 208
San Gimignano *Tuscany* 321
San Giovanni in Venere (Abbey)
  Abruzzi 83
San Giovanni Rotondo *Puglia* 228
San Giulio, Isola di (Island)
  Piedmont 189
San Leo *Marches* 323
San Lorenzo della Costa *Liguria* .. 279
San Marino, Repubblica di 323
San Martino della Battaglia
  Lombardy 194
San Martino di Castrozza
  Trentino-Alto Adige 147
San Martino , Villa Napoleone
  Tuscany 148
San Nicola *Puglia* 353
San Pelino, Basilica di *Abruzzi* ... 332
San Pellegrino Terme (Baths)
  Lombardy 107
San Piero a Grado,
  Basilica di *Tuscany* 272
San Pietro in Valle, Abbazia di
  (Abbey) *Umbria* 334
San Remo *Liguria* 323
San Rocco, Belvedere di *Liguria* .. 279
Sansepolcro *Tuscany* 324
San Severino Marche *Marches* ... 339
Sant'Antioco, island *Sardinia* 394
Santa Caterina del Sasso
  (Hermitage) *Lombardy* 189
Sant'Agata sui Due Golfi
  Campania 330
Santa Margherita Ligure
  Liguria 279

Santa Maria a piè di Chienti
  Marches 152
Santa Maria Capua Vetere
  Campania 128
Santa Maria del Casale *Puglia* 121
Santa Maria di Canneto *Molise* ... 224
Santa Maria di Cerrate *Puglia* 198
Santa Maria di Leuca *Puglia* 252
Sant'Angelo in Formia,
  Basilica di *Campania* 128
Sant'Antimo, Abbazia di (Abbey)
  Tuscany 268
Sant'Antonio di Ranverso,
  Abbazia di (Abbey) *Piedmont* .. 351
Santa Severina *Calabria* 141
Sant'Elia, Antonio 58
Santis, De 72
San Vigilio, Punta di *Veneto* 194
San Vincenzo al Volturno
  Molise 224
San Vito di Cadore
  Trentino-Alto Adige 147
San Vivaldo *Tuscany* 322
Sardinia 386
Sarre, Castello di *Valle d'Aosta* 90
Sarto, Andrea del 163
Sarzana *Tuscany* 129
Sassari *Sardinia* 395
Savigliano *Piedmont* 320
Savoldo 55
Savona *Liguria* 294
Savonarola, Girolamo 161
Savoy, House of 340
Scanno, Lago di (Lake) *Abruzzi* 82
Scarlatti, Alessandro 70
Scarlatti, Domenico 69
Sciascia, Leonardo 68
Scilla *Calabria* 122
Scipio 31
Scola, Ettore 72
Sculpture 62
Scuola romana 59
Segantini, Giovanni 58
Segesta *Sicily* 419
Sei di Torino 59
Selinus, ancient city *Sicily* 419
Sella, Passo di (Pass)
  Trentino-Alto Adige 144
Selva di Val Gardena
  Trentino-Alto Adige 145
Serra San Bruno *Calabria* 123
Sesto *Trentino-Alto Adige* 146
Settignano, Desiderio da 52
Severini 138
Severini, Gino 58
Severus dynasty 32
Sforza, The 210
Sica, Vittorio de 72
Sicilian School 65
Sicily 396
Siena *Tuscany* 325
Sighignola, Belvedere di
  Lombardy 190
Signorelli, Luca 138, 247
Signorini 58
Sila, Massiccio della (Massif)
  Calabria 29
Siracusa *Sicily* 420
Sirai, Monte *Sardinia* 394
Sirmione *Lombardy* 194
Sluderno *Trentino-Alto Adige* 375
Smeraldo, Grotta dello (Cave)
  Campania 85
Solferino *Lombardy* 194

Solimena, Francesco 232
Solunto, ruins Sicily 417
Sorrentina, Penisola
    (Peninsula) 330
Sorrento Campania 330
Spello Umbria 98
Sperlonga Lazio 176
Spluga, Strada del Passo dello
    (Road) Lombardy 133
Spoleto Umbria 330
Staffarda, Abbazia di
    (Abbey) Piedmont 320
Stanghe, Cascate di (Waterfall)
    Trentino-Alto Adige 380
St Francis 292
Stilo Calabria 124
Strà Veneto 116
Stresa Piedmont 189
Stromboli, volcano Sicily 407
Stupinigi, Palazzina di caccia di
    (Palace) Piedmont 350
Subiaco Lazio 331
Sulmona Abruzzi 331
Superga, Basilica di Piedmont 350
Susa Piedmont 351
Susa, Val di (Valley) Piedmont .. 350
Svevo, Italo 67

T

Taggia Liguria 294
Taormina Sicily 423
Taranto Puglia 332
Taranto, Villa Piedmont 189
Tarquinia Lazio 333
Tartini, Giuseppe 70
Tasso, Torquato 66, 153, 330
Taviani brothers 72
Temples, Valley of Sicily 400
Termoli Molise 224
Terni Umbria 334
Terracina Lazio 334
Tetrarchy 32
Tharros Sardinia 395
Tiepolo 364
Tiepolo, Giandomenico 380
Tiepolo, Giovan Battista 58
Tindari Sicily 424
Tintoretto 55, 364
Tirano, Santuario
    della Madonna di Lombardy 335
Tirolo Trentino-Alto Adige 209
Titian 55, 364
Tivoli Lazio 335
Toblino, Lago di (Lake)
    Trentino-Alto Adige 355
Todi Umbria 338
Todi, Jacopone da 338
Tofano di Mezzo Veneto 138
Toirano, Grotte di (Caves)
    Liguria 294
Tolentino Marches 339
Tondi di Faloria Veneto 138
Torbole Trentino-AltoAdige 194
Torelli, Giuseppe 70
Torgiano Umbria 265
Torino Piedmont 340
Tornatore, Giuseppe 72
Torno Lombardy 192
Torre Annunziata Campania 245

Torrechiara, Castello di
    (Fortress) Emilia-Romagna 260
Torre del Greco Campania 245
Torrigiani, Villa Tuscany 203
Tortoli Sardinia 395
Toscanini, Casa
    Emilia-Romagna 259
Tovel, Lago di (Lake)
    Trentino-Alto Adige 355
Trani Puglia 285
Trapani Sicily 424
Trasimeno, Lago di (Lake) 28
Tratalias Sardinia 394
Tre Cime di Lavaredo
    Trentino-Alto Adige 146
Tremezzo Lombardy 192
Tremiti, Isole (Islands) Puglia 352
Trentino Alto-Adige 27
Trento Trentino-Alto Adige 353
Trevignano Romano Lazio 132
Treviso Veneto 355
Trieste Friuli-Venezia Giulia 356
Triple Alliance 36
Troia Puglia 286
Troisi 73
Tropea Calabria 122
Trulli, Terra dei
    Friuli-Venezia Giulia 358
Tura, Cosmè 153
Tura, Cosimo 53
Tuscania Lazio 359
Tuscany 27
Tuscolo Lazio 131

U

Uccello, Paolo 52, 163
Udine Friuli-Venezia Giulia 360
Umbria 28
Ungaretti, Giuseppe 67
Urbino Marches 361
USTICA Sicily 425

V

Vaga, Perin del 182
Val d'Ega, Gola della (Gorge)
    Trentino-Alto Adige 142
Valeggio sul Mincio
    Trentino-Alto Adige 194
Valle d'Aosta 26, 89
Vallone di Furore Campania 85
Valmarana ai Nani, Villa
    Veneto 380
Vanvitelli, Luigi 130
Varallo Piedmont 190
Varenna Lombardy 192
Varese Lombardy 191
Vasari, Giorgio 56, 91, 162
Velia Campania 134
Velletri Lazio 131
Veneto 27
Venezia Veneto 362
    Arsenale 373
    Burano 374
    Ca' Dario 372
    Ca' d'Oro 372
    Canal Grande 370
    Ca' Pesaro 372

Ca' Rezzonico 372
Collezione Peggy Guggenheim 374
Fondazione Querini
  Stampaglia 372, 374
Ghetto 373
Giudecca 373
I Frari 373
Libreria Sansoviana 369
Lido 374
Murano 374
Museo Correr 369
Palazzo Ducale 369
Palazzo Grassi 372
Palazzo Labia 371
Palazzo Vendramin Calergi 371
Piazza San Marco 368
Ponte dei Sospiri 369
Ponte di Rialto 372
San Giorgio Maggiore 373
San Sebastiano 373
Santa Maria della Salute 373
San Zaccaria 373
San Zanipòlo 373
Torcello 374
Torre dell'Orologio 369
Venosta, Val 374
Ventimiglia *Liguria* 294
Verdi, Giuseppe 71
Verdone, Carlo 73
Verga, Giovanni 67, 402
Verna, Convento della
  (Monastery) *Tuscany* 325
Vernazza *Liguria* 135
Verona *Veneto* 375
Veronese 364
Veronese, Paolo 55
Verrocchio 163
Vesuvio *Campania* 244
Vettica Maggiore *Campania* 84
Vezzolano, Abbazia di (Abbey)
  Piedmont 352
Viareggio *Tuscany* 272
Vicenza *Veneto* 378
Vico Equense *Campania* 245
Vico, Lago di (Lake) *Lazio* 381
Vico, Giambattista 66

Victor Emmanuel II 35
Vieste *Puglia* 177
Vietri sul Mare *Campania* 86
Vigevano *Lombardy* 261
Vignola, Giacomo da 54
Vigo di Fassa
  Trentino-Alto Adige 143
Villa Cicogna Mozzoni,
  Bisuschio *Lombardy* 191
Villa Opicina
  Friuli-Venezia Giulia 358
Villa San Giovanni *Calabria* 122
Vinci *Tuscany* 273
Viotti, Giovanni Battista 69
Vipiteno 380
Virgil 204
Visconti, The 210
Visconti, Luchino 72
Viterbo *Lazio* 381
Vittoriale, Il *Lombardy* 193
Vittorio Veneto *Veneto* 356
Vivaldi, Antonio 69, 364
Volpedo, Pellizza da 58
Volterra *Tuscany* 382
Vomano, Valle del (Valley)
  Abruzzi 80

W

War of Independence, First 35
War of Independence, Second 35
War of Independence, Third 36
Wine 75

Z

Zagare, Baia delle (Bay) *Puglia* ... 177
Zevio, Stefano da 51
Zimbalo 196
Zinzulusa, Grotta (Cave) *Puglia* .. 252